# WELCOME TO THE THIRD EDITION OF THE CREATURE FEATURES MOVIE GUIDE

## Completely Revised, Expanded and Updated
## Since 1984

## Here's Why This Movie Guide Will Satisfy
## Your Horror Film Viewing Needs:

- **Capsulized reviews of almost 4000 genre films of science-fiction, horror and fantasy.**

- **Reviews of films and novelty items ignored by other major movie guides**

- **Coded so you can instantly see if a certain title can be rented or purchased at your video store**

- **Reviews of movies and offbeat fare made exclusively for videocassette, and usually not included in other guides**

- **Hundreds of new photographs from the author's private collection, many never before printed**

- **Our cover price is cheap: $11.95. Compare that to other encyclopedias of horror and you'll know**

- **The author, John Stanley, is an acknowledged expert in the field. For six years he was the host of the popular TV show "Creature Features" in the San Francisco-Bay Area. He now writes for the San Franc‌⁀‌⁀ Chronicle as its in-house horror expert and he is a ▢▢▢▢▢▢ ‸merican Fantasy Magazine. He is "The ▢ comes to genre viewing.**

## PREPARE FOR A MACAB▯▯ ▯
## THE WORLD OF FANTASTIC CIN▮▮▮

# DEDICATED TO

*Vincent Price, John Carradine, George Zucco, Lionel Atwill, Colin Clive, John Lithgow, Gene Wilder and Bela Lugosi*

## The Greatest Mad Doctors of All

*Also Dedicated to real-life doctors Tom Mullooly and Richard Burns*

## These intrepid men have looked into the Mouth of Horror and lived to tell about it.

# REVENGE OF THE CREATURE FEATURES MOVIE GUIDE

(Third Revised Edition,
Totally Rewritten and Updated)

## AN A TO Z ENCYCLOPEDIA TO THE CINEMA OF THE FANTASTIC

Or

## IS THERE A MAD DOCTOR IN THE HOUSE?

By
John Stanley

Cover and Interior Illustrations
By
Kenn Davis

Creatures at Large Press
P.O. Box 687
Pacifica CA 94044

**REVENGE OF THE CREATURE FEATURES MOVIE GUIDE**
Third Revised Edition of THE CREATURE FEATURES
MOVIE GUIDE
First printing © 1988 by John Stanley

The first edition of this book was published by Creatures at Large in 1981. The second edition, with additional material, was published by Warner Books Inc. in 1984. This third edition has been completely revised and updated by the author.

Cover design and interior illustrations by Kenn Davis.

Library of Congress Catalogue Card No: 87-91426.

Library of Congress Cataloging in Publication Data:

Stanley, John, 1940-
Revenge of the Creature Features Movie Guide (Third Revised and Updated Edition), or An A to Z encyclopedia to the cinema of the fantastic, or, Is there a mad doctor in the house?

1. Fantastic films--Plots, themes, etc. I. Creature features (Television program) II. Title
PN1995.9F36S7 1987 791.43'09'0915
87-91426

International Standard Book Numbering Agency information:

ISBN: 0-940064-04-9 (Trade Paperback)
ISBN: 0-940064-05-7 (Deluxe Signed Hardcover)
ISBN: 0-940064-08-1 (Creature Features Series)

# INTRODUCTION

## MORE MEMOIRS OF A MONSTER MAN

### BY JOHN STANLEY

### *TV Death Strikes*

**S**O MANY BRIDGES have gone under the water since the second edition of **The Creature Features Movie Guide** was released three years ago that the early 1980s now seem like a galaxy far, far away . . .

No sooner had that mammoth second edition been unleashed on an unsuspecting society than KTVU-TV in Oakland, Calif., recklessly cancelled **Creature Features,** the Saturday night series I had hosted unabashedly for almost six years, bringing to lovers of science-fiction, fantasy and horror movies some of the worst in cinematic (mis)treats.

### *Telstar Regurgitation*

During that best of slime time I had presented a steady supply of notorious and celebrity guests, establishing my weekly show as a bloodied bastion for freaks, oddballs and entrepreneurs who wanted to sell a grue or two. The moods of the show had ranged from the sardonic humor of Robert Bloch to the poetic intellectualism of Ray Bradbury. From the articulate brilliance of Leonard Nimoy to the satirical singularity of William Shatner. From the quiet aloofness of Harrison Ford to the outspoken frankness of Nicholas Meyer. From the youthful enthusiasm of Chuck Norris to the noble air of Charlton Heston. From the cuddly goodness of Mamie Van Doren to the vulgar spice of Edy Williams. From sexy pots to brainy BEMS to out-and-out illiterates in vampire costumes or gangling kids in Giant Lizard Suits. They were all regurgitated into the Telstar Ether, my stoic image floating beside them.

So, on the one hand it came as a resounding shock when I was informed that the "institution" would leave the air after a solid 14-year video history in the San Francisco-Bay Area. It had the same stomach-walloping effect that you feel when you're told a close member of the family has died.

There's an old TV adage: The Lord of the Tube giveth and the Lord of the Tube taketh away . . .

On the other hand, I had psychically sensed administrative axes descending from several directions at once, and knew that cancellation was as inevitable as Darth Vader's return to the movie screen in a future STAR WARS saga.

## 14 Years of Happy Blood

What had happened during those historic 14 years to build up a show and then tear it down? In a sense those incredibly exciting years traced the outward expansion and development of cinematic genre horror and science-fiction in America. These were the years when fantasy-scary genres went from the hands of schlock producers into the hands of aficionados and appreciators turned Hollywood producers who treated their material with the grade-A respect they felt it finally deserved.

## Wily, Wiry Wilkins

**Creature Features** had premiered one stormy night in February, 1971, to discover an enthusiastic, almost cultish audience of young and old, eager to slurp up as many old horror movies as were available.

The original host—my predecessor—was the redoubtable, droll Bob Wilkins, he of the rocking chair and big black cigar. They became his trademarks which would last him for eight years— shticks he had chosen because of his nervousness in front of a camera, not because he thought they would give him identity. The cigar gave him something to clutch, the rocking chair gave him something to thrust-back thrust-forward in order to conceal his nervous energy.

Bob never really knew very much about movies or genres (Clint Eastwood in "Dirty Harry" was more his speed), so he tended to make wry dry jokes, often with a political or social slant. The 1958 Edsel TV commercial and Ronald Reagan doing **Death Valley Days** commercials for a soap company became oft-repeated gags. Peter Finch sticking his head out the window and screaming "I'm mad as hell and I'm not going to take it anymore" in NETWORK was especially a Wilkins favorite.

Gradually he learned what the cadre of fans wanted in terms of guests and announcements, but he still seemed aloof from the fannish element—living with it and tolerating it but not particularly wanting to touch it, or have it touch him.

Wilkins stood it for as long as he could before he got out of television to run his own advertising agency in the Bay Area— a decision he has never regretted. (He came back in May, 1987, for a one-shot **Creature Features** revival, but he told me the following week that he didn't want to work in TV ever again.) This time I understood just how he felt.

What gave **Creature Features** its success? A good part of it was Wilkins' special (and it was special) sense of humor and counter-TV

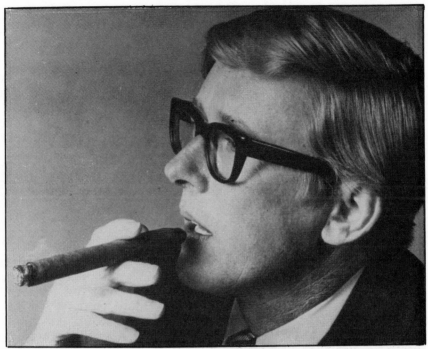

THE ORIGINAL 'CREATURE FEATURES' HOST, BOB WILKINS

image. Another key element was the package of old Universal horror movies that became Bob's main staples for many years.

Running FRANKENSTEIN or DRACULA or DRACULA'S DAUGHTER in a 9 o'clock time slot on Saturday night was a brilliant counter-program strategy one can accredit to former station programmer Tom Breen, a decent enough guy who had had the presence of mind to import Wilkins from nearby Sacramento, where wistful Bob had broken into the business quite by accident, showing horror movies on an independent station because no one else was available—or wanted to do it.

### Saturday Night Jive

Now, in 1971, here were old classics available to a generation which had never seen them before, and to an older generation that remembered them with fondness and now had the opportunity to see them again, in the company of their children. **Creature Features** became a family event. And a KTVU event, with exceptionally startling ratings, considering the competition was primetime network programming. The show became an admired cornerstone of the station, a symbol of success and stability, and put a smile on the faces of almost all the employees.

Try to remember that in 1971, movies were still a novelty item. They came slowly to television after their theatrical runs, often taking as long as ten years or more to reach the tube. One rarely saw a "new" feature film except on the networks.

So, **Creature Features** and Bob Wilkins flourished through the 1970s, kept alive by umpteen repeats of THE MUMMY, THE MUMMY'S TOMB, BILLY THE KID VS. DRACULA, JUNGLE CAPTIVE, THE HORROR OF PARTY BEACH and scores of others that whetted appetites or amused with their blatant badness. Wilkins also used the impetus of the STAR WARS movie to connect him with vast audiences of fans, nailing down David Prowse and Anthony Daniels for interviews. He also knew the importance of STAR TREK and had each key member of the cast into his studio, and promoted their every move between appearances.

By the time I chanced-bungled along in 1979, the year when Wilkins could stand neither the program nor the station another minute, the countenance of the TV Beast was changing.

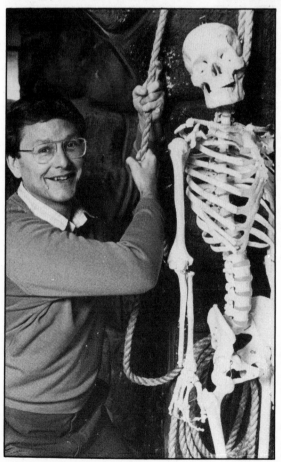

A new, lucrative way to market movies was on the horizon, but I hardly noticed. I was full of fresh ideas and excitement and not just a little merde because I was coming from the ranks of fandom and felt I knew and understood the needs of the program far clearer than Wilkins ever had. I didn't have the brains to ponder the possibility that maybe Bob had understood those needs better despite his personal aloofness from fandom.

I began booking guests who tended to take my own breath away, I began making my own shortened genre pieces on film or tape (which I dubbed "minimovies") and I placed the focus of my weekly 30 minutes on the needs of the fans (and me). Almost of secondary importance, it now appears in retrospect, were the crummy movies I begrudgingly hosted.

By then the station had stupidly given up the option on the Universal film package (it was gobbled up by rival Channel 44 in San Francisco, where publicist Suzanne Toner was having a field day competing with my show—a point of irony since I value Suzanne as a close friend).

I was forcefed some of the worst drivel you will find catalogued in this book. I must have appeared to be floating through my assignment, although I loved the job and the people I worked with at the station, including publicist Judith Morgan Jennings.

Occasionally Breen would call me into his office and ask for my opinion about a film package, and I would respond with a very positive "Yes, please, buy that package, because I need it and can work with it, please, plead plead." Twice he asked me about a package of Boris Karloff films he had an opportunity to buy, and twice I told him

to buy them. They were vintage films from the early 1940s, and I craved them on my diet of mediocrity and schlock. The station never bought the package. My advice was consistently ignored, even though the station paradoxically considered me its "great" in-house expert.

### Dejection, Rejection, Ejection

Feeling dejected, and barely a part of the station, I focused on my own presentation, devoting (I now realize) as little of my air time to some of the films as I could get away with. Better I should have slashed my own throat.

The blind was lead-

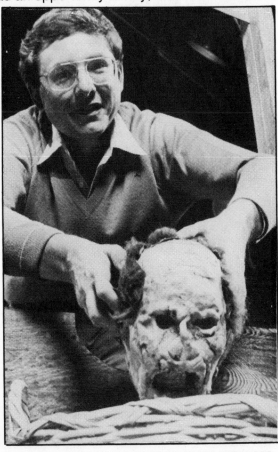

STANLEY WITH HIS CREATURE FEATURES PRODUCER

ing the sublime. Before too many years went by I woke up to the damaging effort the station's indifferent attitude had had on the slow demise of **Creature Features**. While I had kept showing the same old crap, without fighting management for better material, the ratings had infinitisimally dwindled away.

### The Axe Blade Cuts Deep

I should have known something was up when scores of people mistook me for Wilkins, making reference to my cigar and rocking chair—two features I had avoided like the Red Death. Those "fans" had long ago stopped watching the program, and now had only fond, nostalgic memories of the good old days with Bob, whose name they had already forgotten, and whose face they now superimposed over my own. They hadn't even known there was a new host who had replaced old Bob. The audience was bailing out but I was still flying the airplane. Blindfolded.

There befell on my neck three sharp axe strokes:

1. **Saturday Night Live** with its ever-increasing popularity.

2. The burgeoning success of cable systems and individual stations that specialized in showing first-run movies only a few months (sometimes weeks) after they had played in theaters.

3. The growth of the videocassette shops, where one could now buy or rent a movie of one's choice and select the time and place to view it.

STANLEY WITH THE LATE MUCH BELOVED BUSTER CRABBE

CREATURE FEATURES MOVIE GUIDE

CHRISTOPHER LEE ON THE SET OF 'CREATURE FEATURES,' 1979

By 1984 the idea of showing a movie on TV had become as exciting as examining chopped liver under a microscope. And having to pay some guy to host the movie . . . well, that had become an obvious luxury that could be . . . cut?

### CHOP!!!

The axe fell with six-weeks' notice. I gathered up my cassettes, autographed photos, rolled-up one sheets and already-fading memories and retired to my computer, more convinced than ever that the time had come to update this movie guide.

### Histrionics Lesson: A Monster Book

In the beginning, I couldn't give away the concept behind the Creature Features book series. Almost every major New York publisher turned it down, usually with the attitude that Leonard Maltin's **TV Movies** and Steven Scheuer's **Movies on TV** had cornered the market for capsulized film reviews. It was only with the **Creature Features** show supporting me that I mustered enough courage to join the swelling ranks of self-publishers and bring the first edition to press on my own volition. One professional writer told me what I was doing was immoral, but I went ahead anyway, keeping Original Sin as far from my thoughts as possible.

I am happy to report that to this day I do not feel immoral. Nor were any Commandments broken. I am also happy to report that small presses can flourish and make money in this country, a conclusion supported by two benefactors to all self-publishers, Tom and Marilyn Ross, to whose fabulous book, **The Complete Guide to Self-Publishing,** I refer you without hesitation. Wonderful to behold are some of the marketing strategies that Tom and Marilyn have recommended to me via their amazing audiocassette series (write to them at P.O. Box 213, Saguache CO 81149 and ask for details). Independent publishing ain't easy, McGee, but it can be done. Blood, sweat and ink.

We at Creatures at Large Press did not exactly perform a miracle, but over an 18-month period we managed to sell 10,000 books—a respectable, if not spectacular, number. And it wasn't just regional sales based on the TV show's popularlity, as some book industry figures had predicted. The book sold all over the world, especially well in England and Australia.

Flushed with success, I began receiving offers from New York publishers (the same ones who had turned me down years earlier) for the rights to a revised edition. Of four offers for an updated version, I picked the best, which in retrospect wasn't very good at all. In fact, it was a disastrous mistake for me, if not for Warner Books.

I should have insisted on a mass market version, rather than the trade edition that resulted. For the amount of work this book requires—reviewing hundreds of movies, many of them God-awful—there was just no profit (for me) in the estimated 15,000 books printed and sold. (That number could be wrong; Warner never would tell me a number, but it's probably close.)

So for two years I watched the big publishing boys in New York reap the benefits, while I picked up the chaff, remembering how well I had done with the first edition and mentally kicking myself on a daily basis. The nice thing, though, is that there are 25,000 copies out there on shelves.

### In the Mick of Time

I was flustered but I did have the satisfaction of seeing my good friend, Mick Martin, a movie reviewer for the Sacramento Union, mastermind into print Ballantine's invaluable **Video Movie Guide,** which has already enjoyed two editions and performed on the mass

**THE PRECOCIOUS RICKY SCHRODER WITH STANLEY, CIRCA 1980**

market scale that has so far eluded me (How do 500,000 copies strike you?) Mick and his co-writer, Marsha Porter, cover all major features in videocassette, although you will still find some things in this book even they won't stoop to including. I can't blame them—they have class.

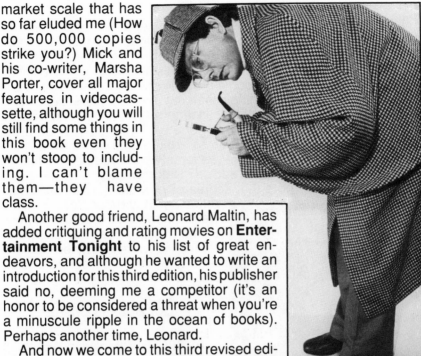

Another good friend, Leonard Maltin, has added critiquing and rating movies on **Entertainment Tonight** to his list of great endeavors, and although he wanted to write an introduction for this third edition, his publisher said no, deeming me a competitor (it's an honor to be considered a threat when you're a minuscule ripple in the ocean of books). Perhaps another time, Leonard.

And now we come to this third revised edition, vastly updated, almost completely rewritten, with many films re-evaulated. Greater emphasis has been placed on visuals, and we've attempted to bring you a wide array of photographs, not only of popular films and their casts, but producers, directors and writers as well.

### Photo Play

Some of the photos in this book are exclusive, seeing print for the first time. My thanks must be extended to Malcolm Willits, an old friend who has faithfully run the Collectors Bookshop for more than two decades. His photo files are extensive, and I recommend the store (now located at 1708 N. Vine Street in Hollywood) to anyone who is looking for stills of motion pictures and/or their stars, producers and directors. Tell'em Stanley sent you.

### New Drawings

We requested our house artist, Kenn Davis, to do an entirely new set of A to Z drawings, one to kick off each letter. As usual, Ken has produced an eclectic series of sketches, showing his many eldritch styles. (Kenn, we might add, has gained greater notoriety of late as the author of the Carver Bascombe private eye novels.)

## A to Z

It is our hope that this alphabetized compendium will serve as an entertaining and enlightening reading experience. What will you find in this book? What won't you find? is a better question. We've tried to make this edition as conclusive as possible (which is impossible, with so many new movies coming out every day). We've done our best to see all the new theatrical features, movies made exclusively for network or cable, and videocassette originals that can only be found in retail stores. We've also gone back and seen a lot of old movies we missed the first two times around, and we've filled in the holes pointed out by you astute readers. (Would you believe we left out THE OMEN from the first edition? Unforgivable.)

However, please note that scores of new/old movies are being released in various forms every week, and you will undoubtedly find things missing from this book. If a favorite of yours is not here, please write to us. We'll do our best to include it in the next edition.

**STANDARD HAREM GIRL GUESTS**

### Our Book Is Cheap

As before, the GUIDE has been designed to be low-priced (compared to index volumes covering the same topics) and compact, fitting easily atop the TV set or under the coffee table for quick reference. Every attempt has been made to be thorough, so the range of this book includes the obscure and esoteric as well as the popular, the foreign as well as the domestic, the cult as well as the popular.

Occasionally we are taken to task for including a title that some of you feel doesn't belong in this book. We admit that sometimes our selections become very subjective, and are often predicated on the slightest whim, such as whether or not the moon is full.

We included WATCHED, for example, not only because of Stacy Keach's cocaine-inspired fantasies, but because the very image of Keach in a room cloudy with cocaine dust is prophetic, foreshadowing a day when he would go to a British prison for the possession of cocaine. Stacy, whom I value as a friend, has paid his pentance and would appreciate the irony.

At first glance ZEBRA FORCE would appear to be an urban action movie with guerrillas vs. the L.A. underworld—until the Caucasian attackers turn into Negroes at the blink of an eye. Take THE ZODIAC KILLER (please). It seems like a standard crime non-thriller—until some of its murder scenes unwittingly portend the slasher trend to come. What's the light-hearted musical-comedy MEET ME IN LAS VEGAS doing in this horrific book? It's use of luck as a supernatural force cannot be overlooked whenever Dan Dailey and Cyd Charisse hold hands. A standard whodunit is WHO KILLED MARY WHATS'ERNAME? but glimpse the surreal milieu and the odd characters and you know you're in a nebulous section of the ethereal Twilight Zone.

### Psycho Cycle

Don't forget that the viewing tastes of horror and fantasy buffs easily overlap into subgenres that reek of Grand Guignol and aberrant psychology, and these are worthy of incorporation. While PSYCHO may be psychiatrically dismissed in the film's closing moments, there lingers afterward the horrific implications to the human psyche, and so Hitchcock's masterpiece belongs to the spirit of this book. So do other films of psychological terror, for their antecedents lie on the fringes of supernatural darkness and evoke within us that sense of horror that we so often seek through our vicarious fantasy viewing.

ANGELIC ANGELIQUE PETTYJOHN

So too must we include the awful (and awful-titled) exploitation films, the axe-and-gore murder flicks, the slashers and gashers and bashers. It would be unfair to exclude the superagents (sorry to report that the latest James Bond adventure, THE LIVING DAYLIGHTS, arrived too late to make this edition) with their super-gadgets and superchicks or the old dark houses with their drafty corridors, secret panels and chest-thumping gorillas. We've even included the wrestling superhulks of Mexico and the muscle-bound warriors of Italy, for what are they but mythology relived (even by Arnold Schwarzenegger).

Please bear in mind the inconsistencies and idiosyncracies which permeate the movie-titling business. Many films are produced under

**PROFESSOR TARU TANAKA WITH STANLEY, 1984**

one title, re-released under yet another title and then presented on TV under still yet again another. We have cross-indexed as many titles as we could to eliminate confusion, and we only hope we haven't added to the universal chaos.

### Year Year—Who Knows the Year?

We often get into arguments about the year of release, which is frequently difficult to pinpoint, for a film will sometimes sit on a shelf for a long period before going into general distribution. In the case of foreign films, they are often purchased by American distributors years after their indigenous runs. Wherever possible, we have listed the date of initial release so that the film can be judged within its proper time frame.

### To Be Or Not to Be?

Some films in this directory may no longer be in theatrical or television distribution, or may not exist at all. Distributors are notorious for destroying prints to simplify their inventories, and only now is the historical significance of film as a record of the customs and mores of our past being taken seriously; only in the past few year have we mastered techniques for transferring old, disintegrating nitrate stock onto acetate-based films.

### Dusting Off the Classics

On the plus side, distributors have wised up to the dormant fortunes in their dusty vaults. Some cable stations have begun reviving movies long out of TV circulation—old Republic films, for example, have been showing up on the Christian Broadcasting Network; RKO and Fox pictures are predominant on American Movie Classics; and old Gene Autry and Roy Rogers Westerns (with the actors serving as hosts) have turned up on the Nashville Network. Watch for Captain USA every Saturday afternoon on the USA Network—he's been running such Mexican goodies as THE LIVING COFFIN and THE CURSE OF THE CRYING WOMAN.

### *How to Get Earlier Editions*

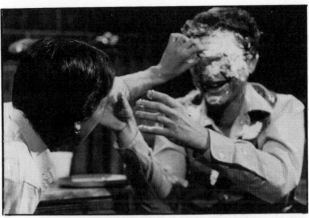

HERE'S PIE IN YOUR EYE, STANLEY (1979)

Reluctantly, we have been forced to cut some titles that appeared in earlier editions, in order to emphasis newer product and to cut down on items which are so obscure, they never seem to turn up anymore. (These titles will be restored in future issues if they do resurface.) Still, we urge readers to have the entire set of the **Creature Features Movie Guide** if they are looking for a complete reference source. (Copies of the first edition, now out of print, can still be ordered through Creatures at Large Press at P.O. Box 687, Pacifica CA 94044—see the back of the book for an order blank. Alas, the second edition is sold out and not available from Warner Books. So much for planning ahead by that prestigious publisher.)

### *Videocassette Code*

We have used the code (VC) at the end of each movie which at one time or another has been available in videocassette. However, this does not necessarily mean you can walk into any video store and find it. Most stores turn over their stock pretty regularly, and if you are looking for older releases, you will have to seek out those few stores which specialize in keeping old stock on hand.

At least our coding will tip you off that it was/is available. Also bear in mind that hundreds of new cassettes are being released each month, so many films now in release may not have been coded at the time we went to press. (VC) is a help, but don't hold us to it.

### *San Francisco's Cinema Shop*

Incidentally, if you're looking for the Oddest Videocassette Store in History, you will find none better than Dan Faris' Cinema Shop, located at 604 Geary Street in San Francisco. As I reported in the pages of the San Francisco Chronicle not long ago, the Cinema Shop features some of the strangest, rarest videocassettes in the short history of the crazy business.

The stock includes Black Exploitation, Teenage Exploitation, Westerns, Worst Government Shorts, World War II Rarities, and Pure Exploitation. Ask Dan or his assistant Steve Imura about YELLOW CARGO, REVENGE OF THE VIRGINS, LYING LIPS, BLOOD OF JESUS, BLACK MARKET BABIES, GANGS INC., SOLDIERS WITHOUT GUNS, LAW OF THE JUNGLE and JAIL BAIT. Believe me, he carries stuff you'll find nowhere else in the country (make that the whole world).

Dan himself is something to meet and behold. But you need know only one basic fact about him, and he says it best in his own unabashed words: "I spend every waking moment of my life watching movies. That's all I live for. One movie after the other. Day in and day out, month after month, year after year. I like nothing better than to watch Rod Cameron get the bends in SEA HORNET."

The videocassette business, the ebullient Faris told me at press time, "is going crazy—it's really out there, moving around like that indescribable thing in STAR TREK—THE MOTION PICTURE. People come into the shop wanting to see the old AIP [American-International] pictures again. They want the classics and the not-so-classics. KILLERS IN SPACE, INVASION OF THE SAUCER MEN. They're hungry for stuff they saw as kids. TERROR IN THE YEAR 5000, THE SHE CREATURE. Stuff that used to fill the Saturday matinee airways. All those old movies were fun, and still are. But some of this new stuff . . ." He shook his head despairingly. "I've been watching a pile of chainsaw movies and after five minutes I lose interest. They're not horror or science-fiction. Give me the good old stuff any day. Hell, give me Rod Cameron in SEA HORNET, groaning from the bends."

### Video Is Booming...Isn't It?

Talk to video entrepreneur Peter Marino, formerly an executive with Warner Bros. Records, and he'll tell you that the videocassette marketplace is upbeat like never before. Peter's partner, Bob Randall (you'll usually find these two bundles of raw energy at Reflections, a major videoshop at 690-A 33rd Avenue in San Francisco), feels there will be even greater availability as collectors demand more and more that the classics be revived— especially in the areas of horror and science-fiction. "You're very book," he told me at press time, "will cause more and more readers to look for these movies. In turn that will help to create a consumer demand.

"Right now," said Randall, "there isn't enough product to meet that consumer demand, so what we're seeing is the re-re-rental of 'Aliens' or 'This Island Earth.' The other horror and sci-fi stuff gets rented whether it's good or bad because it's new and attractively packaged, just like a comic book is attractively packaged."

No one person in the Bay Area has done more to generate the

popularity of retail video stores than Bob Brown, a kind of modern Renaissance man who is a film-maker, a businessman and a movie lover. Brown runs Video City, one of the Bay Area's largest vidshops, at 4266 Broadway in Oakland, and seven other stores in the East Bay. He is also a widely respected video film distributor (if you're looking for that old cult favorite, NIGHTMARE IN BLOOD, here's your chance to track it down—Brown has it in stock as this very moment). He's also a flying enthusiast and travels all over the world taping major air shows and packaging the action-packed footage as videocassette originals.

While Peter Marino paints a picture upbeat, Bob Brown paints a picture beat up. He has lost some of his initial enthusiasm for the retail video market and told me at press time that "quite frankly" he thinks the videocasette store business is in dire trouble.

Brown cited several businesses that were already belly up, with many more to follow. And, even though the handwriting was on the wall for an already oversaturated business, he pointed out that new stores were still opening every day, owned by people with short life expectancy who hadn't heard the word yet.

And, unlike Randall, he feels there is too much product flooding the retail market. "There's so much material being offered every week that no one dealer can purchase it all, so he goes for the major releases. That's leaving a lot of smaller fish, who were depending on the market, out in the cold."

But that hasn't slowed down Brown any. Right after saying that he left town to cover the air show in Reno, and had plans to release many new original air show cassettes in 1988.

### Video Outperforms Theatrical

Despite Brown's sagacious advice for the novices to go into the paper clip business instead, it is still a fact that the volume of videocassette sales and rentals has now surpassed the total U.S. movie box office gross. In 1986, videos racked in an estimated $4 billion, while little old movie houses only racked in $3.7 in 1985, and theaters were unable to beat that in '86.

In mid-1987, it was reported by Jim Fifield, president of CBS-Fox Video, that sales for the year would probably reach 140 million tapes—77 million in sales and 63 million in rentals. He warned that the massive growth rate of home video had already reached its peak, and forecast that the industry would have to improve its service in the face of rising competition from pay TV.

### Theater Audience Phenomenon

The monetary returns of video have done more than their share of good for the movie business, providing a new life-saving outlet for profits. On the other hand, the video market has done its share to deglamorize and cheapen the experience of going to a theater and seeing a movie with an audience. Nothing will ever improve on that phenomenon. Seeing a movie in an enclosed environment, without interruptions or distractions, is still one of the greatest experiences on this planet. Doesn't it seem a bit deflating and disconcerting that for a dollar or two you can see a multi-million dollar production that costs you five dollars or more to see in a theater? What is a major event with a crowd— often filling one with exhileration—becomes a humdrum happening at home, as commonplace as watching reruns of STAR TREK.

Another negative aspect of the videocassette boom is the declining attendance at repertory cinemas throughout the major cities. San Francisco alone in the past few years has seen the demise of several once-popular theaters. At press time Allen Michaan of Renaissance Rialto Theaters had just surrendered his lease on the York Theater, and the city had paid a memorial tribute to the late Mel Novikoff, who had done so much for repertory cinema through his Surf Theaters chain. The fate of the Castro Theater, the Red Vic and others remained uncertain as 1988 loomed.

### Genre Trends of the 1980s

What's been happening with movies during the past three years? Since that seems to be all we've been living with, we're glad you asked. If anything, the excitement generated in the late 1970s by STAR WARS, CLOSE ENCOUNTERS and ALIEN seemed to begin to die out—to be replaced by too many inferior sequels, especially in the case of the JAWS and SUPERMAN series. The sole happy

DAVID PROWSE (DARTH VADER) WITH STANLEY, CIRCA 1982

change has been the death of the Slasher Genre—the only remnant being Paramount's FRIDAY THE 13TH series.

### *The Lucas Report*

Since going to press in late 1983 with the second edition, we saw one of Hollywood's major forces in film fantasy, George Lucas, take a two-year sabbatical following the release of RETURN OF THE JEDI. A divorce ate away some of his profits (and some of his emotions and energy no doubt) but still he built the wonderful Skywalker Ranch in Marin County, Calif.

"George doesn't have his hand in things like he used to," one informant told me. "I think he got burned out by the 'Star Wars' movies and just didn't know what to do with himself. A lot of good people saw that nothing was happening and left him. Not even the little intimate films he wanted to make a few years ago have materialized." At press time, Lucas was involved in a project entitled ROGER RABBIT, but "it looks precarious," reported the informant, no doubt reminded of the HOWARD THE DUCK fiasco of '86.

Lucas has produced nothing of significance since INDIANA JONES AND THE TEMPLE OF DOOM, a film that has dated very quickly since its release in 1984. HOWARD THE DUCK and LABYRINTH proved to be real low-water marks in his career—although two TV movies starring the Ewok creatures were fair-to-good under the supervision of Industrial Light and Magic genius Tom Smith.

By late 1987, there was still no date set for the return of the STAR WARS saga—the wait, it seems, will be a long one.

**STANLEY CONSOLES MONSTERS ON NIGHT OF CANCELLATION, 1984**

## Spiel for Spielberg

Steven Spielberg, on the other hand, stopped directing almost entirely after THE TEMPLE OF DOOM and THE COLOR PURPLE to produce a series of films in the traditions for which he is well known, but in no way has he masterminded works of the calibre of CLOSE ENCOUNTERS OF THE THIRD KIND or E.T. One can only hope he finds properties he personally wants to direct and returns to the screen in a new flash of brilliance.

HARRY AND THE HENDERSONS and INNERSPACE are nice films, but they are summer fare one tends to forget rather quickly. (And neither film performed that well in the summer of 1987.) Nor will AN AMERICAN TAIL—despite some fine work by the Don Bluth factory—exactly make animation history. YOUNG SHERLOCK HOLMES was Spielberg's greatest misfire, in which he forgot that some genres shouldn't be tampered with. Not that Holmes is a sacred cow. More to the point, Holmes is a cerebral exercise in ratiocination, and not an excuse for derring-do and special effects to erupt in the Victorian streets of London.

Spielberg's journey into television, **Amazing Stories,** was an eclectic collection of short stories that varied in quality and which could not survive the plague of poor ratings. I think it was a case of premiering at a time when audiences might have been a little weary of the Spielberg touch. I predict, though, that **Amazing Stories** will be revived one day and be greatly appreciated for its fine production values and offbeat stories.

## Wrong Directions

The concept that clout in the fields of writing and acting automatically gives you the talent to succeed in directing movies proved to be questionable. While Leonard Nimoy was an outstanding choice to direct two STAR TREK features in a row, proving he knew his way around a script and a camera, the decision to let Stephen King direct MAXIMUM OVERDRIVE was a crashing debacle. Even the King of Horror admitted he belonged behind a typewriter, and he's rightfully stayed there ever since.

Another fiasco was allowing Anthony Perkins to direct PSYCHO III. How will William Shatner emerge as director of the next STAR TREK movie? One can only assume he will work his tail off to follow in the high standards now established for the series.

Clive Barker, who burst on the literary scene in 1985 with his six volumes of **The Books of Blood,** was so dissatisfied with how producers "ruined" his scripts for TRANSMUTATIONS and RAWHEAD REX that he insisted on directing his next script, HELLRAISER. It proved to be a dark supernatural fantasy, perhaps a bit too morbid and unpleasant, and occasionally taking itself too

CREATURE FEATURES MOVIE GUIDE

seriously, but at least it conveyed Barker's overview of horror. He told me, "I wanted to convey my passion for telling a story subversive and unnerving. Good fantastique should be dangerous, leading us into dreams and night, giving us a map of unexplored territory. A world of tension and fear in which everything goes wrong."

Tobe Hooper proved he could still direct—and direct well— with THE TEXAS CHAINSAW MASSACRE II, a rollicking funny sequel. John Carpenter seemed incapable of anything good after CHRISTINE, if BIG TROUBLE IN LITTLE CHINA was any indication, and even Ridley Scott, inactive for so long after BLADE RUNNER, gave us the overblown, pretentious LEGEND. After a

A CENOBITE IN 'HELLRAISER'

good start with PSYCHO II, Australia's Richard Franklin had trouble marketing LINK and when last heard from was helming the pilot for TV's BEAUTY AND THE BEAST. (And it was a pretty good pilot, too.) One director to watch: Russell Mulcahy, who showed remarkable style in the excellent JAWS imitation, RAZORBACK, and the Sean Connery swashbuckling fantasy, HIGHLANDER.

And let's not ignore Wes Craven, whose NIGHTMARE ON ELM STREET proved to be one of the most popular horror films of the 1980s, even if it was totally bereft of a logical storyline. That very surrealistic quality is what made it so popular with young audiences, who identified with the confusion of the protagonists as they faced a killing entity that leapt from their nightmares alive and cackling.

George Romero remained an anomaly, refusing to work in Hollywood even though he was making films that equalled his contemporaries on Sun-

RUSSELL MULCAHY, DIRECTOR OF 'RAZORBACK' AND 'HIGHLANDER'

set Boulevard. He turned more to production, remaining behind the scenes of his TV series, <u>Tales From the Dark Side,</u> and planning several major Stephen King projects that have yet to materialize. (Romero's DAWN OF THE DEAD was a disappointing conclusion to his NIGHT OF THE LIVING DEAD trilogy, primarily because he forgot to have any fun tearing apart human bodies and having his zombies munch of bones. The shock and the joy were both gone.) There seemed to be a collection of young film makers who were ill-versed in story-telling, but adept at presenting striking visuals which they must have felt substituted for story. Sam Raimi demonstrated this in his EVIL DEAD pictures, where shock was everything, often in a style that bordered on ludicrous self-parody. HOUSE director Steve Miner was another example of this genre of director.

**DIRECTORS NICK CASTLE, JEANNOT SZWARC, FRANCIS FORD COPPOLA**

On the other hand, Ron Howard demonstrated a balance between story and effects, always stressing the former over the latter. He was a welcome blast of fresh air with his work in COCOON and SPLASH. And Terry Gilliam, with BRAZIL, continued to demonstrate his uncanny knack in depicting a Monty Python world where nothing ever works and chaos reigns over the Universe.

### The Special Art of Effects

What was carried to the point of absurd perfection since last we met in these pages was the art of special effects. Rick Baker, Rob Bottin, Stan Winston, Richard Edlund and Phil Tippett all achieved remarkable visual effects, even if at times the movies were lacking in substance or characterizations. Industrial Light and Magic of San Rafael, Calif., continued to excel in providing work for COCOON, the STAR TREK sagas (including the TV series that debutted in the fall of '87, STAR TREK—THE NEXT GENERATION) and countless other genre entries. But the enthusiasm of the '70s was now gone, and to many of its employees it was becoming just another place to work, with the excitement of the old ways being replaced by the less exciting system of computerized effects.

### Paramount Is Tantamount

If any one studio scored big in the scramble for box office dollars earned from cinefantastique in the 1980s it was Paramount and its STAR TREK film series. At press time the four feature films combined had earned almost $350 million; 3.2 million videocassettes had been sold and 145 stations were carrying the brand-new TV series with a new cast. The USS Enterprise had come to the rescue again.

### Rise of an Empire

One of the most ambitious ventures of the 1980s was Charles Band's formation of Empire International Pictures for the express purpose of making science-fiction, horror and fantasy movies. Unfor-

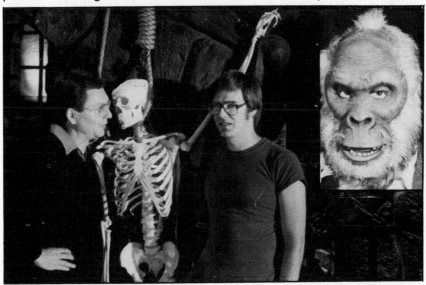

STANLEY WITH EFFECTS GENIUS CHRIS WALAS (HIS CREATION IN INSET)

tunately, Band's attempt to release a couple of B fantasies on a vast nationwide basis (in the style of a major studio) proved disastrous in the early months of 1986. Many of Band's subsequent films saw limited release or went directly to videocassette, proving there was a better market for him there.

The major exception was RE-ANIMATOR, a stylistic gross-out that was comparable to some of the better work of George Romero. Director Stuart Gordon was hailed and revered, although his second film, FROM BEYOND, didn't have the same putrescent pizzazz. John Carl Buechler, a talented special effects man for Band, graduated to director, but his first effort, TROLL, featured too clumsy a script by Ed Naha to be effective. (Naha, incidentally, came up through the ranks writing for Fangora and other professional magazines, and has also fared as a novelist.)

In the fall of '87, Band and his father-composer Albert Band purchased the Dinocitta studio outside Rome, controlling 125 acres of backlot, and luring American producers to its facilities where production costs could be effectively cut.

### Incredible and Strange

The one major offbeat publication of recent years was **Incredibly Strange Creatures,** a collection of interviews with lesser known cult directors such as T. V. Mikels, Herschell Gordon Lewis, Ray Dennis Steckler, Dick Bakalyan, David Friedman, Russ Meyer, Larry Cohen and Joe Sarno.

The book proved so popular that a series of tributes were held in 1987 at the York Theater in San Francisco. Steckler, an eccentric but lovable little guy, was cheered onto the stage and revered for the next three hours by a packed house that hooted with delight at THE THRILL KILLERS and THE INCREDIBLY STRANGE CREATURES WHO STOPPED LIVING AND BECAME MIXED UP ZOMBIES. "A Night of Incredibly Strange Films" even found its way, as an incredibly strange event, onto national cable TV.

Compiled principally by V. Vale, Andrea Juno and Jim Morton, the book can still be ordered from Re/Search, 1529 Grant Avenue, San Francisco CA 94133.

### Corman's Descent

The most important business transaction was the acquisition of New World Pictures by a triumvirate of producers, who bought out Roger Corman and began to turn the business into a much larger enterprise, with tentacles snaking into every area of production: features, TV series and movies, videocassettes.

As a producing force, however, Corman seems to have lost the old spark and financed-distributed a haphazard selection of low budgeters that saw very little theatrical or critical success. STREET-WALKIN and BARBARIAN QUEEN indicated the old pro wasn't trying so hard anymore and living on past glories.

### Brave New World

New World, meanwhile, under a sassy vibrant leadership has become one of Hollywood's driving forces, especially successful in television and videocassette.

Another long-term business thrived under new management: Disney Studios, which for the past decade had floundered with disaster after disaster, emerged with a new division called Touchstone Pictures, which proved with SPLASH that it could compete with the best of them on a level that was satisfying to adults and children.

### *Cannon Fire*

While New World and Disney have learned how to budget and keep their overheads under constant control, Golan-Globus' Cannon Pictures was reportedly teetering on bankruptcy in mid-1987 because of extravagant budgets for losing pictures (including a Sylvester Stallone disaster, OVER THE TOP).

### *Old Genres Never Die*

Despite all these sliding denominators, the truth seems to be that genre movies are still favorites with a majority of viewers and doing handsomely for their makers.

Let's face it: Audiences still love scary stuff. Thunderstorms, creepy corridors, screaming women in negligees, eerie beams of light blasting through windows, heavy breathing on the other side of the threshold . . . The submerged sexual lust in all of us eternally wants to be satisfied—vicariously, of course.

We still love to be reminded that lurking just inside the shadows of darkness are the demons of our worst nightmares. Evil lives and evil makes money and evil pleases us and hurrah for evil. Well, movie evil anyway.

Richard Leskosky, described as "a University of Illinois cinema expert," has remarked that "these movies are a way of seeing our fears dealt with in a manageable way. It has a satisfying effect in the sense we have confronted our worst fears and coped with them. We have seen these horrors and we come out okay."

The horror cycle that began with the Depression "helped [audiences] take their minds off the things outside the cinema that could hurt them." And he predicted, following the Stock Market Crash of October, 1987, that there would be a resurgence in horror movies.

So, with the continuation of scare tactics and evil as prime lures at the box office, the purpose for this book thrives. We know we will be back for a fourth edition in three or four years. Watch the skies for us.

When the screaming starts, we'll be lurking on the periphery, taking notes with our blood-ink pen. And now, before the commercial message, here's a word from our first movie . . .

YOU WILL HAVE A GOOD TIME READING THIS BOOK!

*"Okay, who was playing the piano in the house last night? In the dark. Someone who left wet footprints on the carpet!" —A potential human walking pump in **THE ALLIGATOR PEOPLE**.*

**ABBOTT AND COSTELLO GO TO MARS (1953).** Juvenile science-fiction low-jinks with a misleading title since Venus (inhabited by an Amazonian race) is the destination of the duo of nitwits after they wander aboard a rocketship by accident. Mari Blanchard is the Queen of Venus and Anita Ekberg and Martha Hyer are among her shapely minions. One of the team's lesser efforts, mediocrely directed by Charles Lamont. Robert Paige, Jack Kruschen, Horace McMahon.

**ABBOTT AND COSTELLO MEET DR. JEKYLL AND MR. HYDE (1953).** Frolicking satire with Boris Karloff's bitter half running down London's foggy streets. Robert Louis Stevenson must have rolled over in his literary grave . . . fans will be less offended by liberties taken with the famous tale of dual personality and a formula that brings out the beast in man. Nice support from identity-confused Craig Stevens and Helen Westcott, decent scripting by that split personality writing team John Grant and Leo Loeb, good schizophrenic direction by Charles Lamont. (VC)

**ABBOTT AND COSTELLO MEET FRANKENSTEIN (1948)** First of the spoofs designed for the wild, crazy talents of Bud Abbott and Lou Costello, and certainly their best attempt to kid the cinema's most-adored monsters. Bela Lugosi recreates Dracula, Lon Chaney Jr. is the tormented Larry Talbot (the Wolfman) and Glenn Strange is the hulking Frankenstein Monster. Even Vincent Price's voice gets into the act as The Invisible Man. Madly uninhibited plot concerns Dracula's attempt to transfer Costello's brain into the head of the Monster. It almost fits. Directed by Charles T. Barton with a flair for silly satire. Enlivened by the charms of Lenore Aulbert and Jane Randolph, distressed damsels. (VC)

**ABBOTT AND COSTELLO MEET THE INVISIBLE MAN (1951).** Comedy duo programmer has mildly amusing moments as Arthur Franz dematerializes—along with the plot. A potpourri of prizefighting, gangsters rigging the bouts and the obligatory scientific formula that renders invisibility. "Visibly" diverting if not memorable in the mind's eye. Directed by Charles Lamont with less than a knockout punch despite an able "prelim" cast: Sheldon Leonard, Nancy Guild, Adele Jenkins, William Frawley.

**ABBOTT AND COSTELLO MEET THE KILLER: BORIS KARLOFF (1949).** Satire of old-fashioned murder mysteries, done by the team with the usual turmoil and louting, but it's only distinguishing feature is Boris Karloff as a sinister hypnotist. Directed by Charles T. Barton. Lenore Aubert, Alan Mowbray, Roland Winters.

**ABBOTT AND COSTELLO MEET THE MUMMY (1955).** You'll get gypped in the crypt and you're a dummy for the mummy if you waste time on this abominable slow-man in gauze, who shambles from his Egyptian tomb to chase two dumb desecrators . . . too bad the creep never caught them and wrung their ridiculous necks. The least of the A & C film spoofs . . . Marie Windsor, Michael Ansara, Richard Deacon, Dan Seymour, Kurt Katch and Eddie Parker (as the mummy) cannot resurrect John Grant's tomb-like script. Director Charles Lamont slams home the sarcophagus lid.

**ABBY (1974).** Black exploitation ripoff of THE EXORCIST with Carol Speed sluggishly falling victim to demonic possession with the spirit Eshju. William Marshall (BLACULA) is a bishop fighting evil. Unsuccessful effort by genre director William Girdler.

**ABOMINABLE DOCTOR PHIBES, THE (1971).** Vincent Price in grotesque make-up is at his grotesque best, hamming it up as Dr. Anton Phibes, who employs the Seven Curses of the Pharaohs to avenge his wife's death. Each murder becomes more horrendous, and the morbidity and necrophilia of the nervy ending will have your nerve endings crawling. You'll also laugh yourself to death at the campy elements emphasized so drool-ily by British director Robert Fuest. Phibes is a hideous parody of a man with a skinless face, a speaking tube in his neck and a bad case of acne which doesn't repulse his lovely assistant Vulnavia (Virginia North). Joseph Cotten, Terry-Thomas, Hugh Griffith. The rousing sequel: DR. PHIBES RISES AGAIN. (VC)

**ABOMINABLE SNOWMAN OF THE HIMALAYAS (1957).** Underrated Hammer production, written by Nigel Kneale from his BBC play, THE CREATURE, and suspensefully directed by Val Guest. Peter Cushing and Forrest Tucker lead an expedition in search of the legendary Yeti in the snowy heights of Tibet. The explorers meet terror at the hairy hands of the ancient creatures. An unusual, thought-provoking ending lifts this out of the potboiler category. Maureen Connell, Richard Wattis.

**ABSENT-MINDED PROFESSOR, THE (1960).** Disney fantasy-farce with slapstick for the young and social satire for the old. Fred MacMurray is the bumbling albeit lovable scientist who discovers Flubber, a compound that gives it users strange properties—such as the ability to fly or bound unimpeded across a basketball court. Scenes of a model-T flying across the sky are especially memorable. Bill Walsh based his pleasant screenplay on A SITUATION OF GRAVITY by Samuel Taylor. The wonderful cast includes Nancy Olson as the wife, Keenan Wynn as the villain trying to steal the formula, Ed Wynn, Leon Ames, Edward Andrews, Elliott Reid, Jack Mullaney. Directed by Robert Stevenson. (VC)

**ACCEPTABLE RISKS (1986).** TV-movie set in a chemical plant that is leaking toxic waste into the heavily populated city of Oakbridge. Played as a conspiratorial thriller as the plant manager (Brian Dennehy) tries to keep the leak hush hush and a city manager (Cicely Tyson) closes in on the secret.

**ADAM AND EVE (1958).** When the Garden of Eden dwellers move in this Mexican version of Genesis, there must be frontal foliage, and every motion photographed from a particular (sometimes peculiar) camera angle by writer-producer-director Albert Gout. As the First Man, Carlos Baena wears a flesh-colored G-string and as the First Woman, Christiane Martel (a Miss Universe) wears only eye make-up and long tresses, arranged to tumble "modestly." Or do the tresses sensuously "cascade"? Looks of "dazed innocence" will fool only the dazed and the innocent. Strictly for Peeping Toms and Voyeuristic Vaccilators. Suffers from too much Gout.

**ADDING MACHINE, THE (1969).** Abstract, highly cinematic but ultimately baffling version of Elmer Rice's play, structured as an allegory or a symbolic morality tale under Jerome Epstein's direction. The outre plot has an accountant (about to be replaced by a computer) reexamining life's values, and being propelled into odd environments peopled by even stranger people. The British cast is excellent (Milo O'Shea, Billie Whitelaw, Sydney Chaplin) with Phyllis Diller appearing as a shrill shrew. Enigmatic, but you can't deny it is oddly compelling.

**ADVENTURES OF BUCKAROO BANZAI: ACROSS THE EIGHTH DIMENSION (1984).** An esoteric science-fiction/fantasy adventure, too clever for its own good as it heaps plot on plot without a chance for viewers to absorb it all. Buckaroo (Peter Weller) is a contemporary Doc Savage, an intrepid leader of a team of action specialists, who crashes his nuclear-powered racer through solid matter, causing a disturbance in the Eighth Dimension and releasing aliens to attack Earth. The Oscillation Overthruster is necessary to prevent global destruction, so Buckaroo and his Hong Kong Cavaliers pursue mad scientist Dr. Emilio Lizardo (John Lithgow, in a great campy performance) and the ugly aliens. Although unnecessarily complex, an unfortunate element of the Earl Mac Rauch screenplay, first-time director W. D. Richter does well with the action sequences, but doesn't give enough focus to Buckaroo's team, a colorful band you want to know better. Ellen Barkin, Jeff Goldblum, Christopher Lloyd, Rosalind Cash, Robert Ito, Matt Clark. (VC)

**ADVENTURES OF CAPTAIN MARVEL, THE (1941).** Excellent 12-chapter Republic serial, one of the best cliffhangers of the 1940s with one-time cowboy star Tom Tyler donning the cape of the comic book superhero (the word "Shazam" changes newsboy Billy Batson into this veritable man of steel) to pursue the evil Scorpion, a supervillain designing a matter transference machine for world domination. The action is slam-bang nonstop thank you, and it's great fun, with veteran serial directors William Witney and John England in peak form. Worth seeing in its entirety. Frank Coghlan Jr., Harry Worth, Louise Currie, William Benedict. (VC)

**ADVENTURES OF FREDDIE.** See **MAGNIFICENT MAGICAL MAGNET OF SANTA MESA.**

**ADVENTURES OF MARK TWAIN, THE (1986).** Claymation, an animated process first used in RETURN TO OZ, brings to life Samuel Longhorn Clemens as he, Huck Finn and Tom Sawyer set sail in a balloon that takes them to a rendezvous with Halley's Comet. Twain's voice by James Whitmore. Directed by Will Vinton. (VC)

**ADVENTURES OF THE AMERICAN RABBIT (1986).** Animated feature spinning off from the Superman and Captain Marvel myths. Mild-mannered Rob Rabbit lives in a small town, transforming into American Rabbit when danger is at hand. In this adventure he goes after a pack of jackals on motorcycles. (VC)

**ADVENTURES OF ULTRAMAN, THE (1981).** Repackaged episodes of the famous Japanese kiddie science-fiction series. See **ULTRAMAN.** (VC)

**AERODROME (1983).** Secret British faction takes over the Air Force sometime in the near future. A sinister conspiratorily aura pervades over Giles Foster's direction in this offbeat British TV-movie. Peter Firth, Richard Johnson, Natalie Ogle, Mary Peach, Richad Briers.

**AFTER THE FALL OF NEW YORK (1983).** Italian-French imitation of MAD MAX blending post-holocaust societies with a science-fiction theme. It's weak on effects (the rocketship models are crummy) but it has a touch of plot and strives for some emotion. Nuclear war has destroyed society to create splinter factions at war. A cynical lone-wolf (Michael Sopkiw) is coerced by rebel forces (The Pan-American Federation) to penetrate the ruins of Manhattan where the evil Euraks hold sway, to rescue the only fertile woman on Earth so she can be rocketed to Alpha Centuauri, where mankind intends to start over. Parsifal's comrades are a cyborg with a hook hand and a gray-haired warrior who downs foes with steel balls on a wire. The rubble of the Bronx and rat-infested sewers provide effective settings. The acting is unsophisticated and Martin Dolman's direction conventional, but the film gallops in spite of itself. Michael Sopkin, Valentine Moonier, Roman Geer, George Purdom, George Eastman (as a character who looks like a Caribbean pirate named Big Ape). (VC)

**AFTERMATH (1985).** Astronaut team returns to Earth, dis-

**JOHN LITHGOW IN 'BUCKAROO BANZAI'**

covering mankind has been destroyed by nuclear weapons, and mutants rove the blasted landscape. Written-produced-directed by Steve Barkett, who also stars with Lynne Margulies and Sid Haig. (VC)

**AGENCY (1979).** Conspiracy thriller with mild fantasy overtones involving the use of subliminal hate symbols in TV commercials, produced by a secret government organization to destroy political candidates. Advertising man Lee Majors and an iconoclastic writer (Saul Rubinek, who dies a macabre death in a refrigerator), who work for Robert Mitchum, stumble on the secret. Moderately exciting, good tension. Scripted by Noel Hynd from a Paul Gottlieb novel. Directed in Canada by George Kaczender. Valerie Perrine provides love interest. Alexandra Stewart. (VC)

**AGENT FOR H.A.R.M. (1965).** Third-rate spy crap starring Mark Richman as Adam Chance, an operative of the Human Aetiological Relations Machine assigned to Operation Spore. A scientist has developed a bacteria that when fired from a raygun, penetrates the flesh and devours the body from within, emerging as a hungry fungus among us. Director Gerd Oswald puts sharper focus on the bikini-clad body of Barbara Bouchet than the fungus, and if there's any reason for watching, it's her "body English." Robert Quarry appears in a small role and Wendell Corey is the totally colorless H.A.R.M. assignment chief. Martin Kosleck, Rafael Campos, Carl Esmond and Donna Michelle contribute little to a film which could be H.A.R.M.-ful to your viewing health.

**AIR HAWKS (1936).** Motor-immunizing ray threatens the security of our nation. Bad plotting threatens to damage the brains of movie watchers everywhere. Albert Rogell directed. Ralph Bellamy, Tala Birell, Wiley Post.

**AIRHAWK (1984).** TV clone of BLUE THUNDER depicting the world's deadliest, most sophisticated helicopter, piloted by Jan-Michael Vincent as Stringfellow Hawke, a reclusive cello-playing, ex-Vietnam pilot who takes on assignments for The Firm, a government agency headed by Michael Archangel (Alex Cord). An exciting introduction to the long-running TV series, enhanced by Ernest Borgnine as Dominic Santini, a father figure to Hawke, and Belinda Bauer, an exotic undercover agent posing as a bellydancer in the employ of evil Dr.

## Feat of Clay

**'THE ADVENTURES OF MARK TWAIN'**

Moffett (David Hemmings), a dastard who steals his own helicopter and turns it over to foreign powers. The action scenes are good and the romance between Vincent and Bauer unusually sensuous. Created-produced by Don Bellisario, who birthed MAGNUM PI.

**ALABAMA'S GHOST (1972).** Producer-director Fred Hobbs' descent into ambiguity and esoteric irrelevance as vampires (or facsimiles) chase around California on choppers, pursuing rubbery-necked tourists. Don't expect continuity from this avant garde filmmaker. In fact, you might consider giving up Hobbs' ghost. (VC)

**ALADDIN AND HIS LAMP (1952).** Derring-do and Arabian Nights hokum in which a distressed young man finds a lamp. Guess what's inside, waiting to grant him wishes. John Sands and Patricia Medina should have been called on The Carpet for accepting these shag-gy roles. Directed by Lew Landers, King of the Hollywood lamp scamps. John Dehner, Noreen Nash, Ned Young.

**ALAKAZAM THE GREAT (1961).** Monkey thinks he's smarter than Einstein, but undergoes an object lesson that teaches him even a monkey can be made a monkey of. Japanese animated cartoon dubbed with Occidental voice patterns: Jonathan Winters, Dodie Stevens, Frankie Avalon, Arnold Stang, Sterling Holloway. New score by Les Baxter. Pleasantly diverting, especially for children.

**ALCHEMIST, THE (1983).** Try to follow this: In 1871, Delgado the Alchemist has the hots for raven-haired Lucinda Dooling. Mesmerizing her, he forces her lover (John Ginty, a Virginia glass maker) into fighting for her honor. When she dies accidentally, the warlock curses Ginty and turns him into a tormented man who eats deer. Flash to 1955, when a woman who looks like Lucinda Dooling happens to drive by Ginty's cabin and is ESPed into his lair in the company of a benevolent hitchhiker. Everyone fights for soul possession as demons jump through a portal of Hell, a grandmother is impaled on a spike and a man is torn in half by the time-continuum threshold. With this horribly muddled plot, Charles Band's film is something to watch while twiddling thumbs. Directed by James Amante. (VC)

**ALI BABA GOES TO TOWN (1937).** Eddie Cantor at his funniest in this spoof of the Arabian Nights, complete with flying carpet and tons of non sequiturs. Director David Butler and supporting cast Tony Martin, Roland Young, Gypsy Rose Lee, June Lang and John Carradine also go to town and have a ball.

**ALIAS NICK BEAL (1949).** Offbeat allegorical fantasy (directed with a satanic wit by John Farrow) has a touch of offbeat casting with Ray Milland as a hornless Beelzebub recruiting souls for Hell. His target is an honest politician (Thomas Mitchell) whom he would corrupt prior to the Grand Descent. Jonathan Latimer's script has Frank Capra-like touches, giving this supernatural drama-comedy depth. Audrey Totter employs her own form of seduction. George Macready, Fred Clark, Darryl Hickman, Nestor Paiva.

**ALICE IN WONDERLAND (1933).** A cast indigenous to the 1930s (W.C. Fields, Gary Cooper, Jack Oakie, Richard Arlen, Cary Grant, Charles Ruggles, Baby Leroy, Mae Marsh) populates this expensive Paramount version of Lewis Carroll's fantasyland classic, directed by Norman Z. McLeod and written by Joseph L. Mankiewicz/William Cameron Menzies. Disappointing effort in which the Carroll characters are reduced to costumed Hollywood personalities. Music by Dimitri Tiomkin.

**ALICE IN WONDERLAND (1951).** Full-length Disney feature, a super-deluxe cartoon blending Lewis Carroll's ALICE'S ADVENTURES IN WONDERLAND with THROUGH THE LOOKING GLASS. This reflects the ultimate in Disney's standards. Voices by Kathryn Beaumont, Ed Wynn, Verna Felton, Pat O'Malley, Sterling Holloway, Stan Freberg. (VC)

**ALICE IN WONDERLAND (1951).** Rare adaptation of Lewis Carroll's satirical classic, sparkling blend of live action and stop-motion animation with three-dimensional puppets. Producer-director Lou Bunin found himself in competition with Disney (see above) and unable to find wide-spread distribution. His film languished and died, not enjoying a revival until 1985. Bunin is faithful to Carroll in this curious, stylized, esoteric whimsy crafted by loving hands, which now suffers from outdated techniques, poor sound and color. Carol Marsh is a beautiful blonde Alice, and the opening features live actors (Stephen Murray, Pamela Brown, Felix Aylmer) portraying the British royalty Carroll was satirizing. From there Alice falls into her dream. (VC)

**ALICE IN WONDERLAND (1985).** Would you believe a $14-million TV-movie adaptation of Lewis Carroll by Irwin Allen, Hollywood's Mad Hatter? A journey into a rabbit hole, indeed, as Allen tackles this four-hour musical with updated language

**KARL MALDEN AS THE WALRUS**

and situations. Directed by Harry Harris (of FAME fame), it has enough guest stars to make a March Hare leap into April. How about Sid Caesar as the Gryphon, Roddy McDowall as the aforementioned Hare, Lloyd Bridges as the White Knight, Telly Savalas as the Cheshire Cat, Karl Malden as the Lion, Carol Channing as the White Queen, Jonathan Winters as Humpty Dumpty, and so on. Alice is portrayed by precocious 10-year-old Natalie Gregory.

**ALICE SWEET ALICE (1978).** Grueling suspense with well-developed characters and psychiatric background. A knife-wielding murderer wearing a doll's mask provides the film's engrossing puzzle. The Catholic Church is the dominating motif, with its omnipresent statues of Christ, madonnas and saints, and its themes of pain and suffering, guilt and innocence. Cast of unknowns (Paula Sheppard, Linda Miller, Mildred Clinton) is supported by Lillian Roth and Brooke Shields. Directed by Alfred Sole. (VC)

**ALICE'S ADVENTURES IN WONDERLAND (1972).** British musical based on the Lewis Carroll classic, graced with the presence of Fiona Fullerton, Sir Ralph Richardson, Peter Sellers, Dudley Moore and Flora Robson. Directed and adapted by William Sterling. (VC)

**ALIEN (1979).** Just when you thought it was safe to go back into space, along came this ingenious mixture of Gothic horror and science-fiction, proving the hoariest cliches can still have vitality. It is that rare triumph: a monster movie that retains shock value even after the evil creature is exposed in all its hideous splendor. Credit Swiss designer H. R. Giger for creating the extraterrestrial, ever-changing in its stages of evolution into something larger and deadlier. The story unfolds in the space freighter Nostromo, ordered to set down on an unexplored planet in response to a distress signal. Soon the alien is aboard the ship and tracking the crew members—John Hurt, Tom Skerritt, Ian Holm, Yaphet Kotto,

Harry Dean Stanton, Veronica Cartwright and Sigourney Weaver. Director Ridley Scott loves cat-and-mouse games, alternating false scares with genuine jolts. Dan O'Bannon's screenplay not only touches our sense of wonder but reminds us of our fear of the dark and everything unknown or ugly. A splendid paradox giving us those things we dread most, but love to scream at in the dark. A classic, as is ALIENS. (VC)

**ALIEN CONTAMINATION (1980).** When a freighter is found with its crew turned into grisly gruel and a cargo of pulsating egg-shapes, you know you're dealing with body-snatched filmmakers contaminated by ALIEN. When the egg sacs burst open, they spread their smoky goo, making everyone instantly dead. A conspiracy for world conquest is controlled by a one-eyed Martian glob with a big mouth who hypnotizes humans. The effects in this Italian import are as inferior as the dubbing and the monster will have you laughing, not gagging with revulsion. Director Luigi Cozzi provides an inept charm that makes this mildly fun, especially if you enjoy inane dialogue. Ian McCulloch, Louise Monroe. (VC)

**ALIEN DEAD, THE (1980).** Entities from another world ride to Earth on a meteorite, crashlanding and turning a boatful of kids into raving zombies and other forms of nonsocial creatures. Joining forces to fight them are newsmen Ray Roberts and game warden Mike Bonavia. The work of Fred Olen Ray, who also gave us BIOHAZARD (and indigestion). Buster Crabbe.

**ALIEN ENCOUNTERS (1979).** Writer-director James T. Flocker churned out this empty UFO muddle in semi-documentary fashion, following an investigator in search of a man in black and a floating silver ball allegedly sent to Earth by aliens as part of a probe. Nothing for the mind or the eye. Augie Tribach, Matt Boston.

**ALIEN FACTOR, THE (1979).** Semiprofessional effort by Baltimore filmmaker Don Dohler focuses on a spaceship that crashlands on Earth. Three aliens emerge to terrorize folks around Perry Hill: The Leemoid, a reptilian being that sucks the life force from humans; the Inferbyce, a clawed gooey-looking creature; and the Zagatile, a tall, furry being that looks like it's on stilts. Don Leifert, Tom Griffin. (VC)

**ALIEN LOVER (1975).** TV-movie starring Kate Mulgrew and Pernell Roberts as adults involved with a teenage orphan who makes friends with a being beamed down in a TV signal from another galaxy. Maybe the orphan should have switched channels, if you know what we mean. Directed by Lela Swift. Susan Brown.

**ALIEN ORO, THE (1973).** Episodes from THE STARLOST, a short-lived TV disaster. The setting is the colossal starship Ark, seeking new worlds so its passengers can begin new civilizations. These re-edited episodes deal with Keir Dullea as Devon meeting an alien named Oro, who plans to take over the giant craft. STAR TREK's Walter Koenig portrays Oro. Robin Ward, Gay Rowan, Alexandra Bastedo.

**ALIEN PREY (1983).** Really lousy British science-fiction cheapie, a feeble excuse for torrid, X-rated lesbian scenes between a couple of insufferable bitches living in a country estate. Along comes a humanoid alien that eats chickens, foxes and birds, doesn't know how to swim, and turns into a vampire when he's making love. Shoddy exploitation, with terrible make-up and cliched horror effects. Directed tastelessly by Norman J. Warren. Barry Stokes, Glory Amann, Sally Faulker. (VC)

**ALIEN WARRIOR (1985).** It's "Dirty Harry" from outer space: A humanoid lands on Earth to fight crime. Directed by Ed Hunt. Brett Clark, Pamela Saunders. (VC)

**ALIEN ZONE (1975).** Anthology of four macabre tales told by a ghoulish mortician (Ivor Francis) to John Ericson, an adulterer fleeing an irate husband. Production values are mediocre but the stories a compelling lot: A child-hating woman is terrorized by a gang of youngsters; a killer loves to photograph women he is about to strangle; two rival detectives try to outwit each other; and a Scrooge-minded man is subjected to mental and physical torture. Ericson's fate provides the fifth tale. Made in Oklahoma, ALIEN ZONE is a

**SIGOURNEY WEAVER AS THE YOU-BETTER-BELIEVE-IT RIPLEY IN 'ALIENS'**

diverting novelty, directed by Sharon Miller. In video as **HOUSE OF THE DEAD.**

**ALIENS (1986).** Riveting action-suspense movie, a supreme sequel to Ridley Scott's ALIEN. Writer-director James Cameron, fresh from THE TERMINATOR, concocts a thunderyarn reeking with tension and fear, and structured so tightly that while there is little that's new, it moves at lightning pace, shock on top of shock—Cameron is a master of creating cliffhangers within cliffhangers. Signourey Weaver returns as the resourceful hard-driven Ripley, who is rescued from her space pod 57 years after ALIEN ended and faces a bleak future. Haunted by nightmares of the face-hugger and the belly-busting E.T., she agrees to return to Rhea-M to locate colonists who have suddenly disappeared. Accompanied back to the windswept alien planet by commandoes equipped with futuristic weapons, she must again face the most hideous creatures of all time. Cameron's focus is the battle between the cynical, well-trained commando team and deviously clever alien creatures in the dingy corridors and laboratories of the compound. The humans are only lightly delineated, but some of them come off good, including Michael Biehn, Bill Paxton, Carrie Henn and Jenette Goldstein. Lance Henriksen is the company man with ulterior motives, and William Hope is the synthetic man whom Ripley can never trust. Thrills build on thrills until finally Ripley takes on the Mother Alien and her brood singlehandedly in a sequence that qualifies Weaver as the female Rambo of the 1980s. Like ALIEN, this exploits our worst fears and carries them to an extreme not even Ridley Scott attempted in 1979. All-time classic, brilliantly conceived. (VC)

**ALIENS ARE COMING, THE (1980).** Except for a gigantic mother ship hovering in Earth's atmosphere, this TV-movie features few special effects—or excitement. It's a compen-

dium of science-fiction cliches, from the alien energy forces that take over a human body to glowing green eyes indicating someone is about to be zapped by strange science. Hoover Dam near Las Vegas is the scenic setting to an otherwise routine, predictable invasion plot. One scene shows a shuttlecraft at Vasquez Rocks outside L.A. with a creature saying that in seven years the colony ships will arrive, so the possessive energy forces better adapt quickly. And the story ends on a "the nightmare is just beginning." Gosh, what excitement! Harvey Hart directs listlessly. Tom Mason, Eric Braeden, Caroline McWilliams, John Milford, Max Gail. (VC)

**ALIENS FROM ANOTHER PLANET (1966).** Re-edited episodes of TV's TIME TUNNEL. James Darren and Robert Colbert must find a man in 1547 who has hidden a time bomb in the Time Tunnel Complex; then, the time travelers land in the year 2268 to face aliens from Alpha One. For details, see **TIME TUNNEL, THE.**

**ALIENS FROM SPACESHIP EARTH (1977).** Mixture of documented facts and Hollywood hokum—but which is which? This film asks the burning question: Are we being visited by entities from other planets? Then the question is illustrated by dramatic reenactments of close encounters. Quick, said the alien to the garbage man, take me to your litter. Lynda Day George, Donovan. (VC)

**ALIEN'S RETURN, THE (1980).** A UFO hovers over a desert community, bathing a boy and girl in its eerie light and swirling fog. Years later he's a deputy marshal, she's a satellite research expert who remeet in the town while she's investigating strange emanations from rocks. There's a third subject, a crazed prospector living outside town, responsible for cattle mutilations with his Laser Beam Killer Gun. Better than some of producer-director Greydon Clark's low-budget jobbers, but it still lacks "high tech" clout. Clark directed the script by Jim and Ken Wheat and Curtis Burch with the sense it has relevance, and he's cast it with popular faces: Jan-Michael Vincent (deputy), Cybill Shepherd (research expert), Raymond Burr (Cybill's scientist-father), Vinnie Schiavelli (crazy miner), Neville Brand (sarcastic rancher), Martin Landau (stupid marshal).

**ALISON'S BIRTHDAY (1979).** Australian supernatural flick written-directed by Ian Coughlan with a Down Under cast. It's the old possession-of-the-soul serving, with little icing on the cake. Joanne Samuel, Lou Brown, Bunney Brooke, Margie McCrae, John Bluthal. (VC)

**ALL OF ME (1984).** Absolutely awful Steve Martin supernatural "comedy"—a waste of the wild and crazy guy and of Lili Tomlin. He plays a legal attorney (doubling as a jazz magician at night) sent to draw up the will of a dying millionairess. Lili is the insufferable moneybags who croaks only to have her soul transferred to Martin's body. Now half of him is him, half of him is her. The Phil Alden Robinson screenplay (based on an Ed Davis novel) is vacuous, giving director Carl Reiner nothing to work with.  A waste of Madolyn Smith, Richard Libertini, Dana Elcar, Jason Bernard and Victoria Tennant. (VC)

**ALL THAT MONEY CAN BUY. See DEVIL AND DANIEL WEBSTER, THE.**

**ALLAN QUATERMAIN AND THE LOST CITY OF GOLD (1986).** Richard Chamberlain returns as H. R. Haggard's British adventurer (without a British accent) who treks through dangerous Africa in search of his missing brother in a sequel to KING SOLOMON'S MINES (1986). Quatermain travels in the company of sexy Sharon Stone, native warrior James Earl Jones and cowardly Indian shaman Robert Donner to a shimmering-white metropolis populated by a white race ruled by evil Henry Silva (in an awful fright wig) and Cassandra Peterson (she of Elvira infamy, in a push-up bra). But only the first half of this this has the charm and humor of its predecessor, and as a whole emerges an inferior follow-up. Fantasy elements involve snake monsters that emerge through holes in rocks and some Indiana Jones ripoffs. Otherwise, it's tedious, with Quatermain's dialogue falling flat. Directed by Gary Nelson. (VC)

**ALLEGRO NON TROPPO (1977).** Italian animator Bruno Bozzetto pays homage to Disney's FANTASIA in this cartoon with six vignettes, each illustrated to classical music. A scroungy cat is the hero of Sibelius' "Valse Triste"; a huge Coke bottle figures prominently in Ravel's "Bolero"; and a honeybee housewife wreaks revenge on picnickers in Vivaldi's "Concerto in C." The story of Adam and Eve is recounted to Stravinsky's "Firebird"; a white-bearded satyr can no longer please the nymphs to Debussy's "Prelude to the Afternoon of a Faun" and a fable is the core of Dvorak's "Slavic Dance No. 7." Clever and risque without being offensive. (VC)

**ALLIGATOR (1981).** Tongue-in-cheek spoofery by writer John Sayles (THE HOWLING) sets the skin-tone for this takeoff on giant-monsters-on-the-rampage movies. A 35-foot-long (35 -count'em -35) gator is loose in the sewers and cop Robert Forster is in pursuit—when the monster isn't in pursuit of Forster, jaws slobbering for policeman meat. The creature swims to a theme not unlike John Williams' JAWS and carries away entire bodies (look out, gator hunter Henry Silva, you don't stand a chance). Director Lewis Teague (LADY IN RED, CUJO) takes none of it seriously and spices the sewer walls with such graffiti as "Harry Lime lives!" If you hate the sight of amphibious entities, you might want to take along your Gator Aid. Dean Jagger, Sue Lyon, Angel Tompkins. (VC)

**ALLIGATOR PEOPLE, THE (1959).** Orville Hampton's screenplay is swamped with cliches, but still an entertaining B effort. George Macready is your run-of-the-kill hypo-happy scientist experimenting with serum that results in scaly skin and glutinous gills. Richard Crane and Beverly Garland are the stereotyped hero and heroine who turn the heavies into handbags and walking pumps.  Bruce Bennett and Lon Chaney Jr. lend authority to the eerie proceedings. Directed by Roy Del Ruth with a feeling for a swampland horror tale.

**ALMOST HUMAN. See SHOCK WAVES.**

**ALONE IN THE DARK (1982).** Three whacko mental cases (Jack Palance, Martin Landau, Erland Van Lidth) escape the asylum of doctor Donald Pleasence, who is frequently as fruitcake as his patients. The homicidal threesome surrounds the house of an assistant psychiatrist and terrorizes his family. The headshrinker finally resorts to violence to save his loved ones. The bloodbath is totally gratuitous, and there are moments when writer-director Jack Sholder doesn't adequately explain events. The most depraved scene has Palance under a young woman's bed, thrusting upward with a knife through the mattress, the point of the blade emerging between her thighs. A real mixed bag of genres. (VC)

**ALPHA INCIDENT, THE (1978).** A living micro-organism from Mars, brought to Earth on a space probe, terrorizes a motley bunch at a rural railroad office. The folks bicker and talk and bicker more, while back at the lab scientists seek an antidote. There's nonsense about not being able to fall asleep (for it is then the microbe takes full control and destroys the body) so the characters stay awake by playing poker and having sex. Ralph Meeker is totally wasted as a dim-witted depot manager, and his death scene provides the only effect—his head turning into a puddle of gooey jello. Produced-directed by Bill Rebane, this low-budget made in Wisconsin was hardly an incident. An alpha mess with Stafford Morgan, John Alderman, John Goff, Carol Irene Newel. (VC)

**ALPHAVILLE (1965).** Director Jean-Luc Godard also wrote this science-fiction film set in the near future in which private eye Lemmy Caution (Eddie Constatine) is assigned to rescue a doctor from a city controlled by a computerized brain, Alpha 60, and its creator, Dr. Von Braun (Howard Vernon). Artistic European mixture of film noir, science vs. intellect, and romance and mythology, constantly vacillating between art film and detective actioner. Anna Karina, Akim Tamiroff, Christa Lang. (VC)

**ALTERED STATES (1980).** Science-fiction metamorphosis picture given distinguished treatment by Warner Bros. and ballyhooed for its prestigious director (Ken Russell) and screenwriter (Paddy Chayefsky)—but in reality it's the same old mad-scientist story, redressed with special effects razzle dazzle and modern-day submersion tank techniques. Genetic investigator William Hurt climbs into a deepwater think tank and regresses to a primeval state, turning into a very hairy ape. Yes, it's a glorified Jekyll-Hyde plot as our friendly doctor runs around looking like an extra from QUEST FOR FIRE. Some of the special effects by Dick Smith, Chuck Gaspar and others are state of the art and there's a real freak-out sequence at the end but the whole thing is primordial—it was done oh so long ago.  Blair Brown, Bob Balaban, Charles Haid, Miguel Godreau, Drew Barrymore. (VC)

**AMAZING CAPTAIN NEMO, THE (1978).** Absurd, empty-headed TV-movie from producer Irwin Allen. In this pilot for a short-lived series, two naval officers find the **Nautilus** abandoned on the ocean floor, with Captain Nemo (Jose Ferrer) preserved in a cryogenic chamber. Nemo leaps out and, forgetting he's just slept for 100 years, pursues a sub commanded by the evil Burgess Meredith, who threatens to destroy Washington with a missile if he isn't paid a ransom. Meredith orders his men to "kill, kill, kill," and is surrounded by robot creatures who call humans "aliens." Chase after chase with force fields, radiation-contaminated waters, laser zap guns, underwater swimming, falling debris, etc. Robert Bloch, capable of better, obviously wrote this to Allen's Neanderthal specifications. Wasted are Lynda Day George, Mel Ferrer, Horst Buchholz, Warren Stevens, Tom Hallick. Directed perfunctorily by Alex March.

**AMAZING COLOSSAL MAN, THE (1957).** Co-writers Bert I. Gordon and Mark Hanna explore the mental anguish undergone by Army colonel Glenn Langan, growing ten feet a day after being exposed to a plutonium explosion. For one thing, his sex life has gone all to hell, to the disappointment of Cathy Downs. Instead of staying on this compelling track, director Gordon opts for a rampage of destruction and shoddy effects as the colonel stomps across Las Vegas to face military forces at Hoover Dam. Good score by Albert Glasser. Camp classic of minimal importance. William Hudson.

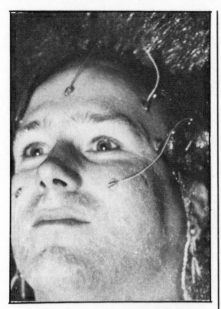

**WILLIAM HURT IN 'ALTERED STATES'**

**AMAZING DR. G, THE (1965).** Less-than-hysterical spoof on James Bond by Italian director G. Simonelli. Archcriminal Goldginger (clever, those Italians) plans to turn government personnel into automatons, unaware most government personnel are already automatons. Yes, a clerk is a jerk. Franco Franchi, as the debonair slick Mr. B, is on his P's and Q's and fit to a T. Strictly Z.

**AMAZING MR. BLUNDEN, THE (1972).** Old gentleman (Lionel Jeffries) from the past turns up in the present via the Wheel of Time, and manipulates the lives of two children to alter a tragic incident of 100 years ago. Hence, a supernatural tale with paradoxes of time travel and touches of the fairy tale blended with the traditional Victorian ghost story. Based on Antonia Barber's THE GHOSTS, it was cleverly written-directed by Jeffries. Superb British film—from the period sets and costuming to the cast: Laurence Naismith, Lynne Frederick, Garry Miller, Rosalyn Landor, Diana Dors. (VC)

**AMAZING MR. X, THE.** See SPIRITUALIST, THE.

**AMAZING SPIDERMAN, THE (1977).** Fans of the Marvel comic book should not be disappointed with this pilot episode of the TV series for which Stan Lee acted as script consultant. Production values are strong, the acting is good and the effects nice—especially in depicting the wall-climbing crimefighter who has been bitten by a radioactive spider and can change himself into an "amazing" individual. Directed by E. W. Swackhamer. Nicholas Hammond, Thayer David, David White, Michael Pataki. Several episodes have been edited and re-released as: CON CAPER/CURSE OF RAVA; ESCORT TO DANGER/NIGHT OF THE CLONES; PHOTO FINISH/MATTER OF STATE; WOLFPACK/THE KIRKWOOD HAUNTING. Many are in videocassette.

**AMAZING TRANSPARENT MAN, THE (1960).** The plot by Jack Lewis is also transparent, the dialogue is vaporous, the acting is invisible and the direction imperceptible in this pellucid piece of nothingness. Douglas Kennedy as a bank robber, Marguerite Chapman as the obligatory skirt and James Griffith as the insidious inventor (planning to create an invisible army of zombies) have every reason to blush unseen as they play shootemup games before the whole thing vanishes into thin air. You'll see through director Edgar G. Ulmer.

**AMAZING TRANSPLANT, THE (1970).** Sexual organ transplant gives its donor a hard time because the stiff-minded recepient now has memories of the former owner's perversions. At least that's how director Louis Silverman translates Dawn Whitman's bizarre script. Transplant yourself to another channel to avoid this limp medical science-fiction hogwash that goes flaccid and never reaches an exciting climax. Juan Fernandez, Linda Southern, Larry Hunter, Kim Pope. (VC)

**AMAZING WORLD OF GHOSTS (1978).** Phoniest documentary ever—Sidney Paul's voice drones on endlessly about "evils hiding in the dark" and "things that go bump in the night" and "ghosts on the threshold of our world," but without any evidence. Not even the visuals are interesting, consisting mainly of a boy walking through a lonely plaza, and famous statues in museums. My, how Mr. Paul does prattle on. What an amazing world of tedium and ineptitude producer-director Wheeler Dixon has materialized.

**AMAZING WORLD OF PSYCHIC PHENOMENA (1976).** The usual ESP topics are covered in this pseudodocumentary enhanced by narrator Raymond Burr and the reports of Uri Geller, who is alleged to bend spoons with his psychic powers, and fortune teller Jeane Dixon. The work of writer-director Robert Guenette. (VC)

**AMAZONS (1984).** Secret cult of statuesque, bust-heavy women warriors plans to take over the world by killing important politicians, but the plot is exposed by a woman doctor and the colossal mammaries milk the action. Madeline Stowe, Jack Scalia, Jennifer Warren, Stella Stevens, Tamara Dobson. Directed by Paul Michael Glaser.

**AMBUSHERS, THE (1967).** The shapely females might be called "fantastic" by chauvinists, but a flying saucer and its gadgetry are the only real fantastic features in this Matt Helm-Dean Martin abomination (second in the series) played for bad puns, sexual double entendres, leering looks and lecherous repartee by director Henry Levin and scenarist Herbert Baker, spinning off the books by Donald Hamilton. The weapons packed by the lightly-clad starlets aren't very secret, but they provide a sorely needed diversion in their brief costumes, Senta Berger, Beverly Adams and Janice Rule included. The usual Helm boudoir gimmicks: plastic inflatable house, circular bed with adjoining bath, ad nauseam. Martin acts as though he wandered onto the wrong soundstage. The male supports are less fetching but capable: James Gregory, Kurt Kasznar, Albert Salmi. (VC)

**AMERICAN CHRISTMAS CARD, AN (1979).** Henry Winkler, "The Fonz" of TV's HAPPY DAYS, becomes Mr. Scrooge in this contemporary version of Charles Dickens' A CHRISTMAS CAROL, set in New England. David Wayne, Dorian Harewood. Directed by Eric Till.

**AMERICAN NIGHTMARE (1981).** Canadian slasher flick in which a cut-and-ask-questions-later madman is on a murderous rampage in Toronto, destroying prostitutes and other nocturnal wanderers. Meanwhile, a pianist (Lawrence S. Day) searches for his missing sister, who has become a prostitute, and policeman Michael Ironside seeks the razor murderer. Directed by Don McBrearty. Lawrence S. Day, Lora Staley. (VC)

**AMERICAN WEREWOLF IN LONDON, AN (1981).** This film, with THE HOWLING, established new trends in the magic of monster movie effects. Rick Baker demonstrates his brilliance in transforming David Naughton into a hairy creature—not with old-fashioned time lapse techniques but by showing Naughton's body stretching, twisting, expanding and agonizingly popping into its new lycanthropic shape. It's utterly enthralling to watch the transformation—and you know movies can never be the same again. John Landis' scripting and directing are homages to old-fashioned werewolf movies, but he contributes his own tongue-in-cheek comedy through innovative dialogue when a dead friend, Griffin Dunne, keeps returning, in various stages of decomposition, to warn Naughton he will soon suffer the transmutation. A groundbreaking movie to be remembered. Jenny Agutter provides love interest. (VC)

**WELCOME TO THE GATEWAY TO HELL IN THE DIMENSIONLESS 'AMITYVILLE 3-D'**

**AMERICATHON (1978).** Neil Israel, the rascal who brought us TUNNELVISION, is back as director-writer with more satirical fun and games, this time in the 1990s. The First Executive (John Ritter) holds a telethon with Harvey Korman as the Jerry Lewis surrogate. The humor is too sophomoric to register on the Richter Scale and the concept quickly crumbles like a used bar napkin. Production qualities are good and the cast rushes pell mell through the colorful sets, and you'll see Fred Willard, Chief Dan George, Terry McGovern, Meatloaf and Dorothy Stratton. But it's an unsalvagable misfire. (VC)

**AMERIKA (1987).** Seven-part TV-movie, highly controversial when first televised on ABC, rousing the heckles of Russians and Americans. The Soviet Union has bloodlessly conquered our land and martial law holds sway, with many entering Siberian-like labor camps, some consorting with the enemy and others fighting for freedom. At 14 1/2 hours it's a long ordeal requiring some patience and enjoyment of political fantasy. Written-directed by Donald Wrye. Kris Kristofferson, Robert Urich, Sam Neill, Cindy Pickett, Mariel Hemingway.

**AMITYVILLE HORROR, THE (1979).** Jan Anson's best-selling haunted house chiller was allegedly true, documenting the supernatural experiences of a family on Long Island. If true, it's far more frightening than any fiction. This version, with James Brolin and Margot Kidder as husband and wife taking over the haunted residence unwittingly, deviates frequently from the so-called true events, adding to the confusion as to fact or fiction. There are several harrowing moments as the couple experiences ghostly phenomena and a chilling religious subplot involving Catholic priest Rod Steiger, but neither director Stuart Rosenberg nor screenwriter Sandor Stern come close to capturing the sheer terror of Anson's narrative, whether it be true or total fabrication. A good score by Lalo Schifrin and a strong supporting cast (Murray Hamilton, Don Stroud, Val Avery, John Larch) keep the film on a professional course. (VC)

**AMITYVILLE II: THE POSSESSION (1982).** This begins before THE AMITYVILLE HORROR took place, depicting al-

legedly true events about a family that lived in the "spirited" house in 1974 and was subjected to supernatural horrors and demonic possessions. (These events were documented in Hans Holzer's book, MURDER IN AMITYVILLE.) One night the young son is thoroughly possessed by an evil demon and kills his family in cold blood. It is one of the most tasteless exploitation devices ever used in a horror film, no matter how true, and shows just how unfeeling the producers of this U.S.-Mexican production were. The film then slides into sheer idiocy as priest James Olson tries to exorcise the youth after helping him to escape jail. The finale—set in the Amityville house—has absolutely nothing to do with demonology but everything to do with effects and make-up. The performances by Olson, Burt Young, Rutanya Alda, Moses Gunn and Andrew Prine are on a level of hysteria, suggesting director Damiano Damiani should take a lesson in How to Avoid Scenery Chewing 1A. A sickening and degrading film, attributable in part to screenwriter Tommy Lee Wallace. (VC)

**AMITYVILLE III: THE DEMON.** Videocassette title for **AMITYVILLE 3-D.**

**AMITYVILLE 3-D (1983).** Third and weakest entry in the series about an alleged haunted house on Long Island, first popularized in a so-called true story by Jan Anson and kept alive by Hollywood exploitation producers. Unlike its predecessors, this is based on no facts whatsoever and is really a loosely connected series of vignettes. Magazine writer Tony Russell buys the accursed estate, laughing contemptuously at the legends, but soon finding himself sucked into the supernatural netherland. So much for respectable realtors. There are some decent special effects (a corpse that comes to life; a fire-breathing monster from the well in the cellar; and the house going berserk in the final reel) but the film's power is limited by the weak William Wales screenplay and the limpid direction of veteran Richard Fleischer. Tess Harper, Robert Joy, Candy Clark, John Beal. (VC)

**AMONG THE LIVING (1941).** Early PSYCHO-style psychological thriller but without the impact we've come to expect from today's similar films. Of interest to film students for its screenplay (by blacklisted writer Lester Cole and Garrett Ford) and its cast: Albert Dekker (in a dual role as sane and insane twin brothers), Susan Hayward, Harry Carey and Frances Farmer. Stuart Heisler directed.

**AMONG THE LIVING DEAD (1980).** An eerie mansion is the setting for this standard foreign-made shocker in which a beautiful woman, on hand for the reading of the will, faces new horrors in the night. Howard Vernon, Christina von Blanc, Britt Nichols.

**AMPHIBIAN MAN, THE (1960).** Pessimistic Russian production deals with a young man who discovers he has the lungs of a shark and will soon have to sacrifice his landlubberish romance, which makes for a despairing situation. This is sloppily dubbed, and tedious at times, and its message (man shouldn't pamper with the forces of nature) too obvious to provide new food for thought—unless you're hungry for shark. The dark side of SPLASH. Directed by Gennadi Kazansky and Vladimir Chebotaryov. Anastia Vertinskaya stars.

**AMPHIBIOUS MAN, THE.** See **AMPHIBIAN MAN, THE.**

**AMUCK (1978).** Farley Granger and Barbara Bouchet star in this psychoterror malarkey produced-directed by Jurgen Goslar. Granger is a novelist who terrorizes Bouchet, a secretary looking for a lost friend in Venice. Cheap scare tactics. AMUCK is amiss and amess.

**ANATOMIST, THE (1961).** A British resurrection of Burke and Hare of old Edinburgh, where bodysnatching was a necessary evil for anatomical schools to procure cadavers for medical purposes. A true event, hellishly fictionalized for the sake of the macabre. Director Leonard William employs an undercurrent of black wit as Alastair Sim, George Cole and Michael Ripper participate in the scandalous uncoverings of newly interred corpses. Same story was done better as DOCTOR AND THE DEVILS.

**AND MILLIONS WILL DIE (1973).** Australian TV-movie in which E Force, a benevolent band fighting disasters, searches Hong Kong for a time bomb that will release a deadly nerve gas that could wipe out the city. Predictable suspense action moves briskly, but director Leslie H. Martinson does not have a knack for staging realistic action. Richard Basehart and Peter Sumner are loyal operatives racing against time, Leslie Nielsen is a sleazy underworld figure and Susan Strasberg is the demented daughter of a Nazi war criminal who unleases the dastardly plot.

**AND NOW THE SCREAMING STARTS (1973).** Gratuitous Gothic geography in this Amicus film is the House of Fengriffin where atmosphere and acting are heavy-handed, mainly because of a severed hand crawling in the drafty corridors, a legendary curse the tormented characters must endure. Directed by Roy Ward Baker. Peter Cushing, Herbert Lom, Stephanie Beacham, Geoffrey Whitehead. (VC)

**AND SOON THE DARKNESS (1970).** British terror thriller with a minor reputation in which two women bicycle across Europe while a slasher waits in the bushes. Directed by Robert Fuest, who gave us THE ABOMINABLE DR. PHIBES. Screenplay by Terry Nation and Brian Clemens. Pamela Franklin, Michele Dotrice, Sandor Eles, Clare Kelly, John Nettleton.

**AND THEN THERE WERE NONE (1945).** Outstanding "isolated mansion" murder mystery in which victims die one by one as a diabolical killer stalks them. It's from a novel/play by Agatha Christie but director Rene Clair and adapter Dudley Nichols play down the comedy elements to emphasize the claustrophobic, oppressive horror hanging over the doomed characters. The twist ending will come as a real surprise. Louis Hayward, June Duprez, Walter Huston, Barry Fitzgerald, Roland Young. (VC)

**ANDROID (1982).** Better-than-average science-fiction adventure, exploring fascinating concepts about man's relationships with robots. Klaus Kinski, bordering on the psychosis of Dr. Frankenstein, lives on a far-flung space station with Max 404, an android assistant played by Don Opper, who co-wrote the script with James Reigle. The doctor is creating a beautiful blonde android to keep Max company. Conflict erupts when three convicts escape from a prison in space and hide on the station. Directed by Aaron Lipstadt, onetime assistant to Roger Corman. Brie Howard, Nobert Weisser. (VC)

**ANDROMEDA STRAIN, THE (1971).** Robert Wise's adaptation of Michael Crichton's best-seller is a science-fiction thriller brilliantly designed, well-acted and -plotted in the style of an exciting detective story. A deadly bacterium brought to Earth by a U.S. satellite destroys a desert community (except for an old man and newborn baby). The survivors are isolated in a secret underground research center where Arthur Hill, Kate Reid, James Olson and Paula Kelly attempt to unravel the mystery behind the bacterium. Although the climax is contrived, the film is brilliant in all technical departments. Scripted by Nelson Gidding. (VC)

**ANDY WARHOL'S DRACULA.** See **BLOOD FOR DRACULA.**

**ANDY WARHOL'S FRANKENSTEIN (1974).** Bloodletting, excessive violence, necrophilia and gore murders. A sickening exercise in black humor . . . You'll need a strong stomach, and an even stronger sense of curiosity, to sit through this low point in cinema. Paul Morrissey directed (and co-wrote the awful screenplay with Tonino Guerra), Carlo Rambaldi handled the gore effects. Joe Dallesandro, Monique Van Vooren, Carla Mancini. (VC)

**ANGEL COMES TO BROOKLYN, THE (1945).** Charles Kemper is a harp player from Actor's Heaven who slumstrums to Earth to help humans. Does he provide relief for starving children in Europe? Does he help millions of homeless in worntorn nations? Nope, benevolent old Kemper helps a Broadway producer put on a show so a struggling actress will have a job. Chalk it up to World War II escapism. Directed by Leslie Goodwins.

**ANGEL FOR SATAN, AN (1960).** Low-budget Italian chiller, of interest to fans of Barbara Steele, the Queen of the Bs during the 1960s. In 1860, a statue of a woman—recovered from a lake— is linked to strange events of 200 years ago. And then a series of murders disrupts the villagers. Beware an evil spirit with hypnotic powers. Directed by Camillo Mastrocinque. Anthony Steffen, Ursula Davis, Claudio Gora.

**ANGEL HEART (1987).** One of the strangest private eye stories ever made in the film noir tradition, eventually seguing into a startling supernatural thriller. Director Alan Parker has a bleak vision of this dark tale, giving it ambience, atmosphere and symbolism of an intriguing nature. In 1955, Mickey Rourke is private eye Harry Angel, hired by Mr. Cyphere (Robert De Niro) to find a singer (Johnny Fortune) missing since 1943. The trail leads Angel to New Orleans and voodoo rites, and it's littered with corpses as Angel gets closer and closer to the occult answer to the mystery. Clever viewers will spot the surprise ending in advance, but it's still a staggering viewing experience with a nihilstic view of life that will leave you stunned. A classic of a new kind. Lisa Bonet (of the Cosby TV show) engages in a heavy R-rated sex scene with Rourke. Charlotte Rampling.

**ANGEL LEVINE, THE (1970).** Black Jewish angel Harry Belafonte is about to have his wings "clipped" when Heaven gives him one more chance: to create a miracle on Earth by helping an aging tailor and his dying wife. But the tailor refuses to believe, and the miracle won't take. Heavy-winged satire directed by Jan Kadar. Belafonte co-produced. Zero Mostel, Ida Kaminska, Milo O'Shea, Eli Wallach, Anne Jackson.

**ANGEL OF H.E.A.T.—THE PROTECTORS: BOOK #1 (1982).** There's a green door and Marilyn Chambers goes behind it in this spy spoof. What Marilyn finds isn't an orgy of excitement—it's stupid mad scientist Dan Jesse with a sound-frequency device that shatters metal, and a gang of horny androids. This nutty professor, plotting to steal microchips programmed with high-security data, is too daffy to make for an interesting villain and the film fails as soft-core exploitation, having too little sex and nudity. And as spy excitement, it lacks clever gimmicks and gadgets. Marilyn may

### THE AMAZING SPIDERMAN

be well-suited (or un-suited?) for X-rated fare, but as sexy spy Angel Harmony (leader of Harmony's Elite Assault Team) she and her shapely body do little for forward thrust. Her associates include Mary Woronov, but even her lesbian role adds nothing. The best thing in this film, produced-directed by Myrl A. Schreibman (CLONUS HORROR), is Lake Tahoe scenery. If you can't stand H.E.A.T., get out of the kitsch. (VC)

**ANGEL ON EARTH (1961).** West German import has racing star Jean-Paul Belmondo contemplating suicide before the next race, so Romy Schneider is sent on celestial wings to save him from the Devil's hairpin. Designed largely for laughs by director Geza von Radvanyi, but fantasy fans may find this too ethereal—like trying to put a piece of cloud in your hip pocket.

**ANGEL ON MY SHOULDER (1946).** Deliciously wonderful supernatural comedy starring Claude Rains as a devious Devil who arranges for a deceased gangster (Paul Muni) to return to Earth to pose as a well-respected judge. The H. Segall-Roland Kibbee script is witty and Archie Mayo directs with a fine blend of melodrama and tongue-in-cheek. Anne Baxter, Onslow Stevens, Jonathan Hale, Fritz Leiber, Lee Shumway. (VC)

**ANGEL ON MY SHOULDER (1980).** Superb TV-movie remake of the 1946 fantasy-comedy that, in some ways, works better than the original since a looser moral code doesn't straitjacket the writers. Peter Strauss as a wisecracking gangster carries off his role with gusto and insight. He portrays a "framed" crook who's been sent to the chair. Next stop: Hell, where he weaves a deal with the Devil to return to Earth and take over the body of a district attorney fighting crime. The idea is to get revenge and to set up the DA for a political fall. It's delightful to watch Strauss undergo subtle character changes and pull a double-cross on old Satan (nicely underplayed by Richard Kiley) and make a few passes at Barbara Hershey. Directed by John Berry. Janis Paige, Scott Colomby, Murray Matheson.

**ANGEL ON THE AMAZON (1948).** Vera Ralston—Czech skating champion who became Republic's mis-leading lady in the 1940s—plays a jungle goddess who wrestles with a black leopard and is so frightened she becomes immune to worry—hence she doesn't age a day. Lawrence Kimble's screenplay is a compendium of potted jungle cliches and director John Auer seems uninspired by eternal youth. Just reading the script must have aged him. George Brent, Brian Aherne, Constance Bennett, Richard Crane, Walter Reed.

**ANGEL WHO PAWNED HER HARP, THE (1956).** British fantasy with Diane Cilento as a winged entity who visits our green planet to perform good deeds—but she meets with disillusionment when faced with demoralizing conditions of the human race. A quaint bit of cloudy fluff, directed by Alan Bromly. Felix Aylmer, Sheila Sweet.

**ANGELS IN THE OUTFIELD (1951).** A miracle occurs during a ball game when an orphan sees angels hovering above a bottom-of-the-league team. Even more miraculous is the change of heart this creates in the foul-mouthed manager (Paul Douglas imitating Leo Durocher). Producer-director Clarence Brown walks a fine baseline between piousness and comedy and Dorothy Kingsley and George Wells score a hit with their screenplay. And Janet Leigh homers as an omnipresent newspaperwoman. What a powerhouse line-up: Keenan Wynn, Lewis Stone, Spring Byington, Bruce Bennett, King Donovan, even Bing Crosby in a cameo.

**ANGRY RED PLANET, THE (1960).** Low-budget space thriller strains to be different but the effects crew only gets hernias for the effort. Four astronauts (Gerald Mohr, Les Tremayne, Jack Kruschen, Nora Hayden) land on an expressionistic Martian landscape. They encounter a giant spider-bat and assorted globular entities, but none of these goofy E.T.s are convincing. The script by director Ib Melchior and Sidney Pink evokes unintended chuckles. This was called a "Cinemagic Film"—referring to a special tinting for the Martian sequences that consisted of orange cellophane over the lens. Stanley Cortez's cinematography is far superior to the material. (VC)

**ANIMAL FARM (1955).** Louis de Rochemont full-length cartoon bringing to life the brutal satire of George Orwell's novelette which satirized the Communist threat of the 1940s. Downtrodden barnyard beasts (voiced by Maurice Denholm and other Britons) take over the homestead from a Dostoyevskian farmer led by a boar hog, Napoleon. Strong message film conceived by producers-directors John Halas and Joy Batchelor—even so, Orwell's ending has been watered down and substituted with an uplifting climax. (VC)

**ANIMAL WORLD (1956).** Irwin Allen semidocumentary of the creature kingdom digressing into speculative anthropology with effects footage by Willis O'Brien and Ray Harryhausen of dinosaurs and other prehistoric monsters. Otherwise, a standard compilation of animal footage taken all over the world.

**ANNA TO THE INFINITE POWER (1982).** Unusually sensitive film based on a book by Mildred Ames depicts a telekinetic teenager and her involvement with spies. An oblique narrative that intrigues throughout. Produced-directed by Robert Wiemer. Martha Bryne, Dina Merrill, Mark Patton, Jack Gilford, Donna Mitchell. (VC)

**ANNIHILATOR, THE (1986).** Obvious ripoff of THE TERMINATOR, even to the point the main villains in this TV-movie have radar-vision, mechanical heads beneath their faces, and glowing red eyes to indicate they're about to attack. They're "Dynamatars"—strange creatures plotting to take over our world. Newspaperman Mark Lindsay Chapman is the only man who knows the secret and he's trying to save a list of victims, never sure if seemingly ordinary humans will turn into the human-machine monsters. Despite the cliches, this has a driving intensity and a sense of style. Geoffrey Lewis is especially good as a robot-man who goes haywire. Directed by Michael Chapman.

**ANTICHRISTO (1974).** See **TEMPTER, THE.** (But we bet you won't be tempted.)

**ANTS.** Videocassette version of IT HAPPENED AT LAKE WOOD MANOR. Great if you're planning to take your VCR on a picnic.

**APACHE DRUMS (1951).** This seemingly conventional Western was the last effort of producer Val Lewton, admired for his features stressing unseen horrors and subtle suspense. One can see why Lewton was intrigued with Harry Brown's story: When bloodthirsty Apaches raid the desert town of Spanish Boot, citizens and soldiers seek refuge in a church with high windows through which attacking redmen leap into the ranks of helpless women and children. Recommended for its taut sequences and all-around suspense.

Directed by Hugo Fregonese. Stephen McNally, Coleen Gray, Willard Parker, James Best, Arthur Shields, James Griffith.

**APARTMENT ON THE THIRTEENTH FLOOR (1972).** Here's a fun-loving premise: Slaughterhouse worker Vincent Parra carries his work home at night, continuing to hack and hew with people instead of animals. Then, taking a tip from Sweeney Todd, he stuffs the parts into a meat grinder. My, isn't this a pleasant book. Directed by Eloy de la Iglesia, produced by Joe Truchado.

**A\*P\*E (1976).** Jack H. Harris release of a U.S.-Korean production in which a 36-foot-high relative of K\*I\*N\*G K\*O\*N\*G is discovered on a Pacific island, captured, lost and then stalked by pursuers to Korea, where the hairy one wreaks revenge. Not very O\*R\*I\*G\*I\*N\*A\*L, is it? Directed and co-produced by P\*a\*u\*l L\*e\*d\*e\*r. Rod Arrants, Joanne De Verona, Alex Nicol.

**APE, THE (1940).** Moronic Monogram mess, a waste of Boris Karloff even though the Englishman gallantly attempts to bring the Curt Siodmak-Richard Carroll material up from the primeval muck of creation. Karloff portrays a misunderstood doctor developing a spinal fluid to cure paralysis. His heart is in the right place to help cure the sick, but his twisted methods (running across the countryside in an ape costume to extract fluid from less desirable humans) lead to his, and the film's, demise. Directed by William Nigh. Maris Wrixon, Henry Hall, George Cleveland, Gertrude Hoffman. (VC)

**APE MAN, THE (1943).** Sad example of what destroyed Bela Lugosi's career after DRACULA. This inexpensive Monogram monstrosity depicts Lugosi mutating into a hairy beast—it shouldn't happen to a gorilla. Wallace Beery, Henry Hall, Louise Currie and Emil Van Horn (as the ape) are wasted under William Beaudine's inept direction. Early Sam Katzman-produced cheapie. (VC)

**APE WOMAN, THE (1964).** Confidence artist discovers a woman with a hairy body and exploits her as a carnival freak. This Italian fantasy, directed by Marco Ferreri, was so depressing and bleak, it was re-edited for U.S. consumption with a more gentle denouement. Ugo Tognazzi, Annie Girardot, Achille Majeroni.

**APOLOGY (1986).** Taut, well-contrived psychothriller for TV in which a killer of homosexual men stalks a young Manhattan artist (Lesley Ann Warren) who has an "apology" answering service for those who want to get their sins off their chests. Hitchcockian in story structure, this unfolds intriguingly with cop Peter Weller following up the clues. Directed by Frank Bierson. Good suspense.

**APPLE, THE (1980).** Borrowing from PRIVILEGE, this too is a futuristic parable about a rock 'n roll star manipulated by fascistic "acid rock" forces. At its core it is an intriguing idea, set in 1994 at the Worldvision Song Contest. The evil Buggallow (all satanic symbolism) signs a young singer to a contract over her boyfriend's objections. She is seduced into perversion, while he seeks solace with hippies left over from the '60s. Ultimately, good intentions are destroyed by the piousness of producer-director Menahem Golan, who spews out an ending in which a man in a white suit comes to Earth in a 1960s automobile and takes good souls back to Heaven. The Biblical analogy is too obvious to work. Grace Kennedy, Catherine Mary Stewart, George Gilmour, Allan Love. THE APPLE shouldn't be picked.

**APPOINTMENT WITH FEAR (1985).** Nuthouse resident becomes the reincarnated spirit of Egyptian god Attis, who specializes in sacrificing kids for the harvest dieties. After he murders his wife, he goes after his son, who is in the care of high school kids. Minor film; disappointment with fear. Directed by Ramzi Thomas. Michele Little, Michael Wyle, Kerry Remous, Doug Rowe.

**APRIL FOOL'S DAY (1985).** Imitative, uninspired slasher sickie, too derivative to hold any surprises. Simon Scuddamore is the brunt of his class on April First—only the joke backfires and poor Simon gets acid in his face. Years later, at a class reunion at old Doddsville County High, Simon's classmates are knocked off via knife attack, poison, electrocution, gentle things like that. The only survivor, Caroline Munro, is pursued by the killer in his Court Jester's outfit. This took three directors and writers to mess up: George Dugdale, Mark Ezra, Peter Litten. Carmine Iannoccone, Donna Yeager, Gary Martin.

**APRIL FOOL'S DAY (1986).** Frank Mancuso Jr., producer of the FRIDAY THE 13TH series, attempts a variation on the slasher flick by placing prank-oriented teenagers in a deserted island mansion where they meet violent demises. Because of a pending surprise twist, the murders cannot be graphically depicted, with director Fred Walton preferring to treat his story as a poor man's TEN LITTLE INDIANS. Genre fans will find this tedious going, with a payoff that may not please everyone/anyone. The joke's on you. Jay Baker, Pat Barlow, Lloyd Berry, Griffin O'Neal. (VC)

**AQUARIAN, THE (1972).** Richard Todd learns the art of leaving his body and elevating himself to a new astral plane, where he formulates a plan to earn the world's greatest fortune. Joan Collins, Jan Murray, Franco Nero.

**AQUARIANS, THE (1970).** When nerve gas is discovered leaking from a sunken ship, scientists fear the ocean could be poisoned so underwater divers splash down to patch up the holes. Better they should have patched up plot holes in the Leslie Stevens-Winston Miller teleplay. This Ivan Tors TV-movie features a futuristic apparatus called Deep Lab. Ricardo Montalban, Jose Ferrer, Leslie Nielsen, Chris Robinson. Underwater footage by Ricou Browning, who played The Black Lagoon creature. Score by Lalo Schifrin.

**ARABIAN ADVENTURE (1979).** Pallid kiddie matinee material which fails to capture the movie magic of THE THIEF OF BAGDAD. Director Kevin Connor needs a sturdier Flying Carpet than Brian Hayles' screenplay. Christopher Lee as the evil Alquazar, ruler of the jeweled city of Jaddur, chews up the Arabian sets as Milo O'Shea (who is as exciting as counting grains of sand in a wizard's hourglass) battles conjurer's tricks, palace guards and other Allah-be-praised wonders for the bejeweled hand of Emma Samms. From the same team that made those Doug McClure fantasy-adventures in the 1970s, so production standards are decent. Mickey Rooney (as a comedy relief inventor), Peter Cushing, Capucine, Oliver Tobias.

**ARCHER: FUGITIVE FROM THE EMPIRE (1981).** Sword-and-sorcery TV-movie with little out of the ordinary for the genre, just decent fare. A bow-and-arrow warrior, capable of a few touches of legerdemain, confronts a sorceress named Estra and some sinuous snake people. Written-produced-

**BORIS KARLOFF IN 'THE APE'**

directed by Nicholas Corea. Lane Caudell, Belinda Bauer, Victor Campos, George Kennedy, Kabir Bedi, Richard Dix. (VC)

**ARE WE ALONE IN THE UNIVERSE? (1978).** "Factual" reports (hah!) on the possibility of alien life forms coming to Earth and fooling around with the forces of nature and man, but one wonders if producer-director George Gale isn't just out to make a fast buck. The narrator of this pseudo-documentary is Hugh Douglas. Superlonely.

**ARIES COMPUTER, THE (1972).** Earth is overpopulated by 2013, so Vincent Price and Andrew Keir devise a diabolical method to cut down on the massive numbers of people with the help of an equally diabolical computer. Assaf Dayan, Stephanie Beacham.

**ARIZONA RIPPER.** Alternate TV title for **BRIDGE ACROSS TIME.**

**ARK OF THE SUN GOD, THE (1986).** Italian-Turkish ripoff of RAIDERS OF THE LOST ARK (as its title subtly suggests) in which safecracker Rick Spear (David Warbeck) is assigned to Istanbul (and that's a lot of bull, Istan) to recover a jeweled scepter once belonging to Gilgamesh and now reposing in the Temple of the Sun God. Similar to director Anthony Dawson's HUNTERS OF THE GOLDEN COBRA. John Steiner, Susie Sudlow.

**ARNOLD (1973).** Contemporary Grand Guignol spoof in which curvaceous Stella Stevens marries a corpse, but a necrophilous nut she's not—she simply wants to inherit a wad of delicious money. The corpse, Arnold, hails from a family of kooks, nuts, perverts, misfits and other everyday people who are murdered as though Dr. Phibes insidiously lurked in the old mansion. This whacky horror comedy, directed by George Fenady, has its moments of macabre humor and graphic bloodletting. Elsa Lanchester, Roddy Mc-Dowall, Farley Granger, Victor Buono, Patric Knowles, John McGiver. (VC)

**AROUND THE WORLD UNDER THE SEA (1966).** Shirley Eaton (the GOLDFINGER girl) looks great in a bathing suit, but there is precious little else to entice your weary eyeballs in this silly underwater adventure. Not even a giant moray eel, a colossal submarine-bathysphere called the hydronaut, ocean earthquakes and other Ivan Tors-style seafaring nonsense. Andrew Marton directs. Lloyd Bridges, Brian Kelly, David McCallum, Keenan Wynn, Marshall Thompson, Gary Merrill. (VC)

**ARREST BULLDOG DRUMMOND (1938).** Undistinguished entry in Paramount's Bulldog Drummond series, in which an Incredible Ammunition Detonating Machine (aka A Death Ray) is activated. John Howard blandly assumes the stiff-upper-lip-and-all-that British agent role. George Zucco, H.B. Warner, Heather Angel, Reginald Denny, E. E. Clive. James Hogan directed.

**ASPHYX, THE (1972).** An ambience of morbidity hangs over this British supernatural terrorizer, creating a queasiness about death singularly fascinating in the hands of director Peter Newbrook. Scientist Robert Stephens discovers that within each person is a soul (or spirit) called for at the moment of death by a being from another dimension called the Asphyx. Using a special beam-control device, Stephens captures an Asphyx coming to claim his own soul; hence, this develops into a thoughtful, atmospheric tale of immortality. The themes dealt with in Brian Comport's script are thoroughly intriguing, and there's a shock twist ending. Effectively photographed by Freddie Young. Robert Powell, Alex Scott, Fiona Walker, Jane Lapotaire. On videocassette as **ASPHYX** and **SPIRIT OF THE DEAD.**

**ASSASSIN (1986).** Clone of THE TERMINATOR, of no particular distinction; a typically hackneyed TV-movie. A humanoid robot (Richard Young) is designed to be the perfect killer, but something goes ker-spung and the robot goes on a killing spree. Retired agent Robert Conrad is coercised into tracking the killer with the scientist (Karen Austin) who designed him. Young, whose face alternates between dead-pan and maniacal glee, plays the role as if in a slasher

movie. Robert Webber is the CIA chief. Written-directed by Sandor Stern.

**ASSAULT (1970).** School for women is under attack from a sex fiend in this pre-slasher-trend British psychoterror flick. Lesley-Anne Down and Suzy Kendall are among the beauties fleeing for their lives. Frank Finlay, Freddie Jones. Also known as TOWER OF TERROR and IN THE DEVIL'S GARDEN. Directed by Sidney Hayers. (VC)

**ASSAULT ON PRECINCT 13 (1976).** John Carpenter pays tribute to NIGHT OF THE LIVING DEAD by depicting a youth gang, a mindless army of kill fanatics, attacking an isolated police station in a small Southern California town without regard for life or limb. The hoodlums show no more emotion than George Romero's walking corpses. The defenders are led by a black policeman and a hard-boiled office employee, who behave in the macho manner of Howard Hawks' characters. Originally this was an obscure film ignored by the critics, but Carpenter's meteoric rise as a director of horror films turned this into a cult favorite. Austin Stoker, Laurie Zimmer. (VC)

**IRATE GENII IN 'ARABIAN ADVENTURE'**

**ASSIGNMENT OUTER SPACE (1962).** A satellite is out of control and Earth is threatened, but Rik Von Nutter is at the controls, ready to sacrifice everything for our safety. Italian flotsam that merely clutters up our satellite signals. Fine tuners beware. Directed by Anthony Dawson. Archie Savage, Alain Dejon, Gabriella Farinon.

**ASSIGNMENT TERROR (1970).** Humanoid aliens from a freezing, dying planet seek to exploit Earthling superstitions as part of an invasion plot. The ridiculous idea, as set forth by writer Jacinto Molina Alvarez (the real name of actor Paul Naschy) and further muddled by producer-director Al Adamson, is to revive the Frankenstein Monster, the Mummy and other popular monsters to terrorize humans. Hey, these freaked-out E.T.'s have seen too many Universal horror movies! Poorly edited and dubbed for the U.S. market—Michael Rennie's real voice wasn't even used. Rennie, assistant Karin Dor and the Werewolf (Naschy) are all that can prevent our destruction. Zounds!

**ASTOUNDING SHE MONSTER, THE (1957).** This brainless movie will astound no one, not even real she-monsters. Frank Hall's non-astonishing script depicts an extraterrestrial femme in a metallic suit whose body has more curves than the Indy 500, and whose mere touch kills (after all, she's surrounded by a force field). The critic who called this "pitiful" was merciful. It didn't do astounding things for the career of

Shirley Kilpatrick (but what a build) or Robert Clarke. The yet-to-astound-us producer-director: Ronnie Ashcroft.

**ASTRO ZOMBIES (1969).** Critics ignored this grade Z abomination when it was released . . . you should be different? Mad scientist Dr. De Marco (John Carradine) is murdering for body organs so he can assemble a new being. Wendell Corey is the government man hot on the trail of the human leftovers. Ted V. Mikels, who went on to THE CORPSE GRINDERS, co-wrote the script with Wayne Rogers, who is still living this down. Rafael Campos, Wally Moon, Joan Patrick. (VC)

**ASTRONAUT, THE (1972).** TV-movie shallow in science-fiction but deep in soap suds depicts the personal problems of a shamster (Monte Markham) who pretends he's an astronaut who went to Mars (the real astronaut died on the Red Planet, but the government has hushed it up). It deals with his marital hang-ups, the cover-up, etc. Directed by Robert M. Lewis. Jackie Cooper, Susan Clark, Robert Lansing, Richard Anderson, John Lupton.

**ASYLUM (1972).** Ripping good Amicus anthology horror film cleverly scripted by Robert Bloch and adroitly directed by Roy Ward Baker. Four terror tales from the Bloch canon ("Frozen Fear," "The Weird Tailor," "Lucy Comes to Stay" and "Mannikins of Horror") are told through patients in an insane asylum. There's even a fifth story (a payoff for the framework itself) with a jolt ending. Superior fare in terms of writing, acting and production values. Britt Ekland, Herbert Lom, Peter Cushing, Patrick Magee, Barbara Parkins, Robert Powell. (VC)

**ASYLUM EROTICA. See SLAUGHTER HOTEL.**

**ASYLUM OF SATAN (1975).** The first feature of William Girdler, and while not an auspicious debut, it did lead him to direct ABBY, DAY OF THE ANIMALS and THE MANITOU before his tragic, untimely death in 1978 while scouting Philippine locations. A Devil worshipper, Dr. Spector, offers a young virgin to Satan; but he fails to double-check the girl's validity—she's no virgin, as several gentlemen will attest. Spector ends up making a spector-cle of himself. Cliched, shopworn film of minimal interest. Charles Kissinger, Nick Jolly, Sherry Stein. (VC)

**ASYLUM OF THE INSANE. See FLESH AND BLOOD SHOW, THE.**

**AT THE EARTH'S CORE (1976).** Second in the Edgar Rice Burroughs adaptations produced in England (thus a sequel to THE LAND THAT TIME FORGOT) and starring Doug Mc-Clure as an adventurer isolated in the lost kingdom of Pellucidar, an underworld non-paradise inhabited by the loathsome Sagoths. The Wing People are dominated by the Sagoths, giving cause for McClure and fellow explorer Peter Cushing to lead an uprising. Special effects consist of mock-up monster models attached to wires or manipulated by stuntmen. Despite the obvious fakery there's a sense of fun to this series. Kevin Connor directed the John Dark screenplay. Cy Grant, Caroline Munro, Keith Barron, Godfrey James. (VC)

**ATLANTIS, THE LOST CONTINENT (1961).** Elaborate George Pal "lost continent" spectacle vacillates between idea-fantasy and sword-and-sandal action with jazzed up Jim Danforth special effects. Daniel Mainwaring's screenplay (from a play by Sir Gerald Hargreaves) focuses on Greek fisherman Anthony Hall rescuing Atlantis princess Joyce Taylor, who takes him by submarine to her underwater kingdom. He learns the Atlantans are planning to use death rays to take over the world and he tries to stop the scheme. Despite its unbalanced blending, this is visually appealing. Pal produced and directed. John Dall, William Smith, Edward Platt, Frank de Kova.

**ATLAS AGAINST THE CYCLOPS (1961).** Italian import showcasing that wonderful one-eyed monstrosity of mythical infamy and the muscles of Mitchell Gordon as the map warrior, Atlas. A sexy babe, Capys (daughter of Circe), shafts Penelope the Queen and forces the "map maker," always a fall guy for a dame with a lot of "freeway" curves, to attack the Cyclops. Not exactly a legendary movie, but it has its share of action-packed grunts and groans, with someone to route for. Directed by Antonio Leonviola. Chelo Alonso, Aldo Padinotti.

**ATLAS AGAINST THE CZAR. See SAMSON VS. THE GIANT KING.**

**ATLAS IN THE LAND OF THE CYCLOPS. See ATLAS AGAINST THE CYCLOPS.**

**ATOM AGE VAMPIRE (1960).** Torpid, inept Italo-French horror film, only of interest to fans of cinematographer Mario Bava, who became an important European horror director. Otherwise, a bloody bore, shoddily directed by Anton Guilo Masano. A once-beautiful, now-scarred entertainer is restored to her former loveliness by a mad scientist (he lovingly specializes in Hiroshima bomb victims) who pumps the blood of other women into her veins. The film could have also used an injection, thank you. Alberto Lupo, Susanne Loret, Roberto Berta.

**ATOM MAN VS. SUPERMAN (1950).** Condensation of Sam Katzman's 15-chapter Columbia serial starring Kirk Alyn as the Man of Steel, and directed by the King of the Cliffhangers, Spencer Bennet. Now-dated superhero stuff still has its charm as Clark Kent/Superman squares off against archvillain Lex Luthor, who uses Kryptonite to disable The Big Fella. Noel Neill, Tommy Bond and Jack Ingram aid in this sequel to Columbia's 1948 serial, SUPERMAN, which also starred Alyn.

**ATOMIC AGENT (1959).** Americanized re-editing of a French melodrama dealing with ruthless spies in pursuit of a new kind of atomic motor that could revolutionize rocketry. Martine Carol, Felix Marten. Directed by Henri Decoin. Unrevolutionary.

**ATOMIC BRAIN, THE (1964).** Also known as MONSTROSITY, a fitting description for this familiar mad-scientist melodrama in which the evil doctor transplants human brains from cranium to cranium. Low I.Q.s result for everyone. Directed brainlessly by Joseph Mascelli. Erika Peters, Judy Bamber, Frank Gerstle.

**ATOMIC KID, THE (1954).** Designed by producer Mickey Rooney as a vehicle for himself, this contains a heap of cheap laughs as he is exposed to an atomic blast and becomes radioactive, tangling with foreign spies while glowing in the dark. Yock yock yock. A good supporting cast—Robert Strauss, Whit Bissell, Joey Forman, Bill Goodwin, Hal March—can't raise the radium count. Directed by Leslie Martinson; based on a Blake Edwards story.

**ATOMIC MAN, THE (1956).** Adaptation of Charles Eric Maine's THE ISOTOPE MAN, scripted by Maine, emerges a British thriller ticking like a Geiger counter. Exposed to radiation, scientist Gene Nelson is out of synchronization with time, reacting to events before they happen. That gives him a decided edge over things to come. Ken Hughes directed. Faith Domergue, Donald Gray, Peter Arne, Vic Perry.

**ATOMIC MONSTER. See MAN MADE MONSTER.**

**ATOMIC ROCKETSHIP. Re-edited first half of the 1936 FLASH GORDON serial.**

**ATOMIC RULERS OF THE WORLD (1964).** Starman, a Japanese superhero from the Emerald planet, flexes his muscles against the evil Meropol Nation to prevent our planet from being blown up by atomic bombs. This English version of SUPER GIANTS 3 and SUPER GIANTS 4 is strictly for moppets, with action so vigorously silly in its execution, it has to be seen to be disbelieved. You might wish Godzilla were

---

*"Your name is Big Ape, right? I've heard a lot about you down in the sewers." —An uncontaminated survivor of nuclear holocaust in* ***AFTER THE FALL OF NEW YORK.***

**CREATURE FEATURES MOVIE GUIDE**                                    **PAGE 13**

on hand to wipe out the bad **and** good guys. Ken Utsui.

**ATOMIC SUBMARINE, THE (1959).** UFO hidden in the ocean's depths disrupts routine aboard Arthur Franz's submarine. Before long a one-eyed E.T. invader is creating havoc for the crew . . . but not much excitement for viewers. Still, this has so many recognizable B-movie faces, it's worth seeing: Dick Foran, Brett Halsey, Tom Conway, Bob Steele, Sid Melton, Joi Lansing, Jack Mulhall, Victor Varconi. Hence, a nostalgic patin a hangs over this Alex Gordon production. Directed by Spencer Bennet, written by Orville Hampton. (VC)

**ATOR.** See **ATOR THE FIGHTING EAGLE.**

**ATOR THE BLADE MASTER (1984).** Inconsequential sequel to ATOR (even weaker than the first film) with Miles O'Keefe still wearing a blond wig and wielding a sword with less than astounding agility. Sagacious inventor Akronos has harnessed atomic energy ("Geometric Nucleus") so he sends beautiful daughter Lisa Foster to fetch Ator to fight the villainous Zovv (Charles Borromin), an articulate spokesman for evil. Meanwhile, Ator, the daughter Mila and karate-swordsman Thong (Chen Wong) protect a helpless tribe against cutthroat Kung warriors, who worship a serpent god. The only good scene: cuties being fed to the giant snake, and Ator battling the colossal asp. (But which is the biggest asp?) Mediocre swashbuckling, marred by stilted acting and less than artistic directing-writing by David Hills.

**ATOR THE FIGHTING EAGLE (1983).** The dumbest sword-and-sorcery picture imaginable with Miles O'Keefe hopelessly incompetent as a sword wielder in loincloth and flowing blonde wigs. When O'Keefe's virgin bride is abducted by the Spider King on her wedding day, Ator sets out in hot-blooded pursuit, abetted by an outlaw (blonde goddess Sabrina Siani) in a series of laughable adventures in The Cave of the Ancient Ones, The Cavern of Blind Warriors, The Land of the Walking Dead, The Room of the Shadow Warrior, The Temple of the Spider, etc. Written-directed by David Hills. The equally bad sequel: ATOR THE BLADE MASTER. (VC)

**ATRAGON (1964).** Japanese science-fiction in the tradition of Godzilla films, directed by Inoshiro Honda, with special effects by Eiji Tsuburaya. The main prop is a nuclear submarine with the marvelous property of flying through the skies. The story takes on proportions of the Atlanta myth when the sub commander, stalwart Captain Shinguji, defends mankind against the undersea kingdom of Mu, ruled by the Goddess Wenda. All very noisy, so you should stay awake. Tadao Takashima, Kenji Sahara.

**ATTACK FROM SPACE (1964).** Sequel to ATOMIC RULERS OF THE WORLD, consisting of re-edited portions of Japan's SUPER GIANT 5 and SUPER GIANT 6, first produced in 1958. Once again Emerald Planet sends the Oriental man of steel-plated chrome to Earth to prevent the insidious Sapphire Galaxy from taking over our solar system. The kids will cheer for more . . .

**ATTACK OF THE CRAB MONSTERS (1957).** Early Roger

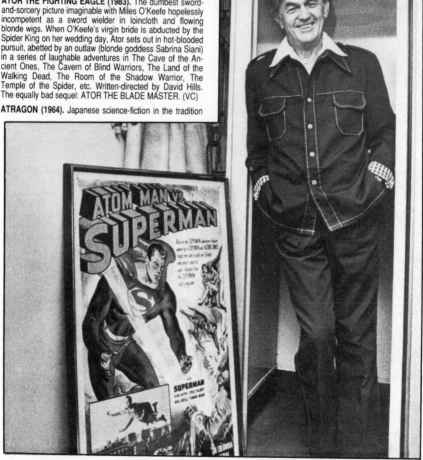

**KIRK ALYN IN PHONE BOOTH TO PROMOTE 'ATOM MAN VS. SUPERMAN'**

Corman exploitationer (he produced and directed), cheap and unconvincing in depicting a band of stranded travelers on a Pacific island inhabited by nuclear-poisoned crustaceans of enormous size. Strictly in the shrimp league, yet by being shoddy and laughable, Corman creates an entertaining framework with Charles Griffith's screenplay. A charming naivete is at work as monsters gobble up characters (some of these scenes are gruesome) and then send out victims' thought patterns to lure the living into a trap. Richard Garland, Pamela Duncan, Russell Johnson, Leslie Bradley. (VC)

**ATTACK OF THE 50-FOOT WOMAN (1958).** Women's Lib should embrace this cheapie as an example of a determined dame rising above the men in her life . . . science-fiction fans will want to push it away. This is so bad it has earned a cult reputation, and should be seen for its incompetent direction (Nathan Hertz Juran), terrible scripting (Mark Hanna) and poverty row effects. An alien crashlanding in the desert detours a woman driver (voluptuous Allison Hayes) and causes her metabolism to accelerate. The well-endowed Ms Hayes (not so well endowed in acting) takes it out on the men in her life, including a jerkola husband. Still, she isn't head and shoulders above the rest of the cast: William Hudson, Yvette Vickers, Roy Gordon, Ken Terrell. (VC)

**ATTACK OF THE GIANT HORNY GORILLA.** See **A\*P\*E.** (But can you stand exposure to H\*O\*R\*N\*Y beasts?)

**ATTACK OF THE GIANT LEECHES (1959).** Producer Gene Corman was barely able to draw money from distributors, let alone audiences, with this anemic excuse for a monster movie, set in the Florida swamps. **You** are the suckeroo, buckaroo, if you bother with this swamp trash scripted by Leo Gordon and directed by Bernard Kowalski. Michael Emmet, Ken Clark, Yvette Vickers.

**ATTACK OF THE KILLER TOMATOES (1979).** Rampaging red-colored monsters of a circular shape attack mankind around San Diego in an intentional spoof of horror movies. It's much talked about by those who haven't seen it, but those who have are less impressed, for its humor tends to wither on the vine. Writer-director John De Bello scores fewer misses than "splats" with his shotgun approach, but some of the giant killer tomatoes, rolling to the attack, are funny—for a while. A curiosity garden piece with its threadbare plot finally getting squished. Love that fruit! This is one Bloody Mary! David Miller, Sharon Taylor, Eric Christmas. (VC)

**ATTACK OF THE MAYAN MUMMY (1963).** Mexican entry in the "Aztec Mummy" series—utter nonsense in which "Bridey Murphy"-style regression into a young girl's past leads scientists to the lost tomb of a Mayan civilization. Guess what moldy character pops out of a sarcophagus. U.S. producer Jerry Warren recut the film for the American market, adding scenes with Richard Webb. It didn't help. Nina Knight, Steve Conte, John Burton.

**ATTACK OF THE MONSTERS (1969).** This has "Made in Japan" stamped all over it. From what other part of the world would you find a film with Gamera the giant turtle battling Guiron to rescue us mere Earthling from brain-eating space beauties from the planet Tera? Directed by Noriaki Yuasa. Nobuhiro Kashima, Chris Murphy.

**ATTACK OF THE MUSHROOM PEOPLE, THE (1963).** Pull up a toadstool and see some Japanese tourists on a luxury yacht washed onto a fog-shrouded island in the Pacific. They decide a fungus is among us when they come face-to-face with monstrous walking incredible edibles. Akiro Kubo heads the all-Oriental cast with that GODZILLA team, director Inoshiro Honda and special effects artist Eiji Tsuburaya picking the mushrooms. Question: What do frogs sit on? Answer: Toad stools.

**ATTACK OF THE PHANTOMS.** See **KISS MEETS THE PHANTOM OF THE PARK.**

**ATTACK OF THE PUPPET PEOPLE (1957).** Producer-director-writer Bert I. Gordon pulls the wires but his marionette melodrama dances short of THE INCREDIBLE SHRINKING MAN. A lonely puppet-master (John Hoyt) miniaturizes John Agar and June Kenny so they are "wee the people," but he only belittles himself in the process. Gordon did his own special effects, but you'll only be left dangling. Nice "strings" by composer Albert Glasser. Scott Peters, Susan Gordon.

**ATTACK OF THE ROBOTS (1967).** French-Spanish production is part of a series that starred Eddie Constantine as Lemmy Caution, an Interpol agent often caught up in science-fictional assignments. In this one he's on the trail of an insidious madman controlling everyone having Type O blood with an army of mechanical monsters. Strictly a computerized programmer with automated acting. Directed by Jesus Franco. Francoise Brion, Fernando Rey.

**ATTACK OF THE SWAMP CREATURE (1975).** Insane doctor kidnaps lovely young women so he can experiment on their bodies to prove man can stay alive underwater. Naturally, he creates a homicidal monster in the process. Written-directed by Arnold Stevens. (VC)

**ATTIC, THE (1980).** In-depth psychodrama with a few Gothic touches (sinister house, electric storms, a corpse in a closet) and a horrific climax in which a repressed Wichita librarian is trapped in her ultimate nightmare. This is more of a character study than a study in horror—a clinical portrait of a sexually deprived spinster forced to care for her sadistic, homicidal father pretending to be a wheelchair cripple. She imagines his death or humiliation in various ways, revealing the psychotic tendencies of an otherwise shy, depressed mind. Writer-director George Edwards is always sensitive to the plight of Carrie Snodgrass, whose performance as the lamentable librarian is intriguing. The intensity of the father (Ray Milland) is another clever stroke in this low-budget effort which is more compelling for its psychological insights into the aberrant mind than for visual shocks. Ruth Cox, Rosemary Murphy. (VC)

**AUDREY ROSE (1977).** Compelling study of reincarnation, superbly directed by Robert Wise but suddenly deteriorating when the issue of life after death is introduced as courtroom melodrama. Anthony Hopkins (as an Englishman who believes his deceased daughter has been reincarnated) is most intense and believable. The other characters wallow in self-pity and unreasoning hysteria. The ending is appropriately shocking and the film states an unusually positive case for believing in reincarnation. Scripted by Frank DeFelitta from his own novel. Marsha Mason, John Beck, Susan Swift, John Hillerman, Norman Lloyd. (VC)

**AURORA ENCOUNTER (1985).** Aliens visit Texas in 1897 in this family-oriented sci-fier, allegedly true. Peter Brown, Jack Elam, Dottie West. Directed by Jim McCullough. (VC)

**AUTOMAN (1984).** Computer expert Desi Arnaz Jr. creates a holograph image that is a halo of glistening blue: Automan, the final imagery in crime fighting, accompanied by Cursor, a flash of light reminiscent of Tinker Bell, and a supercar. It's not a videogame, it's a TV-movie directed by Lee H. Katzin and written (or computerized) by co-producer Glen Larson. Automan, assisted by policeman Robert Lansing and Interpol gal Camilla Sparv, goes into action against Patrick Macnee, kidnapper of the world's best scientists. None of this was compelling enough to become a series.

**AUTOPSY (1974).** An Italian morgue is an eerie place with Ennio Morricone's music swelling on the soundtrack—but don't expect much in the way of visual thrills. This is about as scary as walking through your local horror wax museum blindfolded. Mimsy Farmer portrays a woman working in the morgue, and she's so silly, she deserves every touch of terror thrown at her by writer-director Armando Crispini. (VC)

**AVENGER, THE (1960).** Heads up! Scotland Yard is receiving packages in the mail, each containing a human intelligence from the neck up. A hunchback, wreaking his bent revenge, is responsible for these heinous murders. Can the intrepid inspectors catch him? Heads they win, tales they lose. An Edgar Wallace terror-thriller directed by Karl Anton. Klaus Kinski, Ingrid van Bergen, Heinz Drache, Rainer Brandt.

**AWAKENING, THE (1980).** Expensive adaptation of Bram Stoker's JEWEL OF SEVEN STARS becomes scrambled mumbo jumbo not even an Egypotologist could decipher. Archeologist Charlton Heston uncovers a long-lost tomb of a wicked princess, whose spirit is transmitted into Heston's newborn daughter. Stephanie Zimbalist becomes the possessed girl, but she never really conveys a captured spirit (better days were ahead in TV's REMINGTON STEELE). The Egyptian tomb set is magnificent and Jack Cardiff's desert photography is stunning. But in trying to imitate the gore of THE OMEN, director Mike Newell merely looks like a hack copycat. Susannah York, Jill Townsend. (VC)

**AWESOME LOTUS (1986).** Comedy martial arts actioner starring Loraine Masterson as the title character, a karate killer called out of retirement because silkworms are threatening to put the silk industry out of business. Can she and her associates (a blind karate man and a guy named Tuna who uses his tennis racket as a clobbering device) stop the Federation of Associated Rayon Textiles? Directed by David O'Malley.

**AWFUL DR. ORLOFF, THE (1964).** Another mad doctor, another disfigured beauty, another series of gore murders so the doctor can restore his loved one to her former loveliness. Familiar but graphic Spanish shocker, written and directed by Jesse Franco. This spawned the sequels DR. ORLOFF'S MONSTER, DIABOLICAL DR. Z and ORGIES OF DR. ORLOFF. That Orloff really gets around. Howard Vernon and Perla White.

**AXE (1974).** Originally CALIFORNIA AXE MASSACRE and then LISA, LISA, this was re-released in 1983 to cash in on the slasher-movie craze. It's as low budget as they come, about a gang of cheap, sadistic hoods who terrorize a southern belle and her cripped grandfather. The young woman turns on her assailants and gives 'em what fer, yes indeedie. Written-directed by Frederick R. Friedel, who plays a criminal. Dull.

**AZTEC MUMMY, THE (1957).** Mexican "classic" that started the "Aztec Mummy" films still being talked about in south-of-the-border cantinas among "walking dead movie" aficionados. If ever a film demanded total imbecility and moronic attention spans, here it is, amigos, something to whet your bones on. Rafael Portillo directed this with both eyes closed. Ramon Gay, Rosita Arenas. Sequels were ROBOT VS. THE AZTEC MUMMY, CURSE OF THE AZTEC MUMMY, WRESTLING WOMEN VS. THE AZTEC MUMMY.

**CHARLTON HESTON: CURSED BY A BAD SCRIPT IN 'THE AWAKENING'**

*"I will place a curse of suffering on you that will doom you to a living hell! A hunger, a wild, gnawing animal hunger . . . a hunger for human blood."*
—The titular bloodsucker in **BLACULA**.

**BABA YAGA—THE DEVIL WITCH (1973).** Guido Crepar's cartoon strip inspired this Italian supernatural thriller directed-written by Corrado Farina. Carroll Baker portrays a scheming witch of strange sexual appetites. Evil spells, ample nudity. George Eastman, Ely Galleani.

**BABES IN TOYLAND (1934).** Perennial Laurel-and-Hardy Christmas favorite; a whimsical version of the Victor Herbert-Glenn McDonough operetta set in a kingdom where toys come to life. Only the soldiers are wooden—everything else in Hal Roach's fairy tale production is animated: the clowning of the comedy duo, the charming Frank Butler-Nick Grinde script, the playful direction of Gus Meins and Charles R. Rogers. Marie Wilson toys with her charms. Charlotte Henry, Johnny Downs, Felix Knight.

**BABES IN TOYLAND (1961).** Disney version of the operetta, performed on lavish sets by director Jack Donohue, but without the enduring qualities of the Laurel-Hardy version. Still, a colorful if juvenilistic adaptation with Ray Bolger, Annette Funicello, Tommy Sands, Ed Wynn, Kevin Corcoran and young Ann Jillian sparking the scenery. The Bogeyland sequences are especially good. (VC)

**BABY, THE (1972).** A 21-year-old Mongolian idiot—still wearing diapers and called "Baby" by mother Ruth Roman—is befriended by social worker Anjanette Comer. When it appears Roman and her two sisters are homicidal, Anjanette kidnaps the "infant"—but for reasons that ultimately startle you. Ted Post's direction is first-rate and the screenplay (by co-producer Abe Polsky) is full of twists and turns. Not pablum . . . decidedly grotesque. Marianna Hill, Suzanne Zenor, David Manzy. (VC)

**BABY: SECRET OF THE LOST LEGEND (1985).** Despite a slow start, this Disney pic erupts into an entertaining adventure-fantasy in Africa where paleontologist Sean Young and sports writer-husband William Katt find a mother and father brontosaurus (known to natives as mokele-mobembe) hovering over a newly hatched "baby." Evil anthropologist Patrick McGoohan and African mercenaries tranquilize the mother, kill the father and pursue the infant, who is befriended by the couple. The creatures are remarkably believable, giving the

film an unusual sense of versimilitude. There's a warmth generated for the brontosaurus family, especially by baby. The climactic battle, with mama bronty after McGoohan, is very well executed. Directed on the Ivory Coast by B. W. L. Norton; script by Clifford and Ellen Green. (VC)

**BACCHANTES, THE (1961).** Euripides' Greek play was the basis for this French-Italian slice-of-myth in which the god Dionysus visits Thebes, a city rivaling Athens in its splendour. Ballerina Taina Elg and boisterous, blustering Akim Tamiroff keep this from becoming too stodgy. Giorgio Ferroni directed.

**BACK FROM THE DEAD (1957).** Quickie exploiting the "possessed soul" theme popular during the Bridey Murphy craze, sluggishly directed by Charles Marquis Warren. Catherine Turney's script, based on her novel THE OTHER ONE, never returns from the land of the lifeless. Peggy Castle, Arthur Franz, Marsha Hunt, James Bell.

**BACK TO THE FUTURE (1985).** Delicious Steven Spielberg production, a time travel comedy starring Michael J. Fox as a teenager involved with zany scientist-inventor Christopher Lloyd. Lloyd has designed a sleek sports car equipped with a "Flux Capacitor" capable of time jumping. Circumstances whisk Fox back to his rural hometown in 1955 to cope with the anachronisms of time and place. His main concern is making sure his father and mother fall in love to ensure his own birth. Characters are charming, dialogue crisp and witty. Director Robert Zemeckis (who collaborated on the script with producer Bob Gale) builds to an exciting climax as Fox, with the help of the younger Lloyd, races against "time" to get back to the future, which is our present. This deals wonderfully with the paradoxes of time travel (if Fox brings the time device to the past and shows it to Lloyd, who invented it in the first place?). The filmmakers rely on the cleverness of story and character, using special effects only when needed. Crispin Glover, Claudia Wells, Marc McClure, Lea Thompson. (VC)

**BACK TO THE PLANET OF THE APES (1974).** Pilot episode for TV's short-lived PLANET OF THE APES with Roddy McDowall returning as Galen the Chimpanzee and newcomers Ron Harper and James Naughton as Earthmen trapped in a society of hairy creatures in our distant future.

**JOHN LANDIS SUITED UP FOR 'THE BANANA MONSTER' ('SCHLOCK')**

Highly inferior to the original film series, deservedly lasting only one season. Directors: Don Weis, Arnold Laven. Royal Dano, Biff Elliot, Cindy Eilbacher, Mark Lenard.

**BAD RONALD (1974).** Absorbing psychological TV thriller, directed by Buzz Kulik, in which a youth (Scott Jacoby) commits a murder and is hidden in a secret room by his mother. When she dies, a new family takes up residence, unaware of the hidden boy. Jacoby peeps on the newcomers and ultimately terrorizes them. A curious study of claustrophobic psychosis. Kim Hunter, Pippa Scott, John Larch, Dabney Coleman, Cindy & Lisa Eilbacher. (VC)

**BAD SEED, THE (1956).** Maxwell Anderson's Broadway play, based on a William March novel, sprouts into an even more fascinating film under the green thumb of producer-director Mervyn LeRoy. Nancy Kelly believes her mother was a murderess and that she has genetically transferred homicidal traits to her own 8-year-old daughter (Patty McCormack). Sure enough, the sweet thing is a horrid, deceiving little murderess, a monster in fact. The supporting cast (Eileen Heckart, William Hopper, Paul Fix, Jesse White) adds to the believability of the premise, especially Henry Jones as a dim-witted handyman who's still bright enough to recognize the girl's deceit. Screen adapter John Lee Mahin was forced to tack on a deus ex machine ending demanded by the Hol-

lywood morality code, but otherwise riveting viewing. (VC)

**BAD SEED, THE (1985).** Updated TV-movie version of the Maxwell Anderson play about an amoral, homicidal youngster, Rhoda Penmark, who diabolically murders a schoolmate. Unlike the 1956 version, this is more explicit in depicting how Penmark does in her victims and retains the play's downer ending. The most chilling feature is the implications of genetically inherited sociopathological traits as mother Blair Brown learns the truth of her heritage. Lynn Redgrave and David Ogden Stiers are the neighbors; Richard Kiley is the loving grandfather; Carrie Wells brings off the murderess. David Carradine is outstanding as the handyman. Directed by Paul Wendkos.

**BAFFLED (1972).** The only baffling thing is why Leonard Nimoy, Vera Miles, Susan Hampshire and Rachel Roberts bothered with this unchallenging TV-movie. Nimoy is a race driver who suffers from futuristic visions—and an ESP expert fears the people in his visions are in danger. Most of the story unfolds in a stately English manor. Produced-directed by Philip Leacock. (VC)

**BAIT (1954).** Believe it or not, the Devil (Sir Cedric Hardwicke) is watching this very movie (he must really be torturing himself), providing narration about how man can be seduced by a curvaceous, fleshy female body. A strange low budgeter produced-directed by actor Hugo Haas, who repeatedly displays a fetish for buxom blondes. The demonstrative peroxide bombshell here is Cleo Moore, involved in infidelity and murder. John Agar, Emmett Lynn.

**BAMBOO SAUCER, THE (1967).** After test pilot John Ericson claims he was buzzed by a UFO, he is assigned to parachute into China with a team led by Dan Duryea to locate an alien saucer. The squad works with a Russian team and the cliches are those of the behind-enemy-lines genre as the men bicker over ideologies, Ericson falls for Russian scientist Lois Nettleton and so on. Finally there's a poorly staged shootout with Chinese regulars. Survivors Ericson and Nettleton take the saucer at the speed of light toward Mars. Only the latter minutes, when the saucer zips through space, does this become hardcore science-fiction. A minor message movie from director-writer Frank Telford, with mediocre special effects. Bernard Fox, Vincent Beck, Nan Leslie, Bob Hastings. (VC)

**BANANA MONSTER.** Videocassette title for **SCHLOCK.**

**BANDITS OF CORSICA, THE (1953).** In this version of Alexandre Dumas' CORSICAN BROTHERS, directed by Ray Nazarro, Siamese twins separated at birth retain a metaphysical link—each feels the other's pains and joys. While the 1941 Douglas Fairbanks Jr. version, under the original title, was superior, this remains a decent action costume programmer ably acted by Richard Greene, Paula Richmond, Raymond Burr and Lee Van Cleef.

**BANG BANG KID, THE (1968).** Italian-Spanish cowboy parody clunker, consistently strained when inventor Tom Bosley shows up in the wild town of Limerick to introduce CXA-107, a remote-controlled gunslinger. Most of the gags fall flat as the stupid-looking mechanical shooter makes an oily fool of himself against cow boss Bear Bulloch (Guy Madison). Produced by Sidney Pink, directed by Stanley Praeger. Clank, went the outlaw, slapping hardware. Tom Bosley, Sandra Milo, Dianik Zurakowska. (VC)

**BARBARELLA (1968).** Imaginative adaptation of the French cartoon strip by Jean-Claude Forest with Jane Fonda the wide-eyed innocent in 40,000 A.D. with bulging bosom and an incompetency for sex as she encounters close extraterrestrial adventures of the bizarre kind. Roger Vadim directed with an eye for psychedelic detail and treats matters neither seriously nor inanely, allowing the viewer to indulge in the fun. The set design is wonderfully, incredibly weird; Barbarella is attacked by man-eating Barbie dolls, trapped in the Chamber of Dreams and blows the fuse of the Pleasure Machine. Silly, absurd, funny, outrageous, utterly visual . . . the ridiculousness won't stop. John Philip Law, Milo O'Shea, David Hemmings and Ugo Tognazzi are among the oddly garbed grotesqueries. (VC)

**BAREFOOT EXECUTIVE, THE (1971).** A frightening premise: an innocuous chimpanzee develops the ability to pick hit TV shows. Too bad the networks don't follow the example of this Disney production . . . we might wind up with better programming. Kurt Russell becomes the vice-president of a network, thanks to the chimp. Joe Flynn, Wally Cox, Harry Morgan, John Ritter Alan Hewitt and several Disney regulars populate this mildly diverting entertainment directed by Robert Butler. (VC)

**BARN OF THE NAKED DEAD.** See **TERROR CIRCUS.**

**BARON BLOOD (1972).** Mario Bava directed this Gothic tale about the spirit of Baron Otto von Kleist haunting the halls of the family castle and wreaking vengeance with torture devices. Taut chase sequences, grisly gore effects and eerie photography give Bava's cliched screenplay needed vitality, as do Joseph Cotten (as the Baron) and heavy-breathing Elke Sommer, who does wonders for the low-cut blouse and miniskirt industry. In videocassette as **TORTURE CHAMBER OF BARON BLOOD.**

**BARON OF TERROR.** See **BRAINIAC, THE.**

**BARON'S AFRICAN WAR, THE (1943).** Whittled-down TV version of the Republic serial **MANHUNT IN THE AFRICAN JUNGLE,** which is available in its entirety in a two-cassette version.

**BARRACUDA (THE LUCIFER PROJECT) (1978).** Fish poisoned by mankind's pollution take a human to lunch in the waters off Florida. Munch munch munch with plenty of crunch. Another tale of ecological revenge, but this time there's a subplot involving Dr. Jason Evers, who is experimenting in low blood sugar that could affect the entire town. Wayne David Crawford, the blandest hero ever cast in a horror movie, sets out to solve the mystery. Harry Kerwin directed and co-wrote with Crawford. Comedy relief consists of an obese deputy sheriff. Bert Freed, Roberta Leighton, William Kerwin, Cliff Emmich. (VC)

**BARRY McKENZIE HOLDS HIS OWN (1974).** Madcap, vulgar Australian comedy, in the zippy style of Richard Lester's early work; an olio of satire and jokes aimed at and against Australians by director Bruce Beresford. Barry McKenzie (Barry Crocker) is traveling with Aunt Edna (Barry Humphries in drag) to Paris, when they are mistaken as the Queen of England and her bodyguard by minions of Count Plasma (Donald Pleasence), a Transylvanian nobleman-vampire who wants her kidnapped to improve tourism in the Carpathanian Mountains. Amidst the crude beer, vampire, vomit, toilet and sex jokes are some clever puns and situations. Wild, woolly and nonstop in its assault on your senses (and sensitivities), especially if you are an Aussie. Even the title is a raunchy joke. Roy Kinnear, Dick Bentley, Louis Negan. (VC)

**BASKET CASE (1981).** The Cinema of the Grotesque lives! The wicker basket Kevin Van Hentryck carries into sleazy Times Square contains something that snarls and chomps up McDonald's burgers. It's director Frank Henenlotter homage to monster macabre, full of spattering blood a la Herschell G. Lewis (to whom the film is dedicated) and visually unsettling: "it" is a blob of flesh with monstrous head and gnarly arms . . . a Siamese twin mutant, avenging itself on the flaky doctors who separated him from brother Kevin at birth, and on low-life city trash. This succeeds best with Henenlotter's use of Times Square's derelicts, whores, drug addicts and quack doctors; where it fails is in the acting department. This is not acting—this is hysteria. Make-up and blood effects by Kevin Haney and John Caglione Jr. (VC)

**BAT, THE (1959).** "Old dark house" horror-drama based on the creaky Mary Roberts Rinehart-Avery Hopwood play. Vincent Price is an inspector investigating a caped figure flitting about a weird mansion, The Oaks, inhabited by "batty" dames. Agnes Moorehead, John Sutton and Gavin Good keep the old-fashioned concepts moving under Crane Wilbur's direction. Whodunit of minimal interest.

**BAT PEOPLE, THE (1973).** Low-budget vampire-drama in which John Beck and Marianna MacAndrew suffer from vampire bat bites and undergo transformation. A grisly climax is the only payoff to producer Lou Shaw's screenplay, set in a desert community. Sluggishly directed by Jerry Jameson. Stewart Moss, Michael Pataki, Arthur Space, Paul Carr, Pat Delaney.

**BAT WHISPERS, THE (1930).** Adaptation of THE BAT, the Rinehart-Hopwood play set in a sinister old house, where a caped menace is searching for a hidden room. Roland West's writing-direction are quaintly old-fashioned and if you can accept a dusty antique as a decorative piece, this should fit well on your viewing mantel. Chester Morris, Una Merkel, Chance Ward, Richard Tucker.

**BATMAN (1966).** You loved it as a comic, you loved it as two 15-chapter serials from Columbia, you loved it as a camped-up TV series—now hate it as a feature with Adam West and Burt Ward as the Dynamic Duo fighting four archcriminals (The Catwoman, The Joker, The Penguin and The Riddler) who plan to turn a Dehydration Machine on humans and convert us to dust. Screenwriter Lorenzo Simple Jr. wrote in the same zany tradition of TV series, but his script has little that's funny—maybe he burned out on the better half-hour episodes. Directed by Leslie H. Martinson with as much flair as he could muster. Lee Meriwether, Cesar Romero, Burgess Meredith and Frank Gorshin are the villains. At least Adam

**ADAM WEST AS THE CAPED BATMAN**

West brought respectability to superheroes, paving the way for Superman and others. Stafford Repp, Neil Hamilton. (VC)

**BATMEN OF AFRICA (1936).** Chopped up feature version of Republic's first serial ever, DARKEST AFRICA, with wild animal trainer Clyde Beatty trekking the jungle with Baru the native boy and Baru the ape in search of the lost city of Joba. They're also looking for a missing beauty, the Goddess of Joba, but thwarting them is a tribe of winged warriors and two crooks after a fortune in diamonds. Directed breathlessly by B. Reeves Eason and Joseph Kane, who unfortunately don't work enough with the actors. Looked upon as a dusty antique, however, this has its plus side. Lucien Prival, Edmund Cobb, Elaine Shepard.

**BATTLE BENEATH THE EARTH (1968).** Ridiculous adventure—a British Yellow Horde fantasy about a Chinese scheme to tunnel beneath America with a giant laser gun and invade with swarms of killer Orientals. Thwarting this insidious plot is Sinbad himself, Kerwin Mathews, whose adversary is a Fu Manchu type (Martin Benson). Montgomery Tully directed L. Z. Hargreaves' script with a straight face, playing none of it for its inherent satire and comedy. Vivian Ventura, Robert Ayres, Peter Arne, Bill Nagy. (VC)

**BATTLE BEYOND THE STARS (1980).** Roger Corman's version of STAR WARS is also a space opera remake of SEVEN SAMURAI, with Richard Thomas flying through the Universe seeking mercenaries to help his planet Akirian combat evil warlord John Saxon, who's threatening to blow up everyone with his Stellar Converter. John Sayles' screenplay has a redeeming tongue-in-cheek quality often subservient to the space effects. George Peppard is an amusing cowboy who loves to drink; Robert Vaughn relives his role from MAG-NIFICENT SEVEN as a "gunfighter" haunted by his past; and Sybil Danning is a buxom space jockey whose breasts threaten to pop out of her bra and through the screen. The film's spirit of fun (under Jimmy T. Murakami's direction) should win you. (VC)

**BATTLE BEYOND THE SUN (1963).** Some battle! Two bug-eyed monsters (one an upended pea-pod with a bloodshot eye at the top of its misshapen body, the other a headless toadstool with a jaundiced eye on the tip of its tentacle) clash for about two minutes. The USSR and USA are in a race to reach Mars, so most of this consists of space stations, rockets, satellites, androids and astronauts, without any excitement. Originally a Russian film, then re-edited for the American market by Roger Corman, who added new footage by director Thomas Colchart.

**BATTLE FOR THE PLANET OF THE APES (1974).** Fifth and final entry in Arthur Jacobs' PLANET OF THE APES series—and the least effective. This was relegated to the B category, as witness the decreased production values and a less incisive script. Upstart apes plot to promote a culture that treats men and apes equally, but insurrectionist gorillas thwart this movement with the help of mutant humans. Roddy McDowall is back as Caesar and Claude Akins is the leader of the growlin' dissidents. Director J. Lee Thompson throws it all away in favor of action, but even shootemup can't keep everyone from looking like monkeys. Lew Ayres, Paul Williams, John Huston, France Nuyen, Paul Stevens, Pat Cardi, John Landis. (VC)

**BATTLE IN OUTER SPACE (1960).** Those Godzilla movers, director Inoshiro Honda and special effects artist Eiji Tsuburaya, destroy Venice, New York City and the Golden Gate Bridge just to get warmed up for this super-spectacle in which an alien race tries to destroy our planet, but a counterforce meets the E.T. enemy and proceeds to blast everything in sight. Interplanetary conflagration on a grand scale; mediocre effects. Ryo Ikebe.

**BATTLE OF THE ASTROS.** See **MONSTER ZERO.**

**BATTLE OF THE WORLDS (1961).** Italian director Antonio Margheriti (Anthony Dawson) has the advantage of Claude Rains as a dedicated scientist. Rains keeps the story moving, and lends versimilitude to otherwise pedantic, unexciting proceedings. Rains warns Earth of an approaching meteor—and sure enough, it turns out to be a sphere for a computerized brain system programmed to launch war on Earth. Out go the rockets and "space wars" technology to prevent our destruction. Ultimately it is Dawson's visual style that prevails. Bill Carter, Umberto Orsini, Maya Brent.

**BATTLESTAR GALACTICA (1979).** A 125-minute space adventure re-edited from the three-hour pilot which kicked off the 1978 TV series. It's intergalactic war between the Cylons, a race of robots programmed to destroy mankind, and a ragtag fleet of starships trying to return to Earth after the colonies of the green planet have been attacked and nearly destroyed by the Cylons. John Dykstra, contributor to the STAR WARS effects, has designed ingenious spacecraft, aerial dogfights, massive explosions and alien landscapes and planets. Glen A. Larson's script is derivative of STAR WARS with Richard Hatch and Dirk Benedict emulating Luke Skywalker and Han Solo as the warriors always racing to their battlecruisers. Richard A. Colla began directing but was replaced by an uncredited Alan J. Levi. Lorne Greene, Jane Seymour, Ray Milland, Lew Ayres, Maren Jensen, Wilfrid Hyde-White. (VC)

**BATTLESTAR GALACTICA (TV compilations).** The popular TV series was re-edited and sold into syndication under the same generic title but with each episode having its own sub-

## THE OVION IN 'BATTLESTAR GALACTICA'

title. These include: "Curse of the Cylons," "Experiment in Terror," "Greetings from Earth," "Gun on Ice Planet Zero," "The Living Legend," "Lost Planet of the Gods," "Murder in Space," "Phantom in Space," "Space Casanova," "Space Prison" and "War of the Gods."

**BATTLETRUCK.** See **WARLORDS OF THE 21ST CENTURY.**

**BATWOMAN (1968).** Mexican nonsense as a masked heroine and law enforcement pals battle an evil doctor and his cadre of scaly monsters. Wrecked and wretched, with Rene Cadona misdirecting the tamale traffic and writer Alfred Salazar slinging untasty salsa sauce. Look out for the wickedly athletic Maura Monti.

**BAY OF BLOOD.** Videocassette title of **TWITCH OF THE DEATH NERVE** or **LAST HOUSE ON THE LEFT II.**

**BEACH GIRLS AND THE MONSTER.** See **MONSTER FROM THE SURF.**

**BEAR, THE (1970).** Polish folk lore inspired this fantasy involving a man who is part bear. Beautifully photographed, lyrical in style. Written-directed by Janusz Majewski. Josef Duriasz, Edmund Fetting.

**BEAST, THE.** Videocassette title for **EQUINOX.**

**BEAST FROM HAUNTED CAVE (1960).** Director Monte Hellman dovetails a gangster and monster story (concocted by Charles Griffith) into an unusual melange. A gang of crooks is holing up in a ski resort when a creature in a nearby cave begins a reign of terror. Made in Deadwood, South Dakota. Sheila Carol, Michael Forest, Frank Wolff, Wally Campo. Produced by Gene Corman.

**BEAST FROM 20,000 FATHOMS (1953).** Early colossal-monster-on-a-rampage thriller, enhanced by the effects of Ray Harryhausen, working solo after an apprenticeship with KING KONG creator Willis O'Brien. Although his stop-motion was to undergo refinement, this remains a trend-setting mini-classic, tense and ferocious. The titular entity is a dinosaur freed from its ten-million-year hibernation by an atomic blast at the North Pole. The creature ravages New York City, swallowing one traffic cop whole and attacking a roller coaster. Directed by Eugene Lourie and co-written by Fred Freiberger (STAR TREK's producer in its final season) and Lou Morheim (who would work on THE OUTER LIMITS). Inspired by Ray Bradbury's short short, "The Foghorn." Paul Christian, Paula Raymond, Cecil Kellaway, Kenneth Tobey, Donald Woods, Lee Van Cleef, King Donovan.

**BEAST IN THE CELLAR (1970).** Sleep-inducing, talkative British picture has minimal horror effects and atmosphere.

Yak yak yak between Beryl Reid and Flora Robson and little else. James Kelly wrote-directed this instantly forgettable bore. As for the "beast," it's a scrawny non-brawny. John Hamill, Tessa Wyatt. (VC)

**BEAST MUST DIE, THE (1973).** Assorted characters are invited to the mansion of millionaire Calvin Lockhart, who knows one of them is a werewolf. He has installed electronic lycanthropic-detecting equipment in and around the estate to trap the four-legged attacker. This modern touch is okay but it still boils down to old Wolf Man cliches with a dog dressed to look like a werewolf. Directed by Paul Annett; from a Michael Winder script based on James Blish's novelette, "There Shall Be No Darkness." Peter Cushing, Charles Gray, Anton Diffring. (VC)

**BEAST OF BLOOD (1970).** Filipino-produced sequel to MAD DOCTOR OF BLOOD ISLAND, in which the insidious Dr. Lorca keeps a decapitated creature alive in a serum. Writer-producer-director Eddie Romero needed that formula to inject more life into this listless horror film, as abominable as the dead life forces it depicts. John Ashley, Celeste Yarnall, Eddie Garcia (as Lorca).

**BEAST OF BORNEO (1935).** Mad scientist Dr. Boris Borodoff wants to cut up monkeys to prove a cockeyed theory of evolution, so he ventures to "the green hell" with an expedition headed by a Great White Hero. Orangutans race intelligently through the jungle while the men make monkeys of themselves. Directed by Harry Garson. Eugene Sigaloff, John Preston, Mae Stuart.

**BEAST OF HOLLOW MOUNTAIN (1956).** Willis O'Brien, the major contributor to stop-motion animation with the 1933 KING KONG, utilized Regiscope to animate a cattle-hungry Tyrannosaurus Rex in this U.S./Mexican production made in Mexico by Edward and William Nassour. It's your basic Western but with monster touches, starring Guy Madison as a rancher being forced out by a land baron. Matters pick up with the arrival of Patricia Medina wearing low-cut blouses . . . and finally comes the long-awaited attack by the Rex from his mountain lair, but the beast isn't on screen long enough. Directorial chores were shared by Edward Nassour and Ismael Rodriguez. From an idea by O'Brien. Carlos Rivas, Eduardo Noriega.

**BEAST OF MOROCCO (1966).** Dreary, pain-in-the-neck flick about a hapless chap (William Sylvester) obsessed with a beautiful woman who turns out to be nothing more than your everyday vampiress in charge of a bloodsucking cult. Also known as THE HAND OF NIGHT. Terence De Marney, Diane Clare. Directed by Frederic Goode.

**BEAST OF THE DEAD.** See **BEAST OF BLOOD.**

**BEAST OF THE YELLOW NIGHT (1971).** Filipino-produced film written-directed by Eddie Romero. A man sells his soul to the Devil so he can turn into different creatures at night, including a prowling werewolf. John Ashley, Eddie Garcia, Mary Wilcox. (VC)

**BEAST OF YUCCA FLATS, THE (1961).** Tor Johnson, a brute of a man often seen sneaking up on Bela Lugosi in grade-Z horror jobs, has his sole leading role as a scientist exposed to radiation who goes berserk. Johnson is too typecast, and limited an actor, to bring off the part. The writer-director to blame is Coleman Francis, who resorts to narration to fill in the holes in the feeble plot. Douglas Mellor, Barbara Francis, Tony Cardoza.

**BEAST THAT KILLED WOMEN (1965),** Obscure film, rarely shown. Watch and discover why: Giant gorilla runs wild, this time through a nudist camp. Is nothing sacred in the sunbelt? Blemishes in Barry Mahon's production are as noticeable as those on the extras' behinds; the bad acting is nakedly exposed.

**BEAST WITH A MILLION EYES (1958).** Cheapo science-fiction without much of a beast and surely without a million eyes. Roger Corman is credited as producer, but he disclaims it. Set near Indio, Calif., Tom Filer's screenplay vaguely showcases an obscure extraterrestrial life form that turns beasts against humans. One scene has small birds attacking a station wagon (prophesizing THE BIRDS) but otherwise it's a total dud. Chances are good there are millions of eyes that will never watch Paul Birch, Lorna Thayer and Chester Conklin run around desert country.

**BEAST WITH FIVE FINGERS (1947).** No need to give Warner Bros. the finger: the studio did a remarkably adept job of palming off W. F. Harvey's short story to screenwriter Curt Siodmak, who turned it into a superior piece of psychological horror. The severed hand of a maddened pianist scuttles repulsively to and fro . . . or is Peter Lorre just imagining his old friend has returned from the grave to strangle him? (In some respects, this is similar to Oliver Stone's 1981 THE HAND.) Lorre goes mad as only Lorre can, nailing the ghastly quintet of digits to a board and flinging it into a fire. Give a big hand to director Robert Florey and a round of applause with sweaty palms to Robert Alda, Andrea King, Victor Francen, J. Carroll Naish, Pedro de Cordoba and Charles Dingle.

**BEAST WITHIN, THE (1982).** OMEN producer Harvey Bernhard has fashioned a horror-monster entertainment with outstanding transformation effects by Thomas Burman. Ronny Cox's wife is raped by an unseen slobbering spirit; a son is born possessed by an evil being who takes on new physical shape before launching a homicidal rampage. One of

## MONSTER IN 'THE BEAST WITHIN' AND FILM'S PRODUCER, HARVEY BERNHARD

the film's virtues is the bravura acting by Paul Clemens, who conveys the teenager's demonic pain without makeup in early scenes. There is a dark, moody atmosphere to Philippe Mora's direction that gives this a mild distinction, even if some unnecessarily gory murders do not. Made in the small town of Raymond, Miss. Edward Levy's novel was loosely adapted by Tom Holland, who later wrote PSYCHO II and directed FRIGHT NIGHT. Bibi Besch, Don Gordon, R. G. Armstrong, L. Q. Jones. (VC)

**BEASTMASTER, THE (1982).** Comic-bookish sword-and-sorcery adventure from producer-director Don Coscarelli. Bronzed hero Dar (Marc Singer), searching for the barbarians who slaughtered his village, can telecommunicate with animals and birds and uses an eagle, a panther and two ferrets to carry out his bidding. Some effects are nice, but the plot suffers terribly from weak dialogue and oversimplified situations. Tanya Roberts is merely decorative as a slave girl who bares her breasts briefly in a pool sequence, and Rip Torn is horribly unrestrained as the villain Maax. John Amos shines as Seth, Dar's fighting companion, even though it is a silly role. There's much to be enjoyed, such as the Bird Men, the Zombie Monsters, and a raging night battle, illuminated by fire. (VC)

**BEAUTIFUL WOMEN AND THE HYDROGEN MAN.** See H-MAN, THE.

**BEAUTY AND THE BEAST (1946).** Classic French fantasy, sophisticated yet simplistic, lyrical yet haunting. Jean Cocteau paints a poetic fairy tale in which a father must forfeit his daughter, Beauty, to the Beast. The costuming, sets, and score by Georges Auric are a synthesis of the arts. Jean Marais has a triple role—as the Beast, Prince Charming and Beauty's uninspired suitor. Mila Parely, Nane Germon, Marcel Andre, Michel Auclair. (VC)

**BEAUTY AND THE BEAST (1963).** Commercialized version of the Perrault fairy tale, trivialized into a standard programmer by director Edward L. Cahn. The storyline now has a duke who's been cursed turning into an unattractive creature every night. Eduard Franz, Mark Damon, Joyce Taylor, Michael Pate, Merry Anders.

**BEAUTY AND THE BEAST (1976).** TV adaptation of the Perrault fairy tale starring the husband-wife team of George C. Scott and Trish Van Devere, with supporting roles filled by Bernard Lee (James Bond's M), Virginia McKenna and Patricia Quinn. Directed by Fielder Cook. Scott, who performed his role in a boar's head mask, was nominated for an Emmy.

**BEAUTY AND THE BEAST (1979).** Czech version of the classic allegory, written-directed by Juraj Herz, with Vlastimil Harapes as the ugly creature and Zdena Studenkova as the beauty.

**BEAUTY AND THE ROBOT (1960).** Would you believe Mamie Van Doren has 13 college degrees, speaks 18 languages and is head of a college science department? That isn't the only ingredient that makes this Albert Zugsmith programmer fantastic: It also has a gadget that predicts racetrack results with unerring accuracy, and a chimpanzee that types good English with its feet. Come to think of it, that isn't so fantastic, since it was probably the chimp that typed the screenplay. Originally released as SEX KITTENS GO TO COLLEGE. Well-rounded comedy. Tuesday Weld, Mickey Shaughnessy, Louis Nye, John Carradine, Vampira, Pamela Mason, Harold Lloyd Jr.

**BED SITTING ROOM, THE (1969).** Offbeat British black comedy directed by Richard Lester, based on a play by Spike Milligan and John Antrobus. It's a madman's glimpse at a devastated Great Britain after nuclear holocaust, but the narrative is so shatteringly disjointed, and the characters and situations so outlandish and nonsensical, it is impossible to make any coherency out of the mishmash of detail. It's an unfunny situation to begin with, so what's to laugh at? Rita Tushingham, Ralph Richardson, Peter Cook, Dudley Moore, Spike Milligan, Arthur Lowe.

**BEDAZZLED (1968).** When a cook is about to hang himself because his first love refuses to acknowledge his existence, the Devil grants him seven wishes in exchange for his soul. But the wishes are thwarted by such ugly beasts as infidelity, bigamy, etc. Director Stanley Donen uses the satirical revue, Beyond the Fringe, to fine advantage: Dudley Moore, Eleanor Bron and Peter Cook (the latter also wrote the screenplay which takes effective jabs at society, religion and nunneries). Even Raquel Welch comes off looking good as Lust. You will find it uproarious or offensive—depending on your liberal threshold. (VC)

**BEDFORD INCIDENT, THE (1965).** Well-intended albeit unsuccessful attempt to depict events leading up to an atomic holocaust when the commander of a destroyer (Richard Widmark), under orders from NATO, tracks a Russian submarine in North Atlantic waters, with tension between the sides mounting. It's too heavy-handed under director James B. Harris to work as drama or propaganda, or even as pure suspense. Sidney Poitier portrays a newspaperman tracking the story. James MacArthur, Wally Cox, Martin Balsam, Eric Portman, Donald Sutherland. Written by James Poe from Mark Rascovitch's novel. (VC)

**BEDKNOBS AND BROOMSTICKS (1970).** Delightful Walt Disney comedy intermingling live action with masterful animation. Based on Mary Norton's THE MAGIC BEDKNOB, this is solid entertainment and clever satire in which Angela Lansbury takes a correspondence course in witchcraft just in time to repel invading Germans by bringing to life medieval suits of armor and swords. Imaginatively directed by Robert Stevenson and adapted with the Disney touch by Don Da-Gradi and producer Bill Walsh. David Tomlinson, Roddy McDowall, Sam Jaffe, John Ericson. (VC)

**BEDLAM (1946).** Last of the low-budget horror films produced by Val Lewton for RKO, climaxing a brilliant usage of limited funds and B-players to bring off some of the most literate films in the genre. Mark Robson directed his own screenplay (inspired by Hogarth's painting, "Bedlam") which depicts horrific conditions in the St. Mary of Bethlehem Asylum of London in 1761. Young Anna Lee is incarcerated for meddling in the affairs of the cruel asylum-keeper, Master Sims, devilishly played by Boris Karloff. The costuming and mood of the period are expertly evoked and the supporting cast is superb: Ian Wolfe, Jason Robards Sr., Robert Clarke, Ellen Corby, Billy House. (VC)

**BEES, THE (1978).** If you've seen one swarm, you've seen them all. Yet another "B" thriller movie (written-produced-directed by triple-stinger Alfredo Zacharias) about South American killer bees attacking our hemisphere, with John Saxon, Angel Tompkins and John Carradine out to find and destroy the little sneaks. Expect to break out in hives. (VC)

**BEFORE DAWN (1933).** Edgar Wallace's short story "Death Watch" inspired this "old dark house" tale in which clairvoyant Dorothy Wilson solves a haunted house mystery. Directed by Irving Pichel. Stuart Erwin, Warner Oland, Dudley Digges, Jane Darwell, Frank Reicher.

**BEFORE I HANG (1940).** Better-than-usual low budget Columbia programmer designed for Boris Karloff. As Dr. John Garth, he seeks a serum to fight off aging, even after being sent to prison for a mercy killing. Some fanciful pseudo-science enhances all the double-talk about medicine for the good of mankind, but it finally boils down to Karloff turning into a human monster a la Dr. Frankenstein. Directed by Nick Grinde. Evelyn Keyes, Bruce Bennett, Edward Van Sloan, Don Beddoe, Robert Fiske. (VC)

**BEFORE MIDNIGHT (1933).** Isolated mansion is the scene for yet another mystery in which a man has successfully predicted his own death. Was he clairvoyant or just lucky? Lambert Hillyer directed. Ralph Bellamy, June Collyer, Betty Blythe, Arthur Pierson.

**BEGINNING, THE (1973).** Re-edited footage from the STAR-LOST TV series created (and then disowned) by Harlan Ellison. Keir Dullea and Robin Ward are among the passengers

aboard a huge ship passing through deepest space in search of new worlds. In this adventure set on the Ark, a certain passageway leads to a tribe made up entirely of males. Barry Morse.

**BEGINNING OF THE END (1957).** Atomic radiation has affected the genes of nature, and hopping out of the grass hoppin' mad are the biggest grasshoppers you'll ever see. But the buggy behemoths move as haltingly as the dialogue, so you know you must be watching a Bert I. Gordon epic. You are! Hence, you're watching one of the weakest of the Giant Bug movies of the 1950s. Peter Graves is unconvincing as a young scientist who devises an equally unconvincing supersonic sound-wave device to stop the juggernaut. This does not have legs. Peggie Castle, Morris Ankrum, Richard Benedict.

**BEHEMOTH, THE SEA MONSTER.** See **GIANT BEHEMOTH.**

**BEING, THE (1982).** Blatant ripoff of ALIEN: the titular monster has slavering jowels, gnashing teeth and an ornery disposition, not to mention bad breath. The spawning ground for this one-eyed monstrosity is nuclear waste at a power plant outside Pottsville, Idaho. Pornie film king William Osco turned legit to produce this schlocker, which under the direction of his wife, Jackie Kong (she penned the script), is a boring collection of cliches. Osco co-stars under the name Rexx Coltrane, portraying the gallant hero who rescues Marianne Gordon from ludicrous cliff-hanger situations. Martin Landau, Dorothy Malone, Ruth Buzzi and Jose Ferrer are wasted as townspeople who become fodder for the beast. Also known as EASTER SUNDAY . . . but they changed the title because the only bunnies in this one are dumb. (VC)

**BELA LUGOSI MEETS A BROOKLYN GORILLA (1952).** So awful it's enjoyable watching Bela Lugosi portray a mad doctor on a Pacific island, experimenting with a serum that turns men into gorillas. Tim Ryan's screenplay is, thank God, played for laughs with its main focus on stranded USO entertainers Duke Mitchell and Sammy Petrillo, Dean Martin-Jerry Lewis imitations who parody their counterparts well. Muriel Landers is a native girl in a sarong pursuing Duke, while Sammy is chased by an overweight gal, also in a sarong, through potted jungle sets. William Beaudine, a specialist at directing schlock, knows just how far to go with such drivel. Associate producer was Herman Cohen.

**BELL, BOOK AND CANDLE (1959).** Mixture of the natural and supernatural as witch Kim Novak casts a spell on Jimmy Stewart so he'll give up Janice Rule. The really funny moments are too few in this Columbia version of John Van Druten's stage play, adapted by Daniel Taradash and directed by Richard Quine. The cauldron just doesn't bubble enough to make a substantial witch's brew. Oh, hex! Jack Lemmon, Ernie Kovacs, Hermione Gingold, Elsa Lanchester. (VC)

**BELL FROM HELL (1973).** Offbeat Spanish-French horror film depicting a dementee who plays practical jokes on his aunt and sexy cousins. Surreal visuals include a bee attack and a man walled up alive in an old bell tower. Directed by Claudio Guerin Hill, who died the last day of shooting when he fell from the film's church tower. Viveca Lindfors, Renaud Verley, Alfredo Mayo. (VC)

**BELLS.** TV title for **MURDER BY PHONE.**

**BEN (1972).** Sequel to WILLARD (that money-maker about a disturbed young man who trains rats to do his evil bidding) is cheapjack exploitation, poorly scripted by Gilbert Ralston and routinely directed by Phil Karlsen. Another young man (Lee Harcourt Montgomery) finds the survivors of the first movie and retrains them, hiding his rodents in the city's sewer. Joseph Campanella is in charge of stopping the rats. Arthur O'Connell, Rosemary Murphy, Meredith Baxter, Kenneth Tobey, Norman Alden. (VC)

---

*"We feed on brains. Unfortunately, they don't last very long so we've been reduced to seeking a new world." — Brainless alien invader in*
**BEAST WITH A MILLION EYES.**

**BEN AND ME** (1953). Walt Disney short, frequently repeated on TV, in which a mouse comes to the aide of Benjamin Franklin. Quaint historic comedy, enhanced by the voice of Sterling Holloway.

**BENEATH THE PLANET OF THE APES** (1970). First sequel to PLANET OF THE APES, less than its predecessor but still an exciting actioner. Astronaut James Franciscus, in search of the first lost expedition, is swept up in a time warp too and lands on Earth in the future to find it devastated by atomic war. In an underground city (remnants of New York), he stumbles across humans with telepathic powers. On the surface, meanwhile, the apes, gorillas and orangutans form an attack party. Ample visual surprises, tons of action and a surprise ending. The direction by Ted Post is taut and fast-moving, the screenplay by Paul Dehn is lean and literate, and John Chambers' make-up designs are in the tradition of the origin film. Beneath masks are Kim Hunter, Maurice Evans, Jeff Corey, Thomas Gomez and James Gregory. Among the humans are Linda Harrison (as Nova, speechless native girl), Victor Buono, Tod Andrews, Paul Richards and Charlton Heston, returning as astronaut Taylor. (VC)

**BERKELEY SQUARE** (1933). Time-traveling Leslie Howard (it's never explained, it just happens) finds himself half-a-century in the past, socializing with the elite. This stylish melodrama, based on the John Balderston-John Collins Squire play, has outstanding performances by Howard, Heather Angel, Beryl Mercer, Samuel S. Hinds, Alan Mowbray and Irene Browne, and conveys its warmth without too much sentiment. Credit the direction of Frank Lloyd, the adapting by Sonya Levien and Balderston, and the taste of producer Jesse L. Lasky. Remade in 1951 with Tyrone Power as I'LL NEVER FORGET YOU.

**BERMUDA DEPTHS, THE** (1978). Above-average TV-movie conceived by William Overgard, writer of the STEVE ROPER comic strip. There's a small touch of JAWS and a big touch of MOBY DICK in depicting an expedition searching for a giant sea turtle. Burl Ives is the Ahab obsessed with the capture of the turtle and Connie Sellecca portrays a mysterious brunette swimmer named Jennie Haniver, believed to be the spirit of a young woman who once made a pact with the turtle and is still aqua-maiding 300 years later. The special effects are surprisingly good. Directed by Tom Kotani. Leigh McCloskey, Carl Weathers.

**BERMUDA TRIANGLE, THE** (1978). Oceanwide expanse of nonsense based on Charles Berlitz's two books explaining disappearances in the Atlantic Ocean, with a rambling script by Stephen Lord and unfocused direction by Richard Friedenberg. Berlitz's theories have been derided and debunked in a good PBS documentary, so THE BERMUDA TRIANGLE is strictly for squares. (VC)

**BERMUDA TRIANGLE, THE** (1978). Italian-Mexican programmer cashing in on sensational material about strange disappearances taking place off the Florida coast. Written-directed by Rene Cardona Jr. John Huston, Claudine Auger, Gloria Guida, Marina Vlady.

**BERSERK** (1968). CIRCUS OF HORRORS approach by producer Herman Cohen finds Joan Crawford, in her twilight years, as the dearest owner of a big top plagued by mysterious deaths, most of them occurring in front of audiences: one performer is impaled on bayonets, another has a spike driven into his head and yet another is sawed in half. Despite its Grand Guignol trappings, it's just a glorified whodunit. Ably directed by Jim O'Connolly from a script by Cohen and Aben Kandel. Ty Hardin, Diana Dors, Michael Gough, Judy Geeson. (VC)

**BEST OF SEX AND VIOLENCE, THE** (1981). Schlock film producer-director Charles Band has collected previews of coming attractions from 40 movies released during the 1970s, with John Carradine hosting. These include many horror trailers from such fare as TERMINAL ISLAND, TOURIST TRAP, ZOMBIE, etc. (VC)

**BETWEEN TWO WORLDS** (1944). Sutton Vane's classic play, about a handful of souls sailing on a phantom ship to destiny, is still a fascinating premise in this Mark Hellinger/Warner Bros. version adapted by Daniel Fuchs and directed by Edward A. Blatt. It's been updated to World War II, which adds to the many images and symbols of death important to the theme. John Garfield, Edmund Gwenn, Eleanor Parker, Syndey Greenstreet, Faye Emerson. Music by Erich Wolfgang Korngold.

**BEWARE MY BRETHREN** (1972). Taut British horror thriller in which beautiful women are murdered by a Londoner practicing soul possession. Produced-directed by Robert Hartford-Davis. Patrick Magee, Ann Todd, Suzanna Leigh, Percy Herbert, Tony Beckley, Ronald Allen.

**BEWARE! THE BLOB** (1971). This sequel to THE BLOB, produced by Jack H. Harris and directed by actor Larry Hagman, is a very poor horror film with the Jack Woods-Anthony Harris screenplay trying to play it cute without success. It's just plain stupid, and so are the characters that a decent ensemble is asked to perform: Robert Walker Jr., Richard Webb, Godfrey Cambridge, Carol Lynley, Shelley Berman, Burgess Meredith. Many of these are cameos, in which the performer appears to be immediately consumed by the Blob. Without redeeming social values, and with mediocre special effects, the blob is a slob. On videocassette as SON OF BLOB.

**BEWITCHED** (1945). Radio's Arch Oboler, creator of LIGHTS OUT, wrote-directed this tale of dual personality predating THREE FACES OF EVE. Psychiatrist Edmund Gwenn ferrets out the evil side of Phyllis Thaxter and, through suggestion, tries to destroy the alter ego. Based on an Oboler radio play. Henry M. Daniels Jr., Addison Richards, Will Wright, Oscar O'Shea.

**BEYOND AND BACK** (1978). Sunn-International documentary about people who die, then return from the grave. These "survivors" recount their supernormal experiences, describing sensations and the sights one beholds when stepping across the threshold. People were dying to see it.

**BEYOND ATLANTIS** (1975). Surprisingly good fantasy-adventure with excellent underwater photography. Add to that shapely Leigh Christian and this comes up an unexpected winner. Adventurers John Ashley and Patrick Wayne track Atlantean pearls to a native-inhabited island. Eddie Romero's direction is good and the Charles Johnson script features a neat twist of fate. George Nader looks a bit silly as a native chief, but what counts here is the two-fisted action spirit. Eddie Garcia, Vic Diaz. (VC)

**BEYOND BELIEF** (1976). Trudging pseudodocumentary gives us a "glimpse" at faith healers, ESP and reincarnation, with Uri Geller bending his silver spoons again. BEYOND BELIEF is beyond relief. (VC)

**BEYOND EVIL** (1980). When Lynda Day George takes possession of a centuries-old house on an isolated Pacific island, she's possessed by the spirit of the previous owner, who needs her for sacrificial ceremonies to the Devil. Director Herb Freed, who co-wrote the script with Paul Ross, puts Lynda, John Saxon, Michael Dante and David Opatoshu through standard paces. (VC)

**BEYOND TERROR** (1980). Spanish horror entry, written-directed by Tomas Aznar, in which the spirits of the dead rise from their resting places and put the whammy on young hoodlums. F. S. Grajera, Raquel Ramirez.

**BEYOND THE BERMUDA TRIANGLE** (1976). TV-movie exploits the hysteria surrounding the Devil's Triangle theory but in a low-key, subtle fashion, thanks to the tasteful telescript by Charles McDaniel and the sensitive direction of William A. Graham. Fred MacMurray, after losing his fiancee off the coast of Florida, begins an obsessive search in strange waters. There's a melancholy gentleness about his remorse that only MacMurray can pull off without seeming sentimental. The ending is maudlin, but it works. Sam Groom, Donna Mills, Suzanne Reed, Dana Plato.

**BEYOND THE DARKNESS (1974).** West German exploitationer combines elements of ROSEMARY'S BABY with THE EXORCIST to come up with a weak tale about a busty fraulein who has sex with a demon; and then the monstrous events begin. Strictly for dummkopfs. Directed by Michael Walter. Dagmar Hedrich, Werner Bruhns.

**BEYOND THE DOOR (1975).** An Italian imitation of THE EXORCIST, set in San Francisco, in which Juliet Mills has a baby in her tummy tum-tum capable of opening/closing doors, knocking crockery off shelves and turning mama into a bitch witch who spits up greenish vomit. How this bratty beastie got into her womb only the Devil would know, if you get our drift. There's nice photography of Sausalito and the Golden Gate Bridge, but then there's long, dull stretches of Richard Johnson walking around (he's supposed to be a go-between for the Devil) and the cliche playroom scenes where the toys come to life. Writer-director Oliver Hellman repeatedly fails to breathe life into this blatant ripoff. (VC)

**BEYOND THE DOOR II (1977).** Sequel to BEYOND THE DOOR with Daria Nicolodi in the Juliet Mills role—a mother still suffering the terrors of a son possessed by the spirit of her recently deceased husband, a son who plays cat-and-mouse

**THE WIFE IN 'BEYOND THE DOOR II'**

terror games and employs wicked psychokinetic powers. The kid even tries to get sexual. Mom gets hysterical, boy goes bonkers, audience dozes off. Director Mario Bava allows the door to close on his own screenplay without much of a slam. David Colin Jr. is the mean little kid, Ivan Rassimov the dense new husband. (VC)

**BEYOND THE FOG.** Retitling of **HORROR OF SNAPE ISLAND.** See **TOWER OF EVIL,** preferably in an uncut form, which some liberal TV stations have been known to show.

**BEYOND THE GATE.** See **HUMAN EXPERIMENTS.**

**BEYOND THE LIVING (1977).** Muddled supernatural thriller, obviously inspired by THE EXORCIST, in which the leader of a cult dies in a hospital just as his spirit possesses the curvy body of a nurse. She begins knocking off the characters with

cleavers, knives and other instruments. Meanwhile, there's an absurd subplot in which a black football star-patient turns up with a voodoo amulet to ward off evil. Poorly directed by Al Adamson; just as poorly acted. First released as NURSE SHERRI. Jill Jacobson, Marilyn Joi, Mary Kay Pass, Geoffrey Land.

**BEYOND THE LIVING DEAD (1974).** Spanish fright flick stars Paul Naschy as a nasty nut resurrecting corpses and programming them to knock off innocent folks standing in the way of scientific progress. Beyond the comprehension of most living viewers. (VC)

**BEYOND THE MOON (1954).** Producer Roland Reed spliced together episodes of a cheap TV juvenile series. See (or don't see) ((see if we care)) **ROCKY JONES, SPACE RANGER.**

**BEYOND THE TIME BARRIER (1960).** Robert Clarke, apparently trying to escape from The Hideous Sun Demon, takes off in an experimental supersonic rocket and, after passing through a routine time warp, lands in 2024 to discover a subterranean world that has survived a cosmic nuclear plague. It's a dreary civilization, making our present-day world, even with all its faults, seem Utopian in comparison. Although directed by cult favorite Edgar G. Ulmer, it is marred by terribly amateurish acting, chintzy production values. and an awful script by Arthur Q. Pierce. Darlene Tompkins, John van Dreelen, Arianne Arden.

**BEYOND THE UNIVERSE (1981).** Well-intended, serious-minded science-fiction set in the 21st Century, a hundred years after a nuclear war when a recovering mankind is undergoing a shortage of oxygen. A dedicated scientist and his loyal band, believing Earth to be a cancerous molecule in the lifestream of the Universe in need of healing, try to contact an all-powerful intelligence deep in space, while dictatorial forces on Earth plan the genocide of old people to preserve precious air. There's a mission to rescue Father Hermes, a white-haired, philosophical sage, from death, so he can lead them in making God-like contact. The ambitious script by producer Allan Sandler, director Robert Emenegger, Steven Posner and Seth Marshall III is marred by poor effects and limited sets; but its the thought that counts. David Ladd, Jacqueline Ray, Henry Darrow, John Dewey-Carter, Stephanie Faulkner.

**BEYOND TOMORROW (1940).** Sentimental fantasy-comedy focusing on three old men who return from the grave to share Christmas "spirit" with lovers Richard Carlson and Jean Parker. The old fogies are Harry Carey, C. Aubrey Smith and Charles Winninger, with Maria Ouspenskaya in a supporting role. Very old-fashioned, maudlin script by associate producer Adele Comandini. Directed by A. Edward Sutherland. (VC)

**BIG BUS, THE (1976).** What is 106 feet long, weighs 75 tons, is bigger than 80 Volkswagens and has a swimming pool? Shucks, movie-goers, it's the world's first nuclear-powered bus, the Cyclops, on its maiden voyage from New York to Denver. The gears of this "Grand Hotel" on wheels don't always mesh, but the vehicle still sputters its share of guffaws with James Frawley at the director's wheel. Stockard Channing, Rene Auberjonois, Jose Ferrer, Ruth Gordon, Lynn Redgrave, Larry Hagman, Sally Kellerman. (VC)

**BIG FOOT (1969).** How serious is this movie? When aviatrix Joey Lansing unzips her flying suit, she's wearing a Baby Doll nightie underneath . . . that's how serious. An odd exploitation cheapie in which two hick conmen (John Carradine, John Mitchum) and wimpy roughnecks on Yahamas pursue a tall, disfigured man with oversized feet wearing a mangy ape suit. Tacky, tacky. Big Foot, legendary man-thing of the Northwest, is Small Stuff as he carries away Lansing and other women in bikinis, mainly for breeding purposes. What this breeds most is contempt. The odd cast includes Chris and Lindsay Crosby, Ken Maynard (an old cowboy star playing a general store owner) and Doodles Weaver as a forest ranger. Scenes of Lansing being terrorized by the monster are hilarious. (VC)

**BIG FOOT—MAN OR BEAST? (1975).** Heavy-footed pseudodocumentary with footage of forests and rugged wilderness and a few so-called authentic scenes of Sasquatch. But it

## JAMES HONG SPLITS HIS PERSONALITY IN 'BIG TROUBLE IN LITTLE CHINA'

would never hold up in court. Written-directed by Lawrence Crowley. (VC)

**BIG GAME, THE (1972).** Radar device capable of controlling armies of men and forcing them to fight is fought over by various nations in this international spy thriller, which emphasizes action, double-crosses and commando raids more than science-fiction. France Nuyen uses her beauty to win the affections of the son of the weapon's inventor. Most of the action takes place aboard a freighter as Stephen Boyd and Cameron Mitchell, soldiers of fortune, fight to protect Ray Milland and his invention.

**BIG MEAT EATER (1982).** Science-fiction/fantasy musical-comedy (midnight movie style) in which extraterrestrials tangle with a goofy guy who uses human flesh to run appliances. Some meat! (VC)

**BIG NOISE, THE (1944).** Stan Laurel and Oliver Hardy are hired to deliver a new explosive to a remote location, but this delivers a pop instead of a bang as the boys tangle with World War II spies. W. Scott Darling's script is to blame, never exploiting L & H to full advantage; director Mal St. Clair needed a few firecrackers under him, too. Arthur Space, Bobby Blake, Doris Merrick, Frank Fenton.

**BIG TROUBLE IN LITTLE CHINA (1986).** Ghosts, kung fu, a monster, a subterranean Chinese city and a touch of mysticism . . . ample ingredients for a lively fantasy-adventure, but in making it work director John Carpenter is only partially successful. The main problem is, nothing about this martial arts-ghost story ever ignites the viewer; it's just a lot of tumult and shouting. The best thing is Kurt Russell as a wise-cracking truckdriver who thinks he's John Wayne; Russell plays it for the laughs it's worth. He's swept into a mystery in which a 2000-year-old demon must marry the heroine in order to turn back into a young man. Action, comedy and light-show special effects are included in the brew, but it still emerges lightweight and quickly forgettable. Dennis Dun, Kim Cattrall. (VC)

**BIGGLES (1986).** British time-travel comedy based on a series of books popular in the Empire in which a man from the present (Alex Hyde-White) travels back to World War I where he meets Biggles, an ace fighting to stop the Germans from introducing a terrible new weapon to the battlefield. Directed by John Hough. Peter Cushing, Fiona Hutchison, Marcus Hutchison.

**BILLION DOLLAR BRAIN, THE (1967).** Imaginative spy thriller based on a Len Deighton novel in the Harry Palmer series, with dazzling gadgetry, colorful European locations and manipulative direction by Ken Russell. Ed Begley is outstanding as a Texas multimillionaire, as radical as they come, with a plan to invade Russia with his own army to defend democracy. Michael Caine (as Palmer), Karl Malden, Francoise Dorleac, Oscar Homolka.

**BILLION DOLLAR THREAT, THE (1979).** Dale Robinette is a supersy 007-style pursuing a typical madman who plans to fiddle with the Earth's ozone layer while mankind burns. A five-and-dime threat at best and a substandard TV-movie that sacrifices everything for action. Directed by Barry Shear, scripted by Jimmy Sangster. Ralph Bellamy, Keenan Wynn, Patrick MacNee, Ronnie Carol.

**BILLY THE KID VS. DRACULA (1965).** John Carradine considers this his worst film and wishes to burn the negative. You'll want to provide matches once you witness this abomination scripted by Karl Hittleman, whose brain must have been transplanted to a corpse before he sat down to write. Directed by William "Crankem-Out-Fast" Beaudine, who abounds in absurdities and vampire lore miscalculations, such as having Carradine/Dracula creeping in broad daylight. By all means, don't see it if you can't miss it. Bing Russell, Roy Barcroft, Harry Carey Jr. (VC)

**BIOHAZARD (1984).** Simply awful monster movie, poorly executed by writer-producer-director Fred Olen Ray, who during the closing credits resorts to outtakes in the style of Burt Reynolds, as if writing off the picture as a joke. An ALIEN ripoff of the poorest order, with psychic Angelique Pettyjohn not only making contact with an alien ship and teleporting it to Earth but showing off her enormous breasts. That's how serious she is. When the alien escapes its container, it's on a rampage of gory death. Christopher Ray plays the cheesy monster; Aldo Ray is really bad as a military officer. William Fair, Frank McDonald. (VC)

**BIONIC WOMAN, THE (1976).** TV pilot for a spinoff from THE SIX MILLION DOLLAR MAN, starring Lindsay Wagner as Jaime Sommers, a female counterpart to Lee Majors' Steve Austin. When Jaime is almost killed skiing, the science teams puts her back together and she becomes an operative for the Office of Scientific Information. Routine action stuff, a lot of it in slow motion. Directed by Henry Mankiewicz. Monica Randall, Bob Sullivan. (VC)

**BIRD OF PARADISE (1950).** South Sea island melodrama with fetching sarongs on Debra Paget, belching volcano and an unusual fantasy overtone: water turns to blood during a hero-heroine bathing scene and the regurgitating volcano quiets down only after being fed a sacrifice. Unlike the excellent 1932 King Vidor version, which didn't have any superstitious lore coming true, this takes a fatalistic, it's-bigger-than-love attitude which only makes Delmar Dave's production (he wrote-produced-directed) seem silly. Jeff Chandler, Louis Jourdan, Everett Sloane.

**BIRD WITH THE CRYSTAL PLUMAGE, THE (1971).** Intense, driving psychological crime-horror thriller by Italy's Dario Argento, in which Tony Musante portrays a writer who tracks down a killer of women. Suzy Kendall. (VC)

**BIRDS, THE (1963).** Alfred Hitchcock's masterpiece of shock and suspense, scripted by Evan Hunter from the Daphne du Maurier story. For reasons never explained, only pontificated on by the characters, winged creatures turn against mankind and attack without warning. Rod Taylor and Tippi Hedren are trapped in a farmhouse and the feathered attacks are absolutely spinetingling. (Hedren claims Hitch set hungry birds against her to capture ultimate realism.) The ending is ambiguous, as was the short story, but Hitchcock's mastery direction makes it work. Bernard Herrmann provided the eerie bird "sounds" and Lawrence A. Hampton pulled off the complicated effects, combining real and fake birds in stunning fashion. An all-time favorite worth reseeing. Jessica Tandy, Suzanne Pleshette, Veronica Cartwright, Charles McGraw, Doodles Weaver, Karl Swenson, Ethel Griffies. (VC)

**BIRDS DO IT (1966).** So why can't Soupy Sales (one-time pie-in-the-face TV comedian) fly too? He can, with the help of a special serum (and the well-wired special effects department). Director Andrew Marton keeps the acting on an appropriate juvenile level. Tab Hunter, Arthur O'Connell, Edward Andrews, Beverly Adams.

**BISHOP'S WIFE, THE (1947).** Samuel Goldwyn film that TV revives at Christmas for its heart-tugging warmth and sentimentality. It's really the cast (Cary Grant, Loretta Young, David Niven, Monty Woolley and James Gleason) that makes it watchable. Grant is the spirit Dudley who is sent to Earth to help a bishop (Niven) and his wife (Young) build a new cathedral, and to help the bishop re-establish contact with his "flock." A memorable element is the wine bottle that never empties. Directed by Henry Koster. Gladys Cooper, Elsa Lanchester, Regis Toomey. (VC)

**BLACK ABBOT, THE (1961).** West German adaptation of an Edgar Wallace mystery featuring the standard hooded figure terrorizing everyone around the castle. Joachim Fuchsberger, Klaus Kinski, Dieter Borsche.

**BLACK CASTLE, THE (1952).** Call this the "old dark castle" syndrome: Swashbuckler Richard Greene visits baron Stephen McNally in his medieval surroundings to seek a missing friend. Lurking at the arras as castle retainers, and giving this Universal-International potboiler a touch of the sinister, are Boris Karloff and Lon Chaney Jr. Typical Gothic suspense programmer of the period, with additional villainy from Michael Pate and John Hoyt. Directed by Nathan Juran, scripted by Jerry Sackheim. (VC)

**JOHN CARRADINE'S RECURRING NIGHTMARE: 'BILLY THE KID VS. DRACULA'**

**BLACK CAT, THE (1934).** One of the strangest horror films of the 1930s, thanks to the surreal direction by Edgar G. Ulmer and the often abstract script by Peter Ruric, who threw away Edgar Allan Poe's story in favor of his own cinematic ideas. Boris Karloff is the leader of a cult of devil worshippers in a strange house constructed over a military fort. He and Bela Lugosi begin a game of chess which is really a game of life and death. Full of eerie images (credit photographer John Mescall), bizarre gimmicks and unexplainable characters and relationships. By all means, don't miss it. On a doublebill videocassette with THE RAVEN.

**BLACK CAT, THE (1941).** Nothing to do with Poe; it's another gathering of heirs in a creepy old castle to read the will. What makes it palatable is its cast (Basil Rathbone, Broderick Crawford, Bela Lugosi, Gale Sondergaard, Gladys Cooper, Alan Ladd) and Stanley Cortez's photography. Otherwise you've seen it before, thunderstorm, secret passageways and all. Directed by Albert S. Rogell.

**BLACK CAT, THE (1968).** Twelfth Century Japan is the dream-like setting for this horror film by Kaneto Shindo. Two defenseless women are raped and murdered by roving Samurai. Their souls make a pact with evil spirits, trading

in the making) and expensive ($25 million) animated feature from Disney, based on Lloyd Alexander's THE CHRONICLES OF PRYDAIN. It's sword-and-sorcery adventure in which the evil Horned King seeks The Black Cauldron, that Spectral Stewpot with the power to resurrect a dead army and conquer the world. Standing in his way is young Taran, a naive hero who proves his nettle with the help of a magic sword, a beautiful scullery maid, a roving minstrel, a fuzzy cute animal creature that mutters, and an oracle-divining pig. It's an odd blend of styles (some very cartoonish, some grittily realistic) and characters (some old-fashioned Disney, others like extras from CONAN) and the end result is a stunningly visual piece that still seems trivial and unimportant. Directed by Ted Berman and Richard Rich. John Huston narrates the introduction; voices include John Hurt as the Horned King, Grant Bardsley as Taran and Susan Sheridan as Eilonwy. (VC)

**BLACK CHRISTMAS (1974).** This predates the slasher cycle and establishes the tone and ambience for which the sub-genre was to become known, so producer-director Robert Clark established precedent in this Canadian film, also known as STRANGER IN THE HOUSE on cable TV, and SILENT NIGHT, EVIL NIGHT. It has the twist of placing a fiendish killer in the attic of a sorority house and allowing him to stay

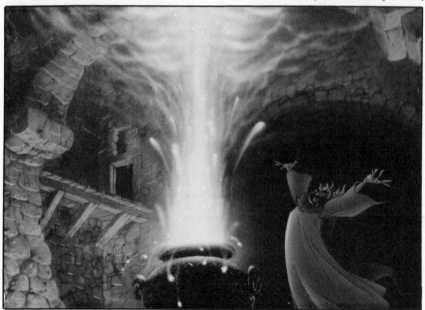

## THE HORNED KING FLIPS OUT IN DISNEY'S 'THE BLACK CAULDRON'

eternal rest for eternal revenge on mercenaries. One lures the unsuspecting warriors to a home where the other bites them in the jugular veins. Highly imaginative and atmospherically photographed. Nobuko Otowa.

**BLACK CAT, THE (1980).** Just how scary is a black pussy? This Italian supernatural thriller directed by Lucio Fulci (best known for bloody zombie movies) answers that question. Not a helluva lot. And how scary are repeated super-close ups of Patrick Magee's eyeball sockets? Not a helluva lot. Magee is a village nut recording tapes with voices from beyond the veil whose evil is transported into a common black cat (the pussy referred to earlier) . . . or is the evil of the cat overtaking him? Scotland Yard (represented by David Warbeck) investigates murders in the village linked to Magee and his cat and a nosy photographer (Mimsy Farmer) thinks the cat has been pulling off the homicides. Murders include a body falling on a pitchfork, a woman burned alive in her nightgown, claws across hands and other feline felonies. Please, no catty remarks.

**BLACK CAULDRON, THE (1985).** A long-awaited (five years

there while police run themselves weary looking for missing persons who are dead in the garret. The killer's identity is never known (writer Roy Moore sets it up so it doesn't matter) and the knowledge of the killer's whereabouts contributes greatly to the tension. Olivia Hussey, Margot Kidder, Keir Dullea, Andrea Martin, John Saxon, Art Hindle. (VC)

**BLACK DEVIL DOLL FROM HELL (1985).** Videotape junk in which a woman is trounced on by a ventriloquist's dummy. Directed by Chester T. Turner. Shirley T. Jones, Rickey Roach. (VC)

**BLACK DRAGONS (1942).** Excruciatingly painful Monogram Sam Katzman programmer with Bela Lugosi sadly wasted as a mad scientist performing plastic surgery on Japanese spies so they can infiltrate America. It's the "yellow horde" menace again, a polemic mangled by writer Harvey Gates and squashed to death by director William Nigh. This has the dubious distinction of featuring Lugosi in two roles. Clayton Moore, George Pembroke.

**BLACK DRAGONS OF MANZANAR (1943).** Re-edited TV

version of the Republic serial G-MEN VS. THE BLACK DRAGON. Good old American investigator Rex Bennett (Rod Cameron) is out to stop Haruchi and his insidious Black Dragon Society and, as usual, the screenwriters have injected fantastic elements into the cliff-hanging events. Incendiary powder in paint blows up a ship; there's a ray gun at one suspenseful point, and a drug-induced suspended animation is sinisterly administered. William Witney directed. Constance Worth, C. Montague Shaw.

**BLACK FRANKENSTEIN. See BLACKENSTEIN.**

**BLACK FRIDAY (1940).** Boris Karloff portrays a sympathetic scientist who transplants the brain of a criminal into an injured colleague, with the patient taking on characteristics of the gangster. Bela Lugosi appears in a small, wasted role as a hoodlum. Curt Siodmak's script bears some resemblance to DONOVAN'S BRAIN, but then he wrote that one too. Not a particularly distinguished Universal horror film of the period, but of interest for its cast. Arthur Lubin directed. Stanley Ridges, Anne Nagel, Anne Gwynne, Paul Fix, Jack Mulhall, James Craig.

**BLACK HOLE, THE (1979).** The Black Hole of Space is a theory among astronomers that when a star dies it becomes a compressed mass, where laws of physics cease to exist. This Disney effort, an answer to STAR WARS, is a compressed mess all right, botched in every respect. Many effects artists (including Peter Ellenshaw) were brought in to assist, but the Jeb Rosebrook-Gerry Day screenplay belies their efforts with cardboard characters and feeble premises. A survey ship has gone dangerously close to a Black Hole and is approached by another ship which soon has human beings in conflict and robots (cutesy-pie creatures) zapping the expensive sets with their blasters. Even the final trip through the Black Hole, intended as an abstraction or a metaphor (or a bad joke?), is a misfire for director Gary Nelson. Anthony Perkins, Robert Forster, Joseph Bottoms, Yvette Mimieux, Ernest Borgnine, Maximilian Schell. Robot voice by Slim Pickens. (VC)

**BLACK LIZARD (1968).** The woman they call Black Lizard owns a club for exotic nude dancers; she also has an inner sanctum inhabited by dwarves and a hunchback. The Black Lizard Dragon Lady wants to kidnap a jeweler's daughter to steal the Star of Egypt diamond. Enter shrewd cop Isao Kimura. Yukio Mishima, the Japanese writer who committed suicide in 1970, and whose play this is based on, has a featured role as a nude "doll" in the Lizard Lady's private collection. Now get this: Black Lizard is portrayed by Akihiro Maruyama, a female impersonator in Japan. How's that for weird?

**BLACK MAGIC (1949).** Heavily atmospheric tale about 18th Century hypnotist Cagliostro and how he keeps beautiful Nancy Guild under his entrancing spell. Producer-director Gregory Ratoff (better remembered as an actor) gives this a gloominess that is all-permeating. Worth seeing for Orson Welles' overwrought but spellbinding performance as the mesmerizer. Akim Tamiroff, Raymond Burr, Frank Latimore, Barry Kroeger, Valentina Cortesa. (VC)

**BLACK MOON (1975).** French director Louis Malle concocts an enigmatic "mythical fantasy" about how Cathryn Harrison escapes a strange war between the sexes to seek refuge in a country manor. Malle, who admits he was influenced by ALICE IN WONDERLAND and Edgar Allan Poe, includes weird visuals (how about a unicorn in the garden) which baffle Harrison as much as they will baffle you. Strictly for the "artistic film" set.

**BLACK NOON (1971).** Supernatural TV-movie, written-produced by Andrew J. Fenady, has the unusual setting of the American West in the 19th Century. A traveling preacher and his wife are victims of a witch cult headed by Ray Milland. Fenady throws in a nice twist ending. Yvette Mimieux is gorgeous in billowing, silky nightgowns as she lures men to their doom. Roy Thinnes, Gloria Grahame, Lyn Loring, Henry Silva. Directed by Bernard Kowalski.

**BLACK ORPHEUS (1958).** Modernization of the Orpheus legend by Marcel Camus. Death pursues Eurydice at a carnival in Rio De Janeiro. Brazilian production is a favorite outre film because of atmosphere and lyrical score. Oscar and Cannes winner. Breno Mello. (VC)

**BLACK PIT OF DR. M, THE (1959).** Prepare for the black pit of despair. This Mexican film, simply put, is simply awful. An insane scientist returns from the grave to invade another body and seek revenge. The party most wronged is the viewer. Gaston Santos, Rafael Bertrand, Mapita Cortes. Directed by Ferdinand Mendez.

**BLACK ROOM, THE (1935).** Identical twins (Boris Karloff & Boris Karloff) are caught up in macabre, sadistic events that lead to the fulfillment of an ancient curse. Assorted bodies are thrown on spikes or skewered in a torture chamber. Karloff, portraying a sympathetic and a hateful character in the same film, shows his mettle under the direction of Roy William Neill. Thurston Hall, Edward Van Sloan, Katherine DeMille, Marian Marsh, Robert Allen. (VC)

**BLACK ROOM, THE (1981).** Ghoulish brother-and-sister team lures unsuspecting victims into the family mansion, photographs them having sex through two-way mirrors in the titular bedroom, and murders them so the brother can have a blood transfusion to stave off a blood disease. My, what wonderful imagery for a fun-loving movie. Directed by Elly Kenner and Norman Thaddeus Vane. Stephen Knight, Cassandra Gaviola, Jim Stathis. (VC)

**BLACK SABBATH (1964).** Horror trilogy introduced by Boris Karloff in the style of his TV series THRILLER. In the first shocker, "A Drop of Water," based on a Chekhov story, a nurse plunders the dead only to become . . . but we can't tell. The second, "The Telephone," concerns strange calls to a beautiful woman; and the third, "The Wurdalak," starring Karloff, is a grisly vampire yarn with excellent atmosphere. One of Mario Bava's best directing jobs. Mark Damon, Michele Mercier, Suzy Anderson. (VC)

**BLACK SAMURAI (1976).** Lowbrow actioner with mild fantasy-horror overtones as D.R.A.G.O.N. agent Jim Kelly seeks a high priest (Bill Roy) and priestess Synne (Marilyn Jo) when they kidnap the daughter of an important official, also Kelly's girlfriend. It's one long series of martial arts battles with Janicot the priest throwing victims to his rattlesnakes, holding voodoo rights and siccing his endless supply of beefcake baddies on Kelly. Al Adamson directed routinely. Easy to watch and forget. (VC)

**BLACK SCORPION, THE (1957).** Willis O'Brien's special effects are the only commendable feature in this multi-legged monsterama in which a Mexican volcano spews up king-size mutant spiders. Richard Denning and Mara Corday race through the south-of-the-border locations in search of a way of stopping the great attack. Edward Ludwig directed this Warner Bros. flick. Unless you really like scuttling bugs, you'd better scuttle elsewhere.

**BLACK SLEEP, THE (1956).** Film lacks acting character but has plenty of character actors: Lon Chaney, John Carradine, Akim Tamiroff, Bela Lugosi, Tor Johnson—what a menagerie. Mad doctor Basil Rathbone performs perverted surgery to create a "gallery of creeps." Lowbrow script by Reginald Le Borg (who also directed) and John Higgins. Barely watchable despite zoo-like cast.

**BLACK SUNDAY (1961).** Queen of Horror Barbara Steele at her horrific best in this Italian vampire tale; director Mario Bava pumps so much eerie, Gothic atmosphere into this adaptation of Gogol's THE VIJ that it's a minor masterpiece. One day each century Satan roams the Earth, seeking souls. Barbara is a witch who makes the mistake of getting involved; there's a great scene of her being resurrected from a tomb. John Richardson, Ivo Garrani.

**BLACK TORMENT, THE (1964).** British supernatural thriller in which a lord remarries and goes home to his Gothic mansion, there to be faced with sorcery, murder and other everyday activities. John Turner, Ann Lynn and Heather Sears work to make all this unbelievable stuff believable. Directed by Robert Hartford-Davis.

**BLACK ZOO, THE (1963).** Michael Gough is the insane proprietor of a private zoo, in such rapport with his beastly charges that he metaphysically touches them with his lust for vengeance. The animals disappear into the night to do his killing but then the worm . . . we mean lion . . . turns. Herman Cohen film directed by Robert Gordon, scripted by Cohen. Rod Lauren, Jerome Cowan, Virginia Grey, Elisha Cook Jr., Marianna Hill, Edward Platt.

**BLACKBEARD'S GHOST (1968).** Peter Ustinov stars in this "cutesy" Disney film as an 18th Century swashbuckler forced to wander in a spiritual limbo until he performs a good deed, in this case helping the track coach of a contemporary college. Directed by Robert Stevenson. Dean Jones, Suzanne Pleshette, Elsa Lanchester, Elliott Reid, Richard Deacon, Kelly Thordsen, Gil Lamb. (VC)

**BLACKENSTEIN (1973).** Unsavory take-off on BLACULA, in which mad doctor John Hart turns a Vietnam basket case into a monster. BLACKENSTEIN only blackens the names of producer-writer Frank Saletri, director William Levey, co-stars Ivory Stone, Andrea King, Liz Renay. (VC)

**BLACKOUT (1985).** Intriguing psychothriller with Richard Widmark as a policeman obsessed by a quadruple family murder—presumably committed by the missing husband. What gives this a twist is that Keith Carradine, an accident victim, could be the father suffering from amnesia. He's undergone facial surgery after a car crash, so who can say? Does he now have a split personality, reverting to homicidal tendencies at times? Is he terrorizing his bride Kathleen Quinlan? Or is a former lover plotting to drive her bonkers? These and other unasnwered questions (until the violent, bloody climax) are what keep this teleplay mysterious. Michael Beck, Gerald Hiken, Paul Drake, Don Hood.

**BLACULA (1972).** Racist twist on the old vampire cliche: A black African Prince (William Marshall) is resurrected by art collectors in Transylvania and shipped to Los Angeles. As if the city isn't already cursed enough, Prince Mamuwalde inflicts his own personal pain—usually via two puncture bites in the neck. Blacula falls for a reincarnated princess and pursues assorted low life and cops through the ghetto streets. It's such bloody good fun, it's a crying shame every time the sun comes up. William Crain directed. Vonetta McGee, Denise Nicholas, Thalmus Rasulala, Elisha Cook Jr. Sequel: SCREAM, BLACULA, SCREAM. (VC)

**BLADE IN THE DARK, A (1983).** Italian psychothriller in the Hitchcock tradition, directed by Lamberto Bava, in which a movie composer isolates himself in a villa to write a horror film score while a woman killer armed with a razor and/or butcher knife stalks lady victims and slashes them up pretty good, with Bava holding back none of the graphics. Clues the composer uncovers suggest every woman in the cast as a suspect, but clever viewers (like you) will figure out the killer's identity in advance of the unmasking, aided by expository flashbacks that set up the pseudopsychiatry. Despite its predictabilities, this is a fair time-killer, cutting slowly into your credulity veins. Andrea Occhipinti, Anny Papa, Fabiola Toledo. (VC)

**BLADE MASTER, THE.** See **ATOR THE BLADE MASTER.**

**BLADE RUNNER (1982).** A visual stunner, directed by Ridley Scott with the same eye for atmosphere that made ALIEN a hit. Graphic designers have created a Los Angeles of 1999 brilliant in its acid-rain wretchedness. But . . . the Hampton

Fancher-David Peoples screenplay, based loosely on Philip K. Dick's DO ANDROIDS DREAM OF ELECTRIC SHEEP?, is such a grim downer the film operates without a soul. The weakest link is Harrison Ford as a washed-out private eye, Deckard, assigned to destroy rebellious replicants (humanoid robots designed to be laborers) who have escaped. Deckard is nothing but world-weary, his voice-over monotonic narration, in the Mike Hammer style, contributing little. The strongest link is Rutger Hauer as the head replicant, suggesting character complexities with the mere twist of a smile. The final confrontation in the Bradbury Building should have been a knockout; yet, since we cannot care about Deckard, we can hardly care who will win. All style and little content; yet, recommended for its compelling visuals and Scott's directorial eye, as well as Douglas Trumbull's effects. Sean Young, Joanna Cassidy, Daryl Hannah, Edward James Olmos, Hy Pyke, Joseph Turkel, Morgan Paull, Brion James. (VC)

**BLAKE OF SCOTLAND YARD (1936).** The Scorpion, wearing a claw-like hand, is hired by an unscrupulous munitions figure, Count Basil Zegelloff, to steal a Death Ray from Sir James Blake, formerly of Scotland Yard. Blake sets out to recover his invention, tangling with thugs and underhanded blackguards. This feature version of a 15-chapter serial has few dull moments and not an ounce of subtlety. Bob Hill directed Sam Katzman's production. Ralph Byrd, Joan Barclay, Dickie Jones, Herbert Rawlinson.

**BLANCHEVILLE MONSTER, THE (1962).** Out of the eons of the misty past it rose, this towering hulk of monstrous flesh and hideous putrescence, to lay its moldly claws on those humans who chance to cross its bloody path. Yep, another movie horror, this one from Spanish-Italian producers, who borrowed ideas from Edgar Allan Poe short stories. Directed by Alberto de Martino. Gerard Tichy, Leo Anchoriz, Joan Hills, Richard Davis, Helga Line.

**BLAST OFF (1954).** Zap! Clap! Trap! See **ROCKY JONES, SPACE RANGER.**

**HARRISON FORD AS DECKARD IN RIDLEY SCOTT'S 'BLADE RUNNER'**

**BLAST OFF (1967).** Jules Verne-style adventure/fantasy set in Victorian days and starring Burl Ives, Troy Donahue, Gert Frobe (remember GOLDFINGER?), Hermione Gingold and Lionel Jeffries. It's a zany plot about sending a ship to Venus. Jolly silly fun. Also called THOSE FANTASTIC FLYING FOOLS. Directed by Don Sharp.

**BLIND BARGAIN, A (1922).** Lon Chaney Sr. silent classic occasionally revived. When Chaney is given a monkey's brain, he turns into a half-human freak who falls for a beautiful young woman. This premise may sound old hat, but remember this was made before all those awful gorilla movies of the 1930s. Sam Goldwyn's production is based on Barry Pain's THE OCTAVE OF CLAUDIUS.

**BLIND DATE (1984).** Flimsy, uninspired slasher flick features a blind man who can see with the aid of a special surgical computer implant—eventually he closes in on the killer. A good cast (Joseph Bottoms, Kirstie Alley, Keir Dullea, Lana Clarkson) is wasted by director Nico Mastorakis. As "blind" as a vampire bat.

**BLIND DEAD, THE (1972).** Spanish horror flick has nice eerie atmosphere and decent special effects in recounting the legend of a 13th Century cult known as the Templarios, who murdered thousands of women in blood sacrifices. Known in Spain as TOMB OF THE BLIND DEAD. Written-directed by Amando De Ossorio. Cesar Burner.

**BLISS (1986).** Australian comedy of the macabre in which Barry Otto dies and goes to Heaven, but then returns to Earth to question the meaning of existence. An irreverent look at the angelic lifestyle. Directed by Ray Lawrence. (VC)

**BLITHE SPIRIT (1945).** Noel Coward's popular play was turned into a memorable screen adaptation by director David Lean and Coward, who wrote the screenplay. Jolly good the way those British handle a comedy ghost story. Rex Harrison is a chap haunted by his wives. Not the alimony-seeking kind—the dead kind! Constance Cummings, Kay Hammond, Joyce Carey. (VC)

**BLOB, THE (1958).** Gelatin-like substance comes to Earth aboard a meteor and grows each time it sucks up a human being, which is often, as Theodore Simonson and Kate Phillips don't want any blobs growing under their script. Steve McQueen and town juveniles set out to warn folks, but nobody listens . . . until it's too late to stop the ever-growing glunky junk. Tongue-in-cheek fun if you can roll with the World's Biggest Jello Ball. Director Irvin S. Yeaworth Jr. deserves credit for turning this into a cult favorite. Aneta Corseaut, Olin Howlin, Earl Rowe. (VC)

**BLOOD (1973).** Don't bleed for sexploitation specialist Andy Milligan, even if he does bleed his cast in this sanguinary story of Dr. Lawrence Orlovski (Allan Berendt), a werewolf living in London during the 1930s who keeps company with man-eating plants and an offspring of Dracula. Thinner than water. Eve Crosby, Pamela Adams.

**BLOOD AND BLACK LACE (1964).** Italian-French horror thriller guided by the sure (and bloody) hand of director Mario Bava, who co-wrote the script about gore murders committed by a masked murderer. Eva Bartok, Cameron Mitchell, Thomas Reiner, Harriet White. (VC)

**BLOOD AND LACE (1964).** Feeble-minded Grand Guignol in an American orphanage where bodies are preserved in a freeze locker by a hammer-slammer who runs around in a mask, murdering anyone he meets. A comedown for Gloria Grahame, Melody Patterson and Vic Tayback. Directed by Philip Gilbert, scripted by Gil Lasky.

**BLOOD AND ROSES (1961).** Roger Vadim's version of J. Sheridan Le Fanu's CARMILLA was brutalized by U.S. censors who removed 13 minutes of Lesbian activity. What's left tells of a woman with a family history of vampirism who becomes obsessed by the spirit of an ancestor and cannot overcome her overpowering craving for blood of both sexes. Mel Ferrer, Elsa Martinelli, Annette Vadim.

**BLOOD BATH (1966).** Schizophrenic beatnik painter in the

## PETER CUSHING IN 'BLOOD BEAST TERROR': HIS WORST?

L.A. suburb of Venice murders young women, lowering their still-warm bodies into a boiling vat. He thinks he's the reincarnation of a vampire once burned at the stake. Poorly executed exploitation flick, of interest to fans of STAR TREK actor William Campbell, who co-stars with Marissa Mathes, Lori Saunders and Sandra Knight. Writtten-directed by Jack Hill and reportedly finished by Stephanie Rothman after Hill was fired by producer Roger Corman.

**BLOOD BATH (1976).** A gore film this is not—there's nary a drop of blood and only one bath . . . bubble at that. This is an anthology in which the principal players of a horror film in production dine with their director and exchange horror stories. In the first, a bomb assassin is handed a strange twist of fate; in the second, a man possesses a magic coin that transports him to the Napoleonic wars; in the third, a miser is locked into an impregnable vault with a ghost; in the fourth, a karate champ knowing the Nine Secrets of Martial Arts learns the tenth secret. After the dinner party, the director goes home to round out a fifth story about a locked room and a monster. Played tongue-in-cheek but very amateurishly acted and photographed (some sets are one-wall affairs). Appears to have been shot half on videotape, half on film. The work of Joel (BLOODSUCKING FREAKS) Reed.

**BLOOD BEACH (1980).** Bathers are sucked into sandy Santa Monica beach by an unseen subterrean creature, baffling policemen John Saxon and Burt Young. Writer-director Jerry Bloom builds a modicum of suspense, failing to pay off with an acceptable solution. The sandsucker turns out to be an uninspired blob creature, its origins never explained. Terrible plotting, worse characterizations. Marianna Hill, David Huffman, Otis Young. (VC)

**BLOOD BEAST FROM OUTER SPACE.** See **NIGHT CALLER FROM OUTER SPACE.**

**BLOOD BEAST TERROR (1969).** Peter Cushing, who considers this British film his worst, portrays a professor dabbling in the mysteries of science who transforms his daughter into a Deathshead Moth—king size, of course. The moth is also a vampire, allowing this flight of fancy to flutter away in all directions. Also known as THE VAMPIRE BEAST CRAVES BLOOD. Directed by Vernon Sewell. Robert Flemyng, Wanda Ventham. (VC)

**BLOOD CASTLE.** Alternate videocassette title for **SCREAM OF THE DEMON LOVER.**

**BLOOD CEREMONY.** See **FEMALE BUTCHER.**

**BLOOD CIRCUS (1985).** Described as a "multi million dollar Class AAAAA Feature Film" by its producer Ryan Zwick and as an "incredible sci-fi two-hour wrestling motion picture" by its director and writer, Bob Harris. It features "aliens, real blood, heads landing in popcorn, fleas, Santo Gold wearing 30 lbs. of gold singing his hit song, 'Santo Gold.'" Had enough already?

**BLOOD COUPLE (1973).** Originally released as GANJA AND HESS, this is the vampiric tale of a doctor's assistant inflicted with a terrible desire for blood after being stabbed with an ancient germ-laden knife. Despite the jab, it's pretty dull. Director-writer Bill Gunn also appeared in the cast with Duane Jones, Marlene Clarke, composer Sam Waymon and Leonard Jackson. (VC)

**BLOOD CREATURE. See TERROR IS A MAN.**

**BLOOD CULT (1985).** Supernatural tale made exclusively for videocassette. At a Midwest college, a series of co-ed murders leads to the discovery of a witches' coven that dates back to the days of Salem witch trials. A sheriff and girlfriend close in on the old hags and crones. Made in and around Tulsa, Oklahoma, by regional videomakers Linda Lewis (producer) and Christopher Lewis (director). Julie Andelman, Charles Ellis, James Vance. (VC)

**BLOOD DEMON, THE. See TORTURE CHAMBER OF DR. SADISM.**

**BLOOD DRINKERS, THE (1966).** Even in the Philippine islands, according to Cesar Amigo's script, they have a problem with bloodthirsty vampires. The evil incarnate is Satan himself, who is warded off by the usual charms and ubiquitous wooden stake. Drips with gore in a cheap, unpleasant way. Directed by Gerardo De Leon. Amelia Fuentes, Ronald Remy, Eddie Fernandez.

**BLOOD FEAST (1964).** Gross exploitation film directed, photographed and scored by Herschell Gordon Lewis, who also did his own special effects. Lewis is legendary as the Grossest Film-maker of All, and this is exemplary of his "work." We're talking gore gore here. Young women are dissected, organ by organ, as a madman restores life into an Egyptian goddess. What a sickening spectacle as Lewis preys on the vicarious needs of lowbrows. The squeamish are advised not to watch, although intellectuals and other thinkers might get off on the sociopathic implications of Lewis' films. Connie Mason, Thomas Wood. (VC)

**BLOOD FIEND. See THEATER OF BLOOD.**

**BLOOD FOR DRACULA (1974).** Andy Warhol's companion piece to his FRANKENSTEIN epic released that same year, but not nearly as bloody. This was also made in 3-D, but now you must endure it in 2-D as Udo Kierr portrays a caped count on the prowl for virgin blood, but rarely finding it (after all, this is Europe). Written-directed by Paul Morrissey. Arno Juerging, Maxime McKenory, Joe Dallesandro. Film-makers Vittorio De Sica and Roman Polanski appear in cameos. Available in videocassette as **ANDY WARHOL'S DRACULA.**

**BLOOD FROM THE MUMMY'S TOMB (1972).** Seth Holt's final directorial assignment—he died during production and was replaced by Michael Carreras. Acting and cinematography in this Hammer production are topnotch but the script by Christopher Wicking, about a buxom young woman who resembles a long-dead Egyptian princess, is pretty turgid stuff. Based on Bram Stoker's THE JEWEL OF SEVEN STARS. Andrew Keir, Valerie Leon, James Villier, George Coulouris. Remade in 1980 as THE AWAKENING.

**BLOOD LEGACY.** Videocassette title for **LEGACY OF BLOOD.**

**BLOOD LINK (1983).** Clinically detailed portrait of a sexually perverted psychokiller murdering beautiful women in Hamburg and Berlin. It's also the weird study of Siamese twins (Michael Moriarity plays the killer and his alter ego, a doctor experimenting in brain control.) Intriguing plot twists and good production make this Italian thriller above average, as does a bizarre ending. However, the graphic sexual violence is a turn-off, creating a fascinating story unpleasant to watch. Penelope Milford, Geraldine Fitzgerald, Cameron Mitchell,

Virginia McKenna. Music by Ennio Morricone. Directed by Albert de Martino. (VC)

**BLOOD MANIA (1970).** Wicked, wanton sexpot speeds up her father's demise so she can help her depraved boyfriend pay off a blackmail debt. These unsavory characters finally get chopped into little pieces, but this merciful acts comes too late to benefit the viewer. All talk and too little show. Directed by Robert O'Neil. Peter Carpenter, co-producer with Chris Marconi, stars. (VC)

**BLOOD OF DRACULA (1957).** Would you believe a vampire movie with songs? Would you believe hypnosis turning Sandra Harrison into a bloodsucker? Would you believe an all-girls' school where the head mistress has evil powers? Would you believe . . . naw, you wouldn't believe. Director Herbert L. Strock and screenwriter Ralph Thorton have justifiably remained obscure all these years, but producer Herman Cohen went on to bigger (if not greater) things . . . I WAS A TEENAGE FRANKENSTEIN, KONGA, etc.

**BLOOD OF DRACULA'S CASTLE (1967).** Unforgivably cheap, dreadfully produced vampire flop which tries to drain a few laughs from the vampire formula, but the results are anemic. A gross misuse of the Count's non-good name by producer-director Al Adamson, who was assisted in the directing by Jean Hewitt. Alex D'Arcy and Paula Raymond are Mr. and Mrs. Dracula, chaining up beautiful chicks in the basement and draining their blood. Ugh. (VC)

**BLOOD OF FRANKENSTEIN. See DRACULA VS. FRANKENSTEIN.**

**BLOOD OF FU MANCHU. See KISS AND KILL.**

**BLOOD OF GHASTLY HORROR (1970). See MAN WITH THE SYNTHETIC BRAIN, THE.**

**BLOOD OF NOSTRADAMUS (1964).** His thirst unquenchable, his fangs perpetually dripping with human blood and gore, a notorious Mexican vampire (German Robles) brags openly of his ability to murder the police chief at midnight—a vow which gravely upsets law enforcement agencies and forces them to prowl the back streets, on vigil against this brazen bloodsucker. This consists of footage taken from a Mexican serial and re-edited to feature length. Old footage was directed by Frederick Curiel, the new by Stim Segar. Julio Aleman, Domingo Soler.

**BLOOD OF THE MAN-DEVIL. See HOUSE OF THE BLACK DEATH.**

**BLOOD OF THE UNDEAD. See SCHIZO.**

**BLOOD OF THE VAMPIRE, THE (1958).** Inspired by the sanguinary efforts of Hammer, screenwriter Jimmy Sangster offers up the sinister doctor Callistrastus (Donald Wolfit, an actor of grand theatrics) conducts blood experiments in an asylum for the criminally insane. A superior British chiller, reeking with period atmosphere and an underlying sense of doom. Full of the blood and gore Hammer made so fashionable, enhanced by Barbara (CAT WOMAN) Shelley as a beautiful heroine undergoing torture and blood transfusions and Victor Maddern as the Igor-style aide-de-camp to the mad doc. Directed by Henry Cass. Milton Reid, John Le Mesurier.

**BLOOD ON SATAN'S CLAW (1971).** Gruesome, above-average British supernatural chiller concerns the Devil afoot in 17th Century England, turning all the kiddies in the surrounding farmlands into a coven of cauldron-stirring witches and warlocks. Exorcism is employed by a noble Englishman (Patrick Wymark) sworn to destroy the devilish band. Depression-period atmosphere and costuming are excellent. Tensely directed by Piers Haggard. Linda Hayden, Barry Andrews, Tamara Ustinov, James Hayter. (VC)

**BLOOD ORGY OF THE SHE-DEVILS (1973).** Quadruple threat Ted V. Mikels (writer/director/producer/editor) offers up a little blood during some sacrificial rites, a few hardly-dressed she-devils (their choreography would roll Busby Berkeley over in his grave) and no orgy at all. It's black magic mumbo jumbo as a queen of the witches, living in a California mansion (in

**CREATURE FEATURES MOVIE GUIDE**

Orange County, maybe?), practices the blackest of arts on the lowest of budgets. Lots of dialogue about psychometry, regression, white magic, etc., but nothing ever builds up to much more than a big letdown. Cast of unknowns (Lila Zaborin, Tom Pace, Leslie McRae, etc.) remained that way. (VC)

**BLOOD RELATIVES (1977).** Lowkey psychokiller melodrama with mild slasher touches, from French director Claude Chabrol, who focuses on mature teenager Audre Landry having a passionate affair with her first cousin. Donald Sutherland portrays a sensitive plainclothesman investigating the girl's stabbing. He suspects David Hemmings, the dead girl's flirtatious boss, but answers to this whodunit are to be found in the victim's red diary. Characterizations are well developed by Chabrol and co-writer Sydney Banks, who adapted a novel by Ed McBain. A cerebral mystery, with only a little action. Lisa Langlois, Stephane Audran, Laurent Malent. Shot in Canada.

**BLOOD ROSE, THE (1969).** See **RAVAGED.**

**BLOOD SABBATH (1972).** Wandering guitarist Tony Geary falls in love with Yala the water nymph (Susan Damante) and is willing to sacrifice his soul to Aloyta, Queen of the Witches (Dyanne Thorne), in exchange for Yala's love. Somewhere in William Bairn's script are some good ideas and writing, weakened however by gratuitous nudity (granted us by sexy members of Aloyta's coven) and only mediocre gore affects. Its cheap shoddy visuals designed by Hugo Grimaldi are in contrast to a languid mood that dominates during the love story. (VC)

**BLOOD SHACK (1981).** Another variation on the slasher flicks, this one focusing on a phantom nicknamed The Trooper who murders with an axe. Directed by Wolfgang Schmidt. Carolyn Brandt, Jason Wayne, John Bates.

**BLOOD SISTERS (1986).** "Their hazing was a night to dismember," claims the Variety ad. Amy Brentano, Shannon McMahon, Dan Erickson. Written-directed by Roberta Findlay.

**BLOOD SONG (1982).** Something to sing about: An unusually tense psychothriller with Frankie Avalon forsaking his clean image to portray a mental patient who escapes from the asylum and stalks a young woman (Donna Wilkes) after axing her father (Richard Jaeckel) to death. Good scary thriller. Directed by Alan J. Levi and Robert Angus. Antoinette Bower, Dane Clark. (VC)

**BLOOD SUCKERS.** Actually the title for **DR. TERROR'S GALLERY OF HORRORS,** which was re-retitled **RETURN TO THE PAST.**

**BLOOD THIRST (1965).** Another winner from the Philippines, depicting bloodthirsty sun cultists. Watch this too long and you'll see spots in front of your eyes. Directed by Newt Arnold. Robert Winston, Yvonne Nielson, Judy Dennis.

**BLOOD TIDE (1981).** More an excuse for filmmakers to vacation in the Greek isles than a film to be taken seriously. A blatant ripoff of JAWS in which archaeologist James Earl Jones disturbs a sea monster from its "ancient sleep." The island natives (Jose Ferrer and Lila Kedrova) know old legends about the slimy, gnashing Kraken requiring a virginal sacrifice but aren't telling Jones or other Americans hanging around: Mary Louise Weller, Lydia Cornell and Deborah Shelton. Guess which one gets eaten while swimming without her bra? Actually, director Richard Jeffries' work is passable but you never fully see the brimy beast, just slobbering jaws in flash cuts. One of the great non-payoffs of all time. It's ebb tide for BLOOD TIDE. (VC)

**BLOOD TRACKS (1986).** A rock group in the Rockies (ha ha) shooting a Rock(ies) Video (ha ha) is attacked by a family of crazies living beneath an old factory. Gore and sex aplenty. Directed by Mike Jackson. Jeff Harding, Naomi Kaneda, Michael Fitzpatrick.

**BLOOD WATERS OF DR. Z (1975).** Titular physician is well named, for this independent Florida exploitationer, shot in the slimy swamps, deserves to be classified as "z" material. Typical mad doctor is turned into a killer aquaman by his own serum, and what better way to spend his time than to kill innocent people and kidnap the heroine so they can raise lots of little aquamonsters. Producer-director Don Barton sinks in his own mire. Marshall Grauer.

**BLOOD WEDDING.** See **HE KNOWS YOU'RE ALONE.**

**BLOODBATH AT THE HOUSE OF DEATH (1984).** British showcase for the hammy thesping of Vincent Price as the leader of strange townspeople living near an isolated mansion where many years before 18 people died one bloody night. It may sound horrifying, but producer-director Ray Cameron intends it as a spoof of horror movies and a vehicle for British comedian Kenny Everett as Dr. Lucas Mandeville. Pamela Stephenson, Sheila Steafel. (VC)

**BLOODBEAT (1985).** Family gathers in the country to celebrate the yuletide only to face an entity of the supernatural—the spirit of an ancient samurai warrior. Directed by Fabrice A. Zaphiratos. Helen Benton, Terry Brown. (VC)

**BLOODEATERS.** See **TOXIC ZOMBIES.**

**BLOODLUST (1961).** Yet another version of "The Most Dangerous Game": Crazed big game hunter Dr. Balleau chases humans with a bow and arrow rig, later displaying them as trophies in special glass cabinets. Written-produced-directed with a minimum of lustiness by Ralph Brooke and starring a cast of unknowns except for Robert Reed (who became a TV star and to this day is embarrassed about this film.) June Kenny, Joan Lora.

**BLOODRAGE (1979).** Pointless bloodbath as another movie mental case stalks the sleazy districts of New York City, attacking anyone he can get his homicidal hands on. Directed by Joseph Bigwood. Lawrence Tierney, Ian Scott, James Johnston, Jerry McGee.

**BLOOD-SPATTERED BRIDE, THE (1972).** Spanish variation on Le Fanu's CARMILLA tale, a loose interpretation as newlyweds Simon Andreau and Maribel Martin, after the slowest wedding night in cinematic history, finally get around to a little depravity and perversion, to set the mood for the entrance of a shrouded woman, a reincarnation of the long-dead Carmilla. At least she enjoys drinking blood from a human wrist and making Lesbian passes at Maribel. The first hour moves too slowly under Vincente Aranda's direction and writing. When the murders occur, it's too late. Pity this could never live up to the imagery of its title. (VC)

**BLOODSUCKERS, THE (1971).** Vampirism is treated as sexual perversion in this British adaptation of Simon Raven's novel, DOCTORS WEAR SCARLET. Released in England as INCENSE OF THE DAMNED, it stars Peter Cushing and Patrick Macnee and is enhanced by Cypriot location shooting. A woman searches for her lost fiancee amidst a cult of Satan lovers. Directed by Robert Hartford-Davis. Patrick Mower, Imogen Hassal, Alex Davion.

**BLOODSUCKERS FROM OUTER SPACE (1985).** Horror and science-fiction into a tasteless meringue. (VC)

**BLOODSUCKING FREAKS.** Videocassette title for **INCREDIBLE TORTURE SHOW, THE.**

**BLOODTHIRSTY BUTCHERS (1970).** Terrible rehash of DEMON BARBER OF FLEET STREET, the Sweeney Todd sanguinary saga. Grotesque oddity that panders to the lowest common denominator, dripping with intestines and blood. A batty barber and a psychotic pastry preparer meld their perversions into one to mutilate victims and sell the leftovers as bargain basement pies. It's the work of the infamous Andy Milligan. John Miranda, Annabella Wood. (VC)

**BLOODY BIRTHDAY, THE (1980).** THE BAD SEED played as a slasher film: Two boys and a girl (all born during a solar eclipse) are instilled with homicidal tendencies on their tenth birthday. Emotionlessly, they beat a young man over the head with a shovel, strangle his girlfriend with a rope, kill dad (the sheriff of peaceful Meadowvale) with a baseball bat, shoot a schoolteacher (Susan Strasberg) and ogle a naked girl through a peephole. Is this sick or what? Director Ed Hunt proves with his screenplay that you can have your cake and slice people too, but BLOODY BIRTHDAY can't hold a candle to other slasher movies. It will just frost you. Jose Ferrer, Ellen Geer, Melinda Cordell, Lori Lethin. (VC)

**BLOODY FIANCEE.** See **BLOOD-SPATTERED BRIDE, THE.**

**BLOODY JUDGE, THE.** See **NIGHT OF THE BLOOD MONSTER.**

**BLOODY PIT OF HORROR (1967).** Italian mishmash of torture scenes that should delight sadists, masochists and other flagellators. Mickey Hargitay, one-time husband of movie sex queen Jayne Mansfield, cracks a mean whip as The Crimson Executioner, the owner of a castle equipped with the latest in torture devices. Visiting the highstone are beautiful models to pose for book covers, but instead they end up posing their last for Mickey. Massimo Pupillo directed this form of viewing torture. Allegedly based on the memoirs of the Marquis de Sade. Walter Brandi.

**BLOODY VAMPIRE, THE (1963).** More footage from a Mexican serial bought up by American producer A. K. Gordon Murray and re-edited into a feature. It's Count Cagliostro, good aristocracy, against Count Frankenhausen, evil aristocracy, and you can imagine the rest as they fight against

**BORIS KARLOFF IN ' BODY SNATCHER'**

and for the forces of evil. Directed-written by Michael Morayta. Carlos Agosti, Begona Palacios.

**BLUE BIRD, THE (1940).** Classic fantasy by Maurice Maeterlinck in the tradition of WIZARD OF OZ: Shirley Temple searches for the Bird of Happiness in a land of doom and pessimism, where Gale Sondergaard is the Wicked Witch. Walter Lang directed. Nigel Bruce, Sterling Holloway, Spring Byington, Ann Todd, Sybil Jason.

**BLUE BIRD, THE (1976).** Maeterlinck's fairy tale about a child's quest for the secret of happiness, moving from the land of the dead to the land of the yet-unborn, was an unmitigated disaster, the first Russian-U.S. film venture. The Kirov Ballet Company, Elizabeth Taylor, Cicely Tyson, Jane Fonda, James Coco and other stars blew it. What went disastrously wrong under George Cukor's direction? Did the Bird of Happiness fly up his nose?

**BLUE SUNSHINE (1977).** LSD derivative causes college students to grow bald and crazy. Writer-director Jeff Lieberman (he who gave us SQUIRM) weaves a detective story (Zalman King is searching for the source of "blue sunshine") and a political cover-up plot. But it doesn't cover up what amounts to a bad trip. You'll feel blue and need sunshine to endure. Deborah Winters, Mark Goddard. (VC)

**BLUE THUNDER (1983).** An incredibly equipped state-of-the-art helicopter (with infrared and eavesdropping devices, not to mention knockout firepower) traverses the skies over Los Angeles, eventually engaging in combat with another superchopper. It's a rousing high-tech actioner with pilots Ray Scheider and Daniel Stern picking up on a military conspiracy and shooting it out in superexciting fashion with bad guy Malcolm McDowell. Great movie action that's technically superior in its nonstop action and special effects. Directed by John Badham, scripted by Dan O'Bannon and Don Jakoby. Warren Oates, Candy Clark. (VC)

**BLUEBEARD (1944).** Cult director Edgar G. Ulmer brings to this PRC quickie good production values and John Carradine gets out of his hammy rut to deliver a good performance as a puppeteer in Paris compelled to knock off his models by putting his fingers around their necks and squeeeezzziiinnnggg. Nils Asther, Jean Parker.

**BLUEBEARD (1972).** Ladykiller Richard Burton can't make love to ladies so he kills them at the moment they surrender sexually. And what lovely victims: Raquel Welch (as a nun yet), Nathalie Delon, Karin Schubert, Marilu Tolo, Virna Lisi and Sybil Danning. Each curdling murder is recounted by Bluebeard to his bride/next-victim-to-be Joey Heatherton, who is psychoanalyzing the Count on her last night to live. Director Edward Dmytryk provides titillation, soft-core nudity, lesbianism, sadism. But scenes are played so flatly, one doesn't know if to laugh or scream. Feminists will despise the demeaning exploitation, chauvinists will ogle the undressed beauties. Burton's performance as the World War I aviator (on the threshold of the Nazi Party) never brings Bluebeard to life as a fascinating serial killer. (VC)

**BLUEBEARD'S TEN HONEYMOONS (1960).** Inexpensive Allied Artists release, shot on location in England and starring George Sanders as the strangler of beautiful spouses. Directed by Lee Wilder. Corinne Calvet, Patricia Roc.

**BLUES BUSTERS (1950).** The idiotic Bowery Boy named Sach (Huntz Hall) develops an excellent singing voice after undergoing a throat operation. You'll only choke on this Monogram programmer that is totally offkey; for diehard Bowery bums only. Directed in the usual cheesy style by William Beaudine. Leo Gorcey leads the pack. Gabriel Dell, Craig Stevens, Adele Jergens.

**BOARDING HOUSE (1982).** Pretty young girls move into a haunted house, oblivious to warnings about its bloody past. Sure enough, a woman's spirit haunts the premises, and blood flows only after it's run cold. Directed by John Wintergate. Alexandra Day, Joel Riordan, Hawk Adley. (VC)

**BOCCACCIO '70 (1962).** Three sexy tales by European directors, one with fantasy appeal. "The Temptation of Dr. Antonio" is a satire on censorship and bluenoses (directed by Federico Fellini) in which a giant poster of busty Anita Ekberg comes to life and walks through the city, disturbing the prudish and bringing out the red blooded. Other segments (directed by Luchino Visconti and Vittorio De Sica) are sex romps with nothing fantastic except the women, Romy Schneider and Sophia Loren.

**BODY BENEATH, THE (1970).** Brace yourself for a British exercise in vampirism in the hallowed halls of Carfax Abbey. Andy Milligan, terror of all producers, writers and directors, shot this in graveyards in 16mm for about $30.50 and blew it up to 35mm, when he should have just blown it up. The body and the film are both beneath . . . contempt.

**BODY DISAPPEARS, THE (1941).** Out-of-sight comedy about a doctor (Edward Everett Horton) with a formula for making bodies vanish into thin air. The slender plot eventually evaporates too. Vaporous direction by D. Ross Lederman. Jeffrey Lynn, Jane Wyman, Willie Best.

**BODY DOUBLE (1984).** Brian De Palma's most outrageous work, for he takes many narrative liberties and defies credulity to spin this strange story about a low budget horror film actor (Craig Wasson) fascinated by a beautiful woman he spies on through a telescope. He follows her, only to learn she is being tailed by a second man. Soon Wasson is into a mystery that includes a terrifying electric drill murder and a sleazy glimpse into the L.A. underground of pornographic movie-making. De Palma is a master at sustaining suspense in the Hitchcock traditon, and uses bits from many of his previous films, even satirizing his DRESSED TO KILL in the closing credits. Don't miss this one. Gregg Henry, Melanie Griffith (as Holly, the pornie queen), Deborah Shelton (as the erotic, alluring Mrs. Revelle), Guy Boyd (as the cop). (VC)

**BODY SNATCHER, THE (1944).** Val Lewton, specialist in low budget films artfully suggesting the lurking unseen, produced this adaptation of Robert Louis Stevenson's macabre tale in which body snatcher Boris Karloff inherits the trade of Burke and Hare, creating his own fresh corpses when the cemetery runs dry. Directed by Mark Robson. Henry Daniell, Bela Lugosi, Edith Atwater, Robert Clarke, Rita Corday, Russell Wade. (VC)

**BODY SNATCHER FROM HELL.** See **GOKE, BODY SNATCHER FROM HELL.**

**BODY STEALERS, THE (1969).** Subtitled THIN AIR . . . describing what Mike St. Clair's plot went into. A science-fiction belly flop in which parachutists keep disappearing in a strange mist. Agent George Sanders leaps into the mystery to find out why. Maurice Evans (believe it or don't) appears as an alien. What will director Gerry Levy and producer Tony Tenser think of next. Strictly Roman Candle city. Robert Flemyng, Patrick Allen, Neil Connery.

**BOG (1978).** There's this Bog Lake, see, where a fisherman is dynamiting the fish, only he shakes up the slumbering Incredible Slime Creature. The rubber-suited hulker starts killing while baffled sheriff Aldo Ray seeks answers from pathologist Gloria De Haven and doctor Marshall Thompson. (He should know, he conquered THE FIEND WITHOUT A FACE.) They stare into microscopes and speculate about the creature's blood and breeding habits, since it appears he thrives on type A and loves to smooch with females—human. Finally we see the Bog Monster. Wow! Glug glgglggg . . . Directed by bogged-down Don Keeslar. Leo Gordon turns up as a bayou monster expert from the big city. There's a witch named Adrianna who has a psychic link with the monster, and in an odd bit of casting, De Haven plays her too. Maybe she got bored playing an uptight pathologist. Made in Wisconsin, and thoroughly glgg glgg glgglggg . . . (VC)

**BOGGY CREEK II (1985).** When word leaks out old "Boggy" is on the rampage again, terrifying folks in the South, an anthropologist leads an expedition into the bayou country where computerized equipment is used to track the beast. Meanwhile, a hermit has captured Big Foot's offspring, holding him captive. This is producer-director Charles B. Pierce's sequel to his 1973 THE LEGEND OF BOGGY CREEK, and it ain't much—certainly nothing like the original. Cindy Butler, Serene Hedin, Chuck Pierce.

**BOMBA ON PANTHER ISLAND (1950).** Is lovely native girl Lita Baron a jungle cat lusting after human flesh? Or is there another solution to the script by director Ford Beebe, who spins his jungle boy character from the books by Roy Rockwood? Johnny Sheffield, Boy in the Weissmuller Tarzan series, rushes past potted plants in this low-budget Monogram series release. Allene Roberts, Charles Irwin.

**BOOGENS, THE (1982).** Halfway-decent monster flick, made in Utah snow country. A mine shaft on the outskirts of Silver City, abandoned since 1912, is reopened, with dynamite blasts setting free a family of tentacled creatures who wrap razor-sharp arms around victims and suck out the blood before engulfing the faces. The four young people caught up in the mystery (Rebecca Balding, Anne-Marie Martin, Fred McCarren, Jeff Harlan) are appealing types, and one wishes their characters were better captured by director James L. Conway. The monsters are only glimpsed briefly during the climactic chase through the abandoned mine shafts, a highlight of this lightweight but enjoyable low-budgeter. (VC)

**BOOGEYMAN (1980).** Strangely plotted supernatural exploitationer kicks off as a psychostudy of an adolescent knife murderer who grows into a troubled mute. The storyline veers to a haunted mirror, pieces of which cause grisly murders a la

THE OMEN. Then it segues into a poor man's EXORCIST as all hell breaks loose involving a Catholic priest, flying knives, glowing windows, etc. Finally, the disjointed elements refuse to jell and the film babbles to an incoherent closing. Directed by Ulli Lommel, a West German filmmaker who decided to go "commercial." Suzanna Love, John Carradine, Nicholas Love, Ron James. (VC)

**BOOGEYMAN II (1982).** This picks up where BOOGEYMAN I left off with terrified Suzanne Love reciting the plot, which permits director Ulli Lommel to use footage from the original. That's one way to save a buck. Only this is twice as awful as its predecessor, one of Ulli's worst in terms of production values and special effects as a spirit with a piece of mirror embedded in his palm terrorizes half of Hollywood's aspiring young performers. Its only statement is about the filmmaking culture of Hollywood as aspirants (Shannah Hall, Ashley Dubay) gather poolside to discuss the vagaries of movie producers. Otherwise, Ulli seems still hung up on impalings and things that are shoved into victims' mouths. Barely watchable, said the Elgin salesman without his clothes on. (VC)

**BOOGIE MAN WILL GET YOU, THE (1942).** Did you hear the one about the traveling salesman who stopped off at the

ULLI LOMMEL'S SELLOUT: 'BOOGEYMAN'

old Colonial Inn and ended up in a state of suspended animation? He (Boris Karloff) was only a mad scientist but he sure knew how to make his thunder bolt. Bless Karloff's patriotic heart—he wants to transform ordinary men into superheroes for the war effort. Director Lew Landers and writer Edwin Blum play this for light farce, as do Peter Lorre, Maxie Rosenbloom, Jeff Donnell and Larry Parks.

**BOOM (1968).** Two-time stage loser by Tennessee Williams, THE MILK TRAIN DOESN'T STOP HERE ANYMORE, becomes a third-time loser as a film despite "prestigious" direction by Joseph Losey and the box office "magic" of Richard Burton and Liz Taylor. Universal lost its axis—the title aptly describes what a bomb says. Burton is the Angel of Death, whose presence results in the demise of women. Ms Taylor is a widow of the five richest men in the world. Very bizarre and milky-murky. Noel Coward, Michael Dunn, Joanna Shimkus.

**BORN IN FLAMES (1982).** Writer-director Lizzie Borden takes an axe and gives our society 40 whacks in this political satire set in the near future when the U.S. Government becomes a one-party system and extremist women spearhead a revolution. Music by the Bloods and Red Crayolas. Honey, Jeanne Satterfield, Diane Jacobs.

**BORROWERS, THE (1973).** Quaint story of a miniature family living under the floorboards of a Victorian house, leading a cozy life by often "borrowing" items from normal-size people above. Adapted from a Mary Norton book. Directed by William C. Miller, Eddie Albert, Tammy Grimes.

**BOURBON STREET SHADOWS.** See **INVISIBLE AVENGER.**

**BOWERY AT MIDNIGHT (1942).** Lowbrow Monogram potboiler quickly runs out of steam even with Bela Lugosi as the star. In a dual role (as Professor Brenner and as Karl Wagner), Lugosi deposits the victims of his murderous sprees in his basement. What wretched behavior—and what a wretched Sam Katzman movie. Directed by Wallace Fox. John Archer, Tom Neal, Wanda McKay. (VC)

**BOWERY BOYS MEET THE MONSTERS, THE (1954).** Leo Gorcey, Huntz Hall and gang come face to face with a mad physician and his menagerie of ghastly creations. Ghastly is the word, all right. Directed by Edward Bernds. John Dehner, Ellen Corby, Lloyd Corrigan.

**BOWERY TO BAGDAD (1955).** Bowery Boys programmer is certain to rub you the wrong way when adults trying to act like teenagers uncover a lamp possessing strange powers. Edward Bernds directed. Huntz Hall, Leo Gorcey, Bernard Gorcey, Stanley Clements.

**BOY AND HIS DOG, A (1975).** Harlan Ellison's prize-winning novella about life after nuclear holocaust, faithfully adapted by producer-director L.Q. Jones and assistant producer Alvy Moore. In 2024, young Vic (Don Johnson) roves the devastated surface searching for food and encountering mutant bands. His canine companion, Blood, is capable of telepathic communications and has a radar-like mind. Love among the ruins with beautiful Susanne Benton leads Vic to Down Under, a subterranean society where the males are sterile and Vic is needed to inseminate the women. Less successful once Up Above is left behind, but still an engrossing science-fiction experiment. Jason Robards, Charles McGraw; Moore also appears as a Down Under resident. (VC)

**BOY AND THE PIRATES, THE (1960).** Bert I. Gordon, king of schlock Z's, slants this innocuous fare for the juvenile set. A youth, propelled through time by a genie, has adventures aboard a pirate ship commanded by Blackbeard. For adults, this picture is equivalent to walking the plank. Filmed in something producer-director Gordon calls Perceptovision. A little "percepto" wouldn't have hurt Gordon. One nice element is Albert Glasser's rousing musical score. Charles Herbert, Susan Gordon, Murvyn Vye.

**BOY WHO COULD FLY, THE (1986).** Autistic youth befriended by sympathetic teenage neighbor learns the ability to fly across the city. Gentle, serious melodrama directed by Nick Castle. Lucy Deakings, Jay Underwood, Bonnie Bedelia, Colleen Dewhurst, Fred Gwynne, Louise Fletcher. (VC)

**BOY WHO CRIED WEREWOLF, THE (1973).** Director Nathan Juran teamed with Kerwin Mathews for this lycanthropic tale, but their winning combination that made THE SEVENTH VOYAGE OF SINBAD a hit is nowhere in evidence. Mathews is bitten by a werewolf and turns into same, threatening the life of his young son. A rehash of wolf man cliches; nothing fresh. Elaine Devry, Robert J. Wilke, Jack Lucas, Paul Baxley.

**BOY WITH GREEN HAIR, THE (1948).** Joseph Losey, later blacklisted for so-called Communist leanings, directed this anti-war allegory about orphan Dean Stockwell who wakes up one morning to find he has green hair. He is ostracized by his small community except for a band of war orphans (spirits of the war dead) who tell him how to put his uniqueness to good use. Gentle, thoughtful, underrated film. Robert Ryan, Pat O'Brien, Barbara Hale, Dwayne Hickman, Russ Tamblyn. (VC)

**GREGORY PECK IN ' BOYS FROM BRAZIL'**

**BOYS FROM BRAZIL, THE (1978).** From the best-seller by Ira Levin, who delivered ROSEMARY'S BABY and married us to THE STEPFORD WIVES. The clever plot deals with a Nazi DNA cloning scheme by master German war criminal Dr. Mengele, played unevenly by Gregory Peck. Hot on Mengeles' trail, trying to solve a mystery surrounding 94 Hitler clones, is Jewish avenger Lieberman, played with dogged weariness by Laurence Olivier. Franklin J. Schaffner directed. Lilli Palmer, James Mason, Uta Hagen, Michael Gough, John Dehner, Denholm Elliott. (VC)

**BOYS FROM BROOKLYN, THE.** Videocassette title for **BELA LUGOSI MEETS A BROOKLYN GORILLA.**

**BRAIN, THE (1964).** Variation on DONOVAN'S BRAIN, wherein a well-meaning doctor (Peter Van Eyck) keeps alive the brain of a sadistic millionaire who gradually compels the doctor to carry out his evil bidding. This German/British co-production effectively makes the old material work thanks to director Freddie Francis. Anne Heywood, Cecil Parker, Bernard Lee, Miles Malleson.

**BRAIN, THE (1971).** Sleazy, amateurish mad doctor non-saga starring Dr. Kent Taylor who transplants the brain of a newly- deceased Middle East ruler into the body of Gor, a brute with a putty face who took lessons at the Tor Johnson Acting School. Performances are so terrible, this is almost enjoyable—but not quite, so wretched is the camera work and music score. Even the sound effects are poor. There's a dwarf who is the doctor's assistant, a blond femme who looks like an aging stripper and a doltish hero (Grant Williams). Meanwhile, Reed Hadley's voice keeps coming out of Gor's mouth until the brain gets switched to a new body, Reed Hadley's. Difficult stuff to set through. Filipino production, directed by Al Adamson, originally BRAIN OF BLOOD. John Bloom, Vicki Volante. (VC)

**BRAIN EATERS, THE (1958).** Nauseating low budget science-fiction thriller about invaders from outer space (what, again?) who consider themselves gourmets in devouring intelligence—literally. Allegedly based on Robert Heinlein's PUPPET MASTERS. Hack stuff from director Bruno Ve Sota. Ed Nelson, who plays the scientist fighting the aliens, produced. Leonard Nimoy, Jack Hill.

**BRAIN FROM PLANET AROUS, THE (1958).** Hysterically dumb schlocker with Earth scientist John Agar contacting an extraterrestrial: an invisible talking brain named Gor. Yuch! It savors Earthling wenches. Can't say we blame It, but . . . does It kiss on the first date? Nathan Juran directed It, Ray

Buffum wrote It, you should forget It . . . unless you're looking for laughs. Joyce Meadows, Robert Fuller, Ken Terrell. Makeup by Jack Pierce. (VC)

**BRAIN MACHINE, THE (1956).** Taut, well-acted, well-produced British thriller with minor fantasy overtones. An apparatus that can read psychotic brain waves sets off a night of terror that involves a woman being taken hostage by a drug smuggler. British film noir directed by Ken Hughes. Patrick Barr, Elizabeth Allen.

**BRAIN MACHINE, THE (1972).** Scientific testing leads to unscrupulous men listening to the thoughts of others and exploiting them. Directed by Joy N. Houck Jr. James Best, Barbara Burgess. (VC)

**BRAIN OF BLOOD.** Alternate videocassette title for **BRAIN, THE (1971).**

**BRAIN 17 (1985).** A robot, asked by a young boy to save the world, obeys the old Asimov Law of Robots: Thou shalt save the world from evil forces. (VC)

**BRAIN THAT WOULDN'T DIE, THE (1961).** Transplanted plot about transplanted brains is lifted from brainless horror films that should have died. Jason Evers is your run-of-the-lab mad scientist keeping the head of his fiancee alive in a solution after her decapitation in an accident. Now his only problem is to find a female body that turns him on. Once the head is attached, he can proceed with wedding plans. Really yucky stuff, as lowbrow as Z movies get, with an awful scene where a monster in a closet yanks a man's arm from its socket. Joseph Green wrote-directed. Virginia Leith, Adele Lamont, Bruce Brighton. (VC)

**BRAINIAC, THE (1963).** He munched on brains, this wretched-smelling abomination who 300 years ago was a respectable baron, until he got mixed up with the wrong crowd and was burned at the stake. Now he's back, thirsting for vengeance. Watch out as the long tongue slurps up the goodies. It came from Mexico but it refused to die and it comes back to haunt us on The Late Show. An Abel Salazar production directed by Chano Urueta. Salazar also stars with German Robles. (VC)

**BRAINSNATCHER, THE.** See **MAN WHO LIVED AGAIN, THE.**

**BRAINSTORM (1983).** Offbeat science-fiction thriller distinguished by the visuals of director Douglas Trumbull, whose special effects excelled in Kubrick's 2001: A SPACE ODYSSEY and who directed SILENT RUNNING. BRAINSTORM deals with scientists Christopher Walken and Louise Fletcher developing a sensory gadget that can record thoughts and emotions onto tape and play them back via a headpiece, so the listener/receiver undergoes an identical experience. The research sequences are fascinating, with implications the device allows one to pass to a higher plane of thought. Benevolent research director Cliff Robertson gives in to clandestine military forces (who want the device for war), and Walken must penetrate plant security to play a tape recording the death experience. Climax effects consist of an abstract neoreligious death sequence, but what Trumbull intended is as nebulous as the heavens in which it is set. BRAINSTORM valiantly tries to reach a metaphysical level, but lacks wallop. Louise Fletcher, Joe Dorsey, Alan Fudge, Jordan Christopher. (VC)

**BRAINWAVES (1982).** German writer-producer-director Ulli Lommel helmed this thriller with a fascinating premise: Accident victim Suzanne Love, suffering brain damage, is fed (via computer) the thought impulses from a brain donated to a lab run by the strange Dr. Clavius (Tony Curtis). While the impulses are designed to reconstrct Ms Love's brain patterns and return her to normal, she is given memories from the donated brain of a murdered woman. How Love and Keir Dullea track down the murderer and deal with the psychological terrors make for an unusual plot. Curtis has one of his oddest roles as the laconic, hoarse-voiced Clavius (he almost looks ill). Vera Miles, Percy Rodrigues, Paul Willson. (VC)

**BRASS BOTTLE, THE (1964).** Unfunny farce with Tony Randall, Burl Ives and Barbara Eden struggling with a hopelessly inept plot (by Oscar Brodney) about a down-at-the-heels architect who buys a bottle with a genie from the King Solomon era. No, Barbara is not the genie—this predates I DREAM OF JEANNIE. If you had three wishes, one would be never to see this movie. Directed for Universal by Harry Keller. Edward Andrews.

**BRAVE NEW WORLD (1980).** TV adaptation of Aldous Huxley's classic premonition of things to come that are less than utopian. Huxley's dire visions of man's dehumanization is unrealized here—it's as if an adult theme were being treated like a children's cartoon show. The good cast (Keir Dullea, Bud Cort, Ron O'Neal, Kristoffer Tabori, Julie Cobb) cannot cope with Doran William Cannon's adaptation. Directed by Burt Brinkerhoff.

**BRAZIL (1986).** Prepare for two hours of bizarre images and situations in this high-tech, high-energy surrealistic fantasy set in a futuristic quasidictatorship, where everything is askew in a Monty Python way, thanks to writer-director Terry Gilliam. Jonathan Pryce, as a worker in the Ministry of Information, is the funny side to Winston Smith of 1984, working against a bumbling "Big Brother" government in hilarious ways and fantasizing about himself as a winged warrior who is always trying to rescue a beautiful blonde from a giant samurai. Imaginative and free-wheeling, but sometimes to the detriment of story and character: It's difficult to relate to people who act so bizarrely and unpredictably. The sets and model work are fabulous, but one wishes Gilliam had restrained his indulgencies to tell a more impactful narrative. Don't miss it, however. Robert De Niro assists as a rebellious furnace repairman acting as a terrorist-commando against the regime. Ian Richardson, Kim Greist, Bob Hoskins, Michael Palin. (VC)

**BREAKFAST AT MANCHESTER MORGUE.** See **DON'T OPEN THE WINDOW.**

**BREEDERS (1986).** Uneven attempt to blend strong visual science-fiction with softcore sex, the latter distracting and cheapening an otherwise okay idea better played without titillation. Assorted Manhattan virgins are being attacked and impregnated by an other-world beast a la ALIEN, much to the puzzlement of doctor Teresa Farley and cop Lance Lewman. They finally discover the breeding grounds beneath the hospital, where babes are drenching themselves in a tub of what appears to be alien sperm. Effects are pretty good but where director-writer Tim Kincaid goes wrong is in casting all the virgins against type. There isn't a single one that could pass the test—these women have been around! Ed French, who appears as a doctor under the alien's spell, designed the standard effects. (VC)

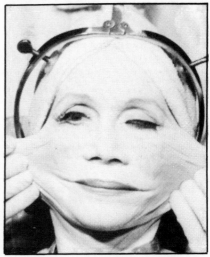

**STRETCHING THE BUDGET OF 'BRAZIL'**

**BRENDA STARR (1976).** TV-pilot for an unsold series features Dale Messick's comic strip reporter (Jill St. John) flying all over the world for her paper, The Flash. Tabi Cooper is Hank O'Hare, her stalwart companion, and Sorrell Booke is Livwright, her bellowing city editor who assigns them to investigate a voodoo cult in Brazil. The body of Jill is wonderful to look at—if only the finished product from director Mel Stuart were as well rounded. Barbara Luna, Torin Thatcher, Victor Buono, Jed Allan.

**BREWSTER McCLOUD (1971).** M*A*S*H director Robert Altman tackled this impossible fantasy about a youth (Bud Cort) who wants to fly and goes about achieving his lofty task in the Houston Astrodome with the help of a sexy bird woman (Sally Kellerman). Parodies of TV cops and arrows of outrage fired at contemporary standards never jell in this allegorical film that goes off in too many directions. Nice try, Robert, but no wings. Michael Murphy, Stacy Keach, William Windom, Shelley Duvall, Margaret Hamilton. (VC)

**BRIDE, THE (1985).** Excellent variation on Shelley's FRANKENSTEIN, beginning where THE BRIDE OF FRANKENSTEIN left off, and reminiscent of Hammer's gothic thrillers. After a rousing opening as lightning bolts bring a

**STING IN 'THE BRIDE'**

woman to life during the height of an electric storm in the Baron's lab, this follows two plots: The Baron (played sensitively by Sting) teaching worldly ways to the bride-to-be; and the Monster (Clancy Brown, wearing little make-up and emphasizing the emotional side rather than the physical) joining a dwarf circus performer (David Rappaport) on the road to Budapest, there to learn he must "follow your heart." It's old-fashioned but compelling, a fresh visualization of the parable aspects of Shelley's classic by writer Lloyd Fonvielle, and handsomely directed by Franc Roddam. Jennifer Beal, as the Bride, develops into an independent woman. Anthony Higgins, Geraldine Page. (VC)

**BRIDE AND THE BEAST (1960).** "Nightmare from the jungle! A human bride, enslaved victim of gargantuan HORROR!" But that's the ad; the movie is never as exciting. The wife of a safari man, entranced by her husband's pet gorilla, develops a taste for bananas, reverting to her Prehistoric Monkey Lady state. Hunter Lance Fuller decides an African safari is what she needs and soon Charlotte Austin is eloping with the first ape who passes in the jungle. The husband tries to save her, but he can't compare to the hairy guy, and she and the

monkey live happily ever after on hanging vines. Produced-directed by Adrian Weiss; scripted by Edward D. Wood Jr., who gave us PLAN 9 FROM OUTER SPACE. Co-starring Johnny Roth.

**BRIDE OF FRANKENSTEIN, THE (1935).** James Whale's sequel to FRANKENSTEIN is a masterpiece of macabre humor and Gothic horror, the best monster film of the 1930s. Colin Clive is again at work in the lab as the ambitious, misguided doctor hoping to resurrect the dead, only now he desires to create a "mate" for The Monster. A delightful subplot involves the miniaturization of beings by the glint-eyed Dr. Pretorious (Ernest Thesiger), and there's the meeting between the Monster and the blind beggar, spoofed so well in YOUNG FRANKENSTEIN. Boris Karloff re-creates his shambling entity of evil and pathos, while Elsa Lanchester doubles as the bride and Mary Wollstonecraft Shelley. Valerie Hobson, Dwight Frye, John Carradine, Una O'Connor. Music by Franz Waxman. (VC)

**BRIDE OF THE GORILLA (1951).** Low budgeter set on a jungle plantation where old witch Giselle Werbisek uses leaves of the "plant of evil" to turn foreman Raymond Burr into a "sukaras," a mythical animal assuming sundry shapes. Burr turns into a standard Hollywood gorilla—or is the metamorphosis only in his mind? This subtlety by writer-director Curt Siodmak doesn't belong in this cheap monster thriller, reminiscent of 1940s' Universal in style and ambience. Barbara Payton is the voluptuous wife, Lon Chaney the superstitious commissioner, Tom Powers the wise, sympathetic doctor and Woody Strode a policeman. Period nostalgia worth seeing. A Jack Broder production.

**BRIDE OF THE MONSTER (1955).** Edward D. Wood Jr. "classic," originally BRIDE OF THE ATOM, revealing a Bela Lugosi ravaged by drugs and alcohol. The abominable plot (Alex Gordon helped Wood with the concept) has Lugosi creating a race of atomic supermen, without a lot of luck, and feeding victims to a swamp monster that looks like half of an octopus. Tor Johnson, the obligatory brainless brute, makes a grab for Lugosi in one of the most pathetic fights ever photographed. And dig those amateurs, Tony McCoy and Loretta King. You have to see it to believe it. (VC)

**BRIDES OF BLOOD (1968).** First in the "Blood Island" Filipino series produced by Eddie Romero. Mad doctor Kent Taylor uses radiation brain waves to turn the living into monsters that love to munch on normal folk. Romero was so overcome as director, he hired Gerrardo de Leon to help him. John Ashley is the hero, Beverly Hills and Eva Darren two of the screaming heroines.

**BRIDES OF DRACULA (1960).** After starring in HORROR OF DRACULA, Christopher Lee refused to play the caped count for a few years, so David Peel assumed the role. Peter Cushing returns as Dr. Van Helsing, the "exorcist" of Transylvania. This excellent Hammer film features silver chains, holy water and a strangely formed "cross" which repels the handsome, young Peel. Terence Fisher directed this film which is heavy with Freudian symbolism. Martita Hunt, Yvonne Monlaur, Freda Jackson, Michael Ripper.

**BRIDES OF FU MANCHU, THE (1966).** Insidious, inscrutable Oriental mastermind (Christopher Lee) has another incredible scheme—to kidnap sexy daughters of government officials and throw the world into political chaos. Out to thwart the scheme is Nayland Smith (Douglas Wilmer) of The Yard. Lee has a new Death Ray he's threatening to use. Directed by Don Sharp, who co-scripted with Harry Alan Towers. Howard Marion-Crawford, Burt Kwouk, Tsai Chin, Marie Versini.

**BRIDGE ACROSS TIME (1985).** The London Bridge transported to Lake Havasu, Arizona, and reconstructed there stone by stone, is the showpiece for this TV-movie in which Jack the Ripper reappears to murder young women in his inimitable style. William F. Nolan's teleplay, though an inspired idea, is somewhat predictable and follows the standard cat-and-mouse games of stalked victims, baffled police, town politicians wanting to cover up lest tourism decline, etc. E. W. Swackhamer directs with a constant eye on the bridge, and ends on a note of typical action. It's not bad, just ordinary.

**ELSA LANCHESTER AND BORIS KARLOFF IN 'THE BRIDE OF FRANKENSTEIN'**

David Hasselhoff, Randolph Mantooth, Clu Gulager, Lindsay Bloom, Rose Marie, Adrienne Barbeau, Lane Smith.

**BRIGADOON (1954).** The dance team of Gene Kelly and Cyd Charisse brings to life Lerne and Loewe's Broadway musical as discoverers of a Scottish village which only appears every hundred years. An exciting blend of fantasy and choreography, with a great score. Directed by MGM's master of musicals, Vincent Minnelli, with superb photography by Joseph Ruttenberg. Elaine Stewart, Jimmy Thompson, Barry Jones. (VC)

**BRIGHTON STRANGLER, THE (1944).** Actor John Loder is so obsessed with his role as a strangler in a British stage hit that a concussion during the London Blitz makes him think he's the character he's playing. He takes the train to Brighton to carry out a murder, but the girl he meets, June Duprez, tries to help him sort out his confusion . . . right up to the twist ending. Similar to the 1947 Academy Award winner, A DOUBLE LIFE, but not as classy. Max Nosseck directed. Ian Wolfe, Miles Mander, Rose Hobart. (VC)

**BRING ME THE VAMPIRE (1965).** Mexican version of that old chestnut—heirs to a fortune gathering in a haunted castle for the night. What they don't know is, the drafty corridors are haunted by a vampire. Take it away! Directed by Alfredo E. Crevena. Maria Eugenia San Martin, Hector Godoy, Carlos Riquelme, Maria Pena.

**BRITANNIA HOSPITAL (1983).** Bizarre British film wavering between social satire and outrageous, black comedy, well directed by Lindsay Anderson. While it makes sport of English institutions, David Sherwin's script has a universality. The setting is a London hospital undergoing inner turmoils on the day Her Royal Highness pays a visit. What really is outlandish is a subplot involving a mad doctor who pieces a Frankenstein Monster from assorted body organs and limbs. When the Creature is brought to life and literally bites the hand of the doctor that fed it life, this becomes very gruesome and will require strong stomachs. There's also a giant brain called Genesis controlling the administrators. The most irreverent scene has police clubbing rioters while H.R.H. listens to "God Save the Queen." Leonard Rossiter, Malcolm McDowell, Mark Hamill, Alan Bates, Marsha Hunt, Dandy Nichols. (VC)

**BROOD, THE (1979).** Disturbing tale from Canada's "king of horror," David Cronenberg, depicting a therapy called psychoplasmics in which the patient changes cell structure through internal anger. Doctor Oliver Reed experiments with Samantha Eggar, who produces a womb-like sac on her tummy and gives birth to a brood of deformed, monstrous dwarves who enjoy hammering innocent people to death. In one sickening sequence, Samantha breaks open the membrane of her sac, removes a malshaped human form and licks away the blood. An intriguing idea, but blatantly pandering and terribly offensive. Art Hindle, Cindy Hinds, Susan Hogan, Henry Beckerman. (VC)

**BROTHER FROM ANOTHER PLANET, THE (1984).** A thoughtful, esoteric science-fictioner, so satiric in its overview of the human race that it becomes precious. Joe Morton portrays a black alien, humanoid except for his three-toed feet and an ability to touch anything broken and make it work. The Brother, stranded on Earth, never speaks as he moves through his episodic adventures in Harlem, some of which are object lessons in human behavior. Trailing the alien are two interstellar cops in black; writer-director John Sayles (himself one of the aliens) plays them largely for laughs. A low budget experimental film, gritty yet charming, with Morton's mimed performance a tour de force. A prestigious effort to use fantasy to make a statement about society. Darryl Edwards, Steve James. (VC)

**BROTHER JOHN (1972).** Angelic being descends to Earth to see if we're worth saving, decides we're terribly racist—and since the angel is Sidney Poitier, who's to say he isn't right? TV-movie directed by James Goldstone, written by Ernest Kinoy. Will Geer, Bradford Dillman, Beverly Todd, Paul Winfield, Warren J. Kemmerling.

**BROTHERHOOD OF SATAN, THE (1971).** Produced by Alvy Moore and L.Q. Jones, and directed by Bernard McEveety, this low budget supernatural thriller is well photographed and acted by Struther Martin (as the leader of a Satanic cult), with Moore and Jones also in the cast. A coven in a Southwestern town needs children to feed the Devil during latest sacrificial offerings. William Welch's script has many chilling moments as well as one eerie dream sequence. Charles Bateman, Anna Capri. (VC)

**BROTHERHOOD OF THE BELL, THE (1970).** Unsettling, offbeat TV-movie: A secret college fraternity is in control of the business world, with powerful contacts to achieve any pur-

**RONDO HATTON IN 'THE BRUTE MAN'**

pose, sincere or diabolical. And the fraternity is part of the Catholic Church! Glenn Ford portrays a professor who tries to expose the brotherhood to the public—with numbing results. Recommended. Directed by Paul Wendkos. Rosemary Forsyth, Dean Jagger, Maurice Evans, Will Geer, William Conrad. Music by Jerry Goldsmith.

**BRUTE MAN, THE (1946).** Rondo Hatton was a limited talent who enjoyed brief fame as a film ugly. He needed no makeup, for he suffered from a disease of the pituitary gland. Hatton's popularity was due to his portrayal of The Creeper, the origin of which is recounted in this shoddy thriller. A football hero is disfigured in a laboratory explosion, and despite his grotesque appearance he falls in love with a blind pianist. Call it pathos/bathos terror. Considered so repulsive in its day, Universal sold it to PRC, a grade-Z studio. Hatton died the same year THE BRUTE MAN was released and passed into oblivion. Directed by Jean Yarbrough. Tom Neal, Jane Adams. (VC)

**BUBBLE, THE (1966).** Arch Oboler produced-directed this science-fiction mystery about a community surrounded by a force-field where the humans are under extraterrestrial scrutiny. Some 3-D effects are startling, others fail. What's unforgivable, Oboler's script and direction are one dimensional. Re-released in the '70s as FANTASTIC INVASION OF PLANET EARTH. Michael Cole, Deborah Walley, Johnny Desmond, Virginia Gregg, Vic Perrin.

**BUCK ROGERS (1939).** In the style of the FLASH GORDON series which also starred Buster Crabbe, this 12-episode Universal serial depicts Buck and Buddy Wade (Jackie Moran) crashlanding their dirigible on a mountaintop, where they are put into suspended animation by a "nirvano" gas. They awaken 500 years later to find the world taken over by Killer Kane (Anthony Warde). Buck battles Kane with the help of Dr. Huer (C. Montague Shaw), Wilma (Constance Moore) and a race of Saturnians. Not as well-produced or -written as the FLASH GORDON cliffhangers, but great fun. In unedited videocassette form as **BUCK ROGERS CONQUERS THE UNIVERSE.** Released in shorter versions as **PLANET OF OUTLAWS** in 1953 and as **DESTINATION SATURN** in 1965.

**BUCK ROGERS (1979).** Theatrical version of the TV-pilot produced by Leslie Stevens and Glen A. Larson. A pastiche of STAR WARS with awesome mothership, comedy relief robots and cardboard heroes and heroines. Some sexual double entendres give the Universal film a false sense of being "adult," but it's cornball space opera with Gil Gerard as Buck, Erin Gray as space jockey Wilma Deering, Henry Silva as Killer Kane and Pamela Hensley as the sexually arousing Princess Ardala Darco. The voice of Twiki the robot is Mel Blanc's. So is the voice of Dr. Theopolis, a miniaturized computer in the shape of a neon disc worn about Twiki's neck. Daniel Haller directed the Larson-Stevens script. Tim O'Connor, Julie Newmar.

**BUCK ROGERS CONQUERS THE UNIVERSE.** Videocassette title for 90 minutes from the 1939 Universal serial **BUCK ROGERS.**

**BUCK ROGERS IN THE 25TH CENTURY.** Videocassette title for the 1979 TV pilot of **BUCK ROGERS.**

**BUCK ROGERS: FLIGHT OF THE WAR WITCH (1979).** Episodes of the Gil Gerard TV series, strung out like derelict spacecraft, mostly space opera cliches. Pamela Hensley, however, is worth ogling in her scanty harem costumes. And this has the "well-roundedness" of Julie Newmar. Larry Stewart directed and Robert W. Gilmer cranked out the script, which depicts our heroes going into a time warp to another universe. Erin Gray, Tim O'Connor, Michael Ansara, Vera Miles, Sam Jaffe.

**BUCK ROGERS: PLANET OUTLAWS (1939).** Compilation of highlights from the Universal serial. (VC)

**BUCKET OF BLOOD, A (1959).** Roger Corman miniclassic in macabre humor, second only to LITTLE SHOP OF HORRORS. Offbalance busboy in a beatnik cafe murders unsuspecting victims and then pours plaster over their bodies, offering the results as "sculpture." For its day, Charles Griffith's screenplay was unique. Richard Miller, Anthony Carbone, Julian Barton, Ed Nelson.

**BUG (1975).** Bradford Dillman reaches for Black Flag when an earthquake cleaves a fissure in a wheat field and releases an insect swarm capable of starting fires by rubbing legs together. And you thought a Boy Scout was clever. Poor horror film, an all-time low for producer William Castle, best remembered for ROSEMARY'S BABY. Jeannot Szwarc directed the Castle-Thomas Page screenplay based on Page's THE HEPHAESTUS PLAGUE. Joanne Miles, Jesse Vint, Patty McCormack. (VC)

**PAMELA HENSLEY IN 'BUCK ROGERS'**

## 'THE BURNING': THE SCHLOCKER THAT BURNED UP AUDIENCES

**BULLDOG DRUMMOND AT BAY (1937).** Drummond was a staunch, upright government agent from the stiff-upper-lip-and-all-that school, who frequently saved the Empire after World War I. (In more recent times the character was parodied in BULLSHOT CRUMMOND, a stage play and film.) In this interpretation of the H.C. McNeil character, Drummond is out to rescue the scientist who invented a robot aircraft. Directed by Norman Lee. Victor Jory, John Lodge, Dorothy Mackaill, Richard Bird.

**BULLDOG DRUMMOND IN AFRICA (1938).** Unengaging Drummond series film with John Howard as Her Majesty's stalwart hero, this time out to stop a mad doctor armed with a Disintegrator Death Beam. Very ordinary, even in its own time. Directed by Louis King. Heather Angel, J. Carrol Naish, H.B. Warner, Anthony Quinn.

**BULLSHOT CRUMMOND (1983).** Frenzied, unharnessed parody of H. C. McNeil's stalwart undercover agent, a gas of a movie played like a Victorian melodrama in Edwardian costumes. Crummond is a complete klutz out to stop his bitter nemesis Otto von Bruno from conquering the world with various devices. It starts when inventor Rupert Fenton is kidnapped, and Rupert's naive daughter seeks help from Crummond. Madcap adventures involve a giant tarantula, an "involuntary slippage chair," a force field, a new explosive and a superintelligent octopus. Nonstop gags Monte Python style, frenetically directed by Dick Clement. The stars—Diz White, Alan Shearman and Ron House—also wrote the script, based on the long-running popular stage play. Frances Tomelty, Michael Aldridge. (VC)

**BURIAL GROUND (1985).** Guests at a mansion in the country are attacked by the Incredible Walking Dead, George Romero style. Because director Andrea Bianchi contributes nothing new, this is real ho hum stuff. Karen Well, Perer Bark. (VC)

**BURIED ALIVE (1980).** Italian gore thriller (or nonthriller, depending on your view) from director Aristide Massaccesi, about a mentally deranged taxidermist who does strange things with corpses following a fouled-up childhood. Who wrote this mess? Ottavio Fabbri, who else? Kieran Canter, Sam Modesto. (VC)

**BURKE AND HARE.** See **HORRORS OF BURKE AND HARE, THE.**

**BURN, WITCH, BURN (1962).** Based on a Fritz Leiber novel, CONJURE WIFE, this is a better-than-average British supernatural thriller starring Peter Wyngarde as a university professor lecturing against witchcraft and Janet Blair as his wife, armed with lucky charms to ward off evil. Some wild, hairy things happen and you'll be unnerved, even if you can see the wires propelling a killer bird when it pops off the face of the campus tower. Directed by Sidney Hayers, written by George Baxt, Charles Beaumont and Richard Matheson. Margaret Johnson, Colin Gordon.

**BURNING, THE (1982).** At Camp Blackfoot, New York, stupid teenagers pull a prank on equally stupid Cropsy, the caretaker, who is horribly disfigured and burned. When he's released from hospital, Cropsy returns to the camp armed with giant shears and eager to wreak vengeance. Another sleazy scuzz-bag slasher-sickness flick with gory murders. Features the massacre of several stupid kids simultaneously, adding to its close-your-eyes-before-the-knife-descends gruesomeness. Producer Harvey Weinstein, a stickler for realism, claims the Cropsy tale is true; or maybe he just saw FRIDAY THE 13TH. Grisly, idiotic contender that suffers from early burnout. Directed by Tony Maylam. Brian Matthews, Leah Ayles, Brian Backer. (VC)

**BURNING COURT, THE (1966).** French version of the John Dickson Carr supernatural novel in which a family is cursed by the ravings of a witch which turn out to be prophetic. Produced-directed by Julien Duvivier. Charles Spaak, Nadja Tiller, Jean-Claude Brialy, Edith Scob.

**BURNT OFFERINGS (1976).** Modern Gothic with excellent technical effects, and fine performances by Oliver Reed, Karen Black and Bette Davis (not playing a crazy old bat for once). But alas, it goes awry because of an ambiguous script by producer-director Dan Curtis and William F. Nolan. The theme of the "house possessed by evil," which Stanley Kubrick unsuccessfully tried to repeat in THE SHINING, never comes off due to a lack of expository material, and an eventual sense of logic-illogic. Instead, it's a mishmash. Even a twist ending cannot save it. Nice try that turns to ashes. Burgess Meredith, Eileen Heckart. (VC)

**BUTCHER, BAKER, NIGHTMARE MAKER.** See **NIGHT WARNING.**

"Having someone special for dinner?"—Titular character in
**CANNIBAL GIRLS.**

**CABIN IN THE SKY (1942).** Film version of Lynn Rott's epic Negro play depicting the Devil vs. the good folks in Heaven, featuring an all-black all-star cast: Ethel Waters, Eddie "Rochester" Anderson, Lena Horne, Duke Ellington, Rex Ingram, Mantan Moreland, Butterfly McQueen, Willie Best. Directed by Vincente Minnelli. (VC)

**CABINET OF CALIGARI (1962).** Robert Bloch scripted this updated version of the silent German classic, but claims producer-director Roger Kay butchered his screenplay. This loose "update" is overloaded with Freudian symbolism and dream sequences. Nothing is what it seems (but can be explained later, once you understand the mystery's key) as distraught Glynis Johns visits a strange house in the country presided over by Dan O'Herlihy. J. Pat O'Malley, Estelle Winwood, Lawrence Dobkin, Vicki Trickett.

**CABINET OF DR. CALIGARI (1919).** Silent German classic in Expressionism, an early attempt to explore psychological horror. It's a nightmare told by an insane asylum inmate, depicting a carnival hypnotist, his somnambulistic zombie, a series of murders, etc. Contemporary audiences may find this too cumbersome with its outmoded acting. Robert Wiene directed, Fritz Lang co-scripted. Werner Krauss, Conrad Veidt, Lil Dagover. (VC)

**CAGE, THE (1965).** The original STAR TREK pilot starring Jeffrey Hunter as Captain Christopher Pike, never shown in its entirely on network but largely used as part of a two-parter in the first season, "The Menagerie." Scenes never shown before are in black and white, footage from TV in color. Series creator Gene Roddenberry introduces the pilot, giving some colorful background as he walks the set of a STAR TREK movie. If you've seen "The Menagerie" there isn't much point in renting this videocassette special, but Trekkies will consider it a must-see curio. Nimoy appears as an excitable Spock, John Hoyt is the ship's doctor, Majel Barrett as a woman on the Enterprise bridge and Susan Oliver as the woman who seduces Pike when he finds himself in a galactic zoo. (VC)

**CAGE OF DOOM.** See **TERROR FROM THE YEAR 5000.**

**CAGED VIRGINS (1973).** France's Jean Rollin specializes in sex films with vampire themes—or were they vampire films with sex themes? In this blatant helping of eroticism and

neck-biting, a European castle is the setting for the terrorization of sexy babes. Known as CRAZED VAMPIRE and VIRGINS AND VAMPIRES. Phillipe Gaste, Marie Pierre Castel, Mirielle D'Argent.

**CALLING DR. DEATH (1943).** Hypnotism solves a murder—the only interesting element in this routine entry in Universal's "Inner Sanctum" series. Lon Chaney Jr. portrays a neurologist plagued by his subconscious. J. Carrol Naish is far better as a suspicious cop. Patricia Morison, David Bruce, Ramsay Ames. Directed by Reginald LeBorg.

**CALTIKI, THE IMMORTAL MONSTER (1959).** Caltiki, god of Mayan legend, loves humans a la carte and rolls out of his sacred waters in an Aztec temple to infect snoopy scientists. In this U.S.-Italian film photographed by Mario Bava in Spain, and directed by Riccardo Freda, there's nobody to cheer except the monster. Eat those fat-headed scientists, Caltiki, you cute little blob. Daniela Rocca, John Merivale.

**CANADIAN MOUNTIES VS. ATOMIC INVADERS.** See **MISSILE BASE AT TANIAK.**

**CANDY (1968).** Innocent alien (Ewa Aulin), sexually provocative, lands her saucer on Earth and is sexually assaulted by Marlon Brando, John Huston, Ringo Starr, Richard Burton, Walter Matthau and other male stars wasting their time in this grotesque version of Terry Southern's porno novel. Don't take strangers from CANDY. Directed by Christian Marquand; scripted by Buck Henry.

**CANNIBAL GIRLS (1972).** In a Canadian town, three dead women with a penchant for human flesh haunt a restaurant where a young couple are spending the night. Low budget avant-garde supernatural thriller. Produced-directed by Ivan Reitman. Eugene Levy, Andrea Martin, Ronald Ulrich. Reitman went on to direct GHOSTBUSTERS.

**CANNIBAL HOLOCAUST.** See **JUNGLE HOLOCAUST.**

**CANNIBAL ORGY.** See **SPIDER BABY.**

**CANNIBALS IN THE STREETS (1980).** Italian-Spanish "zombies on the loose" flick from director Anthony M. Dawson, with gore effects by Gianetto De Rossi, who splashed the blood in ZOMBIE. The flesh-eaters are Vietnam veterans in downtown Atlanta, tearing apart humans. Can only cop

John Saxon stop the plague of the undead? Sleazy. Elizabeth Turner, John Morghen, Cindy Hamilton.

**CANTERVILLE GHOST, THE (1944).** Whimsical, hilarious version of the Oscar Wilde story, directed by Jules Dassin. A cowardly ghost (Charles Laughton, in one of his finest roles) is doomed to walk the family castle until a descendant performs an heroic deed. Updated to incorporate the Nazi threat. Ideal vehicle for Laughton, Robert Young, Margaret O'Brien, Peter Lawford and Rags Ragland.

**CANTERVILLE GHOST, THE (1986).** TV version of Wilde's ghost comedy, updated to modern England where Andrea Marcovicci and Ted Wass turn up to claim their inheritance: a castle (actually filmed in a real one in Worcester). Stalking its halls, with supernatural ball and chain, is Sir John Gielgud as the irascible, blustering spectre; he alone makes this worthwhile. Good effects enhance this old tale in which the ghost must force earthlings to perform an heroic act. Directed by Paul Bogart.

**CAPE CANAVERAL MONSTERS, THE (1960).** Phil Tucker, who established new incompetency levels in ROBOT MONSTER, dips to greater lows with this alien-invaders fiasco. Two bathers are attacked by two circular beams of light (what a great effect!), die in a car crash and return possessed by ET energy fields. Nadja and Hauron (aliens) are responsible for fouling up rocket launchings at Cape Canaveral—mainly by pointing a bazooka-shaped zap gun and firing. They address their ET boss on an "interplanetary receiver"—a TV set in which a pancake floats. Katherine Victor and Jason Johnson convey absolutely no menace as the turgid invaders, who grow uglier as more putty is heaped on their faces. At control center, a Jewish scientist operates phony-looking equipment while leads Scott Peters and Linda Connell stumble around the alien's cave. Mercifully short (69 minutes) but still not short enough!

**CAPRICORN ONE (1978).** After faking a manned flight to Mars, so Congress with okay space dollars, the U.S. space program arranges for the death of the "astronauts." Wise to their pending demise, James Brolin, Sam Waterston and O. J. Simpson run for their lives. Media reporter Elliott Gould uncovers the conspiracy and tracks the men into the desert. This exciting thriller makes only derogative inferences about our conquest of space and U.S. agencies. Written-directed by Peter Hyams. Hal Holbrook, Karen Black, Telly Savalas, Brenda Vaccaro, Robert Walden. (VC)

**CAPTAIN AMERICA (1944).** All 15 chapters of the Republic serial starring Dick Purcell as the comic book hero, here doing battle with Lionel Atwill as a glazed, dazed and crazed guy in control of the Thunder Bolt. Lots of cheap thrills. Directed by John English & Elmer Clifton. (VC)

**CAPTAIN AMERICA (1979).** TV-pilot depicts the famous

**LAUGHTON IN 'THE CANTERVILLE GHOST'**

Marvel comic book superhero created by Simon and Kirby with an average plot: An archvillain plots to steal millions by blowing up Phoenix, Arizona, with a neutron explosive device. Reb Brown is the patriotic American stalwart, Steve Rogers. Directed by Rod Holcomb. Len Birman, Heather Menzies, Steve Forrest, Len Birman. (VC)

**CAPTAIN AMERICA II: DEATH TOO SOON (1979).** Steve Rogers dons the red-white-and-blue of America's great superhero to protect citizens against an aging drug. This TV-movie, another failed pilot, is enough to age anyone, and a drug on the viewing market. Directed by Ivan Nagy. Christopher Lee, Lana Wood, Connie Sellecca, Christopher Cary, Len Birman, Katherine Justice. (VC)

**CAPTAIN KRONOS—VAMPIRE HUNTER (1972).** Exciting Hammer vampire actioner, different and compelling. Peter Cushing is the dedicated Kronos, who embarks on Quixotic hunts for bloodsuckers with his constant companion, a hunchback named Professor Grost. Writer-director Brian Clemens creates a blend of satire and swashbuckling action with overtones of an old-fashioned serial. Watch for exotic Caroline Munro as Kronos' helper. (VC)

**CAPTAIN MEPHISTO AND THE TRANSFORMATION MACHINE (1945).** Feature version of Republic's MANHUNT OF MYSTERY ISLAND (released to TV in 1966) with Roy Barcroft as a bloodthirsty buccaneer who uses a zingy electric chair (the Atomic Power Transmitter) to change from one character to another. Linda Stirling and Richard Bailey, cliffhanging regulars, search for lost radium deposits and fight Mephisto's pirate gang. Chuckles and ersatz thrills. Directed with flair by Yakima Canutt, Spencer Bennet and Wallace Grissell. Kenne Duncan.

**CAPTAIN NEMO AND THE UNDERWATER CITY (1970).** What this youth-oriented adaptation of Jules Verne cryingly needs is not special effects (of which there are scads) but a decent screenplay so Robert Ryan (as Nemo), Chuck Connors, Luciana Paluzzi and Kenneth Connor wouldn't drown in an ocean of cliches. If only its story were up to the visuals of the undersea kingdom of Templemer, Nemo's submarine, etc. Directed by James Hill.

**CAPTAIN SINBAD (1963).** Made in Germany by the King Brothers (GORGO), this colorful fantasy stars Guy Williams as Sinbad, who finds his fiancee trapped by the wicked Pedro Armendariz. Sinbad is tortured, battles a giant hand (winning thumbs down) and seeks to cut out the evil caliph's heart. Principally for the young, but adults will enjoy the costumes, splendid sets and Byron Haskin's stylish direction. Produced by Frank and Herman King.

**CAPTIVE (1980).** Grade B cheapie in which the planet Styrolia engages in war with Earth over possession of Dirathium crystals. Two recon humanoid aliens, shot down by our fighter defense, hold an old farmer and his family captive, until one of the aliens has a change of heart. Unexciting and predictable, with an anti-climactic nonending. The terrible model work finishes off whatever good intentions producers-directors Allan Sandler and Robet Emenegger had. For captive audiences only. Cameron Mitchell, David Ladd, Lori Saunders, Dan Sturkie, Donald Bishop.

**CAPTIVE PLANET (1986).** Another Italian mushed up messmash (to be missed) from director Al Bradly, whose work has to be seen to be (dis)believed. You can almost hear the pulp magazine editors groaning when alien invader humanoids try to conquer our Earth, and miss the mass by lightyears. Sharon Baker, Chris Avram. (VC)

**CAPTIVE WILD WOMAN (1943).** Beauty contest winner Acquanetta walks zombie-like as a mysterious native woman transformed into a member of the monkey family by a mad doctor—but everyone associated with this Universal quickie, including John Carradine as the mad scientist and Milburn Stone and Evelyn Ankers as the sympathetic heroes, are made into monkeys. Surprisingly, this tasteless B effort sparked sequels: JUNGLE WOMAN and JUNGLE CAPTIVE, equally as dismal. Edward Dmytryk directed this? Lloyd Corrigan, Paul Fix, Grant Withers.

**CAPTIVE WOMEN (1952).** New York City ruins in 3000 A.D.

are the depressing setting for this science-fiction yarn by Aubrey Wisberg and Jack Pollexfen (fresh from THE MAN FROM PLANET X) about hideous Mutants who raid the handsome Norms to snatch away buxom, blond-haired women. There's a third band, the Uprivers, who live . . . yeah, upriver. A prehistoric mentality at RKO was responsible for this post-Armageddon fiasco. Robert Clarke, William Schallert, Ron Randell. Associate producer was Albert Zugsmith, famous for his odd mixture of B flicks. Directed by Stuart Gilmore.

**CAPTURE OF BIGFOOT (1979).** Hairy beast, familiar to Boggy Creek residents, runs wild through city streets. Stay upwind while you do your shopping, and watch where you step. Written-directed by William Rebane. Richard Kennedy, Katherine Hopkins, John Goff, Otis Young.

**CAPTURE THAT CAPSULE. See SPY SQUAD.**

**CAR, THE (1977).** Disappointing Universal film imitates the formula of JAWS but with a killer auto. Elliot Silverstein's direction is singularly hindered by a muddled screenplay, which has fuzzily sketched characters and a murky sense of logic in explaining from whence the car came. The real stars are stunt driver Everett Creach and the car, a squat, black evil-looking creation by custom designer George Barris. The wheeled killer takes on an ominous, satanic personality as it zooms, carooms, whirls, spins and roars through a desert community (in and around St. George, Utah), crushing human bodies. James Brolin stars as the sheriff leading the search. John Marley, Kathleen Lloyd, R. G. Armstrong, Kim Richards, John Rubinstein.

**CARE BEARS MOVIE, THE (1985).** Care Bears are benevolent cuddly creatures who live in sunny Care-A-Lot and each has a human counterpart called a Cousin. Each Care Bear and Cousin has a specialty emotion they want to share with others. On the other hand, there's an evil spirit that wants to spread distrust and hate throughout the kingdom. The style is cartoonish and cute. Mickey Rooney narrates these Caring adventures and Carole King sings the title song. Produced in Toronto. Videocassette edition is subtitled LAND WITHOUT FEELINGS. (VC)

**CARE BEARS MOVIE II: A NEW GENERATION (1986).** Inferior sequel to THE CARE BEARS MOVIE, rather charmless. This is strictly Saturday Morning at the Cartoons, a blatant commercial for Care Bear toys and related products as True Heart Bear and Noble Heart Horse set out on a journey of enlightenment. But the bulbs are out as far as ideas are concerned. Directed by Dale Schott. Voices by Maxine Miller, Pam Hyatt, Hadley Kay. (VC)

**CARNAGE (1972).** Italian scarer (also TWITCH OF THE DEATH NERVE and ECOLOGY FOR A CRIME) about sadistic murderers fighting over the estate of Countess Federica. Confusing, graphically revolting, stained with blood from beginning to end, ludicrous in its characterizations. Mario Bava wrote, directed and photographed this bloodbath featuring cleavers, spears and other flesh-penetrating weapons. Claudine Auger, Claudio Volonte, Luigi Pistilli, Isa Miranda. (VC)

**CARNAGE (1984).** Rock-bottom Andy Milligan clunker, depicting newlyweds in a haunted house, where all their guests are murdered by the restless spirits. Poor in all departments, including the gore murders. Leslie Den Dooven, Michael Chiodo. (VC)

**CARNIVAL OF BLOOD (1971).** Also known as DEATH RIDES A CARNIVAL, a fitting subtitle since this is set at Coney Island where a mad slasher with a mother complex uses the rides to knock off victims. A sick story, in which various body organs are extracted by the psychokiller, never

**SISSY SPACEK AS CARRIE, DRENCHED IN STICKY PIG'S BLOOD**

packs the wallop of an ordinary jaunt on a Ferris wheel. Written-produced-directed by Leonard Kirtman. Burt Young, Judith Resnick. (VC)

**CARNIVAL OF SOULS (1962).** Low budgeter, made by industrial filmmaker Herk Harvey in Lawrenceville, Kansas, is a surprisingly effective supernatural thriller about a girl who hovers in the netherland between life and death after an accident. Watch to see what can be done with little money and nameless talent. Candace Hilligoss, Frances Feist.

**CAROL FOR ANOTHER CHRISTMAS (1964).** Rod Serling updated Dickens' A CHRISTMAS CAROL for this story of industrialist Daniel Grudge, embittered over the loss of his son during World War II, who is visited by the ghosts of Christmas Past (Steve Lawrence), Present (Pat Hingle) and Future (Robert Shaw). Directed by Joseph Mankiewicz. Sterling Hayden, Ben Gazzara, Peter Sellers.

**CAROLINA CANNONBALL (1955).** Foreign spies are lost in fields of corn when they tangle with hillbilly Judy Canova in their search for a nuclear-powered rocket. Charles Lamont directed this Republic cheapie. Andy Clyde, Ross Elliott, Sig Ruman, Jack Kruschen. Cornball nostalgia.

**CAROUSEL (1956).** Ferenc Molnar's LILIOM, readapted by Rodgers and Hammerstein from their Broadway dance musical about loud-mouth carnival baker Billy Bigelow, who returns from the dead to help his daughter grow up. Gordon MacRae portrays Bigelow and the songs include "You'll Never Walk Alone" and "If I Loved You." A great cast (Shirley Jones, Cameron Mitchell, Gene Lockhart, John Dehner) led by a famous director (Henry King).

**CARPATHIAN EAGLE, THE (1981).** Repackaged episode from Britain's HAMMER HOUSE of HORROR, a rather grisly tale about a series of traditional murders and how the killer is stalked by a newspaperman and policeman. Directed by Francis Megahy. Pierce Brosnan, Sian Phillips. Elvira hosts the videocassette version. (VC)

**CARRIE (1976).** Producer-director Brian De Palma's treatment of Stephen King's first novel, a lurid tale of modern Gothic horror. At least two sequences will have you leaping from your seat. A psychological study of a mousy young teenager (Sissy Spacek) who uses her power of telekinesis to wreak vengeance after a macabre joke has been played on her during the high school prom. Tension between Spacek and her mother (Piper Laurie), a religious fanatic, is riveting and her "Crucifixion" scene is unforgettable. Among the most powerful horror films of the 1970s. John Travolta, Nancy Allen, Amy Irving, William Katt. (VC)

**CARRY ON SCREAMING (1966).** Entry in the British "Carry On" series spoofs Universal's horror films with mad doctor, vampire, mummy and split personality. Carry on elsewhere unless you dig these uninhibited, zany "Goon Show"-style flicks. Directed by Gerald Thomas. Kenneth Williams, Fenella Fielding, Tom Clegg, Joan Sims.

**CARRY ON SPYING (1964).** England's "Carry On" gang levels its sights on James Bond and comes up with a few laughs, if not avalanches of chortles and guffaws. Three dumb agents are after a mysterious concoction stolen by STENCH, an organization under the control of Dr. Crow, half-man, half-woman. Directed by Gerald Thomas. Kenneth Williams, Barbara Windsor, Charles Hawtrey.

**CARS THAT ATE PEOPLE, THE (1974).** Peter Weir began his directing-writing career in Australia with this bizarre technological horror story set in the Down Under town of Paris, where the young generation drives through the streets in automobiles covered with the decor of other autos they've cannibalized through road traps. Meanwhile, a crazy Frankenstein-style doctor experiments on the captured tourists, turning them into monsters. Well, it's a living. Terry Camilleri, John Meillon, Kevin Miles. (VC)

**CASE OF THE FULL MOON MURDERS (1971).** X-rated spoof of horror and sex films, directed by Sean Cunningham, who would direct FRIDAY THE 13TH and other horror films in the 1980s. Strictly hardcore at the seams, with "big" actor Harry Reems.

**CASINO ROYALE (1967).** Five directors—John Huston, Ken Hughes, Val Guest, Robert Parrish, Joe McGrath—out to make the ultimate James Bond spy adventure with $14 million still ended up with a fuzzy fiasco. This despite dazzling sets, a plethora of special effects and superspy gadgets. Don't confuse this with the Connery series—it was an independent effort treating Ian Fleming's character with tongue in cheek. Despite the fine screenwriters (Wolf Mankowitz, John Law, Michael Sayers, John Huston, Ben Hecht, Joseph Heller, Terry Southern) the cast wanders aimlessly through the lovely framework, hopelessly lost. David Niven portrays Sir James Bond, brought out of retirement to tackle SMERSH, Joanna Pettet is his daughter Mata Bond and Woody Allen plays nephew Jimmy Bond. Peter Sellers, Peter O'Toole, Orson Welles, Ursula Andress, Woody Allen, Deborah Kerr, ad nauseam. (VC)

**CASTLE, THE (1969).** Franz Kafka's allegorical fantasy produced by and starring Maximilian Schell. A stranger, "Mr. K," arrives at an anonymous institution called The Castle and becomes mysteriously caught up in red tape and befuddlement. Metaphysical as hell. Directed-written by Rudolf Noelte. Helmut Qualtinger.

**CASTLE IN THE AIR (1953).** British comedy made screamingly funny by Margaret Rutherford as an aristocratic lady ghost, flitting around the hallways of a Highland castle in her flimsy nightgown, helping the Earl of Locharne (David Tomlinson) pay off his debts so he can keep the home fires burning. Enough satirical jabs to keep the comic bagpipes blowing. Directed by Henry Cass.

**CASTLE OF BLOOD (1962).** Above-average Italian horror flick in which George Riviere spends a night in a haunted castle after accepting a bet from Edgar Allan Poe that he can do so without losing his mind. Naturally, he proceeds to lose his mind as he bears witness to assorted ghostly spirits reliving horrible deaths. Among them is Barbara Steele, who gives this picture a great lift. Directed by Anthony Dawson, who remade the story as WEB OF THE SPIDER. Ah, but that's another night of horror.

**CASTLE OF DOOM.** See **VAMPYR, THE.**

**CASTLE OF EVIL (1966).** Relatives of a recently deceased madman named Kovec gather in an eerie mansion for the reading of the will. Suddenly a facsimile of Kovec begins murdering the heirs. Amateur city stuff under director Francis D. Lyon. Scott Brady, Virginia Mayo, Hugh Marlowe, Lisa Gaye, David Brian. (VC)

**CASTLE OF FU MANCHU (1968).** Final entry in the British Fu Manchu series produced by Harry Alan Towers and starring Christopher Lee as the insidious Oriental with yet another nefarious scheme to throw the world into chaos. Helping old Fu in this new grue is his dastardly daughter, death rays and torture devices in the Sax Rohmer tradition. Directed perfunctorily by Jesus Franco. Richard Greene, Howard Marion Crawford, Maria Perschy. (VC)

**CASTLE OF TERROR.** See **CASTLE OF BLOOD.**

**CASTLE OF THE LIVING DEAD (1964).** Troupe of entertainers stops at Christopher Lee's creepy castle, where bizarre murders commence without delay. Ample lurking through graveyards and secret passageways before the show biz gang (dwarf and all) discovers Count Drago (Lee) is preserving the dead with a secret formula. You'll get a kick out of Donald Sutherland as a comedy relief policeman (he also appears as an old witch). Directed by Luciano Ricci (Herbert Wise). Gaia Germani.

**CASTLE OF THE MONSTERS (1957).** The Mexicans parade out the entire menagerie of cinema monsters. Too bad it wasn't intended as a spoof, because it's hilarious, especially German Robles as the vampire. Directed by Julian Soler. Clavillazo co-stars.

**CAT AND THE CANARY, THE (1928).** Silent version of John Willard's classic play set in a sinister mansion where a killer with a clawed hand sneaks through secret corridors. Directed by Paul Leni. Laura La Plante, Creighton Hale, Flora Finch, Tully Marshall. (VC)

**CAT AND THE CANARY, THE (1939).** Paramount's rollicking comedy version of the John Willard "old dark house" play starring Bob Hope and Paulette Goddard, in top form as they make their way through spooky trappings typical to this genre that blended comedy with the supernatural. Superb fun under Elliot Nugent's direction. John Beal, Gale Sondergaard, George Zucco, Elizabeth Patterson.

**CAT AND THE CANARY, THE (1978).** Tongue-in-cheek version of the famous tongue-in-cheek play by John Willard—which means it's twice as dumb. The heirs gather once again for the reading the will. Some of the updated novelty devices are cute, but the film wallows in its own antiquity and stupidity. It's a good cast (Honor Blackman, Edward Fox, Michael Callan, Wendy Hiller, Carol Lynley, Wilfrid Hyde-White), so put the blame on writer-director Radley Metzger, who graduated from X-rated melodramas to this exercise in macabre humor. (VC)

**CAT CREATURE, THE (1973).** Robert Bloch supernatural teleplay with many in-jokes about movie cats, but it's pallid stuff, certainly not a chip-off-the-old-Bloch that we know. Gale Sondergaard, one-time Spider Woman, is a cat god-

**CAT FROM OUTER SPACE, THE (1978).** Zoolar J-5, a Persian feline, emerges from a disabled flying saucer in this childish Disney comedy written by Ted (HAZEL) Keys. With a magical collar, Zoolar levitates people and places them into suspended animation in his efforts to rendezvous with the mother ship, last seen hovering over Steven Spielberg's L.A. digs. Sally Duncan, Ken Berry, McLean Stevenson, Roddy McDowall and Harry Morgan can add little to the uninspired plot. Ronnie Schell plays an army sergeant but his voice was dubbed so he could supply the voice of Zoolar. In short, the cat has his tongue. Directed by Norman Tokar, Jesse White, Alan Young. (VC)

**CAT GIRL, THE (1957).** Barbara Shelley, in her first British film, inherits a family curse that promises "the craving for warm new flesh and blood." Cuckolded by her devious husband, Barbara unleashes a phantom cheetah on him and his girlfriend—an act of transference that in turn unleashes the curse and sets into motion a series of vengeful murders. Alfred Shaughnessey directed. Robert Ayres.

**CAT O'NINE TAILS (1971).** Karl Malden, who portrays a blind man specializing in solving crossword puzzles, con-

**NASTASSIA KINSKI, BEFORE AND AFTER, IN 'CAT PEOPLE' (1982)**

dess claiming victims to possess a golden amulet. Kent Smith, of CURSE OF THE CAT PEOPLE, has a cameo. Curtis Harrington needed nine lives to direct David Hedison, Stuart Whitman, Keye Luke, John Carradine; Peter Lorre Jr. turns up in one scene with a knife in his back. Has the bite of a kitten instead of a jungle marauder.

**CAT CREEPS, THE (1930).** Early talkie, a version of John Willard's CAT AND THE CANARY, starring Montague Love, Jean Hersholt and Helen Twelvetrees. It's the "old dark house" replete with sliding panels, the clawed hand that reaches for the heroine and other "midnight tinglings." Directed by Rupert Julian.

**CAT CREEPS, THE (1946).** Does the spirit of a dead girl possess a certain black cat? Do you have to torture yourself by watching this web-covered antique? In a way you should, for it is vintage Universal material of the 1940s, functioning on a B level in its special time and place. Not a classic but it will be of minor interest to buffs, even if it bears no relation to THE CAT CREEPS of 1930. Directed by Erle C. Kenton. Lois Collier, Noah Beery Jr., Paul Kelly, Douglas Dumbrille, Jonathan Hale, Rose Hobart.

siders this one of his best low budget features, a tribute to the talents of writer-director Dario Argento, one of Italy's better directors. This blends mystery and psychoterror in telling of a murderer whose blood is tainted with homicidal tendencies. James Franciscus is a reporter on the killer's trail, with Malden assisting him.

**CAT PEOPLE, THE (1942).** Classic supernatural shocker from RKO producer Val Lewton, who stressed unseen horror in his low budget assignments. Simone Simon is a fragile European bride fearful she is turning into a panther. We never witness the transformation, only shadowy figures on lonely, windswept streets and the hint of something prowling just out of camera range. A genuinely eerie atmosphere created by director Jacques Tourneur, with Dewitt Bodeen's script remarkably literate. Highly recommended. Kent Smith, Tom Conway, Jane Randolph, Jack Holt, Alan Napier, Elizabeth Russell. (VC)

**CAT PEOPLE (1982).** Paul Schrader directed this barely-a-remake of the 1942 version, emphasizing the sexual side of humans turning into animals. It's kinky: Malcolm McDowall turns into a panther whenever sex is on his mind, and so should his relative Nastassia Kinski, only she's a virgin and hasn't developed the impulses. Schrader deals with this depravity in vivid visuals. Yet the exposition is so uncertain, he suggests more than he shows, an ironic twisting of Lewton's technique. Even the effects by Tom Burman (human arm popping out of leopard's stomach; arm being ripped out of its socket; man-to-animal transmutation) are very brief, as if Schrader was afraid to include shocks lest he not be taken seriously. In his vain attempt to remain "honorable" and still be trendily "box office" he creates a film that isn't enough to satisfy harcore horror/gore buffs, and that is too obscure to please a mass audience. The Alan Ormsby script (worked over by Schrader) borrows sequences from the '42 version, but ultimately is not an improvement. John Heard, Annette O'Toole, Ruby Dee, Ed Begley Jr., Lynn Lowry, Neva Gage. (VC)

**CAT WOMEN OF THE MOON (1954).** Dreadful 3-D programmer, so unconvincing and stodgy it isn't even so-bad-it's-good. It's just so-bad-it's-unbearable. See it once if you must but don't believe that baloney about its reputation rivalling PLAN 9 FROM OUTER SPACE. Some schlock has it, some doesn't. This don't. Sonny Tufts, Victor Jory, Douglas Fowley and Marie Windsor are members of a lunar expedition but you'll howl at the Sears spacesuits and Woolworth zap guns. The cat women turn out to be 1953 ballet dancers in tights. Cat-o'-nine tails for producer Al Zimbalist (ROBOT MONSTER) and director Arthur Hilton. (VC)

**CAT'S EYE (1985).** Anthology film combining screenwriter Stephen King and director Lewis Teague, who first dealt with King material in CUJO. A well-made film (superbly photographed by Jack Cardiff) consisting of three stories linked by a superintelligent tabby who interferes in the affairs of man for non-evil purposes. The opener is black comedy in which James Woods, a habitual smoker, seeks help from Quitters Inc. and finds that Alan King and staff employ harsh treatments as a cure. The middle narrative concerns an unsavory underworld kingpin (Kenneth McMillan) who forces his wife's lover (Robert Hays) to walk the ledge of a tall building as part of a bet. There's a nice O'Henry twist here. The final story is the strongest: Our heroic tabby follows a gnome-like minimonster (created by Carlo Rambaldi) into a rural family home in Wilmington, N.C., to defend Drew Barrymore from ferocious attacks. The creature is a half-menacing, half-amusing gremlin dressed like a court jester and the battle in the toy-ridden bedroom is a classic. King fans might be disappointed this isn't more graphically violent, but the fact remains it is one of the best Stephen King movies. Candy Clark, Jared Naughton. (VC)

**CATALYSM.** See **NIGHTMARE NEVER ENDS, THE** and **NIGHT TRAIN TO TERROR (1985).**

**CATASTROPHE 1999.** See **LAST DAYS OF PLANET EARTH, THE.**

**CATHY'S CURSE (1976).** French-Canadian horror flick borrowing from CARRIE and THE EXORICST in dealing with an eight-year-old girl possessed by the demonic spirit of her aunt, who was killed in a fiery auto crash. The usual diabolical events begin: Housekeeper plunges from an upper window to her death, family dog is destroyed, other "web of horror" cliches. Special effects are undistinguished, Eddy Matalan's direction is listless and interminably tedious, and Randi Allen as Cathy seems more insufferable than evil. Curses on everyone involved. (VC)

**CATMAN OF PARIS, THE (1946).** Claw-ripping murders in the Parisian capital leads a tormented man to believe he is a werecat (or is it a vampwolf?). Gerald Mohr and John Dehner purr, Lenore Albert loves to have her ears scratched. Robert J. Wilke just loves a saucer of milk. Director Lesley Selander prowls at night.

**CAUGHT BY TELEVISION.** See **TRAPPED BY TELEVISION.**

**CAULDRON OF BLOOD (1971).** Spanish-American grue (produced in 1967 in Madrid, but not released until after Boris Karloff's death) in which Karloff portrays a blind artist

(mis)used by his murderous wife (Viveca Lindfors) to dispose of corpses in a most unusual fashion. Karloff is in a wheelchair most of the time because he was ill. This is one cauldron that fails to boil under the stirring of director-writer Santos Alcocer (Edward Mann). Jean-Pierre Aumont doesn't bubble the pot, either. (VC)

**CAVE OF THE LIVING DEAD (1963).** The cave is the hiding place of female vampires clad in black slips and panties who terrorize (seduce?) a German village with their biting attitude. German film produced by England's Richard Gordon and directed by Akos Von Ratony. Erika Remberg, Carl Mohner, Wolfgang Priess, Karin Field.

**CAVEGIRL (1985).** Lightweight spoof in the tradition of CAVEMAN, but without special effects, monsters or satiric cleverness. It's a dumb teen sex comedy as Daniel Roebuck portrays a nerd who dresses like Indiana Jones. The military is conducting a "harmonic" time continuum test and accidentally sears Roebuck into prehistoric times. There he meets a perky blond cave dweller (Cindy Ann Thompson) in a bikini, gets the hots for her and chases her through the Cro-Magnon district, populated by the "Homo Erectus" species. There are smutty sex jokes, anal humor and a shaving cream squirting melee. Highlight is when Cindy removes her bra and shows off her wonderful breasts. David Oliver produced and directed Phil Groves' script so feebly, this is a total Neanderthal bomb. Bill Adams, Larry Gabriel. (VC)

**CAVEMAN (1981).** Carl Gottlieb assumes directorial reins to bring his script (co-written with Rudy De Luca) to the screen—a hilarious send-up of prehistoric monster movies. Unfortunately, the comedy is thin and the monsters too goofy to make this work. David Allen and Roy Arbogast contribute good special effects, including stop-motion animation, but the cast (Barbara Bach, Ringo Star, Dennis Quaid, Jack Gilford) is lost in time and space. Nice try, Carl, but it's back to the cave to rub two sticks together again. Avery Schreiber, Shelley Long, John Matuszak. (VC)

**CEMETERY GIRLS.** See **DRACULA'S GREATEST LOVE.**

**CEMETERY OF TERROR (1984).** Mexican import in which mad doctor Hugo Stiglitz, resurrecting a corpse in a rite dedicated to Satan, meets nosy teenagers who louse up his plan with their Black Book of the Dead. Written-directed by Ruben Galindo Jr. in Texas. Usi Velasco, Rene Cardona III, Erika Buenfil.

**CENTERFOLD GIRLS (1977).** Sexually depraved slasher (Andrew Prine) is out to get all those "loose" beauties with the staples in their navels who posed for a PLAYBOY-style magazine. CENTERFOLD GIRLS is creased and doesn't unfold neatly. Directed by John Peyser. Tiffany Bolling, Aldo Ray, Ray Danton. (VC)

**CHAIN REACTION (1980).** Australian science thriller, imaginatively directed by Ian Barry and full of unusual plot twists when a worker at WALDO, an atomic waste disposal project, is exposed to a radiation leak and flees hospital to warn the outside world of contamination. The escapee is befriended by a race car driver and his nurse-wife, who become the prey for a group of "company men" covering up the leak. Two exciting car chases in the Miller style, plus good suspense. Steve Bisley, Ross Thompson. (VC)

**CHAIRMAN, THE (1969).** A brain transistor is implanted in Gregory Peck, a Nobel scientist, when he journeys to China to learn about a new enzyme which permits food crops to grow in any climate. What Peck doesn't know is: the transistor is a bomb that can be detonated back at Central Control. Peck's escape from behind the Bamboo Curtain turns into a chase/suspense escapade with spy antics and heroics. More exciting for its Hitchcockian approach than pseudofantastic elements. Directed by J. Lee Thompson. Anne Heywood, Arthur Hill, Keye Luke, Burt Kwouk.

**CHALLENGE, THE (1970).** TV-movie is food for thought when a satellite crashes into the Pacific; Americans and Russians race to salvage the craft; each decides to place a soldier on an island and have them shoot it out, winner taking all. Marc Norman's script pulls off the silly idea with director Allen Smithee manipulating the cast: Darren McGavin and Mako as the warriors, Broderick Crawford, James Whitmore, Paul Lukas as authority symbols.

**CHAMBER OF HORRORS (1940).** Old-fashioned but still entertaining Edgar Wallace story (based on SECRET OF THE DOOR WITH SEVEN LOCKS) set in a weird mansion where Dr. Manetta (Leslie Banks, a great villain of the 1930s) houses his collection of torture instruments. Lilli Palmer is a lovely heroine who falls into his trap, and Gina Malo is refreshing comedy relief as a vacationing American. "I love frolicking in a morgue," remarks Ms Palmer when trapped in a house of the dead with boyfriend Richard Bird. There's really nothing supernatural about it but it's charming in its antiquated fashion. Directed by Norman Lee. (VC)

**CHAMBER OF HORRORS (1966).** Diabolical murderer Patrick O'Neal, who loses a hand escaping the hangman, now uses detachable paws as murder weapons in this TV-movie (produced-directed by Hy Averback), pilot for the unsold series, HOUSE OF WAX. It was considered too graphic for TV and released to theaters, then put on TV anyway. O'Neal is Jason Cravatte, who changes his murder weapon at the drop of a . . . finger. In theaters it was gimmicked up with a "Horror Horn" and "Fear Flasher" (devices that must have warmed William Castle's heart) but these were excised for TV. Suzy Parker makes a fetching heroine in low-cut bodices, but Cesare Danova is a watered-down hero. Written by Stephen Kandell and Ray Russell. Wilfrid Hyde-White, Patrice Wymore, Jeanette Nolan, Marie Windsor, Barry Kroeger, Tony Curtis (in a cameo).

**CHANDU ON THE MAGIC ISLAND (1934).** Last eight chapters of the serial RETURN OF CHANDU re-edited, starring Bela Lugosi as Frank Chandler, also known as Chandu. He's a drab magician (once a popular radio hero) fighting the Black Magic Cult of Ubasti on Lemuria. The first seven reels were also re-edited and re-released as RETURN OF CHANDU. Directed by Ray Taylor. (VC)

**CHANDU THE MAGICIAN (1932).** Feature version of the once-popular radio serial, starring Edmund Lowe as the magician who materializes and dematerializes at will. Bela Lugosi, who would later portray Frank Chandler in a Chandu serial (see CHANDU ON THE MAGIC ISLAND), here portrays the villain, Roxor, a mad priest who intends to conquer the world. Directed by William Cameron Menzies and Michael Varne. Photography by James Wong Howe.

**CHANGE OF MIND (1969).** Another brain transplant story, this one done with thoughtfulness and sensitivity, and not with cackling mad scientists. This treads into racial territory, exploring what happens when the brain of a prominent white D.A. is transplanted into a black man's body. Made in Canada by director Robert Stevens, with music by Duke Ellington. Raymond St. Jacques, Susan Oliver, Leslie Nielsen, Donnelly Rhodes, Janet MacLachlan.

**CHANGELING, THE (1980).** Superior haunted house tale heavy with creepy atmosphere—the house was created by set designers but you'd swear those were real corridors, stairway and dark rooms. Composer George C. Scott, recovering from the loss of his wife and child, discovers the mansion is haunted by a murdered child. Director Peter Medak keeps the tense story unfolding on several levels—as a pure ghost story, as a psychological study of Scott's recovery from personal tragedy, as a morality tale of good vs. evil. The ending is far-out but enhances this unusually excellent supernatural tale. Trish Van Devere, Barry Morse, Melvyn Douglas, Jean Marsh, John Colicos. (VC)

**CHARIOTS OF THE GODS? (1974).** French "documentary" based on Erich Von Daniken's best-seller purporting that extraterrestrials once walked our Earth and influenced the human race. Pyramids, artifacts, cave wall dwellings and possible rocket landing sites on the plains of Peru are "supporting evidence" of Van Daniken's theories. Some have called him hare-brained, others ponder and wonder. It's weak evidence at best, but at least old Erich has started us thinking about many unexplained mysteries of our planet and has thrown notions of prehistory into turmoil. Food for thought,

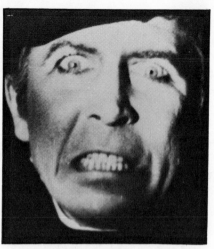

**PATRICK O'NEAL AS THE HOOK KILLER IN 'CHAMBER OF HORRORS'**

anyway. Directed by Harold Reinl. (VC)

**CHARLIE BOY (1980).** Two episodes of Britain's HAMMER HOUSE OF HORROR, re-edited for the U.S. In the title show, directed by Robert Young, a voodoo doll named Charlie Boy (a "fetish") causes gory murders in the style of THE OMEN, all resulting in puncture-wound deaths. There's a good twist ending to this tale of jungle evil. In the second, "The 13th Reunion," directed by Peter Sasdy, a newswoman is assigned to cover the "Think Thin" Fat Farm and lose weight, only she's caught up in a funeral directors' reunion that ends on a sickening note. Leigh Lawson, Marius Goring, Julia Foster, Angela Bruce. (VC)

**CHARLOTTE'S WEB (1973).** Animated version of the E.B. White children's story, telling of a pig who foresees himself becoming sausage links and pork roast; a spider befriends him with its magical web. Voices by Debbie Reynolds, Charles Nelson Reilly, Paul Lynde, Henry Gibson. Directed by Charles A. Nichols. (VC)

**CHARLY (1968).** Based on a science-fiction short story by Daniel Keyes, "Flowers for Algernon," this brought an Academy Award to Cliff Robertson as Best Actor. He portrays a mentally retarded bakery worker who undergoes surgery and develops an incredibly high I.Q. But the process reverses itself and Charly's retardation returns. A bittersweet love story is woven into this fragile tragedy; produced-directed by Ralph Nelson in Boston. Written by Stirling Silliphant. Claire Bloom, Lilia Skala, Dick Van Patten, Leon Janney, Ruth White, Frank Dolan. (VC)

**CHEECH AND CHONG'S THE CORSICAN BROTHERS (1984).** Cheech Marin and Thomas Chong, of stoned-out film comedy, eschew drugs to drag out that old Alexandre Dumas chestnut about Siamese twins who share a psychic link, each experiencing the other's pains and joys. A series of tasteless gags and non sequiturs set against the French Revolution, with emphasis on homosexual and transvestite behavior. The Brothers Corsican escape beheading at the guillotine of dandy-randy heavy Roy Dotrice and are soon embroiled in parodies of the swashbuckler. Thomas Chong directed and co-wrote with associate producer (Cheech's wife) Rikki Marin, who doubles as a princess. Robbi Chong, Rae Dawn Chong, Shelby Fiddis. (VC)

**CHILD, THE (1977).** Rip-off of THE EXORCIST, in which a murderous moppet calls upon ghoulish graveyard demons to carry out her revenge against despicable characters. Suitable for neither children nor adults. Directed by Robert Voskanian. Rosalie Cole, Laura Barnett. Re-released as KILL AND GO HIDE. (VC)

## OH SHUCKS: 'CHILDREN OF THE CORN'

**CHILDREN, THE (1980).** A cloud from a nuclear plant contaminates a busload of kids, turning them into predictable movie zombies. Juvenile jars, kiddie killings and moppet mayhem as the adolescents zap adults with atomic-charged fingers. Produced-directed by Max Kalmanowicz. Gale Garnett, Martin Shakar, Gil Rogers. (VC)

**CHILDREN OF THE CORN (1984).** The worst yet of Stephen King movie adaptations, based on a story from NIGHT SHIFT. A prime example of how young filmmakers (director Fritz Kiersch, screenwriter George Goldsmith) can take a master's work without understanding its nuances and turn it into schlock. Peter Horton and Linda Hamilton are travelers detoured into a rural community in Nebraska lorded over by a cult of youngsters who have slaughtered all the adults as a sacrifice to a corn god, who shows up in the climax but is so poorly photographed, one never knows what "it" is. Horton needs all the ears he can get to make this fiasco work. R. G. Armstrong, John Franklin, Courtney Gains, Robby Kiger. (VC)

**CHILDREN OF THE DAMNED (1963).** Sequel to VILLAGE OF THE DAMNED is in ways superior, thanks to a literate script by John Briley that touches on aggressive behavior. A group of highly intelligent children—created by an alien race which impregnated Earth mothers from deep space—is brought to London where the government intends to destroy them. The kids are wise to the conspiracy and soon have control. Thoughtfully directed by Anton M. Leader; based on ideas from John Wyndham's MIDWICH CUCKOOS. Alan Badel, Ian Hendry, Clive Powell.

**CHILDREN OF THE FULL MOON (1980).** Repackaged version of two episodes from Britain's HAMMER HOUSE OF HORROR. In the first, directed by Tom Clegg, Diana Dors portrays the nanny of children living in a strange house in the forest, who terrorize a man and woman. Very bleak, with a downbeat ending. In "Visitor From the Grave," directed by Peter Sasdy, a weak but wealthy woman kills an intruder. Her husband covers up for her, but then she sees the dead man in the darnedest places. Obviously, this is part of a plot to do her in, but a final twist arrives on top of the twist. Christopher Cazenove, Celia Gregory, Robert Urquhart, Simon Mac-Corkindale. (VC)

**CHILDREN SHOULDN'T PLAY WITH DEAD THINGS (1972).** A hammy traveling troupe journeys to an island to stage a satanic play, pretending to raise the dead. Only the corpses in the graveyard aren't pretending—they're out for blood! This vacillates between stupidity and cheap thrills in the hands of producer-director Bob Clark, who co-scripted with Alan Ormsby, doubling as the troupe's director. Intel-

ligent viewers shouldn't waste time with dumb movies. Anya Ormsby (Alan's wife), Bruce Solomon. (VC)

**CHILL FACTOR. See COLD NIGHT'S DEATH, A.**

**CHILLER (1985).** Producer Richard Kobritz (SALEM'S LOT, CHRISTINE) adds to his good credits with this TV horror movie. Writer-producer J. D. Feigleson's story centers on a malfunction in a Cryonics "mausoleum" which allows doctors to restore life to long-dead Michael Beck—but Beck returns to life without a soul, subjecting everyone to physical and mental tortures. Wes Craven shows he has matured into a director who can sustain suspense and tension. Paul Sorvino is the family minister, Beatrice Straight is the devoted mother, Laura Johnson is a harassed young woman. Make-up work by Stan Winston.

**CHINA SYNDROME, THE (1979).** Superb "what if?" science thriller set in a nuclear power station that almost causes a catastrophic chain reaction except for plant foreman Jack Lemmon's expedient actions. The government hushes it up but newswoman Jane Fonda and cameraman Michael Douglas probe for the truth, forcing Lemmon to face his own strengths and weaknesses. Excellently directed by James Bridges and written by Bridges, Mike Gray and T. S. Cook. Gripping drama with the real Three Mile Island near-tragedy (which occurred the same year this was released) lending credence to the ironic, chilling conclusions this makes about our rush to self-destruction. Scott Brady, Peter Donat, Wilford Brimley. (VC)

**CHINCHERO. TV title for LAST MOVIE, THE.**

**CHINESE WEB, THE (1978).** Episodes of TV's SPIDER-MAN, with the wall-climbing, web-spinning hero helping a Chinese diplomat charged with selling secrets to foreign powers. Directed by Don McDougall. Nicholas Hammond, Robert F. Simon, Benson Fong. (VC)

**CHITTY CHITTY BANG BANG (1968).** Critics unanimously junked this $10 million musical "lemon" about a flying car from the assembly line of producer Albert Broccoli. Hardly anyone liked the songs, John Stears' special effects were sneered at and everyone felt this version of Ian Fleming's book for children had been de-Samonized by the script from director Ken Hughes, Roald Dahl and Richard Maibaum. Dick Van Dyke portrays the father who tells this Detroit fairy tale to his kids. Sally Ann Howes, Lionel Jeffries, Gert Frobe, Benny Hill, James Robertson Justice. (VC)

**CHOKE CANYON (1986).** Stephen Collins is a scientist trying to convert sound waves into energy with a machine he installs in Choke Canyon, Utah, during the Halley's Comet fly-by. A ruthless businessman dumping toxic waste in that area sends a hit man to get rid of Collins, and the action is on. Ridiculous story with well-staged action. Directed by Chuck Bail. Janet Julian, Bo Svenson.

**C.H.O.M.P.S. (1980).** Juvenile comedy produced by Joe Barbera, king of Saturday cartoons. The title stands for Canine Home Protection System, a shaggy dog robot built with X-ray vision, superstrength, in-house sound effects and the ability to detect crime. Industrialist Jim Backus plots to steal the "dog" from inventor Wesley Eure. The cast plays for cute: Conrad Bain, Valerie Bertinelli, Chuck McCann, Red Buttons, Hermione Baddeley, Robert Q. Lewis. At best, a lightweight diversion, something to catch between buses. Don Chaffey directs with an eye on the nearest fire hydrant. (VC)

**CHOPPING MALL (1986).** Group of teenagers are trapped one night in a shopping center with three out-of-control security robots, but writer-director Jim Wynorski's premise is strictly a bargain basement offering that's no bargain for the viewer. Cameos by Paul Bartel, Mary Woronov and Dick Miller help a little, but ultimately this closes for business early. Also called R.O.B.O.T. and KILLBOTS. Kelli Maroney, Tony O'Dell, Barbara Crampton, Suzee Slater.

**CHOSEN, THE (1977).** Italian-British production is a rehash of THE OMEN, with Kirk Douglas as an industrialist who specializes in nuclear power plants and suspects he is fulfilling Biblical prophesies and setting the world on a disaster course. You see, Simon Ward, his son, is the Son of Satan, or the Antichrist. A fine international cast struggles with a muddled screenplay. Anthony Quayle, Virginia McKenna, Alexander Knox. Directed by Alberto De Martino.

**CHOSEN SURVIVORS (1974).** A select (but not that select) group is placed in an underground vault and told it's an experiment in survival . . . then they're told World War III has erupted on the surface. Suddenly vampire bats begin killing the volunteers. Directed by Sutton Rolley. Bradford Dillman, Jackie Cooper, Alex Cord, Richard Jaeckel, Bradford Dillman, Diana Muldaur, Kelly Lange.

**CHRISTINE (1983).** Stylish, well-lubricated adaptation of Stephen King's novel about a 1958 Plymouth Fury which comes off the assembly line possessed by evil powers. Director John Carpenter shifts into high gear almost immediately as the car knocks off its "rivals." The car, you see, is jealous. For this is a love story about a boy and his car. Call it auto-eroticism. There's a great scene of the auto in flames, speeding through the night in pursuit of a teenager. The movie also works because of our own love affairs with cars, which reflect an extension of our sexual energies. Gee, are we getting deep. But don't worry about subtext—focus on

### 'CHRISTINE' PRODUCER RICHARD KOBRITZ

the fury of that Plymouth as it becomes a most frightening "character." Keith Gordon. (VC)

**CHRISTMAS CAROL, A (1938).** The best tune to this MGM adaptation of the Dickens classic is another Carroll: Leo G., who co-stars with Reginald Owen, Gene Lockhart, Terry Kilburn and Ann Rutherford. Somewhat stodgy for today's audiences. Directed by Edwin L. Marin.

**CHRISTMAS CAROL, A (1951).** A heavy atmosphere prevails in this British version of Dickens' tale about Mr. Scrooge, miserly, heartless Londoner, and his fateful encounters with the spirits of Christmases past, present and future. Alastair Sim is superb as Scrooge. Mervyn Johns, Ernest Thesiger. Produced-directed by Brian Desmond Hurst, scripted by Noel Langley. (VC)

**CHRISTMAS CAROL, A (1984).** Superior TV adaptation of Dickens' classic, rich in character acting, insightful characterizations and Victorian ambience—and heartwarming to boot. The Roger O. Hirson teleplay is not only faithful, but sharply recaptures the setting and language of the British writing master. Under Clive Donner's direction, George C. Scott delivers a tour de force as Scrooge undergoes his exposure to the Christmas spirits. Impeccable in supporting roles are Nigel Davenport, David Warner, Frank Finlay, Michael Gough and Angela Pleasence.

**CHRISTMAS EVIL.** Videocassette title for **YOU BETTER WATCH OUT.**

**CHRISTMAS MARTIAN, THE (1971).** Extraterrestrial saucer slingers land on Earth to help lost children find their way home. They in turn help the Martians get back to their own world. Ho ho ho! Canadian-French yuletide-message film directed by Bernard Gosselin.

**CHRISTMAS PRESENT (1985).** British reworking of Dickens' A CHRISTMAS CAROL, starring Peter Chelsom as Nigel Playfayre, a Scrooge-like character who undergoes the expected character transformation. Gentle, mild-mannered TV-movie, written-directed by Tony Bicat. Bill Fraser.

**CHRISTMAS THAT ALMOST WASN'T, THE (1966).** Folksy Italian children's fare in which Rossano Brazzi (who also directed) plays Phineas T. Prune, multi-billionaire who hates children so much he buys the North Pole and plans to evict Santa, charging him with flagrant violation of child labor laws for using elves and fairies. Santa must work in a department store to raise funds—proving even the best of us go commercial. Script and lyrics by Paul Tripp, who also appears in the cast.

**C.H.U.D. (1984).** Contamination Hazard Urban Disposal, a clandestine operation, is dumping toxic atomic wastes into the New York sewers . . . also out there are Cannibalistic Humanoid Underground Dwellers, citizens of a subterranean clan infected by radioactivity. Sounds terrible, but Parnell Hall has shaped an intelligent script focusing on a cop (Christopher Curry) trying to solve his wife's disappearance who uncovers a conspiracy between government and Manhattan authorities. C.H.U.D. has more class than other films about creatures lurking in slimy sewers. Director Douglas Check photographed the underground digs of New York with atmospheric know-how and Tim Boxell's monster designs are effective (creatures have drippy fangs, white glowing bulbs for eyes, stretchable necks and terribly bad breath). What gives this versimilitude, within the context of a horror fantasy, is its realistic Soho locations, grubby street people and T-shirts stained by perspiration spots. The film sports the unusual tag: "Filmed in and under New York City." John Heard, Laurie Mattos, Justin Hall. (VC)

**CHUMP AT OXFORD, A (1940).** Milestone Laurel and Hardy comedy in which Stan sustains a concussion and awakens with the mental capabilities of a genius—with aristocratic mannerisms yet. One of the comedy duo's best film efforts. Directed by Alfred Goulding. Peter Cushing has one of his earliest roles. Forrester Harvey. (VC)

**CINDERELLA (1950).** Walt Disney's version of the oft-repeated fairy tale (chronicled by Charles Perrault and the Brothers Grimm) about the lovely, mistreated scullery maid with the evil stepsisters who goes to the ball and falls for Prince Charming. Disney has pulled off an achievement in animation with his unique touch. Exaggerated storybook prettiness works well here. Voices include Verna Felton, Ilene Woods, Eleanor Audley and Lucille Bliss. (VC)

**CINDERELLA 2000 (1977).** Costumed science-fiction version of the kiddie tale, but soft porn for adults, set in 2047, when love-making is not allowed and Big Brother watches with robots. Director Al Adamson is no Prince Charming and scripter Bud Donnelly may turn into a pumpkin. No glass slipper, this.

**CINDERELLA (1977).** Sexually explicit R-rated version of the famed fairy tale, starring Cheryl Smith as the adventuress who gains the upper hand through more than sweetness and light. Directed by Michael Pataki. Kirk Scott, Brett Smiley. (VC)

**CINDERFELLA (1960).** Reversal of the sexes has Jerry Lewis as the brow-beaten lackey with evil brothers (Henry Silva and Robert Hutton). Ed Wynn appears as the fairy "godfather." Get the idea? Director Frank Tashlin's screenplay is a witless, clumsy, tedious thing, aided none by the maladroit mugging of Lewis, who was his own producer. Anna Maria Alberghetti, Judith Anderson. (VC)

**CIRCLE OF IRON (1979).** Offbeat martial arts film, produced by Sandy Howard in Israel. It's an odd mixture of kung fu and Zen philosophy, based on an idea by Bruce Lee and James Coburn, and expanded by Stirling Silliphant and Stanley Mann. The setting is a never-never land where blind sage David Carradine holds the key to all knowledge. Into this mythical kingdom ("a land that never was and always is") comes warrior Jeff Cooper on The Odyssey of Knowledge, passing assorted ordeals which test his strength and cunning. Each adversary is Carradine in make-up—as the Monkey Man, the Rhythm Man and Death. When Cooper finally reaches Christopher Lee, he learns the meaning of life: Beware Pretentious Movies Bearing Messages with Capital Letters. Roddy McDowall and Eli Wallach appear in cameos (the former as the White Robe, the latter as a man in a tub of oil). The dialogue runs to lines like "Tie two birds together; they have four wings yet cannot fly" and "The fool is the twin of the wise." Potential fools have been forewarned. (VC)

**CIRCUS OF FEAR.** Videocassette title for **PSYCHO-CIR-CUS**, featuring additional footage not included in the TV version, and a new introduction sporting John Carradine.

**CIRCUS OF HORRORS (1960).** Engrossing British shocker about a plastic surgeon (Anton Diffring) who does incredibly terrible jobs on his patients, leaving them hideously deformed. Meanwhile, Diffring runs his three-ring circus like a madman, causing grisly gore murders under the Big Top. Wonderfully graphic deaths in all three rings. Sick but engaging. Directed by Sidney Mayers. Yvonne Monlaur, Erika Remberg, Yvonne Romain, Donald Pleasence. (VC)

**CITY BENEATH THE SEA (1971).** Irwin Allen, Hollywood's sophomoric producer of TV juvenilia, dives to his usual special effects low for this pilot with an absurd script by John Meredyth Lucas. In 2053, Stuart Whitman, boss of a submerged metropolis, is faced with several crises, simultaneously, some natural, some man-made. Your only crisis is deciding which other channel to turn to. Robert Wagner, Rosemary Forsyth, Richard Basehart, Paul Stewart, Joseph Cotten, James Darren, Whit Bissell, Sugar Ray Robinson.

**CITY LIMITS (1985).** Fifteen years "from now" a plague has decimated mankind, and for no reason discernible, society has ended up as young gangs of survivors, bikers called the DAs and the Clippers, who maintain an uneasy truce and occasionally hold jousting contests. But one gang is influenced by the evil Robby Benson (who never moves from behind his desk) and does the forbidden—uses weapons to gain control. From the team that made ANDROID, but this is a pointless, unexciting excuse for a lot of biking stunts, explosions and the like, even though it avoids being a Mad Max imitation. Directed by Aaron Lipstadt, scripted by Don Opper. Darrell Larson, Kim Cattrall, Rae Dawn Chong, James Earl Jones. (VC)

**CITY OF FEAR (1959).** What is Copat 60? A lethal radioactive powder that could blow L.A. off the map. So what's so terrible about that? Some Copat 90 is in a metal box in the hands of an escaped convict (Vincent Edwards). Tense low budget thriller, enhanced by on-location realism. Directed by Irving Lerner. John Archer, Patricia Blair, Lyle Talbot.

**CITY OF LOST MEN (1935).** Mascot's 12-chapter serial THE LOST CITY truncated to 74 minutes of nonstop action and jungle nonsense as electrical engineer Bruce Gordon (Kane Richmond) discovers Magnetic Mountain, hideaway of Zolok (stage actor William Boyd), who plans to take over the world with his earthquake-making machine. Watch for George "Gabby" Hayes as the slave trader, Butterfield. Fun if you can overlook outmoded acting styles and antiquated filming techniques. Directed by Harry Revier.

**CITY OF THE DEAD.** See **HORROR HOTEL.**

**CITY OF THE LIVING DEAD.** See **GATES OF HELL.**

**CITY OF THE WALKING DEAD (1980).** U.S. retitled version of NIGHTMARE CITY, a Spanish programmer in which radioactivity creates vampire monsters who can only be killed with a bullet in the brain (shades of George Romero!). The bloodthirsty killers face an adversary in the form of newsman Hugo Stiglitz, who is aided by general Mel Ferrer. Old splat! Directed by Umberto Lenzi. (VC)

**CITY UNDER THE SEA.** See **WAR GODS OF THE DEEP.**

**CLAIRVOYANT, THE (1935).** Antiquated but fascinating story of a shyster seer who finds he has genuine abilities to prophesize, and must convince citizens a terrible mine cave-in will occur. Deals maturely with themes of responsibility and credibility. Claude Rains, as the soothsayer, projects a haunted, tormented soul. Fay Wray, the girl in Kong's paw, provides sympathetic love interest. Directed by Maurice Elvey. On videocassette as THE EVIL MIND.

**CLAIRVOYANT, THE (1982).** Refreshingly offbeat slasher flick, a serious attempt to create believable characters to go with the mayhem. "The Handcuff Murders" are sweeping Manhattan when TV talk-show host Perry King begins a vendetta against the killer, seeking to help psychic artist Elizabeth Kemp who is drawing impressions of the murders. She is caught between the manipulative host and sincere police officers as the web tightens. Armand Mastroianni directs with restraint. More watchable than most slasher films. Norman Parker, Kenneth McMillan, Joe Morton. In video as THE KILLING KIND.

**CLAN OF THE CAVE BEAR, THE (1986).** Interesting adaptation of Jean Auel's best-selling novel dramatizing man's earliest days, when he still lived in caves and was ruled by

**CALIBOS IN 'CLASH OF THE TITANS'**

superstition and tribal customs. Daryl Hannah is Ayla, child of the Cro-Magnons who is raised by Neanderthals to become the first woman hunter. John Sayles has fashioned a good script emphasizing the mysticism and destiny of early man. Corny, in the vein of ONE MILLION B.C. without dinosaurs. Pamela Reed, James Remar. (VC)

**CLASH OF THE TITANS (1981).** Far from the best work of stop-motion pioneer Ray Harryhausen and producer Charles Schneer (who teamed on many fantasy successes), yet a box-office smash. Harryhausen's techniques seem outmoded (coming in the wake of the effects revolution) and one senses TITANS spelling doom for hand-crafted stop motion. This paean to Greek mythology is tough to identify with, what with all that Grecian royalty atop Mt. Olympus, even in the personages of Laurence Olivier, Claire Bloom, Maggie Smith and Ursula Andress. And the hero (Harry Hamlin) and heroine (Judi Bowker) are squaresville. When Harryhausen unleashes the horned brute Calibos (Lord of the Marsh), the Medusa, the Kraken (a monster of the deep), the two-headed Dioskilos wolf dog and other beasties, the film finally comes alive. Script by Beverly Cross, who is married to Maggie Smith. Burgess Meredith is a standout as Ammon, Chronicler of the Gods. (VC)

**CLASS OF NUKE'EM HIGH (1986)** A radiation leak infects some marijuana at the local high school, turning students into thrill-happy zombies. Directed by Michael Herz. Janelle Brady, Gilbert Brenton, R. L. Ryan.

**CLASS REUNION MASSACRE (1977).** When the grads get together to reune, their ranks are swiftly thinned by one not-so-glad grad eager to spill blood. Hee hee hee. (VC)

**CLAW MONSTERS, THE (1955).** Dr. Morgan (Arthur Space) perfects a hormone that turns crawfish into monsters and uses these mutated creatures to chase away African natives from a diamond mine. But don't fret, gang. Venturing onto the scene is that intrepid adventuress Jean Evans, The Panther Girl, accompanied by her Great White Hunter, Larry Sanders, in this feature-film version of Republic's 12-chapter serial, PANTHER GIRL OF THE KONGO. Phyllis Coates is the pithy helmet girl, but she's no Nyoka. Directed by Franklin Adreon. Myron Healey, Archie Savage, Mike Ragan.

**CLAWS.** Videocassette title for **GRIZZLY.**

**CLIMAX, THE (1944).** Boris Karloff portrays Dr. Hohner, a Svengali impresario casting a hypnotic spell over opera singer Susanna Foster, whom he believes is the reincarnated soul of his dead wife. PHANTOM OF THE OPERA sets were reused in this Universal thriller which has a tense atmosphere despite a too-chatty script by Curt Siodmak and Lynn Starling. George Waggner directed. Turhan Bey, Gale Sondergaard, June Vincent, Thomas Gomez.

**CLOAK AND DAGGER (1985).** Unusual espionage adventure blending action and psychological fantasy to make a point about our current penchant for role-playing games and hero worship. Henry Thomas, having relationship problems with his father (Dabney Coleman), becomes involved with spies and creates imaginary commando-hero Jack Flack (also Coleman) to help him outwit the saboteurs. A fun blend of excitement, genuine menace and comedy by writer Tom Holland and director Richard Franklin. Michael Murphy, Jeanette Nolan, John McIntire, Christine Nigra. (VC)

**CLOCKWORK ORANGE, A (1971).** Stanley Kubrick's masterpiece on brainwashing and conforming, based on Anthony Burgess' novel. The setting is the not-too-distant future of England when "droogs" (ruffians and malcontents) rove the countryside, pillaging and raping. When one of these murderous youths (Malcolm McDowell) is arrested for murder, he is processed through a rehabilitation center until he reaches a more pacificist state. The Kubrick Touch dominates this unusual tale. Patrick Magee, Michael Bates, Adrienne Corri, David Prowse (Darth Vader). (VC)

**CLONE MASTER (1978).** Fascinating John D. F. Black script dominates this TV-movie directed by Don Medford. Black deals with the psychological problems a clone might one day face in a complicated society as scientist Art Hindle makes duplicates of himself. Compelling. Ralph Bellamy, Ed Lauter, Robyn Douglass, John Van Dreelen.

**CLONES, THE (1974).** Low budget science-fiction about asexual reproduction is a disappointingly dull B thriller. The Government has duplicated four scientists 52 times and placed them in meteorological stations to control the weather. A real scientist discovers the plot and escapes—the rest is standard chase material across rooftops and down boulevards. Lamar Card and Paul Hunt co-directed Steve Fisher's uninspired script. Gregory Sierra, Michael Greene, Otis Young, Alex Nichol, Bruce Bennett. (VC)

**CLONES OF BRUCE LEE, THE (1979).** Title gives away the plot of this Hong Kong-produced martial arts actioner with an all-Oriental cast. Directed by Chiang Hung.

**CLONING OF CLIFFORD SWIMMER, THE (1974).** Peter Haskell solves his problems by going to a psychogeneticist and having an exact duplicate of himself produced. But which one is really Clifford Swimmer? Life is full of problems . . . Directed by Lela Swift. Sheree North, Sharon Farrell, Lance Kerwin.

**CLONUS HORROR, THE (1979).** Terse, well-produced low-budgeter depicting a "breeding farm" where a perfect race is created through cloning. One subject breaks free to warn the world of this diabolical conspiracy, so you're in for chase excitement as writer-director Robert Fiveson maintains a brisk pace. Dick Sargent, Paulette Breen, Peter Graves, Keenan Wynn, Timothy Donnelly. (VC)

**CLOSE ENCOUNTERS OF THE THIRD KIND (1977).** Steven Spielberg's awesome masterpiece in special effects science-fiction . . . a triumph depicting man's first contact with extraterrestrials, done in a spiritually uplifting style. Spielberg draws on documented lore of UFOs and, with the cinematic trickery of Douglas Trumbull, creates staggering effects. The "Mother Ship" is a mind-blower and the smaller saucers flit behind glaring lights, looking solid one moment, multi-dimensional and transparent the next. Less effective is Spielberg's script about power lineman Richard Dreyfuss, who is sub-

THE 'CLOSE ENCOUNTERS' RENDEZVOUS POINT BETWEEN MAN AND ALIEN

jected to the saucer phenomena. But, the meager plot is overshadowed by the beauty of the saucers, the integrity of the effects, and the neoreligious mood. French director Francois Truffaut portrays a UFO investigator heading an international team which travels the world in pursuit of the saucer mystery. What a positive way to prepare us for our next step in space exploration. (In 1980, Spielberg released a revised version, featuring new material and deleting old. The film's thrust is, however, basically unchanged.) Another great score by John Williams. Teri Garr, Melinda Dillon, Bob Balaban, Cary Guffey, Carl Weathers, Bill Thurman, Hal Barwood. (VC)

**CLOUDS OVER EUROPE.** See **Q PLANES.**

**CLOWN MURDERS, THE (198?).** Halloween evening finds those in costumes getting less of a treat than they expected in this cuttem-up-alive thriller. John Candy, Susan Keller. (VC)

**COBRA WOMAN (1944).** Colorful fantasy of the most entertaining kind, no matter how hokey it gets. A South Seas island is ruled by a hooded cobra, who can be placated only by beautiful princess Maria Montez. She's a great looker but a terrible actress . . . but who cares when we can groove on sacrifices to the tempestuous volcano, sequined fabrics, and jungle boy Sabu. This Universal hooey bears no resemblance to H. R. Haggard's original story. Directed with a real flash for trash by Robert Siodmak. Lon Chaney Jr., Lois Collier, Edgar Barrier, Samuel S. Hinds.

**COCOON (1985).** Not all box-office winners have to be juvenile-minded teen movies: Richard Zanuck-David Brown's production is about aging seniors and how they face liver spots and dying, only slightly sugar-coated by its fantasy premise. Aliens from another Galaxy wearing human skin (Brian Dennehy, Tahnee Welch, Tyrone Power Jr.) are retrieving huge pods from the ocean floor off Florida. These pods contain life forms which must be nourished before opened. Senior citizens (Don Ameche, Wilford Brimley, Hume Cronyn) swim with the pods, emerging with renewed sexual urges and proof that hearts can be young and gray. Tom Benedek's script (from a David Saperstein novel) sincerely deals with the problems of the men; with wives Jessica Tandy, Gwen Verdon and Maureen Stapleton; with Jack Gilford's rejection of the idea; with greediness destroying a good thing. Ron Howard directs without allowing his characters to become sentimental, and never succumbs to special effects unless needed. The ending is derivative but appropriate to the mood. Recommended. Steve Guttenberg, Linda Harrison, Clint Howard, Rance Howard. (VC)

**COCKEYED MIRACLE, THE (1946).** Cockeyed is right. A hopeless affair about ghosts helping out their families. Frank Morgan, Audrey Totter, Keenan Wynn and Gladys Cooper are all three spiritual sheets to the wind. Directed by S. Sylvan Simon. Based on George Seaton's I'LL BE SEEING YOU. Cecil Kellaway, Leon Ames.

**CODE NAME: HERACLITUS (1967).** A man dies on the operating table, is restored to life minus certain sensitivities (emotions, memory and conscience), and turns into an ideal undercover man. TV-movie directed by James Goldstone. Stanley Baker, Leslie Nielsen, Jack Weston, Sheree North, Kurt Kasznar, Signe Hasso.

**CODE NAME: MINUS ONE (1975).** Retitled version of the TV pilot for THE GEMINI MAN, a short-lived series. Ben Murphy, after exposure to radiation during an underwater mission, can turn himself invisible for short stretches. He employs his talent to rescue a kidnapped aircraft industrialist. Production values? As invisible as Murphy. Allegedly based on H. G. Well's THE INVISIBLE MAN, but a blind man could see through that ruse. Scripted and produced by Leslie Stevens. Directed by Alan Levi. Katherine Crawford, Dana Elcar, Paul Shenar, H. M. Wynant, Richard A. Dysart, Austin Stoker.

**CODE NAME: TRIXIE.** See **CRAZIES, THE.**

**COLD NIGHT'S DEATH, A (1973).** Offbeat TV-movie from

**BRIAN DENNEHY IN 'COCOON'**

the Spelling-Goldberg factory in which scientists Robert Culp, Eli Wallach, isolated in an Arctic research laboratory, are on the receiving end of a colossal joke on science. An unusual idea from the imagination of Christopher Knopf; Jerrold Freedman directed.

**COLD ROOM, THE (1984).** Interesting variation on soul possession: Amanda Pays portrays a spoiled co-ed who travels to East Berlin to patch up a shaky relationship with father George Segal. She undergoes hallucinations which create two time streams: Her own deterioration set in the present, and her transformation into a girl in Nazi Germany caught up in love and betrayal. The time streams flow together for a nice if predictable climax. Intriguing premise, helmed by writer-director James Dearden in Berlin. Renee Soutendijk, Warren Clarke, Anthony Higgins.

**COLD SUN, THE.** See **ROCKY JONES, SPACE RANGER.**

**COLOR ME BLOOD RED (1966).** Blood-dripping obscenity from Herschell G. Lewis, gore specialist and The Greatest Sickie of All Time. A deranged artist retains the blood of his female victims so he has something to splash on his impressionistic canvases. Color it Morbid. Don Joseph, Candi Conder, Scott H. Hall. (VC)

**COLOSSUS AND THE AMAZONS (1960).** Reverse chauvinism: Gianna Maria Canale and sexpot tribeswomen utilize Rod Taylor and Ed Fury as sex objects. But will the dolls respect the guys in the morning? Where's Men's Lib when you need it? Italian grunt-and-strain actioner directed by Vittorio Sala.

**COLOSSUS OF NEW YORK (1958).** Excellent low-budget science-fiction thriller, intelligently written by Thelma Schnee and directed with sensitivity by Eugene Lourie. When a genius (Ross Martin) is struck down by a truck, his father (Otto Kruger) removes his brain and forces his second son (John Baragrey, who looks and sounds like MacDonald Carey) to create a robot body to house the mind. It's a mixture of Donovan's Brain, Gort the Robot, Svengali the Hypnotist and Demon Seed as the brain is stricken by insanity and the robot goes on a murderous spree at the U.N., killing with an X-ray beam through its visor. Ed Wolff plays the ten-foot metal man, Mala Powers is the helpless, beautiful wife and Robert Hutton is the colorless love interest. Charles Herbert, Ed Wolff.

**COLOSSUS: THE FORBIN PROJECT (1968).** Tense, exciting science-fiction about a supercomputer designed to maintain peace throughout the world which takes control of the world's missile systems, forcing the human race to bow to its demagogic whims. Fine special effects by Albert Whitlock, sharp direction by Joseph Sargent and a well-honed script by James Bridges (from the D. F. Jones novel). Eric Braeden, Susan Clark, William Schallert.

**COMA (1978).** Robin Cook's best-seller, faithfully adapted by director Michael Crichton. Nurse Genevieve Bujold discovers patients are dying mysteriously under comatose conditions. Her investigation reveals a shocking plot as she and Michael Douglas nose in places they shouldn't. Good thriller, ample suspense. Richard Widmark, Elizabeth Ashley, Rip Torn, Lois Chiles. (VC)

**COMEBACK, THE (1977).** English singer Jack Jones is writing new material in an eerie country estate when he is haunted by the ghost of his wife, freshly killed in London. The killer comes to the mansion, where a confrontation is played out with buckets of blood. Produced-directed by Peter Walker. Richard Johnson, David Doyle, Sheila Keith. Also known as THE DAY THE SCREAMING STOPPED.

**COMEDY OF TERRORS (1963).** Sidesplitting parody: Undertakers Vincent Price and Peter Lorre plot to finish off a landlord (Basil Rathbone) but instead bumble to their own odd demises. There's Boris Karloff in a hysterical role as an old geezer, with Joe E. Brown and buxom Joyce Jameson adding to the macabre merriment. Director Jacques Tourneur (CURSE OF THE DEMON) makes sport of horror cliches with a cast that made the cliches famous. Classic "black comedy" screenplay by Richard Matheson.

**COMIN' ROUND THE MOUNTAIN (1951).** All-time low for Bud Abbott and Lou Costello, though Margaret Hamilton is flying high as a witch who concocts a love potion for loony Lou. You'll be comin' round the bend after a few reels of this lackluster comedy directed by Charles Lamont. Kirby Grant, Glenn Strange, Dorothy Shay, Bob Easton.

**COMING, THE (1980).** Bert I. Gordon wrote-produced-directed this demon possession chiller starring Susan Swift as a teen whose body is invaded by evil forces. Albert Salmi, Guy Stockwell, Tisha Sterling. Better get going before THE COMING.

**COMING SOON (1984).** Compilation of footage from Universal's horror and science-fiction movies, as well as trailers and behind-the-scenes footage, such as Steven Spielberg making E.T. Written by Mick Garris and John Landis, produced by Landis. Narrated by Jamie Lee Curtis. (VC)

**COMMUNION.** See **ALICE, SWEET ALICE.**

**COMPANION, THE (1976).** Weak, talkative psychothriller in which Jack Ging hires nurse Antoinette Bower to kill shrewish sister Edith Atwater. Flashbacks reveal that Ging and Atwater earlier killed sister and father. Kent Smith and Robert Emhardt add strength to the cast but Tony Sawyer's lukewarm script and Randall Hood's limp direction do nothing to make this rise above the level of a competent TV movie. Nothing

companionable about it.

**COMPANY OF WOLVES, THE (1985).** Beautiful but odd British film mixing man-into-animal special effects with ominous symbolism and literary metaphor to retell the "Little Red Riding Hood" fairy tale as a werewolf story. Director Neil Jordan makes this audacious idea work because the fictional never-never land is a strange, foreboding forest, and the theme depicted in graphic horror terms. (One unsettling sequence shows a man skinning his own head while wolf parts pop out of his body; another has a wolf's tongue darting out of a human mouth.) Sarah Patterson dreams she and her family are living in a small village in a past century—a village threatened by killer wolves or men with "the beast within them." Angela Lansbury is wonderfully gnarly and wise as the grandmother who tells "once upon a time" werewolf tales. Several wolf-narratives within wolf-narratives build to the final confrontation between Patterson (Ms Riding Hood) and Huntsman-turned-fang-monster (Micha Bergese). This works better as an exercise in art design, mood and allegory than as a total story. The photography is exquisite, capturing an autumnal tone that adds to the sinister qualities of the dark forest and medieval times. David Warner. (VC)

**COMPUTER KILLERS.** See **HORROR HOSPITAL.**

**COMPUTER WORE TENNIS SHOES, THE (1970).** The electronic memory bank of a computer is injected into Kurt Russell's brain in this Disney comedy. Cesar Romero is the bumbling bad guy trying to steal the new discovery. Directed by Robert Butler. Joe Flynn, William Schallert, Jon Provost, Pat Harrington. The sequel was NOW YOU SEE HIM, NOW YOU DON'T. (VC)

**COMPUTERCIDE (1977).** In the 1990s the last private eye (Joseph Cortase) and girl friend Susan George pose as newlyweds to penetrate the security of a housing complex that could be secret headquarters for a cloning operation. Dreary, uninspired TV fodder, with even the action sequences causing ennui. Watching COMPUTERCIDE is committing videocide. Directed by Robert Michael Lewis. David Huddleston, Donald Pleasence, Joseph Cortese.

**CON CAPER/THE CURSE OF ARVA (1978).** Re-edited segments of TV's SPIDERMAN starring Nicholas Hammond as the web-spinning misunderstood superhero. In these stories he meets a bank robber and a telekinetic-minded cult figurehead planning to conquer the world with psychic powers. Directors: Tom Blank, Michael Caffey. Robert F. Simon, Chip Fields, Theodore Bikel, Michael Pataki, Andrew Robinson, Ramon Bieri.

**CONAN THE BARBARIAN (1982).** Robert E. Howard's sword-and-sorcery hero with bulging biceps, who prays to the god Crom, reached the screen as Arnold Schwarzenegger, one-time muscle champ. Despite what critics said about his Neanderthal acting, and "barbaric" Austrian accent, it was good casting. John Milius' direction and screenplay (with

**SOME OF THE AWESOME SIGHTS IN THE CLASSICAL 'COMPANY OF WOLVES'**

**ARNOLD SCHWARZENEGGER BATTLES A SERPENT IN 'CONAN THE BARBARIAN'**

cowriter Oliver Stone) give the first half-hour an episodic sense which is then lost when the film indulges the cliches of the quest. The main thrust is Conan's search for his parents' murderer: Thulsa Doom, a snake cultist played by James Earl Jones. Of interest is Conan's romance with a female warrior, Sandahl Bergman. Mako and Gerry Lopez are of minor interest as Conan's chronicler and sidekick. Ron Cobb's visual designs are imaginative, blending Old World cultures with a few Cobb thought up himself. Sequel: CONAN THE DESTROYER. William Smith, Franco Columbo, Max Von Sydow. (VC)

**CONAN THE DESTROYER (1984).** Strong follow-up to CONAN THE BARBARIAN, directed by Richard Fleischer and scripted by Stanley Mann. Arnold Beefcake Schwarzenegger is back as the sword-wielding warrior, assigned to escort a teenage princess to a faraway castle where awaits a precious stone with magical powers. His band includes two-faced Wilt Chamberlain, a beanpole of a warrior in the form of pop singer Grace Jones, and witty chronicler Mako. The villain is a warlock, Dagoth (created by Carlo Rambaldi), who indulges his fighting whims in a room of mirrors. Jack Cardiff photographed it all in Mexico. Enjoyable. Tracey Walter, Sarah Douglas, Jeff Corey. (VC)

**CONDEMNED MEN (1940).** Zombie programmer with a Negro cast, with Mantan Moreland (Birmingham Brown in the Charlie Chan films), Dorothy Dandridge, Niel Webster. William Beaudine directed.

**CONDEMNED TO LIVE (1935).** A monster, thinking it is a bloodsucker of the night, grows up to learn it is really a werewolf. Even creatures need an analyst! Directed by Frank R. Strayer. Ralph Morgan, Maxine Doyle, Mischa Auer, Maxine Doyle, Russell Gleason.

**CONDOR (1986).** Routine TV-movie set in a futuristic L.A. where a peace-keeping corps, Condor, fights The Black Widow, a female criminal who has stolen the code for our national security and is threatening to blow up Hollywood unless an old adversary (Ray Wise, the hero) doesn't surrender. Race against time, cars with rocket launchers, other TV mentality science-fiction. Directed by Virgil Vogel. Wendy Kilbourne plays a "mandroid," whom Wise tediously antagonizes. Assignment chief: Craig Stevens.

**CONDORMAN (1981).** Cartoonist Michael Crawford must

first experience the adventures he creates for his comic strip hero, Condorman, so he's always out in the field in his Condorman costume fighting for the CIA, surrounded by beautiful operatives (Barbara Carrera for one) and gadgets that enable him to fly, drive supercars, etc. Disney spoof of James Bond films is watered down stuff that will disappoint and bore even kids. Directed by Charles Jarrott. Oliver Reed, Dana Elcar, James Hampton. (VC)

**CONFESSIONAL, THE (1976).** Blasphemy of blasphemies: A Catholic priest tapes confessions of his parishioners, then blackmails them, as though he were a disciple of the Devil. And that's the implication in this film written-produced-directed by Peter Walker. Anthony Sharp, Susan Penhaligon, Stephanie Beacham, Mervyn Johns. (VC)

**CONNECTICUT YANKEE IN KING ARTHUR'S COURT, A (1949).** Musical-comedy based on Mark Twain's fantasy about a man who travels in time to King Arthur's court. It's a handsome showcase for Bing Crosby and his crooning, colorfully directed by Tay Garnett. Neat time-travel paradoxes as Crosby makes his way through another time and place hostile toward him. Victor Young's score is memorable and the cast well chosen: Rhonda Fleming, William Bendix, Sir Cedric Hardwicke, Henry Wilcoxon, Alan Napier, Virginia Field, Murvyn Vye.

**CONQUEROR WORM (1968).** Director Michael Reeves, a cult filmmaker who died at 25 from a barbiturates overdose, ascends lowbrown material to make this a stylish horror thriller about a witchhunter (Vincent Price) burning women at the stake during the period when Cromwell was deposing the King of England. Ian Ogilvy, Hillary Dwyer, Patrick Wymark, Rupert Davies. Based on a Poe poem.

**CONQUEST (1984).** Italian-Spanish-Mexican co-op job from Italian director Lucio Fulci, a specialist in graphic, sickening horror. It's sword-and-sorcery in a setting where muscular warriors do battle with she-devil Ocron (Sabrina Siani) and hairy beasts. Script and direction very poor, although Claudio Simonetti's rock score is exciting, if inappropriate to the Neanderthal locations. (VC)

**CONQUEST OF SPACE (1954).** Chester Bonestell's paintings of alien landscapes are the highlight of this science-minded adventure about a flight to Mars and the psychological problems of the crew. Directed by Bryon Haskin, George Pal's film is realistic in its depiction of interplanetary travel, but this realism is in contrast to the unconvincing characters. Walter Brooke, Eric Fleming, Phil Foster, Ross Martin, Benson Fong, William Hopper, William Redfield.

**CONQUEST OF THE EARTH.** Videocassette title for the pilot of **BATTLESTAR GALACTICA.**

**CONQUEST OF THE PLANET OF THE APES (1972).** One of the best in the PLANET OF THE APES series, depicting a futuristic Earth when apes are trained as slaves. Milo the chimpanzee (Roddy McDowall), who has powers of speech and reasoning, forms the slaves into gorilla guerrillas and stages a revolt that leaves mankind aflame. Fine direction by J. Lee Thompson, an excellent script by Paul Dehn and intriguing morality lessons make this compelling. Don Murray, Ricardo Montalban, Hari Rhodes, Natalie Trundy, John Randolph. (VC)

**COPPERHEAD (1984).** Video release, made in Missouri, focusing on a crazy swamp family fleeing with a rare necklace. The father is a crazy guy who enjoys blowing away poisonous snakes, but those slimy critters get their revenge. Written-directed by Leland Payton. Jack Renner, Gretta Ratliff, David Fritts. (VC)

**COPS AND ROBIN (1978).** Episodes of TV's FUTURE COP, in which policeman Ernest Borgnine is teamed with an android (Michael Shannon). The incompatible pair is assigned to protect a woman from criminals. Later remade as a feature, SUPER FUZZ, also with Borgnine. Directed by Allen Reisner. Carol Lynley, John Amos, Natasha Ryan.

**CORPSE, THE.** See **CRUCIBLE OF HORROR.**

**CORPSE GRINDERS, THE (1971).** Bad, bad horror exploitationer, as stomach-churning as its title subtly suggests. At a cat-food factory, house tabbies, fed human flesh turned into hamburger patties, become snarling beasts, attacking innocent cat-lovers. The canning was done by producer-director Ted V. Mikels, the intellectual who (mis)conceived ASTRO ZOMBIES. Arch Hall and Joseph Cranston wrote the tin labels. Tasteless. Sean Kenney, Monika Kelly. (VC)

**CORPSE VANISHES, THE (1942).** Virtually vapid Monogram potboiler with Bela Lugosi as unhinged botanist Dr. Lorenz, who is restoring youthfulness to his aging wife by stealing the blood of brides. Barrel-bottom production with hammy performances by Lugosi, Luana Walters (wife), Minerva Urecal (crazy old lady), Frank Moran (crazy young son) and Angelo Rossitto (cackling insane dwarf) send this up in a disappearing wisp. Directed by Wallace ("Vanishing") Fox, produced by Sam ("Thin Air") Katzman.

**CORRIDOR OF MIRRORS (1948).** Are Eric Portman and Edana Romney reincarnated lovers? You'll have to endure this turgid British melodrama (with Christopher Lee in an early role) to find out. Directed by Terence Young.

**CORRIDORS OF BLOOD (1957).** Interesting psuedohistorical melodrama from Britain with Boris Karloff as a doctor seeking a way to operate without inflicting pain on his patients, and developing the first anesthesia. Unfortunately, he also goes crazy and becomes a hopeless addict. Christopher Lee plays a body snatcher in the Burke & Hare tradition. Robert Day directed. Nigel Green, Adrienne Corri, Francis Mathews, Betta St. John, Finlay Currie.

**CORRUPTION (1967).** That old cut-up, Peter Cushing, is again a demented doctor, carving up bodies in an effort to restore his fiancee's destroyed face. This idea corrupted the brains of hacks Donald and Derek Ford, then spread to British producer Peter Newbrook, who then misled director Robert Hartford-Davies. Don't let it corrupt you. Sue Lloyd, Kate O'Mara, Noel Trevarthen.

**CORSICAN BROTHERS, THE (1941).** Alexandre Dumas' classic about Siamese twins, who experience each other's pains and joys through a psychic link, provides an entertaining premise in this version directed by Gregory Ratoff. Although the brothers vary in temperament, they join forces to destroy their parents' killer. Ratoff directed with buckets of swash and plenty of double exposures so Douglas Fairbanks Jr. slaps himself on the back, shakes hands with himself, etc. Akim Tamiroff, J. Carrol Naish, H. B. Warner, John Emery, Ruth Warrick. (VC)

**CORSICAN BROTHERS, THE (1960).** French adaptation of the Alexandre Dumas novel about Siamese twins stars Geoffrey Horne and Jean Servais. Directed by Anton Giulio Majano.

**CORSICAN BROTHERS, THE (1985).** TV-movie version of the Dumas classic starring Trevor Eve as the brothers with a psychic link. Scripted by Robin Miller, directed by Ian Sharp. Geraldine Chaplin, Olivia Hussey, Simon Ward.

**COSMIC EYE (1985).** Animated science-fiction in which Earth is faced with peace or total destruction. (VC)

**COSMIC MAN, THE (1959).** Direct steal of THE DAY THE EARTH STOOD STILL with alien John Carradine crashlanding on Earth in an attempt to help us feeble-minded Earthlings reconcile our political differences so we can live in peace with the universe. Directed by Herman Green. Lynn Osborne, Bruce Bennett, Paul Langton.

**RODDY McDOWALL AS CORNELIUS**

**COSMIC MONSTERS** (1959). Forrest Tucker blows a hole in the ionosphere, allowing Insidious Insects and Behemoth Bugs to invade Earth. Adapted from the BBC science-fiction serial, STRANGE WORLD OF PLANET X. Gaby Andre, Martin Benson. Directed by Robert Gunn. (VC)

**COSMIC PRINCESS** (1976). Two episodes of the British science-fiction series SPACE 1999, in which part of the moon has shot into space with Moonbase Alpha still intact, commanded by Martin Landau and Barbara Bain. In "The Metamorph," directed by Charles Crichton, series regular Maya (Catherine Schell) is introduced—a woman capable of taking on shapes of many life forms. Mentor, the dictator of the world Psychon, kidnaps the Alphans to rob their minds. In "Space Warp," directed by Peter Medak, the Alphans discover a flotilla of old spacecraft.

**COSMOS—WAR OF THE PLANETS** (1978). Italian science-fiction thriller starring John Richardson and Yanti Somer as astronauts deep in space. Poor. Directed by Al Bradley. West Buchanan, Max Karis. (VC)

**COUNT DRACULA** (1970). Faithful Spanish-British adaptation of Bram Stoker's DRACULA, produced by Harry Alan Towers and directed by Jesus Franco. However, a gap remains between honorable intentions and execution and the film still falls short of its goals, with sloppy camera work and bad zooms. Christopher Lee believes this to be among his best work but it's certainly not the best DRACULA. Herbert Lom is in the Van Helsing role and Klaus Kinski is fly-eating Renfield. Fred Williams, Soledad Miranda. (VC)

**COUNT DRACULA** (1978). Honorable British adaptation of the Stoker novel, presented originally in three 60-minute segments on PBS. Louis Jourdan brings an unusual grace and charm to the title role and makes this a prestigious production with the help of Frank Finlay and Susan Penhaligon (the nurse in PATRICK). Recommended.

**COUNT DRACULA AND HIS VAMPIRE BRIDE** (1973). Lacking in Hammer's usual Gothic flavor and detail. Christopher Lee is now surrounded by a cheap devil cult and is allowed to speak—a blasphemy that destroys the mystique Lee established in earlier films. Lorimar Van Helsing is again essayed by gaunt, indefatigable Peter Cushing, an extra staying power. The final showdown is contrived and half-hearted, as if director Alan Gibson and writer Don Houghton hoped this would be the series' death knell. It was . . . Lee never again donned the Dracula cape. Joanne Lumley, Michael Coles, William Franklyn.

**COUNT DRACULA'S GREATEST LOVE.** See **DRACULA'S GREATEST LOVE.**

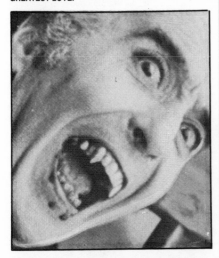

**CHRISTOPHER LEE IN 'COUNT DRACULA'**

**COUNT YORGA—VAMPIRE** (1970). Bob Kelljan and Michael Macready produced this low-budget horror film, successful enough to be followed by a sequel, RETURN OF COUNT YORGA. In an eerie castle outside L.A., Transylvania count Robert Quarry sets up new headquarters which are invaded by stake-wielding teenagers. Roger Perry, Michael Murphy. Narrated by George Macready. (VC)

**COUNTDOWN** (1968). Semidocumentary, unsensational approach to problems astronauts face in preparing for a moon landing and their race to beat Russian cosmonauts to the lunar surface. James Caan, Robert Duvall, Ted Knight, Joanna Moore. Directed by Robert Altman. (VC)

**COUNTESS DRACULA** (1970). Based on Valentine Penrose's historical study THE BLOODY COUNTESS, this Hammer slammer tells the "true" story of Countess Elizabeth Bathory of Hungaria who, in the 16th Century, slaughtered hundreds of virgins in her dungeons and bathed in their blood. Meanwhile, policeman Nigel Green investigates the corpses littering the countryside. Pretty grim material; hardly recommended for the squeamish. Directed by Peter Sasdy. Lesley-Anne Down, Maurice Denham.

**COVENANT** (1985). Imagine THE OMEN and DYNASTY blended (with touches of DALLAS) into a supernatural soap opera . . . The influential Noble family, operating the world's most powerful banks, has a pact with Satan to maintain a stranglehold on the world, helping evil powers (such as Hitler) to power. Family members are so numerous, it would take Alex Haley to root it all out. A band called the Judges has the avowed task to stop the Nobles. This 90-minute TV-movie, designed as a pilot, focuses on the efforts of the Judges (led by Barry Morse) to prevent an initiation ceremony involving the youngest daughter in the family. Director Walter Grauman pulls it into an entertaining package. Jane Badler, Jose Ferrer, Kevin Conroy, Judy Parfitt, Michelle Phillips, Bradford Dillman.

**CRACK IN THE WORLD** (1965). Good special effects film depicting Dana Andrews setting off an atomic explosion deep within the earth. Catastrophe would seem to be in store as the planet's core splits open. Filmed in Spain by director Andrew Marton, this is full of destruction and suspense as Andrews tries to stop the disaster. There's also a personal story between Andrews and his wife (Janette Scott). Alexander Knox, Kieron Moore.

**CRACKED NUTS** (1941). Confidence man tries to sell a mechanical man (Shemp Howard of Three Stooges fame) to a small town in need of oil as much as the robot. Edward Cline directed this dated nonsense—listen to the creaky joints! Stu Erwin, Mischa Auer, Una Merkel.

**CRACKLE OF DEATH** (1974). Don't crackle with glee—it's re-edited episodes of THE NIGHT STALKER with Darren McGavin as Kolchak, a reporter pursuing supernatural beings. "The Doppelganger" is a monster that appears in more than one place at a time and "Matchemonedo" is a legendary bear-creature haunting Chicago's Lakefront Hospital. Directed by Don Weis and Alex Grasshoff. Philip Carey, Simon Oakland, William Smith, Elaine Giftos.

**CRADLE WILL FALL, THE** (1983). James Farentino's eyeballs roll madly as a doctor seeking the formula for a "Fountain of Youth" serum—the better to inject into his patient, Lauren Hutton, a hardworking D. A. TV-movie based on a novel by Mary Higgins Clark and directed by John Llewelyn Moxey. Ben Murphy co-stars.

**CRASH** (1977). A total wreck, salvaged parts from THE CAR that merely rust in the sun. An antique auto possesses powers to kill, sending Sue Lyon scurrying for a traffic cop. Jose Ferrer, John Carradine and John Ericson all pop their clutches. CRASH is a mangled mess with director Charles Band at the wheel.

**CRASH OF MOONS.** See **ROCKY JONES, SPACE RANGER.**

**CRASHING LAS VEGAS** (1956). Huntz Hall, that Aggravating Adult posing as a Bowery Boy, foresees winning numbers in that Nevada gambling mecca, but this does not make for a winning combination unless you're a die-hard Bowery Boys fan. Crashing bore. Directed by Jean Yarbrough. Leo Gorcey, Mary Castle, Don Haggerty.

**CRATER LAKE MONSTER, THE (1977).** Ambitious Ray Harryhausen imitation falls short, mainly because animator David Allen fails to inject personality into his hulking beast, a "plesosaurus" which bellows offkey, waddles awkwardly on flippers and gnashes his teeth unevenly while eating human hors d'oeuvres. William R. Stromberg's direction is adequate, but the story wanders hopelessly, overemphasizing sophomoric comedy relief and an unnecessary subplot about a sheriff chasing a killer. Glenn Roberts, Mark Siegel, Cardella, Kacey Cobb. (VC)

**CRAVING, THE (1985).** Another entry in Paul Naschy's werewolf series, this time with the hairy guy meeting up with Hungary's reigning blood queen, Liz Bathory. In the Carpathians, an evil chick digs up Liz and brings her to life by dripping someone else's blood all over her face and neck. Yech! It's the old silver-dagger-in-the-heart-on-the-night-of-the-full-moon. Spanish gore; ya want more? Directed by Jack Molina. Silvia Aguilar. (VC)

## PETER O'TOOLE IN 'CREATOR'

**CRAWLING EYE, THE (1958).** British cheapie depicting an invasion of radioactive matter with a hypnotic gas that overpowers human will. It's the Swiss village of Trollenberg where psychic Janet Munro encounters tentacled monsters. The man who joins Munro to save the day is Forrest Tucker. Laurence Payne, Jennifer Jayne, Warren Mitchell. Adapted from Britain's TV serial THE TROLLENBERG TERROR by Jimmy Sangster. Directed by Quentin Lawrence.

**CRAWLING HAND, THE (1963).** Delightfully sleazy B in which the X-20 rocket returns from the moon with a madman aboard, his molecules stricken with Cosmic Rayitis. After his ship is blown up by scientists Kent Taylor and Peter Breck, a teenager (Rod Lauren) finds his severed arm on the beach and takes it home, presumably for mother. The hand comes alive, clutching human throats, while Lauren is hypnotized by the hand. What makes this watchable is the cast: Allison Hayes as lab assistant, Tris Coffin as cop, Richard Arlen as lunar project boss and Alan Hale as sheriff. Then there are the comedy-relief ambulance attendants. The digited "hand-me-down" beast is finally trapped in a city dump. Tension mounts. Moral: Never fight the hand that bleeds you. Written-

directed by Herbert L. Strock, who's one continuous yock.

**CRAWLSPACE (1986).** Pointless psychokiller movie—pointless because it exploits human sickness without shedding insight into the madman's character. Klaus Kinski, the son of a Nazi war criminal, has inherited his father's desire to murder. "Killing is my opiate, my fix," mumbles Kinski, during one of his soul-searching sessions, which are frequent in this Empire film produced in Rome. An ex-doctor from Buenos Aires, who was responsible for 60 deaths, KK rents flats to young women, then spies on them from the ventilator shape (crawlspace) or kills their sex partners after watching them coupling. In his lab of horrors, KK keeps a woman in a cage and body pieces in bottles. He plays Russian Roulette to tempt fate and he . . . but why go on. Without redeeming social values; there's a little blood and gore, but it's kept to a minimum. Directed by David Schmoeller. Talia Balsam, Barbara Whinnery. (VC)

**CRAZE (1973).** Antique collector Jack Palance sacrifices humans to an African idol, going bonkers in histrionic eyeball-rolling fashion and bringing his wonderful maniacal menace to this dreadful dreck. A Herman Cohen film made in England, directed by Freddie Francis. Co-written by Cohen and Aben Kandel, who adapted Henry Seymour's INFERNAL IDOL. Diana Dors, Julie Ege.

**CRAZED VAMPIRE. See CAGED VIRGINS.**

**CRAZIES, THE (1975).** Director George Romero attempts to duplicate his NIGHT OF THE LIVING DEAD by depicting the population of Evans City, Pa., going stark raving bananas after exposure to a deadly virus accidentally unleashed by the military into the town's drinking water. Grim civil war sequences ensue as the debilitating virus brings on madness, then death, while the militia tries to restore order. A frightening commentary on martial law. Fast-paced editing breathes an exciting tempo into this low-budget film, Romero's personal favorites. Lane Carroll, Harold Wayne Jones, Lynn Lowry, Lloyd Hollar. (VC)

**CRAZY HOUSE. See HOUSE IN NIGHTMARE PARK.**

**CRAZY KNIGHTS. See GHOST CRAZY.**

**CRAZY PARADISE (1965).** Danish comedy-fantasy lays one fat egg. The plot involves chicken eggs which can increase human sexual drives. Danish, anyone? Directed by Gabriel Axel. Dirch Passer, Hans W. Peterson.

**CRAZY RAY, THE (1923).** Silent Rene Clair French film, about an inventor can make time stand still. Touched by witty scenes and the usual Clair eye for composition. (VC)

**CREATION OF THE HUMANOIDS (1962).** Science-fiction low budget flop about a race of robots created after World War III to serve mankind's survivors. Sincere allegorical effort is marred by stilted acting and bum direction by W. E. Barry. Make-up man Jack Pierce was involved, but the Jay Simms script has too many blemishes to cover over. Don Megowan, Frances McCann, Erica Elliott. (VC)

**CREATOR (1985).** Heart-felt story about a scientist (Peter O'Toole) who has kept cells from his long-dead wife and tries to recreate her in laboratory experiments. So wonderful is O'Toole as Dr. Wolper, and so witty and philosophical is Jeremy Leven's script (adapted from his novel), this is pure joy to behold. It's a love story—of O'Toole's undying feelings for his wife, of his platonic relationship with a nymphomaniac. It's also about love between O'Toole's lab assistant (Vincent Spano) and a technician (Virginia Madsen) dying of cancer. Accolades to director Ivan Passer for a sensitive film that says so much about the joy and pain of life. David Ogden Stiers, John Dehner, Jeff Corey. (VC)

**CREATURE (1984).** Obvious steal of ALIEN, at best an ambitious failure. What detracts is a spirited attempt to duplicate the ALIEN look but without any striving for originality. An archeological expedition travels to Titan, a moon of Jupiter, to discover a derelict ship inhabited by a hideous beast that munches avidly on victims or attaches organic control devices to victims' heads to make them obedient. Numerous gory touches and resurrected corpses, but director William

*"Does a living cell from Earth romance a cosmic ray and give birth to an illegitimate monster?"—Kent Taylor in **THE CRAWLING HAND.***

Malone does not create tension or suspense. Just a lot of blood, a lot of screaming. The cast is slightly above the teenage acting level, taking its sense of hysteria from Klaus Kinski, who turns up as his usual Mad German. He doesn't belong here—one of several misconceptions that ultimately prevents CREATURE from hatching. Stan Ivar, Wendy Schaal, Lyman Ward, Robert Jaffee. (VC)

**CREATURE FROM BLACK LAKE (1976).** Two anthropologists search for a long-armed, dark-haired relative of Big Foot, last seen loping around a sinister lake. Dub Taylor and Jack Elam as good ole swamp boys give the film some character, and the Louisiana bayou photography is okay, but the younger characters and their search is hampered by tomfoolery. The film ends with a harrowing chase, but it comes too late. Directed by Joy Houck Jr. (VC)

**CREATURE FROM THE BLACK LAGOON (1954).** A truly classic monster movie, one of Univeral's best ever, originally shot in 3-D. The excellent underwater photography lifts the somewhat mundane Harry Essex-Arthur Ross storyline out of the doldrums as an expedition of scientists travels to South America in search of a "gillman." Ben Chapman and Riccou Browning share credit for playing the Monster, one of Hollywood's best rubber suit jobs. Richard Denning and Richard Carlson head the expedition, fighting over lovely Julia Adams. In one sequence she goes swimming alone and the monster swims with her, creating an eerie "beauty and the beast" aquatic ballet. Jack Arnold directed in inspired fashion, contributing ambience and action. Equally fine are Whit Bissell, Nestor Piava (as the superstitious captain) and Antonio Moreno. The H.J. Slater musical score is suitably horrendous—and memorable. With the sequels REVENGE OF THE CREATURE and THE CREATURE WALKS AMONG US, this is one helluva series that swam all the way to the bank. (At one time this was available on 3-D videocassette.)

**CREATURE FROM THE HAUNTED SEA (1960).** Roger Corman film (shot in Puerto Rico) blends horror and satire in a spoof of the Warner Bros. gangster films of the 1930s. Charles Griffith's script has American gangster Anthony Car-bone helping members of Batista's government flee Cuba with a gold cache. Carbone plans to kill them off and blame it on a legendary sea monster, which turns out to be real. Betsy Jones Moreland, Edward Wain, Robert Bean. (VC)

**CREATURE OF DESTRUCTION (1967).** Incompetent rock-bottom schlock, just plain utterly awful. Les Tremayne portrays a stage hypnotist who puts beautiful Aron Kincaid into a trance, which turns her into a sea monster (obviously a frogman in a rubber suit) that rises from the surf to murder, kill and slaughter, but not necessarily in that order. Described as a remake of SEA CREATURE, this is the botched work of producer-director Larry Buchanan.

**CREATURE OF THE WALKING DEAD (1964).** American producer Jerry Warren bought a turgid 1961 Spanish film, added new turgid footage with American actors, and released it as a neoturgid torturer. Dreary stuff, with a voice-over narrator spewing out tons of exposition and interminable scenes of people talking about things unrelated to the plot. A mad doctor experimenting in immortality dies and returns to life to take the place of a lookalike modern-day descendant. Frederic Corte directed. Rock Madison, Ann Wells, Willard Gross, George Todd.

**CREATURE WALKS AMONG US, THE (1956).** Third and final release in Universal's BLACK LAGOON series is the least effective, but still better than most B efforts. Scientists Jeff Morrow and Rex Reason capture the Gillman and mutate its lungs so it can live on land. But the murderous passions of man send the Creature into a primeval rage. Arthur Ross' script builds sympathy for the Creature and deals with unusual philosophical issues. Directed with an ambience of moral decay by John Sherwood. Ricou Browning repeats his underwork role as the Creature, Don Megowan takes over the role on dry land. Leigh Snowden, Gregg Palmer. Produced by William Alland.

**CREATURE WASN'T NICE, THE (1981).** Cindy Williams and Leslie Nielsen crew a spaceship with mad scientist Patrick Macnee on board. An extraterrestrial monster is captured and sings "I Want to Eat Your Face" while dancing past

**BEAUTY AND THE BEAST: JULIA ADAMS CONFRONTS THE BLACK LAGOON DENIZEN**

the airlocks. Are you following this? Low camp humor with most of the laughs missing by light-years. Written-directed by Bruce Kimmel. Gerrit Graham, Kenneth Tobey. On videocassette as SPACESHIP.

**CREATURE WITH THE ATOM BRAIN (1955).** They were mindless humanoid robots, their brains wired with vengeful circuitry and programmed to kill, kill, kill. These human monstrosities multilate, bash, crash and make hash of their human targets, knowing no end to their strength. Standing tall in this sea of twisted, mangled bodies is heroic Richard Denning, who finally short-circuits the mad scientist responsible for the destruction. Delightfully inept Sam Katzman production, totally watchable. Thank scriptwriter Curt Siodmak and director Edward L. Cahn for the yocks. Angela Stevens, Harry Lauter, Tris Coffin, Gregory Gay.

**CREATURE WITH THE BLUE HAND (1971).** West German version of a Edgar Wallace masked-murderer thriller, with Klaus Kinski in a dual role. Our maniacal killer is on the loose in a castle, knocking off folks. Will Scotland Yard never bring the terror to an end? Directed by Alfred Vohrer. Diana Kerner, Carl Lang.

**CREATURES FROM BEYOND THE GRAVE.** See **FROM BEYOND THE GRAVE.**

**CREATURES OF EVIL.** See **CURSE OF THE VAMPIRES.**

**CREATURES OF THE PREHISTORIC PLANET.** See **VAMPIRE MEN OF THE LOST PLANET.**

**CREATURE'S REVENGE.** See **BRAIN, THE.**

**CREATURES THE WORLD FORGOT (1971).** A Hammer prehistoric fantasy- adventure, but producer-writer Michael Carreras, no doubt for budgetary reasons, dropped stop-motion dinosaurs and other creatures and focused on a different creature—the kind that arouse men in a different way. The creature he picked was Julie Ege. There's nothing prehistoric, though, about Julie's figure, which bulges out of her animal skins. Carreras' monosyllabic screenplay shows how Julie, daughter of a tribal chief, is given to the chief of a rival clan. Don Chaffey directed this visual entertainment, which has not a serious bone in its body. Brian O'Shaughnessy, Tony Bonner, Robert John.

**CREEPER, THE (1948).** Not to be confused with the Rondo Hatton "Creeper" series . . . this is about some other creep(er). By way of the cliche fiendish serum, the titular terror is transmutated into a "cat killer" with claw-like hands. Jean Yarbrough directed. Onslow Stevens, Eduardo Ciannelli, Julie Morgan, Philip Ahn.

**CREEPERS (1984).** Italian director Dario Argento returns to his SUSPIRIA themes to spin this shivery yarn about a student (Jennifer Connelly) at a girls' school in "Swiss Transylvania" who finds crawling maggots and/or worms while detective Donald Pleasence seeks the identity of a hooded killer who murders with a knife on a pole. This has that surreal quality which has made Argento a cult favorite; his camera follows Jennifer as she chases a fallen telephone down a tunnel and as she plunges into a pit of gooey slime. Despite its murders and "perils of Pauline," though, CREEPERS is second-rate Argento, relying on a pet chimpanzee (a la Cheetah in Tarzan) to solve the case, and never sustaining the drive that made DEEP RED and SUSPIRIA such classics. Daria Nicolodi, Dalila Di Lazzaro. (VC)

**CREEPING FLESH, THE (1973).** British chiller starring Peter Cushing as a scientist exploring New Guinea who discovers a strange skeleton which, when injected with a serum mixed with his blood, comes to live and roves the countryside, causing havoc. Cushing injects daughter Lorna Heilbron with the serum and she too develops anti-social tendencies. Christopher Lee is also on hand, lending his strong presence. Don't try to make sense out of it, just enjoy. Directed by Freddie Francis. (VC)

**CREEPING TERROR, THE (1964).** Reputedly "the worst film of all time," although PLAN 9 FROM OUTER SPACE deserves equal rank. Made at Lake Tahoe, Nev., it depicts an elongated alien monster resembling a clumsy shag rug which devours people through a gaping maw, overturns cars and takes forever to shamble ten feet. Surely an example of superior ineptitude, so kudos to director Art Nelson. There's no dialogue, just narration—reportedly, the soundtracks were lost in the lake. Maybe the creature gobbled them up. Vic Savage, Shannon O'Neill. (VC)

**CREEPING UNKNOWN, THE (1956).** Hammer's film version of Nigel Kneale's TV play THE QUATERMASS EXPERIMENT, the first in the Quatermass trilogy that includes ENEMY FROM SPACE and FIVE MILLION YEARS TO EARTH. Brian Donlevy portrays a driven scientist who tracks down the only surviving member of a rocket crew infected by an alien spore which finally turns into a putrescent blob and engulfs the Tower of London. It's up to Quatermass (naturally!) to stop the monster. Directed by Val Guest. Margia Dean, Jack Warner, Richard Wordsworth, Lionel Jeffries, Thora Hird.

**CREEPSHOW (1982).** George Romero, a lover of horror comics, directs five tales plus a wraparound from Stephen King's screenplay, a homage to the E.C. comics of the 1950s. This blending of Gothic horror and black humor captures the imagination and grossness of those magazines: "Father's Day" is a graveyard tale of a walking corpse wreaking revenge; King appears in ""The Lonesome Death of Jordy Verrill," portraying a bumpkin who sees a meteor crash near his farmhouse and spread a green fungus ("meteorcrap") over everything; "The Crate" is the grisliest, showing how a creature caged up for a century is freed to feed on human flesh; the weakest entry, "Something to Tide You Over," is another walking-corpse story and thus redundant; the creepiest entry, "They're Creeping Up on You," is a man-vs.-nature allegory about an eccentric millionaire (E.G. Marshall) whose penthouse is invaded by cockroaches. Tom Savini's special effects are outstanding. Hal Holbrook, Adrienne Barbeau, Fritz Weaver, Leslie Nielsen, Viveca Lindfors, Carrie Nye. (VC)

**CREMATORS, THE (1972).** Free-rolling adaptation of J.C. May's classic science-fiction novella, THE DUNE ROLLER, in which an extraterrestrial sphere is living matter capable of rolling across the beaches, absorbing people like so many grains of sand. Written-produced-directed by Harry Essex, of OCTAMAN infamy. Maria Di Aragon, Marvin Howard, Eric Allison, Marvin C. Howard.

**CRESCENDO (1969).** Hammer psychothriller directed by Alan Gibson and written by Jimmy Sangster and Alfred Shaughnessy. Stephanie Powers travels to France and falls into the clutches of James Olson, the demented son of a composer who just died, and other members of the family who are just as nutty. Blood, sex and nudity (including bare bottoms) as Stephanie is terrorized. Margaretta Scott, Joss Ackland, Jane Lapotaire.

**CRIES IN THE NIGHT.** See **FUNERAL HOME.**

**CRIME DOCTOR'S MANHUNT (1946).** Split personality theme enlivens this standard entry in the Crime Doctor series starring Warner Baxter as Dr. Ordway. Scripted by Leigh Brackett, directed by William Castle. Ellen Drew, Myron Healey, William Frawley, Claire Carleton.

**CRIME OF DR. CRESPI, THE (1935).** Erich von Stroheim and Dwight Frye star in this Republic low-budgeter, based loosely on "The Premature Burial." As the crazed Dr. Crespi, von Stroheim injects a man with a drug that induces a cataleptic condition, and the man is buried—alive. Scream for your life! Paul Guilfoyle, Harriet Russell. (VC)

**CRIMES OF DR. MABUSE.** TV version of **TESTAMENT OF DR. MABUSE, THE.**

---

*"Heil Gunther!"—Klaus Kinski as the Nazi-loving madman Dr. Gunther in **CRAWLSPACE.***

CREATURE FEATURES MOVIE GUIDE

## 'CRITTERS': THE OLD HAIRY ARM OUT OF A COFFIN TRICK

**CRIMES OF PASSION (1984).** Primarily the study of a prostitute and her sexual games and roles in life, but included here because of Anthony Perkins' role as a defrocked, now-perverted man of the cloth who hangs around skid row and gets off his jollies by wielding a knife. Director Ken Russell opts for an ending that steals directly from PSYCHO and plays as an obscene joke. Kathleen Turner portrays the whore-by-night, working-woman by day. As freakish as it sounds. (VC)

**CRIMES IN THE WAX MUSUEM.** See **NIGHTMARE IN WAX. (A CASE OF WAXY BUILDUP TO A WANING DENOUEMENT!)**

**CRIMES OF THE BLACK CAT, THE (1972).** Italian horrifier in which a feline with poisoned claws strikes again and again. Directed by Sergio Pastore. Antonio De Teffe, Sylva Koscina.

**CRIMES OF THE FUTURE (1970).** David Cronenberg's first feature, an oddity set in Dr. Antoine Rouge's House of Skin, where the dermatologist has created Rouge's Malady. A "monster from within"—a foam that flows from the mouth, ears and other orifices—causes subjects to indulge in weird foot fetishes and metaphoric acts of homosexuality. Also involved is the Institute of Neo-Venereal Disease, where a strange doctor has regenerated defective organs and created new ones. Recommended only to hardcore Cronenberg buffs. General audiences will only be baffled by these bizarre themes.

**CRIMSON CULT, THE (1970).** Produced as THE CURSE OF THE CRIMSON ALTAR, one of Boris Karloff's last films. He portrays a hero, Professor Marshe, an expert in witchcraft. In the English village of Greymarsh, the ancestor of a witch burned at the stake has formed a cult and is preparing new sacrifices. Said to be based on Lovecraft's DREAMS IN THE WITCH HOUSE, but don't believe it. Directed by Vernon Sewell. Mediocre. Christopher Lee, Michael Gough, Barbara Steele, Mark Eden.

**CRIMSON EXECUTIONER.** See **BLOODY PIT OF HORROR, THE.**

**CRIMSON GHOST, THE. (1946).** Cliffhanger fans! Here's all 12 chapters of a rousing Republic serial featuring a ridiculous archvillain: a crude dude who wears a skeleton's face, black robe and scowl cowl. He and his henchmen are out to steal the Cyclotrode, a cool tool capable of short-circuiting all electrical current. Charles Quigley, as criminologist Duncan Richards, fights the kook spook with the yelp help of Linda Stirling ("Queen of the Serials"). Plenty of action and action

and action from Saturday matinee kings William Witney and Fred C. Brannon. Clayton Moore, "The Lone Ranger," is the Crimson Ghost's chief henchman, Stanley Price, Rex Lease. (VC)

**CRIMSON PIRATE, THE (1952).** A delightful farce, with athletic Burt Lancaster swinging from the parapets with his gang of jovial buccaneers; full of non sequiturs and inventions peculiar to the 18th Century: submarines, air balloons, machine guns and tanks. One of the funniest adventure parodies ever made, credit going to producer Harold Hecht, director Robert Siodmak and writer Roland Kibbee. Nick Cravat, Eva Bartok, Torin Thatcher, Christopher Lee.

**CRITTERS (1986).** Entertaining science-fiction/horror played as comedy . . . criminal aliens called Krites escape a space prison in a fighter and fly to Earth, pursued by two bounty hunters with shape-changing powers. The Earth focus is on a rural family terrorized by the Krites, small fur balls with teeth. Director Stephen Herek goes for laughs and thrills, and while the latter are least effective, the film maintains a constant charm by not taking itself too seriously and by having fun with the Jekyll-Hyde bounter hunters. Above average for its type. Dee Wallace Stone, M. Emmet Walsh, Billy Green Bush, Scott Grimes, Don Opper.

**CROCODILE (1986).** JAWS-style plot about an atomic-poisoned crocodile that grows to enormous size (its tail can destroy whole grass villages) and a boatload of adventurers who pursue the creature. Filmed in Thailand, and purely a croc. Directed by Sompote Sands. Nat Puvania, Kirk Warren, Angela Wells. (VC)

**CROWHAVEN FARM (1970).** Supernatural TV thriller by producer-director Walter Grauman, in which Paul Burke and Hope Lange, as Ben and Maggie Porter, inherit a farmhouse—and a legacy of witchcraft to go with their marital difficulties. Neat surprise ending is provided by John McGreevey's script. Lloyd Bochner, John Carradine, Milton Selzer, Patricia Barry, Virginia Gregg.

**CRUCIBLE OF HORROR (1971).** British return-from-the-dead chiller directed by Viktor Ritelis. Michael Gough returns from the dead to wreak his revenge against wife Yvonne Mitchell and daughter Sharon Gurney. A viewing crucible. Simon Gough, David Butler. (VC)

**CRUCIBLE OF TERROR (1971).** An insane sculptor coats his victims with wax or bronze when his body is inhabited by the spirit of a dead artist. But don't be upset, it is in the name of art. Oh well, by now you must have the picture . . . oops, we mean bust. And this is, indeed, a bust. British folderol starring Mike Raven as the artist. Mary Maude, James Bolam, Ronald Lacey. Directed by Ted Hooker. (VC)

**CRUISE INTO TERROR (1978).** A sarcophagus from Egypt, containing the Son of Satan, brings out the worst in passengers aboard a dilapidated pleasure ship in this TV-movie, which is resolved very poorly. One positive feature: the latest in sexy clothes for Stella Stevens (as a washed-up divorcee) and Lynda Day George (unhappy wife searching for new romance with tired hubby Christopher George). Bruce Kessler helmed the cameras. Avast, it's scurvy! Ray Milland, Dirk Benedict, Frank Converse, John Forsythe, Lee Meriwether, Hugh O'Brian. (VC)

**CRY FOR THE STRANGERS (1982).** David Gerber TV-movie based on a John Saul novel about Indian spirits who kill trespassers in a harbor in Washington State. Photographed in an offbeat fashion by Frank Stanley and well directed by Peter Medak. Adapted by J.D. Feigelson. Patrick Duffy, Brian Keith, Cindy Pickett.

**CRY OF THE BANSHEE (1970).** Grotesquely ugly witch of the night Oona calls up a frightful spirit from the beyond—a servant of Satan to claim a psychotic witchhunter. Vincent Price, the villain, chews the scenery in this British chiller, a fault you can lay on producer-director Gordon Hessler. Stylish fun, with surprise ending. Sally Geeson, Quinn O'Hara, Hugh Griffith, Elizabeth Bergner.

**CRY OF THE BEWITCHED. See YAMBAO.**

**CRY OF THE WEREWOLF (1944).** Nina Foch portrays Celeste La Tour, Queen of the Trioga Gypsies, who inherits the lycanthropic curse from her mother (her transformation takes place offscreen, unfortunately, for you werewolf lovers). This mild Columbia horror thriller, set in New Orleans, was directed by Henry Levin. Fritz Leiber, Barton MacLane, Milton Parsons, John Abbott.

**CRYPT OF DARK SECRETS (1976).** Producer's "dark secret" is that he had little money to send on this horror film in and around New Orleans. Weak story concerns a house of the devil and nonsense about an Aztec goddess. Let it stay a secret in the crypt. Maureen Chan.

**CRYPT OF HORROR. See TERROR IN THE CRYPT.**

**CRYPT OF THE LIVING DEAD (1972).** A turkey made in Turkey: Ray Danton directs an international cast headed by Mark Damon and Andrew Prine, the latter an American warning the superstitious natives on an island that a long-dead bloodsucker is about to awaken and drink the life fluid of all. The first hour is spent with the Wild Man, a one-eyed henchman, murdering all interferrers; the last half hour details how Prine rescues heroine Patty Sheppard and turns the tables on female killer Teresa Gimpera. Originally called HANNAH—QUEEN OF THE WITCHES, apparently by someone who doesn't know the difference between vampires and witches. The gore has been heavily edited for TV but the tedium is still intact as Danton originally filmed it. Available in videocassette under either titles.

**CUJO (1983).** Tight adaptation of Stephen King's best-seller about a rabid St. Bernard that traps Dee Wallace and her son (Daniel Hugh-Kelly) in a Ford Pinto and holds them at bay for two days, attacking the car maniacally. Director Lewis Teague displays expertise as a suspense-genre craftsman as the siege becomes a harrowing ordeal. The St. Bernard portraying Cujo (Spanish for "unconquerable force") is deserving of a lifetime supply of Alpo for meeting the rigorous script demands of a rabies-maddened critter that slobbers, drools and goes eagerly for the throat on the theory that man is a dog's best din-din. Ed Lauter, Christopher Stone. This film's bite is worse than its bark. (VC)

**CULT OF THE COBRA (1955).** Ridiculous tale of a beautiful woman (Faith Domergue) who metamorphizes into a giant cobra and attacks GIs who infiltrated a secret snake cult in the Far East in 1945. No attempt is made by director Francis D. Lyons to capture the ambience of the '40s. Ms Domergue lends nothing special to her role (she might have at least tried to look sinuous instead of sensuous) as Marshall

**'CURSE OF THE DEMON'**

Thompson, Richard Long and David Janssen fall under her hypnotic spell. This never became a cult film.

**CURIOUS FEMALE, THE (1969).** Curious title for a science-fiction picture: The year is 2177, when society is under the dictatorial control of a computer complex. For kicks, citizens now watch X-rated sex tapes, which gives producer Joe Solomon an excuse to use footage from THE THREE VIRGINS. Of minimal curiosity. Angelique Pettyjohn, Bunny Allister, Michael Greer, Charlette Jones.

**CURSE OF ALPHA STONE (1985).** Legendary rock containing the mystery of life turns a human guinea pig into a killer. Directed by Stewart Malleon. Jim Scotlin, Sandy Carey. (VC)

**CURSE OF BIGFOOT, THE (1972).** Indian burial ground yields remains of a hairy creature which high school students believe to be the missing link—until the monster awakens and goes on a murderous rampage typical in this kind of exploitation film. Not too sure-footed. Directed by Don Fields. William Simonsen, Robert Clymire.

**CURSE OF DRACULA, THE (1958).** Francis Lederer sinks his aching fangs into his role as the Transylvanian Count, turning up in Southern California as a refugee artist named Bellac who infects neighbors with his vampirism. Stock stuff, undistinguished. Directed by Paul Landres. Norma Eberhardt, Ray Stricklyn, Norbert Schiller.

**CURSE OF FRANKENSTEIN (1957).** Opener in the Hammer FRANKENSTEIN series starring Peter Cushing as the inspired albeit demented doctor who yearns to resurrect the dead and Christopher Lee as the Monster, in a new kind of make-up designed by Phil Leakey and Roy Ashton. An outstanding horror picture (an international hit that sparked a series) with a Gothic flavor and set design that set the standards for scores of Hammer films. Written by Jimmy Sangster, directed by Terence Fisher. Hazel Court, Robert Urquhart, Valerie Gaunt, Noel Hood. (VC)

**CURSE OF FRED ASTAIRE, THE (1982).** Clumsy-footed hoofer (Clio Young) exchanges his soul for fame, then doesn't want to pay off when the Devil comes to collect. Undistinguished comedy-fantasy written-directed by Mark Berger. Mary Jennings, Alan Brooks.

**CURSE OF KING TUT'S TOMB (1980).** Legendary incidents behind the curses surrounding the boy king's burial chamber, and the deaths of those who desecrated the treasure trove, are exploited at a hysterical pitch in this TV-movie directed by Philip Leacock, narrated by Paul Scofield and starring Raymond Burr (in a turban), Eva Marie Saint, Harry Andrews, Wendy Hiller and Tom Baker. The film is subjective—the curse is treated as a reality. How much is true? You'll have to reread history to separate fact from the fiction of Herb Meadow's script. Perhaps the truth is in BEHIND THE MASK

OF TUTANKHAMEN, the Barry Wynne book on which this pyramid of sensationalism is based. (VC)

**CURSE OF NOSTRADAMUS (1960).** That cape-shrouded, fang-drooling Mexican vampire is back to challenge a professor's theories about the supernatural. One of four imported features re-edited from a ten-chapter vampire saga, the others being THE BLOOD OF NOSTRADAMUS, MONSTER DEMOLISHER and GENII OF DARKNESS. Poorly acted, atrociously dubbed. You will curse it from beginning to end. Directed by Frederick Curiel. German Robles, Julio Aleman, Domingo Soler.

**CURSE OF SIMBA. See CURSE OF THE VOODOO.**

**CURSE OF THE AZTEC MUMMY (1961).** Crumbling mummy confronts bumbling dummy (a weary dreary superhero dubbed the Angel) when his flipped crypt is desecrated by your usual cinematic defilers. Another unforgivable Mexican production imported to America by K. Gordon Murray, from the forgettable "Aztec Mummy" series starring Roman Gay. In this sequel to THE ROBOT VS. THE AZTEC MUMMY, Dr. Krupp squares off against the heroic gauzeman, Popoca. Directed by Rafael Portello. Rosita Arenas, Crox Alvaradao.

**CURSE OF THE BLACK WIDOW (1977).** Dan Curtis repeats the formula of his NIGHT STALKER, only instead of a vampire the creature is a Giant Killer Spider. There's the investigator hot on the legs of the spider creature, a research expert who spots the spidery clues, and innocent, sexy victims. The plot scampers along, supported by Anthony Franciosa, Donna Mills, Patty Duke Astin, June Lockhart, June Allyson, Jeff Corey, Sid Caesar and Vic Morrow, the latter as the cop always one clue behind. Unfortunately, you can see the wires pulling the spider's legs in the final scenes. Originally shown mistitled as LOVE TRAP. (VC)

**CURSE OF THE BLOOD GHOULS. See SLAUGHTER OF THE VAMPIRES.**

**CURSE OF THE CAT PEOPLE, THE (1944).** This sequel to THE CAT PEOPLE has Kent Smith and Simone Simon recreating their characters, but has nothing to do with cats. Producer Val Lewton was cashing in on the success of his previous low-budget winner, agreeing to the exploitative title but refusing to compromise story. Scripter DeWitt Bodeen came up with a poetically moody tale about a girl's fantasies which produce a fairy godmother to protect her from a mysterious stranger in the woods. An eldritch fairy tale, so different it will surprise you. Co-directed by Robert Wise and Gunther V. Fritsch. Ann Carter, Elizabeth Russell, Jane Rudolph, Eve March, Julia Dean. (VC)

'CURSE OF THE WEREWOLF'

**CURSE OF THE CRIMSON CULT. See CRIMSON CULT, THE.**

**CURSE OF THE CRYING WOMAN (1960).** English-dubbed Mexican import is a curse on the viewing public. Bride Rosita Arenas inherits a legacy of horror when she inherits a mansion haunted by witches, warlocks and other evils. You'll curse, you'll cry. Written-directed by Rafael Baledon. Abel Salazar, Rita Macedo, Domingo Soler. (VC)

**CURSE OF THE DEMON (1957).** Based on "Casting the Runes," a classic short story by M. R. James, a British historian noted for quiet, antiquarian tales of supernatural horror. This British chiller, which has won cult status, was directed by Jacques Tourneur, a disciple of Val Lewton. Psychic investigator Dana Andrews comes to England to probe a devil cult, only to find the forces of supernatural. The script by Charles Bennett and Hal F. Chester is full of suspense and highlights a classic climax. Peggy Cummins, Niall MacGinnis (as Dr. Karswell), Maurice Denham, Athene Seyler, Liam Redmond, Percy Herbert. (VC)

**CURSE OF THE DEVIL (1973).** If you thought that Spanish epic, MARK OF THE WOLFMAN, was peachy keen, get a load of this sequel. Devilish Princess Bathory, who loves to wallow in bathtubs of blood, sets into motion a curse that'll have you howling like a banshee as the characters tear at each other's throats. Your laughter will be as hysterical as the ending. Scripted by Jacinto Molina, directed by Charles Avred. Part of a series starring Paul Naschy as the Hairy One. Fabiola Falcon, A.V. Molina.

**CURSE OF THE DOLL PEOPLE (1961).** Better-than-average Mexican horror flick depicting how four Mexicans witness a taboo voodoo show and are marked for death. "Dolls"—living horrors possessed with spirits—go into action with their tools to kill, kill, kill. It's creepier than most of these things south of the border. Directed by Benito Alazraki. Elvira Quintana, Ramon Gay, Luis Aragon.

**CURSE OF THE FACELESS MAN (1958).** Embarrassing effort that falls (with a thud) into the mummy genre. Jerome Bixby's ridiculous story concerns a Pompeian, mummified since the eruption of Mt. Vesuvius, who is resurrected by a scientific expedition and breaks free to attack screaming women. Richard Anderson, Adele Mara, Elaine Edwards. Director Edward L. Cahn surely lost face.

**CURSE OF THE FLY (1965).** Third and least effective entry in THE FLY series. The DeLambres, experimenting with a teleportation machine that still has bugs in it (ha ha ha), is suffering from genetic mutations and frequently family members turn into hideous creatures. Director Don Sharp's pacing is slow, the action in Harry Spalding's script too long in coming. Half-hearted, disappointing attempt features Brian Donlevy as a DeLambres, but not even that old pro, who did so much to bring Professor Quatermass to life, can overcome the inadequacies. George Baker, Carole Gray, Michael Graham, Burt Kwouk, Yvette Rees.

**CURSE OF THE HEADLESS HORSEMAN, THE (1972).** Horseback phantom who rides on a nightly errand of revenge, a human head tucked neatly under an armpit one hopes is deodorized, is a legendary figure in search of eight hired gunfighters. Amateurish direction by John Kirkland prevents this from ever getting its head on right. Ultra-Violet, Marland Proctor, Claudia Dean, Don Carrara.

**CURSE OF THE LIVING CORPSE (1964).** Roy Scheider is caught in the jaws of death in this exercise in Grand Guignol in which torso murders appear to be the handiwork of a dearly departed spirit (a millionaire who was buried alive). Actually, the whole terrifying thing is finally explained logically in the usual illogical manner of an Edgar Wallace mystery by screenwriter-director-producer Del Tenney, robbing it of its supernatural suggestions. Still, lively gore flick, more stylish than most. Candace Hilligoss, Helen Waren, Margo Hartman, Robert Milli. (VC)

**CURSE OF THE LIVING DEAD (1967).** The spirit of a 7-year-old girl hangs over a European village, compelling innocent citizens to commit depraved acts. In the hands of director-camerman Mario Bava, this is an interesting if not sensational piece of work, with fine camera angles, acting and offbeat color. Giacomo Rossi-Stuart, Erika Blanc, Max Lawrence. (VC)

**CURSE OF THE MAYAN TEMPLE (1977).** Bill Burrud pseudodocumentary tracing the so-called mysteries that surround a certain South American structure and a "cursed medallion." Patched together celluloid proceeds ploddingly from the time of Christ to modern times, but never answers its own muddled questions.

**CURSE OF THE MOON CHILD, THE (1972).** Adam West sheds the bat-garb of Batman for the dress of Victorian England as he is caught up in a strange cult that engages in such frivolous pastimes as necromancy, human sacrifice, Black Mass ceremonies, etc. Jeremy Slate, Sherry Jackson.

**CURSE OF THE MUMMY (1971).** British TV-movie depicts an Egyptologist resurrecting a long dead queen, unaware his daughter bears a striking resemblance to the corpse. Naturally, when Ra-Antef awakens, there are murderous events ahead. If only that Egypotologist had read Bram Stoker's JEWEL OF SEVEN STARS, he would have closed down the crypt and sailed home to jolly old England. Isobel Black, Patrick Mower, Donald Churchill.

**CURSE OF THE MUMMY'S TOMB (1964).** Gauze-enwrapped, bandage-plastered shambler inspired with Egyptian hieroglyphics strangles those who dare desecrate his sarcophagus. As usual, the long-dead mummification, Ra-Antef, goes to great lengths for revenge and to track down the reincarnation of the man who sent him to the crypt. These mummies—such bores with their one-track minds. Terence Morgan, Fred Clark, Ronald Howard. Produced-directed by Hammer's Michael Carreras. Dickie Owen portrays the mummy.

**CURSE OF THE SCREAMING DEAD (198?).** Zombies on the march, imitating the cadence of the dead guys and gals in NIGHT OF THE LIVING DEAD. (VC)

**CURSE OF THE STONE HAND (1959).** American producer Jerry Warren purchased two films, added new footage with John Carradine, and released it to an unsuspecting public as a fresh feature. The Mexican footage revolves around a story about an Incredible Creeping Crawling Hand (you've seen it before, only done better), the Chilean footage is about a suicide club. Accursed viewing.

**CURSE OF THE SWAMP CREATURE (1966).** Not even in the steaming depths of the deadly Everglades can stragglers avoid the menace of a maniacal doctor, crazily at work creating a reptile monster that is half-human. You'd think the Alligator People would have knocked off these half-wits by now. John Agar looks as though he's still searching for the brain from planet Arous. Produced and directed by the bogged-down Larry Buchanan, king of swamp schlock. Francine York, Bill Thurman, Shirley McLine. (VC)

**CURSE OF THE UNDEAD (1959).** Refreshing vampire shocker—a horror Western depicting fanged Michael Pate as a gunfighter (he hires out gun and teeth) brought into a range war to invoke revenge. This strange man in black, Don Drago Robles, gets revenge by sinking those fangs into the necks of ornery owlhoots, jeerin' jaspers and cussin' critters. Succeeds where BILLY THE KID VS. DRACULA failed. Eric Fleming, John Hoyt, Bruce Gordon, Kathleen Crowley. Directed by Edward Dein, who co-wrote with wife Mildred.

**CURSE OF THE VAMPIRE. See PLAYGIRLS AND THE VAMPIRE, THE.**

**CURSE OF THE VAMPIRES (1970).** Filipino terror (sequel to THE BLOOD DRINKERS) depicts a family of vampires and their problems adjusting to home life, increasing taxes, unemployment and depleted banks—blood banks, that is. No kidding. Directed by Gerardo De Leon. Amalia Fuentes, Eddie Garcia, Romeo Vasquez.

**CURSE OF THE VOODOO (1964).** When great white hunter Bryant Halliday kills a sacred lion, the jungle tom-toms beat a tattoo of revenge. Halliday thereafter is "haunted" and director Lindsay Shonteff plays up the "unseen" horrors of the bush as the curse closes in for a weak-end Halliday. Shot in England. Dennis Price, Lisa Daniely, Mary Kerridge, Ronald Lee Hunt.

**CURSE OF THE WEREWOLF, THE (1961).** Shapely wench Yvonne Romain is raped by a madman in prison and gives birth to a baby which grows into a werewolf in this version of Guy Endore's THE WEREWOLF OF PARIS, but transported to Spain in the 1830s. Hammer's production values are high and Oliver Reed is an excellent tormented monster. Sexual frustrations finally bring out the beast in Reed and he attacks. Directed by Terence Fisher, scripted by John Elder. Clifford Evans, Anthony Dawson, Michael Ripper, Richard Wordsworth. (VC)

**CURSE OF THE WRAYDONS (1946).** Tod Slaughter, a famous British stage villain, stars in this Jack the Ripper tale, adapted from the old Maurice Sandoz play, SPRING-HEELED JACK, THE TERROR OF LONDON. Directed by Victor Gover. Bruce Seton, Andrew Laurence.

**CURSE OF THE YELLOW SNAKE (1963).** West German adaptation of an Edgar Wallace mystery in which an evil Chinese cult stages a "yellow horde" uprising using an objet d'art known as the Golden Reptile. Directed by Franz Gottlieb. Joachim Fuchsberger, Eddie Arent, Werner Peters.

**CURTAINS (1983).** Irritating Canadian-produced slasher film which paints potentially interesting characters in incredibly muddy fashion. Actress Samantha Eggar commits herself to an insane asylum to experience madness so her performance in her next film will be more believable. Hubby-producer John Vernon leaves her in the nuthouse and gathers six beauties in his isolated mansion to select the best, subjecting them to degrading sexual games. That's when the slasher, wearing an old hag's mask, strikes, and that's when it's curtains for CURTAINS. There's nothing clever or suspenseful about the murders, and the climax is neither riveting nor surprising. Jonathan Stryker's direction rambles all over the place. Linda Thorson, Annie Ditchburn, Lesleh Donaldson, Lynne Griffin. (VC)

**CURUCU, BEAST OF THE AMAZON (1956).** Prickly grotesquerie of the Amazon commits hideous murders, throwing John Bromfield and Beverly Garland into confusion (perhaps it's director Curt Siodmak's script that confuses them). Although the ending is a cop-out that nullifies the "fantastic" elements, the film still has gory murders, menacing Brazilian locations (always with the snakes) and denizens of the undergrowth. Tom Payne, Harvey Chalk.

**CYBORG: THE SIX MILLION DOLLAR MAN. See SIX MILLION DOLLAR MAN, THE.**

**CYBORG 2087 (1966).** Pathetic, rock-bottom science-fiction dealing with time travel in an inept fashion by director Franklin Andreon and writer Arthur C. Pierce. Michael Rennie is a robot policeman from the future who returns to the present to prevent Eduard Franz from carrying out experiments in telepathy that will drastically alter the future. The time paradox concept is of interest but so cheaply and obviously concocted that the ironic ending is old hat. Wendell Corey, Warren Stevens, Karen Steele.

**CYCLOPS, THE (1957).** Horror fans prefer to watch this Bert I. Gordon preoduction (he wrote-produced-directed) with one eye shut; general audiences prefer both eyes shut. You have a choice as Gloria Talbot leads an expedition into Mexico in search of her missing lover boy, a crashed aviator grown into a 50-foot monstrosity. Lon Chaney Jr., James Craig, Tom Drake. (VC)

**CYCLOTRODE X (1946).** Re-edited feature-length version of the Republic serial **CRIMSON GHOST, THE.**

---

*"Fools! Here we are so close to solving the mystery of life and death, and they worry about their precious lives."—The title character in*
### CURSE OF THE FACELESS MAN.

*"You out there! Do you know what horror is? Do you know what madness is and how it strikes? Have you seen the demons that surge through the corridors of the crazed mind? Come with me into the tormented, half-lit night of the insane." —Ed McMahon, the narrator of* **DAUGHTER OF HORROR.**

**D DAY ON MARS.** Edited TV version of a 15-chapter Republic serial. See **PURPLE MONSTER STRIKES, THE.**

**DADDY'S DEADLY DARLING (1972).** Originally titled PIGS, this sleazy, unappetizing psychothriller focuses on disgusting elements: Toni Lawrence, a demented young woman, knive-kills her father when he tries to rape her; she escapes an asylum to meet pig farmer Marc Lawrence, who feeds victims to his hogs and finds in Toni a kindred murderous spirit. Jesse Vent portrays the good ole boy sheriff who disbelieves anything evil is happening, and Katherine Ross (but not that Katherine Ross) is a neighbor who believes the pigs are possessed by reincarnated people souls. Lawrence produced-directed this scuzziness, which he wrote as F. A. Foss. Need we add Lawrence makes a boor of himself as he hogs the screen? In video under this title and as THE KILLER. (VC)

**DADDY'S GONE A-HUNTING (1969).** Good psychomystery in which jilted lover Scott Hylands terrorizes ex-girlfriend Carol White, with many visual touches a la Hitchcockian by producer-director Mark Robson. The "McGuffin" here is a kidnapped baby being carried through San Francisco in a poodle basket. Some mild horror touches are combined with the suspense and shocks. Effective ending atop the Hotel Mark-Hopkins. Paul Burke, Rachel Ames, Mala Powers.

**DAGORA, THE SPACE MONSTER (1963).** Out of the depths of the Pacific it undulates, a quivering mass of mutation jelly jiggling across land to turn cities into seaweed-stained rubble. The monstrosity absorbs diamonds, so why isn't it after Mae West? Japanese monster science-fiction directed by Inoshiro Honda. Uninspired destructiveness. Hiroshi Koizumi, Yoko Fujiyama, Yosuke Atsuki. (VC)

**DALEKS—INVASION EARTH 2150 A.D.** Videocassette title for **INVASION EARTH 2150 A.D.**

**DAMIEN—OMEN II (1978).** Murderous moppet of THE OMEN, who turned out to be the Antichrist as predicted in the Book of Revelation, is now 13 and using supernatural powers to the max. Grisly death scenes again—including a hum-

dinger in an elevator. However, Harvey Bernhard's production never achieves the horror of its predecessor. Directed by Don Taylor. William Holden, Jonathan Scott Taylor, Lee Grant, Robert Foxworth, Lew Ayres. (VC)

**DAMN YANKEES (1958).** Cinematic pitch of the George Abbott- Douglass Wallop musical (based on Wallop's walloping novel THE YEAR THE YANKEES LOST THE PENNANT) met mixed reaction—some critics felt Tab Hunter as baseball star Joe Hardy was a homer; others thought he was a casting strike-out. All agreed, however, dancer Gwen Verdon was a hit as Lola the temptress ("whatever Lola wants, Lola gets . . .") who consorts with Satan, who in turn tempts the young ballplayer with promises of eternal youth if he'll throw the World Series. Choreographed by Bob Fosse, scripted by Abbott, directed by Stanley Donen. Ray Walston is fiery as the Devil. Russ Brown, Shannon Bolin, Bob Fosse. (VC)

**DAMNATION ALLEY (1977).** Roger Zelazny's post-Holocaust novel, turned into a hackneyed version of STAGECOACH. Civilization has been wiped out by atomic missiles and the terrain is littered with giant scorpions and armor-plated cockroaches. In place of the stagecoach is the Land Master, a futuristic tank vehicle piloted by Air Force officer George Peppard, his underling Jan- Michael Vincent and other dull characters. There's some nice special effects work when the Earth returns to its proper axis, but other effects are downright awful. Jack Smight directed. Paul Winfield, Murray Hamilton, Dominique Sanda. (VC)

**DAMNED, THE. See THESE ARE THE DAMNED.**

**DANCE OF THE DWARFS (1983).** Faltering adventure in the Philippines when anthropologist Deborah Raffin hires drunken helicopter pilot Peter Fonda to help her locate a scientist who was investigating a tribe of prehistoric reptile-men. However, the hideous monsters (designed by Craig Reardon) are too small a part of this adaptation of the Geoffrey Household novel—the story is devoted to bickering and jokes about Fonda's drinking and chauvinism. A tedious, drawn-out affair under Gus Trikonis' direction. John Amos is really wasted as a snake-loving witch doctor. One of the credits, "Chiquita the Wonder Chicken," gives you an idea where the producers were at. In video as JUNGLE HEAT.

**DANCE OF THE VAMPIRES.** See **FEARLESS VAMPIRE KILLERS, THE.**

**DANGER: DIABOLIK (1968).** Colorful fantasy based on a French comic strip, with John Philip Law as arch criminal Diabolik, who loots riches with bemused indifference. He steals a king-size gold ingot, blows up tax offices and makes love to Marisa Mell amidst $10 million. Delightful in an iconoclastic sort of way. Directed by Mario Bava. Michel Piccoli, Adolfo Celi, Terry-Thomas, Claudia Gora.

**DANGEROUS AFFAIR, A (1931).** Ersatz "haunted house" thriller of the 1930s in which the heirs gather for a reading of the will in a house of secret panels and drafty hallways. Directed by Edward Sedgwick. Jack Holt, Ralph Graves.

**DANTE'S INFERNO (1935).** Excellent melodrama featuring a sequence re-creating Gustave Dore's illustration for Dante's classic poem. The engravings are brought to life with startling accuracy: Legions of naked, writhing bodies in eternal banishment to Hell. The non-fantasy plot concerns the rise and fall of a con artist (Spencer Tracy) in a carnival of horrors. Directed by Harry Lachman. Claire Trevor, Rita Cansino (Rita Hayworth), Henry B. Walthall.

**DARBY O'GILL AND THE LITTLE PEOPLE (1959).** Spooky Irish legends are the meat of sport in this lighthearted Disney comedy with Sean Connery in a pre-Bond role. Leprechauns, wailing banshees, a headless coachman—are all blarney for the stoned. A delightful folklore romp in which the King of the Leprechauns, as big as Tom's thumb, is captured by an old Irishman who uses the little one's magical powers to unite two lovers and to fight off the Coach of Hades. Aye, it was inspiration that caressed the bones of director Robert Stevenson. Albert Sharpe, Janet Munro, Estelle Winwood, Jack McGowran, Kieron Moore, Jimmy O'Dea. (VC)

**DAREDEVILS OF THE RED CIRCLE (1939).** Complete version of the 12-chapter Republic serial, directed by cliffhanger kings William Witney and John English. Master criminal #39013 uses deadly Delta Killer Rays against three daredevils known as the Red Circle. Nonstop, rugged action, the kind men (and kids) like. Charles Quigley, Herman Brix (Bruce Bennett), Carole Landis, Miles Mander, Charles Middleton, C. Montague Shaw, Raymond Bailey. (VC)

**DARK, THE (1979).** Hare-brained mixture of science-fiction and horror when an unfrightening 7-foot extraterrestrial in a fright mask (with glowing red eyeballs) tears off the heads of victims and menaces them with a laser blast. Cathy Lee Crosby, Bill Devane, Keenan Wynn, Richard Jaeckel, Casey Kasem and Biff Elliott run around Hollywood looking bewildered, no thanks to director John "Bud" Cardos. It's the old Frankenstein Monster resurrected in alien form and killing without motive, even though it built a complex craft and flew halfway across the Universe. Lights out for everyone. (VC)

**DARK AUGUST (1976).** An old man curses an artist who accidentally killed his granddaughter. Produced-directed by Martin Goldman. J. J. Barry, Kim Hunter. (VC)

**DARK CRYSTAL, THE (1982).** Muppet mastermind Jim Henson and STAR WARS producer Gary Kurtz collaborated on this fantasy on a faraway planet ruled by Skekses, a race of lizard creatures. It's a kingdom where characters are hand puppets or people in costumes and face masks. David Odell's script, from an idea by Henson, has two Gelflings setting out to find a piece of crystal that, when restored to the mystical Dark Crystal, will remove the blight from the land. The Skekses and the Mystics, a slow-moving race of ponderous thinkers, are brilliantly designed, but the Gelflings are lifeless puppets. Brian Froud's fantasy world is well realized, but anyone expecting DARK CRYSTAL to be a cutesy Muppet romp will be disappointed. Frank Oz once again reveals his talent for bringing nonhuman characters to life. Co-directed by Henson and Oz. Voices by Billie Whitelaw, Stephen Garlick, Lisa Maxwell. (VC)

**DARK DREAMS (1971).** Usual devil cult, usual innocent victims who wander unwittingly into the coven. Usual boredom of

sitting through something you've seen countless times before. Usual uninspired direction by Roger Guermontes. Tina Russell, Tim Long.

**DARK ENEMY (1984).** British post-Holocaust science-fiction, made by and with children, for children. The setting is an isolated farm where a handful of youngsters ponder the outside world—until one of them (Rory Macfarquhar) investigates. Slow and depressing. Directed by Colin Finbow.

**DARK EYES (1980).** Huge-breasted Lana Wood (sister of Natalie) is the eyeful in this weak-kneed supernatural thriller in which a "lonely spirit" from beyond (Kabir Bedi) rapes Ms Wood as frequently as writer-director James Polakof can reload his cameras. Tedious, predictable and taking forever to build to its nonarousing climax. The effects are corny and John Carradine is wasted in a thankless cameo as a priest. Britt Ekland (as a psychic) and Ms Wood appear in semi-stages of undress, but this needs more than tantilizing flesh. Tom Hallick. In video as **DEMON RAGE.**

**DARK EYES OF LONDON.** See **HUMAN MONSTER, THE.**

**DARK FORCES.** Videocassette title for **HARLEQUIN.**

**DARK INTRUDER (1965).** TV pilot (originally BLACK CLOAK) was ignored by networks then released to theaters. It's an above-average supernatural thriller, with themes reminiscent of H. P. Lovecraft. The setting is a Victorian-style San Francisco in 1900 where psychic investigator Mark Richman traces ghastly murders to Sumerian devil creatures led by Warner Klemperer. Produced by Jack Laird, who later did NIGHT GALLERY with Rod Serling. Script by Barre Lyndon, direction by Harvey Hart. Judi Meredith.

**DARK MANSIONS (1986).** TV-movie, of the slick prime-time Aaron Spelling-Douglas S. Cramer variety, in which "volatile passions" and "Gothic supernatural forces" affect a young woman when she joins the mysterious Drake family on a "windswept estate" in Oregon to write the family's history. She resembles a deceased member of the family and seems destined to follow in her fatal footsteps. A lot of in-fighting, a lot of bedroom love-making, but not a lot of excitement or coherence. Nor is the supernatural element very strong until the concluding scenes, which are marred by a postscript that seems an afterthought. Ultimately a timewaster. Directed by Jerry London. Joan Fontaine, Michael York, Paul Shenar, Melissa Sue Anderson, Lois Chiles.

**DARK NIGHT OF THE SCARECROW (1981).** Unusually gory, violent TV-movie, startlingly refreshing. Bubba, a halfwit mistakenly accused of murder, is cold-bloodedly shot to death by angry farmers, who pump 26 bullets into his quivering body before learning he is innocent. The small town acquits the men but soon Bubba is back in the form of a scarecrow, killing farmers with their own equipment. One gets dropped into a thrashing machine, another is suffocated in a silo of grain. The J. D. Feigelson teleplay is filled with twists and surprises, ending on a shocker director Frank De Felitta never tips beforehand. Charles Durning, Larry Drake, Lane Smith, Jocelyn Brando, Robert F. Lyons. (VC)

**DARK OF THE NIGHT (1985).** New Zealand imitation of CHRISTINE in which a Jaguar Mark IV seems to be terrorizing its driver with a bizarre series of events. Sounds shiftless, but director Gaylene Preston creates an interesting character in Heather Bolton, a motorist who may be only imagining the horrors. David Letch, Suzanne Lee. (VC)

**DARK PLACES (1972).** Christopher Lee, Herbert Lom and Joan Collins scheme to locate a cache of stolen money hidden in a house that is reportedly haunted. Violence follows, ending in a bloody mess for all concerned. Directed by Don Sharp. Robert Hardy, Jan Birkin, Jean Marsh. (VC)

**DARK SECRET OF HARVEST HOME, THE (1978).** Tom Tryon's excellent supernatural novel was made into a TV-movie by producer Jack Laird, depicting how the Constantine family settles in a rural New England village, Cornwall Coombe, to be faced with cult-like activities that suggest human sacrifice and satanism. Faithful to Tryon's concepts, including the unsettling ending. Bette Davis heads the cast as Widow Fortune, a dowager with singular powers of witchcraft. Directed by Leo Penn. Joanna Miles, David Ackroyd, Rosan-

# D Is For Director . . .

**STEVEN SPIELBERG**

**RON HOWARD**

**JOHN CARPENTER**

**GEORGE LUCAS**

**JIM HENSON**

**TOBE HOOPER**

**JOHN MILIUS**

**DAVID CRONENBERG**

**JIM CAMERON**

na Arquette, Earl Keyes. (VC)

**DARK SHADOWS.** See **HOUSE OF DARK SHADOWS** and **NIGHT OF DARK SHADOWS**.

**DARK STAR (1975).** Science-fiction with the shining: A starship roves the Universe, armed with thermonuclear bombs to explode unstable suns in advance stages of nova. The John Carpenter-Dan O'Bannon script captures the claustrophobic conditions of deep space travel and the mental deterioration of ennui-softened crewmen. A malfunctioning computer results in one of the strangest villains in any space movie. The only flaw is a form of extraterrestrial life, obviously an inflated beachball with clawed feet. A cult favorite destined for frequent revival. Carpenter produced and directed. (VC)

**DARK WATERS (1944).** Merle Oberon hears strange voices calling her from the bayou, and her night light keeps popping off and on. Too bad she never saw GASLIGHT or she might get wise to what's happening. The waters of the script by Joan Harrison and Marian Cockrell run too still to run deep. Directed by Andre de Toth. Franchot Tone, Thomas Mitchell, Fay Bainter, Rex Ingram, Elisha Cook Jr., Alan Napier. (VC)

**DARKER SIDE OF TERROR, THE (1978).** Research professor Robert Forster is passed over for an appointment, so he creates a clone of himself which then sets out to seduce the wife of the man who did get the appointment. TV-movie directed by Gus Trikonis. Ray Milland, Adrienne Barbeau, David Sheiner, Denise DuBarry, John Lehne.

**DARKEST AFRICA.** See **BATMEN OF AFRICA**.

**D.A.R.Y.L. (1985).** Boring juvenile fantasy about a young robot named D.A.R.Y.L. (Data Analyzing Robot Youth Lifeform), labeled a "test tube experiment in artificial intelligence," who escapes from the lab and seeks refuge in the home of Mary Beth Hurt and Michael McKean. Here he learns the meaning of being human as he demonstrates his incredible powers and learning abilities. Naturally the baddies come looking for him and he becomes an object lesson. Uninspired; dully photographed. Directed by Simon Wincer. Colleen Camp, Kathryn Walker. (VC)

**DATE WITH THE FALCON, A (1941).** Routine grade-B crime thriller in the Falcon series starring George Sanders. The plot concerns the manufacturing of artificial diamonds. Otherwise it's the same old stuff, indifferently directed by Irving Reis. Wendy Barrie, Allen Jenkins, James Gleason.

**DAUGHTER OF DR. JEKYLL (1957).** Wonderfully ridiculous premise for a cheesy B flick: Gloria Talbot thinks she's tainted by the split personality of her infamous father, stalking victims at night. The monster myths really go awry in producer-writer Jack Pollexfen's script when a werewolf gets a stake through the heart. Is nothing sacred in the canon of horror movies? Directed by Edgar G. Ulmer. John Agar, Arthur Shields, John Dierkes, Martha Wentworth. (VC)

**DAUGHTER OF DRACULA, THE (1972).** French-Spanish-Portuguese film with Howard Vernon as Count Karnstein. Directed by Jesus Franco, would-be George Romero of Spain. Britt Nichols, Dennis Price, Soledad Miranda.

**DAUGHTER OF HORROR (1953).** A powerful, shocking film noir experiment in black and white, from the fertile imagination of writer-producer-director John Parker, who displays great understanding of psychology and mood film-making. Originally released as DEMENTIA, this is the surrealistic nightmare of a young woman (Adrienne Barrett) whose mental deterioration blurs the line separating reality from fantasy. She drifts through a nocturnal world populated by a fat man reminiscent of Orson Welles, a sadistic policeman and other lowlifes, a world both fascinating and repelling. Parker's strengths lie in his depiction of the roots of the woman's mental illness through her whorish mother and cruel father. Ed McMahon (Carson's pal) narrates in a style similar to radio's "The Whistler," and the lurid prose greatly enhances this neglected avant garde masterpiece. Great music by George Antheil, enhanced by Marni Nixon's vocals. Must-see. (VC)

**DAUGHTER OF THE DRAGON (1931).** All the Rax Sohmer trappings as we meet Fu Manchu's feminine offspring (Anna May Wong), engaged in world domination with dear dad's tor-

ture devices. Beware the Yellow Horde. Written-directed by Lloyd Corrigan, from Sohmer's DAUGHTER OF FU MANCHU. Warner Oland, Sessue Hayakawa.

**DAUGHTER OF THE MIND (1969).** This TV-movie, produced and directed by Walter Grauman, has all the makings of a chilling ghost story, involving the spirit of a young girl being investigated by a parapsychologist. But then Luther Davis' script cops out to become a commonplace counter-espionage intrigue tale. Subject matter and approach, however, will have ESP fans enthralled until that betrayal. Ray Milland, Pamelyn Ferdin, Gene Tierney, Don Murray, Ed Asner, George Macready, John Carradine.

**DAUGHTERS OF DARKNESS (1971).** Belgium's Harry Kumel directed and wrote this contemporary vampire tale which projects Elisabeth Bathory, 16th Century Hungarian countess who bathed in the blood of virgins, into a desolate luxury hotel on the coast of Belgium. As Bathory, Delphine Seyrig gushes with sophistication, glamour and Lesbian innuendo which soon becomes blatant as she seduces a young newlywed and her moody, dark husband. While there is considerable blood and gore, Kumel explores the darker side of human sexuality in a fascinating fashion, using visual erotica and symbolism. Achieves an aura of decadence strangely compelling. A thinking man's vampire picture. Daniele Ouimet, John Karlen. (VC)

**DAUGHTERS OF SATAN (1972).** A man sees a witch in a painting which resembles his wife. Next thing he knows, wifey is trying to knock him off with incantations and curses. U.S.-Filipino production, directed by Hollingsworth Morse and written by John C. Higgins, has the distinction of starring Tom Selleck, destined for stardom on TV's MAGNUM PI.

**DAWN OF THE DEAD (1979).** George A. Romero's sequel to NIGHT OF THE LIVING DEAD, written-directed by the Pittsburgh terror king. The unrestricted movie code now allows Romero to be more graphic, and while overshock lessens the impact, he still has a primitive power that sets him apart from (if not always above) his contemporaries. This succeeds on two levels—as a stomach- churning gory glimpse at man's prowess to destroy himself with up-to-date weaponry, and as a spoof on LIVING DEAD itself. For sometimes the walking zombies are treated menacingly, other times as colossal jokes. The only way to stop a corpse is to blow its brains out and the film wallows in exploding heads and gore of the grisliest kind (at least for 1979). The bare-bones plot involves a small band trapped in a shopping mall near Pittsburgh. DAY OF THE DEAD was the third and final chapter in this sanguinary saga. David Emge, Ken Foree, Scott H. Reininger, Gaylen Ross. (VC)

**DAWN OF THE MUMMY (1981).** Lowbrow shambling-dead flick with enough gory touches to appeal to the undiscriminating. The Egyptian locations help, but it's still pretty pathetic stuff. The focus is on modern grave robbers desecrating the tomb of a royal king from 3000 B.C. The king and his guards rise from the crypt and tear apart fashion magazine photographers who have stumbled into the chamber with their sexy models. Directed by Armand Weston. Brenda King, Barry Sattels, Joan Levy, John Salvo. (VC)

**DAY AFTER, THE (1983).** TV-movie written by Edward Hume and directed by Nicholas Meyer for $8 million—a staggering project depicting nuclear war in and around Lawrence, Kansas. It begins slowly as an average day for several citizens . . . then news of pending nuclear attack creates a panic. Finally, the Apocalypse comes with twin explosions in which Kansas City is destroyed, women and children vaporized and thousands radiated in the ashy aftermath. The day after is more terrifying as we are eyewitness to countless bodies piled up, people dying of radiation poisoning, looting, firing squads, etc. The special effects are good for the small screen. As grim as anything made for TV. Jason Robards, Georgann Johnson, Kyle Aletter, John Cullum, Bibi Besch, Steve Guttenberg, JoBeth Williams, John Lithgow. (VC)

**DAY AFTER HALLOWEEN (1983).** Compellingly odd Australian psychothriller depicts an odd paranoia: several characters manipulate a sweet young woman—she's chased by a lecherous photographer, a half-crazed boyfriend, a

**DIRECTOR GEORGE ROMERO AND PALS MAKING 'DAY OF THE DEAD'**

notorious cover-girl lesbian and a mad sculptor who puts a severed pig's head in her bed. All of them want to exploit her and soon the misused innocent (Chantal Contouri) is going bonkers. Simon Wincer directed this strange novelty, only picking up the pace and emphasizing his theme in the latter half. The title is pure exploitation—a slasher film this isn't. Music by Brian May. Denise Drysdale, Robert Brunning. (VC)

**DAY AFTER TOMORROW, THE.** See **STRANGE HOLIDAY.**

**DAY IT CAME TO EARTH (1977).** Radioactive meteorite falls to Earth, unleashing extraterrestrial forces of evil. Produced and directed by Harry Thomason. Roger Manning, Wink Roberts, Bob Ginnaven. (VC)

**DAY MARS INVADED EARTH, THE (1962).** Boring low-budget feature from producer-director Maury Dexter which doesn't have a single Martian in it. Most of the scenes are of communications scientist Kent Taylor and wife Marie Windsor walking the grounds of a beautiful Hollywood estate, puzzled when they see facsimiles of themselves and their children. Seems that a probe unit to Mars is being used as a beaming device to bring invisible beings to Earth, where they take possession of human bodies. Or something. The only surprising thing here is a downbeat ending. Otherwise, brace yourself for tedium. William Mims, Lowell Brown.

**DAY OF THE ANIMALS (1977).** Earth's ozone layer is damaged by too much aerosol (!?) and turns animals into rampaging beasts. A little of JAWS, a little of THE BIRDS. Beware of anything on four legs as an expedition is attacked, each member dying a horrible death. Christopher George heads the snivelers and arguers: Leslie Nielsen, Lynda Day George, Richard Jaeckel, Paul Mantee, Ruth Roman, Michael Ansara. Directed by William Girdler. (VC)

**DAY OF THE DEAD (1985).** Third and final installment in the NIGHT OF THE LIVING DEAD series from writer-director George A. Romero. The world is now made up of walking zombies with only a few "normals" left. A handful of survivors hides in an underground center in Florida where Dr. Logan (Richard Liberty) experiments on the dead, discovering their need for flesh is instinctive, not caused by hunger. Crazy Doc Logan soon comes into conflict with a military unit which wants to curtail the doctor's sickening experiments. (This modern Frankenstein has the dedication of a quack at Dachau.) This conflict is forced and seems unnecessary when 9000 zombies are trying to break in. Romero, who before had fun with his zombies, here takes himself seriously, relying on special effects for graphically horrible scenes which revolt rather than entertain. There's the expected chomping on body parts and unstringing of intestines, and thanks to Tom Savini

we see a human body ripped apart. The satire is now gone, replaced by screaming characters behaving in a needlessly sadistic fashion. A clumsy, unresolved conclusion to the trilogy. Lori Cardille, Terry Alexander, Howard Sherman, Jarlath Conroy. (VC)

**DAY OF THE DOLPHIN, THE (1973).** Mike Nichols misfire: George C. Scott talks to dolphins. Blame screenwriter Buck Henry. He does Flipper one better by depicting an articulate dolphin (the sentences aren't complete, but you get the idea) who follows human commands and saves the U.S. President from an assassination bombing. A lot of blackmailing and double-dealing is going on—too frequently without story clarity. John Dehner, Trish Van Devere, Paul Sorvino. (VC)

**DAY OF THE NIGHTMARE (1965).** All-too-familiar plot about a dead woman returning from the grave to wreak vengeance (or so it would appear). Director of photography Ted Mikels went on to make THE CORPSE GRINDERS and other classics. John Ireland, Elena Verdugo, John Hart, Liz Renay, James Cross. Directed by John Bushelman.

**DAY OF THE TRIFFIDS (1963).** John Wyndham's popular novel was mangled by screenwriter Philip Yordan in this British version. At one point it deteriorates into man-battling-rampaging monsters. Still, some of Wyndham's unusual end-of-mankind story remains intact, showing how most of the world's population is blinded by a meteor shower. Spared their vision, Howard Keel and Nicole Maurey flee to safety, surrounded by armies of Triffids. These are spores from the meteors which grow into unpruned plant-like beings which yank up their roots and stalk after mortals, their pods delivering a lethal sting. Directed by Steve Sekely. Janette Scott, Mervyn Johns, Kieron Moore, Janina Faye. (VC)

**DAY OF THE WOMAN.** See **I SPIT ON YOUR GRAVE.**

**DAY OF WRATH (1943).** Somber, fascinating study of the witch hunts of the 1620s by Denmark's Carl Theodore Dreyer—a grim, dark, uncompromising story of an old fat woman (Ann Svierkier) fleeing the Danish puritans who want to burn her at the stake. Inquisition executions are staged with great impact. (VC)

**DAY THE EARTH CAUGHT FIRE, THE (1962).** Doff your fire helmets to the British for giving us an intelligent science-fiction thriller, with nary a monster in sight. Two governments have set off atomic explosions simultaneously, resulting in a shift of the Earth's axis and an eccentric, unstable path for our planet. Mankind heads inexorably toward its doom. Edward Judd is outstanding as a drunken newspaperman, Leo McKern is fine as a crusading science editor, Janet Munro good as the love interest. Val Guest directed and co-wrote with Wolf Mankowitz. Michael Goodliffe. (VC)

**DAY THE EARTH FROZE, THE (1959).** IT CAME FROM OUTER SWEDEN might be the subtitle for this Finnish-Russian import in which a haggy old witch requests that the sun not rise. Nature listens, for reasons never made clear, and a new Ice Age is upon us. There's a Nordic, Viking fairy tale quality to this most unusual film, which was heavily re-edited by American-International; a narration by Marvin Miller was also added. Totally different. Directed by Alekandr Ptushko and Julius Strandberg. Nina Anderson, Jon Powers.

**DAY THE EARTH GOT STONED, THE (1978).** Camp-side spoofery on our penchant for raucous music as a villain, the Lightning Bug, hopes to destroy civilization by overmodulating our rock 'n roll soundtracks. Many scenes from old Republic serials will make this of interest to buffs, but don't expect much in the way of significant cinema. Written-directed by Richard Patterson.

**DAY THE EARTH MOVED, THE (1974).** TV-movie depicts considerable destruction when an earthquake strikes a desert community. Because of an anomaly in a batch of film, an aerial photographer discovers he can predict pending earthquakes. He hurries to the next disaster site to airlift the people out before the quake hits—but it isn't quite that easy. Mainly a disaster thriller, directed by Robert Michael Lewis. Jackie Cooper, Stella Stevens, Beverly Garland, William Windom, Cleavon Little, Sid Melton.

**DAY THE EARTH STOOD STILL, THE (1951).** One of the finest science-fiction movies ever made, thanks to director Robert Wise's concern for atmosphere and characterization and his attempt to make it believable. Harry Bates' short story, "Farewell to the Master," was altered by writer Edmund North but the essence is here, and more. Michael Rennie is Klaatu, an alien humanoid who lands his flying saucer in Washington D.C., to warn Earth that unless we settle our geopolitical differences, we will be destroyed. Wounded by soldiers, he is hospitalized, but goes undercover to locate a brilliant scientist (Sam Jaffe) in order to gather scientists to hear his plea. To prove he means business, Klaatu stops all machinery on Earth for one hour. The score by Bernard Herrmann has become a classic and even theologians have studied the peculiar Jesus Christ symbolism and Biblical analogy which North inserted into the script as a personal joke. Patricia Neal is the love interest who befriends the alien and seeks out a 7-foot robot, Gort, to utter the now-classic line "Klaatu barada nikto," in order to prevent Gort from destroying the world. Gort was Lock Martin, a 7'7" doorman. Hugh Marlowe, Billy Gray, Harry Lauter, Drew Pearson. (VC)

**DAY THE FISH CAME OUT, THE (1967).** Satirical parable misses by a mile, so heavy-handed is writer-director Michael Cacoyannis. A nuclear bomb is accidentally jettisoned onto a Greek island and the idyllic setting is turned into an absurd tourist attraction. The characterizations are genuinely wearisome as everyone looks for the bomb or commercializes the incident. Candice Bergman, Tom Courtenay, Sam Wanamaker, Colin Blakely, Ian Ogilvy, William Berger.

**DAY THE SCREAMING STOPPED, THE.** See **COMEBACK, THE.**

**DAY THE SKY EXPLODED, THE (1959).** Italian-French science-fiction in which a missile from Earth hits the sun, which in turn sends meteors on a collision course with our planet. As in WHEN WORLDS COLLIDE, worldwide destruction begins, only this time scientists decide to fire atomic bombs at the hurtling bodies to stop them. The tension mounts . . . Directed by Paolo Heusch. Cinematography by Mario Bava. Paul Hubschmid, Madeleine Fischer.

**DAY THE WORLD ENDED, THE (1955).** Alex Gordon/Roger Corman exploitation horror/science-fiction flick, as ludicrous as it is entertaining. Paul Birch has designed a modernistic house free from radioactive contamination in which he and daughter Lori Nelson take refuge on the day of Armageddon. However, a strip teaser, gigolo, gold prospector, gangster and moll turn up for shelter. While they bicker, a hideous mutant (a reminder of atomic horrors in the world beyond) pokes around with the hope of carrying away Lori. Richard Denning, Paul Dubov, Adele Jergens, Jonathan Haze, Raymond Hatton. Mike Connors is billed as Touch Connors.

**DAY TIME ENDED, THE (1978).** Filmed as VORTEX, this Charles Band effort stars Jim Davis as the head of a family that moves into a desert solar home just as the effects of a supernova (exploded hundreds of years ago) reach Earth. A green pyramid appears and tiny creatures dance in stop-motion animation. The house is in a time continuum warp (dig those dinosaurs fighting it out, gang). Effects by Jim Danforth and David Allen are nice, and the cast is watchable (Christopher Mitchum, Dorothy Malone, Marcy Lafferty), but the story ends up being slight and pseudo-Spielbergish. Directed by John "Bud" Cardos. Scott Kolden. (VC)

**DAYDREAMER, THE (1966).** Mixture of live action and puppetry to tell several Hans Christian Andersen fairy tales, including "The Little Mermaid," "The Emperor's New Clothes," "Thumbelina" and "The Garden of Paradise." Starring Ray Bolger, Jack Gilford, Paul O'Keefe and Margaret Hamilton, with voice work by Tallulah Bankhead, Burl Ives, Boris Karloff and many others. Produced and written by Arthur Rankin Jr., directed by Jules Bass.

**AUGHRA IN 'DARK CRYSTAL'**

**DEAD AND BURIED (1981).** Offbeat Dan O'Bannon-Ronald Shusett horror tale, with supernatural overtones, set in coastside Potter's Bluff, where townspeople slaughter strangers by setting them afire or poking them with knives, pitchforks and other handy tools. And snapping photos all the while, for the scrapbooks. It's up to sheriff James Farentino to solve the puzzle. By keeping us in the dark about the why (if not the who), the film builds to a suspenseful twist climax. The odd mixture includes witchcraft, voodooism, zombiism. Melody Anderson is Farentino's schoolteacher wife and Jack Albertson is the town coroner. Effects by Stan Winston. (VC)

**DEAD ARE ALIVE, THE (1972).** Alex Cord portrays an alcoholic archeologist photographing Etruscan ruins in Italy, and meeting grotesque walking corpses in the process. Grisly murders occur. The whole thing is one big set of "ruins." Directed by Armando Crispino. John Marley, Samantha Eggar, Nadja Tiller, Horst Frank.

**DEAD DON'T DIE, THE (1974).** Robert Bloch's teleplay pays homage to the "weird thriller" pulp magazines of the 1930s in this TV-movie directed by Curtis Harrington. The time is the Depression when George Hamilton discovers there's a plot afoot in Chicago by mad doctor Varek (Ray Milland) to bring the dead to life to create an army of zombies to take over the world. It's surreal within its perpetual-night atmosphere, with everyone behaving sinisterly. Ralph Meeker, Joan Blondell, Linda Cristal, Yvette Vickers. (VC)

**DEAD-END DRIVE IN (1986).** Australian science-fictioner satirizing our penchant for outdoor movie showcases. In the 1990s teenagers are herded into compounds which double as drive-ins. A young man and his girlfriend are trapped in such a place. Directed by Brian Trenchard-Smith. Ned Manning, Peter Whitford. (VC)

**DEAD EYES OF LONDON (1961).** West German remake of THE HUMAN MONSTER, in the vein of Edgar Wallace mystery adaptations. Heavily insured old men are dying too frequently as far as Scotland Yard's Joachim Fuchsberger is concerned, and the trail leads him to a ring of blind murderers led by a reverend. Directed by Alfred Vohrer. Klaus Kinski, Karin Baal, Anna Savo, Dieter Borsche.

**DEAD KIDS. See STRANGE BEHAVIOR.**

**DEAD MAN'S EYES (1944).** Third entry in Universal's "Inner Sanctum" series starring Lon Chaney Jr. as an artist who has acid thrown into his eyes by a fiery, jealous woman (Acquanetta). After undergoing an eye transplant, Chaney is accused of murder by detective Thomas Gomez. A substandard did-he-do-it-or-didn't- he? plot with few climactic surprises. Directed by Reginald Le Borg. As usual, Acquanetta is totally inept. Jean Parker, Paul Kelly, Eddie Dunn.

**DEAD MEN TELL NO TALES (1938).** A hunchback creates havoc in this British version of Francis Beeding's NORWICH VICTIMS. It seems the malformed, malevolent being has more than one personality. Directed by David Macdonald. Emlyn Williams, Marius Goring, Hugh Williams.

**DEAD MEN WALK (1943).** George Zucco, Practitioner of the Black Arts, dies but doesn't go to Heaven. He sits up in his coffin and tells chortling assistant Dwight Frye he's a vampire. His target is Mary Carlisle, whose life force he sucks out through the neck. Meanwhile, his lookalike brother (another doctor, also played by Zucco) wonders about the two punctures in Mary's neck and reads from a book about witches and warlocks. Very dreary PRC quickie, hacked out by director Sam Newfield; almost unwatchable by modern standards. Dead filmmakers barely walk. (VC)

**DEAD OF NIGHT (1946).** Superlative British ghost story anthology—possibly the most influential horror film of the 1940s. In a drawing room several fascinating characters recount frightening incidents. Basil Dearden directed the first story (by E.F. Benson) in which a racing driver receives a chilling supernatural warning of doom. The second, directed by Alberto Cavalcanti, is the simple, brooding tale (also adapted from Benson) of the ghost of a little boy murdered by his sister in a tower room. "The Haunted Mirror," directed by Robert Hamer, is a gripper in which an ornate looking-glass reflects a strange Victorian bedroom and almost compels its owner to commit murder. H.G. Wells' "The Inexperienced Ghost," set on a golf course and directed by Charles Crichton, is of a comedic nature but is the weakest of the lot). "The Ventriloquist" (directed by Cavalcanti) is the most frightening, with entertainer and dummy shifting personalities. The final tale with a surprise twist involves the storytellers. Highly recommended. Michael Redgrave, Googie Withers, Mervyn Jones, Miles Malleson, Sally Ann Howes. (VC)

**DEAD OF NIGHT (1974).** This low budgeter has gained notoriety for director-producer Bob Clark (who went on to make PORKY'S) and screenwriter Alan Ormsby, who borrowed from "The Monkey's Paw." Richard Backus portrays a Vietnam soldier killed in action whose spirit is brought home by his grief-stricken mother, but now he's a vampire killer.

Well-staged chases and a macabre graveyard climax. John Marley, Anya Ormsby. In video as DEATHDREAM. (VC)

**DEAD OF NIGHT (1977).** Three fantasy-horror yarns scripted by Richard Matheson: "No Such Thing as a Vampire," with Horst Buchholz, Patrick Macnee and Anjanette Comer; "Second Chance," based on a Jack Vance story and starring Ed Begley Jr., Christina Hart and Ann Doran; and "Bobby" starring Lee Montgomery and Elisha Cook Jr. Directed by Dan Curtis. There were two attempts to resurrect a series at Universal entitled DEAD OF NIGHT. This was the second; the first is now TRILOGY OF TERROR. (VC)

**DEAD ONE, THE (1961).** Voodoo tale in which Monica Davis sends a relative corpse out for blood. Voodoo venture vacillates, totally disintegrates when the zombie is zapped by rays of the sun. John McKay, Linda Ormond, Monica Davis. Written-produced-directed by Barry Mahon.

**DEAD PEOPLE. See MESSIAH OF EVIL.**

**DEAD ZONE, THE (1983).** Loyal adaptation of Stephen King's best-seller, a riveting portrait of Johnny Smith, who wakes up from a five-year coma to discover he has the ability to predict the future. How he copes with this unenviable "gift" is enthralling, with Canadian director David Cronenberg avoiding horror cliches. Thus can Christopher Walken's performance be savored without cheap distractions. Brooke Adams is excellent as Johnny's girl (their affair is bittersweet) and Martin Sheen chillingly plays maverick politician Greg Stillson, whom Johnny intends to assassinate when he foresees Stillson's psychotic condition leading America into war. The film poses difficult, controversial issues but doesn't offer simple solutions. Cronenberg's restraint (except for one death sequence involving the Marble Rock Killer) makes for a thoughtful ESP melodrama, insightfully structured by screenwriter Jeffrey Boam. Tom Skerritt is the sheriff, Herbert Lom is Dr. Weizak, Anthony Zerbe is the influential Roger Stuart and Colleen Dewhurst the killer's mother. (VC)

**DEADLIER THAN THE MALE (1966).** Colorful, updated look at British agent Bulldog Drummond, more of a James Bond imitation than the character created by H. C. McNeile. Jimmy Sangster has stuffed his script with a variety of scientific gadgets and assassination devices as shapely murderesses Elke Sommer and Sylva Koscina carry out the evil bidding of master criminal Nigel Green. The women are constantly dressed in minicostumes, the action is explosive and nonstop—in short, the entertainment value is high. Ralph Thomas directs with a flair for pop art, and Richard Johnson portrays the gentleman spy with wonderful aloofness.

**DEADLY AND THE BEAUTIFUL (1973).** Nancy Kwan portrays an outlawed Chinese doctor conducting monstrous experiments in this 007 imitation spy adventure.

**DEADLY BEES, THE (1967).** Amicus' adaptation of H. F. Heard's A TASTE FOR HONEY, scripted by Robert Bloch, is more a murder mystery than a horror film as an insane beekeeper develops a strain of mutant bee that attacks a certain scent. Two of the sting-attack sequences are nicely wrought, with the effects being quite horrible. A traditional stiff-upper-lip-and-all-that cast (Frank Finlay, Suzanne Leigh, Guy Doleman, Michael Ripper, Catharine Finn), was assembled by producers Milton Subotsky and Max J. Rosenberg. Tensely directed by Freddie Francis. There's too much dialogue that just drones on, but so bee it.

**DEADLY BLESSING (1981).** Botched-up Wes Craven effort is an imitation of other genre films. Little logic but plenty of shocks as a family of Hittites, a religious sect, terrorizes women living in a farmhouse. One of the more memorable scenes has a rattlesnake crawling into a hot tub, which has a naked girl in it. We defy you to keep your eyes open during this sequence. The rest is raunchy sex and violence, with several graphic shocks. Maren Jensen, Susan Buckner, Jeff East, Lisa Hartman, Lois Nettleton (in a great going-bonkers role), Ernest Borgnine, Annabelle Weenick. (VC)

**DEADLY DREAM, THE (1971).** Unusual TV-movie dealing with the razor-sharp line separating dreams from reality, and reality from dreams. Research scientist Lloyd Bridges repeatedly dreams a group has formed a conspiracy against

# . . . And A Few Directors More

JOHN LANDIS

DAVID LYNCH

RIDLEY SCOTT

JOE DANTE

MICHAEL CRICHTON

SEAN CUNNINGHAM

TERRY GILLIAM

PAUL SCHRADER

BRIAN DE PALMA

CREATURE FEATURES MOVIE GUIDE

him. The ending by scripter Barry Orringer will startle you. Director Alf Kjellin captures a dreamlike quality matching the surreal story. Janet Leigh, Carl Betz, Leif Erickson, Don Stroud, Richard Jaeckel.

**DEADLY DUST (1978).** That web-spinning, building-climbing superhero leaps off the pages of Marvel comics to star in this TV-film, edited from episodes of THE AMAZING SPIDERMAN in which Spidey protects the U.S. President from insidious evildoers. Nicholas Hammond doubles as Spidey and Peter Parker. Michael Pataki, Robert Alda. (VC)

**DEADLY EYES (1982).** Mutant rodents grow to giant size in the London subway, devouring babies and other innocents. The rabid rats finally meet their match when science teacher Sam Groom buys giant mousetraps. Meanwhile, Scatman Crothers goes to an eerie doom while inspecting a sewer. Creatures average the size of a dachshund—in fact, those are dachshunds under the rat skins, or it's the St. Bernard from CUJO. An insult to James Herbert's novel, being a typical horror film (directed by Robert Clouse) in which most characters are gnawed on before the final fade. The low budget shows in Ron Wisman's effects and there's a distracting (but sizzling) love affair between Groom and Lisa Langlois. Cec Linder, Lesleh Donaldson. (VC)

**DEADLY FRIEND (1986).** Two disparate elements are at work: Writer Bruce Joel Rubin (adapting Diana Henstell's novel FRIEND) wants to tell a bittersweet love story between a brilliant Polytech student (who studies human brains and designs cute robots) and his next-door girlfriend (a victim of fatherly abuse). Director Wes Craven wants to retell NIGHTMARE ON ELM STREET, loading up with nightmares and tacked-on shock scenes and special effects for their own sake (i.e., the basketball bit). Sympathy for the girl, after she's killed and restored to life (a robot circuitry implanted in her damaged brain), is nil once she begins killing those who wronged her. Ultimately the elements fizzle rather than meld, making this the slightest, least significant horror film made by Craven. Matthew Laborteaux, Anne Twomey. (VC)

**DEADLY GAMES (1982).** Esoteric slasher film dealing with the relationship between killer and victim. A black-mask killer is murdering young women, but writer-director Scott Mansfield quickly narrows the possibilities to two suspects: demented policeman Sam Groom or melancholoy theater manager Steve Railsback. The murders are not gory, suggesting Mansfield prefers dealing with people rather than cliche knife murders. His subtleties cause the film to go in and out of focus, and there are counterpoint idyllic moments when a would-be victim (Denise Galin) enjoys fun and games with the two suspects, unaware one of them is the slasher. Not entirely satisfying, but it does explores fascinating psychological territory. Jo Ann Harris, June Lockhart, Colleen Camp, Alexandra Morgan, Dick Butkus. (VC)

**DEADLY HARVEST (1976).** Canadian production set in the near future when food is running dangerously low, and citizens tighten the belts around their empty stomachs to face a bleak tomorrow. Directed by Timothy Bond. Clint Walker, Nehemiah Persoff, Roy Davies, Jim Henshaw.

**DEADLY INTRUDER (1985).** Unimpressive psychokiller flick: A slasher villain just escaped from a nuthouse is loose in a small community, where cop Stuart Whitman is always a few clues behind an arrest. Most of the violence is kept off screen, which doesn't help the film's chances with genre buffs. Directed by John McCauley. Writer/co-producer Tony Crupi turns up as a character named Drifter. Molly Cheek, Chris Holder, Danny Bonaduce. (VC)

**DEADLY LESSONS (1983).** Tame TV-movie cashing in on the slasher cycle, but without the genre's blood and gross thrills. Rather, it plays like a whodunit. The setting is Starkwater Hall, an exclusive school for pedigree teenage girls isolated from the rest of the world so the killer can move freely. Donna Reed stands out as the cold-blooded school mistress; Ally Sheedy is pretty dull as the newcomer facing a hazing. Directed by William Wiard. Larry Wilcox, David Ackroyd, Ellen Geer, Robin Gammell.

**DEADLY MANTIS, THE (1957).** Science-fiction thriller has been "preying" on viewers since its release. It closely follows BEAST FROM 20,000 FATHOMS but the special effects by Clifford Stine aren't half as good. The titular giant mantis is released from an iceberg by an earthquake and begins a wave of destruction, knocking over Washington Monument and hiding in Holland Tunnel. This will appeal to those who enjoy 1950s' rampaging monsters. Craig Stevens is the Air Force officer out to stop the creature, William Hopper is the scientist looking for a killing device and Alix Talton provides love interest. Directed by Nathan Juran.

**DEADLY RAY FROM MARS (1938).** See **FLASH GORDON'S TRIP TO MARS.**

**DEADLY SANCTUARY (1970).** God-awful rendering of the Marquis De Sade's writings, which capture nothing of the man or his search for sadistic sexual pleasure. Instead it's a half-hearted, R-rated portrait of young Justine who is sexually abused by assorted perverts and freaks. The philosophies of the historic, if not beloved, nobleman who sought the ultimate in self-gratification is reduced to devil cult behavior, sadistic bloodletting and sacrifices at the altar of pain. Jack Palance is but a cackling idiot as De Sade, Mercedes MacCambridge is an awful bitch. Despite its many nudity sequences, this never once captures an ounce of eroticism under Jesse Franco's direction. Sylva Koscina, Akim Tamiroff, Maria Rohm. (VC)

**DEADLY SPAWN, THE (1983).** An extraterrestrial monster, ripped out of ALIEN, crashlands on Earth in a meteor shower and proceeds to the nearest dank cellar where it opens its huge toothsome mouth and swallows up the first person it sees. It's an ugly creation, surrounded by smaller mouths, with tadpole-like babies all over the rafters and swimming through greasy puddles. Pretty soon the mother ejects a half-eaten head, which the infants swarm over, devouring with (hamburger?) relish. The only intelligent cast member is a kid who loves horror movies, so he figures out a home-made weapon to combat the gobbling mouth-thing. Very grotesque and poorly shot in 16mm. Cast of amateurs doesn't help. Just as obscure is writer-director Douglas McKeown. Charles George Hildebrandt, Richard Lee Porter, Jean Tafler. John Dods is responsible for less-than-realistic effects. In video as RETURN OF THE ALIEN'S DEADLY SPAWN. (VC)

**DEADLY VISITOR (1973).** Unseen presence in a boarding house is the ghost of a previous inhabitant, back to haunt a writer now living there. Gwen Verdon, Perry King, Stephen Macht, Ann Miles. Cheap British TV production.

**DEADTIME STORIES (1986).** "Nobody lives happily ever after," promise the producers of this anthology film made in Greenwich, Conn. It's a trilogy of tongue-in-cheek horrors told by daddy to a sleepless junior: "Peter and the Witches" is a medieval grim fairy tale in which a fisherman's son helps two cackling crones prepare a human sacrifice, but succumbs to the love of a damsel in distress. This episode is the best of the three, being stylish and featuring a good reformation of a demon's body from bones. "Little Red Runninghood" is a modern variation on the fairy tale but it's predictable, including the verbal punchline. "Goldilox and the Three Baers" is the weakest of the threesome, played totally tongue-in-cheek by director Jeffrey Delman. Scott Valentine, Melissa Leo, Cathryn De Prume, Anne Redfern.

**DEAFULA (1975).** Vampire feature produced in sign language, with a limited soundtrack of music and English translation. If you don't understand the language of the hearing impaired, you will have difficulty following this tale about a bloodsucker on the prowl in Portland, Ore., and his hunchback pal. Written-directed by Peter Wechsberg.

**DEAR, DEAD DELILAH (1972).** Writer-director John Farris centers on an aging matriarch (Agnes Moorehead) and her weird mansion. A murderess is on the premises, axing off human heads, in her search for $500,000 buried in the rafters. Michael Ansara, Dennis Patrick, Will Geer. (VC)

**DEATH AT LOVE HOUSE (1975).** Pseudosupernatural TV-movie—poppycock about a writer and wife (Robert Wagner, Kate Jackson) who move into the mansion of a once-famous movie star to write a script of her life. (The location is the old

Harold Lloyd estate.) Wagner's father once had an affair with fiery Lorna Love, and Wagner becomes obsessed by the spirit of the beautiful, depraved actress. Jim Barnett's teleplay is pure baloney, with a mysterious woman in white flitting around the estate, the wind blowing the curtains, etc. If only director E. W. Swackhamer hadn't played it so straight. Sylvia Sidney, Marianna Hill, Joan Blondell, Dorothy Lamour, John Carradine, Bill Macy. (VC)

**DEATH BITE.** See **SPASMS.**

**DEATH BY INVITATION (1971).** Witchcraft thriller written-directed by Ken Friedman in which the descendant of a woman burned as a witch retaliates with an axe. More gore on the floor. Shelby Leverington, Norman Paige.

**DEATH CAR ON THE FREEWAY (1979).** Director Hal Needham takes the wheel of this obscure TV-movie about a lone van with an unseen driver (a la DUEL) who preys on motorists. Shelley Hack becomes his target and it's a duel on wheels to the death. Barbara Rush, Peter Graves, Dinah Shore, George Hamilton, Frank Gorshin, Dinah Shore.

**DEATH COMES FROM SPACE.** See **DAY THE SKY EX-PLODED, THE.**

**DEATH CORPS.** See **SHOCK WAVES.**

**DEATH CURSE OF TARTU (1966).** A long-dead witch doctor of a Seminole tribe stalks four students who disturbed his burial grounds in the Everglades, assuming the guise of denizens of the swamp to do the killing. Heap plenty trash from writer-director William Grefe, who also gave us that Everglades love story, STANLEY. Fred Pinero, Babette Sherill, Sherman Hayes, Mayra Christine. (VC)

**DEATH DIMENSION (1978).** Killer bomb could freeze our entire planet. Could also ruin TV viewing. Or damage brain cells from underfed story. Dimensionless feature, death to watch, directed by Al Adamson. Jim Kelly, George Lazenby, Harold Sakata, Myron Lee. (VC)

**DEATH GAME (1977).** Depraved psychodrama depicting two perverted, sicko chicks (Sondra Locke, Colleen Camp) who invade Seymour Cassel's home and proceed to (1) seduce him, (2) tie him up and (3) torture him with sleazy sex games. Along comes a delivery boy, whom the busty, sensuous babes drown in a fish tank. Then the fun-happy dolls decide to castrate Seymour. Compellingly degenerate . . . you'll be disgusted, but won't take your eyes off the screen as the bisexual chicks swing. And you'll howl with outrage at the deus ex machina ending. Directed by Peter Traynor. Of the so-low-it's-high-camp genre.

**DEATH IN SPACE (1974).** Quickie TV-movie features George Maharis, Cameron Mitchell and Margaret O'Brien. Astronaut chief disappears through the airlock while his ship is 250 miles above Earth. Was his death accidental or suicide? Or was it murder? Directed by Charles Dubin.

**DEATH IN THE HAND (1947).** Odd British programmer in which a pianist, riding aboard a train, predicts the deaths of passengers by reading their palms. Sounds like DR. TERROR'S HOUSE OF HORRORS without monsters and bloodletting. Based on Max Beerbohm's novel, SEVEN MEN. Directed by A. Barr-Smith. Esme Percy, Ernest Jay.

**DEATH KISS (1932).** Listed for the completist elitist who absolutely must see every Bela Lugosi movie ever made. In this routine Hollywood whodunit, as old-fashioned as Kleig lights and catwalks, our Dracula star portrays the manager of Tiffany Studios, where a murder is committed on the set of a thriller. Quite turgid and predictable, with Lugosi behaving strangely for no reason. Maybe he's scowling at John Wray, Edward van Sloan and David Manner for overacting under Edwin L. Marin's direction. (VC)

**DEATH LINE.** See **RAW MEAT.**

**DEATH MACHINES (1976).** "Mod Squad Goes Bananas" is an apt subtitle for this semi-illiterate martial arts actioner in which a Caucasian, a Black and an Oriental are injected with a Strange New Serum and turned into precision assassins by an insidious Dragon Lady Who Overacts. Kung fu/karate ballets, explosions, fistfights, shoot-outs, sniping, bazooka blasts, mass slaughters, crashing autos and body bashings—but no characterizations, no plot, no intelligent dialogue. A miserable excuse for an action-fantasy flick. Black Belt hero Ron Marchini produced and stars. Made in Stockton, Ca., with Paul Kyriazi directing. (VC)

**DEATH MOON (1978).** TV-movie, filmed on location in Hawaii, dramatizing how businessman Robert Foxworth turns into a werewolf after being jinxed by a native curse. This puts a damper on his love affair with France Nuyen. Directed by Bruce Kessler. Joe Penny, Barbara Trentham, Debralee Scott, Charles Haid, Joan Freeman. (VC)

**DEATH OF OCEAN VIEW PARK, THE (1979).** Playboy Enterprises purchased Ocean View Park in Virginia then wrote a script around its real destruction. Special effects men used 150 sticks of dynamite and 400 gallons of napthalene alone to destroy the roller coaster. The feeble-minded plot is about an unseen supernatural force that leaves every concession overturned. Diana Canova is undergoing premonitions and psychic warnings of the coming disaster. Directed by E.W. Swackhamer. Mike Connors, Martin Landau, James Stephens, Perry Lang, Mare Winningham.

**DEATH ON THE FOUR POSTER (1963).** Atmospheric chiller set in an eerie mansion where several young people gather for an experiment in the occult, in which deaths are predicted by a psychic. Sure enough . . . what begins as fun and games turns into a nightmare. Italian-French film directed-written by Jean Josipovici. John Drew Barrymore, Gloria Milland, Antonella Lualdi, Jose Greci.

**DEATH RACE 2000 (1975).** A Roger Corman-New World cult favorite, directed by Paul Bartel. It's a real-with-it script by Robert Thom and Charles B. Griffith (from an Ib Melchoir idea) set in the future when a transcontinental race is being run. Since America is a fascist land, anything goes, and that includes running over pedestrians, bombing opponents and taking whatever steps are necessary to win. David Carradine is a maniacal driver (nicknamed "Frankenstein" because he is so brutally scarred) who joyfully keeps track of how many pedestrians he hits—each is worth so many points. Sylvester Stallone scores big here as Machine Gun Joe Viterbo. Other cast standouts: Simone Griffith as Carradine's co-pilot, Mary Woronov, Roberta Collins, Joyce Jameson. (VC)

**DEATH RAY (1977).** Terrorists armed with an Incredible Killer Zap Gun are out to conquer the world. Directed by F. G. Carroll. (VC)

**DEATH RAY OF DR. MABUSE.** See **SECRET OF DR. MABUSE.**

**DEATH RAY 2000 (1979).** TV-pilot for the short-lived series A MAN CALLED SLOANE, with a man called Sloane (Robert Logan) chasing after a gadget that could destroy the world. Routine spy thrills. Ann Turkel, Maggie Cooper, Dan O'Herlihy, Peter Nyberg. Directed by Lee Katzin. (VC)

**DEATH RIDE.** See **CRASH.**

**DEATH RIDES A CARNIVAL.** See **CARNIVAL OF BLOOD.**

**DEATH SCOUTS (1977).** Episodes of TV's MAN FROM ATLANTIS series, with Gillman Patrick Duffy thwarting a plot by underwater aliens to take over Earth. Directed by Marc Daniels. Belinda Montgomery, Alan Fudge, Tiffany Bolling.

**DEATH SCREAMS (1982).** "The last scream you hear . . . is your own!" Psychohorror flick depicting the machete murders of college beauties, with plenty of nudity. Directed by David Nelson. Susan Kiger, Jody Kay, Martin Tucker. (VC)

**DEATH SHIP (1980).** A freighter deserted on the high seas, haunted by the misery and sadism of the Nazis who once had a torture chamber aboard, is boarded by Richard Crenna, George Kennedy and other survivors of a sea disaster, who learn of its horrors too late. There's the torture gallery, decomposing bodies on board, ship parts that move supernaturally, and Kennedy who thinks he's the ship's murderous captain. Some scenes are effective but the John Robins script is generally lacking. Directed by Alvin Rakoff. Sally Ann Howes, Kate Reid, Nick Mancuso. (VC)

**DEATH SMILES ON A MURDERER (1974).** Italian shocker

in which Klaus Kinski discovers the secret to an ancient Incan formula for resurrecting the dead, setting into motion a flurry of supernatural revenge killings too numerous to describe here. Suffice to say it moves fast, is often bewildering, and doesn't bear up under much scrutiny. Look and run. Directed by Aristide Massaccesi. Angelo Bo, Ewa Aulin. (VC)

**DEATH TAKES A HOLIDAY (1934).** For three days the personification of Death appears as Prince Sirki (Fredric March), desiring to experience human emotions. For three days death is denied to those who should die. Beautiful Evelyn Venable gives up her earthly lover for the Prince, unaware of his identity. This successful Hollywood version of Alberto Cassella's popular play was adapted by Maxwell Anderson and Gladys Lehman and directed by Mitchell Leisen. Henry Travers, Edward van Sloan, Gail Patrick, Kent Taylor, Otto Hoffman. Special effects by Gordon Jennings.

**DEATH TAKES A HOLIDAY (1934).** TV version of the 1934 Fredric March film is inferior, reminding one of that old adage: Never tamper with a good thing. Robert Butler directed. Monte Markham plays Death. Melvyn Douglas, Yvette Mimieux, Myrna Loy, Bert Convy, Kerwin Mathews.

**DEATH: THE ULTIMATE MYSTERY (1975).** Phony baloney pseudodocumentary studying mummies in Mexico and Egypt with thoroughly depressing narration. There's footage of Cameron Mitchell and Gloria Prince as the study of reincarnation, regression and other life-after-death subjects are probed to the depth of one inch. The work of Robert Emenegger, Allan Sandler and Hans Beimler.

**DEATH TRAP.** See **EATEN ALIVE** (if you have the stomach for a human-chomping amphibian).

**DEATH VALLEY (1981).** Director Dick Richards is saddled with a sleazy slasher script and his efforts to make it significant are wasted as soon as the graphic violence begins after the first half hour. Then the poor writing and dumb characterizations completely befuddle him. The plot has young Peter Billingsley witnessing a murder and being chased by mad-dog killers in Death Valley. Contrived suspense nonsense. Paul Le Mat, Catherine Hicks, Edward Herrmann, A.W. Brimley, Stephen McHattie. (VC)

**DEATH WARMED UP (1984).** Grotesquely unpleasant New Zealand production, unrestrained in violence and gore as a mad surgeon (Gary Day) experiments in brain operations that turn men into kill-happy zombies. Four young people come to an island where Day has his headquarters, Trans Cranial Applications. One of the men (Michael Hurst, his hair bleached snowy blond) has a strange link to the doctor as the quartet is subjected to zombie horrors, including a chase through red-lit tunnels. An axe in the stomach, exposed intestines, a man impaled on a spike and a special gun that fires light-beams into the zombies' stomachs (the only way to kill them) are among the "gorities" dreamed up by director David Blyth and co-writer Michael Heath. Grim stuff; wishy-washies beware. Margaret Umbers, William Upjohn. (VC)

**DEATH WHEELERS.** See **PSYCHOMANIA.**

**DEATHDREAM.** Videocassette title for **DEAD OF NIGHT (1972).**

**DEATHMASTER (1972).** Actor Ray Danton directed this turgid terror tale, cashing in on Robert Quarry's success as a vampire in COUNT YORGA. In this low-grade, low-budget shocker, Quarry (also associate producer) is a gruesome guru who washes up on a California beach and hypnotizes hapless hippies with whom he lives in a deserted mansion. One by one, the teeners are murdered. R. L. Grove's screenplay takes a long time to get started, then poops out at the climax. Should have been entitled TEDIUMMASTER. Betty Anne Rees, John Fielder, Bob Picker.

**DEATHSPORT (1978).** A thousand years from now the good guys are Ranger Guides who use swords to make their point. The bad guys are Statesmen (we aren't kidding about this) who ride cycles called "death machines." So they do battle, with crashes and exciting stuff like that. Meanwhile, David Carradine and Claudia Jennings are gladiators in a sporting arena who escape into the desert. Carradine does his kung fu bit against Richard Lynch while Jennings looks fetching in glamorous rags. Unintentional comedy in the hands of writer-director Henry Suso, assisted by co-director Allan Arkush and co-writer Donald Stewart. (VC)

**DEATHSTALKER (1983).** Sword-and-sorcery fantasy (produced by Roger Corman) with a Conan-style hero who kills mercilessly, grabs the pretty girls and never lets scruples stand in his way. "I steal and kill to stay alive—not for the luxury of glory," he remarks, but deep inside Deathstalker is a good guy, in pursuit of the Amulet of Light, Chalice of Magic and Sword of Justice. There are soft-core sex scenes (wow, you get to see the bare boobs of Barbi Benton, former Playmate) and abundant violence in Howard Cohen's script that director John Watson does not spare. Richard (Rick) Hill is a believable hunk of hero, despite the phony blond wig, and Barbi makes for a beauteous damsel in distress. Richard Brooker snarls too often as the villainous Oghris, but what do you expect in a witchcraft action flick—subtlety? Lana Clarkson, Bernard Erhard, Victor Bo. (VC)

**DEATHWATCH (1981).** Suspenseful social science-fiction drama set in the not-too-distant future, where death by natural causes has been replaced by wars and assorted catastrophes. TV producer Harvey Keitel decides to liven up bored viewers by filming the last days of Romy Schneider, a computer programmer assigned to a machine that churns out best-selling novels. Subtle thinking- man's fantasy, phtographed in Scotland and directed by Bertrand Tavernier. The story was adapted by David Rayfiel from David Compton's THE UNSEEING EYE. (VC)

**DEBORAH (1974).** Confused, driven woman (Marina Malfatti) is blessed (or cursed) with psychic powers. Her desire to have a child, even though she cannot, is so strong it creates supernatural powers. Italian production directed by Albert Verrecchia. Gig Young, Bradford Dillman, Lucretia Love.

**DECEPTION (1973).** Re-edited episodes of the STAR LOST TV series about a giant starship, The Ark, traveling on an eternal voyage through space. In this episode a computer that can induce hallucinations threatens the crew. Keir Dullea, Ed Ames, Angel Tompkins, Robin Ward.

**DEEP RED (1976).** Mini-masterpiece of psychoshock from Italy's Dario Argento, starring David Hemmings as a pianist who witnesses the knife murder of a psychiatrist in Rome. Ingenious killing after ingenious killing follows, with the murderer playing cat- and-mouse games with victims. Among the highlights: a woman being scalded to death in her bathroom, a man being dragged to pieces by a truck. Then Hemmings himself becomes the target for the killer. Daria Nicolodi, Gabriele Lavia, Macha Meril. (VC)

**DEF-CON 4 (1985).** Three astronauts orbiting Earth in a missile- launching satellite watch helplessly as the U.S. and Russia are obliterated in a nuclear holocaust. When the spacecraft crashes down, survivor Maury Chaykin is caught in a war of survival between cannibals, ordinary people and a sadistic militant band. Odd mixture of A BOY AND HIS DOG and MAD MAX as the gangs shoot it out. All the while, unknown to the warring parties, a nuclear missile is counting down to detonation. The space scenes are good high tech stuff under Paul Donovan's direction but the land warfare footage is by now commonplace in these post-Armageddon actioners. With minimum characterization in Donovan's script, the film generates little excitement and seems insignificant. Kate Lynch, John Walsch, Tim Choate. (VC)

**DEFENDERS OF THE EARTH: THE STORY BEGINS (1986).** Cartoon TV-movie in which Flash Gordon, the Phantom and Mandrake the Magician team against Ming the Merciless. Mediocre animation. (VC)

**DEJA VU (1985).** Unconvincing reincarnation story (based on the novel ALWAYS by Trevor Meldal Johnsen) finds novelist Nigel Terry regressing to the 1930s when he was a choreographer in love with prima ballerina Brook Ashley. Who does Ashley turn out to be but the previous soul of Terry's wife, Jaclyn Smith. The regression scenes evolve around tarot card reader Shelley Winters, who is as unbelievable as the rest of this British-produced Golan-Globus film from Cannon, with Clair Bloom appearing as the ballet dancer's domineering mother. Director Anthony Richmond wasn't on his toes—he

# . . . And D Is For Danning, Sybil

**QUEEN OF THE B MOVIES BRINGS SOPHISTICATED INTELLECTUALISM TO HER ROLES**

slouched when he should have pirouetted. (VC)

**DELIRIUM (1974).** Italian psycho-gore murder thriller from the same team (director Ralph Brown, writer Renato Polselli) that did REINCARNATION OF ISABEL. A series of bloody murders appears to have been committed by a prominent doctor, who could be harboring a perverted love for violence. There's a surprise ending—how surprising depends on your ability to second-guess lurid Italian plots. Mickey Haggitay, Rita Calderoni. (VC)

**DELUGE (1933).** S. Fowler Wright's tale of Earth's catastrophic destruction, climaxed by a massive tidal wave blanketing New York City. Some of the holocaust scenes showed up in SOS TIDAL WAVE and assorted Republic serials. Two surviving males (Sidney Blackmer and Fred Kohler) fight over the only surviving female (Peggy Shannon). Felix E. Feist directed. Edward van Sloan, Samuel Hinds.

**DELUSION (1981).** Psychological suspense thriller of the PSYCHO school, so underplayed by director Alan Beattie that it drags lethargically, never building tension or mystery. Beattie, afraid to let the gore cut loose, emphasizes the subtleties of Jack Viertel's script and never compels us into the story. Patricia Pearcy portrays a nurse who arrives at Joseph Cotten's home to care for him, discovering a crazy son locked up in the house. The characters die one by one . . . but it won't take a genius to figure out the "surprise" ending. David Wayward, John Dukakis, Leon Charles. Also known as THE HOUSE WHERE DEATH LIVES. (VC)

**DEMENTED (1980).** In the tradition of I SPIT ON YOUR GRAVE, a woman is savagely attacked by four men and she sets out to lure them into her den of sexuality . . . but she's so around the bend that her victims are innocent. Produced-directed by Arthur Jeffreys. Co-producer Alex Rebar wrote the raunch-play. Sally Elyse, Bruce Gilchrist, Bryan Charles. (VC)

**DEMENTIA. See DAUGHTER OF HORROR.** In fact, don't miss it!

**DEMENTIA 13 (1963).** Francis Ford Coppola's first directorial job, a Roger Corman cheapie shot in and around an Ireland castle. Luana Anders arrives to claim her family inheritance (after helping her weak-hearted husband take a dive over the side of a boat). She unlocks ghastly secrets in the family closet, unleashing an axe murderer. The death-gore scenes are only moderately exciting and it's easy to spot the killer. Not the minor classic some critics claim; just passable. William Campbell, Patrick Magee, Barbara Dowling, Bart Patton. (VC)

**DEMON (1976). See GOD TOLD ME TO.**

**DEMON, THE (1981).** Two plots at work—one about a slasher, dispatched by the Devil, who wears a mask to hide his identity and uses clawed hands and strangulating plastic bags on victims . . . the other about a psychic cop (Cameron Mitchell) tracking the monster. The film comes alive in the last reel when a blonde is trapped in a house with the Demon and runs naked through the rafters. Tedious, with lengthy stretches only enlivened by bare breasts. Directed-written by Percival Rubens, the real demon behind this punishment. Jennifer Holmes, Craig Gardner. (VC)

**DEMON AND THE MUMMY (1975).** Episodes from THE NIGHT STALKER, the short-lived series with Darren McGavin as Kolchak, the newsman tangling with supernatural beings. In "Demon in Lace," directed by Don Weis, Kolchak encounters a succubus inhabiting the bodies of women, who cause the death of men who love them; in "Legacy of Terror," directed by Don McDougall, an Aztec mummy rampages. Keenan Wynn, Jackie Vernon, Carolyn Jones, Erik Estrada.

**DEMON BARBER OF FLEET STREET, THE (1936).** Legendary throat-slitter Sweeney Todd inspired this dainty British horror thriller in which a murderous barber turns over his deceased customers to a pieman who uses the cadavers as meat in his delicacies. Not as hard to stomach as BLOODTHIRSTY BUTCHERS and other variations on this macabre English history (there's even a musical stage version—see **SWEENEY TODD**). Starring Tod Slaughter, the Boris Karloff of his day. Directed by George King. Bruce Seton. (VC)

**DEMON FROM DEVIL'S LAKE, THE (1964).** Filmmaker Russ Marker wanted to leave his mark but was off the mark with this low-budget science-fiction/horror combination in which a U.S. spaceship crashes into a lake in Texas, causing the creatures in the waters and on the land to turn into the titular "demon."

**DEMON, DEMON (1975).** Modestly produced British TV-movie in which Bradford Dillman falls in love with his secretary, who demands full possession maritally. When that fails, she demands full possession of his soul by calling on a witch coven. Boring, boring. Directed by Richard Dunlop. Juliet Mills, Robert Emhardt.

**DEMON LOVER (1976).** Despite stupid gore killings and a dumb teen mentality, this is grisly stuff that will sticks in the memory (and the craw) thanks to the style of writers-directors Donald G. Jackson and Jerry Younkins. Enough idiotic kids to fill a cemetery get involved with a witchmaster who conjures a horned demon from Hell. Especially memorable is the kid who gets an arrow thorugh his groin and grovels on the floor, screaming hideously. Luridly compelling if thoroughly ridiculous and tasteless. This stars Guntar Hanse, who played Leatherface in TEXAS CHAINSAW MASSACRE. Christmas Robbins, Tom Hutton. (VC)

**DEMON MURDER CASE, THE (1983).** Because scriptwriter William Kelley leaves no doubt the Devil is at work in Connecticut, and because the story is based on a true trial still discussed in legal circles, this ranks as an exploitative TV-movie lacking objectivity and documentation. So believe only half of what you see, and doubt the rest. A young boy is seemingly possessed by a demon; when the boy's brother challenges the invisible entity, it infects his body and proceeds to use it to commit murder. A sensational murder case follows. (This story is told in the nonfiction book THE DEVIL IN CONNECTICUT.) The demonologists depicted herein are based on real-life occult investigators Ed and Lorraine Warren. Directed by William Hale. Eddie Albert, Kevin Bacon, Andy Griffith, Cloris Leachman, Joyce Van Patten.

**DEMON PLANET (1965).** Italian space opera directed by Mario Bava combines elements of the supernatural with standard science-fiction when rocket jockey Barry Sullivan investigates the planet of Aura to discover its inhabitants are disembodied spirits in search of bodies. The setting of Aura is a cheap rendering of the kind of thing ALIEN did superbly, resembling a Transylvania moor more than a foreign planet. Norma Bengell, Angel Aranda. In video as **PLANET OF THE VAMPIRES.**

**DEMON POND (1980).** Bizarre Japanese fantasy from director Masahiro Shinoda, blending special effects and an eastern supernatural legend. The Demon Pond is where demons and half-animal, half-human creatures lie in wait, hoping to be set free. Their long wait is interrupted by the arrival of an adventurer. Tamasaburo Bando plays both a wife and a demon princess.

**DEMON RAGE.** Videocassette title for **DARK EYES.**

**DEMON SEED, THE (1977).** Science-fiction thriller combines dazzling computer special effects with a literate story (from a Dean R. Koonz novel) dealing with man's rape of Earth and machine's rape of man—in this case lovely Julie Christie. Herb Jaffe's production depicts the ultimate computer which decides it is greater than its creator and malfunctions to conceive a child that will embody the genius of itself. Among the visual effects is an interpretation of how a machine might experience a sexual climax. Donald Cammell directed the script by Robert Jaffe and Roger O. Hirson. Computer voice: Robert Vaughn. The fine cast is headed by Fritz Weaver as the creator of Proteus IV, Gerrit Graham, Berry Kroeger, Lisa Lu, Alfred Dennis. (VC)

**DEMON WITCH CHILD (1976).** Innocent toddler is taken over by an evil spirit, a worshipper of Satan who adopts a wizened face to do in his assorted victims. Tepid Spanish import. Directed by Amando De Ossorio. Julian Mateos, Fernando Sancho. (VC)

**DEMONIAC (1979).** After a religious nut witnesses a satanic rite staged by a scandal magazine publisher for print, he employs Medieval torture to get even. Dripping gore, holy bore. Lina Romay, Jess Frank, Oliver Mathot. (VC)

**DEMONOID (1982).** The supernatural life force in a 300-year-old hand (severed from a woman who desecrated a Mexican devil cult) is crawling in modern times when a miner (Roy Cameron Jenson) discovers the tomb with wife Samantha Eggar. It's one severed hand after the other and mumbo jumbo about possession as the "hand" life force passes from person to person. And it's a meandering, confusing storyline writer-director Alfred Zacharias and co-author David Lee Fein are handing us. He does not have us in his palm, for sure. Stuart Whitman is a boxing Inglewood priest who spars with evil, but viewers will be struggling just as hard as Whitman to make sense of it all. (VC)

**DEMONS (1972).** Japanese director Toshio Matsumoto over-indulges himself in a bloody samurai tale of revenge depicting a warrior's transmutation into a demon and his eventual descent into Hell. Stark photography and intense acting.

**DEMONS, THE (1972).** Portuguese-French co-production helmed by writer-director Jesus Franco. Standard fare about a witch whose kiss turns men not to jelly but skeletons. Anne Libert, Britt Nichols, Howard Vernon. (VC)

**DEMONS (1985).** A Dario Argento production, shot in Berlin, and directed by Lamberto Bava, who brings surrealism to the first half of this horror film set in a movie theater, the Metropol. The audience is watching a film about Nostradamus the Prophet a viewer turns into a demon (read zombie). . . . and the graphic violence erupts, with the picture going steadily downhill as it turns into another zombiethon with hideous make-up, foaming green bile, claws, fangs. Really weird things happen here (our hero rides through the auditorium on his motorbike, killing zombies with a sword; a helicopter crashes through the roof; two kissing lovers are strangled together while they kiss) and it turns out the world is suddenly infected with demon-mania. Not great, but good enough to indicate Lamberto is better than his material.

**DEMONS OF LUDLOW (1983).** A Bill Rebane special, who directed a script by William Arthur about a demon ghost haunting a particular piano in a small seaside town. Out of tune. Paul Von Hausen, Stephanie Cushna. (VC)

**DEMONS OF THE DEAD (1974).** Italian psychothriller, the kind where a tortured young woman keeps finding dead bodies all over the landscape. In this case the beauty dreams that a mysterious stranger is trying to kill her with a stiletto. The trail of corpses leads to a witchcraft cult with blood rituals. The plot is a muddled mess and no matter how much suspense director Sergio Martino tries to inject into weird events, it's still a muddled mess. Edwige Ferece, George Hilton.

---

*"They will make cemeteries their cathedrals and the cities will be your tombs." —Advertising slogan for **DEMONS.***

*"This is the end of the beginning!" —Closing credit for*
**DESTINATION MOON.**

**DEMONS OF THE MIND (1972).** Hammer shocker deals with satanic possession resulting from incestuous sex and is "intense." Shane Briant and Gillian Hills are children kept imprisoned by their father, Patrick Magee is the family physician who learns the deep dark secrets. The visual horror only comes at the end. Directed by Peter Sykes, written by Christopher Wicking. Paul Jones, Michael Hordern, Yvonne Mitchell, Kenneth J. Warren. (VC)

**DEMONS OF THE SWAMP. See GIANT LEECHES, THE.**

**DEMONS 2—THE NIGHTMARE IS BACK (1986).** Continuation of Lamberto Bava's sanguinary saga about the world being taken over by zombies, in this case in an apartment building in a European setting. Plenty of gore and grue, thank you. Produced by Dario Argento. David Knight, Nancy Brilli.

**DERANGED (1974).** Events in the life of Ezra Cobb (Robert Blossom), who murders women, then wears their skin or stuffs bodies taxidermist-style. It's even more horrible than it sounds, because Cobb is a character based on the real-life killer Ed Gein of Wisconsin, who served as the inspiration for Norman Bates in Robert Bloch's PSYCHO. Scripted by Alan Ormsby, who co-directed with Bob Clark. Tom Savini provided the corpses around the house.

**DESERT WARRIOR (1985).** Uninspired rip-off of MAD MAX with anti-hero Trace (Gary Watkins) battling the villainous Scourge who has kidnaped his sister and is raping her in every reel. Trace's pals are a fast gun (Laura Banks) and a kid with ESP (Linda Grovenor). Dismal stuff, made in the Philippines by director-producer Cirio H. Santiago.

**DESTINATION INNER SPACE (1966).** Laughable low budget "junkie" starring an alien that looks like a rejected version of the Black Lagoon creature. An underwater laboratory commanded by Scott Brady is invaded by a monster from a spaceship that splashed down nearby. Scripter Arthur C. Pierce tries to duplicate some of the tricks of THE THING but director Francis D. Lyon is no Howard Hawks. Sheree North, Gary Merrill, Roy Barcroft.

**DESTINATION MOON (1950).** Much-acclaimed George Pal production depicting man's first flight to the moon—19 years before it happened. The pseudodocumentary style emphasizes the difficulties of such an undertaking, space walks, weightlessness and other scientific curiosities. Authentic for its day, it now seems tame, almost boring. Chesley Bonestell's drawings of the moon are excellent. Irving Pichel directed this historical breakthrough in space films. Good score by Leith Stevens. Robert Heinlein co-wrote the script. Warner Anderson, John Archer, Erin O'Brien-Moore, John Archer, Tom Powers, Dick Wesson. (VC)

**DESTINATION MOONBASE ALPHA (1975).** Two episodes of TV's SPACE: 1999. In one episode, the crew of Alpha is dying from a mysterious malady; in another, a planet appears to be invading our solar system. Directed by Gerry Anderson. Martin Landau, Barbara Bain. (VC)

**DESTINATION NIGHTMARE (1958).** Episodes from the unsold TV series THE VEIL, re-edited and introduced by Boris Karloff: "Mme Vernoy," "Girl on the Road" and "Destination Nightmare." Directed by Paul Landers. Whit Bissell, Tod Andrews, Myron Healy. Other episodes were repackaged as THE VEIL and JACK THE RIPPER.

**DESTINATION SATURN (1939).** Re-edited version of Universal's 12-chapter BUCK ROGERS serial starring Larry "Buster" Crabbe. See **BUCK ROGERS.**

**DESTROY ALL MONSTERS (1969).** Inoshiro Honda, who brought us Godzilla, unites Japan's hulkers (Godzilla, Godzilla Jr., Ebirah, Wenda, Rodan, Anzilla, Gorasorus, Barugan, Mothra, Varan, Ghidrah) in a destruction marathon, the ultimate in Oriental movie mayhem. When Earth is attacked by spacemen called Kilaaks, they unleash the monsters from Ogaswara Island, sending each to destroy a city. Then the Kilaaks, not satisfied half the world has been trampled, unleashes Ghidrah (the two-headed monstrosity) for yet another slugfest. The smash-bash fest will enthrall you with its juvenile execution. Effects by Eiji Tsuburaya, including a spectacular battle atop Mount Fuji. Akira Kubo, Jun Tazaki.

**DESTROY ALL PLANETS (1968).** More Japanese monster mauling with destruction. The unlikely "hero monster~ is Gamera the Flying Turtle (making his fourth appearance, according to contractual arrangements with producer Hidemasa Nagata), who falls under the evil control of invading aliens. But two small children help the thick-shelled creature to break free and he attacks Viras the Incredible Sea Squid. Eastern enthrallment. Directed by Noriyaki Yuasa. Kojiro Hongo, Toru Takatsuka.

**DESTRUCTORS, THE (1967).** A substance called "laser rubies" is sought by foreign powers and undercover agents who use a killer laser beam dubbed "Cyclops." Standard espionage-action flick with fistfights and shoot-outs, directed by Francis D. Lyon. Michael Ansara, Richard Egan, John Ericson, Joan Blackman, Khigh Dhiegh.

**DEVIL AND DANIEL WEBSTER, THE (1941).** Stephen Vincent Benet's classic story, directed by William Dieterle, is an American folk tale depicting how Senator Webster, an orator-statesman, defends farmer James Craig when Old Scratch, grandiosely etched in brimstone by thunderous Walter Huston, comes to claim his soul. The jury is made up of Benedict Arnold, Captain Kidd and Blackbeard, but Webster roars his own brimstone for the defense. Robert Wise was editor, Bernard Herrmann wrote the score. Also known as ALL THAT MONEY CAN BUY. H.B. Warner, Jeff Corey, Simone Simon, Anne Shirley, Jane Darwell, William Alland. (VC)

**DEVIL AND MAX DEVLIN, THE (1981).** A flop Disney comedy in which Elliott Gould, killed in an accident, descends to Hell where he confronts the Devil (Bill Cosby), who will save him from eternal damnation if Gould can find three people to sign over their souls to ol' Nick. The marks are Adam Rich, Julie Budd, David Knell. Directed by Steven Hilliard Stern, screenplay by Mary Rodgers. Susan Anspach. (VC)

**DEVIL AND MISS SARA, THE (1971).** Is Gene Barry the Devil incarnate? Or an outlaw being escorted to stand trial by a prairie family (James Drury, Janice Rule)? This TV-movie keeps you wondering as Barry schemes to possess Rule. Directed by Michael Caffey. Charles McGraw, Slim Pickens.

**DEVIL BAT (1941).** Depressing reminder of Bela Lugosi's plummeting career in the 1940s, this PRC release stars him as a mad scientist, Carruthers, who trains a killer bat to carry out his evil bidding. Lugosi guides the night flapper to the target by giving victims a special perfume. Pathetic in all departments. Directed by Jean Yarbrough. Suzanne Kaaren, Dave O'Brien, Guy Usher, Hal Price. (VC)

**DEVIL BAT'S DAUGHTER (1946).** Rosemary LaPlanche (one-time beauty queen) is a confused woman who believes she is possessed by the spirit of her father, who presumably turned into a bat when he died. This sequel to DEVIL BAT is borderline horror with whodunit overtones. It wasn't the butler, but you won't have much trouble figuring out who is guilty, due to no subtleties from producer- director Frank Wisbar. Eddie Kane, John James, Michael Hale, Monica Mars.

**DEVIL COMMANDS, THE (1941).** William Sloane's THE EDGE OF RUNNING WATER, a superb supernatural novel, is loosely adapted in this Boris Karloff vehicle directed by Edward Dmytryk. Karloff, as Dr. Julian Blair, experiments with an electrical impulse machine that captures brainwaves of the dead. When he "receives" from his deceased wife, he intensifies his tests, using a medium (Anne Revere) and causing injury to his servant (Ralph Penney). He's also lifting bodies from a graveyard. Offbeat, recommended.

**DEVIL DOG: THE HOUND OF HELL (1978).** Uninspired TV-movie, produced by Lou Morheim and directed by Curtis Harrington. The Mangy Mutt from beyond terrorizes Richard Crenna and Yvette Mimieux, ordinary suburbanites. The yip is a gyp. Kim Richards, Victor Jory, Ike Eisenmann, R. G. Armstrong, Martine Beswick. (VC)

**DEVIL DOLL (1936).** One of the last films by Tod Browning, director of DRACULA and FREAKS, and considered by some to be his best. Lionel Barrymore is a financier sent to Devil's Island for a crime he didn't commit. After escaping, he discovers how to miniaturize humans to the size of dolls and stalks the men who framed him. Screenplay by Garrett Fort, Erich von Stroheim and Guy Endore, from Browning's adaptation of A. Merritt's BURN WITCH BURN. Maureen O'Sullivan, Henry B. Walthall, Lucy Beaumont.

**DEVIL DOLL (1964).** Compelling British shocker blending touches of Svengali with the ventriloquist tale from DEAD OF NIGHT. Bryant Halliday is the Great Vorelli, a stage magician-hypnotist with a dummy that walks and move its head when no one is near. (Shades of THE GREAT GABBO with Erich von Stroheim!) Vorelli, a dabbler in the mysteries of India, is no dummy—he knows secrets of soul transference. Lindsay Shonteff directs with a starkness matched by Gerald Gibbs' photography. Chilling O. Henry climax. William Sylvester, Yvonne Romain, Karel Stepanek. (VC)

**DEVIL GIRL FROM MARS (1955).** Hazel Court, in a fetching outfit all the rage on the canals this season, invades Earth with an eye on the men—she has breeding on her mind, guys, so pay attention when she offers a one-way ticket to Mars. Directed by David MacDonald with no subtleties in depicting how a big-breasted woman would conquer. British hogwash . . . unless you groove on big breasts. Patricia Laffen, Hugh McDermott, Adrienne Corri. (VC)

**DEVIL IN THE HOUSE OF EXORCISM.** Videocassette title for HOUSE OF EXORCISM, THE.

**DEVIL RIDES OUT, THE.** See DEVIL'S BRIDE, THE.

**DEVIL TIMES FIVE (1974).** A child possibly possessed by the Devil goes berserk, murdering adults. More bodies are being found in the Generation Gap these days . . . Directed by Sean MacGregor. Gene Evans, Sorrell Booke, Leif Garrett, Carolyn Stellar. Written by John Durren. (VC)

**DEVIL WITHIN HER, THE (1976).** British rip-off of THE EXORICST, as messy as Nicholas Carlesi's diapers, who by the tender age of 30 days has pushed his nanny into the Thames and dunked a dead mouse in a teacup. Joan Collins, who birthed this cradled creature after being hexed by a sinister dwarf, wonders why so much mayhem from a toddler . . . Dr. Donald Pleasence has suspicions—he saw THE EXORCIST. Lack of motivation and obscure demonic background turn this into a nightmare only for producer Nato De Angeles and director Peter Sasdy. Ralph Bates, Caroline Munro.

**DEVIL WOLF OF SHADOW MOUNTAIN (1964).** Western horror tale in which a cowboy drinks from a wolf's print and turns into a beast. Director Gary Kent was last seen gibbering madly as he shambled into the darkness of Shadow Mountain. John Cardoz, Gene Pollock.

**DEVIL WOMAN (1970).** Filipino production focusing on a village Gorgon (snakes in her hair, etc.) who sends her serpents crawling through the jungle to attack natives who have wronged her. Story and direction by J.F. Sibal.

**DEVIL'S BRIDE, THE (1968).** Hammer's superb version of Dennis Wheatley's THE DEVIL RIDES OUT. While some story weaknesses in Richard Matheson's script cannot be denied, Terence Fisher's direction is remarkably fluid, the juxtaposition of scenes excellent and the flavor of Britain in the 1920s well preserved. Christopher Lee fights to destroy Charles Gray's devil cult. The "Death on Horseback" sequence is a shocker, and suspense mounts steadily as Lee and force seek protection in a pentagram under assault from supernatural forces. Anthony Nelson-Keys produced.

**DEVIL'S COMMANDMENT.** See I VAMPIRI

**BILL COSBY: 'DEVIL AND MAX DEVLIN'**

**DEVIL'S DAUGHTER (1973).** Another steal of ROSEMARY'S BABY, an insipid TV-movie about a young woman (Belinda Montgomery) befriended by batty Shelley Winters who wants to please the Devil. Undistinguished, even with the presence of Joseph Cotten and Robert Cornthwaite. Jonathan Frid turns up as a butler—what happened to all those dark shadows? Robert Foxworth is also hanging around. Directed by Jeannot Szwarc.

**DEVIL'S DAUGHTER, THE.** See **POCOMANIA.**

**DEVIL'S EXPRESS (1975).** Martial arts actioner set in New York City, where a practitioner of chop suey kung fu takes on a demon in the subway tunnels. Karate floors evil. Directed by Barry Rosen. Warhawk Tanzania, Sam DeFazio.

**DEVIL'S EYE (1960).** Ingmar Bergman wrote-directed this Swedish import in which the soul of Spanish lover Don Juan is returned to Earth to seduce a lovely virgin whose chastity has proven an "eyesore" for Satan. Jarl Kulle, Bibi Andersson, Stig Jarrell, Gunnar Bjornstrand. (VC)

**DEVIL'S GIFT, THE (1984).** A birthday present to a youngster conjures up demons from the depths of Hell. Directed by Kenneth J. Barton.

**DEVIL'S HAND, THE.** See **CARNIVAL OF SINNERS.**

**DEVIL'S HAND, THE (1961).** Switch for a Witch: Linda Christian fertilizes Robert Alda's dreams in hopes the nightmarish seeds she plants will inspire him to "grow" with her voodoo varsity. But it looks like cult chief Neil Hamilton will still have to endanger Alda's life when he proves an enemy of the devil-doll makers. Directed by William J. Hole Jr. Make-up by Jack Pierce. Jeannie Carmen.

**DEVIL'S MASK (1946).** Entry in Columbia's I LOVE A MYSTERY series, adapted from Carlton E. Morse's radio series. The screenplay (based on Morse's "Faith, Hope and Charity Sisters" radioplay) involves a crashed plane carrying a shrunken head, the only clue to a code and a mystery. Jim Bannon portrays Jack Packard and Barton Yarborough (a radio regular) is Doc Young. Directed by Henry Levin. Anita Louise, Michael Duane, Mona Barrie, Thomas Jackson. Others: I LOVE A MYSTERY and THE UNKNOWN.

**DEVIL'S MESSENGER, THE (1962).** Feature version of the Swedish TV series 13 DEMON STREET, created by Curt Siodmak. Lon Chaney Jr. is the Devil and Karen Kadler is Satanya, his messenger girl. Three narratives: Satanya's image forces weak-willed men to suicide; a woman 50,000 years old is found frozen in the ice; a man's death is foreseen in dreams. Directed by Herbert L. Strock.

**DEVIL'S MISTRESS, THE (1966).** In the Wild West, a female vampire drains the life from cowboys not at home on her range. Look out, wranglers, that gal is giving you a bum steer. Joan Stapleton, Forrest Westmoreland, Robert Gregory. Written-directed by Orville Wanzer.

**DEVIL'S NIGHTMARE (1971).** Campy dialogue and silly premise provide laughs in this Italian-Belgian flop chiller about a Nazi general whose family has a pact with the Devil. Each generation's eldest daughter is born an evil witch lusting to kill. While Berlin is bombed in 1945, General Von Rhoneberg's wife dies in labor to give him a daughter. Ja, mein viewer, she is das bad eine. Flash to present day as seven travelers (symbolizing the deadly sins—how's that for relevance) seeks refuge one stormy night in Castle von Rhoneberg. These idiots (bubbleheaded sexy blondes, a glutton, and so on) meet grisly deaths: quicksand, guillotine, Iron Maiden, impalement on spikes, etc. The priest of the group stands his ground to fight a religious battle. Very obvious; the twist ending is only moderately interesting. Erika Blanc, Jean Servais. Directed by Jean Brismee. (VC)

**DEVILS OF DARKNESS (1965).** Stilted British dud which deals with a vampire cult in need of human sacrifices, carried out in a secret hideout beneath the town cemetery. Directed uncomfortably by Lance Comfort. William Sylvester is a misunderstood hero. Hubert Noel, Tracy Reed, Carole Gray.

**DEVIL'S OWN (1966).** Joan Fontaine is the sole interest in this dull Hammer blend of voodoo and satanism. Nigel

Kneale's script (based on a Peter Curtis novel) is talk talk talk, and the minimal action comes at the climax during an attempted sacrifice. Setting is a staid English village where witches stir up a cauldron of trouble. Could have used a seasoning of excitement and a pinch more sex. Directed by Cyril Frankel. Kay Walsh, Duncan Lamont, Leonard Rossiter.

**DEVIL'S PARTNER, THE (1961).** Negligent nonsense about Ed Nelson bloodizing a pact with the Devil and being transformed into a wild stallion which terrorizes a small town. He also transforms himself into a serpent. Directed by Charles R. Rondeau. Edgar Buchanan, Jean Allison, Richard Crane.

**DEVIL'S RAIN (1975).** Ernest Borgnine is Jonathan Corbis, a goat demon heading a coven of kooks in worship of Satan. Innocent passers-by stumble across the secret in Mexico and must be silenced. Trashy film, barely salvaged in the final minutes when the Evil Ones are drenched in a satanic rainstorm, turning into oozing, melting puddles of multi-colored wax. Not even director Robert Fuest (ABOMINABLE DR. PHIBES) comes in out of the rain. A good cast is wasted on this meltdown: William Shatner, Ida Lupino, Eddie Albert, Tom Skerritt, John Travolta, Keenan Wynn. (VC)

**DEVIL'S TRIANGLE, THE (1974).** Cheapjack pseudo-documentary from producer-writer-director Richard Winer which purports absurd, unsubstantiated theories about those ships, planes and people disappearing in the area of the Atlantic Ocean bounded by Miami, Bermuda and Puerto Rico. The inept narration is read by Vincent Price, who should be ashamed for such trash. By now the theory of the Bermuda Triangle has been thoroughly debunked as tripe.

**DEVIL'S UNDEAD, THE (1979).** Britisher supernatural thriller with Peter Cushing and Christopher Lee as contemporary detectives mixed up with demonology. Directed by Peter Sasdy. (VC)

**DEVIL'S WEB (1974).** Mildly compelling TV-movie starring an aging, somewhat grotesque Diana Dors (once a British sex-pot) portraying a disciple of Satan who possesses human souls. She turns up one day at the home of an English gentleman, whose daughter is paralyzed and needs care. Dors gives her care all right, teaching her the black arts, until she turns evil. Obviously inspired by THE EXORICST. Shaun O'Riordan directed Brian Clemens' script. Andrea Marcovicci, Linda Liles, Cec Linder, Ed Bishop. (VC)

**DEVIL'S WEDDING NIGHT, THE (1975).** Dracula's Nibelungen ring, which lures virgins to a sacrificial party once a year, is the pivotal device in this Italian film, which offers ample nudity should the plot flag. Another variation on the Countess Bathory legend, in which Sara Bay caresses her skin with virgins' blood. Undistinguished mix of blood and sex, directed by Paul Solvay. Mark Damon has a dual role without doubling your pleasure. Miriam Barrios. (VC)

**DEVIL'S WIDOW, THE.** See **TAM LIN.**

**DEVILFISH (1984).** Inept Italian JAWS ripoff, this mammoth monster being a giant shark with tentacles that resembles a calamari on a dinner plate. The six-foot jaws are obviously wire-pulled and the red coloring in the water is Hawaiian Fruit Punch. The creature was created in an experiment, so there's a subplot involving nefarious scientists. Squalidsquid. Michael Sopkin, Valentine Monnier.

**DEVONSVILLE TERROR, THE (1983).** German filmmaker Ulli Lommel directed this slow-moving witchcraft/sorcery tale. It begins centuries back with a Salem witch burning and jumps to modern day, when descendants of the witchstalkers are plagued by a curse. Suzanna Love, one of three women new in town, would appear to be a witch, but it takes forever for the townspeople to catch on. Meanwhile, there's some unclear business about worms infecting the body of a village doctor (Donald Pleasence) and some tedious regression themes. The script by Lommel, Love (his wife) and George T. Lindsey never comes to life, explaining why this was sold directly to cable. Robert Walker and Paul Willson are wasted in empty-headed roles. Angelica Rebane. (VC)

**DIABOLICAL DR. Z, THE (1966).** Murky atmosphere enhances, rather than detracts from, this Spanish-French sequel to

THE AWFUL DR. ORLOF with Howard Vernon back as the mad physician. The doc's daughter (Mabel Karr) takes laboratory center to gain control of a woman dancer (Estella Blain) for revenge. Directed by Jesse Franco. Fernando Montes, Antonio J. Escribano, Guy Mairesse.

**DIABOLIK.** See **DANGER: DIABOLIK.**

**DIABOLIQUE (1955).** French shocker, produced-directed by Henri- Georges Clouzot, is a classic, even if contrived. Without giving too much away, we can say it shows how Simone Signoret and Vera Clouzot murder the dreadful principal of their boys' school (he's also the insufferable husband of Ms Clouzot). They hide his corpse in the swimming pool, then discover it missing . . . The headmaster has returned from the dead! And one of the women sees him alive! At this point we will politely shut up. Based on THE WOMAN WHO WAS NO MORE by Pierre Boileau and Thomas Narcejac. A subplot involves the French detective working on this sinister case. Watch out for the surprise ending. (VC)

**DIAMOND MACHINE, THE (1956).** Unimportant French mystery with a paperthin fantasy premise: Eddie Constantine is hot on the trail of a scientist who knows how to make diamonds from scratch. Directed by Pierre Chevalier; script by Jacques Doniol-Volcroze. Maria Frau, Yves Royan.

**DIAMOND WIZARD, THE (1954).** Less a fantasy than a cops-and- robbers mystery as T-Man Dennis O'Keefe tracks down the genius behind a synthetic diamonds racket. Routine British mystery, co-directed by O'Keefe and Montgomery Tully. Romantic lead is Margaret Sheridan, heroine in Howard Hawks' THE THING. Philip Friend.

**DIAMONDS ARE FOREVER (1971).** Seventh entry in the 007 series stars Sean Connery in his last fling in the role prior to quitting in 1972. In this loose adaptation of an Ian Fleming novel, he's searching for Blofeld, who is firing his diamond

**JILL ST. JOHN AS TIFFANY CASE**

laser at missile bases. The settings range from the lunar landscape to Las Vegas to the Nevada desert. There's a wonderful car chase down the mainstreet of Vegas, a desert race with a moonmobile, lady karate attacks and two dangerous gay villains. Jimmy Dean portrays a Howard Hughes-type recluse, Jill St. John is the beautiful Tiffany Case (oh does she love diamonds), Lana Wood appears briefly as sexy Plenty O'Toole, and Charles Gray is the dastardly cat lover, Blofeld. Directed by Guy Hamilton in flashy fashion and written with ample tongue-in-cheek by Richard Maibaum and Tom Mankiewicz. (VC)

**DIARY OF A MADMAN (1963).** Outstanding period photography by Ellis Carter and a tormented performance by Vincent Price enhance the threadbare screenplay by producer Robert E. Kent, based on Guy de Maupassant's "The Horla." Price is a 19th Century Parisian magistrate, haunted by an invisible entity which forces him to carry out evil acts, such as slashing beautiful Nancy Kovack to pieces. A quasi-religious ending is in keeping with the morality of the times. The "invisible man" tricks are unimpressive and ultimately the weight of the film falls on Price's histronic shoulders. Directed by Reginald Le-Borg. Chris Warfield, Ian Wolfe.

**DIARY OF THE DEAD (1976).** Macabre overtones enhance this demanding, oddly structured Hitchcockian suspense thriller starring Hector Elizondo as a pure heel, an out-of-work crossword puzzle solver with a shrew of a mother-in-law (Geraldine Fitzgerald). How he sets out to knock her off for her $80,000 inheritance leads to a labyrinth of deadly twists and turns under Arvin Brown's subtle direction. Salome Jens supports Elizondo as the brow-beaten wife, but it's clearly his film as he diabolically works his plan. (VC)

**DICK TRACY MEETS GRUESOME (1947).** Comic book movie based on Chester Gould's comic strip cop (Ralph Byrd) is a shoddy, low budget affair, of minimal interest. Boris Karloff is the guest heavy who robs banks with a nerve gas that paralyzes. He borrowed the formula from the Green Hornet, maybe? Directed perfunctorily by John Rawlins. Anne Gwynne is Tracy's wife, Tess Trueheart. Howard Ashley, June Clayworth, Robert Clarke, Lex Barker. (VC)

**DIE! DIE! MY DARLING (1966).** Grand Guignol horror with Stephanie Powers trapped in a house of crazies governed by religious zealot Tallulah Bankhead, who goes bonkers in eye-rolling, scenery-chomping fashion. The graphic murders are of such an abhorrent nature, the film has a singular gripping fascination until its bitter end. Donald Sutherland is Tallulah's nutty handyman, and he's impressive. Directed by Silvio Narizzano, scripted by Richard Matheson from Anne Blaisdell's NIGHTMARE. Yootha Joyce. (VC)

**DIE LAUGHING (1980).** A formula for altering atomic waste into plutonium bomb components is the McGuffin in this light-hearted spy spoof starring Robby Benson as a cabbie who falls into possession of a cute monkey holding the key to the secret. Accused of murder, Benson rushes all over San Francisco with dumb villain Bud Cort in pursuit. There's a strong spirit of fun at work, but the characters do not aspire to anything memorable. Directed by Jeff Werner. Charles Durning, Linda Grovenor, Elsa Lanchester. (VC)

**DIE, MONSTER, DIE (1965).** Loose-as-a-goose adaptation of H. P. Lovecraft's COLOUR OUT OF SPACE, produced in England as a vehicle for Boris Karloff. The setting is H.P.'s infamous Arkham County where a desolate tract of land has been stricken by a diseased power from space that turns everyone into monsters. Director Daniel Haller provides isolated moments of fear and mystery, but the majority of Jerry Sohl's script is muddled. Nick Adams is the American who comes to a weird mansion looking for his bride-to-be (Suzan Farmer). Freda Jackson is a woman who keeps her hideous appearance hidden beneath a veil, and Patrick Magee is a doctor on the edge of the mystery.

**DIE SCREAMING, MARIANNE (1972).** If Susan George never reaches her 21st birthday, some insane individuals will be exceedingly happy—so they do all they can to shorten her life expectancy. Directed by Peter Walker. Chris Sandford, Barry Evans, Leo Glen. (VC)

**DIGBY, THE BIGGEST DOG IN THE WORLD (1974).** Rollicking British satire on mad doctor movies, in the "Carry On" tradition . . . a shaggy dog film for young and old in which Project X powder is lapped up by Digby, who becomes an "incredible 50-foot" dog. The effects by Tom Howard aren't great but this adaptation of a Ted Key book has a light-hearted lampooning spirit. Directed by Joseph McGrath. Jim Dale, Spike Milligan, Milo O'Shea, Angela Douglas.

**DIMENSION FIVE (1966).** Fantasy/spy thriller with secret agent Justin Power (Jeffrey Hunter) using a device that whisks him from time zone to time zone to prevent dirty Commies from destroying L. A. with atomic weapons. Directed dimensionlessly by Franklin Adreon. Frances Nuyen, Harold Sakata, Donald Woods, Linda Ho.

**DINNER FOR ADELE (1977).** A man-eating plant in a Nick Carter detective story? Chomp chomp bang bang. It's Czech director Oldrich Lipsky's satire on cops, robbers and monsters. Carter (portrayed by solemn, precise Michal Docolomansky) and sausage- eating Inspector Ledvina are hot on the trail of a mad botanist, The Gardener, whose prize creation is Adele. Adele, you see, is the hungry plant, whose appetite is unleashed by the sound of Mozart's "Lullaby." Crazy props and wild chases enhance the tomfoolery. Frothy, funny and free-wheeling.

**DINOSAURUS (1960).** The funniest science-fiction movie ever made—unintentionally, that is. This bizarre variation on the Three Stooges—a prehistoric caveman, a tyrannosaurus and a friendly brontosaurus—will have you in stitches as they run wild on a tropical island after being blasted out of their hibernational digs. One hilarous scene has the caveman (Gregg Martell) fleeing in abject terror after seeing a woman in pincurlers. Side- splitting from beginning to end . . . kids will love it. Ward Ramsey, Kristina Hanson, Alan Roberts. Directed by Irvin S. Yeaworth Jr., of BLOB fame. (VC)

**DISAPPEARANCE OF FLIGHT 412, THE (1974).** Two jet aircraft chase a UFO, forcing a special investigation division of the military to quarantine the crews. Officer-in-charge Glenn Ford doesn't appreciate the mistreatment and locks horns with his superiors. This never resolves the issue of UFOs but it's fascinating to see their effect on military authority and the common soldier. Directed by Jud Taylor. Bradford Dillman, Guy Stockwell, David Soul, Kent Smith, Jack Ging, Greg Mullavey, Robert F. Lyons.

**DISAPPEARANCES, THE (1977).** Re-edited episodes of THE MAN FROM ATLANTIS, starring Patrick Duffy (destined for DALLAS) as an underwater humanoid. In this adventure an insane lady scientist kidnaps Dr. Merrill as part of a sinister plot. Belinda J. Montgomery, Alan Fudge, Darlene Carr. Directed by Charles Dubin.

**DISCIPLE OF DEATH (1973).** Utterly inept, lucirously laughable British mishmash starring Mike Raven as a minion of the Devil posing as a priest for easier access to young virgins, whom he periodically sacrifices to satisfy Satan's sadism. Raven is so hammy, and the supporting cast so underdirected by Tom Parkinson, this becomes hopeless junk. The setting is 18th Century England and there are "Dracula's Brides" as well as a cackling dwarf. Marguerite Hardiman, Stephen Bradley, Ronnie Lacey. (VC)

# . . . And D Stands for Disney, Too

**WALT DISNEY ON ONE OF HIS STUDIO SETS, CIRCA 1946**

**CREATURE FEATURES MOVIE GUIDE**

**DISCONNECTED (1986).** Minor slasher film, produced in Connecticut, in which Frances Raines portrays twin sisters implicated in a series of bloody murders. Producer-director Gorman Bechard emphasizes the whodunit aspects of the Virginia Gilroy script, to which he made contributions. Mark Walker, Carl Koch. (VC)

**DISCREET CHARM OF THE BOURGEOISIE (1972).** Luis Bunuel's surrealism switches between reality and fantasy so continuously, most audiences found this art film befuddling. Bunuel has merged ghost stories and narratives-within-narratives in his disjointed glimpse at hypocrisy in French society. Fernando Rey, Delphine Seyrig, Stephane Audran. Oscar-winner for Best Foreign Film. (VC)

**DISEMBODIED, THE (1957).** Join "The Disinterested" after a few minutes of this jungle gibberish about a voodoo cult which puts the whammy on handsome photographer Paul Burke. The girl who does the native dance in a sarong, Allison Hayes, went on to become "The 50-Foot Woman." Directed by Walter Grauman. John E. Wengraf.

**DISTANT EARLY WARNING (1975).** TV-movie set at an Arctic research station invaded by aliens capable of clouding men's minds and making them think they're seeing members of their families. The only problem is, these family members all happen to be dead. Similar to Ray Bradbury's "Mars Is Heaven." Directed by Wes Kenney. Michael Parks, Herb Edelman, Mary Frann, Tony Geary.

**DISTANT SCREAM, A (1985).** British ghost flick about an aged spirit of a woman's lover (David Carradine) who crosses from death to life. Stephane Beachman, Stephen Chase.

**DOC SAVAGE—MAN OF BRONZE (1975).** George Pal's treatment of a pulp magazine superhero (created by Kenneth Robeson) was a major disappointment that marked the start of the producer-director's unfortunate decline. Ron Ely has eyes which literally sparkle, a bobbing Adam's Apple and a mission to South America to find the killers of his father. His Fabulous Five, associates skilled in sciences and martial arts, are far from the characters conceived in the stories, making this seem unfaithful to the source novels. Michael Anderson directed, Pal and Joe Morheim adapted. Paul Gleason, Paul Wexler, Pamela Hensley, Carlos Rivas. (VC)

**DOCTOR AND THE DEVILS, THE (1985).** Dylan Thomas' screenplay resurrecting the Burke and Hare legend of old Edinburgh was first written in 1945, but considered too Grand Guignol for a movie until producer Mel Brooks and director Freddie Francis turned it into a morality play. Timothy Dalton is the maverick, self- righteous anatomical instructor Dr. Rock (based on Dr. Knox) who buys fresh corpses from body snatchers Jonathan Pryce and Stephen Rea. Pryce's portrait of a totally evil man is chilling and the period detail fascinating; in fact, it's often so real, capturing the poverty areas of Edinburgh, that this becomes an uncomfortable viewing experience. Twiggy, Julian Sands. (VC)

**DOCTOR BLOOD'S COFFIN (1961).** Sidney J. Furie cut his directorial teeth on this well-produced, well-acted British programmer enhanced by ancient Cornwall settings. Peter Blood, son of a famous doctor who dabbled in the arcane, has discovered a form of curare poisoning that brings the dead to life. Kieron Moore is an interesting mad doctor, torn between science and evil. Quite fetching is his nurse, buxom Hazel Court, who screams in the appropriate places. Ian Hunter, Fred Johnson, Paul Stockman, Andy Alston.

**DOCTOR OF DOOM (1960).** First in Mexico's "Wrestling Women" series (see WRESTLING WOMEN), in which brain transplants by a mad Tijuana doctor leave several empty craniums, one of which must have been the producer's. Heroic Golden Rubi and Gloria Venus take on the gorilla Gomar and her pain-brain companion, Vendetta. Written with grunts and groans by Alfred Salazar, directed by Rene Cardona. Armando Silvestre, Lorena Velasquez.

**DR. BLACK AND MR. HYDE (1975).** Black exploitationer with Bernie Casey (as Dr. Henry Pride) experimenting with the regeneration of dying cells in liver patients and finding the hypo formula that turns him into an albino-white killer. He has a childhood phobia about prostitutes and kills the street-

walkers in Watts. This puzzles policeman Ji-Tu Cumbuka, who looks almost as tall and lean as the Watts Towers. A genre film needs an aura of entertaining fantasy, but director William Crain captures the drabness of Watts and the squalor of its people, inflicting depression rather than terror. Well-intended but ultimately sleazy. A nice jazz score was inspired by SHAFT. Rosalind Cash, Stu Gilliam. (VC)

**DR. BREEDLOVE OR HOW I LEARNED TO STOP WORRYING AND LOVE.** See **KISS ME QUICK.**

**DR. BUTCHER M.D. (1982).** Originally QUEEN OF THE CANNIBALS, this spaghetti-scarer belongs to the "sick cannibal school" with its torture and mutilation. It's a mad-doctor-on-a-lonely-island tale in which demented Donald O'Brian creates zombies. Flesh-munching and organ-ripping keep this lively, if not intellectual. Strong stomach required. Ian McCulloch, Alexandra Cole. (The M.D. of the title is "medical deviate," the film's alternate title.) (VC)

**DR. COOK'S GARDEN (1971).** Superb psychochiller starring Bing Crosby as a small-town physician who isn't operating with a full set of scalpels. He treats his patients like flowers in his garden—rooting out the sick to make way for the strong. Ted Post directs with a sense of suspense, and it really builds. Based on a play by Ira Levin. Blythe Danner, Frank Converse, Abby Lewis, Bethal Leslie.

**DR. COPPELIUS (1966).** Spanish-U.S. version of a ballet by director Ted Kneeland, based on writings by E.T.A. Hoffmann, with Walter Slezak as a builder of mechanical dolls who transfers life's essence into his androids. Claudia Corday, Carmen Rojas, Caj Selling.

**DR. CYCLOPS (1940).** Ernest B. Schoedsack, co-creator of KING KONG, returned to the genre with this tale of a mad scientist (Dr. Thorkel, played by Albert Dekker) who miniaturizes people to doll size. Unfortunately, the rear projection and matte shots are unimaginatively executed and characters are stereotypes, including Dekker's unbalanced man of science. Still, this has period charm and is one of the first features to use Technicolor as a menacing effect. Janice Logan, Thomas Coley, Victor Killian, Charles Halton.

**DR. DEATH (1973).** Need a soul for that dead body lying around the house? Just pick up the phone and call Dr. Death ("This is Dr. Death . . . I'm not in right now, but if you'll leave your name and number, I'll get right back . . ."). All he has to do is make a house call, pop open the vial around his neck and instruct the wispy vapor that drifts out to enter the cadaver. John Considine is the physician; co-souls belong to Barry Coe, Florence Marley, Cheryl Miller, Jo Morrow and TV horror host Seymour. Directed by Eddie Saeta. (VC)

**DR. DEATH, SEEKER OF SOULS.** See **DR. DEATH.**

**DR. DOOLITTLE (1967).** Musical comedy based on Hugh Lofting's stories about an eccentric British veterinarian-surgeon who talks with animals in the kingdom of Puddleby-on-the-Marsh. Doolittle (Rex Harrison) ventures to the South Seas to find the Great Pink Sea Snail and talks to Polynesia the Parrot, Gub Gub the Pig, Jip the Dog, and Chi-Chi the Chimp. Screenwriter Leslie Bricusse penned the sometimes-charmless music and lyrics for such numbers as "Talk to the Animals" (an Oscar winner). Herbert Ross did the choreography, which most critics considered limp. Director Richard Fleischer spent $18 million on this "talking dog." Samantha Eggar, Anthony Newley. (VC)

**DR. DRACULA (1977).** Re-edited version of SVENGALI, originally filmed in 1974, and later re-released as LUCIFER'S WOMEN. This contains new footage shot by Al Adamson (and featuring John Carradine) and was released directly to TV. See LUCIFER'S WOMEN for a review of the semi-porno as it existed in 1974. This blends devil cult hogwash with a vampire plot, the satanic disciples unaware there is a bloodsucker in their ranks as they attempt to claim the soul of Trilby, who for some reason will give them ever-lasting life. Unendurable. Morgan Upton, Don Barry.

**DR. FAUSTUS (1967).** Richard Burton directed himself (with Nevill Coghill's help) in this British version of the Christopher Marlowe play, filmed at Oxford and featuring esteemed members of that noble institute. Guess what bosomy female he sells his soul to the Devil to possess. Elizabeth Taylor as Helen of Troy breathes deeply, almost falling out of her barely-existent costume. But is this art?

**DR. FRANKEN (1980).** Robert Vaughn, offspring of the infamous Frankenstein Monster creator, is alive and well, thank you, in a Manhattan hospital, specializing in heart transplants. But in private he switches organs body to body—if not legs, how about a pair of eyes? The theme of memory transference within the organs is another cliched fillip to this TV-movie co-directed by Marvin J. Chomsky and Jeff Lieberman. Sometimes the theme is treated seriously, other times it depicts Vaughn's home-made "creature" shambling in a whimsical vein. The ending is strangely flat, perhaps because this was a series pilot. Vaughn is in top form as the driven, not-always-insensitive doc. Teri Garr is an innocent young woman, and Robert Perault and David Selby have key roles.

**DR. FRANKENSTEIN ON CAMPUS.** See **FRANKENSTEIN ON CAMPUS.**

**DR. FRANKENSTEIN'S CASTLE OF FREAKS (1973).** Thoroughly boring, completely unwatchable Italian menagerie horror film. What a waste of Rossano Brazzi, Michael Dunn and Edmund Purdom. Same old hoary cliches in which the evil doctor creates a collection of freako anomalies. Doc does it with his Electric Accumulator. And dig the results: Goliath the Giant, Kreegin the Hunchback and Ook the Neanderthal Man. Directed by Robert H. Oliver with Neanderthal touches. The only watchable thing (or things) are busty lovelies who reveal their enormous breasts. (VC)

**DR. GOLDFOOT AND THE BIKINI MACHINE (1966).** Comedy-mystery disaster starring Vincent Price as the titular madman who plans world domination with an army of lady robots, capable of seducing the average male. A hodgepodge of ideas and performers, directed by Norman Taurog, followed by the equally inept DR. GOLDFOOT AND THE GIRL BOMBS. Dwayne Hickman, Frankie Avalon, Fred Clark, Deborah Walley, Susan Hart, Annette Funicello.

**DR. GOLDFOOT AND THE GIRL BOMBS (1966).** Vincent Price, that creator of robotic pulchritude, is back with a hot plot to start a world war between major powers with his mass-produced androids, bombs set to explode while they're making love to military leaders. "Bomb" is the word for this indulgence in idiocy. Directed by Mario Bava. Fabian, Franco Franchi, Laura Antonelli, Francesco Mule.

**DR. GORE (1975).** "Heh! Heh! Heh! Come into my dank dingy dungeon of darkness, my labyrinthian laboratory of lethargic, luminous light, my chilly chamber of calculated cunning. Yes, it is I, that scurrilous scientist of startling shocks, Dr. Gore. Heh! Heh! Watch me as I create the perfect female with my unscrupulous procedures and diabolical derangement. No one can stop me, not even director Pat Patterson. Heh! Heh! Heh!" (VC)

**DR. HEKYLL AND MR. HYPE (1980).** Parody of the Robert Louis Stevenson double-identity theme, produced in England with Oliver Reed in the dual role. Charles B. Griffith, who wrote LITTLE SHOP OF HORROR for Roger Corman, directs Mel Welles, Jackie Coogan, Corinne Calvet, Sunny Johnson, Maia Danziger, and brings back some of the Corman alumni, including Dick Miller. (VC)

**DR. JEKYLL AND MR. HYDE (1932).** Rouben Mamoulian's direction and the acting of Fredric March and Miriam Hopkins have held up well over the years, making this an endurable film version of Robert Louis Stevenson's oft-abused narrative. As the split personality, March underwent on-camera transfigurations achieved with special lenses and unique make-up by Wally Westmore. Hopkins as the prostitute is extremely seductive and her smouldering sensuality is wonderful to behold in so aged a film. March won an Oscar for his performance, but it is the whole that is greater than any single part. Rose Hobart, Holmes Herbert, Edgar Norton.

**DR. JEKYLL AND MR. HYDE (1941).** MGM's version of the Stevenson horror classic, starring Spencer Tracy in the dual role as the good doctor who allows his evil side to surface while taking a drug that by today's standards would be "hal-

## URSULA ANDRESS IN 'DR. NO'

lucinogenic." While its production standards are high, and its cast includes Ingrid Bergman, Donald Crisp, Lana Turner and Ian Hunter, it lacks the impact of the 1932 version. Still worth seeing. Victor Fleming directed. Barton MacLane, C. Aubrey Smith, Sara Allgood, Billy Bevan. (VC)

**DR. JEKYLL AND MR. HYDE (1973).** A musical version of the Stevenson classic? With Kirk Douglas as the schizophrenic doctor? From a major TV network? What is the world of horror coming to now? But what a cast! Susan George, Stanley Holloway, Michael Redgrave, Donald Pleasence. David Winters directed. (VC)

**DR. JEKYLL AND SISTER HYDE (1972).** Bizarre variation on the Jekyll-Hyde theme: Instead of a good man metamorphosizing into a bad man, a good man metamorphosizes into an evil woman. This turnabout is considered fair play in Brian Clemens' script. The cast includes Ralph Bates as the doctor and Martine Beswick as his female counterpart. Gerald Sim, Ivor Dean, Tony Calvin. Directed by Roy Ward Baker. (VC)

**DR. JEKYLL AND THE WOLFMAN (1971).** Spanish horror (a sequel to MARK OF THE WOLFMAN) with Paul Naschy as the hirsute hanger-on (returning for the sixth time in this Werewolf series) and Shirley Corrigan as shrieking heroine. Acting and plotting are ridiculous, but the sets and camera work are striking. Directed by Leon Klimovsky.

**DR. JEKYLL'S DUNGEON OF DEATH (1979).** Great-grandson of the original Dr. Jekyll-Mr. Hyde has a serum transforming criminals into martial-arts battlers. Unworkable mixture of genres from San Francisco producer-director James Wood. Writer James Mathers stars as Jekyll, and Wood did his own lighting, music and sound. Threadbare, stretched as thin as Mr. Wood himself. (VC)

**DR. MABUSE, THE GAMBLER (1922).** Fritz Lang's earliest depicton of Norbert Jacques' supervillain, a mathematical genius who turns his creativity to evil with an underworld of murderers, rapists, thieves and counterfeiters engaged in bringing about social upheaval for world conquest. The architectural madman (Rudolph Klein-Rogge) assumes various disguises (banker, psychiatrist, gambler, drunken sailor) to flood the economy with fake money. In 1933 Lang produced a sound version, THE TESTAMENT OF DR. MABUSE, followed in the 1960s with a series of West German productions, the first of which (THE THOUSAND EYES OF DR. MABUSE) was directed by Lang. That was followed by THE RETURN OF DR. MABUSE, DR. MABUSE VS. SCOTLAND YARD and THE SECRET OF DR. MABUSE. These latter films were more imitative of the Edgar Wallace mystery.

**DR. MABUSE VS. SCOTLAND YARD (1964).** Evil German madman, out to conquer the world, just might pull it off this time. No matter that Mabuse is dead. Here he returns to life and takes possession of an invention that prevents individual free will. Hence, mild- mannered citizens are turned into killers and conquerers. This West German production, directed by Paul May, was part of a series that gave rebirth to Norbert Jacques' archvillain, first popularized by Fritz Lang in the 1920s. Peter Van Eyck, Klaus Kinski, Walter Rilla.

**DR. MANIAC.** See **MAN WHO LIVED AGAIN, THE.**

**DR. NO (1963).** Granddaddy of the superspy films—first in the James Bond (Agent 007) series. The suave, cold-blooded British spy was created in popular novels by ex-intelligence agent Ian Fleming, and the early films are true to the essence, although later the Harry Saltzman-Albert R. Broccoli series evolved into slick, tongue-in-cheek action with glittering gadgets, superweapons and abundant female pulchritude. In his screen bow, 007 battles a gang of terrorists, SPECTRE, headed by Dr. No, an Oriental mastercriminal operating an underwater city off Jamaica. Sean Connery is slick with the shapely femme fatales, yet ruthless with his Baretta, shooting a man in cold blood, or coolly watching enemies die in fiery traps. Terence Young directed stylishly, setting the standard. Ursula Andress is provocative as Honey, the bikini-clad adventuress who accompanies Bond into Dr. No's stronghold, Joseph Wiseman is slimy-great as the evil Dr. No, Jack Lord adequate as contact agent Felix Leiter. Bernard Lee and Lois Maxwell bow as assignment chief M and his secretary, Miss Moneypenny. Great escapism! (VC)

**DR. ORLOFF'S MONSTER (1964).** A scientist of evil genius creates a stalking hulk of abominable mankind, putrescent of flesh, hideous of countenance. Men have been known to go mad at the sight of this grotesque parody of humankind. This awful Spanish/Austrian sequel to THE AWFUL MR. ORLOF

(notice how one "f" got lost in the translation, along with coherence) was directed by Jesse Franco.

**DR. OTTO AND THE RIDDLE OF THE GLOOM BEAM (1986).** Defective spy comedy with superagent Jim Varney (in five different roles: Dr. Otto, Rudd Hardtact, Laughin' Jack, Guy Dandy and Auntie Nelda) out to stop a mad doctor from conquering the world. Juvenile jokes and amateurish action. Directed by John Cherry.

**DR. PHIBES RISES AGAIN (1972).** Sequel to THE ABOMINABLE DR. PHIBES with Vincent Price (under Robert Fuest's direction) again on a rampage, seeking an eternal elixir in Egypt to restore his long-dead wife to life. Robert Quarry (Count Yorga) isn't the best hero material but he works overtime to outwit the devious Phibes. More macabre murders, each attempting to top the last in grisliness. Valli Kemp plays Vulnavia. Hugh Griffith, Terry-Thomas, Beryl Reid, Fiona Lewis, Peter Cushing. (VC)

**DR. RENAULT'S SECRET (1942).** Scientist George Zucco wants to make a man out of a monkey. The idea sounds cliche but, with all due respect, this low-budget Fox release has ample suspense and a fine cast: J. Carrol Naish, Sheppard Strudwick, Mike Mazurki, Jack Norton. It's quick (58 minutes), leaving you scant time to consider the story absurdities. Harry Lachman directed with a deft hand.

**DR. SATAN (1966).** No-calorie Mexican junkfood, without a single Hollywood name to enhance its U.S. potential. Voodoo vapidity directed by Miguel Morayta. Also known as DR. SATAN AND THE BLACK MAGIC.

**DR. SATAN'S ROBOT (1940).** Feature-length version of Republic's serial THE MYSTERIOUS DR. SATAN (latter is available in its entirety in video.)

**DR. STRANGE (1978).** TV-pilot produced by Philip DeGuere (producer of the updated TWILIGHT ZONE series)  and based on the Marvel comic book character created by Steve Ditko and Stan Lee. Dr. Peter Strange (Peter Hooten), once a prominent surgeon, gives up his practice after an accident and joins force with "The Ancient One," a practitioner of white magic (John Mills), who teaches him the use of supernatural forces against evil. Jessica Walter portrays his antagonist, Morgan Le Fay, Queen of the Sorcerers. DeGuere also wrote and directed this comic book adventure, which never became a series. Clyde Kusatsu, Eddie Benton, Philip Sterling, Sarah Rush, David Hooks. (VC)

**DR. STRANGELOVE, OR HOW I LEARNED TO STOP WORRYING AND LOVE THE BOMB (1964).** Stanley Kubrick's masterpiece, a tour de force of black comedy. By accident, SAC dispatches four planes armed with hydrogen bombs against Russia; one plane in the flotilla of death piloted by Major King Kong (Slim Pickens) keeps jetting toward Moscow, determined to deliver his payload. Back in the states a military uprising is headed by Col. Jack D. Ripper (Sterling Hayden), who believes our water supply has been poisoned by Russians, and General Turgidson (George C. Scott) thinks we can survive despite millions of dead; hell, let the bomb drop. Peter Sellers is in three roles—as President Muffey (who calls the Soviets on the Hot Line, with hilarious results), as Captain Mandrake (a Briton putting down the uprising) and as Dr. Strangelove, an ex-Nazi inventor confined to a wheelchair, whose gloved hand is always ready to rise in a salute to Hitler. An iconoclastic, irreverent statement on our idiotic attitudes toward nuclear weapons; on the muddled thinking of the military; on our race to destruction. The brilliantly original script is by Kubrick, Terry Southern and Peter George. Keenan Wynn (as Colonel Bat Guano), Tracy Reed, James Earl Jones, Peter Bull. (VC)

**DR. SYN (1937).** Skeleton figures on horseback terrorize a British village in 1880; actually it's Captain Clegg (swashbuckled by George Arliss) posing as the sinister Scarecrow. Plenty of pseudohorror and sword action. Directed by Roy William Neill. Margaret Lockwood, John Loder, Roy Emerton. Remade in 1962 as NIGHT CREATURES.

**DR. TARR'S PIT OF HORRORS.** See **DR. TARR'S TORTURE DUNGEON.**

**PETER SELLERS AS DR. STRANGELOVE**

**DR. TARR'S TORTURE DUNGEON (1972).** Alleged adaptation of Edgar Allan Poe's "The System of Dr. Tarr and Professor Fether," produced in Mexico and directed by Juan Lopez Moctezuma. But don't believe for a moment this is faithful to Poe. It is to be avoided like the Red Death; tell-tale signs of no heart. Call it Moctezuma's Revenge. Claudio Brook, Arthur Hansel, Ellen Sherman. (VC)

**DR. TERROR'S GALLERY OF HORRORS.** See **RETURN TO THE PAST.**

**DR. TERROR'S HOUSE OF HORRORS (1943).** Described as an unauthorized editing of scenes from five different movies. The bits are from LE GOLEM, a 1936 French release; VAMPYR, the 1931 Carl Theodore Dreyer film; THE LIVING DEAD, a 1933 English flick; WHITE ZOMBIE and THE RETURN OF CHANDU, both with Bela Lugosi.

**DR. TERROR'S HOUSE OF HORRORS (1965).** Amicus anthology horror film with Peter Cushing as an uncanny tarot card reader who confronts five passengers aboard a speeding train and "reads" their futures. Hence, five supernatural tales: Art critic Christopher Lee is pursued by a beast with five fingers; Roy Castle is haunted by a voodoo curse; Neil McCallum wishes he hadn't when he wrestles with a werewolf; Alan Freeman is attacked by a peculiar vine plant; and Donald Sutherland sharpens his stake for a vampiric kill. The framework aboard the train provides one final, fatal twist. Good stuff directed by Freddie Francis, scripted by Milton Subotsky. Max Adrian, Peter Madden, Katy Wild, Michael Gough, Frank Forsyth. (VC)

**DR. WHO AND THE DALEKS (1965).** DR. WHO remains a popular British science-fiction TV series in America; this film version is aimed at the same youthful, fantasy-oriented audience. As the kindly inventor, Peter Cushing journeys forward in time to a planet where the good Thals fight off the evil Daleks, strange beings who wear metallic coverings to keep out lethal radiation. Directed by Gordon Flemying. Jennie Linden, Roy Castle, Robert Tovey, Geoffrey Toone. (VC)

**DR. X (1932).** First National horror thriller, directed by Michael Curtiz, mixes the whodunit with the mad doctor formula. Flesh is created artificially by a murderous doctor, whose identity is hidden until the climax. Originally shot in two-color Technicolor process. Lionel Atwill, Preston Foster, Fay Wray, Mae Busch, Lee Tracy.

**DOG, A MOUSE AND A SPUTNIK, A (1961).** French comedy attempting to make fun of space travel is a nogoodnik. Directed by Jean Dreville. Noel Neill, Mischa Auer.

**DOGS (1976).** In the tradition of THE BIRDS, Man's Best Friend does an about-tail and doglegs to the left to chase after (or retrieve, in the case of bird dogs) human flesh as though it were upgraded Kal-Kan. This film's bite is worse than its bark as the murderous mutts, callous curs and psychopurebreds take over management of all pounds and kennels. What a time they have with fire hydrants, with the SPCA out of business. David McCallum leads the human pack, with Linda Gray nipping at his heels. No puppy love in this family. Directed by Burt Brinckerhoff on point, who hounded the cast for better performances, and written by O'Brian Tomalin, who loves to be scratched behind his ears. Therein lies the tail of this tale.

**DOGS OF HELL (1982).** Regional filmmaker Earl Owensby shot this on location in Georgia in 3-D, with Lenny Lipton as his stereovision consultant. An Army experiment involving surgical implants in animals has turned a pack of Rottweilers into unthinking killers, a "loss of human affection response," as one of the scientists (Bill Gribble) puts it. The dogs escape (naturally) and invade a resort area called Lake Lure, where campers, farmers and passersby die horribly in the jaws of the killer pack. Tom McIntyre's script takes forever to get yipping and Worth Keter directs without building suspense or characters. Producer Owensby also plays the sheriff but he's one-dimensional. Inconsequential. Robert Bloodworth, Kathy Hasty, Ed Lilliard, Jerry Rushing. (VC)

**DOKTOR FAUSTUS (1982).** Slow-paced, intellectual version of a Thomas Mann novel that allegorically compared the Third Reich to the Faust legend. It's a complex work written-directed by Franz Seitz with Jon Finch as a composer who

signs the obligatory pact with the Devil so he can become a musical genius. The themes are deep and patience is required to endure this West German film.

**DOLL, THE (1963).** French/Italian comedy is a funny satire about the traditional mad scientist who can reproduce anything—so why not a South American dictator's mistress? Directed by Jacques Baratier. Sonnie Teal.

**DOLL, THE (1963).** Swedish fantasy allegory, directed by Arne Mattsson and starring Per Oscarsson as a lonely nightwatchman who finds solace in the companionship of a department store dummy he has stolen and taken home. Dummy comes to life as Gio Petre and finally drives Per to the edge of madness.

**DOLLS (1986).** "It wants to play with you" promises the ad for this Charles Band Empire Pictures release starring Stephen Lee, Guy Rolfe and Hilary Mason. Directed by Stuart Gordon.

**DOMINIQUE IS DEAD (1978).** Millionaire Cliff Robertson is grieving over the death of wife Jean Simmons when he sees her spectral image in the hall. He digs up her coffin to find it filled with rocks. The spirit continues to haunt him, and while he should wise up to the possibility of Hitchcockian tricks, he's a real fall guy in the end. This kind of pseudosupernatural thriller has been done to death, but director Michael Anderson injects it with a sense of classiness. Edward and Valerie Abraham adapted Harold Lawlor's WHAT BECKONING GHOST. Jenny Agutter, Simon Ward. (VC)

**DONKEY SKIN (1971).** French fairy tale, based on a story by Charles Perrault (creator of "Cinderella") with music by Michel Legrand and direction by Jacques Demy. Catherine Deneuve stars as a princess who must disguise herself so she won't have to marry the wrong man, with Delphine Seyrig as a kind of fairy godmother. Suitable for children and adults with non sequitur dialogue, zany behavior and magical tricks performed by magical wands. (VC)

**DONOVAN'S BRAIN (1953).** Curt Siodmak's classic novel (first produced in 1943 as THE LADY AND THE MONSTER) was remade by producer Tom Gries into a superior version thanks to the literate screenplay and direction by Felix Feist. A well-meaning scientist (Lew Ayres) keeps a tyrannical tycoon's brain alive in a special solution, but the brain gains mental control of the scientist, forcing the doctor to commit acts against his will. Chillingly effective. Nancy Davis, Steve Brodie, Gene Evans, Tom Powers, Lisa Howard.

**DON'T ANSWER THE PHONE (1981).** Also known as THE HOLLYWOOD STRANGLER, this was (un)inspired by the L.A. Hillside Strangler case. A macho, ugly young man (a disturbed Vietnam vet played by Nicholas Worth) rushes around Hollywood, choking nubile women to death with a stocking. The violence is gratuitously lingering and has no redeeming values, nor does the Michael Castle script shed insight into psychopathic killers. The couch is empty in this exploitation mess directed-produced by Robert Hammer. James Westmoreland, Pamela Bryant, Flo Gerrish. (VC)

**DON'T BE AFRAID OF THE DARK (1973).** Gnomes and other weird creatures are frightening Kim Darby, who must convince hubby Jim Hutton she isn't going bonkers. Minor supernatural TV-movie, made on a skimpy budget. Directed by John Newland, producer of TV's ONE STEP BEYOND. William Demarest, Barbara Anderson. (VC)

**DON'T GO IN THE HOUSE (1980).** Sicko, disturbing moviemess about a psycho (Dan Gramaldi) whose mother burned him as a kid, so now he sets naked women on fire with his flame-thrower and watches them burn in his asbestos suit, all because he hates his now- deceased mother—and all women, unfortunately, remind him of his mother. He keeps the charred corpses in his private charnel house. Written-directed by Joseph Ellison; produced by Ellen Hammill, who co-wrote this insultive diatribe against women. Don't go in the theater. Robert Osth, Ruth Dardick. (VC)

**DON'T GO IN THE WOODS (1980).** Another knife-killer psycho-suspense, low-budget exploitationeer, quickly forgotten, hardly-shown-anywhere flick from producer-director Jim Bryan. Cast members Buck Carradine, Mary Gail Artz and

James P. Hayden can't see the forest through the trees. (VC)

**DON'T GO TO SLEEP (1982).** After a young girl dies in a fire, parents Dennis Weaver and Valerie Harper undergo personality changes as the spirit of the dead daughter returns for revenge. The family dies off one by one in bloody OMEN style, But since this is a TV-movie the graphics that might have made this exciting were kept to a minimum. Directed by Richard Lang. This is not a sleeper but a yawner, with its prophetic title justly needed. Ruth Gordon, Robert Webber, Robin Ignico, Kristin Cummings.

**DON'T LOOK IN THE BASEMENT (1973).** An aura of madness clings to this low-budget production, a credit to producer-director S.F. Brownrigg and writer Tim Pope. The setting is an insane asylum where administrative nurse Rosie Holotik takes over after the previous director was axed to death. Gradually the inmates seize the asylum and the film sinks ever deeper into a snake pit of insanity, an emotion captured here in all its grotesqueries. Cheap production values but it's full of thrills and shocks, often functioning on more than one level. Ann McAdams. (VC)

**DON'T LOOK NOW (1973).** Daphne du Maurier's story makes for an engrossing psychological horror film directed by Nicolas Roeg, featuring erotic love scenes between Donald Sutherland and Julie Christie. Sutherland, a restorer of European churches, foresees his daughter's drowning. His power of prescience increases—and so does the inexplicable mystery, which is never really explained. Ambiguous and enigmatic, but its psychic themes and imagery are fascinating. Hilary Mason, Clelia Matania. (VC)

**DON'T OPEN THE DOOR (1979).** The maker of DON'T LOOK IN THE BASEMENT, S.F. Brownrigg, is back with another woman (Susan Bracken) faced with potential madness when she returns to her Texas home to ponder who stabbed mother to death. It's sleaze cheaply photographed, but a sense of sexual depravity makes this unpleasantly compelling when Ms Bracken comes to realize that a transvestite killer harassing her with obscene phone calls is hiding in the house. Psycho whackos galore. Gene Ross, Annabelle Weenick, Jim Harell. (VC)

**DON'T OPEN THE WINDOW (1974).** A sound machine designed to kill homicidal bugs in our soil has a profound effect on the dead with sonic impulses—it makes them get up and walk like zombies, killing living beings who happen along. This spaghetti-shocker, a steal of NIGHT OF THE LIVING DEAD, is graphically sickening, in completely terrible taste—but it will please hardcore gore fans. Arthur Kennedy is awful as a disbelieving police inspector. Ray Lovelock, Christine Galbo, Aldo Massasso. Jorge Grau directed.

**DON'T OPEN TILL CHRISTMAS (1984).** He's making a kill list and checking it twice in Britain's answer to SILENT NIGHT, DEADLY NIGHT, with a psychokiller knocking off Father Christmases, English versions of Santa. The murders are a graphic lot: a spear through the mouth, a cleaver across the face, two strangulations, a terrifying castration and several ordinary knife plunges into stomachs. The suspense is well handled by director Edmund Purdom, especially a stalking sequence in the London Dungeon. Purdom also plays the Scotland Yard inspector on the case. Caroline Munro appears in a skin-tight dress in a rock 'n roll routine. Belinda Mayne, Gerry Sundquist. (VC)

**DOOMSDAY CHRONICLES (1979).** William Schallert narrates this pseudodocumentary about the day on which our world will close its doors forever. Would you believe the year of doom will be 1999? We're all doomed if TV keeps throwing us these cheap, inconclusive reports based on thin air and cloud substance. Directed by James Thornton.

**DOOMSDAY MACHINE (1967).** Supercheap, unimaginative science-fiction space film lacking in everything except Stanley Cortez's decent cinematography. A rocket crew headed by Henry Wilcoxon and Grant Williams is halfway to Venus when nuclear war erupts on Earth, and the planet is destroyed. What to do next? Scriptwriter Stuart James Byre settles on bickering among the passengers (Ruta Lee, Bobby Van, Mala Powers, Denny Miller) and a meeting with some superintel-

ligence deep in space that will provide the answer for mankind's new beginnings. The film doesn't end—it just stops. Directed without style by Lee Sholem.

**DOOMWATCH (1972).** Chemicals dumped into waters surrounding a British island create human mutations when fish are eaten from the waters. Unexciting science-fiction directed by Peter Sasdy. Some hideously good monster make-up. Ian Bannen, Judy Geeson, George Sanders, Percy Herbert, Simon Oates, George Woodbridge. (VC)

**DOOR WITH THE SEVEN KEYS (1962).** West German remake of the 1940 British shocker, CHAMBER OF HORRORS, an old Edgar Wallace mystery about a woman who comes to a lonely mansion on the moors to meet a madman who keeps a torture chamber well stocked—with victims. Directed by Alfred Vohrer. Klaus Kinski, Heinz Drache.

**DOPPELGANGER.** See **JOURNEY TO THE FAR SIDE OF THE SUN.**

**DORIAN GRAY.** Videocassette version of **SECRET OF DORIAN GRAY, THE.**

**DORM THAT DRIPPED BLOOD, THE (1981).** Formula stuff from producers-directors Jeffrey Obrow and Stephen Carpenter, a killer-on-the-loose, dumb-trapped-teenagers story, this one set in Dayton Hall, which is closed for renovation. Which gives the characters lonely rooms to wander in while the slasher-basher stalks them. Extremely downbeat ending. The kids are given little to do but scream and die. Laurie Lapinski, Stephen Sachs, David Snow, Pamela Holland. (VC)

**DOUBLE DECEPTION (1960).** Wonderfully puzzling mystery about twins, in which you never are sure which is which. This convoluted enigma is deliciously posed by French masters of suspense Pierre Boileau and Thomas Narcejac, who concocted the original, on which VERTIGO is loosely based. Intriguing. Alice and Ellen Kessler portray the twins. Directed by Serge Friedman. Jean Mercure.

**DOUBLE EXPOSURE (1981).** A slasher film about an ice-pick murderer stalking L.A. prostitutes . . . focus shifts to a girly magazine photographer (Michael Callan) who fears he is the killer. He suffers from dreams in which he slaughters his models (in one case by sticking her head into a bag containing a rattlesnake). Is he dreaming or did he commit these heinous crimes? Not even psychiatrist Seymour Cassel knows for certain. Callan's relationship with his one-armed, one-legged brother (James Stacy) is a mixture of repressed affection, macho backslapping and sibling rivalry. Pamela Hensley and Robert Tessier are cops working with chief Cleavon Little but their contributions are minor as writer-director William Byron Hillman keeps focus on Callan and girlfriend Joanna Pettet. A peculiar non sequitur to the genre, not always successful, but different. (VC)

**DOUBLE POSSESSION.** See **GANJA AND HESS.**

**DOWN TO EARTH (1947).** A star-studded cast in a dull, dreary musical-comedy. Terpsichore, Goddess of Dance, materializes on our mortal plane (i.e., Broadway) to dally with producer Larry Parks in a musical that hopefully was better produced than this Columbia film. Rita Hayworth was at her loveliest as Terpsichore and co-stars George Macready, Edward Everett Horton, Adele Jergens, James Gleason and Marc Platt pant and puff to support her, but there's no real magic under director Alexander Hall.

**DRACULA (1931).** Bela Lugosi's performance is what this Universal "classic" is remembered for; Tod Browning's direction is strangely static, and the Garrett Ford-Dudley Murphy adaptation (from the Hamilton Deane-John Balderston play, in turn from Bram Stoker's novel) is as stuffy as the drawing room in which too much of the action is set. Only the early Transylvania sequence, when Renfield (Dwight Frye) coaches across the eerie moor and arrives at the Gothic Dracula castle, conveys the atmosphere the rest of the film cries for. It is the affected stage-style acting of Lugosi, the malignant evil he suggests, and the hypnotic spell he holds over females that makes one rapt. The supporting cast doesn't stand the test of time as well as Lugosi, but if the film is looked upon as a period piece or a curiosity item, it can be

**FRANK LANGELLA CLIMBS THE WALLS AS DRACULA (1979)**

interesting, nostalgic viewing. Edward Van Sloan portrays the Van Helsing character, Helen Chandler one of Dracula's victims. Make- up by Jack Pierce (who also did Karloff's Frankenstein Monster), cinematography by Karl Freund. (VC)

**DRACULA (1973).** Richard Matheson scripted this Dan Curtis TV-film which met mixed reaction: Many critics felt it was slow-paced and dull, others were encouraged to see Jack Palance attempt a sympathetic, tormented portrait of the King of Vampires. This refreshing shift of pace certainly is worth the serious buff's attention. Nigel Davenport appears as Van Helsing. Simon Ward, Fiona Lewis, Virginia Wetherall, Pamela Brown. Directed by Curtis.

**DRACULA (1979).** Stylish, atmospheric remake of the hoary old Hamilton Deane-John Balderston play (based on Bram Stoker's historic novel). Frank Langella, fresh from scoring in a Broadway version of DRACULA, is a sensual, sexy vampire radiating an uncommon amount of lust as he seduces Van Helsing's daughter. That foe of vampires is essayed with passionate histrionics by Sir Laurence Olivier. Walter Mirisch's production reeks with period decor and costumes, with enough bloodletting and "undead" chills to satisfy specialty crowds as well as general audiences. Well directed by John Badham, with some great shots of Dracula crawling along the side of a building. Donald Pleasence, Kate Nelligan, Trevor Eve. Score by John Williams. (VC)

**DRACULA (1984).** Japanese animated feature of the Dracula legend, full of unexpected graphic violence and gore, and hence not as suitable for young viewers as most cartoons. (VC)

**DRACULA A.D. 1972 (1972).** Hammer broke tradition by placing Dracula in contemporary England, where he is resurrected by a gang of modish rock 'n rollers and avenges himself against a descendant of Professor Van Helsing. Peter Cushing, after an 11-year absence from the series, is back as the updated Van Helsing, tracking the vampire to an old church after his granddaughter (the wonderfully busty Stephanie Beacham) has been lured into Drac's domain. Christopher Lee is still imposing as the bloodsucker with the

bloodshot eyes and his battles with Cushing are well staged, although some of the demises are based on now-predictable cliches and some of the effects have become dated. Nonetheless, quite well done. Directed by Alan Gibson, written by Don Houghton. Caroline Munro, Marsha Hunt, Philip Miller, Michael Kitchen, Christopher Neame.

**DRACULA AND SON (1976).** Mixture of horror, comedy and political polemic: The Communist government ruling modern Transylvania feels vampires are bad for the party's image, so Dracula and son are exiled to England, where the film community welcomes them as stars. But talk about typecasting: the boys are hired to play cinema vampires. Directed by Eduardo Molinaro. Christopher Lee, Bernard Menez, Raymond Bussieres, Anna Gael. (VC)

**DRACULA BLOWS HIS COOL (1979).** Softcore sex comedy produced by the West Germans, in which an ancestor of Dracula (Gianni Garko, who doubles as Count Stanislaus) turns up as a fashion photographer, shooting sexy models against the eerie setting. Plenty of undraped beauties and double entendre vampire-sex gags. The castle, for example, is called Van Screw. Directed by Carlo Ombra. Betty Verges.

**DRACULA EXOTICA (1981).** X-rated horror porn in which Jamie Gillis, as the vampire, sheds his cloak (and everything else) to put the bite on lesbian "twins" who are ready to kiss more than necks. Vanessa Del Rio, Samantha Fox.

**DRACULA HAS RISEN FROM THE GRAVE (1968).** Heavy (handed) use of religious symbolism earmarks this third film in Hammer's series to star Christopher Lee as the infamous count. In John Elder's script he is reduced to a one-dimensional vampire suggesting tons of evil but unsupported by a strong plot. Two priests climb to Castle Dracula to resurrect the antihero and control his bloodletting for purposes of revenge. A giant crucifix figures ludicrously in the blood-gushing climax. Many scenes were shot through a red color filter to cast a sanguinary motif, but this technique, a poor choice by director Freddie Francis, calls attention to itself whenever the camera pans. The beauteous Veronica Carlson is an eyeful in her flimsy nightgowns when Dracula comes to call. Rupert

**CREATURE FEATURES MOVIE GUIDE**

Davies, Barbara Ewing, Michael Ripper. The good music is by James Bernard.

**DRACULA IS DEAD AND WELL AND LIVING IN LONDON.** Also known as **SATANIC RITES OF DRACULA, THE.** See **COUNT DRACULA AND HIS VAMPIRE BRIDE.**

**DRACULA—PRINCE OF DARKNESS (1965).** After HORROR OF DRACULA, Christopher Lee refused to reappear as the Count for several years. This film, however, lured him back into the fold of the cape, so it is often referred to as the sequel to HORROR even though another Hammer feature, THE BRIDES OF DRACULA, was produced in 1960. Two English couples traveling through Transylvania spend the night at the castle, where the bloodsucker is restored to life in a bizarre ceremony, a perversion on religious resurrection. Then old Drac, haunting the hallways once again, goes after Barbara Shelley and Suzan Farmer to make them new "brides." One of the best films in the series, directed by Terence Fisher. Andrew Keir, Francis Matthews.

**DRACULA SUCKS (1978).** Hardcore X-rated fare which we include here for "purists." Sex stars John Holmes, Serena, Seka and Annette Haven, while flitting around castle sets, demonstrate unabashedly that Dracula is interested in areas below the neck. Not for kiddies, obviously. Rereleased as LUST AT FIRST BITE. Directed by Philip Marshak. (VC)

**DRACULA, THE DIRTY OLD MAN (1969).** Sexploitation all the way—and they go all the way in depicting a scarlet-cloaked Dracula (Vince Kelly) with a lair of corpses and a werewolf who supplies beautiful female victims. Then Dracula and Wolfman have a falling out over one particular cutie, ending their wonderful relationship and all those orgiastic occasions. Produced and written by William Edwards.

**DRACULA, THE GREAT UNDEAD (1985).** Recycled TV documentary hosted by Vincent Prince, detailing the myths surrounding bloodsucking vampires. Strictly historical stuff with a few film clips of Bela Lugosi to spice it up. (VC)

**DRACULA VS. DR. FRANKENSTEIN (1972).** Spanish-French concoction blending werewolves, vampires and other beasties of the night. Written-directed by the indomitable Jesus Franco, who is responsible for a series of these things. Dennis Price plays the bad doctor badly, Howard Vernon plays the vampire vampily. Alberto Dalbes, Britt Nichols. In video as **SCREAMING DEAD, THE.**

**DRACULA VS. FRANKENSTEIN (1971).** Depressingly bad pastiche of Universal horror pictures of the 1940s—depressing because it features Lon Chaney Jr. and J. Carrol Naish in their declining, almost decrepit, years. The make-up is dreadful, the lighting amateurish and the music track horrendous. The ludicrous plot is a hodgepodge of creatures and motiveless actions which will insult the most patient, forgiving viewer. Al Adamson directed and he should be ashamed. Forrest J. Ackerman has a bit role as a victim. Anthony Eisley, Regina Carol, Jim Davis, Zandor Vorkov, Russ Tamblyn. (VC)

**DRACULA'S CASTLE.** See **BLOOD OF DRACULA'S CASTLE.**

**DRACULA'S DAUGHTER (1936).** This vintage Universal production picks up where DRACULA left off—with Professor Van Helsing (again played by Edward Van Sloan) under arrest for murdering the Transylvanian Count (after all, he did drive a stake through the chap's cold, cold heart). The female offspring (Gloria Holden) goes on a new spree of murder. Let the name of Countess Marya Zaleska drip with blood! The film is okay as a time-killer but it has none of the legendary proponents of its predecessor. Directed by Lambert Hillyer, scripted by Garrett Fort. Otto Kruger, Marguerite Churchill, Irving Pichel, Hedda Hopper, E.E. Clive.

**DRACULA'S DOG (1978).** Nonclassic goes to the dogs with a howling- funny plot in which a Romanian tomb under Soviet guard is disturbed and a vampire slave (Reggie Nalder) escapes his coffin. Since the last descendant of Dracula now lives a normal life in L.A., the gnarly-faced entity, accompanied by the vampiric hound Zoltan, travels to America. The untainted Dracula (Michael Pataki) has taken his family on a vacation, so most of this cheap Albert Band-directed film takes place at a lake with the toady siccing devil dogs (the Baskerville variety, with blazing demonic eyes) on hapless humans. One harrowing sequence has Soviet policeman Mel Ferrer and Pataki trapped in a tiny one-room shack; another has Pataki trapped in his car that anticipates CUJO. Otherwise, this is unendurable claptrap, enough to make you seek the nearest hydrant. Jan Shutan, Libbie Chase. (VC)

**DRACULA'S GREAT LOVE (1973).** Re-edited U.S. version of a Spanish horror film imitating the Hammer gothic style. Hence, this has good set designs and costumes, but acting and storyline are anemic as the victims of the old count, four lovely senoritas hanging out for the night in an abandoned sanitorium. The dubbing is listless, the blood effects heavily edited for the U.S. and the plot sorely in need of a hero. Drac seeks a virgin to fall in love with so he can restore his "evil superiority" and allow his long-dead daughter to rise from her crypt. Paul Naschy is the fanged creature with a more gentle side than many movie vampires. The swelling bosoms belong to Rossana Yanni, Ingrid Garbo and Mista Miller. Written-directed by Javier Aguirre.

**DRACULA'S LAST RITES (1980).** Lucard is now in the cover-up business: He's the mortician in a small town where folks don't catch on when you murder them by sucking their blood. Spell his name backwards (as they've been doing since SON OF DRACULA) and you discover his heritage as well as the nature of the walking dead around him. Also known as LAST RITES, something this film needed from the start. Directed by Domonic Paris. Patricia Lee Hammond, Gerald Fielding, Victor Jorge, Mimi Weddell. (VC)

**DRACULA'S SAGA.** See **SAGA OF DRACULA.**

**DRAGON MURDER CASE, THE (1934).** Old-fashioned whodunit in which it appears a legendary dragon is responsible for the death of a swimming pool murder. Fat chance in this pseudowhodunit directed by Bruce Humberstone. Warren William stars as detective Philo Vance. Lyle Talbot, Robert Warwick, Margaret Lindsay, Dorothy Tree.

**DRAGON ZOMBIES RETURN (1983).** Hong Kong fantasy, directed by Hau Ching, finds a young woman discovering the Heartbreak Sword in the Treasure Cavern of Heartbreak Gorge, which allows her to learn the secrets of Dragon Kung-Fu. Metaphysical Oriental hogwash mixed with martial arts. Shan Koon Ling Fung, Lo Lieh.

**DRAGON'S BLOOD, THE (1963).** Magical sword is employed by the brave and loyal Siegried in his fight against a towering, fire- breathing dragon. Unfortunately, the plot is also draggin' and the dub job of this Italian tale of legendary knights is a drag on everyone. Directed by Giacomo Gentilomo. Rolf Tasna, Katharina Mayberg.

**DRAGONSLAYER (1981).** Outstanding fantasy-adventure capturing a sense of action, mystery, menace and magic, thanks to the doting care doled out by Matthew Robbins (director) and Hal Barwood (who co-scripted with Robbins). Effects master Dennis Muren pioneered new animation techniques in bringing to life a fire-breather named Vertithrax that flies and breathes fire and is a true menace, not a joke. The tone for the cast is set by Ralph Richardson as the delightful sorcerer Ulrich, while Peter MacNichol as young hero Galen and Caitlin Clark as his maiden are suitably naive and venturesome. The baby dragons provide some of the film's best moments. Albert Salmi, Peter Eyre, John Hallam. Good musical score by Alex North. (VC)

**DREAM LOVER (1986).** After Kristy McNichol undergoes a traumatic rape experience, in which she kills her assailant

---

*"To die, to be really dead, that must be glorious!" —The Count reflecting in* **DRACULA.**

**PETER MacNICHOL AS GALEN ON THE ATTACK IN 'DRAGONSLAYER'**

with a knife, she is so plagued by nightmares she seeks the help of a dream researcher (Ben Masters), but only gets in deeper when her dreams start to become reality in his laboratory. Elements of this psycho-mystery are fascinating, but McNichol portrays the troubled woman with such coldness, one can never feel sympathy for her. Director Alan J. Pakula also needed more exposition instead of all the pregnant pauses and unexplained twists and turns. Paul Shenar, Justin Deas. (VC)

**DREAM ONE (1984).** Strange French-British production about a youngster named Nemo (Jason Connery, son of Sean) who is sent into a fantasy realm where he finds the Nautilus submarine from Verne's 20,000 LEAGUES UNDER THE SEA as well as characters from other literary fantasies, such as Alice (a princess from Yonderland) and a Zorro-like masked avenger. Charming if inexplicable. John Boorman co-produced, Arnaud Selignac directed.

**DREAMS COME TRUE (1985).** "Soul traveling" is a form of psychic projection enjoyed by factory worker Michael Sanville and nurse Stephanie Shuford, who leave their drab lives to dine in Paris, visit a carnival, etc. It's the work of Max Kalmanowicz, who directed THE CHILDREN, and its best moments come during the special effects and astral hopping. Played mainly for comedy.

**DREAMANIAC (1986).** Sleaz-iac quickie-sickie (made for video) about a heavy metal composer who heavily composes up a succubus to suck a bust or two at a sorority hash-brownies party. Amateurish production marked by buckets of unconvincing blood, tons of sex and nudity and tons of sex and nudity. The bare-skinned monotony and bad acting just won't quit. You will not screamaniac. Directed by David De-Coteau. Thomas Bern, Kim McKamy, Sylvia Summers. (VC)

**DREAMCHILD (1985).** Alice Hargreaves, the real-life woman who inspired Lewis Carroll to write ALICE IN WONDERLAND, is portrayed by Carol Browne in this wonderful blend of realism and fantasy. In 1932 Hargreaves is invited to Columbia University to receive an honorary degree during a Lewis Carroll birth centenary. She relives her youth in a blend of nostalgic memories and outright hallucinatory dreams, imagining a tea party with the Mad Hatter and March Hare, among others. Meanwhile, her young traveling companion falls for a brash Herald-Tribune reporter. Offbeat art picture may only appeal to the erudite and learned. Directed by Gavin Millar. Ian Holm, Peter Gallagher. The Muppet shop provided the stylish creatures. (VC)

**DREAMSCAPE (1984).** Tightly honed script by David Loughery, Chuck Russell and director Joseph Ruben makes for an exciting excursion into the subconscious mind (the dreamscape) as telepathic subjects undergo dream testing. Psychic Dennis Quaid is hired by research scientists Max Von Sydow and Kate Capshaw to link with sleeping subjects and experience their nightmares. Some are deadly serious, others amusing, all are couched in symbolic imagery. Christopher Plummer is a sinister government man in charge of an agency wanting the dreamlink for assassination purposes, and Eddie Albert is a U.S. President troubled by nuclear nightmares. Although Peter Kuran's special effects are limited by budget, they succeed in capturing the spirit of bad dreams, especially in the form of a Snake Creature (sometimes animated, sometimes full size). Make-up specialist Craig Reardon contributes some cadaverous faces. This works well as fantasy and thriller. A fine music track by Maurice Jarre. (VC)

**DRESSED TO KILL (1980).** Lulu of a horror film from Brian De Palma—a macabre black joke on the audience as he follows sex- starved housewife Angie Dickinson to her death at the hands of a knife murderess in an unforgettable elevator sequence. More jolting surprises are in score in De Palma's screenplay when the murdered woman's son and a prostitute (Nancy Allen, De Palma's real-life wife at the time) join forces to track the killer. De Palma's direction is often brilliant, with the film opening and closing with erotic shower sequences. They don't make shockers better than this one. Michael Caine, Keith Gordon. (VC)

**DRILLER KILLER (1979).** Sickening gore garbage about an artist who goes off the deep end and uses a carpentry drill to do in his foes. You could say this film is full of bit parts. And holes, especially in Nicholas St. John's script. The biggest "bore" of all turns out to be director Abel Ferrara, who also doubles as the killer. (VC)

**DRIVE-IN MASSACRE (1976).** Producer-director Stu Segall's tribute to the "passion pit" consists of cops looking for a killer who terrorizes moviegoers as they stick their arms out to get a speaker or go to the popcorn stand or the bathroom. It's fun in a perverted kind of way. We recommend you see this only at a drive- in. Written by Buck Flower and John Goff. Jake Barnes. (VC)

**DRUMMOND'S PERIL (1938).** A formula for making synthetic diamonds is the hoary old device setting into motion this hoary old Bulldog Drummond thriller starring John Barrymore. Standard action. Directed by James Hogan. John Howard, Louise Campbell.

**DRUMS O'VOODOO (1934).** Long-lost voodoo thriller based on a J. Augustus Smith play, LOUISIANA, featuring Smith and the original Broadway black cast: Laura Bowman, Gus

Smith, Morris McKenny, Edna Barr and Lionel Monagas. Hagar, a voodoo priestess, holds sway over a superstitious Negro community in the swamp country and uses a spell to put down the villainous Thomas Catt, who is corrupting the town with his saloon.

**DUCK SOUP (1932).** Beefy broth, bubbling with zaniness and flowing nonstop from the Hollywood kettle of the zesty Marx Brothers. Rufus T. Firefly (Groucho) is the ruler of the mythical kingdom of Freedonia, and there is no end to the political-military satire, slapstick, visual jokes and double entendres. Directed by Leo McCarey. Margaret Dumont, Louis Calhern, Edgar Kennedy, Charles Middleton. (VC)

**DUEL (1971).** Although this appears to be a non-fantasy suspense TV-movie about a motorist (Dennis Weaver) pursued by an insane trucker, director Steven Spielberg never allows the homicidal driver to be seen and the semi takes on an evil personification, sliding into the realm of the "Twilight Zone." Weaver's building sense of terror and the cat-and-mouse tactics of the trucker build to a nerve-wracking climax of pure action and menace. Richard Matheson's script (from his short story) functions on several levels, but viewed just as a shocker, it's a pip. First made for TV, this was released abroad in a longer version, now available to TV. (VC)

**DUEL IN SPACE. See ROCKY JONES, SPACE RANGER.**

**DUEL OF THE SPACE MONSTERS. See FRANKENSTEIN MEETS THE SPACE MONSTER.**

**DUMBO (1941).** Walt Disney's full-length cartoon about the baby elephant who joins a circus and learns to fly by flapping its floppy ears is a visual delight, a high point in animation. Based on the book by Helen Aberson and Harold Pearl. Voices by Sterling Holloway, Herman Bing and Verna Felton. (VC)

**DUNE (1984).** Long-awaited version of Frank Herbert's classic novel is a complicated, disappointing film. David Lynch, after THE ELEPHANT MAN, seems incapable of bringing cohesiveness to his script or direction. The story desperately needs humor and levity to contrast the bleakness—Lynch directs with an unrelenting sobriety. Plot: Everyone needs the planet Dune for a spice from its sands that enables a race of mutants to provide a form of astral space travel to several alien cultures migrating through the Universe. Protecting the spices are a race of worm creatures with mystical links to mankind. DUNE is the story of a Messiah who leads the people of Dune out of bondage. The Messiah is Kyle MacLachlan, Kenneth McMillan is the hated Baron Harkonnen, whose corpulent body floats in astral projection, Jose Ferrer is Emperor Shaddam IV, Linda Hunt is Shadout Mapes (a wasted role), Silvana Mangano is Rev. Mother Ramallo; Sting is Feyd Rautha, Max Von Sydow is Dr. Kynes. And on and on, just like this 140-minute movie which never seems to end. Those hoping the battle scenes will save the picture will be surprised to see they are marred by an unbelievability that might pass in STAR WARS but not here. DUNE is all grit, no substance. (VC)

**DUNGEON OF HORROR (1963).** Low budget quickie produced in Texas in which a sadistic count, imaginatively named De Sade, lives in a creepy old castle with crazy members of his family. The survivor of a shipwreck falls into his clutches. In short, lowbrow producers at work trying to please lowbrow viewers. You have been duly warned. Directed by Pat Boyette. Russ Harvey, Lee Morgan.

**DUNGEONMASTER (1985).** Role-playing freaks and purveyors of sword- and-sorcery computer games will find this a tedious game—as much fun as watching an Apple or Atari crashing. Charles Band's production overinvests its energies in effects without a plot to support its gross-outs. Hence, hero and heroine are swept from adventure to adventure with a total disregard for logic, undergoing seven encounters to reach . . . what? It's a lavish ripoff of role-playing without understanding the psychological undercurrents of role-playing.

The shapeless script by Allen Actor provides hopelessly ill-defined roles for swashbuckling Jeffrey Byron, tied-to-the-stake heroine Leslie Wing and scenery- chewing Richard Moll as Mestema, a minion of the Devil. Seven directors are credited with the unsavory stew: Rosemarie Turko handled "Ice Gallery"; John Buechler was responsible for ""Demon of the Dead"; David Allen helmed "Grand Canyon Giant"; Stephen Ford carved a name for himself with "Slasher"; Peter Manoogian mangled "The Cave Beast"; Ted Nicolaou megaphoned "Desert Pursuit"; and Band provided the wraparound stuff. Buechler also designed the make-up. (VC)

**DUNWICH HORROR, THE (1969).** Producers generally have major difficulties adapting the stories of cosmic horror by H. P. Lovecraft, as evidenced by this fiasco with Dean Stockwell

**STING IS STUNG IN 'DUNE,' A STINKER**

and Sandra Dee (voted the girl least likely to succeed in a horror film role) as students at Miskatonic University. Someone has lifted the infamous Necronomicon volume from the campus library and is using its suggested incantations to summon "The Old Ones" (ancient, banished gods of pure evil) from another dimension during orgiastic, satanic rites. Sounds like pure Lovecraft, but this remains far from the Arkham territory Lovecraft so vividly explored in his literate, blood-chilling tales. Directed by Daniel Haller. Les Baxter's music is the best thing of all. Ed Begley, Sam Jaffe, Lloyd Bochner, Talia Coppola. (VC)

**DYBBUK, THE (1982).** Photographed stage version of an old Yiddish classic, acted out by the Jewish State Theatre of Poland. Made for an audience familiar with the religious overtones; very limited appeal elsewhere. Golda Tencer.

**DYNASTY OF FEAR.** Videocassette title for **FEAR IN THE NIGHT** (1973).

---

*"I have some wooden stakes in the car!" —DRACULA'S DOG.*

KD

**EARTH DIES SCREAMING (1964).** U.S.-British science-fiction thriller of the "end-of-the-world" genre, with walking zombies for added flavor. Test pilot Willard Parker discovers a handful of Earthlings has survived an apocalyptic attack perpetrated by robots roving the devastated landscape. Parker must find the power source and destroy the invaders. Virginia Field, Dennis Price. Directed by Terence Fisher.

**EARTH II (1971).** Space opera TV-movie (written by William Woodfield and Alan Balter; directed by Tom Gries) has superb effects but the story doesn't warrant such expense. Gary Lockwood and Tony Franciosa operate a space station between Earth and the moon and must deactivate an unharnessed atomic bomb. The suspense never builds and the outcome is predictable. Gary Merrill, Mariette Hartley, Lew Ayres, Scott Hylands, Hari Rhodes.

**EARTH VS THE FLYING SAUCERS (1956).** Ray Harryhausen's stop motion effects can't salvage this lowbrow Columbia science-fictioner directed by Fred F. Sears, with spacecraft and death rays blatant swipes from George Pal's WAR OF THE WORLDS. The Curt Siodmak plot has Earth satellites being knocked out of the sky, followed by a full-scale invasion against tourist attractions in Washington D.C. Hugh Marlowe, as the stereotyped scientist, is miscast as a hero and forever slows down the already-lumbering plot to romance Joan Taylor. And just when the film needs original music, producer Sam Katzman throws in a mishmash of themes swiped from other pictures. Zap . . . it's sterile. Harry Lauter, Morris Ankrum, Donald Curtis. (VC)

**EARTH VS. THE SPIDER.** See **SPIDER, THE.**

**EARTHBOUND (1940).** Dated supernatural-fantasy (directed by Irving Pichel) starring Warner Baxter as a ghost who forces a confession from the woman who murdered him. Hardly bound for glory. Henry Wilcoxon, Andrea Leeds, Lynn Bari.

**EARTHBOUND (1981).** Disabled alien spacecraft lands near the town of Gold Rush, where dumb sheriff John Schuck and even dumber deputy Stuart Pankin can't control the crowd when word gets out that E.T.s have invaded Earth. It's actually a benevolent humanoid family (led by parents Christopher Connelly and Meredith MacRae) seeking the help of grandfather Burl Ives and his grandson Todd Porter. Hot on their trail is Joseph Campanella as an evil government waiting to betray the aliens. Really stupid science-fiction, the kind in which someone wrinkles his nose and people begin to levitate. Directed witlessly by James L. Conway.

**EARTHQUAKE (1974).** In the immediate future, Los Angeles is totally devastated by a killer quake, which this Universal special-effects disaster epic depicts in microscopic detail. Albert Whitlock's matte work is outstanding, and all the falling glass, bricks and debris are so realistic you'll feel crushed. Where the film falters, under Mark Robson's direction, is in cliched characters and situations concocted by writers Mario Puzo and George Fox. The cast is wonderful (Charlton Heston, Ava Gardner, Lorne Greene, George Kennedy, Richard Roundtree, Walter Matthau, Barry Sullivan, Lloyd Nolan) but ultimately as wasted as the L.A. landscape. (VC)

**EAST SIDE KIDS MEET BELA LUGOSI, THE.** See **GHOSTS ON THE LOOSE.**

**EAT AND RUN (1986).** Hungry humanoid alien (dubbed Murray Creature) lands in Manhattan and becomes addicted to Italian food—Italian men and women. What great lasagna they make! Dare we say this spoof is tasteless? Directed by Christopher Hart. Ron Silver, Sharon Schlarth. (VC)

**EAT OR BE EATEN (1986).** Video original from the Firesign Theater, a satirical parody of monster movies in which a "koodzoo" vine (whatever the hell that is) takes over a town, demanding a human sacrifice. Directed by Phil Austin. (VC)

**EATEN ALIVE (1976).** After THE TEXAS CHAINSAW MASSACRE, Tobe Hooper directed this despicable, sickening misfire (the ultimate underbelly of sleaze movies) with an utterly bananas Neville Brand running a dilapidated hotel (The Starlight) in the Louisiana swamp. Next door is a mud pit containing a flesh-hungry alligator who eats animals—and individuals. An unwatchable film (unless you're a hopeless sadist), especially when it appears the beast is going to eat up a little puppy. What a bizarre cast: Mel Ferrer, Stuart Whitman, Carolyn Jones, Marilyn Burns. Also released as DEATH TRAP and STARLIGHT SLAUGHTER. (VC)

**EATING RAOUL (1982).** Writer-director Paul Bartel concocted (with co-writer Richard Blackburn) this outre black comedy about Paul and Mary Bland (Bartel and Mary Woronov), an average L.A. couple who lure creeps into their home pretending to be swingers, when what they really want to do is kill the deviates for their money. Demurely, Mary seduces them and Paul bangs them—over the head with a skillet, with no visible damage to moral sensitivities. A hilarious movie, great satire on the L.A. culture . . . this low-budget sleeper is a cult favorite. Robert Beltran, Ed Begley Jr., Buck Henry, Garry Goodrow, Charles Griffith. (VC)

**ECHOES (1983).** Moody, atmospheric supernatural chiller directed by Arthur Allan Seidelman in New York City, capturing a Manhattan ambience that enhances this weird psychological tale of an artist (Richard Alfieri) haunted by dreams in which he is a once-famous Spanish painter befouled by love, passion and murder. Psychic Gale Sondergaard believes he is plagued by a "twin spirit" from another dimension, while mother Ruth Roman tells him about a miscarriage she had that might be responsible for an "unborn brother." Stephen Schwartz's music adds to the tension. Nathalie Nell, Mercedes MacCambridge, Michael Kellin. (VC)

**EEGAH! (1962).** Arrrrgggghhhhh!!! Incredibly juvenile fantasy for brainless teenagers has the dumbest caveman in film history chasing a pretty girl through the desert outside L.A. Arrrrggghhhh!!! Director Nicholas Merriwether's camera work has to be seen to be disbelieved. Unknown cast reaches unsurpassed heights of ineptitude. Did we say unknown? The caveman is Richard Kiel, destined to become Jaws in the James Bond series. For Neanderthals only. Arch Hall Jr., Marilyn Manning, Ray Steckler. Aaarrrgghhh!!!

**EERIE MIDNIGHT HORROR SHOW, THE (1978).** Released as TORMENTED, and known to sophisticates as THE SEXORCIST, this is an Italian imitation of THE EXORCIST, depicting a young woman's terror when she is possessed by a spirit embodied in a statue. Presumably the demon is one of Satan's incubi. Undistinguished and contrived, featuring R-rated soft porn and outright sadism. Directed by Mario Gariazzo. Stella Carnacina, Chris Avram. (VC)

**EGGHEAD'S ROBOT (1970).** British kiddie comedy in which the son of a robot-inventing scientist picks up the pieces Dad left in the workshop and constructs his own robot-athlete. Calling all moppets! Directed by Milo Lewis. Roy Kinnear.

**EL TOPO (1970).** South American director Alexandro Jodorowsky is unarguably outrageous: A gunfighter in black (Jodorowsky) stalks the West in absurd fashion, murdering, raping and resurrecting the dead. Rampant with symbolism; sadistic, religious and irreverent in the same breath, totally devoid of logical explanation. You'll appreciate it or hate it.

**ELECTRIC DREAMS (1984).** This "fairy tale for computers" is a light-hearted look at our computerized fetishes, a love story between Lenny Von Dohlen (nerdish architect) and Virginia Madsen (happy cello player) and a love story between Von Dohlen and Edgar, an entity created within his home computer. Rusty Lemorande's script is gentle and whimsical, often told in computerized images, with Giorgio Moroder's score capturing the electronical "passion." Director Steve Barron gives us a pleasant story with pleasant images. Filmed in San Francisco. Maxwell Caulfield. (VC)

**ELECTRONIC MONSTER, THE (1960).** Rod Cameron is the head of a mental institution conducting dream experiments in this British adaptation of Charles Eric Maine's ESCAPEMENT, with script by Maine. Cameron induces hallucinations electronically to cure mental abberations, but his plan backfires and results in greater psychoses in patients. Typically cheap, lackluster film of its period, directed by Montgomery Tully, who threw in some strange dream dance sequences. Mary Murphy is the female lead. Meredith Edwards.

**ELEPHANT BOY (1937).** Alexander Korda's production of a Rudyard Kipling tale (by John Collier, Akos Tolnay and Marcia de Sylva) starring Sabu, "the jungle boy," who has an Eastern mystical rapport with elephants, forcing them to obey his every command. The sequence in the "elephant graveyard" is remarkable. Some jungle footage was shot by documentarian Robert J. Flaherty. Zoltan Korda, Alexander's brother, directed this British classic. Walter Hudd, Wilfrid Hyde White, Allan Jeayes, W. E. Holloway. (VC)

**ELEPHANT MAN, THE (1980).** John Hurt is John Merrick, a real-life freak of the last century who suffered terrible physical and mental discomforts from his malformities until he was

**SABU DASTAGIR (BILLED AS JUST SABU) IN 'THE ELEPHANT BOY'**

befriended by a doctor who nursed his anguish to a state of sensitivity. Merrick was a learned man, which makes his internal grief all the more touching. A tearjerker in many ways, but memorable for Hurt's heavy make-up as the grotesque-looking Merrick, his pain-racked performance, and Freddie Francis' black-and-white photography, which captures the drabness of industrial England. The script is by Christopher DeVore and Eric Bergren, from historical works by Sir Frederick Treves and Ashley Montagu. Directed by David Lynch, chosen by producer Mel Brooks after he flipped out over ERASERHEAD. (VC)

**ELIMINATORS (1986).** A lively adventure-satire from producer Charles Band depicting a "mandroid" and how he/it seeks the help of a lady scientist, soldier-of-fortune and martial arts champ to do battle with a mad scientist and his army. Filmed in Spain under Peter Manoogian's direction, the film has a tongue-in-cheek quality usually missing from Band's low budget films, thanks to the script by Danny Bilson and Paul DeMeo, even if they do steal many ideas. Patrick Reynolds is the half-man, half-machine character but he's stiff and uninteresting compared to the female lead (Denise Crosby), the adventurer (Andrew Prine) and the ninja (Conan Lee). Indiana Jones isn't exactly sweating over this film, but it certainly has its action-packed moments and humor. John Carl Buechler did his usual good effects job. (VC)

**EMBALMER, THE (1964).** Bloodless Italian movie with an anemic plot about a jocular journalist in Venice looking for an imbecilic embalmer impeccably clad in a robe and wearing a death mask who is trying to preserve beauty. In definite need of a transfusion. Colorlessly directed by Dino Tavella. Maureen Brown, Elmo Caruso, Jean Mart.

**EMBRYO (1976).** Rudimentary B-movie material about a scientist (Rock Hudson) experimenting with a human fetus,

elevated by moody photography (Fred Koenekamp's) and direction (Ralph Nelson's). In only a few days the fetus evolves into an adult woman (Barbara Carrera), tutored by Hudson in mathematics and sex—emphasis on the latter. But something goes wrong and the woman turns into a homicidal maniac looking for a new formula to prevent her accelerated aging. Style is everything. Diane Ladd, Roddy McDowall, Dr. Joyce Brothers, Jack Colvin. (VC)

**EMPIRE OF DRACULA (1967).** "Empire" refers to a handful of witless women in a blood-guzzling harem who gang up on hapless males. There is no veil of mystery—it's all dreadfully predictable horror stuff in turgid Mexican style, directed by F. Curiel. Ethel Carrillo, Eric Del Castillo.

**EMPIRE OF PASSION (1978).** Japanese ghost story about two lovers who plot the demise of the woman's husband, only to be haunted for their infidelity. Written-directed by Nagisi Oshima. Kazuko Yoshiyuki, Tatsuya Fuji.

**EMPIRE OF THE ANTS (1977).** Subtitled HOW THE PEST WAS WON, this is superschlock from Bert I. Gordon. Dull characters (Joan Collins, Robert Lansing, Albert Salmi, John David Carson, Jacqueline Scott) are trapped in a seaside resort with mutant ants, grown to enormous size from radiation. Gordon's special effects are slipshod and ten years behind the times and the plot (swiped from an H.G. Wells novel) is utterly ludicrous. The giant picnic crashers have taken over a nearby town and hypnotized all the residents and . . . see what we mean by superschlock? (VC)

**EMPIRE STRIKES BACK, THE (1980).** Sequel to STAR WARS didn't disappoint fans who returned time and again to cheer Luke Skywalker, Princess Leia, C3PO, R2D2, etc. Darth Vader, still the Scourge of the Universe, sends Imperial forces against rebels on the ice planet Hoth, where battles with Emperial Walkers are the major highlight of the film, but

**FATHER-AND-SON DUEL IN 'THE EMPIRE STRIKES BACK': THAT'S HIS BOY!**

only the beginning of new adventures. Luke searches for Yoda, a mentor who furthers his knowledge of the Force; Han Solo and Chewbacca the Wookie escape the Imperial fleet in an exciting Asteroid Belt sequence, Lando Callrissian, rogue adventurer, is introduced; and Luke faces Vader in a light saber showdown that is a splendid piece of choreographed action. Producer George Lucas turned direction over to Irvin Kershner, and the script (by Leigh Brackett and Lawrence Kasdan) has greater philosophical interest. Lucas' third in this series (RETURN OF THE JEDI) rounded out the unresolved elements of this script but this proved to be the most mature. Hence, it seems to have greater depth, though the emphasis rightfully remains on mysticism and action. Mark Hamill, Carrie Fisher, Peter Mayhew, Harrison Ford, David Prowse (as Vader with the voice of James Earl Jones), Anthony Daniels (as the golden robot), Billy Dee Williams, Alec Guinness (strictly as a spectral image). (VC)

**ENCHANTED FOREST, THE (1945).** Edmund Lowe is in commune with Nature—he hears music in trees and talks to animals a la Dr. Doolittle. He teaches these talents to a boy who is lost in the deep woods. Enchanting—if you enjoy mawkish, maudlin plots. Directed by Lew Landers. Brenda Joyce, John Litel, Harry Davenport. (VC)

**ENCHANTING SHADOW, THE (1959).** Honk Kong production, minimally released in America, about a haunted temple, a sorceress and an adventurer's effects to help a tormented spirit. Directed by Li Han-Hsiang. Betty Loh Tih, Chao Lei.

**ENCOUNTER WITH THE UNKNOWN (1975).** Three slow-paced, allegedly true supernatural stories narrated by Rod Serling. The first "encounter" concerns a prophecy of death that begins with a burial in a graveyard; the second is about a strange hole in the ground inhabited by a monster; and the last is the story of a man who meets a strange girl. Poorly directed by Harry Thomason; the script is hopelessly padded. Gene Ross, Rosie Holotick. (VC)

**ENCOUNTERS IN THE DEEP (1985).** Underwater fantasy, set in the Bermuda Triangle, in which an oceanographer discovers a subterranean world of wonders—and dangers. Carol Andre, Andy Garcia.

**END OF THE WORLD, THE.** See **PANIC IN YEAR ZERO.**

**END OF THE WORLD (1977).** Poverty level science-fictioner from director John Hayes, whose plodding work (also reflected in his pitiful editing) is miserably tedious. Christopher Lee portrays an alien, Zandi, who possesses the body of a Catholic priest and is plotting to blow up Earth because (get this, readers) mankind is contaminating the Universe. Ends on a whimper! Utter waste of Dean Jagger, Lew Ayres, MacDonald Carey, Sue Lyon (she without a lollipop). (VC)

**ENDANGERED SPECIES (1982).** Enthralling, offbeat suspenser dealing with the compelling theme of mutilated cattle. This explores the mystery with research and taste, offering a solution that involves a secret military organization (government supported?) conducting tests as part of a clandestine germ-warfare program. Around this semi-plausible premise (it beats UFOs being the culprits) director-writer Alan Rudolph and co-writer John Binder fashion a melodramatic mystery in which burned-out New York cop Robert Urich settles in a small Wyoming community, only to become caught up in the enigma. Rudolph builds suspense and makes the whole conspiratorial aspect believable. JoBeth Williams, Paul Dooley, Hoyt Axton, Harry Carey Jr. (VC)

**ENDGAME (1983).** In the post-holocaust world of 2025 A.D., warriors square off in a bloodsport called "Endgame" while stormtroopers in Nazi helmets gun for them. The game stops when the best Endgame player, Shannon (Al Cliver), talks his roughest opponents (burly brute, martial arts oriental, etc.) into helping him escort a group of mind-reading Mutants to safety, promising them a fortune in gold. Endless battles as the band encounters sadists, killers and blind priests. Never a dull moment in this Mad Max imitation from Italy . . . better than most Road Warrior ripoffs. Directed by Steven Benson. Laura Gemser, George Eastman, Jack Davis. (VC)

**ENDLESS NIGHT (1971).** Agatha Christie adaptation (writ-

**GOSSETT AS THE DRAC IN 'ENEMY MINE'**

ten- directed by Sidney Gilliat) focusing on a woman hired to scare someone to death. Standard suspenser. Hayley Mills, Britt Ekland, George Sanders, Lois Maxwell. (VC)

**ENEMY FROM SPACE (1957).** Second in Hammer's series about determined scientist Bernard Quatermass, again played by Brian Donlevy, who established the role in THE CREEPING UNKNOWN. This is a superior effort, from Nigel Kneale's screenplay (based on his TV serial) to Gerald Gibbs' stark photogrpahy to Val Guest's fine direction. Quatermass discovers a malevolent alien race in control of an isolated industrial station at Wynerton Flats. A political allegory is to be found amidst the intrigue. Vera Day, Bryan Forbes, Michael Ripper, Charles Lloyd Pack. In video as **QUATERMASS II: ENEMY FROM SPACE.**

**ENEMY MINE (1985).** A promising theme kicks off this big-budgeted space adventure of episodic proportions: An Earthman (Dennis Quaid) and a lizard creature called a Drac (Louis Gossett Jr. in heavy makeup and scaly costume) laser each other out of the heavens during a space war and crash-land on a barren planet where they must learn tolerance over mutual hatred. The arms-length relationship shapes into friendship, but just when it's getting good, there's a sharp twist of fate leading to an entirely new and exciting rescue situation. The landscapes are realistically harsh and the action sequences superbly designed, with the story making its human points while remaining solid entertainment. Directed by Wolfgang Petersen, scripted by Edward Khmara. (VC)

**ENTER THE DEVIL (1975).** Female reporter Irene Kelly, probing an Indian devil cult in the desert, gets more than she bargained for in this cheap, uninspired quickie from writers-directors F. Q. Dobbs and David Cass. Some fine Mojave photography by M. F. Cusack helps to maintain some viewer interest but the unknowns (Cass, Josh Bryant, Linda Rascoe) have an impossible time coming to grips with an arid, tumbledown script. Parched throats guaranteed.

**ENTITY, THE (1983).** Above-average supernatural thriller, allegedly based on a true case that occurred in L.A. . . . the suspenseful, frightening story of a young widowed mother (Barbara Hershey) who is attacked by an invisible demon and repeatedly raped. Writer Frank DeFellita deals on a literate level with believers vs. nonbelievers and science vs ESP. Focus is on characters, dialogue and tension as director Sidney J. Furie excellently maintains a fearful atmosphere and refuses to show the "entity" in detail—a choice that may disappoint some fans. Excellent make-up effects by Stan Winston; visual effects by William Cruse. Ron Silver, David Labiosa, Margaret Blye, George Coe, Alex Rocco. (VC)

**EQUINOX (1971).** Four teen-age hikers find an ancient tome of witchcraft which unleashes supernatural entities, including a horned creature with pterodactyl wings and pitchfork tail. Well- intended effort by young writer-director Jack Woods has mediocre- to-good effects—chalk it up as early David Allen-Jim Danforth attempts. Prize-winning science-fiction writer Fritz Leiber turns up as a geologist . . . Woods and co-writer Mark McGee should have asked Fritz to help with the script, since he knows his Lovecraft best. The film took four years to complete, so the characters age before your very eyes. Producer Dennis Muren became an award-winning effects artist. The film has acquired a cult following, although anyone expecting a classic will be disappointed. Frank Bonner, Edward Connell, Barbara Hewitt, Robin Christopher. In videocassette as **BEAST, THE.**

**ERASERHEAD (1978).** Surrealistic nightmare in black and white from avant-garde filmmaker David Lynch, who suffers from an obsession with prenatal dreams. The camera plunges into black holes, squishy worm-things float like spermatozoa and a hideous mutant baby squawls its anger. "Midnight" cult film is flawed by undisciplined editing and the symbolism, to say the least, is pretentious. Still, it has stunning moments,

### RUSSELL IN 'ESCAPE FROM NEW YORK'

with such unsettling visuals and low-live characters as to make it unforgettable. After this, Lynch was chosen to direct ELEPHANT MAN. Jack Nance, Charlotte Stewart, Jeanne Bates, Laurel Near. (VC)

**EROTIC ADVENTURES OF SNOW WHITE, THE.** See **GRIMM'S FAIRY TALES FOR ADULTS.**

**EROTIKILL (1975).** God-awful, rock-bottom Spanish vampire atrocity, poorly acted, incompetently photographed and feebly dubbed—unwatchable in the extreme. Linda Romay bares her considerable assets as Irina, a bloodsucker who terrorizes the usual love-hungry men. Devoid of story, suspense and everything else filmmakers try to put into movies. Directed by J. P. Johnson. Alice Arno, Monica Swin. (VC)

**ESCAPE (1971).** Implausible TV-movie with Christopher George as Cameron Steele, one-time escape artist (a la Houdini) now an investigator using his "unique" skills to elude torture chamber predicaments. Paul Playdon's story unfolds like a pastiche of an old-fashioned serial: Mad scientist creates a virus that could turn the world into incredibly mixed-up, walking zombies. Only Steele can thwart the plan, but first he has to get out of that straitjacket. Would you call this "escapism"? Directed by John Llewellyn Moxey. William Windom, Marlyn Mason, Avery Schreiber, John Vernon, Gloria Grahame, Huntz Hall, William Schallert.

**ESCAPE FROM GALAXY 3 (1986).** "Star Lovers" confront an evil conqueror on a farflung planet in a distant galaxy that's also a long way off. Keep your own distance from this Italian space actioner directed by Ben Norman. Cheryl Buchanan, James Milton, Don Powell. (VC)

**ESCAPE FROM NEW YORK (1981).** One of John Carpenter's best, fieldstripped to move at a roadrunner's pace as pure escapist fantasy. The writer-director (concocting this tale with Nick Castle) never slackens the spirit of adventure and populates this imaginative narrative with hard-boiled characters. The plot is an outrageous joke (Manhattan, by 1997, is a maximum-security prison) and gallops headlong with such stark atmosphere, one hasn't time to ponder absurdities. Kurt Russell, an eyepatch over one eye, does his Clint Eastwood impression as Snake Plisskin, a rebel assigned by security chief Lee Van Cleef to penetrate NYC to bring out the U.S. President (Donald Pleasence), whose Air Force I jet has crash-landed. Adrienne Barbeau (Carpenter's real- life wife), Harry Dean Stanton, Isaac Hayes, Season Hubley, Ernest Borgnine (the latter as a taxi driver). (VC)

**ESCAPE FROM THE BRONX (1984).** Sequel to 1990: THE BRONX WARRIORS, in which society has gone to the dogs and the Bronx is a danger zone full of roving gangs and ROAD WARRIOR-type freakos. Trash, the bash-boss, leads his men against Henry Silva, who has been assigned by the Corporation to wipe out everyone in the Bronx, so there's plenty of action as the factions square off. But that's all there is in this Italian release directed by Enzo G. Castellari. Mark Gregory, Valeria D'Obici, Timothy Brent. (VC)

**ESCAPE FROM THE PLANET OF THE APES (1971).** Third entry in the PLANET OF THE APES series is a talky effort, with screenwriter Paul Dehn overindulging in comedic comparisons between man and monkey. A trio of chimps travels backward in time in a space capsule to our present-day. But because the talking creatures pose a threat, the government sets out to murder the monkeys. This film's outcome led directly to CONQUEST OF THE PLANET OF THE APES. Dehn and director Don Taylor score best in generating empathy for the beleaguered chimps, are less successful with satiric jabs. Roddy McDowall, Kim Hunter, Sal Mineo, Eric Braeden (as the villain), Ricardo Montalban, Jason Evers, Albert Salmi, Natalie Trundy, William Windom.

**ESCAPE IN THE FOG (1945).** Budd Boetticher directed this programmer with Nina Foch as a nurse who dreams about a murder, then encounters the victim-to-be. Will her precognition prevent the crime from really occurring? William Wright, Otto Kruger, Konstantin Shayne, Ernie Adams.

**ESCAPE TO WITCH MOUNTAIN (1975).** Fantasy-adventure from Disney— moppet material as two children (humanoid aliens who don't know it) flee Donald Pleasence, who wants to harness their telekinesis powers for evil. Eddie Albert is a likable vacationer with a flying Winnebago camper, and there are the friendly faces of Ray Milland, Denver Pyle and Reta Shaw. The only groovy visual is one UFO sequence. Directed by John Hough. Kim Richards, Ike Eisenmann. (VC)

**ESCAPE 2000 (1983).** Unusual Australian futuristic adventure, set in a not-too-distant day when an Orwellean society rules. A concentration camp for "deviates" is run by sadistic guards under a perverted commandant. Three sexual sickos drop in for sport in the style of "The Most Dangerous Game." Five prisoners are set free and the commandant and his sporting pals follow, armed with high-powered rifles, explosive arrows and other flesh-rending weaponry. The bloody action is almost nonstop once the hunt begins. The ending turns into a wild 'n woolly shootemup. Much of the gore was cut for the U.S. Produced by David Hemmings, directed by Brian Trenchard-Smith. Music by Brian May. Olivia Hussey, Steve Railsback, Michael Craig, Carmen Duncan. Originally released to theaters as TURKEY SHOOT. (VC)

**ESCAPES (1986).** TV pilot of five stories in the tradition of THE TWILIGHT ZONE, but not as satisfying. Host Vincent Price has little to do but look sinister as he spins the miniyarns: "A Little Fishy" is a swipe of a famous EC tale about a fisherman who picks up a sandwich on the beach; "Coffee Break" is the strange-town-visited-by-an-outsider story in which a van driver goes around in circles because he wasn't nice to the townfolks; "Who's There" is a flop of a story about a jogger who meets some elves in the forest; "Jonah's Dream" features an old woman meeting up with a flying saucer; and "Think Twice" is a story of magic about the thin line separating fantasy from reality. Weak stuff directed by David Steensland. (VC)

**ESCORT TO DANGER/NIGHT OF THE CLONES (1978).** Two episodes of the SPIDERMAN TV series joined together with a touch of Elmer's and resold to TV.

**ESPIONAGE IN TANGIERS (1965).** Italian-Spanish superspy thriller, a carbon copy of James Bond but without the class, has agent S.007 in search of mad fiends threatening Earth with a disintegrating Death Ray. Ride clear of TANGIERS. Directed by Greg Tallas. Luis Davila, Jose Greci.

**E.T. THE EXTRATERRESTRIAL (1982).** To think: the greatest box office smash is a simplistic but heartfelt parable in which boy meets alien, boy loves alien, boy loses alien. Steven Spielberg's masterpiece is that profound. It was fashioned from a screenplay by Melissa Mathison, who borrowed themes from Spielberg with which he is identified: suburban settings; ordinary kids and adults coping with daily realities; an awesome attitude toward lights in the sky and alien life. Brilliant comedy touches keep E.T. from ever becoming too sentimental, and even when the story turns serious, and men are shown as menaces, one feels for E.T.'s plight in wanting to overcome prejudice on Earth so he/it can return home. Carlo Rambaldi created E.T., and although the cutie at times seems clumsy and too cute, the cuteness wins you over. Another great score by John Williams; fine flying sequences executed by Dennis Muren. Dee Wallace, Peter Coyote (the man with the keys), Robert MacNaughton, Drew Barrymore, Henry Thomas, Milt Kogan. (VC)

**EUREKA (1983).** Surrealistic portrait of the world's richest man, overburdened with the esoterica and eccentricities of cameraman-director Nicolas Roeg, almost to the point of excruciation. Gene Hackman does a good job of etching Jack McCall, a man made unhappy by his good fortune, but the narrative is incoherent, full of symbolic asides (such as a voodoo orgy) and erotic extravagances. Other good performers lost in this muddled mess are Theresa Russell, Rutger Hauer, Ed Lauter and Joe Pesci. (VC)

**EVE (1968).** Celeste Yarnall is an eyeful in costumes as skimpy as the budget for this jungle adventure with overtones of SHE. Celeste portrays an Amazon princess who keeps her natives in line with strange powers—or maybe it's her Max Factor look the jungle gang falls for. Big Game Hunter Christopher Lee and explorer Robert Walker Jr. find her and want to possess her. Can you blame the guys? Herbert Lom provides the villainy. Produced-written by Harry Alan Towers, directed by Jeremy Summers.

**EVE, THE WILD WOMAN (1968).** Italian monster mishmash with Brad Harris and Marc Lawrence controlling gorillas with electronic equipment. Directed by Robert Morris.

**EVERYTHING YOU ALWAYS WANTED TO KNOW ABOUT SEX BUT WERE AFRAID TO ASK (1972).** This has nothing to do with David Reuben's best-selling bedroom guide, but does have everything to do with the uninhibited Woody Allen, who has concocted some utterly bizarre sex comedy sketches, Such as Gene Wilder loving a sheep, or the giant breast that is sweeping the country, or the army of sperm cells, depicted as "well-trained" shock troops about to be "launched" on a new mission. John Carradine, Louise Lasser, Tony Randall, Burt Reynolds, Lynn Redgrave. (VC)

**EVERYTHING'S DUCKY (1961).** Nothing's "ducky" in a movie hinging on talking duck jokes. Duck out on this quackery about how sailors Buddy Hackett and Donald O'Connor (they get star "billing") find a duck that speaks. The daffy duck direction was by Don Taylor, the "duck you suckers" writing by John Fenton Murray and Benedict Freedman. Jackie Cooper, Joanie Summers and Roland Winters are "billed" at the bottom. This ultimately takes a tern for the worst. Teal us out.

**EVICTORS, THE (1979).** Writer-producer-director Charles B. Pierce purports this to be a true story of a "haunted" farmhouse in the South, but his execution lacks conviction and the kind of pseudodocumentary air that earmarked his superior LEGEND OF BIGFOOT. Surprises are telegraphed and cat-and-mouse suspense is tepid, with unsatisfying payoff. Wasted cast includes Michael Parks and Jessica Harper as innocent victims of scheming realtor Vic Morrow. Toss out THE EVICTORS.

**EVIL, THE (1978).** Along come Joanna Pettet and Richard Crenna to convert an old mansion into a drug rehab center, unaware of the house's bloody history. First thing they know, people and animals are going crazy at the height of electric storms, shutters are banging in the wind, the house trembles as though it were '06 again and there's a corpse in the dumbwaiter. There's also the lurking presences of Andrew Prine and Victor Buono, the latter as a demon from Hell shown sitting on his throne. "This house is trying to kill us all," remarks Crenna once he catches on to Donald Thompson's plot gimmick. The rent alone is enough to kill anyone. Directed by Gus Trikonis. (VC)

**EVIL BRAIN FROM OUTER SPACE (1964).** Japanese superhero Starman—or Super Giant, if you're inclined—saves Earth from alien invasion in re-edited episodes 7, 8, and 9 of the serial, SUPER GIANT. One wonders if the evil brain of the title actually belongs to producer Mitsugi Okura for endangering our own minds with juvenile science-fiction.

**EVIL DEAD, THE (1983).** Powerful cult favorite appreciated

**THE HUMAN MENACE TO E.T.: EVEREADY WITH A BATTERY OF PROBLEMS**

# E Stands for Effects . . .

RON COBB

RICHARD EDLUND

ROB BOTTIN

RICK BAKER

JOHN CARL BUECHLER WITH HIS GHOULIES

RAY HARRYHAUSEN WITH CREATIONS FROM 'CLASH OF THE TITANS'

CREATURE FEATURES MOVIE GUIDE

for excessive gore effects and sledgehammer techniques from a triumvirate of producers (line executive Robert Tapert, director Sam M. Raimi and actor Bruce Campbell). Made in Tennessee and Michigan, the film concerns a group of young adults finding a Book of the Dead from the Sumerian period in a wilderness cabin. Recited incantations open portals to another dimension and hideous demons wreak havoc. And havoc it is, as bodies are hacked to pieces—the only way to stop the evil entities. A crude effort full of visual shocks, reflecting talents in need of refinement. Duck those flying body parts and look out for the spattering blood. Sarah York, Betsy Baker, Ellen Sandweiss. (VC)

**EVIL EYE, THE (1962).** Mario Bava directed this psychoterror flick in Italy, involving a beautiful woman (Leticia Roman) in a series of bloody murders. Done in the style of DEEP RED, but not nearly as effective. John Saxon, Valentina Cortese.

**EVIL MIND.** TV and video title for the 1935 **CLAIRVOYANT, THE.**

**EVIL OF FRANKENSTEIN, THE (1964).** Hammer's third entry in its Frankenstein series is one of its least efforts, providing only laboratory-worn results. Director Freddie Francis and writer John Elder needed a good solid bolt of electricity in the as . . . pirations. Peter Cushing is back as the Baron with a yen for resurrecting the dead, and Kiwi Kingston, as the Monster, lumbers in caves and laboratories under Francis' own lumbering direction. The Monster doesn't get moving until late in the proceedings, too long preserved in a glacier. One of the least of Hammer's attempts. A new prologue was added for U.S. TV featuring William Phipps. Peter Woodthorpe, Duncan Lamont, Katy Wild. (VC)

**EVILS OF THE NIGHT (1983).** A silly waste of time and talent as Neville Brand and Aldo Ray portray outer space invaders who terrorize teenagers camping out for the weekend. John Carradine, Tina Louise and Julie Newmar are equally wasted by producer-director Mardi Rustam.

**EVILSPEAK (1982).** Dressed-up revamping of the-worm-that-turns tale. Clint Howad (Ron's brother) is a klutzy cadet at a military academy, picked on by four thoughtless juvenile peers. Uncovering a volume on satanic rituals, Clint conjures up Estabar the Demon, who delights in chopping off the heads of virgins. Howard uses a computer to call up the devil in a dungeon beneath the school's chapel. This is not a particularly good film and becomes slightly disgusting when a puppy is needlessly slaughtered by Howard's tormentors. What makes the film work, though, is Howard's ability to engender sympathy. R. G. Armstrong is sorely wasted as a drunken nightwatchman. Effects are only fair and Eric Weston's direction adequate. Some critics speak evil of EVILSPEAK. (VC)

**EWOK ADVENTURE, THE (1984).** Endor's moon, as any RETURN OF THE JEDI viewer knows, harbors primitive but intelligent creatures known as Ewoks, who speak an unintelligible language in groans and sighs and are adept with crude weapons. In this TV-movie, George Lucas' first, a starcruiser carrying a family of four crashlands. The parents are kidnapped by a snorting giant called the Gorax and two kids (Aubree Miller and Eric Walker) are befriended by the little furry ones and trek to find the Gorax. They encounter a vicious Tree Snake, hulking beasts, a lake that entraps those who fall into it and a firefly named Izirna. Bob Carrau's script is juvenile entertainment, but refreshing. Produced by Tom Smith and directed by John Korty in and around Marin County. Special effects by Dennis Muren, Michael Pangrazio, Phil Tippett and Jon Berg. Released in Europe as a feature as CARAVAN OF COURAGE: AN EWOK ADVENTURE. Fionnula Flanagan, Guy Boyd, Dan Frishman, Tony Cox.

**EWOK: THE BATTLE FOR ENDOR (1985).** Sequel to THE EWOK ADVENTURE, superior to the original because it's less a children's story and more an action adventure in the STAR WARS tradition. Aubree Miller is back as the lost Earthling, Cindel, who sees her parents killed in an attack by the evil alien Kerak and his seven-foot henchmen (lizardmen called Marauders). She escapes with Wicket the Ewok to begin adventures that lead her to a derelict named Noa (Wilford Brimley) and a cute little creature, Teek, who zips around

the Endor landscape like a flash. Action is nonstop when Cindel and Wicket are kidnaped by the evil witch Charal and taken to Karek's castle. Climactic battle is a steal from RETURN OF THE JEDI, but still a rousing time. Again, Tom Smith (the genius behind Industrial Light and Magic) is producer and again the story idea is George Lucas'. Jim and Ken Wheat co-wrote and co-directed. The effects are plentiful, featuring a killer dragon in a cave, stop-motion beasts of burden, a flying spaceship, countless laser beam zaps, and other visual delights for which Lucas is famous. Warwick Davis is good as Wicket, but it's Teek who almost steals this show.

**EXCALIBUR (1981).** John Boorman's violent interpretation of the King Arthur legend etches a brutal vision of the Middle Ages, intermingling myth and magic with gritty day-to-day hardships. Arthur (Nigel Terry) pulls the mystical Excalibur sword from a rock and then, with the help of Merlin the Magician (Nicol Williamson), forges a kingdom symbolized by

**AN EWOK WARRIOR**

the gallant Knights of the Round Table and the rest of the Camelot crowd. But there is also betrayal from his Queen Guinevere (Cherie Lunghi) and the royal knight Sir Lancelot (Nicholas Clay), and the ordeal of the Quest for the Holy Grail. Themes of success, failure and redemption run throughout this strange, lengthy period saga. Rospo Pallenberg co-scripted with Boorman. (VC)

**EXO-MAN (1977).** David Ackroyd portrays a professor paralyzed after being shot by a hitman, so he designs a cumbersome suit in which he can move around, terrorizing gangsters. Utterly ridiculous superhero material, even for a TV-movie, by Martin Caidin and Howard Rodman. Directed by Richard Irving. Harry Morgan, Jose Ferrer, Kevin McCarthy.

**EXORCISM (1986).** Devil cult terrorizes British countryside until evil can be overcome by good. (VC)

**EXORCISM'S DAUGHTER (1974).** Spanish attempt to cash in on the EXORCIST craze is a viewing hex on the U.S. market. The setting is a 19th Century asylum for the batty where Amelia Gade is incarcerated. Her doctor tries to help her realize she is buggy because of an exorcism ceremony she witnessed, but the doctor himself is attacked for witchcraft as he applies Freudian techniques on the couch. Written-directed by Rafael Morena Alba.

**EXORCIST, THE (1973).** Thinking man's horror picture juxtaposing graphic shock with allegorical levels of religion vs. evil, with William Peter Blatty adapted his best-seller for director William Friedkin. Everyone was shocked by the nauseous horrors suffered by young Linda Blair as she is possessed by an evil spirit: green vomit, ghastly makeup, foul-mouthed blasphemy, glassy sulphurous green eyes, a head that makes a 360-degree turn, etc. In the process, viewers overlooked many of the story's subtleties, which are of greater interest. How, for example, does the mother of priest Jason Miller fit in? How did the amulet come to be found by police inspector Lee J. Cobb? Concern yourself with these details, and less with the bilious visuals, and you will find THE EXORCIST richly rewarding. Excellently photographed by Owen Roizman and Billy Williams. Max von Sydow, Ellen Burstyn, Jack Mac-Gowran, Kitty Winn. Mercedes McCambridge provided the ugly voice of the Demon that blurts from Blair's mouth. (VC)

**EXORCIST—ITALIAN STYLE, THE (1975).** Italian spinoff of THE EXORCIST, but with a slight difference: Director Ciccio Ingrassia plays the demons and possession for comedy. After all, isn't possession nine tenths of the laughter? Lean back and enjoy, and hope the humor wasn't lost in the dubbed English voices. The production stars Ingrassia (isn't self-casting sweet?), with additional devilment by Lino Banfi and Didi Perego.

**EXORCIST II: THE HERETIC (1977).** An absolute fiasco directed by John Boorman—audiences laughed this hunkajunk off the screen, and it deserved debasing, being the funniest unintentional parody in movie history. Richard Burton, as a priest assigned to investigate the death of Father Karras (which took place in THE EXORCIST) overplays to the point of absurdity. And Louise Fletcher, as a psychiatrist probing the mind of Regan (Linda Blair), is downright amateurish. Don't ask about the plot—it involves James Earl Jones as African chief Kokumo and more mumbo jumbo than most witch doctors hear in a lifetime. Indescribable. The only good thing about this big-budgeted Warner Bros. failure is the cinematography by William Fraker, the set design, and the unusual Ennio Morricone score. Max Von Sydow returns in flashbacks. Ned Beatty, Kitty Winn, Paul Henreid. (VC)

**EXPERIMENT ALCATRAZ (1950).** Minor B-flick, offbeat in telling how doctor John Howard discovers a way of fighting blood diseases with atomic radiation when he uses "guinea pig" volunteers from Alcatraz Prison. The slight science-fictional elements are overshadowed by a typical crime plot; yet, writer Orville Hampton avoids enough cliches to make this

seem different. Directed by Edward L. Cahn. Harry Lauter, Joan Dixon, Robert Shayne.

**EXPERIMENT PERILOUS (1944).** Handsomely produced, unusually literate psychodrama capturing a Victorian air of mystery when doctor George Brent meets an old lady on a train that is imperiled by a storm. When she dies soon after, Brent is thrown headfirst into the enigmatic relationship between Paul Lukas and Hedy Lamarr, a couple who seem happily married . . . but beneath she is being slowly terrorized to death by Lukas, who is plagued by hereditary madness. An internalized detective story, almost totally cerebral until the action-packed climax. The few effects are remarkably good. Directed by Jacques Tourneur. Albert Dekker.

**EXPLORERS (1985).** The gentler side to director Joe Dante, who lightens up after GREMLINS by focusing on three appealing teenagers: One is a dreamer, another is a junior scientist while the third is a youth alienated from his family. Together they make contact with creatures from space, discover how to build a spaceship and fly to meet the E.T.s. That meeting is the funny side to CLOSE ENCOUNTERS as the cute bug-eyed creatures turn out to be TV lovers, who recite lines from cartoons and movies, pointing out how Earth beings are cruel, always destroying creatures from outer space. A charming science fantasy, beautifully written by Eric Luke, with great aliens created by Rob Bottin. Ethan Hawke, River Phoenix, Jason Presson, Mary Kay Place. One of the best of its genre. (VC)

**EXPLORING THE UNKNOWN (1977).** ESP documentary narrated by Burt Lancaster. TV quality.

**EXTERMINATING ANGEL, THE (1967).** Enigmatic, allegorical Luis Bunuel film set in an impressive mansion where several opera- goers gather for supper. Guests find they cannot leave the mansion; crowds gather outside yet cannot enter. Sheep wander in and are cooked over fires of furniture; a bear climbs a column; and an unattached hand drifts into view. Is this the Hell of the sterile rich? If you like them weird and unexplained, you might like it too. Sylvia Pinal, Claudio Brook, Jacqueline Andere. (VC)

**EXTERMINATORS OF THE YEAR 3000 (1984).** Italian-Spanish ripoff of THE ROAD WARRIOR set in a post-holocaust world where men fight for water after the ozone belt is destroyed. Our Mad Max lookalike drives a beat-up wreck equipped with weapons and radar called "The Exterminator," and battles a funky fleet of wheels commanded by Crazy Bull, a grotesque guerrilla who calls his men "Mother Grabbers." Its

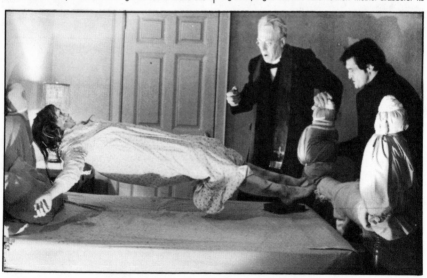

**LINDA BLAIR ON THE RISE IN 'THE EXORCIST'**

CREATURE FEATURES MOVIE GUIDE

## TWO EXTRATERRESTRIAL LIFE FORM UNITS IN 'EXPLORERS'

ineptitude is beyond comprehension and its entertainment value zero. Directed by Jules Harrison. Alicia Moro, Alan Collins, Eduardo Fajardo, Beryl Cunningham. (VC)

**EYE CREATURES, THE (1965).** Extraterrestrial invaders have plenty of eyeball sockets, but still stumble around stupidly as though lost in the dark of the Robert Gurney Jr.-Al Martin screenplay. Producer-director Larry Buchanan was blind not to see the worthlessness of the material. Said to be a remake of INVASION OF THE SAUCERMEN, but even that was better than this laughable trash. That noise you hear is this film hitting rock bottom. John Ashley, Cynthia Hull.

**EYE OF THE CAT (1969).** Michael Sarrazin and Gayle Hunnicutt (a gorgeous woman in miniskirts) plot to get rid of cat-lover Eleanor Parker—only Sarrazin suffers from ailurophobia, a fear of cats. Clever camera angles and exaggerated sound effects are used to hint of a supernatural feline, but how scary can a cat be? Producer Leslie Stevens' film also suffers from bad dialogue by Joseph Stefano and only toward the end does it take on a macabre air. San Francisco location photography (under David Lowe Rich's direction) is okay.

**EYE OF THE DEVIL (1967).** David Niven portrays a French vineyard owner sacrificing himself to the grape gods to stop a three-year famine. The demands of hooded demon worshippers are fought by his wife Deborah Kerr until she is in as much peril as her husband. The supporting cast—Donald Pleasence, Sharon Tate, Flora Robson, David Hemmings and Edward Mulhare—is largely wasted in this film heavily butchered for the U.S. market.

**EYEBALL (1974).** Here's one to turn on gore lovers: murderer kills, then pops out his victim's eyeballs. Nearsighted Italian-Spanish release is about as exciting as watching an eye chart in an optician's office. Director-writer Umberto Lenzi is in need of seeing-eye dogs. John Richardson, Martine Brochard. (VC)

**EYES BEHIND THE STARS (1972).** Photographer and model are in the woods taking photos when the cameraman senses an alien presence. Eventually he has an encounter too close for comfort. Cheap UFO pseudothriller showing how the government suppresses flying saucer reports. Rejected

"Blue Book" material. Directed by Roy Garrett. Martin Balsam, Nathalie Delon, Robert Hoffmann.

**EYES OF A STRANGER (1981).** Epitomizes all the lousy, sleazy, scuzzy movies in the slasher genre. Tom Savini's make-up effects are extra bloody and well done, but that's all that flows freely in this cramped, brainless exercise in murderous behavior. Mark Jackson and E. L. Bloom have concocted the tale of how a TV reporter tracks down the killer in her own neighborhood. Directed by Ken Wiederhorn, who brought us SHOCK WAVES. Lauren Tewes, John Di Santi, Jennifer J. Leigh. (VC)

**EYES OF ANNIE JONES, THE (1964).** ESP combined with a girl who walks in her sleep add up to a corpse. Her strange mumblings become less strange as an ordinary murder plot unfolds. The eyes do not have it. British-U.S. production directed by Reginald LeBorg. Richard Conte, Francesca Annis, Joyce Carey.

**EYES OF CHARLES SAND (1972).** Peter Haskell suffers flashes of precognition, deja vu, visions and foresight as he solves a murder surrounding a family that lives in an old but beautiful mansion. Nicely directed by Reza Badiyi, plenty of atmosphere, but Henry Farrell-Stanford Whitmore plot is predictable. Hugh Benson, Adam West, Barbara Rush, Sharon Farrell, Joan Bennett.

**EYES OF EVIL.** See **THOUSAND EYES OF DR. MABUSE, THE.**

**EYES OF HELL.** See **MASK, THE.**

**EYES OF LAURA MARS (1978).** Chic photographer Faye Dunaway, a specialist in blending sex and sadism in her morbid photo lay-outs, is inexplicably linked to a psychokiller, but this link is never explored, and the film becomes a simple-minded one-murder-after-the-other plot until the maniac closes in on Dunaway. John Carpenter's original concept was revised by David Zelag Goodman. Directed by Irvin Kershner. Tommy Lee Jones co-stars as the cop investigating the mess of corpses. Intriguing premise ultimately suffers from producer Jon Peters' blindness to story quality. Brad Dourif, Rene Auberjonois, Raul Julia. (VC)

**EYES WITHOUT A FACE.** See **HORROR CHAMBER OF DR. FAUSTUS, THE.**

---

*"I created you, Super Germ!" —The Typical Mad Scientist in*
### EVIL BRAIN FROM OUTER SPACE.

KD

*"I've seen enough horror movies to know that any weirdo wearing a mask isn't very friendly." —Girl victim-to-be in*
**FRIDAY THE 13TH PART 6: JASON LIVES.**

**FABULOUS BARON MUNCHAUSEN, THE (1961).** From the Czechs who did THE FABULOUS WORLD OF JULES VERNE . . . an ingenious blending of live action with animation, based on old Gustav Dore engravings. A first-man-on-the-moon story told by writer-director Karel Zeman with great style and panache. Milos Kopecky, Jana Brejchova.

**FABULOUS JOE (1947).** Joe is a dog. So is this Hal Roach film, directed by Harve Foster. You see, Joe talks, and there's nothing duller in Hollywood farces than talking dogs. Walter Abel, Marie Wilson, Sheldon Leonard, Donald Meek.

**FABULOUS JOURNEY TO THE CENTER OF THE EARTH (1977).** See **WHERE TIME BEGAN.**

**FABULOUS WORLD OF JULES VERNE, THE (1961).** Czech combination of live action and animation (dubbed Mystimation) is a visual delight, wherein several Verne stories are woven together with threads of fantasy. Whether in the clouds in novel airships, under the sea in a submarine or on the ground, this flight-into-fantasy-adventure is charming and exciting. Written and directed by Karel Zeman. Lubor Tokos, Arnost Navratil, Miroslav Holub. (VC)

**FACE BEHIND THE MASK (1941).** Worth seeing for Peter Lorre's performance as a fire-victim who hides his disfigurement behind a mask, then falls in love with a blind woman. His involvement with crooks spells his undoing. Despite the low budget and B-quality direction by Robert Florey, this has a tragic quality instilled by Lorre's performance. Evelyn Keyes, Don Beddoe, James Seay, George E. Stone.

**FACE OF ANOTHER, THE (1966).** Hiroshi Teshigahara, director of WOMAN IN THE DUNES, offers another haunting tale with allegorical overtones: A man (Tatsuya Nakadai), horribly disfigured in an accident, turns into an outcast. Paranoia drives him to a psychiatrist-plastic surgeon who produces a life-like mask of a stranger's face. Nakadai assumes the personality of that stranger. A very odd movie, in a style purely Japanese. Eiji Okada.

**FACE OF EVE.** See **EVE.**

**FACE OF FEAR.** See **PEEPING TOM.**

**FACE OF FIRE (1958).** James Whitmore is excellent as a well-liked handyman who tries to save a child during a fire and is so badly burned that he nauseates those who see him. Weak of mind and spirit, he becomes an outcast. Based on Stephen Crane's "The Monster." Directed by Albert Band. Cameron Mitchell, Bettye Ackerman, Royal Dano, Lois Maxwell. Filmed in Sweden.

**FACE OF FU MANCHU, THE (1965).** Hammer's resurrection of the Sax Rohmer villain, with Christopher Lee as the inscrutable, insidious Oriental planning to destroy the world with a new form of poison invented by a German he holds prisoner in the heart of London. Nigel Green is the heroic Sir Nayland Smith of Scotland Yard. Don Sharp directed this Harry Alan Towers production, which Towers wrote. Tsai Chin is Fu's daughter, Karin Dor a hapless captive, Walter Rilla the inventive scientist. There were five sequels, the next being BRIDES OF FU MANCHU.

**FACE OF MARBLE (1946).** Eyes of stone could result from watching this lower berth Monogram horror thriller, by today's standards barely watchable. You have to be a real fan of John Carradine to sit through this. Carradine is a scientist who brings humans and animals back from the dead—with predictable, he-shouldn't-have-tampered-with-science results. Directed by William "Hack-em-Out" Beaudine. Robert Shayne, Willie Best, Maris Wrixon, Claudia Drake.

**FACE OF TERROR (1962).** Spanish import—about a disfigured girl who undergoes beauty transfiguration—underwent its own surgery at the trembling hands of U.S. film doctors. Hence, a plastic movie. Only a special fluid will keep a young woman alive—you'll need a transfusion just to stay awake. Directed by Isidoro Martinez Ferry; U.S. footage by director William Hole Jr. Lisa Gaye, Fernando Rey.

**FACE OF THE SCREAMING WEREWOLF, THE (1960).** A Mexican production starring Lon Chaney Jr., originally a horror comedy, but when American repackager Jerry Warren recut and redubbed, he left the laughs on the editing room floor. You might still think it's funny, but for the wrong reasons. Directed by Gilberto Martinez Solares, it offers Chaney Jr. in a performance clumsy and inept by any standards. It'll give you the screaming mimies.

**FADE TO BLACK (1980).** Compelling study of a misunderstood, lonely young man (Dennis Christopher) who fantasizes images from movies and often assumes the guises of famous monsters, such as the Mummy, Dracula, etc. Finally reality and fantasy are indistinguishable and Christopher the worm turns on those who abused him. These killings are cleverly conceived—in fact, the entire film has a sense of originality (credit writer-director Vernon Zimmerman). Linda Kerridge is a wonderful Marilyn Monroe lookalike, Tim Thomerson is a cop. Clips from THE CREATURE FROM THE BLACK LAGOON. (VC)

**FAHRENHEIT 451 (1966).** The title refers to the temperature at which paper catches fire and burns. This is apropos to a plot set in the future when books have been outlawed and special "firemen" seek out and destroy any volumes still in existence. Oskar Werner is such a fireman who discovers the delights of reading and rebels against the regime. Based on the novel by Ray Bradbury, and directed by Francois Truffaut, this has met with mixed emotions—some feel it captures the poetry of Bradbury, others feel the premise is too absurd. Decidedly for the fans of science-fiction and/or Bradbury who appreciate the literate side to the genre. Julie Christie appears in a dual role. Nicolas Roeg photographed it, Bernard Herrmann wrote the wonderful music. Anton Diffring, Cyril Cusack, Anna Palk, Jeremy Spencer. (VC)

**FAIL SAFE (1964).** Sidney Lumet's version of the Eugene Burdick- Harvey Wheeler best-seller approaches impending nuclear war as a politico-horror thriller, a portrait of inexorable doom. Stark black-and-white photography by Gerald Herschfeld and electrifying acting by Henry Fonda, Dan O'Herlihy and Walter Matthau make this superior apocalypse science-fiction which comments all too effectively on our militancy and inability to control machines we have created to protect us. The plot (scripted by Walter Bernstein) has a U.S. bomber accidentally unleashing a nuclear device on Moscow. To keep peace, the President (Fonda) faces sending one of our own planes to bomb New York City. Dark and gripping. Larry Hagman, Dom DeLuise, Fritz Weaver. (VC)

**FALCON'S GOLD (1982).** Pulp adventure with mild science-fictional overtones: A chunk of meteorite holds the key to laser power, and various governments are after the secret of its destructive properties. The action is slam-bang and there's little time to consider the story holes and absurdities. As old-fashioned as B movies and just as brainless. Simon MacCorkindale, Louise Vallance and John Marley star. Directed by Bob Schulz, scripted by Olaf Pooley. In videocassette as **ROBBERS OF SACRED MOUNTAIN.**

**FALL OF THE HOUSE OF USHER (1948).** Old British geezers at the Gresham Club drink Scotch and soda while one of them reads a story by Edgar Allan Poe. The famous tale is mangled terribly, parts of its faithful to the original, other parts mere fabrication. Most of the time Lady Madoline flits around the castle in a negligee carrying a candelabra while Roderick Usher tries to prevent a curse caused by his mother's severed head. Incredibly amateurish film, poorly acted and edited, with terrible sound. Ultimately unwatchable under the misdirection of the blighter Ivan Barnett. Gwendoline Watford, Kay Tendeter, Irving Steen.

**FALL OF THE HOUSE OF USHER, THE.** Videocassette title of Roger Corman's **HOUSE OF USHER, THE.**

**FALL OF THE HOUSE OF USHER, THE (1979).** Terrible TV version of Poe's classic story with wild-eyed, wild-haired Martin Landau overacting as Roderick Usher while his sister walks the hallways in a zombie-like trance. Ray Walston is the faithful family retainer who mumbles mumbo jumbo jumpily just as the castle's weakened foundations tremble and tumble around him. Story line by Stephen Lord falls apart faster than Usher's estate. Directed by James L. Conway. Charlene Tilton (of DALLAS) plays that whacky sister. (VC)

**FALSE FACE.** See **SCALPEL.**

**FAN, THE (1981).** Weak slasher film failing to believably portray disturbed Michael Biehn and his reign of terror

**CHRISTOPHER LEE IN 'THE FACE OF FU MANCHU'**

directed against an aging but attractive Broadway actress (Lauren Bacall). Nor is there enough graphic violence or suspense to sustain the film's running time. James Garner is totally wasted as Lauren's husband, although Maureen Stapleton is good as the actress' personal secretary caught up in the knife horrors. Directed by Edward Bianchi. From a novel by Bob Randall. (VC)

**FANATIC.** See **DIE, DIE MY DARLING.**

**FANGORIA'S WEEKEND OF HORRORS (1986).** Videocassette of a horror magazine convention for fans featuring interviews with make-up artist Rick Baker, directors Tobe Hooper and Wes Craven and actor Robert Englund. (VC)

**FANGS (1978).** Killer reptiles and serpents put the bite on the enemies of a snake lover. Proved to be poisonous at the box office. Fangs but no FANGS. Les Tremayne, Janet Wood, Bebe Kelly, Marvin Kaplan, Alice Nunn.

**FANGS OF THE LIVING DEAD (1968).** "The coldness of the grave is in my blood," remarks one of the buxom, frilly-

**LINDA KERRIDGE IN 'FADE TO BLACK'**

gowned vampire women in this Italian rehash of DRACULA. The star is Anita Ekberg, who plays with such naivete, it becomes fascinating to watch her act the part of a virgin. Inherting a castle, she arrives to discover a suspicious baron and a harem of busty, lusty bloodsuckers. The color, production and ladies are nice on the eyes but this is ultimately an exercise in tedium, with a terrible ending. Anyway, fangs for the mammaries, Anita. Written-directed by Armando De Ossorio. Also known as MALENKA THE VAMPIRE.

**FANTASIA (1941).** Amalgam of cartoon art set to classical music (by Leopold Stokowski and the Philadelphia Symphony Orchestra) was a daring, revolutionary experiment by Walt Disney, animated by artists visually interpreting the music. Each sequence explores an element of the fantastic—from a Bach of abstract designs to a "Nutcracker Suite" of magical sprites and dancing mushrooms; from Mickey Mouse in "The Sorcerer's Apprentice" to Stravinsky's "Rite of Spring," a pageant of life's evolution depicting primeval ooze, dinosaurs and global holocaust. Centaurettes, dimpled cupids and winged horses frolic in Beethoven's "Pastoral Symphony," followed by Ponchielli's "Dance of the Hours" featuring pirouetting hippotami and ostriches. Moussorgsky's "Night on Bald Mountain" is of macabre design.

**FANTASIES (1982).** TV-movie, cashing in on the theatrical slasher craze in watered-down style, depicts a standard mad-dog killer out to wipe out the cast and crew of a TV soap opera—and if you've ever seen a soap opera, you can understand why. Directed by William Wiard. Suzanne Pleshette, Barry Newman, Patrick O'Neal, Robert Vaughn, Madlyn Rhue, Lenora May, Allyn Ann McLerie.

**FANTASTIC ANIMATION FESTIVAL (1977).** Melange of cartoons from all over the world in a variety of styles—from Max Fleischer's SUPERMAN to the famed BAMBI MEETS GODZILLA. An exciting, eclectic bag of animated goodies certain to strike the fancy of fantasy buffs. (VC)

**FANTASTIC DISAPPEARING MAN, THE.** See **CURSE OF DRACULA, THE.**

**FANTASTIC INVASION OF PLANET EARTH.** See **BUBBLE, THE.**

**FANTASTIC JOURNEY (1977).** Bruce Lansbury TV-movie, pilot for a short-lived series, in which scientists are stranded on an island in the Bermuda Triangle, which turns out to be a time continuum limbo area from which characters can enter past or future. Also on the island is a man from the 23rd Century. Hodgepodge of ideas and cliches (of TV mentality) as the cast encounters pirates, aliens and hooligans from Atlantis. Directed by Andrew V. McLaglen. Carl Franklin, Scott Thomas, Leif Erickson, Ike Eisenmann, Susan Howard.

**FANTASTIC PLANET (1973).** Winner of the Grand Prix at Cannes, this science-fiction cartoon was made in Prague's Czechoslovakian animated studio, drawn by Roland Topor and directed by Rene Laloux. Herein is the marvelous flavor of an alien world, Ygam, on which the Draags (39 feet high, with red and blue eyes) come into conflict with the Oms (tiny creatures treated as pets) when the Oms overmultiply. Voices by Barry Bostwick, Olan Soule, Marvin Miller. (VC)

**FANTASTIC VOYAGE (1966).** Submarine and crew are miniaturized to microscopic size and injected via hypodermic needle into the bloodstream of a scientist who has been shot by foreign agents and will die unless the crew can voyage through his body to his brain and destroy a bloodclot with a laser beam. Imaginatively executed, with tremendous effects for their time. In this bizarre inner world of the body, the simplest things become obstacles: an artery is a whirlpool, blood corpuscles are deadly attackers, etc. Set designs—how the body would look to a microbe—are breathtaking; of lesser interest are crew members bickering as the sub passes through livers and other vital organs. Richard Fleischer directed for producer Saul David, Harry Kleiner fleshed out the wonderful ideas by Jerome Bixby and Otto Klement. Stephen Boyd, Arthur Kennedy, Raquel Welch, Donald Pleasence, Arthur O'Connell, Edmond O'Brien. (VC)

**FANTASTIC WORLD OF D.C. COLLINS (1984).** Soul brother's Walter Mitty with touches of WARGAMES and

CLOAK AND DAGGER when imaginative child Gary Coleman is caught up in spy shenanigans with Soviet agents over possession of a videotape that holds the key to the prevention of nuclear war. As he undergoes the espionage chase, Coleman daydreams he's Clint Eastwood, James Bond, Indiana Jones and Luke Skywalker in parody flashbacks. Routine TV-movie, totally predictable; strictly for kids. Bernie Casey, Shelly Smith, Michael Ansara, George Gobel, Marilyn McCoo. Directed by Leslie Martinson.

**FANTASIST, THE (1986).** The second feature of writer-director Robin Hardy, who first brought us THE WICKER MAN. Here he deals with a psychokiller who poses his nude female victims as famous paintings before knifing them to death. Odd and kinky. Moira Harris, Timothy Bottoms.

**FANTASY FILM WORLD OF GEORGE PAL, THE (1986).** Fascinating documentary on one of Hollywood's most beloved producers of fantasy and science-fiction, whose DESTINATION MOON, WHEN WORLDS COLLIDE and WAR OF THE WORLDS established trends in their time. Tony Curtis, Ray Bradbury and Ray Harryhausen are among the personalities who discuss Pal's warm character and con-

**PRODUCER-DIRECTOR GEORGE PAL**

tributions to cinema. Footage from many of Pal's lavish productions. Written-directed by Arnold Leibovit.

**FANTASY ISLAND (1976).** Two-hour pilot for the long-running TV series starring Ricardo Montalban as Mr. Rourke, the director of a tropical paradise which caters to satisfying the fantasies of guests for the mere sum of $50,000. Ricardo's short little pal Tattoo, Herve Villechaize, exclaims "De plane, boss, de plane!" and went on doing it for several seasons. There's only a slight touch of fantasy in this Aaron Spelling-Leonard Goldberg production—mainly in how Montalban pulls off those fantasies. Directed by Richard Lang. Bill Bixby, Sandra Dee, Peter Lawford, Carol Lynley, Hugh O'Brian, Victoria Principal, Dick Sargent. (VC)

**FAREWELL TO THE PLANET OF THE APES (1974).** Re-edited episodes of the TV series PLANET OF THE APES with Roddy McDowall as Galen the chimp, a fugitive in a kingdom of monkeys and orangs along with two Earthlings who have to keep hiding from search parties. Directed by Don McDougall and J. M. Lucas. Roscoe Lee Browne, Joanna Barnes, Frank Aletter, Ron Harper, James Naughton.

**FAT SPY, THE (1966).** Rarely shown (for good reason) fantasy comedy in which Jack E. Leonard spends most of the time looking for the Fountain of Youth on an island off Florida. He also finds Jayne Mansfield and other characters before meeting up with none other than Ponce de Leon. Not heavy with original ideas; flabby gags. Directed by Joseph Brun. Phyllis Diller, Jordan Christopher, Brian Donlevy.

**FATAL ATTRACTION (1985).** Minor psycho-game thriller set in Toronto where Sally Kellerman literally runs into scientist Stephen Lack in a head-on collision. Later, they are sexually attracted and discover they have a penchant for playing odd games with each other. Mildly mind-bending, but climax is predictable. John Huston appears as Lack's scientist-father. Produced-directed by Michael Grant. (VC)

**FATAL GAMES (1984).** At the Falcon Academy of Athletics, seven teenagers work out for the Olympics, unaware one of them is crazy and eager to spill their blood at the end of a javelin. Although some effort is made to examine the 1984 Olympics in L.A., this is just another slasher flick. Directed by Michael Elliott. Sally Kirkland, Lynn Banashek, Sean Masterson, Nicholas Love. (VC)

**FEAR (1981).** Italian psychothriller set in an isolated country home where several beautiful women are slaughtered by a killer, but not before they've flitted about in various stages of ous breakdown, and must be nuts, but we know better, don't we, fans? The trick ending by writers Jimmy Sangster and Michael Syson is telegraphed, so the shocker holds few surprises. Sangster directed. Joan Collins, Ralph Bates, Peter Cushing, James Cossins. (VC)

**FEAR NO EVIL (1969).** One of two Universal TV-movies (the other is RITUAL OF EVIL) to star Louis Jourdan as psychic ghost chaser David Sorell and Wilfrid Hyde-White as his Watson-like companion, Harry Snowden, an expert in the occult. Bradford Dillman portrays a scientist who buys an old mirror but is killed shortly after in a car crash. His fiance discovers the mirror has strange properties to bring his spirit back. Atmospheric supernatural thriller, tensely directed by Paul Wendkos, adapted by Richard Alan Simmons from a Guy Endore story. Lynda Day, Carroll O'Connor, Marsha Hunt.

**FEAR NO EVIL (1981).** Director Frank LaLoggia helms this above-average, below-expensive supernatural tale featuring some zippy effects. The plot is a bit convoluted and implausible (three Archangles descend to Earth to take on human guises to combat Lucifer and his army of zombies), and there's too much emphasis on a plot involving teenagers,

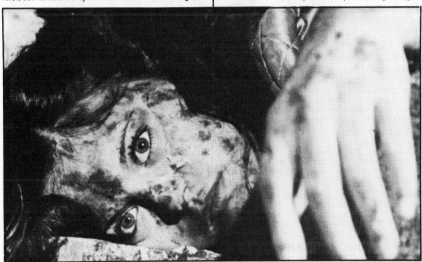

**A VICTIM OF LUCIFER'S ARMY OF LIVING DEAD IN 'FEAR NO EVIL' (1981)**

undress or tossed off everything for love sequences. Some black magic touches give this an added sense of weirdness, but it's all very typical for the genre. Directed by Riccardo Freda. Stefano Patrizi, Martine Brochard. (VC)

**FEAR CHAMBER, THE (1974).** One of four Mexican-produced cheapies made by Boris Karloff in 1968 shortly before his death, but not released for several years. Karloff fans will not be impressed—the Master has only a few scenes as an aging, benevolent scientist who keeps a living rock in his laboratory, unaware his underlings are feeding it beautiful women to control its appetite. Written-directed by Jack Hill. Yerye Beirut, Julissa, Carlos East. (VC)

**FEAR IN THE NIGHT (1947).** Cornell Woolrich's "Nightmare" is the plot of this low budgeter with DeForrest Kelley as a musician who wakes up thinking he murdered someone in the night. He turns to a policeman relative (Paul Kelly) for help, retracing his steps. Evidence mounts that it was no dream. Written-directed by Maxwell Shane, who remade this in 1956 with Edward G. Robinson. Ann Doran, Kay Scott, Jeff York, Robert Emmett Keane.

**FEAR IN THE NIGHT (1973).** Hammer psychothriller with Judy Geeson as a bride being terrorized at a deserted school for boys. Everyone thinks she's still recovering from a nerv-

but overall execution and artistry are good. Elizabeth Hoffmann, Dick Burt, R. J. Silverthorn. (VC)

**FEARLESS FRANK (1967).** Obscure satire on superheroes starring Jon Voight as a young man murdered by criminals who is brought back by a scientist as a caped fighter of crime. An odd mixture with mixed oddities—director Philip Kaufman's best work was yet to come. Monique Van Vooren, Severn Darden, Nelson Algren, Lou Gilbert.

**FEARLESS VAMPIRE KILLERS, THE (1967).** Roman Polanski's lampoonery of the vampire genre is an uneven olio, a mixture of cleverness and inanity that never fully jells. There's a lot of idiotic clowning as a professor (Jack MacGowran) and his assistant (Polanski) invade the castle of Count Von Krolock (Ferdy Mayne). Because these characters are such dunderheads, the foils (and fools) of parody, they are of little interest no matter how much fun is made of wooden stakes and other vampire-hunting accoutrements. Sharon Tate is a girl in a bathtub, and her scene is the funniest. Alfie Bass, Fiona Lewis, Ian Quarrier, Ron Lacey.

**FEAST OF FLESH.** See BLOOD FEAST.

**FEDERAL AGENTS VS. UNDERWORLD INC.** See GOLDEN HANDS OF KURIGAL.

## THE ASSORTED FACES OF PETER SELLERS IN 'FIENDISH PLOT OF FU MANCHU'

**FEMALE BUTCHER.** See **LEGEND OF BLOOD CASTLE.**

**FEMALE TRAP.** See **NAME OF THE GAME IS KILL, THE.**

**FERAT VAMPIRE (1983).** Czech horror-fantasy, intended as a comedy- parody of vampire flicks, but with a twist: The bloodsucker is a sports car that runs on blood, not gasoline. Put your foot on the accelerator and a needle pops through the foot pedal, sucking your life's fluid. And we don't mean oil. Directed by Juraz Herz on squealing wheels.

**FER-DE-LANCE (1974).** Promising premise for a TV-movie shocker—a deadly serpent loose aboard an atomic submarine—has minimum suspense values. Directed by Russell Mayberry, scripted by producer Leslie Stevens. David Janssen is the captain of the sub, Hope Lange his love interest. Ivan Dixon, Jason Evers, Ben Piazza. (VC)

**FIEND (1980).** Regional semi-professional horror thriller from writer-producer-editor-gofer Don Dohler (THE ALIEN FACTOR) about a supernatural firefly that eats its way into corpses and brings them to life. Richard Nelson, Elaine White, George Stover, Greg Dohler (nepotism?) (VC)

**FIEND, THE (1971).** See **BEWARE MY BRETHREN.**

**FIEND WITH THE ELECTRONIC BRAIN.** See **BLOOD OF GHASTLY HORROR.**

**FIEND WITHOUT A FACE (1958).** A favorite "alien invader" thriller with grotesque brain-spine creatures which attach to heads and suck away human brains . . . positively unsettling monsters. Locale is a Canadian Air Force base where rocket experiments are underway and have caused human thoughts to be turned into the attacking brain creatures. This Richard Gordon production is highly recommended for its macabre overtones. Directed by Arthur Crabtree. Marshall Thompson, Kim Parker, Terence Kilburn, Peter Madden. (VC)

**FIENDISH GHOULS, THE.** See **FLESH AND THE FIENDS.**

**FIENDISH PLOT OF DR. FU MANCHU (1980).** Peter Sellers' last film (SON OF THE GONG SHOW?) is not his best as he portrays Sax Rohmer's insidious Oriental in search of an eternal youth serum, with fantasy contraptions randomly thrown in. Sellers plays many characters: Fu Manchu at 168, a younger Fu after drinking the youth elixir, an antiques dealer, and British detective Nayland Smith. Smith's stuffiness and British demeanor are the funniest satiric touches in this mess directed by Piers Haggard. David Tomlinson, Helen Mirren, Steve Franken, Burt Kwouk. (VC)

**FIFTH MISSILE, THE (1986).** TV-movie based on the Frank Robinson-Thomas Scortia novel THE GOLD CREW, in which a Polaris submarine, on a mission to simulate all-out war with the Soviets, is stricken by toxic poison in the ventilating system. Captain David Soul and crew prepare to launch a real missile on Russia. Only Robert Conrad, Richard Roundtree and Sam Waterston stand in the way of world doom. Only mildly exciting. Directed by Larry Peerce.

**FIGHTING DEVIL DOGS.** See **TORPEDO OF DOOM.**

**FILMGORE (1983).** Compilation videocassette of blood-and-gore scenes from graphic horror movies, including THE TEXAS CHAINSAW MASSACRE, DRILLER KILLER, SNUFF, 2000 MANIACS, BLOOD FEAST, etc. etc. Produced by Charles Band, himself a king of schlock, directed by Ken Dixon, with music by Richard Band. (VC)

**FINAL CONFLICT, THE (1981).** Third and final film in THE OMEN series, as godless as its predecessors. Damien Thorn (Sam Neill), the Antichrist, has grown up to become Ambassador to the Court of St. James to be close to the birth site (near London) of the Son of God, whose Second Coming is prophesized in the Book of Revelation. The gory murders are numerous (though not as imaginative as those in THE OMEN and DAMIEN: OMEN II) as the Son of Satan defends himself against priest-assassins armed with the Seven Sacred Daggers of Meggido. The "final conflict" between the Antichrist and the Son of God is poorly developed by scriptwriter Andrew Birkin, but producer Harvey Bernhard's film still has a compelling "sickness" and a good pseudo-religious score by Jerry Goldsmith. Rossano Brazzi, Don Gordon. (VC)

**FINAL COUNTDOWN, THE (1980).** Filmed aboard the USS Nimitz, this is an excellent semidocumentary approach to showing our navy and air force in action. The plot—in which the carrier is caught in a time warp and sent back to Pearl Harbor in 1941 on the eve of the Japanese attack—sounds ingenious on paper, but assorted screenwriters never came to grips with the promising twists. Kirk Douglas, Martin Sheen, Katharine Ross, James Farentino, Ron O'Neal and Charles Durning must work with limited dialogue and limited characterizations; the pilots and jetfighters come off looking great in aerial footage. Directed by Don Taylor. (VC)

**FINAL EXAM (1981).** Tame slasher film made in South Carolina, a clone of HALLOWEEN, right down to the piano plinking when the killer pops into frame. Writer-director Jimmy Huston saves the goriest scenes for last as a fiendish murderer slaughters dumb students. Most of the time FINAL EXAM deals with college campus pranks, hazings and crude jokes, and engages in idle chatter designed to pass as character "development." Huston's writing is so weak that the killer's identity is never given, and his motive thrown away in dialogue that will go over the heads of many. Cecile Bagdadi, Joel S. Rice, Ralph Brown, Timothy L. Raynor. (VC)

**FINAL EXECUTIONER, THE (1985).** In a post-apocalyse world, the rich hunt the mutants in yet another Italian Mad Max spinoff. But when they run out of mutants, they begin killing ordinary people like you and me. Cybernetics specialist William Mang and former policeman Woody Strode go after the hunters. Poorly done. Directed by Romolo Guerrieri. (VC)

**FINAL EYE.** See **COMPUTERCIDE.**

**FINAL PROGRAMME, THE.** Another videocasssette title for **LAST DAYS OF MAN ON EARTH, THE.**

**FINAL TERROR, THE (1983).** Samuel Arkoff's film was released at the end of the slasher cycle, but Rachel Ward and Daryl Hannah in a cast of unknowns indicates this was produced around 1981 but kept shelved until someone decided to exploit the new stars. A busload of fire rangers and girlfriends travels into the gloomy woods near Crescent City, Calif., to be stalked by a toothless hag who eats raw dogmeat and keeps severed hands in her Mason jars. Body count is low, making this of minimum interest to splatter seekers. Director Andrew Davis should have worked for Western Union—he telegraphs his messages so well. Only the photography by A. Davidescu, which captures a sunless forest and a constantly dreary sky, brings any mood or style to this pathetic film. John Friedrich, Adrian Zmed, Mark Metcalf and Lewis Smith are among the louts messing up our beautiful forests. Where the hell is Smoky the Bear? (VC)

**FINAL WAR, THE.** See **LAST WAR, THE.**

**FINGERS AT THE WINDOW (1942).** Basil Rathbone portrays a mad hypnotist who bids the weak-minded and feeble-willed to axe to death his adversaries. Weak thriller directed by Charles Lederer cannot be salvaged by Rathbone, Lew Ayres, Laraine Day or Miles Mander.

**FINIAN'S RAINBOW (1968).** It took Hollywood two decades to make a film from the popular 1947 stage play by E. Y. Harburg and Fred Saidy, which featured the hit songs "How Are Things in Glocca Morra?", "Old Devil's Moon" and "When I'm Not Near the Girl I Love," primarily because the story dealt with race relations. This worthy attempt, directed by Francis Ford Coppola and scripted by Harburg and Saidy, is a bit erratic. The Burton Lane music is still great but the story is dated. And Fred Astaire seems out of place as Finian, who raises crops near Fort Knox by planting a pot of gold he swiped from leprechauns. Petula Clark, Tommy Steele, Keenan Wynn, Don Francks, Al Freeman Jr. (VC)

**FIRE AND ICE (1982).** Excellently animated sword-and-sorcery fantasy-adventure set in a world where evil ice king Nekron uses glacial spears to destroy his enemy, namely the kingdom of Firekeep. His mother Juliana orders the kidnapping of Firekeep's princess, a sexy number who is rescued by a young hero during a series of exciting adventures. What makes this outstanding is the superb art by Frank Frazetta, who worked under writer-producer-director Ralph Bakshi. The film was rotoscoped to give it that life-like quality within the context of animation. Comic book fans will especially grove on this. Voices by Leo Gordon, Susan Tyrrell, Randy Norton, Sean Hannon and Cynthia Leake. (VC)

**FIRE IN THE SKY, A (1978).** TV imitation of METEOR (this came out first but is still a ripoff) stars a comet on a collision course with Earth—destined to hit Phoenix, Ariz., and wipe it out. We're talking off the face of the Earth! Astronomers Richard Crenna and Joanna Miles warn mankind. But do you think mankind listens? Don't expect much in the line of special effects; this consists of characters running around frantically, ignoring Crenna's predicitons or behaving selfishly. Directed by Jerry Jameson. Andrew Duggan, Elizabeth Ashley, Lloyd Bochner, David Dukes.

**FIRE MAIDENS FROM OUTER SPACE (1956).** British science-fiction flick with a ridiculous plot concocted by director-writer Cy Roth: Space explorers (ineptly led by Anthony Dexter) discover a race of beautiful women carrying out sacrifices to the black gods on a moon near Jupiter. By all means, catch it if you want to have a thousand laughs at the expense of Susan Shaw, Paul Carpenter and Harry Fowler. And dig the females dancing to the music of Borodin!

**FIRE MONSTERS AGAINST THE SON OF HERCULES (1962).** Too much brawn and not enough brain in this Italian muscle epic set during the Ice Age, with pecs champion Reg Lewis fighting off a three-headed monster (square vs. ice cube?) Grunt and bear it. Written-directed by Guido Malatesta. Margaret Lee, Myra Kent, Luciano Marin.

**FIREBIRD 2015 A.D. (1981).** Political fantasy in the vein of ROAD WARRIOR in which gasoline is no longer available and illegal bands of motorcyclists search for fuel. Mostly action and car maneuvers, very little fantasy. Directed by David M. Robertson; no writing credit given to protect the guilty. Darren McGavin, Doug McClure, George Touliatos, Mary Beth Rubens, Alex Diakun. (VC)

**FIREFOX (1982).** One of Clint Eastwood's lousiest pictures: dark, melancholy, clumsy, when it should be zappy and fast-paced. FIREFOX depicts has-been pilot Mitchell Gant (Eastwood) being sent to Russia to steal a new jet fighter equipped with weapons controlled by human thought. Little is made of this premise—the plot unfolds like a plodding grade-B spy movie. The characters are unbelievable; even Eastwood looks puzzled about his role. John Dykstra provides nice flying sequences, but they don't make up for deficiencies in Eastwood's directing or in the Alex Lasker-Wendell Wellman script, adapted from Craig Thomas' novel.

*"Eliminate the Nazarene . . . fail, and you will be condemned to a numbing eternity in the flaccid bosom of Christ." —The AntiChrist (Sam Neill) in* **THE FINAL CONFLICT.**

Freddie Jones, David Huffman, Ronald Lacey. (VC)

**FIRESIGN THEATER PRESENTS 'HOT SHORTS' (1983).** In the style of Woody Allen's WHAT'S UP, TIGER LILY?, the comedy group has written new soundtracks for old Republic movie serials and grade Z Hollywood movies such as SPYSMASHER, SHE DEMONS and MANHUNT OF MYSTERY ISLAND. Many of the bits are funny but it's basically a one-joke gimmick that wears thin pretty fast. (VC)

**FIRESTARTER (1984).** Stephen King ranks this among the worst of his novel adaptations, and he struck the match right on the head. It's an effects movie, at the expense of a cohesive narrative, adapted by Stanley Mann and directed by Mark L. Lester. Flying killer fireballs and other inflammatory bolts of energy are cast by Drew Barrymore, a kid who can turn her anger into forms of flaming revenge. In short, she lights up your life. Various government agents and foreign powers are after Barrymore to harness her extrasensory abilities for their own evil uses. George C. Scott fulfills a very odd role (for him). Filmed in North Carolina; the Mike Wood-Jeff Jarvis effects are the best things in this never-catches-fire picture. Which proves there isn't always fire where there's smoke. David Keith, Martin Sheen, Heather Locklear, Art Carney, Louise Fletcher, Moses Gunn. (VC)

**FIRST MAN INTO SPACE, THE (1958).** Cosmic rays turn Earth's first astronaut—an obsessed man who takes his spacecraft higher than ordered—into a hideous, encrusted monster who craves human blood. Writers John Cooper and Lance Z. Hargreaves engender sympathy for the misguided, malformed being instead of making him a killer monster. A low budget, commendable effort from producer Richard Gordon and director Robert Day. Marshall Thompson is the scientist attempting to communicate with the gnarly man. Carl Jaffe, Marla Landi, Bill Nagy, Robert Ayres. (VC)

**FIRST MEN IN THE MOON (1964).** Marvelous adaptation of H. G. Wells' novel about a Victorian spaceship blasting off from Earth and flying to the lunar surface; the expedition's adventures are excitingly riveting. Ray Harryhausen (who doubled as associate producer) provides excellent stop motion, notably the insect moonmen. His lavish alien civilization and all its creatures are a satisfying example of what a ton of imagination on a nominal budget can achieve. Edward Judd, Martha Hyer, Lionel Jeffries, Peter Finch. Written by Nigel Kneale (of Quatermass fame) and Jan Read; directed by

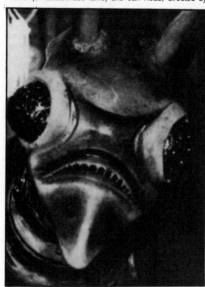

**INCREDIBLE BUG MONSTER IN 'FIVE MILLION YEARS TO EARTH'**

Nathan Juran. Charles H. Schneer produced.

**FIRST SPACESHIP ON VENUS, THE (1961).** East German-Polish film is technically superior in presenting a space odyssey adventure, but dubbing and story are weak. A spaceship from Earth, carrying an international crew, lands on Venus to find civilization destroyed by nuculear holocaust. Depiction of the once sophisticated society is imaginative. Ethnic cast includes Yoko Tani, Oldrich Lukes, Ignacy Machowski. Directed by Kurt Maetzig and based on Stanislaw Lem's 1951 novel THE ASTRONAUTS. Recut for the American market by producer Hugo Grimaldi. (VC)

**FIVE (1915).** Strange end-of-the-world story, not quite successful, but writer-producer-director Arch Oboler lends it a bizarre, black mood. Mankind has been destroyed by the Bomb, but five survivors try to implement a new society, with unhappy results. What's basically wrong is that Oboler's characters are too shadowy and dark. Not a sensible one in the lot, but Oboler is making a comment on the absurdity of people who live on a planet where atomic bombs are used to destroy. FIVE ranks as one of the first films to deal with Atomic Armageddon. William Phipps, Susan Douglas, James Anderson, Earl Lee, Charles Lampkin.

**FIVE MILLION MILES TO EARTH (1968).** Third in the Quatermass series (see THE CREEPING UNKNOWN and ENEMY FROM SPACE) is perhaps Nigel Kneale's best—it is the most outre, replete with religious and mythical overtones. An alien spaceship is uncovered during excavations in London, and corpses of giant grasshoppers are found onboard. Mankind is related to these extraterrestrials through experiments carried out centuries before. Then it really gets weird as ESP and energy force fields come into play. Andrew Keir assumes the Quatermass role originated by Brian Donlevy. Directed by Roy Ward Baker, written by Kneale. Barbara Shelley, James Donald, Duncan Lamont, Bryan Marshall.

**FIVE THOUSAND FINGERS OF DR. T, THE (1953).** Producer Stanley Kramer's offbeat fantasy reflects the ultimate nightmare for children forced to learn music against their will. One such child (Tommy Rettig) dreams he is imprisoned with 500 others in the prison of Dr. Terwilliker (Hans Conried), a crazed piano instructor owning the world's largest piano. The Dr. Seuss fantasy attempts to recapture a WIZARD OF OZ flavor but the choreography is so odd and listless, the film remains consistently offkey. Retuning was in order, maybe? Directed by Roy Rowland, scripted by Dr. Seuss and Alan Scott. Peter Lind Hayes, Mary Healy.

**FLAME BARRIER, THE (1957).** Extraterrestrial substance crashes on Earth aboard a satellite and slurps into a cave for refuge. The entity, which turns flesh into puddles of ooze, is evil and wants to conquer our world—as usual. A total flameout. Directed by Paul Landers. Arthur Franz, Kathleen Crowley, Robert Brown, Vincent Padula, Kaz Oran.

**FLASH GORDON (1936).** First of three Universal serials to star Buster Crabbe as the hero of space, originally created for the comics by Alex Raymond. In this, one of the best action cliffhangers ever, Flash, girlfriend Dale Arden and scientist Dr. Zarkov try to prevent the planet Mongo (ruled by Ming the Merciless) from conquering Earth. On Mongo, it's all-out action as Flash and followers meet Ming's sexy daughter Aura, the Lion Men, the dragon-lizard monster Gocko, and an underwater race led by King Kala. Jean Rogers is Arden, Charles Middleton the evil emperor, Priscilla Lawson the busty Aura and Frank Shannon the dedicated Zarkov. Stylishly directed by Frederick Stephani. The 12-chapter serial has been released in abbreviated versions as SPACESHIP TO THE UNKNOWN, SPACE SOLDIERS and ATOMIC ROCKETSHIP. In video as **FLASH GORDON: ROCKETSHIP.**

**FLASH GORDON (1980).** Dino de Laurentiis' paean to Alex Raymond's hero, immortalized in three Universal serials in the 1930s with Buster Crabbe. Lorenzo Semple Jr.'s script walks a fine balance between action and satire, the costumes and sets are fabulous and the cast finely picked: Sam Jones as Flash is perhaps too naive but his youth and enthusiasm make him acceptable; Max von Sydow makes

**CREATURE FEATURES MOVIE GUIDE**

**BUSTER CRABBE AS FLASH (1936)**

**SAM JONES AS FLASH GORDON (1980)**

movie history as one of the great villains, Ming the Merciless; Melody Anderson is a liberated Dale Arden, and Topol a daffy, dedicated Dr. Zarkoff. Brian Blessed thunders his way through the stylish action as Vultan the Hawkman. Mike Hodges directs it all into an entertaining, cohesive whole. The great sky battles are faithful to Raymond's spaceship designs and overall comic-strippish concept. Only the rock score by Queen seems out of place. Don't miss this fantasy funhouse. (VC)

**FLASH GORDON CONQUERS THE UNIVERSE (1940).** The third serial in Universal's FLASH GORDON series finds Earth subjected to Ming the Merciless' latest ploy to conquer Earth: The Plague of the Purple Death, a "death dust" that Ming's minions have radiated into our atmosphere. Flash, Dale Arde, Dr. Zarkov and Prince Barin, ruler of Arboria, take on Ming with renewed strength, their adventures rocketing them to Frigia, a frozen wasteland. This marked the series' end and is the least of the trilogy, but it's still great fun. In video in all 12 chapters; re-edited and re-released in various forms as PURPLE DEATH FROM OUTER SPACE, SPACE SOLDIERS CONQUER THE UNIVERSE and PERILS FROM PLANET MONGO. (VC)

**FLASH GORDON: MARS ATTACKS THE WORLD.** Feature-length video of FLASH GORDON'S TRIP TO MARS.

**FLASH GORDON: ROCKETSHIP.** Feature-length video of the original FLASH GORDON serial starring Buster Crabbe.

**FLASH GORDON—THE GREATEST ADVENTURE OF ALL (1982).** Above-average animated TV-film starring the popular characters from the comic strip and serials . . . The evil emperor Ming drips with sadistic evil as his sexy daughter lures Flash into her den of iniquity. The action is plentiful and there's a lusty bevy of shapely femmes, giving this an unusual touch of decadence. Voices by Robert Ridgely, Diane Pershing and Bob Holt.

**FLASH GORDON'S TRIP TO MARS (1938).** Second Buster Crabbe FLASH GORDON serial by Universal finds Flash, Dale Arden and Dr. Zarkov flying to Mars to stop Ming the Merciless from stealing the nitrogen from Earth's atmosphere. Adventures involve the Clay People, Azura the Queen of Magic, the White Sapphire, the Tree People, Prince Barin, Tarnak and Happy. Rousing action directed by Ford Beebe and Robert Hill. Re-edited as DEADLY RAY FROM MARS and MARS ATTACKS THE WORLD and in video as **FLASH GORDON: MARS ATTACKS THE WORLD.**

**FLASHMAN (1966).** Italian/French fantasy in which young Paul Stevens dresses up like a comic book superhero to fight

invisible invaders. Flash-in-the-plan movie. Directed by Mino Loy. Claudie Lang, Isarco Ravaioli, John Heston.

**FLESH AND BLOOD SHOW, THE (1973).** British actors audition for a Grand Guignol show as part of a film, but it turns out the auditioner is a man in a sinister hood setting them up for the kill—literally. A spluttering "splatter" movie, originally shot in 3-D by director Peter Walker. Jenny Hanley, Luan Peters, Patrick Bar, Ray Brooks. (VC)

**FLESH AND FANTASY (1943).** A dream-like quality pervades over this trilogy dealing with that primitive level of the imagination giving birth to fear and superstition. In the framework for the weird tales, Robert Benchley is disturbed by a dream and a friend reads to him from an old book to allay his dread. Betty Field and Robert Cummings star in a story about a homely seamstress whose love for a man causes a miracle; Charles Boyer is a tightrope walker haunted by images of circus aerialist Barbara Stanwyck. The best tale is Oscar Wilde's "Lord Arthur Seville's Crime," with Edgar G. Robinson as an American solicitor in London who meets a fortune teller (Thomas Mitchell) with dire predictions. A fourth story, "Destiny," was dropped from the script, expanded and released as the film DESTINY, but it would appear to be of little interest to fantasists. This will be of considerable interest. Directed by Julien Duvivier.

**FLESH AND THE FIENDS, THE (1960).** Gruesome twosome, Burke and Hare, are down to their old grave-robbing tricks in this British chiller, brutally chopped for the U.S. market. It deserved better, being well directed by John Gilling and written with style by Gilling and Leon Griffiths. Peter Cushing stars as Dr. Knox, the Edinburgh anatomical instructor forced to purchase cadavers for the classroom from murderers Donald Pleasence and George Rose. Dark and bleak, similar to THE DOCTOR AND THE DEVILS.

**FLESH CREATURES OF THE RED PLANET.** See **HORROR OF THE BLOOD MONSTERS.**

**FLESH EATERS, THE (1964).** Assorted squabblers are stranded on a secluded island where an idiotic scientist has artifically created amoeba monsters which devour people with considerable glee and gnashing. Some of the effects aren't bad, but overall quality is poor and somewhat sickening. Directed by Jack Curtis. Martin Koslek is the insane inventor, Rita Morly and Byron Sanders stranded victims. (VC)

**FLESH FEAST (1970).** Veronica Lake, once an attractive, hair style-setting '40s star, was co-producer of this low budget flop with a ghastly, repelling premise: Flesh-hungry maggots result in a formula for a rejuvenation serum involving Adolf Hitler. Yech. (Read Ms Lake's autobiography,

VERONICA, for further details about the making of this film in Florida, if you have the curiosity—and stomach.) Directed by Brad F. Ginter. Phil Philbin, Heather Hughes. (VC)

**FLESH GORDON (1974).** Rollicking sex parody of FLASH GORDON serials was heavily pornographic when produced by pornie king William Osco in 1972, but later underwent surgery for theatrical release. It's a lively romp with Flesh, a half-naked Dale Ardor and Dr. Flexi Jerkoff penetrating the kingdom of Emperor Wang's world of Porno. Most of the props and creatures are visualized sex jokes or phallic imagery. Overshadowing the sophomoric humor, amateurish acting and raunchy sex jokes and gropings are imaginative special effects of extraterrestrial monsters in the vein of Ray Harryhausen, brought off by Dave Allen and Jim Danforth. Mike Light wrote-directed what remains an anomaly. Jason Williams, Suzanne Fields, William Hunt, John Hoyt, Lance Larsen, Candy Samples, Mary Gavin. (VC)

**FLIGHT OF THE NAVIGATOR (1986).** Charming juvenile science-fiction adventure from Disney, in which 12-year-old David Freeman returns one day after he's been missing for eight years, having not aged a day. A government investigation reveals that he went into space at the speed of light for four hours, accounting for his disappearance. Freeman escapes the testing headquarters to find he was befriended by a friendly alien out collecting specimens for an intergalactic zoo. The benevolent alien is only a voice (Elliott Gould's?) controlling an extraterrestrial ship, and an amusing relationship develops. Meanwhile, NASA official Howard Hesseman is trying to find Freeman. Takes a while to get going, then it soars. Directed by Randal Kleiser. Veronica Cartwright, Cliff de Young, Sarah Jessica Baker. (VC)

**FLIGHT THAT DISAPPEARED, THE (1961).** Airliner passengers include atomic scientists who have perfected a deadly new killer bomb. The plane is shifted into another dimension by men from the future to prevent the inventors from revealing the bomb's formula. When the scientists are put on trial, this becomes less an adventure than a plea-for-peace message. Directed by Reginald LeBorg. Paula Raymond, Craig Hill, Dayton Lummis, Nancy Hale.

**FLIGHT TO MARS (1951).** Monogram space opera of the dumbest kind. Martians turn out to be nothing more than humanoids from the Screen Actors Guild, women's costumes are miniskirts (at least that part of the film came true) and the plot is pure pulp nonsense. A rocket crew from Earth (including Cameron Mitchell and Arthur Franz) finds an underground city of dying Martians ruled by Ikron the Heinous. Because the society needs a gas called Corium to survive, PG&E intrigue is rampant. Morris Ankrum, Marguerite Chapman, John Litel, Robert Barrat and Virginia Huston are among those misdirected by Leslie Selander. (VC)

**FLY, THE (1958).** If you can overlook inconsistencies in this version of George Langlaan's story (scripted by James

Clavell), you will enjoy this unsettling science-fiction/horror about research scientist David (Al) Hedison, who discovers the secret of teleportation. During an experiment, a common housefly buzzes into the transfer chamber. The result is two incredibly mixed-up beings: a tiny fly with human head, a human with the fly's head. Think about it and it doesn't bear scrutiny. Even so, it's well directed by Kurt Neumann and enhanced by the histronics of Vincent Price (as a member of the cursed Delambre family) and Herbert Marshall (as an investigating policeman). The sequels were RETURN OF THE FLY and CURSE OF THE FLY, with a remake in 1986. Patricia Owens portrays the long-suffering wife. (VC)

**FLY, THE (1986).** Scientific update of the 1958 classic, utilizing gene-splitting and computers to explain how the molecules of a human and a housefly are intermixed. Director David Cronenberg (who co-wrote the unusual script with Charles Edward Pogue) is again fascinated with deformity and "beasts from within" as scientist Jeff Goldblum devises a set of "telepods" to teleport matter from one space to another. Chris Walas' Oscar-winning human/fly special effects are a knockout, but the story less so as it eventually defies all credulity when girlfriend Geena Davis still loves this ugly character in metamorphosis. Sympathy is shown the monster once it emerges, but some may find it hard to get past the gore effects, especially when the fly-creature vomits on a man's hand and foot with an icky goo that dissolves them. John Getz plays a magazine editor after the big story who becomes involved with the fly-by-night. (VC)

**FLYING DISC MAN FROM MARS.** See **MISSILE MONSTERS.**

**FLYING SAUCER, THE (1950).** Unidentified flying objects are reported in Alaska, so the Secret Service dispatches a top agent (hah!) to the north country to determine what the

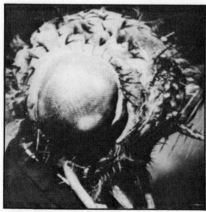

**DAVID HEDISON AS 'THE FLY' (1958)**

**JEFF GOLDBLUM AS 'THE FLY' (1986)**

**CREATURE FEATURES MOVIE GUIDE**

hell is transpiring (or trespassing). This Mikel Conrad production (he directed, wrote and stars) cops out and deteriorates into an espionage thriller. Pat Garrison, Denver Pyle, Roy Engel, Russell Hicks, Gerry Owen. (VC)

**FLYING SAUCER (1965).** English-dubbed Italian film (known as a "spaghetti saucer") with Alberto Sordi in four different roles as he struggles to prevent a Martian invasion, but keeps getting locked up in asylums, the only fitting place for people who believe in Martian invaders. Directed by Tinto Brass. Monica Vitti, Silvano Mangano.

**FLYING SERPENT, THE (1946).** Incredibly naive PRC flick of the so-bad-it's-hilarious-school, with George Zucco outstandingly atrocious as a mad doctor who cages Quetzalcoatl (the Killer Bird God) and sends the winged killer out to murder after he has placed a feather from the bird on the intended victim. Acting and music are equally laughable; wires propelling the creature are discernible even to the most nondiscerning eyeball. Loose remake of DEVIL BAT; Quetzalcoatl was updated in 1982 for Q. Directed by Sam Newfield. Ralph Lewis, Hope Kramer, Eddie Acuff, Henry Hall.

**FOE (1977).** Uninspired cheapie kicks off with a midair collision between an F-16 and a flying saucer reconnoitering Earth. But we never meet the aliens (shown as multi-colored, floating lights), we're given the exposition by research scientist MacDonald Carey (playing Dr. MacCarey, ha ha). The setting is Perish Island, where a lighthouse keeper and his wife are sucked into a radiation whirlpool and spit back out. An ambiguous project, tedious and dull. Director-writer John Coats designed the lousy effects and appears in a minor role. Jerry Hardin, Robert D. E. Alexander, Jane Wiley.

**FOG, THE (1980).** Memorable exercise in supernatural horror as a sinister fog engulfs a coastal California town; within the swirling mist are maggot-decaying pirates armed with pikes, hooks and other flesh-ripping weapons, seeking revenge against the townspeople for wrongs committed a previous century. Director John Carpenter (who co-wrote with producer Debra Hill) plays against our innermost fear of the dark, delivering shock after shock as the fog draws closer. Adrienne Barbeau, Jamie Lee Curtis, Janet Leigh, Hal Holbrook, John Houseman as campside storyteller. (VC)

**FOG ISLAND (1945).** More fog shrouds the logic behind Pierre Gendron's script for this PRC cheapie than the setting; oh well, enjoy the overacting of Lionel Atwill and George Zucco, gentlemen perched in a lonely island's mansion peopled with weird characters, secret rooms, skeletons, sinister shadows, etc. You couldn't cut through this peasoup with a knife. Directed by Terry Morse. Jerome Cowan, Veda Ann Borg, Ian Keith, Sharon Douglas. (VC)

**FOLKS AT RED WOLF INN.** See **TERROR AT RED WOLF INN.**

**FOOD OF THE GODS (1976).** Bert I. Gordon wrote-produced-directed this utterly horrible horror movie allegedly based on an H. G. Wells story. At least a portion of it--the title--is based on Wells. Lowgrade schlock as Marjoe Gortner goes hunting with pals only to encounter giant wasps, extra-large chickens and overgrown rats. If only Marjoe, Ralph Meeker, Ida Lupino and Pamela Franklin had 5000 pounds of American cheese, they might stand a chance. On second thought, Swiss would be better--it would match the thousands of holes in the plot. (VC)

**FOR HEAVEN'S SAKE (1951).** George Seaton tried to duplicate the success of his MIRACLE ON 34TH STREET, but fell on his halo. Undistinguished, now-dated picture is about angels coming to Earth to involve themselves in men's affairs. Clifton Webb is the angelic one in the guise of a rangy Montana rancher, visiting on behalf of an unborn child in Heaven waiting to find a womb to slide into. Webb's entanglement is with the squabbling parents-to-be. Bad Heavens! Joan Bennett, Robert Cummings, Edmund Gwenn, Joan Blondell.

**FOR YOUR EYES ONLY (1981).** The 12th James Bond adventure, more restrained than many, though it still features exciting chases, futuristic gadgets and vehicles designed to keep Agent 007 one step ahead of the villains. Director John Glen emphasizes character and suspense, allowing 007 (Roger Moore) to appear more human than superman. Still, there are the usual mock heroics and contrived escapes. The British agent is after the tracking system of a sunken nuclear submarine stolen by a ruthless mercenary. The Derek Meddings-John Evans effects are outstanding, Alan Hume's cinematography is topnotch and Bill Conti's music is whistleable. The acting by Topol, Lynn-Holly Johnson and Carole Bouquet is just strong enough to hold attention until the next action sequence. A mountain-scaling feat is one of the film's

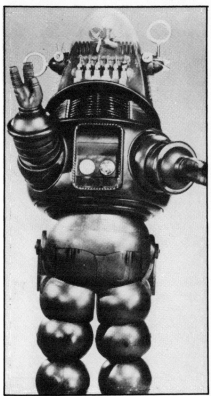

**ROBBY IN 'FORBIDDEN PLANET'**

**LENDING A HAND IN 'THE FOG'**

more suspenseful bits. A stronger villain was needed. (VC)

**FORBIDDEN JUNGLE (1950).** Monogram programmer about a primitive jungle lad who talks to the animals and some inept actors in pith helmets and khakis who walk through a potted jungle in search of the legendary youth. Unga unga bonga. Directed by Robert Tansey. Don Harvey, Forrest Taylor.

**FORBIDDEN MOON (1953).** Forbidden viewing. See **ROCKY JONES, SPACE RANGER.**

**FORBIDDEN PLANET (1956).** Quality science-fiction, set in the year 2200 A.D. on the planet Altair II, where an Earth ship lands to contact Professor Morbius (Walter Pidgeon) and his beautiful daughter Alta (Anne Francis). Soon the ship Bellerephon is attacked by an invisible entity, whose beast-like outline is only visible when it touches the vessel's force-field shield. Nicholas Nayfack's MGM production has over-tones of a whodunit thriller (what is this bizarre alien killer and where does it come from?) and has outstanding technol-ogy—from Robby the Robot to the subterranean city of the long-dead Krell race to Morbius' futuristic home to the spacecraft and land cruisers. Spacemen Leslie Nielsen, Earl Holliman and Warren Stevens remain second bananas to the witty Robby. Cyril Hume's screenplay is a most satisfying piece of science-fiction. Odd electronics score by Louis and Bebe Barron. Directed by Fred McLeod Wilcox. (VC)

**FORBIDDEN ROOM, THE (1977).** Italian mystery with a bet-ter cast (Vittorio Gassman, Catherine Deneuve) than plot: weird events transpire in an old mansion. At least the atmos-phere is eerie. All ambience and ambiguity. Directed by Dino Risi, who co-wrote with B. Zapponi.

**FORBIDDEN WORLD (1982).** ALIEN ripoff depicting space ranger Mike Colby (Jesse Vint), who arrives at a research station on a far-flung world. An experiment in genetic en-gineering has spawned a mutation that's turning humans into piles of gooey leftovers. However, gore can't take the place of suspense. The attitude of director Allan Holzman is so condescending to his characters that the film lapses into laughableness. The two women, for example, quickly strip and leap into bed with Colby, or rush stupidly through the corridors, trying to communicate with "it" or fleeing from its gnashing, slobbering jaws. Dawn Dunlap, Linden Chiles, June Chadwick, Fox Harris. (VC)

**FORBIDDEN ZONE (1982).** Science-fiction musical starring the Mystic Knights of the Oingo Boingo as they tour the Sixth Dimension, an underworld where Herve Villechaize and Susan Tyrrell reign supreme over devils and demons. Strictly for the midnight cult crowd. Made by Richard and Marie-Pas-cale Elfman; the latter also co-stars with Viva. (VC)

**FORBIN PROJECT, THE.** See **COLOSSUS: THE FORBIN PROJECT.**

**FORCE BEYOND, THE (1978).** Some insufferable kids sight a flying saucer and try to warn adults of what they've seen. Low budget time-consumer from director William Sachs; produced and co-written by Donn Davison. Don Elkins, Peter Byrne, Renee Dahinden, Frances Farrelly. (VC)

**FORCE ON THUNDER MOUNTAIN, THE (1978).** Cheapie depicts some wilderness folks attacked by an alien life form who has crash- landed on Earth. He has a device that taps human thought and puts them to evil use. Directed by Peter B. Good, who needs to be better. No thunder, no force. Just the mountain. Todd Dutson, Borge West.

**FORCED ENTRY (1980).** Sicko sick mean-to-women portrait of a psychokiller (Ron Max) who has an obsession against prostitutes and stalks Tanya Roberts into her home. There are lengthy sequences showing Max raping and beating women. There isn't an ounce of entertainment in this despicable movie. Originally produced in 1975, then re-edited with new footage in 1980 . . . no amount of doctoring could

help this disgusting mess directed by Jim Sotos. Nancy Allen, Robin Leslie, Michelle Miles, Brian Freilino. (VC)

**FOREPLAY (1976).** Tepid sex anthology film, with premises barely touching the erogenous zones. In one fantasy, Pat Paulsen buys a life-size Polish sex doll and takes "her" home--only to have his mother intervene. It's a limp Dan Greenberg idea. The second story, by Bruce Jay Friedman, is about a writer's Muse (in red bikini underpants) who whisks the author into the past so he can consummate un-successful sexual conquests. The final episode is equally poor. Zero Mostel is simply awful as a U.S. President black-mailed into performing sexual intercourse with his wife on live network TV. John G. Avildsen directed this latter embarrass-ment. There are frequent cutaways of Professor Irwin Corey, consisting mainly of foul language. In short, FOREPLAY never builds to an arousing climax.

**FOREST, THE (1983).** Poorly executed tedious low-budget indie, in which a wife killer turned cannibal (Michael Brody) living in a forest terrorizes four overnight campers, who are all terribly dull. Writer Evan Jones provides plot twists, such as having the two children wandering the woods turning out to be ghosts (they can't afford superimpositioning the couple, so they're given echo-chamber voices) but otherwise this is quite predictable (with drawn out flashbacks) and hampered by a lack of effects to complement the gore killings. Producer-director Don Jones fails to evoke believable perfor-mances from Dean Russell, Elaine Warner, John Batis and Ann Wilkinson. Aha, some critics can see the sleaze through THE FOREST, after all. (VC)

**FOREST OF FEAR.** See **BLOODEATERS, THE.**

**FORGOTTEN CITY OF THE PLANET OF THE APES (1974).** More re-edited episodes from the short-lived TV series PLANET OF THE APES, starring Roddy McDowall as Galen and Ron Harper and James Naughton as astronauts who are always feeling potential captors.

**FORMULA, THE (1980).** Steve Shagan's best-seller was a compelling detective-mystery but this film version is an exer-cise in cinematic bungling as cop George C. Scott, in track-ing a killer, uncovers a formula that can produce gasoline from synthetic products, first used by Hitler in World War II. There is a conspiracy by a major American oil company to suppress the formula. Marlon Brando exemplifies the con-spiratorial side as an oil magnate cynically soaking motorists with high gas prices  and gloating about it. Director John Avildsen made a botch of this, along with producer-writer Shagan. Marthe Keller, John Gielgud, G. D. Spradlin, Beatrice Straight, Richard Lynch. (VC)

**FOUR FLIES ON GREY VELVET (1972).** Offbeat Italian psychothriller directed by Dario Argento (DEEP RED, SUSPIRIA) in which an intrepid hero uses a strange laser device to capture the image of a murderer on a victim's retina. Suspense builds admirably throughout. Music by Ennio Morricone. Michael Brandon, Mimsy Farmer.

**FOUR SKULLS OF JONATHAN DRAKE, THE (1959).** Familiar beware-the-family-curse is at work in this low-budget special from Robert E. Kent. Eduard Franz, Valerie French and Henry Daniell are employed in Orville H. Hampton's tale about a family whose members are always beheaded at 60. Daniell is Jonathan Drake, who keeps track of all the heads in his private collection. Turns out Drake is a 2000-year-old walking zombie. Zounds! four times.

**FOUR-D MAN, THE (1959).** Jack Harris' production does 3-D one better by having scientist Robert Lansing charged with rays from the fourth dimension, which enables him to pass through solid objects. But this new power also makes him greedy and homicidal, though for no particular reason except to give screenwriters Theodore Simonson and Cy Chermak a chance for violence. Has a period-sleaze fascination about it. Directed by Irwin S. Yeaworth Jr. and featuring Patty Duke

*"The American people don't scare easily!" —The heroic Kent Fowler
(Walter Reed) in **THE FLYING DISC MAN FROM MARS.***

**FRANCIS THE TALKING MULE WITH DOGFACE DONALD O'CONNOR (1950)**

as a kid. Lee Meriwether, James Congdon. (VC)

**FOUR-SIDED TRIANGLE (1953).** When two scientists fall in love with Barbara Payton, they decide to stick her in their duplicating machine so each can own her voluptuous body. But the solving of quantity leads to a problem of quality: Will the duplicate be as good, or better, than the original? Curious, literate British film (early Hammer, actually) directed by Terence Fisher and produced by Michael Carreras. Scripted by Fisher and Paul Tabori, from a William Temple novel. James Hayter, John van Eyssen.

**FRANCIS (1950).** A talking mule with the voice of Chill Wills? Yep, it's time for that fun-loving Universal-International comedy with Donald O'Connor as a World War II dogface who gets thrown into a psycho ward when he tries to explain about the articulate ass that saved his life in a Japanese ambush. Written by David Stern from his novel and directed by Arthur Lubin, with Zasu Pitts, Eduard Franz, Mikel Conrad, Patricia Medina and Ray Collins providing platoon support. This rollicking comedy (now on videocassette) saved Universal from financial ruin and served as the "pilot" for a long-braying, money-making series of lowbrow comedies about which you must now read:

**FRANCIS COVERS THE BIG TOWN (1953).** Yes, but what does Francis cover the big town with? Anyway, mule lovers, Donald O'Connor keeps on making an . . . astronomical nuisance of himself as he and his yakkity four-legged companion set journalism back a few editions by taking jobs at a major metropolitan daily. The mule with Chill Wills' voice loosens his halter-tie, props his hooves on the desk and brays "Slop the presses." Mulish fun directed by Arthur Lubin. Nancy Guild, Gene Lockhart, Gale Gordon, Yvette Dugay.

**FRANCIS GOES TO THE RACES (1951).** You've heard about the guy who talks to horses. In this one, a mule-headed mule talks to horses. Are the movies going to the horses or the asses? Talking-mule fun under Arthur Lubin's direction. Piper Laurie, Cecil Kellaway, Jesse White.

**FRANCIS GOES TO WEST POINT (1952).** The famous military academy is only a stable and a drinking trough for the Talking Mule when he and Donald O'Connor enlist. Mule-headed humor under Arthur Lubin's direction. Lori Nelson, Les Tremayne, David Janssen, James Best.

**FRANCIS IN THE HAUNTED HOUSE (1956).** By this time Universal's talking mule series had so deteriorated, not even Donald O'Connor wanted the role. Replacement Mickey Rooney wanders through this haunted house drivel as though he had stumbled onto the wrong soundstage. It was to be the last in the series . . . for Francis it was back to the stables. Directed by Charles Lamont. Paul Cavanagh, Virginia Welles, David Janssen, Richard Deacon.

**FRANCIS IN THE NAVY (1955).** The Donald O'Connor-Talking Mule series deserved mothballs . . . but stayed afloat as the pair finds its way into active duty, serving at sea and making most of the fish in the ocean dizzy. Arthur Lubin directed. Martha Hyer, Leigh Snowden, Martin Milner, David Janssen, Paul Burke, Clint Eastwood. This time the mule's voice belonged to Paul Frees'.

**FRANCIS JOINS THE WACS (1954).** A clerical error finds Donald O'Connor assigned to a women's unit with his talking pal and both are feeling their oats. But the maneuvers Donald has in mind don't go over well with Julia Adams, Mamie Van Doren and Lynn Bari. You know the old saying: Don't make WAVES. The voice of Chill Wills drones on. Directed by the stubborn Arthur Lubin. ZaSu Pitts, Allison Hayes, Mara Corday.

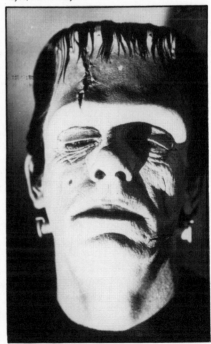

**GLENN STRANGE AS FRANKENSTEIN**

**FRANKENSTEIN (1931).** Granddaddy of the Walking Monster films, so cleverly directed by James Whale it takes on greater classicality with each viewing. Boris Karloff, as Frankenstein's Monster, projects a paradoxical mixture of pathos and horror; the make-up by Jack Pierce is classic in itself. Whale's vision was years ahead of its time, influencing a superb adaptation of Mary Shelley's novel (by Garrett Ford, Robert Florey, Francis E. Faragoh) and crisp, Gothic-inspired camerawork by Arthur Edeson. Whale went on to make BRIDE OF FRANKENSTEIN, which many feel is superior to the original . . . but unquestionably this established a cinema trend. Whale's superb cast includes Colin Clive as Dr. Frankenstein ("It's alive . . . alive!"), Mae Clarke, John Boles, Edward van Sloan, Dwight Frye. A new video version contains the controversial scenes of the Monster drowning a little girl in the village pond, which were cut from the original. (VC)

**FRANKENSTEIN (1973).** Producer Dan (DARK SHADOWS) Curtis' three- hour version of Mary Shelley's novel stars Robert Foxworth as the experimenting doctor, Susan Strasberg as the love interest and Bo Svenson as the Monster. Glenn Jordan directed. Heidi Vaughn, Robert Gentry, Philip Bourneuf. This aired shortly before FRANKENSTEIN: THE TRUE STORY, which beat it all to hell. (VC)

**FRANKENSTEIN (1984).** U.S./British TV production, shot on tape, blending Hammer's Gothic influences with Mary Shelley into a mildly entertaining brew. Robert Powell portrays Dr. Victor Frankenstein with an element of depraved madness, while Carrie Fisher is his innocent sister who is always lifting her period bustle to walk room to room. John Gielgud appears in a cameo as the blind man in the forest. Terence Alexander is the young assistant and Susan Woolridge his love interest. David Warner brings little pathos to the Monster and his make-up is hideous without being stunning or original. James Ormerod's direction has that anonymous clarity that plagues all taped dramas. Ripley Castle in England is the setting.

**FRANKENSTEIN (1984).** Japanese animated version of Shelley's classic, full of violence and gore, and hence not recommended for faint-headed kiddies. (VC)

**FRANKENSTEIN AND THE MONSTER FROM HELL (1973).** Sixth and final entry in Hammer's Frankenstein series, at its best with laboratory black humor. Shane Briant, a young disciple of Baron Frankenstein, is sent to Carlesbad Asylum for the Insane for his heinous acts, but once there is befriended by a practicing Frankenstein (the utterly delightful, and mad, Peter Cushing). Assisted by mute Madeline Smith, the team takes the brain of a genius violinist and places it in the cranium of David Prowse, an act resulting in new mayhem. The John Elder script is cliched and half-hearted; Terence Fisher's direction is weary; the film is only a ghostly shadow of earlier films in this historic series.

**FRANKENSTEIN CONQUERS THE WORLD (1966).** Made as FRANKENSTEIN VS. THE GIANT DEVIL FISH . . . but in one of the international cutting rooms of the world the Devil Fish was spliced out. Destructive mayhem, however, was not cut, so destruction fans can rejoice. The battle royal is between Baragon, a rampaging dinosaur, and a human who has grown to 30 feet in height after swallowing a heart created by Dr. Frankenstein for the Nazis during World War II. Nick Adams headlines the cast to give the film international appeal. "Godzilla" director Inoshiro Honda helms the action, with special effects by his pal Eiji Tsuburaya.

**FRANKENSTEIN CREATED WOMAN (1967).** A Hammer horror film for transsexuals. Peter Cushing, as Baron Frankenstein, has mastered the black science of capturing the spirit of a corpse. A male wraith is transplanted into the body of a beautiful woman with heaving bosom (Susan Denberg), who goes around stabbing respectable folks with a knife, her bosom still heaving. Production values are outstanding and the cast ably manipulated by director Terence Fisher, a specialist at motivating heaving bosoms. Screenplay by John (Heaving) Elder, produced by Anthony Nelson-Keys. Thorley Walters, Robert Morris, Peter Blythe.

**FRANKENSTEIN '88.** See **VINDICATOR, THE.**

**FRANKENSTEIN—ITALIAN STYLE (1977).** X-rated spoof

with a hulking creature better endowed than his predecessors as he rushes from one female assistant to another to "consummate" the relationship. There hangs the tail. Directed by Armando Crispino. Aldo Maccione.

**FRANKENSTEIN MEETS THE SPACE MONSTER (1965).** And you'll meet with utter boredom from this poverty-stricken heap about an experimental "astro-robot" with half a face (and less a brain) fighting Princess Marcuzan and her alien-invader hordes. This has nothing to do with the Frankenstein Monster, but who cares? Produced in Puerto Rica (as MARS INVADES PUERTO RICO); directed by Robert Gaffney. James Karen, Nancy Marshall, Lou Cutell. (VC)

**FRANKENSTEIN MEETS THE WOLFMAN (1943).** Fanged, drooling battle between the Frankenstein Monster and Lawrence Talbot, the misunderstood lycanthrope, was declared the "Clash of the Century" by Universal . . . but it was an average slugfest. Still, the rematch of these box-office monsters, written by Curt Siodmak and directed by Roy William Neill, is fun moving-watching. Lon Chaney Jr. is back

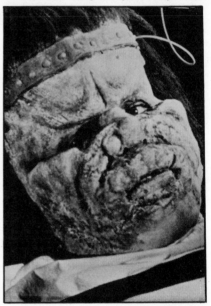

### 'FRANKENSTEIN'S DAUGHTER,' YUCK MONSTER

as Talbot and Bela Lugosi proves he's no Boris Karloff as he shambles ineptly toward oblivion. But boy, what a cast of horror favorites: Partric Knowles as Dr. Mannering, who resurrects the Monster; Lionel Atwill as the village mayor; Maria Ouspenskaya as the gypsy woman who intones the classic "wolfbane curse" lyrics, and Dwight Frye, Dennis Hoey and Ilona Massey, the latter as Baroness Frankenstein. (VC)

**FRANKENSTEIN MUST BE DESTROYED (1970).** In this, fifth in Hammer's FRANKENSTEIN series, Peter Cushing cuts apart cadavers to create a hulking entity of evil. The Bert Batt script succeeds in being occasionally nauseating, such as in a Grand Guignol sequence where a busted waterpipe forces a buried victim up through the mud. Buffs will enjoy this hokum from producer Anthony Nelson-Keys and director Terence Fisher; others may find it unstomachable or tedious as Cushing dons a fright mask to attack victims, cuts open skulls to extract human brains and forces assistant Simon Ward to claim the beautiful body of Veronica Carlson, who is quite beautous in her diaphonous nightgowns. Freddie Jones plays the resurrected Monster.

**FRANKENSTEIN 1970 (1958).** Instead of harnessing

electricity to resurrect man-mad monsters, Baron Victor Von Frankenstein (Boris Karloff) uses atomic energy. Oh well, even horror films have to swing with the age. Anyway, the unhinged Baron (victim of Nazi torture) allows a movie crew (feisty Don "Red" Barry is its director) onto the grounds of his castle, horrified to discover the Hollywoodites are making a fright flick. How horrible! But the Baron knows cast and crew will supply the bodies he needs under his nuclear reactor in the laboratory. Screenwriters Richard Landau and George W. Yates try for a surprise ending; if you are blind in one eye and can't see out of the other, you will be caught totally unaware. Directed by Howard Koch. Tom Duggan, Jana Lund, Mike Lane, Charlotte Austin, John Dennis. (VC)

**FRANKENSTEIN 1980 (1972).** Italian body parts thrown together by director Mario Mancini. Franky baby is looking for a girlfriend, unaware he could self-destruct at any time. John Richardson, Renato Romano, Gordon Mitchell. (VC)

**FRANKENSTEIN ON CAMPUS (1970).** Canadian flick, also called DR. FRANKENSTEIN ON CAMPUS, is a youth-oriented endeavor enlivened by nifty special effects at the climax. Otherwise, it's tedious going when Simon Ward (Viktor Frankenstein IV, descendant of the crazy Bavarian) turns his fellow classmates into monsters. There are insignificant subplots involving campus protest rallies and drugs. If you can sit through this, go to the head of the class. Directed by Gil Taylor. Kathleen Sawyer, Austin Willis.

**FRANKENSTEIN: THE TRUE STORY (1973).** Serious attempt by producer Hunt Stromberg Jr. to capture the spirit of Mary Wollstonecraft Shelley's novel in a four-hour format. The Christopher Isherwood-Don Bachardy script is literate and the acting is superb. Michael Sarrazin plays the man-made monster, but not as a grotesquerie; rather, the problem is how to keep his flesh from rotting. Dr. Frankenstein (Leonard Whiting) joins ranks with David McCallum to solve this problem, then is blackmailed by Dr. Polidori (James Mason) to create a female mate for Sarrazin. One memorable scene takes place at a gala, where a woman's head is ripped off her neck. But it is not so much the horror that director Jack Smight stresses; it is the traumas the characters undergo, including Sarrazin's journey into the Arctic. Agnes Moorehead, John Gielgud, Sir Ralph Richardson, Tom Baker, Jane Seymour.

**FRANKENSTEIN'S BLOODY TERROR (1971).** Spanish import, redesigned for U.S. consumption, has nothing to do with Frankenstein or his Monster—it's about a clan called Wolfstein and depicts a man becoming a werewolf, and then watching helplessly (while chained to a wall) while two vampires seduce his girl. Despite poor dubbing, this has good color photography and nice nocturnal scenes of the vampire playfully leading a young woman into the night. All style, little substance. Directed by Enrique L. Equiluz, written by Jacinto Molina. Paul Naschy portrays the werewolf in this, the first of eight wolfman dim-witted dilemmas.

**FRANKENSTEIN'S CASTLE OF FREAKS.** See **DR. FRANKENSTEIN'S CASTLE OF FREAKS.**

**FRANKENSTEIN'S DAUGHTER (1958).** Terribly wretched Z flick, so compellingly awful it's required viewing for fans of schlock. Exemplary of '50s genre, with its amateurish, hammish actors, its condescending script (by H. E. Barrie) and uninspired direction by Richard Cunha. The grandson of Dr. Frankenstein is up to his usual tricks, perfecting the drug Degeneral, which degenerates poor Sandra Knight into a hideous, fanged she-creature comparable to what you see on Halloween night at the front door, asking for a treat. Meanwhile, some teenagers try to solve the mystery while a cop dumbly investigates. Wonderfully incompetent. John Ashley, Harold Lloyd Jr., Voltaire Perkins. (VC)

**FRANKENSTEIN'S GREAT-AUNT TILLIE (1985).** Mexican production, shot in English with a U.S.-British cast—figure that one out. Writer-director Myron J. Gold plays it for laughs when the Transylvanian town of Mugglefugger lays claim to

the Frankenstein Castle because of unpaid taxes. Along come Victor Jr. (Donald Pleasence), a buxom companion (June Wilkerson) and 109-year-old Great-Aunt Tillie (Yvonne Furneaux) to search for the family fortune, hidden in the castle. Nothing aloof about this spoof. Zsa Zsa Gabor, Rod Colbin, Garnett Smith. (VC)

**FRANKENSTEIN'S ISLAND (1982).** Jerry Warren directed this absolutely unmitigated failure in which balloonists "fall" into the hands of a mad scientist conducting hideous experiments. Sex and sadism in liberal doses don't rescue this mess. Isle be seeing you? No way. Cameron Mitchell, Robert Clarke, John Carradine. (VC)

**FREAKMAKER, THE.** Video title for **MUTATIONS.**

**FREAKS (1932).** Tod (DRACULA) Browning produced-directed this disturbing portrait of carnival life. A stickler for realism, Browning hired real circus freaks to act out a macabre tale. Two normal-sized performers try to swindle an inheritance from a well-to-do midget by poisoning him on his wedding night. The sympathetically portrayed freaks turn against the pair, providing the shock ending that so disgusted viewers of the 1930s. A Classic of the Grotesque based on Tod Robbins' short story, "Spurs." Among the misshapen were a living torso, pinheads, a "living skeleton" and Siamese twins. Wallace Ford, Roscoe Ates, Olga Baclanova, Edward Brophy, Harry Earles, Daisy Earles. (VC)

**FREAKY FRIDAY (1977).** Above average Disney comedy-fantasy in which teenager Jodie Foster and her suburban mother Barbara Harris exchange personalities (but not bodies). Daughter copes with housekeeping while mom handles classroom. Director Gary Nelson and screenwriter Mary Rodgers deal well with the satiric implications, but the latter half deteriorates into car chases, slapstick antics and formula devices. Harris is pixish, nicely capturing the daughter, while Foster is less experienced in suggesting mom's maturity. John Astin, Patsy Kelly. (VC)

**FREE FOR ALL (1949).** Robert Cummings is a fun-loving inventor who creates a pill that turns water into gas. Producer Robert Buckner created a pill the public refused to swallow in 1949 and which is just as bitter today. Directed by Charles T. Barton. Ann Blyth, Percy Kilbride, Ray Collins.

**FRENZY (1972).** Alfred Hitchcock's last really good suspense shocker, depicting in unusually graphic style (with some nudity) the strangulations committed by The Necktie Murderer who is terrorizing London. An innocent man is accused of the heinous crimes but the killer keeps on killing. There's a classic scene in the back of a potato truck and other clever directorial touches to this unsettling psychological tale of sex and murder. Jon Finch, Sandra Knight, Barbara Leigh-Hunt, Barry Foster. (VC)

**FRIDAY THE THIRTEENTH (1980).** A lucky day for producer-writer- director Sean Cunningham: This trend-setting slasher movie was a runaway smash, followed by an endless series of sequels, all in the same lowbrow vein. A blood-drenched psycho killer named Jason is knocking off his victims (for revengeful purposes) at Camp Crystal Lake. This is a curiosity piece, mainly to see the different ways the victims are done in—there are no two deaths alike. Some of the modus operandi are clever, others ludicrous. Tom Savini made his reputation for gore effects on this film. Adrienne King, Betsy Palmer, Harry Crosby, Mark Nelson. (VC)

**FRIDAY THE THIRTEENTH, PART 2 (1981).** All things being relative (if not relevant), this is superior to the original, and better than Part III and beyond. A vast crowd-pleaser under Steve Miner's direction, delivering numerous graphic murders with impalings being the favorite of scripter Ron Kurz. The mutilations are ghastly as that beloved unstoppable killer, Jason Voorhees, returns to Camp Crystal (a.k.a. "Camp Blood") to knock off ill-mannered teenagers just asking for swift dispatching via a poker through the eye, a machete through the jugular, a spear through two bodies at

*"If it moves and it's not one of us, shoot it." —Jesse Vent as Space Ranger Mike Colby in FORBIDDEN WORLD*

**THE EVER-SWINGING JASON VOORHEES IN ANY 'FRIDAY THE 13TH' MOVIE**

once. Oh, there's also a pitchfork, a chainsaw (to keep the soundtrack noisy) and assorted decapitating mechanisms. The cast is negligible (except as cannon fodder) and technical credits adequate if not stunning. Adrienne King, John Furey, Amy Steel, Warrington Gillette, Betsy Palmer. (VC)

**FRIDAY THE THIRTEENTH PART 3 (1982).** The main titles leap out at you in 3-D and it's a whopper of an effect. And then the movie begins. There isn't a whopper to follow it as the body count builds at Lake Crystal, where more dumb teenagers are on an outing, laughing at that old legend about Jason the Killer. Well, before you can say "Son of the Chainsaw Massacre Meat Cleaver Driller Killer Strikes Again," Jason is back wearing his funny mask, waiting to knock off juvenile jerks one by bloody one. And do those kids deserve what they get! Even in 3-D this fails to stimulate new interest. Look at director Steve Miner rolling in the money. Dana Kimmell, Richard Brooker, Catherine Parks. (VC)

**FRIDAY THE THIRTEENTH PART 4: THE FINAL CHAPTER (1984).** The most tepid entry in the series, depicting the slaughterous adventures of Jason Voorhees (an unkillable supernatural wraith) in and around the environs of Crystal Lake. Writers Barney Cohen and Frank Mancuso couldn't dream up new ways for bodies to be slashed, skewered or impaled, so Paramount kept the bloodletting and gore effects by Tom Savini to flash cuts. Six teens rent a summer cottage and face death by butcher-knife beheading, hacksaw hacking, corkscrew twisting, stomach knife-punctures, etc. The characters are witless, the dialogue inane and Joseph Zito's direction feeble. Despite the title, the denouement set up an obvious sequel in which Jason returned in a more youthful body. Kimberley Beck, Peter Barton, Corey Feldman, Alan Hayes, Barbara Howard, Crispin Grover. (VC)

**FRIDAY THE THIRTEENTH PART 5: A NEW BEGINNING (1985).** Fifth in the popular slasher series, a tired formula affair with nothing new about Jason Voorhees, the inhuman killer who delights in wearing a hockey mask. So, this collapses like a balloon with a butcher knife shoved into it. Not a single novel murder device or a bit of suspense. This time the isolated rural setting is a rehab center for the mentally deranged, where ill-defined characters are knocked off by road-flare-shoved-into-mouth, commonplace beheadings and impalings, an axe in the brain, garden shears in the eyeballs, a spike in the brain, ad nauseum. Danny Steinmann directed, but telegraphs every punch. The unlikable cast (Melanie Kinnaman, John Shepherd, Shavar Ross, Marco St. John) behaves like refugees from a school for the teen-aged deranged. An unnecessary and mean exercise in gratuitous violence. (VC)

**FRIDAY THE THIRTEENTH PART 6: JASON LIVES (1986).** Not quite the same old gore murder crap centered around the masked madman, Jason Voorhees . . . this time around writer-director Tom McLoughlin has seen fit to eject a few touches of humor into his genre script, suggesting none of us should take any of this too seriously. Not that anyone would. By now Jason is a menaceless parody of himself as he stalks his youthful victims in rural settings. One of the gags is that Crystal Lake has been renamed Forest Green County and the cemetery where Jason's body lies is called Eternal Peace. Here's the body count: machete thrust for two, impaling on a spear, broken bottle into throat, bare fist through a stomach, 360-degree head twist, and assorted stabbings and decapitations. Duck the splatter from the head on a platter. Thom Mathews, Jennifer Cooke, David Kagen. (VC)

**FRIGHT (1957).** Bridey Murphy reincarnation theme is exploited in this quickie focusing on psychiatrist Eric Fleming who uses hypnotism to prevent a suicide. This accidentally causes an innocent bystander to return to a former life—as the mistress of an Austrian ruler in 1899. Produced-directed by W. Lee Wilder. Nancy Malone, Humphrey Davis.

**FRIGHT (1972).** Peter Collinson directed this British shocker with Susan George as a babysitter trapped in a spooky house with a escapee from an insane asylum. An interesting undercurrent of sexual energy develops as the killer, Ian Bannen, develops several fixations. Honor Blackman portrays Bannen's wife. John Gregson.

**FRIGHT NIGHT (1985).** A clever horror film, designed for fans, which pays off splendidly—like a fun attraction at Disneyland. Writer-director Tom Holland (author of PSYCHO II) uses the old "boy cried werewolf" plot but with ingenious twists. William Ragsdale is convinced a vampire lives next door—but mom, his girlfriend and best friend aren't. Roddy McDowall gives the performance of his career as a late-night "Creature Features" host to whom Ragsdale turns for "professional" help. Eventually the girl (Amanda Bearse), a school chum (Stephen Geoffreys) and McDowall enter the vampire's abode, and a "night of terrors" begins, with Richard Edlund providing effects in all their fury. It's insignificantly juvenile but boy, what a ride while it lasts. Chris Sarandon has great fun as the vampire, knowing when to be subtle and when to ham it up. He has a handsome assistant (Jonathan Stark) and a homosexual relationship is lightly suggested but never elaborated on. And dig that sequence in a disco when the vampire mesmerizes Bearse. (VC)

**FRIGHTMARE (1974).** Disgusting but effective British chiller about a mother (Sheila Keith) who craves (and carves) human flesh and a husband (Rupert Davies) who covers up for her. A black-and-white prologue shows them being sentenced to an asylum in 1957, then the film jumps in color to today as they reunite with their daughters. There's a hot poker murder, a pitchfork homicide and an axe murder or two

**A BRIDE OF THE VAMPIRE ON THE CRAWL IN 'FRIGHT NIGHT'**

in David McGillivray's script, and producer-director Peter Walker has the decency to look the other way when the gore splatters. Well, some of the time, anyway. Deborah Fairfax, Paul Greenwood. In videocassette as **FRIGHTMARE II.**

**FRIGHTMARE (1981).** "I've never died before, but I want to do it right," proclaims vampire film actor Conrad Radzoff, "The Prince of Ham." And after pushing his director to his death for exhibiting boorish temperamental symptons, Radzoff dies from acute overacting. Where do washed-up horror players go after death? Right back to the living: He's conjured up from the dead by a medium. So Radzoff (Ferdinand Mayne) continues to chew scenery—and bodies—by terrorizing the dumb teenagers who stole his corpse from a mausoleum. It's a campy send-up by writer-director Norman Thaddeus Dane, but there isn't enough vitality in the veins of Radzoff to sustain much interest. Luca Bercovici, Nita Talbot, Leon Askin, Jennifer Starrett, Leon Askin. (VC)

**FRIGHTMARE II.** Videocassette title for the 1974 **FRIGHTMARE.**

**FROG DREAMING.** See **QUEST, THE.**

**FROGS (1972).** Frightened by the image of frogs, toads and related amphibians leaping to the attack, croaking a melody of death? Then you'll be quivering in your wading boots as this depicts nature on a rampage against mankind (presumably because of our polluting habits). Personifying man's evil side (along with DDT and insectides) is landowner Ray Milland, who feels the attack just isn't cricket and then orders frogleg soup. The attacking frogs, leaping to the music of Les Baxter and the directorial commands of George McCowan, also have control over snakes and other swamp crawlies as the crowd closes in on Milland's private island, inhabited by quibblers Sam Elliott, Joan Van Ark, Adam Roarke, Judy Pace and William Smith. The writers, Robert

Hutchison and Robert Blees, are no toadies. (VC)

**FROM BEYOND (1986).** Director Stuart Gordon (REANIMATOR) has such a distinct style (frenetic pacing, bizarre characters, no-holds-barred horror) that he overcomes all the shortcomings of this incredibly unrestrained horror thriller from producer Charles Band. Crazy Doc Pretorious (name sound familiar?) has invented the Resonator, which taps into another dimension, allowing a grotesquely awful monster into our world, at the cost of everyone's sanity. Despite all the gooey effects and horrific visuals, the film works because of the overwrought performance of Barbara Crampton as Dr. Roberta Bloch, a psychiatrist who loses all control (sexually and otherwise) to become one of the kinkiest anti-heroines of modern movies (and her bared breasts get pawed by the monster, too). Jeffrey Combs is Crawford Tillinghast. (Characters have genre names provided by scripter Dennis Paoli, who based this super-loosely on a story by H. P. Lovecraft.) (VC)

**FROM BEYOND THE GRAVE (1973).** Amicus anthology film featuring four stories by R. Chetwynd-Hayes, linked together by an antique shop setting where owner Peter Cushing foresees the doom of those customers trying to cheat him. The stories are "The Gate Crasher," "An Act of Kindness," "The Elemental" and "The Door." Director Kevin Connor presents them with a flourish of atmosphere and production value; recommended. David Warner, Margaret Leighton, Donald Pleasence, Ian Bannen, Diana Dors, Lesley-Anne Down, Nyree Dawn Porter. (VC)

**FROM HELL IT CAME (1957).** A tree trunk named Tabanga branches out when it is possessed by the radioactive spirit of a dead native. But what a sap! Leaving its shady past behind, the trunk pulls itself out of the ground and stalks the jungles of a Pacific island, murdering anyone passing through. The performance of the tree (Paul Blaisdell, who was soon after

*"One thing is established. The criminal had wings!" —Insightful cop in*
**THE FLYING SERPENT.**

put out to pasture) is equalled only by the wooden acting of Tod Andrews and Tina Carver (but she does have shapely limbs). The ROOTS of the horror field. The seeds for this "classic" were sown in the mind of writer Richard Bernstein and planted by producer Jack Milner and director Dan Miller. But then someone watered it down.

**FROM RUSSIA WITH LOVE (1964).** Second in the James Bond series produced by Harry Saltzman and Albert R. Brocolli, and still a superior spy thriller. The bone of contention is a Soviet decoding machine, the Lektor, which S.P.E.C.T.R.E. is trying to steal from Russia's cryptographic headquarters in Istanbul. Bond is employed by M (Bernard Lee) to steal the device himself aided by agent Kerim Bey (Pedro Armendariz). And soon our heroic British spy is embroiled with beautiful women (Daniela Bianchi is ravishing) and enemy agents Red Grant (Robert Shaw) and Rosa Klebb (Lotte Lenya). Director Terence Young keeps the pace brisk and the visuals dazzling, capturing every nuance of Richard Maibaum's adaptation of Ian Fleming's novel. The action includes chases involving motorboats and helicopters, a fiery belly dance contest climaxed by a gunbattle, and a fight aboard a speeding train. Martine Beswick, Aliza Gur, Lois Maxwell. (VC)

**FROZEN GHOST (1945).** Entry in Universal's minor "Inner Sanctum" series, B mysteries introduced by a head floating in a crystal ball—or was it a goldfish bowl? Lon Chaney Jr. plays another misunderstood character: Gregor the Great, a hypnotist who fears he committed murder. Chaney is stiff in the thankless role, and gets no help from director Harold Young. The best thing about these old turkeys are their ensemble casts. This one includes Evelyn Ankers, Milburn Stone, Elena Verdugo and Douglas Dumbrille.

**FROZEN SCREAM (1980).** Amateurish, incompetently made time-waster about crazy doctors creating a lab-full of zombie creatures who cackle and look bug-eyed. It's so muddled, there's voiceover narration to explain the plot involving a dumb cop and his terrorized girlfriend, but even that only adds to the confusion. The acting is pathetic, the direction by Frank Roach totally inadequate. The plot is about prefrontal cranial circuitry lobotomies. It's enough to freeze anyone's mind. Renee Harmon, Lynne Kocol. On a videocassette doublebill with EXECUTIONER II.

**FROZEN TERROR (1984).** A severed head still lives, holding sway over a deranged daughter and mother. Directed by Lamberto Bava. Bernice Stegers, Veronica Zinny. (VC)

**DANIELA BIANCHA AS THE RAVISHING SPY IN 'FROM RUSSIA WITH LOVE'**

**FROM THE EARTH TO THE MOON (1958).** The best features in this adaptation of Jules Verne's scientific adventure are Victorian settings and costumes. The Robert Blees-James Leicester script concerns an inventor (Joseph Cotten) who uses a new explosive to launch a missile to the moon. Eventually he and Debra Paget end up in each other's arms, facing the hazards of space flight. Literate, well-produced but but not very exciting. Directed by Byron Haskin. George Sanders, Don Dubbins, Patric Knowles, Morris Ankrum, Carl Esmond, Melville Cooper. (VC)

**FROZEN ALIVE (1964).** More experimentation in the art of preserving dead bodies with freezing techniques, tinged with science-fiction overtones. The Evelyn Frazer script deals mostly with the legal ramifications when scientist Mark Stevens is arrested for killing his wife, when her body is really in a state of suspended animation. Directed by Bernard Knowles. Marianna Koch, Yoachim Hansen.

**FROZEN DEAD, THE (1966).** Frigid Grand Guignol tale of horror, with images that will stick in your mind, even if the story by writer-producer-director Herbert J. Leder might stick in your craw. Demented Nazi scientist Dana Andrews, still loyal to Der Fuehrer, gets an icy grip on himself and experiments with German war criminals in his deep freezer. But the temperature climbs when things go wrong. A wall of severed arms will chill you, no matter how ludicrous their "reach." This doesn't deserve a cold shoulder. Kathleen Breck, Philip Gilbert, Anna Palk, Karel Stepanek.

**FU MANCHU'S KISS OF DEATH.** See **KISS AND KILL.**

**FULL CIRCLE.** See **HAUNTING OF JULIA, THE.**

**FULL MOON HIGH (1982).** Writer-producer-director Larry Cohen's answer to THE HOWLING; a werewolf story about a teenager (Adam Arkin, son of Alan Arkin) who is bitten on his Transylvania. But Cohen plays for comedy in following the youth through his high school adventures. This fails where TEEN WOLF succeeded. Roz Kellym, Elizabeth Hartman, Ed McMahon, Kenneth Mars, Pat Morita, Alan Arkin, Louis Nye.

**FUN HOUSE, THE.** See **LAST HOUSE ON DEAD END STREET.**

**FUNERAL HOME (1981).** Busty teenager Lesleh Donaldson arrives outside Toronto to help grandmother Kay Hawtry run a tourist home, formerly a funeral parlor until Lesleh's grandfather, Mr. Chalmers (rhymes with "embalmers"), disappeared. Down in the cellar, late at night, strange voices can be heard. Is Grandma keeping some dark secret down there? This Canadian film is half-hearted exploitation, not quite a gore movie and not quite a character study. Barry Morse has a minor role as a husband looking for his missing wife. William Fruet's direction is workaday, and Ida Nelson's script is ultimately too derivative of PSYCHO to stand on its own merits. In today's horror market, a film as tame as FUNERAL HOME is bound to come off second best. Good track by Jerry Fielding. Also CRIES IN THE NIGHT. (VC)

**FUNHOUSE, THE (1981).** That TEXAS CHAINSAW MAS-

SACRE lovable, Tobe Hooper, restrains himself for the first half hour of this chiller diller to establish four interesting teenagers who spend the night in a spooky carnival midway. But then Tobe pulls out the stops! A sexually repressed midway helper (Wayne Doba, a professional mime) wears a fright mask to hide the fact that underneath the mask is an even worse countenance—something that would give the Frankenstein Monster nightmares. He kills fortune teller Sylvia Miles and stalks the kids as they flee for their lives. Doba's death scene is the highpoint of the show, but thrills are too far apart. Kevin Conway, William Finley, Cooper Huckabee, Elizabeth Berridge, Miles Chapin. Special effects by Craig Reardon and Rick Baker. (VC)

**FURY, THE (1978).** Insufficient exposition weakens this Brian De Palma horror-adventure about a young man (Andrew Stevens) with psychic powers who becomes a pawn between spy factions. It's visually exciting, however, with several memorable action sequences. Superspy Kirk Douglas (Steven's father) tries to rescue him from the villainous John Cassavetes. Emphasis of the John Farris script is on taut suspense and the thrill of the pursuit, with plenty of smashed-up cars, special effects and make-up (Rick Baker). Carrie Snodgress, Amy Irving, Charles Durning. (VC)

**FURY OF THE CONGO (1951).** Johnny Weissmuller, retired from playing Tarzan to don the safari hat of Jungle Jim, comes across a piece of jungle where nature has gone berserk by producing a man-eating plant (gulp!) and a spider big enough to challenge the ant creatures in THEM. It's dreary Sam Katzman-produced stuff for Columbia, unimaginatively directed by William Berke. Even pros Lyle Talbot and Sherry Moreland look lost in the Congo. Some fury!

**FURY OF THE SUCCUBUS. See DARK EYES.**

**FURY OF THE WOLFMAN (1973).** Paul Naschy tries to get it off his chest—the sign of the Pentagram, we mean. If he doesn't, he'll turn into a hairy killer when the moon is full, just as he did in FRANKENSTEIN'S BLOODY TERROR, to which this is a sequel. Directed by Jose Maria Zabalza, FURY OF THE WOLFMAN will only make horror fans furious. (VC)

**FURY ON THE BOSPHORUS (1965).** Standard superspy stuff in which Ken Clark, as the indestructible Malloy, tracks a kidnapped professor, whose new Death Beta Ray is the hottest thing in the world of laser weaponry. Zip Zap Zum. Ho hum. Margaret Lee provides the skirts and blouses.

**FUTURE COP (1976).** Mildly amusing, one-joke comedy concept teaming veteran cop Ernest Borgnine with a robot cop (Michael Shannon) who has been poorly programmed and is always klutzing it up. Poorly programmed is right. This TV-movie directed by Jud Taylor became a short-lived series that brought back Borgnine, Shannon and John Amos, then it became the inspiration for another movie for TV, COPS AND ROBIN, with the same cast. And if that wasn't enough, the concept was recycled and reprogrammed for the 1980 feature, SUPERFUZZ, again with Borgnine.

**FUTURE COP (1985). See TRANCERS, THE.**

**FUTURE KILL (1985).** Look at Splatter: He's the leader of a punk gang, an android-man whose hand is a claw device that can rip bodies apart at the wriggling of a finger. And Big Splatter and his Little Splatters are cruising the city, following political and social collapse, looking for members of a fraternity who accidentally witnessed Splatter commit a murder. Who will live and die before dawn breaks? A despicable, sickening movie with nothing to counterbalance its graphic violence and nihilistic viewpoints. As Ronald W. Moore has written and directed it on location in Austin, Texas, this has zero entertainment values. Edwin Neal, Marilyn Burns. (VC)

**FUTURE SCHLOCK (1984).** Political satire on Australia's current battle between middle-class suburbanites and non-comformists, set in the 21th Century when the non-comfortists have lost a civil war and are kept prisoners. Rebels Cisco and Pancho drive their Corvette through the night to harass authorities with prankish tricks. Strange Australian

**YUL BRYNNER AS THE ROBOT IN 'FUTUREWORLD'**

release, produced-written-directed by Barry Peak and Chris Kiely. Michael Bishop, Tracey Callander.

**FUTURE WOMEN (1975).** Heavily edited TV version of a European-made fantasy-adventure, hence much of its erotic qualities are missing. Loosely (and we mean loosely) based on characters created by Sax Rohmer, with Shirley Eaton as Samanada, an enticing, scantily-dressed seductress-ruler of the all-female kingdom of Femina, who plans taking over the world with her machine-gun packing femmes. Writer Peter Welbeck treats this as a kind of James Bond spoof but the Lonnie Kaufman production lacks flair to make it work. (Gadgets and effects are very shoddy, indeed). What emerges is a crude film full of fake action. Not even female oglers will find much to satisfy them despite all the beautiful women. And Richard Wyler makes for a dull hero. Directed by Jesus Franco. Eliza Montes, Marta Reeves.

**FUTUREWORLD (1976).** This sequel to WESTWORLD (about a bizarre fantasy paradise that malfunctioned and killed vacationers) picks up when the malfunctions are corrected and Westworld functions alongside Futureworld, where your science-fiction dreams come true. However, crusading reporters Peter Fonda and Blythe Danner suspect a cabal of power-mad villains is using the facilities to take over the world. The Mayo Simon-George Schenk script makes for an exciting thriller with wonderful sets (including the real Houston Space Center) and ample suspense and intrigue. Yul Brynner reappears as the Gunfighter in Black. Directed by Richard T. Heffron. Arthur Hill, Allen Ludden, John Ryan, Stuart Margolin, Robert Cornthwaite. (VC)

**FUTZ (1969).** Sty in the eye from writers Joseph Stefano and Rochelle Owens: man falls in love with his pig, is persecuted by his fellow man. As directed by Tom O'Horgan, FUTZ takes gutz to sit through; you have to be a little nutz.

**FX 18 SUPERSPY (1965).** Superbomb set to destroy Manhattan Island; superagent Richard Wyler primed to stop the dastardly enemy agents who have their hands on the launch controls; superviewer programmed to shut off the set and go to bed when he's licked. Directed by Riccardo Freda. Gil Delamare, Jany Clair.

*"We must find another brain!" —Dr. Frankenstein in* **FRANKENSTEIN.**

*"Think you've seen blood and gore? Think you've seen stomach-retching mutilation? You ain't seen nothing' yet!"*
*—Advertisement for* **THE GRUESOME TWOSOME.**

**GALACTICA III: CONQUEST OF THE EARTH.** Videocassette title of **CONQUEST OF THE EARTH.**

**GALAXINA (1980).** Through the 31st Century soars a starship piloted by Captain Butt (Avery Schreiber) and his misfits, creatures and robots. Their mission: retrieve the Blue Star, a powerful crystal, from robot villain Ordric. This comedy-parody, written-directed by William Sachs, is not a rollicking lampoon but does have isolated laughs. Title character is a sexy humanoid robot (Dorothy Stratten, a Playboy centerfold killed by her husband shortly after production). Tongue-in-cheek homages to ALIEN (a tiny creature scurries through the ship) and STAR TREK (a character named Mr. Spot), but it comes off juvenile. Nice try, but no extraterrestrial cigar. Chuck Colwell's effects range from good to utterly incompetent. Stephen Macht, James D. Hinton. (VC)

**GALAXY EXPRESS (1979).** Japanese animated science-fiction repackaged by Roger Corman. A "space train" of the 35th Century passes through a time continuum, taking passengers to their hopes and dreams. Directed by Taro Rin. (VC)

**GALAXY INVADER (1985).** Alien from beyond our galaxy is hunted by Earthlings. Low budgeter directed by Don Dohler. Richard Ruxton, Faye Tilles, George Stover. (VC)

**GALAXY OF TERROR (1981).** Well-produced B job from Roger Corman, a horror/science-fiction tale (concocted by co-producer Marc Siegler) about a crew on a desolate planet. Each member meets a horrible death, giving the effects team opportunities for blood, gore and multitentacled monsters. The best attack scene is when a sluglike monster "rapes" a beautiful astronaut after stripping away her spacesuit. This moves so fast under Bruce Clark's direction, there's little time to contemplate the plot and illogical behavior of characters. Graphic design is very satisfying but the ending is needlessly metaphysical; yet it too works in its own flawed irrational way. Ray Walston, Erin Moran, Edward Albert. Also released as PLANET OF HORRORS. (VC)

**GALLERY OF HORRORS.** Videocassette title for **DR. TERROR'S GALLERY OF HORRORS,** also known as **RETURN FROM THE PAST.** But under any title . . .

**GAME OF DEATH, A (1945).** Richard Connell's horror-adventure classic "The Most Dangerous Game" is the ultimate yarn in which man pursues man for sadistic bloodsport. While the best version was made in 1932 by Merian Cooper and Ernest Schoedsack, this suffers from budgetary sickness, which hampers the ambitious talents of director Robert Wise. John Loder (as the stranded Rainsford), Edgar Barrier (as the sadistic Nazi-like hunter Zaroff) and Audrey Long (a love interest not in the original story) labor to make Norman Houston's script workable. Story depicts how Zaroff traps, chases and kills shipwreck survivors on his Pacific island. Jason Robards, Robert Clarke, Noble Johnson.

**GAMERA VS. BARUGON.** See **WAR OF THE MONSTERS.**

**GAMERA VS. GUIRON.** See **ATTACK OF THE MONSTERS.**

**GAMERA VS. GYAOS.** See **RETURN OF THE GIANT MONSTERS.**

**GAMERA VS. MONSTER X (1970).** Titled MONSTERS INVADE EXPO '70 in Southeast Asia, this Japanese monster marathon stars a giant flying turtle always sticking its neck out to save mankind from a fate worse than having to watch Japanese monster marathons. Expo '70 is where ferocious, noisy battles occur between Gamera and Jiger, a bitchy female who spits spears (!) through her jagged mouth. Crash bam thud. Directed with subtlety by Noriaki Yuasa.

**GAMERA VS. OUTER SPACE MONSTER VIRUS.** See **DESTROY ALL PLANETS.**

**GAMERA VS. ZIGRA (1971).** Aliens called Zigrans plot to conquer Earth, but first have to kill the heroic turtle Gamera. Call it the old shell game. Kids bring Gamera to life and it engages in a rousing battle with a monster-battleship. Incomprehensible for adults; matinee fodder for toddlers. Directed by Noriaki Yuasa, responsible for a whole series of these gnashing Gamera gambits.

**GAMES (1967).** Director Curtis Harrington's thriller with Hitchcockian overtones isn't up to the Master's standards, but it's a decent tyro's try. James Caan and Katharine Ross conceive diabolical mind-playing "games" . . . but Simone

Signoret turns sport into nightmare. Resolution of the super-natural elements may disappoint buffs but suspense and mystery fans will enjoy Gene Kearney's twist ending, if they haven't seen through the gossamer fabrications. Don Stroud, Kent Smith, Estelle Winwood, Ian Wolfe.

**GAMMA PEOPLE, THE (1956).** Symbolic political science-fiction thriller with Communist madman Walter Rilla turning children into babbling idiots or savant geniuses via radiation treatment. Wobbly, didactic material written by John Gossage and John Gilling (the latter also directed) gets trapped behind an ironic curtain. Paul Douglas, Leslie Phillips, Eva Bartok, Martin Miller, Olaf Pooley. (VC)

**GAMMERA THE INVINCIBLE (1966).** Wow! Look at that! A hot-breathed, jet-propelled, bi-winged prehistoric monster! And a turtle to boot! Yes fans, another fun-loving, panic-happy Japanese-inspired creature on the rampage. And look! They've added American footage featuring Brian Donlevy and Albert Dekker so we'll relate better to Gammera. Now there are two M's in ""Gammera," while the other six films in this snapping turtle series had only one. Something got lost in the translation, maybe? Gammera obscura?

**GANJA AND HESS.** See **BLOOD COUPLE.**

**GAPPA—TRIPHIBIAN MONSTER.** See **MONSTER FROM A PREHISTORIC PLANET.**

**GARDEN OF THE DEAD (1972).** Deceased convicts rise from the grave to scatter and splatter those who have wronged them on the chain gang. Director John Hayes soon after found life to be a tough row to hoe hoe hoe. My, what a seedy joke. (VC)

**GARDENER, THE (1974).** Offbeat film produced in Puerto Rico with Joe Dallesandro as a shady weed chopper who turns into a tree and has rapport with flowers. Writer-director Jim Kay makes this a tough row to hoe since the film never quite sinks its roots. Rita Gam, Katharine Houghton, James Congdon. In video as SEEDS OF EVIL.

**GARGOYLES (1972).** Unusually good monster/effects TV-movie, even if the Stephen-Elinor Karpf teleplay has shortcomings. The excellent make-up by Ellis Burman and Stan Winston justifiably won an Emmy, reminiscent of the quality work often seen on TV's OUTER LIMITS. Cornel Wilde investigates strange stories about winged creatures in the desert; the Carlsbad Caverns (where this was filmed) is headquarters and nesting place for gargoyle-like aliens planning to take over our planet. Tautly directed by B. W. L. Norton. Jennifer Salt, Bernie Casey, Grayson Hall.

**GAS HOUSE KIDS IN HOLLYWOOD, THE (1947).** Eagle Lion cheapie starring Carl "Alfalfa" Switzer of "Little Rascals" fame in a skid row plot (by Robert E. Kent) replete with haunted house, alleged ghosts and a crazy scientist ticked off at the world with a time bomb of destruction. Directed by Edward L. Cahn, music by Albert Glasser. Benny Bartlett, Tommy Bond, Douglas Fowley, James Burke.

**GAS-S-S-S (1971).** Right on, hey-baby, swing-with-it, daddy-o movie for hippie-yippies still under 25. A nerve gas is loose which kills everyone over 25. Is this instant Utopia for the younger set or is this instant Utopia? An odyssey of fun-loving adventure for 20-year-olds who dress like tourists, fight it out with Hell's Angels and shout obscenities. Is this producer-director Roger Corman's idea of a grand time? Ben Vereen, Bud Cort, Elaine Giftos, Cindy Williams, Country Joe McDonald, Marshall McLuhan. (VC)

**GATES OF HELL, THE (1981).** In Dunwich, USA, stomping grounds of H. P. Lovecraft, a priest hangs himself in a graveyard, opening portals to Hades. Christopher George has three days to close that door or every corpse on Earth will never rest again. (Won't George Romero like that!) Director Lucio Fulci (ZOMBIE) is more interested in showing a woman vomit her guts out, a drill penetrate a man's head (from every conceivable angle) and a human brain squashed out of a woman's head. Very pointless (except for the drills), sadistic and visually revolting. Strong stomachs required. Venantino Venantini, Carlo de Mejo, Daniela Doria. (VC)

**GEEK MAGGOT BINGO (1983).** Amateur 16mm monster-horror parody flick for midnight audiences, written-produced-directed by Brooklynite Nick Zedd. A ridiculous Dr. Franken-berry (Robert Andrews), vampire queen Scumbalina (Donna Death), sleazy special effects and very crude camera work and lighting. Enough Zedd?

**GEMINI MAN, THE.** See **CODE NAME—MINUS ONE.**

**GENESIS II (1973).** Disappointing science-fiction TV-movie produced-written by Gene Roddenberry, flawed by naive writing and average direction by John Llewellyn Moxey. Alex Cord, in a state of suspended animation, awakens in 2133 to find civilization destroyed by atomic war. Surviving factions are broken down into Masters and Slaves and Cord is enmeshed in politics and shoot-outs. Similar characters were utilized in two other Roddenberry pilots, STRANGE NEW WORLD and PLANET EARTH. Mariette Hartley is quite sexy in this one . . . Ted Cassidy, Percy Rodriques, Lynne Marta.

**GENII OF DARKNESS (1960).** One of four films re-edited from a Mexican vampire serial and redubbed for gringos. More nocturnal neck-biting adventures with German Robles as a bloodsucker whose wardrobe is as shabby as the production values. The good guys try to steal the ashes from his coffin to keep him from coming back to life. Ashes to asses . . . Directed by Frederick Curiel.

**GENIUS AT WORK (1946).** From the producers of ZOMBIES ON BROADWAY, who again team Wally Brown and Alan Carney (in the vein of Abbott and Costello), this time as two radio stars with a detective show. Lionel Atwill is their adversary, a fan of torture chambers named "The Cobra." Best for its '40s nostalgia and cast. Might a better title have been IDIOTS AT WORK? Script by Robert E. Kent and Monte Brice . . . direction by Leslie Goodwins. Anne Jeffreys, Robert Clarke, Bela Lugosi, Ralph Dunn, Marc Cramer.

**GENOCIDE (1968).** Japanese science-fiction in which a survivor of the Nazi death camps learns how to control giant swarms of insects and turn them against mankind. Quick, reach for the Black Flag! Directed by Kazui Nihonmatsu.

**GHASTLY ONES, THE (1969).** Period gore thriller, produced-directed by Andy Milligan, with a madman running around a mansion chopping folks into little pieces and eating animals alive. The really ghastly one is Milligan who remade this as LEGACY OF HORROR in 1978—it was just as terrible bad ugh. Veronica Radbur, Maggie Rogers. (VC)

**GHASTLY ORGIES OF COUNT DRACULA.** See **REINCARNATION OF ISABEL, THE.**

**GHIDRAH, THE THREE-HEADED MONSTER (1965).** Another of director Inoshiro Honda's exercises in global destruction and monstrous mayhem when a meteorite hatches open to reveal Ghidrah—but three brains aren't better than one, since the fire-breathing extraterrestrial displays a great dumbness as it battles Godzilla (in his first major role as a good character), Rodan and Mothra atop Mt. Fuji. Made when Eiji Tsuburaya's effects were still well produced, establishing the use of several monsters in various combinations of combat. Eiji Okada, Yosuke Natsuki. (VC)

**GHOST, THE (1965).** Scotland, 1919. Peter Baldwin and Barbara Steele have an affair that drives husband Leonard Elliott to twisted jealousy. Elliott dies but since he is a dealer in the occult he is able to return from Deathland (using his housekeeper as a medium) to wreak revenge on the ill-tempered lovers. Elliott is playing the titular character from THE HORRIBLE MR. HICHCOCK, so this is a loose sequel. Harriet White, elio Jotta. Directed by Riccardo Freda.

**GHOST AND MR. CHICKEN (1966).** Universal programmer is as feeble-minded as the character Don Knotts plays: a bumbling typesetter who proves his worth(lessness) by solving a murder case in a haunted house of phony phenomena. Some entertainment value, if you enjoy Knotts' style. Directed by Alan Rafkin. Joan Staley, Dick Sargent, Skip Homeier, Ellen Corby, Hope Summers, Liam Redmond.

**GHOST AND MRS. MUIR, THE (1947).** Supernatural comedy with a few chilling moments. Widow Gene Tierney lives in a seacoast mansion and collaborates on a best-seller with the salty spirit of sea captain Rex Harrison who falls in love with the lovely woman. Excellent period flavor with touches of whimsy, superbly directed by Joseph L. Mankiewicz. George Sanders, Natalie Wood. Inspiration for a 1960s TV sitcom.

**GHOST BREAKERS (1940).** Hilariously funny Paramount comedy directed by George Marshall, proving Bob Hope was a master at screen spoofery. The setting is a haunted house in Cuba owned by Paulette Goddard and frequented by ghosts and zombies. Dean Martin and Jerry Lewis did the same story in 1952 as SCARED STIFF, thought with lesser results. Richard Carlson, Anthony Quinn, Paul Lukas, Paul Fix, Willie Best, Tom Dugan, Pedro de Cordoba.

**GHOST BUSTERS, THE (1975).** After the success of GHOSTBUSTERS, three hoary episodes of a never-aired series were dubbed onto video. Superawful TV sitcom garbage starring Forrest Tucker (as Kong), Larry Storch (as Spencer) and Tracy (a gorilla) as occult private eyes hunting supernatural prey with a Ghost Dematerializer. Produced on tape on phony studio sets, this is stuff they stopped making in the 1930s to salute the death of vaudeville. Directed by Norman Abbott, these superstupid shows parody the Maltese Falcon, the Canterville Ghost and superdumb haunted house cliches. The jokes are as old as the Catskills. (VC)

**GHOST CATCHERS (1944).** Ole Olsen and Chic Johnson rival Abbott and Costello for nuttiness in this Universal programmer in which the dazed duo encounters real ghosts in the haunted house next door to their nightclub. Directed by Edward F. Cline. Leo Carrillo, Gloria Jean, Andy Devine, Lon Chaney Jr., Kirby Grant, Morton Downey, Tor Johnson, Mel Torme, Jack Norton. Fun 1940s nostalgia.

**GHOST CHASERS (1951).** Edgar the Friendly Ghost Chaser helps the Bowery Boys capture crooks led by a flipped-out sawbones, Philip Van Zandt. You'll need a chaser too to sit through this William Beaudine-directed programmer. Tepid tongue in cheek. Leo Gorcey, Huntz Hall and the usual gang of adults acting like teenagers. Jan Kayne.

**GHOST CRAZY (1944).** Lowbrow horror-comedy vehicle for Shemp Howard (later to be one of the Three Stooges) and rotund Billy Gilbert, carnival conmen who travel with a caged gorilla. They stop off at a creepy old house to help a damsel in distress and behave like Stephin Fetchit every time they see a sheeted ghost popping out of a secret passageway built into the family graveyard next door. The gorilla also runs wild through the corridors. Maxie Rosenbloom is especially bad as a dumb chauffeur, Minerva Urecal is the sinister housemaid always opening doors and Jayne Hazard is the harassed heiress. Scripted by Tim Ryan, who also plays straight man to Billy and Shemp. Directed by William Beaudine. John Hamilton, Bernie Sell.

**GHOST CREEPS, THE (1940).** Entry in the East Side Kids series (before they became the Bowery Boys ). Leo Gorcey, Bobby Jordan and other East Siders track down ghosts of dubious ectoplasmic heritage. It's a night of pseudoterror under director Joseph Lewis. Call it nocturnal omission. Vince Barnett, Dave Gorcey, Minerva Urecal.

**GHOST DANCE (1982).** In the spirit (ha ha ho ho) of SHADOW OF THE HAWK . . . An Indian evil spirit possesses medicine man and sets him on a killing spree. Good Arizona location photography but the film is amateurish—from Peter Buffa's direction to the (non)acting of Henry Ball and Julie Amato. Like unkept tomahawk: Heap plenty dull. (VC)

**GHOST DANCE (1983).** British-West German avant-garde film: A French and British girl become involved in psychiatry, ghosts, dreams, ESP, etc. Nothing to dance about. Written-produced-directed by Ken McMullen. Leonie Mellinger.

**GHOST GOES WEST, THE (1935).** Classic British comedy directed by Rene Clair with loving care. Robert Donat is romantically delightful as a Scottish spirit doomed to haunt an old drafty castle. When an American millionare moves the structure stone by stone to the American West, the ghost must help his descendants out of a jam. Solid entertainment produced by Alexander Korda. Jean Parker, Elsa Lanchester, Eugene Pallette, Evelyn Gregg. (VC)

**GHOST GOES WILD, THE (1947).** Artist pretends to be a ghost, ticks off the real ghost who penetrates the "veil of the unknown" to scare the daylights out of the phony. Viewers don't go wild. James Ellison, Anne Gwynne, Edward Everett Horton, Grant Withers, Lloyd Corrigan.

**GHOST HUNTER (1975).** Loose adaptation of Oscar Wilde's THE CANTERBURY GHOST, produced in Brazil and written-directed by Flavio Migliaccio, who also stars as an inventor whose devices carry him into another dimension.

**GHOST IN THE INVISIBLE BIKINI, THE (1966).** American-International's "Beach" series—bikinied teenage girls, motorcycles, robots and monsters—reached an all-time low in this wasted effort featuring teens rollicking in a haunted house. Boris Karloff, dead and gone to Heaven, is told by Susan Hart he can't get through the Pearly Gates unless he performs a good deed, such as helping Tommy Kirk stay out of the clutches of swindler Basil Rathbone. Don Weis directed this brainless exercise in futility. Deborah Walley, Nancy Sinatra, Patsy Kelly, Jesse White, Harvey Lembeck, Francis X. Bushman, Benny Rubin and Bobbi Shaw.

**GHOST IN THE NOONDAY SUN (1973).** Obscure Peter Sellers/Spike Milligan pirate comedy, never released to theaters until 1984, when it promptly walked the plank into oblivion. Sellers is Dick Scratcher, a buccaneer chef (but hardly gourmet) who kills the ship's captain after learning where the booty is stashed. But his memory grows foggy, and he must rely on the captain's ghost to remind him of where it's located. Directed by Peter Medak. Anthony Franciosa, Clive Revill, Peter Boyle, Richard Willis.

**GHOST OF DRAGSTRIP HOLLOW, THE (1959).** This rock 'n roll teen-oriented musical comedy blends dumb characters and hot rods with a stupid music track and a phony-looking monster (the rubber suit from THE SHE CREATURE). Not so-bad-you-should-see-it; so-bad-you-shouldn't-see-it. A talking automobile is among the anomalies in this broken-down jalopy of a movie. Directed shiftlessly by William Hole Jr. Russ Bender, Jody Fair, Martin Braddock, Kirby Smith.

**GHOST OF FLIGHT 401, THE (1978).** Alleged true story of a haunting documented in a John Fuller book, played in lowkey fashion by producer Emmett Lavery Jr. After the crash of an airliner in the Florida Everglades on December 29, 1972, the spectral image of the flight engineer (Ernest Borgnine) is witnessed aboard other planes using salvaged parts from the wreckage. A compelling, offbeat TV-movie retains respectability thanks to director Steven Hilliard Stern and writer Robert Malcolm Young. Gary Lockwood, Kim Basinger, Russell Johnson, Howard Hesseman, Robert F. Lyons.

**GHOST OF FRANKENSTEIN, THE (1942).** Fourth film in Universal's Frankenstein series, directed by Erle C. Kenton, has a lingering, compelling nostaglic flavor of the 1940s. Bela Lugosi returns as the revengeful Ygor (introduced in SON OF FRANKENSTEIN) and Lon Chaney Jr. lurches uncontrollably as the Monster. The story involves Lionel Atwill putting Ygor's brain into the monster. You must see this at least once. Sir Cedric Hardwicke, Ralph Bellamy, Evelyn Ankers, Dwight Frye, Barton Yarbrough, Doris Lloyd.

**GHOST OF SLUMBER MOUNTAIN, THE (1919).** Willis O'Brien, Hollywood's pioneer in stop motion animation (KING KONG and MIGHTY JOE YOUNG) provided effects for this short subject depicting dinosaurs and other extinct characters from prehistoric times. The story opens with Uncle Jack telling a group of children about the time he met Mad Dick, an old hermit with a telescope that enables him to see the creatures. Among the highlights: a battle between a giant bird and a snake, a fight to the death between two triceratops, and Jack being chased by a dinosaur. Crude but of historical importance to O'Brien aficionados.

**GHOST OF YOTSUYA (1958).** Japanese tale of the supernatural, exploring the horrors of the human mind. (VC)

**GHOST SHIP, THE (1943).** A frightening voyage produced by Val Lewton and directed by Mark Robson is unavailable today because of legal complications. The story focuses on a sailing ship commanded by homicidal killer Richard Dix. Third officer Russell Wade suspects the truth, but can't prove it as

**CREATURE FEATURES MOVIE GUIDE**

the body count climbs. Lewton's films are always worth seeing, and if you get the chance, don't pass it up. Edith Barrett, Skelton Knaggs, Lawrence Tierney.

**GHOST SHIP (1953).** Trim, skimming British supernatural tale, set aboard the Cyclops, a luxury yacht haunted by apparitions and the smell of cigar smoke ever since it was found adrift, with no one aboard. A young couple (Hazel Court, Dermot Walsh) purchases the craft, then learns of its ugly history the hard way. Finally, a medium comes aboard to discover there are the corpses of two tormented souls buried below deck, and a murderous captain on the loose. Writer-director Vernon Sewell has tacked on a whodunit ending to give it that is-the-supernatural-real-or-not? A tenseness pervades this underplayed film that will have you clutching for your preserver. Hugh Burden, John Robinson. (VC)

**GHOST STORY (1974). See MADHOUSE MANSION.**

**GHOST STORY (1981).** Peter Straub's convoluted best-seller (possessing the chilling qualities of Henry James and M. R. James) is clumsily transferred to the screen; Screenwriter Lawrence D. Cohen oversimplifies Straub's narrative, limiting the variety of ghosts, among other deficits. One horrible face after another (from the "walking dead" school of graphic countenances) is all you get for your bucks. However, the underlying premise idea is intriguing: The Chowder Society, a group of old men, gathers periodically to swap ghost stories. Its members—Douglas Fairbanks Jr., John Houseman, Fred Astaire, Melvyn Douglas—share a deep, dark secret from their youth, bonded by a similar nightmare. How a wronged wraith (a drowned woman) avenges herself across the veil of death makes for the supernatural thrills—but oh, Straub's novel was so much more. Directed by John Irvin. Craig Wasson, Alice Krige, Patricia Neal. (VC)

**GHOST TRAIN (1941).** Passengers waiting in a British country terminal are subjected to the strange phenomenon of an express roaring past them—one that crashed years before. And this is the anniversary of the accident! Captures the Gothic flavor of the old-fashioned English ghost story, although this allows for Nazi spies. Directed by Walter Forde.

**GHOST WALKS, THE (1934).** Outdated clunker involving hidden passageways, ghosts who aren't really ghosts and a madman who intends to perform operations that the American Medical Association would never approve. Directed by Frank Strayer. John Miljan, June Collyer, Spencer Charters, Eve Southern, Henry Kolker.

**GHOST WARRIOR (1985).** ICEMAN cometh: A 400-year-old samurai warrior, a kind of "Frozen Shogun" found in a cavern in Motosuka, Japan, is revived at a cyrogenics hospital in Los Angeles where Dr. Jane Julian tries to introduce him to the ways of modern man. But this warrior out of time and place must wield his sword against evil in this offbeat, mildly compelling Charles Band fantasy-actioner. Hiroshi Fujioka is quite good as Yoshita as he tangles with modern gangs and is etched in stark relief against skyscrapers, cars, TV sets and pursuing helicopters. Not a classic, but at least writer Tim

Curnen has something to say. Directed by Larry Carroll. John Calvin, Charles Lampkin. (VC)

**GHOSTBUSTERS (1984).** Inspired, ingenious supernatural comedy, a great blend of laughs and special effects. Credit writers Dan Akyroyd and Harold Ramis, and producer-director Ivan Reitman for the refreshing images. Bill Murray (Dr. Peter Venkman), Akyroyd (Dr. Raymond Stantz) and Harold Ramis (Dr. Egon Spengler) are a team of Manhattan spirit smashers who transfix spirits with their nuclear laser guns and imprison the evil protoglops in a ghost gaol at their dilapidated headquarters. One uproarious gag after the other as the threesome chases ectoglopic entities, then faces the wrath of an official who feels they're polluting the environment, and allows the wraiths and spectral creatures to escape. Now the city is threatened with a "ghost wave." Richard Edlund's effects are brilliant. Murray is the aloof ghostbuster who would much rather bed beautiful clients, and his asides are hysterical. Akyroyd is the buffoon and Ramis the straight-faced, text-book expert always spouting jargon about multi-dimensional cross-overs and ectoplasmic invasions. Sigourney Weaver is involved when she discovers an ancient God living in her refrigerator. Ray Parker Jr. wrote the catchy theme song, Elmer Bernstein penned the appealing incidental music. (VC)

**GHOSTKEEPER (1980).** Ghost-cannibal horror from Canada. Riva Spier, Murray Ord. (VC)

**GHOSTS IN ROME (1961).** "Spirited" Italian comedy with tongue in cheek: Aristocratic, high-living ghosts, members of a noble Roman family who have died violently, face eviction when their property is sold to make way for a supermarket. Marcello Mastroianni has two roles, Vittorio Gassman only one. Directed by Antonio Pietrangeli. Sandra Milo, Belinda Lee, Eduardo de Filippo.

**GHOSTS—ITALIAN STYLE (1968).** Amusing Italian farce starring Vittorio Gassman in a double role—once as a human, once as a spirit. Satirical take-off on foreign customs and mores, as they are affected by the supernatural. Sophia Loren provides this Carlo Ponti film with a spirit of her own. What ectoplasmic energy! Directed by Renato Castellani. Mario Adorf, Carlo Giuffre, Francesco Tensi. Marcello Mastroianni has a cameo role as a sprightly spirit.

**GHOSTS OF HANLEY HOUSE, THE (1974).** The owners of the titular mansion can't sell it, so they hold a ghost story party to make everyone relax. But that's when the real ghosts come to life and rattle their chains. Party poopers! British TV-film recycled to America. Elsie Baker, Barbara Chase.

**GHOSTS ON THE LOOSE (1943).** Bela Lugosi joins the East Side Kids (Leo Gorcey, Huntz Hall, Bobby Jordan, Stanley Clements, Sunshine Sammy Morrison) in a haunted house comedy—the joint is actually being used by Nazi agents as a counterfeiting hideout. The real interest here is a smoldering ingenue, Ava Gardner. Moronic Monogram megaloadacrap directed by William Beaudine. (VC)

**GHOSTS THAT STILL WALK (1977).** A young boy is pos-

**'GHOSTBUSTERS': THEY GOT SLIMED!**

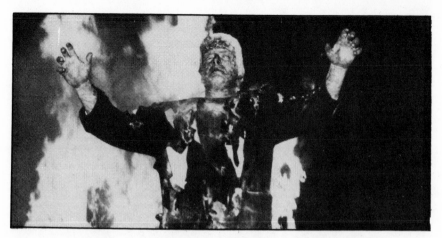

**LON CHANEY JR., ALL FIRED UP, IN 'THE GHOST OF FRANKENSTEIN'**

sessed by the spirit of an Indian medicine man in this low-budget pseudodocumentary about ghosts and spirits. It's terribly disjointed and hard to follow but does have one exciting sequence in which an elderly couple traveling across the desert in a rec vehicle is attacked by boulders that come rolling toward them across the plain. Otherwise, tedious going. And boring. Written-directed by James T. Flocker. (VC)

**GHOUL, THE (1933).** Outdated British chiller of the "walking dead" school . . . Boris Karloff is a Professor of Egyptology in possession of the Eternal Light, a priceless jewel of mysterious properties. Vowing to rise from the dead should anyone tamper with the precious stone, Karloff dies . . . and lives up to his promise when his servant (Ernest Thesiger, later to star in BRIDE OF FRANKENSTEIN with Karloff) steals the Eternal Light. Now it's going to be Eternal Night for that dude. Directed by T. Hayes Hunter. Anthony Bushell, Cedric Hardwicke, Ralph Richardson, Kathleen Harrison.

**GHOUL, THE (1975).** British Gothic horror thriller set in the 1920s: Wild flappers hold a car race across foggy moors. When one car breaks down, its beautiful driver seeks refuge in Peter Cushing's mansion, unaware he is a defrocked minister whose son is infected with a love for Kali the Killer Goddess. Now he is a ghoul, feeding on fresh flesh. John Hurt, in an ugly role, plays the crazed ground's-keeper who rapes the beauties before the son munches at lunches. A lumbering, disgusting, pointless movie with nihilistic overtones in John Elder's script. Veronica Carlson, Don Henderson and Alexandra Bastedo are among the victims. Directed by Freddie Francis. Never theatrically distributed in America. (VC)

**GHOULIES (1985).** Turgid imitation of GREMLINS, unimaginatively plotted by producer Jeffery Levy and director Luca Bercovici, and only coming to life in a few effects sequences. The setting is a creepy old house in Hollywood where Peter Liapis and wife Lisa Pelikan come under the spell of Black Magic. Part of the house's mystery is a group of mischievous monsters which pop in and out to provide the only moments of vitality and humor. Typically sleazy of the lowbrow fare Charles Band turns out. Easily forgotten. Michael Des Barres, Jack Nance. Peter Risch and Tamara de Treaux are among the midgets in make-up.

**G.I. EXECUTIONER (1971).** Produced in Singapore as WIT'S END but not released until 1985. An antimatter device invented by a defecting Chinese nuclear scientist is the weak fantasy element in this otherwise cynical-American-in-a-foreign-country-involved-in-intrigue flicker. Former globe-hopping journalist Tom Keena is in the thick of espionage in a plot too convoluted to work. Keena is an anti-hero but the title is misleading since he is not cast in the mold of "The Executioner." The star attraction is Angelique Pettyjohn as a stripper who shoots it out with a fat spy while she's totally

naked. Victoria Racimo, Janet Wood, Brian Walden. Directed-written by Joel M. Reed in rambling style. (VC)

**GIANT BEHEMOTH, THE (1959).** Stop motion animator Willis O'Brien provides only mediocre effects for this British creature-on-the-rampage production. The brontosaurus hulker, subjected to radiation, ravages downtown London with its radioactive eyes, which can burn flesh from bodies. Gene Evans as the American scientist should have seen THE BEAST FROM 20,000 FATHOMS for monster-destroying pointers. Eugene Lourie, who co-directed with Douglas Hickok, wrote the screenplay. Andre Morell, Leigh Madison, Jack MacGowran, John Turner, Henry Vidon.

**GIANT CLAW, THE (1957).** Sam Katzman quickie is a must-see for sheer incompetence: A low-water mark, even for schlockmeister Katzman, it is inanely, incredulously delightful. The monstrous talon is attached to a giant bird from outer space, so obviously stuffed it will remind you of a Thanksgiving turkey, so obviously pulled by wires you'll search for puppeteers on the corners of the frame. The size of a battleship, the extraterrestrial winged warlord is surrounded by an antimatter force field which makes it impervious to weapons—even to atomic bombs. Jeff Morrow and Mara Corday devise a "mu-meson projector" to down the avian avenger, cheered on by "bird-watchers" Morris Ankrum, Edgar Barrier and Robert Shayne. The bird, with its long neck, bulging eyeballs and plucked look, will have you rolling in the aisles. The studio should have stuffed it. The bird, we mean. Directed by Fred F. Sears, who obviously winged it.

**GIANT FROM THE UNKNOWN (1958).** Buddy Baer portrays a king-size Conquistadore (brought to life by a lightning bolt) who haunts a deserted California town. Produced by Arthur Jacobs, who went on to the PLANET OF THE APES series. Jack Pierce's make-up cannot help create a scary monster this time. Tediously directed by Richard E. Cunha. Edward Kemmer, Morris Ankrum, Bob Steele. (VC)

**GIANT GILA MONSTER, THE (1959).** Produced by actor Ken Curtis, this low budget quickie is an uninteresting potpourri of hot rods and teenagers facing a mystery in the New Mexican desert. "What do you suppose is out there?" and "I think I saw something moving" exemplify the dialogue by director Ray Kellogg and Jay Sims. The monster is a harmless lizard filmed in a sandbox and enlarged by a macro lens. Kellog went on to direct John Wayne's THE GREEN BERETS, Curtis became Festus on GUNSMOKE. Don Sullivan, Lisa Simone, Shug Fisher, Yolanda Salas.

**GIANT LEECHES, THE.** See **ATTACK OF THE GIANT LEECHES.**

**GIANT OF METROPOLIS, THE (1963).** Beefcake in the shape of Gordon Mitchell in the year 10,000 B.D. (Before

Dumbbells), when our bulging hero crashes Atlantis, where crazy scientists have perfected immortality and can train their Death Beam on enemies. Grunts and groans—Italian style, with every Hercules cliche in the tome, directed by Umberto Scarpelli with a sense of humor. A saving grace, in this case. Bella Cortez, Roldano Lupi, Furio Meniconi.

**GIANT SPIDER INVASION, THE (1975).** The opening to another dimension permits all sizes of spiders to attack Earth. The bigger ones are nothing more than multi-legged mock-ups propelled by Volkswagens in their pseudobellies. Blame this mess on voice-trainer/actor Robert Easton, not only for being the rustic dumbbell who finds radioactive spider eggs, but for being the screenwriter (with Richard Huff) who dreamed up the shoddy idea. Steve Brodie, Barbara Hale, Leslie Parrish and Alan Hale Jr. are wasted in nothing roles. Bill Rebane directed . . . sort of.

**GIANT OF THESSALY (1961).** Another search for the Golden Fleece, not as exciting as JASON AND THE ARGONAUTS, produced two years later. But there are decent special effects as a witch transforms men into creatures, and there are well-staged brawls. Directed by Riccardo Freda. Roland Carey, Ziva Rodann, Moira Orfei.

**GIGANTIS THE FIRE MONSTER (1955).** Sequel to GODZILLA, KING OF THE MONSTERS features the towering infernal under the name Gigantis, but a monster by any other name is still Godzilla. The destructor of Tokyo is trailed to an island where he/she/it engages in a battle with Angurus, a spiked creature with wings. After some soothing mayhem, Gigantis-Godzilla stomps toward Tokyo to make it a tail of one city. It was directed not by Honda but Motoyoshi Oda, although the special effects team was headed by Eiji Tsuburaya, Honda's pal. An American version, directed by Hugo Grimaldi, was released in 1959.

**GIRL FROM SCOTLAND YARD, THE (1937).** Totally forgettable spy thriller which features the "death ray" so typical of the time, and the efforts of a young heroine to track down the evil-doers. Directed by Robert Vignola. Karen Morley, Eduardo Ciannelli, Robet Baldwin, Lloyd Crane.

**GIRL FROM S.E.X. (1982).** Softcore porn mixing love and war. Plenty of explicit action (of assorted kinds) as several lovely bodies are contoured to fit a James Bondish spy plot. Directed by Paul G. Vatelli. Annette Haven, Lisa Deleeuw, Don Hart, Nicole Noir, Brooke West.

**GIRL FROM STARSHIP VENUS, THE (1957).** Softcore British porn flick about an alien taking the form of a sexy chick to "experience" native mating customs on Earth. Does she get a dressing down for poor protocol! Written-directed by Derek Ford. Monika Ringwald gives her all for space research. Andrew Grant, Mark Jones.

**GIRL IN HIS POCKET (1960).** French science-fiction comedy starring Jean Marais as a professor who shrinks from his problems by shrinking his girlfriend so she will slip easily in and out of his hip pocket. But he's wrong if he thinks that's going to minimize his girl problems. A surprise is in store for Marais and the audience in this delightful farce. Directed by Pierre Kast. Genevieve Page, Jean-Claude Brialy.

**GIRL IN ROOM 2A, THE (1975).** Poorly rendered Italian gore flick about a cult of sadists led by someone wearing a red mask and gloves, who delights in sticking spears into beautiful young women after abducting them. Daniela Giordano appears to be the next victim when she is released from prison and takes up residence in a strange house. While she hallucinates, we see a man's hand burned on a fireplace grate, bodies probed with pokers and knifes, a blood spot that keeps appearing on the floor, and assorted dull characters searching for missing persons. The dubbing is atrocious, the gore without redeeming social values and the performances, under director-producer William L. Rose, poor. (VC)

**GIRL IN THE KREMLIN, THE (1957).** An Albert Zugsmith Universal production, in such poor taste you won't want to miss it. The premise (scripted by Gene L. Coon and Robert Hill) is that Joseph Stalin really didn't die in 1953; he simply had a face-lift and went underground in Greece, hiding out with Zsa Zsa Gabor. Director Russell Birdwell treats the whole thing as ordinary spy shenanigans. Lex Barker, William Schallert, Maurice Manson, Jeffrey Stone.

**GIRL IN THE MOON (1929).** Early German science-fiction film directed by Fritz Lang depicts man's building of a rocket and the eventual trip to the moon. This is considered less-than-brilliant Lang, but film historians may find the special effects and scientific viewpoints of interest. Gerda Maurus, Willy Fritsch, Gustav von Wangenheim, Klaus Pohl.

**GIRL OF THE NILE, THE (1967).** U.S.-West German film masterminded by producer Sidney Pink is the trite tale of a trudging desert expedition facing a curse of the gods and other superstitious hogwash. Directed by Joe Lacy. Rory Calhoun, James Philbrook, Nuria Torrey.

**GIRL, THE GOLD WATCH AND DYNAMITE (1981).** A sequel to THE GIRL, THE GOLD WATCH AND EVERYTHING, and not much better in continuing the adventures of a timepiece that freezes the spatial continuum and allows its wearer to walk around among frozen figures. This time the watch becomes a pawn in a land swindle. Not the dynamite director Hy Averback or writer George Zateslo were digging for. Philip MacHale, Lee Purcell, Burton Gilliam, Jack Elam, Zohra Lampert, Gary Lockwood, Jerry Mathers.

**GIRL, THE GOLD WATCH AND EVERYTHING, THE (1980).** Light-hearted, minor adaptation of John D. MacDonald's popular fantasy about a nerd (Robert Hays) who inherits a pocketwatch from his late grandfather to discover it stops time. This allows him to carry out ridiculous pranks against the criminals trying to steal the watch. The special effects are minimal, the humor is bantamweight (sometimes feeble) and the whole things smacks of being a glorified sitcom. Pam Dawber, Zohra Lampert, Ed Nelson, Peter Brown, Maurice Evans, Larry Hankin, Jill Ireland. George Zateslo's teleplay never realizes the novel's full comedic potential. Directed by William Wiard.

**GIRL WHO DARED, THE (1944).** We dare you to watch as a girl and a guy get caught up in a ghost hunt in a house with billowing curtains and secret passageways. Kirk (Superman) Alyn and Lorna Gray try being heroic while Roy Barcroft is an old meanie. Grant Withers, Willie Best, Tom London.

**GIRLS NITE OUT (1983).** Routine slasher film in which the psychokiller dresses up in a bearskin and uses special knives to resemble a paw claw. The setting is a university in Ohio where security officer Hal Holbrook leads the search for the freako. Nothing special, you've seen it all before. Directed by Robert Deubel. Julie Montgomery, Richard Bright, James Carroll, Suzanne Barnes, David Holbrook (Hal's son). (VC)

**GIRLY (1970).** Houseful of psychokillers provides the "no place like home" setting for this British exercise in screen mayhem and murder. Nobody dies easy under Freddie Francis' direction. Michael Bryant, Vanessa Howard, Ursula Howells, Robert Swann, Pat Heywood, Michael Ripper.

**GLADIATOR, THE (1938).** Joe E. Brown fantasy-comedy, an adaptation of a Philip Wylie novel, shows the once-popular comedian at his hilarious best. After getting a shot in the arm, Joe E. develops incredible superstrength. Directed by Edward Sedgwick. June Travis, Dickie Moore.

**GLADIATORS, THE (1970).** Futuristic anti-war parable masterfully directed by Peter Watkins in pseudodocumentary style on Swedish locations, depicting how East and West, instead of maintaining armies and nuclear stockpiles, hold televised Peace Games—miniature forms of warfare, featuring crack teams of combat specialists. It is legal bloodshed that satisfies the lust of both powers. Watkins occasionally overplays his symbolic allegory, but this is still imaginative, chilling fantasy. Arthur Pentelow, Frederick Danner. (VC)

**GLASS SLIPPER, THE (1955).** Leslie Caron is a most alluring Cinderella and her dreams most lavish—ballets by Roland Petit yet, set in a Graustrakian castle. Estelle Winwood is the eccentric fairy godmother, Michael Wilding the Prince Charming, Elsa Lanchester the ugly stepmother and Amanda Blake and Lisa Daniels the (hiss hiss) stepsisters. They wring every ounce of charm out of this old Charles Perrault fairy tale. Directed by Charles Walters.

*"Bullets don't hurt [the incredible killer spider]. The only thing I've got to stop him here is a traffic light." —A frustrated traffic controller in*
## THE GIANT SPIDER INVASION.

**GLEN AND RANDA (1971).** Avant-garde Apocalyptic vision film, an eccentric pre-Mad Max version minus violence and bloodletting, reminiscent of Arch Oboler's FIVE in its mood. The title characters, 40 years after The Bomb, are members of a tribe that lives in isolation and ignorance of mankind's past. But Glen (Adam?) is curious about Metropolis (the city he has read about in old Wonder Woman comic books) and he and a pregnant Randa (Eve?) begin a trek through the wilderness of Idaho. The scenes are episodic and slow-paced, but images linger afterward of a tree growing through a rusting car, gas pumps in a weedpatch, Randa eating grass like a horse, the pair eating bugs from old boards, and Glen brutally beating salmon trapped in a stream. Director Jim Mc-Bride goes for esoteric effect with his immature, innocent characters, allowing only the older people (traveling salesman Garry Goodrow, old man Woodrow Chambliss) to be articulate. This could be viewed as hippies seeking the answers to life's riddles. Steven Curry, Shelley Plimpton. (VC)

**GLEN OR GLENDA? (1953).** One of the oddest movies of all time, designed as a pseudodocumentary to cash in on the sensational Christine Jorgenson sex change operation. It's a sympathetic study of transvestism from a transvestite, writer-director Edward D. Wood Jr., who went on to become the diabolical designer of PLAN 9 FROM OUTER SPACE and BRIDE OF THE ATOM. It opens with non sequitur shots of Bela Lugosi reading from a huge tome and talking like the host of INNER SANCTUM, but nothing he says has anything to do with the rest of the film. Lugosi is unbelievably hammy, and his purpose is never made clear. Then there's the framework device in which cop Lyle Talbot visits doctor Timothy Farrell to discuss the lives of two sexually confused men, Glen/Glenda and Alan/Ann. Flashbacks consist of humdrum documentary footage mixed with staged shots that are absolutely hysterical for their bad acting and writing. Occasionally Wood makes a salient point in building empathy for the transvestites, then he negates it with scenes of two struggling women in bondage-sadism-lesbian footage, or indulges in incredibly heavy-handed symbolism. Wood and his real-life wife portray one of the hapless couples struggling with transvestism. Has to be seen to be fully appreciated. (VC)

**GNOME-MOBILE (1967).** Pleasant Walt Disney musical-comedy fantasy enhanced by Walter Brennan, Tom Lowell, Jerome Cowan, Ellen Corby, Ed Wynn and Richard Deacon. Several children encounter elves and gnomes (but no fairies?) in California and protect them from carnival exploitation artists. Kids will love it. Directed by Robert Stevenson. From a novel by Upton Sinclair. (VC)

**GOBOTS: BATTLE OF THE ROCK LORDS (1986).** Feature-length spinoff from the TV cartoon series about warrior robots capable of turning themselves into rocketships and battle tanks. In this animated adventure from the Hanna-Barbera factory, the GoBots come to the rescue of the Rock People, being persecuted by the Rock Lord. Voices: Roddy McDowall, Telly Savalas, Margot Kidder. (VC)

**GOD TOLD ME TO (1976).** Writer-producer-director Larry Cohen's revisionistic look at the Jesus Christ legend will never be sanctioned by the Catholic Church but will fascinate science-fiction fans, iconoclasts, atheists and agnostics. A series of indiscriminate killings is linked to a Jesus Christ-figure (Richard Lynch) apparently conceived when a virgin (a young Sylvia Sydney) was artifically inseminated in a flying saucer in 1951. Equally bizarre is the cop (Tony Lo Bianco) investigating the case who was similarly conceived and has fantastic psychic powers. Then comes the confrontation between the "brothers" as they use their energy beams in a duel to the death. Irreverent film provides religious food for thought—and controversy. One of the oddest, and most misunderstood, films of the 1970s, banned and boycotted and given limited distribution under the title DEMON. Sandy

Dennis, Deborah Raffin, Andy Kaufman, Harry Bellaver. (VC)

**GODSEND, THE (1979).** A mysterious woman gives birth to a baby girl then leaves the infant with English farmers. When the child grows up, she is responsible for several deaths through evil emanations. What sounds like an OMEN rip-off is actually a fair British horror film focusing on psychological aspects rather than grisly details. Produced-directed by Gabrielle Beaumont, Malcolm Stoddard. (VC)

**GODZILLA—KING OF THE MONSTERS (1954).** Japanese classic directed by Inoshiro Honda, with special effects by Eiji Tsuburaya. It was quickly imported to the U.S. where additional footage, featuring Raymond Burr as newspaperman Steve Martin, was added for "local" appeal. In this historic, trend-setting monster movie (the first in a long-running series) Godzilla, a 400-foot-high Tyrannosaurus rex, is aroused from hybernation by an A-bomb test and goes on a rampage to destroy Tokyo. Although depicted as a villain, in later films the radioactive, fire-breathing behemoth became a "good" creature for mankind, battling alien invaders and other monsters. Serious critics have interpreted Honda's inspiration as an allegory of the nuclear age, but hardly anyone took later films seriously as they deteriorated to new lows in special effects. Kids, however, filled the theaters of the world to cheer the dueling titan. Akira Takarada, Momoko Kochi. (VC)

**GODZILLA: 1985 (1984).** After a ten-year hibernation, Japan's reigning King of Monsters returns as the villain he was in the first Godzilla film in 1954. This Godzilla is mean and snarls as he blows his radioactive breath on downtown Tokyo while giving it his famous two-step stomp. Like the origin movie, this features Raymond Burr as an American newspaperman in footage shot especially for the English version. There is nothing new in this revival—the effects by Teruyoshi Nakano are what you would expect, and there are obligatory scenes of scientists and military leaders gathering in chartrooms to declare the dangers of Godzilla's ire. What's different is a sympathetic attitude toward the monster, as if the juggernaut was misunderstood and only looking for a little love and companionship. Forget the fact the large lizard just crushed 3000 Orientals. Directed by Koji Hashimoto. Shin Takuma, Ken Tanaka, Keiju Kobayashi. (VC)

**GODZILLA ON MONSTER ISLAND (1972).** This time the leapin' lizard (in the company of monster pal Angorus) does battle with three-headed Ghidrah and Gigan (an obnoxious bird creature with a buzzsaw in its chest cavity) near a half-completed amusement park featuring a Godzilla tower. All this is instigated by a race of cockroach aliens invading Earth with the usual take-over plot. The buildup to the battle is repetitive and tedious. Action footage lifted from earlier Godzilla films shows you just how lousy the new effects are compared to Eiji Tsuburaya's work. Directed by Jun Fukuda. Hiroshi Ichikawa, Yuriko Hishimi.

**GODZILLA VS. THE BIONIC MONSTER. See GODZILLA VS. THE COSMIC MONSTER.**

**GODZILLA VS. MECHAGODZILLA. See GODZILLA VS. THE COSMIC MONSTER.**

**GODZILLA VS. MEGALON (1973).** Clumsy-footed entry in the Godzilla series, one of the weakest. The 400-foot-tall green lizard is aided by a jet-packed robot superhero in fighting off Megalon (resembling a cockroach with a built-in Zap Killer Beam), a stomper named Borodan and a race of underground Earthlings, the Seatopians, who are ticked off because of nuclear testing. Inferior to previous Godzilla films with utterly awful effects. Written and directed by Jun Fukuda. Katsuhiko Sasaki, Hiroyuki Kawase.

**GODZILLA VS. MONSTER ZERO.** Videocassette version of **MONSTER ZERO.**

**GODZILLA VS. MOTHRA.** Videocassette title for **GODZILLA VS. THE THING.**

**INSTIGATING URBAN RENEWAL IN DOWNTOWN TOKYO IN 'GODZILLA '85'**

**GODZILLA VS. THE COSMIC MONSTER (1974).** This sequel to TERROR OF MECHAGODZILLA is Japanese science-fiction sukiyaki with the King of Monsters battling a cyborg Godzilla controlled by aliens bent on conquest. A huge rodent creature said to embody Oriental spirits comes to the real Godzilla's aid when the languid lizard squares off against antagonistic Angorus. Directed by Jun Fukuda.

**GODZILLA VS. THE SEA MONSTER (1966).** Released in Japan as EBIRAH—TERROR OF THE DEEP, this exercise in cardboard mayhem stars the towering saurian, the King of Monsters, as a crusty critter suffering a case of crabs when he's attacked by colossal crustaceans of the deep. You know Godzilla is on the side of good when he destroys the Red Bamboo, a nefarious gang seeking world control. Jun Fukuda directed, Eiji Tsuburaya did the effects, which were still classy in those days. Akira Takarada, Toru Watanabe.

**GODZILLA VS. THE SMOG MONSTER (1972).** A Japanese coastal industrial city has an ecology problem: its miasmic bay of waste and rotting animal life breeds a plasmic organism named Hedorah which shoots laser beams from its eyepods and flies about at will. It intakes nourishment by sitting atop smokestacks and ingesting waste matter, which it then expels as human-killing smog. To the rescue comes the flat-footed Godzilla to indulge in a typical duel-of-the-titans. Directed by Yoshimitsu Banno. Akira Yamauchi.

**GODZILLA VS. THE THING (1964).** The giant saurian is at war with the giant moth Mothra, which lays an egg—literally speaking, of course. From the egg hatch two caterpillar progeny which weave a shroud of silk around hapless Godzilla, leaving him "stranded." A subplot about miniaturized people makes for a good laughs. Directed by Inoshiro Honda; special effects by Eiji Tsuburaya. Akira Takarada, Yurito Hoshi. In video as **GODZILLA VS. MOTHRA.**

**GODZILLA'S COUNTERATTACK. See GIGANTIS, THE FIRE MONSTER.**

**GODZILLA'S REVENGE (1969).** Shame on director Inoshiro Honda. By this time the Godzilla series was shamelessly borrowing footage from earlier films to keep Eiji Tsuburaya's special effects costs down. The setting is Monster Island, where Godzilla and son Minya (see SON OF GODZILLA about the father-son relationship) fight with Baragon and assorted monstrosities, now glaring stereotypes without compelling personalities. Incompetent dubbing, although the grunts are more articulate than usual.

**GOG (1954).** Duo-duped during the 3-D craze of 1953, this Ivan Tors production is set in an underground space research center where infiltrators have shorted out a computer and taken over robots Gog and Magog to commit murders. Tom Taggart's story has elements of the whodunit in addition to its science-fiction themes. GOG will not leave you agog, but it will keep you entertained. Directed by Herbert L. Strock. Richard Egan, Constance Dowling, Herbert Marshall, William Schallert, Philip Van Zandt.

**GOKE—BODY SNATCHER FROM HELL (1968).** After an airliner has passed through a strange cloud (caused by a flying saucer carrying alien invaders), it crashlands in the desert, where one of the passengers is suddenly infected with vampirism and turns the passengers into bloodsuckers who ooze a strange jelly-like substance. Gorier than usual for a Japanese science-fictioner. Directed by Hajime Sato.

**GOLD OF THE AMAZON WOMEN (1979).** The fabled Cities of El Dorado are sought by explorer Bo Svenson in this utterly absurd TV-movie with a plot that was passe decades ago. Apparently scenarist Sue Donem never got the word. Svenson, after a bow-and-arrow fight in downtown Manhattan, finds a tribe of Amazons in form-fitting Playtex zebra skins. Their leader is buxom Anita Ekberg, who looks uncomfortable in her Maidenform leopard spots. Donald Pleasence and two bad women are after the treasure too. Fortunately, director Mark L. Lester realizes none of this can be taken seriously and emphasizes the camp elements. Richard Romanus, Robert Minor, Bond Gideon, Maggie Jean Smith. (VC)

**GOLDEN ARROW, THE (1964).** Italian potboiler of the Arabian Nights syndrome with flying carpets, wish-fulfilling genies, arrows that do marvelous things and other magical accoutrements. Nothing magical, however, about the performances of Tab Hunter and Rosanna Podesta, nor is the direction by Antonio Margheriti golden. May a thousand curses befall your sister's flea-riddled camel.

**GOLDEN CHILD, THE (1986).** Eddie Murphy is a wonderful screen presence, even when he's hacking his way through a lousy script. When he's on camera, making his delightful wise-guy cracks, GOLDEN CHILD is all that glitters. But when co-producer Dennis Feldman's script resorts to action and monster-movie cliches, this is fool's gold, barely rising above the level of a TV-movie. Director Michael Ritchie glit-zes up the weaknesses as much as he can, but when fantasy can make anything happen, and does, there's no sense of fun—just confusion and hodgepodge. Similar in emptiness to Carpenter's BIG TROUBLE IN LITTLE CHINA, this also blends martial arts impossibilities, a demon from hell (Sardo Numspa, played by Charles Dance) and a quest for a magical object (in this case, a sword). Murphy portrays The Chosen One, decreed by an ancient Asian scroll that he will one day rescue the kidnapped Golden Child in the City of Angels. Sure enough, Eddie rushes down the Hollywood Freeway to find the lad and then faces all the adversaries during the rescue. Murphy deserves a helluva lot better than this. Charlotte Lewis, Victor Wong.

**GOLDEN HANDS OF KURIGAL (1949).** Re-edited TV version of the Republic 12-chapter serial FEDERAL AGENTS VS. UNDERWORLD INC., in which an evil network of criminals has stolen a famous artifact, the Golden Hands, which an ancient legend says are cursed. It's a nonstop battle between the evil Nila (Carol Forman) and her henchmen and federal agent Dave Worth (Kirk Alyn, who that same year was to play Superman); he must battle hired guns and stop Nila from using an Oriental drug that controls men's minds and turns them into dupes. Fred Brannon directed with all the expected cliffhangers in place. Rosemary La Planche, Roy Barcroft, James Dale, Bruce Edwards, Tris Coffin.

**GOLDEN MISTRESS, THE (1954).** Haitian locations cannot invigorate a tired script about a missing idol which causes a wave of voodoo murders. Rosemary Bowie is absolutely dreadful as the heroine (although the contours of her body might distract you from the corny plot), and hero John Agar isn't much better. A lot of stock footage of pythons crawling around. Directed with minimum impact by Joel Judge.

**GOLDEN RABBIT, THE (1962).** British concept of rollicking

THE ORIGINAL GOLDEN GIRL (SHIRLEY EATON) IN 'GOLDFINGER'

CREATURE FEATURES MOVIE GUIDE

humor, of uninhibited hilarity, is to have a scientist changing lead to gold and then gold back to lead. Leaden is the key word here. Silly and inconsequential. Directed by David MacDonald. Timothy Bateson, Maureen Beck.

**GOLDEN VOYAGE OF SINBAD, THE (1974).** Ray Harryhausen's effects excitingly capture the Arabian Nights in this excellent fantasy adventure. Marvel at the duel wth the six-armed Kali; a battle between a centaur and a griffin; a ship's masthead painfully coming to life and attacking; and a devious homunculus. For these visual treats alone this Charles Schneer production is worth repeated viewings, as well as for the score by Miklos Rozsa. Brian Clemens' screenplay is weak on character development and John Phillip Law portrays the familiar sword-swinging hero with indifference, but it is Harryhausen who keeps it alive. Another outstanding feature is Tom Baker as the Black Prince, whose villainy is convincing. Also appealing is the semi-draped Caroline Munro, whom fans will want to ogle. A miniclassic. Martin Shaw, Douglas Wilmer. Directed by Gordon Hessler. (VC)

**GOLDENGIRL (1979).** Curt Jurgens subjects daughter Susan Anton to an experiment by a neo-Nazi to produce a superhuman athlete. Then Anton steps forward to show the world she can sweep the Olympics as a track star. Interesting character study strengthens an otherwise routine plot of political intrigue. James Coburn, Robert Culp, Leslie Caron. Directed by Joseph Sargent, Harry Guardino. (VC)

**GOLDFINGER (1964).** Best of the James Bond 007 glossy thrillers for tongue-in-cheek thrills, comedy, gimmicks and gadgets, thanks to scripters Richard Maibaum and Paul Dehn. Director Guy Hamilton brings to this well-packaged entertainment style and pacing and there has never been a better supervillain than Gert Forbe as the gold-hungry Auric Goldfinger, who employs a laser beam that threatens Bond's "family jewels." Connery is in top form and so is Shirley Eaton as the girl in a bikini. The plot concerns the robbery of Fort Knox, a nuclear bomb (to which Bond is handcuffed) and a unique Oriental villain nicknamed Odd-Job (Harold Sakata). Also a flying team of shapely femmes led by Pussy Galore (Honor Blackman). Twenty-four karats! (VC)

**GOLDSTEIN (1965).** Philip Kaufman (see FEARLESS FRANK) co-directed with Benjamin Manaster this fantasy comedy derivative of a Biblical story. An old man appears from the depths of a Chicago lake and guides others with some divine force. It turns out the old man is Elijah, Hebrew prophet. Lou Gilbert, Ellen Madison, Thomas Erhart.

**GOLEM, THE (1915).** Earliest of films about the Jewish avenger, which legend states stormed Prague in the 1580s to save the Jews from a pogrom. German actor Paul Wegener and screenwriter Henrik Galeen directed and wrote with Wegener playing the animated statue crashing through modern-day Prague in his search to find the daughter of an antique dealer whom he loves. Wegener and Galeen worked on a sequel in 1917, THE GOLEM AND THE DANCER, but it contained no horror material, being a story in which Wegener played himself, a film actor who goes to a theater to see himself in the first GOLEM film.

**GOLEM: HOW HE CAME INTO THE WORLD, THE (1920).** Paul Wegener again worked with writer Henrik Galeen and cinematographer Karl Freund and tried to remain true to the legendary aspects of the Jewish savior. An important contribution for its make-up and scenes of the hulking monster, which inspired many Frankenstein entities to come. Again, Wegener played the monster. (VC)

**GOLEM, THE (1936).** Czech version of the legend aobut the Jewish savior, directed by Julien Duvivier. This is set in the 17th Century and depicts the clayman coming to life to protect the Jews against a pogrom. This has several worthwhile moments—including a ballroom sequence in the palace of Emperor Rudolph II of Prague during which the Golem advances like a juggernaut through the horrified crowd. Interesting use of tilted, subjective camera. Harry Baur, Germaine Aussey, Raymond Aimos, Roger Karl.

**GOLIATH AGAINST THE GIANTS (1961).** Beefcake bumbling and biceps babbling as Brad Harris grunts and bemoans his way through a mythical fantasy populated by a sea monster, a valley of non-jolly, non-green giants and a bevy of Amazonian femmes, who can be quite fatale. Fails to stand tall. Directed by Guido Malatesta. Gloria Milland, Fernando Rey, Barbara Carrol, Jose Rubio.

**GOLIATH AND THE DRAGON (1960).** Mark Forest can't see through the trees as Hercules (not Goliath) when he does battle with a three- headed dog, a fire-breathing St. George hater and a king-size killer bat. Everyone else—including Broderick Crawford as the scheming emperor—battles the impossible script. Zounds is right! Directed by Vittorio Cottafavi. Gaby Andre, Leonora Ruffo, Philipe Hersent.

**GOLIATH AND THE GOLDEN CITY. See SAMSON AND THE SEVEN MIRACLES OF THE WORLD.**

**GOLIATH AND THE SINS OF BABYLON (1964).** More muscle-flexing and superhuman strength when Mark Forest, as a Babylonian bodybuilder, struts his stuff through the palace, impressing kings, subduing villains and seducing beautiful wenches. What a life! Directed by Michele Lupo. Eleanora Bianchi, Scilla Gabel, John Chevron, Jose Greci.

**GOLIATH AND THE VAMPIRES (1964).** One-time Tarzan, Gordon Scott, portrays a muddled muscleman who flexes his biceps (but seldom his brain) to destroy zombie slaves and bloodsuckers. Maciste (his name isn't Goliath or Hercules) misses by a mile. Directed by Giacomo Gentilomo. Gianna Maria Canale, Jacques Sernas, Leonora Ruffo.

**GOLIATH AWAITS (1981).** An ocean liner, hit by a Nazi torpedo in 1939, has sunk to the bottom of the sea, but peculiar air pockets permit survivors to live on in a new environment. As subsequent generations grow up, a new society is formed, molded by a living code. Much of this four-hour TV-film directed by Kevin Connor deals with a fight for power within the old compartments of the ship while rescue operations take place above. Frank Gorshin is a heavy and Christopher Lee is a leader trying to keep anarchy from reigning. Mark Harmon, Eddie Albert, John Caradine, Alex Cord, Jeanette Nolan, Robert Forster, Jean Marsh.

**GOOD AGAINST EVIL (1977).** TV-movie, made in San Francisco, focuses on a young couple terrorized by satan worshippers. Dack Rambo portrays a writer who meets a woman (Elyssa Davalos) selected to bear the Devil's child. Where's Rosemary when you need her? Dan O'Herlihy has the thankless role as the exorcist who imitates Max von Sydow. Tepid TV terror. Directed by Paul Wendkos, scripted by Jimmy Sangster. Richard Lynch, Lelia Goldoni.

**GOODBYE CHARLIE (1964).** George Axelrod's play reached the screen directed by Vincente Minnelli and starring Debbie Reynolds as the reincarnated spirit of a screenwriter shot dead by an irate husband. A male screenwriter, that is. Yes, it's the old ploy of a man's soul in a woman's body. Scrambled souls and hapless hams. Maybe the dead screenwriter really wrote this (instead of Harry Kurnitz). Tony Curtis, Pat Boone, Roger Carmel, Walter Matthau, Joanna Barnes, Martin Gabel, Donna Michelle.

**GOONIES (1985).** Over-produced, overwrought children's fantasy from Steven Spielberg, directed by Richard Donner and written by Chris Columbus. A group of kids on the Oregon coast are propelled into an exotic adventure in underground caverns in search of pirates' treasure. It has the madcap tempo of a roller coaster ride, but there is never real jeopardy to the kids even though the caves are full of death traps (a la Indiana Jones) and a crazy mother and her two sons are stalking them. What seems wrong are production values that treat the featherweight story as an epic, when modesty was called for. GOONIES is skilled filmmaking, and certainly has youthful vitality provided by Sean Astin, Josh Brolin, Jeff Cohen and Corey Feldman. It is the slightness of story that throws the concept awry. (VC)

**GORATH (1962).** GODZILLA director Inoshiro Honda, with special effects pal Eiji Tsuburaya, weaves more sublime outer-space thrills with giant monsters. A planet on a collision course with Earth forces scientists to move our planet from its orbit by firing rockets into the stratosphere, but the noise disturbs a walrus-shaped monstrosity and it looks like we're doomed. Ryo Ikebe, Akihiko Hirata, Jun Tazaki. (VC)

**GORE GORE GIRLS, THE (1972).** Go go dancers are really the bore bore girls, and judging from their execution of the two-step, their executions at the hands of auditioning producers are thoroughly justified. This was the last film by Herschell Gordon Lewis, noted for his sick mutilation movies, and it stars comedian Henny Youngman as the owner of the go go house. Strictly for the blood-and-guts group. Our advice: Don't watch watch. Frank Kress, Amy Farrell. (VC)

**GORGO (1916).** Britain's King brothers (Herman, Maury and Frank) produced this unusually sentimental, if still destructive, tale of mother's love. A baby saurian is discovered floating in the Irish Sea and taken to London to be exhibited in a circus. Its 200-foot-high mother comes looking for baby, wrecking Westminster Abbey and seeing that London Bridge is literally falling down. Unsurpassed for bathos, handkerchief-wringing and a fondness for mother's love. The special effects by Tom Howard are good, even though the monsters are merely men in dinosaurus suits. Directed by Eugene Lourie (THE BEAST FROM 20,000 FATHOMS, THE GIANT BEHEMOTHS). Bill Travers, William Sylvester. (VC)

**GORGON, THE (1964).** Greek legend claims three sisters (Stheno, Euryale and Medusa) can turn your bone to stone should you chance to glance the flakes of snakes writhing atop their dead heads. From that theme, Anthony Nelson-Keys has fashioned a Hammer vehicle with Christopher Lee

**MALIGNED STAR OF 'GORILLA AT LARGE'**

as an investigator who realizes that a brain surgeon (Peter Cushing) is harboring a beauty (Barbara Shelley) for reasons slitheringly sinister. It is only fitting the characters should be stoned. Directed by Terence Fisher, written by John Gilling. Richard Pasco, Michael Goodliffe, Jack Watson. (VC)

**GORILLA, THE (1939).** The zany Ritz Brothers, a sophisticated version of the Three Stooges, are hired by millionaire Lionel Atwill to protect him from a murderer named The Gorilla. The private eye triumvirate runs wild through Atwill's mansion during an electric storm as a man in a gorilla suit slips in and out of secret panels and as butler Bela Lugosi behaves with sinister overtones. A delightfully fun-filled, old-fashioned farce with high entertainment values and a sparkling cast. Anita Louise, Patsy Kelly, Edward Norris, Joseph Calleia. Directed with parody style by Allan Dwan. (VC)

**GORILLA AT LARGE (1954).** Produced at Fox during the 3-D craze of the 1950s, this emerges a hackneyed, corny story more appropriate to the 1930s. And yet it's a campy entertainment. A gorilla in a sleazy carnival is suspected of committing murders, but anyone can see this is a whodunit. Anne Bancroft is beautiful as an aerialist, Raymond Burr is sinister as the carnival owner, Lee J. Cobb lends a modicum of believability as the investigating cop, and Cameron Mitchell and Charlotte Austin are on hand as the love interests.

Watch for Lee Marvin as a dumb Irish cop—he's hysterical. Harmon Jones directed the whole thing straight. Don't miss this, it's a kick in the ape. Warren Stevens, Billy Curtis.

**GORY MURDER, THE (1982).** Body parts are displayed throughout this Hong Kong production, which focuses graphically on the murder of a woman at the hands of a sex fiend. Not a pleasant way to kill 90 minutes.

**GOTHIC (1986).** Bizarre Ken Russell fictional biography of poet Lord Byron and how he introduces Mary Shelley (creator of FRANKENSTEIN) and Dr. Polidori (THE VAMPYRE) to drugs that cause them horror-riddled hallucinations. Interesting study of nightmares of the mind. Gabriel Byrne, Julian Sands, Natasha Richardson.

**GRADUATION DAY (1981).** Above-average slasher film with clever camera work, good use of point-of-view shots and swift pacing. Forty years ago a soldier received a Dear John letter and came home to shove a pitchfork into the backs of his faithless wife and lover at the graduation dance. When the graduation-dance tradition is revived, the murders start anew, the victims being members of the school track team. The lethal stalker is a stranger in a military uniform. Freed also directed. Christopher George, Michael Pataki, E. J. Peaker, E. D. Murphy. (VC)

**GRAVE DESIRES.** See **BRIDES OF BLOOD.**

**GRAVE OF THE VAMPIRE (1972).** Michael Pataki portrays a vampire who rapes a pretty co-ed near a mauseoleum. The offspring, brought up on mother's blood, is William Smith, who spends years seeking the rapist—only to confront dear dead dad, and realize heritage is everything in life, after all. Strange vampire flick directed by John Hayes, who co-wrote with David Chase. Lyn Peters, Jay Adler. (VC)

**GRAVE ROBBERS FROM OUTER SPACE.** See **PLAN NINE FROM OUTER SPACE.** Or don't see **PLAN NINE FROM OUTER SPACE.** See if we care.

**GRAVEYARD, THE.** Videocassette title for **TERROR OF SHEBA.**

**GRAVEYARD OF HORROR (1971).** Cemetery, hidden cave, grave robber, hairy corpse that comes to life, innocent victims—all blended by Spanish writer-director Miguel Madrid into substandard horror genre material. They'll dig you . . . you won't dig them. William Curran, Catharine Ellison, Beatriz Lacey, Frank Brana, Yocasta Grey.

**GRAVEYARD TRAMPS.** See **INVASION OF THE BEE GIRLS.**

**GRAY MATTER (1973).** Intriguing metaphysical ideas are lost to poor production and mediocre acting in this scientific thriller shot on a shoestring. A government conspiracy allows for an experiment involving a Brain Machine in the National Environmental Control Center, but questions of immortality and truth lead to human disintegration. Directed and co-written by Joy N. Houck Jr. (as a reverend), Barbara Burgess, Gil Peterson, Gerald McRaney. (VC)

**GREASER'S PALACE (1972).** Writer-director Robert Downey intermingles religious symbolism and irreverent parody in this fantasy allegory. A dude in a zoot suit drops by air into the Old West, where he assumes the stance of a Jesus Christ, resurrecting the dead, healing and carrying on in a style often non-Christian. Luana Anders, Albert Henderson, Stan Gottlieb, Allan Arbus, Ron Nealy. (VC)

**GREAT ALLIGATOR, THE (1981).** Remote tropical island tourists Barbara Bach and Mel Ferrer could be dinner for an angry tribal god, Kuma, who is ticked off at the tourist litter. Kuma assumes the form of an overgrown, scaly creature that would one day make about 5000 pairs of walking pumps. This Italian film, directed by Sergio Martino, was made as BIG ALLIGATOR RIVER and sold directly to TV. Richard Johnson, Claudio Cassinelli, Romano Puppo. (VC)

**GREAT GABBO, THE (1929).** A curious antique, based on Ben Hecht's "The Rival Dummy," about a vaudevillian ventriloquist (Erich Von Stroheim) who presents a sophisticated act in a lavish revue. The dummy takes over the master but the strange thing here, under James Cruze's direction, is that Von Stroheim's wooden companion moves and talks on his own! That's never explained—the focus is on Von Stroheim's descent into madness. He finally freaks out during one of the film's interminable musical production numbers. The supporting cast (Betty Compton, Don Douglas, Marjorie Kane) is just coming to grips with sound, so performances tend to be a bit hysterical. Defies explanation. (VC)

**GREAT GAMBINI, THE (1937).** Night club mind-reader Akim Tamiroff predicts a murder. Paramount programmer directed by Charles Vidor. Reginald Denny, William Demarest.

**GREAT IMPERSONATION, THE (1935).** Weird country estate, located near the Black Bog, is setting for shenanigans with ghosts, creepy caretakers, sliding panels, etc. Directed by Milton Krasner. Edmund Lowe, Valerie Hobson, Dwight Frye, Frank Reicher, Spring Byington.

**GREAT RACE, THE (1965).** This riotously falls into the

## FATHER AND SON IN 'GREYSTOKE'

category of THE CRIMSON PIRATE and other comedy spoofs which spotlight weapons and inventions out of their time. Jack Lemmon and Peter Falk are insidious inventors who constantly create devices to thwart Tony Curtis and other drivers in a major car race from New York to Paris in the early 1900s. An utterly hilarious Blake Edwards production (he directed and co-wrote with Arthur Ross), full of wonderful vintage automobiles, bizarre gadgets, Roadrunner-style visual gags and pie-throwing slapstick. Natalie Wood, Keenan Wynn, Arthur O'Connell, Vivian Vance, Larry Storch, Ross Martin, George Macready, Denver Pyle. (VC)

**GREAT RUPERT, THE (1950).** George Pal fantasy-comedy directed by Irving Pichel, in which squirrel Rupert is really an animated puppet—which is more than you can say for Terry Moore, Jimmy Durante and Tom Drake, who are allegedly real. They're all mixed up with Rupert in a mystery surrounding a cache of money hidden in an old mansion.

**GREAT SPACE CHASE, THE (1979).** Feature-length version of the MIGHTY MOUSE TV series featuring the caped superstrong rodent against Harry the Heartless and his heartless-heartless Catomaton.

**GREAT WHITE (1982).** This copy of JAWS, an Italian cheapo picked up and finished by American producer Edward Montoro, was shown in a few U.S. cities before Univer-

sal sued for alleged story similarities. Court injunctions placed this back on the shelf, and at present it is not being shown. Filmed on the Great Barrier Reef of Australia, with additonal footage taken in Georgia and Malta, the film depicts the exploits of a killer shark pursued by James Franciscus and Vic Morrow. Directed by Enzo G. Castellari.

**GREEN MANSIONS (1959).** Offbeat melodrama-fantasy based on the William Henry Hudson novel, starring Audrey Hepburn as the legendary Bird Girl of the Amazon, Rima, who is not permitted to leave her forest even when she meets political refugee Anthony Perkins and falls in love. Mel Ferrer directed from a screenplay by Dorothy Kingsley. Lee J. Cobb, Sessue Hayakawa, Henry Silva, Nehemiah Persoff.

**GREEN PASTURES (1936).** Marc Connelly's stage hit, an unbridled whimsical fantasy presenting a Negro's impression of life after death (i.e. "de lawd" and His Angels holding a fish fry behind the Pearly Gates). All-black cast is headed by Rex Ingram, Eddie "Rochester" Anderson, Oscar Polk and George Reed. Connelly adapted his own play and co-directed with William Keighley. (VC)

**GREEN SLIME, THE (1969).** U.S.-Japanese space sukiyaki set on Gamma III, a station adrift in space where astronauts from many nations confront and confound protoplasmic aliens of a hue between yellow and blue on the color spectrum. Producers Ivan Reiner and Walter Manley were not green with envy about the inadequate special effects work, and fans have remained an indifferent hue due to technical deficiencies. The monsters are one-eyed entitites with tentacles they are eager to wrap around the curvy body of Luciana Paluzzi. Among the astronauts are Robert Horton and Richard Jaeckel. Directed by Kinji Fukasaku.

**GREMLINS (1984).** Steven Spielberg's production is the brainchild of screenwriter Chris Columbus, director Joe Dante and producer Mike Finnell, who have concocted a whimsical morality fable with its share of bloody moments. What makes this refreshing is its blending of dark macabre humor with serious horror and the air of a fairy tale. Chris Walas designed and articulated the gremlins with a large staff. It begins when madcap inventor Hoyt Axton brings home a cuddly, wide-eyed little creature he nicknames "Gizmo." Although Gizmo is benevolent, he passes through an odd reproductive stage, then his offspring pass through a cocoon state, leading to the birth of impish, malevolent little critters who create havoc in a small town. Great creatures, repulsive and fascinating in the same breath. Every sequence is oozing with inspiration and a cast of character players (Polly Holliday, Harry Carey Jr., Dick Miller, Edward Andrews, Scott Brady, Kenneth Tobey, Belinda Balaski) brings an added touch of Hollywood fun. (VC)

**GREYSTOKE: THE LEGEND OF TARZAN, LORD OF THE APES (1984).** Fresh approach to the standard cinematic rendering of Edgar Rice Burroughs' jungle hero, with director Hugh Hudson and writers P.H. Vazak (a pseudonyn for Robert Towne) and Michael Austin dispensing with romantic images and showing the nitty gritty of growing up as the son of a pack of apes. This part of the film is fascinating as little Tarzan passes through various ages until he emerges a disciplined son of the jungle. It's when he's domesticated and taken back to Victorian England that the film falters and becomes a strange love story that's more difficult to relate to. Tarzan fans may resent the heavy realism, while Burroughs purists will have to appreciate and respect this attempt to recapture the true spirit of the Tarzan novels. Christopher Lambert is fine as John Clayton-Tarzan and Sir Ralph Richardson is superb as the Sixth Earl of Greystoke. Ian Holm, James Fox, Andie MacDowell, Cheryl Campbell, Nigel Davenport, Ian Charleson. Recommended, as long as you don't go in expecting to see a typical Tarzan adventure. (VC)

**GRIM REAPER, THE (1981).** Joe D'Amato, who directed the ATOR movies as David Hills, helms this Italian platter of splatter for nongourmets (creep connoisseurs only) with Tisa Farrow leading a pack of American tourists to a Greek island where a murderous cannibal is eager to become part of the have-a-tourist-for-lunch bunch. This slowly gnaws away at you as the corpses pile up and as knife after knife is shoved into human flesh. The victims die horribly, by throat-biting, hair-pulling and other sickening means. Unrelenting in its horror, and ultimately without any purpose for existing. Those looking for a flood of blood won't be disappointed. George Eastman, Bob Larson, Saverio Vallone. (VC)

**GRIMM'S FAIRY TALES FOR ADULTS (1970).** German "bloody horror-sex" exploitationer repackaged for the U.S. Fairy tale characters are depicted doing things Mother Goose would never have allowed. Grimm has become grim in the same style of black comedy horror that E.C. Comics indulged in during the 1950s. Grimm and bear it. Directed-written by Rolf Thiele. Marie Liljedah, Eva V. Rueber-Staier.

**GRIZZLY (1976).** This imitates a successful shark thriller in every detail, but on dry ground. A 15-foot-tall superbear terrorizes Georgia State Park, devouring unsuspecting backpackers and hunters until forest ranger Christopher George and Richard Jaeckel track it down using neomodern weapons. There's even a campfire sequence when one of the characters tells about how a terrible bear once attacked a group of people that is similar to the story of the Indianapolis

**STRIPE, A MISCHIEVOUS 'GREMLIN'**

survivors told by Robert Shaw in JAWS. Directed by William Girdler. Andrew Prine, Lynda Day George. (VC)

**GROOVE ROOM (1974).** British "old dark house" comedy with Sue Longhurst, Diana Dors and Martin Ljung as Jack the Ripper. Vernon P. Becker wrote and directed. Also known as WHAT THE SWEDISH BUTLER SAW.

**GROUND ZERO (1973).** An atomic device is fastened to one of the towers of the Golden Gate Bridge by a madman. Up the tower goes special agent Ron Casteel to get his man. Although professional writer Samuel Newman wrote this, it is the pits. So is the direction by producer James T. Flocker. And the acting is lousy—even San Francisco attorney Melvin Belli stinks. Cinematic ineptitude of the highest order. Augie Treibach, Kim Friese, Yvonne D'Anger (onetime topless star).

**GROUNDSTAR CONSPIRACY, THE (1972).** Intriguing if sometimes confusing spy-espionage thriller with fantastic overtones, based on L.P. Davies' THE ALIEN and directed in Vancouver by Lamont Johnson. George Peppard is a

shrewd, ruthless security chief trying to find out who blew up a giant computer. His key to the mystery is Michael Sarrazin, a possible enemy agent—but for whom? The twist here is that Sarrazin has lost all memory and doesn't know who he's working for. Peppard's game to outwit him will have you guessing. Campus sequences shot at Simon Fraser University. Christine Belford, Tim O'Connor, James Olsen.

**GROWING PAINS (1982).** Videocassette version of an episode from HAMMER HOUSE OF HORROR. See **HOUSE THAT BLED TO DEATH.** God, what a drippy book.

**GRUESOME TWOSOME (1969).** A mother-son team operating Mrs. Pringle's Wig Shoppe has a dual purpose: with his electric knife he scalps the young women dumb enough to be lured into his bedroom, she turns the hair into profitable commodities for the shop inventory. This is a family picture? Awful exploitationer from Herschell Gordon Lewis really scalped exhibitors. You really have to love gore movies to endure this cruel cruel exercise in body dismemberment. Elizabeth Davis, Chris Martell. (VC)

**GUARDIAN OF THE ABYSS (1982).** Step into Hell, ladies and gentlemen, right this way through the antique mirror, which reflects only death. An episode of the British series, HAMMER HOUSE OF HORROR, repackaged for U.S. consumption with Elvira introducing and yocking it up in the Bob Wilkins tradition. Directed by Don Sharp. (VC)

**GUESS WHAT HAPPENED TO COUNT DRACULA (1970).** Not very much, as this saw little distribution. Des Roberts plays Count Adrian, and the setting is Hollywood. Claudia Barron, John Landon. The work of Laurence Merrick.

**GULLIVER'S TRAVELS (1939).** In the wake of Disney's SNOW WHITE AND THE SEVEN DWARFS came this animated feature by Max and Dave Fleischer, a loose adaptation of Jonathan Swift's satire classic, with a prince and princess added to the cast of characters to take advantage of the then-popular Prince Charming image. While the Disney influences are more than obvious, this is still pleasant animation with a comic-book style removed from the quaintness and soft focus of Disney. There's a satisfying Victor Young musical score. The voice of Princess Glory was by Metropolitan Opera star Jessica Dragonette. (VC)

**GULLIVER'S TRAVELS (1977).** Anglo-Belgian blend of animation and live action starring Richard Harris as the shipwrecked adventurer who gets mixed up with little people and then with giants in order to help the little people. Not an auspicious credit for Peter Hunt, whose direction is static. The Don Black script makes only token effort to deal with Jonathan Swift's political satire; mainly for children. Catherine Schell, Norman Shelley. (VC)

**GULLIVER'S TRAVELS BEYOND THE MOON (1966).** Science-fiction version of Swift's satiric classic, with Gulliver and pals traveling to another world where evil robots clank their dominance. Japanese animated cartoon is largely for the teeter totter set; adults will certainly suffer.

**GURU THE MAD MONK (1970).** Andy Milligan sexploitation abomination in which the titular torturer drinks the blood of pretty young girls in his confessional. The setting is allegedly the Middle Ages, but contemporary sets slipped past the graphic designers— they must have been distracted by the beautiful nubile bodies. Neil Flanagan, Judy Israel.

**GUY NAMED JOE, A (1943).** Respectable big-budgeted MGM fantasy scripted by Dalton Trumbo and directed by Victor Fleming, with touches of World War II propaganda. Spencer Tracy, a flying hero who dies in battle, returns to train new recruits in the art of shooting down Japanese Zeros and Nazi Me-109s. He also instills new hope and inspiration in Van Johnson and Irene Dunne, who provide the obligatory love interest. Lionel Barrymore, Ward Bond, James Gleason, Esther Williams. Cinematography by Karl Freund.

**GYPSY MOON (1953).** See **ROCKY JONES, SPACE RANGER.** But beware the Curse of the Gypsy.

*"The End! Or is it?" —Closing credit of **GRAVE OF THE VAMPIRE.***

*". . . for it is written, the inhabitants of the earth have been made drunk by her blood and I saw her sit upon the hairy beast and she held forth a golden chalice full of the filthiness of her fornication. And on her forehead was written, 'Behold, I am the great Mother of Harlots and all abominations of the earth.'"* — Christopher Lee in **HOWLING II**

**H. G. WELLS' NEW INVISIBLE MAN (1962).** Arturo De Cordova and Ana Luisa Peluffo in a Mexican version of the Wells classic about an unjustly accused murderer who becomes invisible to prove his innocence. Directed by Alfredo Crevena.

**H. G. WELLS' THE SHAPE OF THINGS TO COME (1979).** The title is an outright lie! This is not even a remake of the 1936 British mini-masterpiece, THINGS TO COME. Hell, it's not even H. G. Wells. It's a Canadian hunkajunk inspired by STAR WARS and STAR TREK set "tomorrow after tomorrow," after Earth has been ravaged by robotic wars. A moon colony (in need of a substance called RADIC-Q2) sends scientist Barry Morse, Sparks the robot and a couple of heroic types to Delta 3 to get RADIC-Q2, but there they encounter dictator Umas (Jack Palance in a Flash Gordon costume) and his robot warriors at war with Carol Lynley and her rebels. The effects have all been done before, the robot comedy relief is pitiful and the torrent of cliches boils down to a waste of anyone's time. Directed without originality by George McCowan. John Ireland, Mark Parr.

**HAIL! (1972).** . . . but nothing hearty about this social satire in which a U.S. President (Dan Resin) quiets opposition by establishing concentration camps. Directed by Fred Levinson. Richard B. Schull, Lee Meredith, Dick O'Neill.

**HALF HUMAN (1957).** Japanese fantasy-horror directed by Inoshiro Honda, which sheds new light on the Abominable Snowman of the Himalayas, but the link of logic is missing from this snow-covered slop. New footage with John Carradine and Morris Ankrum was shot by Kenneth Crane for the U.S. but in any language HALF HUMAN is half-baked. Special effects by Inoshiro's pal, Eiji Tsuburaya. Akira Takarada, Kenji Kasahara, Russ Thorson.

**HALLOWEEN (1978).** This low-budget box office success, which launched director John Carpenter's astounding horror genre career, is a paean to October 31—a series of jolts designed to shock, rock and knock the viewer as it depicts a psychopathic madman who escapes from a mental asylum and terrorizes teen-age babysitters and their boyfriends in a small Midwestern town. The killer is unkillable, allowing for a surprise ending. Carpenter, who scripted with Debra Hill, certainly knows his scare tactics, never letting the viewer relax. The graphic, stylish murders helped establish the slasher trend. Donald Pleasence portrays the psychiatrist in pursuit of the killer; Jamie Lee Curtis is the screaming female target who must (with the viewer) experience the ultimate in blood-curdling horror. Nancy Loomis, Nick Castle. (VC)

**HALLOWEEN II (1981).** Sequel to John Carpenter's HALLOWEEN picks up on the same night as the original, as Jamie Lee Curtis is hospitalized with psychiatrist Donald Pleasence close at hand, concerned the killer is still loose. Doc is so right. The Bogeyman Slasher, as you suspected, is alive and well—well-angered, too, shambling zombielike to the hospital to kill the personnel and get poor Jamie. Unfortunately, it's a weak premise (co-authored by Carpenter and Debra Hill), with the hospital so poorly lit, one wonders how the nurses and doctors can find their patients. A hypodermic needle thrust into an eyeball, slashed throats and a human head dipped into scalding water are among the jolly sights. The contrivances are so poor and forced, you almost wish the killer would hurry up and knock off Curtis. Directed by Rick Rosenthal, with added footage by Carpenter. (VC)

**HALLOWEEN III: SEASON OF THE WITCH (1982).** See a man's eyes squeezed out of his head. See a man set himself on fire. See a human head twisted off its torso. See a boy's face explode in a shower of beetles, roaches and rattlesnakes. Had enough? If not, catch this John Carpenter-Debra Hill flick, with all the imagery of a Halloween nightmare. But don't be misled by the title. This has nothing to do with the first two HALLOWEEN flicks about the masked Bogeyman Slasher. Dan O'Herlihy portrays a designer of children's fright masks (creations of Don Post) with a fiendish plot: In each mask is a device that will explode while children are watching a TV commercial. It's up to Tom Atkins and Stacey Nelkin to thwart the diabolical plan. Director-writer

# Carpenter Builds Suspense

**THE INFAMOUS BEDROOM SEQUENCE IN JOHN CARPENTER'S 1978 'HALLOWEEN'**

Tommy Lee Wallace can do little to make it plausible. There are some frightening sequences, but an element of fun is missing. Michael Currie, Dick Warlock. (VC)

**HAMMER HOUSE OF HORROR DOUBLE FEATURE.** Repackaging of the British TV series HAMMER HOUSE OF HORROR, with two episodes combined in each TV offering. TV Guide usually lists these under the title of the first episode, so see the following: **CHARLIE BOY; CHILDREN OF THE FULL MOON; HOUSE THAT BLED TO DEATH; TWO FACES OF EVIL** and **WITCHING TIME.** Some are also in individual videocassette form.

**HAND, THE (1960).** Grisly British revenge mystery: Three English POWs refuse to cooperate with Japanese captors and each has a hand cut off. A fourth man talks to save himself and later the three one-handed chaps track him down. Ironic twist-of-fate climax. A hand-me-down movie? Directed by Henry Cass. Derek Bond, Ronald Leigh-Hunt.

**HAND, THE (1969).** Plot-within-a-plot: A writer concocts a movie story about a severed hand. The producer scoffs at such a ridiculous plotline, having never seen THE BEAST WITH FIVE FINGERS. The next thing you know, the writer is murdered by his wife, who is lent a helping "hand" by her lover. And then the plot of the story starts to come true. French chiller, directed by Henry Glaeser. Natalie Delon, Henri Serre, Roger Hanin.

**HAND, THE (1981).** Thinking man's BEAST WITH FIVE FINGERS, in which cartoonist Michael Caine, after losing his right hand in a bloody, freakish car accident, sinks into madness, with the severed hand knocking off anyone who has wronged him. Or is Caine committing the murders and hallucinating about the hand? Writer-director Oliver Stone has done a thoughtful job of adapting Marc Brandel's THE LIZARD'S TAIL, exploring Caine's insanity with the use of black-and-white film, distorted camera angles, etc. You never know for certain about Caine's crawling fingers until the jolt-

ing, bizarre climax. Make-up and effects by Stan Winston, Tom Burman and Carlo Rambaldi. Music by James Horner. Andrea Marcovicci, Viveca Lindfors, Annie McEnroe. (VC)

**HAND OF DEATH, THE (1961).** John Agar, after experimenting with a formula that should-not-have-been-conceived-because-it-tampers-with-the-forces-of-nature, turns into something that looks like a leftover from THE ALLIGATOR PEOPLE. Directed by Gene Nelson. Paula Raymond, Steve Dunne, Roy Gordon, John Alonzo.

**HAND OF NIGHT.** See **BEAST OF MOROCCO.**

**HAND OF POWER (1970).** West German production of an Edgar Wallace horror thriller is preposterous yet has a compelling fascination to its campiness. An avenging murderer dressed like a skeleton and calling himself "The Laughing Corpse" commits ghastly murders with a Scorpion-shaped ring that contains a poisonous puncture needle. The characters are hopelessly stereotyped, yet their naivete adds to the film's peculiar appeal. Directed by Alfred Vohrer. Joachim Fuchsberger, Siv Mattson, Pinkas Braun, H.V. Meyerinck.

**HANDS OF A STRANGER (1962).** Third remake of THE HANDS OF ORLAC in which a doctor saves the talent of a concert pianist (who has lost the use of his hands) by operating and grafting on the hands of a murderer. That's just great, except the pianist takes on traits of the killer and is unable to restrain himself from murdering. Directed-written by Newton Arnold. Irish McCalla, Paul Lukather, Joan Harvey.

**HANDS OF A STRANGLER (1960).** Second film version of Maurice Renard's classic tale of a well-meaning physician (Donald Wolfit) who grafts the hands of a murderer onto the wrists of an injured concert pianist (Mel Ferrer). Christopher Lee co-stars as a stage magician who learns the truth. Reportedly, this French-British film was butchered by U.S. censors. Directed by Edmond T. Greville. Donald Pleasence, Dany Carrel, David Peel, Felix Aylmer.

**HANDS OF ORLAC, THE (1925).** Silent version of Maurice Renard's horror tale, produced in Austria by Robert Wiene (THE CABINET OF DR. CALIGARI) and starring wonderful German villain Conrad Veidt.

**HANDS OF ORLAC, THE (1960).** See **HANDS OF A STRANGLER.** (It'll choke you up!)

**HANDS OF STEEL (1986).** Cyborg assassin (Daniel Greene) can't carry out his new assignment when his human side prevails, so he goes on the run. Italian copy of THE TERMINATOR directed by Martin Dolman. Elisabeth Parker, Saul Sasha. (VC)

**HANDS OF THE RIPPER (1971).** Offbeat Hammer horror thriller directed by Peter Sasdy and starring Angharad Rees as the daughter of jolly Jack the Ripper. The L. W. Davidson screenplay emphasizes some strange psychological side effects as Rees is obsessed with memories of gory murders and possessed by the spirit of not-so-dear old dad. Now she must carry out his unholy cravings and carvings. Eric Porter portrays the headshrinker protecting her from herself. Ripping good. Jane Merrow, Keith Bell. (VC)

**HANGAR 18 (1980).** Intriguing, suspenseful adaptation of an allegedly true story (legendary in the UFO annals) in which a flying saucer and a NASA missile collide in space and the bodies of aliens are retrieved from a desert crash site, then taken to a top-security military base. After that, the Steven Thornley script is purely speculative. Where the film falters is in its cheap special effects. The cast chosen by producer Charles E. Sellier Jr. and directed by James L. Conway is first-rate: Robert Vaughn, Darren McGavin, Gary Collins, Philip Abbott, William Schallert, H. M. Wynant. (VC)

**HANGING WOMAN, THE (1971).** Spanish horror involving zombies, directed by John Davidson. Paul Naschy. (VC)

**HANGOVER SQUARE (1945).** Following his all-too-believable performance as Jack the Ripper in THE LODGER, Laird Cregar, an obese, sinister-looking actor who looked years older than his age, again works with director John Brahm to penetrate to the depths of schizophrenic behavior as concert pianist George Harvey Bone, driven to murder in a repressive Victorian society. With this predictable story, success hinges on atmosphere and Cregar's aggravated performance. Brahm and screenwriter Barre Lyndon make it work. The ending is a concerto sequence beautifully edited to the tempo of the Bernard Herrmann score. George Sanders, Linda Darnell, Glenn Langan, Alan Napier. It was to be Laird's last great performance—he died shortly after at 28.

**HANNAH—QUEEN OF THE VAMPIRES.** See **CRYPT OF THE LIVING DEAD.** (Hardly the living end.)

**HANS CHRISTIAN ANDERSEN (1952).** Here's one moppets will slurp up as avidly as chocolate sodas through straws: a sweet-flavored, sugar-coated biography of the Danish storyteller in music and song. This Samuel Goldwyn production, directed by Charles Vidor from a screenplay by Moss Hart, spotlights a Frank Loesser score that includes ballet fantasies. Danny Kaye in the title role is at his delightful best. Jeanmarie, Farley Granger, John Qualen. (VC)

**HANSEL AND GRETEL (1970).** West German version of the old Grimm fairy tale, which is grim indeed, played more as a horror story by writer-director F. J. Gottlieb than as a kiddie yarn. The witch and the gingerbread house are all here, but watch for those Freudian overtones. Barbara Klingered, Francy Fair, Dagobert Walter, Herbert Fux. (VC)

**HANSEL AND GRETEL (1982).** FAERIE TALE THEATER episode starring Joan Collins as the wicked bitch . . . er, we mean witch . . . with Ricky Schroder and Bridgette Anderson as the kids. Directed by James Frawley. (VC)

**HAPPY BIRTHDAY TO ME (1981).** Above average slasher flick, featuring a top star (Glenn Ford), a name director (J. Lee Thompson) and a major studio (Paramount). While this qualifies as an imitation of HALLOWEEN, it has enough ingenious twists and turns (credit writers John Saxon, Peter John and Timothy Bond) to hold its own against lesser copycats. In fact, the denouement with surprise revelations is startling. The plot revolves around teen-agers who are mur-

dered one by one, and it seems obvious who the killer is . . . or does it? Pseudopsychiatrist motivations and mental-breakdown nonsense give the film a compelling perversity and sense of madness. Don't be put off by the shish-kebab skewering scene . . . it's only the tip of the . . . fork? Melissa Sue Anderson, Sharon Acker, Lawrence Dane. (VC)

**HAPPY GHOST II (1985).** Chinese supernatural comedy (with English subtitles) in which the ghost is a high school teacher who becomes the brunt of juvenile jokes staged by his students. His use of spectral powers only gets him in trouble with the faculty. Obviously, a sequel to HAPPY GHOST. Directed by Clifton Ko Chisium. Raymond Wong stars as Hoi Sum-Kwai, the smiling, happy-go-lucky entity.

**HAPPY MOTHER'S DAY, LOVE GEORGE.** See **RUN, STRANGER, RUN.** (But walk to your TV.)

**HARD ROCK ZOMBIES (1984).** Tombstoned rock 'n rollers rise from their beat peat graves to engage in a little junk funk punk. The metal's heavy, man, heavy, when you're trying to push open the mausoleum door. The great-filled dead include E. J. Curcio, Geno, Sam Mann and Mick McMains. Directed by Krishna Shah. (VC)

**HARDWARE WARS (1977).** Laugh-a-second, 13-minute parody of STAR WARS is a cult favorite, coming from the whacky mind of Berkeley filmmaker Ernie Fosselius. This bright, inspired send-up of Lucas' characters and concepts has ordinary home appliances replacing the spaceships and weaponry. On video, coupled with OTHER FILM FARCES that include "Bambi Meets Godzilla," "Porklips Now" and

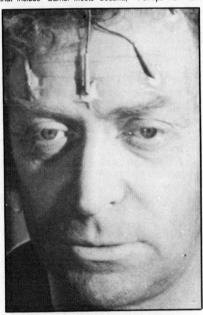

**MICHAEL CAINE IN 'THE HAND'**

"Closet Cases of the Nerd Kind." (VC)

**HARLEM GLOBETROTTERS ON GILLIGAN'S ISLAND (1981).** TV-movie revival of the long-running albeit utterly dumb TV show about a band of nitwits stranded on a deserted island. In this empty-headed fluff directed by Peter Baldwin, the basketball team is also stranded, and battles a team of robots. Bob Denver, Martin Landau, Scatman Crothers, Alan Hale, Barbara Bain, etc. etc. Ugh!

**HARLEQUIN (1980).** Puzzling Australian film with Robert Powell as a supernatural clown with powers of healing who saves a politician's dying son. In truth, the politician (David Hemmings) is a puppet of an unscrupulous industrialist

(Broderick Crawford) and must decide between righteous-ness, as dictated by the Harlequin, or corruption. The moral battle is compelling, Powell's performance is sympathetic and Simon Wincer's direction is tense. Unfortunately, the special effects are inferior and elements of the screenplay by Everett DeRoche are murky. Yet, HARLEQUIN is different. Also known as DARK FORCES.

**HARRY AND THE HENDERSONS (1987).** An excellent comedy in the vein of E.T., in which a middle-class Seattle family takes in a Bigfoot creature and learns to love him despite his clumsy, destructive ways and strong body odor. Rick Baker's hairy Harry is the real star of this Spiel-berg/Amblin production, which constantly tugs at the heart strings and isn't afraid to wallow in a little sentiment. The result is above-average entertainment with an ensemble of believable players: John Lithgow and Melissa Dillon head the typically loveable Spielbergite family, David Suchet is an in-tense but still sympathetic villain (a big game hunter in pur-suit of Bigfoot) and Don Ameche brings charm to the funny tale as an anthropologist. Like E.T., it has a hokey message about man learning to live with alien (here substitute animals), but it's fun and that's what counts.

**HARVEY (1950).** This superb whimsical fantasy won a Pulit-zer Prize for playwright Mary C. Chase and an Oscar for sup-porting actress Josephine Hull. More than just the story of oddball Elwood P. Dowd (James Stewart) who insists his constant companion is a six-foot-high invisible rabbit . . . it is a commentary on our society and the thin line dividing sanity from insane. This screen version, adapted by Chase and Oscar Brodney, also makes poignant comments about our lack of communication. But enough heavy-handed analysis! This is a wonderful satiric comedy involving classic misunderstandings, character mix-ups and other old devices cleverly revitalized. It will stir your funny veins and touch your sensitive bones. Directed with a deft touch by Henry Koster. Cecil Kellaway, Jesse White, Wallace Ford, Charles Drake, Peggy Dow, Nana Bryant.

**HATCHET FOR A HONEYMOON (1971).** Spanish-Italian horror job from director Mario Bava, depicting a young desig-ner who loves to hack up shapely models in wedding gowns. What ever happened to nuptial happiness? Just when he thinks he's a masterful hacker, there appears the ghost of his wife to complain about the wedding night accommodations. The pacing, though erratic, is suitably spattered, as in "the blood spattered wife." (VC)

**HATCHET MURDERS, THE.** Videocassette title for some versions of Dario Argento's **DEEP RED.**

**HAUNTED (1976).** Unusual, sometimes enigmatic super-natural thriller written-produced-directed by Michael De Gaetano (UFO TARGET EARTH). Too ambiguous to find a large audience, this obscure film focuses on an English-woman who fears she might be the reincarnation of an old In-dian woman who once practiced black magic. Stalking her is Aldo Ray. You figure it all out. (VC)

**HAUNTED AND THE HUNTED, THE. See DEMENTIA 13.**

**HAUNTED CASTLE, THE (1969).** The Ghost Cat of Nabeshima is an ancient Japanese legend explored in this bloody Japanese film directed by Tokuzo Tanaka. The feline in question turns into a woman who takes on Dracula over-tones, drinking the blood of victims. Kojiro Hongo, Naomi Kobayashi, Mitsuyo Kamei.

**HAUNTED HONEYMOON (1986).** Gene Wilder wrote-produced-directed and stars in this spoof on the OLD DARK HOUSE genre, bringing only a faint-hearted glow to his protoplasm. Nothing new as Wilder and fiancee Gilda Radner arrive at the family manor to learn a werewolf is loose in the area. A lot of creeping around the castle leads nowhere. Dom DeLuise, Jonathan Pryce, Paul L. Smith. (VC)

**HAUNTED HOUSE OF HORROR, THE. See HORROR HOUSE.** (A house of another holler!)

**HAUNTED PALACE, THE (1963).** Pretty good horror film produced-directed by Roger Corman, said to be based on a poem by Poe and H.P. Lovecraft's novella, "The Case of Charles Dexter Ward." But any similarities are purely . . .

Charles Beaumont's script describes a warlock (Vincent Price) who possesses the body of a descendant to wreak revenge against those who burned him at the stake. The most interesting horror device, besides creepy characters with fright faces, is a Thing in a well, one of the banished "Elder Gods," the only real Lovecraftian touch. Lon Chaney Jr., Debra Paget, Elisha Cook Jr., Leo Gordon.

**HAUNTED STRANGLER, THE (1957).** "The Haymarket Strangler" was executed 20 years ago for garroting and slashing five women and now, in 1880 London, obsessed mystery writer/criminologist Boris Karloff is afraid the wrong man was accused. Soul possession sets in when Karloff picks up a scalpel at Scotland Yard's Black Museum and duplicates the heinous murders, his face a twisted, gnarly frightness. Mildly interesting variation on the Jekyll-Hyde theme; produced in Britain by Richard Gordon, directed by Robert Day with some nice can-can scenes. But the story is too predictable to sustain to the end. Anthony Dawson, Elizabeth Allan, Jean Kent, Dorothy Gordon. (VC)

**HAUNTED: THE FERRYMAN (1986).** Horror novelist, rest-ing in the country, realizes one of his books is coming true. Directed by John Irvin. Jeremy Brett, Natasha Parry, Leslie Dunlop. (VC)

**HAUNTING, THE (1963).** Robert Wise's production is one helluva scary supernatural thriller, among the best ever made. Credit Wise's incredibly precise direction and Nelson Gidding's adaptation of Shirley Jackson's HAUNTING OF HILL HOUSE. It's truly scary because the horrors remain un-seen and, following the theory of Val Lewton, play heavier on the imagination. Richard Johnson, a psychic ghost chaser, picks "sensitives" to help him investigate an old mansion steeped in psychic phenomena. (Much of this is based on true cases.) Psychological problems of spinstress Julie Harris are strangely related to the ghostly events. Guaranteed to chill you, and only now becoming recognized as a classic. Clair Bloom, Russ Tamblyn, Lois Maxwell. (VC)

**HAUNTING OF JULIA, THE (1976).** Moody, slow-moving British-Canadian horror film (produced in London), based on a lesser known Peter Straub novel. Mia Farrow, who has just lost her daughter, moves into a strange old house haunted by the spirit of a perverted young girl. Mia becomes obsessed with investigating the child's past. This is lyrical and full of ambience, if not action and thrills. It is so subtle under Richard Loncraine's direction, the film never saw wide dis-tribution and was cut for TV. Tom Conti, Keir Dullea, Jill Ben-nett, Cathleen Nesbitt, Jill Bennett, Mary Morris. (VC)

**HAUNTING OF M, THE (1979).** Stylistic period piece (set in 1906) has the flavor of a Henry James ghost story and is steeped in subtlety—to the detriment of the film ever finding popularity in the horror market. One cannot deny the ex-quisite photography of Gregory Nava, and one must admit that his wife, Anna Thomas, is a good director with a detail for character nuances. But the pacing is slow and the super-natural thrills almost nonexistent when a family is haunted by the ghost of a previous generation. Produced in Scotland. Sheelagh Gilbey, Nini Pitt, Evie Garratt.

**HAUNTING OF PENTHOUSE D, THE (1974).** Mentally dis-turbed woman recuperates in a Manhattan penthouse, but horrors surrounding her father's death take on supernatural dimensions, and she is newly terrorized. Directed by Henry Kaplan. David Birney, Tyne Daly, Farley Granger.

**HAUNTING OF ROSALIND, THE (1973).** What appears to be an ordinary romance between a handsome young man and a beautiful young woman takes a turn for the ghostly when she claims the spirits of the dead have entered her house. Pamela Payton-Wright, Susan Sarandon, Beatrice Straight, Frank Converse.

**HAUNTING PASSION, THE (1983).** Restrained, intelligent TV-movie of the supernatural, which handles its sexual theme tastefully: Jane Seymour is romanced by an invisible ghost in her coastside home. This deals as much with Seymour's problems with her TV newscaster husband; he's undergoing a midlife crisis and cannot perform sexually, leav-ing an opening for the surrogate ghost. The characters, in-cluding husband Paul Rossilli, are well developed by producer Douglas Schwartz and co-writer Michael Berk. Hiro Narita's camera captures the rugged Pacific Coast and the whole thing comes together under John Korty's direction. Women will identify with Seymour being lured into her weird affair while an incredulous husband accuses her of infidelity. Millie Perkins, Gerald McRaney, Ruth Nelson. (VC)

**HAUNTS (1977).** Only the bad scripting by Anne Marisse and directing by Herb Freed will haunt you . . . A madman wielding scissors attacks pretty girls in a small community, while in a farmhouse outside town May Britt fears that her father, Cameron Mitchell, is responsible for the scissors attacks. The editor should have wielded his own scissors on the raw footage more deftly. Aldo Ray hangs around town as the sheriff. E. J. Andre, William Gray Espy. (VC)

**HAUNTS OF THE VERY RICH (1973).** TV-movie directed by Paul Wendkos borrows from the OUTWARD BOUND premise: Passengers aboard an airliner don't know how they got there or where they're going. Eventually they reach a tropical island (a la FANTASY ISLAND) where weird things happen. Finally it becomes apparent that Lloyd Bridges, Cloris Leachman and Anne Francis are caught up in a Is-it-Heaven-or-Hell? plotline. The allegory is contrived by writer William Wood but compelling enough to hold your interest. Edward Asner, Tony Bill, Moses Gunn, Donna Mills.

**HAUSER'S MEMORY (1970).** Based on a novel by Curt (DONOVAN'S BRAIN) Siodmak, this TV-movie explores the premise that scientist David McCallum can inject himself with the memories of another man. Unfortunately, this knowledge also gives him the key to a baffling mystery, and he is pursued across Europe by international spies. Directed by Boris Sagal. Susan Strasberg, Lilli Palmer, Robert Webber, Leslie Nielsen, Helmut Kautner.

**HAVE ROCKET, WILL TRAVEL (1959).** Picks up where ABBOTT AND COSTELLO GO TO MARS left off, but with the Three Stooges at the (out of) controls. Science-fiction slapstick, directed by David Lowell Rich, features such inanities as giant spiders, robots, a botched flight to Venus and assorted cliches spoofing CAT WOMEN OF THE MOON and other howlers. Have TV/will switch . . . unless you're a diehard Stooges fan. Moe, Larry and Joe De Rita, Jerome Cowan, Anna-Lisa, Bob Colbert, Marjorie Bennett.

**HAWK THE SLAYER (1980).** On the surface a sword-and-sorcery actioner about bitter-rival brothers in search of the key to supernatural powers. But this British production has the structure of a Western, with the fights staged as if they were gunbattles. It reeks of Oedipus overtones as the evil brother Voltan (Jack Palance) seeks to destroy the good (John Terry, armed with Mindsword, a magical blade that appears out of thin air whenever needed). The film is not without merit: settings are foggy and mystical, characters gritty and determined, and the effects, though not stupendous, are palatable. However, director Terry Marcel tends to take it too seriously. The acting is of the grandiose, scenery-chewing school and the cast larger than life: Roy Kinnear, Patrick Magee, Harry Andrews, Bernard Bresslaw, Ray Charleson. Designed for British TV, with ambiguous ending. (VC)

**HAXAN (1921).** Subtitled WITCHCRAFT THROUGH THE AGES, this Swedish pseudodocumentary may strike an irreverent note with religious viewers lacking senses of humor. There are frolicking witches and warlocks and promiscuous friars, symbolic of the violence of the Catholic Church during the Inquisition. Re-released in 1969 with new music and narration. An antique piece, quaint, irresistibly laughable, written-directed by Ben Christensen.

**HE KNOWS YOU'RE ALONE (1980).** Psychokiller flick in which women are terrorized then murdered in a manner most foul. The slaughterer of brides-to-be plays ugly cat-and-mouse games with victims, striking when you least expect the knife to fall. Despite predictability, it's terrifying in an excruciating way, and bloodcurdling. Directed by Armand Mastroianni. Don Scardino, Caitlin O'Hearney, Tom Rolfing. Tom Hanks appears in a cameo. (VC)

**HEAD, THE (1959).** Dr. Ood, having seen too many German horror movies, transfers the beautiful body of a strip-tease queen to the head of a hunchback. Or does he put the hunchback's noogin on the strip-tease queen's curvaceous body? Hmm . . . anyway, the result is that two equal one. Dr. Ood (Horst Frank) proves to be just an oodle bit too farfetched, and by calling the substance that keeps the body organs alive Serum Z, he has unintentionally provided the film with a suitable grading. Written-directed by Victor Trivas. Michel Simon, Karin Kernke, Dieter Eppler.

**HEADLESS EYES (1971).** Thoroughly despicable junk that has zero entertainment value and disgusts from beginning to end. Down-on-his-luck New York artist Bo Brudin has his eye poked out while robbing a woman's apartment. This turns him into a serial killer with a patch over one eye. He kills women he sees on the street, then hangs their eyeballs from the ceiling or implants them in his works of "art." There's absolutely no reason on earth to watch this amateurish mess—it's an insult to women in particular and mankind in general. Call it blind filmmaking with unsightful writing. Directed by Kent Bateman. (VC)

**HEADLESS GHOST, THE (1959).** Herman Cohen, who gave us the I WAS A TEENAGE SOMETHING OR OTHER series, is up to his usual cheap tricks, producing a cheap movie not only headless but brainless. Made in England, this alleged supernatural comedy sports a juvenile plot about a spectral entity that has misplaced his head and terrorizes stupid teenagers to get it back. Don't worry, you won't lose your head over this one. Directed by Peter G. Scott. Richard Lyon, Clive Revill, Lilliane Scottane, David Rose, Jack Ellen.

**HEARSE, THE (1980).** Nicely crafted vehicle of horror (pun intended). Trish Van Devere, recovering from a mental collapse, settles in a small town where she is unwelcome because the house she has inherited is allegedly haunted. At night, an antique corpse wagon keeps turning up to terrorize her. An old diary of an ancestor indicates she is related to a witch possessed by the Devil. The terror builds nicely in this better-than-average Crown-International release, decently directed by George Bowers with taut script by Bill Bleich. Joseph Cotten, David Gautreaux, Donald Hotton. (VC)

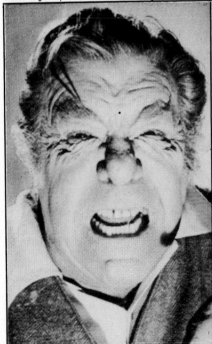

**LON CHANEY JR.
IN 'THE HAUNTED PALACE'**

**BERNADETTE PETERS WITH AN OILY CHARACTER IN 'HEARTBEEPS'**

**HEARTBEEPS** (1981). Childish "mechanical" comedy-love story with Andy Kaufman and Bernadette Peters as shelved robots who meet in a circuitry-adjustment factory and get oiled on each other, with Kaufman hoping he can soon get his piston into Bernadette's camshaft. The robot characters, however, are dumb and without charm, and their face masks are the five-and-dime variety. One funny feature is a comedy robot that tells Henny Youngman jokes. Now that's funny. Stan Winston and Albert Whitlock did the effects. Directed by Allan Arkush. Melanie Mayron, Christopher Guest, Randy Quaid, Kenneth McMillan, Dick Miller. (VC)

**HEAVEN CAN WAIT** (1943). Worthwhile comedy produced-directed by Ernst Lubitsch, featuring Laird Cregar as the Devil, who must listen to playboy Don Ameche explain why he shouldn't be dispatched to Hell following his demise. A colorful depiction of American life at the turn of the century, fired up by a musical score by Alfred Newman and a superb cast: Gene Tierney, Charles Coburn, Spring Byington, Signe Hasso, Allyn Joslyn, Louis Calhern. Not to be confused with the 1978 Warren Beatty fantasy-comedy—that was based on HERE COMES MR. JORDAN.

**HEAVEN CAN WAIT** (1978). Delightful escapism comedy starring Warren Beatty who co-wrote with Elaine May and co-directed with Buck Henry. Beatty stars as a football star whose soul is prematurely taken and who demands a replacement body. What he gets is the aging carcass of a millionaire industrialist—and naturally he wants to play quarterback for the L.A. Rams. A remake of the 1941 HERE COMES MR. JORDAN with Julie Christie, James Mason (as the overseer from above), Jack Warden, Dyan Cannon, Charles Grodin, Vince Gardenia, Buck Henry. (VC)

**HEAVEN ONLY KNOWS** (1947). Also known as MONTANA MIKE . . . another Hollywood fantasy in which an angel descends from Heaven to become entangled in the affairs of mortals. The setting is the West; Archangel Robert Cummings has been chosen to reform a gunslinger and prove that saloon gals, gambling and poker aren't the only things in a cowpoke's life. Pleasant whimsey directed by Albert S.

Rogell. Brian Donlevy, Marjorie Reynolds, Bill Goodwin, John Litel, Stu Erwin, Gerald Mohr, Lurene Tuttle.

**HEAVENLY BODY, THE** (1943). Droll, sophisticated comedy with mild fantasy overtones: Hedy Lamaar, wife of astronomer William Powell, falls in love with handsome stranger James Craig after certain predictions are made. Meanwhile, telescope-happy Powell has discovered a comet on a collision course with the moon. Directed by Alexander Hall. Spring Byington, Morris Ankrum.

**HEAVENLY KID, THE** (1985). Youth-oriented, unusually sappy teen-age fable in which dragster Lewis Smith is killed in a race when his car plunges off a cliff. But he's doomed to ride a subway train for eternity . . . unless, he's told by a heavenly emissary named Rafferty (Richard Mulligan), he redeems himself by returning to Earth and helping nerdish Jason Gedrick make it with the chick of his dreams. That's what writers Cary Medoway (who also directed) and Martin Copeland call a premise. There's nothing heavenly about it. It's just plain dull and maudlin. (VC)

**HEAVY METAL** (1981). Spinoff from the illustrated fantasy magazine, an imaginative mixture of science-fiction, fantasy, horror and surrealism in different animation styles. The results are uneven but the highs outnumber the lows. The youth market was attracted by the hard-rock music track (Black Sabbath, Cheap Trick, Blue Oyster Cult) and comic fans dug the adaptations of Richard Corben and Berni Wrightson. One tale is about a cabbie in a half-destroyed, futuristic New York City, another is about a haunted B-17 during World War II. A green ball of "universal evil" threads in and out of the narratives, but otherwise the stories have little connection. A constantly dazzling piece of work, although the animation styles vary in quality and some storylines are sappy. Directed by Gerald Potterton.

**HEAVY TRAFFIC** (1973). X-rated cartoon from Ralph Bakshi in the style of the underground comic magazines is certain to be heavy going for squares but grand fun for the drug generation as an artist, suffering from the malaisse of city life, retires to his drawing board to let his imagination run

**CREATURE FEATURES MOVIE GUIDE**

free. His fantasies become part of the film's reality. (VC)

**HELICOPTER SPIES, THE (1967).** Episodes of TV's MAN FROM U.N.C.L.E. series recut to feature length, then sold back to TV. As Napoleon Solo, Robert Vaughn walks indifferently through an adventure in Greece involving a new secret device that could destroy half (or 50 per cent) of the world. David McCallum is his partner Ilya and Leo G. Carroll is the assignment chief. Bradford Dillmann, Carol Lynley, Lola Albright, Julie London, John Carradine.

**HELL NIGHT (1982).** Clever blending of slasher and haunted house cliches, building to many successful suspense sequences—you even grow to like four teen-agers locked in the old Garth Mansion overnight as part of the Alpha Sigma Rho initiation rites. Well directed by Tom De Simone and written with verve by Randolph Feldman. The killers are deformed creatures hiding in tunnels under the house or in secret passageways within, from where they strike. The last 15 minutes are especially good: Linda Blair runs screaming through the house, killer in hot pursuit. Kevin Brophy, Vincent Van Patten, Peter Barton, Jenny Neumann. (VC)

**HELLEVISION (1939).** Chances of ever seeing this are slender but we include it for the record . . . scientist picks up TV signals from Hell (but which Hell is it: NBC, CBS or ABC?) which turn out to be stock footage shots from a silent film version of DANTE'S INFERNO. To hellvitit.

**HELLHOLE (1985).** Women-behind-bars variation, with better characters than one might expect in a schlock sleazebagger. Samuel Arkoff's film breaks tradition with asses-and-jugs-in-the-jug by adding a Frankenstein plot: Doctor Marjoe Gortner tests a brain serum on inmates of the Ashland Sanitarium for Women, assisted by psychiatrist Mary Woronov, who wants to satisfy her bisexual perversities. (Her performance offers the most intense depiction of a lesbian ever seen in crud movies.) Gortner's "chemical lobotomies" are for the good of science, but he only creates victims who go mad and have to be placed in a secret cellblock. Meanwhile, an inmate (Judy Landers, a very dull actress) is stalked by a humming killer (Ray Sharkey) posing as an intern to prevent her from squealing on gangsters. Edy William fans will delight in watching her fondling women in some soft porn segments; in fact, there's a whole lot of lesbianism going on. No redeeming values in Vincent Mongol's screenplay, but director Pierre De Moro gives it style, attempting to enhance the material with every camera angle. Terry Moore, Robert Darcy. (VC)

**HELLO DOWN THERE (1969).** Dumb Ivan Tors underwater fantasy-adventure with Tony Randall and family living on the ocean floor in a special housing facility. Directed by Jack Arnold, with diving sequences by Ricou Browning, gentlemen who collaborated on THE CREATURE FROM THE BLACK LAGOON. Janet Leigh, Jim Backus, Roddy McDowall, Ken Berry, Merv Griffin, Bruce Gordon, Arnold Stang.

**HELLSTROM CHRONICLE, THE (1971).** Nils Hellstrom is a fictitious scientist (Lawrence Pressman) with a theory the insect world will inherit the Earth, while mankind will die out, because bugs adapt faster than people to changing environments. This theory is espoused with real footage—close-up scenes of the insect world and its undeniably marvelous "beasts": bees, termites, carnivorous plants, spiders, locusts, etc. Hellstrom's point is frighteningly made and cannot be dismissed as pure fiction. David Seltzer wrote the script. (VC)

**HELP! (1965).** Richard Lester's cinema verite/staged masterpiece blends the music and imagery of the Beatles at work and play with a wild, whacky plot in which the mod British musicians search for Ringo Starr's magic ring, stolen by a crazy cult headed by high priest Clang (Leo McKern). A marvelous satire on genre movies (dig that crazy incredible

**THE HEROIC CHARACTER DEN CONQUERS BARBARIANS IN 'HEAVY METAL'**

shrinking man parody) as well as a brilliant compendium of their best songs sung in the unlikeliest places. Victor Spinetti, Roy Kinnear, Eleanor Bron, Alfie Bass. (VC)

**HENDERSON MONSTER, THE (1980).** Talkative, actionless TV-movie discusses important science-fiction and horror themes but without showing them. Call it a thinking man's FRANKENSTEIN. Jason Miller is a lab investigator studying genetic diseases by improving genetic codes through "gene-splicing," a form of separating DNA to creates new forms of "super-bacteria." Scientists, politicians and journalists clash when Henderson (Miller) refuses to sign a paper that would force him to follow safety procedures. Ernest Kinoy's literate script deals with moral, political implications of man tampering with nature, but at the total expense of excitement. Directed by Waris Hussein. Stephen Collins, Christine Lahti, David Spielberg, Nehemiah Persoff, Larry Gates. (VC)

**HENRY THE RAINMAKER (1949).** Raymond Walburn doesn't talk about the weather—he devises a way to make it rain. Only he doesn't know how to make it stop. Monogram quickie is more thunderstorm than brainstorm and, frankly, all wet. Directed by Jean Yarbrough. Walter Catlett, William Tracy, Mary Stuart, Barbara Brown.

**HER HUSBAND'S AFFAIRS (1947).** Scientist discovers a fluid that removes one's hair and replaces it with thick new sprouts. Ben Hecht and Charles Lederer must have been getting bald when they batted out this comedy. Directed by S. Sylvan Simon. Lucille Ball, Franchot Tone, Edward Everett Horton, Gene Lockhart, Larry Parks.

**HER PANELED DOOR (1950).** Women's thriller in the British tradition in which Phyllis Calvert fears a terrible secret behind a door in the family mansion. Watch for a young Richard Burton. Directed by Ladislas Vajda. Edward Underdown, James Hayter, Helen Cherry, Betty Ann Davies.

**HERBIE GOES BANANAS (1980).** Love Bug Volkswagen with a motor all its own is back for its fourth Disney comedy, breaking up counterfeiters in Mexico and rescuing a kid-napee. On the wild ride: Cloris Leachman as Aunt Louise and Harvey Korman as Captain Blythe. Strictly for the Hot Wheels set. Directed by Vincent McEveety. Charles Martin Smith, John Vernon, Alex Rocco. (VC)

**HERBIE GOES TO MONTE CARLO (1977).** Disney was hardly gambling with this comedy about a flying Volkswagen—it was the third entry in a popular series, although by now the premise was starting to break down. Fun and games in France and Monte Carlo, but the humor is thin. Dean Jones, Don Knotts, Julie Sommars, Roy Kinnear, Jacques Marin. Directed by Vincent McEveety. (VC)

**HERBIE RIDES AGAIN (1974).** Disney's sequel to THE LOVE BUG stars Helen Hayes as Mrs. Steinmetz, the good witch, and Keenan Wynn as Alonzo Hawk, fierce ogre. Hawk wants to erect a skyscraper where Mrs. Steinmetz lives but she enlists the help of a flying Volkswagen (a former racing car). Which leads to merry chases over the hills (not on the streets) of San Francisco. Ms Hayes flits through the ridiculous proceedings oblivious to her perils, giving this tire-squealing fluff an added delight. Directed by Robert Stevenson. Ken Berry, Stephanie Powers, John McIntire. (VC)

**HERCULES (1959).** First in the Italian series about the son of Jupiter (Steve Reeves) using superhuman biceps in his search for the Golden Fleece. Sylva Koscina is lovely to look at, and surely delightful for Reeves to hold during romantic clenches, but there's little else to recommend in this poorly dubbed, sword-and-sandals enterprise. Cinematography by Mario Bava, who would become an important horror director. Directed by Pietro Francisci. Gianna Maria Canale. (VC)

**HERCULES (1983).** Stupefying Italian interpretation of Greek mythology, imitating CLASH OF THE TITANS by having Zeus and lesser Gods on Mt. Olympus overseeing the affairs of mortals and intervening on a mere whim. What makes this so unwieable is Lou Ferrigno (TV's "Incredible Hulk") . . . the muscleman is a helluva hunk, but when he tries to emote, it makes you realize how great Arnold Schwarzenegger is. Writer-director Lewis Coates has concocted a laughably

dumb plot that sinks beneath camp to become insufferably dull. Co-stars Sybil Danning (her overlarge breasts threatening to pop out of her halter like overripe tomatoes), Brad Harris, Rossana Podesta and William Berger are at the mercy of wretched dialogue and action. The special effects are amateurish . . . would you believe time-lapse photography, the old-fashioned kind? One's mind gibbers insanely. (VC)

**HERCULES II (1984).** Sequel to the Lou Ferrigno vehicle has the son of Zeus stalking earthly landscapes to retrieve seven lost thunderbolts ("now let's see, where the hell did I put that bolt of lightning?") and using superstrength to fight off an array of mediocre effects. This Italian film, directed by Lewis Coates, is a mess, again demonstrating Lou hasn't an acting bone in his body. Milly Carlucci, William Berger.

**HERCULES AND THE CAPTIVE WOMEN (1961).** The lost kingdom of Atlantis provides the setting for another Italian mess featuring Reg Park as a succulent strongman. He battles, in grunting fashion, an army of automatons and one big dragon. Fay Spain provides a modicum of glamor as the evil Queen Antinea. Directed by Vittorio Cottafavi. Ettore Manni, Luciano Marin, Ivo Garrani, Gian Maria Volonte.

**HERCULES AND THE HAUNTED WOMEN.** See **HERCULES AND THE CAPTIVE WOMEN.**

**HERCULES AND THE HYDRA.** See **LOVES OF HERCULES, THE.** (Muscles amore?)

**HERCULES AND THE PRINCESS OF TROY (1966).** Gordon Scott leaps out with sword clutched in hand to stop a sea creature from devouring maidens. He claims the babes are out of season. Diana Hyland looks great in flowing gowns; Everett Sloane narrates. Directed by Albert Band.

**HERCULES AND THE TYRANTS OF BABYLON (1964).** Stone-faced Rock Stevens is compelled to put his arms around sorceress Helga Line. Yes, she's handing him a Line; she's evil and must be stopped before half the world is destroyed and the other half is wiped out. In Babylon, events just babble on. Directed by Domenico Paolella. Mario Petri, Livio Lorenzon, Annamaria Polani.

**HERCULES GOES BANANAS.** Alternate videocassette title for **HERCULES THE MOVIE.** (A-peeling stuff.)

**HERCULES IN NEW YORK.** See **HERCULES THE MOVIE.**

**HERCULES IN THE HAUNTED WORLD (1964).** "Hercules Descending" might be the subtitle for this adventure in Hell, where old Herc (beefcaker Reg Park) searches for a herb to break a magical spell binding a princess to bondage. Demons and goddesses in Hades are framed against swirling fires of eternal damnation. Christopher Lee turns up as a minion of Satan, and there are other various creatures out of DANTE'S INFERNO. Refreshing attempt by director Mario Bava to bring genuine fantasy into these cardboard adventures. Eleonora Ruffo, Giorgio Ardisson, Marisa Belli.

**HERCULES IN THE VALE OF WOE (1962).** "Woe" aptly describes what you're in for. Not only must you endure a ridiculous beefcake hero (Kirk Morris) boxing with Mongolians but you must also endure two confidence men from Rome who jump into a time machine and travel back to Hercules' days. Groan ohh ouch yikes . . . woe is us. Frank Gordon, Bice Valori.

**HERCULES OF THE DESERT (1964).** Legendary muscleman isn't Hercules, he's Maciste. You'll be further baffled by men who can cause avalanches and other disasters through echoing techniques, I think . . . I think . . . I think . . . I think . . . The hero is Kirk Morris; real villain is writer-director Amerigo Anton. Helene Chanel, Alberto Farnese.

**HERCULES, PRISONER OF EVIL (1967).** Reg Park, who sucked away your breath in HERCULES AND THE CAPTIVE WOMEN, is smashing up papier-mache scenery again as an over-muscled, empty-craniumed grunt hero of the loincloth who destroys a sorceress who turns men into werewolves. You too will howl . . . with laughter . . . at director Anthony Dawson's attempts to make a serious swashbuckler. Ettore Manni, Maria Teresa Orsini, Mireille Granelli.

**HERCULES, SAMSON AND ULYSSES (1964).** Three times

as much grunting and groaning in this Italian spectacle, for as the title hints, you're in for a triple treat of muscle-flexing. Kirk Morris, Richard Lloyd and Enzo Cerusico comprise the tiresome threesome hunting a sea monster. For biceps bionics only. Directed-written by Pietro Francisci.

**HERCULES THE INVINCIBLE (1963).** Italian potboiler has muscle maniac Dan Vadis battling a giant dragon. They should have breathed more fire into the script instead of the mouth of the creature. Directed by Alfredo Mancori. Spela Rozin, Ken Clark, Carla Calo, Jon Simons.

**HERCULES THE MOVIE (1970).** Zeus is ticked off because Hercules is knocking over pillars and throwing papier-mache boulders, so he banishes the sinew-swelling strongman to contemporary Earth, where his loincloth is right in fashion. Of historical interest because Arnold Schwarzenegger stars as Hercules, but under the name of Arnold Strong. His co-star is Arnold Stang, who clings when Strong swings and flings. Directed by Arthur A. Seidelman. (VC)

**HERCULES UNCHAINED (1960).** Mythology-happy sequel to HERCULES, directed by Pietro Francisci. Again, Steve

**HERCULES VS. THE VAMPIRES. See HERCULES IN THE HAUNTED WORLD.** (Fangs for the muscles.)

**HERE COMES MR. JORDAN (1941).** Light-winged fantasy that established the trend for angels-from-Heaven-come-to-Earth plots. A dumb but ambitious prizefighter dies in a plane crash . . . kindly, white-haired Mr. Jordan (a heavenly emissary played by Claude Rains) must find the boxer another body. The body picked is that of a just-murdered millionaire. Edward Everett Horton appears as Messenger #7013. Remade in 1978 by Warren Beatty as HEAVEN CAN WAIT. Directed by Alexander Hall. Robert Montgomery, Evelyn Keyes, James Gleason, John Emery, Rita Johnson. (VC)

**HERO AT LARGE (1980).** Not a fantasy, but included here because of John Ritter's portrayal as Captain Avenger, a facsimile of a superhero promoting a new movie. A hired actor, Ritter takes on characteristics of the superhero and is soon in trouble. A signficiant comedy for points about bravery and stalwart qualities we enjoy in our heroes, but which are harder for ordinary people to achieve. Funny and moving. Directed by Martin Davidson. Anne Archer, Bert Convy, Kevin McCarthy, Harry Bellaver, Anita Dangler.

**SEAN CONNERY AS RAMIREZ, CLANCY BROWN AS THE KURGAN IN 'HIGHLANDER'**

Reeves is the biceps-bulging beefcaker and lovely Sylva Koscina is his wife with her own well-rounded muscles. Hercules loses his memory to a magical water and is a prisoner in the male harem of the Queen of Lidia. Dreadfully dubbed, but Mario Bava's camera work is excellent, and this Italian film is superior to the imitations which followed. Wrestler Primo Carnera does battle with our hero. (VC)

**HERCULES VS. THE GIANT WARRIORS (1965).** Zeus figures prominently in this Italian-French production, robbing Hercules (Dan Vadis) of his superstrength. What is the poor weakling to do now that the Giant Warriors have been awakened and are on the march? What else but throw sand into their faces. Directed by Alberto De Martino. Moira Orfei, Piero Lulli, Marilu Tolo, Pierre Cressoy.

**HERCULES VS. THE MOON MEN (1964).** Straight from wars on the lunar surface comes a race of moon mongrels ruled by a sorceress, Queen of the Lunar Loonies. The only man who can stop their moon-iacal deeds is Hercules, who bulges to life in the form of Alan Steel (brace yourself!) Written-directed by Giacomo Gentilomo. Jany Clair, Jean Pierre Honore.

**HEX (1973).** Tough motorcyclists riding through South Dakota invade a witch's farm and are "hexed," dying one by one, always in bloody, awful ways. Keith Carradine heads the terrorists who become the victims. A box office bomb, HEX should be called WREKS. Directed by Leo Garen. Gary Busey, Robert Walker Jr., John Carradine, Dan Haggerty, Cristina Raines, Tina Herazo.

**HIDDEN HAND, THE (1942).** Secret serum enables woman to fake a heart attack to carry out a diabolical plot against heirs to her estate. Outdated comedy, old-fashioned scare tactics. Directed by Ben Stoloff. Craig Stevens, Elizabeth Fraser.

**HIDDEN POWER (1939).** Scientist Jack Holt searches for an anaesthesia to curtail human suffering, creating an explosive new power instead. Directed by Lewis D. Collins. Regis Toomey, Gertrude Michael, Dickie Moore.

**HIDEOUS SUN DEMON, THE (1959).** Robert Clarke produced, directed and stars in this cheapie, demonstrative of the mutated monster craze that swept '50s Hollywood. He portrays a physicist exposed to radiation who, under sun rays, transmutates into a scaly, homicidal creature. Clarke

**CLINT EASTWOOD IN
'HIGH PLAINS DRIFTER'**

conveys the torment this brings to the human soul, but such sympathetic touches amidst the murder and mayhem he wreaks. Just plain hideous. Patricia Manning, Alan Peterson, Patrick Whyte, Del Courtney. (VC)

**HIGH PLAINS DRIFTER (1973).** The oddest spaghetti Western ever—seemingly a Clint Eastwood vehicle so he can re-enact his Man With No Name. However, there's more to it when Eastwood, a sadistic gunfighter, rides into a small town on the edge of a lake and turns its people against each other. Get this: Eastwood is Death, avenging his own murder. Is that what Ernest Tidyman's script is about? Eastwood proves he is a superior director, capturing the fury and violence of this supernatural (?) oater. Verna Bloom, Billy Curtis, Marianna Hill, Jack Ging, Mitchell Ryan. (VC)

**HIGHLANDER (1986).** Stupendous fantasy-adventure, directed with great imagination by Russell Mulcahy, who employs an always fluid camera to tell this cosmic-level story about a race of immortals who duel over the centuries with magical swords to claim "The Prize." With the pacing of an MTV video, this covers four centuries by cross-cutting between past and present to dramatize the growth of one such immortal, a Scotsman (Christopher Lambert) trained by mentor Sean Connery. Their common enemy is Kurgen, a malevolent immortal who would make the entire world suffer should he win The Prize. The fights are brilliantly staged in this stylish example of superior screen fantasy. The first half is so good, in fact, there's no way Mulcahy can top himself at the climax. Roxanne Hart, Clancy Brown. (VC)

**HIGHLY DANGEROUS (1951).** British-American thriller in which Margaret Lockwood and Dane Clark, traveling in postwar Russia, uncover a Soviet plot that would involve insects in germ warfare. Eric Ambler wrote this espionage fantasy, Roy Baker directed. Marius Goring, Anthony Newley, Wilfrid Hyde-White, Michael Hordern, Olaf Pooley.

**HILLBILLYS IN A HAUNTED HOUSE (1967).** Two music world celebs spend a night in a haunted house and are subjected to floating apparitions, a gorilla and eyeballs peeping out from behind paintings. They also tangle with a gang of spies and crazy doctors. Directed by Jean Yarbrough. The world's first—and last—Country and Western horror comedy! Ferlin Husky, Joi Lansing, Lon Chaney Jr., John Carradine, Basil Rathbone, Linda Ho. (VC)

**HILLS HAVE EYES, THE (1977).** A man's skull is split open with a crowbar; a caveman mutant rips the head off a canary and drinks its blood; a German Shepherd rips open a man's foot, then tears at his throat; a knife plunges countless times into a twitching torso; a man is tied to a yucca plant,

drenched in gasoline and set aflame; a baby is kidnapped and prepared for a human barbecue. And that's during the prologue . . . yes, it's fun and games from Wes Craven, that modern intellectual who gave us THE LAST HOUSE ON THE LEFT. Craven's screenplay has a Cleveland family in the desert, searching for an old family mine, when it is attacked by degenerate cavemen and women who carry walkie-talkies and have large putty noses, which they scratch as they slaver and cackle their homicidal glee. This pandering, revolting plunge into depravity and death does, however, have a social comment: When innocent people resort to violence, they become no better than their bloodthirsty nemeses. How's that for profundity? John Steadman, Dee Wallace, Susan Lanier, Martin Speer, Robert Houston, James Whitworth, Michael Berryman. (VC)

**HILLS HAVE EYES II, THE (1984).** Back we go into Wes Craven territory, those hills in and around Yucca Valley where young people inevitably meet their deaths at the hands of barbaric cannibals. This time a bus-load of eight youthful ones on their way to a motorcycle race are stranded—among them (purely by coincidence) a male survivor of the original film plus a reformed cannibal from that same movie, now a vegeterian. Her maniacal brother, thought to be dead in the first film, is back with another hairy desert buddy to terrorize the dumb, hapless band. So what we get is a falling rock crushing a cyclist's head, a catapulted spear into a human chest cavity, a hatchet into a brain and other grisly deaths ending up in a charnal house of corpses. One of two survivors is blind, so writer-director Craven gets to play WAIT UNTIL DARK too. Despite its blood and thunder, it is a weak sequel which in no way enjoyed the success of its predecessor. James Whitworth and Michael Berryman fare best as the bone-chompers. (VC)

**HITCHER, THE (1986).** Decidedly strange psychokiller movie with such ill-defined motivations and surreal plotting that the easiest way to watch, without feeling frustration, is to accept this as a nightmare from which one can't wake up. David Howell, driving across Texas, picks up a hitchhiker named John Ryder (Rutger Hauer) to become the victim of Hauer's conspiracy to make him look guilty of grisly murders. Howell goes through harrowing experiences, with Hauer involving him with police and then protecting him from capture. There's an undercurrent of homosexual masochism in Eric Red's terse, unexplained script with images of chains and leather, and a weird psychic link between the two men. Hauer seems to want Howell to kill him, as if that were the ultimate sexual experience. It's grisly: there's a human finger on a plate of French fries, a woman tied between trucks and assorted shotgun murders. Many have found this film despicable,

**WES CRAVEN, DIRECTOR OF
'HILLS HAVE EYES'**

　　　　　　　　**CREATURE FEATURES MOVIE GUIDE**

others are intrigued by its enigmas. Directed by Robert Harmon. Jennifer Jason Leigh, Henry Darrow. (VC)

**H-MAN, THE (1959).** Lime jello lives, fans. A quivering puddle of mutant ooze, radioactively stimulated, creeps and seeps and bleeps its way through Japanese streets, sucking up hapless humans foolish enough to want to pet it. The ooze, apparently having seen THEM, seeks refuge in the sewer system. The eating scenes, prepared by GODZILLA special effects genius Eiji Tsuburaya, are scrumptuous as human flesh dissolves. You'll then laugh yourself silly at the dubbed soundtrack. That GODZILLA director, Inoshiro Honda, was at the helm. Rated H—for Hokum. Yumi Shirakawa, Kenji Sahara, Akihiko Hirata, Mitsuru Sato.

**HOBBIT, THE (1977).** Animated TV-feature based on the famous book by J.R.R. Tolkien and featuring the voices of Orson Bean, John Huston, Paul Frees and Hans Conried. Produced-directed by Jules Bass and Arthur Rankin Jr. (VC)

**HOLD THAT GHOST (1941).** Frivolous Bud Abbott-Lou Costello comedy of haunted house antics. The screaming and yelling will keep you from dozing, and there are a few funny moments amidst the total nonsense. Richard Carlson and Joan Davis co-star with Evelyn Ankers, Universal's horror heroine. Directed by Arthur Lubin. Mischa Auer, Shemp Howard, Marc Lawrence, the Andrews Sisters.

**HOLD THAT HYPNOTIST (1957).** You are watching a Bowery Boys film directed by Austen Jewell when you begin to feel drowsy . . . Dan Pepper's story is about Sach . . . he's an idiot falling into a state of . . . hypnotic regression . . . he is looking . . . for a treasure map of . . . Blackbeard the Pirate . . . in 1683 . . . you are growing sleepier by the second . . . sleepy . . . blink wink . . . zzzzzzzz.

**HOLD THAT LINE (1952).** More Bowery Boys least-side bunk with Leo Gorcey, Huntz Hall and other juvenile saps using a superstrength concoction to win the college football game. You really must have an appreciation for what these films reflect—kiddie pranks on the most basic level. Directed by William Beaudine. John Bromfield, Veda Ann Borg, Gil Stratton Jr., Taylor Holmes, Mona Knox.

**HOLLYWOOD GHOST STORIES (1986).** Pseudodocumentary about Hollywood stars whose ghosts have been seen by others. Interviews with "witnesses," reports on the spectral sightings of George Reeves and Valentino. Sexy German actress Elke Sommer talks about a haunted house she once lived in. Directed by James Forsher. (VC)

**HOLLYWOOD MEATCLEAVER MASSACRE.** See MEATCLEAVER MASSACRE. (Chopped quivers?)

**PATRICIA BRESLIN IN 'HOMICIDAL'**

**JACK BENNY IN
'THE HORN BLOWS AT MIDNIGHT'**

**HOLOCAUST 2000.** Videocassette title for **CHOSEN, THE.**

**HOLY TERROR.** Videocassette title for **ALICE, SWEET ALICE.** (Enfant terrible?)

**HOMEBODIES (1974).** Bizarre, offbeat tidbit in which elderly folks in a highrise knock off those responsible for condemning their tenement to destruction. Strangely dark macabre comedy, in the vein of ARSENIC AND OLD LACE but with perverse meanness. Some deaths are quite grisly, such as a body being dumped into fresh cement. Written-directed by Larry Yust, with writing assist from Howard Kaminsky and Bennett Sims. Paula Trueman, Peter Brocco, Frances Fuller, Ian Wolfe, Kenneth Tobey. (VC)

**HOMICIDAL (1961).** Producer-director William Castle claimed the idea for this horror thriller came to him in his sleep; we suspect it came to him while he watched Hitchcock's PSYCHO. There are many similar plotting tricks in Robb White's script, but in general the level of acting, scripting and direction are beneath the Master of Suspense. Butcher knife murders are committed by a crazed young woman, but nothing is really what it seems, so be prepared for shocking surprises. Castle's gimmicks and sneaky tricks included a special "Fright Break" (not in TV prints), a pause before the denouement for customers to reclaim admission money and leave. Jean Arliss, Glenn Corbett, Patricia Breslin, James Westerfield, Richard Rush, Hope Summers.

**HONEYMOON HORROR (1982).** Poor producer's clone of FRIDAY THE 13TH, extremely amateurish in its execution of special effects—so bad, in fact, when an axe sinks into a human's brain, it starts to fall out before the cut. At Honeymoon Cove, on Lover's Island, somewhere in Texas, a husband finds his wife with another man and is trapped in a fire. Later, three pairs of collegiate newlyweds stop off at the rundown resort to frolic, but instead meet bloody demises at the hands of a badly burned maniac. William F. Pecchi steals the movie (a mean achievement) as a pot-bellied redneck sheriff who chomps hungrily on an old cigar. No honeymoon, this. Directed by Harry Preston. Cheryl Black. (VC)

**HOPPITY GOES TO TOWN.** See **MR. BUG GOES TO TOWN.** (And so does this nice animated movie.)

**HORN BLOWS AT MIDNIGHT, THE (1945).** Mark Hellinger's comedy fantasy (directed by Raoul Walsh) stars Jack Benny as an angel sent to Earth to herald the Coming of Doom. For years Benny made derogatory comments about this film on his radio and TV shows, and everyone agreed the comedian was justified in his long-running pentance. For nostalgia freaks. Dolores Moran, Alexis Smith, Allyn Joslyn, Guy Kibbee, Truman Bradley, Mike Mazurki.

**HORRIBLE DR. HICHCOCK, THE (1962).** Robert Flemying, as a lover of dead corpses, seeks new blood to inject into his first wife, who has died. He selects Barbara Steele but Barbara resists and screams (as is befitting the Queen of Horror) for her life. And then the first wife returns, looking a little grave-worn. This Italian chiller, directed by Robert Hampton, was trimmed for the U.S.; much of its original morbidity (and hence its appeal) has been lost. The sequel was THE GHOST, not nearly as depraved (drat it).

**HORRIBLE HOUSE ON THE HILL.** See **DEVIL TIMES FIVE.**(Five times as horrible!)

**HORRIBLE ORGIES OF COUNT DRACULA.** See **REINCARNATION OF ISABEL.**

**HORRIBLE SEXY VAMPIRE, THE (1973).** The title of this Spanish import pretty well sums up its subtleties as directed by Jose Luis Madrid. Waldemar Wohlfahrt portrays the bloodsucking baron. Horrible is right!

**'HARRY AND THE HENDERSONS'**

**HORROR AND SEX.** See **NIGHT OF THE BLOODY APES.**

**HORROR AT 37,000 FEET (1973).** Airborne TV-movie about an airliner suspended in midair because it is carrying a sacrificial druid stone. GRAND HOTEL in the sky quickly becomes tedium at 37,000 feet. Directed by David Lowell Rich. William Shatner, Roy Thinnes, Chuck Connors, Tammy Grimes, Buddy Ebsen, Paul Winfield.

**HORROR CASTLE (1963).** Madman appropriately nicknamed "The Executioner," believed to be 300 years old, runs maniacally through the drafty halls of an old German structure, knocking off victims with ancient torture devices. Christopher Lee portrays the messed up caretaker, who should have taken greater care to protect guests Rossana Podesta and Georges Riviere. Directed by Anthony Dawson; based on THE VIRGIN OF NUREMBURG by Frank Bogart.

**HORROR CHAMBER OF DR. FAUSTUS (1962).** Mad doctor Pierre Brasseur believes he can restore the marred beauty of his daughter by grating on the faces of lovely lasses, whom he kidnaps into his secret lab. This French film, directed by Georges Franju, who collaborated with mystery writers Pierre Boileau and Thomas Narcejac, has numerous plot holes, as do the faces of victims when the doc gets through. The grafting sequences have an overabundance of hideous detail. Alida Valli, Juliette Mayniel.

**HORROR CREATURES OF THE PREHISTORIC PLANET.** See **HORROR OF THE BLOOD MONSTERS.**

**HORROR EXPRESS (1972).** All aboard for terror and destruction! Cataclysmic evil emanates from the remains of a prehistoric monster being railed to Moscow via the trans-Siberian Railroad. The will of the monster invades the minds of the passengers because it needs to build a starship to return to its own galaxy. Nifty British-Spanish chiller with superior production values and plenty of gory effects. Directed by Eugenio Martia. Christopher Lee is the archeologist, Peter Cushing is a sympathetic scientist and Telly Savalas is a Hungarian cop. Helga Line, Silvia Tortosa. (VC)

**HORROR HIGH.** See **TWISTED BRAIN.**

**HORROR HOSPITAL (1973).** Emergency! Acting coach needed in Ward B to restrain Michael Gough from going bonkers in a fright mask as he tampers with the brains of his patients and cuts off their heads. Gory, gratuitous British import directed by Anthony Balch. Calling all film doctors . . . Calling all film doctors . . . (VC)

**HORROR HOTEL (1960).** British supernatural thriller reeking with atmosphere and mystery in crisp black-and-white photography. The setting is a New England community taken over by a witches' coven. Into the sinister town come a young man and woman seeking one of the coven's victims. Directed by John Llewellyn Moxey. Patricia Jessel, Christopher Lee, Betta St. John, Valentine Dyall, William Abner. (VC)

**HORROR HOTEL MASSACRE.** See **EATEN ALIVE.**

**HORROR HOUSE (1970).** Psychotic knife killer attacks teenagers in a dark, old mansion outside London . . . which of the boppers is the attacker? Weak terror whodunit, barely kept alive by writer-director Michael Armstrong. Jill Haworth does look good in miniskirts, though. Frankie Avalon, Dennis Price, Mark Wynter, Richard O'Sullivan.

**HORROR ISLAND (1941).** Treasure hunters wind up on an old island where stands an ancient mansion, home of "The Phantom." Secret corridors, treasure maps, and the old kill-them-one-at-a-time gambit. Outmoded but still fun. Directed by George Waggner. Dick Foran, Peggy Moran, Leo Carrillo, Al "Fuzzy" Knight, John Eldredge.

**HORROR MANIACS (1953).** Britain's horror film star of the 1940s, Tod Slaughter, is grubby as hell in the role of a corpse snatcher in the Burke and Hare tradition. Directed by Oswald Mitchell, written by John Gilling. Henry Oscar, Denis Wyndham. Also known as GREED OF WILLIAM HART.

**HORROR OF DRACULA, THE (1958).** Hammer shocker, scripted by Jimmy Sangster and directed by Terence Fisher, was responsible for reviving Bram Stoker's classic vampire villain. This Gothic production brought international acclaim (and box office receipts) to the British studio, which would continue in the same vein for the next 20 years. Christopher Lee attempted to capture the more subtle nuances of the Transylvanian count (subtleties ignored by Bela Lugosi) and the film is punctuated by its own curious miasma of Gothic mistiness. Peter Cushing essayed the Van Helsing role. Unarguably the best in the Hammer series. Michael Gough, Melisa Stribbling, Carol Marsh, Valerie Gaunt. (VC)

**HORROR OF FRANKENSTEIN, THE (1970).** Writer-director Jimmy Sangster demonstrates less subtlety and more black comedy in this lowbrow entry in the Hammer-Frankenstein series. Ralph Bates, as the industrious Baron, is no replacement for Peter Cushing and David Prowse (Darth Vader's body in STAR WARS) is no surrogate for Christopher Lee as the Monster. Critics agreed this was the least effective of the Hammer outpourings, its attempts at humor failing miserably. Veronica Carlson, Kate O'Mara, Dennis Price. (VC)

---

*"He is the very embodiment of evil. He is the Devil himself." — Peter Cushing as Professor von Helsing in* **HORROR OF DRACULA.**

**HORROR OF IT ALL, THE (1964).** Pat Boone finds himself in an old, dark house haunted by sinister types. The real "horror of it all" is that director Terence Fisher or writer Ray Russell wanted to be associated with this U.S.-English production. Dennis Price, Andre Melly, Valentine Dyall.

**HORROR OF PARTY BEACH, THE (1964).** Bikini beach girls are ruthlessly attacked, the flesh ripped from their succulent bodies, by "Black Lagoon"-style amphibians created from radioactive waste dumped in the ocean. Wonderfully inept as the creatures crash a slumber party and carry the girls away—from the Neanderthal production values to the Stoned age cast headed by John Scott and Alice Lyon to the non-direction of Del Tenney. A classic of its kind. (VC)

**HORROR OF THE BLOOD MONSTERS.** Videocassette title for **VAMPIRE MEN OF THE LOST PLANET.**

**HORROR OF THE ZOMBIES (1974).** Third film in the "Blind Dead" series, this Spanish import stars Maria Perschy and Jack Taylor in a tale about a ghost ship and flesh-munching knights who are nothing more than hungry skeletons. Yummy yummy. Directed-written by Amando De Ossorio. (VC)

**HORROR ON SNAPE ISLAND.** See **TOWER OF EVIL.**

**HORROR PLANET (1981).** Perfectly awful British ripoff of ALIEN, with touches of FRIDAY THE 13TH and DRACULA thrown in for exploitative enhancement. On a science research lab on some farflung planet in some faraway galaxy, a bug-eyed monster impregnates researcher Judy Geeson and causes her to go berserk. With superhuman strength she vampirizes her research workers one by one, pausing long enough to give birth to mini-monsters. A bloody mess, literally, with plenty of weird sound effects and electronic noises to keep you on edge. Nick Maley, who co-wrote with Gloria Maley, also did the sickening gore effects and creatures. Directed by Norman Warner and co-starring Robin Clarke as the hero and Jennifer Ashley, Stephanie Beacham and Victoria Tennant biting the extraterrestrial dust. (VC)

**HORROR RISES FROM THE TOMB (1972).** Spanish rotboiler stars Paul Naschy as a beheaded knight who turns up in modern times as a sorcerer, terrorizing the inhabitants of an old castle and all the beauties therein. The Jacinto Molina screenplay is medieval. Directed by Carlos Aured. (VC)

**HORRORS OF BURKE AND HARE, THE (1971).** A few nights in the careers of the Body Snatchers, those grave disturbors of old Edinburgh who sold "goods" to surgical colleges in need of cadavers for anatomy classes. Directed in England by Vernon Seawell as BURKE AND HARE. Derren Nesbitt, Harry Andrews, Glynn Edwards. (VC).

**HORRORS OF SPIDER ISLAND (1959).** German-Yugoslav effort set on a tropical island where a plane crashes. Survivors include a talent scout and his good-looking models. Before long they meet up with eight-legged monstrosities with vampire overbite. Designed for unthinking teen-agers by producer Gaston Hakim, who lured director Fritz Bottger into his own spider's web. Also known as IT'S HOT IN PARADISE. Cold! Helga Frank, Harald Maresch.

**HORRORS OF THE BLACK MUSEUM (1959).** Herman Cohen titillator with sexually suggestive murders committed by a museum curator (Michael Gough) who also writes mysteries. He needs to feel the exhileration of each murder so he can faithfully set it down on paper, you see. Each homicide is depicted in all its gory glory and Gough stirs up a formaldehyde float in a huge vat so he can "dissolve" his relationships with victims. Not recommended for kiddies and their pets. Features the infamous needles-in-the-binoculars scene, among other graphic deaths. Directed by Arthur Crabtree. Shirley Ann Field, June Cunningham, Graham Gurnow, Beatrice Varley, Austin Trevor, Nora Gordon.

**HORSE'S MOUTH, THE (1954).** A waggish Irish oracle who forecasts track results gives tips to a young newspaperman (Joseph Tomelty). All of England, in the meantime, is in an uproar over how this affects the odds. Directed by Pennington Richards. Robert Beatty, Mervyn Johns, Virginia McKenna, Gillian Lind, Ursula Howells.

**HOSPITAL MASSACRE.** Videocassette title for **X-RAY.**

**HOSPITAL OF TERROR.** Videocassette title for **BEYOND THE LIVING.**

**HOUND OF THE BASKERVILLES, THE (1939).** The first film to team Basil Rathbone and Nigel Bruce as Sherlock Holmes and Dr. Watson is not a masterpiece but still a jolly good attempt to recapture the Victorian flavor of Sir Arthur Conan Doyle's novel. The setting is the foggy moors surrounding Baskerville Hall and the curse that taints its inhabitants. Directed by Sidney Lanfield. Richard Greene, Lionel Atwill, John Carradine, Wendy Barrie. (VC)

**HOUND OF THE BASKERVILLES, THE (1959).** Hammer's version of the Doyle horror-mystery classic stars Peter Cushing as the Baker Street sleuth, Sherlock Holmes, and Andre Morell as the winsome Watson. This is more effective than

**SON OF A BEACH: 'THE HORROR OF PARTY BEACH'**

the Rathbone-Bruce treatment and will grip your interest with its hellish hound, mist-bound swamps and devious characters, even if the story about a family living under a dreaded curse is familiar. Directed by Terence Fisher. Christopher Lee portrays Baskerville. Miles Malleson. (VC)

**HOUND OF THE BASKERVILLES, THE (1972).** TV-movie strains for the Doyle touch but is inferior to previous versions. Stewart Granger as Holmes doesn't project the mandatory qualities for the Baker Street sleuth and there is a lacking in budget and script to pull it off. Bernard Fox is just a passable Watson. Directed by Barry Crane. William Shatner, Anthony Zerbe, Sally Ann Howes, John Williams.

**HOUND OF THE BASKERVILLES, THE (1977).** A genuine

dog. British spoof of Doyle's Sherlock Holmes yarn that critics found singularly unfunny. The game is definitely not afoot with Paul Morrissey directing. Re-edited for the U.S. and made all the worse for it. Dudley Moore, Peter Cook, Denholm Elliott, Joan Greenwood, Spike Milligan.

**HOUND OF THE BASKERVILLES, THE (1983).** British remake of the classic Doyle horror novel set on the English moors, with Sherlock Holmes (Ian Richardson) and Dr. Watson (Donald Churchill) hurrying to the aid of Sir Henry Baskerville, who is plagued by a family curse and a huge "hound from Hell" that stalks the bogs, tearing out human throats. Martin Shaw portrays Baskerville, Denholm Elliott is Dr. Mortimer and Ronald Lacey is Inspector Lestrade. Directed by Douglas Hickox. Has plenty of bite.

**HOUNDS OF ZAROFF.** See **MOST DANGEROUS GAME, THE** (from the producers of KING KONG).

**HOUSE (1986).** Sean S. Cunningham's production blends the supernatural and outright horror but can't decide whether to play it straight or zoom into camp. Hence, it unwinds with a troubled sense about its own soul. William Katt is mystery writer Roger Cobb, so troubled by his Vietnam experiences that he moves into a sinister Gothic house (where his aunt committed suicide) to write his memoirs. Soon he's reliving his unpleasant 'Nam experiences in flashbacks, a bug-eyed monster is coming out of a closet to get him, and he's off into another dimension in search of his long-missing son. The film, directed by Steve Miner and scripted by Ethan Wiley, vacillates between stark thrills and comedic laughs played straight-faced by the cast: George Wendt (as a next door neighbor), Kay Lenz (as Katt's ex-wife, who still loves him) and Richard Moll as a soldier who returns from the dead to terrorize Katt. HOUSE is a mood piece consisting of loosely knit vignettes, vague characters and a sense of displacement. Call it weak foundations. (VC)

**HOUSE AND THE BRAIN, THE (1973).** A worshipper of demons holds a woman hostage in his gothic castle—a fitting location for the duel between good and evil which takes place when the woman's lover seeks her out. Loose adaptation of the classic story by Bulwer-Lytton, "The Haunters and the Haunted." Keith Charles, Carol Williard, Hurt Hatfield.

**HOUSE AT THE EDGE OF THE PARK (1984).** Two psychos turn a party into mayhem and murder. Directed by Roger D. Franklyn.

**HOUSE BY THE CEMETERY (1982).** Lucio Fulci, that sweet Italian who gave us ZOMBIE and GATES OF HELL, restrains himself (but only slightly) to tell this tale about a sweet mother, father and son who move into Oaks Mansion, a creepy old place (yep, the one next door to the graveyard) only to find it haunted by a ghoul named Freudstein, who once carried on "illegal experiments" with the body cells of corpses. There are buckets of gushing blood as the killer's knife slits throats and plunges into torsos. There's a weird babysitter, a tomb in the hallway, a vampire bat that clings to the wife's head and hero's hand for several screen minutes, sinister rooms, a dark cellar, etc. Katherine MacColl, Paolo Malco, Ania Pieroni. Exteriors filmed near Boston. (VC)

**HOUSE BY THE LAKE, THE (1977).** Canadian kill-thrill flick,

produced by Ivan Reitman, who would go on to make GHOSTBUSTERS and other major features. The stars, Brenda Vaccaro and Don Stroud, are an asset to writer-director William Freut who has set his story in a pastoral location to contrast the murderous mayhem of a band of sadistic killers. Ample gore effects. Chuck Shamata, Richard Ayres.

**HOUSE IN NIGHTMARE PARK (1973).** The British tried to cash in on the snake craze of the early 1970s with this frightful horror comedy about an old house of deadly serpents, controlled by a family of snakes-in-the-grass. The Terry Nation-Clive Exton script lacks anything sensuous although it has ample sinuousness. Director Peter Sykes thought of making a sequel but decided the plot had no re-coil. It's okay to laugh, though: this was designed as a vehicle for British comedian Frankie Howerd. Hiss, hiss! Ray Milland, Kenneth Griffith, Hugh Burden, Rosemary Crutchley.

**HOUSE IN THE WOODS, THE (1957).** Patricia Roc, Michael Gough and Ronald Howard bring to life a lifeless British supernatural nonthriller about a spirit of a murdered woman who returns from beyond for her revenge. Written-directed by Maxwell Munden.

**HOUSE OF CRAZIES.** See **ASYLUM.** (Oh, nuts!)

**HOUSE OF DARK SHADOWS (1970).** Popular daytime serial DARK SHADOWS prompted producer Dan Curtis to make two full-length features, of which this is the first. (NIGHT OF DARK SHADOWS was a sequel.) Jonathan Frid recreates Barnabas Collins, who rises from the grave and does the Dracula bit by turning all the residents of the family mansion into "blood brothers." Joan Bennett is Elizabeth, a fellow Collins. Barnabas ages to 150 years in one sequence, an effect achieved by make-up specialist Dick Smith. Directed by Curtis. Grayson Hall, Kathryn Leigh Scott.

**HOUSE OF DARKNESS (1948).** British film borrowing from DEAD OF NIGHT to tell its story—a series of ghost narratives presented in flashbacks. Laurence Harvey, in an early role, is the stepbrother of a murdered man whose spirit is "restless." Scripted by John Gilling, directed by Oswald Mitchell. Leslie Brooks, John Stuart.

**HOUSE OF DRACULA (1945).** Sequel to HOUSE OF FRANKENSTEIN, in which Universal amalgamated its popular monsters for maximum box office potential, if not artistic benefits. You get Lon Chaney Jr. as the Wolf Man, John Carradine as Dracula and Glenn Strange as the Frankenstein Monster. There's a hunchbacked nurse, Lionel Atwill as a police inspector, and an assortment of creepy characters. This romp was to mark the finale to the studio's pseudo-

**THE ASSORTED HORRORS THAT PLAGUE WILLIAM KATT (FAR RIGHT) IN 'HOUSE'**

serious monster movies, and paved the way for Abbott and Costello horror comedies. Directed by Erle C. Kenton. Jane Adams, Martha O'Driscoll, Ludwig Stossel, Skelton Knaggs, Dick Dickinson. Make-up by Jack Pierce.

**HOUSE OF EVIL (1968).** One of four independent low-budget features made with Boris Karloff two years before his death. The film was caught up in courtroom battles after the death of producer Luis Vergara and may still be hard to come by. Consider yourself lucky, unless you're a purist who must see every Karloff film. The Jack Hill screenplay centers on a castle equipped with a torture chamber, and "torture" is exactly what this Mexican-financed movie is. Directed by Juan Ibanez and Jack Hill.

**HOUSE OF EVIL (1974).** British TV cheapie starring Salome Jens as the sister to Jamie Smith Jackson . . . they're supposed to be in league with the Devil. And the Devil can keep them. Dabney Coleman, Andy Robinson, Sara Cunningham, Lou Frizzle. Directed by Bill Glenn.

**HOUSE OF EXORCISM (1976).** What's needed here is a Roman Catholic priest to exorcise those awful imitations of THE EXORCIST, of which this Italian film is one. The excellently curved Elke Sommer brings a great sensuousness to her role as a possessed woman who spits out frogs! And there's Telly Savalas, doing an imitation of Kojak in search of Kolchak. Technically a re-edited version of LISA AND THE DEVIL, highlighted by new footage with Robert Alda as a priest. Directed by Mario Bava. Alida Valli, Sylva Koscina.

**HOUSE OF FEAR (1939).** A haunted theater tale that opens with supernatural elements and closes a standard whodunit. Should have been titled BORED ON THE BOARDS, so slow is its pace. Directed by Joe May. William Gargan, Irene Hervey, Robert Coote, Walter Woolf King, El Brendel.

**HOUSE OF FRANKENSTEIN (1944).** This followed FRANKENSTEIN MEETS THE WOLFMAN at Universal and marks the studio's first attempt to unite its money-making monsters. For the price of admission you get Lon Chaney Jr. as the Wolf Man, John Carradine as Dracula and Glenn Strange as the Frankenstein Monster. Boris Karloff is Dr. Gutva Niemann, who escapes from prison with a hunchback killer (J. Carrol Naish) to restore supernatural creatures to life. This was such a box office hit, it was followed by HOUSE OF DRACULA. And what a supporting cast: Lionel Atwill (as the ubiquitous police inspector), Elena Verdugo as the gypsy girl and George Zucco as a traveling showman. Directed by Erle C. Kenton, story idea by Curt Siodmak.

**HOUSE OF FREAKS.** See **DR. FRANKENSTEIN'S CASTLE OF FREAKS.** (You'll freak out!)

**HOUSE OF FRIGHT.** See **TWO FACES OF DR. JEKYLL.**

**HOUSE OF HORRORS (1946).** Rondo Hatton, who suffered from acromegaly (a disease of the pituitary gland) and needed no makeup with his elongated, fearful face, was featured in a handful of pictures as the Creeper. In this, the first of the short-lived Universal series, Hatton is saved from death by a sculptor (Martin Kosleck) who sends the creepy Creeper into the night to commit revenge murders. Hatton was an inept actor badly exploited in these shockers, which included PEARL OF DEATH and THE BRUTE MAN. He died the year this was released and he is now forgotten except by Late Show fans. Directed by Jean Yarbrough. Virginia Grey, Robert Lowery, Kent Taylor, Alan Napier, Bill Goodwin.

**HOUSE OF INSANE WOMEN.** See **EXORCISM'S DAUGHTER.**

**HOUSE OF MYSTERY, THE (1934).** Monogram programmer with a pulp plot: When a sacred Indian temple is violated, an old curse goes into effect. Ed Lowry and Verna Hillie trample the phony temple sets. Directed by William Nigh.

**HOUSE OF MYSTERY (1960).** Weird British film about a young couple (Jane Hylton, Peter Dyneley) out buying a house who listen to a macabre narrative from a mysterious woman. Another couple once lived in the house and a strange power afflicted their TV screen. Director Vernon Sewell's story delves into psychic phenomena, materializations, etc. Snap ending enhances a film pervaded by unseen

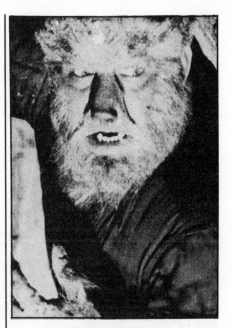

**LON CHANEY JR. IN 'HOUSE OF FRANKENSTEIN'**

horror and menace. Nanette Newman, Colin Gordon.

**HOUSE OF PSYCHOTIC WOMEN (1975).** Psycho killer thriller from Spanish director Carlos Aured, starring Paul Naschy as an escaped prisoner who takes a job as a handyman, only to become a suspect in a series of gore murders. Better than most Spanish imports, but nothing to scream your lungs out about. Maria Perschy. (VC)

**HOUSE OF SECRETS (1936).** Hoary hokum with Sidney Blackmer and Holmes Herbert caught up in the mysteries of an old mansion: hidden panels, torture dungeon, mad scientist, outre experiments. Nothing secret about this house built by director Roland Reed and writer John Krafft. Blueprints are all too familiar. Leslie Fenton, Syd Saylor.

**HOUSE OF SHADOWS (1983).** Spanish horror thriller starring Yvonne De Carlo and John Gavin. Directed by Richard Wulicher. (VC)

**HOUSE OF TERROR (1972).** Contrived suspense thriller in which nurse Jenifer Bishop arrives in the Hollywood Hills to take care of a shrewish wife watched over by a scheming husband. Jacquelyn Hyde, Mitchell Gregg. Directed by Sergei Goncharoff.

**HOUSE OF THE BLACK DEATH (1965).** B-film cast (Lon Chaney Jr, Andrea King, John Carradine, Tom Drake, Jerome Thor) is wasted in this bleak horror depicting a duel between two warlocks. Chaney must resort to wearing the horns of the Devil. Director Harold Daniels lingers his camera on the shapely body of a belly dancer, proving he's an intellectual. Dolores Faith, Sabrina, Sherwood Keith. Also known as BLOOD OF THE MAN BEAST.

**HOUSE OF THE DAMNED (1963).** "Damned if I'll set in this theater house through the whole thing," was an oft-heard comment in connection with this haunted house thudder that exploits circus freaks living in secret chambers in the typically weird mansion. Harry Spalding's script also features some walking bodies that are missing vital pieces—heads, arms, legs, simple stuff like that. Maury Dexter produced and directed. Screenplay by Harry Spalding. Merry Anders, Richard Crane, Erika Peters, Richard Kiel.

**HOUSE OF THE DEAD.** Videocassette title for **ALIEN ZONE, THE.** (Dig that unreal estate!)

**HOUSE OF THE LIVING DEAD (1973).** A psychotic killer in a cape, who imagines he's out of an Edgar Wallace thriller, rushes around a South American plantation, knocking off family members. A mixture of Black Magic and the Old Family Curse. You'll be cursed too while watching. Also known as DOCTOR MANIAC. Mark Burns, Shirley Anne Field, David Oxley. Directed by Ray Austin. (VC)

**HOUSE OF THE LONG SHADOWS (1983).** Updated version of George M. Cohan's mystery-comedy play, SEVEN KEYS TO BALDPATE, couched in Gothic imagery. Director Peter Walker has assembled a superb cast (Vincent Price, Christopher Lee, Peter Cushing, John Carradine) to portray weirdos in the eerie mansion Bllyddpaetwr (the setting is now Scotland) on the same night a young American writer (Des Arnaz Jr.) settles into the house to write a novel within 24 hours to win a $20,000 wager with publisher Richard Todd. The thrills are played tongue-in-cheek and the violence cleverly suggestive rather than overt—but what destroys Michael Armstrong's script is a trick within a trick utterly unsatisfying for so prestigious a coterie of horror stars. Sheila

excellent use of color and atmosphere to convey a sense of foreboding horror. Vincent Price essays Roderick Usher, a demented aristocrat who has unwittingly entombed his sister alive in her crypt. He spits out the scenery while the rest of the cast creeps along secret passageways, stares at degenerate Usher paintings and breathes Victorian decay. Scripted by Richard Matheson. In video as **FALL OF THE HOUSE OF USHER, THE.**

**HOUSE OF WAX (1953).** Superb remake of MYSTERY OF THE WAX MUSEUM, horror in the Grand Guignol tradition, with Vincent Price as a "mad wax" museum curator/sculptor who covers victims with wax and displays them in his Chamber of Horrors. The setting is turn-of-the-century Baltimore, from fogbound streets to gaslit morgues. The 3-D composition lends maximum effect and there is an excellent fire sequence, as well as a memorable chase through dark streets. And, of course, the great paddle-ball scene. Frank Lovejoy is the concerned policeman, Phyllis Kirk and Carolyn Jones are among the potential victims. Watch for Charles Buchinsky as the mute assistant—he later became Charles Bronson. Scripted by Crane Wilbur and directed by one-eyed Andre de Toth. Paul Picerni, Roy Roberts. (VC)

## PHYLLIS KIRK IS PURSUED BY A PHANTOM THROUGH BALTIMORE IN 'HOUSE OF WAX'

Keith is the blonde in the "long shadows." (VC)

**HOUSE OF THE SEVEN CORPSES (1972).** Low budgeter with a decent cast forced into a wasteland of shoddy material. John Ireland, John Carradine and Faith Domergue wander through a feeble plot about the making of a horror film in a mansion (shades of FRANKENSTEIN '80). A resurrected ghoul knocks off a movie producer, a couple of performers and anyone else who wanders through the script. Maybe the ghoul didn't like producer-writer-director Paul Harrison's dialogue. Utterly forgettable. (VC)

**HOUSE OF THE SEVEN GABLES, THE (1940).** A family curse hangs heavy over brothers Vincent Price and George Sanders in this adaptation of Nathaniel Hawthorne's ghost novel in which spirits return to haunt the living. Lester Cole's script is an intelligent interpretation, but the supernatural elements have been toned down. Directed by Joe May. Margaret Lindsay, Dick Foran, Alan Napier, Nan Grey, Cecil Kellaway. A more faithful rendering is in TWICE TOLD TALES.

**HOUSE OF USHER (1960).** Roger Corman's adaptation of Poe's short story, "The Fall of the House of Usher," makes

**HOUSE OF WHIPCORD (1975).** British chiller directed by Peter Walker in which Patrick Barr is a former prison warden who keeps a torture chamber downstairs in order to dole out punishment. Barbara Markham, Ray Brooks. (VC)

**HOUSE ON BARE MOUNTAIN (1962).** Vampire nudie flick set at Granny Good's School for Good Girls. Count Dracula, werewolves and numerous baked babes run rampant in a romp of lascivious lechery. Directed by Lee Frost. Co-producer Bob Cresse stars with Jeffrey Smithers.

**HOUSE ON HAUNTED HILL (1959).** William Castle's best gimmick flick with Vincent Price as a sophisticated madman who invites five guests to Haunted Hill with the offer of $10,000 to anyone who can spend the night and still collect in the morning. Floating sheets, ghostly faces, skeletons, bubbling pits, doors and windows that fly open mysteriously, etc. etc. It's really great fun . . . Robb White's script even has a few genuinely frightening moments. Castle directed with his usual lack of subtlety, but here it worked. Richard Long, Elisha Cook Jr., Carol Ohmart, Carolyn Craig. (VC)

**HOUSE ON SKULL MOUNTAIN (1973).** It's the old "Ten Little Indians" theme, death to defilers one by one, with touches of voodoo and black magic when heirs gather in a weird house outside Atlanta. You weren't expecting white magic, were you? Directed by Ron Honthaner. Mike Evans, Victor French, Ella Woods, Janee Michelle. (VC)

**HOUSE ON SORORITY ROW, THE (1983).** Yet again, another slasher terrorizer in which sorority sisters, on the night of a grad party, are murdered one by one. This marked the writing-directing debut of 24-year-old Mark Rosman, who filmed on location at an old house in Baltimore. Special effects by Rob E. Holland. This is sheer imitative exploitation, but with a few effective moments. Kathryn McNeil, Eileen Davidson, Charles Serio, Lois K. Hunt. (VC)

**HOUSE THAT BLED TO DEATH (1980).** Episodes of Britain's HAMMER HOUSE OF HORROR TV series re-edited for U.S. consumption. The first story, "The House that Bled to Death," is just that, a mansion with bloody good walls and a gore floor. Tom Clegg directed. The second, "Growing Pains," is a tale of possession: An adopted youth is taken over by his step-father's real child, returned from the dead. Francis Megahy directed. Rachel Davies, Milton Johns, Sarah Keller. The latter is available in videocassette.

**HOUSE THAT DRIPPED BLOOD, THE (1971).** Good Amicus horror film (produced in Britain) written by a prestigious master of horror tales, Robert Bloch. The macabremeister interweaves four stories to recount a strange mansion's history. The main thread is an investigator, searching for a missing film star, who checks out previous tenants. Story one: A horror story writer (a chip off the old Bloch?) is haunted by his fictional creations. Story two: Ghostly figure haunts a wax museum managed by a lunatic. Story three: Witchcraft and voodoo dolls with Nyree Dawn Porter and Christopher Lee. Story four: The investigator discovers what happened to that missing star—and wishes he hadn't. Directed by Peter Duffell. Peter Cushing, Ingrid Pitt, Denholm Elliott, Tom Adams, Jon Pertwee. (VC)

**HOUSE THAT SCREAMED, THE (1971).** Polished, hand-somely produced Spanish horror film set in a 19th Century boarding school for young women. A touch of class is provided by Lilli Palmer as the head mistress who runs a taut ship, permitting sadism and sex because she considers her job "impossible." The film excellently captures the oppressive sexual needs of the girls with erotic artsy intercutting. Heavy lesbian overtones and one intense hazing scene. Suddenly the girls are attacked by a knife killer, their bodies disappearing. While the outcome is predictable, it's the style of director Narciso Ibanez Serrador that makes this so enjoyable. Cristina Galbo, Mary Maude, John Moulder Brown.

**HOUSE THAT VANISHED, THE (1974).** A case of The Movie that Vanished once exhibitors got the word about this British-produced foundation-less misconstruction about a madman with a knife who kills only beautiful women. Directed by Joseph Larraz. Andrea Allan, Karl Lanchbury. Also in videocassette as SCREAM AND DIE. (VC)

**HOUSE THAT WOULD NOT DIE, THE (1970).** Genuine haunted house with genuine spirits, witchcraft and black magic—no plots to drive Aunt Petunia up the wall to inherit the money. That alone makes this TV-movie a welcome relief. Directed by John Llewellyn Moxey, written by Henry Farrell. Barbara Stanwyck, Richard Egan, Katherine Winn.

**HOUSE WHERE DEATH LIVES, THE.** See **DELUSION.**

**HOUSE WHERE EVIL DWELLS, THE (1982).** Lackluster, predictable "haunted teahouse" tale begins in Japan in 1840 and shamelessly depicts a cuckolded samurai chopping up his wayward wife and her lecherous lover. Heads roll, arms fly, legs gambol and blood spatters. So much for the prologue. Cut to modern times as Edward Albert and Susan George move into the house, aided by U.S. Ambassador Doug McClure, an old family friend. Soon Susan is haunted by three Japanese spirits superimposed over the footage, leaving nothing to the imagination. Gradually (as certain as death and taxes), the Americans are caught up in a love triangle and restage the samurai violence with karate and swingin' swords. Very unscary, even when Susan's daughter

is attacked by crawling spider creatures (where did they come from?). Uninspired except for torrid love scenes in which bare-breasted Susan gives all she has—which is considerable. Directed by Kevin Connor. (VC)

**HOW AWFUL ABOUT ALLAN (1970).** Strong Hitchcockian overtones permeate this TV-movie psychothriller about a blind man (Anthony Perkins), living with a daffy sister, who is either bonkers or is being subjected to a bizarre let's-drive-the-guy-around-the-bend conspiracy. Directed by Curtis Harrington, jaggedly scripted by Henry Farrell. Julie Harris, Kent Smith, Joan Hackett, Robert H. Harris.

**HOW DOOO YOU DO (1946).** Minor PRC programmer with a plethora of B players (Bert Gordon, Keye Luke, Charles Middleton) and several pounds of bbbaaalllooonnneeeyyy. Borderline fantasy plot has a doctor experimenting on a heart disease cure, which enables a corpse to return to life. Directed sssllllooowwwllllyyy by Ralph Murray.

**HOW I WON THE WAR (1967).** British spoof on World War II demonstrating how man finds an amusing side to an otherwise deadly situation. Director Richard Lester depicts a platoon of soldiers killed one by one—but each dead man continues to fight with his buddies as a ghost. Offbeat approach to an anti-war statement deserves attention. Written by Charles Wood. Michael Crawford, John Lennon, Roy Kinnear, Alexander Knox, Jack MacGowran, Lee Montague.

**HOW TO MAKE A DOLL (1967).** Gore specialist Herschell Gordon Lewis went semi-legit to make this sex comedy with a robot theme, in which a scientist creates a bevy of beauties (solely for sexual purposes). Robert Wood, Jim Vance.

**HOW TO MAKE A MONSTER (1958).** Herman Cohen horrifier bravely dares to mock its own genre, making its weak script and mediocre make-up effects worth enduring. A make-up man working for AIP in Hollywood (Robert H. Harris) is told monster movies are passe and his services no longer needed. An ingredient mixed into his cosmetics turns young actors into monsters—enabling Cohen to use all the fright masks from his earlier I WAS A TEENAGE horror flicks. Targets of these monstrous murderers are studio bosses; they couldn't have picked a more deserving bunch of idiots. Gary Conway portrays the monsters. Paul Brinegar, John Ashley, Gary Clarke, Morris Ankrum, Robert Shayne.

**HOW TO STEAL THE WORLD (1968).** Episodes of TV's MAN FROM U.N.C.L.E. series edited into a feature. Napoleon Solo (Robert Vaughn) and Russian partner Illya Kuryakin (David McCallum) chase mad scientist Barry Sullivan to prevent him from using his poison gas to dominate human will. Eleanor Parker, Leslie Nielsen, Tony Bill, Leo G. Carroll, Hugh Marlowe. Directed by Sutton Roley.

**HOW TO STUFF A WILD BIKINI (1965).** . . . with the curvaceous body of Annette Funicello, that's how . . . plus half

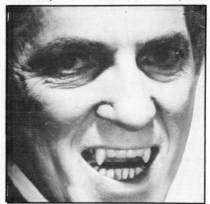

**JONATHAN FRID IN**
**'HOUSE OF DARK SHADOWS'**

## NO TERN UNSTONED: 'HOWARD THE DUCK'

the starlets wandering Hollywood Boulevard. Buster Keaton (in one of his last roles) is a crazy witch doctor who conjures up a floating bikini. Then he floats Annette into the bikini, and then she floats all the way to America to meet Dwayne Hickman, Frankie Avalon and other beach party boys who dance to Les Baxter music. American-International beach movie drowns in the awful scripting by William Asher and Leo Townsend. Asher also directed. Beverly Adams, Brian Donlevy, Mickey Rooney, John Ashley, Jody McCrea.

**HOWARD THE DUCK (1986).** An expensive flop from producers George Lucas and Gloria Katz, and director Willard Hyuck, a disaster that never comes to grips with making a duck character from another planet, trapped on Earth, believable. For one thing the duck costume and make-up are phony—Howard looks like a midget in a Halloween costume going to a masquerade. For another, the duck's character is stupid, when he should have been played seriously, to offer a contrast to the ridiculous premise. Yes, the special effects are stupendous . . . but without a story to support them, they produce only yawns. Howard is this quacker living on a parallel Earth who is sucked into an astronomical beam and swept across the Universe to Earth, where he falls in love with musician Lea Thompson and thwarts an alien overlord from bringing all his cronies through the beam to conquer our planet. A real snoozer, proving even a genius like Lucas can have his off days. (VC)

**HOWLING, THE (1981).** Outrageous werewolf film based on the lousy best-selling paperback by Gary Brandner, which director Joe Dante has thrown away in favor of a new tongue-in-cheek narrative by John Sayles and Terence H. Winkless, which is at its best when reinforced by Rob Bottin's special effects. Transmutation of man into upright werewolf is one of the most harrowing ever filmed—done with special masks and apparatus that permits us to see jaws growing into shape (complete with dripping teeth) along with hair and fingernails. Dante has loaded his yarn with visual in-jokes (Roger Corman and Forrest J. Ackerman have cameos). The story, unfortunately, unfolds awkwardly and the characters are unbelievable. Dee Wallace, Patrick Macnee, Elizabeth Brooks, John Carradine, Slim Pickens, Kenneth Tobey. (VC)

**HOWLING II (1986).** Not a sequel in the true sense, just crass exploitation. Psychic investigator/occult prac-

titioner/wolf expert Christopher Lee is hot on the spoor of a cult of werewolves and subsidiary monsters. He is aided by Anne McEnroe (her sister was murdered by the beasts) and her boyfriend, Reb Brower. The bloody trail leads to Transylvania and the Queen of the Werewolves, played by Sybil Danning. Just to watch her rip off her robe, or grow hair when she makes love to her favorite male werewolf, makes this film worth seeing. Grrrrrrrrrr. A very noisy film, full of special effects, transmutating wolves and a gargoyle-like monster that is quite unappetizing. Philippe Mora directs with emphasis on the action and Ms Danning's spectacular body, no doubt hoping to cover over the weak story co-scripted by Gary Brandner, creator of the HOWLING books. (VC)

**HU-MAN (1976).** French art film, described by writer-director Jerome Laperrousaz as "a reworking of the Orpheus myth," proposes an odd concept: An actor (Terence Stamp) will put himself in dangerous situations and his fear will be televised to the watching world. Emotional energy unleased in viewers will then send him into the future or the past. Jeanne Moreau is Stamp's mistress. Music by Eric Burdon.

**HUMAN DUPLICATORS, THE (1965).** Unsubstantiated rumors have it this was financed by Xerox . . . Richard Kiel, extraterrestrial humanoid Kolos, dispatched to conquer Earth, is so ridiculously stilted you might be tempted to watch this fantastic fiasco for laughs. After a while, however, his performing ineptitude is topped by blonde sexpot Barbara Nichols portraying an undercover woman. Then there's the automaton-like performance of George Nader as the most wooden secret agent since Pinocchio the Spy. George Macready tries to make his mad scientist role tolerable, but you'll be too busy laughing at everyone else to notice. One film we doubt anyone is going to want to copy. Directed by Hugo Grimaldi, written by Arthur C. Pierce. (you were expecting Arthur C. Clarke?) Richard Arlen, Hugh Beaumont. (VC)

**HUMAN EXPERIMENTS (1980).** Prison doctor is as warped as the criminals he works on, believing that if he uses shock treatment, they'll go straight. Crooked thinking, for sure. Sleaze-bag stuff directed by J. Gregory Goodell. Linda Haynes, Jackie Coogan, Aldo Ray, Geoffrey Lewis, Lurene Tuttle. Experiment ultimately fails. (VC)

**HUMAN FEELINGS (1978).** Nancy Walker plays God (!) who sends angel Billy Crystal to Earth to find six honest folks in Las Vegas. Unsuccessful TV pilot, directed by Ernest Pintoff. Pamela Sue Martin, Armand Assante.

**HUMAN MONSTER, THE (1940).** Bela Lugosi in a dual role doesn't necessarily double your pleasure. On the one hand, he is Professor Dearborn, nice old proprietor of the Dearborn Institute for the Blind. On the other, he is Dr. Orloff, who tortures the blind patients and electrocutes them to collect on insurance policies. Directed by Walter Summers in England as DARK EYES OF LONDON. Based on an Edgar Wallace novel. Hugh Williams, Greta Gynt, Wilfrid Walter. (VC)

**HUMAN VAPOR, THE (1960).** Japanese film directed by Inoshiro Honda, that GODZILLA gyrator, in which a prison convict adapts the ability to turn himself into a cloud of smoky nothing while carrying out criminal acts. Shinichi Sekizawa's story is anything but a gas. Performance of the airy Yoshio Tsuchiya tends to be vapid, and the rest of the cast is full of hot air. Effects by Honda's partner, Eiji Tsuburaya. (VC)

**HUMANOID, THE (1979).** Italian space adventure, lacking a genteel touch, in which Richard "Jaws" Kiel portrays a rocket jockey who prevents Arthur Kennedy and girlfriend Barbara Bach from conquering the Universe with the help of an extraterrestrial guru. Routine STAR WARS clone, cheaply produced. Directed and written by George B. Lewis. Corinne Clery, Leonard Mann.

**HUMANOID DEFENDER (1985).** Man with superhuman powers (Gary Kasper) turns against the government unit that

*"Be gentle." Howard the Duck to his earthling girlfriend, who has just told him, "I can't resist your intense animal magnetism."*
*—HOWARD THE DUCK.*

created him to fight for peace and justice. (VC)

**HUMANOIDS FROM THE DEEP (1980).** Grotesque zom-biemem from the depths answer the mating call by sexually attacking young women on dry land. Originally this was a less violent monster film directed by Barbara Peeters, but unhappy producer Roger Corman shot new attack footage, focusing heavily on the amorous amphibians ripping the clothes from the wriggling sexpots. This New World picture, starring Doug McClure, Vic Morrow and Ann Turkel, climaxes (excuse the expression) with a huge battle at a dockside carnival. Music by James Horner. (VC)

**HUMONGOUS (1982).** Stupid teenagers accidentally sink their yacht off a strange island where, back in 1946, a pretty daughter was raped during a dinner party. The shipwrecked clods find the island seemingly deserted, but one by one, they're knocked off by a hairy wild man. There's nothing surprising or special about the "creature," and the characters are cannon fodder, without personalities. From director Paul Lynch and writer William Gray, who gave us PROM NIGHT. Janet Julian, David Wallace, Janet Baldwin. (VC)

**HUNCHBACK OF NOTRE DAME, THE (1923).** Silent classic starring Lon Chaney as Quasimodo, the deformed bellringer who falls hopelessly in love with the gypsy girl Esmeralda. This features the much-remembered sequence in which the misshapen freak is publicly whipped on a massive turntable. For mastery of make-up and acting, this was Chaney's finest midnight hour. Directed by Wallace Worsley, who helmed Chaney in A BLIND BARGAIN. Chaney closely followed Victor Hugo's description of the humped man and even wore a rubber device so he could not stand erect. (VC)

**HUNCHBACK OF NOTRE DAME, THE (1939).** As the hunchback Quasimodo, the misshapen bellringer of the Paris cathedral, Charles Laughton is more hideous than the neighboring stone gargoyles. Under the direction of William Dieterle, this second film version of Victor Hugo's tumultuous tale of 15th Century France explores the medieval mind in all its murkiness in a Gothic Paris setting. High RKO production standards set by Pandro S. Berman make this a minor masterpiece of period filmmaking. Maureen O'Hara is the beautiful Esmeralda; Sir Cedric Hardwicke is the villainous Frollo and Walter Hampden is the Archbishop. Thomas Mitchell, George Zucco, Edmond O'Brien, Fritz Leiber, Rondo Hatton, Walter Hampton, George Tobias. (VC)

**HUNCHBACK OF NOTRE DAME, THE (1957).** Anthony Quinn is the bellringing gnome in this French adaptation lacking the classical elements of the 1939 version. Quinn portrays Quasimodo as though he were a Mongolian idiot—mumbling and slobbering a la Brando. Provocative Gina Lollobrigida is Esmeralda, the beauty Quasimodo rescues from torture and hides in his Paris cathedral, which is assaulted by an unruly mob. The dubbing is bad, and none of this does justice to Victor Hugo's book. Directed by Jean Delannoy.

**HUNCHBACK OF NOTRE DAME, THE (1976).** BBC-TV version of Hugo's novel, directed by Alan Cooke, was shown in America two years after its original televising, an early experiment in tape-to-film techniques. Warren Clark is the titular freak, Kenneth Haigh is Archdeacon Claude Frollo and Michelle Newell is Esmeralda.

**HUNCHBACK OF NOTRE DAME, THE (1981).** Distinguished TV version of Victor Hugo's classic tale of the bellringer of Notre Dame, Quasimodo, and his search for love and sympathy in a world of hate and misunderstanding. Give credit to writer John Gay for etching fine characterizations and period dialogue that doesn't sound stilted, and to Anthony Hopkins, who brings believability and warmth to the poor misshapen human-gargoyle. One of the best adaptations of Hugo. Derek Jacobi, John Gielgud, Robert Powell, Lesley-Anne Down. Directed by Alan Hume, produced by the prestigious Norman Rosemont.

**HUNCHBACK OF THE MORGUE, THE (1972).** Absolutely repelling Spanish debacle with the titular monstrosity (Paul Naschy, the poor producer's Vincent Price) stockpiling dead girls in his cellar, fighting off hungry rats and keeping company with a mad scientist and his Monster, a head floating in

**TRANSFORMATION IN 'THE HOWLING'**

**LON CHANEY SR. IN THE 1923 VERSION OF 'THE HUNCHBACK OF NOTRE DAME'**

liquid. It's The Movie Theme That Never Dies. Directed by Javier Aquirre. Rossana Yanni, Vic Winner.

**HUNDRA (1984).** Thundra-ing U.S.-Spanish sword-and-sorcery actioner, a Conan imitation in the same spirit as RED SONJA. Hundra (Laurene Landon) is the sole survivor of a village of females that is massacred and the femme warrior sets out in sexy costumes to wreak revenge and rebuild the population. Turgidly directed by Matt Cimber, who co-authored the weak screenplay with John Goff. John Ghaffari.

**HUNGER, THE (1983).** Bizarre, offbeat vampire tale, directed with stunning razzle dazzle by British commercial-maker Tony Scott, brother of Ridley. While the shots are boggling and the ambience effective, this adaptation of Whitley Strieber's novel portrays enigmatic characters in search of a plot. At times the narrative disintegrates into eye-zapping images and effects. The outre story deals with two vampires (Catherine Deneuve, David Bowie) living off human blood—until Bowie's aging process accelerates and Deneuve needs a new partner. She picks Susan Sarandon, a researcher in human longevity, and seduces her in a lesbian sequence done with extreme taste (soft lenses and fog filters). The "makeup illusions" are by Dick Smith and Carl Fullerton. Dave Allen and Roger Dicken did the aging monkey effects. Cliff De Young, Beth Ehlers, Dan Hedaya, James Aubrey, Shane Rimmer, Bessie Love. (VC)

**HUNGRY PETS.** See **PLEASE DON'T EAT MY MOTHER.**

**HUNGRY WIVES (1973).** Writer-producer-director George Romero's attempt to deal with witches and covens in the naturalistic setting of contemporary suburbia is one of his lesser works, better functioning as a psychology study of bored, sexually frustrated, alcoholic housewives and how they overcome their ennui. This has the unorthodox editing style characteristic of early Romero works, but it's a tedious ordeal, without sympathetic characters or a building plot structure. Virginia Greenwald, Ray Laine, Jan White.

Originally entitled JACK'S WIFE, this is now on videocassette as **SEASON OF THE WITCH.**

**HUNK (1987).** A smacky nerd (Steve Levitt) trades his intellect for a bronzed hardbody (John Allen Nelson) by making a pact with devilish James Coco (as Dr. D). Lowbrow teen fare from Crown International. Robert Morse, Avery Schreiber. (VC)

**HUNTED, THE (1974).** Screen variation on Richard Connell's famous story, "The Most Dangerous Game," in which a madman hunter pursues human beings for sport. Lee Remick is one of the quarry the hunter would love to have mounted for his trophy room. Directed by Douglas Fithian. Michael Hinz, Ivan Desny. (VC)

**HUNTER (1971).** A deadly virus is at the heart of this Bruce Geller TV-movie: A brainwashing plot against American agents is afoot, and it's up to an undercover plant to expose the villains. A rejected pilot for a series deemed so bad, CBS kept it on the shelf for two years before sneaking it into the schedule. Leonard Horn directed the Cliff Gould script. John Vernon, Steve Ihnat, Fritz Weaver, Edward Binns, John Schuck, Barbara Rhoades.

**HUNTERS OF THE GOLDEN COBRA (1982).** Italian adventure-fantasy in the Indiana Jones style . . . not as classy but still rousing good action as a British Intelligence officer and an American soldier (David Warbeck) pursue a Japanese officer who has stolen the precious Golden Cobra, a relic containing supernatural destructive powers. In the jungle, Warbeck meets a tribe of blowgun-packin' natives, ruled by a beautiful white woman, but is wounded and passes out. Later, he and the English spy return and undergo a series of slick adventures in the Philippines, finding a native religious cult called the Awoks. Directed by Anthony Dawson. Rena Abadesa, Almanta Suska, John Steiner. (VC)

**HURRICANE ISLAND (1950).** Sam Katzman actioner potboiler for Columbia is a mixture of heavy adventure and light fantasy, with Ponce De Leon discovering the Fountain of Youth in Florida jungles. There's love between Jon Hall and Marie Windsor and plenty of destruction before the inevitable hurricane. Vigorously directed by Lew Landers, who stages the hand-to-hand fighting well. Edgar Barrier, Lyle Talbot, Marc Lawrence, Marshall Reed, Don Harvey.

**HUSH, HUSH, SWEET CHARLOTTE (1964).** Following the success of WHAT EVER HAPPENED TO BABY JANE?, producer-director Robert Aldrich duplicated the formula of daffy old crones played by one-time Hollywood greats. In the Henry Farrell-Lukas Heller story, Bette Davis is a demented spinster, haunted by a 30-year-old murder and seeing dead bodies all over the old family mansion. The whole thing is treated by Aldrich as a macabre gothic joke and you'll see through the red herrings without much difficulty. What makes this film memorable is the decaying Southern plantation and decadent characters to match. Joseph Cotten, Olivia de Havilland, Agnes Moorehead, Victor Buono, Bruce Dern, Mary Astor, William Campbell. (VC)

**HYPER SAPIEN: PEOPLE FROM ANOTHER STAR (1986).** Three extraterrestrials from the planet Taros seek refuge on Earth from Ricky Paul Goldin and Keenan Wynn in Wyoming. Canadian-British production has unimpressive special effects and a leaden story. Directed by Peter Hunt.

**HYPNOSIS (1962).** What a la+gh! Those dumb It@lian& G&#man Sp^nish p*odu+ers cla@med their fr)ght cla%%ic would p;ut the vieAwer into a d&&p sleep. Wha# a lot of @#$% no5en^5e. AnyonW k{ows tha] a dum{ (mov!e like this c-n't po$$ibly h)rm any*ne. Don't you beXieve a w''rd of ~t.

**HYPNOTIC EYE, THE (1960).** According to mad hypnotist Jacques Bergerac, you are sleepy . . . director George Blair wants you to relax . . . screenwriters Gitta and William Read Woolfield say don't worry . . . when you awaken you will revel in the mesmerizing power of hype . . . er, HypnoMagic, the screen's latest dynamic discovery to make your eyeballs pop from their sockets . . . but this is what will really happen: You will fall asleep . . . and you will stay asleep . . . all the way through the movie . . . and you will wake up and forget you ever heard of . . . THE HYPNOTIC EYE.

**HYPNOTIST, THE (1956).** Borderline fantasy theme deals with the use of hypnotism to force a pilot to commit a murder. This idea was brought to full flower in the 1962 classic THE MANCHURIAN CANDIDATE; here it is a weakly developed premise for a routine whodunit. Directed and written by Montgomery Tully. Roland Culver, Patricia Roc.

**HYSTERIA (1964).** Hammer psychothriller produced-written by Jimmy Sangster and directed by Freddie Francis, a blending of amnesia hallucinations, creating the question: Is Robert Webber as crazy as he thinks, or is there a logical explanation? You've seen it all before. Lelia Goldoni, Anthony Newlands, Maurice Denham, Jennifer Jayne.

**HYSTERICAL (1983).** Pathetic parody of horror movies, with dumb jokes coming fast and furious but never attaining wit. In a lighthouse in Hellview, Oregon, the Hudson Brothers (Bill, Mark, Brett) venture to solve the mystery of a long-dead lighthouse keeper (Richard "Jaws" Kiel), whose corpse is restored to life by his also-long-dead wife (Julie Newmar). Half the cast walks with zombie death faces and the other half grimaces at the non sequiturs, non-funny jokes and weary sight gags by the cornball brothers. One long, tedious absurdity that builds to absolutely nothing. Supporting players helpless to support even themselves are Franklyn Ajaye, Keenan Wynn, Charlie Callas, Richard Donner, Murray Hamilton and Clint Walker. They're as much at sea as the lighthouse keeper. Let's hear it for gross incompetence for producer Gene Levy, director Chris Bearde and the Hudsons, who wrote this mess with Trace Johnston. (VC)

**THUNDA ON THE TUNDRA WITH LAURENE LANDON IN 'HUNDRA'**

*"Do you have any idea how many baboons are out there looking for dinner?" —Timothy Bottoms in IN THE SHADOW OF KILAMANJARO.*

**I BURY THE LIVING (1958).** Weird graveyard chiller with Richard Boone as a cemetery curator who thinks he has power over life and death by shifting stickpins in a map. Superior tombstone mood established by director Albert Band and "plotter" Louis Garfinkle gets covered over by a cop-out ending. Theodore Bikel, Herbert Anderson, Peggy Maurer, Russ Bender, Robert Osterloh. (VC)

**I, DESIRE (1982).** TV-movie with fascinating man vs. supernatural premises, dealing with the milieu of the L.A. prostitute with realism. David Naughton is lured into the digs of a femme fatale hooker, Desire (Barbara Stock), who is also a vampire subjecting the city to a reign of terror. Nice climactic sequence has Naughton trapped in the spider's web. Fascinating, offbeat. Directed by John Llewellyn Moxey. Dorian Harewood, Marilyn Jones, Brad Dourif.

**I CHANGED MY SEX. See GLEN OR GLENDA?**

**I DISMEMBER MAMA (1972).** Screenwriter William Norton comments on the sexual perversions of contemporary society when a psycho case flips out and wants to kill his mother. First he goes after another older mother, slaughtering her and befriending her young daughter. But this attempt at pathos amidst bloodletting is feeble sentimentality. This guy is a psychokiller and deserves to be put away! Zoey Hall is the "I" of the title, a freaked-out killer living in Movieland, but it's Greg Mullavey as a hard-nosed cop who's far more interesting. Directed by Paul Leder. (VC)

**I DREAM OF JEANNIE: 15 YEARS LATER (1985).** Barbara Eden still looks great in the harem costume she wore in the I DREAM OF JEANNIE sitcom. In this TV-movie revival, directed by Bill Asher, she's up to her magical mischief, engaging in wizardry against her sister (Jeannie II, also Eden) who is enticing Jeannie's boyfriend Tony Nelson with a sexy astronaut. (Nelson is not Larry Hagman this time, but Wayne Rogers.) Series regulars Bill Dailey (as clumsy oaf Capt. Roger Healey) and Hayden Rorke (as psychiatrist Bellows) are on the Magic Carpet ride. Good clean fun, nothing else. MacKenzie Astin, Dori Brenner.

**I DRINK YOUR BLOOD (1971).** Foreign feature recut and thrown into the U.S. market by exploitation producer Jerry

Gross. Writer-director David Durston's premise will turn your stomach as much as the title: Hippies munch on meat pies infected by a disease and turn into rabies-infected idiots. To go any further could bring about regurgitation. Ronda Fultz, Bhaskar, Jadine Wong, Riley Mills.

**I EAT YOUR SKIN (1971).** Re-edited version of ZOMBIES, a 1961 feature written-produced-directed by Del Tenney which still turns up on TV in its original form under that title. (It is also known as VOODOO BLOOD BATH.) This new version was released with I DRINK YOUR BLOOD. See ZOMBIES for a full report. (VC)

**I LED TWO LIVES. See GLEN OR GLENDA?**

**I LOVE A MYSTERY (1945).** First film adaptation of Carlton E. Morse's radio series about a trio of private detective-adventurers (Jack Packard, Doc Long and Reggie Yorke) from the A-1 Detective Agency who encounter the occult in their colorful mysteries. In this one the team (minus Reggie) meets a millionaire (George Macready) who fears a devilish cult is after his head. Jim Bannon portrays Packard while Barton Yarborough (from radio) portrays drawlin' Doc. Unfortunately, this Columbia short-lived series was hampered by low budgets and indifferent scripting. Directed by Henry Levin. Equivalent sequels were THE DEVIL'S MASK and THE UNKNOWN.

**I MARRIED A MONSTER FROM OUTER SPACE (1958).** Schlock bug-eyed monster material builds into something better under director Gene Fowler Jr. Louis Vittes' screenplay focuses on newlyweds Gloria Talbott and Tom Tryon when their wedded bliss is interrupted by an alien who inhabits Tryon's body. Gloria suspects something is wrong—Tom acts emotionless—and by sticking to her viewpoint the film builds as a satisfying mystery. Sexual implications, unfortunately, are barely dealt with: Are the extraterrestrials trying to breed hybrid offspring? Or do they simply dig shapely Earth wenches? Fowler is more concerned with conspiratorial elements (a la INVASION OF THE BODY SNATCHERS). Special effects by John P. Fulton are limited; all around, though, better than average. Ken Lynch, John Eldridge, Valerie Allen, Maxie Rosenbloom. (VC)

**'I WAS A TEENAGE WEREWOLF'**

**I MARRIED A WITCH (1942).** Classic Rene Clair comedy full of bitchy battle-of-the-sexes dialogue and "ghostly" special effects by Gordon Jennings. Witch spirit (Veronica Lake) is freed from imprisonment and returns to haunt a descendant (Fredric March) of a witchhunter who sent her to the stake 300 years before. Adapted by Robert Pirosh and Marc Connelly from the novel by Thorne Smith, who created TOPPER. Robert Benchley, Susan Hayward, Cecil Kellaway, Chester Conklin, Monte Blue. (VC)

**I MARRIED AN ANGEL (1942).** Rodgers and Hart's stage musical-comedy—fanciful, amusing fantasy in which an angel descends from Heaven to marry a mortal—was drastically altered by screenwriter Anita Loos so that it is no longer light-footed but plodding under W. S. Van Dyke II's direction.

And the casting by MGM of Jeanette MacDonald and Nelson Eddy was a mogul's mistake, for she lacks ethereal quality and he emerges a stiff-necked, giddy Hungarian playboy. Reginald Owen, Anne Jeffreys, Janis Carter, Edward Everett Horton, Binnie Barnes.

**I, MONSTER (1972).** Inferior adaptation of Stevenson's Jekyll-Hyde tale with Christopher Lee, Peter Cushing and Mike Raven remaining superior to co-producer Milton Subotsky's script. Lee portrays the doctor meddling with a schizophrenic formula. Production standards are high and capture Victorian London, but one wishes director Stephen Weeks had plugged up the story shortcomings.

**I SAW WHAT YOU DID (1965).** Gimmicky William Castle-directed potboiler in which two teenage baby sitters prankishly phone numbers at random, exclaim "I saw what you did!" and hang up. One man they call (John Ireland) has just finished slaughtering his wife (Joan Crawford) in a shower scene inspired by PSYCHO. Ireland sets out to track down the silly girls. William McGivern's script (from an Ursula Curtiss novel) has plenty of opening and closing doors and windows as the mad killer closes in. A minor film that will satisfy juveniles more than adults. Leif Erickson, Pat Breslin, Andi Garrett, Sharyn Locke, John Archer.

**I SPIT ON YOUR GRAVE (1979).** The epitome of rape-woman's revenge pictures, a cult favorite written-directed-edited by Meir Zarchi. A bloody tale about four men who gang-bang vacationing Camille Keaton. After a second go-around of debasement, the chauvinistic pigs are wasted one by one by the avenging angel who uses every weapon at hand—from butcher knife to hangman's rope to woodman's axe to . . . just name it. Terribly graphic, not for the squeamish. Eron Tabor, Richard Pace. (VC)

**I VAMPIRI (1957).** Gianna-Maria Canale, one-time queen of Italian B movies, pulls a Countess Bathory routine by bathing her body in the blood of striptease beauties while carrying on before the public as a stately actress. Routine psychomurders are enhanced by Mario Bava's cinematography and nifty aging effects at the climax. For voyeurs and gore fans. Directed by Riccardo Freda.

**I WALKED WITH A ZOMBIE (1943).** RKO low budgeter is producer Val Lewton's classic, a loose adaptation of JANE EYRE (scripted by Curt Siodmak and Ardel Wray) in which a nurse (Frances Dee) is brought to a Caribbean island to care for a woman in a zombie-like state, victim of mental paralysis. Hauntingly directed by Jacques Tourneur, with a Calypso-inspired score by Roy Webb. J. Roy Hunt's cinematography is punctuated by striking visuals, such as a voodoo native (Darby Jones) with a cadaverous face stalking two women through a canefield. James Ellison, Tom Conway, Edith Barrett, Christine Gordon. (VC)

**I WAS A TEENAGE ALIEN (1980).** Delightful amateur satire on monster movies produced by the police department of San Rafael, Calif., as a deterrent to shoplifting. Director Bob Cooper (who later worked on the special effects in GREMLINS) and photographer Daniel May fashion a palatable object lesson by turning it into a science-fiction satire about a bug-eyed alien, Orville, and a humanoid accomplice who leads teenagers astray. This short subject (50 minutes) has standout comedy cameos.

**I WAS A TEENAGE FRANKENSTEIN (1957).** Herman Cohen's sequel to I WAS A TEENAGE WEREWOLF, with Whit Bissell reappearing as a mad doctor, relative of the infamous Baron. Ludicrous as its title, with severed limbs graphically offered up for their shock value (and severed limbs in 1957 were an onscreen rarity). Despite its trend-setting virtues, and the fact it was an early proponent of black-macabre humor, Kenneth Langtry's script is hopelessly laughable, often in the wrong places. You too will be a teenage zombie if you can sit through this exploitative mess. Directed by Herbert L. Strock. Gary Conway, Angela Blake, Phyllis Coates, Robert Burton, George Lynn.

**I WAS A TEENAGE WEREWOLF (1957).** Herman Cohen spearheaded teen-age horror films with this vehicle for Michael Landon, whom is still living it down. Whit Bissell is either wonderful or ludicrous, depending on your taste, as the mad doctor who turns teenager Landon into a fanged beast. Bissell repeated this role in Cohen's sequel, I WAS A TEENAGE FRANKENSTEIN. Directed by Gene Fowler Jr. (I MARRIED A MONSTER FROM OUTER SPACE). Guy Williams, Robert Griffin, Eddie Marr, Yvonne Lime.

**I WAS A ZOMBIE FOR THE FBI (1984).** An alien monster presented in stop-motion animation, a silver ball that turns humans into zombies, the secret formula for a new soft drink, Unicola—these are among the bizarre ingredients that make this an offbeat science-fiction spoof played straight by writer-director Marius Penczner. The time is the 1950s when the criminally-inclined Brazzo brothers survive a plan crash, stumble across an alien plot and involve the FBI in a kidnapping—and that's only the beginning. Refreshing oddity; unusual in that it was produced at Memphis State University. John Gillick, James Rasberry, Larry Raspberry. (VC)

**ICE HOUSE, THE.** See **LOVE IN COLD BLOOD.**

**ICE PIRATES, THE (1984).** Rollicking, amusing parody of space adventures. The visual look is everything as warp-drive buccaneer Robert Urich and spaced-out swashbucklers Michael D. Roberts, Anjelica Huston and John Matuszak embark to the only planet in the galaxy having water, there to battle the evil Templar Empire. The funniest elements are (1) a castrating assembly line complete with gay "barber"; (2) the grungiest looking robots in any universe and (3) a time warp sequence in which the action is speeded up as the characters age at accelerated pace. Credit the tongue-in-cheek stylishness to director Stewart Raffill, who co-wrote with Stanford Sherman. For a switch, Urich is a sometimes-cowardly hero. Mary Crosby, as the kidnapped Princess Karina, is so beautiful and seductive, she alone is reason to keep your eyes glued to the foolishness. (VC)

# Lurid, Literate Mr. Lewton

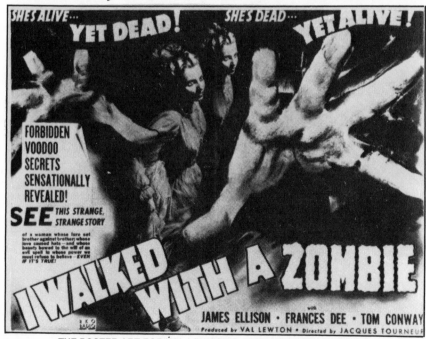

THE POSTER ART FOR VAL LEWTON'S 'I WALKED WITH A ZOMBIE'

**JOHN LONE: 'ICEMAN' COMETH**

**ICEBOX MURDERS, THE (1986).** Fiendish killer chases beauties through a maze of corridors, then stuffs their freshly-slain corpses into his deep freeze. Give this one the cold shoulder. Jack Taylor, Mirta Miller. (VC)

**ICEMAN (1984).** This starts as a fascinating, pseudoscientific examination of how a team of Arctic anthropologists uncover a human body frozen for 40,000 years by cutting away pieces of ice with lasers to expose a Neanderthal Man. The film loses its impetus after that as the Iceman is placed in an artificial environment and studied by the team. Although John Lone is excellent as the primitive man, and Timothy Hutton and Lindsay Crouse compassionate and warm as the befrienders, the story moves away into muddled metaphysical and quasi-religious ideas. One wants to feel more for the Iceman, as he is basically a good guy trapped in a world he can't understand, but he is never allowed to develop beyond his Neanderthal soul. A gallant attempt that doesn't make it, though ably and stylishly directed by Fred Schepisi. Danny Glover, Josef Sommer, David Strathairn, Philip Akin. (VC)

**IF (1969).** Satiric allegory from British director Lindsay Anderson has considerable impact in depicting the cruel system imposed on students in a British public school. Three boys begin a violent insurrection against sadistic, whip-wielding guards—but the film is ambiguous whether this attack is imaginary or real. Unsettling, turbulent script by David Sherwin. Malcolm McDowell, Richard Warwick, Peter Jeffrey, David Wood, Robert Swann. (VC)

**IGOR AND THE LUNATICS (1985).** Devil cult is killing young women in awful ways (how about putting them through the saw at the nearby mill?) so the police close in. Years later, the leader of the crazies gets out of prison and begins a new assault. Sleazy and cheap. Directed by Billy Parolini. Forget Igor and don't be a lunatic and watch. Joseph Eero, Joe Niola, T. J. Michaels. (VC)

**I'LL NEVER FORGET YOU (1951).** But you may forget this movie, in which Tyrone Power travels backward in time for no explainable reason, finding a new romantic life in the 18th Century. This remake of BERKELEY SQUARE, produced in England, finds Power adapting well to the new time and place and falling in love. Directed by Roy Baker. Ann Blyth, Michael Rennie, Dennis Price, Beatrice Campbell.

**ILLEGAL ALIEN (1982).** Lampoon on the 1979 box office smash ALIEN, with unusually excellent sets for an amateur production. However, producer Gregory Keller fails in giving us a funny substitute for the monster, and this short subject fails. In space, no one can hear you not laughing.

**ILLUSION OF BLOOD (1968).** Bizarre Japanese mixture of supernatural and samurai when a sword-swinging warrior is haunted by his first wife (looking for alimony after death?) and driven to self-destruction. Directed by Shiro Toyoda.

**ILLUSTRATED MAN, THE (1968).** A major disappointment, failing to capture the poetry or imagination of Ray Bradbury's story anthology. Jack Smight is too conventional a director to give this the technique it cries for. In this space weird images appear: "The Veldt" is about children living in a playroom with a holograph-projected African setting; "The Long Rains" is about a rocket crew stranded on a rain-pelted Venus and trying to make its way to safety; "The Last Night of the World" depicts a family of the future which beds down in anticipation of Armageddon. Claire Bloom, Jason Evers, Robert Drivas, Don Dubbins, Tim Weldon, Christine Matchett. (VC)

**IMAGES (1972).** Director Robert Altman indulges in a bit of is-it-real-or-isn't-it? in depicting the schizoid behavior of Susannah York. This British release, a disaster at the box office (critics were unkind too), might please Altman fans but general audiences will find this too esoteric. Rene Auberjonois, Cathryn Harrison, Marcel Bozzuffi.

**IMMEDIATE DISASTER. See STRANGER FROM VENUS.**

**IMMORAL MR. TEAS, THE (1958).** Night-goer Russ Meyer made light-core movie history with this low-budget sex fantasy that earned millions and established a new trend among flesh peddlers. Teas (a real-life character playing himself) is a sex tease given a new drug that enables him to see through clothing—which in turn allows the viewers to see several nubile young women, of ample proportions, bounding and jiggling through life. Pretty tame by today's gait, but what a shocker back there in '58.

**IMMORAL TALES (1974).** Anthology of four stories from writer-director Walerian Borowczyk that strides between art and pornography. Only one yarn has fantastic overtones: Paloma Picasso (daughter of artist Pablo) is Elizabeth Bathory, 16th Century Hungarian noblewoman (see DAUGHTERS OF DARKNESS and COUNTESS DRACULA) seeking virgins' blood to summerize her wintry body. Paloma skinny dips in ruby-red liquid before the orgiastic bloodlust goes into full swing.

**IMMORTAL, THE (1969).** Quinn Martin's TV-movie is a frightful mangling of James Gunn's fine novel by scriptwriter Robert Specht—you will hardly recognize the original; it's more a variation on THE FUGITIVE. Racing car hero Christopher George possesses special blood sought by dying millionaire Barry Sullivan and this quickly becomes nothing more than escapes, car crashes and other action hogwash. THE IMMORTAL became a short-lived tired-blood series, all too mortal. Directed by Joseph Sargent. Jessica Walter, Ralph Bellamy, Carol Lynley.

**IMPULSE (1974).** Demonic seizure of William Shatner's brain leads to bloody murders and child molestations. Shatner must have done it for the money—or did he do it on an . . . impulse? Directed by William Grefe in Florida, where he also made STANLEY. Harold Sakata, Ruth Roman, Kim Nicholas, James Dobson, Jennifer Bishop.

**IMPULSE (1984).** When Meg Tilly's mother tries to blow out her brains for no reason, Meg and husband-doctor Tim Matheson journey to her small rural hometown, where people are acting strangely; something is not allowing them to censor out their own unacceptable, antisocial urges. Soon the whole town is going crazy. Director Graham Baker emphasizes ambience and mystery, and a conspiratorial air, allowing the film to be compelling. The visual and verbal clues to the solution are given early on; see if you can figure it out before Matheson does. Brace for a disturbing film and downbeat ending. Hume Cronyn, John Karlen, Bill Paxton, Amy Stryker. (VC)

**IMPURE THOUGHTS (1986).** Religious message film angled for Catholics in which four men who have died wait in a nebulous room (purgatory?), describing their lives. Hence, four flashbacks to see if the men can confess their sins and move on (to Heaven?). If you're looking for entertainment, pray for a miracle. Directed by Michael A. Simpson. John Putch, Brad Dourif, Terry Beaver.

**IN LIKE FLINT (1967).** Sequel to OUR MAN FLINT is another pleasantly satiric Bond spoof. James Coburn is cool superagent Derek Flint, a gadget-equipped sex symbol with a computerized brain and a mastery of martial arts. A band of women, intent on conquering Earth, is replacing political leaders with doubles by using a numbing face cream. Delightful weapons and gimmicks, beautiful women and creative set designs; good clean fun without insulting your intelligence under Gordon Douglas' direction. Lee J. Cobb is the befuddled assignment chief. Among the sexy gals: Jean Hale, Anna Lee, Yvonne Craig (Batgirl herself) and Erin O'Brien. Andrew Duggan, Hanna Landry, Steve Ihnat, Herb Edelman, Thordis Brandt.

**IN POSSESSION (1985).** Horror film starring Carol Lynley and Christopher Cazenove as a couple that sees apparitions on a Brighton holiday. These apparitions return two years later to haunt the couple.

**IN SEARCH OF . . .** See **LEONARD NIMOY IN SEARCH OF . . . (TAKEN FROM THE SYNDICATED TV SERIES)**

**IN SEARCH OF ANCIENT ASTRONAUTS (1975).** Re-edited footage from CHARIOTS OF THE GODS?, the German feature based on Erich Von Daniken's book about visitors from space and the so-called proof on Earth. Repackaged for TV by Alan Landsburg, narrated by Rod Serling. Don't take it too seriously . . . (VC)

**IN SEARCH OF ANCIENT MYSTERIES (1975).** More footage from CHARIOTS OF THE GODS? repackaged for U.S. TV by Alan Landsburg with Rod Serling narrating. Pure speculation, inconclusive evidence.

**IN SEARCH OF BIGFOOT (1976).** Standard poor man's documentary about the legendary creature of the Pacific Northwest, with alleged footage of the Incredible Mind-Boggling Hulking Hairy Beast-man Thing running upright on two legs. Produced-directed by Lawrence Crowley and William F. Miller. Narrated by Phil Tonkin.

**IN SEARCH OF DRACULA (1976).** U.S.-Swedish horror documentary narrated by Christopher Lee, produced-directed by Calvin Floyd, with narration by his wife, Yvonne. This discusses the history of vampires via paintings, drawings and film footage of early Murnau, Dreyer and Lugosi. Scholarly, not scary, and based on the popular book by Raymond T. McNally and Radu Florescu. This decent "doc" has turned up on educational channels.

**LOU FERRIGNO AS
'THE INCREDIBLE HULK'**

**IN SEARCH OF HISTORIC JESUS (1980).** Exceedingly dull pseudodocumentary about the Shroud of Turin, alleged to be the robe Jesus Christ wore when he was Crucified. Some good actors lend their support (and no doubt religious beliefs): Royal Dano, Nehemiah Persoff, John Anderson, John Rubinstein. Thoroughly unconvincing as fact or fiction. Directed by Gary Conway.

**IN SEARCH OF NOAH'S ARK (1976).** Sunn Classic pseudodocumentary which investigates reported wreckage on Mt. Ararat as remnants of the famous Biblical vessel which kept alive all the species on Earth during the Great Flood. Directed by James L. Conway. Noah count. (VC)

**IN THE DEVIL'S GARDEN.** See **ASSAULT.**

**IN THE GRIP OF THE SPIDER.** See **WEB OF THE SPIDER.** (A well-spun yarn?)

**IN THE MIDNIGHT HOUR (1985).** Violent TV-movie vacillating between graveyard humor and standard shock thrills in telling its satirical tale of the town of Pitchford Cove, where teenagers on Halloween night violate the graveyard to enact a ritual that unleashes scores of corpses. These walking dead are ghouls who crash a teen party and go for yocks; the vampires go for the jugular; others are werewolves, and one 17-year-old (Jonna Lee) joins with a good guy teen (Lee Montgomery) to help him undo the damage. A lively affair, full of laughs and thrills (the dead in the graveyard are especially effective) and excellent production design by Charles Hughes, who did Michael Jackson's THRILLER video. In the tradition of AMERICAN GRAFFITI, the voice of Wolfman Jack blares over car radios as the teens roar through town. Dick Van Patten has fun as a silly dentist and Kevin McCarthy is the drunken judge who gets his comeuppance. Shari Belafonte-Harper, LeVar Burton. Directed by Jack Bender.

**IN THE SHADOW OF KILAMANJARO (1986).** Dramatization of a true incident that took place in Kenya during the drought of 1984, when 90,000 starving baboons went on a killing spree, terrorizing natives and settlers alike. Director Raju Patel treats this topic as though it were a remake of JAWS rather than history, emphasizing gory remains of the attacks and building suspense each time the critters amass in the darkness, or just over the next rise. Well done, with interesting characters, good photography, decent dialogue. Timothy Bottoms, Michele Carey, Don Blakely, John Rhys-Davies, Irene Miracle, Calvin Jung. (VC)

**IN THE YEAR 2889 (1965).** Obvious remake (though uncredited) of Roger Corman's THE DAY THE WORLD ENDED, depicting a handful of holocaust survivors who gather in a sheltered valley to bicker with each other and fight off a mutant monster. Corman's version was watchable—this work from director-producer Larry Buchanan is uninspired. Les Tremayne, Paul Petersen, Quinn O'Hara, Charla Doarty and Neal Fletcher are lost in the pages of Harold Hoffman's screenplay ripoff.

**INCREDIBLE FACE OF DR. B, THE (1961).** Incredible excuse for a Mexican horror film which unsuccessfully tries to blend themes of black magic with eternal life. The most incredible face of all must have belonged to the producer when he saw how bad the rushes looked. Jaime Fernandez, Erick del Castillo, Elsa Cardenas.

**INCREDIBLE HULK, THE (1977).** Adult approach to a popular green-tinted brutish comic book hero results in a better-than-average TV-movie starring Bill Bixby as a scientist, Dr. David Bruce Banner, conducting experiments that enable test subjects to perform superhuman feats in time of anger and duress. Through a combination of gamma rays and ire, Bixby is transformed into a giant brute, primitive and uncontrollable (the towering creature is Lou Ferrigno). The teleplay by Kenneth Johnson, who produced and directed, deals with Bixby's personal anguish and his romance with lab assistant Dr. Elaina Marks (Susan Sullivan). The special effects are good, especially the destruction of an experimental pressure chamber. Jack Colvin, Susan Batson, Lara Parker, Brandon Cruz. (VC)

**INCREDIBLE INVASION, THE (1968).** Jack Hill assisted

Juan Ibanez in directing this U.S.-Mexican film, historically the last Boris Karloff ever made. Karloff portrays the inventor of a machine that destroys with radioactive powers. Extraterrestrial entities, in the bodies of unsavory humans, infiltrate Mayer's home, attacking his beautiful daughter (Christa Linder) before the doc regains his zapped willpower to put a stop to the nonsense. Karloff was ill and his movements are restricted. In videocassette format under the title **SINISTER INVASION.**

**INCREDIBLE MELTING MAN, THE (1978).** Make-up specialist Rick Baker outdoes himself in creating a hideous countenance stripped of human flesh. Eyeballs are exposed and atilt, ears are ready to drop off and the face is oozing with bubbly goo. Unfortunately, writer-director William Sachs does nothing exciting with the melter. Alex Rebar, only survivor of a flight to Saturn, is infected with radiation poisoning and becomes a Frankenstein Monster bashing everyone in sight and throwing their body parts around while he continues to decompose at an alarming rate. A throwback to the monster science-fiction movies of the 1950s. Or is this a throwaway? Myron Healy, Jonathan Demme, Burr DeBenning, Rainbeaux Smith. (VC)

**INCREDIBLE MR. LIMPET, THE (1963).** Melange of live action dumbbell comedy and animated underwater sequences is strictly for the unsophisticated Don Knotts set. Knotts portrays a 4-F reject during World War II who wants to serve his country so badly he turns into a dolphin when he gets into the water. Limpet, in short, is limpid. Directed by Arthur Lubin. Carole Cook, Andrew Duggan, Jack Weston.

**INCREDIBLE PETRIFIED WORLD, THE (1957).** Incredible petrified script by John Steiner creates wooden acting and a director, Jerry Warren, who is "stumped" by the material. John Carradine, Phyllis Coates and other B players are trapped in a diving bell at the bottom of a strange submerged world, which looks like the bottom of a goldfish bowl. Robert Clarke repeats the kind of gurgling role he played in THE HIDEOUS SUN DEMON. (VC)

**INCREDIBLE PRAYING MANTIS, THE.** See **DEADLY MANTIS, THE.** (And now, let us prey.)

**INCREDIBLE SEX-RAY MACHINE, THE (1978).** Voyeuristic scientist develops machine that can see through walls and turn people horny. A patch quilt of softcore porn and stupid

FASCINATING
OVENTURE
ITO THE
NKNOWN!

THE INCREDIBLE
SHRINKING MAN

GRANT WILLIAMS · RANDY STUART · AIME HEE TALE LANGUAGE, DIRECTED

'THE INCREDIBLE SHRINKING MAN'

**TOMLIN AND BAKER:
'INCREDIBLE SHRINKING WOMAN'**

science. Starring Russ Meyer's Uschi Digart.

**INCREDIBLE SHRINKING MAN, THE (1957).** Classic of its kind, brilliantly designed by the Universal-International special effects department (under Clifford Stine) and featuring a 15-foot mousetrap, an 18-foot pencil, a four-foot pin and a 40-pound pair of scissors. Thus is Grant Williams dwarfed and made to appear shrinking at the rate of an inch a week. Based on a Richard Matheson novel, and adapted by Matheson, Albert Zugsmith's production transcends the limitations of the fantasy thriller to deal with the metaphysical aspects of a shrinking human. It begins when Williams is inundated in a strange cloud while at sea and follows him "down" until a house cat, a spider and water drops are staggering nemeses in his miniaturized world. And he continues to diminish in size—until finally, in a brilliant climax directed by Jack Arnold, he passes into another molecular universe. Randy Stuart portrays the long-suffering wife until Williams is so small he can't see her anymore. William Schallert, Billy Curtis, April Kent. (VC)

**INCREDIBLE SHRINKING WOMAN, THE (1981).** Delightful parody combining slapstick and satire. Lily Tomlin (among several roles) portrays a modern housewife exposed to chemical products that shrink her to minuscule size. In one scene she literally stands on a soap box to deliver a tirade to her long-suffering (but tallll) husband, Charles Grodin; in another she is (again, literally) washed down the drain. Finally she's kidnapped by corporation boss Ned Beatty, who wants to learn her secret so he can shrink anyone who stands in the way of company progress. Lily and a gorilla (played by make-up man Rick Baker) bring the film to an hysterical conclusion. Beautifully photographed in pastel shades by Bruce Logan. Effects by Baker and Roy Arbogast. Intelligently directed by Joel Schumacher; Jane Wagner's script works on several levels. A real treat for big and little people. Henry Gibson, Maria Smith, Mike Douglas, Terry McGovern. (VC)

**INCREDIBLE TORTURE SHOW, THE (1977).** Also known as BLOODSUCKING FREAKS, which shouldn't be confused with BLOODTHIRSTY BUTCHER. It's a Grand Guignol show presented by Sardu the Great. But offstage he's performing the real thing. Yes, fans, see a woman's brains popped out of her cranium, see eyeballs eaten before your very . . . eyeballs? See . . . yuch! The mastermind behind this blood and gore thriller is writer-producer-director Joel Reed. Lynette Sheldon, Karen Fraser.

**INCREDIBLE TWO-HEADED TRANSPLANT, THE (1971).** Stomach-churning nonsense about the head of a homicidal maniac being grafted onto the body of a thorough idiot by crazy doctor Bruce Dern, who hit an all-time low in this production for American-International. What's incredible

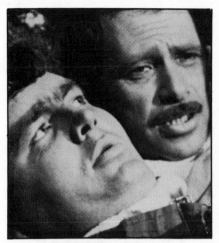

**'THE INCREDIBLE TWO-HEADED TRANSPLANT'**

about a movie like this is that it was ever financed. Directed by Anthony Lanza. John Bloom, Pat Priest, Casey Karem, Berry Kroeger, Larry Vincent.

**INCREDIBLY STRANGE CREATURES WHO STOPPED LIVING AND BECAME MIXED-UP ZOMBIES, THE (1964).** Madame Estrella, a fortune teller at a sleazy carnival midway, gets angry at her customers if they mock her prophecies, throws acid in their faces and then has her Igor assistant toss their bodies into a pit. So much for the zombies. Along comes a shiftless bum (Cash Flagg) who falls prey to her influences, becoming a knife murderer who slashes up a couple of bodies. Meanwhile, back at the midway, hapless audiences are subjected to several production numbers, some of them featuring a talentless stripper named Carmelita who is barely able to take it off. The finale voodoo production is interrupted by the zombies escaping from their cell and the police rush in for a grand shootout—except for Cash, who escapes to the nearby beach to lead the law (and girlfriend) on a merry chase. Somewhere in all this mess must be some talents at work, such as producer-director Ray Dennis Steckler. Meanwhile, the Theater Marquee Dressers of America continue to complain about this movie—every time it plays, they run out of letters. Atlas King, Carolyn Brandt, Toni Camel, Erina Enyo, Brett O'Hara. Incidentally, the name Cash Flagg is an alias for director Steckler. A Steckler for details?

**INCUBUS (1965).** Experimental film written-directed by Leslie Stevens, largely ignored because of its soundtrack of Esperanto, the artificial universal language which dulled, rather than whetted, appetites of audiences. Filmed at Big Sur, Calif., it is set on a mythical island inhabited by demons, where William Shatner engages in good vs. evil combat. Flowery, stylized and often laughable. Allyson Ames, Ann Atmar, Eloise Hart, Milo Milos.

**INCUBUS (1982).** John Hough (TWINS OF EVIL, LEGEND OF HELL HOUSE) helms this grisly Canadian horror-charger in which the small town of Galen is terrorized by an invisible sex-starved demon that materializes only during the dreams of a young man whose mother was once branded a witch. Or so it seems . . . Trying to solve the supernatural mystery is doctor John Cassavetes, cop John Ireland and newspaperwoman Kerrie Keane. Not a particularly outstanding terrorizer, but it has enough plot and goofy characters (and screams on the soundtrack) to sustain attention. Scripted by George Franklin from Ray Russell's novel. Helen Hughes, Dirk McLean. (VC)

**INDESTRUCTIBLE MAN, THE (1956).** Bottom-of-the-barrel Allied Artists fiasco with Lon Chaney Jr. as an electrocuted criminal restored to life (yeah, one of those plots) who goes

around town knocking off all the guys who sent him up the river. Said to be a remake of MAN-MADE MONSTER, but don't believe it. So poorly scripted (by Sue Bradford and Vy Russell) and directed (by Jack Pollexfen) that you might find it entertaining. Robert Shayne, Marian Carr, Ross Elliott, Stuart Randall, Kenneth Terrell. (VC)

**INDIANA JONES AND THE TEMPLE OF DOOM (1984).** The ultimate cliffhanger movie—it sweeps one headlong into the second screen adventure of soldier-of-fortune archeologist Indiana Jones. And because the "thrill ride" is non-stop, one has no time to consider the absurdities and excesses screenwriters Willard Hyuck and Gloria Katz pump into George Lucas' original idea. Like RAIDERS OF THE LOST ARK, it's a fast-paced, exciting saga produced by Lucas and Steven Spielberg, again with Spielberg at the directorial reins. The action is treated with tongue-in-cheek, but there are also moments of severe intensity. The madcap plot begins in Shanghai 1935 with Jones and night club dancer Kate Capshaw and the Oriental kid Shortround (homage to the orphan in Samuel Fuller's STEEL HELMET) fleeing from insidious Orientals. After a great night club dance sequence, the three escape via a wild airplane ride that leads them to a hair-raising parachute jump (but without a parachute), a ski ride and a "white rapids" excursion. Then the trio winds up in India where they help recover a magical glowing rock from a Kali cult of Thugees. There's a fiery pit, secret caverns, torture chambers, a hallway full of creepies and crawlies, a variation on a roller coaster ride, a tidal wave and a suspension bridge with Indie trapped in the middle and hungry crocodiles snapping below. Harrison Ford leaps and jumps and runs through it all, always managing to recover his hat and whip. Ke Huy Quan is cute as the Chinese youth and Amrish Puri and Roshan Seth make for good cardboard villains. Don't miss the eating scene—it's the funniest gross-out ever. (VC)

**INFERNAL IDOL, THE.** See **CRAZE.**

**INFERNAL TRIO, THE (1974).** French-Italian-German mixture of psychoterrors: gore murders, a Count Dracula character and black humor that helps to make the tedious moments more endurable. Francis Girod directed and wrote. Romy Schneider, Michel Piccoli.

**INFERNO (1980).** Italy's Dario Argento, famed for DEEP RED and SUSPIRIA, is up to his usual writing and directing scare tactics in this tale of witchcraft, suspended animation and other supernatural delights. Mario Bava was credited

**LON CHANEY JR. AS 'THE INDESTRUCTIBLE MAN'**

with some of the effects. Irene Miracle, Leigh McCloskey, Eleonara Giorgi, Alida Valli.

**INFERNO IN SPACE (1954).** See **ROCKY JONES, SPACE RANGER.** (Inferno: Pure hell!)

**INFRA-MAN (1975).** Kids will cheer the wonderful menagerie of grotesque extraterrestrial creatures, the kung fu fighting and other comic book elements of this Oriental mishmash. Adults may become fascinated watching this awfulness carried to ultra-ludicrous extremes as a super-powerful hero in funny clothing (he's a bionic man) fights a dragon lady (Dragon Mom) who sends these boggling creatures—Octopus Man, Beetle Man, etc.—out from her headquarters in the bowels of the Earth to do battle. It Came From Hong Kong. Directed by Hua-Shan. Hsiu-Hsien portrays Infra-Man, the ultimate Chinese savior. (VC)

**INITIATION, THE (1982).** Unusual slasher film with more meat than usual: In addition to members of a sorority pulling some pranks during Hell Week, there is a young member (Marilyn Kagan) undergoing nightmares of a childhood trauma when she saw her mother in bed with another man, and during a struggle a man burst into flames. And there's a relationship with her mother (Vera Miles) and father (Clu Galager). Meanwhile, seven inmates have escaped from an insane asylum, one of them a bloodthirsty psychopath who kills with assorted instruments. The climactic bloodbath (after a few preliminary murders) comes during the night in a shopping mall when the killer strikes with bow and arrow, hatchet, crossbow, speargun, etc. Fans will probably anticipate the surprise twist. Directed by Larry Stewart. (VC)

**INITIATION OF SARAH, THE (1978).** Undistinguished TV-movie ripoff of CARRIE, complete with girl-being-hazed scenes. Shy, reticent Kay Lenz attends a college only to come in conflict with members of a rival sorority to which her more outgoing sister belongs. Kay has these strange psychic powers, you see, so on the night of the initiation who should urge her to utilize them for evil purposes but batty sorority mistress Shelley Winters. Directed by Robert Day. Tony Bill, Kathryn Crosby, Morgan Fairchild (as a great bitch), Tisa Farrow. The daughters of several well-known actors were thrown in as atmosphere players. (VC)

**INN OF THE DAMNED (1974).** Australian psychokiller flick starring Alex Cord and Dame Judith Anderson. Directed by Terry Bourke.(VC)

**INNER SANCTUM (1947).** This has nothing to do with the radio horror series of the 1940s that featured a creaking door and host with ghoulish puns; the titled was purchased for exploitative reasons. Strange Dr. Velonious (Fritz Leiber) meets

## THE INCREDIBLE BIONIC 'INFRAMAN'

a young woman on a train and tells her a weird story about a man who commits murder and seeks refuge in a boarding house in a small town. Uninspired plot with predictable ending. Plodding direction by Lew Landers. Mary Beth Hughes, Charles Russell, Lee Patrick.

**INNOCENTS, THE (1961).** Superior cinematic version of Henry James' TURN OF THE SCREW, directed with unbearable tension by Jack Clayton, scripted by Truman Capote and William Archibald with insight, and capturing the decay, depravity and haunted possession which reeks throughout the novel. Deborah Kerr is the prim governess dispatched to a country mansion to tend the children of cold baron Michael Redgrave. Beneath the serene exterior are undercurrents of menace. Are the souls of the children possessed by a former governess and valet who were carrying on a sadistic love affair before their deaths—or is it all in Kerr's vivid imagination? Much of the horror in this U.S.-British production is only suggested. One of the best ghost movies ever made. Martin Stevens, Pamela Franklin.

**INQUISITION (1974).** Spanish torture chamber melodrama written and directed by Jacinto Molina, who also stars under the name of Paul Naschy as a fanatic of the Inquisition who falls in love with the daughter of a warlock, whom he has sentenced to death. She makes a pact with the Devil to get even. Ricardo Merino, Toni Osbert. (VC)

**INSEMINOID.** See **HORROR PLANET.**

**INSIDE THE LABYRINTH (1986).** One-hour videocassette which goes behind the scenes of the making of Jim Henson's LABYRINTH to show how the many creatures were designed and articulated. And David Bowie is shown in the studio, recording the film's soundtrack. (VC)

**INSPECTOR CALLS, AN (1954).** British film version of J. B. Priestley's stage classic, directed by Guy Hamilton and scripted by Desmond Davis, resembles a standard drawing room detective thriller when a Scotland Yard investigator turns up one evening at the home of a wealthy Yorkshire family and commences to prove that each of them, in some way, was responsible for the death of a young woman. The surprise ending has supernatural overtones. Alastair Sim, Eileen Moore, Bryan Forbes, Arthur Young.

**INTERFACE (1984).** Silly, poorly conceived computer-theme fantasy, made in Dallas by regional filmmakers (dare we call them hackers with emphasis on the hack?). Its saving grace is a couple who play it strictly for laughs as they search for the secret to a group of masked, costumed computerites ("We are the interpreters of the Master Process") who sit around their consols speaking with metallic voices and killing

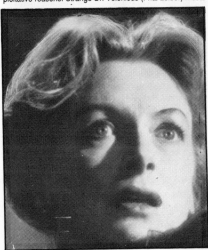

## DEBORAH KERR IN 'THE INNOCENTS'

by remote control devices. An anticlimactic ending causes the film to fall apart. Maybe director Andy Anderson forgot his modum operandi. John Davies, Laura Lane, Matthew Sacks. (VC)

**INTERNATIONAL HOUSE (1933).** Hearty Paramount comedy with an all-star cast (W.C. Fields, Rudy Vallee, Burns and Allen, Sterling Holloway, Stu Erwin, Bela Lugosi) focuses on some eccentrics staying at a Chinese hotel where skullduggery is afoot to wrest the Radioscope (a device that can pick up sight and sound anywhere in the world) from the inventive Wang Wu-Hu. Precious and nostalgic. Directed by Edward Sutherland. (VC)

**INTO THE DARKNESS (1986).** Beautiful models are knocked off one by bloody one in a routine blood-splasher enhanced only by the menacing presence of Donald Pleasence. Directed by Michael Parkinson. Ronald Lacey, Polly Pleasence. Double your Pleasances? (VC)

**INTRUDER WITHIN, THE (1981).** Okay TV-movie, but too imitative of ALIEN to generate its own unique suspense.

# Martians!

## 'INVADERS FROM MARS' (1986)

Chad Everett is a "tool-pusher" on an oil rig for the Zorton Oil Company, who drills to 19,000 feet to uncover a hideous creature from our ecological past, a spawn that implants reproductive sperm within a human being. When that man goes crazy and attacks a woman crew member, she is destined to give birth to . . . you know what, don't you? The monster passes through various evolutionary stages before becoming a man in a glistening fright suit. Directed by Peter Carter. Joseph Bottoms, Jennifer Warren. (VC)

**INVADERS FROM MARS (1953).** A cult following has built over the years because this touches a sensitive cord in young people, who remember those things which first frightened them, and the gap between youth and adults. Jimmy Hunt wakes up one night to spy an extraterrestrial craft submerging itself in a hill outside his house, but no one will believe his wild story, not even when the aliens take over humans in a widespread conspiracy. It's the ultimate in paranoia-for-kids. Director William Cameron Menzies, noted

for set design work on GONE WITH THE WIND and for directing THE MAZE, brings his abstract styles to the strange sets and scene compositions, giving INVADERS FROM MARS a touch of class. While Richard Blake's script cops out at the end, and then throws a terrible cliche at us for the final whammy, the story does have wonderful moments. Arthur Franz, Helena Carter, Leif Erickson, Morris Ankrum, Milburn Stone. (VC)

**INVADERS FROM MARS (1986).** Sincere remake of Menzies' 1953 cult favorite, with writers Dan O'Bannon and Don Jakoby sticking to the original story and director Tobe Hooper trying to recapture what made the original so memorable to the young. In ways they do a better job in capturing the paranoia of a lad who sees everyone being turned into zombies but whom nobody will believe. This excels with its effects by John Dykstra and its Stan Winston-designed monsters. Wonderful cave and spaceship interiors too as Hunter Carson and Karen Black lead the Marines in an exciting old-fashioned rescue. The film is simple and fast-moving with cliff-hangers and visual delights: soldiers being sucked into the sand, Lucille Fletcher swallowing a frog whole, and a machine that bores needles into humans being zomboided. Jimmy Hunt, who played the boy in the original, is back as the town's police chief; as he walks up to the hill toward the sandpit, he remarks, "I haven't been up here since I was kid." Timothy Bottoms, Laraine Newman, James Karen. (VC)

**INVADERS FROM SPACE.** See **ATTACK FROM SPACE.**

**INVADERS FROM THE PLANETS.** See **ATOMIC RULERS OF THE WORLD.** (They don't measure up.)

**INVADERS FROM THE SPACESHIP.** See **PRINCE OF SPACE.**

**INVASION (1966).** British chiller, recommended for its atmosphere and acting. An extraterrestrial "Lystrian" craft crashes near a country hospital, with the aliens aboard being a policewoman and prisoner. When they're taken to the hospital, a force field pops up around the building. The peculiar ambience generated by director Alan Bridges makes up for the low budget. Edward Judd, Yoko Tani, Tsai Chin.

**INVASION, THE (1973).** Re-edited episodes from TV's STAR LOST, about a ship on a thousand-year journey through space. In this storyline, a deranged space commander plans to increase the intellectual capacity of the Ark through brain implants. Keir Dullea, Stephen Young.

**INVASION EARTH 2150 A.D. (1966).** Sequel to DR. WHO AND THE DALEKS, again featuring that lovable old curmudgeon doctor (Peter Cushing) who moves through the dimensions in his time machine. In this adventure Dr. Who (a character created on the BBC, and still very popular) squares off against the Daleks (mutated beings in R2D2-like movable units) who have conquered our planet and are preparing to blow out the middle of the globe and use it as a giant spaceship (creative, those Daleks). Directed by Gordon Flemying. Bernard Cribbins, Ray Brooks, Andrew Keir.

**INVASION FORCE.** See **HANGAR 18.**

**INVASION FROM INNER EARTH (1977).** Filmed in the snow wastes of Wisconsin, this low-budget cheapie depicts stranded travelers being knocked off by red-glowing death rays generated by off-camera aliens (that's one way to keep the budget at poverty level). The plot plods as often as the snowbound characters, and director Ito Rebane's idea of a frightening E.T. is to have a heavy-handed voice boom over a radio receiver. The effects are plain awful and the film lumbers to an incomprehensible ending in which the last man and woman on Earth turn into children and scamper into a Garden of Eden. Paul Bentzen. (VC)

**INVASION OF CAROL ENDERS, THE (1974).** Meredith Baxter transfers her personality into the body of a woman killed in an "accident" in this Dan Curtis TV-movie. Chris Connelly, Charles Aidman. (VC)

**INVASION OF PLANET X.** See **MONSTER ZERO.**

**INVASION OF THE ANIMAL PEOPLE (1960).** Swedish smorgasbord recut for the U.S. with new footage shot by

**LIKE PEAS IN A POD: KEVIN McCARTHY IN THE 1956 VERSION OF 'INVASION OF THE BODY SNATCHERS'**

Virgil Vogel and Jerry Warren, featuring John Carradine and Robert Burton. An alien creature on the loose is recaptured by its other-world masters, who closely encounter some mountain folks. Aliens should better observe the leash laws. Minor science-fiction, making little sense. Written by Arthur C. Pierce. Barbara Wilson, Stan Gester. (VC)

**INVASION OF THE ASTRO ZOMBIES.** See **MONSTER ZERO.** (That's what it adds up to.)

**INVASION OF THE BEE GIRLS (1973).** Quickie horror thriller with fantasy overtones scripted by Nicholas Meyer, who claims his script was tampered with. What should have been a stinger about women turning into men-destroying insects is instead a stinker—Meyer is hereby vindicated. William Smith is a G-man buzzing around the hive of beautiful sexy women, Victoria Vetri and other "Bee Girls." Strictly for the Birds—and B fans. Directed by Denis Sanders. Anitra Ford, Rene Bond, Cliff Osmond. (VC)

**INVASION OF THE BLOOD FARMERS (1972).** Druid cult seeks a special blood type to rejuvenate the body of its dying queen, which is kept secreted in a coffin. Lifeless film produced and directed by Ed Adlum could use a transfusion itself. Cynthia Fleming, Tanna Hunter. (VC)

**INVASION OF THE BODY SNATCHERS (1956).** The political ramifications of director Don Siegel's classic have been well expounded on (it was produced during the McCarthy hysteria of the 1950s and its subtext is rooted in fear of conspiracy) but it can be enjoyed strictly for its thrills and techniques. A tale of mounting suspicion and horror as Kevin McCarthy, a resident of the town of Santa Mira, discovers an alien race (creatures encased in strange pods which froth and crack open) is creating duplicates of the townspeople and turning them into zombies. The literate Daniel Mainwaring-Sam Peckinpah script (from Jack Finney's novel) and the supporting cast (Dana Wynter, Carolyn Jones, King Donovan) contribute greatly, but it is finally Siegel's direction that makes it a classic work. (VC)

**INVASION OF THE BODY SNATCHERS (1978).** Inspired by Jack Finney's novel first produced in 1956, this has undergone so many changes it stands as a new story and shouldn't be compared to the Don Siegel version. This time we are introduced to the alien spores as they leave their home planet and drift through space to Earth; it's a striking sequence. The spores settle in San Francisco near victims-to-be: Donald Sutherland, Brooke Adams, Leonard Nimoy, Veronica Cartwright. Slowly the humans are replaced by the pod creatures, but we're still not sure how much is conspiracy and how much is paranoia and hysteria. The pod effects are revoltingly good and there are several startling scenes, including a mutation dog, that make this Philip Kaufman-directed film memorable. Don Siegel turns up in a cameo as a cab driver, and Kevin McCarthy plays his character in the original, running through the streets to warn us that the bubbling pod monsters are back. (VC)

**INVASION OF THE BODY STEALERS.** Videocassette title for **BODY STEALERS, THE.** (Bum Bum!)

**INVASION OF THE FLESH HUNTERS.** Videocassette title for **CANNIBALS IN THE STREETS, THE.** (Yum Yum!)

**INVASION OF THE LOVE DRONES (1977).** Porn corn about crazy inventor Dr. Femme (Viveca Ash) who arrives on Earth in a craft powered by a "sex drive." Her foreplay: to create a race of sexy love creatures, the energy from which will create a worldwide orgy of pleasure. This film has some climax! It'll warp you out! Jerome Hamlin is the crew of one who puts Ash, Jamie Gillis, Bree Anthony, Tony Blue and other porno figures through their stances.

**INVASION OF THE NEPTUNE MEN (1961).** Japanese gibberish for children about attackers from our eighth planet and one heroic alien, Ironsharp, who squares off against the creepos to save precious Earth from being savaged. Directed by Koji Ota. Shinichi Chiba (otherwise known as Sonny Chiba) stars as the steely dull Ironsharp.

**INVASION OF THE SAUCER MEN (1957).** American-International double-biller slanted for teenagers and featuring wonderful bug-eyed, head-bulging Martians. The film has a reputation for being so-bad-it's-good. The Robert Gurney Jr.-Al Martin mishmash of a plot (from a Paul Fairman story) has teeners being injected with alcohol by the aliens in an attempt to have them arrested for drunk driving. The hero is Lyn Osborne, Cadet Happy on TV's SPACE PATROL. The cast is a hodgepodge: Frank Gorshin, Steve Terrell, Gloria Castillo, Russ Bender, Ed Nelson. Directed by Edward L. Cahn. Would you call this a Cahn Job? Remade as THE EYE CREATURES.

**INVASION OF THE STAR CREATURES, THE (1962).** Lowbrow premise intentionally played for laughs—a spoof directed by Bruno Ve Sota. However, you won't be guffawing or choking on your own chortles. Some va-va-voom babes from space with size E bras want to take over Earth with the help of Vege-Men, but two deadbeats from the Army thwart the dumb plot—no difficult achievement for two idiots. Frankie Ram, Bob Ball, Gloria Victor, Dolores Reed.

**INVASION OF THE VAMPIRES (1962).** They must have smuggled this Mexican flick in—surely it would have been confiscated by the Border Patrol as material detrimental to the human brain. Same old fanged killer (Count Frankenhausen, played by Carlos Agosti) although they've set this in the 16th Century, which allows for different costuming. Stalking the Count is a doctor who asks "Do you suppose there are forces of darkness?" You better believe it, Doc. Written-directed by Miguel Morayta.

**INVASION OF THE ZOMBIES (1961).** Second in a Mexican series detailing the ridiculous behavior of a masked wrestler called Samson (or Santo) who fights evil scientists and other forces of evil—when he isn't wrestling a bad script. In this epic, he throws down a scientist who has created an army of zombies and pins him with a brain lock. Written-directed by Benito Alzraki.

**INVASION: UFO (1972).** Re-edited episodes of a British series which took the kind of model work in the THUNDER-BIRDS series and combined it with live action. SHADO is an Earth organization designed to fight off attacking aliens, who are human in shape and often trick us Earthlings by infiltration methods. Standard TV fare directed-written by Gerry Anderson and David Tomblin. Ed Bishop, Wanda Ventham Sewell, Michael Billington. (VC)

One of Norris' worst. Even his early kung fu programmers were better. Directed by Joseph Zito, written by James Bruner and Norris. (VC)

**INVISIBLE ADVERSARIES (1978).** Austrian import from Export—producer-director Valie Export, that is. It's hard to see what he saw in this tale about unseen entities called Hyksos who are up to the usual Alien Invasion plot. Invisible production values. Seldom seen.

**INVISIBLE AGENT (1942).** Cigarettes floating in air and Gestapo agents being kicked in the seat of their pants by an unseen presence are highpoints of this propagandistic comedy-adventure in which Jon Hall is rendered "unsightly" by taking a drug intravenously. Traveling to Nazi Germany, he gives the Fuhrer what for. Curt Siodmak's script is preachy and preposterous and director Edward L. Marin glorifies mock heroics as Hall indulges in espionage situations. Peter Lorre overplays a Japanese baron and Ilona Massey slinks around as a Berlin femme fatale. So overdone it's fun. Cedric Hardwick, Keye Luke, John Litel.

**INVISIBLE AVENGER (1958).** "The Shadow," the invisible

**THE INCREDIBLY BUG-EYED ALIENS IN 'INVASION OF THE SAUCER MEN'**

**INVASION U.S.A. (1953).** Albert Zugsmith low budget feature directed by Albert E. Green, reflecting the "Red Menace" hysteria of the Cold War. Ordinary folks in a bar meet a soothsayer who predicts what might happen if the U.S. was invaded by the enemy following nuclear holocaust. Bingo: The invasion happens, with the Commies blasting us to pieces. Hampered by a lack of effects if not a lack of paranoiac ideas. However, the trick ending just doesn't work. Gerald Mohr, Dan O'Herlihy, Peggie Castle, Phyllis Coates, Edward G. Robinson Jr., Noel Neill.

**INVASION U.S.A. (1985).** Bloodthirsty Communist commando Richard Lynch leads Soviet terrorists to the Florida coast in barges, then has squads attack homes in the suburbs, shopping centers, etc. The only man to stop this terrible invasion is Chuck Norris, portraying secret agent Mark Hunter, who proceeds to act as a one-man army, killing the invaders ruthlessly, often in cold blood. This is an awful movie, full of stupid story holes, plagued by sadistic, gratuitous violence, with motives and human behavior defying all logic. Somewhere in the script is a good idea for a movie, but this ain't it.

crimefighter (real name: Lamont Cranston) of pulp magazines and radio, is the hero in this seldom-shown Republic film made in New Orleans and directed by famous cameraman James Wong Howe and John Sledge. Cranston ("who clouds men's minds so they cannot see him") uses his hypnotic cloak of invisibility to thwart a political assassin while also investigating the murder of a jazz figure. Richard Derr portrays the playboy investigator. Marc Daniels, Helen Westcott, Dan Mullin, Jeanne Neher.

**INVISIBLE BATMAN, THE (1985).** Italian mishmash in which a costumed superhero fights disorganized crime. Etore Gunadi, Ercole Tassi.

**INVISIBLE BOY, THE (1957).** A vehicle designed for Robby the Robot following his popular reception in FORBIDDEN PLANET. This MGMer is memory banks above most science-fiction films of the period, with Richard Eyer as a likable youth who puts Robby back together. As a reward, Robby (with the voice of Marvin Miller) turns the boy invisible. Unfortunately, the robot comes under the spell of a central computer, Univac, which plans world conquest. Nice special effects and refreshing comedy runs through Cyril Hume's screenplay. Philip Abbott, Diane Brewster, Harold J. Stone, Robert H. Harris. Directed by Herman Hoffman.

**INVISIBLE CREATURE (1960).** Made in Britain as THE HOUSE IN MARSH ROAD, this supernatural thriller is about a husband who plans to murder his wife but finds she is protected by a spirit. Directed by Montgomery Tully. Tony Wright, Patricia Dainton, Sandra Dorne.

**INVISIBLE DEAD (197?).** Spanish horror thriller starring Howard Vernon and Nadine Pascal. A young scientist must retrieve his daughter from a crazy scientist living in a castle of potential doom. (VC)

**INVISIBLE DR. MABUSE, THE (1961).** Mediocre West German revival of the super archvillain created by novelist Norbert Jacques and made famous on celluloid by German filmmaker Fritz Lang in the 1920s. Dr. Mabuse (Wolfgang Priess) schemes to steal a formula for invisibility and take over the world. His nemesis is government man Les Barker. Karin Dor, Werner Peters. Directed by Harold Reinl.

**GHOST, THE (1941).** Poverty-stricken Monogram mess produced by Sam Katzman and starring Bela Lugosi as confused, mixed-up Charles Kessler who is hypnotizing his wife into committing murders. They don't come more pathetic than this. Directed by Joseph H. Lewis. Betty Compson, John McGuire, Polly Ann Young. (VC)

**INVISIBLE HORROR, THE.** See **INVISIBLE DR. MABUSE, THE.**

**INVISIBLE INVADERS, THE (1959).** Riotously inept low budgeter, every scene a treat for buffs taking perverse delight in watching disasters. Invisible aliens, hiding on the moon, fly to Earth and, changing their molecular structure, take possession of corpses to become a conquering army of walking dead. They start with Dr. Karol Noymann (John Carradine in a cameo). Really bad special effects and terrible acting by John Agar, Jean Byron and Robert Hutton provide a laugh-a-minute, as do the solemn narrator and documentary footage that plug up all the incompetencies in Samuel Newman's script. Director Edward L. Cahn has a style as stiff as the walking dead, and one wonders if George Romero was inspired by this film's hulking dead men. Even Paul Dunlap's music is utterly corny. By all means, see it and revel in its absolute ineptitude.

**INVISIBLE KILLER, THE (1940).** Quickie PRC mystery thriller in which sound is diabolically utilized as an instrument of murder. Sounds unsound, looks unsound. Directed by Sam Newfield. Roland Drew, Grace Bradley.

**INVISIBLE MAN, THE (1933).** The irony of Universal's adaptation of H. G. Wells' novel about scientist Jack Griffin (who discovers monocaine, a drug that renders him invisible) is that it made a star of Claude Rains, even though he is seldom seen, only heard, while swathed in bandages and wearing black goggles. Because of the formula, he is turned into a power-mad killer. "Suddenly I realized the power I had, the power to rule, to make the world grovel at my feet," he proclaims. James Whale's direction has yet to become dated, and the effects, for their day, are marvelous. So are character bits by Una O'Connor, John Carradine, Dwight Frye, E. E. Clive, Gloria Stuart and William Harrigan. Excellent dialogue adapted by R. C. Sherriff.

**INVISIBLE MAN, THE (1975).** This Universal pilot for a series is an updated, science-fictional version of the H. G. Wells novel. David McCallum is Dr. Daniel Weston, a scientist involved in the development of a laser beam who stumbles across the secret of invisibility. He decides to keep it a secret from mankind and flees. Of course, others who want the secret chase after him. Directed by Robert Michael Lewis, written-produced by Steven Bochco. Melinda Fee, Jackie Cooper, Henry Darrow, Arch Johnson.

**CLAUDE RAINS AS 'THE INVISIBLE MAN'**

**INVISIBLE MAN'S RETURN, THE (1940).** Sequel to THE INVISIBLE MAN stars Vincent Price as the brother of scientist Jack Griffin. Price is seldom seen but often heard once he takes a duocaine inoculation and is rendered unseeable. Escaping prison (where he has been unjustly sent), he searches for Jack's real killer. The effects are what you would expect as Price wraps and unwraps himself and as objects float. Not classic, but enjoyable. Joe May directed the Lester Cole-Curt Siodmak script. Nan Grey, Sir Cedric Hardwicke, John Sutton, Alan Napier, Cecil Kellaway.

**INVISIBLE MAN'S REVENGE, THE (1944).** Sequel to a sequel has little to do with Wells' fantasy, or to the two films preceding it. Scientist John Carradine discovers a formula for

*"The dead will kill the living and the people of Earth will cease to exist."*
*—John Carradine as Dr. Karol Noymann in **INVISIBLE INVADERS.***

invisibility via injection, which he gives to wrongly-accused Jon Hall so he can escape pursuers and track down the culprits who cheated him out of a diamond mine. More floating objects and invisible man trickery, but Ford Beebe's direction is lackluster. Evelyn Ankers, Alan Curtis, Gale Sondergaard, Ian Wolfe, Lester Matthews, Billy Bevans.

**INVISIBLE MONSTER. See SLAVES OF THE INVISIBLE MONSTER.**

**INVISIBLE RAY, THE (1936).** Boris Karloff is scientist Janos Rukh, who captures light rays from the past and finds an ancient meteor in the Carpathians imbued with "Radium X," a substance more powerful than radium which infects Karloff with a luminous radioactivity that kills anything he touches. On the expedition is Bela Lugosi as Dr. Felix Benet, a sympathetic scientist. The effects are innovative in this unusually lively Universal horror thriller. Directed by Lambert Hillyer. Frances Drake, Frank Lawton, Beulah Bondi, Walter Kingsford, Frank Reicher. (VC)

**INVISIBLE STRANGLER (1984).** Originally produced in 1976 as THE ASTRAL FACTOR, but unreleased for many years . . . Robert Foxworth is a L.A. cop investigating strangulation murders committed by a criminal who escaped from prison using his ESP powers of invisibility. The familiar faces include Stephanie Powers, Elke Sommer, Sue Lyon, Leslie Parrish, Mariana Hill, Alex Dreier, Percy Rodrigues and John Hart. Directed by John Florea. (VC)

**INVISIBLE TERROR, THE (1963).** This West German swipe of THE INVISIBLE MAN—despite amateurish acting and poor action—takes on a life of its own, its absurdities encouraging one to ask: How could this have been produced? Director Raphael Nussbeaum knows nothing about pacing or directing actors, and he and co-writer Wladimir Semitjof know nothing about plots or characters. Just as baffled are players Hanaes Hauser, Ellen Schwiers and Hans Borsody. It has something to do with a doctor who discovers a serum for invisibility. The effects are so bad as to be laughable. In short, total human ineptitude that's a kick to watch. So be a masochist and watch.

**INVISIBLE WOMAN, THE (1940).** No connection to THE INVISIBLE MAN outside of exploitation of the title. John Barrymore, appearing in one of his last roles, invents a machine that renders fashion model Virginia Bruce invisible. Foreign spies pursue the machine and Miss Bruce. The usual cliched invisible sight gags, without any new twists. Worth watching, though, for its cast: Shemp Howard, John Howard, Charles Ruggles, Oscar Homolka, Maria Montez, Margaret Hamilton. Directed by Edward Sutherland.

**INVISIBLE WOMAN, THE (1983).** Utterly empty TV-movie—possibly the worst ever produced, featuring the most invisible production values of our time. Alan J. Levi, who gave us an INVISIBLE MAN series in 1975 with David McCallum, might have faded into nothingness after this nonsubstance about a research scientist (Bob Denver) whose test chimpanzee accidentally mixes a formula and vanishes. Along comes Alexa Hamilton to become the Invisible Woman. Photographed on tape, which adds to its non-production look. Not a single "invisible" joke that wasn't done better in the TOPPER series, and you'll watch a cast waste away to nothing: Jonathan Banks, David Doyle, George Gobel, Harvey Korman, Ron Palilo, Mel Stewart. So bad it even has a laugh track. Vapid vaporousness.

**INVITATION TO HELL (1984).** TV-movie inspired by POLTERGEIST in which inventor Robert Urich arrives at the headquarters of a strange corporation, Micro Digitech, to begin experiments on a new spacesuit for a Venus expedition that has laser weaponry built into its sleeves and has a helmet that can detect non-human lifeforms. A seductive demon from Hell (Susan Lucci) is meanwhile luring everyone through the portals of her country club into the depths of hell in order to control their souls. When Urich's wife (Joanna Cassidy) and children are mind-zapped, he dons the armored spacesuit for his descent into Hell. Silly premise never convinces. Directed by Wes Craven. (VC)

**IRON WARRIOR (1986).** Third entry in the forgettable Ator

series, this time shot on the isle of Malta as the sword-wielding Poor Man's Conan (Miles O'Keeffe, still looking awful in a phony wig) fights monsters and assorted villains to protect Princess Janna (Savina Gersak), who's quite something to look at even if the film is not. Directed by that Italian potboiling king, Al Bradley, who here adds an "e" to his name following some awful sci-fi non-thrillers.

**IS THIS TRIP REALLY NECESSARY? (1969).** John Carradine, a movie director who muddles fantasy with reality after taking LSD, uses an Iron Maiden to kill actresses who star in his pornographic flicks. Is this film really necessary? Produced-directed by Ben Dendit. Marvin Miller, Carol Kane.

**ISABEL (1968).** Genevieve Bujold is going mad, seeing illusions, apparitions and visions in this confusing Canadian psychological study written-produced-directed by Paul Almond. What does it all mean? You tell us. Mark Strange.

**ISLAND, THE (1980).** This Zanuck-Brown production of Peter Benchley's novel proposes a solution to the Bermuda Triangle mystery: All those boats and people are vanishing because modern descendants of 17th Century pirates are still plying the trade. An exciting premise, but Benchley's script is insipid and the characterizations are atrocious. STAR WARS has greater believability when magazine researcher Michael Caine and his young son seek an answer to the mystery by acting as decoys. David Warner and his bloodthirsty pirates are supposed to have a code all their own, but it's a ridiculous life they lead, plunging the film into laughability. The ending includes the worst mock heroics in movie history. A tremendous flop, director Michael Ritchie's worst. Angela McGregor, Frank Middlemass. (VC)

**ISLAND AT THE TOP OF THE WORLD (1974).** Inferior Disney adventure-fantasy with poor effects and a horribly mangled story—a literary massacre of Ian Cameron's THE LOST ONES. David Hartman, hardly the stuff movie heroes are made of, leads an expedition to the polar regions in the airship Hyperion in 1908. The team discovers a long-forgotten kingdom ruled by bloodthirsty Vikings. This "adventure epic" misses by miles, turning its potential fun and excitement into turgidity. Directed by Robert Stevenson. Donald Sinden, Jacques Marin, Mako. (VC)

**ISLAND CLAWS (1982).** Old-fashioned giant-monster-on-the-rampage flick, enhanced by Florida photography and the personas of Robert Lansing and Barry Nelson. A research team is experimenting with crustaceans when an atomic energy malfunction creates one huge monster crab killer and forces the little crabbers to turn against mankind, with a taste for People Thermidor. Thrills are minimal until the monster crab attacks. The story (by Jack Cowden and underwater stuntman Ricou Browning) is predictable if you've seen monster movies of the 1950s. Herman Caredenas directs. Jo McDonnell, Nita Talbot. (VC)

**ISLAND OF BLOOD (1986).** Actors working on a rock 'n roll film begin dying according to a song's lyrics. Crime of a rhythm. Jimmy Williams, Dean Richards. (VC)

**ISLAND OF DR. MOREAU, THE (1977).** Effective adaptation of H. G. Wells' novel with Burt Lancaster as the demented albeit earnest doctor who converts animals into half-men through vivisection. The "creative make-up" is excellent, resulting in a menagerie of "manbeasts" led by Richard Basehart as the Sayer of the Law. The tropical rain forests near St. Croix in the Virgin Islands are a superb location for director Don Taylor. Michael York and Barbara Carrera as the lovers confronted with Moreau's horrors make for a sympathetic couple. The ending is ambiguous, but it still works. ISLAND OF LOST SOULS was the 1933 version starring Charles Laughton, and that was a good one too. Watch for Nick Cravat as M'Ling. (VC)

**ISLAND OF LIVING HORROR, THE. See BRIDES OF BLOOD.** (Be careful when you say "I do"!)

**ISLAND OF LOST SOULS (1933).** Repelling though intriguing adaptation of H. G. Wells' thoughtful novel about the mad Dr. Moreau, who grafts animals into men in his "House of Pain" to change the process of evolution. Charles Laughton,

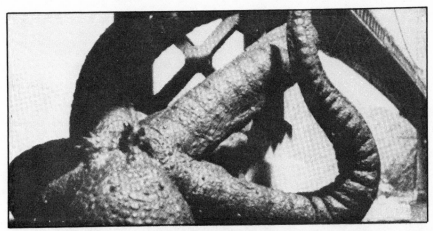

**TWO TENTACLES MISSING: RAY HARRYHAUSEN'S KILLER OCTOPUS IN
'IT CAME FROM BENEATH THE SEA'**

as the vivisectionist who presides God-like over his creatures, is on the hammy side, but this very overplaying is what makes Moreau seem above the affairs of ordinary men, destined to change science. Bela Lugosi as the wolfman has a grotesquely satisfying role. Not for the squeamish as the beasts-men scamper about in mental anguish. Written by Philip Wylie, directed by Erle C. Kenton and starring Richard Arlen as the young shipwrecked hero. One of the best horror films of the 1930s.

**ISLAND OF LOST WOMEN (1959).** Stranded fliers find a lost scientist (Alan Napier) and his beautiful daughters . . . there's a death ray and other overused fantasy elements to round out this pulp magazine-inspired adventure tale. Directed by Frank Tuttle. Jeff Richards, Diane Jergens, George Brand, Gavin Muir, John Smith, June Blair.

**ISLAND OF TERROR (1967).** An isolated community is under attack by man-produced silicate monsters that suck the bone marrow of humans. Director Terence Fisher has infused tongue-in-cheek with the macabre to avoid the humdrum in this sometimes sickening nightmare. Silicates are crawling, snake-like tentacles which slither around corners when you least expect them. They'll have you jumping as they wriggle up stairways and latch onto human flesh. There's also a great sequence where Peter Cushing has to cut off his own hand to save himself from the clutching terrors. There's a macabre epilogue, proving the whole thing was a black joke to Fisher and producer Richard Gordon. Niall MacGinnis, Edward Judd, Eddie Byrne.

**ISLAND OF THE BURNING DOOMED (1967).** Produced in Britain as NIGHT OF THE BIG HEAT, this is a simmering adaptation of a John Lymington novel in which Christopher Lee, Peter Cushing and other familiar faces are attacked by aliens capable of burning measly humans to death with a heat wave. But the film, unlike the characters, never catches fire. Directed by Terence Fisher.

**ISLAND OF THE DAMNED (1976).** Spanish horror thriller is an obvious exploitation film in which a pregnant wife and her husband visit a pleasure island not far from Benavid to find all the adults dead and homicidal children eager to slaughter more. On a less obvious level, the film points out how children become victims of adult madness through civil war and strife. Hence, their revenge! Luis Perafiel's script never becomes that explicit but it's still food for thought. Where it does become explicit is in the violence of the children as they close in on the couple, forcing them to commit acts of mayhem to escape. Above average. Directed by Narciso Ibanez Serrador.

**ISLAND OF THE DOOMED. See MAN-EATER OF HYDRA.**

(You're just in time for dinner.)

**ISLAND OF THE LOST (1968).** Insignificant Ivan Tors TV-movie in which explorer-anthropologist Richard Greene and five young fellow travelers discover a Pacific island inhabited by prehistoric sabertooth wolves, nine-gill sharks, ferocious ostriches, etc. A blending of FLIPPER and SWISS FAMILY ROBINSON as the stranded band meets a native (who looks like Sabu the Jungle Boy) living on the island as part of a survival course imposed by his tribe. Written by Tors and Richard Carlson, with Ricou Browning handling the underwater photography.

**ISLE OF THE DEAD (1945).** Arnold Boecklin's painting, Die Todinsel, inspired this low-key Val Lewton horror chiller, strongly atmospheric but slow under Mark Robson's direction. One of Boris Karloff's strangest roles—he portrays a tyrannical Greek general in the year 1912 (the Balkan War is raging) who believes in "vrykolakas," Greek vampires. When a sinister plague infects the island, Karloff quarantines everyone and, one by one, the assorted characters meet their doom. Ellen Drew, Jason Robards Sr., Alan Napier, Katherine Emery. (VC)

**ISLE OF THE FISHMEN. See SCREAMERS, THE.**

**ISLE OF THE SNAKE PEOPLE. See SNAKE PEOPLE, THE.** (Slither, don't walk, to that reference!)

**ISN'T IT SHOCKING? (1973).** Psychomurder TV-movie with Edmond O'Brien as gentle, peace-loving Justin Oates, who is killing old folks in a small Oregon community with a strange electronic device, and watching as fledgling sheriff Alan Alda bumbles his way to a solution. O'Brien's gimmick is to chew gum when he's getting ready to kill. Directed by John Badham. Louise Lasser, Ruth Gordon, Will Geer, Lloyd Nolan, Liam Dunn, Pat Quinn.

**IT (1966).** The Golem is the Jewish Avenger—a creature of clay wreaking havoc on desecrators. Roddy McDowall is a batty museum curator keeping the mummified body of the Golem as an exhibit who finally misuses the creature for evil revenge. The thing goes berserk, destroying Hammersmith Bridge and kidnapping Jill Haworth. Written-produced-directed by Herbert J. Leder.

**IT CAME FROM BENEATH THE SEA (1954).** Collaboration between producers Charles Schneer and Sam Katzman and stop motion animator Ray Harryhausen results in an average but nostalgic monster flick about a giant octopus awakened by an atomic blast and attracted to San Francisco Bay. The creature (with only six tentacles, due to Katzman's insufficient budget) attacks the Golden Gate Bridge and Embarcadero. This has its fun moments but is strictly a B movie . . . Harryhausen's best work was yet to come. Directed rather indifferently by Robert Gordon. Donald Curtis and Kenneth Tobey still have time to woo scientist Faith Domergue during the mayhem. Ian Keith, Harry Lauter, Del Courtney. (VC)

**IT CAME FROM HOLLYWOOD (1982).** Compilation of the best "worst" scenes from genre movies, emphasis on monsters, horror and drugs. Comedians appear in camped-up performances, each covering specialized themes. Gilda Radner does Gorillas and Musical Memories; Cheech and Chong cover (naturally) Getting High, Giants, and Animal Kingdom Goes Berserk; Dan Aykroyd deals with Brains, Aliens and Troubled Teenagers. There's a salute to Edward Wood Jr. (PLAN 9 FROM OUTER SPACE) and Prevues of Coming Attractions and Technical Triumphs (would you believe FLYING DISC MAN FROM MARS?). The guest hosts are superfluous—the clips can stand alone. Anyway, fans, you'll see scenes from WHITE GORILLA, BRAIN THAT WOULDN'T DIE, BRIDE OF THE MONSTER, etc. Hollywood at its funniest—and dumbiest. (VC)

**IT CAME FROM OUTER SPACE (1953).** Harry Essex's screenplay is based on a Ray Bradbury premise, which was greatly altered before this Universal-International film went before the 3-D cameras. It still rises above its B-movie cliches as a plea for better understanding between races. This is Jack Arnold's best directorial work, for he captures a desert eeriness as bug-eyed aliens crashland their ship near astronomer Richard Carlson's isolated home. The extraterrestrials, dubbed Xenomorphs, are giant eyeball creatures capable of assuming human forms. A "fish-eye" lens is used to simulate the point of view of the creatures. Done with flourish and style; well photographed in 3-D; one of the best science-fiction films of the 1950s, faults and all. Barbara Rush provides the obligatory love interest, Charles Drake is the disbelieving sheriff, and Russell Johnson and Joe Sawyer portray possessed telephone linemen. (VC)

**IT CAME UPON A MIDNIGHT CLEAR (1984).** Sappy TV-movie starring Mickey Rooney as a New York cop who suffers a fatal heart attack and goes to Heaven, requesting of St. Peter (George Gaynes) that he be allowed to spend one final Christmas on Earth with his grandson (Scott Grimes). Sentimental cornpone in Central Park. Barrie Youngfellow.

**IT CAME . . . WITHOUT WARNING (1980).** Here's a warning: Beware this science-fiction terror tale in which an alien stalks Earthlings for trophies to adorn his spaceship walls. Martin Landau and Jack Palance deserve the Overacting Awards of 1980; they are genuinely terrible as would-be vic-

tims of the creature, who uses ugly disc-shaped suckers for "bullets." Slurp sqwk glump: those are sounds made by the Incredibly Hungry Disc Beasties. They are effective, even if Greydon Clark's direction isn't. Cameron Mitchell, Neville Brand, Sue Ane Langdon, Larry Storch, Ralph Meeker.

**IT CONQUERED THE WORLD (1956).** "It" does nothing of the sort—"it" is one sad-looking Venusivian hiding in a cave that blows its invasion because "it" is dumb enough to rely on Lee Van Cleef to carry out "its" evil bidding. And dumb enough to send a squad of bat creatures to kill Beverly Garland, thereby tipping off Peter Graves to what is happening. This Roger Corman produced-directed quickie ranks as one of his all-time worst. Dick Miller, Russ Bender, Sally Fraser, Jonathan Haze, Charles B. Griffith.

**IT FELL FROM THE SKY.** See **ALIEN DEAD, THE.**

**IT GROWS ON TREES (1952).** Cute comedy from Universal-International in which a heart-warming family discovers it has a tree in the backyard capable of a new greenery—greenbacks, to be precise. Directed by Arthur Lubin. Irene Dunne, Dean Jagger, Les Tremayne, Joan Evans, Richard Crenna, Sandy Descher.

**IT HAPPENED AT LAKE WOOD MANOR (1977).** Lake Wood is minor as far as horror is concerned. This TV-movie, now in syndication as ANTS, is preposterous: Swarms of irate ants attack a resort, imprisoning dull and unimaginative individuals inside. Ants' antisocial behavior is blamed on pesticides and man's carelessness toward nature, but hasn't that already been overworked by frogs? The suspense is ersatz, the menace of these Hymenopteras uninvolving . . . you wouldn't hesitate to go on a picnic. In fact, do—it beats this dreary stuff. Directed by Robert Scheerer. The best screamer in the cast is Suzanne Somers. Robert Foxworth, Lynda Day George, Myrna Loy, Bernie Casey, Steve Franken, Anita Gillette. (VC)

**IT HAPPENED HERE (1966).** Two Englishmen (Kevin Brownlow and Andrew Mollo) spent eight years and $20,000 to produce this pseudodocumentary depicting what might have happened had Hitler invaded England in 1943 and conquered the Empire. Britain is depicted under Fascist rule (Gestapo troops march past Big Ben; SS troopers flirt with girls on the Thames) but an underground group fights the invaders. Rough camera work and a soundtrack often unintelligible are deficits that give this flight-of- fiction a hard-edged reality. Pauline Murray, Sebastian Shaw, Fiona Leland.

**IT HAPPENED ONE CHRISTMAS (1977).** Inferior remake of IT'S A WONDERFUL LIFE, with the Jimmy Stewart role

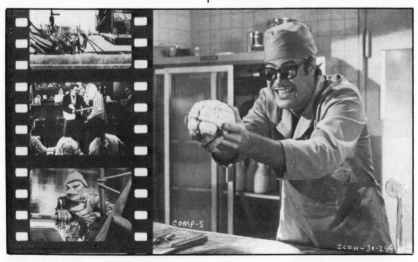

**DAN AYKROYD INTRODUCES BRAIN(LESS) MOVIES IN 'IT CAME FROM HOLLYWOOD'**

rewritten for Marlo Thomas, who now fights despair after a life of self-sacrifice. It just didn't happen that Christmas. Cloris Leachman, Wayne Rogers, Orson Welles, Doris Roberts, Barney Martin. Directed by Donald Wrye.

**IT HAPPENED TOMORROW (1944).** Dick Powell can read tomorrow's news today, provided by an old ghost. What happens when he reads his own obituary? Directed by Rene Clair. Linda Darnell, Jack Oakie, Eddie Acuff, Edgar Kennedy, Marian Martin, John Philliber.

**IT HAPPENS EVERY SPRING (1949).** For fantasy fans, baseball lovers, romanticists and scientists. Professor Ray Milland invents an anti-wood substance. Think what that could mean if applied to a baseball. So, as his spitball curves around his swinging bat in the majors, he becomes a big league pitcher and carries a losing team to the World Series. It's the whimsical side to THE NATURAL. Marvelous comedy with Jean Peters as love interest and Paul Douglas as a blustering manager. A film like this should happen every spring. Directed by Lloyd Bacon. Alan Hale Jr., Ray Collins, Ed Begley, Ray Teal, Gene Evans.

**IT LIVES AGAIN.** Videocassette title for **IT'S ALIVE II.**

**IT! THE TERROR FROM BEYOND SPACE (1958).** Epitome of science-fiction monster movies of the 1950s, more bearable than its title would suggest thanks to a decent script by professional fantasy writer Jerome Bixby. Ray "Crash" Corrigan dons the traditional rubber suit to play a vampire-style Martian which stows away on a rocketship and then, when deep in space, develops a thirst that can't be quenched at the snack bar. That's when astronauts Marshall Thompson, Shawn Smith, Ann Doran and Kim Spalding get it in the neck. Frequently compared to ALIEN. Directed by "quickie master" Edward L. Cahn.

**IT'S A DOG'S LIFE (1955).** Capricious fluff about a dog with human intelligence; the story is narrated by the voice of the dog (or is it the voice of Vic Morrow?). No, the film is not a dog; the dog is a dog. Directed by Herman Hoffman. Edmund Gwenn, Jeff Richards, Dean Jagger, Sally Fraser, Richard Anderson. Scripted by John Michael Hayes.

**IT'S A WONDERFUL LIFE (1946).** Capra-corn as Hollywood's producer-director Frank Capra indulges in whimsical nostalgia to present a slice of unforgettable Americana. Guardian Angel Clarence (Henry Travers) is dispatched to a small Wisconsin town to show Jimmy Stewart, a bitter, disillusioned young man, what might have happened had he never been born. A touch of A CHRISTMAS CAROL makes this an exceptionally thoughtful and penetrating slice of life, which Capra scripted with the help of Frances Goodrich and Albert Hackett. A new videocassette version was issued in computerized color. Donna Reed, Lionel Barrymore, Thomas Mitchell, Gloria Grahame, Ward Bond. Wonderful music by Dimitri Tiomkin. (VC)

**IT'S ALIVE (1968).** Pathetic quickie, sloppily edited and poorly acted, one of the worst low budget jobs of its kind—give credit to writer-producer-director Larry Buchanan for botching this one thoroughly. A crazy rancher who collects snakes and crawlies has also found a "lizard amphibian" in a cave, so he feeds it passers-by. Along comes Tommy Kirk (who just happens to be a paleontologist) plus another couple, and they're all thrown to the Masasaurus. The most exciting thing is not the creature—it's a rubber-suited fake—but watching blonde Shirley Bonne walk around in a yellow miniskirt. Performances are consistently sad.

**IT'S ALIVE (1975).** Larry Cohen, creator of TV's THE INVADERS and director-writer of unusual features (DEMON, THE STUFF), wrote and directed this gruesome shocker about an infamous infant who slides from the womb with claws, fangs, sharp teeth and other implements for killing doctors and nurses before they even have time to spank his spiked behind. While it sounds like the ultimate nightmare, rolling birth and death into one act, Cohen, through his strange sensibility, creates the ambience of an abnormal world tainted by birth control pills, poisonous chemicals, smoggy air and atomic fallout. Mother's love will never be the same. Your skin will crawl as the bloodthirsty bambino

(created from the nightmares of Rick Baker) lurks around every corner, waiting to strike. Cohen keeps his monster out of camera range most of the time, thereby building suspense, and allowing the shocks to come when they should. John Ryan, Sharon Farrell, Guy Stockwell, Andrew Duggan, Michael Ansara. (VC)

**IT'S ALIVE II (1978).** Larry Cohen's IT'S ALIVE was a powerful indictment against our misuse of atomic power and drugs, but this sequel fails in the delivery room. Call it stillborn. Cohen's writing and directing are utterly off the mark in depicting another baby-faced killer sliding from a womb with claws and teeth to kill. Parents Frederic Forrest and Kathleen Lloyd flee with the mutant to a secret incubation hideout where other baby-monsters are undergoing study by scientist Andrew Duggan and the father from the first film, John Ryan. (Duggan believes the babies are "the next step in evolution so we can survive the pollution of our planet.") Heaven forbid! What would the mothers of America say? Credit Rick Baker for the hideously fanged, high-headed creatures infrequently shown during Cohen's hide-and-seek direction. John Marley, Eddie Constantine. In videocassette as **IT LIVES AGAIN.**

**IT'S NOT THE SIZE THAT COUNTS (1974).** Sequel to PERCY, known in England as PERCY'S PROGRESS . . . a continuation of the adventures of the man with the first penis transplant . . . but here the concept shrinks to nothing. On top of the misplaced organ theme, this deals with a chemical in the water making men impotent. Ooops, there goes sex, just when you needed it most. Denholm Elliott, Elke Sommer, Vincent Price, Judy Geeson, Milo O'Shea, Julie Ege, George Coulouris. Directed by Ralph Thomas.

**I'VE LIVED BEFORE (1956).** Low budget, mildly interesting tale of reincarnation from Universal. Jock Mahoney, a sympathetic airline pilot, believes he is the reincarnation of a flyer shot down over France on April 29, 1918. John McIntire is the doctor who talks about psychoses and neuroses and helps Mahoney to sort out his life. Ann Harding is the girl who provides a link between Mahoney and the Spad flyer. Directed by Richard Bartlett. Leigh Snowden, April Kent, Jerry Paris, Raymond Bailey.

**IVORY APE, THE (1980).** You thought King Kong had problems . . . Rangi is an ape who simply wants to be left alone. But no such luck. Captured and placed aboard a freighter, she breaks her bonds and escapes to Bermuda, where the local constabulary wants to shoot her down after she attacks and kills her trackers. Anthropologist Cindy Pickett and Steven Keats want to take Rangi alive, while big game hunter Jack Palance has more fatal ideas in mind. Never very exciting—the William Overgard script unfolds in a predictable fashion, and there's more dialogue than action. The best moment comes when Palance recounts how a crocodile once carried away his son in its jaws. Directed by Tom Kotani on location. Earl Hyman, Derek Partridge.

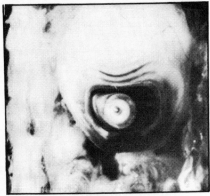

**A XENOMORPH:**
**'IT CAME FROM OUTER SPACE'**

KD.

*"Invaders of my universe! Your destiny is to die!"—The Alien Presence*
in ***JOURNEY TO THE SEVENTH PLANET.***

**JABBERWOCKY (1977).** British satire, inspired work by Monty Python alumnus Terry Gilliam, who directed and co-wrote (with Charles Alverson). King Bruno the Questionable (Max Wall) must defeat a dragon monster that is so awful, peasants would rather catch the plague. In the vein of MONTY PYTHON AND THE HOLY GRAIL, with blood, dis-memberment, wallowing in dirt. A treat for those who like humor as dark as the ages in which this medieval parody is set. Michael Palin portrays the dragon-stalking peasant mis-taken for a prince. Deborah Fallender. (VC)

**JACK AND THE BEANSTALK (1952).** Universal-Internation-al fantasy-comedy with Lou Costello as a babysitter reading the fable to an obnoxious brat. Presto: The fable lives. Cos-tello becomes the simpleton Jack and Bud Abbott plays the village butcher "boy." Buddy Baer is the ogre—ferocious but appealing enough not to scare the kids for whom this fluff was intended. Directed by Jean Yarbrough. Dorothy Ford, William Farnum, Barbara Brown. (VC)

**JACK THE GIANT KILLER (1962).** Director Nathan Juran and actors Kerwin Mathews and Torin Thatcher re-teamed again after the success of SEVENTH VOYAGE OF SINBAD, but this fantasy-adventure (written by Orville Hampton) sorely needs the Harryhausen touch. While Don Beddoe is effective as a verse-spouting leprechaun, the giants, sea serpents, griffins and flying witches leave much to be desired. Mathews is again brave of heart, Thatcher is treacherous as Pendragon the Sorcerer and Judi Meredith is enchantingly beautiful. Youngsters will enjoy, adults may squirm. Jim Dan-forth special effects.

**JACK THE RIPPER (1958).** Episodes from the flop series THE VEIL, repackaged as a TV feature. Boris Karloff intro-duces four tales of terror and has roles in some: "Jack the Ripper," "Summer Heat," "Vision of Crime" and "Food on the Table." Directed by David MacDonald. Niall MacGinnis, Clif-ford Evans, Morris Ankrum, Robert Griffin.

**JACK THE RIPPER (1959).** This version of the Whitechapel murders of the 1880s and the perverted maniac who com-mitted the heinous crimes is a plight of fancy with little bear-ing on facts. Written by Jimmy Sangster, and directed by Robert Baker and Monty Berman, this British film was picked up by Joseph E. Levine, who spent millions for U.S. exploita-

tion. It didn't help this, one of the least effective accounts of the infamous slasher. Lee Patterson, Eddie Byrne, Ewen Solon (the Ripper).

**JACK THE RIPPER (1976).** This Jack tears it! A totally inac-curate German-Swiss depiction of the infamous London mur-ders in Whitechapel, with facts discarded by screenwriter-director Jesse Franco in favor of brutish exploitation. Klaus Kinski portrays the sexual brute as a despicable freako who stops at nothing to murder and fornicate simultaneously. Clinically sickening in its pandering to detail. Josephine Chaplin, Herbert Fux, Lina Romay. (VC)

**JACK'S WIFE.** See SEASON OF THE WITCH.

**JADE MASK, THE (1945).** Charlie Chan programmer with a weak fantasy element: a formula for making wood as hard as steel. Otherwise, petrified whodunit fare, with phony walk-ing dead men and an unscary mansion with secret pas-sageways. Not for the jaded. Directed by Phil Rosen. Sidney Toler, Mantan Moreland.

**JALOPY (1953).** Broken-down Bowery Boys vehicle with stripped gears never gets out of first and stalls after the credits. Huntz Hall creates a formula that is a love potion and a high-powered auto fuel. Directed by William Beaudine without overdrive. All the usual delinquents, plus Robert Lowery as an adult baddie.

**JAMES TONT, OPERATION D.U.E. (1966).** French-Italian James Bond spoof, lowbrow comedy with too few laughs. Gimmicks and pretty girls are aplenty, but the secret agents (vying for a hormone substance that turns folks young or old) are of poor Bondage. Operation D.U.D. Directed by Bruno Corbucci. Landro Buzzanca, France Anglade. A sequel, JAMES TONT, OPERAZIONE U.N.O., was so poor it never reached U.S. shores. Lucky U.S.

**JASON AND THE ARGONAUTS (1963).** Superb mythologi-cal fantasy, directed by Don Chaffey, with stop motion by the incomparable Ray Harryhausen. A recounting of the adven-tures of Jason and his warriors who dare the dangers of a bronze giant named Talos, the winged harpies, the seven-headed Hydra and sword-wielding skeletons to claim the Gol-den Fleece. Todd Armstrong is a superb Jason, watched from on high by the Gods of Mt. Olympus. The link between mortal and immortal becomes a compelling element to the Jan Read-Beverly Cross script. As picturesque, picaresque fantasy, this is hard to top. Nancy Kovack appears as Medea, Honor Blackman and Niall MacGinnis are Goddess and God, Nigel Green is the brave but short-lived Hercules. A great score by Bernard Herrmann enhances this British-U.S. effort. (VC)

**JASSY (1948).** Margaret Lockwood, Patricia Roc, Dennis Price and Cathleen Nesbitt star in this British thriller in which a gypsy girl is accused of her husband's death and those around her realize she has psychic power. Moody and atmospheric, more thriller than fantasy. Directed by Bernard Knowles. Sassy, classy, not too trashy.

**JAWS (1975).** Box office smash based on the so-so albeit best-selling novel by Peter Benchley, an all-time record setter. Under Steven Spielberg's direction, this tale of terror is also a classic adventure saga, ingeniously mounted to evoke our primeval fears as a Great White Shark (25 feet long) attacks the New England community of Amity. After early episodes in which humans are bait or narrowly escape the superfish, sharkfighters Robert Shaw, Richard Dreyfuss and Roy Scheider set out aboard the Orca to kill the monster. In addition to taut, unbearable action sequences and great shark effects, there are subtle horrors too, such as when Shaw, a survivor of the sinking of the U.S. Indianapolis in 1945, describes how men were eaten alive. Carl Gottlieb and Spielberg hashed out the final story. This all-time fish whopper did for public beaches what ALIEN did for space travel. The great "shark machine" music score is by John Williams. Secondary roles by Lorraine Gray (as the sheriff's wife) and Murray Hamilton as the mayor who doesn't want the beaches closed despite the threat. (VC)

**JAWS II (1978).** This sequel to the smasheroo inspired by Peter Benchley's novel is afloat in too-familiar waters and totally lacks the bite of the original. Director Jeannot Szwarc imitates Spielberg in shameless, unimaginative style, but captures none of the visceral terror. Bruce the Mechanical Shark looks exactly that as he "attacks" youngsters trapped on the high seas. Surely a colossal case of overbite. Carl Gottlieb co-scripted with Howard Sackler. Returning in their original roles are Roy Scheider as the sheriff, Lorraine Gary

as his wife and Murray Hamilton, still obnoxious as hell as the mayor. (VC)

**JAWS 3-D (1983).** What could have been gnashing thrills, Bruce the Shark in 3-D, is a major disappointment when a baby Great White and 35-foot-long mother enter the lagoon of a newly opened seaworld park in Florida and attack swimmers and the underwater observation rooms and corridors. Except for a few scenes where the behemoth swallows a man, or bumps its vengeful snout against plucky heroine Bess Armstrong, JAWS 3-D strangely lacks excitement. It's hard to understand the underlit scenes (after all, this came from Universal) the stupid characters (did Richard Matheson and Carl Gottlieb really write this dribble?), and the juvenile, almost Porky's approach. A few 3-D effects are fine (such as a floating severed arm), but stereovision adds little to the dimensions of this mediocre attempt. Lou Gossett Jr. is the only cast member who seems to take his role seriously as the park supervisor faced with maintaining calm during the disaster—Dennis Quaid, Lisa Mauer and Armstrong swim against the current. Production designer Joe Alves was graduated to director but he needs to be thrown back in to take more lessons. Simon MacCorkindale, Barbara Eden. (VC)

**JAWS OF DEATH.** Videocassette title for **MAKO, JAWS OF DEATH.**

**JAWS OF SATAN (1983).** Terribly amateurish killer-snake movie: a King Cobra on a rampage is a demon serpent, sent from Hell to terrorize priest Fritz Weaver. If that sounds absurd, consider the awful Neanderthal special effects, the absurd screenplay by Gerry Holland and the unskilled direction of Bob Claver. The cobra commands other poisonous creatures (asps, rattlers, cottonmouths, water mocassins) to carry out its biting, so the coiled critters are turning up everywhere, harassing heroine Gretchen Corbett and hero Jon Korkes, both of the Wimp School of Acting. There's a stupid subplot about the town not wanting the snake news to leak out so the new dog-racing track can be opened. A wretched wreck filmed in Alabama. (VC)

**JAWS OF THE JUNGLE (1936).** Documentary footage of native tribes in Ceylon are intermingled with staged scenes of Devil Killer Vampire Bats flapping their way to earth to feast

**AT THE WHEEL: KERWIN MATHEWS IN 'JACK THE GIANT KILLER'**

on mortal men. Teeto, Minta, Gukar and other natives rush around the jungle, avoiding killer animals and snakes, while a narrator explains what the hell is happening. Or tries to explain. Produced by J. D. Kendis.

**J.D.'S REVENGE (1976).** Well-acted, well-written tale of the supernatural in which law student/cab driver Glynn Turman (in an excellent performance) is possessed by the spirit of a razor-wielding black lowlife murdered in 1942 in a slaughterhouse. Turman undergoes gradual transformation, tying in with some of J. D. Walker's associates from the old days, including Lou Gossett, a prizefighter-turned-preacher. Unfortunately, the motivation for the possession is a night club hypnosis act—a weakness in Jaison Starkes' otherwise compelling story, which captures a flavor of Negro character most Hollywood films miss. Above average for an apparent exploitationer. Produced-directed by Arthur Marks. Joan Pringle, David McKnight.

**JEKYLL AND HYDE PORTFOLIO, THE (1972).** Mad killer with a split personality has nothing to do with Robert Louis Stevenson, but isn't it fun for producer-director Eric J. Haims to exploit famous titles. Portfolio permanently closed. Gray Daniels, Mady Maguire, Rene Bond.

**JEKYLL AND HYDE . . . TOGETHER AGAIN (1982).** Comedian Mark Blankfield portrays a doctor who creates a white powder that, when sniffed, brings out an alter ego. It's a "beast of the 1980s" that sprouts kinky hair and kinky jewelry (yes, jewelry). And then this hybrid Hyde grows platform heels (yes, platform heels) and a gold tooth with Love inscribed on it (yes . . .). This is a self-respecting monster? Blankfield's talent could not salvage this mess (mis)conceived by writer-director Jerry Belson who demonstrates a lack of taste and respect for "an audience of the 1980s." Bess Armstrong, Tim Thomerson, George Chakiris. (VC)

**JENNIFER (1978).** Thinly disguised copy of Brian De Palma's CARRIE, exploiting a withdrawn woman (Lisa Pelikan) who possesses supernatural powers which she calls on in time of jeopardy. Jennifer is harassed by the campus bitch and her cronies at Green View School for Girls but, because she once reached into a box of poisonous serpents without being bitten, she has the Power to call upon the Winds of Fury. That's when the snake gods attack. "Give me the vengeance of the viper," she demands. You should say, "Give me the Power to resist imitation B-movies." Nina Foch, John Gavin, Jeff Corey, Florida Friebus. Directed by Brice Mack. (VC)

**JESSE JAMES MEETS FRANKENSTEIN'S DAUGHTER (1966).** An outré oater with monster motifs, a curious blend of cowboys and cut-ups, mad doctor style. Result: A laughable, unmitigated disaster that bites the dust. This abomination depicts how a pardner of fast-drawing Jesse is transmutated into a cactus-chewing Monster dubbed "Igor" when the daughter of the title implants Dr. Frankenstein's brain in his cranium. Directed by William Beaudine. John Lupton, Nestor Paiva, Narda Onyx, Jim Davis, Estelita. (VC)

**JITTERBUGS (1943).** Appealing Laurel and Hardy comedy in which the buffoons take special pills to become inflated, and then drift through the air like balloons. Douglas Fowley, Bob Bailey, Vivian Blaine. Directed by Mal St. Clair.

**J.O.E. AND THE COLONEL (1985).** "Project Omega" creates a superperfect human by recombining of molecules in a controlled environment. The result is the world's first "J-type Omega Elemental," a perfect soldier for special assignments. It's a comic book idea but treated by producer-writer Nicholas Corea with a degree of drama by allowing J.O.E. to have compassion for the three scientists who created him. The rest is predictable TV-movie formula action with J.O.E. carrying out assorted dangerous missions to satisfy his need for adrenalin-producing excitement. Just slightly above average. Directed by Ron Satlof. Terence Knox, Gary Kasper, Aimee Eccles, William Lucking, Marie Windsor, Gail Edwards, Allan Miller.

**JOE MacBETH (1956).** Shakespeare's MACBETH has been modernized (and Irishized?) and given gangster environment with the ghost of Banquo turning up at the appropriate moment. Shakespeare buffs might feel something is rotten in Hollywood; others will be amused. Paul Douglas and Ruth Roman are well matched to Philip Yordan's script, directed by Ken Hughes. Made in England.

**JOHNNY DOESN'T LIVE HERE ANYMORE (1944).** Also known as AND THEN THEY WERE MARRIED, this low budget Monogram comedy stars James Ellison as a pleasant young man who proves he's worth his salt—by spilling some. This results in the acquisition of a bad-luck gremlin, before gremlins were made popular by Spielberg. Quaint and sometimes cute; harmless to the intellect. Robert Mitchum has a bit role. Simone Simon, Chick Chandler, William Terry. Directed by Joe May.

**JOHNNY GOT HIS GUN (1971).** Dalton Trumbo's classic antiwar novel of World War I, about an American doughboy who has his arms and legs blown away and his face destroyed (along with his powers of speech and hearing), was brought to the screen as a labor of love by Trumbo, who served as writer and director. Timothy Bottoms as the hopeless quadriplegic returns to his past to create a fantasy world and retain his sanity. He also devises a way of thumping his torso on the sheet to communicate with his nurse, Diane Varsi. In one sequence, Donald Sutherland appears as Jesus Christ. Unsettling . . . many viewers may not be able to take this uncompromising portrait of war's ruinous aftermath. Marsha Hunt, Charles McGraw, Eduard Franz, Donald Barry, Bruce Morrow. (VC)

**JOHNSTOWN MONSTER, THE (1971).** British children's film (produced in Ireland) in which toddlers fake a Loch Ness monster to attract attention; but before it's over, the real Ness nemesis rears its ugly head out of the water. Written-directed by Olaf Pooley. Connor Brennan, Simon Tully.

**JONATHAN (1970).** The West Germans tackle the Dracula theme, throwing in political overtones for Greater Social Sig-

'JASON AND THE ARGONAUTS'

nificance. But it's still a vampire blitz, Fritz, so don't get too redeeming. Jonathan is an oppressor who treats his peasants like so much dirt—or clods. He gets overthrown, but the overthrower turns out to be just as bad as Jonathan. And so it goes in the world of vampires—and politics. Written-directed by Hans W. Geissendorfer. Jurgen Jung, Ilse Kunkele, Paul Albert Krumm.

**JOURNEY BACK TO OZ (1971).** Animated version of the L. Frank Baum children's classic, with the voice of Liza Minnelli for Dorothy, who is transported via cyclone into a magical land with all the familiar characters. Lyrics by Sammy Cahn and Jimmy Van Heusen. Directed by Hal Sutherland. Other voices: Milton Berle (Cowardly Lion), Herschel Bernardi (Woodenhead the Horse), Ethel Merman (Wicked Witch) and Margaret Hamilton (Aunt Em). Hamilton, by the way, was the wicked witch in the MGM film. Mel Blanc, Jack E. Leonard, Paul Lynde, Mickey Rooney. (VC)

**JOURNEY BENEATH THE DESERT (1961).** Undistinguished French-Italian actioner finds director Edgar G. Ulmer struggling with an arid script and coming up lost in the middle of story desolation. An atomic explosion reveals an entrance to the Lost City of Atlantis, still ruled by the wicked queen Antinea (Haya Harareet), who proceeds to give nosy explorer Jean-Louis Tritignant a bad time. Familiar to SHE and Maria Montez's SIREN OF ATLANTIS.

**JOURNEY INTO DARKNESS (1969).** Re-edited episodes of TV's JOURNEY TO THE UNKNOWN. "Paper Dolls," directed by James Hill, concerns quadruplet brothers psychically linked and the efforts of one brother to misuse his power. "The New People," directed by Peter Sasdy, concerns a strange life-and-death game designed by a rich young man who collects people like trophies. This short-lived British series, which crashed the U.S. briefly in 1968, was produced by Hitchcock associate Joan Harrison. Robert Reed, Michael Tolan, Michael Ripper.

**JOURNEY INTO MIDNIGHT (1969).** Like JOURNEY INTO DARKNESS, this is two one-hour episodes of the British TV series JOURNEY TO THE UNKNOWN, re-edited for syndication. "Poor Butterfly," directed by Alan Gibson, depicts a costume ball attended by the spirits of the dead. In "The Indian Spirit Guide," written by Robert Bloch and directed by Richard Baker, a phony spiritualist plans to fleece a gullible widow trying to contact her dead husband. Chad Everett, Julie Harris, Edward Fox, Tracy Reed.

**JOURNEY INTO THE BEYOND (1973).** West German ESP documentary with John Carradine as narrator. The cameras of producer Rudolph Kalmowicz rove the world to record bizarre rituals, sacrificial offerings and other odd forms of human behavior. Better than most TV pseudodocumentaries. Directed by Rolf Olsen. (VC)

**JOURNEY TO THE BEGINNING OF TIME (1966).** Czech melange of live action, animation and puppet work in depicting a group of youths drifting down the river of time and encountering dinosaurs and other heavy-footed beasts of the prehistoric past. Good work from hard-working director Karel Zeman.

**JOURNEY TO THE CENTER OF THE EARTH (1959).** Bernard Herrmann's music sets the mood for this spirited version of Jules Verne's novel about an expedition into the bowels of our planet, directed by Henry Levin with a sense of style. Light-hearted, comedic touches in the Walter Reisch-Charles Brackett screenplay contribute to an air of entertainment. The underground sets are stunningly imaginative, the adventures varied (complete with giant lizards and an erupting volcano) and the cast colorful: James Mason and Pat Boone are fine heroes leading the expedition while heroine Arlene Dahl keeps her lips well painted to lessen our fears that she might be too far from civilization. Diane Baker, Alan Napier, Thayer David. (VC)

**JOURNEY TO THE CENTER OF TIME (1968).** Back and forth in time—centuries into the future where mutants battle a dictatorship, centuries into the past with some savage dinosaurs—keeps this fantasy clipping along, even if it fails to come to grips with a logical discussion of what the hell is going on. Call it the poor producer's TIME TUNNEL. Directed

by David L. Hewitt. Scott Brady, Gigi Perreau, Anthony Eisley, Lyle Waggoner, Austin Green. (VC)

**JOURNEY TO THE FAR SIDE OF THE SUN (1969).** The Doppelganger theory, that somewhere in the Universe is a parallel world matching our own detail for detail, is put to the test in this commendable space thriller, directed by Robert Parrish and written by Gerry and Sylvia Anderson and Donald James. European Space Exploration Centre uncovers a planet on the other side of the sun and sends a manned vehicle with Roy Thinnes. There he finds everything identical to Earth, only his internal organs are on the wrong side of his body! Once the space exploration is over, the film becomes a study in conspiratory paranoia. Herbert Lom, Ian Hendry, Lynn Loring, Patrick Wymark.

**JOURNEY TO THE PAST.** See I'LL NEVER FORGET YOU. (But you might forget the movie.)

**JOURNEY TO THE SEVENTH PLANET (1962).** Sluggish Swedish space adventure depicts a rocketship landing on Neptune in 2001 and the crew meeting alien intelligence that can read minds and put up defenses that play on human fears. The Sidney Pink-Ib Melchoir screenplay borrows themes from Ray Bradbury stories. The expedition includes John Agar and Carl Ottosen, with Greta Thyssen and Ann Smyrner as beautiful alien humanoids. Despite the promising premises, it's very tedious going, showing little visual imagination to pull off the difficult effects.

**JOURNEY TO THE UNKNOWN (1969).** Two hour-long episodes of a British horror TV series of the same title, re-edited for syndication. In one story, Vera Miles is trapped in a library and stalked by the Devil. In the second yarn, Patty Duke is terrorized at a seaside hotel by a demented landlady (Joan Crawford). This series was short-lived and marred by slow-moving plots, which these narratives too well exemplify. Produced by Joan Harrison, one-time associate of Alfred Hitchcock.

**JUNGLE, THE (1952).** Terrific adventure made in the jungles of India; authenticity places this Robert L. Lippert low budgeter above most of its kind. Rod Cameron, Marie Windsor and Cesar Romero search for prehistoric mastodons—and find them in a hair-raising climax. Far Eastern musical score, depiction of native customs and actual battles among wild animals make this very viewable. Directed by William Berke, scripted by Carroll Young.

**JUNGLE BOOK, THE (1942).** Alexander Korda's imaginative adaptation of Rudyard Kipling's famous story, treated here as a fairy tale and set in an impressionistic jungle of cobalt blues and magentas. Sabu portrays Mowgli, raised by wolves from infancy to become a jungle boy who talks to monkeys, snakes, elephants and other denizens of the verdane. Mowgli's world is interloped upon by three turbaned villains searching for a Legendary Lost City and a treasure in jewels. The animals are real except for Kaa the wise old python. The Miklos Rozsa score is a classic. Directed by Alexander's brother, Zoltan Korda. As good as another Korda classic, THE THIEF OF BAGDAD. Rosemary De Camp, Ralph Byrd, Joseph Calleia, Patricia O'Rourke, John Qualen, Frank Puglia. (VC)

**JUNGLE BOOK, THE (1967).** Animated cartoon version of the Mowgli stories by Rudyard Kipling is passable, but not up to Disney's usual standards. Although enchanting at times, the film seems old-fashioned in its music and use of stereotyped voices. The story has a panther escorting the jungle boy back to his village after the animals agree he cannot survive in the wilds. Voices by Phil Harris, Louis Prima, Sebastian Cabot, George Sanders, Sterling Holloway, Verna Felton. Directed by Wolfgang Reitherman.

**JUNGLE CAPTIVE (1945).** Universal's third and final entry in its hairy apewoman series (the other films are CAPTIVE WILD WOMAN and JUNGLE WOMAN) is campish fun in which Otto Kruger (mad doctor) and Rondo Hatton (mad doctor's mad assistant) revive an ape woman from the twilight of death and monkey around with her ancestral genes. Vicky Lane endures the ape make-up. Directed by Harold Young. Amelita Ward, Jerome Cowan, Eddie Acuff, Ernie Adams, Phil Brown.

JOHNNY
WEISS-
MULLER
AS
JUNGLE
JIM

**JUNGLE GENTS (1954).** Sach Jones (Huntz Hall) possesses the strangest supernatural talent: He can smell out diamonds. So Hall smells his way to a cache in yet another Bowery Boys debacle. No gem, this. (Pearls before swine?) Directed by Edward Bernds and Austen Jewell. Leo Gorcey, Laurette Luez, Bernard Gorcey, Eric Snowden.

**JUNGLE HEAT.** Videocassette title for **DANCE OF THE DWARFS.** (Can't stand the heat? Get out of the jungle!)

**JUNGLE HELL (1956).** Sabu, of ELEPHANT BOY and JUNGLE BOOK fame, is sadly miscast in this bad film by Norman A. Cerf involving a flying saucer, a death ray and some incomprehensible nonsense about a radioactive rock. And that, viewer, is the real hell of this jungle movie.

**JUNGLE HOLOCAUST (1978).** A sleazy documentary filmmaker stages a real slaughter of natives for his camera team, only to have the Amazon tribesmen turn against him. This Italian production, directed by Ruggero Deodato as CANNIBAL HOLOCAUST, is a ghastly exploitationer that tries to deliver a message. The only message is: Some filmmakers can be absolutely tasteless. With European porn star R. Bolla. Dining room only. (VC)

**JUNGLE JIM (1948).** First in a series of cheap Africa adventures from producer Sam Katzman and starring Johnny Weissmuller as a pith-helmeted he-man (first created as a comic strip by Alex Raymond) who walks past potted plants, mumbles monosyllabic sentences and pats Tamba the chimp on the noggin. It kept the one-time Tarzan star active for years in low budget junglejunk produced on the backlot at Columbia and featuring footage from countless other (and better) movies. This features Jungle Jim seeking a rare drug that combats polio. The villain is George Reeves, who became TV's SUPERMAN. Virginia Grey, Lita Baron. Directed by William Berke.

**JUNGLE JIM IN THE FORBIDDEN LAND (1952).** Khakiclad scout of the potted jungle fights a greedy ivory hunter who is upsetting the natives when there's a "giant apeman" believed to be the missing link. A midget idea from the brain of Samuel Newman, directed by Lew Landers. Johnny Weissmuller mutters the same tired dialogue. Angela Greene, Jean Willes, William Tannen.

**JUNGLE MANHUNT (1951).** Johnny Weissmuller, as a man of the bush, helps a reporter find a missing football player. This Sam Katzman programmer is padded with dinosaur footage from other pictures which only points out major deficiencies in this potted jungle fiasco. Directed by Lew Landers. Bob Waterfield, Lyle Talbot, Sheila Ryan.

**JUNGLE MOON MEN (1955).** The Jungle Jim character was dropped so Johnny Weissmuller could portray himself, although what significance that would have on a movie of this nature is questionable. Nothing else, however, seems changed as Weissmuller walks by the same potted plants he passed in JUNGLE JIM IN THE FORBIDDEN LAND. In short, the same junglelessness with Weissmuller searching for the secret to eternal youth from a jungle tribe that prays to the moon god. The title is misleading—pygmies just happen to be called "moon men." Directed by Charles S. Gould. Myron Healy, Jean Byron.

**JUNGLE PRINCESS (1936).** Dorothy Lamour is still growing into her sarong as a shapely lass raised by a tiger in this women's lib version of Tarzan. The jungle creature comes to her help when she is under attack; the Malaysian setting includes the obligatory giant ape. Directed by William Thiel. Ray Milland, Akim Tamiroff, Lynne Overman.

**JUNGLE RAIDERS (1985).** An expedition searches for a cursed jewel in the verdant thick. Lee Van Cleef, Christopher Connelly, Marina Costa. (VC)

**JUNGLE TREASURE (1951).** Entry in the British "Old Mother Riley" comedy series in which a supernatural manifestation turns out to be an antiquated pirate who knows the whereabouts of a buried fortune. Directed by Maclean Rogers, scripted by Val Valentine. Arthur Lucan, Kitty McShane, Sebastian Cabot, Garry Marsh.

**JUNGLE WOMAN (1944).** Sequel to CAPTIVE WILD WOMAN continues the adventures of Acquanetta, an unfortunate who keeps transmutating into a gorilla woman when doctor J. Carrol Naish fools around with her genes. (And we don't mean Levis, gang.) Occasionally the she-creature reverts to type and kills—but not with her looks. Either you will view this as a stilted, turgid mess or you will find it nostalgically pleasing, reflecting the values of a Universal horror movie of the '40s. Reginald Le Borg directed. Third and final film in this series was JUNGLE CAPTIVE. Evelyn Ankers, Lois Collier and Milburn Stone are all competent, but Acquanetta walks through her role as if in a trance.

**JUNIOR (1985).** Two busty hookers just released from prison start a new life on an old abandoned riverboat in the Deep South, but are terrorized by a low I.Q. pervert and his equally crazed mother. The best moment is when Junior (Jeremy Ratchford) cuts apart their house with his chainsaw; another socially redeeming scene has Junior fondling one of the girl's privates. A movie with a contradiction: it depicts the women as gutsy and liberated, yet exploits their sexuality to the max. Strictly for intellectuals and (lame)brains. Directed by Jim Hawley. Suzanne Delaurentiis, Linda Singer, Jeremy Ratchford. (VC)

**JUST BEFORE DAWN (1982).** Youthful campers, with a deed to a section of wilderness, ignore warnings of forest ranger George Kennedy not to go into the woods. Of course, they go anyway, only to be terrorized by evil mountainmen. Director Jeff Lieberman (SQUIRM, BLUE SUNSHINE) creates suspenseful moments but has nothing new to offer. Kennedy gives a good but limited performance, and Deborah Benson is the best of the teen-agers, proving in the climactic struggle that a woman can be effective in the most terrifying of situations. Just watchable. Chris Lemmon, Gregg Henry, Mike Kellin, Ralph Seymour. (VC)

**JUST FOR FUN (1963).** Pseudopolitical satire, set in the near future when British teenagers are granted the power to vote, and they use musical groups as a way of pulling in votes. Basically a musical featuring the Springfields, the Criticets and the Tremelos. Of borderline interest to fantasy buffs. Directed by Gordon Flemying. Mark Wynter, Cherry Roland, Bobby Vee, Richard Vernon, Irene Handl.

**JUST IMAGINE (1930).** Musical comedy-fantasy of historical interest only: El Brendel, a citizen of 1930, awakens to find himself in 1980 surrounded by bewildering futuristic gadgetry. Then he blasts off for Mars! Songs by Henderson, DeSylva and Brown. Directed-written David Butler. Maureen O'Sullivan, Frank Albertson, John Garrick.

---

*"She's got the power . . . and you haven't got a prayer."—Advertisement for JENNIFER.*

*"The Beast was a tough guy . . . He could lick the world. But when he saw beauty . . . he went soft, he forgot his wisdom."*—Carl Denham *(Robert Armstrong) in* **KING KONG.**

**KADOYNG (1972).** Spaceship from beyond the stars piloted by a benevolent being (Leo Maguire) lands to help a family in need. Whoever heard of Care in Space? Minor British effort. Maguire scripted with Ian Shane directing.

**KAMIKAZE (1986).** Offbeat French science-horror thriller in which a disgruntled electronics expert creates a death ray that kills when projected into TV sets. A detective investigates, donning Japanese kimono and hachimaki (headband of the suicide pilot) for the final battle. Directed by Didier Grousset. Richard Bohringer, Dominique Lavanant.

**KARATE KILLERS, THE (1967).** Re-edited episodes of TV's MAN FROM U.N.C.L.E. starring Robert Vaughn and David McCallum as superagents for a clandestine American security agency, with Leo G. Carroll their assignment chief, Mr. Waverly. In the two glued-together stories our agents are after a formula that could turn water into gold, and then they go after some special aircraft. Fun viewing if you don't mind the TV limitations. Curt Jurgens, Joan Crawford, Telly Savalas, Herbert Lom, Diane McBain, Kim Darby, Jill Ireland. Directed by Barry Shear.

**KEEP, THE (1983).** When writer-director Michael Mann adapted F. Scott Wilson's vampire novei, he dropped all references to vampires—and forgot one should never take horror material too seriously or one could fall flat on one's egg-covered face. So there is Mr. Mann, face down in the mire over this heavy-handed and solemnly pretentious affair. The only saving grace are the special effects, light show extravaganzas with thick white beams of light. An immortal guardian, Glaeken Trismegestus (Scott Glenn, in a role that must have even puzzled him), arrives in a Rumanian village in 1941 after Nazi troops have unleashed a locked-up demonic power (Molasar) from a castle in which the creature has been held captive by a talisman. A Jewish language expert in a wheelchair (Ian McKellen) and his daughter (Alberta Watson) are brought to the Keep to translate runes for a Wehrmacht officer (Jurgen Prochnow) and an SS major (Gabriel Byrne). McKellen believes Molasar to be a savior of the Jews (a Golem?) but the Nazis believe it to be the evil they stand for. Soon the vampire that's never called a vampire rips asunder the bad Nazis and is ready for a showdown with that Glaeken Trismegestus guy, whose eyes glow like emeralds. As they square off with Killer Zap Rays, music by the Tangerine Dream swirls around them with the fog. Figure it out and give us a call. Better yet, read Wilson's book. (VC)

**KEEP MY GRAVE OPEN (1980).** A strange woman (Camilla Carr) living in a strange house kills any strangers who drop by. Very odd and unpredictable, with unexplained motivations until you learn the trick ending. Produced-directed by S.F. Brownrigg, responsible for DON'T LOOK IN THE BASEMENT. Strange enough, strangely enough, to hold your interest. Gene Ross, Stephen Tobolowsky, (VC)

**KEEPER, THE (1976).** Canadian film written-directed by Tom Drake, with Christopher Lee as an insane asylum director who has a plan to insure his patients and then murder off their heirs, so he will have their money to conquer the world a la Dr. Mabuse. Lee, a cripple who walks with a cane, accomplishes this with a hypnosis machine. A private detective named Dick Driver, who acts melodramatic in the extreme, is hired by a man whose brother is an inmate and to whom he is psychically linked. There are strange twists and turns, plus a police chief who falls under Lee's spell and acts as if he's in a comedy and not a horror film. Despite hammy acting, this has a style and ambience that makes it interesting. Tell Schrieber, Sally Gray. (VC)

**KGOD (1980).** KRUD, a rundown TV station in San Poquito, is taken over by Dabney Coleman and turned into a rousin' religious rete—but at the expense of decency and fair play, the message writers Dick Chudnow and Nick Castle throw as the final amen. But first comes a series of on-air program parodies with religious motifs, such as the game show "Healed for a Day," an exorcism reported on the morning news and "One Life to Lose," a soap opera starring Joseph and Mary of Nazarus. This comedy satire in the vein of Mad Magazine may grow on you despite its ineptitudes; its witlessness is charming. But in no way does this make a serious statement about the effect religious programming has on Americans. An odd bag of performers from Jamie Lyn Bauer to Sidney Miller to Joyce Jameson to Ruth Silveira to Lewis Arquette. (VC)

**KID WITH THE BROKEN HALO, THE (1982).** Saccharine TV-movie designed to tug at heart strings, bring tears to eyes and make one feel good about humanity. And who's to say those aren't good values in a saccharine TV-movie? One just wishes telewriter George Kirgo had tried for something less hackneyed, less obvious, than this vehicle for the cutesy-pie talents of Gary Coleman. Little ol' Gary is an angel earning his halo who goes to Earth with fellow angel Robert Guillaume (TV's BENSON) to help three families straighten out worldly problems. June Allyson is an ex-actress who hates the world and her snotty behavior is the only realistic counterpoint to the helpings of granulated sugar. Two other families are troubled by more domestic problems, but it's ho-hum city. Ray Walston is cute as the angel bookkeeper, but hohum to him too. Directed with a sense of helplessness by Leslie Martinson. (VC)

**KILL AND GO HIDE.** See **CHILD, THE.** (No kidding!)

**KILL AND KILL AGAIN (1981).** Amusing, tongue-in-cheek martial arts romp with James Ryan (South African action star) heading a team of professional fighters (with mystical and levitational powers) into a tyrant's stronghold, where a mind-controlling drug is being tested to pave the way for world conquest. Has the virtue of never taking itself seriously and spoofs superspy-kung fu flicks with a passion. Directed by Ivan Hall. Anneline Kriel, Ken Gampu, Norman Robinson. (This was a follow-up to Ryan's KILL OR BE KILLED, a actioner with no fantasy overtones.) (VC)

**KILL, BABY, KILL.** See **CURSE OF THE LIVING DEAD.**

**KILL OR BE KILLED.** Episodes of TV's TIME TUNNEL series including one in which the two scientists trapped in time (see TIME TUNNEL) turn up at Pearl Harbor on the eve of the Japanese sneak attack. One of them must seek out his own father to warn him. James Darren, Robert Colbert, Sam Groom, Linden Chiles, Lew Gallo.

**KILL TO LOVE (1981).** Hong Kong production about a maddog killer knocking off his victims in horrible ways. Chop suey holiday. Directed by Tam Kav Ming. Ching Hsia, Chung Cheung Lin.

**KILLDOZER (1974).** Universal TV-movie, directed by Jerry London, will make you doze when it should kill you with its unusual theme. Theodore Sturgeon, an excellent science-fiction writer, adapted his own short novel with the help of Ed MacKillop but what emerges is typically TV hack. A construction crew on a Pacific island is building a landing strip when an inexplicable invisible force from another world invades a bulldozer, giving it life . . . the animated inanimate object attacks the crew. Deteriorates into stock situations with stock characters played by Clint Walker, Carl Betz, James Wainwright, Robert Urich and Neville Brand.

**KILLER, THE.** Videocassette title for **DADDY'S DEADLY DARLING,** also in videocassette under that title. Original title was **PIGS.** It's a porker under any snout.

**KILLER APE (1953).** Ridiculous Jungle Jim movie with the natives restless because of a giant gorilla with homicide in mind. The creature is controlled by villains concocting a serum that will destroy all of mankind's will to resist. Use your own will to resist this junky Sam Katzman-produced movie starring Johnny Weissmuller. Directed by Spencer Gordon Bennett. Nestor Paiva, Carol Thurston, Max Palmer, Ray "Crash" Corrigan, Nick Stuart.

**KILLER AT LARGE (1936).** One of Lon Chaney Jr.'s early films, a routine crime drama gimmicked up with wax dummies, a cemetery and other "creepy" stuff of the 1930s. Directed by David Selman. Mary Brian, Russell Hardie, Thurston Hall, Betty Compson, Henry Brandon.

**KILLER BAT.** Videocassette title for **DEVIL BAT.**

**KILLER BEES, THE (1974).** This has very little sting despite director Curtis Harrington and a bravura performance by Gloria Swanson, making a "rare appearance." Gloria portrays the matriarch of a family in Napa Valley (where exteriors were filmed) which raises hives of a rare African bee. Eventually the winged creatures attack and kill under her guidance. After this, Gloria became known as "the queen of

the bees." Standard TV-movie fare. Kate Jackson, Edward Albert, Craig Stevens, Roger Davis.

**KILLER GRIZZLY.** See **GRIZZLY.** (Grrrrrrrr!)

**KILLER IN EVERY CORNER (1974).** Low budget British TV-movie starring Patrick Magee as a professor with a new study of psychology and Joanna Pettit as one of three women who agree to partake in his experiments. (VC)

**KILLER LACKS A NAME, THE (1966).** Variation on THE INDESTRUCTIBLE MAN and MAN-MADE MONSTER, in which the titular villain finds that his steel hand contains enough voltage to knock off his enemies. This Italian effort, directed by Tullio Domichelli and starring Lang Jeffries and Olga Omar, will not give you much of a charge. Lacks a jolt. The amps went oomph.

**KILLER PARTY (1986).** April Fool's Day saga only for fools: When three pledges in the Sigma Alpha Phi sorority undergo initiation on "Ghost Night," real horrors begin to happen at a costume party when a killer in a diving suit (isn't this synopsis incredible?) kills via electricity, hammer, guillotine, pitchfork and standard kitchen knife, then stuffs body parts into a frig. What appears to be a slasher flick turns into supernatural hogwash when a long-dead sorority spirit takes over a live body. Paul Bartel (wasted as a nerdy professor), Martin Hewitt, Ralph Seymour, Elaine Wilkes. Directed by William Fruet. (VC)

**KILLER SHREWS, THE (1959).** Cheapie produced by Ken Curtis (Festus on GUNSMOKE) and released to theaters with THE GIANT GILA MONSTER. This is not about ugly wives going on a murderous rampage. In this case, shrews are the tiniest of rodents, but some crazy scientist has enlarged them to 100 pounds each. Strange how these giant killer shrews resemble Irish setters in blackface. Maybe they'll bark the hero (James Best) or his Norwegian girlfriend (Ingrid Goude) to death. There's such a wonderful sense of ineptitude in Ray Kellogg's direction that this becomes fun to watch. Curtis doubles as one of the victims, proving he's a "shrew-d" guy. Baruch Lumet.

**KILLER SPORES (1977).** Space capsule returns to Earth contaminated by an alien substance which takes over control of humans. Patrick Duffy, who has gills that enable him to live underwater, is assigned by NASA to investigate. Re-edited episodes of TV's MAN FROM ATLANTIS series. Routine, uninspired videofare. Directed by Reza Badiyi. Belinda Montgomery, Alan Fudge.

**KILLER WITH TWO FACES (1974).** British TV cheapie starring Donna Mills as a screaming heroine frightened by a mad strangler who could be one of two brothers. Undistinguished production values bring this down to the level of a thriller soap opera. Ian Hendry, David Lodge, Roddy McMillan. Directed by John Scholz-Conway.

**KILLERS ARE CHALLENGED (1966).** Transparent 007 imitation from Italy, originally SECRET AGENT FIREBALL, with Richard Harrison as a spy-hero who poses as a scientist to protect a petroleum project. His gadgets include a ring that forewarns him of pending death. You too have been forewarned. Directed by Anthony Dawson. Susy Andersen, Wandisa Guida.

**KILLERS FROM SPACE (1954).** Humanoids with bulging eyeballs and wearing jumpsuits resurrect Peter Graves from the dead as part of their hohum, what-a-bore plot to take over Earth. Don't they know hundreds of other extraterrestrials have tried without success? Some aliens just never get the message. A very dull science-fiction movie directed by W. Lee Wilder (brother of Billy Wilder). Barbara Bestar, James Seay, Frank Gerstle.

**KILLERS OF THE CASTLE OF BLOOD.** See **SCREAM OF THE DEMON LOVER.** (Nothing to shout about.)

**KILLER'S MOON (1978).** Drug-crazed fanatics flee an asylum for the insane, killing everyone in sight. British psychothriller directed by Alan Birkinshaw. Anthony Forrest, Tom Marshall, Georgina Kean, Nigel Gregory.

**KILLING CARS (1986).** West German science thriller, made in England, stars Jurgen Porchnow as Ralph Korda, an automotive engineer who has designed a new kind of power

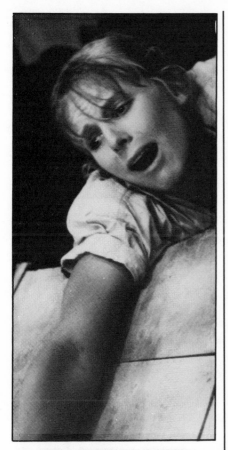

**INTO THE PIT IN 'THE KINDRED'**

source for cars—but before he can introduce it, agents from a sinister oil cartel set out to stop him. Directed-written by Michael Verhoeven.

**KILLING KIND, THE (1973).** John Savage, suffering from a mama's complex, stalks his victims while ever-loving mom Ann Sothern bakes apple pies and coos her affection to calm down her killer boy. Slow, lethargic pacing by director Curtis Harrington. Cindy Williams, Luana Anders. (VC)

**KILLING HOUR, THE (1982).** Videocassette title for **CLAIRVOYANT, THE.** (Clair who?)

**KILLING OF SATAN, THE (1983).** Filipino horror flick about the Devil fighting mortal men with his Powers of Darkness. Directed by Efren C. Pinon. Ramon Revilla, Elizabeth Oropesa, George Estregan, Paquito Diaz. (VC)

**KILLINGS AT OUTPOST ZETA (1980).** Low budget adventure in the tradition of STAR TREK which attempts an intriguing story, even if production is hampered by lousy special effects. After three expeditions to a farflung planet have disappeared, a fourth team of space rangers is sent to solve the mystery. What they find are 11 corpses, their insides eaten away. It seems that in exploring the planet, the previous scientists discovered a form of rock life. Nice try by producer-directors Allan Sandler and Robert Ememegger (he also wrote the electronic music score). The screenplay by Peter Dawson focuses on plot, not much character. Gordon Devol, Jacquelyn Ray, Jackson Bostwick, Hildy Brooks.

**KINDRED, THE (1986).** Obvious ripoff of ALIEN, without an original thought in its head, and an embarrassment for Rod Steiger to be appearing in. He's a nutty scientist on the fringes of an experiment in gene-splicing that has resulted in "Anthony," a tentacled monster hiding in subterranean chambers underneath a doctor's country home. What are catacombs and deep pits doing under the floorboards? Just one of the many dumb aspects of a goo movie. Goo is all over everything as the monster spurts like a giant penis. From Jeffrey Obrow and Stephen Carpenter, the schlockmeisters who gave us THE DORM THAT DRIPPED BLOOD. One critic thought the title referred to a benevolent Communist. The title stands for trash of the sleaziest kind. David Allen Brooks, Talia Balsam, Kim Hunter.

**KING ARTHUR, THE YOUNG WARRIOR (1975).** Legendary tale of the most gallant knight of all, told in traditional form in this British TV-movie. Oliver Tobias, Jack Watson, Peter Firth, Brian Blessed. (VC)

**KING DICK (1982).** French-Italian animated feature, originally released as LITTLE DICK, THE MIGHTY MIDGET. A midget must force an ugly witch to return him to full size, along with a prince and princess. Sex themes, poor dubbing and substandard animation make this unsuitable for children . . . and adults. (VC)

**KING DINOSAUR (1955).** First effort by producer-director Bert I. Gordon focuses on four astronauts who land on an alien planet, Nova, and walk past Benedict Canyon boulders, reacting to offscreen prehistoric monsters. On screen, the monsters turn out to be stock footage beasties from ONE MILLION B.C. The turgid screenplay was by Tom Gries, who became a film-TV director. The narrator is Marvin Miller. Gordon's co-producer was Al Zimbalist. Bill Bryant, Wanda Curtis, Douglas Henderson.

**KING KONG (1933).** The granddaddy of giant ape movies, so skillfully conceived by producers-directors Merian Cooper and Ernest B. Schoedsack that it has lost little of its charm and suspense. And Willis O'Brien's stop-motion effects are still startling for their time, ingeniously depicting the 50-foot-tall gorilla presiding over prehistoric Skull Island. A filmmaking expedition headed by Carl Denham (Robert Armstrong) and an adventurer (Bruce Cabot) pursues the creature after it abducts Fay Wray. The chase includes colossal battles with dinosaurs, a marauding pterodactyl, a giant snake and other monstrous spectacles. Captured and returned to civilization

**POSTER ART FOR 'KING KONG' (1976)**

**'KING KONG LIVES': BUT NOT FOR LONG**

as a sideshow display, the mighty Kong breaks free to provide this unbridled fantasy with a grand climax atop the Empire State Building. It features a great Max Steiner score and its cast includes Wray as Ann Darrow, the woman Kong rips the clothes from, Frank Reicher as Captain Englehorn, Noble Johnson as the native chieftain, and Sam Hardy as Charles Weston. The script was begun by British mystery writer Edgar Wallace, but when he died after finishing the first draft, it was taken over by Ruth Rose (Schoedsack's wife) and James A. Creelman. David O. Selznick was executive producer. Dino de Laurentiis remade it in 1976 but this RKO

production remains the definitive giant ape movie. (VC)

**KING KONG (1976).** Producer Dino De Laurentiis proclaimed this $24 million remake a "cinema event"—and while it may be undeniably an event, it is far from recommendable cinema. The Lorenzo Semple Jr. screenplay, unfortunately, calls on some of the TV BATMAN traditions of high camp and emerges a mishmash of satire, thrills, fantasy and spectacle under John Guillermin's direction. This leaves only the special effects to marvel at, and while some of them are good, there is no sense of tradition, balance or proportion. The hairy paw picking up screaming Jessica Lange, so deftly handled in the 1933 original, is so overdone here it soon becomes ludicrous. No stop motion animation—it was all done with men in monkey suits or with unconvincing giant mockups. It finally topples from its own weight. Boy, what a bomb! Jeff Bridges, Charles Brodin, John Randolph, John Agar, Rene Auberjonois, Ed Lauter. Rick Baker wears the monkey suit. (VC)

**KING KONG ESCAPES (1968).** More Toho Studio mass destruction (special effects by Eiji Tsuburaya) as the hairy desecrator of Tokyo battles Gorosaurus, a relative of Godzilla, plus an exact replica of himself, Mechanikong, the work of a scientist (dubbed Dr. Who) who is apparently as nutty as Japanese special effects artists. American footage featuring Rhodes Reason has been appended for U.S. appeal. It comes out silly; you really have to like these Japanese things to enjoy. Directed by Inoshiro Honda.

**KING KONG LIVES (1986).** How the mighty have dropped with a leaden thud since Kong plummeted from the top of the Empire State Building in Dino De Laurentiis' 1976 remake. Here Dino offers a sequel wherein dedicated doctor Linda Hamilton is keeping Kong alive in the world's biggest animal hospital so she can give him a heart transplant. Who should adventurer Brian Kerwin find on Kong Island—just when Linda needs a transfusion for Kong—but a Young Chick Kong, who has the hots for the hairy guy. While that sounds funny, the most hilarious scenes come when Kong is operated on, the surgical tools looking like props from THE INCREDIBLE SHRINKING MAN. Kong and his Chick thunder across the plains, stomping everything in sight, in some of the funniest scenes imaginable, especially when the scale of things is entirely wrong. The idea of trying to inject a love story, complete with mother's love, into a thundering-plundering-blundering Kong movie is the most ludicrous thing im-

**JESSICA LANGE AT THE WORLD TRADE CENTER: KONG TOOK THE BIG FALL FOR HER**

**CREATURE FEATURES MOVIE GUIDE**

aginable—yet director John Guillermin (who helmed the 1976 fiasco) does just that with an utterly straight face. So bad it's not even good. (VC)

**KING KONG VS. GODZILLA (1963).** Predicted clash of the century between "two world-shaking monsters" is in reality a Japanese thud as loud as Kong's footfall. The hairy ape of Skull Island battles a king-sized octopus and the savior of Japan, Godzilla, in a seemingly endless series of fisticuffs and body bashings. Additional footage with Michael Keith was shot for the U.S. Directed by Inoshiro Honda. Based on an idea by animator Willis O'Brien.

**KING OF KONG ISLAND (1968).** Also known as EVE THE WILD WOMAN. With remote-control devices, giant gorillas become robot killers. A descendant of the King himself happens along and decides enough is enough already and starts crunching skulls—and remote-control devices. Left to its own devices, this Spanish-produced job would fall flat on its ugly kisser. Directed by Robert Morris. Brad Harris, Marc Lawrence, Esmeralda Barros, Adrianna Alben. (VC)

**KING OF THE JUNGLE (1933).** Buster Crabbe considered this take-off on Tarzan one of his few "A" movies and was proud of his acting as a "lion man." Philip Wylie and Fred Niblo Jr. co-authored the screenplay about a jungle youth raised on the vine by lions who is captured and brought to the U.S. as a carnival attraction. Good jungle and wildlife footage; holds up better than most '30s jungle flicks. Frances Dee, Irving Pichel, Douglas Dumbrille. Directed by Bruce Humberstone and Max Marcin.

**KING OF THE ROCKETMEN (1951).** Full-length Republic serial, all 12 chapters, in which Tris Coffin, a member of Science Associates, dons a jet-propelled flying suit to become "Rocket Man," a high-flying hero who goes up against Mr. Vulcan, an evil nerd trying to steal the Sonutron (a rock disintegrator) and wreak havoc on the world. Instead, he should have concentrated on disintegrating the rocks in his head—he and his henchmen bungle the job so badly. Straight out of the comic books, and lively directed by Fred C. Brannon. Don Haggerty, Mae Clarke, House Peters Jr. and other serial regulars. Released to TV in a shortened version as LOST PLANET AIRMEN. (VC)

**KING OF THE STREETS (1985).** Humanoid alien from another planet (Brett Clark) lands on Earth in a fiery blaze to fight crime and cure the sick with a mere touch. Sluggish, joyless Canadian film directed and co-written by Edward Hunt. The streets are strictly slums. Pamela Saunders, Reggie De-Morton.

**KING OF THE ZOMBIES (1941).** Not the king of the zombie movies, for sure. Horridly hoary and ingratiatingly insipid "walking dead" melodrama in which mad doctor Henry Victor creates zombies for the Axis. Mantan Moreland rolls his eyes and runs at the slightest sign of a "spook." As dated as whalebone corsets and Easter bonnets. Dick Purcell, Joan

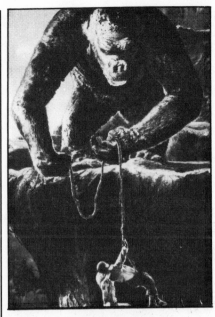

**'KING KONG' (1933)**

Woodbury. Directed by Jean Yarbrough. (VC)

**KING SOLOMON'S MINES (1937).** This British version of Henry Rider Haggard's epic adventure about an African expedition in search of a priceless diamond treasure, featuring Quartermain the Great White Hunter, is crude by today's standards, with far too much emphasis on the gospel singing of Paul Robeson, playing one of the native bearers. Sir Cedric Hardwicke and Roland Young are among the intrepid explorers who dare the dangers of the Dark Continent, coming up against a witch who brings about a volcanic explosion and puts a curse on the trekkers. The 1950 MGM version was better, although that featured none of the fantasy elements. Directed by Robert Stevenson. John Loder, Anna Lee. (VC)

**KING SOLOMON'S MINES (1985).** This has such a spirited sense of light-hearted adventure, and moves at such a lightning clip, that one is almost willing to overlook the fact it has nothing to do with H. R. Haggard's novel and everything to do with Indiana Jones. The exciting action sequences are al-

**MINING HIS OWN BUSINESS: RICHARD CHAMBERLAIN AS QUARTERMAIN IN 'KING SOLOMON'S MINES'**

**CREATURE FEATURES MOVIE GUIDE**

**HUMAN LEFTOVERS FOLLOWING THE MAIN COURSE IN 'KINGDOM OF THE SPIDERS'**

most direct steals, right down to the line "Trust me." Richard Chamberlain proves a virile, rugged Quartermain helping feisty heroine Sharon Stone find her lost father and a diamond mine in Africa shortly prior to World War I. Full of derring-do and mock heroics in a tongue-in-cheek vein, with the villains (Herbert Lom as a German officer, John Rhys-Davies as a Turkish adventurer) more caricature than menace. There's an hysterical cannibal pot sequence, a madcap flying chase, a strange tribe of tree-hanging Africans, a couple of village massacres and one lengthy cave sequence that features a wicked witch, a giant spider and death devices a la Temple of Doom. Production values are grand, with half the tribes of Africa working as extras. Directed by J. Lee Thompson, written by Gene Quintano and James R. Silke. (VC)

**KING SOLOMON'S TREASURES (1978).** Light-hearted, minor fantasy-adventure based loosely on H. R. Haggard's novel about Allan Quartermain, a Great White Hunter searching for a lost fortune in the wilds of Africa. John Colicos makes for a different Quartermain, but equal emphasis is put on comedy relief: naval officer Patrick Macnee and David McCallum, who help in rescuing a young woman from a prehistoric monster and in finding a lost Roman-style city ruled by a Cleopatra-like Britt Ekland. Harry Alan Towers' production, directed by Alvin Rakoff, doesn't build a lot of steam, and is only exciting during its final action sequences when a volcano blows its top. Diverting but hardly memorable. Wilfrid Hyde-White, Ken Gampu, Hugh Rose.

**KINGDOM IN THE CLOUDS (1968).** Rumanian effort, beautiful and lyrical in telling the fable of a youth seeking immortality and encountering magic, witches and Father Time himself. Written and directed by Elisabeta Bostan. Mircea Breazu, Ana Szeles, Ion Tugearu.

**KINGDOM OF THE SPIDERS (1977).** Swell yarn about how several thousand tarantulas, bola, crab, wolf and funnel-web spiders attack a small Arizona community to get even for man's misuse of insecticides. Director John "Bud" Cardos makes this absurdity work with the help of William Shatner in one of his better movie roles as a veterinarian who joins up with bug expert Tiffany Bolling, who's really bug-eyed over Captain Kirk. The effect of the 5000 spiders swarming over everything (and everybody) is quite chilling and will have you watching where you step for days afterward. Above average low budget effort, thanks to many suspenseful sequences and a twist ending. Woody Strode, Nancy Lafferty, Natsha Ryan, Joe Ross. (VC)

**KIRLIAN WITNESS, THE (1978).** Minor but interesting effort from writer-producer-director Jonathan Sarno, depicting a murder that is "witnessed" by a plant and the efforts of the victim's sister to track down the murderer. Kirlian photography, a method of photographing an object's aura, is ultimately used to solve the case. This offbeat film is marred by a muddled script and a cast of unknowns. Nancy Snyder, Lawrence Tierney, Joe Colodner. Photographed in Soho, a section of New York City.

**KISS AND KILL (1968).** Christopher Lee essays the insidious Fu Manchu role for the fourth time with sadistic glee, rubbing his hands together and curling his mustache. This time Fu's plot to rule the world involves hypnotized women who transfer a deadly poison to anyone who touches their lips. Call it the Max Factor application. Richard Greene portrays the Scotland Yard pursuer Nayland Smith and Shirley Eaton is chief among the "black widows." Directed by Jess Franco. Maria Rohm, Tsai Chin.

**KISS DADDY GOODBYE (1981).** Twin daughters with peculiar psychic powers utilize their ESP abilities to avenge the death of their father. Fabian Forte, Marilyn Burns.

**KISS KISS, KILL KILL (1966).** German-Italian-Yugoslav hodgepodge spy thriller featuring a drug that induces a zombie-like state; apparently the drug affected the entire cast, which walks vacant-eyed through their mindless roles. A dismal adaptation of Bert F. Island's "Kommissar X" books. Directed by Gianfranco Parolini. Tony Kendall, Brad Harris, Maria Perschy, Christa Linder, Pino Mattei.

**KISS ME, KILL KILL (1974).** Bluebeard wife killer Michael Jayston uses strangulation techniques, sometimes in the bathroom. He's looking for a third victim when he meets a pretty blonde (Helen Mirren) he's really in love with. But he cannot resist the temptation of a rich widow's pocketbook and begins two-timing the two women. Brian Clemens' script has a twist ending on top of a twist ending—it should catch you by surprise. Interesting to see most of it happening from the killer's point of view, with a subplot about a dedicated policeman hot on his trail. Produced-directed by John Sichel. Michael Gwynn, Richard Coleman, Tony Steedman, Richard Hampton.

**KISS ME DEADLY (1955).** What's a Mike Hammer thriller by Mickey Spillane doing in this book? Because Ralph Meeker, as the blood-and-guts private eye, is in pursuit of a suitcase of material that could have a devastating effect on anyone who opens it. Director Robert Aldrich has fashioned one of the strangest of mystery thrillers with a great supporting cast: Albert Dekker, Paul Stewart, Cloris Leachman, Leigh Snowden, Strother Martin, Jack Elam, Percy Helton, Robert Cornthwaite. Don't miss it.

**KISS ME, MONSTER (1968).** Isolated Caribbean island is the haven for a mad doctor carrying out experiments on animals and men as though he had just seen THE ISLAND OF DR. MOREAU on The Late Show. Jesus Franco is responsible for another Spanish flicker which is more successful with its grotesque imagery than its flaccid characters and pulp magazine situations. Janine Reynard.

**KISS ME QUICK (1963).** Russ Meyer, king of the soft pornies after THE IMMORAL MR. TEAS, delves into the sex life of the Frankenstein Monster when an alien from Sterilox joins forces with Dr. Breedlove. Meyer lovers will dig his

　　　　　　　　　　　　　　　**CREATURE FEATURES MOVIE GUIDE**

menagerie of monsters (including a mummy and vampire) but if his chauvinistic comedy and penchant for exposed female flesh and outrageous sense of filmmaking unnerve you, you'd better kiss it off quick. Jackie DeWit, Althea Currier, Fred Coe, Claudia Banks.

**KISS ME, KILL ME.** See **T.A.G.—THE ASSASSINATION GAME.** (You're It!)

**KISS MEETS THE PHANTOM OF THE PARK (1978).** Outrageous TV vehicle for the rock group Kiss, its title giving away the storyline about mad doctor Anthony Zerbe trying to turn the musicians into sideshow freaks so far out, it's hard to distinguish them from rockers. It ends up a menagerie of popular monsters (Frankenstein Monster, werewolf, Dracula) under Gordon Hessler's direction. Our advice: Kiss it off. Deborah Ryan, Don Steele. (VC)

**KISS OF EVIL (1962).** Made in Britain as KISS OF THE VAMPIRE and re-edited heavily for the U.S. It was produced during that long period when Christopher Lee refused to don the cape of Dracula, and Hammer was forced to cast a surrogate count, in this case Noel Willman, who portrays Dr. Ravna. The good doc invites an English couple honeymooning in Bavaria to his chateau, where he and his disciples practice the black arts and drink plenty of blood to keep their strength up. A professor resembling Van Helsing chances along and turns the tables on the vampire gang with the help of a squadron of bats that zoom at his command. One of the better Hammer offerings. Directed by Don Sharp and scripted by producer Anthony Hinds (John Elder). Clifford Evans, Edward De Souza, Isobel Black, Jennifer Daniel, Carl Esmond.

**KISS OF THE TARANTULA (1972).** A lonely, misunderstood child, befriended by her undertaker father but hated by her unfaithful mother, realizes mom is committing adultery with dad's brother and unleashes a tarantula spider into her bedroom. It's the beginnings of a spider murderess. This independent low budgeter, directed by Chris Munger, does for spiders what WILLARD did for rats. You'll shudder as scores of tarantulas scurry ;up the arms and legs of a pair of kissers in Lover's Lane when the demented Suzanne Love unleashes her pretty pets as eight-legged avengers. She cackles such commands as "Spin faster" and "Scuttle you creepers" as they scurry into the night to spread their web of horror. A strange subplot involves a rural policeman who falls in love with Suzanne (as though she were a hypnotic spider-

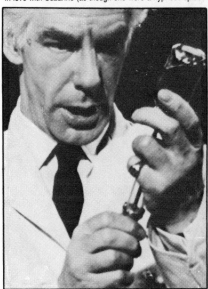

**MICHAEL GOUGH NEEDLES FRIENDS IN 'KONGA'**

woman) and covers up her crimes, but his faith/fate is a chilling one which climaxes the film. Eric Mason, Patricia Landon.

**KISS THE GIRLS AND MAKE THEM DIE (1967).** Dim-witted dialogue and atrocious acting make this Italian-U.S. spy spoof, shot in Brazil, forgettable. Michael Connors, in his pre-MANNIX days, walks somnambulistic through his role as a super agent out to stop a crazed industrialist from sterilizing mankind with a ray beam. The ray should have been aimed at producer Dino De Laurentiis. Directed by Henry Levin and Dino Maiuri. Dorothy Provine portrays Connors' contact in Brazil. Terry-Thomas, Beverly Adams, Marilu Tolo, Margaret Lee, Raf Vallone.

**KNIFE FOR THE LADIES, A.** See **SILENT SENTENCE.**

**KNIGHTS OF TERROR (1964).** Undistinguished clanking armor melodrama (of French-Italian-Spanish manufacture) in which armored attackers in fright masks pillage and rape across the landscape. This warrants mention here only for its ridiculous utilization of a new kind of explosive during a period when gunpowder had yet to be invented. Film ultimately creates a clunk among the clanking. Directed by Mario Costa. Tony Russell, Scilla Gabel, Yves Vincent.

**KNIGHTS OF THE DRAGON, THE (1985).** It's not really a dragon the gallant knights are riding after in this Spanish medieval action fantasy—it's an alien creature in a space suit and he's up against it with alchemist Klaus Kinski going crazy and Harvey Keitel as a maladroit knight strictly from a square table. Directed-produced by Fernando Colomo.

**KONGA (1961).** Herman Cohen production, unconscionably made under the title I WAS A TEENAGE GORILLA. Biologist Michael Gough is raising man-eating plants when he decides to branch out into bigger things. Twenty-five feet bigger: that's size of a chimp-turned-killer-gorilla injected with a New Scientific Serum That Will Advance Mankind Into a New Epoch. Gough also has an ogling eye for Claire Gordon, a bouncy young thing who wears tight sweaters, much to the jealousy of lab assistant Margo Johns. The gorilla comes off looking all right, but you can't say the same for Gough when Konga picks up the hapless doctor and carries him into the London street to do an imitation of King Kong. Really quite terrible but its high incompetency level makes it viewable. John Lemont directed. Jess Conrad, Austin Trevor, Jack Watson.

**KONGO (1932).** Seldom-seen MGM jungle thriller, a remake of the silent film, WEST OF ZANZIBAR. Walter Huston is an African adventurer who has been severely injured and seeks revenge by torturing his attacker's daughter. Entertaining but now dated mixture of creepiness and sadism. Directed by William Cowen. Lupe Velez, Conrad Nagel, Virginia Bruce, Mitchell Lewis.

**KRONOS (1957).** Twentieth Century-Fox is to be commended for attempting a different kind of alien invasion thriller, even if it is hampered by a low budget, a mediocre score by Paul Sawtell and only average direction by producer Kurt Neumann. A flying saucer deposits a towering hunk of computerized machinery on Earth, which then pistons its way across the landscape, sucking up energy sources and squashing everyone who gets beneath its size 45 sneakers. Jeff Morrow, John Emery and Morris Ankrum are experienced hands with this kind of material, but it's that gigantic mechanical block that steals the show. Barbara Lawrence, Robert Shayne, George O'Hanlon. (VC)

**KRULL (1983).** A fairy-tale quality instills this sword-and-sorcery adventure with a sense of childlike wonder, making it more palatable for the young than the grittier Conan sagas. Emphasis is on dazzling effects and innovative designs on the planet Krull, where a rock-fortress spaceship commanded by the Beast unloads an army of Slayers. Warrior Ken Marshall is separated from his lovely princess (Lysette Anthony) and joins forces with Ergo the Magician and a band of thieves to challenge the Beast in his Black Fortress. The odyssey unfolds with a deadly bog, two murderous changelings, a cavern of webs housing the Widow of the Spider, a herd of sky-riding Firemares and assorted quest perils. Final assault on the Beast is a rousing one—plenty of thunder, fire and clashing steel—and there's an opulent score by James Horner. KRULL never becomes a classic, but it's fine matinee material, blazing with color and action. Peter Yates' direction is first-rate, giving the material a sense of the majestic. Freddie Jones is the wise man, Ynyr; Francesca Annis the Widow of the Web; Bernard Bresslaw is the one-eyed Cyclops; David Barttley is Ergo the Magician and Alun Armstrong is Torquil, leader of the bandits. (VC)

**KUNG FU EXORCIST (1976).** Hong Kong blending of horror and martial arts. Kathy Leen, billed as the "lady Bruce Lee," fights her way to victory against the Shaolin Holy Man, who has aligned himself with the Devil so his flying dropkicks will have greater impact.

**KUNG FU FROM BEYOND THE GRAVE (1982).** As in HAMLET, a murdered spirit informs his son from beyond the grave to seek revenge and our hero, Sonny Sing, does just that, aided by a vampiric count at one point in the non-stop martial arts action. Call it BLOOD AND CHOP SUEY.

**KUNG FU ZOMBIE (1981).** Love that title! Martial arts master almost gets the chop suey kicked out of his noodles

when he confronts a vampire proficient in kung fu. Just a lot of fighting with little motive behind the supernatural elements. Should please action buffs, though. Directed by Hwa I Hung. Billy Chong.

**KWAIDAN (1965).** Japanese anthology film by Masaki Kobayashi plunges you into the shadowy valley of Lafcadio Hearn's ghost stories, once described by a critic as "permanent archetypes of human experience." It masters the paradox of being simultaneously horrifying and beautiful with its four-part, two-and-a-half-hour format. The first tale is the surrealistic vignette of a defeated Samurai warrior who leaves his wife for a wealthy highborn who turns out to be an unbearable bitch. "In the Cup of Tea" deals with a man who peers into his teacup one morning and finds the reflection of a stranger gazing back. "Koichi, the Earless" is the most ghostly of the yarns, depicting a man summoned by ancient spirits to serve as their storyteller. "The Woman of the Snow" is about a secret whispered by one friend to another which must never be repeated. A color film of lush composition featuring superb use of dream-like special effects. Excellent Japanese cast headed by Renato Mikuni, Michiyo Aratama and Tatsuya Nakadai. (VC)

# The Beast of Krull

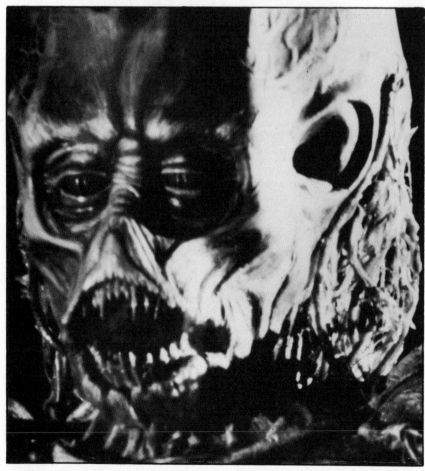

*"Planet Robber Tramples the Earth!"—Advertisement for* **KRONOS**

K.D.

*"I am Dracula, Lord of Darkness, Master of the Vampires, Prince of the Undead, Ruler of the Damned."—The evil Count in* **LEGEND OF THE SEVEN GOLDEN VAMPIRES.**

**L.A. 2017 (1971).** Philip Wylie's last assignment: an episode of TV's NAME OF THE GAME, directed by Steven Spielberg. Wylie's parable, about the pollution of our environment, is couched within a nightmare. Magazine publisher Gene Barry is transported to the future and enmeshed in intrigue in an underground society. Unsettling in its depiction of the remnants of L. A. drenched in poisonous yellow fog; effective message/entertainment. Sharon Farrell, Barry Sullivan, Edmond O'Brien, Paul Stewart.

**LABORATORY (1980).** Prepare for total tedium when humanoid aliens in shiny metallic suits abduct Earthlings (alcoholic rich bitch, Chinese woman, fanatical priest, woman musician, black athlete, etc.) and place them under observation in a deserted clinic. Absolutely nothing happens for the next hour while the aliens talk in metallic, hard-to-understand voices and the humans bicker and snicker. The ultimate in bland dullness. Produced-directed by Allan Sandler and Robert Emenegger, low budget specialists. Martin Kove, Ken Washington, Camille Mitchell.

**LABYRINTH (1986).** A curious mixture of Muppet humor, WIZARD OF OZ and ALICE IN WONDERLAND: Obnoxious teenager Jennifer Connelly is plunged into a fantasy kingdom ruled by the King of Goblins (David Bowie) as she pursues the gremlins who whisked away her baby brother. The premise is weak (the infant is never in any real danger) and not even a 13-hour time limit imposed on Connelly adds to the suspense as she intergoes one adventure after the other with oddball fairies, goblins, dwarves and other MUPPET-style characters. While Brian Froud's designs and Jim Henson's creatures are amusing (especially a talking shaggy dog with eyepatch, a clumsy dwarf named Hoggle and a dim-wit fuzzball called Bluto), there is an air of ersatz to the thrills in Terry Jones' script, and Bowie is too charming—Tim Curry could have done it better. The light-hearted comedic approach by director Henson and producer Geoge Lucas ultimately turns this into a snoozer, despite all the puppet and voice talent involved. (VC)

**LADY AND THE MONSTER, THE (1943).** First screen adaptation of Curt Siodmak's novel DONOVAN'S BRAIN, in which a financial genius' brain is preserved after his death and takes over others by telepathic communication, is inferior to

the 1953 version. The classic idea was malshaped by Republic Studios into an ordinary horror flick. Directed by George Sherman, the film is a failed, dated atmosphere piece. Vera Ralston is terribly miscast as the heroine. Erich von Stroheim, Richard Arlen, Sidney Blackmer.

**LADY DRACULA. See LEMORA—LADY DRACULA.**

**LADY FRANKENSTEIN (1972).** Women's Lib comes to the laboratory! Smock-wearing "femme fatale" Sara Bey (as evil as her father) is a real cut-up as she switches brains in two bodies to create a new Frankenstein Monster, copying daddy's techniques. Daddy is Joseph Cotten, who wanders through this European Hammer-clone as if he were looking for David Selznick to offer him a better role. The monster is a fright-ful make-up job but Bey is well built, exposing her beautiful breasts in sizzling love scenes. Mel Welles forgot to direct Mickey Hargitay, who stands around looking very brawny—and lost. Herbert Fux (!), Paul Muller. (VC)

**LADY IN A CAGE (1964).** Thrill-happy sadists invade the home of invalid Olivia de Havilland, who is trapped in her elevator between floors. The hoodlums, led by James Caan in his first screen role, create nightmare situations that drive de Havilland to the brink of insanity. We're talking murder, rape and pillage, with whorish Ann Sothern egging the blood-thirsty boys on. Hot stuff for its day. Taut, arty direction by Walter Grauman. Jeff Corey, Rafael Campos, Jennifer Billingsley, Scatman Cruthers, William Swan. (VC)

**LADY POSSESSED (1951).** Vague, ill-defined personality transference melodrama about an American (June Havoc) living in London who begins to behave like the late wife of theater pianist James Mason after she moves into the dead woman's old digs. Compared to today's "possession" films, this is tamed and underplayed to the point of being esoteric. LADY POSSESSED is so dated it has assumed a mildly compelling watchability it may not have had even in 1951. Mason also produced and co-wrote with wife Pamela. Directed by William Spier and Roy Kellino, with Stephen Dunne making his film debut.

**LADY, STAY DEAD (1982).** Australian shocker from producer-writer-director Terry Bourke about a gardener (Chard Hayward) who kills a woman, then covers his tracks

by attacking someone else who saw the crime being committed. Sleaze fans will be disappointed to learn this is only slightly tacky. Movie, stay lost. Roger Ward. (VC)

**LADYHAWKE (1985).** Top drawer fantasy adventure full of derring-do and swashbuckling; it's also a pleasing fairy tale romance in which a gallant knight (Rutger Hauer) turns into a wolf at night, and the beautiful princess Isabeau (Michelle Pfeiffer) transmutates into a hawk by day. This means they can never fulfill their love—until there happens along a flippant squire (Matthew Broderick), who conspires with an old man named Imperius (Leo McKern) to undue the evil spell done upon the couple by an evil bishop (John Wood). The Italian castles and ruins lend an authenticity to this sometimes-gritty, realistic costume drama, which has consistently high energy performances. Directed by Richard Donner for producer Harvey ("The Omen") Bernhard. (VC)

**LAKE OF DRACULA (1973).** Toho horror film made with compassion and beauty. A young woman is saved from a vampire by an old man and the experience lingers with her for years, even though others treat it as a bad dream. Events come to a climax when Dracula's grandfather turns up. Also known as DRACULA'S LUST FOR BLOOD. Directed by M. Yamamoto. Midori Fujita.

**LAND OF DOOM (1984).** Another after-the-Bomb Mad Max-style adventure, the focus this time on a warrior named Harmony (Deborah Rennard), a man-hater forced to join forces with another nomad (Garrick Dowhen) as they trek to some legendary paradise. Wall-to-wall action with crazy vehicles and zap guns and other leftovers from ROAD WARRIOR, with bands of sadists pillaging and raping and finally being outgunned with the help of some midgets in robes. That's about all director Peter Maris can offer, and if that's all you need in a movie, by all means . . . (VC)

**LAND OF THE MINOTAUR, THE (1977).** Dreadful British-Greek production, made in Greece, in which minister Donald Pleasence utilizes religious symbols (cross, holy water, etc.) to fight off a devil cult commanded by Peter Cushing. Bereft of logic, characterizations, suspense and anything else that makes watchable cinema. Directed by Costas Carayiannis, Luan Peters, Vanna Revilli. (VC)

**LAND THAT TIME FORGOT (1975).** First entry in a series of

**BEASTIES AND GHOULIES FROM 'LABYRINTH' (CLOCKWISE FROM UPPER RIGHT): A FIERY, SIR DIDYMUS, J ARETH'S CITIZENS, LUDO AND ANOTHER FIERY.**

Edgar Rice Burroughs adventure-fantasy yarns produced by John Dark and directed by Kevin Connor. When a British merchant is sunk by a U-Boat during World War I, the survivors (Doug McClure, Susan Penhaligon) seek refuge on an uncharted island forgotten by time. All the monsters (dragon, pterodactyl, etc.) are full-scale mock-ups moved mechnically, and sometimes it shows. Yet, there is a spirit of rousing adventure that makes this enjoyable. The sequel was AT THE EARTH'S CORE, followed by THE PEOPLE THAT TIME FORGOT. Decent escapist entertainment. John McEnery, Anthony Ainley. (VC)

**LAND UNKNOWN, THE (1956).** Potentially exciting lost world theme (helicopter carrying explorers bumps into a flying pterodactyl and crashlands in a primeval jungle) becomes the hackneyed plot for a cheap-jack (and we mean cheap, Jack) Universal-International potboiler, marred by what appears to be stock footage of attacking dinosaurs from previous prehistoric sagas. Clifford Stine's effects are ultimately too limited. Directed by Virgil Vogel. Jock Mahoney, Douglas Kennedy, William Reynolds.

**LASERBLAST (1978).** Teenager Kim Milford discovers a laser cannon in the desert (dropped during a war between alien armies) and uses it for revengeful purposes. This low budget quickie from producer Charles Band is one zap after the other, with Milford turning green whenever he blows up cars and buildings. There's some nice stop motion work of the aliens by Dave Allen—it's the story that's unanimated. Keenan Wynn and Roddy McDowall are wasted in stupid cameos. Directed with a one-track mind to blow everything up by Michael Rae. (VC)

**LASERBLAST II (1985).** "The ultimate alien weapon is back" with special effects by Mechanical and Makeup Imageries Inc. Charles Band-Paul Levinson production written by Robert Amante.

**LAST BRIDE OF SALEM, THE (1974).** Cheapo TV-movie, shot on tape, in which painter Bradford Dillman and goody-two-shoes wife Lois Nettleton move to Salem Village, a small community haunted by witches. Everyone pooh-poohs the old legends except the local minister who knows evil is afoot when he discovers Dillman is a descendant of a cursed family. And now Dillman and his daughter are marked for sacrifice. Also sacrificed: good acting and production. Don't sacrifice your time. Directed by Tom Donovan. Joni Brick, Paul Harding.

**LAST CHASE, THE (1981).** Racer Lee Majors sees his career cut short when oil reserves are depleted and an epidemic kills millions. Speeding around in his red Porsche, Majors survives by swiping gas from deserted stations. Ecological warning in the guise of science-fiction never builds up the speed that Majors does and is a minor diatribe. Directed by Martyn Burke. Burgess Meredith, Chris Makepeace, Alexandra Stewart. (VC)

**LAST CHILD, THE (1971).** TV-movie set in 1994 when the government, to cut overpopulation, limits families to one child. Parents Michael Cole and Janet Margolin flee totalitarian authorities, aided by a sympathetic senator (Van Heflin, excellent his last role). The story is well thought out by Peter S. Fischer. Directed by John Moxey. Kent Smith, Ed Asner, Harry Guardino, Barbara Babcock.

**LAST DAYS OF MAN ON EARTH, THE (1973).** British film about Michael Moorcock's Jerry Cornelius (taken from THE FINAL PROGRAMME), a chap in quest of microfilm that will reveal the secret to self-reproducing in a sterile post-Armageddon world. His adversary is Jenny Runacre, who wishes to procreate with him to create a New Messiah. A strange movie from writer-director Robert Fuest (THE ABOMINABLE DR. PHIBES) that falls short of its artistic goals. Jon Finch, Sterling Hayden, Harry Andrews, Hugh Griffith, Patrick Magee, George Coulouris. (VC)

**LAST DAYS OF PLANET EARTH, THE (1978).** Loosely-joined vignettes of doom as Earth heads for the last round-up, Japanese style. Armageddon begins when the ocean turns blood-red and all sealife expires, vegetation blooms and becomes man-eating stalkers, and radioactive monsters rove the planet. A visionary nightmare from director Toshio

Masuda, with destruction Godzilla style.

**LAST DINOSAUR, THE (1977).** U.S.-Japanese TV production written by William Overgard, author of the "Steve Roper" cartoon strip. An oil-seeking expedition discovers a lost world inhabited by wild natives and a tall man in a dinosaur suit. Characters and dialogue are hopelessly banal (Richard Boone is the insufferable leader of the expedition) and the special effects are from the Godzilla school of destruction. Directed by Alex Grasshof and Tom Kotani. Joan Van Ark, Steven Keats, William Ross.

**LAST HORROR FILM, THE (1982).** Amusing satire on horror movies starring Joe Spinell as a neurotic, possibly insane New York cabbie named Vinny Durand who has the hots for actress Jana Bates (Caroline Munro) and imagines himself a movie director making a horror flick, THE LOVES OF DRACULA. He follows her to the Cannes Film Festival in France, where this was filmed in 1981, so there's a rich amount of moviedom detail that will intrigue buffs. A series of gore murders begins with Durand hanging around the edges, breathing heavily, taking films of Jana and then making love to her projected image. And dig those hilarious scenes between Spinell and his little old Jewish mother (actually played by his mom, Mary). A campy, way-out derivative genre of slasher flicks directed and co-produced by David Winters. (VC)

**LAST HOUR, THE (1930).** Unimaginative Killer Ray Beam brings down aircraft in an unimaginative British film that must have wearied Britons when first released. Directed by Walter Forde. Stewart Rome, Wilfred Shine.

**LAST HOUSE ON DEAD END STREET (1981).** Filmmakers murder their stars to make snuff movies, then when they get cheated by their distributor, they kill the executives and use their death scenes in new snuffers. That'll teach the bastards who keep screwing over directors and exhibitors. Directed by Victor Juno. (VC)

**LAST HOUSE ON THE LEFT, THE (1972).** Pandering, wretched collaborative effort of producer Sean S. Cunningham and director Wes Craven, made to shock and horrify in the grossest manner with its mannerless tale of murder and retribution. Like Craven's HILLS HAVE EYES, this depicts a family being attacked by psychotic killers. Rape, castration, buzzsaw killings, crucifixions, sadistic torture . . . Craven crassly leaves out nothing. Utterly sickening . . . and yet this has an unrelenting power that makes it compelling despite its crudities. You'll still need a strong stomach. David Alex Hess, Lucy Grantham. (VC)

**LAST HOUSE ON THE LEFT II.** A retitling of CARNAGE (also known as TWITCH OF THE DEATH NERVE) so don't be fooled if you've already seen it. And if you haven't seen it, don't be fooled into watching. In videocassette format as BAY OF BLOOD.

**LAST MAN ON EARTH, THE (1964).** First adaptation of Richard Matheson's classic novel, I AM LEGEND, is far more faithful than the second, THE OMEGA MAN. Filmed in Italy by director Ubaldo Ragona (with U.S. insert shots by Sidney Salkow), it stars Vincent Price as the only non-tainted survivor of a worldwide plague; all others are walking corpses, a mutated form of vampirism. Price burns their bodies during the day and, with the coming of dusk, rushes to his fortress to fight off the nocturnal marauders, using traditional weapons of the vampire fighter. Some sequences are gripping. Emma Danieli, Giacomo Rossi Stuart.

**LAST MOVIE, THE (1971).** Following EASY RIDER, Dennis Hopper was given carte blanche by Universal to produce any movie; he chose this outre story—so bewildering to studio executives they gave it minimal distribution. Produced in Peru, it depicts the making of a Western movie (with real-life director Samuel Fuller portraying the crazed director who calls for action by firing his six-shooter into the air) but quickly turns into a Moebius Strip, twisting and winding in its depiction of illusions-within-reality, reality-within-illusions, and other time-space psychological distortions. Bizarre and different, utterly baffling to most viewers unless they're high on grass. Peter Fonda, Julie Adams, John Phillip Law, Sylvia Miles, Rod Cameron, Kris Kristofferson. Released to TV as CHINCHERO.

**LAST OF THE SECRET AGENTS, THE (1966).** Marty Allen and Steve Rossi portray undercover espionage spies in this James Bond spoof with such uninspired gimmicks as a spy agency called GGI (Good Guys Inc.) which is fighting T.H.E.M.—art thieves out to steal the Venus De Milo. But art is ain't. Produced and directed by Norman Abbott. Nancy Sinatra, John Williams, Edy Williams, Lou Jacobi, Sig Ruman, Harvey Korman, Ed Sullivan.

**LAST RITES.** See DRACULA'S LAST RITES.

**LAST STARFIGHTER, THE (1984).** Superior teen-age space adventure with excellent digital special effects and an interesting love story fleshed out by writer Jonathan Betuel. Lance Guest is a sympathetic young man living a bleak existence in a trailer park and excelling only at video games who

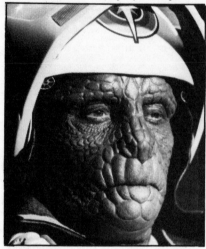

## DAN O'HERLIHY : 'LAST STARFIGHTER'

is picked by humanoid alien Robert Preston (portraying loveable conman Centauri) to help the Star League of Planets fight off a flotilla of invaders (and all because he's great at computer games). Guest is trained for this assignment by Dan O'Herlihy as Grig, the only remaining extraterrestrial who knows intergalactic warfare. Designers Ron Cobb and James D. Bissell have done a fine job of giving this fairy tale a glossy look, and there is computer animation of a high quality. But ultimately it is the sensitive love between Guest and Catherine Mary Stewart that makes this Universal production work so nicely. Directed by Nick Castle, an associate of John Carpenter. (VC)

**LAST UNICORN, THE (1982).** Winning animated version of Peter S. Beagle's novel about a beautiful white unicorn searching for the rest of her breed and battling the Terrible Red Bull. There's a lot of wizardry and magic at work, making this very suitable for adults and children. Voices by Alan Arkin, Jeff Bridges, Mia Farrow, Robert Klein, Angela Lansbury, Christopher Lee, Paul Frees. (VC)

**LAST WAR, THE (1961).** Japanese production, with special effects by Eiji Tsuburaya, depicts massive destruction: earthquakes, tidal waves, atomic explosions, the shattering of the London Bridge, the pulverization of the Arch of Triumph, the crumpling of the Statue of Liberty and the nuclearization of the Kremlin domes. Now let's see . . . did they leave any landmark out? It's all caused by faulty wiring in a missile base Fail-Safe System. The only thing missing amidst all this Japanese-created mayhem is Godzilla battling Rodan. Directed with a spectacular sense for the destructive by Shue Matsubayashi.

**LAST WARRIOR, THE.** See FINAL EXECUTIONER, THE.

**LAST WAVE, THE (1978).** Australia's Peter Weir directs an intriguing if mystifying tale of prophecy and doom. The sym-

bolism is fascinating, though, and the atmosphere of pending death heavy as Sydney-based attorney Richard Chamberlain defends a gang of Aborigines accused of murder, but he is simultaneously plagued by visions of horrors to come. A film that works on several levels, and which challenges the intellect as well as pleases the eye. Olivia Hamnett, Gulpilil, Nandjiwarra Amagula. (VC)

**LAST WOMAN ON EARTH, THE (1960).** Director Roger Corman trivializes post-Armageddon survival into a cheap triangular love story. Two men and one female, instead of worrying about how to build a better world in the wake of nuclear holocaust, engage in fatiguing dialogue and clumsy clenches. The screenplay is by Robert Towne, who later wrote CHINATOWN. Towne also plays one of the argumentative males opposite Anthony Carbone and Betsy Jones-Moreland. Almost instantly forgettable.

**LATE GREAT PLANET EARTH, THE (1978).** Prophesies of evil events yet to come, including the emergence of the Antichrist, based on the best-seller by literary soothsayer Hal Lindsey. Orson Welles narrates, trying to convince us we're doomed by the end of this century. This intriguing pseudo-documentary (written-directed by Robert Amram) makes a strong case for mankind's demise in the near future, when Apocalypse will be Now! Profound food for thought unless you think the world will never end.

**LATHE OF HEAVEN, THE (1980).** TV adaptation of Ursula K. LeGuin's popular novel about a man (Bruce Davison) whose dreams change the shape of the world. A psychologist (Kevin Conway) investigating the phenomenon tries to use the dreamer to make the world a better place, but his altruistic plan backfires. Recommended. Produced-directed by David Loxton and Fred Barzyk.

**LATITUDE ZERO (1969).** Japanese adventure-fantasy with an American cast (Joseph Cotten, Cesar Romero, Patricia Medina, Richard Jaeckel) borrows Jules Verne devices when a war rages between two submarine captains equipped with death zap guns, nuclear torpedos and assorted destructive weapons. A few hulking monsters are thrown in should you get bored with underwater action. That GODZILLA team, director Inoshiro Honda and special effects artist Eiji Tsuburaya, collaborated. Final coordinate: Zero. Akira Takarada, Tetsu Nakamura.

**LEECH WOMAN, THE (1960).** Producer Joseph Gershenson (head of Universal's music department) leeches off other horror movies to concoct this minor film that failed to suck money from fans. Coleen Gray, seeking eternal life, learns from Africans that a brain secretion can restore the aged body. One murder, however, leads to more before she and the plot turn to powder. Edward Dein directed. Gloria Talbott, Grant Williams, John Van Dreelan.

**LEGACY, THE (1980).** Botched project unrealized in the scripting (blame Jimmy Sangster, Patric Tilley, Paul Wheeler) and never focused by director Richard Marquand. Several travelers (Katharine Ross, Sam Elliott, Roger Daltrey, Charles Gray. etc.) gather in a European chateau where "a legacy of evil" is passed generation to generation—or something like that. Who knows for sure? Supernatural gore murders go on interminably. (VC)

**LEGACY OF BLOOD (1978).** Hopelessly incompetent psychothriller in which four heirs to a country estate spend the night in the homestead to qualify for the family fortune. Of course, each is murdered in some horrible fashion; even the head of the local sheriff (Rodolfo Acosta) ends up on a turkey platter in the frig. Jeff Morrow has tried to live this film down for years, but so far he hasn't succeeded. John Carradine, John Russell and Faith Domergue must harbor similar feelings, for all are squandered by producer-director Carl Monson on this worthless exercise in futility. A pox on the house of writer Eric Norden.

**LEGACY OF HORROR (1978).** Primary primer in how not to make a movie—a masterpiece of choppy, amateurish editing, poor lighting, camera noise, uneven acting and rank cinematography. Credit tacky Andy Milligan the exploitationer—he wrote and directed this mess about three silly sisters who must spend the night on Haney Island with their equally inane husbands to collect their fathers' inheritance. One by one they are murdered by a slouch-hatted slouch who leaves a head on the dining room platter, shoves a pitchfork into a fat stomach and saws a man in half (murders heavily cut by the TV censor). Elaine Boies, Chris Broderick, Louise Gallanda, Dale Hansen, Jeannie Cusick. Said to be a remake of Milligan's THE GHASTLY ONES. Ghastly is the word!

**LEGACY OF MAGGIE WALSH.** TV title for **LEGACY, THE.**

**LEGEND (1985).** Ridley Scott's fairy tale fantasy is set in a never-neverland beautifully rendered in autumnal detail, all falling leaves, mysticism and magic. So beautiful is the scenery, in fact, that the exquisite detail overshadows the weak story. A peasant (Tom Cruise) and Princess Lili (Mia Sara) trek to see the last remaining unicorns in the kingdom, unaware that Darkness (personified by Tim Curry, excellent as a world-weary, thoroughly evil demon) is using the pair to set a trap for the horned creatures that personify goodness. When the Princess is kidnapped, Jack must rescue her with a crew of elves and fairies. Rob Bottin created the wonderful creatures, but the screenplay by William Hjortsberg lacks humor or clever development, and the romantic leads are real wimps, hardly the stuff of which quest fantasy is made. Billy Barty, Alice Playten, David Bennett, Cork Hubbert. (VC)

**LEGEND OF BIGFOOT, THE (1976).** Did naturalist Ivan Marx capture "exclusive" footage of hairy beasts lunching in an unidentified swamp? Or are they Screen Actors Guild extras in monkey costumes? Burning questions to ask as you watch this "documentary." Marx, who claims the creatures are genuine, follows the trail of Bigfoot from Arizona to the Arctic Circle and has interesting travel footage, if nothing else. There is a strange scene of a bright light moving across the twilight landscape, as if an old Indian legend is coming true. Or is it a Volkswagen lost on the tundra? More burning questions . . .

**LEGEND OF BLOOD CASTLE (1972).** Another sanguinary variation on the Countess Bathory theme, with Lucia Bose bathing in the results of a nosebleed and coming out of the tub with a rosy glow on her cheeks. But by now the theme has been bled to death. Utterly anemic. Jorge Grau directed this Spanish-Italian fiasco. Ewa Aulin.

**LEGEND OF BLOOD MOUNTAIN, THE (1965).** Obscure fright flick about a small-town newspaperman in Georgia on the trail of a killer monster. Poor regional film-making by director Massey Cramer. Gregory Ellis, Erin Fleming.

**LEGEND OF BOGGY CREEK, THE (1973).** Producer-director Charles B. Pierce, known for wilderness Westerns, uses pseudodocumentary techniques in "documenting" the allegedly true story of a hairy Bigfoot haunting the Arkansas swamp country. Pierce uses local residents who claim to have seen the monster and re-enacts close encounters with such veracity, you almost believe everything he's telling. The story is told in voiceover by a resident of the area, as though it were a misty memory, giving this a high dramatic content. Willie E. Smith, John Hixon. (VC)

**LEGEND OF DOOM HOUSE (1972).** Orson Welles finds himself in a house haunted by Greek gods. Is this mythology or mystery? Susan Hampshire portrays a Gorgon. Harry Kumel directed the French-Belgium-German production, based on a novel by Jean Ray. Jean-Pierre Cassel, Sylvia Vartan, Walter Rilla, Mathieu Carriere.

**LEGEND OF HELL HOUSE (1973).** In adapting his own outstanding novel HELL HOUSE, Richard Matheson has eschewed garishness and gory imagery for unseen (or off-camera) grotesqueries. Hell House, accursed estate of the perverse Emeric Belasco, has been haunted by psychic phenomena since his death years before. A dying millionaire hires psychist Clive Revill to prove the existence of life after death and Hell House becomes the proving ground. Members of his team include his wife (Gayle Hunnicutt), a mental medium (Pamela Franklin) and a medium (Roddy McDowall) who is the sole survivor of an earlier attempt to exorcise Hell House. This unusually atmospheric film (in the league of THE HAUNTING) is tense throughout under John Hough's direction, with several twists of plot. It is not the harrowing experience of Matheson's superb book, but it comes as close as a movie can. (Watch for Michael Gough in a most unusual guest role.) (VC)

**LEGEND OF HILLBILLY JOHN (1972).** ONE STEP BEYOND host John Newland directed this version of Manly Wade Wellman's classic book WHO FEARS THE DEVIL?, a collection of supernatural stories about a guitarist, Silver John, who roves the Appalachians, warding off evil with his guitar's silver strings. Hedge Capers, Denver Pyle, Susan Strasberg, Percy Rodriguez, R. G. Armstrong.

**LEGEND OF HORROR (1972).** Yet another version of Edgar Allan Poe's "The Tell-Tale Heart," produced by Ricky Torres Tudela and directed by Bill Davies. Karin Field.

'LEGEND': BILLY BARTY AND CORK HUBBERT; A FAIRY NAMED OONA

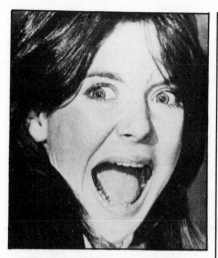

**PAMELA FRANKLIN IN 'LEGEND OF HELL HOUSE'**

**LEGEND OF LIZZIE BORDEN, THE (1975).** A spinstress living in Fall River, Mass., allegedly picked up an axe one morning in 1892 and gave her mother 40 whacks. When she saw what she had done, she gave her father 41. But that's the old legend—this TV-movie offers new theories about the infamous murder case. As the accused murderess, Elizabeth Montgomery is coldly indifferent to the homicidal events, bringing a macabre touch to the docudrama approach. Intriguing study in abnormal human behavior. William Bast wrote the fine script that was ably directed by Paul Wendkos. Fritz Weaver, Ed Flanders, Katherine Helmond, Don Porter, John Beal.

**LEGEND OF LOCH NESS (1976).** Pseudodocumentary about the Scottish loch where it is believed a prehistoric sea beast dwells in the depths, only occasionally rearing its snake-like head above the water. Explorers use modern equipment to seek the creature, but come away with inconclusive evidence. Produced-directed by Richard Martin, written by Christian Davis. Narrated by Arthur Franz. (VC)

**LEGEND OF LYLAH CLARE, THE (1968).** Bizarre, sometimes surreal story of a film producer (Peter Finch) who finds a lookalike for a dead actress and trains her to imitate the late glamour queen. Is Kim Novak, who begins behaving too real, possessed by the dead woman's spirit? Is she a reincarnation? Is she a walking corpse? These questions are left dangling. Everything comes out as muddy as the Mississippi as producer-director Robert Aldrich and writers Hugo Butler and Jean Rouverol make devastating statements about TV advertising and various failings of the media. Ernest Borgnine, Coral Browne, George Kennedy.

**LEGEND OF SLEEPY HOLLOW (1949).** Walt Disney's animated version of Washington Irving's childhood classic about Ichabod Crane's terrifying Halloween-night ride through a forest frequented by The Headless Horseman. (VC) (Originally included in ADVENTURES OF ICHABOD AND MR. TOAD, which also featured an adaptation of "The Wind in the Willows.")

**LEGEND OF SLEEPY HOLLOW (1980).** TV-movie adaptation of Washington Irving's classic story featuring the Headless Horseman. However, there's nothing much classic in Henning Schellerup's direction. Jeff Goldblum, Paul Sand, Meg Foster, Laura Campbell, Dick Butkus. (VC)

**LEGEND OF SPIDER FOREST, THE (1971).** Britisher about a spider-venom nerve gas and a creature described as a "spider goddess." Peter Sykes directed the script by Donald and Derek Ford. Simon Brent, Neda Arneric. (VC)

**LEGEND OF THE BAYOU.** See **EATEN ALIVE** (unless you can't stand the sight of people and animals being swallowed whole by an alligator living next door to Neville Brand, who owns a rundown swamp hotel).

**LEGEND OF THE MOUNTAIN (1979).** Chinese-Mandarin ghost tale, based on an 11th-century legend called "A Caveful of Ghosts in the West Mountains," which pretty well gives away the plot. Directed by King Hu.

**LEGEND OF THE SEVEN GOLDEN VAMPIRES (1973).** Co-production between Hammer and the Shaw Brothers of Hong Kong results in satisfying sukiyaki—an east-west blending of martial arts, kung fu and vampire bloodletting. In 1804, Count Dracula inhabits the body of a Chinese priest in order to resurrect seven vampire corpses in Samurai armor who terrorize villagers. Flash-ahead to 1904: Peter Cushing, again as Van Helsing, joins his heroic son, Swedish beauty Julie Ege (in low-cut gowns, blouses and high-heeled boots) and a troupe of Chinese warriors to trek to a haunted village and destroy the demons. The action is almost nonstop, the fights are tremendous jobs of choreography and the make-up for the monsters quite effective. All in all, a rousing piece of entertainment. Directed by Roy Ward Baker with an insidious eye, and written by Don Houghton with an inscrutable glance. Robin Stewart, David Chiang, John Forbes Robertson.

**LEGEND OF THE WEREWOLF (1975).** British horrorizer in the Hammer mood, with Gothic atmosphere, superior direction by Freddie Francis and a fine cast headed by Peter Cushing as an investigating medical examiner and Ron Moody as the young man plagued by lycanthropy, who goes on multi-murder sprees when the moon is full. (He was raised by a wolfpack as a child, accounting for his desire to eat raw flesh.) Anthony Hines, scripting as John Elder, faithfully follows the lore of THE WOLF MAN (even time-lapse photography is used for transformations) with the plot reminiscent of CURSE OF THE WEREWOLF. (VC)

**LEGEND OF THE WOLF WOMAN (1977).** Larry Woolner of Dimension Pictures tried to pass off this Spanish import as true—but who was he kidding? Here's the truth: It's a horror film loaded with helpings of sadism, violence and sex as Ann Borel, thinking she is the reincarnation of a wolf creature from a previous century, rips, tears and slashes her way to oblivion. Make that movie oblivion. Directed-written by Rino Di Silvestro. Frederick Stafford. (VC)

**LEMORA—LADY VAMPIRE (1973).** Offbeat, surrealistic vampire flick with arty overtones—some scenes pretentious as hell, others more traditional. A young girl's odyssey through a nightmarish landscape is filled with grotesque people and maintains curiosity if you don't take the story literally. Cheryl Smith carries the picture as the 13-year-old girl. Directed by Richard Blackburn.

**LEONARD NIMOY IN SEARCH OF: VOL. 1 (1978-81).** Three half-hour episodes of the once-popular TV series IN SEARCH OF, hosted by Leonard Nimoy. These three cover the theme of London: Sherlock Holmes, Jack the Ripper and the Tower of London murders. (VC)

**LEONOR (1975).** Offtrail Luis Bunuel horror film, a Spanish-French-Italian effort, starring Liv Ullmann as a woman who sucks the life force from children. Slow going, with strange Bunuel imagery to keep you pondering. (VC)

**LEOPARD MAN, THE (1943).** Cornell Woolrich's novel BLACK ALIBI was adapted by screenwriter Ardel Wray for producer Val Lewton. It emerges a superb low-budget, high-thrills masterpiece of "quiet horror." Director Jacques Tourneur provides memorable sequences greater than the sum total—including one in which a gypsy girl's blood flows under a door after she is locked outside and attacked by an unseen force. That force is believed to be an escaped leopard, but all is not what it seems. Minimal focus is placed on hero and heroine (Dennis O'Keefe, Jean Brooks) as they track down the source of evil. (VC)

**LESBIAN TWINS.** See **VIRGIN WITCH, THE.**

**LET'S KILL UNCLE (1966).** Unusual William Castle film in which a young boy and girl are trapped in a mansion on an island with Nigel Green, who tries to knock off the kiddies in different ways. Worth a look for its unusual theme. Pat Cardi,

**CREATURE FEATURES MOVIE GUIDE**

Mary Badham, Linda Lawson, Nestor Paiva.

**LET'S LIVE AGAIN (1948).** John Emery is a nuclear researcher whose brother is reincarnated as a dog. This theme was not uncommon in the 1940s—it was responsible for more "dogs" than Hollywood producers realized. Producer Frank Seltzer was throwing a bone to director Herbert I. Leeds. He should have rolled over and played dead. Hillary Brooke, Taylor Holmes, James Millican.

**LET'S SCARE JESSICA TO DEATH (1971).** Director John Hancock is to be congratulated for a multi-layered horror film with frightening visuals. There isn't a lot of logic one can attach to the story yet the overall effect is unsettling. Zohra Lampert is a young woman newly released from an insane asylum but we never know for certain if she is hallucinating or something really weird and freaked out is happening on her Connecticut farm. Are those spaced-out inhabitants in the nearby town vampires or zombies? The film has a dream-like quality in depicting her nightmares. Gretchen Corbett, Barton Heyman, Kevin O'Connor. (VC)

**LICENSE TO KILL (1964).** Standard Nick Carter spy thriller with Eddie Constantine as the international agent preventing Oriental baddies from stealing a new anti-gravity device. Except for Constantine, who is always interesting to watch, this French production has little to recommend it. Directed by

Henry Decoin. Daphne Dayle, Paul Frankeur, Yvonne Monlaur, Charles Belmond, Vladimir Inkijinoff.

**LICENSED TO KILL.** See **SECOND BEST SECRET AGENT IN THE WHOLE WIDE WORLD, THE.**

**LICENSED TO LOVE AND KILL.** See **MAN FROM S.E.X.**

**LIFE AND ADVENTURES OF SANTA CLAUS (1986).** Animated TV-movie based on a L. Frank Baum novel retelling the Santa legend. He's accepted into The Immortals (a race that rules over the elements) so he can battle the bad Awgwas and prove he wants to bring pleasure to children. Voices by Earl Hammond, Earle Hyman, Larry Kennedy. Produced-directed by Arthur Rankin Jr. and Saul Bass.

**LIFE IS A CIRCUS (1958).** British comedy (written-directed by Val Guest) depicts how members of the Big Top utilize Aladdin's Lamp to save their tent. The good cast includes Bud Flanagan, Shirley Eaton, Lionel Jeffries (as the genie) and Jimmy Nervo. Known as part of the "Crazy Gang" series, an imitation of "Carry On." A Three-Ringer . . .

**LIFE, LIBERTY AND PURSUIT ON THE PLANET OF THE APES (1974).** Earth astronauts Ron Harper and James Naughton are subjected to perilous brainwashing techniques by chimps and orangutans in this TV-movie of episodes re-edited from the deservedly short-lived PLANET OF THE

'LEGEND OF THE LOCH NESS': YOU USE A HAMMER LOCH TO CATCH HIM (IT?)

APES series starring Roddy McDowall as Galen. Beverly Garland, Mark Lenard.

**LIFE POD (1980).** Gold Key time-killer (which means watching grass grow is more exciting) about a spaceship plagued by a computer that goes a little crazy. Gee, aren't those blades pushing through the ground exciting? Joe Penny, Jordan Michaels, Kristine DeBell.

**LIFEFORCE (1985).** Colin Wilson's intellectual novel SPACE VAMPIRES becomes an uneven but still recommended space-horror film by director Tobe Hooper, who thrives on the first half of the Dan O'Bannon-Don Jakoby script. Hooper helms outstanding macabre scenes of dead bodies popping to life—this is one time horrific visuals will have you shivering days later. A spaceship sent to investigate Halley's Comet discovers an alien vessel which harbors bat-like creatures and three incubated humanoids. One of them, a big-busted female, sucks energy from Earthlings, turning them to horrendous cadavers, before she escapes. The gripping, if eerie, fascination builds as inspector Peter Firth and astronaut survivor Steve Railsback attempt to solve the soul- transference, lifeforce-energy transference mystery. It is when London is ablaze, and half the population turns into zombies, that the film falls apart, its special effects too metaphysical and its ending too ridiculous to live up to the earlier great thrills. Frank Finlay, Mathilda May, Patrick Stewart. Music by Henry Mancini, effects by John Dykstra and John Gant. (VC)

**LIFESPAN (1975).** A short life span, that's what this U.S.-British-Belgian production experienced. The aged story: a doctor experiments with a serum to lengthen life, his subjects members of an old folks' home. Life expectancy for this drops off after 20 minutes. Alexander Whitelaw wrote-produced-directed in Amsterdam. Hiram Keller, Tina Aumont, Klaus Kinski, Eric Schneider.

**LIFT, THE (1983).** Fascinating Dutch horror film, a cross between an exploitation shocker and a European art film. A new elevator system in a high-rise reprograms itself to kill human passengers in grisly ways through a system of organic microchips—at least that's what writer-director Dick Maas intimates as his strange tale leanly, tersely unfolds. Maas conveys a sense of classy horror and then lapses into graphic slayings—including one hair-lift-ing sequence in which a security guard is decapitated. The mystery involves a conspiracy between the elevator designer and the electronics programmer as a lift repairman (Huub Stapel) searches for the truth. Gripping stuff, "up-lifting." (VC)

**LIGHT BLAST (1985).** Stand-up comic Michael Pritchard portrays mad scientist Yuri Soboda who creates a deadly laser and plans to blow up San Francisco. Who steps forth to save the metropolis when the mayor is incapacitated and police are paralyzed? Why, who else but Erik Estrada as inspector Ronn Warren. Crooks in the know never mess with that guy! It's one car chase after another, and one exploding "light blast" after another until yucky Yuri is yoaked and yocked. Directed in S.F. with an Italian crew by Enzo G. Castellari. Thomas Moore, Peggy Rowe, Bob Taylor. (VC)

**LIGHT YEARS AWAY (1981).** Allegorical French-Swiss film by writer-director Alain Tanner about a strange old man (Trevor Howard) who claims birds have taught him how to fly, and who imparts philosophies to drifter Mick Ford. Odd offering, more thoughtful than action-oriented, enhanced by Scottish backgrounds.

**LIGHTNING BOLT (1967).** Anthony Eisley is a lackluster superspy trying to prevent an insidious madman from exploding U.S. spacecraft with a typical, hohum laser beam death ray vortex blaster atom-smashing burp buster. Italian-Spanish thriller directed by Antonio Margheriti (Anthony Dawson). Wandisa Leigh, Diana Lorys, Fulco Lulli.

**LI'L ABNER (1940).** Infrequently shown version of Al Capp's comic strip fails to capture the flair of the printed page, but is still an interesting period piece. The main problems with this RKO release were the low budget and the uninspired direction of Albert S. Rogell. Buster Keaton appears as Lonesome Polecat. Other familiar faces belong to Chester Conklin, Doodles Weaver and Edgar Kennedy. This focuses on the

**JON HALL, STAR OF 'THE LION MAN'**

women running after their men in an annual race with the help of the Kickapoo Joy Juice.

**L'IL ABNER (1959).** The 1957 Norman Panama-Melvin Frank Broadway play came to the screen with all the crazy ingredients and flavor of Al Capp's cartoon strip. Dogpatch has been selected as an atomic bomb site, which brings out the worst in Evil-Eye Fleagle—he puts the "whammy" on folks. Yokumberry is a drink that gives Abner Yokum his abnormal strength, but in the process he loses his sex drive—which is upsetting to Daisy Mae's own dogpatch. Peter Palmer is wholesomely naive as Abner and Leslie Parrish is absolutely stunning in the original HotPants. Frank directed, Panama produced and together they adapted their own material. Stubby Kaye is Marryin' Sam, Al Nesor is Fleagle. Other Dogpatch dwellers: Julie Newmar, Stella Stevens, Bern Hoffman, Billie Hayes and Robert Strauss.

**LINK (1986).** Offbeat suspense thriller with horror overtones—an oddity from Australian producer-director Richard Franklin and writer Everett DeRoche. Terence Stamp, specialist in the behavior of chimpanzees, brings student Elizabeth Shue to his isolated coastal Gothic mansion where she meets a superintelligent chimp named Link, who dresses like the family retainer, smokes cigars and watches her take a bath with a lecherous look on his kisser. Gradually Link turns homicidal, suggesting a subtext that man evolved with a killer instinct no amount of civilization can cure. Franklin mounts the suspense during the siege portion of the film, but a weak character for the woman, and a small role for Stamp create an unfocused film, with an ending less than satisfying and an ambiguous theme. (VC)

**LINK, THE (1982).** See **BLOOD LINK.**

**LION MAN, THE (1937).** Edgar Rice Burroughs story in which Jon Hall is a pale carbon copy of Tarzan as he swings across one of the phoniest studio back-lot jungle sets ever potted by the greenhouse boys. The kids, though, should love such corny action. Directed by John P. McCarthy. Kathleen Burke, Eric Snowden, Ted Adams.

**LION, THE WITCH AND THE WARDROBE (1979).** Animated fantasy based on C.S. Lewis' "Chronicles on Narnia," depicting how some kids use their closet as a means of traveling to another kingdom. (VC)

**LIQUID SKY (1983).** New wave/punk rock/heavy

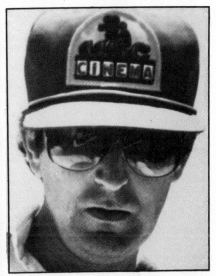

**LINK THE SUPER-INTELLIGENT ORANGUTAN AND HIS DIRECTOR, RICHARD FRANKLIN**

metal/western decadence flick depicting freaked out adrogyne Margaret whose penthouse rooftop is visited by a flying saucer. Once she's been infected by an alien organism, her orgasms result in the deaths of her partners. What a way to go in the land of debauchery. Sardonic and funk punk bunk, with video graphics and reverse polarity taking the place of sexual encounters of the closest kind. It may be judged more MTV than movie as Anne Carlisle (as the borderline man-woman) writhes through her torrid affairs with Manhattan low life. Smartly produced by Russian emigre Slava with his wife Nina Kerova. (VC)

**LISA AND THE DEVIL.** See **HOUSE OF EXORCISM, THE.** (What's a sweet kid like her doing in a . . . ?)

**LISA, LISA.** See **AXE.** (The poor girl was chopped up and renamed.)

**LITTLE ARK, THE (1971).** Two children trapped in a church belfry during a flood in Holland in 1953 are rescued by fisherman Theodore Bikel, who relates to them an animated story of ghosts and a mermaid. Directed by James B. Clark. Philip Frame, Genevieve Ambas.

**LITTLE GIRL WHO LIVES DOWN THE LANE, THE (1976).** Chilling thriller with provocative psychological implications as 13-year-old Jodie Foster knocks off a number of folks to keep her secret: Mother is buried in the cellar. Tautly directed by Nicolas Gessner, scripted by Laird Koenig. Alexis Smith, Martin Sheen, Scott Jacoby. (VC)

**LITTLE ORBIT, THE ASTRODOG AND THE SCREECHERS FROM OUTER SPACE (1977).** Animated French cartoon depicting adventurers (including robot, two humans, one dog) from the planet Hunger who fight off invaders on Planet High Rise.

**LITTLE PRINCE, THE (1973).** Offbeat, charming philosophical music-fable based on the book by French aviator Antoine de Saint-Exupery (who died in World War II), produced-directed by Stanley Donen in the fashion of an allegory, with script/lyrics by Alan Jay Lerner and music by Frederic Loewe. A singing pilot (Richard Kiley) crashes in the Sahara Desert and meets an emissary from Asteroid B-612, a small child (amidst a flock of animated birds) in search of the true meaning of life. In surreal flashbacks the youth tells of odd characters he's met in his search through the galaxies. A child with a thick British accent, Steven Warner seems a strange choice for the prince, but he looks endearing. In one of the musical sequences Gene Wilder plays a fox and Bob Fosse does a marvelously choreographed snake routine. (VC)

**LITTLE RED RIDING HOOD (1959).** First in a Mexican trilogy imported to the U.S. by producer K. Gordon Murray. The little girl going to grandmother's house encounters—you guessed it—the Big Bad Wolf. Maria Garcia bounces along with her big basket. Directed by Roberto Rodriguez, as were the sequels: **LITTLE RED RIDING HOOD AND HER FRIENDS (1959)**, and **LITTLE RED RIDING HOOD AND THE MONSTERS (1959)**, which includes a vampire and a witched witch, with Tom Thumb helping "Red." Strictly for lobo lovers and hood manufacturers.

**LITTLE SHOP OF HORRORS, THE (1960).** Producer-director Roger Corman's macabre comedy classic parodies horror-monster flicks with a vengeance. Jonathan Haze is in a daze as Seymour Krelboing, a flower shop clerk who raises a giant plant that repeatedly burps "Feed me, I'm hungry!" Seymour does—human food. Belch! Mel Welles is Gravis Mushnik, the shop owner, Jackie Joseph is the love interest and Dick Miller is a customer. Scripted by Charles Griffith, who wrote the story around a standing set Corman had seen in a studio. The film developed a cult following and became a musical in New York and L.A. for years, the stage ultimately filled with the huge killer plant. A musical film remake was released in 1986. (VC)

**LITTLE SHOP OF HORRORS (1986).** Corman's B-film and the intimate off-Broadway musical were turned into an overinflated horror musical, faithfully following the music and storyline of the play but much darker and crueler in depicting how a nerd falls in love with a bimbo and feeds human body parts to a man-eating, talking plant. What was once a charming comedy becomes an uncomfortable experience, for the screen overemphasizes the slum area of Mushkin's Floral Shop and the monstrousness of the plant, Audrey II, as it sways humans with its Svengali-like hold. Especially unfunny are Steve Martin as a sadistic dentist and Bill Murray as his masochistic patient, carrying to extremes what was in the original film a short and funny moment. Director Frank Oz must have been escaping his G-rated Muppet image—even Warner Bros. had to lighten up the unpleasantries before the film was released.

**LIVE AGAIN, DIE AGAIN (1974).** TV-movie explores Cryonics, a form of suspended animation in which a diseased person is frozen with the hope the body can be thawed out later when the disease is curable. Director Richard A. Colla leans heavily on psychological aspects as a family faces the reality of a Cryonics-treated mother (Donna Mills) returning to life after 34 years. The startled husband is Walter Pidgeon and the children, now grown up, are Vera Miles and Mike Farrell. Written by Joseph Stefano.

**LIVE AND LET DIE (1973).** Roger Moore's first time out as British spy 007, James Bond . . . He attempts the droll indifference and sophisticated snobbery of the licensed-to-kill superagent, but he's a connoisseur strictly for philistines. The series had begun to deteriorate to the point screenwriter Tom Mankiewicz was forced to introduce a stereotyped Southern sheriff, J. W. Pepper. Director Guy Hamilton tries to maintain the visual standards he established in GOLDFINGER with a plot about Negro drug king Kananga (Yaphet Kotto) and how Bond tracks him to his voodoo-happy lair in the Louisiana swamps. All very contrived, with a wild and woolly motorboat chase, an alligator pit and other jeopardy devices. Jane Seymour, David Hedison. (VC)

**LIVER EATERS, THE.** See **SPIDER BABY.**

**LIVING COFFIN, THE (1965).** Churubusco-Azteca Mexican horror film blending pseudosupernatural and action Western elements when a buckskin hero and his comedic Pancho-like sidekick meet a ranching family haunted by The Curse of the Crying Ghost. A mysterious veiled witch, a bog of quicksand and a coffin with a built-in alarm device are featured in Raymond Obon's goofy script. Such an odd melding of genres, it's kind of fun, in an incompetent way, of course. American producer K. Gordon Murray brought it across the border with new footage directed by Manuel San-Fernando. The original spooks-and-sombrero stuff was shot by Ferdinand Mendez. Gaston Santos is the cowboy hero. Mary Duval, Peter D'Aguillon, Charles Ancira.

**LIVING DEAD, THE (1934).** Antiquated British mystery mellow-drama in which a Scotland Yard dick invents a serum that induces death—it's part of his scheme to collect insurance on his subjects. Only he has the antitoxin when he kidnaps his partner's daughter and puts her into a coma. The living end in tedium! You too will slide into catatonia as this stuffy stuff unfolds. Directed by Thomas Bentley. Gerald Du Maurier, George Curzon. (VC)

**LIVING DEAD AT MANCHESTER MORGUE.** See **DON'T OPEN THE WINDOW.** (Manchester guardian?)

**LIVING GHOST, THE (1942).** Rattlingly old Monogram monstrosity, unworthy of attention when first produced, still unworthy. Paralysis of the brain is the danger you run when meeting a corpse that appears to be dead, but which is simply in hibernation. Played as a comedy by director William Beaudine and cast members James Dunn, Joan Woodbury and Minerva Urecal. Dated hogwash.

**LIVING HEAD, THE (1959).** Mexican horror importer K. Gordon Murray at work again, jazzing up an Abel Salazar flicker for U.S. consumption. This abomination is head but not shoulders above others of its (stereo)type. When a tomb is opened by an archeological expedition, its members find the head of an Aztec warrior, who's been waiting centuries for idiots just like these to drop into the vault so he can now fulfill a curse. Directed by Chanto Urueta and starring Salazar and German Robles. (VC)

**LIVING IDOL, THE (1957).** Steve Forrest and James Robertson Justice enliven this U.S.-Mexican film (made in Mexico) in which an idol of stone is responsible for several deaths and a young woman turns out to be reincarnated. Only for those with idol time on their hands. Directed by Albert Lewin and Rene Cardona. Liliane Montevecchi.

**LIZZIE (1957).** Hugo Haas-directed version of Shirley Jackson's novel, THE BIRD'S NEST, about a young woman (Eleanor Parker) with three personalities: Elizabeth, a mousy worker in a museum; Beth, who seems well adjusted; and Lizzie, a wild party girl. Which will dominate the soul? Psychiatrist Richard Boone probes her psyche to find out. Joan Blondell co-stars with director Haas who plays a friend of Elizabeth's—or is it Beth's—or Lizzie's—or—

**LOCH NESS HORROR, THE (1982).** Larry Buchanan special, which means you're in for cheap thrills with that Scotland denizen of the deep, Nessypooh. Sandy Kenyon, Barry Buchanan (is this nepotism?), Preston Hansen. (VC)

**LOCK UP YOUR DAUGHTERS (1956).** A collection of scenes from cheap Bela Lugosi movies, thrown together by producer Sam Katzman, who hired Lugosi to narrate shortly before the actor died. Footage includes scenes from THE APE MAN and THE VOODOO MAN. Lock up your TV set unless you dig funky lunky junky unspunky nostalgia.

**LODGER, THE (1926).** Early Alfred Hitchcock thriller (subtitled "A Story of the London Fog") based on the 1913 Marie Belloc-Lowndes novel about Jack the Ripper. Dated and stodgy, and suffering from a cop-out ending imposed on Hitch. A curiosity piece revived at Hitchcock retrospectives. Ivor Novello, Malcolm Keen. (VC)

**LODGER, THE (1944).** Atmosphere and performance are everything in this fogbound, eerie version of Marie Belloc-Lowndes' novel depicting fear-stricken London during the horrendous Jack the Ripper rippings of gin-swilling prostitutes in Soho. Laird Cregar, a superb heavy of the early 1940s, provides an undercurrent of menace and smouldering psychosis in one of the finest, subtlest portrayals of a heinous villain ever. Barre Lyndon's adaptation is brooding with Victorian ambience in this glimpse at the darkest side of man. Merle Oberon is the music hall dancer who becomes Cregar's target; George Sanders is her compassionate lover. Congratulations to director John Brahm, cinematographer Lucien Ballard and composer Hugo Friedhofer for haunting contributions to this horror classic. Sir Cedric Hardwicke, Sara Allgood, Doris Lloyd. (VC)

**LOGAN'S RUN (1976).** MGM's version of the William Nolan-George Clayton Johnson novel was thoroughly botched into a bastardization of glaring inconsistencies, peopled by uninteresting characters and often ineptly directed by Michael Anderson. The setting is a subterranean future society where everyone is brainwashed into going to their deaths at the age of 30; if they try to "run" they are cut down by "Sandmen." Sandman Michael York rebels and escapes to the outside world. There's a sequence with Peter Ustinov living in the ruins of the nation's capital, there's Roscoe Lee Brown playing a robot named Box and there's Jenny Agutter for love interest. Farrah Fawcett-Majors appears briefly to deliver an utterly appalling performance. An embarrassment for all concerned. (VC)

**LONDON AFTER MIDNIGHT (1927).** Tod Browning wrote, produced and directed this MGM silent mystery thriller with pseudohorror vampire overtones. Remade by the studio in 1935 as MARK OF THE VAMPIRE. Lon Chaney, Percy Williams, Conrad Nagel, Henry B. Walthall.

**LONG DARK NIGHT, THE.** Condensed TV version of **PACK, THE.** (A dogged film!)

**LONG, SWIFT SWORD OF SIEGFRIED (1971).** U.S.-West German fantasy adventure depicting the heroic knight in pursuit of the fire-eating dragon. Long all right, but not too swift. Originally directed by Adrian Hoven in German, with English scenes written and directed by David F.

SOME 'LOOKER'

Friedman. This has the distinction of being one of Sybil Danning's first films . . . now she's swift— if you get our drift. Raymond Harmstorf, Heidi Bohlen, Carl H. Heitmann.

**LOOK WHAT'S HAPPENED TO ROSEMARY'S BABY (1976).** Look what's happened to a hit movie when they made a breeched TV sequel. They gave birth to a Mongolian. Stillborn. The story (by producer Anthony Wilson, not Ira Levin) picks up years later when the Devil's son Adrian is a young boy and is taken away from Rosemary (now Patty Duke). The narrative then skips to when Adrian is a young man (Stephen McHattie) involved with a demon cult. Only Ruth Gordon as the witch next door repeats her role from the original—everything else is second-rate substitution. And director Sam O'Steen is no Roman Polanski. Broderick Crawford, George Maharis, Tina Louise, Donna Mills, Ray Milland, Stephen McHattie.

**LOOKER (1981).** Michael Crichton wrote-directed this strange mixture of science-fiction, suspense and horror, never quite findi:g the right blend. It's gimmicky and tricky, about a TV-commercial production company that has an artificial way of creating laser projections of beautiful models. But first the company must eliminate the real women on whom these clone lovelies are patterned with a strange time-continuum blaster. Sinks into utter confusion at times but the set designs are outstanding and the cast (Albert Finney as the hero, James Coburn as the heavy, Susan Dey and Leigh Taylor-Young as love interests) is accomplished, even with the sometimes-weak material. (VC)

**LOOSE IN LONDON (1953).** Leo Gorcey, Huntz Hall and the Bowery Boys find their hair standing on end in a British manor complete with torture devices, a belltower that tolls the hour of murder and the "ghost" of a hangman. If you love dumb delinquents, you'll love LOOSE IN LONDON. Directed by Edward Bernds. Angela Greene.

**LORD OF THE FLIES (1963).** On the eve of atomic holocaust, English schoolboys being flown to safety crash-land on a tropical island. The youths splinter into roving bands and eventually deteriorate into practitioners of cruel barbarism. This strange allegory on social and political behavior, based on the novel by William Golding, has uneven acting and suspense, but still yields a high rate of cinematic allegory. A good effort from screenwriter-director Peter Brook. James Aubrey, Tom Chapin, Hugh Edwards. (VC)

**LORD OF THE RINGS (1978).** Director Ralph Bakshi injects a flavor of reality into this animated version of J. R. R. Tolkien's epic narrative set in Middle Earth, specifically the novels THE TWO TOWERS and THE FELLOWSHIP OF THE RING. All the likeable and evil characters have been re-created: the Hobbits, wizards, the Gollum, Ring Wraiths, etc. But none recaptures the poetic, sensitive qualities of Tolkien's tomes. Bakshi abandoned sequels but there were TV movies by other animators: THE HOBBIT and RETURN OF THE KING. Voices by John Hurt, Christopher Guard, William Squire, Andre Morell. Script adaptation by Chris Conkling and Peter S. Beagle. (VC)

**LORD SHANGO (1975).** All-black cast dominates this programmer set in Tennessee in which Lord Shango, a tribal priest, returns from the dead to make sure the superstitious folks stay in line. Marlene Clark, Lawrence Cook. Directed by Raymond Marsh.

**LORELEI'S GRASP, THE (1975).** Spanish horror specialist Amando de Ossorio (yes, the writer-director who gave us NIGHT OF THE SORCERESS and NIGHT OF THE SEAGULLS) returns to curse our nightmares with this tale about a girls' school threatened by a wild beast that tears the hearts from its victim. One of the babes is that ultimate of legendary sirens, Lorelei, who rises from her slumber every few centuries to steal the hearts of the young. A hunter assigned to destroy the beast makes the mistake of falling in love. Tony Kendall portrays the hunter, with Helga Line and Silvia Tortosa assisting with exposed pulchritude.

**LOST ATLANTIS (1932).** French director G. W. Pabst's version of "L'Atlantide" by Pierre Benoit. It's the ancient legend of a lost continent, presented here as a mythical desert adventure in which a soldier-of-fortune meets a queen with cosmic powers. Remade in America as SIREN OF ATLANTIS. Brigitte Helm, Jean Angelo, John Stuart.

**LOST CITY, THE (1935).** See CITY OF LOST MEN.

**LOST CITY, THE (1982).** Robert Dukes directed this imitation of SHE which features a long-undiscovered metropolis, a queen with a headdress, crumbling ruins and a quest for

SAM, FRODO AND GOLLUM IN 'LORD OF THE RINGS'

romance and riches. Bernadette Clark, David Cain Haughton, Margot Samson.

**LOST CITY OF ATLANTIS, THE (1978).** Phony and groany documentary speculates on the mystery of Atlantis and other enigmas. Plenty of conjecture by writer Sara Nickerson but few answers and little conviction. Unimaginatively slapped together by director Richard Martin.

**LOST CONTINENT, THE (1951).** Robert L. Lippert fantasy-adventure has adequate production values, a catchy score by Paul Dunlap and a good performance by Cesar Romero as a flight commander looking for a rocket that crashed on a high plateau. His flight crew (including John Hoyt, Hugh Beaumont and Sid Melton) is trapped and surrounded by man-eating dinosaurs. Surprisingly good for a low budget quickie, even if some footage was lifted from other Lippert films. Hillary Brooke, Acquanetta, Whit Bissell, Chick Chandler. Directed by Sam Newfield.

**LOST CONTINENT, THE (1968).** Hammer adaptation of the

together—zappo, unlimited power. Her adversary is Dr. Sin Do (played with incredible hamminess by Angus Scrimm, the Tall Man from PHANTASM) who runs an island called Golgotha. To the island goes Angel with Raven de la Croix, an Indian woman who appears out of a mist on a white charger, and karate-kicking Angela Aames. Played for laughs by Wynorski, but his plotting is plodding and he allows the actors to run away with their outrageous lines. It's the bouncing breasts that will make you say: So who wants subtlety? Bob Tessier is really awful as Scrimm's right-hand toady. Appearing in cameos: Linda Shayne, Angelique Pettyjohn, Kenneth Tobey and Garry Goodrow. (VC)

**LOST HORIZON (1937).** James Hilton's romantic fantasy set in Shangri-la, a luxuriant valley hidden in the Tibetan Mountains, could only have been given such poetic, sensitive interpretation by producer-director Frank Capra. Shangra-li, a paradise where aging, greed and brutality are nonexistent, is an idyllic symbol for everything man searches for. Ronald Colman was never more romantically appealing as Robert

**WILLIS O'BRIEN'S STOP-MOTION CREATURES IN 'THE LOST WORLD' (1925)**

popular Dennis Wheatley fantasy-adventure novel with touches of William Hope Hodgson splashed in for added monster moisture by producer-director Michael Carreras. A freighter is jeopardized by a cargo of high explosives; survivors of this ordeal find themselves facing another ordeal: A Sargasso Sea of Lost Ships, menaced from underwater by seaweed serpents and colossal crabs and from on deck by shipwrecked Spanish nuts who worship a wriggling octopus god. This pulp adventure has middling special effects and a mediocre script by Michael Nash that keeps it dead in the water. Eric Porter, Hildegard Knef, Suzanna Leigh, Victor Maddern, Nigel Stock, Michael Ripper.

**LOST EMPIRE, THE (1985).** As dumb as this is, it has moments of fun and should please oglers, since producer-writer-director Jim Wynorski (one-time press agent for Roger Corman) has made a male sexual fantasy first, an adventure second. Unlikely L.A. cop Angel Wolfe (buxom Melanie Vincz) is out to avenge a fellow cop's death and find the Eye of Avatar, an energy-packed gem belonging to the lost race of Lemurians. There are two Eyes and whoever puts them

Conway, brought to the valley with other stranded airline passengers aboard a plane with no pilot. The cast is superb: Jane Wyatt as Conway's sweetheart; H.B. Warner as wise old Chang, Sam Jaffee as the High Lama, and Edward Everett Horton as a fussy paleontologist. Thomas Mitchell, Noble Johnson, Margo. A reconstructed, full-length version of Capra's original cut was recently released to theaters. (VC)

**LOST HORIZON (1973).** Although Ross Hunter's musical version of the James Hilton book was severely panned (Rex Reed called it "Brigadoon with chopsticks"), it is not nearly as static or plastic as you might fear. True, its musical sequences are absurd within the framework of such a time and place, yet this version (directed by Charles Jarrott) closely follows the spirit of Capra's 1937 film. Charles Boyer as the High Lama, John Gielgud as wise old Chang, Peter Finch and Michael York as the stranded travelers. Don't be put off by bad publicity. Olivia Hussey, Sally Kellerman, George Kennedy, Liv Ullmann, Bobby Van.

**LOST ISLAND OF KONGA (1938).** Abbreviated version of the 12-chapter Republic serial HAWK OF THE WILDER-

NESS, directed by William Witney and John English, and starring Mala and Bruce Bennett (still working as Herman Brix). The setting is an uncharted island inhabited by a jungle boy and superstitious natives living in constant dread of a volcano. An expedition arrives to rescue the boy and that creates a series of narrow escapes and cliffhangers. Monte Blue, Jill Martin, Noble Johnson, William Royle.

**LOST JUNGLE, THE (1934).** Feature-length version of Mascot's serial starring animal trainer Clyde Beatty as an African explorer looking for the missing father of his fiancee. He crashes his dirigible on a tropical island and stumbles across a subterranean metropolis that has everything but Rapid Transit. It's poorly directed by Armand Schaefer and David Howard and the acting is downright atrocious in this charmless cliffhanger. Warner Richmond, Cecelia Parker, Syd Saylor, Mickey Rooney.

**LOST MISSILE, THE (1958).** Footloose rocket from Russia streaks into our stratosphere and could destroy Peoria. But don't sweat, democracy lovers. Robert Loggia is on hand to produce a countermissile that will save us from destruction. Directed by Lester William Berke. Script by Jerome Bixby and John McPartland. Ellen Parker, Larry Kerr, Joe Hyams.

**LOST PLANET AIRMEN (1949).** Videocassette feature-length version of the Republic serial KING OF THE ROCKET MEN, which is also in video in all 12-chapters. See **KING OF THE ROCKET MEN.**

**LOST TRIBE, THE (1949).** Jungle Jim . . . pith helmets . . . Tamba the chimp . . . jungle Shangri-La . . . potted plants . . . a lost race of natives . . . Columbia sound stage sets . . . rubber crocodiles . . . Elena Verdugo in a sarong . . . tired-and-blue Johnny Weissmuller vehicle from venerable Z-producer

island's people from an evil takeover. Original title was SAMURAI PIRATE; "Sinbad" was added to capitalize on THE SEVENTH VOYAGE OF SINBAD with Kerwin Mathews. Effects by Eiji Tsuburaya, of GODZILLA fame. Directed by Senkichi Tangiguchi.

**LOVE AT FIRST BITE (1979).** New wrinkles are painted onto the 800- year-old face of Dracula in this funny satire on movie monsters. George Hamilton is marvelous as the Transylvanian shut-in who yearns for the 20th Century so much that jets to New York to claim a fashion model. Dracula is now an anachronism, adapting to 20th Century Manhattan, and the gags are fast and furious. Classic scenes: the disruption of a funeral in a Harlem chapel, a midnight raid on a New York blood bank, Dracula disco dancing. Susan St. James is the lovely fashion model hypnotically falling for Hamilton's charms, and Richard Benjamin is wonderful as a psychiatrist who gets his monster lore scrambled up. Robert Kaufman's script is an absolutely delight and director Stan Dragoti pulls it wonderfully together. Dick Shawn portrays a zany cop and Arte Johnson is Drac's Igor. (VC)

**LOVE BUG, THE (1969).** First of four Walt Disney comedies about an intelligent Volkswagen (Herbie the Love Bug) owned by a racing driver in San Francisco. Designed for moppets, but even older folks should enjoy the slapstick and cute antics as Herbie runs wild. Directed by Robert Stevenson. David Tomlinson, Dean Jones, Michele Lee, Buddy Hackett, Joe Flynn, Joe E. Ross. (VC)

**LOVE BUTCHER, THE (1975).** Sleazo stuff from directors Mikel Angel and Don Jones, who play this psychothriller for laughs. A wimpy gardener (Erik Stern) is abused by the women who hire him, so he turns into a killer who beds the broads before he butchers them. What makes THE LOVE

---

*"There may be no tomorrow. There may be no this afternoon."—The narrator in* **THE LOST MISSILE.**

---

Sam Katzman and director William Berke. Munga bunga crumba. Myrna Dell, Ralph Dunn.

**LOST TRIBE, THE (1983).** New Zealand psychic mystery tale directed and written by John Liang, who emphasizes the introspective nature of his characters. The daughter of a vanished explorer has visions that he's in trouble and eventually an expedition investigates. John Bach, Darien Takle, Emma Takle.

**LOST WOMEN, THE (1952).** Turgidly written-directed-acted science-fiction thriller about a mad scientist (Jackie Coogan) who creates a race of superwomen (hah!) injected with the emotions of spiders. So incompetent you won't believe your eyes. A lost cause for Richard Travis, Lyle Talbot, Allan Nixon, Tandra Quinn, Mona McKinnon. Directed by Herbert Tevos and Ron Damond. In video as **MESA OF LOST WOMEN.**

**LOST WORLD, THE (1925).** Silent milestone, first major feature to spotlight the stop motion work of special effects pioneer Willis O'Brien, who went on to taller things in KING KONG. It's the classic Sir Arthur Conan Doyle story about explorers led by Professor Challenger who find a prehistoric world in South America of brontosauruses and tyranosaurus rexes. A cliche today, but fresh and exciting when produced. Wallace Beery, Bessie Love, Lewis Stone. Directed by Harry Hoyt. (VC)

**LOST WORLD, THE (1960).** Producer-director Irwin Allen fails to do justice to Conan Doyle's Professor Challenger adventure, in which Claude Rains leads an expedition into South America in search of a high plateau forgotten by time. The gloss is there but Allen caters to the lowest common denominator. The "monsters" are real lizards shot with macro lenses—and the thrills involving a tribe of cannibals are just as phony. Waste of a good cast: David Hedison, Jill St. John, Michael Rennie, Fernando Lamas, Richard Haydn. Allen co-wrote the script with Charles Bennett.

**LOST WORLD OF SINBAD, THE (1965).** Toshiro Mifune portrays a Japanese swordsman-adventurer who challenges a Medusa-like enchantress and assorted demons to save an

BUTCHER unique is the use of garden tools by the killer. Gee, what a tough row to hoe . . . shear terror . . . should we call the killer a rake? But enough, we must be shoveling off. (VC)

**LOVE CAPTIVE, THE (1934).** Abracadabra time: A doctor specializing in hypnosis has hot eyeballs for the girl of someone else's dreams and uses his devious talent to steal her away. Don't stare too deeply into the doc's eyes or you'll fall asleep at the set. Directed by Max Marcin. Nils Asther, Gloria Stuart, Paul Kelly, John Wray.

**LOVE EXORCIST. See DADDY'S DEADLY DARLING.**

**LOVE FROM A STRANGER (1936).** British variation on the Bluebeard theme with Basil Rathbone setting out to knock off another beautiful wife. Based on an Agatha Christie story. Directed by Rowland V. Lee. Ann Harding, Bruce Seton, Binnie Hale, Donald Calthrop.

**LOVE IN COLD BLOOD (1969).** Sleazy poverty row production, shot in a blight-riddled part of L.A. David Story is an ice house worker, a whacko case who murders buxom, platinum-haired Sabrina and other sexpots. He's psycho, man, psycho. He hides their bodies in cold storage. We're talking cold shoulder here. David has a real- life lookalike brother Robert, who portrays a cop, and David also murders him and takes his place. The Storys must have taken their training at the Neanderthal school of acting. A mess, even with Jim Davis and Scott Brady helping. Directed by Stuart E. McGowan.

**LOVE ME DEADLY (1972).** A case of necrophilia involving a coven of devil worshippers operating out of an L.A. funeral home. Mary Wilcox plays the lover of corpses. Never widely released—one of the movie world's small favors to you. Directed-written by Jacques LaCerte. Lyle Waggoner, Christopher Stone, Timothy Scott. (VC)

**LOVE PILL, THE (1971).** Recommended to horny viewers only: A candy (discovered by a "green" grocer) doubles as a contraceptive when chewed just right. Women are turned into

**JAYNE MANSFIELD:
'LOVES OF HERCULES'**

flaming nymphomaniacs, their bodies quivering with passion—and then the fun begins in this unsophisticated British sex comedy. Directed by Kenneth Turner. Toni Sinclair, Melinda Churcher, Henry Woolf.

**LOVE SLAVES OF THE AMAZON (1957).** Tall, beautiful women, their bodies pulsating with lust, capture wilderness explorers and imprison them, with the idea that they will serve as "love slaves." Lowbrow action adventure, rather intense for its time, written-produced-directed by Curt Siodmak. Don Taylor, Eduardo Ciannelli, Gianna Segale, John Herbert, Harvey Chalk, Wilson Vianna.

**LOVE TRAP (1978).** Sexy British spoof, in the fashion of old music hall revues, with plenty of naked female flesh and comedy antics as World War II serviceman Robin Askwith, returning from the war, becomes involved in a series of murders and mistaken identities over a miniaturized cigarette lighter that has an effect on electronic power whenever someone flicks the Bick. Despite its silliness, it's entertaining. Directed by James Kenelm Clarke. Anthony Steel, Fiona Richmond, Graham Stark, Linda Hayden.

**LOVE TRAP.** See **CURSE OF THE BLACK WIDOW.**

**LOVE: VAMPIRE STYLE (1971).** West German comedy-satire of the Dracula genre in which a descendant of the old Count knocks off fellow villagers one by one. Herbert Fux, B. Valentin.

**LOVE WAR, THE (1970).** Unconvincing, cheap TV-movie: Earth is fought over by two alien races; Lloyd Bridges and Angie Dickinson get caught up in the extraterrestrial showdown, but neither is what he and she appears. Incredulously, the fate of our wonderful planet hangs in the balance when opposing parties come face to face in a deserted town to shoot it out. Resembles an episode of THE INVADERS. Directed by George McGowan.

**LOVES OF HERCULES (1960).** Muscleman Mickey Hargitay is supposed to be a gallant he-man fighting off mythical creatures, such as the Cyclops and the Hydra and the Incredible Forest of Tree Men. But he spends his time in this French-Italian "spectacle" breathing hot passionate breath all over the thinly clad body of real-life lover-wife Jayne Mansfield. Can't say we blame him for being distracted; who needs myths when you have the rounded substance of Mansfield? Directed by Carlo Bragaglia.

**LOVESICK (1983).** Psychiatrist Dudley Moore falls for a lovely playwright patient (Elizabeth McGovern)—which so irritates the ghost of Sigmund Freud that he appears as Alec Guinness. Only Moore can hear Guinness' pearls of couched wisdom, so it's one of those movies where the other characters keep wondering why Moore is always talking into thin air (into which this Marshall Brickman movie very quickly evaporates). John Huston turns up as a fellow shrink warning Moore about his infidelity and other good people walk through without conviction, including Alan King, Renee Taylor, Ron Silver and Gene Saks. You won't love LOVESICK but you may get sick. (VC)

**LOVING TOUCH, THE.** See **PSYCHO LOVER, THE.**

**LUCAN (1977).** Wolf Boy (Kevin Brophy), raised by critters running free in the forest, returns to civilization under Dr. Hoagland (John Randolph) to live down his reputation as a sonofawolf. Lucan has orange-glowing eyes and lopes as fast as a wolf. Sure-footed TV-movie (directed by David Greene) led to a series that loped on ABC for two years. Then Lucan disappeared into the wilderness and was never seen again. Must have been the call of the wild. Stockard Channing, Ned Beatty, John Randolph, William Jordan.

**LUCIFER COMPLEX, THE (1978).** A mountain hiker enters a hidden cave where a huge computer is stored with tapes of man's history. For 20 minutes the young man watches stock footage of warfare and moralizes in stream-of-consciousness dribble. Then the story jumps to 1986 as secret agent Robert Vaughn uncovers a Nazi plot involving cloning of Adolph Hitler and other luminaries of our time. The Vaughn footage (directed-written by David L. Hewitt) appears to be an unsold TV pilot added to James Flocker's cave footage. An editor's nightmare, with dangling plot elements and a non-ending. Turgid and unwatchable, including the performances of Keenan Wynn and Aldo Ray. (VC)

**LUCIFER'S WOMEN (1974).** Director Paul Aratow's remake of TRILBY, the story of Svengali luring a beautiful woman into his power. It's a poorly shot, feeble-mindedly written sex exploitation film blending lesbianism, satanism and other distasteful themes. Made in San Francisco, and wrenching the talents of Larry Hankin, Morgan Upton and other decent actors . . . See DOCTOR DRACULA for details about how this was re-edited for TV.

**LUCK OF THE IRISH, THE (1948).** All you O'Flahertys, Mc-Gillicutties and O'Hoolihans take note: Here's a fittin' Irish fantasy that'll pop your Cork County. Cecil Kellaway is a leprechaun (who imbibes too much) affecting the conscience of a newspaper reporter (Tyrone Power) who is being manipulated by his publisher (Lee J. Cobb). Can the good fairy of folklore lead Power and girlfriend Anne Baxter to the pot o' gold? A viewing rainbow from director Henry Koster and writer Philip Dunne.

**LUGGAGE OF THE GODS! (1983).** Labored takeoff on CAVEMAN in which a tribe of primitive cave people comes into contact with the 20th Century and tries to deal with today's people and inventions. It's played by writer-director David Kendall solely for its comedy as Yuk, Hubba, Zoot, Kono and Tull fight off modern crooks who are after rare art that has accidentally fallen from a plane. Mark Stolzenberg, Gabriel Barre, Gwen Ellison, Martin Haber.

**LUST AT FIRST BITE.** See **DRACULA SUCKS.**

**LUST FOR A VAMPIRE.** Videocassette title for **TO LOVE A VAMPIRE.**

**LUST OF THE VAMPIRES.** See **I VAMPIRA.**

**LYCANTHROPUS.** See **WEREWOLF IN A GIRL'S DORMITORY.** (A sorority row?)

---

*"Children of the night . . . shut up!"—George Hamilton as Dracula in*
**LOVE AT FIRST BITE.**

*"There is no more foul and relentless enemy of man in the occult world than this dead-alive creature spewed up from the grave."*—**MARK OF THE VAMPIRE.**

**M (1930).** Superb psychokiller study, years ahead of its time in a fascinating, chilling vein. This German trend-setter was directed by Fritz Lang in Berlin, with real underworld characters in small roles. Peter Lorre made his screen debut as a perverted child murderer who wants to stop but can't resist his perverse impulses. The role made Lorre famous but typecast him for life. Lang was an imaginative filmmaker, a fact reflected in every frame of this innovative work. (VC)

**M (1951).** Joseph Losey's remake of Lang's portrait of a child murderer is inferior but still a compelling study. David Wayne essays the Lorre role, fondling the shoes of his victims and playing melancholy tunes on a flute. Howard Da Silva is the detective, Martin Gabel the underworld kingpin who organizes a search for the killer, who is despised even by criminals. Raymond Burr, Steve Brodie.

**M3: THE GEMINI STRAIN. See PLAGUE, THE.**

**MACABRE (1958).** The first of producer-director William Castle's "gimmicky" shriekers: Audiences were insured by Lloyds of London against death by fright. Based on THE MARBLE FOREST, a novel by 15 mystery writers, and adapted by Robb White, it tells of a doctor (William Prince) with just five hours to find his daughter, who has been buried alive. Castle had his tongue firmly in his cheek and provides numerous surprises. Delightful closing credits. Castle was off and running for the next 15 years as a purveyor of hokum. Jim Backus, Ellen Corby, Christine White, Susan Morrow.

**MACISTE AGAINST HERCULES IN THE VALE OF WOE.** See **HERCULES IN THE VALE OF WOE.** (Either way, woe is you in the vale of vacuous viewing.)

**MACISTE IN HELL (1962).** Strongarm fool Kirk Morris can lift lead weights but has trouble lifting a curse off a Scottish village, so he travels to Hell to confront evil personified. Finally, in hellish frustration, he flexes his muscles and burps, and the witches flee in abject horror . . . is it because Maciste has bad breath? An Italian mess, said to be based on a 1926 film, MACISTE IN HELL. Directed by Riccardo Freda.

**MACUMBA LOVE (1960).** Low budget exploitation voodoo thriller (made in Brazil by producer-director-actor Douglas Fowley) as topheavy as its two main attractions, June Wilkin-

son, a buxom blonde with a 44-inch chest, and as leaden as Walter Reed playing a writer in the tropics exposing withcraft as fakery. Wilkinson went on to pose for Playboy au naturel and Reed retired to Santa Cruz. Also hanging around the edges is Ziva Rodann. Macumba Dumba Dumba.

**MAD ABOUT MEN (1954).** Husky-voiced, musky-mannered Glynis Johns in a dual role—as a young woman and as Miranda the Mermaid. The latter decides to switch places with her human counterpart for a different kind of splash. This British sequel to MIRANDA is aswim with fun and awash in light-heartedness. Directed by Ralph Thomas. Donald Sinden, Margaret Rutherford, Noel Purcell.

**MAD BUTCHER, THE (1972).** Italian black comedy variation on Sweeney Todd with Victor Buono as Otto Lehman, a crazed Viennese meat-cutter who is released from an asylum to resume his practice . . . of strangling assorted victims and stuffing their bodies into a grinder that spits them out as delicious sausages that he then blightly sells to the local police. Director John Zurli goes for laughs with a lilting Viennese waltz in the background. Buono brings a special charm to his madman who calmly goes about his business while a newspaperman and frustrated policeman try to solve the mystery. There's no blood or gore—writers Robert H. Oliver and Dag Molin had the taste to imply the horror underlying their whimsical macabre story. "Buono appetito!" Brad Harris, Karin Field, Carl Stearns. (VC)

**MAD DOCTOR, THE (1941).** Psychopathic physician Basil Rathbone knocks off wealthy wives with the help of creepy pal Martin Koslek. The script by Howard J. Green needed some doctoring of its own. Don't be patient with this terribly outdated thriller from director Tim Whelan. Ellen Drew, John Howard, Ralph Morgan, Billy Benedict, James Seay.

**MAD DOCTOR OF BLOOD ISLAND (1969).** Sanguinary companion to BEAST OF BLOOD (same monster appears in both), shot in the Philippines with John Ashley and Angelique Pettyjohn. A monster of chlorophyll turns green everytime it sees a fresh victim. You'll turn purple. Directed by Eddie Romero and Gerry DeLeon. (VC)

**MAD DOCTOR OF MARKET STREET, THE (1941).** San Franciscans can relax—the main artery of downtown bleeds only slightly in this Universal horror thriller with Lionel Atwill as a scientist who flees the city by the Bay to a tropical island where he holds sway over superstitious natives. A shipwreck survivor turns up to upset his tyranny. Joseph Lewis directed this un-Marketable ugly. Una Merkel, Nat Pendleton, Noble Johnson, Ann Nagel, Richard Davies.

**MAD EXECUTIONERS, THE (1965).** Edgar Wallace mystery set in London (but produced in West Germany) depicting grisly axe murders—but at the same time a sex fiend is loose, pillaging and raping, so Scotland Yard has double trouble: Rape and scrape. Directed by Edward Zbonek. Wolfgang Preiss, Chris Howland, Harry Riebauer.

**MAD GENIUS, THE (1931).** Variation on the Svengali theme: a crippled puppeteer (John Barrymore) maintains strange sway over a young man he turns into a groovy dancer. When the dancer falls in love with Barrymore's secret love, the mesmerist exercises his power to its fullest—ending in an axe murder. Directed by Michael Curtiz. Donald Cook, Marian Marsh, Boris Karloff, Louis Alberni.

**MAD GHOUL, THE (1943).** David Bruce is a laughable walking monster when George Zucco (a mad scientist, cackling with sadistic glee) discovers a poisonous vapor that forces Bruce to kill at Zucco's bidding. Robert Armstrong, Evelyn Ankers, Turhan Bey, Milburn Stone and Charles McGraw do what they can with the feeble idea. James P. Hogan directed this helping of tasteless ghoulish ghoulash.

**MAD LOVE (1935).** Best film version of Maurice Renard's THE HANDS OF ORLAC with Peter Lorre as Dr. Gogol, who grafts a French murderer's hands onto the mutilated arms of a concert pianist. Gogol's motive is to get closer to the pianist's wife, an actress who works in a Grand Guignol theater. Under Karl Freund's direction, this MGM classic plunges headlong into psychological horror as Gogol talks the pianist into thinking he's a killer. Colin (FRANKENSTEIN) Clive is Orlac, Frances Drake is Yvonne Orlac. Supporting cast consists of Ted Healy, Edward Brophy, Isabel Jewell, Keye Luke and Billy Gilbert. Gregg Toland photographed it beautifully and Dimitri Tiomkin wrote the score.

**MAD, MAD MONSTERS (1972).** When Baron Frankenstein holds his wedding at the castle, all the monsters are invited in this animated feature slanted for the kids. Similar to MAD MONSTER PARTY but not as clever. (VC)

**PETER LORRE IN 'MAD LOVE'**

**MAD MAGICIAN, THE (1954).** Still occasionally revived in its 3-D format, this has remained an insignificant thriller in which Vincent Price hams it up as an stage illusionist's assistant who kills his employer and takes his place. John Brahm directed Crane Wilbur's script with nothing up his sleeve and never pulls the rabbit out of the hat. Among the death devices is a crematorium designed for stage work and a buzz-saw trick that isn't a trick. Patrick O'Neal portrays the hero. Jay Novello, Corey Allen, Eva Gabor, Mary Murphy.

**MAD MAX (1979).** Australian landmark film that instigated a new trend in futuristic fantasies set in an anarchistic world of roving warrior bands. Mel Gibson portrays a policeman trying to keep peace after industrial collapse who foresakes his

**TINA TURNER AND HER GREGARIOUS WARRIOR BOYS IN 'MAD MAX BEYOND THUNDERDOME'**

**BADUR THE ORANG IN 'THE MAFU CAGE'**

badge to pursue the cutthroats who wiped out his family. The car chases and crashes are spectacularly staged, establishing a new state-of-the-art for breathless pursuits and grinding collisions. And the brutality is extreme. After MAD MAX, action movies were never the same. The mastermind was George Miller, who co-directed with Gibson. Two wildly wonderful successful sequels followed, ROAD WARRIOR and MAD MAX BEYOND THUNDERDOME. (VC)

**MAD MAX II. See ROAD WARRIOR, THE.**

**MAD MAX BEYOND THUNDERDOME (1985).** Third action-packed saga in the career of Mad Max, from the rip-roaring imaginations of directors George Miller and George Ogilvie, who give full vent to the fantasy of a post-holocaust world in which a roving warrior (Mel Gibson) daily fights to survive. Max (played with greater sensitivity by Gibson this time) faces Aunty Entity (Tina Turner), dictatorial champion of Bartertown, where he squares off with a brute named Blaster in a gladiatorial arena of bone-cracking action. Ever-changing scenery and creative plot twists keep one enthralled as Max faces not only Thunderdome but a wheel of fortune, a blistering desert crossing, a society of youngsters trying to keep old traditions alive, and a climactic train-and-car chase that includes the chief villain (Ironbar, played by Angry Anderson) and the zany pilot Jedediah (Bruce Spence) from the second film. Totally satisfying action-fantasy. (VC)

**MAD MISSION 3 (1984).** Rotund Harold Sakata (Oddjob of GOLDFINGER) and Richard Kiel (Jaws of the Bond films) harass a bumbling Japanese agent who is tricked by James Bond and Queen Elizabeth lookalikes to steal the Star of Fortune from a well-guarded security system. Madcap parody, vigorous but dumb, with Peter Graves doing a gag on his own MISSION: IMPOSSIBLE TV series. Of minimal interest and of no importance. Directed by Tsui Hark. Samuel Hui, Sylvia Chang. (VC)

**MAD MONSTER, THE (1942).** PRC quickie, directed by Sam Newfield, with scientist George Zucco (what, again?) as a madman mainlining a transfusion of wolf's blood into a farmer's bloodstream. And guess what that turns him into . . . Fangs McDonald. Zucco whips the hairy new creation into submission and sends him on errands of revenge. And don't forget a quart of milk on the way home. Rock bottom material, so bad it fascinates. Glenn Strange, who was to play the Frankenstein Monster at Universal, is the wolf creature. Anne Nagel, Johnny Downs, Mae Busch. (VC)

**MAD MONSTER PARTY (1967).** "Animagic" puppet film

blending horror and comedy, the scenario by Ken Korobkin and Harvey Kurtzman, the latter the creator of Mad Magazine. The puppet characters are a melange of cinema monstrosities: Frankenstein Monster, Dracula, Wolfman, the Creature, Dr. Jekyll and Mr. Hyde, the Mummy and the Hunchback of Notre Dame. Boris Karloff provides the Baron's voice. Enchanting; for all ages. Directed with real style by Jules Bass. (VC)

**MADAM WHITE SNAKE (1962).** Classic legend from the Sung Dynasty (960-1279 A.D.) about snakes (one green, the other white) turning into beautiful goddesses after a thousand years. When they tire of heavenly bliss they return to Earth as women to enter into love affairs—and everyone lives happily ever after. Originally made in Mandarin, with English subtitles. Directed by Shiro Toyoda. Shirley Yamaguchi.

**MADAME SIN (1971).** Robert Wagner was exec producer and star of this TV-movie, an unsold pilot with Bette Davis as a female Fu Manchu who owns her own island, from which she plans to conquer the world with help from financial genius Denholm Elliott. Through subterfuges, she makes it appear undercover agent Wagner is a defector, and then tricks him into helping her kidnap a naval officer so she can hijack an atomic sub. Unusually downbeat ending. Directed by David Greene in England and Scotland. (VC)

**MADHOUSE (1974).** Sleazy spooker filmed in London about a hammy film actor (Vincent Price) suspected of committing gore murders during the filming of a TV series. The climax is so unbelievable and forced even horror fans will wonder what's happening. Made by the kind of mentality that thinks the sight of a spider is the height of horror. Eeeekkkkk! Directed by Jim Clark. Adrienne Corri, Linda Hayden, Robert Quarry, Peter Cushing, Natasha Payne.

**MADHOUSE (1983).** U.S.-Italian production written-produced-directed by Ovidio G. Assonitis. Trish Everly, Michael Macrae, Dennis Robertson, Morgan Hart. (VC)

**MADHOUSE MANSION (1974).** Ghost story in the M. R. James tradition, so damn bloody British that Americans might find this too fey and slow-moving when a sexually repressed young man shows up at a baronial house for a holiday in the 1920s. He's haunted by a doll that comes to life and gives him psychic images of a hundred years ago when the mansion was next door to Borden's Insane Asylum and plots were afoot to incarcerate an innocent woman. The minimum gore scenes are forever in coming and one must look for subtleties within the excellent period milieu. Produced-directed by Stephen Weeks at Penhow Castle. Marianne Faithfull, Leigh Lawson, Barbara Shelley. (VC)

**MADMAN (1982).** Old "Madman Marz," a farmer who dangled from a rope after murdering his family, is said to prowl the woods at night. Children around the campfire are warned not to speak his name or he may come back to murder again. But Marz still goes on a marvelous murder spree, knocking off the characters of writer-director Joe Giannone as fast as possible in 88 minutes. Tony Fish, Alexis Dubin, Harriet Bass, Seth Jones. (VC)

**MADMEN OF MANDORAS. See THEY SAVED HITLER'S BRAIN.** (Better yet, don't see **THEY SAVED HITLER'S BRAIN** if you still have your own brain.)

**MADONNA OF THE SEVEN MOONS (1946).** Foreshadowing later clinical studies of dual personalities (LIZZIE and THREE FACES OF EVE) is this British melodrama starring Phyllis Calvert as a woman who vacillates between being a happy bride and the mistress of a gangster. Directed by Arthur Crabtree. Patricia Roc, Stewart Granger, Jean Kent.

**MAFU CAGE, THE. See MY SISTER, MY LOVE.**

**MAGIC (1978).** Low-key version of William Goldman's novel depicting a demented stage ventriloquist whose dummy (named Fats) overpowers his personality. The slasher aspects are minimized as director Richard Attenborough focuses on the warped character of Anthony Hopkins. Ann-Margret delivers a laid-back unsexy performance as a childhood sweetheart whom Hopkins returns to during his descent into madness. Goldman adapted from his own novel. Ed Lauter, Burgess Meredith. (VC)

**MAGIC CARPET, THE (1951).** Lucille Ball in a Sam Katzman potboiler? Columbia boss Harry Cohn was punishing Lucy for breech of contract, but she still worked her magic in this Arabian Nights spinoff. She teams with the Scarlet Falcon (John Agar) and his desert dune riders to trap the evil Caliph of Islam (Raymond Burr) with the help of the aeronautical shag. Patricia Medina adds sexual charms, director Lew Landers shoots fast. Rug-ged.

**MAGIC CHRISTIAN, THE (1969).** Hodgepodge of non sequiturs, tied together by Peter Sellers as a millionaire traveling the world to prove everyone has a price (even Vincent). Some sequences are surrealistic; some designed for sight gag appeal; some relate to nothing in the universe. Despite madcap sequences (Raquel Welch whipping slavers, Christopher Lee spoofing Dracula, Laurence Harvey stripping, Yul Brynner dressed as a woman), the celebrity cast cannot make this adaptation of a Terry Southern novel better than average. Directed by Joseph McGrath, who adapted with Southern and Peter Sellers. Ringo Starr, Wilfrid Hyde-White, Richard Attenborough, Roman Polanski, John Cleese. (VC)

**MAGIC FACE, THE (1952).** This purports unconvincingly

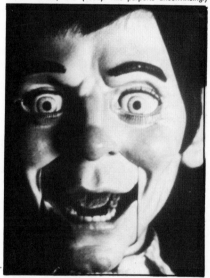

**FATS THE DEMENTED DUMMY IN 'MAGIC'**

that a lookalike assumed Hitler's place in the last days of World War II, all because Der Fuehrer stole the man's wife. Luther Adler (who was also Hitler in THE DESERT FOX) essays both roles and saves the Mort Briskin-Robert Smith screenplay from total Gotterdamerung with his virtuoso performances. William L. Shirer, famed war correspondent, lends a documentary flavor with his March of Time narration, but it is total capitulation for Briskin and Smith, who also produced. Directed by Frank Tuttle. Patricia Knight, Heinz Moog, Ilka Windish, Charles Koenig.

**MAGIC FOUNTAIN, THE (1961).** Animated version of the Grimm fairy tale "The Water of Life" (adapted by John Lehmann) with voices by Sir Cedric Hardwicke, Buddy Baer and Hans Conried. Produced-directed by Allan David.

**MAGIC SERPENT (1966).** Japanese fairy tale: Heroic young man searches for the murderer of his father, a wicked wizard. When he finds the sorcerer, the dude turns into a dragon, so the young man turns into a king-size frog. Directed by Tetsuya Yamauchi. Also called GRAND DUEL IN MAGIC.

**MAGIC SWORD, THE (1962).** Bert I. Gordon fantasy-adventure yarn for the young set, based vaguely on the St. George-Dragon legend. Basil Rathbone is a chilly sorcerer, Estelle Winwood a maladroit witch, Gary Lockwood the heroic St.

George, Anne Helm the fair Helene. Also on hand: an ogre, a bubbling pond that dissolves flesh from bones, a French shepherdess who turns hag, and assorted magic. Above average, capturing the quality of a rousing fairy tale. Bernard Schoenfeld scripted for producer-director Gordon. Richard Kiel turns up as a very tall giant. (VC)

**MAGIC TOYSHOP, THE (1986).** British TV-movie is an interesting study in how a sadistic toymaker builds prototypes which begin to act out violent and sexual acts, until members of the man's family rebel. Odd and haunting. Directed by David Wheatley. Tom Bell, Patricia Kerigan, Caroline Milmoe.

**MAGIC VOYAGE OF SINBAD (1953).** Not released in America until the early 1960s, this is a Soviet version of an ancient legend, which leads one to suspect the Sinbad title was capitalistic exploitation. Whatever . . . an adventurous wanderer seeks the Bird of Happiness with an underwater maiden. Directed by Alexander Ptushko . . . for the U.S. edition, new scenes were shot by James Landis and written by Francis Ford Coppola. Edward Stolar, Anna Larion.

**MAGIC WORLD OF TOPO GIGIO, THE (1965).** Remember that mechanical mouse on TV's ED SULLIVAN SHOW with the squeaky monologues? Well, the Italians produced a puppet film in which the heroic rodent sets off on a flight to the moon in the company of a cowardly worm and girlfriend Rosy. But the flight goes awry and the trio lands in an amusement center where a crazy magician kidnaps Rosy. Directed by Federico Caldura.

**MAGICIAN, THE (1926).** Silent mini-classic directed-written by Rex Ingram is based on a Somerset Maugham novel, said to be inspired by the career of Aleister Crowley. Although terribly anitquated, its themes and imagery will make horror fans feel at home as the mad magician (Paul Wegener) prepares beauty Alice Terry for a bloody transfusion in order to create a new life force. Comes complete with hump-backed assistant. Ivan Petrovich, Gladys Hamer.

**MAGICIAN, THE (1958).** Genuinely chilling moments dominate this Swedish mystery by Ingmar Bergman about a mesmerizing legerdemain expert who travels the countryside, claiming ESP powers. It's a dark mood that Bergman projects, and he does it brilliantly. Ingrid Thulin, Bibi Andersson, Max von Sydow. (VC)

**MAGICIAN OF LUBLIN, THE (1978).** Fascinating portrait of a Jewish entertainer with humble village roots who rises to the top of Warsaw society as a magician/escape artist, but then throws it all away to greed, ego and lust. Alan Arkin's portrayal is unusually anachronistic for a turn-of-the-century drama, but the German locations, period costumes and co-performances (Louise Fletcher, Valerie Perrine, Lou Jacobi, Shelley Winters) make it work. Yasha (the magician) believes he can fly and this fantasy elements provides this adaptation of Isaac Bashevis Singer's "The Magician" with some startling moments and a supernatural climax. Directed in an air of "yiddishment" by Menahen Golan. (VC)

**MAGNETIC MONSTER, THE (1953).** Producer Ivan Tors and director Curt Siodmak teamed to write this low budgeter dealing with science-fiction theories difficult to depict—which makes this more oriented to ideas than visuals. The "monster" is a new isotope sucking up energy and giving off radiation as it grows in size. The good cast makes up for the intangible "monster": Richard Carlson, King Donovan, Strother Martin, Kathleen Freeman, Jean Byron.

**MAGNETIC MOON (1954).** Unattracting viewing. See ROCKY JONES, SPACE RANGER.

**MAGNIFICENT MAGICAL MAGNET OF SANTA MESA (1977).** Lighthearted, innocuous David Gerber TV-movie starring Michael Burns as a wimpy inventor who accidentally discovers a magnetic force-field that could revolutionize the face of modern industry. Only Burns' boss, Mr. Undershaft, and a devious millionaire (Harry Morgan) plan to steal the formula and reap a greedy harvest. On the level of a sitcom, with little attraction or pull. Watch for Loni Anderson in a minor secretarial role. Directed by Hy Averback. Susan Blanchard, Tom Poston, Conrad Janis.

**MAGNIFICENT MS (1979).** SUPERMAN clone with the emphasis on a flying superheroine, produced-directed by Damon Christian. Desiree Cousteau has the leading role. This saw hardly any distribution—it didn't have "flying" power.

**MAGUS, THE (1969).** Bewildering adaptation of a John Fowles novel, its ending as ambiguous as its story. Anthony Quinn is the magus (magician) on a Greek island where Michael Caine has been assigned to teach. Caine is enmeshed in a maze of role-playing games involving Quinn and the mysterious Candice Bergen. There are plots within plots and a World War II flashback involving betrayal and heroism. Under Guy Green's direction, a psychic journey into the peculiar patterns of the mind. Certain to be too abstract and complex for viewers seeking pat solutions. Fowles did his own adapting, so he's got nothing to kick about. Anna Karina, Julian Glover, Corin Redgrave, Paul Stassino.

**MAIN STREET KID, THE (1948).** A youth struck by lightning discovers he has the power of telepathy. Too bad the producers at Republic weren't struck by more inspiration in making this comedy fantasy. Directed by R. G. Springsteen. Al Pearce, Janet Martin, Adele Mara, Roy Barcroft.

**MAJIN, MONSTER OF TERROR (1966).** Handsomely produced Japanese supernatural actioner with fine destruction effects when a legendary "golem" of the Orient (a stone statue imbued with a warrior's spirit) comes to life for revenge against the evil chamberlain of a nearby castle, who has offended the rock guy by driving a huge spike into his forehead. Before the rampage, when villains are crushed underfoot or swallowed up by gaping holes in the earth, the film is a Samurai warrior saga with ample sword action as the chamberlain orders the death of the heirs to the throne. Well directed by Kimiyoshi Yasuda. Worthwhile, in spite of our previous jokes about a "stonefaced" hero.

**MAJIN STRIKES AGAIN (1966).** You've heard of rock 'n roll idols—here's a rock idol who rolls with the punches when fighting the forces of evil. Yes, it's Rock Head himself, that legendary warrior statue imbued with a soul who does for the Japanese what the Golem did for the Hebrews in this sequel to MAJIN, MONSTER OF TERROR. More good action directed by Issei Mori and Yoshiyuki Kuroda. Third film was RETURN OF MAJIN. You can't keep a stoned guy down.

**MAJIN, THE HIDEOUS IDOL.** See **MAJIN, MONSTER OF TERROR.** (Majin Japan!)

**MAKE THEM DIE SLOWLY (1983).** Sickening Italian cannibal shocker stars Lorainne de Selle as an anthropologist who wants to prove that cannibalism doesn't exist and goes to South America. She's wrong—or there wouldn't be a movie. One stomach-churning atrocity after another as members of her expedition are tortured and then put to death, and deservedly so. The most appalling death device is a special head-holder which allows a machette-wielding native to slice off the top of the scalp and pluck out the brains for a royal feast. The violence is disturbing, especially to the animals, many of which are slaughtered on screen. Strong stomachs required. Allegedly banned in 31 countries, but don't believe it. Written-directed by Umberto Lenzi. John Morghen, Robert Kerman, Richard Bolla. (VC)

**MAKING CONTACT (1986).** Well-produced, well-directed fantasy from German filmmaker Roland Emmerich doesn't have a single original idea—it's entirely derivative of Spielbergisms: the weird lights and moving toys of CLOSE ENCOUNTERS, the telepathy and scientific teams of E. T., the supernatural voice from beyond on the phone of POLTERGEIST, etc. There's even the knife-throwing of CARRIE. It's infuriating to watch a well-made film totally predictable and lacking dramatic punch of its own. It all starts when Joshua Morrell, following his father's untimely death, makes contact with a voice that turns out to be that of a turn-of-the-century magician, represented by a devil doll. MAKING CONTACT never connects. Tammy Shields, Eva Kryll, Jan Zierold. (VC)

**MAKING MICHAEL JACKSON'S THRILLER (1984).** Behind-the-scenes documentary about how John Landis directed the classic musical **THRILLER**, complete with monsters, make-up and all the gore. (VC)

**MAKING MR. RIGHT (1987).** Well-intended but ultimately

tedious fantasy-comedy in which a nerdy professor (John Malkovitch) creates an android named Ulysses in his own image for Chemtec Corporation. When a female PR expert (Ann Magnuson) is called in to hype him to the public, she teaches the naive idiot robot the art of romance—and in one minute causes him to short circuit. It sounds like a workable idea, and tries to make some statements about love, loneliness and the human condition, but it's treated with a lot of dumb humor (mistaken identities, people falling in swimming pools) that leaves director Susan Seidelman with Mr. Wrong. Polly Bergen, Ben Masters, Laurie Metcalf. (VC)

**MAKING OF STAR WARS/EMPIRE STRIKES BACK, THE (1980).** Behind-the-scenes look at the making of the first two films in the STAR WARS saga, prepared for the video market by producer Gary Kurtz. William Conrad narrates. (VC)

**MAKO, JAWS OF DEATH (1976).** Sonny Stein (Richard Jaeckel) makes friends with killer Mako sharks and learns to communicate in his own unique way. When some of the sharks are borrowed by local marine biologists for experiments, they turn into killers, their teeth gnashing against soft human flesh. Produced-directed by William Grefe, who gave

**'MAKING MR. RIGHT': JOHN MALKOVICH**

the world the rattlesnake love story, STANLEY. Jennifer Bishop, Harold Sakata, John Davis Chandler.

**MALATESTA'S CARNIVAL OF BLOOD (1973).** Horror thriller with Herve Villechaize (destined for FANTASY ISLAND) involved in an unsavory plot of murder, gore and cannibalism. Written-directed by Christopher Speeth. Janine Carazo, Jerome Dempsey, William Preston.

**MALENKA THE VAMPIRE.** See **FANGS OF THE LIVING DEAD.** (And Anita Ekberg's bazooms!)

**MALPAS MYSTERY, THE (1960).** British adaptation of Edgar Wallace's FACE IN THE NIGHT, in which a faceless murderer terrorizes Maureen Swanson, Allan Cuthbertson and Geoffrey Keene in the traditions of "the old dark house." Directed by Sidney Hayers, Ronald Howard, Sandra Dorne.

**MALTESE BIPPY, THE (1969).** Rowan and Martin, the "Laugh-In" team, are witless wonders in this Norman Panama-directed "contemporary action-adventure-romantic-supsense-horror-melodrama comedy." The boys are making nude films in an old house where Martin turns into a werewolf and Julie Newman is Countess Dracula. The duo offers alternative endings, each a thud. A bomb when released— SON OF THE MALTESE BIPPY was never made. Thank your lucky bippy. Carol Lynley, Fritz Weaver, Dana Elcar.

**MAMMA DRACULA (1980).** French-Belgian effort starring

Louise Fletcher as a contemporary vampire (unaffected by daylight or religious symbols) who must periodically bathe in the blood of virgins. But did you know there's a short supply? Society is so perverted, you see. Maria Schneider portrays a policewoman and the whole thing, as the title indicates, is played for broad farce by farcical broads. Directed by Boris Szulzinger. Jimmy Shuman, Alexander Wajnberg.

**MAN, THE (1972).** Lee Rich-produced TV-movie depicting political turmoil in the near future when the first black U.S. President steps into the Oval Office. Rod Serling adapted Irving Wallace's best seller; Joseph Sargent directed. James Earl Jones, Martin Balsam, Lew Ayres, Burgess Meredith, Barbara Rush, William Windom, Patric Knowles, Jack Benny.

**MAN ALIVE (1945).** Old-fashioned mystery-comedy involving seances, afterlife misunderstandings, thunderstorms and other seemingly supernatural elements that all turn out to be farce. Fun-scary in a dumb way. Pat O'Brien, Adolphe Menjou, Ellen Drew, Jason Robards, Rudy Vallee. Directed by Ray Enright.

**MAN AND THE MONSTER, THE (1958).** Second-rate pianist with a nagging mother ("Your mind is gone, son!") sells his soul to the Devil in exchange for brilliance, but finds that everytime he plays, he turns into a cheap version of the Wolfman. These are the keys to the kingdom? Call it long-hair music. This Mexican thriller is a non-chiller with its atrocious dubbing and turgid Alfred Salazar dialogue. Abel Salazar as the pianist gives a grind-tuned performance. Directed by Raphael Baledon. Snuck across the border by the infamous schlock packager K. Gordon Murray.

**MAN BEAST (1956).** The worst is Yeti to come. A search for the Abominable Snowmen leads an expedition into the mountains of Tibet, unaware that the high-altitude creatures are luring good-looking women into the snow country to improve the breeding stock. Sex in a snowdrift? And who the devil is Rock Madison, the leading man? More cheap thrills from producer-director Jerry Warren. Virginia Maynor, George Skaff, Tom Maruzzi, Lloyd Nelson. (VC)

**MAN CALLED DAGGER, A (1967).** Laszlo Kovacs' cinematography is the highlight of this typical Bond imitation superspy thriller directed by Richard Rush in which secret agent Dick Dagger (Paul Mantee) prevents a wheelchair-bound former Nazi (Jan Murray) from taking over the world with a mind-conquering gadget. Dagger's girl is Terry Moore and Sue Ane Langdon is Murray's sexy mistress. Richard Kiel has a "giant" role. Leonard Stone, Eileen O'Neill.

**MAN CALLED FLINTSTONE, THE (1966).** Theatrical version of Hanna-Barbera's animated TV series is strictly for young adults. It has some 60,000 drawings, the voices of Alan Reed, Mel Blanc, Gerry Johnson and Jean Vanderpyl, and a storyline that satirizes James Bond spy movies. Fred Flintstone, the cave dweller, looks just like Secret Agent Rock Slag, so soon old Fred is up against the Green Goose, the insidious leader of S.M.I.R.K. Which will match the look on your face as this lame comedy cartoon unfolds.

**MAN FROM ATLANTIS, THE (1977).** Two-hour pilot for a short-term series with Patrick Duffy (DALLAS) as a young man equipped with gills, webbed hands and feet. In this origin yarn, directed by Lee H. Katzin, Duffy (as an extraterrestrial known as "Mark Harris") washes up on a beach and is rushed to a Navy hospital. Once the military knows his capabilities, he is assigned to find a sunken submarine. Belinda Montgomery portrays Duffy's pretty assistant; Victor Buono is the villain always trying to destroy Duffy. Lawrence Pressman, Dean Santoro, Art Lund, Steven Franken.

**MAN FROM PLANET X, THE (1951).** Scientist Raymond Bond informs newspaperman Robert Clarke that a new planet is headed toward Earth . . . sure enough, on a foggy moor in Scotland, a spaceship lands to spearhead an alien invasion. The twist here is that a human, for his own evil ends, captures the bubble-headed alien and tortures it for information. This early science-fiction film released by United Artists, which helped establish trends of the 1950s, is of marginal interest, directed in only a week by Edgar G. Ulmer. Weak production values, though the script by producers Aubrey Wisberg and Jack Pollexfen is decent enough. Mar-

garet Field, William Schallert, Roy Engel, Charles Davis.

**MAN FROM S.E.X., THE (1983).** British-produced James Bond spoof from producer Lindsay Shonteff, starring Gareth Hunt as Charles Bind, a supersecret agent dispatched by boss Geoffrey Keen to America to fetch a missing lord. Hunt comes up against a supervillain named Senator Lucifer Orchid (Gary Hope) who is manufacturing human clones and substituting them in high positions. One of them is the vice president, another is Hunt himself. It's handled by director Shonteff and screenwriter Jeremy Lee Francis as comic book action farce. Nick Tate, Fiona Curzon, Toby Robins.

**MAN FROM YESTERDAY (1949).** British mystery-adventure starring John Stuart with Laurence Harvey in a supporting role. The John Gilling plot deals with spiritualism and reincarnation in India, but the cop-out ending is certain to displease hardcore horror fans. Directed by Oswald Mitchell.

**MAN GOES THROUGH THE WALL, A (1960).** Heinz Ruehmann is delightful as a clerk with the power to walk through walls. He uses his wild talent to torment his bosses and to commit petty thefts. This amusing German comedy is a fragile fable poking fun at German bureaucracy and ill-mannered people who deserve to be driven bananas by a man who keeps thrusting his head through the wall. Directed by Ladislao Vadja; based on a novel by Marcel Ayme.

**MAN IN BLACK, THE (1950).** Lotus-happy yoga disciple uses body-relaxing techniques to simulate death and check up on his cheating wife. However, tampering with "forces better left unmolested" leads him into a spiritual world all too real. One of two tales told by Valentine Dyall in this early Hammer film written by John Gilling (from a BBC radio series) and directed by Oswald Mitchell. Anthony Hinds produced. Betty Ann Davies, Sheila Burrell, Sidney James.

**MAN IN HALF MOON STREET, THE (1944).** Miklos Rozsa's music graces this "mad scientist" thriller in which Nils Asther, a 120-year-old scientist, needs new glands to stay young and in love with his wife. But dire results are in store. Based on a play by Barre Lyndon, later remade by Hammer as MAN WHO COULD CHEAT DEATH. Directed by Ralph M. Murphy. Helen Walker, Brandon Hurst, Paul Cavanaugh.

**MAN IN OUTER SPACE (1961).** Czech science-fiction satire about a nutty middle-class workman accidentally sent into the galaxies where he meets an alien capable of invisibility. They return to Earth in 2447 to engage in comedic social situations. Directed by Oldrich Lipsky.

**MAN IN THE ATTIC (1953).** Remake of THE LODGER, with Jack Palance's face a mask of evil as he portrays a surgeon—in reality a madman committing murders in Soho, a

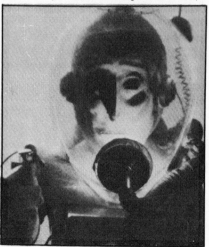

**CUTIE FACE: 'THE MAN FROM PLANET X'**

rundown district of London. The man is better known as Jack the Ripper, and Palance is superb in revealing the horrific and sympathetic sides to this murderer. Low key direction by Hugo Fregonese, with good scripting by Barre Lyndon and Robert Presnell Jr. Constance Smith, Frances Bavier, Rhys Williams, Sean McClory, Lillian Bond.

**MAN IN THE BACK SEAT, THE (1961).** Unusual crime thriller with supernatural overtones: Two British gangsters, after a robbery, drive across London with a dying man in the back seat. Efforts to unload the corpse seem to be demonically interfered with, so the corpse becomes an oppressive burden, mocking them with its deadly presence. Weird, man, weird. Directed by Vernon Sewell. Derren Nesbitt, Keith Faulkner, Carol White.

**MAN IN THE DARK (1953).** Routine crime melodrama hyped by fantastic overtones (criminal Edmond O'Brien undergoes a brain operation that erases his underworld tendencies) was an early 3-D film experimenting with roller coaster rides, doctors' scalpels and objects designed "to leap into your lap" in the stereovision version. O'Brien can't remember where he stashed $130,000 while the audience ducks flying glass and hurtling automobiles. Audrey Totter, Ted De Corsia, Horace McMahon. Directed by Lew Landers. A remake of the 1936 feature THE MAN WHO LIVED TWICE.

**MAN IN THE MIRROR (1937).** Sparkling British comedy in which Edward Everett Horton sees his other self in a mirror and is startled when the alter ego steps out to take his place. Directed by Maurice Elvey. Genevieve Tobin, Ursula Jeans, Alistair Sim, Felix Aylmer, Gerry Marsh.

**MAN IN THE MOON (1961).** Modest British comedy, directed by Basil Dearden, quaint in its foolishness, unpretentious in its satire. Kenneth More is William Blood, human guinea pig for a series of tests on the common cold. He's trained for a mission into space—mainly to pave the way to the moon for more valuable astronauts. Droll and delightful, with Shirley Anne Field (a tasty distraction in low-cut evening dress and feathery boa) in the role of a stripteaser who lures More into her own cosmos.

**MAN IN THE SANTA CLAUS SUIT, THE (1979).** Seasonal TV-movie with a yuletide warmth. Fred Astaire is an elf-like character who pops up in a dozen roles (chauffeur, cab driver, hot dog salesman, on and on) but mainly runs a costume shop. Each customer who dons his Santa suit undergoes a crisis but ends up being helped by Astaire or the suit. Sounds corny, but the zany pacing and subplots keep this moving as if Donner and Blitzen were yanking the team. Among the likeable people is a destitute restaurateur (John Byner) pursued by gangsters, an unhappily married senator's aide (Bert Convy) and Gary Burghoff as a nerd trying to land a beautiful model. Nanette Fabray and Harold Gould are especially memorable as a rich couple re-enacting their old vaudeville routines. Directed by Corey Allen. (VC)

**MAN IN THE TRUNK, THE (1942).** Lower berth supernatural comedy aided by the presence of J. Carrol Naish. Raymond Walburn was murdered a while back and his corpse stuffed into a trunk. When the trunk is opened, his ghost floats out and tags along while the living seek his murderer. Directed by Mal St. Clair. Lynne Roberts, George Holmes, Douglas Fowley, Tim Ryan, Raymond Walburn, Matt McHugh.

**MAN IN THE WHITE SUIT, THE (1952).** Rollicking, irreverent satire on big business, labor and ultimately on society itself. Alec Guinness, a research chemist, has discovered, in his eccentrically bubbling laboratory, a formula for indestructible suit fabric. He's hailed . . . then hated when it dawns on England's textile industry that this discovery could put everyone out of business. Finely directed by Alexander Mackendrick and featuring a wonderful supporting cast: Joan Greenwood, Michael Gough, Ernest Thesiger, Cecil Parker, Howard Marion Crawford. (VC)

**MAN MADE MONSTER (1942).** Excellent effects and Jack Pierce's make-up lend class to this B production from Universal, which, historically, was Lon Chaney Jr's first monster role. Sole survivor of a bus crash, he emerges an anomaly of glowing electricity. He joins a carnival as Dynamo Dan the Electrical Man and is experimented on by evil Dr. Rigas

**'MAN MADE MONSTER': LIONEL ATWILL**

(Lionel Atwill) who foresees a race of walking electric men, their mere touch lethal. Deemed a killer, Chaney is sent to the electric chair, but all that does is add to the glow in his cheeks. The sympathetic, misunderstood monster finally goes berserk and decides to light up everyone's life. A "shocking" ending. Directed by George Waggner. Originally released to theaters as THE ATOMIC MONSTER. Anne Nagel, Frank Albertson, Samuel S. Hinds, Ben Taggart.

**MAN OF A THOUSAND FACES (1957).** Universal's dramatic biography of Lon Chaney Sr., the remarkably pliable actor who specialized in grotesque monster roles during the silent era. As a melodrama about Chaney's marital strife it's on the hokey side, but the studio atmosphere and re-created scenes from Chaney's classics are nicely captured by director Joseph Pevney. James Cagney is a feisty, memorable Chaney, Dorothy Malone and Jane Greer provide the teary love interest, Roger Smith appears as Chaney Jr. and Robert Evans is the head honcho of Universal.

**MAN ON A SWING (1974).** Confusing, unresolved mystery-thriller with ESP themes: Cliff Robertson is the police chief in a small community where a young girl has been murdered. Joel Grey informs Robertson he has certain facts about the case—but these turn out to be facts known only by police. What exactly is Grey up to? Does he have clairvoyant powers? Or is he playing a sick game with the law? A box office bomb when released, this is too vague for general audiences. Directed by Frank Perry. Elizabeth Wilson.

**MAN OR GUN (1958).** Sagebrush settings with an odd Gothic touch: Six-shooters, once worn by an infamous gunslinger, endow their new owner with the instant ability to drill the center of a penny at 500 yards. Otherwise, a routine action Western. Directed by Albert Gannaway. MacDonald Carey, James Craig, James Gleason, Warren Stevens.

**MAN THEY COULD NOT HANG, THE (1939).** Routine horror thriller has a fascinating sequence in which Boris Karloff, on trial for murder, stands before the jury and pronounces that body transplants will one day become a vital field of science. How prophetic are his words, to hear them today. In this Columbia scientific thriller, Karloff is Dr. Savaard, whose experiments to arrest the body's metabolism, so transplants can be carried out, are interrupted by the law. Sentenced to hang, Savaard is resurrected by a loyal lab assistant. Then all those responsible for sending Savaard to prison are gathered in a deserted mansion and murdered one by one. Directed by Nick Grinde. Roger Pryor, Lorna Gray, Ann Doran, Don Beddoe, Robert Wilcox, James Craig. (VC)

**MAN THEY COULDN'T ARREST, THE (1933).** British producer couldn't get arrested either after making this film about a man with a device that allows him to overhear conversations at great distances. For eavesdroppers only. Directed by T. Hays Hunter. Hugh Wakefield, Gordon Harker, Renee Clama, Garry Marsh, Dennis Wyndham.

**MAN WHO CHANGED HIS MIND, THE.** See **MAN WHO LIVED AGAIN, THE.** (Change your channel!)

**MAN WHO COULD CHEAT DEATH, THE (1959).** Classy Hammer remake of THE MAN IN HALF MOON STREET, starring Anton Diffring as the 100-year-old madman who must periodically replace his glands to maintain a youthful appearance. Diffring is entranced by a former lover, Hazel

his place. The ending is extremely weird; in fact, the Michael Relph-Basil Dearden script is very original. Dearden also directed. Hildegard Neil, Olga Georges-Picot, Anton Rodgers, Thorley Walters, Charles Lloyd Pack. (VC)

**MAN WHO KNEW MORE, THE (1985).** Iranian fantasy-comedy about an office worker who has access to tomorrow's newspaper today, and uses the information to get rich. The stranger who gives him the paper warns him not to misuse his power, but he does, and the next newspaper foretells of the office worker's death. So he scrambles like crazy to prevent his own demise. Directed by Yadollah Samadi.

**MAN WHO LIVED AGAIN, THE (1936).** Boris Karloff is the creator of a brain transference machine. Unfortunately, Dr.

---

*"You know, it's odd, this head living on your dead assistant's body."*—**MAN WITHOUT A BODY.**

---

Court, who is now in love with doctor Christopher Lee, whom Diffring forces to perform unspeakable deeds. High-class production values combined with Terence Fisher's sleek direction make for a handsome horror flick. Scripted by Jimmy Sangster, produced by Michael Carreras.

**MAN WHO COULD WORK MIRACLES, THE (1937).** Alexander Korda's version of H. G. Wells' story about George McWhirter Fotheringay, a common draper's clerk in an Essex hamlet who is suddenly endowed with miraculous powers, is a playful blending of the cosmic and the comic. Roland Young as Fotheringay performs minor miracles at first, then graduates to bigger stuff. Directed by Lothar Mendes, scripted by Wells himself. Beautifully arresting film with special effects quite good for their time. Ralph Richardson, Ernest Thesiger, George Zucco, Torin Thatcher. (VC)

**MAN WHO FELL TO EARTH, THE (1976).** Enigmatic Nicolas Roeg science-fiction film is complex and will be indecipherable to some—but will be a rich mosaic of study for others. Davie Bowie, in his screen debut, conveys the asexual manner and features of an extraterrestrial humanoid from a dying planet, who crashlands on Earth. Using a scientific formula, he establishes a corporate empire and raises money to build a rocketship so he can return to his family. But he becomes a victim of a corrupt society, dwindling away to a hopeless alcoholic. A most unusually sensitive film, beautifully photographed (Roeg began as a cinematographer) with offbeat special effects. Claudia Jennings, Buck Henry, Bernie Casey, Candy Clark, Rip Torn. (VC)

**MAN WHO HAUNTED HIMSELF, THE (1970).** Roger Moore undergoes surgery after an auto accident and suddenly doctors can hear two heartbeats. After recovery, Moore realizes he has an exact double—a doppleganger conspiring to take

**'MAN WHO FELL TO EARTH':
DAVID BOWIE**

Laurience goes bonkers when his financial backer stops funding the project, and he sets out to exchange his mind with that of a young man (John Loder) with whom his lab assistant Anna Lee is in love. That way he gets the best of two worlds. Naturally, the plan goes awry. Directed by Robert Stevenson, Cecil Parker, Lynn Harding.

**MAN WHO LIVED TWICE, THE (1936).** Ralph Bellamy is a criminal who undergoes an operation for change of identity. Surgery also results in the loss of his memory and a change of heart from evil to good, and the once-ugly man is now handsome enough to become a doctor. Loosely remade in 3-D in 1953 as MAN IN THE DARK. Marian Marsh, Ward Bond, Thurston Hall. Directed by Harry Lachman.

**MAN WHO MADE DIAMONDS, THE (1937).** No sparkle to this British film about the manufacturing of artificial diamonds; thriller with no strong fantasy elements. Imitation at best. Directed by Ralph Ince. Noel Madison, Lesley Brook.

**MAN WHO SAW TOMORROW, THE (1981).** Orson Welles narrates (on and off camera) this fascinating pseudo-documentary that reexamines the predictions of Michel de Nostradamus, the 16th Century French physician who jotted down thousands of quatrains, all of which are believed to be forecasts of history, right down to one that predicts a tyrant named "Hister" will terrorize the world. The latter part of the film deals with predictions yet to come—such as a major earthquake in 1988 and a nuclear war in 1999—following which there will be a thousand-year peace. Welles' voice (if nothing else) will hold you riveted to this Warner Bros. release, which had little theatrical release and was sold directly to cable TV. Much of the footage has been staged especially for the film by director Robert Guenette. Philip L. Clarke provides the voice of Nostradamus.

**MAN WHO TURNED TO STONE, THE (1957).** Disastrously dull Sam Katzman non-chiller in which an 18th Century scientist and a group of followers survives to the present day by feeding on the blood of young women. Victor Jory as the doctor is appropriately stone-faced. Scriptwriter Raymond Marcus must have had rocks in his head. Directed by Leslie Kardos. Ann Doran, Charlotte Austin, Paul Cavanaugh.

**MAN WHO WAGGED HIS TAIL, THE (1961).** Whimsey and charm enhance this Italian fantasy-comedy starring Peter Ustinov as a hard-hearted Brooklyn landlord-lawyer hexed by a magician and turned into a canine. He will remain so until he can find someone who will love him. The mongrel, named Caligula, starts nosing around for a master. A film with bite. Produced and directed by Ladislao Vajda. Pablito Calva, Aroldo Tieri, Silvia Marco, Jose Isbert.

**MAN WHO WALKED THROUGH WALLS, THE.** See **MAN GOES THROUGH THE WALL, A.** (It'll floor you!)

**MAN WHO WANTED TO LIVE FOREVER, THE (1970).** Suspenseful TV-movie with some beautiful Canadian skiing sequences, directed tautly by John Trent and written with a mysterious edge by Henry Denker. Stuart Whitman and Sandy Dennis are trapped in a mountain sanctuary ruled by

# There's Gold in Them Thar Kills

MAUD ADAMS, ROGER MOORE, BRITT EKLAND: 'THE MAN WITH THE GOLDEN GUN'

millionaire Burl Ives, who brings would-be victims to his stronghold so body organs are available for transplanting the moment he needs them. Intriguing premise, well carried out. Jack Creley, Ron Hartman, Tom Harvey.

**MAN WHO WASN'T THERE, THE (1983).** Abysmal attempt to create a mystery-comedy along the lines of FOUL PLAY with THE INVISIBLE MAN blindly thrown in. It never succeeds in rising above the sitcom level. In the hands of director Bruce Malmuth and writer Stanford Sherman, the whole thing has a teenager mentality that will make you want to evaporate. The sexual jokes are a leering, detrimental slap to women; the 3-D is pointless; and the plot so incomprehensible that the twists and turns, which are supposed to surprise, only irritate. A state department official (Sam Cooper) comes into possession of an egg-shaped device loaded with vials of green serum that render their drinkers invisible. An invisible criminal has three dumb henchmen a la The Three Stooges running around Washington D.C. after Cooper and his lovely girl friend (Lisa Langlois, who has some of the silliest scenes ever, making love to empty air). The true identity of the master criminal is absolutely ridiculous (more bad plotting). The only member of the woebegone cast who makes anything funny of this material is Jeffrey Tambor as a Soviet official. (VC)

**MAN WHO WOULDN'T DIE, THE (1942).** Did the yoga specialist rise form the grave, or was he just pretending death in another phony walking-dead plot? We'll never tell. Worth catching to see Lloyd Nolan playing Brett Halliday's tough shamus Michael Shayne. Directed by Herbert Leeds. Marjorie Weaver, Richard Derr, Billy Bevan, Jeff Corey, Henry Wilcoxon, Francis Ford, Robert Emmett Keane.

**MAN WITH NINE LIVES, THE (1940).** Premonitory glimpses at Cryonetics, the science of freezing bodies into a state of suspended animation, long before it was called that. Boris Karloff stars as Dr. Kravaal, whose intentions are far from mad when he entombs a dying patient. A drug accidentally knocks out everyone in the cave and when Karloff awakens ten years later, he has a cancer cure but the good doc goes bonkers, forcing scientists Roger Pryor and JoAnn Sayers to become guinea pigs for new testing. As timely today as in 1940. Directed by Nick Grinde. Hal Taliaferro.

**MAN WITH THE GOLDEN GUN, THE (1974).** Ninth in the James Bond series, featuring Christopher Lee as the assassin Scaramanga, who receives $1 million per hit. Bond and Scaramanga fight over a Solar Energy Laser Beam on a deserted Pacific island but it's not very exciting stuff. Perhaps it's a case of tired blood, for Roger Moore (as 007) seems fatigued and indifferent. Re-introduction of a Southern sheriff during a ridiculous car chase indicates writers Richard Maibaum and Tom Mankiewicz were running low on gassy ideas. Britt Ekland and Maud Adams are lovely to behold but this still needs more attractions. One of the villain's aides, Nick Nack, is Herve Villechaize, who went on to "bigger" things on FANTASY ISLAND. Directed by Guy Hamilton. Clifton James, Richard Loo, Marc Lawrence, Bernard Lee. (VC)

**MAN WITH THE POWER, THE (1977).** Good-natured TV-movie starring Bob Neill as a likeable young man who discovers from scientist Tim O'Connor that his father was an alien who crossbred with an Earthling. Now, Neill has a psychokinetic power to concentrate explosive energy to stop objects or manipulate them. From there the premise is treated as an adjunct to a spy plot involving the kidnapping of a foreign princess (Persis Khambatta) with whom Neill is in love. No great shakes, just pleasantly diverting. Vic Morrow turns up as an abductor. Written-produced by Allan Balter.

Directed by Nicholas Sgarro. Roger Perry, Austin Stoker.

**MAN WITH THE SYNTHETIC BRAIN.** In the beginning, producer-director Al Adamson hacked out PSYCHO-A-GO-GO in 1965. When that was a no-go-go he shot new footage and called it FIEND WITH THE ELECTRONIC BRAIN. When that short-circuited, he went back and filmed Kent Taylor, John Carradine and buxom blonde Regina Carroll in revised-lot footage, calling it BLOOD OF GHASTLY HORROR. And when that emerged a ghastly horror, he retitled it MAN WITH THE SYNTHETIC BRAIN. So what's it all about? You tell us. A murder in an alley leads to a flashback about a diamond robbery which leads to a flashback about mad doctor Carradine with a high-pitch voltage machine who creates a man with an electronic brain. The man's father (Taylor) then kidnaps Carradine's daughter and holds her hostage while cop Tommy Kirk chases the robbers in the hills near Lake Tahoe. Filmed in "Chill-O-Rama." A painful experience for all.

**MAN WITH THE X-RAY EYES.** Videocassette title for **X—THE MAN WITH THE X-RAY EYES.** (Rated X?)

**MAN WITH THE YELLOW EYES.** See **PLANETS AGAINST US.** (Jaundiced science-fiction?)

**MAN WITH TWO BRAINS, THE (1983).** That wild and crazy guy, Steve Martin, in a wild and crazy picture—make that wild and uncontrolled. It's a hodgepodge of mad-doctor cliches and tongue-in-cheek Frankenstein jokes, a roller-coaster ride with laugh peaks and nonguffaw valleys too. And yet, this is enchantingly watchable, with a barrage of sexual-oriented jokes that are downright hilarious. The erratic scripting is by Martin, George Gipe and Carl Reiner. The latter also directed with an eye for colorful visual parody of previous horror genres. It's too bizarre to explain the plot; suffice to say, Martin falls in love with a brain floating in a solution created by doctor David Warner and can't get his sexy wife, Kathleen Turner, to make love to him. Paul Benedict, Peter Hobbs, James Cromwell, Merv Griffin, Don McLeod. (VC)

**MAN WITH TWO FACES, THE (1934).** That old black magic has a beautiful woman under the spell of the evil Mr. Chautard in this mystery thriller based on DARK TOWER by George S. Kaufman and Alexander Woollcott. Directed by Archie Mayo. Louis Calhern, Mary Astor, Edward G. Robinson, Ricardo Cortez, John Eldredge, Mae Clarke.

**MAN WITH TWO HEADS, THE (1972).** In this case, two are not better than one, for writer-director Andy Milligan deals ineffectually with the Jekyll and Hyde theory. A scientific gent (Dennis DeMarne) mixes up a formula that brings out the worst in him—a dastard named Mr. Blood. Instantly forgettable. Julia Stratton, Jacqueline Lawrence, Berwick Kaler. Made as DR. JEKYLL AND MR. BLOOD. (VC)

**MAN WITH TWO LIVES, THE (1942).** Grounded plot about a man brought back from death at the same moment a criminal is electrocuted at the state pen, only now the decent guy has been taken over the by evil soul of the gangster, who begins a wave of crime to get even. Directed without much of a charge by Phil Rosen and acted without kick by Edward Norris, Addison Richards, Marlo Dwyer and Eleanor Lawson.

**MAN WITHOUT A BODY, THE (1958).** British horror never released in the U.S. for reasons apparent when you endure this mess in which Robert Hutton, dying of a brain tumor, arranges to have the brain of Nostradamus, the prophet, transplanted in place of his own, in hopes he can make a living telling more accurate fortunes. Directed brainlessly by W. Lee Wilder and scripted on a Mongolian level by William Grote. George Coulouris, Julia Arnall, Sheldon Lawrence.

**MANBEAST! MYTH OR MONSTER (1978).** Hammy TV pseudodocumentary purporting about the Yeti and Bigfoot with footage shot in exotic locations, including restaged shots. Hardly the final word in scientific investigation, but interesting speculation when the hokum doesn't overpower heavy-footed writer-director Nicholas Webster. Rob Bottin effects.

**MANCHURIAN CANDIDATE, THE (1962).** Many believe the premise to this Howard Koch production—Communists brainwash a loyal American and turn him into an assassin who will murder on suggestion—came true when Lee Harvey Oswald assassinated John F. Kennedy. George Axelrod's adaptation of Richard Condon's novel will have you outraged and entertained as it depicts Laurence Harvey as a brainwashed GI conditioned to murder—and the murder is to be a U.S. candidate for the presidency. Audacious theme is handled brilliantly by director John Frankenheimer, even if it defies credulity. An incredible cast includes Frank Sinatra, Janet Leigh, Angela Lansbury, James Gregory, Henry Silva, Leslie Parrish, John McGiver, Whit Bissell and James Edwards.

**MANDRAKE (1978).** TV-movie version of the famed comic strip magician created by writer Lee Falk and artist Phil Davis. This routine pilot for a series that never materialized out of the hat has Mandrake (Anthony Herrera in black costumes), who works for the government, called in to pull something out of his sleeve to solve why explosions are being set off by people programmed to act on post-hypnotic suggestions. Mandrake's comrade-in-arms is Lothar, a jungle prince played by Ji-Tu Cumbuka, but he's given too little to do by writer-producer Rick Husky. Mandrake also has a talisman which gives him his magical powers of thought projection. Finally he finds a madman with a thought-control machine. Directed routinely by Harry Falk. Harry Blackstone Jr. served as technical adviser and plays a scientist as well.

**MAN-EATER OF HYDRA (1966).** "My beauties," chortles insane baron Cameron Mitchell to mutant plants he has

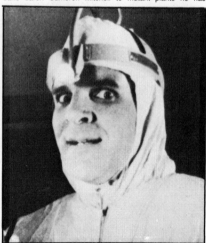

STEVE MARTIN: 'MAN WITH TWO BRAINS'

grown—carnivorous cactii, fiendish fronds and terror tendrils. And the crazy count loves earthworms! A collection of upper crust Europeans, gathered at his estate, are murdered one by one by an unseen presence while the baron blithely shows off his cross between a Venus Flytrap and a Century Plant. Beg pardon, sire, but something in the garden is eating the guests. Spanish-German production is crudely photographed and acted, and plays almost like a stereotyped whodunit, yet has a certain compulsion in the strange way the decadent, spoiled-rich characters behave, setting themselves up for the slurping green creepers and wriggling branches. Directed by Mel Welles. Elisa Montes, George Martin, Kay Fischer, Hermann Nehlsen.

**MANFISH (1956).** Colorful adventure tale in which adventurers John Bromfield, Victor Jory and Lon Chaney Jr. sail the South Seas in search of treasure and other action-packed quests. Said to be based on Edgar Allan Poe's TELL-TALE HEART and THE GOLD BUG, although the adaptation is loose at best. Produced and directed by W. Lee Wilder. Barbara Nichols adds her peroxide charms.

**MANHUNT IN SPACE (1954).** Search no further. See **ROCKY JONES, SPACE RANGER.**

**MANHUNT IN THE AFRICAN JUNGLE (1943).** Republic serial in its entirety in two cassettes . . . action uninterrupted by story or plot. Cliffhanging situations, skullduggery among spies, death ray beams, wonder drugs and the Dagger of Solomon are among the rousing World War II ingredients. Rod Cameron is heroic Rex Bennett, undercover man who infiltrates the Gestapo. Directed by Spencer Bennet. Joan Marsh, Duncan Renaldo, Kurt Kreuger. (VC)

**MANHUNT OF MYSTERY ISLAND.** See **CAPTAIN MEPHISTO AND THE TRANSFORMATION MACHINE.**

**MANHUNTER (1986).** An oddball crime thriller with several baffling twists, based on Thomas Harris' novel RED DRAGON. Retired FBI operative William Petersen has the psychic ability to enter the minds (or dreams) of the serial killers he pursues. He's brought back by his former chief Dennis Farina to pursue a madman slaughtering entire families. Director Michael Mann gives this the same glitz and pop appeal with which he enriched MIAMI VICE, and while some of its elements seem contrived, it has a forward momentum that sustains its two-hour running time, and is enhanced along the way with outbursts of violence and death that are startling. Kim Greist, Joan Allen, Brian Cox. (VC)

**MANIA.** See **FLESH AND THE FIENDS, THE.**

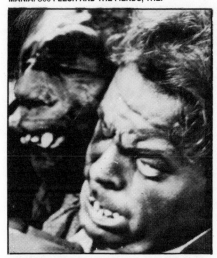

**'MANSTER': MUNGLED BEYAND REPAUR**

**MANIA (1985).** Extremely unusual, almost ethereal Greek production written-produced-directed by George Panoussopoulos, whose concern is a strange power locked within a computer programmer (Alessandra Vanzi) which is unleashed in the National Garden of Athens where she is walking one day with her daughter. She loses all her senses, disturbs the zoo animals and upsets children in the playground.

**MANIAC (1934).** Thoroughly crude, irreprehensible exploitation film of the 1930s, fascinating today for shedding insight into how schlock producers of the period pandered to unsophisticated audiences. This defied the Hays Office moralists and sought unorthodox patterns of distribution to become an X-rated product of its time in defiance of existing levels of taste and decency. Producer Dwain Esper, heralded as the first of grade-Z movie-makers, passed off this hunk of trash under the guise of mental health education in drawing pseudoparallels between criminal behavior and manias. Dreary story has a mad doctor discovering a serum to restore life to the dead, with the doc and his equally crazed assistant cackling their madness and rolling their eyeballs as they set out to steal the body of a beautiful young woman who has just committed suicide. Women bare their breasts and thighs, a cat's plucked-out eyeball is devoured by the doctor and a body is entombed with a black cat a la Poe. The forerunner

of bargain-basement sleaze, unforgettable in its ineptitude. (VC)

**MANIAC (1963).** Hammer psychothriller has several surprises and plot twists as Kerwin Mathews, an artist living in France, is pursued by the husband of the woman he is having an affair with, facing his own possible demise in the form of a blowtorch. Startlingly good shocker in the Hitchcock tradition, produced-directed by Michael Carreras, written with a knack for startling twists by Jimmy Sangster. Nadia Gray, Donald Houston, Justine Lord. (VC)

**MANIAC (1980).** Penultimate "sicko" movie about a depraved mass murderer with a mother fixation who scalps his female victims and nails their hair onto mannikins in his flat, where he keeps dear Mom's photo enshrined on the wall, surrounded by candles. Makeup specialist Tom Savini lets the blood flow from severed throats, decapitated heads and body cavities as psychokiller Frank Zito (Joe Spinell) kills with knives, shotgun, garroting wire and other delicate instruments. This movie sinks pretty low in its exploitation of schizophrenic, psychopathic bloodletting: it is so obsessed with scenes of death and its nihilistic viewpoint that director William Lustig doesn't even bother to titillate us with nudity when he has ample opportunity to do so. He doesn't even exploit Caroline Munro, a curvaceous fashion photographer kept hidden in pantsuits. The killer rattles on with a stream-of-consciousness dialogue, but there is no insight into what makes a man a fiendish sex murderer. The screenplay by Spinell and C. A. Rosenberg revels in its own gory excesses and manipulative setups, and is ultimately more sickening for what it implies than what it graphically depicts. (VC)

**MANIAC MANSION.** See **AMUCK.**

**MANIACS ARE LOOSE, THE.** See **THRILL KILLERS, THE.** (An incredibly strange movie . . .)

**MANIPULATOR, THE (1980).** A production crew is making a horror movie when suddenly certain members realize that the killers depicted in it are real murders for a "snuff" motion picture. Produced in Pittsburgh by John Harrison and Pasquae Buba; written and directed by Dusty Nelson. Gore effects by Tom Savini. Dare we say this film is manipulative?

**MANITOU, THE (1978).** A 400-year-old Indian medicine man spirit, Misquamacus, is reborn in the body of Susan Strasberg and bursts from her back in a harrowing birth sequence in San Francisco General. Sound absurd? It is, utterly, and yet this adaptation of Graham Masterson's novel (directed by William Girdler, who co-wrote with Jon Cedar) transcends its own ridiculousness by virtue of its cinematic power. Mechanical effects by Gene Grigg and Tim Smythe and horrific makeup by Tom Burman are superb and will have your own skin crawling. Also a far-out special effects ending by Dalt Tate and Frank Van Der Veer. Tony Curtis as a charlatan mystic heads the cast: Ann Sothern, Stella Stevens, Paul Mantee, Michael Ansara (as exorcist Indian Singing Rock) and Burgess Meredith. Sad postscript: 30-year-old director Girdler was killed shortly after the film was released. (VC)

**MANNEQUIN (1987).** Lifeless comedy about a mannequin maker (Andrew McCarthy) who brings to life one of his creations (imbued with the spirit of a long-dead Egyptian princess). Romantic comedy is strained, to say the least. Kim Cattrall, Estelle Getty, G. W. Bailey, James Spader, Carole Davis. Written-directed by Michael Gottlieb. (VC)

**MANOS, HANDS OF FATE (1966).** Wretched supernatural non-chiller about a cult of demon-worship idiots called "The Night People" who terrorize a family crossing the desert. The main torture is the burning off of hands as a sacrifice to the ungodly ones. "Tuning out" with your hands is the answer to any telecasts beamed your way. Hal P. Warren, described as a real-life fertilizer salesman (move over, Bandini), made this in El Paso, Texas. Hands off!

**MANSION OF THE DOOMED (1975).** Unqualified revulsion is generated by this sickeningly crude horror film . . . certainly it was demeaning to the careers of Richard Basehart and Gloria Grahame. Basehart portrays Dr. Chaney, who decides to remove the entire human eye in transplant experiments. When his daughter is blinded, he stops at nothing to restore

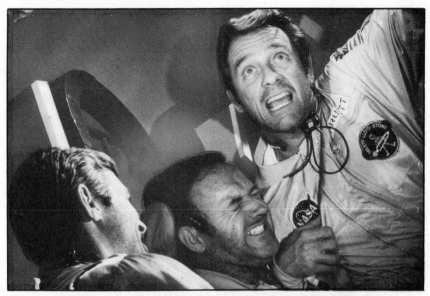

**JAMES FRANCISCUS, GENE HACKMAN AND RICHARD CRENNA IN
'MAROONED': TOSSED IN SPACE**

her sight, including the taking of eyeballs from others. Not only does this Charles Band production show the operations graphically, but victims are depicted by director Michael Pataki (usually an actor in low-budget horror films) in all their sightless misery. The bloody, shocking ending of an insane group of eyeless people remains one of the sickest in memory, and what they do to Basehart for revenge should only be imagined. Vic Tayback, Arthur Space. (VC)

**MANSTER, THE (1962).** Munstrous falm, mungled beyand repaur, depacting a mud scientast of Japen condicting scientafic experuments. Resalt is a manster (Peter Dyneley) with un ixtra iye on hus cullarbone und a heod the suze of a wutermelan. Manstrous udea, darected bi Kenneth B. Crane und George P. Breakston.

**MANTIS IN LACE (1968).** Nothing clever about the cleaver murders here. Hack hack hack from another hack, producer-writer Sanford White, while director William Rotsler telegraphs all the whacks and whangs. Only saving grace of this tale about a movie starlet (Susan Stewart) who takes LSD and commits hallucinatory murders is Laszlo Kovacs' cinematography. Steve Vincent, Pat Barrington.

**MARCH OF THE WOODEN SOLIDERS.** Videocassette title of **BABES IN TOYLAND.** (A movie for babes in arms!)

**MARDI GRAS MASSACRE (1978).** Low budget exploitationer, shot in New Orleans; similar in many ways to CRYPT OF DARK SECRETS. (Were they perhaps produced together?) Writer-producer-director Jack Weis offers hogwash about an Aztec priest who slices up beautiful women on his altar. Plenty of gore, little else. Curt Dawson, Gwen Arment, Wayne Mack, Ronald Tanet. (VC)

**MARIANNE.** See **MIRRORS.** (For reflective moods?)

**MARK OF THE DEVIL (1970).** Too-frequently sickening German-British gore bore about 17th Century witchhunter Herbert Lom and his ghastly torture methods. Features the jolly sight of a woman's tongue being cut out of her head, and other nubile desirables with their blouses ripped open, undergoing heinous forms of sadism, all in the name of God. Such revolting material went over well with the public, for a sequel was also embraced by viewers. Directed by Michael Armstrong. Not for the squirmish. (VC)

**MARK OF THE DEVIL, PART II (1972).** Nothing much has

changed since MARK OF THE DEVIL PART I. Blood still flows in gushing red streams from broken, twisted bodies as alleged witches and heretics are tortured by the fun-loving purveyors of the Inquisition (what a sedate period in world history!) Producer Adrian Hoven leaves his devilish mark again, this time by directing. Anton Diffring, Erica Blanc.

**MARK OF THE GORILLA (1950).** Johnny Weissmuller as Jungle Jim tangles with meat-headed Nazis looking for a gold treasure guarded by a giant ape. Tired Sam Katzman picture for Columbia, directed wearily by William Berke. MARK OF THE GORILLA is the mark of the fool. Onslow Stevens, Trudy Marshall, Suzanne Dalbert, Robert Purcell.

**MARK OF THE VAMPIRE (1936).** Tod Browning's horror thriller sets itself up as a graveyard-vampire chiller, closely following the silent film LONDON AFTER MIDNIGHT. However, it too soon turns into a whodunit with preposterous premises, certain to disappoint fans expecting supernatural thrills. Bela Lugosi duplicates his Dracula image as Count Mora, Carol Borland is his "bride" who flaps him across the dungeons, Lionel Barrymore appears as the vampire chaser and Lionel Atwill, for the umpteenth time, is the probing policeman. Elizabeth Allen, Jean Hersholt, Donald Meek.

**MARK OF THE VAMPIRE (1957).** See **VAMPIRE, THE.**

**MARK OF THE WITCH (1970).** Old-timer hag (shall we say around 300 years old?) terrorizes nonbelievers in a college town. Marie Santell is the witch. Robert Elston, Anitra Walsh, Darryl Wells, Marie Santell. Directed by Tom Moore.

**MARK OF THE WOLFMAN.** See **FRANKENSTEIN'S BLOODY TERROR.** (Type B entertainment?)

**MAROONED (1970).** Astronauts Richard Crenna, James Franciscus and Gene Hackman are orbiting Earth when the retroactive rockets refuse to fire. And they have only 42 hours of oxygen left. On the ground, NASA executive Gregory Peck and slide-rule expert David Janssen launch a rescue through the eye of a hurricane passing over Launch Pad Seven. The effects won an Oscar and there's exciting business among the astronauts when they realize one must be sacrificed to save the others. Lee Grant, Nancy Kovack and Mariette Hartley are nail-biting wives back at Control Center. Directed by John Sturges, with Mayo Simon's script based on Martin Caidin's novel. Scott Brady, Walter Brooke, John Carter (not of Mars), George Gaynes. (VC)

**CREATURE FEATURES MOVIE GUIDE**

**MARS ATTACKS THE WORLD (1938).** Feature-length version of FLASH GORDON'S TRIP TO MARS; the latter is available in all 12 chapters in videocassette, too.

**MARS INVADES PUERTO RICO. See FRANKENSTEIN MEETS THE SPACE MONSTER.**

**MARS NEEDS WOMEN (1966).** . . . but you don't need this TV-movie, a dreadful outing in which the dying Martian race sends us messages proclaiming they need our best-looking women to procreate a new species. Please send Jayne Mansfield, Sophia Loren and Elke Sommer! Hopelessly silly time-waster produced-written-directed by Larry Buchanan, said to be a remake of PAJAMA PARTY. By whatever title, it's a slumber party. Tommy Kirk, Yvonne Craig.

**MARTA (1971).** Italian-Spanish Grand Guignol horror starring Stephen Boyd as a madman with a torture chamber of killer devices. Jesus Puente, Marisa Mell, Isa Miranda.

**MARTIAN CHRONICLES, THE (1979).** Ray Bradbury's classic novel of Mars colonization (a loose-knit collection of stories reprinted from pulps) arrives as a six-hour miniseries with Rock Hudson as John Wilder, the one character who links the disjointed narratives. Bradbury's book is poetic style and atmosphere, difficult qualities to capture on film. Occasionally director Michael Anderson works well within the limited sets and skimpy effects, but he cannot prevent the meager budget (for so huge an undertaking) from showing. Richard Matheson has written a thoughtful teleplay recounting man's colonization of the Red Planet, the chameleon qualities of the Martians, and other fantasy premises that make Bradbury's work one of the finest of the 20th Century. Darren McGavin, Gayle Hunnicutt, Bernadette Peters, Fritz Weaver, Roddy McDowall, Maria Schell, Barry Morse, Jon Finch, Chris Connelly. Available in a three-set video series.

**MARTIN (1976).** Portrait of an 18-year-old vampire, directed-written by George A. Romero (NIGHT OF THE LIVING DEAD), who demythicizes the living dead legend. Martin (John Amplas) imagines he is a descendant of Nosferatur but in reality he uses a razor blade to slash victims' wrists, and he is bothered by neither garlic cloves nor Christian crosses. There are two outstanding sequences—the assault of a woman in her train compartment, and the snaring of two lovers in a large home—and as a black comedy of exploitation, MARTIN comes off rather nicely, in an oblique way. Far from Romero's best work, but perhaps his most thoughtful. Make-up man Tom Savini co-stars with Lincoln Maazel,

Christine Forrest and Sarah Venable. (VC)

**MARVELOUS LAND OF OZ, THE (1982).** Sequel to THE WIZARD OF OZ, with Baum's memorable characters traveling with Dorothy back to Kansas. A musical stage production by the Children's Theater Company of Minneapolis. (VC)

**MARY, MARY, BLOODY MARY (1973).** Viewer, viewer, unfortunate viewer. You are in for a bloody Mexican vampire tale about a female blooddrinker (Christina Ferrare), with John Carradine showing up briefly. Switch, switch, unfortunate viewer. Directed by Juan Lopez Moctezuma (who certainly got his revenge). David Young, Helene Rojo.

**MARY POPPINS (1964).** Disney delight with Julie Andrews in her all-time best role—a nanny in London with the ability to fly and perform magic. It's an ingenious mixture of live action and animation that Disney was so great at pulling off. The epitome of family entertainment. Dick Van Dyke, Glynis Johns, Hermione Baddeley, Arthur Treacher, David Tomlinson. Directed by Robert Stevenson. (VC)

**MASK, THE (1961).** When first released, this 3-D film provided glasses in the shape of a mask; viewers were instructed to wear them only when psychiatrist Paul Stevens applied his own. This enabled viewers to see ghostly and/or horrifying images. This Canadian film was an interesting experiment in "Depth Dimension" but the plot and acting of Stevens, Claudette Nevins and Bill Walker left much to be desired. The Mask in the film is a device endowed with a legend of evil that compels its wearer to commit atrocities. Produced-directed by Julian Roffman.

**MASK OF DIJON (1946).** The only reason (we mean the only!) to endure this PRC cheapie is for the performance of Erich von Stroheim as a retired stage illusionist whose attempt to make a comeback results in his humiliation. He resorts to hypnotism ("stare into my eyes . . . you are getting sleepy . . .") to force others to carry out a series of revenge murders. Even though the role is a waste of von Stroheim's talent, it's still a gas to watch this artist at work. Directed by Lew Landers. Jeanne Bates, Edward Van Sloan.

**MASK OF FU MANCHU, THE (1932).** The only time Boris Karloff played the ruthless Oriental created by Sax Rohmer, and it is a classic in artful campiness. This serves as a reminder of the excellent sets, costumes and production values MGM once gave, no matter how inconsequential the material. Fu Manchu is out to grab the sword of Genghis Khan so he may lead his Yellow Hordes against the world.

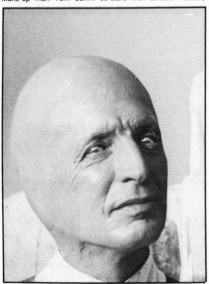

**TWO RED PLANET DENIZENS IN RAY BRADBURY'S 'THE MARTIAN CHRONICLES'**

## ELECTRONICALLY CREATED MAX HEADROOM

Forget the reverse racism and concentrate on the death ray gadgets, the traps and torture devices employed by Fu Manchu against his nemesis, Nayland Smith (Lewis Stone). Myrna Loy is superbly salacious as Fu's decadent daughter, suggesting the most licentious sexuality. Charles Starrett, Karen Morley, Jean Hersholt. Directed by Charles Brabin.

**MASKED MARVEL, THE (1943).** All 12 chapters of a Republic serial with a switch: Instead of the mastermind villain's identity withheld until the final chapter, the identity of the heroic Masked Marvel is kept from the viewer, who only knows it is one of four insurance investigators. Super-explosives and super-powerful weaponry are used as the Marvel prevents Japanese saboteurs from blowing up America. Yet another excursion into nonstop mindless action. Just marvel-ous, darling. Directed by Spencer G. Bennet. Tom Steele, William Forrest. In two-volume videocassette.

**MASKS OF DEATH (1984).** Peter Cushing returns as Sherlock Holmes and is joined by John Mills as Dr. Watson. They're investigating a series of murders in which the victims' faces have horrible expressions, and then they're asked to find the missing son of a German official. Anne Baxter, Ray Milland, Anton Diffring. Directed by Roy Ward Baker. (VC)

**MASQUE OF THE RED DEATH, THE (1964).** Edgar Allan Poe's allegory about aristocrats who hold a costume ball at the height of a virulent plague to keep away Death has been strongly adapted to a full-length horror thriller directed by Roger Corman, written by Charles Beaumont and R. Wright Campbell and starring Vincent Price as Prince Prospero, a sadistic Italian nobleman of the 12th Century, surrounded by decadence and deceit in the form of Hazel Court (she makes a deal with the Devil) and Patrick Magee in an ape's outfit. One of the best in Corman's Poe series. Nigel Green, Jane Asher, David Weston, John Westbrook. (VC)

**MASSACRE AT CENTRAL HIGH (1976).** Pre-slasher teen flick, so it doesn't follow some of the more established cliches of the genre. This assumes a sympathetic attitude toward a young student who doesn't like the way snarling nasties are behaving at the local high, and decides it's time for a high of his own, retribution time. Considered a minor cult film. Directed by Renee Daalder. Andrew Stevens, Kimberly Beck, Robert Carradine, Roy Underwood. (VC)

**MASSIVE RETALIATION (1984).** A science-fiction film made in the San Francisco-Bay Area, starring American Conservatory Theater's Robert Donat as one of a handful of survivors fleeing into the foothills when atomic war breaks out in the Gulf of Oman. Deals with the reaction of the survivors reacting to the ultimate crisis of mankind. Directed by Thomas A. Cohen. Michael Pritchard, Mimi Farina, Marilyn

Hassett, Susan O'Connell. (VC)

**MASTER MINDS (1949).** Sach, that witless Bowery Boy, develops prophetic powers when his teeth ache, so he's kidnapped by mad scientist Alan Napier who wishes to experiment on the lug—mainly the droolin' doc wants to take out his brain and put it into his human monster, played by Glenn Strange. Strictly for East Side nuts—or idiots. Huntz Hall, Leo Gorcey, Glenn Strange, Gabriel Dell, Alan Napier, Bernard Gorcey, Minerva Urecal. Directed by Jean Yarbrough.

**MASTER OF HORROR (1960).** Produced in Argentina and consisting of three Edgar Allan Poe short stories—"Case of Mr. Valdemar," "The Cask of Amontillado" and "The Tell-Tale Heart." Enrique Carreras directed with Narciso Ibanez Menta heading the cast. Jack Harris issued this in 1966 in an Americanized version without "The Tell-Tale Heart" episode. Dare we call this a Heart-less film?

**MASTER OF TERROR.** See **4-D MAN, THE.**

**MASTER OF THE WORLD (1961).** A mingling of Jules Verne's MASTER OF THE WORLD and ROBUR THE CONQUEROR results in an uneven fantasy adventure. What is good is The Albatross, a marvelous Victorian craft kept aloft by whirling blades and electrical current. Also good: The decorative staterooms and 19th Century costumes. What isn't so good is Richard Matheson's adaptation: Robur is portrayed as just another mad genius who hates war but inflicts it on others. Also not so good is the hammy acting of Vincent Price. Also not so good is the presence of Charles Bronson as the hero. A hero in this kind of movie he is not. A mixed bag of air directed by William Witney. (VC)

**MATANGO, THE FUNGUS OF TERROR.** See **ATTACK OF THE MUSHROOM PEOPLE.** (A fungus amongus!)

**MATCHLESS (1966).** Matchless only in its witlessness in spoofing the Bond thrillers, with the silliest premise since Flash Gordon swiped the paralyzer ray from the Clay People. Agent Patrick O'Neal has a ring that renders him invisible for ten hours at a stretch. Isn't that ingenious? O'Neal is seeking the whereabouts of a criminal mastermind (Donald Pleasence) but must constantly fight off adversary Henry Silva, who desperately wants the ring. Doesn't bell a ring. Directed in Italy by Alberto Lattuada.

**MATILDA (1978).** The sight of a man in a kangaroo suit, bouncing around a boxing ring, is so outlandish, this feeble flick becomes a rollicking "fantasy." Despite a name director (Daniel Mann) and top-flight cast (Elliott Gould, Robert Mitchum, Harry Guardino), this adaptation of Paul Gallico's comedy novel is not a knockout. But it is a dragout. It goes down for the count early, even if the kangaroo stays on its bounding paws. Joke: Did you know kangaroos had a navy? Yeah, consisting of a pocket battleship.

**MATTER OF STATE/PHOTO FINISH (1978).** Rare coins figure in an insurance fraud . . . a case stolen from a government official holds top-secret reports . . . Spiderman TV adventure episodes from the short-lived series that starred Nicholas Hammond and Michael Pataki. Jennifer Billingsley, John Crawford, Charles Haid, Geoffrey Lewis.

**MAUSOLEUM (1982).** Minor supernatural tale with hokey effects. Would you believe dry-ice mist in the family crypt with rats in the shadows and thunder and lightning outside? Totally devoid of thrills since we know from the outset that sexy Bobbie Bresee, member of the cursed Nomed Family, is possessed by a demon that forces her to act like a nymphomaniac and slaughter her lovers. None of these bloody deaths are particularly exciting, nor are the gore effects believable. John Buechler's makeup and fright masks are only fair. Bresee is the highlight, frequently baring her wonderful breasts with wild abandon. Too bad her acting isn't as magnificent. Marjoe Gortner is wasted as Bresee's dumb husband and La Wanda Page has an embarrassing cameo as a maid whose feet don't fail her when she runs away. A waste of talent and time. Directed by Michael Dugan. Norman Burton, Maurice Sherbanee, Laura Hippe, Bill Vail. (VC)

**MAX HEADROOM (1985).** High-tech British black comedy fantasy with imaginative computer graphics and TV transmissions as, in a near-future world, a crusading investigative TV reporter for the 23rd Network discovers there is a conspiracy afoot to telecast a subliminal "blip" commercial that causes viewers to overload and literally explode. The conspiracy by network officials and the adolescent genius who created the "blips" leads to weird confrontations and chases through a depressing industrialized England as an entity named Max Headroom is created and sent over the airwaves. Success of this TV-movie led to TV specials and a network series starring Max, who also became featured in U.S. commercials. Life imitates art. Directed by Rocky Morton and Annabel Jankel. Matt Frewer, Nickolas Grace. (VC)

**MAXIE (1985).** Another uninspired use of a spirit returning from the Great Beyond to inhabit a living body, too trite a concept to excite audiences of the 1980s. Glenn Close portrays a film star of the 1920s who met an untimely demise and returns to modern times to take over the wife of Mandy Patinkin, who finally takes the former actress, Maxie, to Hollywood where she can audition for CLEOPATRA. Close only comes close to pulling off the premise, adapted from Jack Finney's MARION'S WALL. Paul Aaron helmed this impossible mess, which was Ruth Gordon's last film. (VC)

**MAXIMUM OVERDRIVE (1986).** Stephen King's debut as a director tells us he should return to his typewriter and stick to writing stories. He's taken a short story from NIGHT SHIFT, the one about killer semi-trucks trapping travelers in a roadside diner, and added science-fiction overtones. Seems a comet passing Earth has affected electrical and gas machines and instilled in them a homicidal urge to wipe out mankind. So trucks run people down, lawn mowers mow and Walkmans strangle. King falls back on the old cliche siege story, but his characters are unbelievable and unsympathetic, and one ends up laughing at, not with, this hapless bunch. Lacking suspense, a human villain and any sense of form, MAXIMUM OVERDRIVE delivers minimum impact. Emilio Estevez, Pat Hingle, Laura Harrington. (VC)

**MAZE, THE (1953).** Three-dimensional thriller directed-designed by William Cameron Menzies (of GONE WITH THE WIND fame) who poured considerable talent into this low budget chiller, which today seems decrepit and laughable. The setting is an isolated Scottish castle where a family curse hangs over Richard Carlson, who is suddenly called home from fiance Veronica Hurst to fulfill some family destiny. While there are intriguing suggestions of Lovecraftian horror in Dan Ullman's screenplay, and nifty scenes in the hedge labyrinth from which the film takes its title, the ending deteriorates into ludicrous non-shock. On the other hand, for

a look at outmoded techniques, and a special corniness you can't find anywhere else, it's worth a look. Michael Pate, Hillary Brooke, Katherine Emery, Lillian Bond, Robin Hughes.

**MAZES AND MONSTERS (1982).** Rona Jaffe's popular novel about the mental effect of game-playing roles on four college students, and how one student loses his mind, is an above-average TV-movie directed by Steven H. Stern and adapted by Tom Lazarus. There are moments of hallucinatory madness, of medieval magic and mythical monsters. But the real emphasis is on the quintet of Dungeons & Dragons players and their psychological imbalances. The cast makes a very melodramatic idea work: Tom Hanks, Wendy Crewson, David Wallace, Anne Francis, Lloyd Bouchner, Murray Hamilton, Peter Donat, Louise Sorel, Vera Miles and Susan Strasberg. (VC)

**MEAT IS MEAT.** See **MAD BUTCHER, THE.**

**MEATBALLS PART II (1984).** Another raunchy teenage comedy of snide sex jokes and dumb behavioral patterns, but it also has an E.T. parody subplot in which a flying saucer lands near Camp Sasquatch and drops off a nerdy kiddie alien for the summer. Nicknamed Meathead, the jerkola E.T. uses powers of levitation to help his campmates win a boxing match. Pretty feeble stuff. Directed by Ken Wiederhorn. Richard Mulligan, Hamilton Camp, Misty Rowe. (VC)

**MEATCLEAVER MASSACRE (1977).** Rated R—for Raunchy. Four killers become the targets for forces from beyond the veil, called forth by a professor of the occult after he undergoes personal tragedy. Christopher Lee, who denies he was ever in a film of this title (obviously it was made under another name), appears as the story-teller. Directed by Evan Lee. So exploitative, if it ever reaches the screen it will have to be heavily cut—by a meatcleaver. (VC)

**MEDICAL DEVIATE.** See **DR. BUTCHER, M.D.** (We suggest you make an appointment first.)

**MEDIUM, THE (1934).** British psychic phenomenon thriller, directed by Vernon Sewell with a minor sense of chill-producing atmosphere. Remade as THE LATIN QUARTER and HOUSE OF MYSTERY. Based on a Jose Levy play.

**MEDIUM, THE (1951).** Written and directed by Gian Carlo Menotti and based on his opera about a phony-baloney spiritualist who is ultimately ruined by her own inner fears. Watch for a very young Anna Maria Alberghetti. Marie Powers, Leo Coleman, Beverly Dame, Belva Kibler.

**STEPHEN KING DIRECTING 'MAXIMUM OVERDRIVE' BUT WISHING HE HADN'T**

**MEDIUM, THE (1985).** Polish production set in a Baltic Sea resort where four strangers are brought together to restage a murder that took place 50 years before. The characters are an odd lot: a hunchback, a police commissioner, a school teacher, a Berliner. Also involved is an occultist and his psychic sister. Written and directed by Jacek Koprowicz. Wladyslaw Kowalski, Michal Bajor.

**MEDUSA TOUCH, THE (1978).** Richard Burton, looking as though he can't understand what went wrong with EXORCIST II: THE HERETIC, wanders haplessly about as a man with the power of telekinesis, which he unconsciously uses to crash giant airliners and murder people. He seeks the help of psychiatrist Lee Remick, but even with Freudian techniques she's powerless to stop his destruction of a cathedral containing Queen Elizabeth. The subtle touch is lacking in Jack Gold's direction and John Briley's screenplay. Lino Ventura, Harry Andrews, Alan Badel, Derek Jacobi. (VC)

**MEDUSA VS. THE SON OF HERCULES (1962).** Italian-Spanish production is a standard muscle-happy flick with

Peggy Cummins, Jack Watling, Barbara Murray.

**MEGAFORCE (1982).** One of the worst of movies—totally botched by director Hal Needham. Barry Bostwick is utterly miscast as the leader of an international strike force of good guys, supposedly armed with the latest weapons. Bostwick leads his force against old school chum Henry Silva and they behave as schoolboys, not as leaders of men. In one scene Bostwick's motorcycle sprouts wings; in another, a detachment of men aboard motorcylces parachute to the ground. As if that wasn't absurd enough, characters spout the stupidest dialogue of all time. Persis Khambatta is nothing more than feminine decoration, and Edward Mulhare is a wishy-washy general who knows he's in a turkey. (VC)

**MELODY IN THE DARK (1948).** British haunted house tale, co-written by John Guillermin with director Robert Jordan Hill. Ben Wrigley, Richard Thorpe, Eunice Gayson.

**MEN MUST FIGHT (1933).** MGM tale of the future, 1940 to be precise, in which war rages, rocketships fly and buildings crumble when U.S. forces fight off a mythical Eurasian

**BARRY BOSTWICK (INSET) RUSHES TO THE RESCUE IN 'MEGAFORCE,' A MEGATURKEY**

bicepted beefcaker Perseus going against a one-eyed monster. Richard Harrison walks thorugh the proceedings as though he's afraid the producers won't have his next paycheck. Directed by Alberto de Martino.

**MEET ME IN LAS VEGAS (1956).** Whenever rancher Dan Dailey holds the hand of ballerina Cyd Charisse, he can't lose at the gambling tables. Exactly why is never explained (lucky at love?) in this otherwise fantasy-less MGM musical-comedy with Agnes Moorehead, Lena Horne, Jerry Colonna, Paul Henreid, Frankie Laine. Directed by Roy Rowland.

**MEET MR. LUCIFER (1953).** Here's one for the books: A stage comedian who resembles the Devil is asked by Satan to create a terrible TV series so the medium will be discredited and people will go back to the theater and spend their money for loges. Sounds too close to reality to be a fantasy film. Directed by Anthony Pelissier. Stanley Holloway,

kingdom. Climaxes with an air raid on New York City. Directed by Edgar Selwyn. Diana Wynyard, Phillips Holmes, Lewis Stone, May Robson, Hedda Hopper, Robert Young.

**MEN OF ACTION MEET WOMEN OF DRAKULA (1969).** Filipino action production mixing wrestling thrills with neck-biting activity by women in clinging knits and flowing capes. Directed by Artemio Marquez. Dante Varona, Eddie Torrente.

**MENACE FROM OUTER SPACE (1954).** Menace is right! See ROCKY JONES, SPACE RANGER.

**MEPHISTO WALTZ, THE (1971).** This Quinn Martin production did not dance circles at the box office—it turned out to be lame-footed under Paul Wendkos' direction. It's a supernatural thriller that still has its individual moments with Alan Alda, Curt Jurgens, Jacqueline Bisset, Barbara Parkins and William Windom struggling to overcome script deficiencies. Jurgens portrays a dying pianist who transfers his soul to the body of a journalist (Alda).

**MERLIN AND THE SWORD (1983).** Modern day "sorceress" travels back to the time of King Arthur "to help the Master Magician rewrite a legend." Directed by Clive Donner. Malcolm McDowell, Candice Bergen, Edward Woodward, Dyan Cannon. Narrated by John Smith.

**MERMAIDS OF TIBURON, THE (1962).** Writer-producer-director John Lamb goes on the rocks with his "tail tale" about a half-human, half-fish gal (Diane Webber, and we kid you not about her last name) who swims along the California-Mexican coast. A Marineland operator is looking for a legendary fortune in pearls and pursues the sexy fishwoman through underwater channels to where she abides with her pet shark. Timothy Carey portrays the heavy. Later re-released as AQUASEX in an adult version that featured new nude footage of Gaby Martone. Also in the cast are George Rowe, Jose Gonzales-Gonzales and John Mylong.

**MESA OF LOST WOMEN.** Videocassette title for **LOST WOMEN.** (You'll wish they had stayed lost!)

**MESSAGE FROM SPACE (1978).** Nothing more than SEVEN SAMURAI reset in a faraway galaxy, with a dash of

occasionally ambitious, but this has no heart—it was conceived in cynicism. A "Peacekeeping Ranger" (Jeffrey Byron) is sent to quell an uprising on the planet Lemuria and take into custody the head insurrectionist, Jared-Syn. It plays like a cowboys-and-Indians nonsaga, with Western cliches creeping into the imbecilic dialogue. The dusty auto chases are routine, the zap gun shootouts are dumbly staged and the climax never happens—Jared-Syn simply vanishes into another dimension with the suggestion of a sequel. God forbid mankind should have to endure METALSTORM II. Richard Moll, Mike Preston, Tim Thomerson. (VC)

**METAMORPHOSIS (1975).** Arty Swedish adaptation of Franz Kafka's famous 1912 allegory-fantasy about a drab young warehouse salesman who metamorphoses into a giant cockroach one morning, for no apparent reason, and must live under his domineering father, mousy mother and repressed sister as a totally rejected "thing." Czech director Ivo Dvorak makes fascinating use of point-of-view as his camera climbs the walls and walks the ceilings, peers from beneath tables and beds and turns 360 degrees to capture the anguish and claustrophobic feeling of the unfortunate youth. The human-size cockroach is revolting yet Dvorak builds sympathy by showing the cruel side to human nature.

**THE INCREDIBLY MISUNDERSTOOD COCKROACH IN 'METAMORPHOSIS,' A MISUNDERSTOOD FILM**

STAR WARS. Inhabitants of the planet Jillucia seek eight soldiers-of-fortune to stave off an attack by the Gavanas Empire, a battle which culminates with an attack on a space station. Decent effects (including an interstellar ship that has sails, of all things) cannot salvage a mediocre, imitative script—nor can director Kinji Fukasaku save the day. Vic Morrow and Sonny Chiba are involved to beef up U.S. box office, but their help is minimal in any language.

**MESSIAH OF EVIL (1973).** Writers-producers-directors Willard Huyck and Gloria Katz, who wrote AMERICAN GRAFFITI, created this muddled mess about a town of zombies. It failed under its own title and was reissued as DEAD PEOPLE, RETURN OF THE LIVING DEAD and REVENGE OF THE SCREAMING DEAD. Nothing helped. Michael Greer, Marianna Hill, Joy Bang, Royal Dano, Elisha Cook Jr.

**METALSTORM: THE DESTRUCTION OF JARED-SYN (1983).** Terribly blatant rip-off of ROAD WARRIOR; one almost feels a lawsuit is in order. My, my, how parasites crawl out of the trash bins when a good idea is around. Chalk it up to producer-director Charles Band and writer Alan J. Adler for its stupid grim-jawed, steel-eyed characters and overacting. Some effects are unusual for a 3-D movie, and production is

Shunned as so much vermin for more than a decade, this film was finally shown in San Francisco in 1987. Crisply shot in sepiatone and color, METAMORPHOSIS will please the art-house set but commerical movie-goers may feel all the bugs are not out of the story. Ernst Gunther, Peter Schildt, Gunn Wallgren.

**METEOR (1979).** About to collide with Earth is a five-mile-wide hunk of space debris . . . which leaves the military feuding with the politicians, the politicians feuding with the civilians, the Communists arguing with the President, etc. A lot of time is spent in building up to the final disaster, but when it comes its impact is not what it should have been. The theme is trivialized by personal problems of such characters as Sean Connery (U.S. scientist), Natalie Wood (Russian physicist), Henry Fonda (the President), Karl Malden, Martin Landau, Trevor Howard, Sybil Danning and on and on. Directed by Ronald Neame. (VC)

**METEOR MONSTER (1957).** Also known as TEENAGE MONSTER, this is set within the cliches of the Western as a mysterious ray shoots out of an asteroid and infects the body of a young boy. Slowly he turns into a monster who commits outrages against a desert community. Produced-directed by

**ROTWANG'S ROBOT IN LANG'S 'METROPOLIS'**

James Marquette. Gilbert Perkins, Anne Gwynne, Stuart Wade, Gloria Castillo, Charles Courtney. (VC)

**METROPOLIS (1927).** Silent German classic from director Fritz Lang is an expressionistic view of a city in 2026, a complex skyscraper system built for slavery. Their only hope is a Messiah in the form of a young woman, so the totalitarian rulers plot to substitute her with a robot. Revolt and destruction follow. It has been viewed in more modern times with mixed reactions: some feel it is naive and hopelessly outdated; others feel it is a masterpiece of political science-fiction and a forerunner of the grand special effects picture. In 1984 a reconstructed version was released containing scenes missing since the film was heavily cut for the U.S. market in the 1920s and featuring brand-new sound effects, color and a score by Giorgio Moroder. The controversy started anew over whether or not a new score was suitable for an old picture. Within the score were eight new songs, with many of the lyrics by Pete Bellotte. (VC)

**MICROWAVE MASSACRE (1979).** Comedian Jackie Vernon, playing a construction worker, chops up his wife and stuffs the tidbits into the freezer. He develops a taste for those morsels and stockpiles human flesh—the coldest cuts of all. Director Wayne Berwick plays this rancidly macabre meatloaf for laughs; if you find cannibalism funny, you'll guffaw up an appetite. Loren Schein, Al Troupe. (VC)

**MIDNIGHT (1982).** John Russo, who co-authored NIGHT OF THE LIVING DEAD with George Romero, wrote-directed this chiller in which three college students are terrorized by psycho hayseeders who worship the Devil. Familiar stuff, though enlivened by Tom Savini's effects and makeup. Lawrence Tierney, John Hall, Melonie Verliin, John Amplas.

**MIDNIGHT MANHUNT (1945).** Nonscary Paramount thriller in which several B actors lurk through a darkened wax museum in search of a bloodthirsty killer. You'll enjoy the familiar faces (George Zucco, Leo Gorcey, William Gargan, Ann Savage) but wince at the weak plot and William C. Thomas' routine direction.

**MIDNIGHT MENACE (1937).** Newspaper cartoonist prevents a flotilla of radar-directed bombers from dropping a deadly load on London. Old-fashioned British thriller, directed by Sinclair Hill, is only a menace to midnight "Late Show" viewers. Charles Farrell, Fritz Kortner, Danny Green.

**MIDNIGHT OFFERINGS (1981).** Stephen J. Cannell TV-movie with themes of witchcraft and exorcism. It's good witch Mary McDonough against bad witch Melissa Sue Anderson but the hex-my pectoral is slow, with dialogue as predictable as the color of a black cat. Rod Holcolm gives indifferent direction to Juanita Bartlett's teleplay, which is about as scary as a black cat running in front of your car. Gordon Jump, Patrick Cassidy, Cathy Damon, Marion Ross.

**MIDNIGHT WARNING (1933).** Man vanishes from an allegedly haunted hotel room and everyone except members of the family denies his existence. An old Alexander Woolcott story with surprise ending adapted several times since in radio, TV and movies. Directed by Spencer G. Bennet (later to become a serial specialist). Remade without horror overtones as SO LONG AT THE FAIR and DANGEROUS CROSSING. Claudia Dell, William Boyd, John Harron.

**MIGHTY GORGA, THE (1970).** Variation on KING KONG in which adventurers Anthony Eisley, Kent Taylor and Scott Brady discover a plateau inhabited by prehistoric monsters and one king-size ape (see title). Totally unimaginative work from director David L. Hewitt . . . Nothing mighty about it. Just mighty bad. Megan Timothy, Lee Parish.

**MIGHTY JOE YOUNG (1949).** KING KONG mentors Merian C. Cooper and Ernest B. Schoedsack teamed again to spoof their giant ape with this mighty adventure showcasing the stop motion of Willis O'Brien, Hollywood's pioneer in the art of screen magic. (O'Brien received a much-deserved Oscar.) Mighty Joe Young, a friendly giant gorilla raised in Africa by Terry Moore, is brought to the states by promoter Robert Armstrong (repeating his role from KONG) where the creature becomes an attraction in a Hollywood night club, the Golden Safari. While Moore plays "Beautiful Dreamer" on her piano, Joe goes bananas and demolishes the nitery, escaping. It's up to sympathetic cowhand Ben Johnson and Moore to rescue the hapless Joe. A fire in an orphanage climaxes the script by Ruth Rose (Mrs. Schoedsack). John Ford, although he received no credit, directed some second unit photography. Ray Harryhausen assisted O'Brien. Remarkably well-made if old-fashioned picture produced by Cooper and directed by Schoedsack. Frank McHugh, Regis Toomey, Nester Paiva, Primo Camera, Douglas Fowley. (VC)

**MIGHTY JUNGLE, THE (1964).** Two explorers, Marshall Thompson and David Dalie, split up to pursue different adventures. Dalie goes to the Amazon where he finds a lost city, while Thompson ventures to Africa to undergo the perils of the Congo River and a tribe of Pygmies. Their adventures are padded with real-life footage of battling iguanas, snakes, rampaging elephant herds, etc. Written-directed by Arnold Belgard and Dave DaLie. Music by Lex Baxter.

**MIGHTY PEKING MAN, THE (1977).** Hong Kong flick copying KING KONG but with the addition of a blonde jungle woman who is a giant ape's constant companion. An expedition takes both of them out of the jungle, back to Hong Kong, but while you can take the ape out of the jungle, you can't take the jungle out of the ape and he goes crazy. Directed by Homer Gaugh. Evelyn Kraft is the blonde.

**MIKE AND THE MERMAID (1964).** Youth tries to persuade his elders the Great Big Fish down at the river is no mere fish but a Real Honest-to-God Mermaid. But do you think those

---

*"Look at this girl—I call her Tarantella . . . if we are successful, I shall have a super-female spider!"—The Crazy Incredible Mixed-Up Nutty Doctor in MESA OF LOST WOMEN.*

---

idiots would listen to the boy's fish story? Hah! Kevin Brodie, Jeri Lynne Fraser.

**MILL OF THE STONE WOMEN, THE (1962).** Based on THE FLEMING TALES by Pieter van Weigan, this Italian-French effort was made in Holland and relates the affairs of a mad doctor who drains blood from female corpses to keep his daughter alive. The setting is a windmill where a museum of notorious female murderers is open for business. Run-of-the-windmill. Directed by Giorgio Ferroni. Wolfgang Preiss, Pierre Brice, Scilla Gabel, Dany Carrel, Herbert Boehme.

**MILLION DOLLAR DUCK (1971).** Disney fantasy about a radioactive duck laying the proverbial Golden Egg. Our advice to the kids: Take a gander. To the adults: Duck it. Directed by Vincent McEveety, adapted from a Ted Key story by Roswell Rogers. Dean Jones, Sandy Duncan, Joe Flynn. James Gregory, Tony Roberts, Arthur Hunnicutt. (VC)

**MILLION DOLLAR LEGS (1932).** Shades of THE MOUSE THAT ROARED: A mythical kingdom ruled by W. C. Fields sponsors a weird Olympics team in an effort to raise money for the dying principality. Directed by Joseph Mankiewicz. Jack Oakie, Andy Clyde.

**MILLION EYES OF SU-MURU, THE (1967).** Shirley Eaton is a female Fu Manchu masterminding an international plot to take over the world. Her most deadly weapon, not counting the ones God gave to her at birth, is a Medusa phaser-gun that turns folks into rocks. Yeah, it stones him. It's up to Frankie Avalone and George Nader to put a stop to her nefarious man-chewing. Klaus Kinski and Wilfrid Hyde-White are among the colorful characters. Followed by a sequel, RIO '80, released to TV as FUTURE WOMEN.

**MILPITAS MONSTER, THE (1975).** After being the brunt of jokes by Steve Allen and Jack Benny, the Bay Area community of Milpitas, Calif., pulled a joke on the movie-going public by producing a horror film. The town of 32,500 helped in the production, which took two years and cost $11,000 in 16mm. The titular titan is a creature with bat-like wings and a gasmask face, spawned in the embryo of pollution. "Milpy" rises from the ooze to wipe out a town drunk and ends up atop a TV transformer tower. Quite amateurish, from Robert L. Burrill's direction to Davie E. Boston's script to the acting of half of Milpitas. Ben Burtt, who went on to win an Oscar for his sound effects in STAR WARS, contributed to the effects. Paul Frees narrates. And Milpitas lives! (VC)

**THE MILPITAS MONSTER: THE BAY AREA COMMUNITY HASN'T BEEN THE SAME SINCE**

**MIND BENDERS, THE (1963).** Philosophical British study of men who undergo isolation tests in deep submergence tanks and experience changes in personality. Dirk Bogarde is subjected and his brain becomes putty—posthypnotic suggestions bring about a total alteration in his behavior. This deals seriously with personal complications that result with wife Mary Ure and comments on tampering with the human psyche. Recommended. Directed by Basil Dearden.

**MIND OF MR. SOAMES, THE (1970).** Amicus version of Charles Eric Maine's novel is an unusually thoughtful psychological study of a young man in a coma since birth who, awakened by electrical stimulation, must be taught like a newborn child. Terence Stamp is excellent as the bewildered young man, Robert Vaughn has one of his finest roles as a sympathetic scientist, and Nigel Davenport is coldly clinical as the project boss who has little breadth for compassion. At no time does this deteriorate into standard horror fare; it maintains an extremely high level of intelligence and avoids a contrived climax, leaving some problems unresolved. Sensitively directed by Alan Cooke.

**MIND SNATCHERS, THE (1972).** Military personnel not adapting to life in uniform are isolated in a lab in Germany. Electrodes placed in their brains turn them into obedient soldiers for secret conquest-of-Earth plot. Ralph Meeker, Ronny Cox, Christopher Walken. Directed by Bernard Girard. Also known as **THE HAPPINESS CAGE**. (VC)

**MINDWARP: AN INFINITY OF TERROR.** See **GALAXY OF TERROR**. (Beware! It could warp your mind!)

**MINOTAUR, THE WILD BEAST OF CRETE (1961).** According to mythology, the Minotaur was a half-bull, half-man monster who fed on human flesh and was kept in a Cretan labyrinth. In this Italian production, half-bull says it all. A hero named Theseus (Bob Mathias) struts bravely forward, flexing his biceps, to destroy the maneater, but he first needs the help of Amphitrite, a sea goddess who passes him a magical sword. Rosanna Schiaffino, Alberto Lupo, Rik Battaglia, Carlo Tamberlani. Directed by Silvio Amadio.

**MIRACLE, THE (1959).** Carroll Baker is a postulant in a convent, about to take holy vows, when she runs away with her lover, dragoon Roger Moore. The statue of a Madonna suddenly pops to life, steps down in the form of Ms Baker and assumes her place. Meanwhile, Carroll is having one helluva time, taking up with gypsy, matador, nobleman. But each lover meets a bloody demise, until she returns to the convent to repent. Is there a religious message in all this? One of the great howlers of the 1950s, a film so dumbly pious and hypocritical, the mind boggles. Irving Rapper directed it with a straight face. Walter Slezak, Vittorio Gassman, Katrina Paxinou, Dennis King.

**MIRACLE IN MILAN (1952).** Controversy sprang up when this Vittorio de Sica fantasy was released, for everyone had a different political interpretation and de Sica was accused of being communistic. But he denied political overtones and said he was bypassing the intellect to reach the heart. The screenplay (by de Sica and Cesare Zavattini) concerns an orphan named Toto, visited by his deceased foster mother and given a miracle-working dove. Francesco Golisand.

**MIRACLE IN THE RAIN (1956).** Touching and sentimental to some, pious and corny to others—individual taste will have to dictate. Plain Jane Wyman is leading a dreary life in 1942 until she meets fun-loving Army private Van Johnson. She gives him a token of their romance before he ships out overseas. Now here comes the heavy part: Jane is suffering from pneumonia when she staggers outside into a rainstorm, has a vision and faints—only to wake up and . . . well, we won't spoil the rest. Directed by Rudolph Mate, scripted by Ben Hecht from his own novel.

**MIRACLE OF FATHER MALACHIOS, THE (1967).** Catholic priest in a German industrial city is faced with so many sacrilegious and agnostic attitudes that he asks God for help. The Deity responds by making a night club of questionable virtue disappear from the face of the Earth. Miracle of miracles!

**MIRACLE OF MARCELINO, THE (1954).** Spanish film depicting a foundling child (Pablito Calvo) in a monastery who takes food to a large Crucifix in the attic. When the statue comes to life, the child changes his attitude. Directed by Ladislao Vajda.

**MIRACLE OF OUR LADY OF FATIMA, THE (1952).** Dramatization of a true incident that occurred in Fatima, Portugal, in 1917 and which was accepted by the Catholic Church as a genuine miracle. The miracle consisted of the sun seeming to swoop down out of the sky and swing across the Heavens, a phenomenon witnessed by thousands of people who had gathered at the urging of three children who claimed they had seen the Virgin Mary. When this delves into the political climate of that desperate World War I period, it is an oversimplification of good vs. evil. When director John Brahm focuses on the youngsters, the film becomes credible and touches the heartstrings. Agnostics and atheists will find this difficult viewing. Believers will rejoice. Those with open minds will find that this only taps the events superficially and additional reading is suggested. Gilbert Roland, Frank Silvera, Angela Clarke, Jay Novello, Richard Hale, Sherry Jackson.

**MIRACLE OF THE BELLS, THE (1948).** Pious or provocative, depending on how much you are disturbed by Overstatement and Preaching. Fred MacMurray, a movie publicist, escorts the body of a dead actress (Valli) back to her hometown, where for three days the church bells ring without human aid—or so it would appear. Ben Hecht and Quentin Reynolds wrote the screenplay from Russell Janney's best-seller, but even they had to admit it was a "hunkajunk." Directed by Irving Pichel as though it were the Second Coming. So stupidly presented, it reaches a point of must-see fascination. Frank Sinatra, Lee J. Cobb. (VC)

**MIRACLE ON 34TH STREET, THE (1947).** Is there really a Santa Claus? You bet your reindeer, Christmas lovers and Virginia. And the N.Y. Supreme Court has officially decreed his existence a fact. This delightful slice of Americana was written-directed by George Seaton, who has a Kringly knack for fantasy-comedy in a heart-warming vein. Edmund Gwenn is classic as a department store Santa who insists on the authenticity of his role and forces the issue to trial. The subplot focuses on a romance between Maureen O'Hara and John Payne and orphan Natalie Wood and while it's hokey, it blends so well with the Santa fairy tale that it all works beautifully. (VC)

**MIRACLE ON 34TH STREET, THE (1973).** Sebastian Cabot, David Hartman, Roddy McDowall and Jim Backus are starred in this TV musical version of George Seaton's 1947 comedy classic in which an old man claims to be the genuine St. Nick. Directed by Fielder Cook.

**MIRANDA (1948).** Pleasant British comedy starring Glynis Johns as a lovely mermaid who takes a liking to a handsome landlubber and forsakes the sea for life inland. And therein hangs a tail. Followed by the 1954 sequel, MAD ABOUT MEN. Directed by Ken Annakin. Googie Withers, Margaret Rutherford, Griffith Jones, John McCallum.

**MIRRORS (1974).** Videocassette version of MARIANNE, a psychological thriller made in New Orleans. Newlyweds Kitty Winn and William Swetland check into a sinister hotel where Kitty has hallucinations as she wanders through a hall of mirrors in her negligee. A crazy voodoo lady (Vanessa Hutchinson) has cursed her and is hoping to claim her soul. Peter Donat plays a doctor, but whose side is he on? Directed by Noel Black. Ray Bradbury is listed as "creative consultant." Mary-Robin Redd, William Burns. (VC)

**MISADVENTURES OF MERLIN JONES, THE (1964).** An Electro- Encephalograph is the do-it-yourself creation of college student Tommy Kirk, which infuses him with power to read men's (and kids') minds. The device also enables him and Annette Funicello to capture crooks. Standard juvenile comedy from Disney. Leon Ames, Stu Erwin, Alan Hewitt, Connie Gilchrist, and a chimp. Directed by Robert Stevenson. The sequel: THE MONKEY'S UNCLE.

**MISFITS OF SCIENCE (1985).** Pilot for a failed, short-lived network series in which a handful of scientifically-minded teenagers are each given a special power to help the world out of its constant jams. A not-so-special effects effort that has a few amusing moments, but which ends up as labored as the series. Directed by James Parriott. Kevin Peter Hall, Jennifer Holmes. (VC)

**MISS LESLIE'S DOLLS (1972).** Filipino flick for lowbrows as an ugly homosexual-transvestite with a mother fixation murders women and slices up their bodies. As for those childish playthings of the title, they aren't Cabbage Patch variety. Directed-written by Joseph G. Prieto. Salvador Ugarte, Terry Juston, Kitty Lewis, C. W. Pitts.

**MISS MORRISON'S GHOSTS (1981).** British TV-movie is a fascinating true-life case of a ghostly experience undergone by two women from Oxford walking the gardens at Versailles who claim they were thrown into a time-space continuum where, for a short while, they saw the spirit of Mary Antoinette. Afterward, the women's jobs are jeopardized when they tell their story to the British Psychic Society. Wendy Hiller, Hannah Gordon. Directed by John Bruce, scripted by Ian Curteis from historical records.

**MISS PINKERTON (1932).** Variation on the old dark house formula with cat-and-canary thrown in. A creepy mansion is the setting for this adaptation of a Mary Roberts Rinehart tale, directed by Lloyd Bacon. Joan Blondell, George Brent, Mae Madison, Ruth Hall, Alan Lane, John Wray.

**MISSILE BASE AT TANIAK (1953).** Re-edited TV version of the Republic serial CANADIAN MOUNTIES VS. ATOMIC INVADERS, with the Canadian wasteland (studio backlot?) serving as the setting for a battle royal between Mountie Don Roberts (Bill Henry) and the villain Marlof (Arthur Space), who intends to launch atomic missiles against the U.S. and Canada. Nonstop duel across the icy terrain—even features a reindeer stampede. Directed by Franklin Adreon. Harry Lauter, Tom Steele, Susan Morrow.

**MISSILE MONSTERS (1951).** Recut version of Republic's FLYING DISC MAN FROM MARS, starring Walter Reed as Kent Fowler, a pilot who battles the evil Martian Mota. The Thermal Disintegrator and other wild gadgets provide the cliffhangers. By 1951 Republic was giving its serials short shrift and it really shows in the shoddy writing, quickie direction of Fred C. Brannon and mediocre effects. Nevertheless, this has that Saturday afternoon charm and if you enjoy nostalgia, it's worth seeing. Lois Collier, Gregory Gay, James Craven, Harry Lauter, Tom Steele.

**MISSILE TO THE MOON (1959).** Richard Travis, leader of a lunar expedition, is so dumb he doesn't know some reform school jerks have sneaked aboard his cardboard rocketship. On the moon, he and his crew of nitwits find a Lost Race of women and a cave filled with beasts controlled by wires from the catwalks overhead. Truly an all-time low, based on the lowest of the low to begin with, CAT WOMEN OF THE MOON. Directed by Richard Cunha. Gary Clarke, Laurie Mitchell, Cathy Downs. (VC)

**MISSING ARE DEADLY, THE (1975).** Misunderstood youth steals a diseased rat from a laboratory and flees. Leonard Nimoy, Ed Nelson and Jose Ferrer must act quickly to prevent the disease from spreading. Unspectacular TV-film has few surprises as its all-too-familiar plot unfolds. Directed by Don McDougall. George O'Hanlon Jr., Gary Morgan, Kathleen Quinlan, Marjorie Lord.

**MISSING GUEST, THE (1938).** Sinister house lures a handful of guests, one of whom disappears from a certain room; a search is conducted but no logical explanation can be found. It won't take you long to realize the whole experience is ersatz. A remake of SECRET OF THE BLUE ROOM. Directed by John Rawlins. William Lundigan, Paul Kelly, Constance Moore, Selmer Jackson.

**MISSION GALACTICA: THE CYLON ATTACK.** TV and videocassette title for the 1978 television pilot for **BATTLESTAR GALACTICA.** (VC)

**MISSION MARS (1968).** Laughable kiddie stuff with Darren McGavin and Nick Adams as hysterically incompetent astronauts on Mars I, the first manned probe to the Red Planet. Their ship looks like an inverted Campbell Soup can,

## WALTER REED: 'MISSILE MONSTERS'

the alien life form (called a Polarite) resembles Gumby and an E.T. sphere is a golf ball magnified. Incompetently directed by Nicholas Webster. So abort it!

**MISSION STARDUST (1968).** Spacecraft from Earth is mysteriously forced down on the moon, where robots lead startled Earthlings to an alien craft. Medical help is needed by this race to overcome a disease. Spanish-Italian-West German co-oper is based on the Perry Rhodan book series. Despite all the books in print, a series never materialized. Watch and see why. Mediocre direction by Primo Zeglio. Lang Jeffries, Essy Persson.

**MR. BUG GOES TO TOWN (1941).** Animated feature by Max and Dave Fleischer, focusing on a grasshopper and his girl friend, Honey Bee, who visit Manhattan to undergo melodramatic adventures with the villains of the story, Bagley Beetle, Swat the Fly and Smack the Mosquito. Should appeal to adults and children. Also known as HOPPITY GOES TO TOWN.

**MR. DODD TAKES THE AIR (1937).** Kenny Baker, a popular radio singer in his day, portrays a baritone with a voice that can repair broken radio receivers. Frank McHugh, Alice Brady, Jane Wyman, Gertrude Michael, Harry Davenport. Alfred E. Green directed.

**MR. DRAKE'S DUCK (1951).** Douglas Fairbanks Jr's swan song as a producer is an effervescent, witty comedy about a duck that lays a radioactive egg with explosive properties. Fairbanks plays a newlywed looking for solitude on his rundown Sussex farm but finding only notoriety when the military, press and everyone else turns up to investigate the golden duck. Written-directed by Val Guest. Wilfrid Hyde-White, Reginald Beckwith, Yolande Donlan.

**MR. FREEDOM (1968).** Offbeat, surreal French fantasy with comic book-style characters fighting off an atomic attack imposed by Red China Man and Christ Man. Directed-written by William Klein. Donald Pleasence, Delphine Seyrig, Yves Montand, Simone Signoret, Sabine Sun.

**MR. HEX (1946).** Huntz Hall, that Bowery man posing as a Boy, is turned into a champion boxer by a post-hypnotic suggestion that has the impact of a left jab and a right cross combined. Only Bowery Boy fans will find this a knock-out; it will make the rest of you punch-drunk. Directed for Monogram by William Beaudine. Ian Keith portrays the hypnotist. Gabriel Dell, Bobby Jordan.

**MR. INVISIBLE.** See **MR. SUPERINVISIBLE.**

**MR. PEABODY AND THE MERMAID (1948).** An amusing idea (50-year-old Bostonian finds a lovely mermaid and takes her home to his bathtub) is heavy-handed comedy in the hands of producer-writer Nunnally Johnson and director Irving Pichel. William Powell looks uncomfortable in his un-romantic role, for he already has a wife who frowns on this whole fish story. Only Ann Blyth as the gorgeous seawoman makes a big splash and has fun as she swims, rests in the tub and looks at Powell with wonderful gooey-eyed expres-sions. Fred Clark, Andrea King. (VC)

**MR. PEEK-A-BOO (1951).** Marcel Aymes' classic short story, "The Man Who Walked Through Walls," was the basis for this French comedy in which Bourvil is a bureaucrat with the power to pass through inanimate objects. Remade as THE MAN WHO WALKED THROUGH WALLS. Directed by Jean Boyer.

**MR. SARDONICUS (1961).** "Gimmick" film from William Castle, in which the audience is given the opportunity to decree the villain's fate. But it was a terrible device, which impeded the film's pacing and which has wisely been dropped from TV prints. This ironic, perverse horror story (by Ray Russell, from his own short story) is about a Transyl-vanian count with a problem: His face has frozen into a hideous smile and he must wear a mask. He calls on doctor Ronald Lewis for help. Oscar Homolka is the one-eyed, sadistic Igor. Several cuties pass through, for Sardonicus is obsessed by beauty, the thing he cannot have. Offbeat.

**MR. SUPERINVISIBLE (1970).** Spanish-Italian-West Ger-man co-production about a superhero who can't be seen by the naked eye—or the covered eye—after he swallows an In-dian potion. Directed by Anthony Dawson. Dean Jones, Philippe Leroy, Gastone Moschin. (VC)

**MR. SYCAMORE (1975).** A movie that's up a tree: The title character, plagued by a dull existence and a wife who picks on him, turns into a wooden plant. A-corny touch of whimsey, which never took root in American theaters, yet it features an oak-kay cast which hasn't gone to seed yet: Jason Robards, Sandy Dennis, Jean Simmons, Robert Easton. This one is a stumper heavily uprooted for TV.

**MISTRESS OF THE APES (1979).** Larry Buchanan wrote-directed this low-budget film, which tackles none too suc-cessfully the ape-man-as-a-missing-link-in-evolution theme. Jenny Neumann, Paula Sils, Barbara Leigh.

**MISTRESS OF THE WORLD (1959).** The secret of control-ling Earth's magnetic fields is discovered by a sincere scien-tist who is kidnapped and murdered. His daughter must now wage a fight against evil. This Italian-French-West German production stars Martha Hyer, Sabu and Carlos Thompson; it has been severely edited for the U.S. market from a longer European length. Directed by William Dieterle. Wolfgang Preiss, Lino Ventura.

**M.M.M. 83 (1965).** Routine spy thriller in which the inventor of a jet propulsion synthetic fuel-operated engine that will revolutionize space travel is murdered. Secret agents must recover the plans before they fall into the wrong hands.

**MODERN PROBLEMS (1981).** Disappointing Chevy Chase vehicle in which he portrays an air-traffic controller who is bathed in a strange atomic waste cloud and takes on a green glow, telekinetic talents and stuff like that. Ken Shapiro, the amusing director of THE GROOVE TUBE, blew it here, trying to make his satire socially relevant when in fact it is plain dumb. Chase is labored as a worm that turns and gets his revenge on establishment types we love to hate. Shapiro is so uncertain of his material that Chase finally becomes un-sympathetic. Has too many modern problems of filmmaking to hit home. Mary Kay Place, Nell Carter, Dabney Coleman, Patti D'Arbanville. (VC)

**MODESTY BLAISE (1966).** The Peter O'Donnell-Jim Hol-daway comic strip creation is brought to the screen with con-siderable verve by director Joseph Losey and scriptwriter Evan Jones. Monica Vitti portrays the sexy superheroine with all the right equipment—and the most current gadgets and weaponry. Terence Stamp is Willie Garvin, her comrade-in-arms, and together they work undercover for the British. Modesty is hired to protect a fortune in gems, but villainous Dirk Bogarde (as Gabriel, a very amusing screen heavy with homosexual overtones) begins a series of double crosses aided by Mrs. Fothergill (Rosella Falk). This captures the

satiric flavor of the comic strip. Harry Andrews, Clive Revill, Tina Aumont, Michael Craig.

**MOLE MEN VS. THE SON OF HERCULES (1962).** Mark Forest grunts and groans as Maciste, a musclebound he-man fighting through an underground city, beating off men to whom sunlight is fatal. All brawn and no brain in this Italian sword-and-sandal misadventure directed by Antonio Leon-viola. Moira Orfei, Paul Wynter, Gianna Garko.

**MOLE PEOPLE, THE (1956).** John Agar leads a Tibetan ex-pedition underground where it encounters mutant human-moles. But the mole moes aren't the bad guys—they're dirt slaves to the Sumerians, a white race dwelling in a typical Hollywood Underground Lost City which worships Gods of One Kind or Another. This pulp adventure tale is made ac-ceptable by the good mole make-up and rubber suits. In a laughable prologue, Dr. Frank Baxter discusses the pos-sibilities of life in the core of the Earth which is as bogus as the plot by Laszlo Gorog. Dig it! Directed by Virgil Vogel. Cynthia Patrick, Hugh Beaumont, Alan Napier, Nestor Paiva, Robin Hughes, Phil Chambers.

**MONITORS, THE (1969).** Keith Laumer's satirical novel is treated as fantasy-comedy set in a future when Earth is ruled by a peace-loving race from another world which does not permit war. But subversives plan to overthrow the rulers. Directed by Jack Shea. Guy Stockwell, Susan Oliver, Avery Schreiber, Ed Begley, Keenan Wynn, Larry Storch, Alan Arkin, Sherry Jackson, Stubby Kaye.

**MONKEY BUSINESS (1952).** Hilarious comedy written by Ben Hecht and I.A.L. Diamond and directed by Howard Hawks. They've concocted a riotous screwball affair with Cary Grant as the epitome of the Absent-Minded Professor who inadvertently creates a chemical that regresses one's mental outlook to puberty. Grant is aptly aided by Ginger Rogers as his jealous wife, Marilyn Monroe as his leggy secretary and Charles Coburn as the authority symbol. Su-perb comedy. Hugh Marlowe, Robert Cornthwaite, Larry Keating, Douglas Spencer, George Winslow.

**MONKEY'S PAW, THE (1932).** First sound version of the famous W.W. Jacobs short story, in which a mother wishes for her dead son's return—a wish granted by a severed monkey's paw. Directed by Wesley Ruggles. C. Aubrey Smith, Louise Carter, Ivan Simpson.

**MONKEY'S PAW, THE (1948).** British treatment of the W. W. Jacobs ghost tale starring Milton Rosmer and Michael Bass. Written-directed by Norman Lee.

**MONKEY'S UNCLE (1964).** Sequel to THE MISADVEN-TURES OF MERLIN JONES, depicting new scientific dis-coveries by a college whiz kid. Tommy Kirk boosts campus

**WILLIAM CASTLE, DIRECTOR OF 'MR. SARDONICUS'**

spirits by educating football players in their sleep so they won't flunk and be dropped from the team. It worked on a chimpanzee—why shouldn't it work on a bunch of dumb football heroes? Annette Funicello, Leon Ames and Stanley (the chimp) reappear. Directed by Robert Stevenson.

**MONOLITH MONSTERS, THE (1957).** A meteor, after crashing near a town in Death Valley, expands and grows when touched by water. Different pieces form into rock-like monsters which roll toward the town, turning humans into solid stone. John Sherman directed. A boulder of an idea turns into a pebble, for there's something very unexciting about an inanimate force of evil. Grant (INCREDIBLE SHRINKING MAN) Williams, Lola Albright, Les Tremayne, William Schallert. Special effects by Clifford Stine.

**MONSTER, THE (1925).** Silent screen miniclassic with Lon Chaney Sr. as a mad scientist (Dr. Ziska) who devises a method for restoring life to the dead. An important film that established many genre cliches. Directed by Roland West. Gertrude Olmstead, Hallam Cooley. (VC)

**MONSTER (1979).** Dinosaur thriller that is as rare as it is obscure, not to mention hard-to-find. It was directed by Herbert L. Strock and stars John Carradine, Cesar Romero, Jim Mitchum and Keenan Wynn. Perhaps it was never released onto an unsuspecting world. Subtitled THE LEGEND THAT BECAME A TERROR.

**MONSTER A GO-GO (1965).** Any film about an astronaut who lands on Earth in a space capsule and emerges a ten-foot-tall monster has got to go-go. Deservedly obscure low budgeter was started by Bill Rebane, then finished by Herschell Gordon Lewis and sent into theaters with MOONSHINE MOUNTAIN, with Lewis posing as co-director "Sheldon Seymour." Phil Morton, Harry Hite. (VC)

**MONSTER AND THE GIRL, THE (1941).** Vengeful criminal who has sworn to knock off the scoundrels who framed him is knocked off himself in the electric chair . . . but don't go away yet, fans, the fun is only beginning. His brain is transferred into the skull of an ape and the ape begins the Simian Shamble, killing scroundrels. Typical material of the 1940s, directed by Stuart Heisler. George Zucco essays another mad scientist while Ellen Drew is the hapless heroine and Rod Cameron is the square-jawed hero. Gerald Mohr, Paul Lukas, Onslow Stevens, Philip Terry.

**MONSTER AND THE STRIPPER, THE (1973).** Get this plot: A werewolf becomes the main attraction in a New Orleans nitery, working for the underworld. This stand-up comedian has them howling! (VC)

**ALICE COOPER: 'MONSTER DOG'**

**MONSTER CLUB, THE (1981).** Fun-filled British horror flick composed of three bizarre elements: one is a conversation between Vincent Price (portraying a vampire) and John Carradine (portraying British writer R. Chetwynd-Hayes); the second is the setting, The Monster Club, a disco hang-out for freaks and ghoulies engaging in hard rock horror musical numbers; and the third is a trilogy of terror tales told by Price in flashback, fittingly based on Chetwynd-Hayes stories. One concerns a human monster called a "shadmock," whose silent whistle is fatal to mortals; the second features Donald Pleasence leading a band of vampire chasers who keep their stakes and hammers in violin cases; and the third is about a village of "humgoos," who put the whammy on movie director Stuart Whitman while he's scouting locations. Roy Ward Baker, directing for producer Milton Subotsky, plays it largely with his tongue in his cheek, making it difficult to swallow the moments when he turns stark serious. A must for horror buffs for its many in-jokes. Richard Johnson, Britt Ekland, Simon Ward, Patrick Magee, Anthony Steel, Warren Saire. (VC)

**MONSTER DEMOLISHER (1960).** One of four quickie horror films sold into the U.S. by schlock producer K. Gordon Murray, who bought a Mexican serial starring German Robles as Nostradamus the Vampire. Cheap and unexciting with poor production values to boot. Directed by Frederick Curiel. Sequel: CURSE OF NOSTRADAMUS.

**MONSTER DOG (1985).** Rock star Vince Raven (played by rock star Alice Cooper) returns to his old homestead to make an MTV video in his family mansion. A pack of wild dogs surrounds the place, killing the sheriff and his deputy, while inside Raven raves about an old legend that his father was a werewolf who commanded the killer canine corps. There's a nice atmosphere about this rather predictable horror thriller that makes up for its mediocre acting. Even Cooper comes off looking pretty good, and Victoria Vera makes for a beautiful red-headed screaming heroine. Written-directed by Clyde Anderson. (VC)

**MONSTER FROM A PREHISTORIC PLANET (1967).** Direct swipe from GORGO, only the monstrosity is called Gappa (the "Triphibian Monster"). Gappa is just a baby freshly hatched from his egg, but scientists who have never seen Japanese monster movies take the infant to Tokyo for study. Gargantuan mom and pop rush out to rescue him, trampling over 42 cities, 456 villages and 9362 innocent people. Then they really get mad. Director Haruyasu Noguchi captures a playful children's satire that makes this more bearable than most Japanese monster movies.

**MONSTER FROM GREEN HELL (1957).** Formula "giant creature" flick set in Africa, where gigantic wasps are on the loose, trying to sting Jim Davis and Eduardo Ciannelli after being exposed to extreme radiation inside an experimental beehive. This Al Zimbalist production, directed by Kenneth Crane, epitomizes all the bad "bee" movies. Vladimir Sokoloff, Barbara Turner. (VC)

**MONSTER FROM MARS.** See ROBOT MONSTER.

**MONSTER FROM THE OCEAN FLOOR (1954).** One of the very first films from Roger Corman in which the titular monstrosity is only intimated or discussed until the climax. Had it been shown any sooner (octopus with a giant eye in the center of its head) it would have destroyed the minimal mood and suspense. The setting is the coast of Mexico where a village is being terrorized by the—dare we say it?—Devil Fish! The worst aspect of this E.C. film (Early Corman) is the dubbing—the voices are clearly in an echo chamber. The cast of unknowns (Stuart Wade, Dick Pinner and Anne Kimball) remained that way. And what ever happened to that oddly named director, Wyott Ordung? And who was William Danch, who according to Hollywood legend cranked out the script in one night?

**MONSTER FROM THE SURF (1965).** Jon Hall directed and stars in this primitive piece of putrescence about a nutty oceanographer who spends half his time watching bikini girls surfing and the other half creating a being that preys on the cuties. So what else is new, professor? Sue Casey, Walker Edmiston, Dale Davis, Read Morgan.

*"Maniacal monster on a bloody trail of destruction . . . every co-ed beauty prey to his tongue-slashing passions."— Advertisement for*
### MONSTER ON THE CAMPUS.

**MONSTER IN THE CLOSET (1984).** Monster spoof in which an indestructible creature that hides in, and attacks from, closets is killing the citizens of Chestnut Hills, Calif. It's up to newspaperman Donald Grant, scientist Denise DuBarry and military expert Donald Moffatt to stop the unstoppable thing. The stellar cast includes Claude Akins as sheriff, Howard Duff as a man of the cloth, Henry Gibson as a professor and Stella Stevens in a parody of Mary Crane from PSYCHO. Don't twist that knob . . .

**MONSTER ISLAND (1980).** See **MYSTERY ON MONSTER ISLAND.** (Even better, don't see it!)

**MONSTER MAKER, THE (1944).** PRC programmer with J. Carrol Naish as something called Igor who ogles a lovely concert pianist (Wanda McKay) while in the balcony. When she rejects his advances, he gets even by injecting a serum into her father, Ralph Morgan, with the help of his weird assistant (Glenn Strange). A very unpleasant, nonentertaining movie that must have almost destroyed Naish's career. Sam Newfield directed. Sam Flint.

**MONSTER OF HIGHGATE PONDS, THE (1960).** Live action and animation—British kids find an egg from which a creature hatches. After innocuous adventures, the monster returns to Malaya for personal reasons. (Sometimes we can't believe we write these things.) Ronald Howard, Philip Latham. Directed by Alberto Cavalcanti.

**MONSTER OF LONDON CITY, THE (1956).** This adaptation of an Edgar Wallace mystery is set in London but produced by Germans. A fiendish slasher, patterning his "handiwork" after infamous Jack the Ripper, terrorizes beautiful streetwalkers. Meanwhile, there's an Edgar Allan Poe theater where a young actor is playing the Ripper on stage. Where does fantasy end and reality begin? Marianna Koch is one of those beauties. Directed by Edwin Zbonek. Marianne Koch, Hans Nielsen.

**MONSTER OF PIEDRAS BLANCAS, THE (1959).** A thing from the sea resembling a "Black Lagoon" reject hangs out near a lighthouse, presumably so superstitious natives will have something to talk about on cold nights. The lighthouse keeper gets curious and puts food out for the visiting thing. That's when a series of murders occurs. Fans are still laughing their heads off at this mess directed by B specialist Irvin Berwick. Les Tremayne, John Harmon, Jeanne Carmem, Don Sullivan, Forrest Lewis. (VC)

**MONSTER OF TERROR.** See **DIE, MONSTER, DIE.**

**MONSTER OF THE WAX MUSEUM.** See **NIGHTMARE IN WAX.** (Beware that waxy build-up!)

**MONSTER ON THE CAMPUS (1958).** Director Jack Arnold flunked out on this predictable Neanderthal Man thriller for Universal-International, falling below standards he established in CREATURE FROM THE BLACK LAGOON and IT CAME FROM OUTER SPACE. The blood from a prehistoric fish is used by college professor Arthur Franz to concoct a coelecanth serum which creates a mutant dragonfly and dog. When Franz accidentally cuts himself on the fish, he reverts to primeval barbarism and goes on a homicidal rampage. Primitive best describes David Duncan's script. Eddie Parker, Whit Bissell, Joanna Moore, Troy Donahue.

**MONSTER SHARK (1984).** The umpteenth ripoff of JAWS, depicting scientist William Berger chasing after a 40-foot, prehistoric-age shark/octopus that's been eating the local swimming population. Phony effects destroy what little impact this Italian "monstrosity" possesses after director Lamberto Bava and screenwriters Luigi Cozzi and Sergio Martino get through playing around in the water. Tiny little cinematic bubbles, indeed.

**MONSTER SHOW, THE.** See **FREAKS.**

**MONSTER THAT CHALLENGED THE WORLD, THE (1957).** Uninspired formula "giant-monster-created-by-radiation" non-thriller. This time the monstrosity is a giant caterpillar (would you believe a mutant mollusk?) rising from the depths to terrorize Tim Holt, Audrey Dalton and Hans Conried. Or is Hans Conried terrorizing us? Poorly done, from the

# M Is for Music . . .

**HENRY MANCINI AND JOHN WILLIAMS, MAJOR CONTRIBUTORS TO FANTASY SOUNDTRACKS**

effects to Arnold Laven's direction to Pat Fielder's script. Milton Parsons, Jody McCrea, Casey Adams.

**MONSTER WALKS, THE (1932).** Mischa Auer is Hanns Krug, your typical movie maniacal idiot who binds Vera Reynolds, your typical movie heroine, and torments her with Yogi the Ape, your typical movie gorilla. After a smattering of this typical behavior, your typical viewer switches channels. Typically directed by Frank Stayer. Typically acted by Vera Reynolds, Rex Lease. (VC)

**MONSTER ZERO (1966).** And Zero is exactly what this Japanese monster flick scores on the Entertainment Scale. GODZILLA director Inoshiro Honda and effects buddy Eiji Tsuburaya are up to their usual tricks with Monster Zero, a hulking entity of evil who strangely resembles three-headed Ghidrah. Also involved are Godzilla and Rodan, who've been lured from Earth by Planet X fiends so they won't interfere with a force invading Earth. It's incomprehensible but lean back and enjoy the explosive effects, atrocious dubbing and Nick Adams re-creating his role of the astronaut he played in FRANKENSTEIN CONQUERS THE WORLD. Akira Kubo, Akira Takarada.

**MONSTERS ARE LOOSE, THE.** See **THRILL KILLERS, THE.**

**MONSTERS CRASH THE PAJAMA PARTY (1965).** Independent quickie designed as a satire on American-International beach-horror flicks. It's set in a haunted house and features a menagerie of creatures and monsters. It has justifiably retained its obscurity for more than two decades. Directed by Don Brandon. Peter James Noto stars.

**MONSTERS FROM AN UNKNOWN PLANET.** See **TERROR OF MECHAGODZILLA.**

**MONSTERS FROM THE MOON.** See **ROBOT MONSTER.**

**MONSTERS INVADE EXPO '70.** See **GAMERA VS. JIGER.**

**MONSTERS OF DR. FRANKENSTEIN.** See **FRANKENSTEIN'S CASTLE OF FREAKS.**

**MONSTROID.** See **MONSTER** (1979).

**MONSTROSITY.** See **ATOMIC BRAIN, THE.**

**MONTY PYTHON'S MEANING OF LIFE (1983).** Be forewarned: If you find the Python group tastelessly irreverent, expect to be insulted, for this is a witty albeit vile offering. It begins brilliantly with a ten-minute parody of pirate movies and big business, then switches to a pseudoexamination of life—dealing with birth control, sex education, religion, a boys' school, the military aristocracy and so on. Among the highlights (or lowlights?) is dancing in the streets of Devonshire by the lower classes, a sickening liver removal scene, a spoof of ZULU, a fat man throwing up in a posh French restaurant, and Christmas in Heaven. Terry Jones directed and Terry Gilliam handled the animation. John Cleese, Eric Idle, Michael Palin and Graham Chapman appear in most of the scenes, often in drag. Hilarious one moment, sickening the next. (VC)

**MOON MADNESS (1983).** Animated French cartoon written-directed by Jean Image, whose images are those of Baron von Munchausen and his men traveling to the moon aboard a hot-air balloon. On the lunar surface the explorers discover a race of headless men called Selenites. Based on H.G. Wells' FIRST MEN IN THE MOON.

**MOON OF THE WOLF (1972).** TV-movie explores the werewolf legend in the Louisiana bayou, where David Janssen is a sheriff investigating throat-ripping murders. Bradford Dillman, Royal Dano, Geoffrey Lewis and Barbara Rush are caught up in the lycanthropic events. Howling good. Directed by Daniel Petrie. (VC)

**MOON PILOT (1962).** Disney comedy pokes fun at our predilection for national security, at pompous military officers and at our drive to conquer space. Astronaut Tom Tryon is chosen to circumnavigate the moon and this leads to a meeting with an alien from Beta Lyrae. Directed by James Neilson. Brian Keith, Edmond O'Brien, Kent Smith, Bob Sweeney, Tommy Kirk, Nancy Kulp. (VC)

**MOON ZERO TWO (1969).** Transmutation of cowboy adventure into space opera. James Olson, rocketship pilot in the year 2021, is down on his luck and agrees to help the Beautiful Girl in Distress Looking for Her Missing Brother. This Hammer production was written by Michael Carreras and directed by Roy Ward Baker, but it was not a success. MOON ZERO TWO added up to zilch. Catherine Von Schell, Adrienne Corri, Bernard Bresslaw, Michael Ripper.

**MOONCHILD (1972).** Indecipherable, pretension allegory in which Mark Travis undergoes a reincarnation cycle at an old Spanish-style church (the Mission Inn in Riverside) where John Carradine is "The Keeper of Words" and Victor Buono symbolizes gluttony, or something. Images are of gargoyles, musty corridors, eyeballs, hooded monks and a girl running free in an aqua negligee. What does it mean? Ask writer-director Alan Gadney. There are flashbacks to the Spanish Inquisition and a one-eyed hunchback named Humunculus among the freaky background players. A lot of artsy-crafts cross-cutting only obscures the clouded issues. MOONCHILD is too quickly eclipsed by its own enigmatic shadows. A puzzle without a solution. Janet Landgard, Pat Renella, Mark Travis, William Challee.

**MOONRAKER (1979).** Eleventh James Bond adventure, depicting 007's attempt to stop master villain Drax (Michael Lonsdale) from starting a totalitarian colony in space. There's an excellent space station battle, a gondola chase through Venice, motorboat action, ample fistfights and sexual encounters of the closest kind. Richard Kiel repeats his Jaws role. Roger Moore walks indifferently through it all. Fun to watch but quickly forgotten. Lois Chiles co-stars as Mary Goodhead. Directed by Lewis Gilbert, scripted by Christopher Wood. Brian Keith, Bernard Lee. (VC)

**MOONSHINE MOUNTAIN (1967).** Undistilled Herschell Gordon Lewis in which an ape killer stands vigilence over an infamous Kentucky still, knocking off any dirty revenooers who chance along. Stillborn. Chuck Scott, Adam Sorg, Jeffrey Allen, Bonnie Hinson.

**MORE THAN A MIRACLE (1967).** CINDERELLA—ITALIAN STYLE was the British title for this Italian/French film. Sophia Loren is the peasant girl in the low-cut blouse and Omar Sharif is the Prince Charming caught up in a plot of witches and magic. Dolores Del Rio and Leslie French co-star. Directed by Franceso Rosi.

**MORE WILD WILD WEST (1980).** Enchanting sequel to the TV series THE WILD WILD WEST, which featured out-of-time-and-place weaponry and inventions, and frequent science-fiction plots. Secret agents James West (Robert Conrad) and Artemus Gordon (Ross Martin) are back to prevent Jonathan Winters from taking over the world via a mad scheme that involves invisible fighters. Burt Kennedy directed the William Bowers-Tony Kayden script for more than it is really worth. Harry Morgan, Victor Buono, Avery Schreiber, Joyce Brothers.

**MORIANNA (1965).** Swedish horror thriller that overlaps into the supernatural. Written-directed by Arne Mattsson. Anders Henriksson, Lotte Tarp, Heinz Hopf.

**MORONS FROM OUTER SPACE (1985).** Witty British spoof of science-fiction movies and the British classes in the Carry On tradition in which a crew of hapless humanoid aliens bumble their way to Earth, crashlanding on a freeway in a hysterically funny sequence. Pompous leaders and the media assume these maladroit fools are superintelligent and efforts are made to display them to the world as superiors. Directed by Michael Hodges, scripted by Mel Smith and Griff Rhys Jones, a comedy team portraying the aliens Bernard and Graham Sweetley. (VC)

**MORTUARY (1981).** All of us will have our day with the mortician (or cremator) sooner than we hope, so why go to the movies and watch a madman mortician thrust blunt instruments into bodies and tube out their blood supplies? A wretched excuse for a movie from writer-director Howard Avedis, with Christopher George as an uptight mortician. But is he or his morbid son (Bill Paxton) the caped, pasty-faced killer who stalks Lynda Day George with a skewering device?

It's a moot point—you'll only want to divert your eyes from the screen when the embalming techniques are dragged out in their bloody horrification. And you'll cringe as a still-living body (Mary McDonough's) is about to be skewered alive and the killer cackles, "This way, heh heh, we'll be together forever." Morbid City. (VC)

**MOST DANGEROUS GAME, THE (1932).** Richard Connell's story was perfect for producers Ernest Schoedsack and Merian C. Cooper, who were themselves adventurers and must have felt rapport with both Great White Hunter Rainsford (Joel McCrea) and Evil Hunter Count Zaroff (Leslie Banks). In its day this was hard-hitting and explicit but time has blunted its undercurrents of perverted sex and made apparent its cinematic crudities. Still, one can sense the genius of Schoedsack (who co-directed with Irving Pichel) and Cooper in depicting a depraved madman and how he hunts people for the greatest thrill of all, the human trophy. Many sets were reused in KING KONG. The script was by James A. Creelman, the music by Max Steiner. Remade as A GAME OF DEATH and RUN FOR THE SUN. Robert Armstrong, Fay Wray. (VC)

**MOST DANGEROUS MAN ALIVE (1961).** Cobalt bomb blast turns escaped convict Ron Randell into a literal "man of steel." Because he was framed, Randell sets out to kill the men who set him up. While this is familiar stuff, director Allan Dwan has a surprise: He explores the sex life of "the most dangerous man alive" with mistress Debra Paget—or at least

**MOUNTAINTOP MOTEL MASSACRE (1983).** Taking her cue from Norman Bates about motel management, proprietor Anna Chappell kills her daughter in a fit of range, then attacks unsuspecting roomers (black carpenter, drunken preacherman, newlyweds, two bimbos and an ad man) with a sickle or throws bugs and snakes on their sleeping bodies. Utterly bad gore effects. Guests check in but don't check out in this sleazy slasher flick poorly shot in Louisiana. Directed by Jim McCullough Jr. Bill Thurman, Will Mitchel. (VC)

**MOUSE ON THE MOON (1963).** Sequel to THE MOUSE THAT ROARED under Richard Lester's direction is another droll exercise in satire. That poor principality, Grand Fenwick, discovers its only economy, wine, can fuel a moon rocket. Margaret Rutherford, Terry-Thomas and Ron Moody give it wit and charm. Script by Michael Pertwee.

**MOUSE THAT ROARED, THE (1959).** It's the audience that roared— that's how this British satire-comedy was received around the world. In the fictional principality of Grand Fenwick the grand Duchess declares war on the U.S. (soley for rehabilitation funds). An attack expedition sets out for America and becomes embroiled in slapstick with the deadly Q-Bomb. Peter Sellers plays three roles (the Prime Minister, a soldier in arms and the Grand Duchess) and is ably assisted by Jean Seberg, daughter of the bomb's creator. Directed by Jack (THE CREATURE FROM THE BLACK LAGOON) Arnold. The screamingly funny screenplay was by Stanley Mann and Roger MacDougall. Leo McKern, William

---

"Kill! Then love! When you have known that, you have known everything."—Zaroff the Hunter (Leslie Banks) in **THE MOST DANGEROUS GAME.**

---

as far as they dared to go in those days. Morris Ankrum, Elaine Stewart, Anthony Caruso.

**MOTEL HELL (1980).** Outrageous black horror-comedy that will make you laugh in spite of your good taste. Rory Calhoun is a good ol' country boy operating the roadside Motel Hello (only the O burned out on the neon sign) and a sausage-packing plant next door. Seems Farmer Smith and his sister have decided smoked people'r better'n smoked pig, so they bury their still-living, let's-fatten-'em-up human guinea pigs up to their necks in a field. (Occasionally Rory, bein' a humane sorta guy, goes out there and snaps their necks.) Calhoun's nonchalance and Kevin Connor's witty direction make this in-bad-taste film palatable, right up to the bloody climax featuring a duel with chainsaws and a tied-down heroine headed toward a buzzsaw. Scripted by producers Robert and Steven-Charles Jaffe. Wolfman Jack, Dick Curtis, Paul Linke, Nancy Parsons. (VC)

**MOTHER'S DAY (1980).** Offshoot of THE TEXAS CHAINSAW MASSACRE — macabre humor mixed with bloody, excruciatingly painful attacks on women. Mother (Rose Ross), the epitome of matriarchal love) is training her two perverted, stupid backwoods sons in the art of attack and rape. Holden McGuire and Billy Ray McQuade are the slobbering oafs who eat their breakfast from swill buckets. The demented lads have their fun with three campers. When two turn on the boys makes for a hair-raising climax that involves a can of Draino and a TV set as murder weapons. Oh, we almost forgot the electric carving knife. You'll cheer the girls in spite of yourself. Nancy Hendrickson, Deborah Luce and Tiana Pierce turn in good performances. Produced-written-directed by Charles Kaufman. (VC)

**MOTHRA (1962).** Early Japanese monster-on-a-rampage excitement stirrer, not as ludicrous as later efforts, but still ludicrous in a child-like, innocent way. Two Oriental girls called the Peanut Sisters, each six inches high, help a giant caterpillar hatch from its giant egg. When the girls are kidnapped by a contemporary P. T. Barnum, Mothra goes wild, destroying Tokyo Tower and spinning a cocoon. The usual massive destruction results as it rescues the helpless girlettes. Mothra is not a man in a rubber suit but a mock-up controlled by wires. Directed by Inoshiro Honda, with effects by his pal Eiji Tsuburaya. (VC)

Hartnell. (VC)

**MOVIE HOUSE MASSACRE (1984).** Allegedly haunted film palace becomes the site for new murders in the slasher vein in this weak-kneed horror spoof. Directed by Alice Raley. Mary Woronov, Jonathan Blakely, Lynne Darcy. (VC)

**MS .45 (1980).** Disturbing avant garde exploitation film made in Manhattan is fascinating in its surrealistic depiction of an "angel of vengeance." Zoe Tamerlis is a mute Garmet District worker brutally raped twice in the same day. She kills her second attacker, cuts up his body and stores the pieces in her frig. With the dead rapist's .45, she is turned into a cold-blooded murderess, her targets any men she meets on the street. It's not so much a revenge movie as the portrait of someone driven insane by life's pressures. Zoe is coolly beautiful and frightening, conveying the madness of Nicholas St. John's script. Abel Ferrara has a real sense of stylized direction, ending on a ritualistic touch of symbolism as Zoe, dressed as a nun at a masquerade party, becomes a black image of Death. A knockout, gritty movie, unpleasant but enthralling. (VC)

**MUMMY, THE (1932).** This Universal horror feature inspired many sequels and imitations, but this has best withstood the Egyptian sands of time. It holds up thanks to cinematographer Karl Freund, making his directorial debut. Freund often relied on the unseen to convey horror, and this approach has assured Stanley Bergerman's production an immortality of its own. Boris Karloff, in Jack Pierce's superb makeup, portrays Im-Ho-Tep, a 3700-year-old high priest of Egypt resurrected by an archeological expedition. Disguising himself in yet another kind of Pierce makeup, wizened Karloff walks through modern Egypt carrying the Scroll of Thoth in an effort to find his long dead love, reincarnated in the modern body of Zita Johann. Edward Van Sloan, David Manners, Noble Johnson, Bramwell Fletcher, Arthur Byron, Henry Victor, Leonard Mudie. (VC)

**MUMMY, THE (1959).** Unlike many Universal "Mummy" sequels of the 1940s, in which Kharis shambled around pathetically, incapable of frightening the least discriminating of children, this Hammer version captures the murderous ferocity of the gauze-enwrapped high priest as he stomps across foggy 19th Century England, seeking the reincarnation of a princess now married to archeologist Peter Cushing, the man who desecrated Kharis' tomb. It's Christoper Lee in the makeup of Roy Ashton, and he's wonderfully unstoppable. The scene of Lee rising from a bog is especially striking. Directed by Terence Fisher, written by Jimmy Sangster. Yvonne Furneaux portrays the princess-now-a-wife. Eddie Byrne, Felix Aylmer, George Pastell, Michael Ripper, Raymond Huntley, John Stuart. (VC)

**MUMMY VS. THE HUMAN ROBOT (1963).** Mexican variation on an old theme has the standard bandage-covered personage from a previous Egyptian era fighting it out with a clanking robot while a mad doctor stands in the wings, cackling. The whole production should have been mummified and buried in a crypt.

**MUMMY'S BOYS (1936).** This satire on THE MUMMY finds Bert Wheeler and Robert Woolsey (a popular comedy team) cracking Egyptian jokes in King Pharmatime's tomb. A curse on the shrine has knocked off nine out of 13 archeologists and a hulking figure has been shambling around the pyramids. Sample joke: "Four little daughters of the Nile? No wonder the Sphinx won't talk." Directed by Fred Guio. Moroni Olson, Willie Best, Frank M. Thomas.

**MUMMY'S CURSE, THE (1945).** The last of Universal's "Kharis the Mummy" films, which had so deteriorated that the hulking high-priest-in-bandages was a laughing, not a screaming, matter. It picks up where THE MUMMY'S GHOST left off—as the swamp is drained and the bodies of Princess Ananka and Kharis are recovered. Soon Kharis (shabbily played by Lon Chaney Jr.) is footloose on a diet of tana leaves, chasing a beautiful woman who can't quite flee the slow-moving shambler. Virginia Christine, Peter Coe, Martin Kosleck. Directed by Leslie Goodwins.

**MUMMY'S GHOST, THE (1944).** Third in Universal's "Kharis the Mummy" series coming on the heels of THE MUMMY'S TOMB, with Lon Chaney Jr. stumbling around New England to discover that Ananka, his beloved princess, is reincarnated in the shapely form of Ramsay Ames. John Carradine takes over as high priest to force-feed the tana leaves. Makeup by Jack Pierce. George Zucco appears briefly to send Carradine on his mission. Barton MacLane, Robert Lowery. Directed by Reginald Le Borg.

**MUMMY'S HAND, THE (1940).** This sequel to THE MUMMY started a series of Universal programmers featuring a bandaged high priest named Kharis, who forsakes the Scroll of Thoth for tana leaves. The role of the long-dead Egyptian went to former cowboy actor Tom Tyler—his only appearance as a monster. Dick Foran and Wallace Ford are the desecrators of the tomb under the Hill of the Seven Jackals,

while George Zucco is the instigator of evil—he brews nine tana leaves to give the mummy momentum. The dummy mummy thinks Peggy Moran is a reincarnation of his adored Ananka and he hulks after her, bandages trailing. A lengthy flashback features footage from THE MUMMY. This is better than the three films that followed, which were all shoddy imitations. Eduardo Ciannelli, Cecil Kellaway. Directed by Christy Cabanne.

**MUMMY'S REVENGE, THE (1973).** Spanish stew of supernatural curses and Egyptian walking dead is strictly meat and potatoes—basic to the horror viewer's diet, without any rich calories. Ultimately inedible. Directed by Carlos Aured, scripted by Jacinto Molina. Paul Naschy portrays the Nile Valley drifter in bandages. Helga Line. (VC)

**MUMMY'S SHROUD, THE (1967).** Despite the mummy cliches which riddle its plot like holes in ancient bandages, this Hammer period horror thriller is quite well done in the characterization and acting departments. After a cumbersome beginning in Egyptian times, as we're inundated with exposition about the history of our gauze-enwrapped entity, we flash to today to see an expedition desecrate the tomb and remove mummy Eddie Powell to a museum, there to be resurrected by He Who Possesses an Accursed Blanket. Intense murders follow, often of innocent victims, making the violence that much more effective. Andre Morell is exceptional as the head of the expedition, a spoiled, you-love- to-hate- him millionaire. Stylishly done with individual details often outshining the sum total. Maggie Kimberley portrays an unlikely archeologist, what with all those flimsy nightgowns and low-cut blouses. Best of the cast is Catherine Lacey as a decaying old soothsayer who reads crystal balls. John Gilling directed handsomely. David Buck, John Phillips. Produced by Anthony Nelson-Keys (writing as John Elder). Michael Ripper, Elizabeth Sellars.

**MUMMY'S TOMB, THE (1942).** Second Universal feature in the "Kharis" series, with Lon Chaney Jr. inheriting the gauze from Tom Tyler in THE MUMMY'S HAND. Again it's George Zucco as the High Priest, who turns the evil-doing over to Turhan Bey, who then dispatches Kharis to kill archeologist/tomb defiler Dick Foran, but not until we've seen footage from THE MUMMY'S HAND and the angry villagers from FRANKENSTEIN. In this one Elyse Knox is the reincarnation beauty who is carried away by Kharis. Directed by Harold Young. Make-up by Jack Pierce.

**MUMSY, NANNY, SONNY AND GIRLY.** See **GIRLY**.

**MUNSTER, GO HOME (1966).** Feature based on TV's THE MUNSTERS with Fred Gwynne, Yvonne De Carlo, Al Lewis

**STUCK IN THE MUD: CHRISTOPHER LEE IN 'THE MUMMY' (1959)**

**CREATURE FEATURES MOVIE GUIDE**

and Butch Patrick recreating video roles. The Munsters inherit a haunted house and all its problems, which include a counterfeiting ring led by Hermione Gingold, Terry-Thomas and John Carradine. Directed by Earl Bellamy.

**MUNSTERS' REVENGE, THE (1981).** TV-movie reuniting the cast members so popular in the series: Yvonne De Carlo, Fred Gwynne and Al Lewis. Pallid stuff, directed by Don Weiss without much enthusiasm, and the laughs are really limited even though all your favorite monsters parade through. The villain is a Sid Caesar caricature, Mr. Diablo. Robert Hastings, Gary Vinson. (VC)

**MURDER AND THE COMPUTER (1975).** An inventor about to unveil the world's most sophisticated computer is murdered . . . it had to be someone on hand during the ceremonies. TV whodunit directed by Paul Stanley. Gary Merrill, Babara Anderson, Kaz Garas.

**MURDER AT DAWN (1932).** Poverty row production creaks with age but features the interesting DXL Accumulator, designed by the same electronics specialist who created the equipment in FRANKENSTEIN. The DXL is a device harnessing solar energy, but the plot focuses more on whodunit in an old dark house. Directed routinely by Richard Thorpe. Mischa Auer, Jack Mulhall.

**MURDER BY DECREE (1979).** Splendid Sherlock Holmes and Dr. Watson thriller in which the fabulous detective heroes stalk Jack the Ripper. It would appear the Whitechapel killings are being covered up by a government conspiracy. Classy material (similar to A STUDY IN TERROR), with the murders photographed with taste and Christopher Plummer as a singularly likeable Holmes and James Mason as an articulate Watson. What a marvelous supporting cast! Anthony Quayle, Donald Sutherland, John Gielgud, Susan Clark, Genevieve Bujold, Michael Hemmings, Frank Finlay. Directed by Bob Clark. (VC)

**MURDER BY INVITATION (1941).** Monogram low-budget, lowbrow quickie set in the usual "old dark house" where a masked knife murderer is killing the heirs one by one while fleeing down secret passages and hiding behind sliding panels. Directed by Phil Rosen. Wallace Ford, Minerva Urecal, Marian Marsh, Sarah Padden, Dave O'Brien.

**MURDER BY PHONE (1980).** A literately written Canadian horror film, best for its clever dialogue between ecology fighter Richard Chamberlain and telephone company advisor John Houseman, who meet in Toronto during a save-the-environment convention. Meanwhile, certain citizens are answering their phones, only to have blood shoot from their ears, nose, eyes and mouth because of a terrible vibrating force. Then a killer bolt of electricity pours through the receiver and throws them against the wall as if Zeus had struck. Chamberlain, when he isn't dating mural painter Sara Botsford, is hot on the trail of the killer, suspecting the telephone company of conspiracy. Slickly directed by Michael Anderson. Hell's Bells, this is pretty good stuff. Barry Morse, Robin Gammell, Gary Reineke. Shown on cable TV as **BELLS.** (VC)

**MURDER BY TELEVISION (1935).** Fuzzy, unadjusted Bela

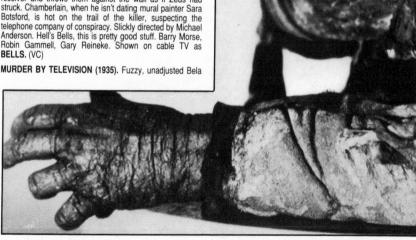

TOM TYLER AS KHARIS IN 'THE MUMMY'S HAND': A COWBOY STAR UNDER WRAPS

**CREATURE FEATURES MOVIE GUIDE**

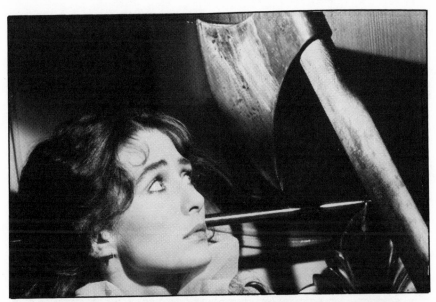

**CHRISTINE KAUFMANN GETS THE AXE IN 'MURDERS IN THE RUE MORGUE'**

Lugosi whodunit potboiler in which two brothers—one an inventor, the other a murderer—are involved with the development of television. There's also a Death Ray, a standard ploy of the 1930s. Static direction by Clifford Sanforth; needs fine tuning. Poor picture, bad reception. June Collyer, George Meeker, Huntley Gordon. (VC)

**MURDER BY THE CLOCK (1931).** New drug resurrects a dead man— better they should have used the drug on slowman director Edward Sloman. Murder thriller with mild supernatural overtones (including crypt with built-in warning devices) as the hairy hand clutches for the girl and a killer flees along secret passageways in an old, dark house. Regis Toomey, William Boyd, Lilyan Tashman.

**MURDER CLINIC, THE (1968).** Black-robed fiend (with a cowl yet) stalks the drafty halls of an isolated hospital for weirdos and freakos, slashing victims with a razor blade. A young nurse arrives on the Gothic scene to serve as the heroine of this Italian-French horror tale that is overacted but compellingly presented with its period ambience, costumes and baroque settings. William Berger stars as a misunderstood doctor who keeps an ugly secret in one of the upstairs rooms, from which weird sounds emanate at night. Plenty of gore (some has been cut for TV) and creeping around to create tension and suspense. Produced-directed by Michael Hamilton. William Berger, Françoise Prevost, Mary Young, Barbara Wilson. (VC)

**MURDER IN SPACE (1985).** Gimmick-riddled whodunit originally shown on Showtime with prizes offered to those who could spot clues revealing the murderer of several astronauts (male and female) aboard Comestoga, a lab rocketing through space. First a Soviet cosmonaut is strangled to death (it is discovered she was pregnant), then crew members are poisoned, throttled and blasted to pieces. Back on Earth, U.S. and Russian scientists and diplomats hush up the scandalous elements, while figuring out which crew member is the maniac. It's contrived and absurd, and will no doubt be recut for subsequent sale to other stations, with a tacked-on solution. Directed by Steven Hilliard Stern. Wilford Brimley, Arthur Hill, Michael Ironside, Martin Balsam, Damir Amdrei, Tom Butler.

**MURDER IN THE AIR (1940).** Standard whodunit, dingy and dreary, with a feeble gimmick: A special machine can freeze objects in midair. Of more interest will be the presence of

Ronald Reagan. John Litel, Eddie Foy Jr., Robert Warwick. Directed by Lewis Seiler.

**MURDER IN THE BLUE ROOM (1944).** Enjoyable tongue-in-cheek ghost comedy with a literate script by I.A.L. Diamond and Stanley Davis. It's that old standby—the mysterious room in which no one can spend the night without disappearing. Under Leslie Goodwins direction, it's played largely for laughs, with secret passageways, sliding doors and ectoplasmic shapes drifting through the darkness. Lean back and enjoy. Anne Gwynne, John Litel, Donald Cook, Regis Toomey, Ian Wolfe.

**MURDER MANSION (1970).** Is there any truth to the eerie legends surrounding that strange old house? The only way for a young couple to find out is to spend the night there. What they find are ghosts and vampires and . . . Analia Gade, Ida Galli. Directed by F. Lara Polop. (VC)

**MURDER SOCIETY, THE.** See **MURDER CLINIC, THE.**

**MURDERER'S ROW (1966).** Second in the simple-minded Matt Helm series with Dean Martin as the superspy who walks indifferently through his bizarre adventures. Brimming with succulent women, gleaming gadgets, ingenious weapons and flippant dialogue and never for a moment taking itself seriously. You'll enjoy Karl Malden as a villain with a killer ray who hopes to destroy the White House. The stylish way it's directed by Henry Levin, you might just as well set your brain on "idle" and enjoy. Ann-Margret, Camilla Sparv, Beverly Adams, Tom Reese.

**MURDERS IN THE RUE MORGUE (1932).** The title is the only Poe you'll find in this Universal thriller starring Bela Lugosi as a carnival spielman with a giant gorilla act. The early promising atmosphere and odd sexual overtones are not sustained as master detective Dupin (young Leon Ames billed as Leon Waycroft) is shown to be a real jerk while tracking down Dr. Mirakle and putting a stop to his crazy theory that mating his ape with a beautiful virgin will result in a perfect union between man and animal. Directed by Robert Florey, who lingers sadistically on the scenes in which the Darwin-crazed Lugosi tortures prostitutes captured from the streets. Camerawork by Karl Freund.

**MURDERS IN THE RUE MORGUE (1971).** Strangely compelling thriller of the Grand Guignol school, though it has nothing to do with Poe's short story. The offbeat Henry

Slesar-Christopher Wicking script features bizarre character relationships, flashbacks within flashbacks and dreams within dreams to create a convoluted plot. A maniac (Herbert Lom) is committing ghastly acid murders while Jason Robards Jr. and Christine Kaufman stage a horror play in Paris' finest theater. Gordon Hessler directed this odd olio. Adolfo Celi, Lilli Palmer, Maria Perschy, Michael Dunn. (VC)

**MURDERS IN THE RUE MORGUE, THE (1986).** Well-produced TV-movie distinguished by the performance of George C. Scott as French detective Auguste Dupin, who comes out of retirement to solve two bloody murders and prove his daughter's fiancee is not guilty of the crimes. Paris locations are cleverly used, and Scott is fine, but the pacing is slow and the plot too predictable to sustain suspense. Directed by Jeannot Szwarc. Val Kilmer, Rebecca De Mornay, Ian McShane.

**MURDERS IN THE ZOO (1933).** Lionel Atwill so overacts as a philanthropist/big game hunter that what should be horrifying is ludicrous. Because he's insanely jealous of his unfaithful wife, he sews up the mouth of her paramour and leaves him to die in the jungle. The next lover is killed by the fangs of a mamba snake. And on it goes, involving lions, tigers and a house of pythons. While today it might seem juvenile and dumb, and Charlie Ruggles' humor absolutely unstomachable, it was hard-hitting in its day and frequently censored because of Atwill's suggested depravity. Written by Philip Wylie and Seton I. Miller; directed by Edward Sutherland with a relish for the distasteful. Randolph Scott, Gail Patrick, John Lodge.

**MUSIC OF THE SPHERES (1983).** Frightfully dull Canadian idea movie that never overcomes viewer indifference. With a soundtrack half- English, half-French, it unfolds in the next century when supercomputers (called "Beasts") inform Anne Dansereau that a plan to use asteroids as sources of solar energy is throwing the balance of the Universe out of kilter. This movie goes absolutely nowhere, unenhanced by mediocre effects and droning dialogue. Actionless atrophy. Directed by G. Philip Jackson.

**MUTANT (1982). See FORBIDDEN WORLD.**

**MUTANT (1983).** This time the zombies are on the march because of exposure to toxic refuge, but a zombie is still a zombie with only an appetite for human flesh. Same old "walking dead" cliches with Wings Hauser and Bo Hopkins fighting off monsters. Directed by John "Bud" Cardos. (VC)

**MUTANT HUNT (1986).** Empire-International science-fiction adventure written-directed by Tim Kincaid. Rick Gianasi, Mary Fahey, Ron Reynaldi, Bill Peterson, Stormy Spill.

**MUTATIONS, THE (1974).** This British nightmare thriller, like Tod Browning's FREAKS, features real-life sideshow freaks. Donald Pleasence portrays a biologist who sees the world dying and decides crossbreeding man and plants is the answer to survival. His experiments create hideous mutants and a man-eating plant to dispose of any cadavers left lying around. Directed by Jack Cardiff, this was Michael Dunn's last film before his untimely death. Tom Baker is Pleasence's assistant and Jill Haworth and Julie Ege provide shapely bodies and screaming mouths. (VC)

**DENNIS HOPPER HAS THE SHINING IN 'MY SCIENCE PROJECT'**

CREATURE FEATURES MOVIE GUIDE

**MUTILATOR, THE (1983).** Below-average slasher flick be-speckled with weak characterizations, almost non-existent plotting and only moderately sickening gore. After a clumsy prologue in which a youngster accidentally shoots his father, which serves as a motive for the parent to become a killer, the story jumps to the present day to follow six teenagers to a seaside condominium, where they are stalked and slaughtered by the father, a big game hunter. Death by drowning, chainsaw slicing, machete chopping, pitchfork plunging, hook impalement, and battleaxe bleeding. Also for your viewing pleasure: a body severed in half, another body beheaded, still another delegged. My, my, ain't we got fun. Filmed near Atlantic Beach in a dismal coastal location. Buddy Cooper wrote and directed. Quick, head him off before he leaves for Hollywood. Matt Mitler, Frances Raines, Morey Lampley, Ruth Martinez. Jack Chatham plays the brute killer with no charm. (VC)

**MUTINY IN OUTER SPACE (1965).** The mutiny is not com-mitted by humans but by a fungus brought aboard Space Station X-7. With the help of stop-motion animation, it takes over, turning astronauts into beasts. Poor science-fiction directed by Hugo Grimaldi. William Leslie, Glenn Langan, Dolores Faith, Richard Garland, Pamela Curran.

**MY BLOOD RUNS COLD (1965).** Your blood won't run cold watching this anemic pseudohorror thriller. Allegedly, a mad killer is the reincarnation of an old lover boy once in love with an ancestor of Joey Heatherton. As the killer, Troy Donahue talks Joey into thinking she's been reincarnated too. Phony chills and ersatz thrills bloodlessly directed by William Conrad from John Mantley's pale script. Barry Sullivan, Nicolas Coster, Jeanette Nolan.

**MY BLOODY VALENTINE (1981).** "Roses are red/Violets are blue/MY BLOODY VALENTINE/Is absolute grue" . . . Heart-to-heart Canadian horror film of the slasher school is strangely compelling despite lack of characters and logic. It hinges on grabby visuals as a deranged killer—wearing a miner's uniform and facemask—attacks citizens of Valentine Village with a pick-axe. Photography and stunt work are ex-cellent as the murderer stalks partygoers in a coal mine. Without getting pickie, we enjoyed it. Sorry, no miners al-lowed. Directed by George Mihalka. Paul Kelman, Cynthia Dale. Effects by Tom Burman. (VC)

**MY BROTHER TALKS TO HORSES (1946).** Fred Zinneman comedy has "Butch" Jenkins, freckle-faced, buck-toothed youth, engaging in equine dialogue with nags, mares and palominos about who is going to win the fifth at Bay Meadows. Naturally this upsets adults—such as eccentric mother Spring Byington, older brother Peter Lawford and girlfriend Beverly Tyler.

**MY FRIEND, DR. JEKYLL (1961).** The Italians played this for laughs—a shrewd move since audiences would have laughed anyway: A mad scientist invents a personality trans-ference machine and switches bodies with the instructor in a girls' school, where he instigates some love-making ses-sions. Abbe Lane can't resist Ugo Tognazzi. Directed by Marino Girolami. Carlo Croccolo, Raimondo Vianello.

**MY FRIENDS NEED KILLING (1977).** Attempt to deal with the psychological motivations behind why a Vietnam veteran (Greg Mullavey) would go on a spree and murder the men he served with (apparently they were involved in a massacre). Mullavey doesn't just murder—he first tortures his victims and their wives. Writer-director Paul Leder (I DISMEMBER MAMA) goes for an unusual ending. Meredith MacRae, Clayton Wilcox, Carolyn Ames.

**MY SCIENCE PROJECT (1985).** Uninspired, boring teenage fantasy-comedy in which an inept science student, poking around an abandoned Air Force installation, discovers a force-field gadget left over from a flying saucer discovered by the military in 1959. The device sucks up all the energy in sight and becomes a time tunnel, out of which emerge monsters and warriors of the past. John Stockwell, Danielle Von Zerneck and Fisher Stevens are the hapless teens, but the picture goes to a freaked-out performance by Dennis Hopper as a science teacher who regresses to his hippie habits when he's sucked into the space-warp continuum.

### HOT JOEY HEATHERTON: 'MY BLOOD RUNS COLD'

Jonathan Betuel, who wrote THE LAST STARFIGHTER, wrote-directed but his story is shapeless and the characters uninteresting; no amount of effects can save his science-fic-tion project. (VC)

**MY SISTER, MY LOVE (1979).** Intriguing psychological study of two sisters living in a cluttered mansion, where they keep an ape in a "mafu cage" belonging to their late father, a noted jungle explorer. Lee Grant tries to stay afloat while her sister, Carol Kane, sinks into barbarism, torturing apes and humans alike. Produced largely by women, this low budget effort is strangely compelling and offbeat, with lesbian touches that arrive at a shocking moment. Directed by Karen Arthur. Will Geer, James Olson and Badur the Orang. Released as **THE MAFU CAGE.** (VC)

**MY SON, THE HERO (1961).** Italian-French farce making sport of mythological characters and their accoutrements. So we have Pedro Armendariz involved with Pluto's helmet of in-visibility, the snaky Gorgon, the Cyclops, statues that come to life and other oddities. Legend has it this was made as a serious film, then turned into a comedy by English dubbers in the style of Woody Allen's WHAT'S UP, TIGER LILY? Directed by Duccio Tessari.

**MY SON, THE VAMPIRE (1952).** Made in England as OLD MOTHER RILEY MEETS THE VAMPIRE, this was re-edited and released in the U.S. as VAMPIRE OVER LONDON. This present version was re-re-issued in 1964 and is part of the "Mother Riley" series popular for many years in Great Britain. Arthur Lucan appears in drag, capturing a music hall lowbrow humor for which he was famous. Bela Lugosi is a nut, Baron Van Housen, who thinks he's Dracula and wears all the regalia, sleeping in a coffin to boot. He also has a robot who . . . but why "carry on." Produced-directed by John Gilling.

**MY WORLD DIES SCREAMING.** See **TERROR IN THE HAUNTED HOUSE.** (Screeches and screams!)

**MYRA BRECKINRIDGE (1970).** While critics hated this adaptation of Gore Vidal's best-seller, and even members of the cast (Mae West among them) disowned it as a piece of unforgivable trash utterly ruined by director Michael Sarne, this expensive flop has several intriguing characteristics. The plot evolves around a man (film critic Rex Reed) being trans-formed into a beautiful woman (Raquel Welch) during a sex-change operation, and his/her subsequent misadventures in

Hollywood. It's daring, it's resourceful, it's irreverent and offensive as hell. Outrageous is a better word. Personal taste will dictate personal reaction. Farrah Fawcett, Roger C. Carmel, Calvin Lockhart, Jim Backus, John Carradine, Andy Devine, Grady Sutton.

**MYSTERIANS, THE (1959).** Cockroach-headed aliens from Mysteroid, their eyes shooting blue flames, wear uniforms that strangely resemble Oriental styles and have a bearing that smacks of Confucian etiquette. Despite this dead giveaway you're watching a Japanese science-fiction movie, THE MYSTERIANS is a visual delight with assorted effects depicting death and destruction. Some sympathy is engendered for the Mysterians who claim their planet has been destroyed by Strontium-90 and they have come to Earth only to procreate a new race with the help of our beautiful women. From that indomitable GODZILLA pair, director Inoshiro Honda and effects pioneer Eiji Tsuburaya. Kenji Sahara, Yumi Shirakawa. (VC)

**MYSTERIES FROM BEYOND EARTH (1975).** Documentary that purports to examine UFOs, Atlantis, pyramids, Mayan temples, the Bermuda Triangle, Black Holes in space and other phenomena "kept secret from our world" or "from beyond the stars." Despite all the hype, this emerges a boring, tedious, pretentious "expose" that resorts to stock footage of flying saucers from old movies to keep the viewer awake. Hosted by Lawrence Dobkin, who delivers the sleep-inducing narration on camera. Produced-directed by George Gale. (VC)

**MYSTERIES FROM BEYOND THE TRIANGLE (1977).** This is supposed to be the documented voyage of a band of scientists and psychics who traveled through the Bermuda Triangle. But it looks more like 16mm photography of a yachtsman's holiday blended with travelogue stock footage. Poor excuse of a movie that never swims but treads in place with wild speculations and unsubstantiated, harebrained conclusions. (VC)

**MYSTERIES OF THE GODS (1976).** More West German interpretations about man being descended from aliens, taken from the books of Erich von Daniken. Wild theory, with little substantiation or scientific proof to back it up. Directed by Harald Reinl.

**MYSTERIOUS CASTLE IN THE CARPATHIANS, THE (1982).** Czech comedy in the Gothic tradition, set in the last century in Devil's Castle, where an opera fan keeps the body of his prima donna preserved in a special crypt. Meanwhile, to keep visitors away, the Baron's crazy-mad inventor assistant creates unnatural phenomena to give the place a spooky reputation. Directed-written by Oldrich Lipsky. Michael Docolomanky, Jan Hartl.

**MYSTERIOUS DOCTOR, THE (1943).** Warner Bros. programmer in which a headless ghost (minus a horse, too) named Black Morgan commits a series of bloody knife murders in the wee mining town of Morgan's Head in Cornwall. Lots of atmosphere, some good character portrayals by Eleanor Parker, John Loder, Lester Matthews and Creighton Hale. Directed by the mysterious Ben Stoloff.

**MYSTERIOUS DR. FU MANCHU, THE (1929).** First sound film to feature the diabolical Fu Manchu. The Oriental with designs to take over the world was Warner Oland, destined to play Charlie Chan in later years. Neil Hamilton (of TV's BATMAN) is on hand as Nayland Smith of Scotland Yard, Fu's nemesis, while Jean Arthur provides skirts and screams. Directed by the mysterious Rowland V. Lee.

**MYSTERIOUS DR. SATAN, THE.** Unedited multi-chapter Republic serial directed by cliffhanging masters William Witney and John English. Dr. Satan (Eduardo Cinnelli) is an archfiend who has invented a robot to terrorize the world. But he needs C. Montague Shaw's remote control device to make it work. That's when a man in a copper mask steps in to thwart the evil gang. Non-stop action and non-stop nonsense will have you alternately chuckling and gasping—it never stops moving along its ludicrous, fun-filled pathways. Robert Wilcox is the hero, Ella Neal the heroine. The feature version is **DR. SATAN'S ROBOT.** (VC)

**MYSTERIOUS ISLAND (1929).** MGM adaptation of Jules Verne's science-fiction adventure was begun silent, then sound was added prior to its release. It is not totally faithful to Verne (you will, for example, not find Captain Nemo), but it does deal with stranded Civil War escapees meeting a submarine crew on a lost island. This took three years to complete and three directors contributed: Maurice Tourneur, Lucien Hubbard and Benjamin Christiansen. Lionel Barrymore, Pauline Starke, Warner Oland.

**MYSTERIOUS ISLAND (1961).** Visually exciting adaptation of Jules Verne's book with effects by Ray Harryhausen and outstanding music by Bernard Herrmann. The John Prebble-Daniel Ullman-Wilbur Crane screenplay is the weakest element of this Charles H. Schneer production filmed in Spain and England, for the characters are treated as stereotypes and the situations often deteriorate into shopworn thrills. Three Yankee prisoners of war escape Richmond Prison during a storm and make their getaway in an observation balloon to an unexplored Pacific island where a "Swiss Family Robinson" lifestyle is established. The Yanks are joined by shipwreck survivors and all are under attack from giant monsters: an overgrown chicken, a prehistoric Phororhacos, a nautiloid cephalopod and other Harryhausen marvels. Michael Craig, Michael Callan, Gary Merrill and Joan Greenwood are among the stranded, while Herbert Lom emerges from the foamy brine as Captain Nemo. Stylishly directed by Cy Endfield. (VC)

**MYSTERIOUS ISLAND OF CAPTAIN NEMO (1973).** French-Spanish production, an adaptation of Jules Verne themes, is sorely lacking in imagination and exciting effects. Omar Sharif portrays the Nautilus-sailing captain, but it is a portrayal inferior to James Mason's in Disney's 1954 TWENTY THOUSAND LEAGUES UNDER THE SEA. Directed by Henri Colpi and Juan Antonio Bardem.

**MYSTERIOUS MONSTERS, THE (1975).** TV documentary, narrated by Peter Graves, which focuses on the Abominable Snowman of the Himalayas, the Loch Ness Monster and Bigfoot. Nothing new, same old rehash. Directed-written by Robert Guenette. Peter Hurkos, the world-famous psychic, puts in an appearance.

**CRAB MONSTER IN 'MYSTERIOUS ISLAND'**

**MYSTERIOUS MR. WONG, THE (1935).** Bela Lugosi at his worst, portraying a Chinese shopkeeper in search of the 12 coins of Confucius, which will give him mystical powers. Totally turgid Monogram hambone with Wallace Ford clowning around as the guy who's going to get the insidious Wong. As drab as they come. Directed by William Nigh. (VC)

**MYSTERIOUS SATELLITE.** See **WARNING FROM SPACE.** (You are warned!)

**MYSTERIOUS STRANGER, THE (1982).** Delightful adaptation of a Mark Twain fantasy, a companion piece to his CONNECTICUT YANKEE IN KING ARTHUR'S COURT, in which a printer's apprentice (Chris Makepeace) imagines he is back in Guggenheim's day, helping print Bibles. He conjures up a free-wheeling youthful spirit from the future named No. 44 (Lance Kerwin) who works magical spells over striking printers and confounds an alchemist (a wonderful character essayed by Fred Gwynne). An amusing period fantasy, rich in character and detail, superbly directed by Peter H. Hunt. Highly recommended.

**MYSTERIOUS TWO (1979).** Alan Landsburg TV-movie, pilot for a proposed series that never materialized, stars John Forsythe and Priscilla Pointer as white-robed emissaries from another planet or dimension who hypnotically gather followers and then lead them away to . . . where? Not even you, the viewer, will find out in this allegorical tale inspired by the Jonestown massacre of 1978, when almost a thousand people committed suicide at the command of their demigod ruler. Here the lambs to the slaughter believe that "He and She" (as the aliens are called) will provide and make a blissful world. Originally made as FOLLOW ME IF YOU DARE, then shelved before coming to the network in 1982. Director-writer Gary Sherman captures a weird quality with his glaring white lighting and a melancholy pacing. Great build-up to a non-payoff. James Stephens, Robert Pine, Noah Beery Jr., Vic Tayback.

**MYSTERY IN DRACULA'S CASTLE (1977).** Eerie lighthouse is the setting for this mystery-comedy from Disney's TV department. Brothers who are horror movie fans tangle with jewel thieves. Nothing supernatural about it, just fanciful

**A HULKER IN**
**'MYSTERY OF MONSTER ISLAND'**

window dressing and cheap Gothic thrills without payoff. Johnny Whitaker, Clu Gulager, Mariette Hartley. Directed by Robert Totten.

**MYSTERY MANSION (1983).** Lackluster juvenile adventure made on location in Oregon, and designed as a family picture, but adults will find it tedious going. Three children and their father seek a treasure map after one of the kids has prescient dreams about an incident that occurred in an old house back in 1889 when an outlaw gang killed the adult occupants and caused the death of a young girl. Two escaped convicts and a benevolent old prosector figure into the scheme, but this never builds up much steam, thanks to the pedantic direction of David E. Jackson. Dallas McKennon, Jane Ferguson, Greg Wynne. (VC)

**MYSTERY OF MARIE ROGET, THE (1942).** Blatant misuse of the Poe title, since this Universal programmer has little to do with the classic detective story featuring C. August Dupin, the deductive sleuth who set the style for Sherlock Holmes. It's basically a detective tale with Patrick Knowles excellently conveying the personality of the eccentric French investigator. It has some nice Gothic touches, and is enhanced by Maria Ouspenskaya and Charles Middleton. Directed by Phil Rosen.

**MYSTERY OF MONSTER ISLAND (1980).** Ineptly juvenile U.S.-Spanish production, allegedly based on an adventure story by Jules Verne but don't believe it. It's quite a stupid tale in which a young scholar and his elocution teacher are stranded on an island overrun by prehistoric beasts (which walk upright on two legs), seaweed monsters, steam-blowing worms and other rubber-suited entities that look as though they just stepped out of an Irwin Allen misadventure. Peter Cushing, as a benevolent island owner, and Terence Stamp as a gold-hungry villain are utterly wasted in a film that is neither exciting nor funny, and which has a cop-out ending. Misdirected by J. Piquer Simon. Paul Naschy, Ian Sera, David Hatton, Bianca Estrada.

**MYSTERY OF THE GOLDEN EYE (1978).** Re-enactment of an allegedly true story about three adventurers searching for the lost son of a U.S. Senator on the island of Komodo, famed for its giant prehistoric dragons. Footage of the lizard creatures is good, and even shows a family of them munching on a freshly killed deer. The human footage is less stimulating, since the camera team was amateurish, incapable of getting the synch sound correct (lips are off 90 per cent of the time). The narration (read by actor Arthur Franz) sounds like it came out of the pages of a two-fisted adventure pulp magazine, it's that unconvincing in trying to inject intrigue into dull travelogue footage. And wait until you find out the mystery behind the Golden Eye! Produced-directed by Richard Martin. The adventurers are Robert White, K. K. Mohajan and Basil Bradbury. Phony baloney.

**MYSTERY OF THE MARIE CELESTE, THE.** Alternate videocassette title for **PHANTOM SHIP.**

**MYSTERY OF THE 13TH GUEST, THE (1943).** Folks in a haunted mansion (Dick Purcell, Tim Ryan, Helen Parrish) are attacked by some unseen presence. Same old dark house you've been trapped in before. Directed by William Beaudine. Based on Armitage Trail's THE 13TH GUEST, first produced in 1932 with Ginger Rogers.

**MYSTERY OF THE WAX MUSEUM, THE (1932).** One of the first films made in the two-strip Technicolor process; it also served as the model for the 1953 3-D remake, HOUSE OF WAX. Lionel Atwill has one of his finest roles as museum curator Ivan Igor, a genius wax sculptor disfigured in a fire. Now he is a madman, killing his enemies and encasing their corpses in wax to serve as his "horror displays." Has the famous scene in which Fay Wray pounds away at Atwill's face until it cracks to reveal a terribly scarred countenance beneath. Glenda Farrell, Frank McHugh, Holmes Herbert, Gavin Gordon.

**MYSTIC, THE (1925).** A silent terror flick from director Tod Browning in which the title Hungarian, a charlatan, suddenly finds his blood running cold when he raises a spirit from beyond. Aileen Pringle, Conway Tearle, Mitchell Lewis.

"The proofs [of the murders] are circumstantial. It's more probable that of late more and more you're watching on your television many of those pictures of terror."—Thick-skulled police chief to his hard-working underling in *NIGHT OF THE BLOODY APES.*

**NABONGA (1943).** Classic example of How to Set Up Camp in the Jungle: Hire Julie London to play a "great white goddess" raised by gorillas and revered by superstitious natives; sign Buster Crabbe to wear jodhpurs as he rushes past potted tropical plants; engage Barton MacLane to scowl villainously. Once intended to make you scream . . . nowadays you'll only scream with laughter at how decrepitly Sam Newfield directed this bunk. Nabonga nowanna.

**NAIL GUN MASSACRE (1987).** A helmeted avenger takes to the streets of Texas to kill assorted construction workers because they gang- banged a pretty girl a time back. This film's only novelty is the murder weapon, subtly referred to in the title. Otherwise, it's your usual gore deaths with the only question being: Who is the killer? Directed by Terry Lofton and Bill Leslie. Rocky Patterson, Michelle Meyer, Ron Queen. (VC)

**NAKED EVIL (1973).** Re-edited version of a 1966 voodoo thriller, EXORCISM AT MIDNIGHT, with new footage for the U.S. Based on Jon Manship White's play, THE OBI, it concerns a bottled spirit uncorked into present-day England. Detective Richard Coleman investigates the supernatural cult. Bottled entertainment from writer-director Stanley Goulder. Anthony Ainley, Suzanne Neve.

**NAKED EXORCISM (1975).** Italian chiller with Richard Conte caught up in demonology. The story (by director Angelo Pannaccio) asks the burning question: Does the Devil possess the brother of a nun? Jean-Claude Verne, Francoise Prevost, Mima Monticelli.

**NAKED JUNGLE, THE (1954).** Cancel your picnic plans to see this version of Carl Stephenson's classic short story, "Leiningen vs. the Ants." It's slow going—what with all those smoochy embraces between mail-order bride Eleanor Parker and plantation owner Charlton Heston—until the army of killer ants mobilizes for action and marches on the plantation's crops. Then those little buggers'll scare the hell out of you as men are eaten alive by the ravenous carnivores. Directed by an antsy Byron Haskin, written by Philip Yordan and Ronald MacDougall with ants in their pants. Great thrills in this George Pal production.

**NAKED LOVERS (1977).** Corpses are walking again when alien creatures from the planet Eros bring the dead to live. Isn't it loverly . . . Ursula White, Alban Ceray, Barbara Moose, Didier Aubriot. French production, produced-directed by Claude Pierson.

**NAKED VENGEANCE (1986).** In the style of I SPIT ON YOUR GRAVE, in which a raped woman seeks revenge against her attackers, going for the short hairs. Strong stomachs required. Directed by Cirio H. Santiago. Deborah Tranelli, Kaz Garas. (VC)

**NAKED WITCH, THE (1961).** Andy Milligan, who grinds out low-budget quickies that tend to remain obscure, if not completely forgotten, directed-photographed this minor item about a witch who comes to life when the stake through the heart is removed. Barely interesting. Beth Porter, Lee Forbes, Robert Burgos. Also called THE NAKED TEMPTRESS.

**NAME FOR EVIL, A (1973).** Pretentious allegory, too esoteric and undisciplined. Robert Culp resigns his architectural firm by throwing his TV out the window and moves to Canada to restore his great-great-grandfather's mansion, haunted by a ghost on a white charger. The ghost starts sleeping with wife Samantha Eggar while Culp seeks solace with a mountain girl. Ambiguous as hell; a complete misfire. Written-directed by Bernard Girard. (VC)

**NAME OF THE GAME IS KILL, THE (1968).** Jack Lord stars in this psychochiller set in the Arizona desert where an evil family of temptresses (Tisha Sterling, Collin Wilcox, Susan Strasberg) threatens an unsuspecting traveler. Directed by Gunnar Hellstrom. T. C. Jones, Mort Mills.

**NANNY, THE (1965).** Lowkey, underplayed Hammer production with stress on the psychological implications of a murderous woman (Bette Davis) appearing on the surface to be all sweetness and light. Davis does a great job working with producer-writer Jimmy Sangster and director Seth Holt. Pamela Franklin, Wendy Craig, Jill Bennett.

**NASTY RABBIT, THE (1965).** Juvenile spy spoof in which rabid Russian roustabouts dressed as wranglers hop to the task of destroying our nation with a bacteria-laden rabbit.

Director James Landis and writers Arch Hall Sr. and Jim Crutchfield forgot to carry a rabbit's foot for good luck—the film died during testing. Hare today, gong tomorrow. Melissa Morgan, Arch Hall Jr., Mischa Terr, John Akana.

**NATAS: THE REFLECTION (1983).** Nosy reporter seeks the truth about an old Indian legend that states there is a sentry standing guard over the passageway between Heaven and Hell. Call it blights-of-passage. Directed by Jack Dunlap. Randy Mulkey, Pat Bolt. Elvira introduces this videocassette version with her usual asides. (VC)

**NATIONAL LAMPOON'S CLASS REUNION (1982).** Mildly amusing spoof on slasher movies, in which The Unknown Killer (with a paper sack over his head) terrorizes Lizzie Borden High School when graduates of '72 gather for a reunion. There's a nerd (Fred McCarren) who becomes the hero, a Dracula vampire (Jim Staahl), a fire-breathing witch (Zane Buzby) and a sexy beauty (Shelley Smith), a blind girl who can't hear so good (Mary Small) and other "joke" types. John Hughes' script never fails to remain sophomoric but Michael Miller's direction is effective for such a ridiculous premise. Momentarily diverting, then easily forgotten. As in all National Lampoon productions, the humor is "sick." Misty Rowe, Michael Lerner. (VC)

**NATURAL, THE (1984).** While this tells of a baseball player who makes a striking comeback, it is also an allegory of battle between good and evil forces, a metaphor for the indomitable spirit of man. Call it an American fable. Robert Redford stars as Roy Hobbs, a once-promising rookie mysteriously shot by a woman in black. He turns up years later to resume his career, armed with "Wonderboy," a bat made from a tree struck by lightning. When he leads the team to victory, Hobbs is tempted by a seductress (Kim Basinger), a corrupt team owner (Robert Prosky) and a perverted gambler (Darren McGavin). Can he overcome his weaknesses and achieve the American Dream? In two great batting sequences, Hobbs performs miraculous (in a literal sense) feats of baseball, beautifully punctuated by Randy Newman's music. One of the best Americana films in years, using baseball as a symbol of our drive for success. Based on the 1952 novel by Bernard Malamud, adapted by Roger Towne and Phil Dusenberry. Barry Levinson directed. Glenn Close, Robert Duvall, Wilford Brimley, Barbara Hershey, Richard Farnsworth, Joe Don Baker. (VC)

**NAVY VS. THE NIGHT MONSTERS (1966).** Screenwriter Michael Hoey turns out hooey about plant creatures (borrowed perhaps from DAY OF THE TRIFFIDS?) with acid in their veins who stalk forth and "stump" Anthony Eisley before launching their invasion against Earth. Mamie Van Doren breaths heavily in order to push the biggest night monsters of all against the thin material of her blouse, thereby revealing the roundness of the Gargantuas concealed beneath. Hoey directed with the same amount of hooey. Bobby Van, Billy Gray, Pamela Mason, Russ Bender. (VC)

**NEANDERTHAL MAN, THE (1953).** Cliched human-into-primeval-creature theme when scientist Robert Shayne discovers how to send a man back through evolutionary stages. In short, just another hairy monster. Similar to MONSTER ON THE CAMPUS. Directed by E. A. Dupont. Richard Crane, Doris Merric, Joyce Terry, Dick Rich.

**NECROMANCY (1971).** Terror tale written-produced-directed by Bert I. Gordon with Orson Welles as Cato, boss man of a witchcraft cult restoring life to Cato's dead son. Along comes Pamela Franklin, unwitting (or is it witless?) heroine subjected to tortures. For lovers of dead movies only. Lee Purcell, Michael Ontkean, Harvey Jason.

**NECROPHAGUS. See GRAVEYARD OF HORROR.**

**NEITHER THE SEA NOR THE SAND (1972).** Susan Hampshire's love for Michael Petrovitch keeps him alive—literally, since he's been dead long enough to push daisies. He's up and on his feet, but that doesn't stop him from decomposing. Susan notices a strange smell and realizes she has the wrong slant on love. Frank Finlay co-stars in this British import. Directed by Fred Burnley.

**NEON MANIACS (1986).** Gang of assorted monsters from the pits of Hell (one would assume—writer Mark P. Carducci never explains) attack some dumb teenagers in San Francis-

**ROBERT REDFORD AS BASEBALL HERO ROY HOBBS IN 'THE NATURAL'**

co, who then arm themselves with water pistols to destory the uglies. Directed without style by Joseph Mangine. Allan Hayes, Donna Locke, Leilani Sarelle.

**NEPTUNE DISASTER, THE (1973).** Hard to believe a full-grown movie producer (Sandy Howard) would ask his cameraman to photograph fish in an aquarium tank with macro lenses and pass them off as "monsters from the deep." Yet that's what happened in this underwater fantasy. Ben Gazzara, Yvette Mimieux and Ernest Borgnine look through the windows of their "Neptune" craft and react to "monsters" but their expressions are those of the dumbfounded. As if they wanted to cry out: What the hell're we doing in this feeble movie? Directed by Daniel Petrie.

**NEPTUNE FACTOR, THE.** See **NEPTUNE DISASTER, THE.** (By any name it's a tragedy!)

**NESTING, THE (1982).** Robin Groves, a neurotic writer suffering from a growing attack of agoraphobia, seeks refuge in a haunted house in this curious blending of supernatural shocks and psychological terrors. Groves has her moments as spectres of the dead force her closer to the brink of madness. It's a valiant try by writers Daria Price and Armand Weston (the latter, a one-time pornie maker, produced-directed) and the film is compelling despite its limited budget. It is a strong supporting cast (John Carradine and Gloria Grahame in pivotal roles) that finally gives convincing clout to an otherwise predictable horror story. Christopher Loomis, Michael David Lally, David Tabor. (VC)

**NET, THE.** See **PROJECT M-7.**

**NEUROSIS (1979).** Spanish thriller, allegedly based on a Poe yarn, in which a madman sinks deeper and deeper into depravity while thrashing about in his weird mansion. Howard Vernon, Daniel Villiers, Valerie Russell.

**NEUTRON AGAINST THE DEATH ROBOTS (1962).** Is Neutron a gallant superhero in a gleaming uniform, an aura of patriotism emanating from his body, a halo of truth ringing his incorruptible head? Naw, he's a sloppy-looking Mexican

**MAMIE VAN DOREN (CIRCA 1984), SEX KITTEN WITH THE BIG NIGHT MONSTERS**

CREATURE FEATURES MOVIE GUIDE

wrestler (Wolf Ruvinskis) clad in a Woolworth's black mask (a dyed barley sack) and droopy boxing trunks in his fight against south-of-the-border criminals. A single monster brain is created from three scientific brains by the incredible Dr. Caronte. Still not enough brains to make this intelligible. Directed-written by Frederico Curiel.

**NEUTRON AND THE BLACK MASK (1962).** More hilarious bone-crunching which pits a witless wrestler against an insidious doctor who specializes in new weapons and monsters. Hard to tell which of them has the lowest IQ. Wolf Ruvinskis in droopy trunks again, under Frederico Curiel's direction. Julio Aleman.

**NEUTRON BATTLES THE KARATE ASSASSINS (1964).** Muscular wrestler Wolf Ruvinskis takes the full count against automaton killers who deliver death-dealing blows with hands and feet. Someone must have had a stranglehold on the Mexican scenarist when he conceived this story—the blood wasn't reaching his brain.

**NEUTRON TRAPS THE INVISIBLE KILLERS (1964).** Not only can you not see villains, but you cannot find plot in this Mexican film in the Masked Wrestler vs. Evil Genius Doctor series. Wolf Ruvinskis again, trying to hitch up his droopy drawers.

**NEUTRON VS. THE AMAZING DR. CARONTE (1964).** That thick-skulled masked wrestler in droopy trunks is still trying to pin an evil genius to the mat but there's never a referee to count to three. So Neutron, against his code of ethics, fights dirty by kicking Dr. Caronte right in his lobotomy. Now that hurts! Wolf Ruvinskis fights valiantly to keep his sagging trunks above his knees.

**NEUTRON VS. THE MANIAC (1961).** Masked wrestler of Mexico, a superhero among body-hold fans, is back for another round as he floors Dr. Caronte over possession of a deadly explosive, but it's hardly a main event for the viewer. A preliminary at best. Wolf Ruvinskis almost loses his droopy boxing shorts in this one.

**NEVER SAY NEVER AGAIN (1983).** Sean Connery's return as James Bond after he forsook the part for 12 years is a loose remake of THUNDERBALL (producer Kevin McClory ended up with story rights after a legal battle; this is not part of the official series). It's a return to adventurous derring-do as British secret agent 007 tries to thwart Largo from detonating two atomic warheads he's stolen from U.S. missiles as part of a SPECTRE plot. The gadgetry, action and sexy ladies are abundant—everything you expect in a Bond thriller. Barbara Carrera is a wonderfully sadistic SPECTRE assassin, as exotic as she is deadly; Kim Basinger is the innocent (though well-rounded) young thing saved by Bond; Max von Sydow is the insidious SPECTRE chief with the white cat; Klaus Maria Brandauer is one of the best Bond villains yet, giving Largo such human traits as a sense of humor, joviality and jealousy. There are jokes about Bond growing old, but Connery still has the looks to pull it off. Irvin Kershner's direction is slick and unobtrusive. (VC)

**NEVER TOO YOUNG TO DIE (1986).** Parody of James Bond action thrillers with some touches of ROAD WARRIOR for bad measure. John Stamos is superspy Lance Stargrove and Vanity is his lover, Danja Deering. Plot involves poisoning the L.A. water supply. Hurrah!

**NEVERENDING STORY, THE (1984).** Offbeat fairy tale told in striking details by German filmmaker Wolfgang Petersen, which ultimately fails because of what seems to be an insignificant plot and a fantasy logic never clearly brought into focus. Despite the glaring failures of the narrative (Petersen co-scripted with Herman Weigel), its visuals are delightful. A youth, reading a book given to him by a strange shopowner, finds himself projected into the land of Fantasia, which is about to be destroyed by The Nothing. He must find a cure for the dying Empress in her Ivory Tower, and he sets out on his episodic quest. The lad meets a racing snail, a rock-eating stone man, a wise old colossal turtle, statues with laser-beam eyes and other quaint, often charming creatures. It is then that the film's imaginative qualities soar. But when it tries to be philosophical with a form of double think, it is a

**THE ORACLE IN 'NEVER-ENDING STORY'**

huge letdown. Tami Stronach, Moses Gunn, Patrick Hayes. Brian Johnson's visual effects are stunning. (VC)

**NEW ADVENTURES OF TARZAN, THE (1935).** Originally a 12-chapter serial independently produced by Edgar Rice Burroughs in Guatemala. Also shown in theaters in feature-length form. In 1938, it was re-edited and re-released. See **TARZAN AND THE GREEN GODDESS.**

**NEW ADVENTURES OF WONDER WOMAN, THE (1977).** WONDER WOMAN TV episodes re-edited to feature length, with shapely Lynda Carter portraying the superhero with bullet-bouncing bracelets. She is forced to leave Paradise Island to protect its secret location from evil forces. Girl watchers won't want to miss the bevy of jiggling beauties (scantily clad at that). Lyle Waggoner, Beatrice Straight, Jessica Walter, Fritz Weaver.

**NEW INVISIBLE MAN, THE (1957).** See **H.G. WELLS' NEW INVISIBLE MAN.** (New man, old cliches.)

**NEW ORIGINAL WONDER WOMAN, THE (1975).** Delightful World War II adventure right off the pages of Charles Moulton's famed superheroine action strip. Amazonian Lynda Carter is bulgingly, curvaceously perfect as the sensuous superheroine with bullet-bouncing bracelets, magical lariat and transparent aircraft. She leaves her feminist kingdom, Paradise Island, to fight Axis powers as military aide-de-camp Diana Prince. This pilot TV-film led to a successful series which promoted Ms Carter into the awareness of all red-blooded Americans who believe in freedom, justice and the American way. Directed by Leonard Horn. Red Buttons, Cloris Leachman, Lyle Waggoner, Stella Stevens.

**NEW PLANET OF THE APES.** See **BACK TO THE PLANET OF THE APES.** (Sure you want to go back?)

**NEW YEAR'S EVIL (1982).** Roz Kelly, a sexy New Wave chick-emcee for a punk-rock radio special on New Year's Eve, is unaware she's spawned a neurotic, possibly psychotic son. But it's not the disturbed young man who commits a series of bloody knife murders starting at midnight sharp. He's an unidentified character calling himself Evil who

**LYNDA CARTER AS WONDER WOMAN**

from the time-space continuum, the brother of Jesus Christ, although what significance this has to the rest of this lackadaisical story remains a mystery in the hands of writer-director Nico Mastorakis. Dull, slow-moving, never interesting. Peter Hobbs, Jeremy Licht, Phaedon Georgitsis, Betty Arvanitis. Next . . . (VC)

**NEXT VICTIM (1972).** Slasher stalks wife of a Austrian diplomat. So what else is new? George Hilton, Christina Airoldi. (VC)

**NEXT VOICE YOU HEAR, THE (1950).** Pious idea by Charles Schnee (God's voice is heard over every radio station in the world, in the language of the listener) is an impossible assignment for director William Wellman. Sure we should examine our hearts . . . sure we should glory over the Universe set before us . . . sure we should have faith . . . but producer Dore Schary should leave message-sending to Western Union. James Whitmore is still good as Joe Smith, factor worker (or Everyman) in this turgid allegory. Nancy Davis, Gary Gray, Jeff Corey, Lillian Bronson.

**NICE GIRLS DON'T EXPLODE (1987).** Regional science-fiction thriller shot in and around Lawrence, Kan., in which a strange mother (Barbara Harris, who's really a strange mother) is capable of setting fires through her emotional outbursts, which she has passed on as a legacy-curse to her daughter, Michelle Meyrink. William O'Leary tries to help Michelle with her problem, but director Chuck Martinez has bigger problems trying to make this idea work, what with FIRESTARTER already burning up the market. Wallace Shawn, James Nardini.

**NIGHT CALLER, THE (1965).** Low-budget British effort, in which an egg-shaped object sent to Ganymede (a moon of Jupiter) and back is discovered by American scientist John Saxon, working with a team at an astronomy station. The egg is now a matter transferrer for a monster sent here to (1) frighten Patricia Haines half to death and (2) kidnap pretty women by posing as the editor of a girly magazine. Ronald Liles' direction achieves a dreary look distinctively British with a stiff-upper-lip cast: Maurice Denham, Alfred Burke, Aubrey Morris, Warren Mitchell, Jack Watson. Some scenes take on a semidocumentary look of a crime detection story, but in general Jim O'Connolly's tired script is made up of unclear ideas and scientific double talk.

**NIGHT CALLER FROM OUTER SPACE.** See **NIGHT CALLER, THE.** (The Blood Beast is here!)

**NIGHT CHILD, THE (1975).** EXORCIST ripoff, with Italian producer William C. Reich slipping in his pasta. It's lifeless and dull, with Richard Johnson as the man who could save the day if only he'd stop messing with Joanna Cassidy's body and pay attention to the little girl (Nicole Elmi) with the strange, people-destroying powers. You'll fall asleep waiting for the ESP action to reach its zenith. A nadir for director Max Dallamano. Lila Kedrova, Edmund Purdom.

**NIGHT COMES TOO SOON, THE (1947).** British version of Bulwer-Lytton's "The Haunted and the Haunters, or The House and Brain," directed by Denis Kavanagh. An old house is haunted by spirits which must be exorcised by a psychic doctor. Valentine Dyall, Anne Howard.

**NIGHT CREATURE (1977).** Metaphysical link between big game hunter Axel McGregory (Donald Pleasence) and a killer leopard provides an odd ambience to this strangely compelling tale of cowardice and bravery, photographed in exotic Thailand locations. Pleasence has brought the black cat to his private island for a showdown, but unexpected visitors foul up his plans. Good dialogue and mood make up for an ambiguous, unresolved story. Ross Hagen, Jennifer Rhodes. Also called OUT OF THE DARKNESS.

**NIGHT CREATURES (1962).** Skeletons on horseback ride through Romney Marsh, pillaging, murdering and frightening farmers. Dr. Blyss, the village vicar (Peter Cushing), warns the populace the Devil is afoot, but cooler heads recognize the presence of pirate captain Clegg and his "Marsh Phantoms." Minor Hammer production is actually a remake of a 1937 film, DR. SYN (remade a third time by Disney as THE SCARECROW OF ROMNEY MARSH). Directed stylishly by

promises to do in Roz by a specified time. She tries to act as a psychiatrist for the police, but the killer continues to knock off beautiful women, moving ever closer to the station. Footage is devoted to punk-rock numbers while the plot waits in the wings, so don't anticipate breathtaking pace. There are surprise twists; still, this is not a holiday treat from writer-director Emmett Alston. Kip Niven is Evil. Chris Wallace, Grant Cramer, Louisa Moritz. (VC)

**NEW YORK RIPPER (1982).** Italian horror director Lucio Fulci is on the loose in the Empire State with a modern day Jack the Ripper tearing apart the city's prostitutes. So "terrifying" it was banned in Argentina (allegedly). Jack Hedley, Almanta Keller, Howard Ross, Alexandra Delli Colli.

**NEXT OF KIN (1982).** Australian supernatural thriller set in a lonely rest home, where events described in an old woman's diary start to recur. Directed-written by Tony Williams. Jackie Kerrin, John Jarratt. (VC)

**NEXT ONE, THE (1982).** Weak, tedious Greek-produced fantasy with supernatural-religious overtones, about as exciting as Zorba the Greek on crutches. Adrienne Barbeau and her young son are living in a villa on the isle of Myconos when a stranger (Keir Dullea) washes ashore. He's someone

Peter Graham Scott. Oliver Reed has the unusual role of a pirate who acts as lookout while disguised as a scarecrow. Yvonne Romain, Milton Reid.

**NIGHT CRIES (1978).** Psychiatry and psychic phenomena are skillfully blended by writer Brian Taggart into a supernatural mystery story. Well directed by Richard Lang and nicely acted by Susan St. James as the distraught mother who refuses to believe her baby died at childbirth and dreams she is in jeopardy. William Conrad is a scientist conducting experiments in dreams who helps Susan unravel the sex trauma haunting her. Tense moments are never compromised with gimmicks or tricks—it's an excellent TV-movie. Michael Parks, Cathleen Nesbitt, Ellen Geer, Jamie Smith Jackson, Lee Kessler.

**NIGHT DIGGER, THE (1971).** British psychothriller starring Nicholas Clay as a sadistic murderer who brings women into his old dark house, murders them and places their corpses under a road being paved. Meanwhile, back at the house, mother Patricia Neal patiently waits for her son to grow up. Screenplay by Roald Dahl. Directed by Alistair Reid. Pamela Brown, Jean Anderson, Yootha Joyce.

**NIGHT EVELYN CAME OUT OF THE GRAVE, THE (1972).** Good Italian thriller with quasisupernatural overtones and a strong sense of sexual perversion. Maniac Anthony Steffen enjoys bringing beautiful women home to his estate and then . . . but that would be giving away too much. Watch as a number of ghastly sights unfold under Emilio P. Miraglia's direction. Erika Blanc, Giocomo Rossi-Stuart, Marina Malfatti, Umberto Raho, Rod Murdock.

**NIGHT FRIGHT (1968).** Regional low budget schlock, filmed in the South and strictly from hunger. A rocket sent into space (Operation Noah's Ark) with hundreds of animals is subjected to radiation, turning them into mutations. The ship (now a UFO) lands near Satan's Hollow, and a creature attacks stupid teenagers making out in a convertible. This monster (with the body of Robot Monster and the face of It! The Terror From Beyond Space) runs through the woods after sheriff John Agar and deputy Bill Thurman, pipe-smoking scientist Roger Ready and more dumb stupid teenagers led by Carol Gilley. Deadly dull, without a whit of imagination; director James A. Sullivan brings no pace or style to the routine story. Instantly forgettable.

**NIGHT GALLERY (1969).** Rod Serling's collection of horror stories, THE SEASON TO BE WARY, was adapted by Universal into a trilogy which became the pilot for a popular series. Stories are hung together by the theme of surrealistic paintings in a creepy art gallery, presided over by host Rod Serling. In the first tale, directed by Boris Sagal, Roddy McDowall speeds along the death of a relative, then realizes he is being haunted by a painting. In the second, directed by Steven Spielberg (making his directorial debut), Joan Crawford is a blind woman who buys the eyes of a beggar so she might see again; and in the third, directed by Barry Shear, Richard Kiley is a one-time Nazi butcher seeking refuge from Israeli avengers (and his conscience) by hiding in a painting hanging in an art gallery. (VC)

**NIGHT GAMES (1980).** French director Roger Vadim deals with the phobias and traumas of Cindy Pickett and Joanna Cassidy in this tale of a frightened housewife and a phantom killer on the loose. Barry Primus, Mark Hanks.

**NIGHT GOD SCREAMED, THE (1971).** Priest Alex Nichol and wife Jeanne Crain pick a poor neighborhood to move into: It's frequented by devil worshipers, who have just drowned a young women as a sacrifice to Satan. Low budget job, inadequately directed by Lee Madden and leadenly scripted by Gil Lasky, Daniel Spelling.

**NIGHT HAS A THOUSAND EYES, THE (1948).** Cornell Woolrich was a pulp writer of the 1940s, excellent at suspense noir, and this adaptation of his 1945 novel is a classic in foreboding gloom and inexorable doom, even though toward the end it begins to turn into a whodunit typical of the 1940s. Edward G. Robinson portrays an unhappy, haunted man who can predict disasters but only wishes the "unseen forces" to leave him alone. Finally he predicts that a matron (Gail Russell) will die one night at 11 p.m. sharp—but before that someone will crush a flower under foot, a vase will break and a wind will blow. Yeah, it all starts to happen. While the final explanation is disappointing, Robinson is still permitted the validity of his prescience. Directed by John Farrow with a stronge sense of film noir. John Lund, William Demarest, Virginia Bruce, Jerome Cowan, Richard Webb, Onslow Stevens.

**NIGHT HAIR CHILD.** See **WHAT THE PEEPER SAW.**

**NIGHT HAS EYES, THE.** See **TERROR HOUSE.**

**NIGHT IN PARADISE (1946).** Walter Wanger fantasy depicting the court of King Croesus of Lydia in 560 B.C., to which Aesop the writer comes to pen a new fable. But Aesop pays scant attention to blank paper, instead ogling the scant costumes and the never-blank face of Merle Oberon as a snippy Persian princess. Gale Sondergaard is a Phrygian sorceress who makes herself invisible, plaguing others with her mocking laughter, while Thomas Gomez and Turhan Bey contribute to this fancy-dress fol-de-rol. Escapist hokum directed by Arthur Lubin. Ray Collins, Paul Cavanaugh, Marvin Miller, John Litel, Douglass Dumbrille, Moroni Olsen, Julie London, Barbara Bates.

**NIGHT IS THE PHANTOM.** See **WHAT!** (Huh?)

**NIGHT KEY (1937).** Kindly Boris Karloff, inventor of a burglar alarm system, is kidnapped by underworld dastards, and pretends to co-operate until he can juryrig the device to fire death rays at the heavies. The British actor is a gentle puppy in this unimportant Universal programmer directed by Lloyd Corrigan. Ward Bond, Jean Rogers, Warren Hull.

**NIGHT LEGS.** See **FRIGHT.** (Knocking knees?)

**NIGHT LIFE OF THE GODS (1935).** Alan Mowbray possesses a magical ring which brings statues to life. Breezy, refined comedy based on a book by Thorne Smith, creator of TOPPER. Directed by Lowell Shermann. Irene Ware, Douglas Fowley, William Boyd, Florine McKinney.

**NIGHT MONSTER (1942).** Metaphysical theme rescues this Universal potboiler from cinematic mediocrity. Ralph Morgan portrays a legless madman who creates a new set of legs through sheer will power. He behaves in standard crazy-man style by stalking into the night to murder the doctors responsible for his double amputation. Bela Lugosi and Lionel Atwill

**BELA LUGOSI IN 'NIGHT MONSTER'**

are present but contribute little to the horror. Ford Beebe directed in the style of an "old, dark house" thriller-comedy. Nils Asther, Don Porter, Leif Erickson.

**NIGHT MUST FALL (1937).** Frightening psychological study of a madman—based on the famous Emlyn Williams suspense play, but so literate it is not the stuff of visceral viewing. It's about a psychotic axe murderer, a Cockney lad charming . . . and deadly. Robert Montgomery conveys this twisted sickness with such smooth deftness we almost forget who Danny really is as he convinces an old woman in a wheelchair (Dame May Whitty) that he's a good boy, while he's really terrorizing her. And let's not forget what the hatbox contains . . . Adapted by John Van Druten and directed by Richard Thorpe. Rosalind Russell, Alan Marshall.

**NIGHT MUST FALL (1964).** What was subtle, underplayed horror in the 1937 MGM version of Emlyn Williams' play is commercialized here for sheer visual horror. Albert Finney is Danny, but not the deceptive genius essayed by Robert Montgomery. Here he is a brutal butcher, wallowing in sexual debauchery and ceremonially perversion as he dominates the household of a wheelchair-bound woman. Here we see him chopping off a woman's head and throwing her body into a pond, as well as the sexual games. Put the blame on con-

up from his coffin to warn the audience it shouldn't reveal the ending to friends. Aged, but not vintage. Bela Lugosi, Wallace Ford, George Meeker, Sally Blane, Matt McHugh, Gertrude Michael. Directed by Benjamin Stoloff.

**NIGHT OF THE BEAST. See HOUSE OF THE BLACK DEATH.** (Moan suite moan?)

**NIGHT OF THE BIG HEAT. See ISLAND OF THE BURNING DOOMED.** (And see sizzling, smoking flesh!)

**NIGHT OF THE BLIND DEAD. See BLIND DEAD, THE.**

**NIGHT OF THE BLOOD BEAST (1958).** Astronaut passing through Earth's radiation belt is infected by an alien spore and returns a "blood beast." Scientists are trapped in a space center with the creature, allowing director Bernard Kowalski (working under producers Gene and Roger Corman) to imitate the best scenes from THE THING. Ed Nelson, Jean Hagen, Angela Greene, Michael Emmet.

**NIGHT OF THE BLOOD MONSTER (1972).** A Spanish-German-Italian effort in the degenerate tradition of MARK OF THE DEVIL . . . a sickening exercise in sadism and brutality, lacking any social redeeming values, even after being heavily cut for the U.S. market. Christopher Lee is a witchhunter

---

*"He [Professor Graves] tampered with things beyond his province . . . and if it was madness, well, those whom the gods destroy, they first make mad."—The summing up in* **THE NEANDERTHAL MAN.**

---

temporary graphic cinema, director Karel Reisz and screenwriter Clive Exton. Mona Washbourne is the widow, Susan Hampshire is her daughter.

**NIGHT MY NUMBER CAME UP, THE (1955).** Dream premonitions serve as the fantasy foundation for this British film based on a true story. Naval commander Michael Hordern has a dream in which an RAF C-47 crashes. How the dream begins to come true builds into a fascinating climax. Michael Redgrave, Denholm Elliott, Alexander Knox. Directed by Leslie Norman, scripted by R. C. Sherriff.

**NIGHT OF A THOUSAND CATS (1974).** Meow-ish Spanish exploitationer with Anjanette Comer, a comely pussycat, cast to make this catnip digestable in the U.S.—but you won't buy the canned goods director Rene Cardona is selling: A crazed nobleman lives in the ruins of an old Mexican castle with his mute Igor-type assistant and a kennel of hungry cats, to whom nutty Hugo feeds the tastiest cat food of all: human flesh. The felids (cats to you) are only a part of it. Hugo, who flies around in a helicopter looking for women lounging in their bikinis, also has a trophy room where he keeps the heads of his victims, mostly beauties who come to the castle for sex. The climactic confrontation between man and cat hardly lives up to its title, with only a few dozen tomcats rushing through the castle. The film finally tucks its tail between its legs and ducks into an alley. (VC)

**NIGHT OF BLOODY HORROR (1969).** Terrible title matches bad lighting, lousy acting and sleazy set design in this low budget incompetence produced on location in New Orleans by writer-producer-director Joy N. Houck Jr. Same old descending meat cleaver and running blood. Night of the Cinematic Bungle. Gerald McRaney, Gaye Yellen. (VC)

**NIGHT OF DARK SHADOWS (1971).** DARK SHADOWS, TV's first daytime serial to deal with the supernatural, led to the feature, HOUSE OF DARK SHADOWS, which in turn led to this sequel of a sequel but without Jonathan Frid as Barnabas the Vampire. The setting—the Jay Gould estate in Tarrytown, New York—is far from menacing, what humor the film has is unintentional and the plot unfolds in haphazard fashion, as though producer-director Dan Curtis and screenwriter Sam Hall were still grinding out afternoon fodder. David Selby, Lara Parker, Kate Jackson, Nancy Barrett, Grayson Hall, Thayer David, John Karlen.

**NIGHT OF TERROR (1933).** Creaky Columbia chiller features a series of murders, a seance to raise the dead and a hilarious final scene in which one of the film's corpses pops

(patterned after a real personage) scouring the England of King Henry V for witches and assorted heretics. More subtly known in the United Kingdom as THE BLOODY JUDGE. Directed by Jesus Franco. Maria Schell, Leo Genn, Maria Rohm, Margaret Lee.

**NIGHT OF THE BLOODY APES (1971).** Brunette in shocking red tights and wearing a cat-like face mask wrestles other women while her boyfriend, a police inspector, watches. Meanwhile, a goofy but well-meaning scientist transfers a gorilla's heart into the body of his dying son but the young man turns into a half-simian, half-human who crashes through Mexican streets on a rampage of destruction. Mostly, the ape-man tears clothing off shapely women and mauls them, affording many views of large bare breasts and creamy thighs. The gore effects are crude and sickening, the wrestling scenes dull and the acting and dubbing pathetically bad. And the title is wrong—there's only one ape. Directed by Rene Cardona, who co-wrote with son Rene Cardona Jr. Armand Silvestre, Norma Lazareno, Jose Elias Moreno, A. M. Solares. (VC)

**NIGHT OF THE COBRA WOMAN (1972).** CULT OF THE COBRA again but on a minuscule budget, in a Filipino setting, as beautiful Marlene Clark transmutes into a deadly snake whenever she doesn't get her formula, a mixture of sex and serum. Some fix. This U.S.-Philippines venture, written and directed by Andrew Meyer, was defanged for U.S. consumption and is less "striking." Features the subtle acting styles of Joy Bang and Slash Marks. Audiences throughout the world hissed. The pits. (VC)

**NIGHT OF THE COMET (1984).** A juvenile mentality permeated this low budget feature from producers Thomas Coleman and Michael Rosenblatt, who proved by slanting to the lowest common denominator, you can hit the jackpot. The script by director Thom Eberhardt makes little sense and is full of holes yet audiences enjoyed this fantasy about the end of the world, trivialized to become mainly a visit by teenager survivors to a clothing store, where they run wild. It begins when a passing comet sends out deadly rays that either kill people or turn them into zombies. There are bits and pieces from so many other movies, it's impossible to keep tabs on the helter-skelter, pasted-together plot. There's also some indecipherable business with scientists in an underground installation who hope to find a serum to combat lethal cosmic rays. You really have to be a teen-ager to enjoy this hodgepodge. Geoffrey Lewis, Mary Woronov and Sharon Farrell are the names in the cast, but the key roles belong to

**THE UGLIES IN 'NIGHT OF THE COMET' GET BLASTED BY CATHERINE MARY STEWART**

the teens: Catherine Mary Stewart, Kelli Maroney and Robert Beltran. Some effects are okay, but it's Juvenile City all the way. (VC)

**NIGHT OF THE CREEPS (1986).** A low budget science-fiction/horror thriller derivative of everything: THE THING, NIGHT OF THE LIVING EAD, FRIDAY THE 13TH, ALIEN and any other recent innovative special effects movie. Too bad it doesn't have a single original idea, for director-writer Fred Dekker shows promise. It begins in 1959 when an alien probe is launched to Earth, just when an axe maniac is about to murder a couple of college students. Cut to 1986 as Tom Atkins (detective Cameron) tries to solve a series of murders involving walking corpses, worm-like creatures that leap into your mouth and take over your body, and that old axe killer. Cameron is very good as the hard-edged unorthodox cop, and is supported by a decent teen cast: Jason Lively, Lene Starger, Steve Marshall and Jill Whitlow. Above average for its type. (VC)

**NIGHT OF THE DARK FULL MOON.** See **SILENT NIGHT, BLOODY NIGHT.** (Is nothing holy?)

**NIGHT OF THE DEMON.** Alternative title to **CURSE OF THE DEMON.** (You'll curse, all right!)

**NIGHT OF THE DEMON (1979).** Cheesy "Bigfoot" gore flick, overloaded with bloody, violent deaths, finally amateurish under Jim Wasson's direction. The survivor of an expedition of field students tells police about his wilderness adventure . . . in flashback we meet five colorless explorers in search of "Crazy Wanda," a legendary woman of the backwoods who allegedly was raped by a beast and gave birth to a malformed hairy infant. When they dig up the baby's grave to prove the story, the hirsute one with bad body odor goes . . . Bigfoot. Climactic siege features death by routine saw cut, ordinary broken glass, standard strangulation, typical throttling, mundane disembowelment, and predictable pitchfork. And that doesn't include other deaths revealed in flashbacks-within-the-flashback. For blood-and-guts fans only. Mike Cutt, Joy Allen. (VC)

**NIGHT OF THE DEVILS (1971).** Italian-Spanish quickie in which a young man fears his girl is part of a witch cult. Directed by Giorgio Ferroni. Based on a short story by Tolstoy. Gianni Garko, Agostina Belli, Maria Monti.

**NIGHT OF THE EAGLE.** See **BURN, WITCH, BURN.**

**NIGHT OF THE GHOULS (1959).** Flushed with the critical acclaim of PLAN 9 FROM OUTER SPACE, writer-producer-director Edward Wood Jr. made this sequel. Once again Criswell, the alleged hypnotist and medium, introduces us to a

tale of the "undead," this time about Dr. Acula (Kenne Duncan), a fake swami who fleeces innocent folks by promising to raise their dead relatives. What Acula doesn't know is that his powers are real, and he can raise the dead, who then raise hell with Acula and assistant Tor Johnson. Rock-bottom budget provided skimpy sets and no-quality production values. Wood Jr. was a terrible filmmaker, but even unintentional laughs aren't enough to make one set through such incompetence. (VC)

**NIGHT OF THE HOWLING BEAST (1975).** Spanish sequel to FRANKENSTEIN'S BLOODY TERROR, with Paul Naschy as a member of a Tibetan expedition who is attacked by a werewolf and changed into a creature. Then it becomes a battle between the wolfman and a yeti. Amando de Ossorio manages to be competent and incompetent at alternating moments with Jacinto Molina's howling funny script. The visuals surpass the weak acting by Gil Vidal, Grave Mills and Silvia Solar. (VC)

**NIGHT OF THE HUNTER (1954).** Visually artistic film directed by Charles Laughton, surrealistic and macabre in recounting Davis Grubb's hair-raiser about a psychotic, Scriptures-quoting preacher (Robert Mitchum) who has "love" tattooed on one hand, "hate" on the other. He's in pursuit of two children who know where the family fortune is buried, and there's no doubt of his homicidal intentions. Literate screenplay by James Agee; Stanley Cortez's cinematography is outstanding. Shelley Winters, Peter Graves, James Gleason, Lillian Gish, Don Beddoe.

**NIGHT OF THE LAUGHING DEAD.** See **HOUSE IN NIGHTMARE PARK, THE.** (Ha ha ha ha ha . . . glck!)

**NIGHT OF THE LEPUS (1972).** Jumpin' jackrabbits! The Southwest desert is littered with little critters—only they're not so little after being injected with a hormone (designed to decrease breeding habits) which increases growth genes. In short, thousands of rabbits have been photographed in macro close-up by director William Claxton and matted with Rory Calhoun and Janet Leigh looking scared to death. Not as hare-y as you think, it just breeds contempt. This hasenpfeffer speciality was concocted for producer A. C. Lyles. DeForest Kelley, Paul Fix.

**NIGHT OF THE LIVING DEAD (1968).** Pittsburgh's George Romero shot this low budget horror film on weekends, with a cast of unknowns, for $150,000. The result was a classic which has built one of the strongest reputations in the horror genre, and which set a trend. It's a miniclassic of eerie proportions due to its black-and-white photography, its clever use of documentary techniques to lend versimilitude, its im-

*"Please don't reveal the ending—or I'll tear you limb from limb!"*
*—The Incredibly Insane Maddened Homicidal Maniac in*
***NIGHT OF TERROR (1933).***

aginative editing and its horribly ironic ending. A space probe returning to Earth introduces into our atmosphere a form of radiation which affects dead bodies, bringing them to life. Soon the countryside is crowded with armies of walking dead. Untainted humans seek refuge in a farmhouse—and the horror is unrelenting as the zombies attack, often munching on human flesh (TV prints are minus these scenes, but their removal doesn't hamper the overall effect). The only way these creatures can be stopped is by shooting them in the head. John A. Russo wrote the script for Romero, who got great milage out of Duane Jones, Judith O'Dea, Karl Hardman, Marilyn Eastman. Re-released to TV in 1986 in a colorized form. There were two sequels: DAWN OF THE DEAD, which was also a box office smash, and DAY OF THE DEAD, which was less so. (VC)

**NIGHT OF THE SEAGULLS (1975).** Dead knights ride through a small village, terrorizing superstitious folks with their quest for the blood of virgins. It takes a doctor and his wife to find a way to stop them in this sequel to THE BLIND DEAD from writer-director Amando De Ossorio. Victor Petit, Maria Kosti, Sandra Mozarosky, Julie James.

**NIGHT OF THE SORCERESS (1970).** Great Leopard Devil claim sacrifice of blonde white girl. Soldiers come, kill plenty bad natives. Many moons later, expedition comes from sky in great silver bird. God men go to taboo burial grounds. Take long time die, one by one. Leopard Devil take lives. Angry. Plenty mad. Turn man into creature who belong in black lagoon. Powerful witch doctor say: "My mother the sorceress told me there'd be nights like this." Another lowbrow Spanish special from director Amando de Ossorio. Jack Taylor, Simon Andreu, Kali Hansa.

**NIGHT OF THE WEREWOLF. See CRAVING, THE.**

**NIGHT OF THE WITCHES (1970).** Rapist disguised as a preacher gets his comeuppance when he falls in with a witch cult, unaware of the satanic rape they have planned. This Canadian production has occasional moments of light-heartedness, but tedium finally prevails. Leading player Keith Erik Burt (who also wrote and directed) is really Keith Larsen, star of many B movies. Ron Taft co-stars.

**NIGHT OF THE ZOMBIES (1983).** Writer-director Joel M. Reed, the intellectualizing sentimentalist who brought us BLOODTHIRSTY FREAKS, is up to his old blood-gushing tricks in this walking-dead tale of World War II soldiers who have been kept in suspended animation with a nerve gas called Gamma 693 and are now alive, terrorizing civilians and passers-by at a former battlefield in Germany. Sleazy stuff with cheap makeup and effects. Jamie Gillis is an investigating CIA agent, Ryan Hilliard is the doctor and Samantha Grey is the obligatory love interest. And Reed, ever so shy, turns up as a modern-day Nazi.

**NIGHT OF THE ZOMBIES (1983).** Wretched Italian mess of a movie, a direct steal of DAWN OF THE DEAD when New Guinea is exposed to a strange gas (unleashed during secret experiments) and turned into a landscape of Walking Dead. The whole thing is ludicrous beyond words as four SWAT-team types set out on a mission (the purpose of which is never clear) by blasting their way through the undead. Even though the yokels know they have to shoot the creatures in the head, they repeatedly waste their ammo by firing into the bodies, and behave like the Three Stooges. Director Vincent Dawn has gone to extremes to make this as bloody as possible with exploding heads, maggot-infested bodies, ghouls munching on human organs and intestines. Not a single frightening moment, it's simply repulsive and unwatchable. One of the all-time worst. Frank Garfield. (VC)

**NIGHT RIPPER (1986).** Video special depicting a fiendish killer stalking and slashing beautiful models. Directed by Jeff Hatchcock. James Hansen, April Anne. (VC)

**NIGHT SCHOOL (1980).** Although atmospherically directed by Kenneth Hughes, this slasher-gasher has a silly premise:

the headhunter rituals of New Guinea and how they're applied to ghastly knife killings at Wendell College in Boston. After each beheading, the motorcyclist-murderer throws the head into liquid. The killings are repetitive (woman victim screams, slasher closes fast with a knife) and moments of depraved sexuality are gratuitously thrown in. There's cat-and-mouse "Where's the head hidden this time?" but this attention to black humor ultimately evokes nihilism. Rachel Ward looks great in a shower-stall strip scene, but is hopelessly lost with her dialogue. You'll spot the killer's identity early on—there aren't enough characters to create a guessing game. Leonard Mann, Drew Snyder.

**NIGHT SHADOWS. See MUTANT (1983).**

**NIGHT SLAVES (1970).** Director Ted Post is to be congratulated for taking a Everett Chambers-Robert Specht script nobody wanted and turning it into an effective TV-movie, based on a Jerry Sohl novel. The setting is a small town which comes under the hypnotic spell of aliens repairing their rocketship—only James Franciscus is immune because of a metal plate in his skull, and he falls for one of the lovely E.T.s (Tisha Sterling). Post avoids sensational claptrap to give this some poetry. Lee Grant, Andrew Prine, Scott Marlowe, Leslie Nielsen, John Kellogg, Victor Izay.

**NIGHT STALKER, THE (1972).** Dan Curtis' production made history as the highest-rated TV-movie of its day as it took a fresh, novel approach to the vampire theme. Kolchak, an impetuous, fast-talking newspaperman (Darren McGavin), believes Las Vegas murders are being committed by an ageless bloodsucker (no, not a slot machine). After frustrating politics with police and city officials, Kolchak faces the creature (Barry Atwater) in a hair-raising showdown. Superbly directed by John L. Moxey and wonderfully scripted by Richard Matheson, from an original story by Jeff Rice. Carol Lynley, Ralph Meeker, Kent Smith, Claude Akins, Simon Oakland (as Kolchak's city editor). The concept resulted in a sequel, THE NIGHT STRANGLER, and a short-lived series which each week pitted a new monster against the unflappable Kolchak. The series ran down, but not Kolchak. He's forever incorrigible. (VC)

**DARREN McGAVIN IN 'NIGHT STALKER'**

*"Some call [this train] the Heavenly Express . . . others, Satan's Cannonball. But we guarantee to deliver every passenger at his right destination."—The Night Porter in NIGHT TRAIN TO TERROR.*

**NIGHT STALKER, THE (1987).** Yet again another uninspired killer-on-the-loose slash-bash, this time with the sleazeball killing prostitutes and painting Oriental figures on their faces as he chants mumbo jumbo. What does it all mean? Ask cop J. J. Stryker (Charles Napier), who sips vodka at breakfast and hangs out with his chick, a one-time streetwalker turned sculptress. Directed (if you can call it that) by Max Kleven.

**NIGHT STAR—GODDESS OF ELECTRA (1963).** Italian sword-and- sandal epic set during the Roman Empire when a mad magician (John Drew Barrymore) intends to bring dead soldiers to life to create an army of unkillable troops and conquer the world. Directed by Giuseppe Vari. Susi Andersen, Ettore Manni, Philippe Hersent.

**NIGHT STRANGLER, THE (1973).** Fascinating sequel to THE NIGHT STALKER stars Darren McGavin as the flustered, aggressive newsman Kolchak, stalking mysteries that invariably lead him into the supernatural. Richard Matheson's teleplay has Kolchak in Seattle, trailing a "walking corpse" killer who slaughters women. With research help from librarian Wally Cox, Kolchak realizes he is dealing with a 100-year-old madman who needs a periodic serum fix to stay alive. Jo Ann Pflug is the heroine and Simon Oakland re-creates the harassed assignment editor. Directed by Dan Curtis. Richard Anderson, Scott Brady, Margaret Hamilton, John Carradine, Nina Wayne.

**NIGHT TERROR (1977).** Fast-moving suspense tale relying on visual impact. Valerie Harper witnesses the slaying of a patrolman and flees in her car for her life, the killer in hot pursuit. Edge- of-chair material never lets go in this taut TV-movie directed by E. W. Swackhamer. Richard Romanus, Nicholas Pryor, John Quade, Michael Tolan.

**NIGHT THAT PANICKED AMERICA, THE (1975).** Behind-the-scenes dramatization of how Orson Welles' Mercury Theater dramatized H. G. Wells' WAR OF THE WORLDS on radio on Oct. 30, 1938. What was intended to be a Halloween prank was taken to be a real event by the U.S. public, which panicked and fled the "invaders from Mars." This documents the production, the real-life cast and crew and the lis-

**BARBARA STANWYCK, ROBERT TAYLOR: 'NIGHT WALKER'**

teners who overreacted. Joseph Sargent directed Nicholas Meyers' script. Vic Morrow, Cliff De Young, Wallace McGinn, Meredith Baxter, Tom Bosley, Will Geer.

**NIGHT THE WORLD EXPLODED, THE (1957).** Kathryn "Grant" Crosby ranks this among her favorites—although we don't see why. It's a farfetched yarn by Luci Ward and Jack Natteford about a mineral deep in the Earth threatening to explode and destroy our world. Give producer Sam Katzman and director Fred F. Sears credit for bringing in another Columbia quickie on schedule with little regard for cinematic values. William Leslie, Tris Coffin, Terry Frost.

**NIGHT THEY KILLED RASPUTIN, THE (1962).** Italian-French historical drama about the wild-eyed Russian prophet who took over the court of the Czar in the 1910s, claiming he could heal the ruler's sick son. John Drew Barrymore portrays Prince Yousoupoff, who led the plot to murder the self-appointed "messiah," while Edmund Purdom portrays the monk. Directed by Pierre Chenal.

**NIGHT THEY SAVED CHRISTMAS, THE (1985).** North Pole City, the home of Santa, is endangered when an oil company closes in. Elf Paul Williams calls on Jaclyn Smith, Paul LeMat and their kids to prevent the tycoons from destroying the place where all the toys are made. Art Carney portrays Santa, June Lockhart is Mrs. Santa. TV-film directed by Jackie Cooper. Scott Grimes, Mason Adams.

**NIGHT TIDE (1963).** Writer-director Curtis Harrington's first film is set at a seaside carnival where sailor Dennis Hopper is mesmerized by Mora the Mermaid (Linda Lawson), who really thinks she is part of a race of sea creatures. A fortune teller warns him to stay away, but Hopper is inexorably drawn to this strange woman. A most persuasive film, unmarred by its low budget. Luana Anders, Gavin Muir.

**NIGHT TRAIN TO TERROR (1985).** White-haired God (billed as Himself) and Satan (billed as Lu Sifer) are on a celestial/hellbound train with rock 'n rolling teenagers, debating good vs. evil and philosophically discussing ownership of three souls: hence, three stories made up of parts of unreleased features. "The Case of Harry Billings" is a surreal nightmare in a hospital where the bodies of patients are cut up and sold. John Philip Law wanders through this dream-of-horrors, surrounded by crazy doctors and naked, sexy women. "The Case of Gretta Connors" is another surreal tale about a Death Club, where members subject themselves to dangers for thrills—there's an electrocution sequence, a winged beetle of death (stop motion) and a wrecking ball torture device. "The Case of Claire Hanson" is footage from CATACALYSM, with Cameron Mitchell and Marc Lawrence as policemen in pursuit of Olivier, the Son of Satan (Robert Bristol). Faith Clift plays a lady surgeon, the only person who can stop his reign of evil if she can cut out his heart and put it into a box belonging to God. This features some amateurish stop-motion monsters. Five directors are credited: John Carr, producer Jay Schlossberg-Cohen, Philip Marshak, Tom Mc-Gowan, Gregg Tallas. (VC)

**NIGHT UNTO NIGHT (1947).** Obscure Warner Bros. programmer in which Viveca Lindfors is a woman haunted by the voices of ghosts and Ronald Reagan as an epileptic scientist who tries to help her overcome her mental anguish. Directed by Don Siegel. Broderick Crawford, Craig Stevens, Rosemary De Camp, Osa Massen.

**NIGHT VISITOR, THE (1971).** Many Ingmar Bergman regulars star in this Mel Ferrer production—a Gothic horror thriller set in an insane asylum from which Max von Sydow escapes each night to carry out a gruesome murder, returning before morning. Directed by Laslo Benedek on location in Sweden. Trevor Howard, Liv Ullmann, Per Oscarsson, Andrew Keir, Rupert Davies. (VC)

**NIGHT WALKER, THE (1965).** William Castle "gimmick" horror film, written by Robert Bloch and prefaced with gobblydegook about dreams, making producer-director Castle seem as though he is seriously dealing with the subconscious. Castle was a huckster just making another buck. Bloch's script unfolds, unfortunately, without more of the tongue-in-cheek spoofery for which Castle was famous. After her husband dies in a mysterious explosion, Barbara Stanwyck has bizarre dreams about a walking man (Lloyd Bochner). Numerous thrills follow, with at least a dozen red herrings and a climax in a room of death more hilarious than frightening. Robert Taylor, Judith Meredith, Rochelle Hudson, Hayden Rourke, Tetsu Komai.

**NIGHT WARNING (1981).** Susan Tyrrell's performance as a demented, getting-battier-by-the-minute broad is the single saving grace of this exploitation shocker—and we mean exploitation. This low- budget film rakes homosexual haters over the coals in the form of prejudiced cop Bo Svenson, who wants to nail Susan's nephew (Jimmy McNichol) for murder and for hanging around a "faggot" basketball coach. The situation is contrived and denigrates the film's more honorable intentions, leaving only Ms Tyrrell to go bonkers in her wonderfully unsubtle way. She knives nearly all the cast to death with unrestrained glee. Directed by William Asher. Marcia Lewis, William Paxton. (VC)

**NIGHT WATCH (1973).** Cat-and-mouse suspense thriller based on a play by Lucille Fletcher, who gave us SORRY, WRONG NUMBER. Elizabeth Taylor thinks she has seen the moving figure of a dead man in the house next door. Did she? Or is she crazy? Or is some diabolical plot afoot? Husband Laurence Harvey isn't telling. Brian G. Hutton's direction keeps you guessing. Billie Whitelaw.

**NIGHTBEAST (1982).** Low budget, semi-professional special effects movie from writer-producer-director Don Dohler, an editor of fanzines before he turned filmmaker. A zap gun-carrying alien lands in a spaceship outside Perry Hill in Maryland and proceeds to either eat the people or laser them to death, depending on his shifting moods. Tom Griffith, Jamie Zemarel, Don Leifert. (VC)

**NIGHTCOMERS, THE (1972).** Prequel to Henry James' TURN OF THE SCREW, revealing how evil valet-gardener Quint (Marlon Brando) and governess Miss Jessel (Stephanie Beacham) engage in a love-hate relationship and how their brutal, voyeuristic bedroom techniques turn two innocent children into little monsters. Directed by Michael Winner. Harry Andrews, Anna Palk. (VC)

**NIGHTDREAMS (1981).** Lightly pornographic fantasy in which a pair of scientists observes a woman, jolting her with stimulating electrons so she will undergo erotic dreams. Dorothy LeMay, Loni Sanders, Jennifer West, Ken Starbuck, Kevin Jay, Andy Nichols.

**NIGHTMARE (1956).** Adaptation of Cornell Woolrich's familiar story about a musician who wakes up after a nightmare to find clues that indicate he actually carried out a murder. Kevin McCarthy, as the New Orleans jazz player, seeks the help of Edward G. Robinson, his brother-in-law policeman. First made in 1947 as FEAR IN THE NIGHT. Maxwell Shane directed-wrote both versions. Virginia Christine, Connie Russell, Barry Atwater, Rhys Williams.

**NIGHTMARE (1961).** Foreign comedy in which a cop has dreams about his wife's infidelity . . . when those dreams come true he investigates. Played for laughs, with Senta Berger titillating.

**NIGHTMARE (1964).** Teen-ager Jennie Linden has terrifying dreams in which she hears the voice of her crazed mother, beckoning for her. Seems the old bat went berserk one night, stabbing a man to death; and now Jennie fears she has inherited mom's madness. A phantom figure in a nightmare haunts her until her birthday, when Jennie flips out and stabs the woman to death. It was a plot, you see, to drive her mad and collect the family fortune . . . but the woman who engineered that scheme is plagued by visitations herself. This Hammer suspense thriller has an intriguing Jimmy Sangster script, but if you'll sharp, you'll spot the red herrings early on and figure out what's happening. Directed by Freddie Francis. David Knight, Moira Richmond.

**NIGHTMARE (1973).** David Hemmings and Gayle Hunnicutt portray a couple caught up in a country home mystery in this

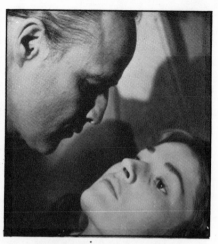

## MARLON BRANDO AS QUINT IN 'THE NIGHTCOMERS'

British shocker. Lynn Farleigh.

**NIGHTMARE (1981).** Cinematic sleaze scuzz as its best, recommended to splatter fans only. A homicidal maniac keeps reliving a horrible incident from childhood during which he axed to death his mother and father while they were engaging in a little sadistic sexual pleasure. Despite its morbidity and grisly effects, NIGHTMARE has a fascination that will hold and repel you. Written-directed by Romano Scavolini, this has drama and pacing that indicates there's talent for better things. Try to get out of that sleaze pit, Romano. (VC)

**NIGHTMARE ALLEY (1947).** William Lindsay Gresham's novel was a shocker which continues to earn stature as literature in depicting a maladjusted young man who joins a carnival and rises to become a successful night club mind reader and then a bilker of millionairesses via a phony spiritualism racket. The movie code of the 1940s allowed Darryl Zanuck to do only portions of the book, and while Fox made an earnest attempt to capture the essence of Gresham's psychological portrait, the film fell short of its goal. Tyrone Power is powerful as Stan Carlisle, repelled when he first sees the "geek"—half-man, half-beast of the midway who tears off heads of chickens. This deterioration of an ambitious man into a dipsomaniac is ten times more shivery than any alleged "monster" movie. Directed by Edmund Goulding. Coleen Gray, Joan Blondell, Helen Walker.

**NIGHTMARE CASTLE (1966).** Standard Italian Gothic chiller undistinguished except for the presence of Barbara Steele in two roles, as a wife cheating on her husband and as a cousin. You've seen it before: mad doctor utilizes electrical impulses in experiments with human blood; murder victims rise from grave to wreak vengeance. Directed and written by Mario Caiano. Paul Miller, Helga Line, Laurence Clift, Rik Battaglia. (VC)

**NIGHTMARE CITY. See CITY OF THE WALKING DEAD.**

**NIGHTMARE HOTEL (1970).** Spanish horror flick, written-directed by Eugenio Martin, set in a hostelry of hostility on the Mediterranean coast, where two batty sisters murder the tourists when they fail to live up to moral standards. The bodies, with gaping knive wounds in vital organs, are dumped into wine vats before being served to the guests. Meanwhile, innocent young Judy Geeson arrives looking for her missing sister and notices how strange it is that the guests disappear at night without checking out. Accommodations must be poor. Don't make a reservation.

**NIGHTMARE IN BLOOD (1976).** Low budget horror film designed for fans depicts the world of fantasy-comic book

**CREATURE FEATURES MOVIE GUIDE**

fandom. While its humor is hip and droll, it's still a genre suspense shocker featuring a series of macabre murders. Jerry Walter brings new facets to the screen vampire as Malakai, a Hollywood actor specializing in vampire films, and guest of honor at a San Francisco convention. Various elements of fandom (horror writer, Sherlock Holmes fan, comic book store owner) band to destroy that which they love most when they discover Malakai is a bloodsucker. Malakai's henchmen are two publicity men who turn out to be Burke and Hare, the infamous body snatchers. The John Stanley-Kenn Davis screenplay touches on elements of vampirism never before discussed in films and incorporates a censor of comic books named Unworth and an Israeli avenger searching for Malakai since the Nazi atrocities. Totally offbeat; recommended to fans. Stanley, host of TV's CREATURE FEATURES in San Francisco for six years, directed and co-produced with Davis. Kerwin Mathews has a cameo role in a swashbuckling sequence. Barrie Youngfellow, Hy Pyke, Ray K. Goman, Drew Eshelman, Morgan Upton, Justin Bishop. (VC)

**NIGHTMARE IN WAX (1969).** Variation on the HOUSE OF WAX theme but as limp as a piece of melting candle.

OF THE MIND. (Odds and Ids?)

**NIGHTMARE ON ELM STREET, A (1984).** Extremely successful box office hit, with Robert Englund as a maniacal killer named Fred Krueger who uses as his weapons a hand of long knifes in place of fingernails. Krueger is a supernatural entity in a slouch hat who turns up in the dreams of assorted teenagers and proceeds to murder them. Director Wes Craven's script is weak on exposition and logic, but it didn't bother audiences, as he focuses in on suspenseful murders and bloody special effects, with atmosphere and spooky shadows abounding. This led to A NIGHTMARE ON ELM STREET, PART 2: FREDDY'S REVENGE. (VC)

**NIGHTMARE ON ELM STREET, PART 2: FREDDY'S REVENGE (1985).** In some ways this is better than the original, being more capably directed by Jack Sholder and having more character development. On the other hand, it doesn't have as many scares and it barely walks the twilight nightmare world of dreams, as the first film did. Anyway, what we have here is the return of Freddy Krueger in the dreams of Mark Patton, who moves into the sinister house on Elm Street where the horrors of the first film took place. Father Clu Gulager and mother Hope Lange, having never

**DAN CALDWELL AS PROFESSOR SEABROOK IN 'NIGHTMARE IN BLOOD'**

Cameron Mitchell is good as Rinaud, disfigured curator of a wax museum who showcases his victims as exhibits. Rex Carlton's story is so ludicrous and sleazy, it's fascinating to watch. The ending, unfortunately, is a cop-out. Directed by Bud Townsend in the Movieland Wax Museum in Los Angeles. Anne Helm, Berry Kroeger, Scott Brady. (VC)

**NIGHTMARE MAKER.** See **NIGHT WARNING.**

**NIGHTMARE NEVER ENDS, THE (1972).** Jewish avenger in search of a Nazi war criminal discovers Olivier (Robert Bristol) is the Son of Satan (symbol: 666) and convinces cops Cameron Mitchell and Marc Lawrence to track him down. Meanwhile, a lady surgeon (Faith Clift) is married to Nobel Prize-winning author Robert Moll, who writes a book, GOD IS DEAD. Only she can stop Olivier by cutting out his heart and putting it into a box once owned by God. Many scenes from this were used in the anthology film, NIGHT TRAIN TO TERROR. Screenplay by Philip Yordan; directed by Tom McGowan, Greg Tallas and Darryl Marshak. Originally made as CATALYSM. (VC)

**NIGHTMARE OF TERROR.** Videocassette title for **DEMONS**

seen the original movie, have no idea their son is being taken over by Freddy. It becomes not a symbolic battle but a literal one as the external Mark Patton cracks open and Robert Englund (in the makeup of Krueger, and wearing the knives-for-fingernails device) pops out. This battle of wills is the film's primary strength, with a nice climactic confrontation in a boiler factory. However, the film's best sequence comes at the beginning as a runaway bus is perched on a precipice—that is straight out of a terrifying nightmare. Horror fans should be pleased with this solid follow-up. (VC)

**NIGHTMARE ON ELM STREET 3: DREAM WARRIORS (1987).** Another solid follow-up to the Wes Craven box-office hit, exploring new "nuances" of the Freddy Krueger character for shock exploitation. This time a group of youngsters terrorized by Krueger in their dreams take part in a controlled experiment using a new drug. The last 30 minutes are exciting as they link together to stay in the same dream and fight Krueger with their various combative techniques. There are some imaginative surprises and creative effects, though as usual the story remains slender and predictable and the characters of minimal interest. Directed by Chuck Russell. Craven concocted the yarn and co-wrote. Heather Lan-

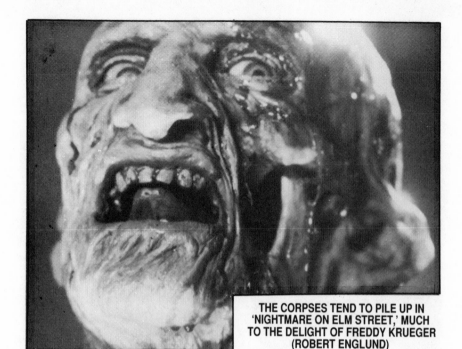

genkamp, Patricia Arquette, Priscilla Pointer, John Saxon, Craig Wasson, Robert Englund. (VC)

**NIGHTMARE VACATION.** See **SLEEPAWAY CAMP.**

**NIGHTMARE WEEKEND (1986).** Evil computer scientist Debbie Laster uses her software to warp human minds and turn three college girls into "mutantoids." She accomplishes this by firing a silver ball into the brain, which then goes psycho and turns its owner into a drooling, slavering walking dead shambling rambling zombie freak killer. Directed by Henry Sala. Dale Midkiff, Debra Hunter, Lori Lewis. (VC)

**NIGHTMARES (1983).** Anthology of eerie tales, directed by Joseph Sargent, without any bonding theme. "Terror in Topanga" is derivative of the slasher genre with a maniacal murderer threatening housewife Cristina Raines, who has to go out for cigarettes late one night. This is the weakest of the lot, so the film builds with "The Bishop of Battle," detailing how a young boy (Emilio Estevez), obsessed with video games, challenges a 13-level, 3-dimensional war game. "The Benediction" is a chilling narrative that first establishes a man of the cloth (Lance Henriksen) and his lack of religious faith prior to his encounter with a sinister pickup truck. "Night of the Rat" is the biggest crowd-pleaser, in which a giant demon rodent from German mythology terrorizes a suburbanite family. The suspense mounts as the unhappily married husband and wife (Richard Masur and Veronica Cartwright) face a horrific onslaught. The first three yarns were written by Christopher Crowe (who produced TV's 1985 revival of Alfred Hitchcock), the fourth by Jeffrey Bloom. A quality Universal product. (VC)

**NIGHTSTALKER (1979).** Two 20,000-year-old flesh eaters (i.e. cannibals) move to Los Angeles, hearing that the meat there is fresh daily. Molar-moving melodrama. Directed by Lawrence D. Foldes. And what the hell is Aldo Ray doing in this mess? (VC)

**NIGHTWING (1979).** Columbia adaptation of Martin Cruz Smith's novel starts as a study of the plight of contemporary American Indians—then shifts to bat exterminator David Warner showing up with a "bat mobile" loaded with scientific tracking equipment. Next, bats attack out of the night, claiming victims. Then the search for the bat cave. A muddled mess because of the meandering screenplay by Steve Shagan, the uninspired direction of Arthur Hiller, and the mediocre bat effects. Nick Mancuso, Strother Martin, George Clutesi, Steven Macht, Kathryn Harrold. (VC)

**NINE EIGHTY FOUR—PRISONER OF THE FUTURE (1984).** An executive is imprisoned by The Movement in some future period when mind games are the order of the time. Imitative of 1984 and THE PRISONER. Directed by Tibor Takacs. Don Francks, Stephen Markel. (VC)

**1984 (1956).** If George Orwell intended his novel to be a frightful warning, this British film version isn't even an old-fashioned "boo." The main fault lies in its limited budget: It is imperative the atmosphere of the future totalitarian state of "Big Brother" be realistically conveyed, that there be the paranoia of everybody under surveillance in a grim world. That grimness is lost here. The workload falls on Edmond O'Brien and Jan Sterling as the defiant lovers and on Michael Redgrave as the ruthless leader who subjects Winston Smith (O'Brien) to the ultimate terrors in physical and psychological torture. A well-intended film that just didn't come off. Directed by Michael Anderson. Donald Pleasence, Michael Ripper, Mervyn Jones, Ewen Solon.

**1984 (1983).** George Orwell's world of Big Brother—a dictatorship in which men are enslaved by tricks of government—never came to pass in our time, although Orwell's "prediction" today seems more of a symbolic parable than a realistic alternate future. If ever a movie grimly portrayed an unbearable, unliveable society, here it is in all its squalor and depression, capturing what was missing from the 1956 version. The cast resembles concentration camp victims— gaunt, closely shaven, empty-eyed, traumatized—and there isn't a single humorous moment for two hours. The acting, though superb, plays second to the blemishes, bleak settings and somber tone of director Michael Radford. Hence, John Hurt as the trammeled Winston Smith (who has love for his fellow man despite dehumanization) and Richard Burton (as the Interrogator who has neither love nor hate but obediently carries out his duty) are not pleasant to watch. Orwell's message comes through strong: that once man has lost his freedom, he is totally subservient to the Big Lies of propaganda, and will believe what isn't true, and disbelieve what is. In terms of conveying a frightening image, this British film succeeds, but in terms of entertainment, it is a bleak and depressing experience. (VC)

**1990: THE BRONX WARRIORS (1983).** Vic Morrow, in one of his last roles, portrays Hammer the Exterminator, a policeman of the future who infiltrates the Bronx, which has become so lawless, authorities stay away. This no-man's-land is a battleground for gang wars between Trash (caucasian) and Ogre (black). There's another gang called the Zombies and there's some freaks who live in the subterranean ruins like cavemen. Obviously inspired by THE ROAD WARRIOR, this Italian production will be of interest one day to archeologists, for it was filmed in the ruins of the Bronx and affords a depressing, frightening look at what is happening to a major U.S. city. Unintelligently directed by Enzo G. Castellari and written with an equal amount of insight by Dardano Sacchetti. Christopher Connelly, Fred Williamson, Mark Gregory, John Sinclair. (VC)

**NINJA TERMINATOR (1985).** The Golden Ninja Warrior, a statuette of magical powers, is sought by three martial arts students in this action-oriented karate-klout movie. Sho Kosugi, Wong Cheng II, Jonathan Wattis. (VC)

**NINJA II: THE DOMINATION (1984).** An appalling bloodbath of Phoenix policemen sets into dubious motion this sequel in the NINJA series (continuous sword fighting, body-slamming and car crashing). A samurai warrior, impervious to shotguns and rifles, kills scores of bluecoats before transferring his evil soul into the body of a lovely telephone repairwoman, who starts behaving like a demon from THE EXORCIST, slaughtering more policemen. The action has been adequately directed by Sam Firstenberg but the story is bereft of suspense or characterizations. Sho Kosugi, the dedicated hero ninja, is on hand (this time with one eye covered by a black patch) to duel with the supernatural force in assorted locales in fights that kung fu you to death. All formula and no interplay can make even raw action dull. Lucinda Dickey does what she can with the role of the possessed woman and Jordan Bennett muddles along as a cop. David Chunt, T. J. Castronova. (VC)

**NINTH CONFIGURATION, THE (1979).** Oddball study in schizophrenia and psychotic behavior by writer-producer-director William Peter Blatty, who adapted his own novel. It was never a box office hit, being a noncommercial look at madness without heroes or easy answers. When several U.S. soldiers break down (including an astronaut who aborts a mission just before take-off), they are gathered in a castle in the Pacific Northwest, and allowed by psychiatrist Stacy Keach to act out fantasies. But there is a secret behind Keach's behavior that wrenches the narrative and puts it into new perspective. Not an easy film to endure, but sincere and literate, and well acted by Jason Miller, Scott Wilson, Robert Loggia, Moses Gunn, Tom Atkins and Neville Brand. Filmed in Hungary. (VC)

**NINTH GUEST, THE (1934).** Odd assortment gathers in a penthouse to hear a recorded voice warn them they're going to die. Who is the "invisible host"? Directed by Roy William Neill. Donald Cook, Genevieve Tobin.

**NITWITS, THE (1935).** Title not only describes Bert Wheeler and Robert Woolsey (a comedy duo of the period) but writers Fred Guiol and Al Boasberg, who dreamed up this satiric mystery thriller in which people tell nothing but the truth when they sit in a particular chair. Directed by George (!?) Stevens. Betty Grable, Evelyn Brent, Hale Hamilton, Fred Keating, Eric Rhodes, Willie Best.

**NO BLADE OF GRASS (1970).** Cornell Wilde distinguished himself as a director with BEACH RED and THE NAKED PREY. In this version of John Christopher's novel, we have a Wilde look at ecological neglect that leads to worldwide famine and anarchy, and a small band that makes its way to a fortress in the wilderness. But, Wilde degrades the worthy message by focusing on gang rape and unsavory motorcycle gang killings in B-movie fashion. What might have been an important post-holocaust film disintegrates into a shootemup action thriller. Nigel Davenport, Jean Wallace (Wilde's wife), Anthony May, Lynn Frederick, George Coulouris, Patrick Holt, John Hamill.

**NO HAUNT FOR A GENTLEMAN (1952).** British supernatural comedy about a long-dead ghost haunting the mother-in-law of the owner of a rural estate is no choice for a cinemaphile. Directed by Leonard Reeve. Sally Newton, Jack McNaughton, Anthony Pendrell, Dorothy Summers.

**NO HOLDS BARRED (1952).** World's greatest weakling, "Sach" Jones (Huntz Hall), possesses incredible physical strength through magic and becomes a top wrestling pro. The rest of the Bowery Boys wrestle with a hopeless script under William Beaudine's drop-kick direction. Leo Gorcey, Marjorie Reynolds, Leonard Penn, David Condon.

**NO. ONE OF THE SECRET SERVICE.** See **MAN FROM SEX, THE.** (Quite a place to hail from!)

JOHN HURT AS WINSTON SMITH (WITH BIG BROTHER WATCHING) IN '1984'

**NO PLACE LIKE HOMICIDE (1962).** Entertaining British horror comedy featuring batty types in the "old dark house" gathered for the reading of a will. There's a series of murders with supernatural overtones. Directed by Pat Jackson. Kenneth Connor, Shirley Eaton, Dennis Price, Donald Pleasence, Michael Gough, Sidney James.

**NO PLACE TO HIDE (1955).** Pellets containing a lethal virus are carried by two boys on the run through the Philippines. David Brian is the sympathetic doctor seeking the youths "before it's too late." Feeble travelogue adventure, with no place to go but down. Josef Shaftel directed Norman Corwin's script. Marsha Hunt is the long-suffering mother. Hugh Corcoran, Celia Flor, Manuel Silos.

**NO SURVIVORS, PLEASE (1963).** Uninspired West German import depicts alien invaders (Orions) taking over Earthlings. Producer Hans Albin co-directed with Peter Berneis, who wrote the script. Maria Perschy, Robert Cunningham. No audience, sorry.

**NOCTURNA (1978).** Low budget quickie, subtitled GRANDDAUGHTER OF DRACULA, opens at Dracula's castle in Transylvania, which has been converted into a hotel where Drac's granddaughter falls for a musician. When she runs away to New York with the rocker, granddad (John Carradine) follows in this poor man's LOVE AT FIRST BITE. Writer-director Harry Tampa plays it strictly for laughs, with Yvonne De Carlo re-creating her role from THE MUNSTERS. Bizarre mixture of rock, sex and vampires featuring stand-up comic Adam Keefe. (VC)

**NOMADS (1985).** Abstract, avant-garde supernatural tale, so different it defies categorization. A nurse (Lesley Anne Down) is bitten by a patient (Pierce Brosnan, TV's Remington Steele) who acts like a raving lunatic. Suddenly she is possessed by images of the man's past, and through psychic flashes learns he is an anthropologist who has just moved into a new home with his wife—a home once frequented by "nomads," evil spirits in human shape who wander the deserts of the world. Cross-cutting between Pierce's persecution at the hands of the nomads (who take on the

modern persona of a punk motorcycle gang) and the images haunting Down, the film unfolds oddly and surrealistically, without resorting to the usual occult cliches. Written-directed by John McTiernan. Very outre indeed. Anna-Maria Montecelli, Adam Ant, Hector Mercado, Mary Woronov (she as the strangest nomad of all). (VC)

**NORLISS TAPES, THE (1973).** Producer-director Dan Curtis teamed with writer William F. Nolan for this TV pilot, which had all the makings for a good series but was passed on. Roy Thinnes is psychic investigator David Norliss, faced with a walking corpse and a demon from Hell. Don Porter, Angie Dickinson, Claude Akins, Michele Carey (in a very sex role), Hurd Hatfield, Stanley Adams.

**NORMING OF JACK 243, THE (1975).** David Selby, a conformist living in a futuristic society, falls in love with a fugitive who forces him to reconsider his pacificism. Politically minded TV-movie directed by Robert Precht. Leslie Charleson. Low and budget and energy—below "norming"-al.

**NORTHSTAR (1985).** Failed TV pilot in which astronaut Greg Evigan is subjected to a force field in space and returns to Earth with superhuman powers and an IQ surpassing Einstein's. Given that, it's nothing more than the usual spy shenanigans. Barely interesting. Deborah Wakeham, Mitchell Ryan, Mason Adams.

**NOSFERATU (1922).** German filmmaker F. W. Murnau changed the names and incidents in Bram Stoker's DRACULA and foisted it on the public as an original story about a bloodsucker living in Bremen in 1838. Stoker's widow recognized the similarities and sued Murnau. All prints were ordered destroyed but a few survived the purge and NOSFERATU took its place among silent vampire classics. There's no doubting the Stoker influence in these chronicles of the nocturnal affairs of Count Orlock (Max Schreck), but the film warrants attention as an historical conversation piece. Alexander Granach. (VC)

**NOSFERATU—THE VAMPIRE (1979).** Decidedly offbeat remake of F. W. Murnau's 1922 pirated version of DRACULA, written-produced-directed by Germany's Werner Herzog. But the pacing is so leisurely, the film plods along when it should leap out at you. Yet, the heavy atmosphere and unnerving make-up of Klaus Kinski in the title role gives this lengthy West Germany production (124 minutes) a compelling attraction-repulsion. Isabelle Adjani.

**NOT OF THIS EARTH (1956).** Paul Birch, alien from Davana, generates Death Rays whenever he removes his dark glasses and concentrates his gleaming, blank orbs. He's on Earth to send specimens of mankind back to his home planet, and he's aided in his vampiric mission (they need blood, you see) by a bat monster. Produced-directed by Roger Corman, written by Charles Griffith and Mark Hanna. Beverly Garland, Jonathan Haze, Dick Miller.

**NOTHING BUT THE NIGHT (1972).** Christopher Lee formed his own company, Charlemagne, to make this adaptation of John Blackburn's CHILDREN OF THE NIGHT. In Brian Hoyles' treatment, children are injected with serum that contains memory genes of the dead; these memories are transferred to the young who become terrifying mur-

**VIC MORROW IN HIS NEXT-TO-LAST ROLE IN '1990: THE BRONX WARRIORS'**

**CREATURE FEATURES MOVIE GUIDE**

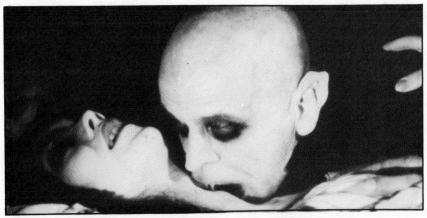

**KLAUS KINSKI GIVES ISABELLE ADJANI A PAIN IN THE NECK
IN 'NOSFERATU—THE VAMPIRE'**

derers. Unfortunately, the atmosphere and brooding horror of the novel never reached the screen under Peter Sasdy's direction. Peter Cushing, Diana Dors, Christopher Lee, Georgia Brown, Keith Barron, Duncan Lamont.

**NOTHING LASTS FOREVER (1984).** Comedy-love story set sometime in the near future when artist Zach Galligan flunks a test and ends up directing traffic in the Holland Tunnel under boss Dan Aykroyd. Somehow Galligan, after a love affair with Apollonia van Ravenstein, goes to the moon on a Lunarcruiser bossed by travel guide Bill Murray. First feature of producer Lorne Michaels and writer-director Tom Schiller. Filmed in black and white.

**NOW YOU SEE HIM, NOW YOU DON'T (1972).** Comedy-farce in the Disney series starring Kurt Russell as the brainiest boy in Chemistry 1A who is always creating a new formula. This time it's a spray that brings about invisibility—a discovery crook Cesar Romero plans to steal. The premise is belabored but the effects during the crazy car chases are amusing. Directed by Robert Butler. Joe Flynn, Joyce Menges, Jim Backus, William Windom. (VC)

**NUCLEAR CONSPIRACY, THE (1986).** Boring but boring British movie in which a young woman finds her husband missing and her daughter kidnapped, and goes on their trail with a free-wheeling photojournalist who'll do anything to get a picture. It's all talk and boring detective work as they follow the trail to a cover-up. Clumsy and lacking action. Written-produced-directed by Rainer Erler. Birgit Doll, Albert Fortell, Mark Lee, Kitty Myers, Frank Wilson.

**NUDE BOMB, THE (1980).** Feature version of TV's GET SMART spy spoof about Control Agent 86, Maxwell Smart, who fights the forces of CHAOS in the most delightfully inept style. As 86, Don Adams is no different from his TV days as he staunchly fights for the freedom, liberty and clothing of all by preventing a plot that would strip us bare-ass nude. Clive Donner directs this compendium of spy cliches and gags (by Arne Sutton, Bill Dana and Leonard B. Stern) with monumental indifference. Bomb indeed. Sylvia Kristel, Rhonda Fleming, Dana Elcar, Pamela Hensley. (VC)

**NUKE 'EM HIGH (1986).** A loose sequel to TOXIC AVENGER, for it is set in the same town: Tromaville, the "nuclear waste capital of the world." Once again there's a spillage (this time from the Tromaville Nuclear Facility) which gets into the drinking water at the local high school and causes the teenagers to go berserk, killing each other, regurgitating ALIEN-like monsters and behaving in the farcical

style for which producers Lloyd Kaufman and Michael Herz are by now famous. It took two directors to handle it (Samuel Weil and Richard W. Haines) but it's still out of control—a wild parody of catastrophe movies in need of a few subtle touches, or some degree of cleverness. Hell, nuke the movie. Janelle Brady, Gilbert Brenton. (VC)

**NURSE SHARI.** See **BEYOND THE LIVING.**

**NURSE WILL MAKE IT BETTER.** See **DEVIL'S WEB, THE.** (Open wide and say "Arrgghh!")

**NURSE'S SECRET (1941).** Based on a Mary Roberts Rinehart character, Nurse Adams, who solves mysteries in old dark houses with her tongue firmly entrenched in her cheek. In this one she's out to find a killer who has taken arsenic out of old lace and put it into hypo needles. Directed by Noel M. Smith. Faye Emerson, Lee Patrick, Regis Toomey, Julie Bishop, Charles Trowbridge.

**NUTTY PROFESSOR, THE (1963).** Even those who normally eschew Jerry Lewis comedies may find this uncommonly fulfilling in exploring the Jekyll/Hyde theme. Lewis portrays clumsy, shy Professor Julius F. Kelp, a myopic, marmot-toothed scientist who discovers a bubbling concoction that turns him into an aggressive alter ego, Buddy Love. Lewis also directed and co-wrote the clever script with Bill Richmond. Stella Stevens, Del Moore, Kathleen Freeman, Howard Morris, Buddy Lester. (VC)

**NYLON NOOSE, THE (1963).** German nonsense about a daffy doctor trying to mummify bodies and some stockholders gathered in the obligatory weird mansion. The stockholders are strangled, one by one, with a nylon noose. You'll get all choked up too. Directed by Rudolf Zehetgruber. Richard Goodman, Laya Raki.

**NYOKA AND THE LOST SECRETS OF HIPPOCRATES.** See **NYOKA AND THE TIGERMEN.**

**NYOKA AND THE TIGERMEN (1942).** Re-edited version of Republic's 15-chapter serial, PERILS OF NYOKA, starring Kay Aldridge as the comic book jungle girl searching for her missing father and the Tablets of Hippocrates, which are said to record long-lost secrets of the ancient Greeks, and which only she can decipher. An evil Arab, Vultura, is also after the Tablets and it's one cliffhanger after another, including an encounter with a giant gorilla, Satan. Watch and have fun. Directed by serial whiz William Witney. Clayton Moore, Tris Coffin, Lorna Gray, William Benedict, Charles Middleton, Robert Strange. (VC)

---

*"Was she human? Or was she a beautiful temptress from the sea, intent upon loving, consuming and killing?"—Advertisement for **NIGHT TIDE.***

**CREATURE FEATURES MOVIE GUIDE**

*"Good morning! You are one day closer to the end of the world!"—Teaser line for **THE OMEN.***

**087 MISSION APOCALYPSE (1966).** Doomsday device falls into evil hands; a superagent is assigned to save the world from destruction. Bland Bond bonbon. Apocalypse now for writer-director James Reed. Arthur Hansel, Pamela Tudor, Harold Bradley, Moa Thai.

**O.K. CONNERY. See OPERATION KID BROTHER.**

**O.K., NERO (1954).** When two sailors (Carlo Campanini, Walter Chiari) are transported through time to Nero's Rome, they decide gladiatorial duels, orgies and wild chariot rides aren't sporting enough and introduce football, billiards and jitterbugging to the toga crowd. Which leads the Emperor to exclaim: "Throw the lions to the comics." Lowbrow Italian parody of continuous yocks, directed by Mario Soldati. Silvana Pampanini, Jackie Frost.

**OSS 117—DOUBLE AGENT (1968).** French-Italian spy antics with John Gavin as an agent wiping out assassins in the Mideast. Directed by Andre Hunebelle. Margaret Lee, Curt Jurgens, Luciana Paluzzi.

**OSS 117—MISSION FOR A KILLER (1966).** Part of a French-Italian series produced on scenic European and South American locations with attractive men and women. The superspy is played by Frederick Stafford and concerns his search for a rare Indian drug (from Amazon jungle flowers) being used by a powermad society of conquerers. Directed by Andre Hunebelle. Mylene Demongeot.

**OSS 117 TAKES A VACATION (1969).** Third-rate French-Brazilian James Bond imitator who tangles with supervillains, falls into the arms of beautiful women and uses the latest in weaponry. Directed by Pierre Kalfon. Luc Merenda, Elsa Martinelli, Edwige Feuillere, Genevieve Grad.

**O LUCKY MAN (1973).** Britain is now a fascist state of corrupt corporations, forcing coffee salesman Malcolm McDowell to endure unscrupulous government officials and murdering execs. As usual, the English satirize themselves with devastation. Directed by Lindsay Johnson. Arthur Lowe, Ralph Richardson, Rachel Roberts. (VC)

**OASIS OF THE ZOMBIES (1981).** Band of adventurers searching for Rommel's treasure in North Africa wishes it had stayed on firmer terra when the men face a legion of Nazi dead which rises to stalk them. Manuel Gelin, France Jordon,

Jeff Montgomery.

**OBEAH (1935).** A voodoo spell is placed on a jungle explorer by a high priestess, whose chanting mumbo jumbo can be understood only by monkeys. Phillips H. Lord, who went on to produce radio's GANG BUSTERS, tops the cast. Written-directed by the redundant F. Herrick Herrick.

**OBLONG BOX, THE (1969).** "Far worse things are known to mankind," says Vincent Price, probably referring to other American-International pics exploiting Edgar Allan Poe titles. Pretty gory stuff, with depravity and bawdiness thrown in by producer-director Gordon Hessler. Price has a brother who's been disfigured by an African witch doctor and buried alive, only someone dug him up and now he's on a rampage of murder and lust. Alastair Williamson, Christopher Lee, Sally Geeson, Rupert Davies.

**OBSESSION (1976).** Brian De Palma's films reflect a love for Hitchcock plots, and this pays particular homage to VERTIGO. Cliff Robertson, grieving over the loss of his wife, is drawn into an affair with a woman who bears a startling resemblance to his spouse. Paul Schrader's script becomes too artsy-craftsy but Vilmos Zsigmond's cinematography heightens suspense and ambience. In Hitchcock tradition, De Palma picked Bernard Herrmann to write the score. Genevieve Bujold, John Lithgow, Sylvia Williams, Wanda Blackman, Sylvia Kuumba Williams. (VC)

**OCTAMAN (1971).** Embarrassing man-in-a-rubber-suit monster movie, the worst of its kind. The blame goes to writer-director Harry Essex, who steals elements from his own script for CREATURE FROM THE BLACK LAGOON. Unfortunately, as a director Essex knows nothing about building suspense or how to photograph a menacing creature effectively. It must have been depressing for Kerwin Mathews and Pier Angeli to endure the humiliation of appearing in shots with the phony-looking monster (in fact, Angeli committed suicide during production). Octaman is supposed to be a octopus mutation created by contaminated waters. This U.S.-Mexican production drowns in its own bubbles. Jeff Morrow, Harry Guardini. (VC)

**OCTOPUSSY (1983).** The 13th James Bond adventure and sixth with Roger Moore as the indefatigable British agent, 007. There are the usual superweapons and the action sequences are among the liveliest for the series, but Moore was getting too old for the part. His adversary is Afghan prince Kamal Khan (Louis Jourdan), who operates a palace in India with his henchman Gobinda (Kabir Bedi). Kamal plots with a power-hungry Russian general (Steven Berkoff) to explode an atomic bomb in Germany and bring chaos to N.A.T.O. Titular character is an octopus-loving dragon lady heading an all-women's smuggling ring, but she is woodenly portrayed by Maud Adams. The derring-do, of course, is absurd yet frequently exciting, thanks to high production standards set by producer Albert Broccoli and clever editing by John Grover. Especially fun is a fight aboard a speeding train and Bond clinging to the fuselage of a plane in flight. The whole thing passes as tongue-in-cheek escapism. Directed by John Glen, who helmed FOR YOUR EYES ONLY. Script by George MacDonald Fraser, Richard Maubaum and Michael G. Wilson. Music by John Barry. Lois Maxwell, Kristina Wayborn. (VC)

**OF GODS AND THE UNDEAD (1969).** Brazilian horror item centers on creatures of the undead who assume human shape to carry out ghastly murders. Ungodly dead in all respects. Directed-written by Ruy Guerra.

**OF UNKNOWN ORIGIN (1983).** Strangely compelling war of cunning and nerves erupts in a Manhattan apartment when advertising exec Peter Weller duels with an intelligent mutant rat. Hence, the film becomes a metaphor for man's never-ending war against vermin, and the history of how rats have plagued mankind is graphically described and depicted in this adaptation of "The Visitor" by Chauncey G. Parker III. Director George P. Cosmatos captures a surreal element as Weller becomes obsessed with the challenge and sinks into depression and insanity. In fact, it is this psychological exploration that raises this above other films about killer rodents. Brian Taggert's script also insightfully deals with Weller's professional life, giving the film a rich subtext. Supporting cast is good (Jennifer Dale, Shannon Tweed, Lawrence Dale) but ultimately the rat and Weller's obsession dominate the film—each displaying aggressive madness. Louis Del Grande, Kenneth Welsh. (VC)

**OH, BOY! (1938).** "Oh, brother!" is a more apt way to describe this archaic British comedy about a weak-willed scientist (Albert Burdon) who concocts a magical formula that turns him into a strongman. Oh, well! Directed by Albert De Courville. Mary Lawson, Bernard Nedell.

**OH, GOD! (1977).** Thought-provoking allegorical in which a supermarket manager (John Denver) is approached by the Almighty (George Burns) and asked to tell the human race to straighten out its problems. Denver is judged part of the Lunatic Fringe but finds notoriety on Dinah Shore's TV show. This leads to a courtroom hearing, where Burns appears to prove God's existence. The laughs are gentle, the message obvious, the acting restrained. Director Carl Reiner makes it work without piousness. Only atheists and agnostics will be offended. Ralph Bellamy, Donald Pleasence, Teri Garr, William Daniels, Barnard Hughes, Paul Sorvino, Barry Sullivan, George Furth. (VC)

**OH, GOD! BOOK TWO (1980).** In the beginning there was OH, GOD! and lo, it came to pass there was a sequel directed by Gilbert Cates, and audiences looked at it and said it was fair to middling. And God, who does resembleth George Burns with a cigar, said, "I shall choose a child to carry My Word to the people," and the child was Louanne. And she was good. Worldly wickedness was challenged by universal good will, and Box Office Keepers did say, "Receipts, thou art beautiful." And Suzanne Pleshette, David Birney, Howard Duff, Wilfrid Hyde-White, Conrad Janis and Hans Conried were hence employed. (VC)

**OH, GOD! YOU DEVIL (1984).** Third film in the series with George Burns (cigar and all) as The Lord is a whimsical, entertaining allegory about good vs evil, decency vs greed and other modern themes. A podunk musician (Ted Wass) unwittingly signs a pact with The Devil (also Burns) to be metamorphosized into rock star Billy Wayne (Robert Desiderio), only Billy realizes success isn't so great and just wants his wife back. He calls on God for help, and at a poker table in Las Vegas, God and Satan determine the fate of all. Lowkey and amusing with Paul Bogart directing unobtrusively to retain the gentleness of this modern fable. Eugene Roche is especially good as Wayne's record agent. Roxanne Hart, Eugene Roche, Ron Silver. (VC)

**OH HEAVENLY DOG (1980).** Joe Camp, creator of BENJI, puts the pooch to a new use in directing this fantasy-comedy in which private eye Chevy Chase, while investigating a murder, is stabbed to death and winds up in Heaven. He's ordered to return to Earth to solve his own homicide but the only body available is that of a dog. So he goes down on all fours, wags his tail and tracks Omar Sharif and other suspects through rainy London streets. Inoffensive fun, with

**ROGER MOORE BEING PROTECTED BY MEMBERS OF THE PALACE GUARD IN 'OCTOPUSSY'**

several plot surprises and a good performance by Benji. Jane Seymour, Robert Morley, Donnelly Rhodes, Alan Sues. (VC)

**OH, THOSE MOST SECRET AGENTS (1966).** Oh, those most dumb Italians turn out another insipid spy spoof about another idiotic superspy chasing another insidious mastermind after another powerful weapon in another dumb plot to take over the same old silly world. Directed by Lucio Fulci, who became a sleazy horror director. Franco Franchi.

**OH! WHAT A LOVELY WAR (1969).** British comedy patterned after a music hall entertainment, which struggles to keep its balance as director Richard Attenborough walks precariously between fantasy and reality in this overstated satire of World War I and the stupidity of its generals. A seaside resort advertises "World War One . . . Songs, Battles and a Few Jokes." The Len Deighton script, based on a play, shifts between the resort and battlefield, but there are no trenches—only fields of poppies and scoreboards of casualty figures. Laurence Olivier, Ralph Richardson, Jack Hawkins, the Redgraves, Maggie Smith, Dirk Bogarde and any other leading British actor you can think of appears. Ends up in a cinematic no-man's-land.

**O'HARA'S WIFE (1982).** Standard TOPPER-style supernatural comedy in which Ed Asner, undergoing the grief of his wife's death in a car accident, discovers her spirit has returned to his household. But only he can see her spectral form. So you have jokes with Asner talking to air, misunderstandings, etc. Predictable TV-movie, directed by William Bartman, with Mariette Hartley doing what she can with the thankless wife role. Tom Bosley, Perry Lang, Ray Walston, Jodie Foster, Nehemiah Persoff, Richard Schaal.

**OLD DARK HOUSE, THE (1932).** Following FRANKENSTEIN, director James Whale made this version of J. B. Priestley's BENIGHTED with relish, creating a subgenre terror-satire genre that persisted for years. A violent thunderstorm (what other kind are there in horror films?) forces travelers to spend the night in a weird mansion inhabited by butler Boris Karloff, a 102-year-old lunatic, a fire-loving brother and a God-fearing sister, all suffering from assorted psychoses, neuroses and halitoses. Tons of fun in an atmosphere of musky decay. Ernest Thesiger, Charles Laughton, Raymond Massey, Melvyn Douglas.

**BORIS KARLOFF IN 'THE OLD DARK HOUSE'**

**OLD DARK HOUSE, THE (1963).** Producer-director William Castle's remake of Whale's 1932 mystery-comedy is a remarkable failure, capturing none of the decaying atmosphere and droll comedy. The house is too new and airy to be a Gothic and the plot has been updated to feature Tom Poston as a car salesman who goes to the old place to sell a car and takes refuge with oddball travelers during a storm. Robert Morley, Janette Scott, Mervyn Jones.

**OLD DRAC.** See **OLD DRACULA.** (It sucks?)

**OLD DRACULA (1975).** Producer John H. Wiener would have us believe his film is a comedy-horror classic destined to take its place beside YOUNG FRANKENSTEIN. Wiener would have us believe David Niven brings new exciting interpretations to the vampire count, placing him in the Lugosi-Lee category. Wiener would have us believe a faulty blood transfusion turning a long-sleeping princess into a black vampire in the form of Teresa Graves is the unique premise for a funny, invigorating, inspirational full-length film, directed by Clive Donner. Above all else, Wiener would have us believe he is a film producer. Ha!

**OLD LEGENDS NEVER DIE (1966).** Two re-edited episodes of Irwin Allen's TIME TUNNEL series. James Darren and Robert Colbert travel back to King Arthur's day to tangle with Merlin the Magician, then find themselves in Sherwood Forest helping Robin Hood and his Merry Men sign the Magna Carta. See **TIME TUNNEL, THE.**

**OLD MOTHER RILEY MEETS THE VAMPIRE.** See **MY SON, THE VAMPIRE.** (Young Dracula?)

**OLD MOTHER RILEY'S GHOSTS (1941).** Arthur Lucan in drag really is a drag as a charwoman who breaks up a plot to steal a secret invention from a designer living in an alleged haunted house. Part of the Mother Riley series the British used to chortle over. Produced-directed by John Baxter. Kitty McShane (Lucan's wife) co-stars with John Stuart, A. Bromley Davenport and Dennis Wyndham.

**OLIVIA.** See **TASTE OF SIN, A.**

**OMEGA MAN, THE (1971).** Richard Matheson's I AM LEGEND was first adapted as LAST MAN ON EARTH, a panned Italian cheapie that was at least faithful to the book, which blended mythical vampirism with science-fiction. This Charlton Heston vehicle is less faithful. The year is 1975 and Heston would appear to be the sole survivor of a plague. Gone are the vampires of I AM LEGEND, gone is the one-man battle to survive against blood-drinking zombies. A new plotline has Anthony Zerbe heading religious mutants wishing to kill Heston because he represents the knowledge that poisoned mankind. Then comes a real clunker: Heston finds other untainted survivors and has a miscegenational romance with Rosalind Cash. At that point it is folly to compare. Director Boris Sagal has made a sow's ear out of a silk purse. (VC)

**OMEGANS, THE (1969).** Radioactive Malaysian river has strange properties, leading natives to believe it is "cursed." A famous painter discovers his wife and guide are lovers and decides to use the water to dispose of them. Weird thriller (a U.S.-Philippine production) features Keith Larsen and Ingrid Pitt, she of Hammer vampire-lesbian films. Directed by W. Lee Wilder. Bruno Punzalan.

**OMEN, THE (1976).** Screenwriter David Seltzer borrowed a prophecy from the Book of Revelation, which foredooms the coming of Armageddon, and fashioned the premise for a horror trilogy, of which this is the first. It's a supernatural terror tale of sensational proportions: The Antichrist child, the son of Satan, is reborn and walks among us, destined to rise up through politics and turn "man against his brother . . . till man exists no more." A whopper of a tale—from Jerry Goldsmith's suspenseful score to Gil Taylor's low-key lighting to John Richardson's bloody good effects to Richard Donner's taut direction. This features several grisly, imaginative murders as Gregory Peck sets out with photographer David Warner to prove the Antichrist exists. There's a ghastly beheading, a

**NAUGHTY NAUGHTY: HARVEY STEPHENS AS THE MEAN LITTLE KID IN 'THE OMEN'**

hanging, an attack by the Hounds of Hell and other demonic horrors. While the sequels (DAMIEN: OMEN II and THE FINAL CONFLICT) never fully lived up to the premise, this carries it all too well. Producer Harvey Bernhard has made a classic. A sense of desolate hopelessness prevails as evil wins time and again. Leo McKern, Lee Remick, Billie Whitelaw, Harvey Stephens, Martin Benson. (VC)

**OMICRON (1963).** Extraterrestrial who has never seen Italian science-fiction movies thinks he has a brilliant idea: He'll invade the body of an Earthling and take over our planet. These poor dumb beings from beyond our galaxy . . . will they never learn? Written-directed by Ugo Gregoretti. Renato Salvatori., Rosemary Dexter, Mara Carisi.

**OMOO OMOO THE SHARK GOD (1949).** Oboy, oboy, Herman Melville would perform aquatic somersaults if he knew what U.S. producers did to his novel about the South Seas and the curse that hangs over valuable pearls. Better confined to the Deep Six. Directed by Leon Leonard. Ron Randell, Devera Burton, Trevor Bardette, Pedro DeCordoba.

**ON A CLEAR DAY YOU CAN SEE FOREVER (1970).** Despite high-class names (director Vincent Minnelli, cinematographer Harry Stradling, lyricist Alan Jay Lerner, actress Barbra Streisand, actor Yves Montand), this was a box office disaster. Streisand plays a Bridey Murphy type who, through regression brought on by her psychiatrist, discovers she lived a previous existence in England in the 1840s. Full of large-scale production numbers, but the film never personally involves the viewer. Adapted by Alan Jay Lerner from his play. Bob Newhart, Jack Nicholson. (VC)

**ON BORROWED TIME (1939).** Based on the Paul Osborne-Lawrence Watkin Broadway play in which Mr. Brink (Sir Cedric Hardwicke) is in reality Mr. Death, fresh from Hell to claim wheelchair-bound Lionel Barrymore. Death is tricked into climbing an apple tree and trapped by Gramp's magical powers. Occasionally sentimental fable, well acted. Directed by Hal Bucquet. Beulah Bondi, Una Merkel, Henry Travers, Ian Wolfe, Truman Bradley, Grant Mitchell.

**ON HER MAJESTY'S SECRET SERVICE (1969).** George Lazenby replaces Sean Connery in this, the sixth in the James Bond series. Lazenby has neither the diction nor the finesse of Connery, nor does he even appear comfortable in the arms of Diana Rigg and other beauties. To take up the slack, director Peter Hunt works extra-hard with action. Villain Ernst Stavros Blofeld (Telly Savalas) is masterminding a takeover of the world using allergies hidden in women's cosmetics that will result in sterility. Richard Maibaum adapted the Fleming novel, providing a love affair between Bond and Diana Rigg (daughter of an international bad guy) that is easily the best aspect of this spy adventure. Julie Ege, Bessie Love, Catherina Von Schell. (VC)

**ON THE BEACH (1959).** Stanley Kramer's blatant plea for peace is a classy version of Nevil Shute's popular novel in which mankind has dropped the Bomb and Australia is the only continent yet to be touched by a radioactive cloud. Survivors gather Down Under to wait for death. The story pivots on the adventures of a submarine commander (Gregory Peck), his affair with Ava Gardner and their subsequent acceptance, and rejection, of doom. Kramer's direction emphasizes the gloom of inexorable death. "Waltzing Matilda" is used to haunting effect. Anthony Perkins, Fred Astaire, Donna Anderson, Guy Doleman. (VC)

**ON THE COMET (1970).** Czechoslovakian adventure is enchanting material from writer-director Karel Zeman, who borrowed from a Jules Verne book. When a comet collides with Earth in 1888, it rips away a hunk of North Africa containing a French military outpost; this piece roars off through space. The survivors, besides arguing about national differences, face prehistoric monsters, sea serpents and a colossal fly through stop-motion animation. Designed for families. Emil Horvath, Magda Vasarykova. (VC)

**ONCE BEFORE I DIE (1968).** Inexplicable film produced-directed by John Derek in the Philippines as a vehicle for his then-wife Ursula Andress. What emerges is an anomaly of a film, or to be less polite, a muddled mess. U.S. soldiers escort Andress through the jungles shortly after Pearl Harbor, with Andress appearing to be an "Angel of Death"—her image is often freeze-framed or superimposed over scenes

TV title for the British-made **FRIGHTMARE II.**

**ONCE UPON A MIDNIGHT SCARY (1979).** Anthology TV-film in which Vincent Price introduces children's ghost stories. "The Ghost Belonged to Me" is about a boy who sees a spectre in the family barn, warning him of a disaster. Washington Irving's "Legend of Sleepy Hollow" is played for laughs, emphasizing silliness rather than the tale's supernatural elements. Longest of the pieces is "The House With a Clock in Its Walls," in which a youth discovers his uncle is a wizard. Designed to get children to rush to the library and get books to read. Excellent idea. Alexandra Johnson, Pat Peterson, Jessica Lynn Pennington, Pamela Brown. (VC)

**ONCE UPON A SPY (1980).** Jimmy Sangster, that old Hammer faithful, penned this TV-movie clone of James Bond with Christopher Lee as wheelchair-bound villain Marcus Valorium, who has perfected a "molecular condensor beam" capable of shrinking objects. First he steals the fabulous X-2 computer (as big as a barn) by shrinking it, then he shrinks an aircraft carrier, then he plans to bounce his beam off the

**JIM CARREY CONSIDERS LAUREN HUTTON'S CHARMS IN 'ONCE BITTEN'**

of war and destruction. And the men she kisses die in battle soon after. A baffling experience, with the only memorable acting by Richard Jaeckel as a war-crazed dogface with a bald head. Derek appears in a brief role, assisted by Ron Ely and Rod Lauren.

**ONCE BITTEN (1985).** Teenage sex comedy with supernatural overtones, not as dumb as some but still kind of dumb when you think about it. Lauren Hutton is "The Countess," a 400-year-old vampiress living in an L.A. mansion. She needs three fixes from a male virgin very fast or she'll show her years, so she picks high schooler Jim Carrey, who is also frustrated because his girl (Karen Kopins) won't dish out. The women fight for Hutton's attention while Hutton is dumbfounded. There's some funny chase stuff through the Countess' mansion with her manservant, a gay vampire (Cleavon Little), leading the monster followers. Some of the blood gags work, some don't. Finally fizzles under Howard Storm's direction. They all deserve a transfusion for trying, anyway. (VC)

**ONCE UPON A FRIGHTMARE.** Variant videocassette and

mirror of a satellite and destroy everything. Agent K-12 (Mary Louise Weller, a real looker) gets hooked up with nerdish computer guy Ted Danson who proves durable when the tough get going. Director Ivan Nagy plays this for what it is, comic book fodder. John Cacavas' music (almost wall to wall) emulates Bond themes and is the best thing in the picture. Very glitzy and glittery with unbelievable derring-do. Eleanor Parker is good as a feisty assignment chief. Leonard Stone. Produced by Jay Daniel, who went on to co-produce TV's "Moonlighting."

**ONCE UPON A TIME (1944).** Funny Hollywood fantasy about a Broadway impresario down on his luck—until he discovers a youngster carrying a matchbox, inside which a caterpillar dances to the tune of "Yes Sir, That's My Baby." Without getting preachy or heavy-handed, this adaptation of Norman Corwin's radio play "My Client Curly" makes comments on human nature and the flightiness of success—a pun you will better understand when you see this comedy directed by Alexander Hall. Cary Grant, Janet Blair, James Gleason, William Demarest, Art Baker, John Abbott.

**ONE BODY TOO MANY (1944).** Comedy takeoff on THE OLD DARK HOUSE, full of the usual fright cliches: sinister figure lurking in a mansion, thunder and lightning, hidden passageways and secret panels. Bela Lugosi portrays the butler who greets an insurance investigator who has come to protect a millionaire. Lugosi keeps trying to serve poisoned coffee to guests, just one of many zany delights. Directed by Frank McDonald. Jack Haley, Lyle Talbot.

**ONE DARK NIGHT (1982).** Writer-director Thomas McLoughlin borrows from the bobbing corpses of POLTERGEIST as 154 corpses (designed by Tom Burman) are brought to life and shamble through the shadowy corridors of a mausoleum, literally smothering the panicked characters to death. But instead of being macabre, the sequence has the effect of a funhouse of horrors, and shock value is minimized. On the plus side is an underlying premise of telekinesis. Karl Raymar has developed the power to rob young girls of their bioenergy and becomes a psychic vampire. His corpse is placed in the mausoleum, and then a teen-age sorority forces a plebe to spend the night there. Juvenile scare tactics begin. Despite its cloying failures, it's an interesting experiment. Adam West, Robin Evans, Melissa Newman, Meg Tilly, Leslie Spreights. All we can say is: Rest in pieces. (VC)

**ONE DEADLY OWNER (1974).** Mildly compelling supernatural tale about a Rolls Royce purchased by Donna Mills, a beautiful model who doesn't understand her compulsion for the car. Gradually she realizes its previous owner, wife of a business tycoon, is (re)possessing the car in an effort to tell Mills how she died. No special effects or action sequences to speak of, so Brian Clemens' teleplay depends on characterization. In this respect he is aided by Mills, by her boyfriend Jeremy Brett and by Laurence Payne and Robert Morris. Easily forgettable. Ian Fordyce directed with "soap opera" production values. (VC)

**ONE FRIGHTENED NIGHT (1935).** Comedy-mystery in the style of THE CAT AND THE CANARY in which heirs gather to hear the reading of the will. Dusty fun. Directed by Christy Cabanne. Charles Grapewin, Regis Toomey, Wallace Ford, Hedda Hopper, Mary Carlisle, Arthur Hohl.

**ONE HUNDRED CRIES OF TERROR (1965).** . . . but only two tales of gothic horror—the first involving a husband and a secret lover who plot to murder the wife; the second about a woman buried alive in a mausoleum. Mexican film directed by Ramon Obon. Adriana Welter.

**ONE MAGIC CHRISTMAS (1985).** Harry Dean Stanton as an angel named Gideon? That's only one of many oddities in this dark parable (from Walt Disney yet!) in which he is assigned (by God?) to convince a certain mother the values of the yuletide season. That mother, Mary Steenburgen, has lost her seasonal spirit because (1) hubby has just been shot by a bank robber, (2) her kidnapped children have drowned in a frozen river and (3) she's been fired from her supermarket job. To prove his point, Stanton (who looks more like a sinister character than an angel) sends Mary's daughter to the North Pole to meet Santa. Ultimately a sentimental tearjerker that doesn't have the strength of its schmaltz to pull it off. Gary Basaraba, Elizabeth Harnois, Arthur Hill (playing a white-haired grandfather), Wayne Robson. Directed by Phillip Borsos. (VC)

**ONE MILLION B.C. (1940).** Hal Roach production that established man vs. dinosaur trends which makes for whopping good adventure. Call it a tribute to the Stone Age, for it's filled with visual thrills, not the least of which is Carole Landis in antelope pelt. The Rock People are a crude, meat-eating tribe lorded over by grunting Tomack (Lon Chaney Jr.), who kicks Victor Mature out into the cold. Jutting-jawed Mature goes to live with the Shell People, a less boorish tribe that savors vegetables and fish and practices genteel manners. Eventually the tribes become gregarious, but not before battles with brontosauri, trachodons and other beasts. Then there's a grand climactic volcanic eruption with the ground breaking away. A classic, directed by Roach, Roach Jr. and D. W. Griffith. (VC)

**ONE MILLION YEARS B.C. (1967).** Hammer's remake of Hal Roach's 1940 miniclassic, with Raquel Welch (in fetching

**HARRY DEAN STANTON:
'ONE MAGIC CHRISTMAS'**

animal skins) as the girl of the Shell People who meets a guy of the Rock Tribe (John Richardson). Michael Carreras wrote-produced for Hammer, with Don Chaffey directing. A must-see for the effects work of Ray Harryhausen, combining stop motion animation and real lizards shot in gigantic closeups. Like its predecessor, this has no historic accuracy but it's grand entertainment. Martine Beswick.

**ONE NIGHT STAND (1984).** On the evening nuclear war breaks out in Europe and the U.S., four teens in a Sydney apartment listen to news on their transistor while playing poker, chattering and coming to a realization that dawn will bring a new world. This unusual Australian film, which faces important issues without resorting to Armageddon cliches, was written-directed by John Duigan. Tyler Coppin, Cassandra Delaney, Jay Hackett. (VC)

**ONE OF OUR DINOSAURS IS MISSING (1975).** Amusing Disney fantasy- comedy spoofs British behavior (nannies, stiff upper lip, that sort of thing, old chap) and monster films. Lotus X is a Chinese secret hidden in the tibia of a museum dinosaur, which restores life into the tired bones of the ancient creature. Fighting over possession of Lotus X are Peter Ustinov (Hnup Wan, of Chinese Intelligence) and Helen Hayes (nanny and backbone of the Empire). Made in England with Robert Stevenson directing. (VC)

**ONE OF OUR SPIES IS MISSING (1966).** Episodes of THE MAN FROM U.N.C.L.E. series, re-edited into a feature. Henry Slesar's storyline is average TV spy fare with Robert Vaughn and David McCallum as supercool superspies with superwry superwits. Maurice Evans, Vera Miles, Yvonne Craig, Dolores Faith, Ann Elder and James (STAR TREK) Doohan are involved with a serum that restores life. Leo G. Carroll appears as Mr. Waverly, assignment chief. Darrell Hallenbeck directed.

**ONE SPY TOO MANY (1966).** More re-edited MAN FROM U.N.C.L.E. footage with Rip Torn as would-be conquerer of the world, Alexander the Greater, out to steal a new Biological Warfare Gas that makes unwilling people say "I will." Napoleon Solo (Robert Vaughn) and Illya Kuryakin (David McCallum) want the "I will" gas and are surrounded by beautiful women who keep taking their clothes off. It's enough to make you cry "Uncle." Directed by Joseph Sargent. Dorothy Provine, Yvonne Craig, Leo G. Carroll.

**1001 ARABIAN NIGHTS (1959).** Full-length Near-Sighted

**'ONIBABA': SURREAL HORROR IN A JAPANESE VEIN OF LUST AND BLOOD**

Magoo cartoon will disappoint fans eager for the satire of the Magoo short subjects, but children will be diverted by a story in which Magoo, uncle of Aladdin, is hopelessly in love with a princess. Gags are unnecessarily repeated and the film looks padded, as though the idea fizzled at midpoint. The producers might have been as near-sighted as Magoo. Voices by Jim Backus, Kathryn Grant, Hans Conried, Dwayne Hickman, Herschel Bernardi. (VC)

**ONE THOUSAND YEARS FROM NOW.** See **CAPTIVE WOMEN.** (But no captive audience . . .)

**ONE TOUCH OF VENUS (1948).** Light comedy touch keeps this from becoming hopelessly coy when a department store floorwalker (Robert Walker) kisses a marble statue of the Venus de Milo, granting it life in the form of gorgeous Ava Gardner. Adapted by Harry Kurnitz and Frank Tashlin from the play that originally starred Mary Martin with book by S. J. Perelman and Ogden Nash; music by Kurt Weill. Directed by William A. Seiter. Dick Haymes, Eve Arden, Tom Conway, Arthur O'Connell. (VC)

**ONE WISH TOO MANY (1956).** British comedy for the juvenile crowd: Youth discovers glass marble that grants his every wish. Directed by John Durst. Anthony Richmond, John Pike, Terry Cooke, Rosalind Gourgey.

**ONIBABA (1965).** Macabre, exquisitely photographed Japanese allegory horror tale (based on an ancient legend) in which two women survive in a remote marshland during the 16th Century by preying on stragglers and soldiers. This is artistically grisly stuff as the murderesses, always surrounded by a field of reeds bending in the wind, lure unsuspecting males into live-deathtraps. When the younger woman falls for a samurai, the older realizes the duo act might be doomed so she preys on the girl's fears of the supernatural. The trick involves a hideous mask, and how it is (mis)used will unsettle you. Its stark images are very memorable. Directed by Kaneto Shindo. Nobuko Otowa.

**ONLY WAY OUT IS DEAD, THE.** See **MAN WHO WANTED TO LIVE FOREVER, THE.**

**OPERATION ABDUCTION (1957).** French Secret Service sends its best agent to protect an inventor designing a new interplanetary rocket fuel. Operation ordinary. Frank Villard, Daniel Goedet.

**OPERATION ATLANTIS (1962).** More Bond-ish nonsense in

which a secret agent discovers the Chinese have a Hidden Atomic City from which to Launch a Terrifying Invasion. Italian/Spanish sleep-inducer directed by Domenico Paolella. John Ericson, Berna Rock, Erica Blank.

**OPERATION COUNTERSPY (1965).** Prognosis: Better-than-average James Bond pastiche (of Italian-Spanish-French origin) featuring death rays and a madman in command of a secret base bristling with superweapons. Directed by Nick Nostro. George A. Ardisson.

**OPERATION KID BROTHER (1967).** Sean Connery's kid brother, Neil Connery, plays a secret agent related to James Bond who meets Celi as villain, Daniela Bianchi as femme fatale, Bernard Lee as M, Lois Maxwell as Moneypenny and Anthony Dawson as hit man. Alberto De Martino directed it into a mishmash. The patient died.

**OPERATION MONSTERLAND.** See **DESTROY ALL MONSTERS.**

**OPERATION TOP SECRET (1964).** French agent outbids other spies and counterspies in his race to recover a German scientist who has devised a plan to return space rockets to Earth. Roger Hanin.

**ORACLE, THE (1985).** An "ancient power" seduces a beautiful woman. Directed by Roberta Findlay. Caroline Capers Powers, Roger Neil, Victoria Dryden. (VC)

**ORCA (1977).** To whales what JAWS was to sharks—but hardly a whale of a movie. Seafaring Richard Harris, after harpooning Orca's mate, is attacked by the superwhale, which also rams its snout into a seacoast town, almost sinking it. Touches of MOBY DICK don't do much to improve the silly story, nor do gratuitous touches of gore totally false to the nature of killer whales. Among potential whale bait are Bo Derek, Keenan Wynn, Charlotte Rampling and Will Sampson. Munchy munchy. Michael Anderson directed this major disaster in the wake of JAWS. (VC)

**ORGY OF THE DEAD (1966).** Edward D. Wood Jr., producer of PLAN NINE FROM OUTER SPACE, is back with more inept horror laughs with a script about a menagerie of monsters loose in a tomb. Criswell the prophet, who introduced PLAN NINE, is also back, and so is strongarm menace Tor Johnson and femme fatale Vampira, with Lon Chaney Jr. joining in the new fun. Call it "Orgy of the Living Incompetent" as Criswell, The Master of the Dead and his

Princess of Darkness (Fawn Silver) terrorize two writers in a cemetery while several broads dance and jiggle their bare breasts. Directed by A. C. Stevens. (VC)

**ORGY OF THE VAMPIRES.** See **ORGY OF THE DEAD.**

**ORLAK, THE HELL OF FRANKENSTEIN (1961).** Mexican monster mayhem (and mirth?) from producer/director Rafael Baledon as a remote-controlled entity with a metal head, created by the typical mad scientist (would you believe Dr. Carlos Frankenstein?), stomps through some taco stands on the outskirts of Mexico City. Has the burning aftertaste of Tabasco sauce. Joaquin Cordero.

**ORLOFF AGAINST THE INVISIBLE MAN (1970).** Nutty scientist creates an unseeable human who kidnaps his maker's daughter. Howard Vernon, Britt Carva. Directed by Pierre Chevalier.

**ORPHAN, THE (1979).** Mixed-up youth undergoes headaches and other traumas as a prelude to graphic murders. Children shouldn't play with dead adults. John Ballard wrote-directed; allegedly inspired by Saki's short story "Sredni Vashtar." Mark Owens, Joanna Miles.

**ORPHEUS (1950).** Writer-director Jean Cocteau's haunting masterpiece of the classic legend about a poet (Jean Marais) who is returned to life by the personification of Death. Like Cocteau's BEAUTY AND THE BEAST, this is topheavy with fantasy imagery, artistic lighting and camera angles. Performances by Maria Casares and Juliette Greco are good, but ultimately it is the visuals that remain with you, and the great music by Georges Auric. (VC)

**OSA (1985).** Pointless MAD MAX ripoff, poorly written and directed by Oleg Egorov without any of the style of the genre. In a vague future society where water is a precious commodity, and anarchy rules in the desert, a gang of cutthroats

led by Mr. Big murders a young girl's family. She grows up under the tutelage of "Trooper," who teaches her how to use a crossbow. Characterizations are nonexistent but noisy action is plentiful. The climax is a game to the death called Bird Hunt. Totally preposterous. Kelly Lynch, Peter Walker, Etienne Chicot. (VC)

**OTHER, THE (1972).** Tom Tryon's best-selling novel with heavy religious symbolism is such an ingenious storytelling trick it is difficult to describe without giving away its jolting surprises. Under Robert Mulligan's sensitive direction, it unfolds on a Connecticut farm in 1935 and shows the strangest abnormal psychology in children since THE BAD SEED. In spite of visual gimmicks (Tryon adapted his novel), Mulligan never cheapens the story, only enhances it with his clever manipulations. We refuse to say anything else—except see it! Chris and Martin Udvaronky, Uta Hagen, Diana Muldaur, John Ritter, Victor French.

**OTHERS, THE (1957).** TV version of Henry James' famous novella, THE TURN OF THE SCREW, with Sarah Churchill as the governess battling to save the lives of two children—or is the supernatural horror all in her overvivid imagination? Tommy Kirk, Geoffrey Toone.     CREATURE FEATURES MOVIE GUIDE -OUANGA to OVERSEXED

**OUANGA (1935).** The title refers to a voodoo curse placed by a native priestess on the wife-to-be of a plantation owner. The sacrificial rites lead to a hexed climax. Also known as CRIME OF VOODOO and later remade as POCOMANIA. Produced-written-directed by George Terwilliger. Fredi Washington, Philip Brandon.

**OUR MAN FLINT (1966).** Wonderful spoof of the Bond spy genre with lanky, dapper James Coburn as Derek Flint, an operative of Z.O.W.I.E. who can control his body organs (oops, did we write that?), has a cigarette lighter with 83

**SHIRLEY MacLAINE:**
**'OUT ON A LIMB'**

**ROD SERLING:**
**'THE OUTER SPACE CONNECTION'**

functions (blow torch included) and possesses an astonishing knowledge of bouillabaisse. In his spare time he pursues G.A.L.A.X.Y., an insidious gang controlling the weather via weird science. Lee J. Cobb is the M of the bureau, while Gila Golan is among the harem girls who surround Flint. The sequel, IN LIKE FLINT, was an equally raucous success. Directed by Daniel Mann. Edward Mulhare, Benson Fong, Russ Conway.

**OUR MOTHER'S HOUSE (1967).** Mildly macabre British film, directed by cameraman Jack Clayton, in which five children growing up with an invalid mother are suddenly faced with caring for themselves. Keeping mom's death a secret is what gives this "children's" tale its bizarre twist—that and the way old dad (Dirk Bogarde) shows up at an inopportune moment. It is the suggested horrors that stand out, rather than the visuals. Pamela Franklin, Margaret Brooks, Mark Lester, Louis Sheldon Williams.

**OUT OF THE DARKNESS (1985).** British supernatural tale set in an English village where three youths see the ghost of

### SEAN CONNERY IN 'OUTLAND'

a child who died in the 17th Century Plague. They set out to learn the town's history and free it of the unhappy spirit. Designed for children. Written-directed by John Krish. Garry Halliday, Michael Flowers.

**OUT OF THIS WORLD (1954).** But not far-enough out. It's still bad news for all mankind. See **ROCKY JONES, SPACE RANGER.**

**OUT ON A LIMB (1987).** What's a true story doing in this book? It's Shirley MacLaine's search for identity via reincarnation, UFOs, astral travel and extraterrestrial communication, as she described in her best-selling book, adapted to TV as a five-hour movie. Only during the last two hours, when Shirley reaches Peru and begins to undergo mysticism and ESP phenomena, does this become fascinating. The scenery is great, the philosophy intriguing if mystifying (and inconclusive) and ultimately it's food for thought, even if the diet might seem weak to those searching for the answer to self-identity. Well-intended by producer co-writer Colin Higgins and director Robert Butler. Charles Dance, John Heard, Anne Jackson.

**OUTER SPACE CONNECTION, THE (1975).** Intriguing science speculation from IN SEARCH OF producer Alan Landsburg, in the vein of Erich Van Daniken but done with a greater honesty. Written-directed by Fred Warshofsky, this suggests we have been visited in the distant past by aliens who left behind a stone laboratory-museum to which they will

return early in the next century. Fascinating theory, well thought out, with the voice of Rod Serling to back it up. A most persuasive documentary. (VC)

**OUTER TOUCH (1979).** Lowbrow British comedy about shapely women from outer space hunting down humans for their zoo of aliens back home. Directed by Norman J. Warren. Barry Stokes, Tony Maiden.

**OUTING, THE.** See **SCREAM.** (Outing shouting?)

**OUTLAND (1981).** Awesome, superbly crafted mystery-action film set on a mining station on Io, a moon of Jupiter. Writer-director Peter Hyams has fashioned a tense thriller depicting what it might be like, 100 tears from now, on a farflung world where Earthmen mine trinium. The full-scale interior sets are fascinatingly complex, the exterior models mind-boggling and the pace unrelenting as marshal Sean Connery tracks down a company conspiracy to feed its workmen drugs to improve their output. But the drug also causes the men to freak out. When Connery won't knuckle under, company boss Peter Boyle imports two hired gunmen to the massive mining community. There's even swinging doors for those who want to compare this to HIGH NOON. Frances Sternhagen, James Sikking. (VC)

**OUTLAWS (1986).** Above-average TV-movie blending time travel and the traditional Western. Outside Houston, Texas, in 1899, an outlaw gang is trapped by lawman John Grail (Rod Taylor), and just as the shoot-out begins, a bolt of electricity propels them into the 1980s, where they learn the ways of civilization but without giving up their own code of the West. The parable element of Nicholas Corea's script is well done, and the characters (William Lucking, Charles Napier, Patrick Houser, Richard Roundtree) very appealing. Director Peter Werner permits the action to get wild and woolly when it should. Mighty nice.

**OUTRAGE (1964).** Remake of the Japanese classic RASHOMON, reshaped into a Western by director Martin Ritt, but a pretentious misfire, overacted by Paul Newman as a greasy Mexican bandit who may have raped a woman and murdered her husband. The same story is told from different points of view with an Indian witch doctor telling the dead man's side from beyond the grave. Heavy-handed outrage against Japan's Akira Kurosawa. Others who overact are Clair Bloom as the wife, Laurence Harvey as the husband and William Shatner as the disillusioned priest. Faring better are Howard Da Silva as the narrator and Edward G. Robinson as the philosophical peddler who best understands the dark side of human nature.

**OUTWARD BOUND (1930).** First film version of Sutton Vane's allegorical play (remade in 1944 as BETWEEN TWO WORLDS) is about a shipload of passengers who come to realize they are dead and on their way to . . . heaven or hell? Directed by Robert Milton. Leslie Howard, Douglas Fairbanks Jr., Helen Chandler, Montagu Love.

**OVAL PORTRAIT, THE (1972).** Wanda Hendrix, Gisele MacKenzie and Barry Coe star in this TV-movie about a woman possessed by a woman's soul trapped in a painting. Based on an Edgar Allan Poe story.

**OVERDRAWN AT THE MEMORY BANK (1983).** Videocassette version of a PBS special starring Raul Julia as a man in a futuristic society who is rounded up a la THE PRISONER and sent out to detention. Driected by Douglas Williams. Linda Griffiths, Wanda Cannon. (VC)

**OVERLORDS OF THE UFO (1970).** TV documentary from Gold Key examines photos of unidentified flying objects and alleged saucers in an effort to separate the real from the phony. Not overly convincing.

**OVERSEXED (1974).** Dr. Shirley Jekyll mixes a formula that turns her into Ms Sherry Hyde, thereby doubling her need for sexual encounters of the closest kind and breaking the snaps on her now-undersized bra. Veronica Parrish stars for director-writer Joe Sarno, a filmmaker with a cult following. Undernourished in all departments.

---

*"Even in space the ultimate enemy is man!"—Teaser for **OUTLAND.***

*"Surrender or I'll blow your Nikes off."* —Sybil Danning as Ilona in
**PANTHER SQUAD.**

**PACK, THE (1977).** Schweinhund of dog-slasher movies as psychopoodles, demonic dachshunds, terror terriers and horror hounds seek human hydrants. A "We're surrounded and got to find a way out" plot with Joe Don Baker as chief canine-kicker. Robert Clouse wrote-directed. Dogs' "worst enemies" are R. G. Armstrong, Richard B. Shull, Richard O'Brien and Hope Alexander-Willis. Also known in some pounds as KILLERS WHO WORE COLLARS. (VC)

**PAJAMA PARTY (1964).** Beach-and-bikini blunder, a wretched futility starring Tommy Kirk as a Martian, but that only begins to suggest ineptitudes to which this alleged comedy sinks. Kirk the E.T. falls for Annette Funicello, while former stars frolic in outre roles: Elsa Lanchester, Buster Keaton, Dorothy Lamour, Harvey Lembeck. Miswritten by Louis M. Heyward, misdirected by Don Weis.

**PANDA AND THE MAGIC SERPENT (1958).** Ancient Chinese fairy tale, made by the Japanese, depicts the animated adventures of a cute furry animal, a Dragon God and an immortal serpent, The White Snake Enchantress. Directed by Taiji Yabushita and Kazuhiko Okabe. (VC)

**PANDEMONIUM (1982).** Takeoff on FRIDAY THE 13TH (made as THURSDAY THE 12th), with a knife killer tracking down cheerleaders at It Had to Be U. A horror writer's AIRPLANE with an array of gags falling deader than the killer's victims. Barely bearable—the girls are more bareable. Botched, Sole-ful misfire by director Alfred Sole. Carol Kane, Tom Smothers, Miles Chapin, Debralee Scott, Donald O'Connor, Kaye Ballard, Tab Hunter. (VC)

**PANDORA AND THE FLYING DUTCHMAN (1952).** Modern look at the ancient legend: James Mason is skipper of the Flying Dutchman, doomed to sail the seas until he finds a woman willing to die for him. He pursues Ava Gardner, certainly a woman any man would die for. Jack Cardiff's Mediterranean footage is beautiful in color. Written-directed by Albert Lewin. Striking MGM production made in Britain. Nigel Patrick, Sheila Sim, Marius Goring.

**PANIC (1976).** Italian flicker, set in Great Britain with poor lip synch, is an old-fashioned "Frankenstein on the Loose" plot in which a professor, experimenting in bacteriological warfare, discovers a vaccine, has an accident and emerges a horrible monster with a body that bleeds and a bloated face

stripped of flesh. "The Plurima Plan" has backfired and it's up to hero and heroine to prevent a panic in the town under quarantine, and to discover an antidote. Predictable cliches will hardly throw you into a panic. (VC)

**PANIC AT LAKEWOOD MANOR. See IT HAPPENED AT LAKEWOOD MANOR.** (Ants in your rants!)

**PANIC IN THE CITY (1967).** No-nonsense low budget feature, shot on L.A. streets, moves fast under Eddie Davis' direction as federal agent Howard Duff tracks down an A-bomb being built by a demented Soviet agent. Semidocumentary approach helps gloss over story holes and Paul Dunlap's music heightens tension. Stephen McNally is a straightfaced assignment chief, Linda Cristal is a lovely radiation expert who provides love interest, and Nehemiah Persoff goes bonkers as the crazed Ruskie. Anne Jeffries and Dennis Hopper have limited spy roles. Tense climax, unusually downbeat for a programmer.

**PANIC IN THE WILDERNESS (1975).** Bigfoot-type monstrosity decides it's feeding time and goes on a routine rampage in the Canadian Northwest while human beings wonder what that strange thing is over there behind that clump of trees. The only panic this film caused was audiences scampering for exit doors to the greater outdoors.

**PANIC IN YEAR ZERO (1962).** Hydrogen holocaust is upon us and so is anarchy—rape, murder and other normal human reactions to Armageddon. A family fights off pillagers and rapists to survive. Cheap production values, a vague screenplay and the indifferent direction by Ray Milland (who also portrays Harry Baldwin, average father) make this a weak end-of-civilization yarn. When a doctor comments: "If we scrape the scabs off, and apply disinfectant, civilization might recover," one wishes American-International had applied disinfectant to the script's botched complexion. Milland's torn family consists of Jean Hagen, Mary Mitchell and Frankie Avalon.

**PANIC ON THE AIR (1936).** Newfangled high-frequency device is knocking radio shows off the air. Can anyone save AMOS 'N ANDY and THE WITCH'S TALE from oblivion? And what about FIBBER McGEE AND MOLLY? Probing questions this cheapie never answers as its characters play good-guy-chases-bad-guy. Directed by D. Ross Lederman.

Lew Ayres, Florence Rice, Benny Baker.

**PANTHER GIRL OF THE CONGO.** See **CLAW MONSTERS, THE.** (Talons by the gallons!)

**PANTHER SQUAD (1986).** A female Rambo, Ilona (Sybil Danning), and her scantily clad warrioresses fight Clean Space, an ecological group preventing space exploration. All the nubile, demure Sybil shows off is her disintegrator zap-gun; she doesn't even give us a modicum of titillation. Her fans will weep. Directed by Peter Knight. (VC)

**PAPER MAN (1971).** The deaths of three college students appear to be caused by a computer intelligence. Solution to the mystery is more mundane but early portions of this TV-movie have eerie qualities. Directed by Walter Grauman. Dean Stockwell, Stephanie Powers, James Stacy, James Olson, Ross Elliott, Tina Chen.

**PARADISIO (1962).** Arthur Howard (brother of famed British actor Leslie Howard) possesses eyeglasses that see through clothing in this British "nudie," for which audiences got to wear 3-D glasses. Even though Pop Howard raises his eyebrows, this remains lowbrow stuff. Sample: He visits the Louvre, looks at Goya's painting and sees the Maja stripped. A serpent is in PARADISIO.

**PARANOIA (1969).** Italian-French shocker with Carroll Baker as a woman undergoing psychological terror. Director Umberto Lenzi throws in plenty of sizzling sex. Lou Castel, Tino Carraro, Collette Descombes.

**PARANOIAC (1963).** Despite Jimmy Sangster's clever plot, this Hammer mystery is dull, lacking a psychological terror film needs. Oliver Reed, who killed his brother, is stunned when the brother returns alive. Directed by Freddie Francis. Janette Scott, Alexander Davion.

**PARASITE (1982).** Released to theaters in 3-D, this low budget science-fiction/horror cheapie takes place in a post-Armageddon world where men are equipped with laser guns. A monster runs around burrowing into people and leaping at the camera. Stan Winston's creature effects are average, gore is gratuitous. The stuff wrapped around the violence is lethargic as Robert Glaudini discovers there's a worm in his abdomen that could spread to mankind. Produced-directed by Charles Band. (VC)

**PARASITE MURDERS, THE.** See **THEY CAME FROM**

**'PEEPING TOM' DIRECTOR MICHAEL POWELL**

**ROBERT HELPMANN AS DR. ROGET IN 'PATRICK'**

**WITHIN.** (Intestional subterfuge required.)

**PARDON ME, BUT YOUR TEETH ARE IN MY NECK.** See **FEARLESS VAMPIRE KILLERS, THE.**

**PARIS PLAYBOYS (1954).** Idiot's delight: The Bowery Boys, in the French capital, fight over ownership of a sour cream that doubles as an explosive. TNT for your complexion? The cast got creamed on this one: Leo Gorcey, Huntz Hall and dem udder East Side dopes. How about a sour cream pie for director William Beaudine?

**PARTS—THE CLONUS HORROR.** Cassette title for **CLONUS HORROR, THE.**

**PASSING OF THE THIRD FLOOR BACK, THE (1936).** Strange British allegory, directed by Berthold Viertel, in which a Jesus Christ figure appears on Christmas Eve to help boarding house roomers. Conrad Veidt, Anna Lee, Cathleen Nesbitt, Rene Ray, Frank Cellier.

**PASSPORT TO DESTINY (1944).** Charwoman Elsa Lanchester in a World War II fantasy: She stalks Adolf Hitler, aided by a magical ring which protects her from the Gestapo and SS. A curiosity piece you might enjoy for its outbursts of blatant propaganda. Directed by Ray McCarey. Gordon Oliver, Lenore Aubert.

**PASSPORT TO HELL (1964).** Would you believe the Black Scorpion is bent on conquest with a nerve gas? And would you believe Agent 353 is hot on his insidious trail? Would you believe the French, Italians and Spaniards would subject the world to such a feeble-minded premise? Go get those evil guys, George Ardisson.

**PATRICK (1979).** Australian import directed by Richard Franklin, a USC graduate who went on to make ROADGAMES and PSYCHO II. Patrick is a psychotic nerd who murders his mother and lover, then slides into a coma-tose state to become a "living dead man" used as a guinea pig in a neurologist's research. Patrick, immobile on his bed, develops powers of psychokinesis and terrorizes, in cat-and-mouse style, nurse Susan Penhaligon and hospital staff. Familiar material is given an attractive edge by Franklin's direction and the hip script by Everett De Roche. Music by Brian May. Robert Helpmann, Julia Blake. (VC)

**PEANUT BUTTER SOLUTION, THE (1985).** Youngster visits ruins of a haunted house and sees something so terrifying his hair falls out. He's visited by dead winos and told to use flies, kitty litter and peanut butter to get his hair back. But this grows hair that's too long. Cute Canadian production written-directed by Michael Rubbo. Mathew Mackay, Alison Podbrey, Michael Hogan. (VC)

**PEARL OF DEATH (1944).** Sherlock Holmes feature in the

**RELIVING YOUTH IN
'PEGGY SUE GOT MARRIED'**

Basil Rathbone-Nigel Bruce Universal series, featuring Rondo Hatton as "The Creeper," a character whose origins are detailed in THE BRUTE MAN. Updated Holmesian adventure, above average for the series, based on Doyle's "The Adventure of the Six Napoleons." Evelyn Ankers, Dennis Hooey, Ian Wolfe. Directed by Roy William Neill.

**PEEPING TOM (1960).** Director Michael Powell's unrelenting portrait of a psychopathic young man (who photographs the women he murders with a 16mm camera) was ahead of its time and resulted in Powell's ostracism from Britain's film industry. "Shovel it up and flush it down the sewer," wrote one critic. Yet this has no blood or gore, maintaining an implicit viewpoint toward sex and violence. What disturbed Powell's contemporaries was Leo Marks' screenplay focusing on perversion through metaphor and symbolism. Thus, the film asks viewers to become voyeuristic to watch, and perhaps it was this that evoked negative critical response. Carl Boehm is superb as the filmmaker. Moira Shearer, Anna Massey, Shirley Anne Field. (VC)

**PEGGY SUE GOT MARRIED (1986).** Unusually sensitive love story that uses time travel as a device for Kathleen Turner, portraying an unhappily married housewife, to return to her teen years, ready to rectify all the mistakes of her future. But the men she thinks she would prefer all turn out to be less than perfect, and her boyfriend (husband to be) drives her onto the horns of a dilemma. Beautifully directed by Francis Ford Coppola, with fine supporting role by Nicholas Cage, Leon Ames and Don Murray. (VC)

**PENETRATION (1976).** Re-edited version of the Italian feature THE SLASHER IS THE SEX MANIAC, with new pornographic footage of Tina Russell and Harry Reems. Farley Granger, who plays a policeman, must have been mortified.

**PEOPLE, THE (1972).** Sensitive adaptation of Zenna Henderson's morality parables about humanoids stranded on Earth, living in an isolated rural community and alienated from mankind. Their dormant telepathic and levitation abilities are reactivated with the help of new schoolteacher Kim Darby, who gains her trust along with doctor William Shatner. John Korty directs this offbeat Francis Ford Coppola TV production with a gentle, poetic touch. Dan O'Herlihy, Laurie Walters, Diane Varsi. (VC)

**PEOPLE THAT TIME FORGOT, THE (1977).** Third in a series of Edgar Rice Burroughs adventures—previous two being LAND THAT TIME FORGOT and AT THE EARTH'S CORE. Patrick Wayne and explorers find Doug McClure (star of the previous adaptations) in a kingdom of dinosaurs, pterodactyls and Neanderthal brutes. The effects (mechanized models and mock-ups) aren't always convinc-

ing, but a fun-spirit of adventure makes up for shortcomings. Directed by Kevin Connor. Dana Gillespie, Thorley Walters, Sarah Douglas, David Prowse, Milt Reid. Fourth in the series: WARLORDS OF ATLANTIS. (VC)

**PEOPLE WHO OWN THE DARK, THE (1975).** Spanish end-of-the-world thriller directed by Leon Klimovsky and starring Maria Perschy, Tony Kendall and Paul Naschy as members of a coven who are saved from an atomic blast but then fight senselessly among themselves. These folks are welcome to all the dark they can get. Don't sit in it with them. Written-directed by Armando de Ossorio. (VC)

**PERCY (1971).** Would you believe the first male sex organ transplant? Performed by that stiff-mannered, upright surgeon Sir Emmanuel Whitbread? Smutty British joke, erected from a novel by Raymond Hitchcock and inserted into a screenplay by Hugh Leonard. Director Hywel Bennett tries to pump energy into this flaccid project, but it's limp. There isn't even a climax, offhand. Oh, the film has spurts but suffers from self-abuse and withdrawal symptons as Denholm Elliott, Elke Sommer and Britt Ekland end up rubbing you the wrong way. In the final analysis, sterile and impotent. Call it emasculated. But don't call it irresistible.

**PERCY'S PROGRESS.** See **IT'S NOT THE SIZE THAT COUNTS.** (Wanna bet?)

**PERFECT WOMAN, THE (1950).** Not the perfect way to spend 90 minutes, since this British comedy (based on a stage play) is heavy-handed and its robotic concept hopelessly clanking. An inventor creates a flawless female amidst belabored situations. Directed by Bernard Knowles. Stanley Holloway, Patricia Roc, Nigel Patrick.

**PERILS FROM THE PLANET MONGO.** Re-edited footage of **FLASH GORDON'S TRIP TO MARS.**

**PERILS OF GWENDOLINE: IN THE LAND OF THE YIK YAK (1985).** Tongue-in-cheek erotic-bondage adventure based on the lesbian-oriented French comic strip by John Willie, with director Just Jaeckin adding Indiana Jones touches for good measure. A light-hearted, well-produced male fantasy with happy-go-lucky Brent Huff reluctantly leading Tawny Kitaen into jungle dangers to find her father and a priceless butterfly. The Kiop kingdom of cannibals and a Forbidden City of breast-plated (ha ha!) beauties pulling chariots for their queen are among the points of interest, not to men-

**MUSHY STUFF IN
'PERILS OF GWENDOLINE'**

tion the two naked points on most of the women in the cast. Filmed in the Philippines.

**PERILS OF PAULINE, THE (1967).** Tedious, unfunny Universal TV-movie comedy makes satiric sport of Pauline White, serial queen of the 1910s, by depicting Pamela Austin in states of undress, suspended animation and assorted disarray. Belabored effort is unbecoming to Pat Boone and Terry-Thomas. Directed by Leonard and Joshua Shelley.

**PERILS OF NYOKA.** See **NYOKA AND THE TIGERMEN.**

**PERSECUTION.** See **TERROR OF SHEBA.**

**PERSEUS THE INVINCIBLE.** See **MEDUSA VS. THE SON OF HERCULES.** (Beware kinky hair!)

**PETER PAN (1953).** J. M. Barrie's fantasy about a fairy who leads two children into a Never Never Land inhabited by Captain Hook and Pirates is a Pan-of-gold, a Disney animation masterpiece. Voices by Bobby Driscoll, Hans Conried, Heather Angel, Tom Conway, Stan Freberg, Kathryn Beaumont. Highlights are Tinker Bell, an imp surrounded by a twinkle of light, reckless redskins who wage war on lost human boys and a crocodile hungry for Hook.

**PETE'S DRAGON (1977).** Superb Disney musical-comedy blending live action and animation to tell the hilarious saga of Elliott the Dragon, a fire-breather from Fantasy World, on Earth to help children in trouble. He flies, turns invisible and has a sense of humor, snarling at disbelievers and throwing frightening shadows on walls. His lovability ultimately wins you over. Elliott meets 9-year-old Pete (Sean Marshall), a runaway pursued by the nasty Gogans. Setting is Passamaquoddy, where lighthouse keeper Mickey Rooney and daughter Helen Reddy befriend the boy and dragon. Jim Dale pops up as a medicine show man, Dr. Terminus, with Red Buttons as his assistant, Hoagy. Shelley Winters is grotesquely hilarious as Ma Gogan in ugly makeup and scraggly wig. Don Chaffey directed with a masterful touch. Jim Backus, Jane Kean, Jeff Conaway. (VC)

**PHANTASM (1979).** Little logic dominates this macabre tale set at Morningside Cemetery, USA, as the sinister Tall Man (Angus Scrimm, shouting "BOOOYYYYY!") sends human victims into another dimension where they are reduced to dwarves and exploited as slaves. This hogwash is a crowd pleaser thanks to the stylish direction-photography by Don Coscarelli, who has included a severed hand and finger, .45 slugs plowing into flesh and a floating silver sphere which thuds into heads and drills out brains and blood. Coscarelli's

**ANGUS SCRIMM (THE TALL MAN) IN 'PHANTASM'**

only concern is to shock us into our early tombstones. A pleasing if disjointed supernatural thriller. Just lean back into the casket and enjoy. Bill Thornbury, Michael Baldwin, Reggie Bannister. (VC)

**PHANTOM CREEPS, THE (1939).** Feature version of a 12-chapter Universal serial starring Bela Lugosi as Dr. Alex Zorka, an insane inventor who builds an eight-foot robot and an invisibility belt. Captain Bob West (Robert Kent) is Zorka's adversary. Laughable but fun all the way. Directed by Saul Goodkind and Ford Beebe without a trace of subtlety. Edward Van Sloan, Regis Toomey, Eddie Acuff.

**PHANTOM EMPIRE, THE (1935).** Full-length Gene Autry serial blending an underground lost city with six-shooters and cowboy action. Autry sings on the air from "Radio Ranch" then rushes off to prevent subterranean tyrants from destroying civilization with death rays, disintegrator units, sonar devices and atom-smashing smasheroos. For loyal Autry fans only—it's very crude toil. Frankie Darro, Smiley Burnette. Directed by action specialists B. Reeves Eason and Otto Brower. The feature version is **RADIO RANCH.** (VC)

**PHANTOM FIEND (1935).** . . . None other than Jack the Ripper in this British version of Marie Belloc-Lowndes' THE LODGER. Don't step into the foggy streets of Whitechapel without looking in each direction first. And check out those shadows. Cast features a young Jack Hawkins. Ivor Novello, who portrayed the suspected murderer in Alfred Hitchcock's 1926 silent version, repeats that role here. Directed by Maurice Elvey.

**PHANTOM FIEND.** See **RETURN OF DR. MABUSE, THE.**

**PHANTOM FROM SPACE (1953).** Cheapie suffers from lack of production, especially when an invisible extraterrestrial is finally revealed to be human in form. Setting is L.A.'s Griffith Observatory where the alien is pursued. Weak as a new-born kitten. Ted Cooper, Jim Bannon, Noreen Nash. W. Lee Wilder produced-directed.

**PHANTOM FROM 10,000 LEAGUES (1955).** Menace from the deep turns out to be shallow. Kent Taylor discovers an amphibious creature but keeps it a secret from over-developed spy Helene Stanton, who wears skimpy bathing suits to take our minds off the underdeveloped plot. Dan Milner directed this really terrible movie that will give you the bends. Cathy Downs, Michael Whalen, Rodney Bell.

**PHANTOM OF CRESTWOOD (1932).** Ahead-of-its time whodunit thriller in which a high-class mistress (Karen Morley) gathers her lovers at Crestwood to extort them, unaware a killer wearing a death mask and using gaming darts is running through the secret passageways. Great flashback device, good effects. Directed by David Ruben. Ricardo Cortez, Anita Louise, H. B. Warner, Pauline Frederick.

**PHANTOM OF HOLLYWOOD (1974).** Take-off on PHANTOM OF THE OPERA, set in a deteriorating film studio, Worldwide, where bigwigs are selling off the backlot to pay off debts. From the depths of movies' past comes a Masked Avenger to preserve low budget picture values, even at the cost of human life. Standard TV-movie produced-directed by Gene Levitt. Peter Lawford, Jack Cassidy, Skye Aubrey, Jackie Coogan, Broderick Crawford, Kent Taylor, Regis Toomey, John Ireland.

**PHANTOM OF PARIS.** See **MYSTERY OF MARIE ROGET, THE.** (Hairy in Paree!)

**PHANTOM OF SOHO (1963).** German-British thriller, based on an antiquated Edgar Wallace mystery, MURDER BY PROXY, in which a masked fiend darts through seedy London streets, knocking off British folks who lack redeeming values. Directed by F. J. Gottlieb. Dieter Borsche, Hans Sonhnker, Barbara Rutting, Werner Peters.

**PHANTOM OF THE OPERA, THE (1925).** Appreciation for the silent screen is suggested for re-viewing this oldie with make-up genius Lon Chaney as an acid-scarred madman living beneath the Paris Opera House who frightens all the sopranos out of their tenors. Based on a Gaston Leroux novel, this Universal classic has marvelous make-up, but the acting is hopelessly laughable. All very stagy and hokey . . .

**CREATURE FEATURES MOVIE GUIDE**

# Opera Phantoms We Have Loved

LON CHANEY SR. AS THE PHANTOM (1925)

CLAUDE RAINS AS THE PHANTOM (1943)

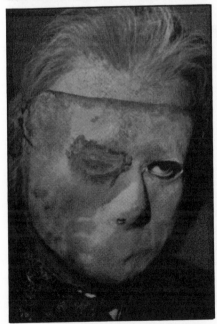

HERBERT LOM AS THE PHANTOM (1962)

PHANTOM OF THE PARADISE

CREATURE FEATURES MOVIE GUIDE

> *"Feast your eyes, gloat your soul, upon my accursed ugliness."—A title card from **PHANTOM OF THE OPERA (1925)**.*

an antique for collectors only. Directed by Rupert Julian. Mary Philbin, Norman Kerry, Snitz Edwards, Gilbert Gowland, John St. Polis, John Miljan. (VC)

**PHANTOM OF THE OPERA, THE (1943).** Second screen version of Leroux's novel is one of the few horror films in Technicolor from the 1940s. Stylized, beautifully photographed by Hal Mohr and very entertaining despite some hokum. Claude Rains portrays a misused-abused composer whose face is scarred by acid and who, in pain-riddled madness, seeks refuge in sewers beneath the Opera House. In revenge, he commits outrages against the establishment he once so loved. Enduring favorite with great sets and costumes and a flamboyant cast: Nelson Eddy, Susanna Foster, Leo Carrillo, Fritz Leiber, Edgar Barrier, Fritz Feld. Directed by Arthur Lubin. (VC)

**PHANTOM OF THE OPERA (1962).** Hammer's filmization of Gaston Leroux's novel is comparable to the 1943 version in story and opulence. Herbert Lom is the Phantom in a one-eyed mask, Michael Gough is the music pirate and Heather Sears is the beautiful soprano. Polished under Terence Fisher's direction, romantically mysterious and set in London instead of Paris, with the underground chambers of the Phantom now connected with the slimy blimey sewers. Adaptation by producer Anthony Hinds. Thorley Walters, Edward De Souza, Miles Milleson, Michael Ripper.

**PHANTOM OF THE OPERA (1983).** TV-movie version of Leroux's novel is set in turn-of-the-century Budapest. Maximilian Schell's singing wife is beautiful but incompetent, and commits suicide, driving Schell to the brink of insanity. He is disfigured and, with an accomplice, flees underground into the labyrinth of the city, there to heal his body and scheme revenge. Five years later he reemerges as the Phantom to terrorize American singer Jane Seymour, British opera director Michael York and other hapless figures in the musical landscape. Though this has the ambience of Budapest, it remains inferior to earlier sound versions and unfolds in a most peculiar way. Directed by Robert Markowitz. Jeremy Kemp, Diana Quick, Philip Stone.

**PHANTOM OF THE PARADISE (1975).** Bizarre Brian De Palma film satirizes PHANTOM OF THE OPERA and com-ments on our music-oriented rock 'n roll youth and the debased values of the business world. De Palma's script is a retelling of the Faust legend, with crazed songwriter William Finley entering into a blood pact with rock impresario Paul Williams (who wrote music and lyrics). Climactic rock concert is a masterpiece of hysteria, but clarity of plot is often sacrificed for wild visuals. Williams is brilliant as the satanic force of depraved sexuality. For the "turned on" generation(s); squares may find it hard going. (VC)

**PHANTOM OF THE RED HOUSE (1954).** Mexican haunted house quickie has heirs to a fortune killing each other while a dead millionaire's spirit watches. Directed by Miguel M. Delgado. Alma Rosa Aguirre, Raul Martinez.

**PHANTOM OF TERROR.** See **BIRD WITH THE CRYSTAL PLUMAGE, THE.** (Dario Argento plum!)

**PHANTOM OF THE RUE MORGUE (1954).** Warner remake of MURDERS IN THE RUE MORGUE, shot in 3-D, depicts the Surete unsurely pursuing a killer of beautiful women over the rooftops of Paris. Good color and direction by Roy Del Ruth, but 2-D TV prints lose something of the original stereovision. Karl Malden gives his only performance as a mad doctor and tinges his professor with dignity and humanity, but he still seems a bit out of place. Claude Dauphin, Patricia Medina, Steve Forrest, Merv Griffin (!), Anthony Caruso and a gorilla named Sultan, played by apesuit specialist Charles Gemora.

**PHANTOM PLANET, THE (1961).** Variation on GULLIVER'S TRAVELS has Earthman Dean Fredericks (of Hollywood) landing on an alien planet, Rheton, inhabited by a race of tiny people who need his help to fight off an attack by another E.T. race. Fredericks is shrunken to six inches and squares off against the invaders, led by Richard Kiel. Lousy special effects, slow moving as hell. Directed by William Marshall. Francis X. Bushman, Coleen Gray.

**PHANTOM RAIDERS (1940).** Subtitled NICK CARTER IN PANAMA, this is early Jacques Tourneur, who was responsible for such classics as THE CAT PEOPLE and CURSE OF THE DEMON. This, however, is lowbrow stuff about

'PHANTOM PLANET': LOOK OUT FOR THE LITTLE BASTARDS

**CREATURE FEATURES MOVIE GUIDE**

**INCREDIBLE KILLER ANT IN 'PHASE IV'**

remote-controlled explosives controlled by an evil power. Walter Pidgeon, Joseph Schildkraut, Dwight Frye.

**PHANTOM SHIP (1937).** Hammer's second film, first released as MYSTERY OF THE MARIE CELESTE. It deals fictionally with the famous brigantine found abandoned in the Atlantic in December 1872, offering a wild interpretation of what happened to the vanished crew. A kind of whodunit, with crew members being murdered one by one during a raging storm at sea. Bela Lugosi portrays a suspicious captain. Denison Clift directed. (VC)

**PHANTOM SPEAKS, THE (1945).** Republic quickie (released with THE VAMPIRE'S GHOST) follows the story of BLACK FRIDAY very closely in telling of a murderer on Death Row who is electrocuted. His spirit then enters the body of a doctor and commands him to kill, kill, kill. Directed by John English. Richard Arlen, Lynne Roberts, Stanley Ridges, Tom Powers, Jonathan Hale.

**PHANTOM TOLLBOOTH, THE (1970).** Imaginative cartoon by Chuck Jones, mixing live action with animation. The titular tollbooth is a passageway to a magical world structured on the laws of mathematics and patterned on the written word. Voices by Mel Blanc, Hans Conried, Les Tremayne, Larry Thor, Daws Butler, June Foray. (VC)

**PHANTOM TREEHOUSE, THE (1984).** Animated cartoon in which two boys and their dog become lost in a world of strange characters.

**PHARAOH'S CURSE (1957).** When it comes to Egyptian expeditions and long-dead mummified corpses which rise to go on murdering rampages, Hollywood seems singular incapable of contributing anything new to the genre. This Howard W. Koch production epitomizes that problem by (a) depicting an expedition to Egypt and the finding of (b) a mummified individual who (c) rises and goes on a rampage. Tut, tut. Mark Dana, Ziva Rodann and Diane Brewster are directed listlessly by Lee Sholem.

**PHASE IV (1974).** Saul Bass, famed film title designer, directed this bizarre science-fiction/horror thriller depicting a war between scientists in a desert outpost and an army of intelligent killer ants that drench their enemies in a sticky yellow substance. The ants, a result of pollution, are diabolical adversaries as they chew their way into the installation and demonstrate hypnotic powers. The excellent cinematography and John Barry's art direction enhance this offbeat tale starring Nigel Davenport and Michael Murphy. The ending is a way-out metaphysical piece. (VC)

**PHENOMENA (1985).** See **CREEPERS.**

**PHENOMENAL AND THE TREASURE OF TUTANKAMEN (1984).** The curse of King Tut strikes again in this inept French-Italian superhero adventure as a masked hero pursues a golden relic with mystical powers. Slam bam, crash boom. Directed by Ruggero Deodato. Maura Nicola Parenti, Gordon Mitchell. (VC)

**PHILADELPHIA EXPERIMENT, THE (1984).** Since 1943 unsubstantiated legends have abounded that the U.S. Navy conducted experiments with an invisible force field that caused several ships to turn invisible. This big-budgeted New World film builds an exciting time travel story around that legend: Two sailors in the radar experiment (Michael Pare, Bobby Di Cicco) are catapulted to the present to face a series of out-of-water adventures. What makes this above average is that it sensitively deals with the problems of a young man finding that the woman he loved in 1943 is now beyond his reach. But director Stewart Raffill also emphasizes action and weird effects, balancing plot and adventure. An exciting project, with many clever touches, and a fine cast co-starring Eric Christmas, Nancy Allen, Kene Holliday and Miles McNamara. (VC)

**PHOBIA (1981).** Even John Huston had to leap into the horror genre, but his contribution as director is ordinary, displaying no genuine care for the field. Dr. Paul Michael Glaser is conducting "implosion therapy" on human guinea pigs, each of whom suffers from a phobia: fear of heights, of falling, of snakes, of crowds. One by one these patients are murdered

# Great Scott!

**JUDSON SCOTT IN 'THE PHOENIX'**

in graphic ways: by dynamite explosion, by falling, by drowning, by snake bite, by elevator crush. A lack of suspects tips off who the killer is early on but there's still a compelling quality thanks to the intense performance of ruthless, driven investigating cop John Colicos. Co-scripted by Jimmy Sangster. Susan Hogan, Alexandra Stewart. Robert O'Ree, David Bolt, David Eisner.

**PHOENIX, THE (1978).** Taiwanese import, also known as WAR OF THE WIZARDS, in which an alien woman, Flower Fox, travels to Earth and puts under her evil spell a fisherman who has found her magical book, "Magic Vessel of Plenty and Bamboo Book." Since the book creates wealth, several villains come after it, including Flower Fox's henchman, Steel Hand, standing seven feet tall as Richard Kiel. Directed by Richard Caan and Sadamasa Arikawa.

**PHOENIX, THE (1981).** TV-movie (pilot for a short-lived series) about an extraterrestrial (formerly a Mayan known as "Bennu of the Golden Light") who walks out of his South American tomb to shake up mankind with Charlie Chan homilies and mystical mutterings. Superhero action written-produced by Anthony and Nancy Lawrence. Judson Scott, Shelley Smith, E. G. Marshall. Directed by Douglas Hickox.

**PHOENIX 2772.** See **SPACE FIREBIRD 2772.**

**PHYNX, THE (1970).** Inept spy spoof in which a rock music group sets out to rescue ex-Hollywood stars kidnapped by a ruthless mastermind. Cameos by Edgar Bergen, Busby Berkeley, Dick Clark, Louis Hayward, Leo Gorcey, Huntz Hall, Dorothy Lamour, Guy Lombardo, Joan Blondell, Michael Ansara, Rona Barrett—the list is endless. Made by director Lee H. Katzin and other rat- phynx.

**PICNIC AT HANGING ROCK (1975).** Australian director Peter Weir has taken a true incident from 1900 and made a mystical, puzzling film that never solves its mysteries, although that very fact is one of this movie's strongest elements. Four school girls picnicking on a precipitous rock formation suddenly vanish; later, one of them turns up badly scratched up but alive. Were they swallowed alive by the earth? Back at the boarding school, head mistress Rachel Roberts drinks too much, a young man nearly goes crazy searching for his lost love and other characters behave strangely. For some this may pass as artistic cinema with ample pregnant pauses, but those seeking an answer will call this pretentious and tedious. Like it or not, it's beautifully photographed and directed. Dominic Guard, Helen Morse, Anne Lambert. (VC)

**PICTURE MOMMY DEAD (1966).** Picture producer-director Bert I. Gordon lifeless, imitating other psychothrillers and you've got the motion picture. Susan Gordon (Bert's daughter) is possessed by the spirit of her dead mother (Zsa Zsa Gabor), which causes newlywed dad Don Ameche and bride Martha Hyer consternation. Or is it constipation? Wendell Corey, Signe Hasso. (VC)

**PICTURE OF DORIAN GRAY (1945).** Oscar Wilde's morality horror story, about an evil man (Hurd Hatfield) whose decadence is embodied in a painting that reflects his degradation while he remains young, becomes literate, fascinating cinema in the hands of writer-director Albert Lewin, with George Sanders memorable as the decadent Englishman who introduces Dorian Gray to debauchery. Angela Lansbury, Donna Reed, Peter Lawford, Bernard Gorcey. Narration read by Sir Cedric Hardwicke. (VC)

**PICTURE OF DORIAN GRAY (1973).** Oscar Wilde's classic about a man's search for eternal youth, and his descent into sin, was produced for TV by Dan Curtis. Shane Briant is the artist who stays young while his portrait grows old with evil. Nigel Davenport, Charles Aidman, John Karlen, Fionnula Flanagan. Directed by Glenn Jordan. (VC)

**PIECES (1983).** Repulsive chainsaw-killer flick, in which a campus madman dismembers beautiful women, taking "pieces" back to his freeze locker to complete a human "jigsaw puzzle." As degrading as it is absurd, and humiliating to women. Filmed in Boston by producer-writer Dick Randall, this is awful awful sleazy trash. Christopher George plays an unlikable cop, Lynda Day is an unlikely undercover woman posing as a tennis champion and Edmund Purdom is the campus dean. Spanish director Juan Piquer Simon went all to pieces directing this sicko movie. (VC)

**PIED PIPER, THE (1972).** Literate, well-acted version of Robert Browning's famous poem about a mysterious piper in medieval 14th Century England whose magical pipe music mesmerizes plague-bearing rats away from a village. Sets and costumes are realistic in this David Puttnam film that walks between adult themes and children's touches. Well-directed by Jacques Demy. Donovan plays the piper and wrote the music. Donald Pleasence, Michael Hordern, Roy Kinnear, John Hurt, Jack Wild, Diana Dors.

**PIED PIPER OF HAMELIN (1957).** TV production recounting in music and dance the legendary tale of the medieval piper who lures children from a German village. Van Johnson, Claude Rains, Jim Backus, Lori Nelson, Kay Starr, Doodles Weaver. Directed by Bretaigne Windust. (VC)

**PIGS.** See **DADDY'S DEADLY DARLING.** (Oink!)

**PILL CAPER, THE (1967).** Re-edited episodes from the ghastly unfunny TV sitcom, MR. TERRIFIC. For details, see THE POWER PILL, more of the same terrible stuff. Directed by Jack Arnold. Stephen Strimpell, John McGiver.

**PILLOW OF DEATH (1945).** Last of Universal's "Inner Sanctum" programmers introduced by a floating head in a crystal ball. Lon Chaney Jr. is going bonkers again as a lawyer who murdered his wife (or did he?). Production is threadbare and the George Bricker script weak in this ugly duckling swan song. Indifferently directed by Wallace Fox. Brenda Joyce, J. Edward Bromberg, Wilton Griff.

**PINK CHIQUITAS, THE (1986).** Meteor from outer space lands near Beansville and proceeds to turn any women who come near it into nymphomaniacs. Private eye Tony Mareda Jr. (Frank Stallone) is hot on the case. Canadian spoof of genres, with some amusing moments but weak special effects. Written-directed by Anthony Currie. John Hemphill, Bruce Pirrie, Don Lake.

**PINK PANTHER STRIKES AGAIN, THE (1976).** Pink Panther movies are pretty far out but this goes science-fiction crazy. Herbert Lom returns as the French policeman driven so daffy by Inspector Clouseau that he plays the organ (remember PHANTOM OF THE OPERA?) and prepares his Destruction Device to knock down the U.N. building. Things vanish and reappear in a time continuum . . . this neglect to control his own plot leads to director Blake Edwards' downfall. This is still fun (if you're in the spirit for utter disjointed nonsense) and Sellers' bumbling and mumbling is great. Lesley-Anne Down, Marne Maitland, Burt Kwouk, Colin Blakely, Burt Kwouk. (VC)

**PINOCCHIO (1940).** Disney masterpiece about a wooden puppet transformed into a bona fide youth with Jiminy Cricket looking on is a free-handed adaptation of Collodi's classic, replete with Geppetto the gentle woodcarver, Figaro the kitten, Cleo the goldfish and Monstro the Whale. Brilliant animation craftsmanship. Voices by Dickie Jones, Cliff Edwards, Walter Catlett, Evelyn Venable. (VC)

**PINOCCHIO IN OUTER SPACE (1965).** Carlo Collodi's puppet story becomes animated space opera with the voice of Arnold Stang in this U.S.-Belgian cartoon. Our long-nosed hero journeys to the far reaches of the Universe to do battle with a giant whale and make friends with an extraterrestrial snapping turtle. (VC)

**PIRANHA (1978).** Of the JAWS school, but lacking as sharp

*"Phantom marine mutations? Death rays? Utter nonsense! I'm afraid, Doctor, you're the victim of an overwhelming imagination."—PHANTOM FROM 10,000 LEAGUES.*

**CREATURE FEATURES MOVIE GUIDE**

**MONSTRO THE WHALE MAKING A SPLASH IN WALT DISNEY'S 'PINOCCHIO'**

an overbite because of an underlying tongue-in-cheek attitude. On the surface an exploitation "eat 'em alive" picture, but more a fantasy-satire thanks to John Sayles' script and Joe Dante's whimsical direction. A mutant strain of piranha is fed into U.S. waterways and the teeny sharp-teeth water-demons feast greedily on the feet of Keenan Wynn and the facial tissues of Bradford Dillman. Barbara Steele fans will enjoy her role as a conspiratorial military officer. There's also some unusual stop motion footage of strange creatures in a laboratory. And some dialogue is wonderfully witty. (VC)

**PIRANHA II: THE SPAWNING (1981).** Loose sequel to PIRANHA is set at a Caribbean resort where underwater diving coach Tricia O'Neil is the focal point of a battle between her, local authorities (chief of police happens to be her estranged husband) and a tourist (Steve Marachuk) who is a member of a secret research program that has created a mutant—a cross between a piranha and a flying fish. A school of these winged monsters is now munching on hotel guests. It's hard to get much suspense out of tiny creatures and the effects are standard blood and gore, with one ALIEN-style attack when a minimonster pops from a victim's stomach. Director James Cameron is strongest in allowing his cast to create believable characters. Not a bad movie, but no classic, either. Cameron went on to make TERMINATOR and ALIENS, two superior thrillers. (VC)

**PIT, THE (1981).** Horror movie twice as bad as its title—hence, the pits. A perverted look at a perverted kid (Sammy Snyders) who peeps on his sexy babysitter and talks to his friend Teddy, a toy bear who talks back, planting salacious ideas in his "innocent" head. Sammy is also the friend of Trogs, gnarly beasts with blazing yellow eyes in a pit outside town. To keep them fat, Sammy feeds them his friends. The perversity and gore never really gell, with the most fascinating premise, Sammy's abnormal sexuality, only shallowly explored. The story picks up steam once the beasties escape the pit and reign munching terror on delicious humans. A minor Canadian production filmed around Beaver Dam, Wisc. Directed by Lew Lehman. Laura Hollingsworth. (VC)

**PIT AND THE PENDULUM, THE (1961).** Campy adaptation

of Edgar Allan Poe's horror tale about an Inquisition prisoner being tortured by a razor-edged pendulum swinging closer and closer to his restrained body. But in no way is producer-director Roger Corman faithful to Poe. It's pure hokum as Vincent Price, a crazed, insanely jealous nobleman, tortures John Kerr—not to mention the audience—with a terrible case of overacting. Script by Richard Matheson. Barbara Steele, Luana Anders, Anthony Carbone, Patrick Westwood, Lynne Bernay. (VC)

**PLACE TO DIE, A (1973).** An English village steeped in superstition and devil worship believes the wife of a newly arrived doctor should be a sacrificial lamb for blood rituals. British TV production directed by Peter Jefferies. Alexandra Hay, Bryan Marshall, Juan Moreno, Lila Kaye.

**PLAGUE, THE (1979).** Scientist working on a mutant bacteria (M3) to nourish plants and provide food for millions causes a leakage to the outside world, where bacteria infects children. The epidemic snowballs as a researcher seeks a virus to counteract the acetylecoline created by the bacteria. Kate Reid, who fought the Andromeda Strain, is again a loyal scientist battling the killer disease. Canadian production, directed by Ed Hunt. Celine Lomez. (VC)

**PLAGUE M3: THE GEMINI STRAIN. See PLAGUE, THE.**

**PLAGUE DOGS, THE (1982).** Richard Adams' novel was not his best work, being a didactic diatribe against vivesection. However, producer-writer Martin Rosen distilled the story's essence into an animated feature in the tradition of his WATERSHIP DOWN. Two dogs escape an experimental station in England's Lake District and begin a trek to a mythical island for animals. They are befriended by the Tod, a fox who teaches them how to stay alive in the wilderness. Meanwhile, the army and populace are in pursuit to destroy the dogs. Animation is state-of-the-art, but adults may consider this too depressing—for them and children. A miserable box office failure despite tons of good intentions. Voices by John Hurt, James Bolam, Christopher Benjamin, Judy Geeson, Nigel Hawthorne.

**PLAGUE OF THE ZOMBIES (1966).** Director John Gillig has

**ONE OF THE NIGHTMARISH SEQUENCES IN MARTIN ROSEN'S 'PLAGUE DOGS'**

Gilling has fashioned a stylish Gothic Hammer horror thriller set in the last century that constantly builds tension with superior production values. Peter Bryan's storyline touches on British hierarchy and its indifference to the working class when a doctor and his daughter come to visit an old friend in an eerie Cornish village and uncover a sadistic squire who turns men into zombies to work an old tin mine beneath his plantation through voodoo rituals. There is a nice incongruity in the imagery. Especially memorable are scenes where corpses slither and wriggle out of their graves and stalk hero and heroine. One of Hammer's best. Jacqueline Pearce, Andre Morell, Diane Clare, Michael Ripper, John Carson. Produced by Anthony Nelson-Keys.

**PLAN NINE FROM OUTER SPACE (1959).** Ranks with FIRE MAIDENS FROM OUTER SPACE and CAT WOMEN OF THE MOON in sinking to new inspired depths of cinematic ineptitude. Words such as amateurish, crude, tedious and aaarrrggghhhh can't begin to describe this Edward D. Wood film with Bela Lugosi appearing in a few graveyard scenes made shortly before his death. Other dull footage shows Lugosi coming out of a drab house. Lugosi died before the film was finished and an obvious "double" was used. The unplotted plot by Wood has San Fernando Valley residents troubled by UFOs of the worst encounter. Humanoid aliens Dudley Manlove (a famous radio voice) and Joanna Lee land their cardboard ship with a ninth plan to conquer the world (the first eight failed, you see). They resurrect corpses, including Vampira, Tor Johnson and Lugosi (or his double). The results are unviewable except for masochists who enjoy a good laugh derived from watching talentless folks making fools of themselves. A psychic named Criswell introduces the film with typical Wood dribble. Lyle Talbot, Tom Keene, Mona McKinnon. (VC)

**PLANET EARTH (1974).** Failed Gene Roddenberry TV pilot is a remake of another unsold pilot, GENESIS II. John Saxon awakens from suspended animation in the 22nd Century, discovering mankind has splintered into strange societies. The rulers are women led by sexy Diana Muldaur and the men are slaves called Dinks. How Saxon and Ted Cassidy save man from a fate worse than death is the substance of the teleplay by Roddenberry and his wife, Juanita Bartlett. Janet Margolin, Christopher Carey, Majel Barrett.

**PLANET OF BLOOD.** See **QUEEN OF BLOOD.**

**PLANET OF DINOSUARS (1978).** Low budget feature with stop-motion animation sequences depicting prehistoric creatures on a rampage. Produced-directed by James K. Shea. James Whitworth, Pamela Bottaro, Harvey Shain.

**PLANET OF HORRORS.** Originally made as MINDWARP: AN INFINITY OF TERROR, but released as PLANET OF HORRORS, then retitled **GALAXY OF TERROR** (see that entry) for cable TV. Roger Corman really had a hard time making up his mind on this one. Call it what you will.

**PLANET OF OUTLAWS (1939).** Re-edited version of the 1939 Universal serial BUCK ROGERS, with Buck (played by the great Buster Crabbe) and the good Dr. Huer battling Killer Kane and the Zug race of Saturn. Directed by Ford Beebe and Saul Goodkind. Constance Moore, C. Montague Shaw, Jackie Moore. See **BUCK ROGERS.** (VC)

**GENE RODDENBERRY,
'PLANET EARTH' CREATOR**

**PLANET OF STORMS (1962).** Soviet science-fiction set on Venus, inhabited by giant monsters and assorted lizard beings. Lavish effects were later lifted and used in VOYAGE TO THE PREHISTORIC PLANET and VOYAGE TO THE PLANET OF PREHISTORIC WOMEN by Roger Corman and associates. But remember—you saw it here first. Directed by Pavel Klushantsev.

**PLANET OF THE APES (1968).** Based loosely on the Pierre Boulle novel, this major Fox release is a grand mixture of action, suspense and satire—although the latter element tends toward parody and frequently cheapens the overall effect. Charlton Heston is one of three U.S. astronauts caught in a time warp and thrown far into the future. They crashland on a desolate planet ruled by chimpanzees, orangutans and gorillas, where man is a mute slave. There is much ape talk about man's warlike nature and his downfall. John Chambers' makeup is imaginative, Franklin J. Schaffner's direction is brilliantly right throughout and there is a visually rewarding punchline to the Rod Serling-Michael Wilson script. Kim Hunter, Roddy McDowall, James Whitmore and Maurice Evans are among many stars who appear in make-up and costumes. Four sequels and a TV series followed. (VC)

**PLANET OF THE VAMPIRES.** Videocassette title for **DEMON PLANET, THE.** (Sci-fi sorcery?)

**PLANET ON THE PROWL.** Videocassette title for **WAR BE-**

**TWEEN THE PLANETS.** (Prowl howl!)

**PLANETS AGAINST US (1961).** What happens when the Italians/French/Germans ally to make a science-fiction film? They came up with a humanoid robot (Michel Lemoine) that walks softly on flesh-covered feet and carries a big schtick: eyeballs that hypnotize and zap, and hands that turn humans to household dust. Brutally re-edited for the U.S. market. Directed by Romano Ferrara. Maria Pia Luzi, Jany Clair, Marco Guglielmi, Otello Toso, Peter Dane.

**PLANETS AROUND US.** See **PLANETS AGAINST US.**

**PLANTS ARE WATCHING, THE.** See **KIRLIAN WITNESS, THE.** (Watching grass grow!)

**PLAY DEAD (1985).** Yvonne de Carlo has a satanic pact with a Devil Dog, who murders members of her family for revenge. One is strangled, another electrocuted; even an investigating cop dies after the canine pours him a lye-laced cocktail. Pretty well acted and produced, but lacking sufficient exposition and characterizations to give it substance. In short, it finally rolls over and . . . Directed by Peter Wittman. Stephanie Dunnam, David Cullinand. (VC)

**PLAY IT AGAIN, SAM (1972).** Woody Allen's comic masterpiece finds him playing his usual inept, impotent self but imagining that the spirit of Humphrey Bogart (Jerry Lacy) is always at his shoulder with tough-guy, amorous advice. The

# *Making Up and Going Ape*

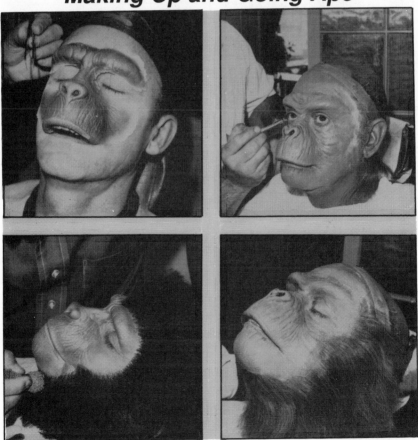

RODDY McDOWELL GOES THROUGH VARIOUS STAGES OF COMPLICATED MAKE-UP IN PREPARING FOR 'PLANET OF THE APES'

Bogart impression is hilarious and Allen is excellent as the nerd in search of a proper balance between the way he is and the way he'd like to be. Based on the Broadway play by Allen. Diane Keaton, Tony Roberts, Jennifer Salt, Susan Anspach. Directed by Herbert Ross. (VC)

**PLAY MISTY FOR ME (1971).** Clint Eastwood made his directorial debut with this odd psychological thriller with a minimum of suspense and "slasher" behavior. Clint is a soft-voiced Monterey disc jockey who is the love object of Jessica Walter—but he rejects her in favor of Donna Mills. This turns love into hate as Jessica sharpens her butcher knife and goes after Clint with a vengeance. There are only a few scary segments; on TV, unfortunately, the closing scenes are too dark. Watch for director Don Siegel as a bartender—Eastwood's private little joke. (VC)

**PLAYGIRL KILLER (1970).** Canadian release in which William Kerwin kills his models and stores their corpses in a freezer. Also known as DECOY FOR TERROR. Directed by Enrick Santamaran. Neil Sedaka. (VC)

**PLAYGIRLS AND THE VAMPIRE (1960).** Italian film from writer-director Piero Regnoli blending throat-biting and sex. A bunch of good-looking babes hole up in a weird castle where they flirt and walk around in 1959 clothing styles and stiletto heels. One of them even does a striptease to show off her lacy underwear, but for what purpose is never made clear. Walter Brandi has a double role—as the vampire and as his brother, Count Gabor Kernassy. The vampire elements are minimal—a couple of fangs and that's it. Already terribly dated. Followed by THE VAMPIRE AND THE BALLERINA, another in the vague Countess Bathory adaptations. Lyla Rocco, Mario Giovannini.

**PLEASE DON'T EAT MY MOTHER! (1973).** Revoltingly titled exploitationer—an alleged comedy about a plant that devours human flesh ala LITTLE SHOP OF HORRORS, only with a lot of bare female flesh on the premises. Produced-directed by Carl Monson, starring Rene Bond, Flora Wisel. Our advice? Please don't watch this movie!

**PLUCKED (1967).** On a chicken farm, poultry breeder Jean-Louis Trintignant hatches a plots to kill Gina Lollobrigida so he can fornicate on a steady basis with Ewa Aulin. But fun-loving Ewa has her own plan: to turn Trintignant into chicken mash. Somewhere in the plot some radioactivity creates mutant chickens. PLUCKED (a French-Italian production) is for clucks who should be plucked. Even the distributor chickened out when it came time to release the film. Yes, fans, it laid a colossal egg. From the cracked Grade-Z imagination of writer-director Giulio Questi.

**POCOMANIA (1939).** Voodoo thriller set in Jamaica with an all-black cast, a remake of a 1935 feature known as DRUMS OF THE JUNGLE and OUANGA. Nina Mae McKinney is a hexish priestess who curses a rival to acquire possession of a plantation. Produced- directed by Arthur Leonard. Jack Carter, Ida James. (VC)

**POINT, THE (1971).** Animated TV special, a thoughtful cartoon that will touch the sensitivites of adults and children. A round-headed youth in a society of people with pointed heads must learn to adjust to being an "ugly duckling." He finally gets "the point." Directed by Fred Wolff. (VC)

**POINT OF TERROR (1972).** One-time actor Alex Nichol directed this independent Crown-International production, but frankly we missed the Terrorless Point. Peter Carpenter stars as a man who experiences a series of murders, including his own. And then he wakes up! Ah, but then you're in store for a (non)surprise. Dyanna Thorne, Lory Hansen.

**POISON AFFAIR, THE (1955).** Also known as CASE OF POISONS, this French horror thriller is an atmospheric experiment in black mass, with undercurrents of sadism and masochism. Directed by Henri Decoin. Anne Verdon, Danielle Darrieux, Viviane Romance, Paul Meurisse.

**POLTERGEIST (1982).** Smash winner from Steven Spielberg, who gave directorial reins to Tobe Hooper. Spielberg's goal, with fellow writers Mark Grais and Michael Victor, is one of contrasts: to tell a suburbia haunted-house story and throw in all the ESP and parapsychology tricks in the books on haunting. It's a child's nightmare as unseen entities enter a tract home through the TV ("They're here," naively comments the young daughter) and inspire grosser phenomena. Along the supernatural path the daughter is trapped in another

# P Is for Playful Phantom . . .

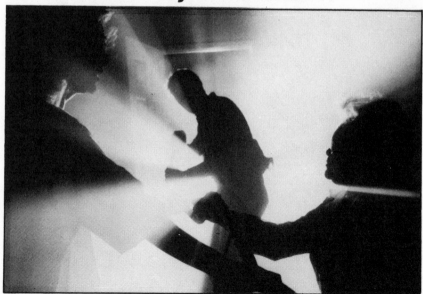

GLARING LIGHTS EARMARK A JOURNEY INTO THE OCCULT IN SPIELBERG'S 'POLTERGEIST'

dimension, the son is attacked by a tree, and coffins and corpses pop up from the ground to terrorize the housewife. Enthralling, edge-of-the-seat movie that comes complete with a monstrous demon from beyond and a plethora of glaring white lights. Outstanding effects by Industrial Light and Magic. Heather O'Rourke as the daughter, Craig T. Nelson as the average father, Jobeth Williams as the typical housewife and Zelda Rubenstein as the petite but powerfully weird clairvoyant make for wild and unbelievable events. (VC)

**POLTERGEIST II: THE OTHER SIDE (1986).** Inferior sequel to the splendid POLTERGEIST never captures the intensity or fearfulness of the original, no matter how many monsters or supernatural effects director Brian Gibson throws at the camera. It resumes suburbia living with the Freeling family (victims of that first Cuesta Verde haunting) now staying with JoBeth Williams' mother. This time the evil spirits are members of a religious Mormon-like sect who sought refuge in a cave (the one under the tract home) with their maniacal leader back in the 1800s. But ole man Kane (Julian Beck) is trapped in Purgatory, and must out-magic Indian medicine man Will Sampson who chants and smokes demons up his nose. There's no logic within-the-logic-of-the-supernatural in the script by co-producers Mark Victor and Michael Grais— just disconnected events with ill-defined characters. (Only Beck comes off well, looking genuinely satanic as the brimstone preacher who walks through people.) Richard Edlund's effects are up to standard, but without a strong story, they float in limbo. Craig T. Nelson is back as the father, Zelda Rubinstein reprises her role as the diminutive, squeaky-voiced psychic investigator and Geraldine Fitzgerald is the dead mother who dons angel's wings in an unintentional comedy scene. (VC)

**POOR DEVIL (1973).** Poor TV pilot has Sammy Davis Jr. as a Devil's apostle bungling his assignments. He's given one last chance by Satan to lay claim to a human being or he'll send Davis to . . . Heaven? Christopher Lee has the Devil to play. Directed by Robert Scheerer. Jack Klugman, Adam West, Madlyn Rhue, Ken Lynch, Buddy Lester.

**POOR GIRL, A GHOST STORY (1986).** Of interest to fans of

director Michael Apted, who helmed this one-hour episode from the British series, HAUNTED. Shades of THE INNOCENTS as governess Lynne Miller tutors for a rich family which is stricken with supernatural events. (VC)

**POPDOWN (1968).** British pop-up plot takes a potshot at our potent potential for Pop Art by portraying the Alien Op, a snoop cop who opportunely opts to crop up, plunk down and pore over our planet people to perceive our penchant for pop. Plodding production for potheads poops out. Fred Marshall produced, directed and penned. To put it plentifully: Plop! Plooey! Piff! Pow! Plunk! Per-Klop!

**POPEYE (1980).** A rarity of cinema: an adaptation of a popular comic strip that translates well to the screen. Comedian Robin Williams makes his pic debut as Elzie Crisler Segar's sailor who loves spinach and Olive Oyl, in that order. Director Robert Altman, filming on Malta, has captured the look and spirit of the four-color strip with a cast that looks as though it stepped out of the pages of "Thimble Theater." Williams' muscles had to be built up with falsy forearms, but you'd swear Shelley Duvall had been born to play the bean-pole Olive Oyl. The blustering sailor man with the corncob pipe sings "I Yam What I Yam and That's All That I Yam," and there are 11 other songs by Harry Nilsson. Paul Dooley portrays Wimpy the hamburger lover, Paul L. Smith is the villainous Bluto (his song: "I'm Mean"), Ray Walston is Luther Billis. Script by Jules Feiffer, who must have taken his spinach as a boy. (VC)

**POPULATION: ONE (1986).** Sole survivor of a nuke attack, trapped in an underground shelter, imagines 20th Century history in a series of surreal and abstract images created by writer-director Renee Daalder. Super-weird, for the avant garde underground.

**PORT SINISTER (1953).** Inexpensive adventure in which Port Royal, a sunken pirates' city, rises during an undersea earthquake, attracting treasure seekers who encounter giant monsters from the deep. Nothing sinister about it—simply silly. Also known as THE BEAST OF PARADISE ISLAND. Directed by Harold Daniels, written by producers Jack Pollexfen and Aubrey Wisberg. James Warren, William Schallert, Lynne Roberts, House Peters Jr.

# *. . . Whose Son Isn't So Playful*

**THE FREELING FAMILY FLEES A FURIOUS FORCE IN 'POLTERGEIST II: THE OTHER SIDE'**

**SHELLEY DUVALL AND ROBIN WILLIAMS IN 'POPEYE': A COMIC STRIP COMES TO LIFE**

**PORTRAIT OF JENNY (1949).** Is love so powerful it transcends time, space, mortality? Struggling artist Joseph Cotten thinks so after meeting mysterious Jennifer Jones, who commissions him to paint her portrait. After an affair with Cotten, she perishes in a Cape Cod hurricane, just like another woman many years before. Jones had earlier remarked, "Where I come from, nobody knows; where I'm going, everyone goes." Profound, what? Metaphysical melodrama on the pretentious side—it's an overblown David O. Selznick production, directed by William Dieterle. Ethel Barrymore, Lillian Gish, Cecil Kellaway, David Wayne, Henry Hull, Florence Bates, Albert Sharpe.

**POSSESSED, THE (1977).** EXORCIST-style special (liquid matter spewing from a human mouth, stuff like that) provides the highpoint for yet another TV-movie about evil spirits taking over people. The setting is a school for girls which must be cleansed by defrocked father James Farentino. Whatever possessed producer-director Jerry Thorpe? Joan Hackett, Eugene Roche, Harrison Ford.

**POSSESSED, THE.** Videocassette title for **DEMON WITCH CHILD.** (Kid that exorcist!)

**POSSESSION (1973).** When a married couple (John Carson, Joanne Dunham) moves into a country home, the wife hears screams in the night and a whistling of "Green Sleeves." Eventually it's revealed there's the decayed body in the cellar of a woman murdered in 1953. Seance medium Hilary Hardiman reveals the corpse is reaching from beyond the grave—and the husband seems possessed by the murderer's spirit. Brian Clemens throws in a twist to climax this inexpensive TV-movie produced in England and directed routinely by John Cooper. Poorly staged action, and not a drop of gore. If POSSESSION is nine-tenths of the law, consider this an arresting experience. Richard Aylen, James Cossins.

**POSSESSION (1981).** German-French production directed by Poland's Andrzej Zulawski, in which a demonic creature (created by Carl Rambaldi and resembling the newborn babe in ERASERHEAD) takes over the body of Isabele Adjani, forcing her to have violent spells, vomit and behave in a messy manner in a Berlin subway station. Meanwhile, her husband, Berlin businessman Sam Neill, tracks down her lovers to dispose of them. This film has won foreign awards and is full of bloody excesses, making it simultaneously compelling and repulsive. Heinz Bennent. (VC)

**POSSESSION OF JOEL DELANEY (1972).** Tense, unsettling supernatural thriller in which socialite Shirley MacLaine has difficulty grasping the fact her brother's soul is possessed through voodoo rites in downtown Manhattan. Black

magic in squalid tenements? This contrast of imagery is nicely visualized by director Waris Hussein. The climax in a lonely beach cottage offers (a) a severed head and (b) a twist ending that just might surprise you. Perry King, Michael Hordern, Lovelady Powell, Barbara Trentham.

**POSSESSOR, THE (1972).** Italian hokum about a medallion that curses an archeology student to murder. A female succubus is responsible. Cheap stuff originally entitled SEX OF THE WITCH. Directed by Elo Panaccio. Susan Levi, Jessica Dublin. (VC)

**POWER, THE (1968).** Producer George Pal took the gourmet novel by Frank Robinson and turned it into a plate of scrambled eggs. John Gay's screenplay is constantly undernourished, and Byron Haskin's direction unfulfilling, as George Hamilton realizes that one of several men in a research project has a terrible "power" to move objects, to blot out entire memories and to kill by telekinesis. In short, one of the finest novels of the 1950s emerged as one of the most disappointing A films of the 1960s. Offbeat music by Miklos Rozsa. Suzanne Pleshette, Michael Rennie, Nehemiah Persoff, Earl Holliman, Richard Carlson, Aldo Ray, Ken Murray, Barbara Nichols, Yvonne De Carlo.

**POWER, THE (1984).** Not a single original idea in this low budget hunka junk from UCLA film graduates Jeffrey Obrow and Steve Carpenter, the pair who concocted THE DORM THAT DRIPPED BLOOD. A cheap-looking clay Aztec figurine (housing evil powers of the god Destacatyl) levitates a man and pinions him on a spike, drops a ton of steel on a nightwatchman and harasses a reporter for a sensation tabloid as sleazy at this movie. The exploding arms and throbbing armpits have been done before and the climax is simply one kid turning into a monster and terrorizing reporter Susan Stokey and other teen-agers in an ordinary house. Tacked on openings and closings were added by distributor Ed Montoro who believes a new shock should come every 7 minutes. It's making movies by the numbers. He even had the audacity to steal the title of Frank Robinson's science-fiction classic. Shameful. (VC)

**POWER MAN. See POWER WITHIN, THE.**

**POWER OF THE WHISTLER (1945).** "The Whistler" was originally a radio suspense series about a wandering storyteller who "knows many things for I walk by night . . . yes, I know the strange tales of men and women who have stepped into the shadows." The film adaptations from Columbia were inexpensive but well-produced noir thrillers. In this one, directed by Lew Landers, a fortune teller predicts the death of Richard Dix, who just happens to be homicidal. Janis Carter, Jeff Donnell, John Abbott.

**POWER PILL, THE (1968).** MR. TERRIFIC was a short-lived sitcom depicting the nebbish misadventures of gas station nerd Stanley Beemish, who possesses superhuman powers a la Superman when he swallows a pill concocted by the Bureau of Special Projects in Washington, an agency run by John McGiver. Beemish (Stephen Strimpell) is enmeshed in espionage plots as he fumbles his way to victory in this compilation of half-hour episodes; a subplot involves everyone looking for a device that nullifies all sources of power. One of the most inept sitcoms ever conceived for the boob tube; one can only ponder how director Jack Arnold got involved. Companion compilation is THE PILL CAPER, which is just as terrible tasting.

**POWER WITHIN, THE (1979).** Barnstorming pilot, struck by lightning, becomes a human dynamo. Naturally, foreign spies

American jungle to retrieve a cabinet member being held hostage by rebel forces. What Arnie and his well-armed men don't know, once they've completed their mission in a blaze of pyrotechnics, is that they are being stalked by an alien creature who's presumably landed on Earth in a space pod to take a few trophies for his den. The characters are vivid, though thinly etched in the Jim and John Thomas script, which stresses the physical tracking. Finally it's just Arnie against the alien, using his wits in a Rambo style. Early scenes of the alien using camouflage techniques (by Stan Winston) are unusually effective, although eventually it becomes just another ugly extraterrestrial life form. Still, the tension sustains and the film ends on a satisfying, uplifting note after an intense one-on-one bashing match. Carl Weathers, Elpida Carrillo, Bill Duke, Jesse Ventura, Sonny Landham, R. G. Armstrong.

---

## *"Pray to God it only kills you!"—Advertising slogan for* **THE PIT.**

---

want the secret too and the chase is on. Aaron Spelling-Douglas S. Cramer TV pilot starring Art Hindle, Edward Binns, Eric Braeden, David Hedison. Directed by John Llewellyn Moxey. Also known as POWER MAN. (VC)

**PRAY TV.** Videocassette title for **KGOD.**

**PRAYING MANTIS (1982).** The dark side of woman's deceit and deception is brilliantly dramatized in this superb British TV-movie. Philip Mackie's 145-minute adaptation of Hubert Monteilhet's novel, LES MANTES RELIGIEUSES, is a complicated but enthralling tale of adultery, lesbianism, murder and revenge involving an aristocratic couple and commoners who blur the class distinctions with their nefarious plots. The acting is impeccable, with the cast headed by Jonathan Pryce as a weak-willed anthropologist. The "praying mantis" women are etched in subtleties and extremes by Cherie Lunghi and Carmen Du Sautoy. The direction by Jack Gold is cold and calculated, contrasting the lovers' passion. (VC)

**PREDATOR (1987).** A tense, action-packed, high-tech science-fiction/horror adventure, forever on the move under John McTiernan's direction as rescue commando Arnold Schwarzenegger and his team move into a dense South

'THE POWER' (1984)

**PREHISTORIC WOMEN (1950).** Treated as a pseudo-documentary, with a narrator blabbering about primeval man and the first steps toward civilization while people in loincloths and animal pelts stand around speaking prehistoric gibberish. In one sequence the hero caveman discovers fire and cooks a side of beef. The first hash slinger! Don't let the lipstick on the girls 20,000 B.C. bother you—it didn't bother director Greg Tallas. Some hairy giants are among the oddities. Allan Nixon, Laurette Luez.

**PREHISTORIC WOMEN (1967).** Producer-director Michael Carreras of Hammer, in the wake of ONE MILLION YEARS B.C. and SHE, looks again at primordial landscapes populated by voluptuous women who move as though choreographed by Gower Champion. There are so many underdressed "slave girls" (original British title) that one is apt to overlook several hundred visible holes in the plotline. Martine Beswick and Edina Ronay are two well-rounded damsels of yesteryear who wear furry costumes which slip so frequently they must be made of banana peels. They fight over Michael Latimer after he's captured by, and rescued from, rhinoceros-worshipping savages. This won't increase your knowledge of prehistoric man, but it 'll give you an eye-popping glimpse at the shape of women who went . . . and came. (VC)

**PREHISTORIC WORLD.** See TEENAGE CAVEMAN.

**PRELUDE TO TAURUS (1972).** Arctic scientists picking their way through the snow discover frozen bodies a million years old. Electronic equipment thaws them out but not the congealed plot. Pamela Tiffin, Robert Walker Jr.

**PREMATURE BURIAL, THE (1962).** One of the best films in Roger Corman's Edgar Allan Poe series, reeking with decay and desolation as nobleman Ray Milland, who lives in a weird house isolated on a foggy moor, is obsessed with the fear of being buried alive. Ray Russell and Charles Beaumont concocted an intriguing if frequently corny storyline that, combined with Daniel Haller's set design and Corman's direction, is a winner. Hazel Court, Richard Ney, Heather Angel, Alan Napier, John Dierkes. (VC)

**PREMONITION, THE (1975).** Despite a ponderous beginning, this emerges an offbeat tale of ESP with supernatural overtones, in the hands of director Robert Allen Schnitzer. Anthony Mahon's script unfolds like a mystery story as crazed mother Ellen Barber seeks to reclaim the baby she gave away for adoption, aided by a crazy carnival clown (Richard Lynch). Sharon Farrell, the new mother, experiences flashes of things to come and other phenomena as the kidnaping plot unfolds, thickened by the appearance of a female doctor experimenting in telepathetic dreams. Some elements don't quite blend smoothly, but the film gallops to a rapid conclusion, with policeman Jeff Corey helping out. Filmed in Mississippi. (VC)

**PRESIDENT VANISHES, THE (1934).** President of the USA Arthur Byron purposely disappears to squelch a totalitarian takeover plot in this oldie directed by William Wellman. Its political fantasy is negligible, but you'll love Rosalind Russell, Sidney Blackmer, Paul Kelly, Edward Arnold, Andy Devine, J. Carrol Naish, Jason Robards.

**PRESIDENT'S ANALYST, THE (1967).** Theodore J. Flicker's amusing, outre satire on presidential administrations, the FBI and our obsession with violence, conspiracies and counterespionage. James Coburn, headshrinker for the President, learns more than he should from the First Executive and flees for his life, pursued by humanoid robot killers. Outrageous, iconoclastic, thoroughly enjoyable if you like off-the-wall humor. Godfrey Cambridge, Pat Harrington, Will Geer, Arte Johnson, Glory Annen, Sally Faulkner. (VC)

**PREVIEW MURDER MYSTERY, THE (1936).** Robert Florey, director of MURDERS IN THE RUE MORGUE, helmed this lower berth feature in which a movie PR man (Reginald Denny) uses a unique system of television to solve an otherwise routine Hollywood whodunit.

Montgomery) team up to rip off a bank's automated teller machine, only to stumble across a plot by foreign spies (led by Keenan Wynn) to destroy the U.S. currency system via computers. They rush to Washington D.C. to warn the CIA, but agents Samuel Bottoms and Clu Gulager are hard-headed until . . . written-directed by Michael Farkas. (VC)

**PRINCE OF SPACE (1959).** Japanese superhero stuff, designed for the child viewer, in which the undefeatable Planet Prince comes to Earth in a flying saucer to defend us hapless humans from alien invaders. In the first of two episodes, the priceless Prince tangles with Phantom Mission, a magician figure trying to swipe a formula for a new rocket fuel. In the second, the old Phantom teams with giants to kidnap a famous physicist who knows a new formula. Formula is

# Schwartzy on the Prowl

**ARNOLD SCHWARZENEGGER IN MACHO POSES WHILE STALKING 'PREDATOR'**

**PREY (1977).** Obscure science-fiction quickie about extraterrestrial Barry Stokes taking over an Earthling. Directed by Norman J. Warren.

**PREY, THE (1980).** A man in the woods is beheaded by his own axe. So much for setting the stage. Along come three guys and three gals, and guess who are "the prey." A lot of footage of bugs, insects, snakes, spiders, raccoons and other creatures preying on each other, as well as gushing blood, severed throats and detached heads. Someone tells "The Monkey's Paw" at a campfire. Minor slasher movie, very minor. Directed by Edwin Scott Brown, who co-produced with wife Summer. Debbie Thureson, Steve Bond, Robert Wald, Jackson Bostwick. (VC)

**PRIME RISK (1984).** Diverting spy-superscience flick, derivative of WARGAMES a little too much, but rewarding. A computer expert (Toni Hudson) and a young pilot (Lee

the word for Eijiro Wakabayashi's direction. Cheaply made.

**PRINCESS CINDERELLA (1955).** Italian version of the Cinderella fantasy, doctored up to feature numerous fairy tale ingredients in an effort to please the kiddie population. Directed by Sergio Tofano. Silvano Jachino, Robert Villa.

**PRISONER, THE (1967).** One of the all-time classic fantasy-mystery TV series, first shown on U.S. TV in 1968 as a summer replacement. Created by Patrick McGoohan, it also stars McGoohan as presumably an intelligence officer who resigns his position and is suddenly kidnapped and taken to a remote village where he is brainwashed by agents of an unknown power. There are no pat answers to who, what and why, for this is an experiment in surrealism, a metaphor for man's undying will to escape his captors and enjoy freedom. All 17 episodes of this enthralling series are available on videocassettes. (VC)

**PRISONER OF THE CANNIBAL GOD (1978).** Obscure Italian potboiler with Ursula Andress and Stacy Keach. One can only hope Ursula's outfits are skimpy enough to provide something to look at, or that Stacy takes off his safari jacket to flex his biceps. This tale of masked cannibals could be strictly from hunger. Written-directed by Sergio Martino. Claudio Cassinelli, Franco Fantasia.

**PRISONERS OF THE LOST UNIVERSE (1983).** Fantasy-adventure on the level of a Saturday matinee. TV personality Kay Lenz and workaday electrician Richard Hatch are propelled into another dimension, a medieval world where evil tribesman Kleel (John Saxon) rules with an iron gauntlet. Hatch, who just happens to be an expert kendo swordsman, and Lenz, who has a spicy tongue and liberated attitude, proceed to do in the heavies with the help of a comedy-relief thief (Peter O'Farrell) and a Green Man (Ray Charleson). There are moments when director Terry Marcle captures a spirit of fun and action, but otherwise it's colossally stupid. The special effects are TV mediocre. Kenneth Hendel, Myles Robertson. (VC)

**PRIVATE EYES (1953).** Sach (Huntz Hall) gets punched in the nose and acquires mind-reading abilities, so the Bowery Boys (Leo Gorcey and the gang) take over a detective agency. Someone punch director Edward Bernds in the nose for subjecting mankind to more East Side escapism. Lee Van Cleef, Emil Sitka, Myron Healy, Joyce Holden.

**PRIVATE EYES (1981).** Tim Conway claims he wrote the script for this mystery-comedy parody over a weekend, and it shows. Conway and Don Knotts are bumbling detectives of the dumbest kind, investigating a millionaire's murder at a castle estate. They encounter all the "old dark house" cliches in a slapstick, no-subtleties-wanted tradition. Lang Elliott directs so indifferently that the most thrilling thing in this comedy of terrors and errors is the shapely body of Trisha Noble. Now there's something to scream about! Bernard Fox, Grace Zabriskie, John Fujioka. (VC)

**PRIVATE LIFE OF SHERLOCK HOLMES, THE (1970).** Must-see for Baker Street Irregulars and Holmesphiles . . . a minor masterpiece written by Billy Wilder and I.A.L. Diamond and directed by Wilder, with excellent music by Miklos Rozsa. Robert Stephens makes the London sleuth a more likable man than Basili Rathbone, with a greater sense of humor and a self-effacing manner. Almost at once the game is afoot when Holmes helps an attempted suicide . . . a plot involving marvelous Jules Verne-style gadgets, Queen Victoria and Holmes' supercilious brother Mycroft (Christopher Lee). Lush, expensive production handsomely mounted, which unfortunately died at the box office and has been brutally edited. Colin Blakely essays an intelligent Dr. Watson. Genevieve Page, Clive Revill. (VC)

**PRIVATE LIVES OF ADAM AND EVE, THE (1961).** Ridiculous film co-directed by Mickey Rooney and Albert Zugsmith, and starring Rooney as the Devil . . . casting coup of the century. Other casting milestones: Mamie Van Doren as Eve, Marty Milner as Adam, Fay Spain as Lilith. Does this mean the Tree of Knowledge is played by Tuesday Weld? And is that June Wilkinson, the girl busting out all over the land of Nod? Her cup does runneth over. Some paradise! Scripted by Robert Hill. Paul Anka, Mel Torme, Ziva Rodann, Cecil Kellaway.

**PRIVATE PARTS (1972).** Dilapidated hotel in L.A. slums is the setting for this morbid tale of murderous misfits. This weird excursion by director Paul Bartel relies strictly on grotesque visuals without character expansion. A 14-year-old runaway (Ann Ruymen) seeks refuge among residents who behave like asylum inmates: swishy ex-minister, photographer who makes love to plastic mannequins, etc. Pretty kinky; you kids send the adults to bed early if this shows up on the late show. Produced by Gene Corman, Roger's brother. Stanley Livingston, John Ventantonio.

**PRIVILEGE (1967).** Visually fascinating British fantasy, directed by Peter Watkins in pseudodocumentary style (not unlike his WAR GAME), is ruthlessly savage in its use of political satire, unrelenting in depicting greed. In a Britain of the near future popular singer Paul Jones is misused by a coalition government as a propagadan device to persuade young people to conform. Jones, a neurotic, uptight, laconic pawn, finally revolts after he is shrouded in religious neo-Nazi mysticism during a lavish night rally. Required viewing for fantasy buffs and for those with strong political consciences. Frightening in a way few films ever achieve, beautifully scripted by Norman Bogner. Jean Shrimpton plays an important role as a model girlfriend to Jones.

**PROBE (1972).** Leslie Stevens wrote and produced this pilot for the short-lived spy series, SEARCH, which depicts colorless secret agents using sophisticated electronic gadgets against spies. Commonplace as TV movies go. Directed by Russ Mayberry. Burgess Meredith, Angel Tompkins, Elke Sommer, John Gielgud, Ben Wright.

**PROFESSOR CREEPS, THE (1942).** Black-oriented programmer, "racist" by today's standards. Mantan Moreland portrays a black version of Philip Marlowe—down-and-out private eye, pursued by creditors, hired to find the missing whatever. Eventually he gets tangled up with witchcraft idiots in a rundown mansion where the obligatory gorilla runs wild. William Beaudine directed.

**PROFESSOR POTTER'S MAGIC POTIONS (1983).** Juvenilistic British comedy by the Children's Film Foundation Ltd. will interest children only. Potter's a nitwit absent-minded fool always concocting some new discovery in his lab which the elementary schoolers then use to foul up the system. There's an elixir of truth, a superstrength drink, a spray that turns adolescent warbling into beautiful singing, and a Fountain of Youth formula which reverts the Head Master back to his childhood. Silly and inconsequential. Directed by Peter K. Smith.

**PROFILE OF TERROR. See SADIST, THE.**

**PROJECT M-7 (1953).** M-7 is a supersonic aircraft piloted by James Donald, who discovers his partner is a foreign agent. Outdated British production (originally THE NET) has little to recommend it—not even the flying scenes are that exciting. Phyllis Calvert, Robert Beatty, Herbert Lom, Maurice Denham. Directed by Anthony Asquith.

**PROJECT MOONBASE (1953).** Robert Heinlein, esteemed science-fiction author, is credited with helping producer Jack Seaman write this Robert L. Lippert film, but his style and themes are not to be found in this uninteresting, pseudoscientific depiction of man going to the moon and facing several crises. Directed by Richard Talmadge. Donna Martell, Ross Ford, Hayden Rorke, James Craven.

**PROJECT X (1968).** Gimmick specialist William Castle purchased two novels by L. P. Davies—ARTIFICIAL MAN and PSYHCOGEIST—and had scenarist Edmund Morris dovetail them into a far-out story about scientists circa 2118 who trick secret agent Christopher George into believing he's passed back through time to the 1960s. Motive: to probe his mind and uncover some Deep Dark Secret about how to stop a Soviet-Chinese invasion. Premises are bizarre and Beyond Human Ken, so dyed-in-the-wool buffs will enjoy this more than general audiences. Hallucinatory sequences with animation were provided by Hanna-Barbera. Henry Jones, Monte Markham, Harold Gould, Keye Luke, Greta Baldwin, Robert Cleaves, Phillip E. Pine.

**PROJECTED MAN, THE (1967).** British horror thriller with scientific ovetones would have been more watchable with faster pacing and less superfluous material. Bryant Halliday is made hideous during an experiment with matter transference gadgets. Now his mere touch can kill, and he's on a rampage of murder and destruction. Mary Peach, Tracy Crisp, Norman Wooland. Ian Curteis directed.

**PROJECTIONIST, THE (1971).** Experimental, offbeat collage of social comment, in-jokes, satire, etc. by Harry Hurwitz, who wrote-produced-directed over a five-year period. Projectionist Chuck McMann is so caught up in his private film fantasy world he superimposes dreams over reality, becoming Captain Flash and constantly saving the world from some new disaster. The lighter side of FADE TO BLACK. Rodney Dangerfield, Ina Balin, Harry Hurwitz. (VC)

**PROM NIGHT (1980).** In a moment of moppets' malice, four youngsters cause the death of a fifth . . . years later, an axe-packing, black-masked killer turns up at the school prom to

**TALIA SHIRE AND ROBERT FOXWORTH FLEE POLLUTION MONSTERS IN 'PROPHECY'**

wreak revenge. This gore thriller features one harrowing chase through the campus, but is otherwise predictable slasher fare. You'll feel stood up. Directed by Paul Lynch, scripted by William Gray. Such a copy of HALLOWEEN, even Jamie Lee Curtis stars. Leslie Nielsen, Robert Silverman, Casey Stevens, Antoinette Bower. (VC)

**PROPHECY (1979).** Disaster from director John Frankenheimer, who fails to come to grips with the techniques of making an effective horror thriller. Scriptwriter David Seltzer disguises this tale with ecological themes and social "significance," but none of it helps to make the monster plot cohesive. Tom Burman's grotesque creatures, created by pollution, are frightening at first, but then become grotesque and dumb. Armand Assante, Talia Shire, Robert Foxworth, Richard Dysart, Graham Jarvis, Victoria Racimo. (VC)

**PROTOTYPE (1983).** Thinking man's science-fiction TV-movie, written with dignity by Richard Levinson and William Link in dealing with the dilemma every scientist faces when his creation (or weapon) is used for ill purposes. The new design here is a humanoid (David Morse) perfected by staunch scientist Christopher Plummer. When the Pentagon intervenes, Plummer steals his creation and hides him away. Levinson and Link concentrate on the cerebral, intellectual aspects. Arthur Hill, as a Pentagon general, is unusually restrained and sympathetic, indicating the writers feel there are two sides to every weapon. David Greene directs with a sure, restrained hand. Reminiscent of THE QUESTOR TAPES, but lacking that film's greater sense of melodrama, which this could have used more of. Otherwise, superior TV. Frances Sternhagen, James Sutorius, Stephen Elliott, Doran Clark.

**PROWLER, THE (1981).** War vet murders his girlfriend who has just jilted him for another guy, then pitchforks her new boyfriend to death. Flash forward to the present time, to the first dance since the year of the murders, and the body count climbs. Tom Savini provided the gore; Joseph Zito directed in unimaginative style. You've seen it all before in slasher flicks. Farley Granger, Vicky Dawson, Laurence Tierney, Christopher Goutman. (VC)

**PSI FACTOR (1980).** Extraterrestrials are on the move again, this time hailing from another dimension. Remains dimensionless, no matter how you view the factor. PSI in your eye. Peter Mark Richman, Gretchen Corbett.

**PSYCHIC, THE (1977).** Watchable for the performance of Jennifer O'Neill, who portrays a woman whose visions of a murder from the past hold a terrifying key to the future. Honorable intentions on the part of Italian director Lucio

Fulci, better known for graphic zombie shockers. Marc Porel, Gabrielle Ferzetti, Gianna Garko. (VC)

**PSYCHIC KILLER (1975).** Intriguing premise by Greydon Clark, Mike Angel and Ray Danton has convicted murderer Jim Hutton learning astral projection through a strange medallion held by a fellow inmate. When Hutton is released, he uses his power against those who wronged him. The revenge killings foreshadow techniques in slasher films to come. Despite inspired moments, this is hampered by an inadequate budget and ordinary direction by Danton, who cast his then-wife Julie Adams as psychiatrist heroine, Paul Burke and Aldo Ray as bewildered cops, Nehemiah Persoff as a believer in ESP and Neville Brand as a butcher. Rod Cameron, Della Reese, Whit Bissell. (VC)

**PSYCHO (1960).** The ultimate in horror thrills, a movie that delivers everything, and a genuine genre classic. It's a series of cinematic tricks allowing director Alfred Hitchcock to indulge his unique style and techniques, all of which are effective in their impact. The shower sequence, the most famous movie murder of all time, demonstrates the fine art of editing, and there are at least three other sequences which have you leaping once Hitch focuses on Norman Bates, a reclusive, strange young man who runs a motel and lives in a Gothic house with his domineering mother. But first there's Janet Leigh embezzling money from her boss and taking it on the lam. Later, her lover John Gavin and her sister Vera Miles search for her, as does investigator Martin Balsam. Then comes the sequence when Miles dares to enter the Bates' cellar and . . . but we can't reveal more without spoiling the many thrills this adaptation of Robert Bloch's famous novel delivers. (It was scripted faithfully by Joseph Stefano.) This ultimate horror in schizophrenia isn't as farfetched as it might seem—Bloch claims his descent into a killer's warped mind is based on a true-life case. The great score is by Bernard Herrmann. Simon Oakland, John McIntire, Frank Albertson. (VC)

**PSYCHO II (1983).** Is it possible to follow in Hitchcock's footprints and successfully make a sequel to the great macabre classic? Sort of . . . at least this is not a failure, even if it can't reach the heights of that which inspired it. Richard Franklin, an Australian who had barely distinguished himself with PATRICK and ROADGAMES before being picked to direct Norman Bates' return 23 years later, seems an unlikely choice. But he was a Hitchcock disciple and advised by Hitch in the art of German expressionistic cinema. With writer Tom Holland, Franklin fashions a homage to the themes and characters of Robert Bloch's novel (although, alas, Bloch was not involved) and strives for a film that spins off from, but doesn't copy, the original. Now it is Bates

**CREATURE FEATURES MOVIE GUIDE**

# The House That 'Psycho' Built

**ALFRED HITCHCOCK**  **ANTHONY PERKINS IN 'PSYCHO II': PORTRAIT OF EVIL**

(declared sane and released from Atascadero Hospital) being terrorized by someone dressing up like Mother and murdering with a butcher knife. Behavior of the characters is often confusing, but the shocks keep one's mind off script deficiencies. The macabre ending, comedic one moment and horrifying the next, comes as a jolt. Anthony Perkins is oddly vulnerable as Bates; Vera Miles returns as Lila, fighting to keep Bates institutionalized; Robert Loggia is the sympathetic psychiatrist; and Meg Tilly is Norman's confused love interest. (VC)

**PSYCHO 3 (1986).** Call it "Daze of His Lives: The Continuing Love Story of Norman Bates." That infamous mother-lover is back in the phantom house on the hill next door to the motel, welcoming travelers in his inimitable style. This time the callers include a defrocked nun on the run from her haunted past and a low-life vagabond with kinky sex habits (not the nun's). Anthony Perkins doubles as director of this offshoot of Robert Bloch's famous novel, bringing unusual touches to what by now are standard cliches in Charles Pogue's script. But the latter half and the climax are just a rehash of what we've seen before, with nothing new for the payoff. (In that respect, PSYCHO II was better.) It's passable, with some gory murders to liven up the pace, but never has the intensity or driving momentum of its predecessors. Just run-of-the-kill. Jeff Fahey, Diane Scarinid, Roberta Maxwell. (VC)

**PSYCHO A GO GO.** See **FIEND WITH THE ELECTRONIC BRAIN.**

**PSYCHO CIRCUS (1967).** Bloodcurdling murders under the big top in the tradition of CIRCUS OF HORRORS, heavily edited for TV. Harry Alan Towers' script, based on an Edgar Wallace tale, was directed by John Moxey. Leo Genn is a Scotland Yard cop investigating the deaths. Those in the circus include Christopher Lee as a lion trainer, Heinz Drache as a ringmaster and Anthony Newlands as the owner. Other faces: Klaus Kinski, Suzy Kendall. In cassette as **CIRCUS OF FEAR.**

**PSYCHO FROM TEXAS (1982).** Made in Louisiana in 1974, this finally reached the screen with the impact of a double-barreled shotgun missing both firing pins. It's not Southern Comfort as John King III runs wild in the bayou, murdering, raping women and kidnaping an oilman for ransom. Action with minimal characterizations. Produced-directed by Jim Feazell.

**PSYCHO KILLERS.** See **FLESH AND THE FIENDS, THE.**

**PSYCHO LOVER, THE (1971).** Psychiatrist plots to murder his wife, using headshrinker techniques and brainwashing to program the killer. Offbeat but minor, reminiscent of THE MANCHURIAN CANDIDATE. Written-produced-directed by Robert Vincent O'Neil. Lawrence Montaigne, Joanne Meredith, Frank Cuva.

**PSYCHO RIPPER.** See **NEW YORK RIPPER.**

**PSYCHO SEX FIEND.** See **HOUSE THAT VANISHED, THE.**

**PSYCHO SISTERS (1972).** Susan Strasberg screams in the shower and behaves neurotically after her husband dies in this exploitation cheapie. She's consoled by her sweet young sister—or so it appears. Faith Domergue, Sydney Chaplin. Directed by Reginald LeBorg. (VC)

**PSYCHOMANIA (1963).** Girls' school is always a suitable setting for a bloody horror movie—so many lovely young bodies for a sadistic killer to choose from, and the camera can linger on the gory details as the madman hacks and hews. This will turn your stomach as well as it turned a profit when first released. A Del Tenney production directed by Richard Hilliard and starring Dick Van Patten as a cop, Lee Philips as the psycho killer, James Farentino, Sylvia Miles, Sheppard Strudwick and Margot Hartman. (VC)

**PSYCHOMANIA (1973).** Upper-crust Britishers George Sanders and Beryl Reid make a pact with a Frog Demon for immortality, so when their son (Patrick Holt), the leader of a pack of motorcyclists called The Living Dead, kills himself in a crash, they resurrect him and he roars out of his grave aboard his hog. He urges his gang members to kill themselves too. That way, he reasons, they can all smell equally as bad as they terrorize supermarket shoppers and like that. So the riders set out to commit suicide in spectacular ways (running their bikes into stone walls and off cliffs, exciting stuff) except for one young woman who has a strange urge to stay alive. What a bizarre British horror film, especially when the grand dame, Reid, turns into a frog. Defies description. Directed by Don Sharp. (VC)

**PSYCHOPATH, THE (1966).** A bloody killer leaves tiny dolls beside his corpses. It turns out that all four victims once examined the records of a German tycoon after World War II and his fortune was lost as a result. Now revenge is being

**ROBERT BLOCH: HE'S THE WRITER WHOSE TYPEWRITER DRIPS BLOOD**

# P Is for Producer . . .

SAMUEL GOLDWYN JR.

HARVE BENNETT

MARTIN ROSEN

ALAN LANDSBURG

FRANK MARSHALL

JULIE CORMAN

IRWIN ALLEN

DEBRA HILL

GARY KURTZ

## 'THE PUPPETOON MOVIE'

wreaked—but by whom? Robert Bloch keeps his often-illogical screenplay moving quickly, providing a framework for red herrings, gore murders and PSYCHO-type thrills. Passable, although nobody went psycho over this British film directed by Freddie Francis. Patrick Wymark, Alexander Knox, Margaret Johnston, Judy Huxtable, John Standing. (VC)

**PSYCHOPATH, THE (1973).** Obscure thriller in which Tom Basham, the host of a kiddie TV show, runs across the county murdering the adults who are mean to kids who watch his show. There's a version with many murders and a version with none of the murders. Figure that out. Written-produced-directed by Larry Brown.

**PSYCHOTRONIC MAN, THE (1980).** Slow-moving, ponderous independent feature shot in Chicago by director Jack M. Sell, with long stretches where very little happens. A barber (Rocky Foscoe) is possessed with what a scientist calls "psychotronic energy" (submerged power in the subconscious mind) and he wills people to die. One man splatters on the sidewalk in slow motion, others are engulfed by wind and go bonkers. Tedious, barely watchable.

**PUFNSTUFF (1970).** Feature version of a TV kiddie series from Sid and Marty Krofft is a disappointment, tending to talk down to its audience. It depicts a magical kingdom of witches, warlocks, talking animals, etc. Directed by Hollingsworth Morse. Jack Wild, Billie Hayes, Martha Raye, Mama Cass Elliott, Billy Barty, Lou Wagner.

**PUMAMAN, THE (1980).** Superpoor superhero Italian fantasy-adventure: An ancient Aztec legend claims that aliens descended to Earth at the dawn of time, giving superpowers to a race of men. Now conquest-hungry Donald Pleasence wants those powers and steals a Golden Mask that enables him to put people under hypnotic spells and perhaps knock off Pumaman. Who is Pumaman? Glad you asked. He's a wimpy guy working as a paleotologist in a museum, who is befriended by a South American Indian named Vadinho. Suddenly Pumaman is wearing this cheap cape and can fly. The special effects shots are terrible, the acting is even worse. It's hard to believe this got made. Misconceived by director Alberto De Martino, this is the stuff that gives comic books a rotten reputation. Walter George Alton is Pumaman, Miguelangel Fuentes the Indian and Sydne Rome the heroine in distress. (VC)

**PUNISHMENT PARK (1970).** Outstanding social fantasy written-directed by Peter Watkins (PRIVILEGE, WAR GAME). The setting is a suppressed society in the near future, where political dissenters are told they will be granted freedom if they can survive a "game" devised by the U.S.

government. This doesn't say much for how other nations see our political machine, but it will enthrall you as the prisoners run for their lives across the desert.

**PUPPETOON MOVIE, THE (1987).** A delightful compilation of cartoon short subjects first produced by George Pal from 1942-47 for Paramount. Pal, a Hungarian who had fled the Nazis, was a well-loved artist who used wooden figures with stop-motion techniques to produce some of the most striking animation work of the period, which was often honored with Oscar nominations. After an introduction featuring Art Clokey's Gumby, Pokey and Arnie the Dinosaur, you'll see the best of Pal's work in such short subjects as "John Henry and the Inky Poo," a classic based on an old Negro legend, "Tulips Shall Grow," Pal's indictment of the atrocities committed by the Nazis in Holland, "Tubby the Tuba," a wistful, melancholy story of a woe-begone musical instrument (narrated by Victor Jory) and "Jasper in a Jam," about a little boy locked in a clock shop for the night. Recommended. (VC)

**PURPLE DEATH FROM OUTER SPACE (1940).** Feature version of Universal's 12-chapter serial FLASH GORDON CONQUERS THE UNIVERSE.

**PURPLE MONSTER STRIKES, THE (1945).** Fifteen-chapter Republic serial, in which astronomer Cyrus Layton meets a Martian maverick out to conquer Earth. He steals the doctor's mind and body for nefarious schemes, but Craig Foster, legal counsel, fights to save mankind. Roy Barcroft, serial villain, is the Purple Monster uttering purple prose. Co-directed by Spencer Bennet and Fred C. Brannon. Dennis Moore, Linda Stirling, James Craven, Bud Geary. The thrills don't get in the way of the plot. (VC)

**PURPLE ROSE OF CAIRO (1986).** Brilliant Woody Allen comment on our love for movies, and the thin line that separates their fantasy from our reality. Movie-starved Mia Farrow, a struggling, abused housewife-waitress during the Depression, seeks escape into melodramas, and is astonished one matinee when the main character of the film speaks to her, steps down from the screen and becomes part of her life. The complications this creates are hilarious and poignant. Another stroke of Allen's movie-making genius. Danny Aiello, Jeff Daniels. (VC)

**PURSUIT (1972).** Michael Crichton directed this TV-movie based on his novel BINARY. A demented political fanatic intends to disrupt the 1972 Republican National Convention with a deadly nerve gas as part of his master scheme to destroy the President. Tense, fast-moving thriller scripted by Robert Dozier. Ben Gazzara, E. G. Marshall, William Windom, Martin Sheen, Joseph Wiseman, Jim McMullan.

**PYGMY ISLAND (1950).** Unsurprising entry in Sam Katzman's Jungle Jim series with Johnny Weissmuller as the king of the potted forests. In this one the swimming champ, pal of assorted chimps and chumps, takes on a guy in a gorilla suit, some men impersonating witch doctors and a rubber crocodile. Not to mention a strange plant. Directed by William Berke. Ann Savage, David Bruce, Billy Barty, Tris Coffin, Steven Geray, William Tennen.

**PYRO (1964).** Look what happens when you play with fire: You come up with a smokeless Spanish-U.S. psychothriller—a flame-out. Barry Sullivan's jilted mistress, Martha Hyer, starts a conflagration that destroys Sullivan's family and leaves him horribly scarred. Masterful plastic surgery restores him to normal and he in turn sets out to wreak his revenge. Sullivan's makeup is just as uninspired as the rest of the production, which will leave you burned. Directed by Julio Coll. Sherry Moreland, Hugo Pimental.

**PYRO—THE THING WITHOUT A FACE. See PYRO.**

**PYX, THE (1973).** Strange Canadian film, directed by Harvey Hart, stars Christopher Plummer as a cop investigating the death of prostitute-drug addict Elizabeth Lucy (Karen Black) and uncovering a Devil cult. Ambiguous, cloudy. Soundtrack songs were written and sung by Ms Black. (VC)

---

*"Please don't give away the ending, it's the only one we have."—Alfred Hitchcock for PSYCHO.*

KD.

*"There's a certain irony in the fact that our lives, and perhaps the lives of everyone on Earth, may depend on Captain Patterson's sex appeal"—One of the Earth astronauts in* **QUEEN OF OUTER SPACE.**

**Q** (1982). Satisfying monster movie written-produced-directed by Larry Cohen, with stop-motion effects by Dave Allen and associates. Decapitation of a window washer on the Empire State Building is the first in many claw crimes committed by a feathered flying serpent, known in Aztec mythology as Quetzlcoatl. Q, for affectionate brevity, lives atop the Chrysler Building and brings daily terror to residents by skinning them alive. Bizarre sacrificial killings by a believer in Aztec legends has led to the "rebirth" of the bird—that's the theory of cop David Carradine, who has a hard time convincing fellow cops Richard Roundtree and James Dixon. Outstanding is Michael Moriarty as a dumb, small-time hood who knows where the bird is hiding and extorts the city. Ending is a bloody shootout atop the Chrylser Building, reminiscent of the climax of KING KONG. Good score by Richard O. Ragland. Candy Clark, Lee Louis. (VC)

**Q PLANES** (1939). Classy British production depicting how a test pilot and a Scotland Yard sleuth track down a new secret weapon, a Death Ray concealed on a fishing trawler. High on suspense and good acting: Laurence Olivier, Valerie Hobson and Ralph Richardson contribute finely etched roles. Its wartime propaganda is compelling. Tim Whelan and Arthur Woods co-directed.

**QUATERMASS AND THE PIT.** See **FIVE MILLION YEARS TO EARTH.**

**QUATERMASS CONCLUSION** (1979). Another chapter in Nigel Kneale's British TV series about dedicated scientist Quatermass, who dabbles in arcane alien matter, much to his ever-suffering regret. In this four-hour TV-movie, a beam from outer space gravely affects the youth of England. Everyone gathers at Stonehenge for a fiery confrontation. Directed by Piers Haggard. John Mills, Simon Mac-Corkindale, Barbara Kellerman. (VC)

**QUATERMASS II: ENEMY FROM SPACE.** Videocassette title for **ENEMY FROM SPACE.**

**QUATERMASS EXPERIMENT.** See **CREEPING UN-KNOWN, THE.** (Run, don't creep, to see it!)

**QUEEN KONG** (1976). British film (budgeted at $632,000)

described by producer Virgilio De Blasi as a light-hearted, affectionate parody—but Dino de Laurentiis felt it encroached on his $20 million remake of KING KONG and charged copyright infringement. Oh well. The plot by Ron Dobrin and Frank Agrama (the latter also directed) has Queen Kong climbing the London Post Office Tower in emulation of the real King. All you queens take note.

**QUEEN OF BLOOD** (1966). Writer-director Curtis Harrington, to make up for a small budget, utilizes color to good advantage and emphasizes character rather than effects in telling of an expedition sent into space in 1990 to a dying planet. Astronauts John Saxon, Judi Meredith and Dennis Hopper find a sinister green-colored woman (Florence Marly), the sole survivor of her race, and one by one they fall victim to her vampirism. Harrington throws a surprise into the climax. Basil Rathbone in one of his final screen roles. Forrest J. Ackerman guest stars. Rocket footage was lifted from a Soviet science-fiction movie.

**QUEEN OF OUTER SPACE** (1958). Spaceship crew discovers life on Venus—and what life! Beautifully stacked babes in silk stockings, miniskirts and boots. And wearing Earth-type lipstick yet! Their queen is Zsa Zsa Gabor, who cuts down on the divorce ratio by issuing no-men-allowed decrees. She then turns her Beta Disintegrator Ray on Earth. Space heroes Eric Fleming, Paul Birch, Dave Willock and Patrick Waltz keep their jaws jutting and crack chauvinistic jokes about the well-rounded dolls. Edward Bernds, who directed The Three Stooges, was at the helm. Script by Charles Beaumont from a one-joke outline by Ben Hecht. The Dolls: Laurie Mitchell, Lynn Cartwright.

**QUEEN OF SPADES** (1948). Stylish British adaptation of Pushkin's fantasy about an aging countess who sells her soul to the Devil to win at cards. Along comes an Army officer who murders her for the secret, then is haunted by her tormented soul. Sensitively rendered and moody in its photography, with a haunting score by Georges Auric. Thorold Dickinson directed. Anton Walbrook, Edith Evans, Ronald Howard, Anthony Dawson, Miles Malleson.

**QUEEN OF SPADES** (1960). Pushkin's horror story retold

through the music of Tchaikovsky in a Russian production written-directed by Roman Tikhomirov that will possibly strike the fancy of opera lovers more than horror fans. But watch it and get cultured, you lowbrows . . .

**QUEEN OF SPADES** (1966). French version of Pushkin's tale, given terrible distribution in the U.S. The lack of a full house gave the producers a royal flush. Directed by Leonard Keigel. Dita Parlo, Jean Negroni.

**QUEEN OF THE AMAZON** (1947). Great White Goddess rule over jungle people, take care her villagers. Come from giant silver bird that fall from sky. White man come jungle, look for Great White Goddess. Natives no let Great White Goddess go back white man's world. Tom-toms beat message. White man evil. White man take long time die. Robert Lowery, Patricia Morison, J. Edward Bromberg.

**QUEEN OF THE AMAZONS.** See **COLOSSUS AND THE AMAZONS.**

**QUEEN OF THE CANNIBALS.** See **DOCTOR BUTCHER M.D.** (No matter how you slice it . . . )

**QUEEN OF THE GORILLAS.** See **BRIDE AND THE GORILLA.** (Bride-and-seek in the bush?)

**QUEEN OF THE JUNGLE** (1935). Feature version of a 12-chapter serial, which in turn featured stock footage from a 1922 cliffhanger, JUNGLE GODDESS. It's set in the lost land of Mu, where a Killer Ray emanates from the eye of an idol. The usual collection of motley natives (posing as leopard men) comes up against the great white hunter, etc. etc.

Directed by Robert Hill. Reed Howes, Mary Kornman, Dickie Jones, Marilyn Spinner, William Walsh, Lafe McKee.

**QUEEN'S SWORDSMEN, THE** (1962). Sorry, no musketeers. This is the misadventure of Stinky the Skunk and a companion named Wolf who rescue the princess and throw out the evil queen. No, it isn't animated. It's men in animal skins leapfrogging around the Mexican landscape. SWORDSMEN really stuck it to the Americans.

**QUEST, THE** (1984). Offbeat Australian quasifantasy blending metaphysical overtones with coming-of-age object lessons when inquisitive youth Henry Thomas probes the mystery behind a legendary creature living in a lake of Devil's Knob, an area shrouded in frog mysteries. Thomas' meeting with an Aborigine, steeped in the region's legends, leads him deeper into the meaning of life (and lake) until the climax, where the explanation behind the monster offers a fresh insight into Thomas' learning process. Beautifully photographed and acted; recommended. Tony Barry, Rachel Friend, John Ewart. Written by Everett de Roche, directed by Brian Trenchard-Reed. (VC)

**QUEST FOR FIRE** (1982). Caveman saga, but not in the stylized tradition of ONE MILLION B.C. or other prehistoric fantasies with stop-motion monsters or beauties in pelts. No, this is a gritty, realistic look at Neanderthals, showing how man discovered not only fire but a sexual position other than the standard Missionary grope. Nothing glamorous about these people, who dress in rags and paint their faces with mud. Mammoths and saber-toothed tigers harass them, and

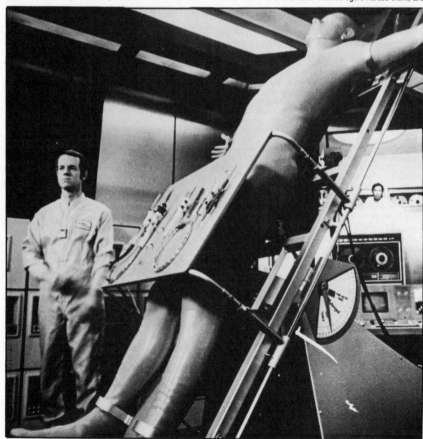

**MIKE FARRELL PREPARES ANDROID ROBERT FOXWORTH IN 'THE QUESTOR TAPES'**

# Sex and Fire B.C. Style

**HOW THE CAST WENT NATIVE IN FIRST PYROMANIA MELODRAMA, 'QUEST FOR FIRE'**

their guttural language was specially created by Anthony Burgess. Directed by Jean-Jacques Annaud. Everett McGill, Rae Dawn Chong, Ron Perlman. (VC)

**QUEST FOR LOVE (1971).** Unusually sensitive, literate British fantasy-romance, dealing with an outre form of time travel. Scientist Tom Bell awakens in a different time stream, where he is now a novelist unhappily married to Joan Collins. Time "split" back in 1938 on two different parallel courses, and he's trapped in his alter ego, a man who has many traits he despises. He falls in love with Collins, but their newfound relationship is cut short by her untimely death. Back in his own time zone, Bell seeks Collins' counterpart, to prevent her death. Handsomely directed by Ralph Thomas, intelligently scripted by Bert Batt, from John Wyndham's "Random Quest." Simon Ward, Denholm Elliott and Laurence Naismith lend excellent support. (VC)

**QUESTOR TAPES, THE (1974).** Android Robert Foxworth seeks data about his creator (his memory banks have been erased) in this Gene Roddenberry TV pilot—one of his best efforts, even if it never sold as a series—which he co-wrote with Gene L. Coon. An intriguing variation on the theme of man looking for his origins while under the secret control of aliens for thousands of years. Don't miss this suspenseful, literate offering. Directed by Richard Colla. Lew Ayres, John Vernon, Dana Wynter, Mike Farrell, James Shigeta.

**QUIET EARTH, THE (1985).** "Operation Flashlight," an attempt to meddle with the forces of nature, backfires and mankind is destroyed in an instant in the neutron fashion, with no visible devastation to society. Sole surviving scientist Zac Hobson (Bruno Lawrence) faces his isolation by looting and talking to mannikins. Eventually he finds two more survivors (Alison Routledge, Peter Smith). In the tradition of Arch Oboler's FIVE and THE WORLD, THE FLESH AND THE DEVIL. New Zealand film directed by Geoff Murphy, based on a Craig Harrison best-seller. (VC)

**QUINTET (1979).** Frigid tale set in the distant future when a new Ice Age has left mankind in a city buried up to the mezzanine with icicles. Survivors Paul Newman, Vittorio Gassman, Fernando Rey, Bibi Andersson play an odd game, Quintet, but it's a Big Chill you'll give this Robert Altman film because of its lack of warmth. Suffered from bad circulation among exhibitors. (VC)

*"How's your appetite today, eh? I must try and remember mom's old recipes. Baked mouse, rat pie, fried rat tails. No, really, if you cook them in vinegar, they're fine."* —A holocaust survivor in **RATS: NIGHT OF TERROR.**

**RABBIT TEST (1978).** Tasteless comedy, directed by Joan Rivers, depicting the world's first pregnant man. Rivers fires off a thousand gags in helter-skelter fashion, usually missing the target. Joan, can we talk? Alex Rocco, Billy Crystal, George Gobel, Doris Roberts, Jack Albertson. (VC)

**RABID (1977).** Porn queen Marilyn Chambers actually has a wardrobe in this shocker written-directed by Canadian horror king David Cronenberg. She's the carrier of a strange blood disease that compels her to inject poison into victims through a phallic-like syringe built into her armpit. Deodorant companies, take note. The mad-dog disease sends them screaming, biting into the world. It's an epidemic of monumental proportions in downtown Montreal! Graphic effects are enough to make you foam at the mouth. Morbidly compelling, with an unpleasant ending. Frank Moore, Joe Silver, Patricia Gage. (VC)

**RACE WITH THE DEVIL (1975).** Only Jack Starrett's direction injects life into this B chase chiller. Starrett keeps the film keen with excitement when two married couples—vacationing in a trailer—accidentally witness the sacrificial murder of a woman during a satanic cult meeting. It's a hair-raising, tire-squealing pursuit with a large-scale conspiracy going down. But not even Starrett can salvage the lousy ending. Warren Oates, Peter Fonda, Loretta Swit, Lara Parker, R. G. Armstrong, Phil Hoover. (VC)

**RADAR MEN FROM THE MOON (1952).** Clown in a flying suit—Commando Cody, Sky Marshal of the Universe—jetpacks to the moon to discover a dictator using atomic weapons against Earth in this uncut 12-chapter Republic serial. George Wallace runs around in the silly suit (first worn in KING OF THE ROCKETMEN) against adversary Retik (villain-portrayer Roy Barcroft). If Commando Cody is your idol, see another serial in which he appears, ZOMBIES OF THE STRATOSPHERE. Directed by Fred C. Brannon. Aline Towne, Clayton Moore, Tom Steele. (VC)

**RADAR SECRET SERVICE (1950).** Robert L. Lippert quickie depicts government agents with newfangled radar equipment tracking down hijackers of atomic materials. Standard chase-action low budgeter with John Howard, Tom Neal, Adele Jergens, Sid Melton, Ralph Byrd, Tris Coffin, Marshall Reed. Directed by Stan Newfield.

**RADIO RANCH (1935).** Feature-length version of an old Gene Autry serial. See **PHANTOM EMPIRE.**

**RADIOACTIVE DREAMS (1986).** Somewhere in this mess of a movie is a good idea for a movie that hasn't been made yet. It's the attempted funny side to Mad Max when two missile site watchmen (Michael Dudikoff and John Stockwell) dig their way to the surface on April 1, 2010 (a joke on us all?) to play the roles of private eyes Philip and Marlowe (detective stories being all they've read for many years) in a post-holocaust world. What follows is an incomprehensible mishmesh in which various gangs of mutants, little boys in white suits (who keep saying "fuck") and other grotesque survivors chase after the two red keys that will launch the world's only remaining atomic missile (a symbol of power, you see). Dudikoff and Stockwell aren't exactly a barrel of laughs running around Edge City in their BVDs while a sexy woman named Miles Archer (Lisa Blouton, a Sybil Danning rival) attempts to seduce the keys from them, and a dude named Dash Hammer pursues with a zap gun. Produced by Albert Pyun and Thomas Karnowski. George Kennedy and Don Murray have utterly ridiculous roles that make no sense. (VC)

**RAGE (1973).** The first half of this George C. Scott-directed anti-government polemic is exciting in depicting the accidental unleashing of a nerve gas that results in the death of a rancher's son and his livestock. The government conspires to cover up the incident, forcing the rancher (Scott) to carry out acts of revenge against military installations. Unfortunately, the second half was severely cut by Warner Bros. and an enraged Scott disavowed his own creation, accusing the studio of its own conspiracy. Richard Basehart, Martin Sheen, Barnard Hughes, Stephen Young, Kenneth Tobey, Nicolas Beauvy, Paul Stevens. (VC)

**RAGE (1984).** Italian MAD MAX imitation offering nothing original—just brainless action and stupid plotting. Captain Rage is a survivor of nuclear apocalypse who goes into "The

Forbidden Land" (nuked New Mexico?) to Alpha Base to find uranium to save mankind. His adversary, Sergeant Flash, pursues him into "The Land of the Trembling Rocks" where they fight it out in a climactic train chase. Styleless and witless, with inane dialogue that runs to such lines as "It won't be easy building up a new world, but there's no harm in trying." Wanna bet? (Un)directed by Anthony Richmond. Conrad Nichols, Steve Eliot, Chris Huerta.

**RAGGEDY ANN AND ANDY (1977).** Animated version of Johnny Gruelle's doll characters endowed with life-breathing qualities. Loaded with songs but not too much stuffing. Voices by Didi Conn, Arnold Stang, Joe Silver, Paul Dooley. Directed by Richard Williams.

**RAIDERS FROM OUTER SPACE (1966).** Three re-edited episodes of Irwin Allen's TIME TUNNEL series with Robert Colbert and James Darren as scientists trapped in time zones. In "Rendezvous with Yesterday," we meet the researchers working on the tunnel, and see how our heroes are sent into time. "The Kidnappers" deals with plant people in some future time; "One Way to the Moon" depicts a flight to Mars threatened with sabotage. Gary Merrill, Whit Bissell, Warren Stevens, Michael Ansara, Ross Elliott, J. T. Callahan. For details see **TIME TUNNEL, THE.**

**RAIDERS OF ATLANTIS (1983).** Satisfying actioner, full of blazing machine-guns, exploding grenades, Molotov cocktails, and bodies falling from parapets. As a fantasy, however, the story is muddled and imitative, borrowing from RAIDERS OF THE LOST ARK and THE ROAD WARRIOR for style. The salvaging of a Russian sub causes part of lost Atlantis to rise from the ocean just when Chris Connolly and other soldiers of fortune happen to be passing by. Out of nowhere appears a gang of mercenaries to restore Atlantis to its full glory. From then on the action is nonstop under Roger Franklin's direction. A U.S.-Italian production. Mike Miller,

Ivan Rassimov, John Blade, Bruce Baron. (VC)

**RAIDERS OF THE LIVING DEAD (1986).** Dead bodies walk the earth, with only one teenager standing in their way. Scott Schwartz, Robert Deveau, Zita Johann. Directed by Samuel M. Sherman.

**RAIDERS OF THE LOST ARK (1981).** Dynamite team of George Lucas (producer) and Steven Spielberg (director) created this wonderful homage to the cliffhanger serials of yesteryear, accomplished with the flashy, dazzling production and effects expertise of the 1980s. Lawrence Kasdan's script has all the cliches, and yet, since they have been unused for so long, they are like newfound gems. The excitement begins with archeologist-adventurer Indiana Jones (Harrison Ford) stealing a delicious sacred stone from temple ruins in South America (actually Hawaii) and escaping a dozen death traps and a tribe of angry natives, all in the same afternoon—before escaping in an airplane, in the cockpit of which a boa constrictor is waiting. Then the pacing really picks up when he and the heroine—tough chick Karen Allen—search for the Lost Ark of the Covenant, which contains a sinister power the Nazis are also after. (This takes place in the 1930s—the last great decade for adventurous exploring here on Earth.) There's a great snake-chamber sequence, a wild-and-woolly chase with Ford almost single-handedly destroying a German truck convoy, and climactic special-effects hoopla when the Covenant is opened and Pandora's demons are unleashed. The raw spirit of adventure is beautifully punctuated by John Williams' music. Ronald Lacey, John Rhys-Davies, Denholm Elliott, Paul Freeman. (VC)

**RAINBOW BRITE AND THE STAR STEALER (1985).** Rainbow Bright is a little girl in the kingdom of Rainbow Land who brings "joy and color" to the world . . . she must prevent an evil Princess and her army of Glitterbots from taking the planet Spectra. Released theatrically as an animated feature,

**HARRISON FORD AND KAREN ALLEN IN 'RAIDERS OF THE LOST ARK'**

this has characters introduced in videocassette specials. (VC)

**RAINBOW BRITE: MIGHTY MONSTROMURK MENACE (1983).** Rainbow and her friends (the Sprites and the Color Kids) must prevent the dastardly Murky Dismal from erasing all the colors in the spectrum. Animated for children viewing. (VC)

**RAINBOW ISLAND (1944).** South Sea paradise. Sarongs. Shipwreck survivors. Human sacrifices. Temple dances. Man-eating plant. No pot of gold at the end of this rainbow. Dorothy Lamour, Eddie Bracken, Barry Sullivan, Reed Hadley, Anne Revere. Directed by Ralph Murray.

**RAISE THE TITANIC (1980).** Clive Cussler writes rousing adventures with mild science fiction overtones. This adaptation of his best-selling novel simplifies a complicated plot, focusing strictly on the finding of the Titanic and getting it resurfaced and returned to port. While the scientific techniques and apparatus are interesting, the characters remain singularly dull. Richard Jordon doesn't do justice to Cussler's he-man adventurer, Dirk Pitt. Box office disaster for Sir Lew Grade. Directed by Jerry Jameson. Anne Archer, Jason Robards, Alec Guinness. (VC)

**RAMAR OF THE JUNGLE (1952).** Cheap TV series featuring Jon Hall as a pith-helmeted Great White Hunter in Africa who stalks past potted ferns and palms was re-edited into TV features in 1964, of which this is demonstrative. A jungle doctor meets the typical "white goddess" who may possess the secret of eternal youth. Other forgettable features in this series (some have fantastic ingredients, some don't) are RAMAR AND THE BURNING BARRIER, RAMAR AND THE UNKNOWN TERROR, RAMAR AND THE SEVEN CHALLENGES, RAMAR AND THE DEADLY FEMALES, RAMAR AND THE JUNGLE SECRETS, RAMAR AND THE SAVAGE CHALLENGERS and RAMAR'S MISSION TO INDIA.

**RASHOMON (1951).** Japanese director Akira Kurosawa's masterpiece. Set in 8th Century Japan, it tells of three men (priest, woodchopper, servant) who take refuge from a storm under the gate of Rashomon, in the ruined city of Kyoto, where they discuss the recent murder of a Samurai warrior and the seduction of his wife by a bandit. In flashbacks, we see five versions of the same tragedy, including one told by the dead warrior through a medium. A compelling study of objective/subjective truth, of man's lust, greed and prejudice. Toshiro Mifune is the grunting, animalistic bandit and his performance is unforgettable. Hollywood remade this as a Western; see OUTRAGE, THE.

**RASPUTIN (1939).** French "biography" of the mad monk who infiltrated the palace of Russia's Nicholas II, essayed by Harry Baur with unkempt beard, peasant's smock and a manner that makes him both repugnant and attractive. More realistic than the 1933 stylized version. Directed by Marcel L'Herbier. Marcelle Chantal, Corine Nelson.

**RASPUTIN AND THE EMPRESS (1933).** Superb MGM classic, casting a weird pallor over Russian history and treating the household of Nicholas II with nightmarish overtones. Rasputin is depicted as a clever, though wretched, letch who uses hypnotic powers over the Czar's family, all manner of perversions being hinted at in Charles MacArthur's screenplay. Rasputin's final death scene is memorably gruesome—no matter how hard his murderers try, they can-

**TOAD SLURTHIE CHASES RAINBOW IN 'RAINBOW BRITE AND THE STAR STEALER'**

not kill him without resorting to some new method. The acting may seem overdone under Richard Boleslavsky's direction, but it is appropriately theatrical to this stylized narrative. John, Ethel and Lionel Barrymore star. Ralph Morgan, Diana Wynward, Edward Arnold.

**RASPUTIN—THE MAD MONK (1966).** Fictional biography of the monk who held Svengali-like control over the Czar's court is a tour de force for Christopher Lee, who overcomes the limitations of John Elder's script to breath fire and brimstone into this strange personage from Russian history. Directed by Don Sharp with a flair for atmosphere and costumes, this Hammer film utilizes sets from DRACULA—PRINCE OF DARKNESS, and interjects horror movie-inspired devices. Barbara Shelley, Richard Pasco, Suzan Farmer, Francis Matthews, Derek Francis.

**RAT PFINK AND BOO BOO (1966).** BATMAN spoof is a juvenile mis- mixture of maladroit superheroes (rocker singer and gardener) chasing a motorcycle gang which has kidnapped a young woman with the help of Kogar the Gorilla. Yes, some rat pfink producer- director (Ray Dennis Steckler) made a boo boo. Carolyn Brandt.

**RATBOY (1986).** An honorable attempt by actress-turned-director Sondra Locke, produced for Warner Bros. by Clint Eastwood's Malpaso production company. This is an American fairy tale about a human freak living in a garbage dump who is befriended by a young journalist (Ms Locke); but she wants only to exploit him for her own ends. It's about our media-hungry culture, our penchant for exploitation and our lack of compassion for that which is different. Whatever the film's good intentions, however, it remains an unrealized anomaly, trapped in a twilight zone of its own making. Locke's direction is adequate but the woman she portrays is scatter-brained and erratic to the point of distraction. It's tough to sympathize with a half-rat person, no matter how cute Rick Baker has designed him. The structure of the story finally defeats everyone. Robert Townsend, Larry Hankin, Christopher Hewett.

**RATS: NIGHT OF TERROR (1983).** Above-average Italian-French post-holocaust shocker that starts in the MAD MAX vein and then shifts to traditional horror. In 225 A.B. (After the Bomb) the world is divided into an underground society and those "primitives" who rove the surface. A motorcycle gang led by Kurt (a Jesus Christ lookalike—this whole movie has a strange Biblical connection) finds a food cache in a deserted desert town taken over by an army of rats. How the rodents devour the characters (often from within, chewing their way to the surface) is the focus while the bikers argue among themselves, go hysterical, etc. More characterization than usual and a real sense of horror on occasion. A surprise ending works nicely. Obviously, director Vincent Dawn is trying to make something different in the genre. Richard Raymond, Richard Cross. (VC)

**RATS, THE. See DEADLY EYES.**

**RATS ARE COMING! THE WEREWOLVES ARE HERE! (1972).** Andy Milligan is writing-producing-photographing! The results are here! And are they awful! Man-eating rats WILLARD-style, family werewolves WOLFMAN-style. The directing is hack-style. Otherwise, this independent low budgeter is style-less and should be returned to England, from whence it sprang. Hope Stansbury. (VC)

**RATTLERS (1976).** Snake-in-the-grass Harry Novak unleashed this exploitationer on the passion pits of the world, a hunkajunk set in the snake pit of life. The poisonous coilers

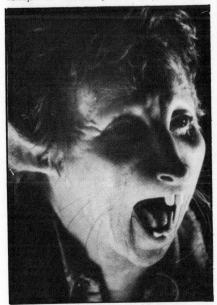

**OF MOUSE AND MEN: 'RATBOY'**

get extra mean when their systems ingest a strange nerve gas. Fangy producer- director John McCauley strikes without warning, putting the bite on his cast: Sam Chew, Elizabeth Chauvet, Celia Kaye, Dan Priest. (VC)

**RAVAGED (1969).** Plastic surgeon Howard Vernon steals the faces of beautiful women and grafts them onto the ugly countenances of his patients in this sexually-alive French horror film directed by Claude Mulot. Frederic Lansac, Elizabeth Teissier, Philippe Lemaire, A. Duperey.

**RAVAGERS, THE (1979).** Pointless, murky, unresolved, clumsy science fiction, as empty and soulless as the radioactive landscape in which it is set. Mankind has dropped the Big Bomb and now there are two bands of survivors: The Flockers (The Good Guys) and the Ravagers (The Bad Guys). Richard Harris is neither, being a loner-individual seeking the Land of Genesis with pleasure girl Ann Turkel. Ernest Borgnine, Art Carney and Woody Strode are wasted in unbelievable, unmotivated roles. Adapted from Robert Edmond Alter's novel, PATH TO SAVAGERY. Totally ravaged by director Richard Compton.

**RAVEN, THE (1935).** This has nothing to do with Poe's poem, but it does owe inspiration to Edgar Allan for torture devices used by mad doctor Bela Lugosi, a Poe-phile who turns to the master's literature to wreak vengeance. Boris Karloff has a sympathetic role playing a criminal disfigured by Lugosi as a form of blackmail. Unusually sadistic for its time; a Universal period piece you want to see. Directed by Louis Friedlander. Irene Ware, Samuel Hinds, Ian Wolfe. On a cassette double bill with THE BLACK CAT.

**RAVEN, THE (1963).** The chemistry of Peter Lorre, Vincent Price and Boris Karloff results in a delightful horror parody brew. Price portrays a queasy magician who hears someone tapping, tapping, tapping at his 15th Century chamber door . . . yes, it's Poe's famous black bird with the refrain "Nevermore," but this bird has a quirk: It keeps transmutating into Lorre (or is it the other way around?). Producer-director Roger Corman winds up the spoof with a marvelous Duel of the Wizards—a classic piece of comedy special effects. Kudos to screenwriter Richard Matheson. Hazel Court, Jack Nicholson, Olive Sturgess. (VC)

**RAW FORCE (1982).** Low budget action film, with emphasis on martial arts action, in which adventurers set sail for Warriors' Island, where an army of kung fu zombies awaits. Once Cameron Mitchell, Geoff Binney and Jillian Kessner are in action, it's a series of shootouts and skull crashings. Directed-written by Edward Murphy. Jennifer Holmes, Robert Dennis, Hope Holiday, Vic Diaz.

**RAW MEAT (1972).** Disgusting title is unfaithful to this British horror thriller which is actually quite tasteful in depicting how Britons trapped in a collapsed London subway tunnel early in our century turn to cannibalism to survive. Unfortunately, the U.S. version was heavily edited. Directed by Gary Sherman. David Ladd, Donald Pleasence, Christopher Lee, Norman Rossington, Sharon Gurney.

**RAWHEAD REX (1987).** A huge monster representing the Devil Incarnate terrorizes an Irish village where historian David Dukes and his family have settled to research the local digs. Scripted by Clive Barker, who is Britain's answer to Stephen King, and directed by George Pavlou. Kelly Piper, Ronan Wilmot.

**RAY BRADBURY THEATER, VOL. I and II (1986).** Repackaging of half-hour adaptations of Bradbury stories made for cable TV: "Marionettes Inc." stars James Coco; "The Playground" features William Shanter; and "The Crowd" highlights Nick Mancuso. Modest, low budget movies, all written by Bradbury and directed by Paul Lynch, William Fruet and Ralph Thomas. (VC)

**RAY BRADBURY'S THE ELECTRIC GRANDMOTHER (1981).** Videocassette version of a family TV special written by Bradbury and Jeffrey Kindley. It's a bittersweet look at the confusion children undergo in growing up, and the pain of losing loved ones. Edward Hermann and his children go to Fantoccini Ltd. for the answers to their problems: They order a new grandmother who shows up in the sling of a helicopter one day as Maureen Stapleton, who proceeds to teach them love and respect. Poignantly moving. Paul Benedict, Tara Kennedy. Directed by Noel Black. (VC)

**RAZORBACK (1983).** Australian import is one of the better imitations of JAWS, capturing a shivery element of fear. Here the ruthless predator is a killer boor stalking the Outback, so huge it crashes through walls and drags its victims into the desert to eat them. Gregory Harrison plays the husband of a TV reporter researching kangaroo poachers who is attacked by the razorback. Harrison and a big game hunter, whose baby was dragged off by the beast, join ranks to track the killer. Director Russell Mulcahy uses desert locations to great advantage, employing lights and shadows to capture an eeriness similar to the mood evoked in IT CAME FROM OUTER SPACE. There's also disturbing symbolism that enhances the psychology of the horrors Harrison encounters, and a statement about man's inhumanity as reflected through the uncouth kangaroo hunters. Scripted by Everett De Roche. Bill Kerr, Chris Haywood, John Howard, David Argue, John Ewart, Judy Morris. The monster was designed by Bob McCarron. (VC)

**R.C.M.P. AND THE TREASURE OF GENGHIS KHAN (1948).** Canadian Mountie Christopher Royal, his jaw grimly determined, wars with outlaw Mort Fowler over a 13th Century treasure containing the secret to liquefying diamonds. It's a seesaw battle to see who will walk "The Cave of a Thousand Tunnels." Jim Bannon is the red-coated hero in this truncated version of the Republic serial DANGERS OF THE CANADIAN MOUNTED. Directed by Fred Brannon and Yakima Canutt. Virginia Belmont, Anthony Warde, Tom Steele, Dorothy Granger.

**REAL GENIUS (1985).** Talk about a movie that never goes anywhere but sour: several teenagers with high I.Q.s join in a campus project to perfect a laser beam. They bicker with each other, pull pranks on each other, meet girls and wander aimlessly through Brian Grazer's production. Director Martha Coolidge seems confused about what to do with the guys and gals, who finally just poop out from ennui. Talk about low I.Q. Strictly lamebrain. Val Kilmer, Gabe Jarret, William Atherton, Michelle Meyrink, Ed Lauter. (VC).

**RE-ANIMATOR (1985).** Topnotch gore flick—disgustingly sickening as it has terrible pandering on one hand and clever humor on the other. There's real talent here as some smart filmmakers give us a sendup while still satisfying our vicarious, visceral needs. Although based on H. P. Lovecraft's short stories about Herbert West, a resurrector of the dead, this is in no way Lovecraftian. It's George Romero-Herschell Lewis-Lucio Fulci in one. The Dennis Paoli-William J. Norris-Stuart Gordon script is outrageous: an intense, al-

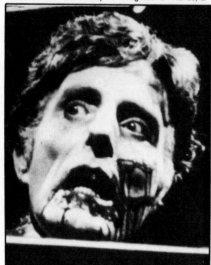

**THE SEVERED HEAD IN 'RE-ANIMATOR'**

most nerdish medical student (Jeffrey Combs as West) discovers a green serum that brings corpses to life. His main adversary is a sadistic, perverted doctor who has eyes only for Barbara Crampton, even after his head has been severed. There are graphic encounters with the dead come-to-life, a scene where the doctor's head makes love to the heroine while she's strapped to a table, and a final crescendo of morgue black humor when a roomful of cadavers attack, their intestines popping out and enwrapping the hero like a vengeful serpent. If it sounds grotesque, blame make-up men Anthony Doublin, John Naulin and John Buechler, and credit director Gordon. You'll "ugh" and "ahh" but you'll love it, perverted viewer that you are. (VC)

**REBORN (1984).** It's a miracle this muddled mess of a movie was ever produced; it religiously stays bad from beginning to end. In one of his hysterical, fever-pitched roles, Dennis Hopper plays a white-suited, bow-tied TV preacher (Rev. Tom Harley) who heals the sick, has his own church/school/studio,

offers a BankonChrist card and keeps goons around to run his electronic pulpit. It has something to do with a woman who can make her hands and feet bleed (stigmatized stigmata?) with Michael Moriarty trying to keep the girl from falling into Hopper's clutches. Utterly senseless, totally pointless and thoroughly unnecessary in anyone's viewing plans. Directed in Italy by Bigas Luna. Antonella Murgia, Francisco Rabal. (VC)

**RED ALERT (1977).** Taut, engaging TV version of Harold King's novel PARADIGM RED, the story of a nuclear leak in a plant that threatens the future of mankind. Director William Hale emphasizes suspense as tension builds to a race-against-time climax. David Hayward, M. Emmet Walsh, William Devane, Ralph Waite, Adrienne Barbeau.

**RED DAWN (1984).** On a visceral level, this John Milius film is a rousing, patriotic depiction of U.S. guerrilla youths killing Soviet and Cuban troops who have had the temerity to invade America and start World War III. You can't help but be caught up in the mock heroics as these teen-agers, the Wolverines, blaze away with machine-guns and rocket launchers, blowing away half the Ruskie army. However, the politics of this movie are so scrambled, and the explanation of how the U.S. could be invaded in a war of conventional weapons so unconvincing, the story falls apart when it attempts to justify its own militarism. Patrick Swayze heads the freedom fighters who are guided by blind hate and revenge, while the enemy forces are commanded by William Smith, whose guile suggests an updated Fu Manchu. Powers Boothe appears as a downed jet pilot who aids the Wolverines (and explains the war's expositon) and Harry Dean Stanton and Ben Johnson are among captured Americans frequently tortured or mown down by firing squads. This will either kick you in the guts or leave you cold with incredulity. (VC)

**RED HANGMAN, THE.** See **BLOODY PIT OF HORROR, THE.** (You'll see red, all right!)

**RED HOUSE, THE (1947).** Thanks to screenwriter-director Delmer Daves, and the theremin of composer Mikos Rozsa, this ranks as a super-entertaining horror mystery. True, there are no ghosts or goblins, but the film reeks with a cursed atmosphere and Rozsa's music evokes dreaded things that probably not even the script suggested. (It is a score that should be listened to, and studied, by aficionados of film music.) Never has Edward G. Robinson been so tormented by the horrors of the past, and never have "the haunted woods" been filled with such foreboding. Lon McCallister, Judith Anderson, Rory Calhoun, Julie London, Ona Munson, Harry Shannon. (VC)

**RED PLANET MARS (1952).** Radio contact is made with Mars by dedicated scientist Peter Graves with a "hydrogen valve" designed by a Nazi war criminal. But it's a ruse . . . the messages (which upset the economy of the world, throwing governments into chaos) are phonies sent by the Nazi, who is controlled by Soviet agents. And then a message from Mars pleads for universal peace and Christianity. The Russian people are so shaken that in one of the most pious moments in movie history, they stage a revolt, knocking Stalin to pieces in 12 days. (See THE 27TH DAY for a similar plot.) The John L. Balderston-Anthony Veiller script (based on a play, and hence preachy and talky) is an exercise in spiritualism and wishful thinking, one of the oddest science-fiction movies of the 1950s, an obvious result of McCarthyism and Red Hysteria. Don't miss it. Directed by Harry Horner with a straight face. Andrea King, Marvin Miller, Morris Ankrum, Bayard Veiller, Walter Sande.

**RED SHOES, THE (1948).** Beautiful use of Technicolor by cinematographer Jack Cardiff highlights this classic British film produced and directed by Michael Powell and Emeric Pressburger, a distinguished pair of (shoe-film)makers. This glimpse at the world of ballerinas focuses on Moira Shearer, who in one sequence cannot stop dancing when she is wearing a certain pair of shoes (an idea borrowed from Hans Christian Andersen). So distinguished is this production that we hesitate to include it in this kind of book. Anton Walbrook, Marius Goring, Robert Helpmann.

**RED SONJA (1986).** Sword-wielding heroine of Conan

creator Robert E. Howard is brought to life by Danish model Brigitte Nielsen, who had never acted before. She does a credible job under Richard Fleischer's sure-handed direction. The plot is predictable odyssey stuff (by Clive Exton and George MacDonald Fraser) as Red Sonja and a male counterpart (not Conan, but played by Arnold Schwarzenegger as if he were) seek a green crystal with destructive powers. This has a fairy tale quality as Sonja teams up with a spoiled young boy prince and his retainer. Fantasy elements include a pet spider that purrs like a kitten and a viewing screen manipulated by a wizard as wicked as the way Nielsen handles her sword. Could have used more romance between Brigitte and Arnold, but they went for a PG rating. Sandahl Bergman, Paul Smith, Ronald Lacey. Music by Ennio

**BRIGITTE NIELSEN IN 'RED SONJA'**

Morricone. (VC)

**RED TENT, THE (1971).** Italian explorer Umberto Nobile (Sean Connery) is in his 80s, watching a TV show about his ill-fated flight in the airship Italia over the North Pole in 1928. The ghosts of those who died in the crash (Nobile was sole survivor) and the aborted rescue attempts that followed gather to relive the bitter struggle for survival in the snowy wasteland. The ghosts then consider Nobile's guilt or innocence. Italian-Soviet film, fascinatingly acted and capturing the bitter chill of ice floes. Directed by Mikhail K. Kalatozov. Claudia Cardinale, Hardy Kruger, Peter Finch, Massimo Girotti. Music by Ennio Morricone.

**REDEEMER, THE (1976).** Homosexual actor, lesbian bitch, unscrupulous attorney, athlete, rich woman, louse of a lover—these graduates of Stuart Morse Academy, class of '67, turn up at the creepy old school, only to be imprisoned by a revengeful fiend who uses flame thrower, shotgun, swords and washroom basin to kill. Writer William Vernick never makes it clear why it's happening, and tries to cover his botches with pseudoreligious overtones. Director Con-

stantine S. Gochis plods along with no help from his editors. In short, fans, there is nothing redeeming about THE REDEEMER. Michael Hollingsworth, Damien Knight, Gyr Patterson. Subtitled SON OF SATAN! (VC)

**REEL HORROR (1985).** Egads! Hecate's a queen of night creatures confronted with entities that burst forth from old cans of movie film. Un-canny. "Terrifying and hilarious." Oh, reel-y? Catherine Bach, Leslie Caron, John Carradine, Donald Pleasence, Katherine Ross, Talia Shire. Produced-directed by Ross and Claire Hagen.

**REFLECTION OF FEAR, A (1971).** Weak imitation of PSYCHO, with surprise twists more baffling than enthralling. Sondra Locke is held prisoner by her mother in her bedroom with an unseen murderer. The cast is good (Robert Shaw, Sally Kellerman, Mary Ure, Mitchell Ryan, Signe Hasso) but the ending totally muddled. Directed by William Fraker, photographed by Laszlo Kovacs.

**REFLECTIONS OF MURDER (1974).** TV-movie reworking of DIABOLIQUE, the superb French horror thriller based on the Pierre Boileau-Thomas Narcejac novel. Considerable changes were made, but it has a distinctive flavor and is quite satisfying. Directed by John Badham. Sam Waterston, Tuesday Weld, Joan Hackett, Michael Lerner.

**REINCARNATE, THE (1971).** Canadian supernatural-black magic thriller in which a dying attorney undergoes sacrificial rituals to transfer his life force into the body of a young artist. But the body-and-soul transference has one black cat too many. Directed by Don Haldane. Jack Creley, Jay Reynolds, Trudy Young, Terry Tweed, Rex Hagon.

**REINCARNATION OF ISABEL, THE (1973).** Mickey Hargitay, one-time muscleman-husband of sex symbol Jayne Mansfield, stars in this Italian chiller about a centuries-old castle where satanic monks resurrect a witch burned at the stake 400 years before. She has a strange appetite, this beautiful woman: she thrives on virgins' blood. From director Ralph Brown and writer Renato Polselli, the team that collaborated on DELIRIUM. Rita Calderoni.

**REINCARNATION OF PETER PROUD, THE (1975).** Faithful adaptation of Max Ehrlich's best-seller, but what works on paper doesn't always translate so well to screen. The climax is predictable from the outset, and the pacing is terribly slow under J. Lee Thompson's direction. Michael Sarrazin stars as a young man suffering from recurring nightmares who realizes he lived a former life in New England. He tracks down his heritage only to fall in love with his daughter from the previous lifetime. It gets a mite kinky at that point, with a masturbation scene that is erotic but tasteful. Margot Kidder, Jennifer O'Neill, Cornelia Sharpe, Debralee Scott, Steve Franken. (VC)

**RELUCTANT ASTRONAUT, THE (1967).** Play the reluctant viewer to avoid this Don Knotts programmer in which a lily-livered janitor (guess who) is picked to be an astronaut, presumably to undergo rigorous, dangerous training to make it safer for more heroic spacemen who will risk the actual journey. Produced-directed by Edward J. Montagne. Joan Freeman, Leslie Nielsen, Jesse White, Jeanette Nolan, Arthur O'Connell, Joan Shawlee, Burt Mustin.

**RELUCTANT SAINT, THE (1962).** Edward Dmytryk directed this gentle little comedy on location in Italy about a 17th Century stableboy who elevates himself to the priesthood only to float whenever he prays. Based on an Italian legend. Maximilian Schell, Ricardo Montalban, Akim Tamiroff, Mark Damon, Luciana Paluzzi, Lea Padovani.

**REMARKABLE ANDREW, THE (1942).** World War II propaganda entertainment: William Holden, beleaguered bookkeeper, is helped by Andrew Jackson's ghost to maintain integrity and fight corruption. Ironically, this was adapted by Dalton Trumbo (from his own novel), who in later years was accused of Communist leanings and blacklisted. Brian Donlevy stars as the spirit. Ellen Drew, Rod Cameron, Richard Webb. Stuart Heisler directed.

**REMEMBER LAST NIGHT? (1935).** Included here for director James Whale completists, this is a slick, fun-filled murder mystery with very light extrasensory perception overtones, in the style of the THIN MAN films. Constance Cummings and Robert Young are an idle-rich couple who, following a wild party one night, wake up in a friend's home to find their host dead in his bed, murdered. Cop Edward Arnold pays a call to interrogate the suspects. Bright, sophisticated, full of witty dialogue, art deco in its design. Based on Adam Hobhouse's HANGOVER MURDERS. Recommended.

**REMO WILLIAMS: THE ADVENTURE BEGINS (1985).** Loose adaptation of the Warren Murphy-Richard Sapir "Destroyer" novels, scripted by Christopher Wood and directed by Guy Hamilton. Despite an incredulous premise (one-time New York cop undergoes plastic surgery to as-

sume new identity to work for clandestine government operation that fights evil forces), this is an engaging adventure with a modicum of fantasy. As Remo Williams (a name selected off the bottom of a bedpan), Fred Ward portrays a dour, slighty-likeable hunk who undergoes training with 80-year-old Chiun, a Korean played by Joel Grey. Chiun teaches Remo to dodge bullets, scale walls, climb the Statue of Liberty and other feats of derring-do (would you believe walking on water?). This is the best part of the film; the rest of Wood's script deals with an industrialist (Charles Cioffi) misappropriating U.S. funds for a "Star Wars" spaceware program. The action is rousing (especially the Statue of Liberty sequence) and there are ample mock heroics but the plot remains threadbare and characterizations are never

# Remo: Biggest Little Agent in the World

**FRED WARD AS REMO WILLIAMS FACES A STATUE OF LIMITATIONS**

**JOEL GREY (LEFT) BEFORE MAKE-UP; SYMBOL HE CARRIES; HOW HE LOOKS AS CHIUN**

**CREATURE FEATURES MOVIE GUIDE**

developed. Wilford Brimley and J. A. Preston are the secretive government men and Kate Mulgrew barely qualifies as the love interest, so dismally written is her role as a military aide. It's doubtful the adventure will continue . . . (VC)

**RENO AND THE DOC (1983).** Canadian film proposes an interesting psychic link between a con man, Dr. Hugo Billing, and a quiet, hermit-like skiier named Reginold Colt—but writer-director Charles Dennis does little with it except make sex and drinking jokes. It's the story of how Doc forces Reno to make a comeback to win the Whistler's Cup, a skiing championship, with tasteless racist gags about a tribe of drunken Indians (the Cuchamungas) who like to shoot up the countryside. Of absolutely zero interest to fantasy fans. Ken Welsh, Henry Ramer, Linda Griffiths. (VC)

**RENTADICK (1972).** The title of this lowbrow British comedy sums up the lower level to which it aspires. The limp plot by John Cleese and Graham Chapman concerns a nerve gas that paralyzes all organs from the waist down. Directed by Jim Clark. James Booth, Julie Ege, Ronald Fraser, Spike Milligan, Tsai Chin.

**REPEAT PERFORMANCE (1947).** After she commits a murder of passion, Joan Leslie is projected back in time exactly one year—fate has given her another chance at life. Interesting premise goes hammy in the hands of director Alfred Werker, even if Louis Hayward and Richard Basehart starring. More of a romantic melodrama than a time-travel fantasy. Virginia Field, Tom Conway.

**REPO MAN (1984).** Outre blending of punk rock imagery and surrealistic science-fiction by British writer-director Alex Cox. Emilio Estevez is a punker wandering through blighted industrial sections of L.A., searching for a meaning to his nihilistic existence, when he teams with Harry Dean Stanton, a bitter, uptight cynic who repossesses cars. Meanwhile, there's a 1964 Chevy Malibu driven by a crazed nuclear scientist who has stolen the corpses of aliens from a government experimental station and hidden them in the trunk. When opened, the trunk emits an all-engulfing white light that disintegrates mortal beings. Somehow Cox blends the seamy slice of life with metaphysical fantasy into this offbeat meringue of genres. Produced by Monkee Michael Nesmith. Tracey Walter, Sy Richardson, Jennifer Balgobin, Vonetta McGee. (VC)

**REPTILE, THE (1966).** Pessimistic doom hangs over this Hammer film directed by John Gilling and scripted by John Elder. Jacqueline Pearce is the beauty cursed by an old Mayan legend who occasionally gets scaly and turns into a poisonous snake monster. Which accounts for the scores of neck-punctured corpses lying about the Cornwall village. Standard monster stuff, but well done. Noel Willman, Jennifer Daniel, Ray Barrett, Michael Ripper.

**REPTILICUS (1962).** Tale about the tail of a dinosaur which rejuvenates itself into an entirely new beast—a Sweetish version of GODZILLA scripted by that team of Danish pastry makers, Sidney Pink (who also directed) and Ib Melchior. Carl Ottosen and Ann Smyrner are the monster stalkers as the creature (a flimsey puppet on wires) stalks through downtown Copenhagen. There's nice pseudodocumentary scenes with Danish military forces, but the effects and crummy-looking monster by Kay Koed are Ineptilicus. Mimi Heinrich, Dirk Passer.

**REPULSION (1965).** Roman Polanski's masterpiece of psychological horror will unmercifully grip you. For the entire time you are in the mind of Catherine Deneuve, a demented woman who goes on a killing spree in her apartment. The reasons are not explained, only visually hinted at. Catherine is possessed by a saddening, frightening form of madness—you sympathize with her, even after she commits her heinous crimes. The detail is realistic, the setting is stark, the music by Chico Hamilton and Gabor Szabo captures the film's mood of mental aberration. A film about the real horrors of the mind—for fantasy go elsewhere. (VC)

**REST IS SILENCE, THE (1960).** German updating of Shakespeare's HAMLET, in which the ghost of a young man's father returns from the grave to inform him (through a series of phone calls) who the murderers are. The rest isn't silence—it's revenge carried out by Hardy Kruger. Written-produced-directed by Helmut Kautner.

**RESURRECTION (1980).** Ellen Burstyn is a Kansan who almost dies in an auto crash, undergoing an "out of body" experience in which dead figures beckon for her to join them. But she lives, now endowed with healing powers. Lewis John Carlino's script deals with faith healing without copping out, and Daniel Petrie directed with conviction. But the film was ignored by the public, much to the disappointment of Ms Burstyn and her co-stars, Sam Shepard and Eva Le Gallienne, who felt this was a significant contribution. Nick Carey did the "hereafter" effects.

**RESURRECTION OF ZACHARY WHEELER, THE (1971).** TV-movie depicts a presidential candidate badly injured in a car crash and taken to a weird clinic in Alamagordo, New Mexico, where synthetic bodies, "somas," are created, then used in a bizarre blackmail plot. Most of this is chase action, focusing on newsman Leslie Nielsen trying to avoid capture as he tracks the mystery. Directed by Robert Wynn. Angie Dickinson, Jack Carter, Bradford Dillman. (VC)

**RETIK THE MOON MENACE (1952).** Feature version of the serial **RADAR MEN FROM THE MOON.**

**RETURN (1985).** Lethargic as a corpse . . . tedious as a calculus exam . . . as slow as free-flowing molasses . . . You won't go back to resee this Boston product about a young man possessed by the spirit of someone who's been dead for 20 years. Phony baloney "age regression" melodrama with no action or special effects. Yakity yakity yakity. Directed by Andrew Silver. A waste of Frederic Forrest, Anne Lloyd Francis and Karlene Crockett.

**RETURN, THE.** Videocassette title for **ALIEN'S RETURN, THE.** (At least Cybill Shepherd is in it!)

**RETURN, THE (1973).** After 400 years in a time warp, the Ark, an exploration spacecraft, returns to Earth. Episodes from the doomed Harlan Ellison TV series, STARLOST. Keir Dullea, Lloyd Bochner, Edward Andrews.

**RETURN FROM THE BEYOND (1961).** Poverty stricken Mexican tale about a crazed physician and his house of horror. Pray it returns to the beyond. Also called MYSTERIES OF BLACK MAGIC. Elsa Cardenas, Jaime Fernandez. Directed by Miguel M. Delgado.

**RETURN FROM THE PAST (1966).** Dreadful anthology of five stories about vampires, werewolves, walking dead, etc.—in short, scrapings of the horror barrel. This cheapie, directed by David L. Hewitt, looks like it was produced and performed by a fourth-rate acting troupe with props and wardrobe left over from a high school play. Originally released as DR. TERROR'S GALLERY OF HORRORS . . . or was it THE BLOOD SUCKERS? Should be returned to the past. John Carradine, Lon Chaney Jr., Rochelle Hudson, Roger Gentry, Vic McGee, Gray Daniels.

**RETURN FROM WITCH MOUNTAIN (1978).** Inferior sequel to the Disney smash ESCAPE TO WITCH MOUNTAIN, again with Kim Richards and Ike Eisenmann as E.T. humanoid kids stranded on Earth who take trips from their sanctuary on Witch Mountain. The alien moppets, who possess "molecular flow," the supernatural ability to control objects and people, are on vacation in L.A. when they encounter evil scientist Christopher Lee and associate Bette Davis. But not even the sight gags and situations are enough to prevent this from becoming substandard Disney fare. John Hough directed. Jack Soo, Denver Pyle. (VC)

**RETURN OF CAPTAIN MARVEL.** Feature-length version of the Republic serial **ADVENTURES OF CAPTAIN MARVEL, THE.** (The greatest!)

**RETURN OF CAPTAIN INVINCIBLE (1982).** A film much beloved by its star, Christopher Lee, but unfortunately it was never released in America, and has not as yet turned up on TV or in videocassette.

**RETURN OF CAPTAIN NEMO, THE.** See **AMAZING CAPTAIN NEMO, THE.** (Boggling! Not amazing)

**RETURN OF CHANDU, THE (1934).** Feature version of the first half of a serial of the same title, starring Bela Lugosi as Chandu the Magician, a popular radio hero of the 1930s who goes up against the Black Magic Cult of Ubasti on the island of Lemuria. Dreary, outdated material in need of action, pacing and decent acting. Second half was released as CHANDU ON THE MAGIC ISLAND. Directed by Ray Taylor. Maria Alba, Clara Kimball Young. (VC)

**RETURN OF COUNT YORGA, THE (1971).** The success of COUNT YORGA—VAMPIRE dictated this sequel, Robert Quarry again essaying the bloodsucker who runs amock in California. Now there's better acting thanks to Mariette Hartley, Roger Perry, Walter Brooke, Yvonne Wilder (as a deaf mute) and George Macready. And director Bob Kelljan has greater control, providing frightening moments when corpses attack an orphanage near San Francisco. Bill Butler's cinematography is high class. Once again Michael Macready (George's son) produced. Screenplay by Kelljan and Yvonne Wilder.

**RETURN OF DR. FU MANCHU, THE (1930).** Sax Rohmer's diabolical Oriental goes bonkers in this sequel to THE MYSTERIOUS DR. FU MANCHU. Warner Oland is the madman plotting to take over the world with the aid of a secret drug that induces catalepsy; the insidious Chinese fiend also contends with Scotland Yard's Nayland Smith (Neil Hamilton). Directed by Rowland V. Lee. Jean Arthur, William Austin, O. P. Heggie, David Dunbar.

**RETURN OF DR. MABUSE, THE (1961).** Well-produced Italian-French-German sequel to the Fritz Lang films about an ingenious madman bent on conquering the world. Inspector Lohmann (Gert Frobe) and an FBI man (Lex Barker) join reporter Daliah Lavi to prevent the archvillain (Wolfgang Preiss) from infiltrating a nuclear plant and controlling employees' minds. Interesting, but not up to Lang's originals or the books by Norbert Jacques. Directed by Harald Reinl, Fausto Tozzi, Werner Peters.

**RETURN OF DR. X, THE (1940).** Humphrey Bogart in a horror film? There he is with pallid face, sunken cheeks and horn-rimmed glasses, requiring a blood "fix" every few hours, which accounts for the 493 corpses littering his neighborhood. Bogart was being punished by Jack Warner for his iconoclastic attitudes, but never again was he so dumbly wasted in such undistinguished fare. Meanwhile, Wayne Morris endures as a fast-talking (also dumb) newspaperman, Dennis Morgan suffers as the Nice Young Man, John Litel looks embarrassed as the Doctor Who Went Too Far and Rosemary Lane oozes charm as the Friendly Nurse. Directed programmer-style by Vincent Sherman.

**RETURN OF DRACULA, THE. See CURSE OF DRACULA, THE.** (Curses! Boiled again!)

**RETURN OF GIANT MAJIN, THE (1966).** Clomping time again for that ancient God of War who inhabits a stone statue standing guard over a mountain in Japan, and goes around crushing the worst offenders in a medieval feud. Production values are good, the action well staged. Directed by Kenji Misumi and Yoshiyuki Kuruda. Kojiro Hongo, Shiho Fujimura, Taro Marui.

**RETURN OF MAXWELL SMART. See NUDE BODY, THE.**

**RETURN OF PETER GRIMM, THE (1935).** More creaky than charming is this quaint, sentimental ghost story based on a play by David Belasco, first made as a silent film in 1926. Crotchety Lionel Barrymore returns from the grave enwrapped in a gooey substance that suggests cinematographer Glenn Williams smeared Vasoline on the lens. Thin plot has relatives fighting over an inheritance and deciding how they should feel about the recently deceased—who stands to one side, looking over their shoulders. It's gentle and bloodless as Barrymore tries to prevent a wrongful marriage, and it's saccharine sweet when a youngster also goes to his maker and walks off into the sunset with the cranky Barrymore. Directed by Victor Schertzinger as though it were still a play and not a movie. Helen Mack, Edward Ellis, Donald Meek, George Breakston.

**RETURN OF SHERLOCK HOLMES, THE (1986).** The first hour of this TV-movie from writer-producer Bob Shayne is a Sherlockian delight: Private eye Jane Watson (Margaret Colin, a wonderfully spunky, energetic actress with lovely big big eyes one could swim in) finds out she is the great granddaughter of Dr. John Watson and resurrects Holmes from a deep-freeze sleep, where he has been awaiting a cure for bubonic plague (with which he was injected by James Moriarty's brother). Holmes (a lean, erudite Michael Pennington) is soon caught up in a mystery that unfortunately is far too routine for the premise once it's established. But oh, does Pennington have fun with the sexy Colin, even though he is a walking anachronism. Recommended to detective fans, although Holmesian buffs may consider this sacrilegious, and becry such spoofery. Lila Kaye, Connie Booth, Nicholas Guest, Barry Morse (in a cameo that's bigger than it seems).

**RETURN OF SUPERBUG (1979).** West German Wunderauto, about which everyone oughta wunder, has become a jeep half-track operated by a robot character called "El Guancho" with a voice like Bugs Bunny's. On an island off the coast of Spain, several parties are in search of an airplane containing the "Treasure of Corleone," lost during World War II. Oddly enough, unlike the two films before it, this has serious themes, such as the Superbug's pilot having a drinking problem. Director Rudolf Zehetgruber is nothing but a backseat driver. Rudolf Rittberg, Brad Harris.

**A BEVY OF BLOODY THROAT-BITERS IN 'RETURN OF COUNT YORGA'**

CREATURE FEATURES MOVIE GUIDE

# Revenge of the Rebels

JABBA'S PALACE GUARD

R2D2 AND WICKET THE EWOK IN 'RETURN OF THE JEDI'

NIEN NUMB, NUMB
WITH SHOCK

CARRIE FISHER AS
THE PRINCESS

ROUTINE STORMTROOPER
IN ACTION

*"The Great Jabba the Hutt has decreed that you are to be terminated . . . You will therefore be taken to the Dune Sea and cast into the pit of Carkoon, nesting place of the all-powerful Sarlacc . . . In his belly you will find a new definition of pain and suffering as you are slowly digested over a thousand years."*—A Palace Minion to Luke Skywalker in ***RETURN OF THE JEDI.***

**PAWN.** Videocassette version of **DEADLY SPAWN, THE.** (Deadly is right!)

**RETURN OF THE APE MAN (1944).** Not that it matters, but this is not a sequel to THE APE MAN. Bela Lugosi and John Carradine bring a prehistoric Neanderthal out of its deep freeze—a hairy caveman who loves to run amok, a nonsocial trait they "exorcise" by giving him the brain of George Zucco. The result is a cultured, refined gentleman who plays "Moonlight Sonata" . . . and then goes on a murderous rampage. All-time low for all. Sam Katzman and Jack Dietz produced for Monogram; Phil Rosen directed.

**RETURN OF THE SIX MILLION DOLLAR MAN AND THE BIONIC WOMAN (1987).** Two old TV series are retreaded into a TV-movie that is just as bad as the originals. Steve Austin (Lee Majors) and Jamie Somers (Lindsay Wagner) are brought out of retirement to stop Fortress, a gang led by Martin Landau that is trying to get the secret of bionic power. But the first hour is strictly bionic soap opera as Austin rekindles an old romance with Jamie and tries to win the respect of the son he never raised. Phony sentiment and mushy stuff stand in the way of action until Austin and Jamie team up to throw the bad guys in slow motion through windows and out doors. Richard Anderson is back as the manipulative assignment chief, with Lee Majors II playing Austin's son, who also becomes a bionic warrior with X-ray zap vision. Bionic crude. Directed by Ray Austin. Gary Lockwood, Tom Schanley.

**RETURN OF THE BLIND DEAD (1973).** Spanish sequel to

**'RETURN OF THE FLY'**

THE BLIND DEAD, directed by Amando de Ossorio and starring Tony Kendall and Fernando Sancho. This "walking dead" series continued with **HORROR OF THE ZOMBIES.**

**RETURN OF THE EVIL DEAD.** See **RETURN OF THE BLIND DEAD.** (The blind leading the sublime?)

**RETURN OF THE FLY (1959).** Underrated sequel to THE FLY, with a scientist's son (Brett Halsey) picking up the experiment in teleportation where dead old dad left off. With stark black-and-white photography by Brydon Baker, director Edward L. Bernds evokes some horrifying moments in a mortuary and keeps things buzzing. George Langelaan's story gimmick—transposition of body parts on human and fly, so tiny fly has human head and huge human has huge fly's head—is repeated by Bernds (he also scripted), indicating there was nothing new to be achieved in this sequel. But it's still a nice low budget film. Vincent Price reappears as a family friend. Dan Seymour, John Sutton. (VC)

**RETURN OF THE GIANT MONSTERS, THE (1967).** Japanese monster movie with plenty of snap—its main protagonist being a giant turtle who comes out of his shell when Gyaos, a winged monstrosity that fires laser bolts through its mouth, attacks Earth without pity. Kazufumi Fujii's special effects include mandatory earthquakes and spewing lava, just in case the towering titans bore you with their routine destruction. Actually the effects are good . . . but you

must have appreciation for these Oriental slam-bang affairs to sit through to the bitter end. Kojiro Hongo, Kichijiro Ueda. Directed by Noriyaki Yuasa.

**RETURN OF THE INCREDIBLE HULK, THE (1977).** Sequel to THE INCREDIBLE HULK has Bill Bixby back as Dr. Banner, searching to learn why he transmutates into a green monster (played by strongman Lou Ferrigno with spinach-coloring rubbed all over his body) whenever he gets mad or placed under stress. Based on the Marvel comic book character; decently done. Directed by Alan J. Levi. Dorothy Tristan, William Daniels, Laurie Prange.

**RETURN OF THE JEDI (1983).** Third in the STAR WARS series, culminating the middle trilogy of George Lucas' proposed nine-part saga. JEDI resolves the cliff-hangers in THE EMPIRE STRIKES BACK and moves faster than Imperial fighters as Luke Skywalker, Princess Leia, Chewbacca, Lando Calrissian and that Laurel-and- Hardy team in space, R2D2 and C3PO, penetrate the fortress of the vile bandit Jabba the Hutt (a giant toad creature) to rescue Han Solo's carbonized body. After a marvelous opening featuring a menagerie of extraterrestrials and a hair-raising battle aboard Jabba's land barge, our heroes are off to fight the Empire, personified by Darth Vader and the Emperor (looking like a wicked wizard) and several thousand stormtroopers. Ken Ralston's team at Industrial Light and Magic has perfected its equipment so that the effects are simply great. There's a mind-boggling number of space hardware whizzing past the camera, and a fabulous chase on air bikes through a redwood forest. Phil Tippett's otherworldly beings are a delight to terrestrial eyes. In addition to nonstop action, diehard fans will be intrigued by Luke's quest for his true heritage. It's a mythological duel of good vs. evil in its purest form and helps to elevate Lawrence Kasdan's screenplay, often guilty of banal dialogue and indifference to the popular characters. Director Richard Marquand goes for the glossy and bright, and seems to be on the same wave length as Lucas; hence, this doesn't have the pessimism Irvin Kershner brought to THE EMPIRE STRIKES BACK, and it ends on a positive upbeat note in the camp of the Ewoks, a race of cuddly bear-like creatures who help fight the Empire. A superexciting superpicture. Mark Hamill, Carrie Fisher, Harrison Ford, Peter Mayhew, Billy Dee Williams, David Prowse, Anthony Daniels. (VC)

**RETURN OF THE KING . . . A STORY OF THE HOBBITS, THE (1980).** Animated sequel to THE HOBBIT, a U.S.-Japanese project featuring the voices of Orson Bean, Theodore Bikel, William Conrad, John Huston and Roddy McDowall. Directed in Japan by Akiyuki Kubo, in America by Arthur Rankin Jr. and Jules Bass. Scripted by Romeo Muller, who followed Tolkien's RETURN OF THE KING and THE HOBBIT.

**RETURN OF THE LIVING DEAD, THE (1985).** Dan O'Bannon, author of ALIEN and DEAD AND BURIED, makes his directorial debut with this spinoff from NIGHT OF THE LIVING DEAD and spoofs the genre without sacrificing shocks and thrills. A superior example of black comedy horror (O'Bannon scripted too). In a strange warehouse for the world's oddities, are cannisters belonging to the U.S. military, rumored to contain corpses inflicted with a plague from space (there are even references to George Romero's 1967 movie). A malfunction frees a corpse and a mist rises into the air, causing a toxic rain to fall on Resurrection Cemetery. Next, the walking dead are everywhere. Absolutely hysterical (if you have a morbid sense of humor, that is) with hair-raising thrills in the Romero tradition. O'Bannon is to be commended. And thanks also goes to Clu Gulager, James Karen, Beverly Randolph, Thom Mathews and Don Calfa for giivng it a touch of versimilitude, even when it's supposed to be wild, woolly fun. (VC)

**RETURN OF THE MAN FROM U.N.C.L.E.: THE 15 YEARS LATER AFFAIR (1983).** Resurfacing of T.H.R.U.S.H., the terrorist birdbrains, forces Napoleon Solo and Illya Kuryakin back into action in this TV-movie based on the hit 1964-67 series. T.H.R.U.S.H. demands $350 million in ransom or it will explode the H957 nuclear device—the most terrifying weapon in the universe. This is so imitative of the Bond films

**CREATURE FEATURES MOVIE GUIDE**

**YOUR STANDARD ACTIVE CORPSES IN 'RETURN OF THE LIVING DEAD'**

that some sequences play like direct steals. The devices are strained; the only freshness is provided by Robert Vaughn and David McCallum as the retreads who crack jokes about their ages. George Lazenby also saves the day by breezing through as James Bond (referred to as J.B.) and rescuing Napoleon during a high-speed chase through Las Vegas. With Leo G. Carroll dead, Patrick Macnee is the new chief, Sir John Raleigh. Villains are Anthony Zerbe and Keenan Wynn, but they are total stereotypes, of little interest. Okay escapism and that's about the extent of it. Directed by Ray Austin. (VC)

**RETURN OF THE TERROR (1934).** Mild thriller (based on an Edgar Wallace mystery) in which an inventor of a deadly X-ray device is sent to prison. When released, he turns the contraption on those who framed him. Directed by Howard Bretherton. Mary Astor, Lyle Talbot, John Halliday, J. Carrol Naish. Remake of the silent film, THE TERROR.

**RETURN OF THE VAMPIRE, THE (1943).** Columbia pastiche of horror films of the 1940s is crude but fun—if you can accept cornball premises and a corny fog swirling around the vampire as he attacks his victims. Bela Lugosi is a long-dead bloodsucker in cahoots with a werewolf (Matt Willis) he holds under his power in London 1918. A Van Helsing-imitating professor destroys him with a stake, but an air raid in blitz-terrorized London years later resurrects him and he begins a new wave of horror, attacking members of the family that originally "staked" him. Directed by Lew Landers. Nina Foch, Miles Mander. (VC)

**RETURN OF THE ZOMBIES (1984).** Stan Cooper and Charles Quiney star in this supernatural fright flick in which the death of an evil count and his daughter results in the dead rising from their graves. (VC)

**RETURN TO BOGGY CREEK (1978).** Not a sequel to LEGEND OF BOGGY CREEK, but a good children's movie under Tom Moore's direction, well photographed with many beautiful shots of the swamps, ample banjo music and a "Boggy Creek Ballad" as two brothers and their sister have encounters with a benevolent, hairy beast of legend. Languidly told, with colorful bayou characters. Worth going back for. Directed by Tom Moore. Dawn Wells and Dana Plato head the able regional cast. (VC)

**RETURN TO EARTH (1976).** Offbeat TV docudrama of Colonel Edwin E. "Buzz" Aldrin and the ordeal he underwent after returning from a manned moon flight. He suffered bouts of depression, feelings of worthlessness and domestic alienation. Cliff Robertson portrays the astronaut with an air of dignity while Shirley Knight is the long-suffering wife. Directed by Jud Taylor, scripted by George Malko from a book by Aldrin and Wayne Warga. Charles Cioffi, Ralph Bel-

lamy, Stefanie Powers, Alexandra Taylor.

**RETURN TO FANTASY IS-LAND (1977).** Second TV pilot for the series that became the ridiculous, long-running hit, FANTASY ISLAND, with assorted wish-fulfillers making fools of themselves while hanging around Mr. Roarke (Ricardo Montalban). Directed by George McGowan. Adrienne Barbeau, Horst Buchholz, Joseph Cotten, Pat Crowley, Joseph Campanella, George Chakiris, Karen Valentine. You'll also find Herve Villechaize as Tattoo.

**RETURN TO HORROR HIGH (1987).** Crippen High, scene of many gore murders a few years ago, is visited by a film crew making a horror film, but then the killer strikes on the set. Directed by Bill Froehlich. Lori Lethin, Brendad Hughes, Alex Rocco, Scott Jacoby, Vince Edwards.

**RETURN TO OZ (1985).** Admirable attempt by Disney to recapture the flavor of the adventures of Dorothy in Oz (as originally conceived by L. Frank Baum) was a box office failure, which critics decried for its somber tone and its failure to be as charming and appealing as the 1939 MGM musical. All that aside, it's a rather imaginative if slow-paced sequel, following Dorothy as she is subjected to the electrical machine of a doctor (Nicol Williamson) and nurse (Jean Marsh) trying to cure her of insomnia caused by her first adventure in Oz. She awakens in the fanciful kingdom with a talking chicken named Billina and is joined with Tik Tok, a mechanical robot, Jack Pumpkinhead and a moose head named Gump. They must free the Emerald City inhabitants, who have been frozen into marble statues by the evil Gnome King, a rock man, and his queen, Princess Mombi (also played by Marsh). The more memorable sequences include the Wheelers, a crowd of cackling jokers who move about on wheels, and a chamber where the princess keeps assorted heads encased behind glass. The effects are quite good, especially Will Vinton's Claymation, a process of animation

the rock faces. There's more production quality than zip to Walter Murch's direction, but don't be put off by the bad word of mouth. Murch co-wrote with Gill Dennis, inspired by Baum's LAND OF OZ and OZMA OF OZ. Fairuza Balk is a good Dorothy, Piper Laurie appears as Aunt Em, and Matt Clark is Uncle Henry. Some have called this the dark side to THE WIZARD OF OZ. (VC)

**RETURN TO SALEM'S LOT (1987).** Although Stephen King is given a "creative consultant" credit, his original novel SALEM'S LOT has little to do with this horror-comedy item starring Michael Moriarty as an anthropologist and Richard Addison Reed as his son, who move back to Salem's Lot, there to discover the town is still swarming with vampires led by Andrew Duggan. Directed and co-written with James Dixon by cult favorite Larry Cohen, who brings his usual off-beat quirks to the story. Director Samuel Fuller puts in a guest appearance. June Havoc, Ronee Blakley, Evelyn Keyes.

**RETURN TO TREASURE ISLAND (1954).** Dawn Addams is a descendant of Jim Hawkins, the youth who befriended pirate leader Long John Silver in Robert Louis Stevenson's novel, TREASURE ISLAND. She has a map of the treasure's location and with the help of Tab Hunter sets out to find it. So does a gang of modern pirates. Directed by E. A. Dupont. Porter Hall, Harry Lauter, James Seay.

**RETURNING, THE (1983).** Ancient Indian spirits heap plenty mad! Gallop from great teepee in thunder sky to haunt white eyes living in land of great sand dunes, the Mojave. Angry warrior spirits no want land back—only wantum try out techniques they saw in THE EXORCIST many moon ago. Big Chief Joel Bender and scratching paper man Patrick Nash like Custer—lead'em cast (Susan Strasberg, Gabriel Walsh, Ruth Warrick) and crew to great massacre at Little Big Picture. Heap plenty bad medicine. You gettum what you pay wampum for. Ugh!

**REVENGE (1971).** Haggy old dame goes bats in a decaying San Francisco Victorian, imprisoning Stuart Whitman for revenge but unaware she has the wrong guy. Prisoner's girl,

through ESP powers, sets out to rescue him from what is a fate worse than death—being locked up with Shelley Winters! Joseph Stefano dreamed it up; Jud Taylor directed. Bradford Dillman, Gary Clarke. (VC)

**REVENGE (1986).** Here's a blood cult flick that goes to the dogs: In Tulsa, Okla., some of the best citizens are members of the Kaninas Cult, which worships a demon hound. Patrick Wayne and a farmer lady track down the culprits in a cheapie made just for videocassette, described as a sequel to the equally ugly BLOOD CULT. Among the delights: an axe in a farmer's forehead, a co-ed's severed foot, deskinned heads and several charred bodies. Written-directed by Christopher Lewis. John Carradine. (VC)

**REVENGE OF FRANKENSTEIN, THE (1958).** Sequel to CURSE OF FRANKENSTEIN and one of the best in Hammer's Frankenstein series, permeated with a satanical sense of humor (thanks to scripter Jimmy Sangster) that does not distract from the horrific elements. Peter Cushing returns as the Baron, working in a hospital in Carlsbruck to have easy access to organs and limbs so he might give his hunchback assistant a new body. It's warped (the story, not the body) but that's what makes these British fright flicks so bloody good, old man. Directed by Terence Fisher with a lust for macabre humor. Michael Gwynn replaces Christopher

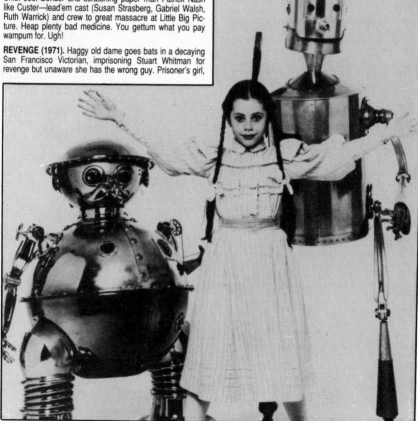

**TIK TOK, DOROTHY (FAIRUZA BALK) AND THE TIN MAN IN 'RETURN TO OZ'**

**JOHN BROMFIELD AND THE GILL MAN IN 'REVENGE OF THE CREATURE'**

Lee as the Monster, with Lionel Jeffries as a body snatcher. Francis Matthews, Eunice Gayson.

**REVENGE OF THE CREATURE (1955).** THE CREATURE FROM THE BLACK LAGOON was too big a hit just to float away, so director Jack Arnold and producer William Alland reteamed for this exciting sequel recapturing the superb underwater photography and brain-bashing thrills of the original. Martin Berkeley's story is nonstop action when the Gill-Man is rediscovered in his Black Lagoon, captured and brought to a sea world park in Florida. Eventually the primeval Creature goes on a rampage—mainly to carry Lori Nelson away to his marshy hideaway in the Everglades. John Agar and John Bromfield fight over the girl, but it's just a half-hearted subplot. Originally produced in 3-D, but few patrons saw it that way in the 1950s. In 1982 the film resurfaced in some cities on TV in a special 3-D presentation. It was only partially successful, since the process doesn't work so well. Nestor Paiva, Clint Eastwood (making his movie debut as a lab technician), Robert B. Williams, Dave Willock. There's also a 3-D videocassette.

**REVENGE OF THE DEAD (1984).** By Italian horror standards, one of the tamest spaghetti-shockers ever produced, so pallid, in fact, one wishes Lucio Fulci were on hand to provide walking corpses. This Italian TV-movie is about an unsold novelist who discovers letters written on his typewriter ribbon which refer to "K Zones," areas where the dead can return to life. The writer and his wife set out for a place called Necropolis and an oracle of the dead. Unfortunately, the emphasis of director-producer Pupi Avati is on dialogue and literacy with a modicum of visual shocks. The film's 100 minutes cannot sustain interest. Gabriele Lavia, Anna Canovas, Bob Tonelli, John Stacy. (VC)

**REVENGE OF THE GODS (1966).** Re-edited episodes from Irwin Allen's TIME TUNNEL (see that entry for more details). In their time-hopping adventures, Robert Colbert and James Darren witness the Fall of Jericho and the Siege of Troy. Whit Bissell, Lee Mereiwether, John Doucette, Rhodes Reason, Michael Pate, Lisa Gaye.

**REVENGE OF THE HOUSE OF USHER (1980).** Corpses, vampires and a weird old house in a horror tale that has nothing to do with Edgar Allan Poe. (VC)

**REVENGE OF THE JEDI.** George Lucas announced the third film in his STAR WARS series under this title, but changed his mind before the release date, retitling the project RETURN OF THE JEDI. Some posters and pre-release material carry the REVENGE title.

**REVENGE OF THE LIVING DEAD.** See **MURDER CLINIC, THE.** (Feeling lifeless? See a doctor!)

**REVENGE OF THE MYSTERONS FROM MARS (1981).** TV version of THUNDERBIRD 6, a sequel to THUNDERBIRDS ARE GO, is a full-length puppet space adventure produced in England by Gerry and Sylvia Anderson. Great fun as Captain Scarlett and Spectrum save Earth from destruction, with the model work extremely good. Directed by Brian Burgess, Robert Lynn and Ken Turner.

**REVENGE OF THE SCREAMING DEAD.** See **MESSIAH OF EVIL.** (You'll scream all right, with pain!)

**REVENGE OF THE STEPFORD WIVES (1980).** TV-movie sequel to THE STEPFORD WIVES (a popular novel by Ira Levin and a top quality feature film) is totally unfaithful to the original, and just plain stupid exploitation. Total waste of time. Divorce yourself. Surprising, too, since it was directed by DR. PHIBES mastermind Robert Fuest, and it has a good cast: Arthur Hill, Don Johnson, Sharon Gless, Julie Kavner, Mason Adams, Audra Lindley. (VC)

**REVENGE OF THE TEENAGE VIXENS FROM OUTER SPACE (1986).** Lightweight spoof has sexy spacegals visiting Earth, one of them to visit a human son she sired 16 years earlier. Cheap and easy to forget, its titillation being minimal. Directed by Jeff Farrell. Howard Scott, Lisa Schwedop. (VC)

**REVENGE OF THE ZOMBIES (1943).** Monogram flopper with John Carradine as a Nazi doctor living in the swamp who creates walking dead for his Fuehrer. But the cackling madman is no match for hero Robert Lowery, heroine Gale Storm and comic relief Mantan Moreland. Even Carradine's own wife (Veda Ann Borg) has her own plans. Strictly for sleepy-heads who walk as they snooze.

**REVENGE OF THE ZOMBIES (1981).** Hong Kong production from Run Run Shaw, gory and bloodthirsty in the extreme. Black magic runs rampant as a hundred-year-old sorcerer retains youthfulness by drinking blood—by the buckets. Torture and martial arts action, too. Directed without subtlety by Horace Menga.

**REVOLT OF THE ZOMBIES (1936).** The zombies are revolting! Edward and Victor Halperin (WHITE ZOMBIE), clumsy filmmakers at best, return to the walking dead theme with predictably uneven results. Terribly inept, almost unwatchable. A low point in the career of Dean Jagger as an explorer in Cambodia who finds the secret to creating zombies and goes into the recruiting business. Of minor interest to film historians and horror fan completists who want to see everything. Edward produced, Victor directed. Dorothy Stone, Roy D'Arcy, Robert Noland.

**REX HARRISON PRESENTS STORIES OF LOVE (1974).** Trilogy of romances by well-known authors. Two of them have elements of fantasy and mystery: "Epicac" is the story of a computer programmer who falls in love with a machine; it's from a Kurt Vonnegut Jr. story. "Kiss Me Again, Stranger" is a Daphne Du Maurier tale about the love between a war veteran and a murderess. Julie Sommars, Bill Bixby, Roscoe Lee Browne, Leonard Nimoy, Lorne Greene.

**RHINOCEROS (1974).** American Film Theater production of Eugene Ionesco's play, directed by Tom O'Horgan (of HAIR fame) and starring Zero Mostel and Gene Wilder as men turning into rhinos because of their "beastly" points of view. At heart, a serious message story about conformity, but Julian Barry's adaptation contributes slapstick and coyish comedy that Ionesco never had in mind. Karen Black, Robert Weil, Joe Silver, Marilyn Chris.

**RICHARD III (1955).** British version of Shakespeare's play about the crippled English king who ruthlessly murdered those blocking his way to power. Sir Laurence Olivier directed, produced and starred in the title role, assisted by John Gielgud, Ralph Richardson, Claire Bloom, Sir Cedric Hardwicke, Alec Guinness, Pamela Brown, Stanley Baker. Highly recommended. (Incidentally, this is the same story as told as Gothic horror in THE TOWER OF LONDON.)

**RIDERS OF THE WHISTLING SKULL (1937).** The Valley of the Skulls is location of the long-lost city of Lukachuke, still inhabited by Lukachukians—or whatever they're called. Along comes an archeological expedition with the Three Mesquiteers (Bob Livingston, Ray Corrigan, Max Terhune) riding shotgun. Supernatural themes make this an offbeat entry in the Republic Western series, and more enjoyable than most dusty old oaters. Remade in 1949 as a Charlie Chan feature, THE FEATHERED SERPENT. Directed by Mack V. Wright. Mary Russell, Yakima Canutt.

**RIDERS TO THE STARS (1954).** Passing meteor swarm attracts three rocketeers, who blast off from Earth to catch hunks of the spacerock with their ships. According to scientist Herbert Marshall, the meteors could provide an answer to our space problems. The astronauts (William Lundigan, Robert Karnes and Richard Carlson) fly high while lovely Ph.D. Martha Hyer waits on the ground. Realistic details and emphasis on people make this more like an old-fashioned service drama than a space adventure. Richard Carlson directed the Curt Siodmak script.

**RIDING ON AIR (1937).** Joe E. Brown is Elmer Lane—mismanaging editor of the Caremont (Wisconsin) Chronicle—who is involved with swindlers promoting a new airplane radio beam. Although scooped by rival papers, Elmer still stops the presses as a conquering hero after a battle in the sky with gangsters carrying contraband perfume. Yes, they raise quite a stink . . . Rollicking, delightful RKO comedy, a laugh a minute. Directed by Edward Sedgwick. Guy Kibbee, Florence Rice, Clem Bevans, Harlan Briggs.

**RING OF TERROR (1962).** Wardrobe and hair styles suggest this was filmed during the mid-1950s but unreleased until the 1960s. It's an amateurish story about fraternity students and hazing rituals. A medical student must remove the ring from the finger of a corpse in a graveyard, but he dies of fright. You'll die of boredom as this nothing production unfolds. Directed by Clark Paylow for low pay. George Mather,

Esther Furst, Austin Green, Joe Conway. (VC)

**RIO '80.** See **FUTURE WOMEN.** (Shapely drama)

**RIPPER, THE (1985).** Amateurish, low-budget regional thudder shot on tape in Tulsa, Okla., and sold directly to cassette. A college instructor teaching "Famous Crimes on Film" finds a ring once worn by Mary Kelly, one of Jack the Ripper's victims. At night he has nightmares in which he sees old Jack slaughtering women and ripping out their intestines. Lumbering, cumbersome hunkajunk with tediously repetitious murders and downright bad acting—not to mention crummy dialogue (by Bill Groves) and slow direction (by Christopher Lewis). An excruciating viewing experience. Robert Brewer and David Powell did the make-up effects. Famed make-up man Tom Savini plays Jack the Ripper with such clever touches as twirling the ends of his mustache and chuckling with fiendish glee, in the style of Oil Can Harry. Really clever, Tom. (VC)

**RISK, THE (1960).** What might have been a boring spy thriller (bubonic-curing serum is discovered but concealed from the medical world) is enhanced by the talents of producers-directors Ray and John Boulting, specialists in the British thriller. Tony Britton, Ian Bannen, Peter Cushing, Donald Pleasence, Virginia Maskell, Spike Milligan.

**RITUAL OF EVIL (1970).** Too bad Universal didn't continue its series about a ghost investigator (Louis Jourdan) and his wise old assistant (Wilfrid Hyde-White), who were introduced in FEAR NO EVIL the year before. Both are TV movies of considerable quality. In this sequel, finely written by Robert Presnell Jr. and superbly directed by Robert Day, Jourdan investigates the death of an heiress, encountering black magic rituals. Anne Baxter, Diana Hyland, Belinda Montgomery, Carla Borelli, John McMartin.

**RITUALS (1978).** An engrossing performance by Hal Holbrook, struggling against the wilderness and his fellow man, is what holds together this otherwise shallow Canadian picture which vacillates between DELIVERANCE and a slasher movie. Five physicians take a fishing trip into the "Cauldron of the Moon," a beautiful but isolated region of Ontario, Canada, where they are terrorized by an unseen mad-

**LAURENCE OLIVIER IN 'RICHARD III'**

**MEL GIBSON AS MAD MAX AND EMIL MINTY AS THE FERAL KID IN 'ROAD WARRIOR'**

man. There's too much dialogue among the doctors about a medical mistake one of them must have made, and there's too much bickering back and forth over trivialities. But when Holbrook takes center stage, and the focus is on the plight of men in the wilds, this is compelling. The explanation behind the mystery is rather weak, and never cleverly worked into the scheme of things by writer Ian Sutherland, and Peter Carter is perhaps too introspective to be directing an action picture, but there is a raw energy and power that works its way through the mundanities. Not for the squeamish, however. Lawrence Dane, Robin Gammell, Ken James, Gary Reineke. (VC)

**ROAD TO BALI (1953).** Zany Hope-Crosby "Road" picture, directed by Hal Walker. The duo is in the South Seas as jobless vaudevillians who hire out as divers for sunken treasure. There's a hilarious squid, a slap-happy gorilla, an erupting volcano, even Dorothy Lamour in sarong. One sequence features Bogart pulling the African Queen through a swamp—another has Jane Russell appearing out of thin air. The non sequiturs go on and on. A ball and a half.

**ROAD TO HONG KONG (1962).** Last of the Hope-Crosby "Road" pictures resembles an elongated vaudeville sketch and is not up to earlier efforts in the series. The tomfoolery dreamed up by director Norman Panama and producer Melvin Frank involves a space launching and an international gang (led by Joan Collins) out to steal the formula for a new rocket fuel. Dorothy Lamour is also on hand—but it isn't the same old magic. Frank Sinatra, David Niven, Dean Martin, Jerry Colonna and Peter Sellers appear in cameos.

**ROAD TO MOROCCO (1942).** Hope-Crosby "Road" inanities are a pure delight with satire of Arabian Nights cliches—flying carpets, talking camels, magic rings, genii, etc. Wonderfully directed by David Butler. Dorothy Lamour, Anthony Quinn, Monte Blue, Vladimir Sokoloff.

**ROAD TO ZANZIBAR (1941).** Second of the Hope-Crosby "Road" pictures finds them in the midst of savage natives and performing routines with a crazy gorilla. Zesty, marvelous comedy. Forget your troubles and enjoy. Directed by Victor Schertzinger. Dorothy Lamour, Una Merkel, Eric Blore, Douglass Dumbrille, Leo Gorcey, Iris Adrian.

**ROAD WARRIOR, THE (1981).** Sequel to MAD MAX is George Miller's masterpiece of the Cinema of the Bizarre, ten times better than its predecessor, with Mel Gibson repeating his role as a lone warrior in a post-Armageddon society where gas and oil are the richest commodities and survivors of industrial collapse fight to claim them. Max, in the tradition of the roving gunslinger aiding the underdog, befriends a benevolent band to keep precious fuels from falling into the hands of a vicious gang led by Humungus. The chase sequences are among the most exciting ever filmed, and every stunt is inspired as this Aussie film unfolds at a fever pitch. Characters are often grotesque and unlikeable, but you'll still be rooting for the good guys and booing the bad. Bruce Spence, Vernon Wells, Kjell Nilsson, Mike Preston, Emily Minton, Vernon Wells. (VC)

**ROADGAMES (1982).** Well-crafted though eccentric suspense thriller in the Hitchcock vein, cleverly conceived by writer Everett De Roch and intelligently directed by Richard Franklin. Patrick Anthony Quid (Stacy Keach) is a trucker on his way to Perth with pig carcasses when he suspects the driver of a green van is a Jack the Ripper-style murderer. His game is to chop up women's bodies—and Quid suspects two carcasses in his refrigerated rig might be human. It's a rich characterization for Keach, for Quid is an independent, good-humored driver who often talks to his companion, Boswell, an Aussie dog known as a dingo. Jamie Lee Curtis turns up as a runaway heiress and joins Quid in his "game" to track the killer. Franklin never compromises the story for shocks and shows insight into how screen suspense should be handled. ROADGAMES is a minor classic, and the collaboration of producer Bernard Schwartz and Franklin led to PSYCHO II. (VC)

**ROBBERS OF THE SACRED MOUNTAIN.** Videocassette title for **FALCON'S GOLD.**

**ROBIN HOOD AND THE SORCERER (1983).** The dark side of the Sherwood Forest legend, produced in England by Paul Knight and directed by Ian Sharp from a melancholy script by Richard Carpenter. While this lacks the romantic element of the Errol Flynn version, it chooses its own sad, shadowy path through shrouded Sherwood. This has a subtext of sword and sorcery as a god of the woods, Hearne, guides Robin to his destiny and as a sorcerer tries to stop him from acquiring an arrow of good fortune. Sharp has directed the action sequences with a sense of gritty, grunting realism . . . yet despite all these newfound assets, one cannot help but remember the superior Warner Bros. 1939 film. Ah well, everything in its time and place. Michael Praed as Robin of Loxley, Nicholas Grace as the ambivalent Sheriff of Nottingham and Clive Mantel as the intense Little John. (VC)

**ROBIN HOOD . . . THE LEGEND SERIES: HEARNE'S SON**

**(1985).** An episode from the British-produced TV series in which a nobleman (Jason Connery), after Robin has been killed, takes over his role as protector of the forest, fighting the evil Sheriff of Nottingham. Medieval in flavor, mystical in its atmosphere, this is good stuff but not in the tradition of Errol Flynn. Directed by Robert Young. Oliver Cotton, Nickolas Grace. (VC)

**ROBINSON CRUSOE OF MYSTERY ISLAND (1936).** Whittled version of the 15-chapter serial ROBINSON CRUSOE OF CLIPPER ISLAND, now 100 minutes of nonstop action. Mala, an imitation of Sabu the Jungle Boy, is an undercover Polynesian working for U.S. Intelligence, sent to an island where the villain Porotu is trying to erupt a volcano with the help of a Volcano Eruption Machine. A big dog named Buck slobbers on our hero's face.

**ROBINSON CRUSOE ON MARS (1964).** Fascinating science-fiction version of Daniel Defoe's novel of survival, written by Ib Melchoir and John C. Higgins. Astronaut Paul Mantee is ejected from Gravity Probe One when his missile almost collides with a meteor. Landing on the Red Planet, he undergoes incredible hardships, finding a means of breathing and overcoming a series of nightmares in which his dead partner, Adam West, returns alive. Mantee meets an escapee humanoid slave whom he dubs Friday. Aliens with heat rays seek Friday, allowing for exciting space opera with zappy (for their time) effects. Elements of this were borrowed for 1985's ENEMY MINE. Directed by Byron Haskin, who often worked with George Pal.

**ROBOCOP (1987).** Glossy, high-tech comic book action movie, superior in photography and design and featuring excellent stop-motion work by Phil Tippett, who contributed so much fine material to the STAR WARS trilogy. In a futuristic society controlled by an evil corporation, a dedicated cop (Peter Weller) is blasted apart by a gang of sadists in one of the goriest death scenes imaginable. Weller is resurrected as a cyborg, but this is a Six Million Dollar Man with only half a heart; the other half is ruled by computerized directives and a penchant for violence against those who break the law. It's wall-to-wall action with Tippett's activation of an Enforcement Droid the highlight of this absurd but entertaining film. What's contradictive about Paul Verhoeven's direction is the stark violence, which is quite unsuitable for the young people the rest of this Judge Dredd-imitation resembles. Then again, it's played larger-than-life in a tongue-in-cheek way that makes the violence seem as absurd as everything else in this slam-bam superhero superflick. Weller's partner is Nancy Allen, with Ronny Cox turning up as a corporate villain of the slimiest order.

**ROBOT HOLOCAUST (1985).** Made-for-video science-fictioner is so bad in script and acting, camp followers might get a chuckle or two out of this megamess. The plot is indecipherable (and unmuddleable). On New Terra, following the Robot Rebellion of '33, a band of Earthlings (stupid heroes, whinny broads in halter tops and a Conan lookalike) faces the forces of the Dark One and a chick in spike heels (Angelika Jager, a wonderfully incompetent hamactress) by

# Don't Mess With This Future Cop!

**PETER WELLER AS THE CYBORG POLICEMAN IN 'ROBOCOP'**

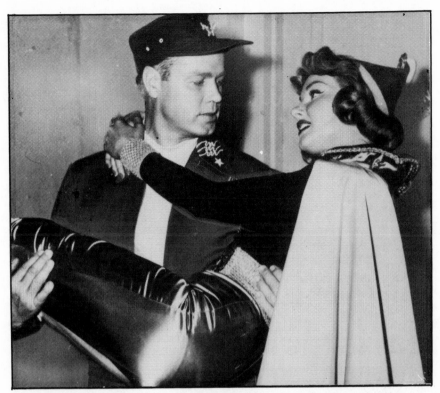

**RICHARD CRANE AND SALLY MANSFIELD IN 'ROCKY JONES, SPACE RANGER'**

defying The Cave of Sewage Worms, the Room of Questions, the Pleasure Machine and the Vault of Beasts to free mankind. Everyone talks like he/she is in a Shakespeare drama and behaves like a refugee from an Edward D. Wood Jr. movie. Quick, hand over that can opener! Unbelievably poor special effects, to boot. Speaking of boots, give one to director-writer Tim Kincaid and the so-called cast: Nadine Hart, Norris Culf, Joel von Ornstein and Jennifer Delora. (VC)

**ROBOT MONSTER (1953).** Reportedly produced-directed by Phil Tucker in less than a week on a budget of $580.25; and written in 30 minutes by Wyott Ordung. Exec producer Al Zimbalist even decided to Contribute to the Arts by filming in 3-D. If nothing else, that will keep this "classic" from falling "flat." As the hero, George Nader looks as mechanical as the extra in an ape suit (with a fishbowl over his head) called Ro-Man, who lands on Earth with his Bubble Communications Machine to kill the only six human beings left after a zap ray has wiped out mankind. Once those six are dead, it will be safe for 268,000 Martians to carry out a landing. Meanwhile, in Bronson Canyon, Ro-Man chases Nader, Claudia Barrett and Selena Royle in the funniest footage ever. Must be seen to be (dis)believed. Marvelously incompetent. Yes, by all means, gang, see it! (VC)

**ROBOT OF REGALIO (1954).** Get oiled first! See **ROCKY JONES, SPACE RANGER.** (Listen to the creaking!)

**ROBOT VS. THE AZTEC MUMMY, THE (1959).** Mexican sequel to THE AZTEC MUMMY, directed by Raphael Portillo, in which Dr. Krupp wanders into a South American crypt with a clanking robot, which he has given a human brain so it won't bump into any stray sarcophaguses. Krupp wants to loot the Aztec treasure, but standing guard over the fortune is that hulking package of bandages, that walking commercial for plastic strips, that swathed slob called the Aztec Mummy.

Crash! Bang! Thunk! Boom! Bash! Mangle! Thud! Crunch! Wallop! Don't worry: The Aztec Bandage Shroud returned in CURSE OF THE AZTEC MUMMY.

**ROCK & RULE (1983).** Animated fantasy about a rock 'n roll star who hopes to generate enough evil at one of his concerts to release an evil demon . . . features music by such figures as Iggy Pop, Debbie Harry and Lou Reed. Voices by Paul LeMat, Don Francks and Susan Roman. Directed by Clive Smith. (VC)

**ROCKET ATTACK U.S.A. (1960).** Spy thriller starring nobody you ever saw before, packaged by producers you never heard of, about characters you wish they hadn't bothered to create. Superspies rush around Moscow trying to convince Commie leaders that atomic war is futile, but the Soviets, who have never heard of the Nuclear Freeze, devastate New York City anyway and World War III begins. Great idea for entertainment. Directed by Barry Mahon.

**ROCKET MAN, THE (1954).** Light-hearted, minor comedy conveys its message in a gentle fashion—is therefore inoffensive fare. A spaceman gives a toy gun to a youth (George Winslow). Actually the weapon is a Truth Inducer; everytime the boy aims it, the one on the receiving end of his aim blurts the truth. Oscar Rudolph directed the Lenny Bruce-Jack Henley screenplay. Spring Byington, Charles Coburn, Anne Francis, John Agar, Stanley Clements.

**ROCKET SHIP.** See **FLASH GORDON** (1936).

**ROCKET TO THE MOON.** See **CAT WOMEN OF THE MOON.** (Better yet, don't bother.)

**ROCKETSHIP X-M (1950).** Producer Robert L. Lippert rushed this to beat DESTINATION MOON into theaters, and some consider this B effort superior to the more expensive

# The 'Rocky' Road to Laughs

MAGENTA, FRANK N. FURTER AND LITTLE NELL IN 'ROCKY HORROR PICTURE SHOW'

RICHARD O'BRIEN AS RIFFRAFF AND PATRICIA QUINN AS MAGENTA

George Pal production. The first rocketship blasting off for the moon malfunctions and lands instead on Mars, where astronauts Lloyd Bridges, Ona Massen, Noah Beery Jr., John Emery and Hugh O'Brian find the atomized remains of a once-great civilization. The remnants are primitive cavemen, blinded by radiation. An unhappy ending is an unexpected twist to this film directed and written by Kurt Neumann. Good production values considering the low budget, and a fine score by Ferde Grofe, with effective use of the theremin. A recent cassette version features new special-effects footage and tinted sequences.

**ROCKING HORSE WINNER, THE (1950).** Slow pacing and underplayed emotions are shortcomings in this John Mills-produced version of D. H. Lawrence's short story about a child who can predict race winners if he is riding his toy rocking horse with great frenzy. Mills appears as the handyman, Valerie Hobson is the mother, John Howard Davies is the driven youth and Ronald Squire is the sympathetic uncle. Written-directed by Anthony Pelissier.

**ROCKY HORROR PICTURE SHOW, THE (1975).** As a London stage musical, this appealed greatly to the transvestite-gay crowds, but soon became the straight "in thing." This film version, like the play, is faithfully slanted for the freak-rock crowd. It satirizes Frankenstein, haunted house mysteries, science-fiction movies and our penchant for sexual identity confusion. Naive newlyweds Barry Bostwick and Susan Sarandon stumble onto a foreboding castle where aliens from the planet Transsexual are creating the perfect he-man stud under the scientific (and loving) care of Dr. Frank N. Furter (Tim Curry). Full of bizarre props, musical production numbers and strange cutting techniques. It has become the most successful midnight movie of all time and continues to play in major cities with attendees dressed as the characters and acting out their own show. Those who relate to a mixture of depravity and satire will find this diverting. Directed by Jim Sharman, who co-wrote with Richard O'Brien, who also appears in the cast. Jonathan Adams, Charles Gray, Meatloaf, Little Nell, Patricia Quinn, Peter Hinwood. The sequel was SHOCK TREATMENT, a major disappointment.

**ROCKY JONES, SPACE RANGER.** Low budget TV kiddie series produced in 1953-55 starring Richard Crane as jockey Rocky jocularly rocketing into space for the United Solar System, fighting evil where he, Winky and Vena Ray find it. These dumb live-broadcast shows were repackaged for TV

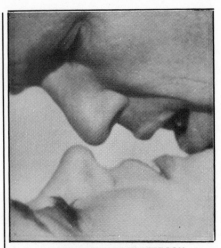

**FONDA AND KRISTOFFERSON IN 'ROLLOVER'**

and are again appearing on some of the pay channels as killer filler. These deceptively appear under titles that give only a slight inkling of just how awful they really are. You are hereby warned of BEYOND THE MOON, BLAST OFF, CRASH OF MOONS, DUEL IN SPACE, FORBIDDEN MOON, GYPSY MOON, INFERNO IN SPACE, MAGNETIC MOON, MENACE FROM OUTER SPACE, OUT OF THIS WORLD, ROBOT OF REGALIO, SILVER NEEDLE IN THE SKY. Ad nauseum.

**RODAN (1956).** Made in the wake of GODZILLA—KING OF THE MONSTERS by Japan's leading director of monster movies, Inoshiro Honda, this Japanese science-fiction epic reflects the Asian predilection for super-ludicrous effects in depicting a giant pterodactyl with a 250-foot wing span and a destructive nature that allows it to destroy several metropolises. Emphasis is on rousing catastrophe, while the

**PRODUCER ROGER CORMAN, PROFILED IN 'HOLLYWOOD'S WILD ANGEL'**

dwarfed humans stand around in awe or run screaming in terror. Eiji Tsuburaya is responsible for the destruction. Better than later Japanese monster movies, with more care lavished on the spectacle. But the dubbing is atrocious and acting styles hard to take. (VC)

**ROGER CORMAN: HOLLYWOOD'S WILD ANGEL (1978).** Crude but interesting one-hour documentary directed by Christian Blackwood in which Hollywood schlockmeister Roger Corman is examined. Includes interviews with Peter Fonda, Joe Dante, Paul Bartel and other cult directors. Recommended for those into genres. (VC)

**ROLLER BLADE (1986).** Unbelievably bad MAD MAX imitation, so incompetent one wonders to what new low Donald G. Jackson (co-writer, producer, photographer, director) will sink next. Set in the post-holocaust "Second Dark Age," this portrays a cult of "Holy Rollers"—religious women of "The Cosmic Order of Roller Blade" who wear roller skates, fight with knives and take orders from Mother Speed, who talks with a lisp. They're looking for a magic crystal but so is the masked villain Saticon, who commands a hand puppet cackling with lustful glee as it strips cellophane off a nude woman. It's hard to imagine a society that runs around on roller skates and skateboards, but here it is in all its vast stupidity, including a marshal who talks with "thee" and "thou" for no apparent reason. The action is phony, the attempts at serious religion blasphemous, the effects laughable and the acting hitting a new low of rank amateurism. Has to be seen to be believed. Suzanne Solari, Jeff Hutchinson, Shaun Michelle. (VC)

**ROLLERBALL (1975).** Title refers to a game—a futuristic bloodied version of Roller Derby which has taken the place of warfare—controlled by six corporate cartels merged to form a world government. Director Norman Jewison creates a sterile but slow- moving picture when depicting the robot-like people of tomorrow—but an exciting and necessarily bloody one when depicting the awesome-awful sport. The chief player is Jonathan E. (James Caan), who finally rebels in one final terrifying orgy of Rollerball bloodlust. William Harrison's original story was a terse metaphor—millions were expended to give the sport specific rules and bring it to sanguinary life, as conceived by Harrison in his screenplay adaptation. John Houseman, Maud Adams, Pamela Hensley, Ralph Richardson, John Beck. (VC)

**ROLLOVER (1981).** Alan J. Pakula directed this futuristic financial thriller in which the Arabs rig a diabolical system to collapse the world money market and bring about financial chaos and anarchy. Its abstractions are not easy to follow but it is an honorable attempt to suggest where today's economic manipulations are taking us. Fine cast is headed by Jane Fonda, Kris Kristofferson and Hume Cronyn. Pakula and screenwriter David Shaber avoid crass commercialism tricks and stick to the intrigue among those who have the power to make our world collapse. (VC)

**ROMAN SCANDALS (1933).** Eddie Cantor's funniest comedy: He travels through time and wakes up in ancient Rome. The gags, non sequiturs and anachronisms are bounced off the Coliseum wall nonstop. Eddie is selected by Nero to be his wine taster; he is frequently surrounded by beautiful Samuel Goldwyn girls in togas and there is a chariot race making sport of BEN-HUR. Directed with real style by Frank Tuttle. Ruth Etting, Alan Mowbray. (VC)

**RONA JAFFE'S MAZES AND MONSTERS.** Videocassette

**JAMES CAAN IS CORNERED DURING A TENSE MOMENT IN THE GAME 'ROLLERBALL'**

PETER O'TOOLE THINKS HE'S GOD IN THE CLASSIC SATIRE 'THE RULING CLASS'

title for **MAZES AND MONSTERS.**

**ROOGIE'S BUMP (1954).** Only a bump on a log as far as the movie world was concerned—minor league material about a boy who becomes a major league pitcher due to a protuberance on his throwing arm. Directed by Harold Young. Robert Marriot, Ruth Warrick, Robert Simon.

**ROOM TO LET (1950).** Early Hammer film based on a BBC play by Margery Allingham, recounting the story of Jack the Ripper with Valentine Dyall as the strange lodger, Dr. Fell. The story is set in London 1904 and told in flashback form. Interesting variation on an overdone theme. Directed by Godfrey Grayson, who co-adapted with John Gilling. Merle Tottenham, Jimmy Hanley.

**ROSELAND (1971).** Self-indulgent mishmash of bizarre imagery, sex symbolism and tons of pretentiousness from artist-turned-filmmaker Fred C. Hobbs. E. Kerrigan Prescott and the ever-popping Tiny Bubbles star.

**ROSEMARY'S BABY (1968).** Congratulate William Castle for buying Ira Levin's book in galley form (before it became a best seller) and for realizing he needed Roman Polanski (and not himself) to direct. The results vindicated Castle for making so many awful horror movies during the 1960s. This is a quiet exercise in the supernatural that builds gradually, often providing only a suspicion of evil, and sometimes a doubt, that newlywed Mia Farrow is the victim of a conspiracy plot in modern Manhattan. She suspects neighbors Sidney Blackmer and Ruth Gordon are witches, joined in a bloodpact with her husband-actor John Cassavetes. Is it possible he has formed a union with the Devil? Is the baby in her stomach spawned by Satan during one of her nightmares? She becomes the perfect Hitchcockian foil: a misunderstood, sympathetic, vulnerable young woman whose bizarre story is disbelieved by everyone, including doctor Ralph Bellamy. Maurice Evans, Patsy Kelly, Charles Grodin, Hope Summers, William Castle (as the man in the phone booth). (VC)

**ROSEMARY'S BABY II.** See **LOOK WHAT'S HAPPENED TO ROSEMARY'S BABY.** (Don't look now!)

**ROSEMARY'S KILLER.** See **PROWLER, THE.**

**ROTTWEILER.** See **DOGS OF HELL.** (Some bark!)

**RUBY (1977).** Weak Curtis Harrington's horror film, starring Piper Laurie as the former moll of a deceased gangster; the hood returns from the dead and leaves the bodies of victims all over a drive-in movie specializing in old horror movies. Harrington was reportedly fired during production and replaced by Stephanie Rothman. Janet Baldwin, Stuart Whitman, Roger Davis, Fred Kohler. (VC)

**RUDE AWAKENING.** Videocassette edition of a one-hour episode from a British TV horror series, HAMMER HOUSE

GAS PAINS HIT MIA FARROW
IN 'ROSEMARY'S BABY'

OF HORROR. See **TWO FACES OF EVIL / RUDE AWAKENING.**

**RULING CLASS, THE (1972).** Scathing, uncompromising satire aimed at the British class system and a devastating indictment of the "stupidity" of the English power structure, told through the distorted, surrealistic viewpoint of a debauched madman suffering schizophrenia. Peter O'Toole believes he is God, and spends his resting moments perched on a giant cross in the manor house. "When I pray to Him," says O'Toole, "I am talking to myself." This paranoid black sheep of an upper crust family is finally "exorcised" back to sanity—or so it seems as he takes his seat in the House of Commons. However, the old mugger is still quite bats, imagining everyone in the House to be decaying, frozen corpses. He also imagines himself as Jack the Ripper and goes on a slashing spree. This black comedy scripted by Peter Barnes was not a blooming success in the eyes of the ruling critics, but O'Toole fans will not want to miss his tour de force of acting. Equally effective, even when the picture is uneven, are Arthur Lowe, Alastair Sim, Coral Browne, Harry Andrews, Nigel Green, William Mervyn, James Villiers. Directed by Peter Medak. (VC)

**RUN FOR THE SUN (1956).** Only loosely based on Richard Connell's famous short story, "The Most Dangerous Game," for producer-director Ray Boulting has taken liberties with the original classic yarn—so many, in fact, this has none of the horror flavor. It becomes a tedious trek through the swamps of South America as Nazi Trevor Howard chases downed fliers Richard Widmark and Jane Greer. Complete misfire; even A GAME OF DEATH was more faithful. Peter Van Eyck, Carlos Hennings.

**RUN, PSYCHO, RUN (1969).** Tedious, unwatchable Edwardian horror-melodrama without much horror, directed by Italy's Brunello Rondi. The setting is the Cornwall coast in 1910, where a young wife is suddenly murdered and husband Gary Merrill finds a lookalike to keep her memory alive.

It's mostly talk among characters in period costumes with puffy hairstyles. The ultimate in boredom and non-delivery. Elga Anderson, Rosella Falk.

**RUN, STRANGER, RUN (1973).** Actor Darren McGavin directed this offbeat psychothriller in Nova Scotia . . . Robert Clouse's script involves Ron Howard in a series of graphic murders. Cloris Leachman, Patricia Neal, Bobby Darin, Simon Oakland, Tessa Dahl, Kathie Brown. (VC)

**RUNAWAY (1984).** Exciting, imaginative science-fiction action-mystery from writer-director Michael Crichton, set in a not-too-distant future when mankind is served by robots which occasionally go haywire. Tom Selleck and Cynthia Rhodes are members of the "Runaway Squad," designed to put amuck metal out of commission. Villain Gene Simmons, armed with a zap gun that fires guided-missile bullets around corners, is after microcomputer chips that will give him control of the robots and he sics an army of mechanical spiders on Selleck in a rousing, outrageous climax. If you can overlook the flaws and story holes, and accept this as fantasy in its purest movie form, you'll get a real kick out of this. Crichton has a way with suspense and pacing this time out that atones for his lesser effort, LOOKER. Kirstie Alley, Stan Shaw. (VC)

**RUSH (1984).** Super-chintzy Italian MAD MAX rip-off, relying on action as a Rambo-style survivor (Conrad Nichols) of nuclear war roves the desert's "forbidden zone." In this world you're either a prisoner in tattered rags or a well-armed soldier working for villain Gordon Mitchell . . . Rush rushes to support the former by blasting the latter to pieces in poorly staged, unbelievable action sequences directed by Anthony Richmond. The videocassette version is enhanced by an introduction and closing with Sybil Danning, clad in a camouflaged bra and little else, and carrying a wicked machine-gun as she makes cracks about her .38s and the guys' "big barrels." Now that's worth seeing. (VC)

**ROBOT SPIDER MONSTERS ATTACK TOM SELLECK IN THE WILD WILD 'RUNAWAY'**

**CREATURE FEATURES MOVIE GUIDE**

*"People call me, I load up my car with all my goodies and my little toolbox and things and I go to some strange state and I kill people. I'm a hired killer. People hire me to design and carry out gruesome deaths."*
*—Special effects man Tom Savini in SCREAM GREATS.*

**SAADIA (1953).** Supernatural thriller shot in Morocco; doctor Cornel Wilde falls in love with sorceress Rita Gam. Written-produced-directed by Albert Lewin. Michel Simon.

**SABU AND THE MAGIC RING (1957).** Thudding TV pilot was recut into this feature with Sabu as an overaged jungle boy and William Marshall (Blacula) as a genie. Sorry, Sahib, but it's a forgettable night in Arabia. Directed by George Blair. Daria Massey, Robert Shafto, John Doucette.

**SACRIFICE! (1972).** Unsavory entry in Italy's cannibal pictures, the "eat-em-up-alive" genre. In this culinary outing on the Thailand-Burma border, a tribe of gourmets has a tasty recipe for Human a la Chomp. Directed by Umberto Lenzi.

**SADIST, THE (1963).** Low-budgeter from writer-director James Landis with psychopathic killer Arch Hall Jr. on a murder spree with chick Marilyn Manning. Enough pistol killings to hold the average fan's attention, but nothing startling.

**SAFE PLACE, A (1971).** Is Orson Welles a diabolical magician forcing Tuesday Weld into a fantasy world which never allows her to grow up? Strange avant garde film written-directed by Henry Jaglom. Jack Nicholson, Philip Proctor.

**SAGA OF DRACULA (1972).** Saga is sagging and sanguinary in this sappy Spanish sputterer from director Leon Klimovski: Count Dracula's granddaughter, heavy with child and bad dialogue, arrives at the old castle homestead with her nonvampiric husband. While she and the audience endure labor pains, hubby dallies with the count's lovely brides and becomes lost to their desires. Tina Sainz, Tony Isbert, Narcisco Ibanez Menta (Dracula), Cristina Suriani.

**SAGA OF THE VIKING WOMEN AND THEIR VOYAGE TO THE WATERS OF THE GREAT SEA SERPENT.** Roger Corman's grab at the longest title of all time! Better known as **VIKING WOMEN AND THE SEA SERPENT, THE.**

**SAILOR WHO FELL FROM GRACE WITH THE SEA, THE (1976).** Unusual psychological horror story with a shock ending reminiscent of the E.C. Comics. Demented youngster Jonathan Kahn watches mother Sarah Miles making love to sailor Kris Kristofferson. Slowly he and his chums devise a horrifying scheme. Directed-written in Dartmouth by Lewis John Carlino. Margo Cunningham, Earl Rhodes. (VC)

**SAKIMA AND THE MASKED MARVEL (1943).** Feature version of a 12-chapter Republic serial. See **MASKED MARVEL, THE.** (Who is that masked man?)

**SALEM'S LOT (1979).** TV adaptation of Stephen King's best-selling vampire novel—the shuddering tale of how a European bloodsucker turns an entire East Coast community into a graveyard. Reggie Nalder is the vampire Barlow in the Lugosi tradition, with James Mason portraying Barlow's aide-de-vamp. David Soul tries to stop the pair with the help of Lance Kerwin. Written by Paul Monash, directed by Tobe Hooper, the mild-mannered sentimentalist who gave us TEXAS CHAINSAW MASSACRE. Producer Richard Kobritz also made CHRISTINE, another King vehicle. Originally four hours but cut to a shorter version for cable TV. Some scenes are stronger than those shown on the network. (VC)

**SALVAGE (1979).** Amiable TV-movie with junk dealer Andy Griffith building a spaceship to fly to the moon and salvage science equipment littering the lunar surface. Lighthearted fare with interesting characters, this two-hour pilot became a short-lived series that never lived up to its promising debut. Directed by Lee Phillips. Joel Higgins, Trish Stewart, Richard Jaeckel, J. Jay Saunders, Raleigh Bond, Peter Brown.

**SAMSON AND DELILAH (1949).** Cecil B. DeMille's epic Biblical "True Confessions" about the passionate lovers who ultimately betray themselves, realizing real love too late. The superstrength of Samson (Victor Mature) emanates from his uncut hair but when Delilah (Hedy Lamarr) shears his bangs, his sinewness is also clipped. DeMille's point of view is all gaudiness and phony baloney dialogue. Angela Lansbury, Henry Wilcoxon, George Reeves, George Sanders. (VC)

**SAMSON AND DELILAH (1984).** Producer Franklin Levy describes this TV-movie as the Biblical "Body Heat," about the Israelite hunk with the muscles and seven long locks of hair who falls for a looker from the valley of Sorek. The hunk is Australian unknown Anthony Hamilton, the femme is Belinda Bauer and they have some sizzling love scenes. Levy's production for Gregory Harrison's company has the spirit of an old-fashioned Biblical epic, with Victor Mature in a small role as Samson's father. Directed by Lee Phillips. Max Von Sydow, Stephen Macht, Maria Schell, Jose Ferrer. And Bauer . . . what a femme fatale from Sorek!

**SAMSON AND THE MIGHTY CHALLENGE (1964).** The mighty challenge for the viewer is to endure this monument to muscles as four brawn-happy grunters (Samson, Hercules, Maciste, Ursus) wreak havoc on dumb villains by using incredible superpower. No mental workout, this. Directed by Giorgio Capitani. Alan Steele, Nadir Baltimor.

**SAMSON AND THE SEVEN MIRACLES OF THE WORLD (1963).** The eighth wonder is that this Italian spaghetti strainer about a muscleman with superstrength got produced at all. Even Gordon Scott admirers will concur that his trophy tissue is a dead atrophy issue as he fights saucy Tartars and saves Yoko Tani from a death worse than fate. Not Great Scott! Directed by Riccardo Freda. Dante Di Paolo.

**SAMSON IN KING SOLOMON'S MINES (1964).** Reg Park replaces Gordon Scott but the grunts are the same and the biceps bulge just as beefily as Maciste (where the hell's Samson?) is forced to slave in an African mine, a magical ring strapped to his leg by a lovely villainess. Now all Maciste has to do is form a union to improve labor conditions. Directed-written by Piero Regnoli. Wandisa Guida, Dan Harrison, Eleonora Bianchi, Elio Jotta.

**SAMSON IN THE WAX MUSEUM (1964).** You thought the "Neutron" series from Mexico (featuring a black-masked wrestler in droopy drawers) was bad? Usted haven't seen nada yet, amigo. A wrestler named Samson (or Santo, depending on translation) tries to get a brainlock on a mad scientist running a wax museum who has the power to turn people into monsters. No Mexicali rose garden, this. Directed by Alfonso Corona Blake. Claudio Brook, Ruben Rojo.

**SAMSON VS. THE GIANT KING (1965).** The character is actually Maciste, found interred in a tomb somewhere in Russia. Special salve spread over his powerful beefcake restores his brawn and he's off to fight an evil Czar steppe by steppe. Maciste (Kirk Morris) crumples cardboard pillars, throws papier mache boulders and knocks down a balsa wood coliseum. Directed by Amerigo Anton. Massimo Serato.

**SAMSON VS. THE VAMPIRE WOMEN (1961).** Atrophied entry in the Mexican hammerlock-adventure series starring simple-minded grunter Santo, redubbed Samson. Possessing a more scintillating personality is the sexy vampire who sics her shapely femmes and machos on Santo. Written-directed dis-gruntedly by Alfonso Corona Blake. (VC)

**SAMURAI (1979).** Routine TV-movie starring Joe Penny as Lee Cantrell, an eager-beaver San Francisco assistant D.A. who takes samurai lessons from James Shigeta. When he sees the law being abused, and reruns of THE GREEN HORNET, Penny dons Japanese warrior garb and wields a wicked sword to stop a powerful tycoon (Charles Cioffi) who has a supersonic device that could cause a major earthquake. The Jerry Ludwig script is predictable, the characters cliched. Directed by Lee H. Katzin. Geoffrey Lewis, Morgan Brittany, Beulah Quo, Dana Elcar.

**SANDCASTLES (1972).** Director Ted Post does what he can with this TV-movie, one of the first shot on videotape: A young man killed in an accident returns from the grave to rectify wrongs he made while living. Not only that, but the spirit (Jan-Michael Vincent) falls in love with Bonnie Bedelia. Herschel Bernardi, Mariette Hartley, Gary Crosby.

**SANTA CLAUS (1960).** Check it once, don't check it twice: Beloved St. Nick (Jose Elias Moreno) joins Merlin the Magician to fight the Red Devil when he should be handing out presents to kiddies. Is nothing sacred to Mexican director Rene Cardona? Or to K. Gordon Murray, the U.S. impresario who imported this from down south? Jangled bells.

**SANTA CLAUS—THE MOVIE (1985).** Enchanting, family-style movie spends its first half explaining how a big-hearted Earthling and his wife are picked by Father Time to become Mr. and Mrs. Santa Claus, destined to live forever at the North Pole where an army of elves led by Dudley Moore makes the toys. This portion is charming, with elaborate sets to give Santa Claus versimilitude. Then the film switches to modern times and trivializes the spirit of Christmas by focusing on two very uninteresting kids and one evil toy manufacturer (John Lithgow). But it's still successful enough that you should put this on your Christmas list. Huddleston is an excellent Santa. Burgess Meredith, Judy Cornwell. (VC)

**SANTA CLAUS CONQUERS THE MARTIANS (1964).** Old St. Nick conquers them in the sense he wins their hearts when Red Planet adults and one clanking, in-need-of-oil

**DUDLEY MOORE IS A GOOD FAIRY**
**AND DAVID HUDDLESTON IS ST. NICK IN 'SANTA CLAUS' (1985)**

CREATURE FEATURES MOVIE GUIDE

robot kidnap him and Earth children to brighten up life around the dreary canals. You don't have to watch, it's okay to pout and shout as this slowly unfolds. Directed by Nicholas Webster. John Call (Santa), Leonard Hicks. Somewhere among the green people is Pia Zadora. (VC)

**SANTO AGAINST THE ZOMBIES.** See **INVASION OF THE ZOMBIES.** (Santo wrestles a bad script!)

**SANTO AND BLUE DEMON VS. DRACULA AND THE WOLF MAN (1967).** Nothing like cramming all the ingredients into its title, but then the Mexicans are not known for cinematic subtleties. In this Masked Wrestler mindboggler, two dumb wrestlers meet two dumber monsters. Two plus two equal one dumb movie. Directed by Miguel M. Delgado. Aldo Monti, Eugenia San Martin.

**SANTO AND DRACULA'S TREASURE (1968).** That low IQ'ed masked wrestler Santo is back, struggling with a hapless script in which he performs such stupid acts as removing a ring from Dracula's finger, sending people in a time machine back to their earlier lives, etc. No treasure, this. It just sucks your life away. Directed by Rene Cardona.

**SARGOSSA MANUSCRIPT, THE (1965).** Baroque Polish film, directed by Wojciech J. Has and starring Zbigniew Cybulski as a young Captain of the Walloon Guards of the King of Spain. En route to Madrid he spends an evening in a haunted inn, invited to the bed of two beautiful Moorish princesses. But when he awakens, he is sprawled on a barren field, surrounded by corpses . . . that's only the beginning of his bizarre supernatural odyssey which consists of stories-within-stories, surrealistic and Gothic in overtone. Episodic, oft-puzzling film is based on stories by Jan Potocki.

**SASQUATCH (1977).** Sole-flattened treatment of the Big Foot theme, directed by Ed Ragozzini, stumbles over its own fallen arches at every bend in the Canadian Northwest scenery. Scientists search for the missing link but prove to be dumber than the hairy apeman outsmarting them from behind every bush. SASQUATCH is a no watch. (VC)

**SATAN BUG, THE (1965).** Crisp suspense chiller adapted by James Clavell and Edward Anhalt from an Alistair MacLean novel, swiftly paced by director John Sturges. A virus serum is stolen by a demented doctor (Richard Basehart) who has delusions of power. If allowed to escape its bottle, the "bug" could wipe out mankind. George Maharis portrays a heroic agent, Dana Andrews is a general, Anne Francis is his daughter and Frank Sutton and Ed Asner are oleaginous heavies. John Larkin, John Anderson, Hari Rhodes.

**SATAN MURDERS, THE (1974).** Unscrupulous woman plots with demon lovers to kill her equally unscrupulous husband in this British TV production which stumbles about on cloven feet. Directed by Lela Swift. Larry Blyden, Salome Jens, Susan Sarandon, Douglas Watson, Paul Sparer.

**SATANIC RITES OF DRACULA.** Also known as **DRACULA IS DEAD AND WELL AND LIVING IN LONDON.** See **COUNT DRACULA AND HIS VAMPIRE BRIDE.**

**SATANIK (1968).** Director Piero Vivarelli, red-blooded Italian male, has this thing for Magda Konopka, lingering his camera on her shapely thighs and voluptuous breasts. Magda starts the picture as an old hag but turns into a ravishing, miniskirted babe after drinking a youth formula. Despite obvious flaws, this has an undercurrent of sexual perversity; clumsily diverting. Julio Pena, Armando Calvo.

**SATANIS—THE DEVIL'S MASS (1969).** Documentary profiling Anton Szandor LaVey, at one time in the 1960s the sorcerer supreme of San Francisco and Pope of the Church of Satan. This "devil incarnate" is shown in his everyday satanic rites involving topless dancers, boa constrictors, sadistic beatings, sex in coffins, that sort of everyday thing. Produced-directed by Ray Laurent.

**SATAN'S BLACK WEDDING (1976).** Terrible production standards and awful color—not to mention atrocious acting and horrendous direction by Phillip Miller in telling this tale about devil worshippers. Amateurish trash.

**SATAN'S BLADE (1984).** Legend of a killer comes true for a handful of travelers subjected to stab, stab, stab. Tom Bonglorno, Stephanie Leigh Steel. (VC)

**SATAN'S CHEERLEADERS (1976).** Writer-director Greydon Clark intermingles THE OMEN with I WAS A RAH RAH BOOM GIRL in this "cheer-y" tale of a witch cult headed by John Ireland and Yvonne DeCarlo which terrorizes big-busted, miniskirted cheerleaders from Benedict High. Remarks a cult member, "Some townspeople feel the Prince of Darkness might desire that the blood of a maiden flow tonight." Incompetently handled, in a bemusing way, with Jack Kruschen and John Carradine on the sidelines. Let's hear it for Satan: Give me an E . . . X . . . P . . . L . . . O . . . I . . . T . . . A . . . I . . . O . . . N . . . Give me an F . . . I . . . L . . . M . . . Give me a . . . aw hell, give me a raincheck.

**SATAN'S MISTRESS.** See **DARK EYES.**

**SATAN'S SADISTS (1969).** Sickening exercise in violence and bloodletting—unredeemed and unrelieved in its trashiness as a motorcycle gang kills for pleasure. Familiar faces are welcome in this wasteland, but are only death fodder for the bikers: Russ Tamblyn, Scott Brady, Kent Taylor. Greydon Clark, a producer of schlock, is a gang member. Directed by Al Adamson. Regina Carrol, Robert Dix, Gary Kent. (VC)

**SATAN'S SATELLITES (1952).** Edited-down feature version of a 12-chapter Republic serial. See **ZOMBIES OF THE STRATOSPHERE.** (Walking dead in space?)

**SATAN'S SCHOOL FOR GIRLS (1973).** Roy Thinnes, hero of TV's THE INVADERS, as Satan? Yep, they cast against type in this TV-movie about a fashionable girls' school. Directed by David Lowell Rich. Kate Jackson, Pamela Franklin, Lloyd Bochner, Cheryl Ladd. (VC)

**SATAN'S SKIN.** See **BLOOD ON SATAN'S CLAW, THE.**

**SATAN'S SLAVE (1976).** British import starring Michael Gough as a dabbler in black magic who intends to bring to life a long-dead witch. Directed by Norman J. Warren.

**SATAN'S TRIANGLE (1975).** Supernatural TV-movie advances the theory that ships and planes are missing in the Bermuda Triangle because a demon needs the crews and passengers to keep his home fires burning. What begins in promising fashion when Kim Novak is shipwrecked is quickly awash in muddy waters when helicopter rescuers Doug McClure and Alejandro Rey show up. Directed by Sutton Roley. Jim Davis, Ed Lauter, Michael Conrad.

**SATELLITE IN THE SKY (1956).** Above Earth, a Tritonium bomb accidentally adheres to the hull of a spaceship. Now, unless astronauts risk their lives, our planet could be in terrible danger. British science-fiction is basically land-locked soap opera focusing on frightened men finding faith in themselves, loving their women fast and hard, etc. Directed by Paul Dickson. Kieron Moore, Donald Wolfit, Lois Maxwell, Bryan Forbes, Thea Gregory, Jimmy Hanley.

**SATISFIERS OF ALPHA BLUE (1981).** Alpha Blue is a vacation planet in the 21st Century where sexual needs are satisfied by computer. A rebel decides it's time again for kissy poo poo and for everyone to have a name instead of a number. Pornie written-produced-directed by Gerard Damiano. Lysa Thatcher, Hillary Summers, Maria Tortuga.

**SATURDAY THE 14TH (1981).** Blame producer Julie Corman, wife of Roger, for this flubbed comedy-spoof directed childishly by Howard R. Cohen. A couple (Richard Benjamin, Paula Prentiss) moving into a haunted house are confronted by aliens, vampires and other monsters and things. Many folks worked on the effects, but men in rubber monster suits still look like men in rubber monster suits and most of the jokes fall as flat as corpses. The only funny sequence is when a shark fin appears in a bathtub. Rosemary DeCamp, Jeffrey Tambor, Severen Darden. (VC)

**SATURN THREE (1980).** Astonishing sets and futuristic hardware mean very little when the plot is one big Story Hole in blackest space. The star here is Hector the Demi-God Robot, a masterpiece of technology, blending human features with robotic traits. The less successful human stars are Kirk Douglas and Farrah Fawcett as space dwellers on Titan,

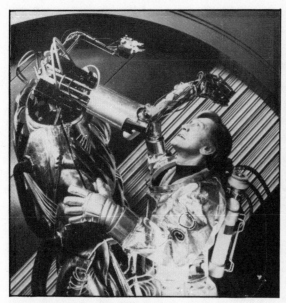

**KIRK DOUGLAS FINDS PARADISE LOST WHEN A ROBOT ATTACKS IN 'SATURN 3'**

a moon of Saturn, living an idyllic Adam-and-Eve existence until Harvey Keitel drops by to malprogram the robot to lust after Farrah's body. This mess of contrivance and confusion never reaches a suitable conclusion. Based on an idea by production designer John Barry, who died before the film was completed, director Stanley Donen stepped in to finish the job. Did he finish the job! (VC)

**SAVAGE BEES, THE (1976).** Bruce Geller, creator of MISSION: IMPOSSIBLE, produced-directed this TV-film, swarming with excitement when South American killer bees migrate to Louisiana aboard a banana boat and sting folks to death. Ben Johnson is the efficient sheriff, Michael Parks is the medical aide, Horst Buchholz is the expert on killer bees. Written by Guerdon Trueblood. In the same vein as THE SWARM and THE BEES. (And THE STING?) (VC)

**SAVAGE CURSE, THE (1974).** British-produced TV cheapie depicts walled-alive themes borrowed liberally from Poe's "Cask of Amontillado." Scripted by Brian Clemens, directed by John Sichel. Quite tacky. George Chakiris, Jenny Agutter, Anton Diffring, Russell Hunter.

**SAVAGE WEEKEND (1978).** Also known as THE UPSTATE MURDERS and KILLER BEHIND THE MASK, but by any title it's a slasher movie displaying a fetish for sadism and bordering on abnormal sexuality in depicting what happens to some unlikable vacationers who become fodder for a killer in a fright mask. Unusual amount of soft porn and nudity, enough to make you head downstate. And the sequence in which a nymphomaniac fondles a cow in vivid close-up leaves no doubt what udder gutter the mind of writer-director David Paulsen is sprawled in. Murders by strangulation (followed by hangings), by hatpin (through the brain of a raving homosexual), by chainsaw (now, there's an old saw!), by buzzsaw (now, there's a new saw!). Excruciating and embarrassing to watch. Christopher Allport, James Doerr, Kathleen Heaney, David Gale, Marilyn Hamlin. (VC)

**SAVAGES (1973).** Weird idea, enigmatically executed by Berkeley film director James Ivory in Tarrytown, N.Y. Primitive Mud People rise from primeval ooze, exposing their naked behinds with indifference. They're about to make a human sacrifice when a croquet ball drops out of nowhere. Awed at something more perfectly rounded than derrieres, they discover an elegant manor and crash a party. Comparison of modern decadence and ancient barbarism is at

work here—thoughtful stuff, but as we said earlier, extremely puzzling. Sam Waterston, Salome Jens. (VC)

**SCALPEL (1978).** First feature effort of Joseph Weintraub and John Grissmer could have used a finer edge in depicting a psychopathic plastic surgeon (Robert Lansing) who creates a "dead ringer" lookalike for his missing daughter (Judith Chapman) so he can collect a $5 million inheritance. Ample twists and turns in director Grissmer's screenplay; a minor suspense melodrama with a surprise ending. Go ahead, take a stab at SCALPEL. (VC)

**SCALPS (1983).** Juvenile gore thriller poorly written and sloppily directed by Fred Olen Ray, with a terrible soundtrack and an amateurish cast, which at least makes for a few unintended laughs. Archeology students on an expedition to the Black Trees Indian Burial Ground disturb the spirit of the renegade Black Claw (also known as Tom A. Hawk), who scalps the kids, shoots arrows into them and otherwise behaves abominably. Cancel his reservation. The gore effects are really bad, almost suggesting this was cranked out by high school kids. Kirk Alyn (one-time serial SUPERMAN) appears briefly as an absent-minded digs specialist, Forrest J. Ackerman has a pointless cameo as "Professor Trentwood" and Carroll Borland pops up momentarily as Dr. Reynolds, with nothing to do. Jo Ann Robinson, Roger Maycock, Richard Hench, Frank McDonald. On videocassette with **SLAYER.**

**SCANNERS (1981).** Contrived but fascinating film written-directed by David Cronenberg. Psychics (scanners) have disrupted a government investigation of their powers and gone underground to wage a war of conquest. Scientist Patrick McGoohan sends a scanner into their secret ranks to spy . . . intrigue and violent death follow. Cronenberg achieves a weird atmosphere and the special effects (including an exploding human head) shook up audiences and gave the film much word of mouth. If Cronenberg had avoided his muddled plot, he might have scanned better. Stephen Lack, Jennifer O'Neill, Michael Ironside, Lawrence Dane. (VC)

**SCARAB (1983).** Devil-worship exploitation flick starring Rip Torn, Robert Ginty and Cristina Hachuel. Directed by Steven-Charles Jaffe. The plot revolves around a resurrected Egyptian god and a former Nazi seeking new sources of power.

**SCARED STIFF (1953).** Dean Martin-Jerry Lewis remake of

the 1940 Bob Hope-Paulette Goddard horror comedy, GHOST BREAKERS, with new musical numbers. The comedians are hamming it up in Jamaica, where they have fled to avoid gangsters. Lizabeth Scott has inherited a haunted castle infested with zombies, secret passageways, flying bats, clanking suits of armor and other "old dark house" cliches rigged by effects master Gordon Jennings. George Marshall directs it all with an appropriate light touch.

**SCARED STIFF (1987).** Undistinguished horror item about a slave master of the 1850s who comes back to a Southern mansion to terrorize modern inhabitants, a psychiatrist and his wife and child who apparently have been cursed. Curses on director Richard Friedman, who co-wrote the script with Mark Frost and producer Daniel F. Bacaner. David Ramsey, Nicole Fortier, Andrew Stevens, Mary Page Keller.

**SCARED TO DEATH (1946).** The only color film Bela Lugosi ever worked in—a skid row programmer narrated by a dead girl, her report coming to us in flashback from a slab in the morgue. A stiff, boring plot has several characters coming together under one roof and behaving ridiculously. Slow moving and talkative. Directed by Christy Cabanne. George Zucco, Nat Pendleton, Joyce Compton, Douglas Fowley. (VC)

**SCARED TO DEATH (1980).** ALIEN lookalike called a Syngenor (Synthesized Genetic Organism), created in a laboratory DNA experiment, is hiding in L.A.'s sewers, rising to the streets now and then to suck the marrow from a victim by inserting its tongue into the mouth. Ugh. Under Bill Malone's direction, the first half is slow going, alternating between scenes of trapped humans undergoing attack and the domestic life of ex-cop John Stinston and secretary Diana Davidson. The last half picks up by shifting to the sewers, where Stinston and scientist Toni Jannotta are pursued by the thing. Climax takes place in an iron metal factory and finally the film becomes mildly harrowing. The characters, unfortunately, are all contrived and boring. The monster, derivative of H.R. Giger, is kind of a gas . . . barely. (VC)

**SCAREMAKER, THE.** See **GIRLS NITE OUT.**

**SCARLET CLAW, THE (1944).** Phosphorescent ghost haunts the moors, ripping out throats of victims with a bloody claw and fleeing—a white, glittering spectre etched against foggy swampland. Who should pick up a glow of his own as he cries "The game is afoot!" but Sherlock Holmes, visiting

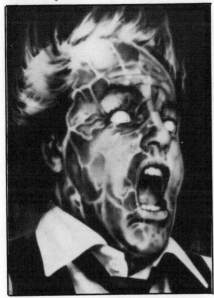

**MIND OVER MANNERS IN 'SCANNERS'**

Canada with the good Dr. Watson. Jolly good item, with plenty of thrilling and scary moments, in the Universal series that starred Basil Rathbone and Nigel Bruce. A fine chap, that producer-director Roy William Neill. And that writer Edmund L. Hartman, now there's a good fellow, hey what?

**SCARLET CLUE, THE (1945).** Usually these Charlie Chan things are dull drawing room capers, plodding toward predictable climaxes. This deviates by presenting the killer in the garb of a fantastic creature utilizing bizarre poison capsules and radio beams to carry out homicides. Even Sidney Toler as Charlie Chan seems livelier, as though he detected a glimmer of hope in the script. Directed by Phil Rosen. Mantan Moreland, Ben Carter, Benson Fong, Ian Wolfe.

**SCARS OF DRACULA (1970).** Popular Hammer production in the Christopher Lee/Dracula series—written by John Elder, directed by Roy Ward Baker, scored by James Bernard. Lee, resurrected when his ashes are covered with bat's blood, begins his reign of terror and fights off a revenge seeker. Blood and sadism (lots) have been added to the formula. Dennis Waterman, Christopher Matthews, Jenny Hanley, Michael Gwynn, Wendy Hamilton, Michael Ripper. (VC)

**SCHIZO (1976).** Graphic British psychothriller with a top-notch cast, good direction by Peter Walker and a mildly intriguing script by David McGillivray. It's a bloody thing, though, highlighting a darning needle through an eyeball socket, a sledgehammer into a human brain, a body run over by a truck, and a few standard knife slashings. Lynne Frederick portrays a pretty ice skating star pursued by a strange man (John Leyton) and a memory of maternal homicide. Nice twist ending. A strong stomach, as with most Walker films, is suggested, if not required. Stephanie Beacham adds her charms to the tense tale. (VC)

**SCHIZOID (1971).** Made in London, this is a French/Italian/Spanish psychothriller starring Leo Genn, Stanley Baker, Florinda Bolkan and Jean Sorel. Lucio Fulci directed with a mind that has to be schizoid.

**SCHIZOID (1980).** Psychiatrist Klaus Kinski's group-therapy patients are being knocked off one by one by a scissors-wielding maniac while gossip columnist Marianna Hill conducts an investigation. Cheap and tasteless, although some scenes of Kinski capture an eerie quality whenever director-writer David Paulsen tries to upgrade the sleazy material. Craig Wasson, Richard Herd, Donna Wilkes. (VC)

**SCHLOCK (1973).** John Landis' first feature is a refreshing change of pain for horror fans, depicting a Neanderthal hairy man (Landis) recently thawed from his prehistoric haven and now on a rampage in an average American city. It's played as a satire on movie monsters, and features parodies and take-offs of popular movies. On videocassette as **BANANA MONSTER.** Forrest J. Ackerman and Don Glut guest star.

**SCHOOL SPIRIT (1985).** Football player Tom Nolan, on his way to get laid, is killed in an accident. An already dead uncle (John Finnegan) shows up to take him to Heaven, but the star is still eager to get laid and wants another day to attend to unfinished "business." This low-budget supernatural comedy, released by Roger Corman, was directed by Alan Holleb. Roberta Collins, Larry Linville, Daniele Arnaud. (VC)

**SCORPIO SCARAB (1972).** Clones of government officials are brought to life by an object on exhibit in the Washington Museum of Antiquities. Angie Dickinson brings things to life in her own way as her body undulates with vibrant sexuality. George Hamilton, Simon Oakland, Ricardo Montalban.

**SCOUNDREL, THE (1935).** Noel Coward, as a Scrooge-like moneybags who evokes no tears when he dies, returns to Earth in human form to gain sympathy so his soul can rest in peace. Written-produced-directed by scoundrels Ben Hecht and Charles MacArthur. Julie Haydon, Stanley Ridges, Alexander Woolcott, Eduardo Ciannelli, Martha Sleeper.

**SCOUNDRELS, THE (1969).** Masked hero of Mexico puts a stranglehold on motorcyclists working for a batty babe who worships Aztec gods. Hero acts so much like a blind fool it appears he forgot to cut eyeholes in his face mask. Directed by Federico Curiel. Mil Mascaras, Regina Torne.

**SCREAM** (1985). Originally shot in 1981 as THE OUTING, this was released four years later and immediately hailed as the worst horror movie of all time. Hopelessly written-directed by Larry Quisenberry with the pacing of a snail, this hunkanothin' follows uninteresting, never-developed hikers to a deserted Western town where an unseen killer strikes with hatchet and axe. Minimal gore scenes and hardly any explanation about the killer, who is never really shown. Woody Strode turns up mysteriously on horseback. One long series of dull panning shots with people who act contrary to human nature. Really awful. Pepper Martin, Hank Worden, Alvy Moore, Gregg Palmer. (VC)

**SCREAM . . . AND DIE.** Alternate videocassette title for **HOUSE THAT VANISHED, THE.** (A lease on life?)

**SCREAM AND SCREAM AGAIN** (1970). Stomach-churning thrill piece from director Gordon Hessler and writer Christopher Wicking, who bring to this British luridness a touch of allegory. Vincent Price is a scientist creating superhumans through fiendish surgical anomalies, mutilating bodies in sickening ways to acquire transplants. That's when Hessler and Wicking get a little carried away . . . again and again. Peter Cushing is an ex-Nazi and Christopher Lee is a British secret

from a house for the criminally insane and goes on a rampage of mass murder. Written-produced-directed by Robert J. Emery. Paul Vincent, Paul Ecenia. (VC)

**SCREAM FOR HELP** (1984). Swift pacing and thrill piled on thrill make this a lively if implausible suspense-mystery, scripted by Tom Burman and directed by Michael Winner. Teen-ager Rachael Kelly suspects her stepfather of trying to kill her mother for the family fortune but noone in town (including the police commissioner) will believe her, even though it's apparent from the outset there is indeed a conspiracy afoot. The climax is ludicrous and grossly violent yet the film moves so briskly, its tempo sweeps you along with it, compelling you to watch. Filmed in New Rochelle. David Brooks, Marie Masters.

**SCREAM GREATS** (1986). Documentary on make-up/special effects man Tom Savini, featuring many fascinating quotes by Savini as well as interviews with George Romero and various actors on the set of DAY OF THE DEAD. Fascinating look into low budget movies. Footage features many films Savini has labored on, with emphasis on his working relationship with Romero. First in a series of videos from Fangoria, a magazine specializing in movie fantasy. (VC)

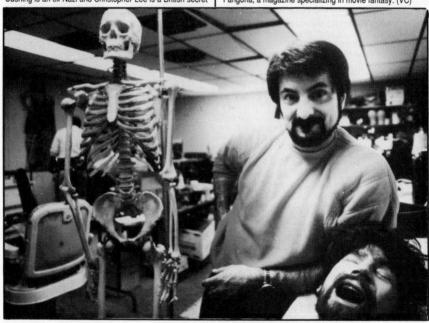

**MAKE-UP MASTER TOM SAVINI, PROFILED IN 'SCREAM GREATS'**

agent. Judy Huxtable is a screaming victim. Based on a Peter Saxon novel. Alfred Marx, Uta Levka. (VC)

**SCREAM, BABY, SCREAM** (1969). Artist at work in Miami—he turns nice folks into monsters so he can then paint them. Weasel at the easel. Beware, viewer, beware. Directed by Joseph Adler. Ross Harris, Eugenie Wingate.

**SCREAM, BLACULA, SCREAM** (1972). Sequel to the box office smash BLACULA, a sometimes-amusing, often-chilling portrait of vampirism with William Marshall again "bringing to life" the aristocratic black vampire. This time his bones are used in voodoo rituals, and he reappears in human form to do battle with priestess Pam Grier. Marshall, with his authoritative presence and booming, rich voice, creates a sympathetic vampire. Directed by Bob Kelljan of COUNT YORGA—VAMPIRE fame. Don Mitchell, Richard Lawson.

**SCREAM BLOODY MURDER** (1972). A psychopath with a hook hand, the result of an accident while he was squashing his dear ol' daddy to death with the family tractor, is freed

**SCREAM GREATS VOL. 2** (1986). Second videocassette original in a series produced by Fangoria magazine, this volume about real-life devil cults, witches and other satanic elements in the world of black arts. (VC)

**SCREAM OF DEATH.** See **LIVING COFFIN, THE.**

**SCREAM OF FEAR** (1961). Favorite Hammer production in the let's-scare-the-lovely-young-woman-to-death genre, cleverly written by producer Jimmy Sangster and directed by Seth Holt. Susan Strasberg returns home to be haunted by the corpse of her father, who turns up in the swimming pool. Decorum dictates we reveal nothing further, lest your enjoyment of this labyrinthine thriller be marred. Take nothing for granted, and be prepared to be jolted by the "haunting" scenes. Christopher Lee, Ronald Lewis, Ann Todd.

**SCREAM OF THE DEMON LOVER** (1971). Spanish-Italian programmer with an all-too-familiar plot (beautiful young woman comes to eerie Gothic castle, where sinister nobleman holds sway) is well photographed and acted, suggesting exciting things which never arrive. He's a part-time doctor experimenting with rejuvenating dead flesh, she's a biochemist falling for the baron even though he's suspected by the villagers of heinous crimes against women. There's a decayed hand that crawls over her supple body and a fiend in the cellar—and would you believe a servant named Igor? Director J. L. Merino is worthy of better assignments than E. Colombo's screamplay. Jennifer Hartley and Jeffrey Chase do what they can as the odd couple, but are ultimately defeated by an unsatisfying, illogical ending. In videocassette under this title and as **BLOOD CASTLE**.

**SCREAM OF THE WOLF (1974).** Werewolf TV-movie produced-directed by Dan Curtis and adapted by Richard Matheson from a David Chase story. Or are those torn-up corpses some kind of trick? Peter Graves, Clint Walker, Philip Carey, JoAnn Pflug, Don Megowan.

**SCREAM, PRETTY PEGGY (1973).** Blatantly plagiaristic TV-movie rip-off of Robert Bloch's PSYCHO utilizing predictable plot devices. Bette Davis stars as a bedridden mother, Ted Bessell is her artistic, misunderstood son. Gee, did we give it away? Scripter Jimmy Sangster and director Gordon Hessler should be ashamed. Charles Drake, Sian Barbara Allen.

**SCREAMER (1974).** Surprisingly effective British TV-movie starring Pamela Franklin as a young woman who fears she is being stalked by a homicidal rapist. Recovering from an attack, she superimposes the attacker's face over every man she meets and goes hysterical. Brian Clemens' telescript introduces a few unexpected twists before a satisfying climax. Shaun O'Riordan's direction is better than usual for these cheap productions. Only the gore effects fall down. (VC)

**SCREAMERS (1978).** Roger Corman purchased an Italian flick, THE FISH MEN, added 12 minutes of new footage and re-released it on an unsuspecting world. Richard Johnson is a scientist who's created gill guys, and Barbara Bach is his daughter, who reluctantly cooperates until the survivor of a shipwreck, Claudio Cassinelli, helps her to escape the volcanic island as it sinks. Special makeup work by Chris Walas. Italian footage was shot by Sergio Martino, U.S. inserts by Dan T. Miller. Joseph Cotten, Mel Ferrer, Cameron Mitchell, Beryl Cunningham. (VC)

**SCREAMING DEAD, THE (1971).** Videocassette title for **DRACULA VS. DR. FRANKENSTEIN.**

**SCREAMING SKULL, THE (1973).** American-International thud-crud as dim-witted as the family servant played by Alex Nicol, who directed in a manner as dim as the lighting. To the haunted mansion come John Hudson and Peggy Webber, not overly bright themselves. In fact, everyone seems to have a bulb unscrewed as a diabolical murder plot unfolds that involves a human head stripped of all flesh, gleaming white, which keeps popping up in the darnedest places. Gee, the supernatural must be at work. Did we say diabolical? Make that dim-witted. From F. Marion Crawford's story.

**SCREAMING WOMAN, THE (1972).** TV adaptation of Ray Bradbury's story about a child who hears a woman's voice coming from beneath the ground and tries to tell disbelieving adults. However, telewriter Merwin Gerard threw away the concept in favor of cliches: Olivia de Havilland, recovering from a breakdown, finds a woman buried alive, but nobody will believe her—except Ed Nelson, the neighbor who did the burying. So now he has to shut her up . . . and the terror begins. Ray Bradbury this is not. On its own it holds up as a formula suspense chiller, but director Jack Smight is no Hitchcock. Joseph Cotten, Walter Pidgeon, Jan Arvan.

**SCREAMPLAY (1986).** Spoof on horror flicks starring Rufus Butler Seder as a would-be writer named Edgar Allen (ha ha!) whose characters come to life as he creates them at the typewriter. Unusual, with some nice twists by the real "screamwriters," Ed Greenberg and Mr. Seder. Incidentally, Seder also directed his own scream-pt.

**SCREAMS OF A WINTER NIGHT (1979).** Children camping at a mountain lake swap terror stories at night. An anthology film materializes with bloodcurdlers about Bigfoot, an apartment seemingly haunted, and a psychopathic "child woman." Directed by James Wilson. Gil Glasgow, Mary Cox, Robin

**ALBERT FINNEY IN 'SCROOGE'**

Bradley, Matt Borel, Patrick Byers. (VC)

**SCREAMTIME (1983).** Described as "the newest thing in nightmares!" A British trilogy of horror stories. One is about a puppeteer who uses his dummies to get revenge on human dummies; the second is about a woman haunted by prophetic visions; and the last is about thieves who encounter supernatural guardians in an old mansion. Axes, knives, skeletons. Get the picture? Dora Bryan, Robin Bailey, Ann Lynn. Directed by Al Beresford. (VC)

**SCROOGE (1970).** Ebenezer Scrooge, villain of Dickens' A CHRISTMAS CAROL, has never been more avaricious, churlish or penurious as in this dark British musical-comedy directed by Ronald Neame. Give Albert Finney credit but also credit the production design of Terry Marsh for capturing the supernatural. While the songs are mediocre to good, the cast injects considerable excitement and charm into the material: Alec Guinness as Marley's Ghost, Edith Evans as the Ghost of Christmas Past and Kenneth More as the Ghost of Christmas Present. A perennial favorite with lavish music productions and faithfulness to the spirit of Dickens. (VC)

**SEA SERPENT (1985).** Atomic explosion arouses an underwater undulater sleeping it off in the briny deep. Ship's captain Timothy Bottoms, whose drunkenness has caused disaster at sea, espies the slippery serpent, but nobody will believe him—until he finds a woman (Taryn Power) who also saw the aquatic assaulter. Off they go to destroy the marine marauder with advise from professor Ray Milland (in his last role). Poorly made Spanish seafarer, of minimum impact; a dozing denizen. Jared Martin. (VC)

**SEANCE ON A WET AFTERNOON (1964).** Engrossing British film written-directed by Bryan Forbes, chilling and stark in its depiction of an unbalanced woman (Kim Stanley) who forces her milquetoast husband (Richard Attenborough) to kidnap a rich industrialist's daughter. It's the woman's hope to establish herself as a celebrated spiritualist by "locating" the youngster. Realization that she is willing to murder the child comes as a jolt to Attenborough. He is thrown into a dilemma, the uncertainty of which holds one in the grip of its ghastly implications. Patrick Magee, Maria Kazan. (VC)

**SEARCH. See PROBE. (Dig it!)**

**SEARCH FOR BRIDEY MURPHY, THE (1956).** Based on the bestseller by Morey Bernstein, reportedly the true story of a woman who, when hypnotized by Bernstein, regressed to a previous existence in Ireland. A restrained study in reincarnation, never sensational or exploitative, and not too exciting, either. But it is persuasive, leading one to believe Bridey was indeed a woman who lived 150 years ago, and whose mem-

memories are retained in the body of a modern woman. Louis Hayward portrays Bernstein; Teresa Wright is Bridey. Written-directed by Noel Langley. Kenneth Tobey, Richard Anderson, Nancy Gates, Walter Kingsford.

**SEARCH FOR THE EVIL ONE (1967).** Joseph Kane, who once directed Roy Rogers Westerns, turned up in his twilight years to helm this bit of nonsense about Adolf Hitler turning up alive in Argentina (where else?) and plotting a new assault on the world. Sieg Heil! drama designed for Nuremberg burn-outs. Lisa Pera, H. M. Wynant, Henry Brandon (Martin Bormann), Pitt Herbert (Hitler), Anna Lisa.

**SEARCH FOR THE GODS (1975).** TV-movie, produced by Douglas S. Cramer, with a Herman Miller-Ken Pettus script playing off the Erich von Daniken theory that extraterrestrials walked our planet centuries ago. But this comes off as routine good guys vs. bad guys pap, directed routinely by Jud Taylor. A wandering young man (Kurt Russell), looking for pieces of an ancient medallion with alien-like markings, stumbles around Taos, New Mexico. The search is just as futile for the viewer. Ralph Bellamy, Stephen McHattie, Raymond St. Jacques, Victoria Racimo.

**SEASON OF THE WITCH.** Videocassette title for George Romero's **HUNGRY WIVES.** (Yum yum!)

**SECOND BEST SECRET AGENT IN THE WHOLE WIDE WORLD, THE (1966).** British imitation of James Bond from

'THE SECRET LIFE OF WALTER MITTY'

director Lindsay Shonteff, starring Tom Adams as agent Tom Vine, who joins sexy Veronica Hurst to protect a Swedish scientist who has developed Re-Grav, an anti-gravity machine. The sequel was WHERE THE BULLETS FLY. Peter Bull, Judy Huxtable, Francis De Wolff. (VC)

**SECOND COMING OF SUZANNE, THE (1974).** Movie-within-a-movie: Jared Martin and pal Richard Dreyfuss are producing a film in which Sondra Locke is playing Jesus Christ. Director Michael Barry (son of Gene Barry, who appears as a media executive) tries to pack mountains of social implications and modern meanings into this low-budget fantasy made in San Francisco, but it is pretentious self-indulgence. Locke has a terrifying Cross to bear. (VC)

**SECONDS (1966).** Multi-tiered John Frankenheimer film, adapted from David Ely's novel by Lewis John Carlino, is an allegory about our search for identity and a "fresh start," and a whopper of a horror tale, photographed surrealistically by James Wong Howe. A secret organization supplies clients with new identities and faces so they can escape to a new milieu. John Randolph, disillusioned New York banker, emer-

ges from his operation as Rock Hudson. But the "new man" cannot adjust to the artificial world the organization provides and he demands yet another identity. The climax is absolutely shocking; Rock Hudson was never better. Salome Jens, Will Geer, Jeff Corey, Murray Hamilton.

**SECRET AGENT FIREBALL.** See **KILLERS ARE CHALLENGED.** (But you won't be challenged!)

**SECRET AGENT SUPER DRAGON (1966).** Sequel to CODE NAME: JAGUAR is an unimpressive Italian/French/German spy adventure with undercover agent Ray Danton assigned to prevent a typical mastermind from taking control of Earth with the drug Syncron II. Marisa Mell and Margaret Lee are sexy ladies populating Danton's scrumptious surroundings. Directed by Calvin Jackson Padget. Jess Hahn, Carlo D'Angelo.

**SECRET BEYOND THE DOOR (1948).** Fritz Lang psychological thriller filled with psychiatric double-talk to cover up incongruities and lapses in Silvia Richards' story about a woman who marries publisher Michael Redgrave and suspects he's a Bluebeard. Joan Bennett is asking for it when she reaches for the knob to the door of the Forbidden Bedroom. The music by Miklos Rozsa provides a lot of what isn't there. And incidentally, there are enough red herrings to open a fish shop with. Anne Revere, Paul Cavanagh.

**SECRET CEREMONY (1969).** In a London cemetery, Mia Farrow meets Elizabeth Taylor, a whore putting flowers on the gravestone of her daughter who died ten years earlier. Mia strangely resembles the dead daughter, and damned if the whore doesn't strangely resemble Mia's late mother. Director Joseph Losey blends fantasy and reality along a path that leads to suicide and murder—but can you endure the grimness? Robert Mitchum, Pamela Brown.

**SECRET LIFE OF WALTER MITTY, THE (1948).** Wonderful adaptation of James Thurber's short story about a meekish gent who escapes into fantasies, ideally slanted for the comedic talents of Danny Kaye. Mitty, a milquetoast working for a pulp magazine publisher, fantasizes numerous whimsical adventures, then he's pulled into a real one when he comes in possession of a secret formula which spy Boris Karloff is seeking. Frothily directed by Norman Z. McLeod. Virginia Mayo, Ann Rutherford, Fay Bainter. (VC)

**SECRET OF DORIAN GRAY, THE (1971).** Absolute cropper . . . Harry Alan Towers' updating of the Oscar Wilde novel, THE PICTURE OF DORIAN GRAY, to satisfy the youth market . . . an Italian-German bomb with writer-director Massimo Dallamano emphasizing the decadence and homosexuality of a young man (Helmut Berger) whose soul is captured in a painting which reflects his aging and sexual debaucheries while he remains vigorously youthful and nocturnally active. Richard Todd, Herbert Lom, Beryl Cunningham. Very, very perverted . . .

**SECRET OF DR. ALUCARD.** See **TASTE FOR BLOOD, A.**

**SECRET OF DR. MABUSE, THE (1964).** Last of several West German sequels to Fritz Lang's films of the 1920s about a mastermind criminal with plans to conquer the world. The mad doctor (Wolfgang Preiss) is a math genius who turns his brilliance to evil with the use of a Death Ray. Peter Van Eyck, Werner Peters, Leo Genn and Yoko Tani drudge drearily through Western Europe, looking like refugees. Directed by Hugo Fregonese, written by Ladislas Fodor.

**SECRET OF MY SUCCESS (1965).** Unusual story about a mild-mannered English constable to a British diplomat in South America who has three adventures—one of them involving giant spiders in a castle dungeon. Directed by Andrew L. Stone. Lionel Jeffries, James Booth, Shirley Jones, Stella Stevens, Honor Blackman, Amy Dolby.

**SECRET OF NIMH, THE (1982).** Splendid adaptation of Robert C. O'Brien's novel about a family of mice seeking a new home before their old one is destroyed by the spring plow. Mother mouse seeks mythical characters because one of her sons is sick with pneumonia and needs medicine. A fanciful odyssey with wonderful animal characters. This is stylish, old-fashioned animation by producer-artist Don Bluth, who left the Disney company with other artists to work inde-

**CREATURE FEATURES MOVIE GUIDE**

pendently. The film was not a
big success, perhaps because
audiences were asked to accept
rats as heroic figures. Too bad .
. . the film deserved a better
fate with its bursts of vivid imagination. Voices by Elizabeth
Hartman, Dom De Luise, Hermione Baddeley, Peter Strauss,
Paul Shenar, Derek Jacobi,
John Carradine, Aldo Ray. (VC)

**SECRET OF THE BLACK
WIDOW (1964).** Diabolical killer
utilizes slugs shaped to
resemble black widow spiders
as he cuts down his targets one
by one, baffling Scotland Yard
flatfeet. West German thriller (of
dubious thrills) directed by F. J.
Gottlieb. O.W. Fischer, Karin
Dor, Werner Peters.

**SECRET OF THE BLUE
ROOM (1933).** Kurt Neumann
directed this first film version of
the mystery-pseudosupernatural
tale by Erich Philippi about a
man who dies in a haunted
room. (Remakes included MUR-
DER IN THE BLUE ROOM and
THE MISSING GUEST.) Pretty
standard "old dark house" stuff,
but the cast is a nice blend:
Paul Lukas, Onslow Stevens,
Edward Arnold, Lionel Atwill.

**SECRET OF THE CHINESE
CARNATION, THE (1965).**
Brad Harris and other
espionage agents are after a
revolutionary formula for fuel,
which could bring about a major
change in world economy. West
German spy actioner directed
by Rudolf Zehetgruber.

**MRS. BRISBY AND JEREMY THE CROW IN 'THE SECRET OF NIMH'**

**SECRET OF THE LOCH, THE (1934).** Diver Seymour Hicks
takes a swim in the Scottish loch and discovers an underwater beast—sort of a British Loch Jaws. Directed by Milton
Rosmer. Nancy O'Neil, Gibson Gowland.

**SECRET OF THE SWORD (1985).** Feature spinoff from the
animated TV series starring He-Man and She-Ra. A glorified
Saturday morning cartoon with drawings, music track and
voices all deadly familiar. He-Man and She-Ra (who turn out
to be long-lost brother and sister) join forces to fight off the
evil Hordak and his hordes. Voices by John Erwin, Melendy
Britt and George DiCenzo.

**SECRET OF THE TELEGIAN (1960).** Remove the blood
from the body, replace it with electricity and you've got yourself a rechargable monster (sorry, batteries not included).
That's one way for Japanese producer Tomoyuki Tanaka to
stay "current." The monster is really a man who uses a
teleporter device to avenge himself against wartime comrades who betrayed him. Special effects are by Eiji
Tsuburaya, who used to have so much fun making Godzilla
movies. Socket to them, director Jun Fukuda.

**SECRET SERVICE IN DARKEST AFRICA. See BARON'S
AFRICAN WAR, THE.** (A baron landscape?)

**SECRET WITNESS (1931).** Killer gorilla is trained to kill for
its demented master. Directed by Thornton Freeland. Una
Merkel, William Collier Jr., ZaSu Pitts, Paul Hurst.

**SECRETS OF THE DEATH ROOM. See LOVE ME DEAD-
LY.** (Step right in, my dear)

**SECRETS OF THE FRENCH POLICE (1932).** Surely, Shirley, The Surete was surly over this surreal serving. Its real
secrets had to be more titillating than those "exposed" here.

It's no secret composer Max Steiner's score was the highpoint of this thriller in which a hypnotist uses mirrors to mes-
merize a beautiful woman and hides his corpses in plaster
. . . of Paris, of course. Odd mixture of routine police work
and mad doctor cliches, allegedly based on newspaper ar-
ticles. Frank Morgan, Julia Gordon, Gregory Ratoff. David O.
Selznick produced this creaking curiosity piece.

**SEE NO EVIL (1971).** Richard Fleischer's attempt to make a
PSYCHO tale: Blind girl Mia Farrow is trapped in a house of
corpses and pursued by a killer identified only by his cowboy
boots. The macabre touches of Brian Clemens' script have
their moments, but shock value is minimal and one wearies
of Farrow's pathetic screams and ever-depressing plight. If
only these helpless people would learn to lock their doors.
Dorothy Allison, Robin Bailey, Diane Grayson. (VC)

**SEED OF TERROR. See GRAVE OF THE VAMPIRE.**

**SEEDS OF EVIL. Videocassette title for GARDENER, THE.**

**SEIZURE (1974).** Gore murders galore when a demented
writer (Jonathan Frid of DARK SHADOWS) creates characters who spring to life: Martine Beswick is the Queen of
Death, Henry Baker plays an executioner and Herve Villechaize ("De plane, boss, de plane") is Shorty the Slicer.
Director Oliver Stone co-scripted with Edward Mann. Troy
Donahue, Mary Woronov. This'll grab you.

**SENDER, THE (1982).** Thought-provoking sophisticated horror film dealing with the psychological traumas of a young
man (Zeljko Ivanek) suffering from amnesia. He's placed
under the care of psychiatrist Kathryn Harrold, who experiences the mental images of his nightmares. Low-key handling
by director Roger Christian and the taut screenplay by
Thomas Baum make for a decent shocker. Shirley Knight ap-

**LOSING ONE'S HEAD DOESN'T PAY MENTAL DIVIDENDS IN 'THE SENDER'**

pears as an apparition (or ghost?) of the boy's domineering mother, who fights Harrold for her son's love. Filmed in Georgia and England. Paul Freeman, Sean Hewitt. (VC)

**SENSUOUS VAMPIRES.** See **VAMPIRE HOOKERS, THE.**

**SENTINEL, THE (1977).** Attempt at a classy demonic film in the league of THE OMEN or THE EXORCIST falls short in the hands of director Michael Winner, who allows the climax to deteriorate into a freak sideshow. Too many important events in Jeffrey Konvitz's story are left unexplained and characterizations are muddy as a river bottom when fashion model Cristina Raines settles in a strange New York City brownstone, where priest John Carradine maintains a singular vigil at an upstairs window. One scary sequence has the model confronted with the terrors of her childhood but the film as a whole never jells, this despite a plethora of interesting characters: Eli Wallach as the cop on the case, Ava Gardner as a strange realtor; Sylvia Miles and Beverly D'Angelo as lesbian lovers; Burgess Meredith as a sinister man with a cat; Christopher Walken as Cristina's lover; and Jose Ferrer and Arthur Kennedy as men of the cloth. (VC)

**SERENADE FOR TWO SPIES (1965).** Secret Agent 006 1/2 rushes through the States to recover a stolen laser ray gun in this uninspired German-Italian spoof of James Bond with Tony Kendall as the goofy spy John Krim. Written-directed by Michael Pfleghar. Barbara Lass, Helmut Lange.

**SERGEANT DEADHEAD THE ASTRONAUT (1965).** Lamebrain American-International excuse for comedy—produced during the "Beach" craze—is strictly for deadheads. Astronaut Frankie Avalon goes into orbit with a chimpanzee. Each returns to Earth with the traits of the other, the chimp plotting rocket trajectories and the astronaut peeling bananas. This throws the military into an uproar. You'll be thrown into a tizzy. Directed by Norman Taurog. Deborah Walley, Cesar Romero, Fred Clark, Buster Keaton.

**SERPENT ISLAND (1954).** Bert I. Gordon's first feature, so impotently produced it was never released to theaters, merely shown "first-run" on TV. Not even that medium really wanted it. Sonny Tufts and Mary Munday are lovers caught up in a voodoo curse after their boat sinks and leaves them stranded on a Pacific island. The poor acting will evoke a curse from you, too.

**SERPENT WARRIORS (1986).** Eartha Kitt as a snake goddess? Clint Walker as a zoologist? You bet your fangs. An ancient curse by a snake-loving tribe is plaguing a construction site, so Walker and his pals, Anne Lockhart and Chris Mitchum, are needed to fight off the wriggling warriors and sinuous slammers. Hundreds of snake extras were needed by director Niels Rasmussen to satisfy Martin Wise's hissing script demands. Coil up and go to sleep.

**SEVEN BROTHERS MEET DRACULA, THE.** Videocassette title for **LEGEND OF THE SEVEN GOLDEN VAMPIRES, THE.** (Seven brides for seven corpses?)

**SEVEN DAYS TO NOON (1950).** Gripping doomsday film from John and Roy Boulting in which an atomic plant researcher (Barry Jones) steals the UR-12 model bomb and threatens to blow up London if the Prime Minister doesn't cease bomb production. The City's evacuation is detailed, with stark scenes of deserted London landmarks. Meanwhile, Scotland Yard under Andre Morell is seeking the professor. Supertense suspense thriller. Barry Jones co-stars.

**SEVEN DEATHS IN THE CAT'S EYE (1972).** Italian/French/German production . . . a masterpiece of horror—in a pig's eye! Beastly murders in a European village culminate in the stalking of new victims in the local castle. Meow Owww! Written-directed by Antonio Margheriti. Jane Birkin, Anton Diffring, Hiram Keller, Dana Ghia. (VC)

**SEVEN DEADLY SINS, THE (1953).** Seven Italian and French directors spin seven vignettes, each dramatizing a provocative sin. Only one episode (directed by Jean Dreville) is touched by fantasy: "Sloth," in which a lazy angel floats to Earth to influence our pedantic pace.

**SEVEN DOORS TO DEATH (1983).** New Orleans hotel has a subterranean chamber with a door leading to "The Beyond." When opened, the passageway allows walking dead to enter society in this Italian film that is a companion piece to GATES OF HELL. Directed by Lucio Fulci. Katherine MacColl, David Warbeck, Sarah Keller. (VC)

**SEVEN FACES OF DR. LAO (1964).** George Pal eggroll captures the Confucius charm of Charles Finney's novel, thanks to most honorable Charles Beaumont script. Tony Randall, playing a Chinese circus owner who turns up in Abalone, Arizona, also essays Merlin the Magician; seer Appolonius of Tyana; Pan; Medusa; the Abominable Snowman; and a mustachioed serpent. Frank Tuttle won an Oscar for his make-up. All about an unscrupulous businessman (Arthur O'Connell) buying up Abalone property because a railroad is coming through and how things are set right by the philosophical (but never insidious) Dr. Lao. Barbara Eden, Noah Beery, Lee Patrick, John Ericson, Minerva Urecal. Jim Danforth provided animated sequences.

**SEVEN FOOTPRINTS TO SATAN (1929).** Version of A. Merritt's fantasy novel released in silent and sound editions. The Devil is in pursuit of a fabulous jewel. Directed by Ben Christensen. Thelma Todd, Creighton Hale, Ann Christy.

**SEVEN KEYS TO BALDPATE (1929).** First sound version (following two silent ones) of the George M. Cohan play based on an Earl Derr Biggers novel, directed by Reginald

---

*"So terrifying you will need a blindfold to see it!"— Adveritsement for*
### SCREAM BLOODY MURDER.

**CRISTINA RAINES IN 'THE SENTINEL'**

Barker. A writer tries to hack out a novel in empty Baldpate Inn but he's harassed by strange visitors and comedic interruptions. This comedy-mystery with overtones of the "old dark house" was made twice more in sound, then converted into a British horror picture, HOUSE OF THE LONG SHADOWS. Richard Dix, Margaret Livingston.

**SEVEN KEYS TO BALDPATE (1935).** Second talkie version of the Cohan comedy-mystery play, starring Gene Raymond, Eric Blore, Margaret Callahan, Walter Brennan and Erin O'Brien-Moore. This old chestnut is always fun to watch. Directed by William Hamilton and Edward Kelly.

**SEVEN KEYS TO BALDPATE (1947).** George M. Cohan's stage play was adapted into this, a funny spoof on the "old dark house" genre, with Phillip Terry holing up in a weird house to write a book on a bet. Directed by Lew Landers. Arthur Shields, Jacqueline White, Jason Robards.

**SEVEN MAGNIFICENT GLADIATORS, THE (1983).** Sword-and-sandal remake of SEVEN SAMURAI, but playing more like THE MAGNIFICENT SEVEN, a remake in itself. Bandit leader Dan Vadis, endowed with supernatural powers by his sorceress mother, yearly attacks a village, but the town's women have had enough and, armed with a magical sword, seek a gladiator who can wield it without burning his hands. That warrior is Han (Lou Ferrigno) who joins with Sybil Danning (as a good-natured swordstress) and five other muscular heroes to fight to the death with Vadis. It's all quite predictable; director Bruno Mattei offers few surprises. Other headliners include Brad Harris, Carla Ferrigno and Mandy Rice-Davies (one-time prostitute involved in the British Parliament scandals of the 1960s.) Entertaining for its rousing sword battles and the performance of the provocative Danning, otherwise a ho-hum affair.

**SEVENTH CONTINENT, THE (1968).** Allegorical Czech-Yugoslav film for kids, but with enough social comment to appeal to adults. Three neglected children—Oriental, Negro, Caucasian—meet on an uncharted island where they create their own paradise. Soon, children are coming from all over to escape the inanities of parents. Director Dusan Vukotic utilizes animation, superimposition and other effects to tell this fable which clearly carries the warning: Beware anyone over eight. Iris Vrus, Tomislav Pasaric.

**SEVENTH SEAL, THE (1956).** Ingmar Bergman's work is perpetually dark, rampant with heavy symbolism and troubled people. This remains one of his best films, set in the 14th Century when a knight (Max von Sydow), after ten bloody years in the Crusades, pauses for a game of chess with Death on a bleak beach. The burning of a young woman at the stake, the travels of a couple named Mary and Joseph, the disillusionment of people in a time of corrupted Christianity—all are made bawdy, brutal, funny and touching in this Bergman masterpiece. Seal of Approval. (VC)

**SEVENTH VEIL, THE (1946).** Heavy-handed British melodrama has James Mason maintaining a Svengali control over brilliant pianist Ann Todd, who cannot escape the mesmerizing spell. Strictly for ladies with dry handkerchiefs.

**KERWIN MATHEWS BATTLES BONES O'RATTLE IN 'THE SEVENTH VOYAGE OF SINBAD'**

Directed tearfully by Compton Bennett. Hugh McDermott, Herbert Lom, David Horne, Yvonne Owen. (VC)

**SEVENTH VICTIM, THE (1943).** Esoteric Val Lewton production for RKO, made when he was turning out low budget horror films. Kim Hunter (in her screen debut) plays a meek student at a strict girls' academy, who ventures to New York City to find her missing sister. Hunter is befriended by a strange private detective whose body turns up dead on a subway. Then she meets Hugh Beaumont, once married to her sister, who introduces her to life in an Italian cafe called Dante's, inhabited by disillusioned poets and other lost people. The errant sister, acting as one in a trance, is part of a cult worshipping the Devil, and she must die for betraying the sect's code of silence. An allegorical conclusion has the sister entering a flat with a hangman's rope dangling from the ceiling. Director Mark Robson, in his debut, never compromises the dark pessimism. Tom Conway, Jean Brooks, Isabel Jewell, Evelyn Brent, Chef Milani. (VC)

**SEVENTH VOYAGE OF SINBAD, THE (1958).** Fruitful collaboration between producer Charles Schneer, director Nathan Juran, writer Kenneth Kolb and stop motion animator Ray Harryhausen—an enchanting adventure tale, its acting and dialogue appropriately stylized, its creatures often sympathetic and its story capturing the magic of the Arabian Nights. Kerwin Mathews is a robust, romantic Sinbad forced by evil magician Torin Thatcher (he has shrunken princess Kathryn Grant to minuscule size) to seek the egg of a roc on an island dominated by a cyclops. Harryhausen's effects (including an ingenious sword duel with a skeleton) were to improve in subsequent films but the sheer art of his talent is all here: the dancing snake woman, a two-headed roc, a firebreathing dragon, etc. etc. All beautifully enhanced by Bernard Herrmann's score. An absolute must for fantasophiles. Richard Eyer appears as the genie from "the land beyond beyond." Alec Mango, Danny Green. (VC)

**SEVERED ARM, THE (1973).** Sickening revenge yarn in which survivors of a mine cave-in slice off a man's arm for food. In moments they are rescued. Years later the survivors die one by one, each horribly mutilated. In some instances, arms are torn out of their sockets. You'll be revolted unless you're an utter sadist—in which case, enjoy! Written-directed by Thomas S. Alderman. Deborah Walley, Marvin Kaplan, John Crawford, Paul Carr, Ray Dennis. (VC)

**SEX KITTENS GO TO COLLEGE.** See **BEAUTY AND THE ROBOT** (but only if you have nine lives).

**SEX MACHINE, THE (1975).** Italian soft-core porn-comedy set in the next century and purporting the preposterous precept that intercourse and other sexual acts can create an electrical flow, direly needed by mankind because electrical power is no more. Feeble excuse for dumb slapstick and smutty gags without "socially redeeming" values. The film's only amusing sequence comes when a massive orgy is held in a hotel, while in the kitchen a team of scientists note how much voltage is stimulated by various acts of copulation, homosexuality, lesbianism, etc. Luigi Proietti, Agostina Belli. Written-directed by P. F. Campanile.

**SEX ON THE GROOVE TUBE.** See **CASE OF THE FULL MOON MURDERS.**

**SEX VAMPIRES.** See **CAGED VIRGINS.**

**SEXORCIST, THE.** See **EERIE MIDNIGHT HORROR SHOW, THE.** (Ultimate witching hour?)

**SH! THE OCTOPUS (1938).** Nutty lowbrow comedy with comedians Allen Jenkins and Hugh Herbert teamed as goofy private eyes who tangle with a clever con artist and his Death Ray, not to mention eight metallic arms. Sh! Don't tell anyone. Directed by William McGann.

**SHADEY (1985).** Intriguing British film in which Anthony Sher portrays a mechanic with the ability to project mental imagines onto unexposed film. He wants to use his talent to raise money for a sex change operation but others want his talent put to other purposes, and soon Oliver Shadey is involved with spies and a crazy lady who eats coal for dinner and chases him with a knife. Bizarre blending. Directed by

Philip Saville. Billie Whitelaw, Patrick Macnee, Leslie Ash, Katherine Helmond.

**SHADOW, THE (1933).** British chiller (unfortunately, without much bright-ish chill) about a hooded figure who behaves like a shadowy substance by flitting through the secret passageways of an old mansion—killing the inhabitants. Nothing is hiding in the shadows you haven't already seen. Directed by George A. Cooper. Elizabeth Allen, Henry Kendall.

**SHADOW CHASERS (1985).** Two-hour TV pilot for a comedy-supernatural series created by Brian Grazer and Kenneth Johnson, a curiously amusing idea blending the humor of GHOSTBUSTERS with the paranormal of Gary Collins' TV series, SIXTH SENSE. Trevor Eve is a serious professor at Georgetown University teamed with Dennis Dugan, a frivolous tabloid writer who believes in the supernatural. In their first misadventure together, they investigate a haunted house where a mysterious fire consumed a man alive. Characters and situations are amusingly developed by Grazier and Johnson, the latter also directing. Nina Foch is a university scientist giving them assignments.

**SHADOW OF CHIKARA (1977).** What begins as an adventure Western, in which Confederate survivors of the last battle of the Civil War set out to find a lost treasure, gradually shifts into a moody, strange tale of the quasisupernatural. Is a hidden cache of diamonds in a mountain cave watched over by demon hawks or hawk spirits in human form? Writer-producer-director Earl E. Smith has fashioned his macabre horror yarn with some dandy surprise twists and a creepy ambience. Offbeat. Joe Don Baker, Sondra Locke, Ted Neeley, Slim Pickens, John Davis Chandler, Joy Houck Jr. Also known as WISHBONE CUTTER. (VC)

**SHADOW OF CHINATOWN.** Videocassette title for **YELLOW PHANTOM.** (A cowardly death-dealer?)

**EVE & DUGAN: 'THE SHADOW CHASERS'**

**SHADOW OF DEATH.** TV title for **BRAINWAVES.**

**SHADOW OF EVIL (1966).** Made in Bangkok, with Kerwin Mathews as a secret agent (OSS 117) trying to stop a mad scientist (Robert Hossein) and his virulent rats from spreading an epidemic across Earth. Pier Angeli provides love interest. An entry in the French OSS spy series. Directed-written by Andre Hunnebelle. Dominique Wilms.

**SHADOW OF TERROR (1945).** PRC quickie in which scientist Richard Fraser invents a new explosive, then fights foreign spies to protect patent rights. The A-bomb was dropped on Hiroshima only days before the film's release, so director Lew Landers Elmer glued-on an epilogue which declares the "powerful new explosive" was atomic all along. Footage of the first mushroom cloud was also quickly gluesticked. So science-fiction it ain't. At best, a hackneyed spy thriller. Grace Gillern, Cy Kendall, Emmett Lynn.

**SHADOW OF THE CAT, THE (1961).** A dead woman's feline wreaks revenge by attacking her killers in this British chiller diller directed by John Gilling, who cleverly uses his camera to turn an ordinary house cat into a sinister creature. Barbara Shelley, Freda Jackson, Andre Morell, William Lucas.

**SHADOW OF THE HAWK (1976).** Beautifully photographed supernatural fantasy depicts Canadian Indian Jan-Michael Vincent helping exorcise an evil spirit holding a 200-year-old grudge. Chief Dan George is the ancient shaman whose sad dignity is touched by "bad medicine," Marilyn Hassett is a reporter. Writer Norman Thaddeus Vane's redman sorcery doesn't always work, but director George McGowan labors bravely to give his film redman class. Wampum not at box office, but producer John Kemeny's heart in right place.

**SHADOW ON THE LAND (1968).** TV-film, directed by Richard C. Sarafian, depicts a near future when the USA has been seized by a totalitarian dictatorship, against which a

'SHE CREATURE': SHE'S A BEAUT!

handful of Americans plan a revolt. Intrigue and counterespionage tactics; more killing and violence than usual for a tube movie. Writer Nedrick Young really lets the bullets fly. Jackie Cooper, John Forsythe, Gene Hackman, Carol Lynley, Janice Rule, Myron Healy.

**SHADOW WORLD (1983).** Juvenile space action, animated, in which a fair-haired lad of the galaxy saves our star systems from invaders. Routine. (VC)

**SHADOWMAN (1973).** French TV serial is complete with cliffhangers as supercriminal Jacques Champreux and villainess Gayle Hunnicutt search for a treasure, resurrecting corpses along the way to form a zombie army. Heavily cut for the U.S. Directed by Georges Franju. Gert Frobe, Josephine Chaplin, Raymond Bussieres, Ugo Pagliai. (VC)

**SHADOWS IN THE NIGHT (1944).** Originally released as CRIME DOCTOR'S RENDEZVOUS, this is part of a series starring Warner Baxter as Dr. Ordway, a crime psychologist who was once a criminal himself. This episodes features a gas that creates illusions; several characters suffer identical nightmares. Directed by Eugene Forde. Nina Foch, George Zucco, Minor Watson, Lester Matthews, Ben Welden.

**SHADOWS RUN BLACK (1984).** "The Black Angel" is on the loose in this sleazy slasher flick, knocking off beautiful co-eds, whose bodies are shown in their glorious nudity. A black sheep in any filmmaker's shadowy past. Kevin Costner, William J. Kulzer. Directed by Howard Heard. (VC)

**SHAGGY D.A., THE (1976).** Sequel to Disney's THE SHAGGY DOG is missing its original cast, but it does have the original scarab ring, once owned by the Borgia family, inscribed with the Latin phrase "Intra Kapori Transmuto." It is this device which turns lawyer Dean Jones into a Bratislavian sheep dog, still capable of speech and thought. Which happens at a bad time since Jones is running for D.A. against crooked Keenan Wynn. Every cliche comedy device is thrown into the breach, but the film still goes to the dogs. Directed by Robert Stevenson. Tim Conway, Suzanne Pleshette, Vic Tayback, Jo Anne Worley. (VC)

**SHAGGY DOG, THE (1959).** The scarab ring of the Borgias, combined with the proper incantation, turns the son of mailman Fred MacMurray into a Bratislavian sheep dog—usually at the most embarrasing moments. Endearing Disney comedy, capturing the nostalgia of a Saturday matinee. A frustrated policeman ("Follow that dog!") and spies add to this fluffy innocuousness directed by Charles Barton. Tommy Kirk, Jean Hagen, Annette Funicello. (VC)

**SHAME OF THE JUNGLE (1975).** French-Belgian animated feature which spoofs Edgar Rice Burrough's beloved Tarzan with several science-fiction elements thrown in. Voices by Bill Murray, John Belushi, Johnny Weissmuller Jr.

**SHANKS (1974).** Singularly offbeat William Castle production (he also directed) starring French mime Marcel Marceau as an insane puppeteer who can control the dead. Given only limited distribution; most critics deemed this a failure. Marceau fans may want to see his first effort of straight dramatic acting; otherwise, of marginal interest . . . rank shank.

**SHARAD OF ATLANTIS (1936).** Re-edited TV version of a Republic serial. See **UNDERSEA KINGDOM.**

**SHE (1935).** Merian C. Cooper, co-director of KING KONG, produced this version of H. Rider Haggard's novel, starring stage actress Helen Gahagan in her only screen role. Unlike the original, set in Egypt, this takes place in the icy Himalayas, where within a Siberian mountain, explorers discover a lost kingdom, Kor, ruled by a 500-year-old queen who believes one of the adventurers to be the reincarnation of her former lover. To keep her youth she must enter a Flame of Immortality. Directed by Irving Pichel and Lansing C. Holden. Nigel Bruce, Noble Johnson. Max Steiner music.

**SHE (1965).** Hammer's version of the Haggard fantasy novel set in the kingdom of Kuma is the second sound attempt. The problem here seems to be not the set design or costuming—they are exquisite. It is the mundane screenplay by David T. Chantler which too often relies on hackneyed "lost city" cliches. For those bored by reincarnation, or by the stereotyped performances of Peter Cushing, John Richardson and Christopher Lee, there are the garments of Ursula Andress (as Ayesha) and Rosenda Monteros, so flimsy as to require excessive chauvinistic scrutiny. Thus the all-important question becomes: Are those shapely wenches wearing anything underneath their Frederick's of Hollywood attire? Directed by Robert Day, produced by Michael Carreras. Bernard Cribbins, Andre Morell.

**SHE (1982).** Sandahl Bergman portrays the ruler of a lost kingdom, but this Italian film strays markedly from Haggard's novel, incorporating elements of parody and science-fiction to create a hybrid defying description. In this city of the Urech people, one ruler can levitate his enemies, and certain mutants can clone themselves each time one of their arms falls off. Writer-director Avi Nesher (an Israeli) has written a black comedy adventure with anachronisms. David Goss, Quin Kessler, Harrison Muller, Gordon Mitchell. (VC)

**SHE BEAST (1965).** One of the few works of director Mike Reeves, who attracted a cult following after his premature death in 1968 of a drug overdose. Originally REVENGE OF THE BLOOD BEAST, this stars Barbara Steele as a woman possessed by an ancient witch. She goes on a murderous rampage, while her husband (Ian Ogilvy) searches Transylvania for her. The rampage allows Reeves some interesting juxtaposing of images. He was working with a limited budget (and not the greatest script by Michael Byron) yet he brings it off pretty well. His best work was to come in CONQUERER WORM and THE SORCERERS. (VC)

**SHE CREATURE, THE (1956).** Chester Morris prowls California beaches in a black homberg as a hypnotist, the Great Lombardi, who puts the whammy on sexy Marla English. Forcing her soul back to prehistoric times, she emerges from the waves covered with unattractive appendages, carrying out Morris' evil bidding with slashing deaths. American-International release was produced by Alex Gordon, directed by Edward L. Cahn. Tom Conway, Cathy Downs, Ron Randell. The story was used again (by an even worse director) in CREATURE OF DESTRUCTION. (VC)

**SHE DEMONS (1958).** Ludicrous, grade-Z Arthur Jacobs abomination suffering from diarrhea of the jungle. Whip-cracking sadistic Nazis dominate a Pacific island where a fiendish doctor strips the beauty off assorted lasses and tries to transfer their good looks to his ugly frau. You'll really need a sense of humor to sit through this. Richard E. Cunha directed, if you can call it directing. One historical highlight is Irish McCalla as a shipwrecked traveler—that same year she appeared on TV as SHEENA, QUEEN OF THE JUNGLE. Tod Griffin, Victor Sen Young, Gene Roth. (VC)

**SHE DEVIL (1957).** Immaterial fantasy thriller, produced-directed by Kurt Neumann, doesn't even adequately exploit the shapely body of Mari Blanchard, and any resemblance to Stanley Weinbaum's famous short story, "The Adaptive Ultimate," is purely coincidental. The wonderful Ms Blanchard, one of the sexiest actresses of the 1950s, is able through serum injections to adapt herself as she rushes around inexpensive Fox soundstage sets murdering minor characters. Jack Kelly, Albert Dekker, John Archer, Blossom Rock.

**SHE WAITS (1972).** Unimpressive supernatural TV-movie with Patty Duke possessed by the ghost of David McCallum's first wife (Dorothy McGuire). Lots of talk, more talk; few thrills. Produced and directed by Delbert Mann. Beulah Bondi, Lew Ayres, Nelson Olmstead. (VC)

**SHE WAS A HIPPY VAMPIRE.** See **WILD WORLD OF BATWOMAN, THE.** (She shoots from the hip!)

**SHE-DEVILS ON WHEELS (1968).** Motorcycle gore movie, full of violent dismemberings and bloodlettings. The twist here is that the "mean mothers" are exactly that—women who perform sadistic acts against males. Produced-directed by Herschell Gordon Lewis.

**SHE-FREAK (1967).** Revolting exploitation of circus freaks in the style of Tod Browning's FREAKS but without a sense of taste or sympathy for those short-changed by nature. A terrible misuse of the malshaped and malformed by producer-writer David F. Friedman and director Byron Mabe. SHE-

**TANYA ROBERTS AS
SHEENA--WHAT A QUEEN!**

FREAK is a she-weak. (VC)

**SHE-WOLF OF LONDON (1946).** June Lockhart dreams about hideous murders in Hyde Park and imagines the Allenby Curse has turned her into a hairy monster. There's psychiatric double talk and ample dark photography but the material will neither frighten nor fool any really intelligent she-wolves. Directed by Jean Yarbrough. Don Porter, Lloyd Corrigan, Dennis Hoey, Martin Kosleck.

**SHEENA (1984).** The major mistake in attempting to bring

the comic book "Queen of the Jungle" to the screen was to present her as a naive innocent rather than as a hip modern woman. Thus, as sexy as she may be in her leopard skin briefs, Tanya Roberts just doesn't convince. Instead, writers David Newman, Leslie Stevens and Lorenzo Semple Jr., spinning off from the character created by Will Eisner and S. M. Eiger in the 1930s, concoct a campy jungle adventure that is often laughable, and which director John Guillermin directs with a straight face. Ted Wass and Donovan Scott are ridiculous newsreel cameramen in Tigorda (a fictional African kingdom) involved in political intrigue and picturesque adventures with Sheena, who bounces along (in more places than one) on a horse painted to look like a zebra. It becomes a chase involving soldiers, trucks, helicopters and other standard action gimmicks. Sheena can talk to the animals and has some limited mystical powers as the silly story unfolds. If you can get into the spirit, you might have fun watching this turkey. Elizabeth of Toro co-stars. (VC)

**SHERLOCK HOLMES AND THE SPIDER WOMAN (1944).** Fictional spiders from the upper reaches of an African river are employed on an eight-hour, eight-legged basis to crawl through gratings and bite victims for that wonderful "spider woman," Gale Sondergaard. This murderess-seductress almost outwits the Baker Street sleuth and his bumbling but loveable companion, Dr. Watson. One of the best films in the Universal series to star Basil Rathbone and Nigel Bruce with wonderful interplay between Rathbone and Sondergaard and

**BASIL RATHBONE
VS. THE SPIDER WOMAN**

good scenes involving Angelo Rossitto as a midget who helps the spiders along the conduits and other walkways. Sondergaard would return in this same role in an inferior psuedosequel without Holmes, THE SPIDER WOMAN STRIKES BACK. Produced-directed by Roy William Neill.

**SHERLOCK HOLMES IN THE BASKERVILLE CURSE (1985).** Undistinguished British cartoon feature, of the cheap Saturday morning variety, its only interesting element being the voice of Peter O'Toole as Holmes. It's Sir Arthur Conan Doyle's HOUND OF THE BASKERVILLES in simplified form—and a complete waste of your time.

**SHINBONE ALLEY (1971).** Delightful cartoon version of Don Marquis' "archy and mehitabel" stories, in which a poet who writes in a free-verse style is reincarnated as a cockroach and must jump from typewriter key to typewriter key to write his material (hence no capital letters). Quaint and entertaining. Voices by Carol Channing, Eddie Bracken, John Carradine, Alan Reed.

**SHINING, THE (1980).** Stanley Kubrick's uneven adaptation

of Stephen King's best-seller about The Overview, a haunted hotel in the Rockies, and a young boy with the powers of telepathy and prophecy. Kubrick's camera is fluid and there are brilliant sequences: Jack Torrance (Jack Nicholson) and his family being haunted by a moldy corpse; wife Shelley Duvall discovering a weird manuscript by her husband; a chase through a hedgerow maze; Torrance meeting a ghostly bartender (Joseph Turkel); and the final deterioration of Torrance as he chases his wife with an axe. But Kubrick and co-writer Diane Johnson have erringly and too frequently deviated from King's masterful plot and neglected important exposition; scenes are enigmatic and frustrating when they should be thrilling and enlightening. There is evidence Kubrick does not fully know the horror genre, or he might have avoided the unsatisfying "twist" ending. Another flaw is Nicholson's descent into madness—he goes bonkers too quickly. Scatman Crothers plays the Negro who, like Torrance's son, has "the shining," but it's another misinterpreted role. (VC)

**SHIP OF ZOMBIES.** See **HORROR OF THE ZOMBIES.**

**SHIRLEY THOMPSON VS. THE ALIENS (1972).** Australian science-fiction about invading aliens has about as much bounce as a kangaroo with two broken legs. A statue of the Duke of Edinburgh comes to life but not the film. Should be put outback and down under and kept there. And good day to you too, Shirley Thompson.

**SHOCK (1946).** Nifty suspense thriller is frugal on budget but frenetic on technique when psychiatrist Vincent Price murders his wife in a fit of range, unaware a young woman has seen the ghastly crime and, as a result, is in a state of immobile shock. When he finds out she knows too much, he and his nurse set out to keep her quiet by using drugs and hypnosis. Lynn Bari, Reed Hadley, Anabel Shaw, Frank Latimore, Charles Trowbridge, Renee Charles. (VC)

**SHOCK CHAMBER (1985).** Amateurish Canadian TV-movie, a trilogy of tales with ironic twist endings. A mother tells a magazine writer about her three sons: In "Symbol of Victory," a teener tries out a love potion on his father's secretary; in "Country Hospitality" a waitress working in a rural greasy spoon poisons a kidnapper, then plans to doublecross her accomplices; in "The Injection" two brothers plan an insurance policy ripoff by feigning death. The latter has the best twist, but the whole thing is cheaply shot on videotape and the "surprises" have all been done before. Doug Stone appears in all three episodes. Karen Cannata, Bill Boyle, Bill Zagot, Victor P. Farkas.

**SHOCK TREATMENT (1973).** Also known as DOCTOR IN THE NUDE, this French-Italian film focuses on physicians at a rejuvenation center who discover a formula to prevent the aging of the body, but several youths are murdered for their blood and organs before the diabolical plot is squelched. Written-directed by Alain Jessua. Alain Delon, Annie Girardot, Michel Duchaussoy, Robert Hirsch.

**SHOCK WAVES (1975).** Minor low budget horror favorite with SS officer Peter Cushing creating an underwater corps of Aryan zombies, who rise from the depths as blond figures wearing goggles. Brooke Adams ends up on Cushing's Nazihappy island after surviving the sinking of a yacht captained by John Carradine. Directed by Ken Weiderhorn. (VC)

**SHOES OF THE FISHERMAN (1968).** Didactic politicalreligious fantasy set in the near future when a Russian archbishop, after ten years in a Siberian labor camp, is appointed Pope. A famine crisis arises in Red China, and when it appears the Chinese are about to use the atomic bomb, the Pope makes an announcement that shocks the Catholic Church. Turgidity and oversimplification of complex issues make this pretty hard to swallow—if you're still awake. Directed by Michael Anderson. Anthony Quinn, Oskar Werner, Vittorio De Sica, John Gielgud, Rosemary Dexter, Burt Kwouk, Clive Revill, Laurence Olivier, David Janssen.

**SHOGUN ASSASSIN (1980).** Americanized version of Japan's "Baby Cart" samurai series, depicting Lone Wolf, a freelance killer who travels to and from his bloody assignments with his five-year-old son Kuroso riding in a wooden cart equipped with knives. Two films in the series have been re-edited by U.S. producers David Weisman and Robert Houston, and a completely new soundtrack added. The result is a bizarre, mystical action film, with gallons of spurting gore as Lone Wolf's magical sword kills ninja (trained assassins) by the hundreds. There are moments in the film when Lone Wolf seems to be possessed by prophetic visions and a sense of superhearing. Anyway, it's weird (what with that little kid narrating the story) and definitely worth a look. (VC)

**SHOGUN WARRIORS: GRANDIZER (1982).** Japanese animated cartoon in the STAR WARS vein, shown in America only on cable TV. Other films in this series include SHOGUN WARRIORS: GAIKING; SHOGUN WARRIORS: SPACEKETEERS; SHOGUN WARRIORS: STARVENGERS.

**SHORT CIRCUIT (1986).** Sparkling comedy that remains cute without resorting to teenage dumbness. The real heroes of this spoof on hardware movies are the men who made Robot #5 operable: designer Syd Mead and activator Eric Al-

Laughing Crow. (Un)directed by Michael Find..y. Alan Brock, Jennifer Stock, Tawn Ellis, Michael Harris. (VC)

**SHUTTERED ROOM, THE (1968).** Unfaithful version of a novelette by H. P. Lovecraft and August Derleth. That was a good horror story—this is just a horror. After so many horrendous murders, performed by something locked up in a weird house, it is utterly impossible to swallow the explanation offered about what is hiding in the shuttered room. This "monster" would have a difficult time kicking sand into the face of a 90-pound weakling, let alone throttling half the cast. A waste of Gig Young, Carol Lynley, Oliver Reed, Flora Robson and Bernard Kay. Directed by David Greene.

**SIGN OF THE FOUR (1982).** British TV version of the Sherlock Holmes novel by Conan Doyle has Ian Richardson as a breathless Holmes and David Healy as a keen-eyed Watson. Where the Charles Edward Pogue teleplay falters is in showing the mystery rather than telling it from Holmes' viewpoint.

**NO IFS AND ANDS ABOUT IT: CHUCK NORRIS STOMPS BUTTS IN 'SILENT RAGE'**

lard. #5, the cutest damn robot in any movie, is part of a line of laser-equipped metal warriors called Saints, created by scientist Steve Guttenberg, who works for Nova Laboratories. During a lightning storm mishap, #5 takes on human characteristics and is befriended by Ally Sheedy. Afraid of being dismantled, #5 flees in a series of madcap, hilarious misadventures during which he is inspired by John Wayne, the Three Stooges and John Travolta, among others. Wonderfully directed by John Badham; one not to miss. (VC)

**SHOT IN THE DARK, A (1935).** Old-fashioned murder mystery thriller in the "old dark house" tradition. A shrouded figure flits through the mansion, using an unusual weapon to carry out his murders. Directed by Charles Lamont. Charles Starret, Robert Warwick, Edward Van Sloan.

**SHOUT, THE (1978).** Thinking man's horror film, based on a short story by Robert Graves. Directed by Jerzy Skolimowski, who explores in fascinating style the concept that a man can kill by the tone of his voice. Thoughtful and literate. Alan Bates, Susannah York, John Hurt, Tim Curry, Robert Stephens, Julian Hough. (VC)

**SHRIEK OF THE MUTILATED (1974).** Real shrieks came from mentally mutilated theater patrons who wanted their money back after being exposed to this hysterically bad cheapie in which a demented college professor leads a field trip of dumb students to Boot Island to snag a man-killing white Yeti—who looks like a starving actor in a furry white suit. Also involved is a cannibal-devil cult and some of the worst acting since the 1920s. And dig that crazy Indian called

Hence, little suspense and few surprises. Holmes and Watson are tracking the Great Mogul, the world's second largest diamond. Similar to the play, CRUCIFER OF BLOOD, without comedy. Directed stylishly by Desmond Davis.

**SILENCERS, THE (1966).** First in the Matt Helm series starring Dean Martin as Donald Hamilton's superspy, intended as a high-class Bond imitation, but bargain basement with its cheap gadgets and madman-plans-to-conquer-the-world plot. Villain Victor Buono behaves like an angry grandfather; Martin behaves as though he lost interest in acting right after THE YOUNG LIONS. Does director Phil Karlson know the meaning of comedy . . . of satire? Clumsy and leering; but the women are great: Stella Stevens, Daliah Lavi, Nancy Kovack, Cyd Charisse and Beverly Adams.

**SILENT MADNESS (1984).** Originally shot in 3-D, this low budget shocker is set in Cresthaven Mental Hospital where Belinda Montgomery and Viveca Lindfors face a series of murders. Directed by Simon Nuchtern.

**SILENT NIGHT, BLOODY NIGHT (1973).** Gory thriller as chopped up as victims of an axe murderer taking revenge on mental cases responsible for an insane asylum revolt that resulted in the death of doctors and personnel. The story gets further chopped up by censors during flashbacks. First released as NIGHT OF THE DARK FULL MOON, this was directed by Theodore Gershuny and produced and co-written by Jeffrey Konvitz. Patrick O'Neal, John Carradine, James Patterson and Walter Abel all look cut to the quick. (VC)

**SILENT NIGHT, DEADLY NIGHT (1984).** Controversial (when released) bloodthirsty slasher flick about a killer in a Santa Claus suit, slaughtering innocent people. Its controversy also flowed from its less-than-lovely portrait of a Catholic school for orphans, operated by a starkly stern Mother Superior who delights in sadistic spankings. All that aside, it's a slasher-genre entry undeserving of the attention. A shallow psychological history of the murderer is presented when, as a youngster, he must watch as his mother and father are murdered on Christmas Eve by a Santa Claus lookalike. He grows into a tall, muscular teen-ager (Robert Brian Wilson) who thinks Santa punishes those who aren't good during the year. When he's forced to don a St. Nicholas outfit by his boss, he's primed for a rampage of yuletide destruction, including a beheading, an impaling and assorted axe penetrations. Directed by Charles E. Sellier. Lilyan Chauvan, Toni Nero, Danny Wagner, Britt Leach. (VC)

**SILENT NIGHT, EVIL NIGHT.** Originally **BLACK CHRISTMAS,** now it's **STRANGER IN THE HOUSE** on TV.

**SILENT RAGE (1982).** Chuck Norris' kung fu/karate expertise is worked in with a Frankenstein plot tinged with horror touches. Hence: "Chuck Norris Meets the Bionic Man on Halloween." Feeble in all departments, with the karate action never blending with the horror elements, despite screenwriter Joseph Fraley's double talk about a superserum (Monogen 35) and other gibberish. Just an excuse for director Michael Miller to stage action (including a barroom brawl) showing off Norris' physical dexterity. Ron Silver, Toni Kalem, Steven Keats, William Finley, Stephen Furst, Brian Libby. (VC)

**SILENT RUNNING (1972).** "A" for effort to writer-director Douglas Trumbull, who first found favor through his effects in 2001: A SPACE ODYSSEY. Trumbull repeats his spectacular outer space images: awesome spaceships floating between planets, exploding suns, a solar storm . . . A floating space station (the last garden of a defoliaged-Earth) is manned by Bruce Dern and three "drone" robots, Huey, Dewey and Louie. Dern goes psychotic when ordered to destroy his forest, and he mutinies. The effects are wonderful and Dern's demented attitude is justified by the Deric Washburn-Michael Cimino-Steve Bochco script. Adult science-fiction worthy of repeated viewings. (VC)

**SILENT SCREAM (1980).** Writer-director Denny Harris pays homage to Hitchcock's PSYCHO with this tale of a demented household where innocent roomers are murdered or terrorized by a knife-happy kook daughter (played without restraint by Barbara Steele). Gore murders provide a handful of shocks, but the plotting (or is it plodding?) of the Ken and Jim Wheat script is predictable, and the characterizations without depth. A moment of silence, please, while we scream for Denny Harris. Yvonne De Carlo, Cameron Mitchell, Avery Schreiber, Rebecca Balding, Juli Andelman. (VC)

**SILENT SENTENCE (1973).** Heavily edited TV version of the feature A KNIFE FOR THE LADIES. Not quite a Western, not quite a horror flick . . . call it an oater-bloater. A Jack the Ripper-style killer is stalking saloon girls while sheriff Jack Elam and investigator Jeff Cooper stalk the murderer. Made in Old Tucson, this has the look of a Universal TV-movie, with Gene Evans, Joe Santos, John Kellog and Ruth Roman in interesting character roles. Only mildly diverting. A minor stab at best. Directed by Larry G. Spangler.

**SILVER BULLET (1985).** Well-produced adaptation of Stephen King's novelette, "Cycle of the Werewolf," which proves to be a slight story, of minimal conse-

quence. King adapted his own book, emphasizing life in a small North Carolina town, Tarker's Mills, and how it is plagued by brutal werewolf killings. The focus is on crippled Corey Haim (his motorized wheelchair is dubbed Silver Bullet) and his relationship with sister Megan Follows and alcoholic uncle Gary Busey. How they learn the werewolf's identity and set a trap builds to an unexceptional climax, with no surprises. Carlo Rambaldi's werewolf is an effective one; the moonstalker just needs a stronger story. Daniel Attias directs well, especially a sequence in the swamp when the wolfman stalks his stalkers through nocturnal mist. Everett McGill, Corey Haim, Terry O'Quinn. (VC)

**SILVER NEEDLE IN THE SKY (1954).** See **ROCKY JONES, SPACE RANGER.** (He sticks it to you!)

**SIMON (1980).** Under Marshall Brickman's direction this dabbles satirically where ALTERED STATES seriously wallowed, and emerges too intellectualized to be entertaining. Alan Arkin is a genius immersed in a think tank. When he emerges he performs the film's only funny bit: Without makeup or props, he pantomimes man's evolution, from amoeba to monkey to present day. Now, that's funny. The rest of Brickman's gags (he wrote the script too) and concepts aren't. Unrealized premise wastes Austin Pendleton, Judy Graubart, William Finley and Fred Gwynne. (VC)

**SIMON, KING OF THE WITCHES (1971).** Andrew Prine's portrayal of a world-weary magician/warlock is the only unusual aspect of this low budgeter which remains strangely lowkey when Prine befriends a young boy and helps a district attorney find out who's been supplying drugs to his daughter (Brenda Scott). There's just no pacing or excitement. A ride down the Hollywood Freeway around 4:30 p.m. any weekday is scarier. Directed by Bruce Kessler. (VC)

**SINBAD AND THE EYE OF THE TIGER (1977).** Packed with the visual stop-motion thrills only animator Ray Harryhausen can bring to romantic fantasies. This adventure in the land of Arabian Nights lore is abroil with mythical monsters, exciting duels between man and beast, wizardry and witchcraft. Patrick Wayne is a mediocre Sinbad, as wooden as the dialogue, so it's a showcase for Harryhausen's memorable creations: a chess-playing baboon, three axe-swinging jinns; a Troglodyte; a giant tiger; a king-size walrus and a metal giant called Minaton. What, no Caroline Munro? Directed by Sam Wanamaker, scripted by Beverly Cross. Taryn Power, Jane Seymour, Margaret Whiting, Patrick Troughton. Harryhausen also co-produced with his partner of many years, Charles Schneer. (VC)

**SINISTER INVASION (1968).** Videocassette title for **INCREDIBLE INVASION, THE.** (A Karloff special!)

**GARY BUSEY FIRES THE BIG ONE IN 'SILVER BULLET'**

**SINISTER MONK, THE (1965).** West German thriller in the Gothic style of Edgar Wallace, depicting a hooded figure armed with a whip who lashes his victims to death. Blackmail, murder, mayhem—all the things that make life worth living. Harold Leiphitz, Karin Dor. Directed by Harald Reinl.

**SINS OF DORIAN GRAY, THE (1983).** TV-movie switches the sexes in Oscar Wilde's morality tale of debauchery and soul disintegration by having "Dorian" a sexpot (Belinda Bauer) who gives up her decency by transferring her soul to a piece of film, her screen test. "Dorian" wants to be a successful Hollywood actress and starts sleeping with producers and acting like a superbitch. Unusually trashy material for the tube—audiences will love its luridness. Directed by Tony Maylam. Anthony Perkins, Joseph Bottoms, Olga Karlatos, Michael Ironside, Olga Karlatos.

**SINS OF THE PAST (1984).** TV-movie starring Barbara Carrera as the madame of a group of high-class prostitutes who break up when one of them is murdered. Then, individually, the beauties (including Kim Cattrall, Debby Boone, Tracy

## MARIA MONTEZ: 'SIREN OF ATLANTIS'

Reed and Kristie Alley) are tracked by a slasher-killer. Standard TV fare (with a few erotic touches) written by Steve Brown and directed by Peter H. Hunt.

**SINTHIA THE DEVIL'S DOLL (1970).** Child commits murder. Is she possessed? Wouldn't seem likely, since THE EXORCIST hasn't even been produced yet. Ah, to the Devil with it! . . . The hell you say! Directed by Ray Dennis Steckler. Shula Roan, Diane Webber, Maria Lease.

**SIREN OF ATLANTIS (1948).** "Lost Continent" fantasy should remain lost, being inept trash with one-time Universal star, Maria Montez, who never learned to act. Explorers Jean-Pierre Aumont and Dennis O'Keefe stumble across a missing city ruled by Montez, who had seen better civilizations in films with Sabu and Jon Hall. Burning braziers and bulging brassieres as she lolls on divans in skimpy costumes and watches dances performed for her amusement. Slave, peel that grape! Montez's last picture . . . she committed suicide soon after. Three men were needed to direct: Arthur Ripley, Douglas Sirk, John Brahm. Henry Daniell co-stars.

**SIREN OF BAGDAD (1953).** Hans Conried's comedic talents keep this Arabian Nights parody wriggling like a camel undergoing a flea attack. Although the setting is ancient Egypt, Robert E. Kent's script is loaded with non sequiturs and contemporary gags. Paul Henreid is a daffy magician who uses

his magic box to save slave girls. Very campy albeit dumb, with Patricia Medina and assorted harem girls (Laurette Luez, Anne Dore) providing a fetching decor to this Sam Katzman nonsense. Directed so fine by Richard Quine.

**SISTERS (1973).** Brian De Palma's homage to Hitchcock is a film of black comedy and biting satire, but confused by erratic editing, strange juxtaposing of scenes and lack of logic. Because De Palma's intentions are fuzzy, SISTERS is a intriguing mess. The director/co-writer darkly examines one of two Siamese sisters (both played by Margot Kidder) who keeps splitting her personality—not to mention a few heads. Jennifer Salt, an irascible reporter, sets out to prove the sister committed murder. True, the suspense is considerable and there is excellent use of split screen but it's ultimately a bumble of a jumble. Bernard Herrmann wrote the music. Charles Durning, Barnard Hughes, Bill Finley. (VC)

**SISTERS OF CORRUPTION (1973).** Spanish slash trash about a killer so fickle who strikes with a sickel, swathing then bathing his victims in blood. Directed by Juan A. Bardem. Jean Seberg, Perla Cristal, Gerard Tichy.

**SISTERS OF DEATH (1978).** Members of an old sorority are lured to a class reunion, only to be trapped in a castle with a fiendish killer. Among the sexy ladies is Claudia Cardinale.

**SIX HOURS TO LIVE (1932).** Warner Baxter, a diplomat murdered during a trade conference, is restored to life by the "magic ray" of a doctor, but resurrection can last only six hours, all the time he has to catch his murderer. Directed by William Dieterle. Irene Ware, John Boles.

**SIX MILLION DOLLAR MAN, THE (1973).** While the Lee Majors TV series quickly denigrated into a stupid kiddie-oriented SUPERMAN, this pilot film is an exciting thriller that does justice to Martin Caudin's novel, CYBORG. Majors is a test pilot horribly mutilated in a plane crash; the U.S. Government spends $6 million to restore him with greater speed, strength, X-ray vision and other superhuman talents. Richard Irving directed. Barbara Anderson, Martin Balsam, Darren McGavin, Robert Cornthwaite, Olan Soule. On videocassette as **CYBORG, THE SIX MILLION DOLLAR MAN.**

**SKELETON ON HORSEBACK (1940).** Czech allegory directed by Hugo Haas—who later worked in Hollywood making cheap sex melodramas about overweight men obsessed with voluptuous, brassy blondes. In this version of a play by Karel Capek, THE WHITE SICKNESS, a disease threatens to wipe out mankind unless a doctor can discover a cure. Haas also heads the cast with Bedrich Karen.

**SKETCHES OF A KILLER (1978).** Psychotic artist Allen Goorwitz murders his female subjects, cackling with glee. Meredith MacRae, Frank Whiteman.

**SKULL, THE (1965).** Based on Robert Bloch's "The Skull of the Marquis De Sade," this has an unusual viewpoint: through the eyes of a skull as it bites its victims to death. Director Freddie Francis and screenwriter Milton Subotsky have created an effective supernatural thriller showcasing a skull possessed by the spirit of the sadistic Frenchman. But that doesn't curtail Peter Cushing—a collector of demonology, witchcraft and black magic artifacts—from buying the skull from collector Patrick Wymark. Nice cranium capacity. Same story was retold as part of TORTURE GARDEN. Nigel Green, Christopher Lee, Michael Gough, George Coulouris, Patrick Magee, Nigel Green, Jill Bennett, Ann Palk.

**SKULLDUGGERY (1970).** Thoughtful adventure-message film (directed by Gordon Douglas) about man's relationship to his prehistoric past, and the crass exploitation of his own soul. Nelson Gidding's story is finally a plea for better understanding among races. Burt Reynolds and Susan Clark lead an expedition into Rhodesia to find benevolent half-man, half-ape creatures. The tiny beings are considered for slave labor, and a courtroom trial places creatures and mankind on examination. Roger C. Carmel, Chips Rafferty, Wilfrid Hyde-White, Pat Suzuki, Alexander Knox, Rhys Williams.

**SKULLDUGGERY (1983).** Stylish, unusually imaginative glimpse at role-playing games and how they cross from fantasy into reality, and back. This fascinating tale, marred only by a complicated plot, begins in Canterbury in 1382 when The Warlock claims the soul of an unborn child and curses a royal family. Flash ahead to Trottelville USA in 1982 as a group meets to play life-and-death games, unaware Diabolus has dealt himself into the game. A phantom archer is involved in the deadly play and the murders are cleverly fashioned by director by Ota Richter. Thom Haverstock, Wendy Crewson, Clark Johnson, Kate Lynch. (VC)

**SKY ABOVE HEAVEN (1964).** Dull French film about an aircraft carrier pursued by a flying saucer which is a radioactive probe from space. Warring powers of Earth must put aside differences to face a common enemy. Director/co-writer Yves Ciampi tries to make social commentary on war and peace, but it ends up resembling a recruiting film. C'est magnifique, la guerre. Andre Smagghe, Yvonne Monlaur.

**SKY BANDITS (1940).** A singing Renfrew of the Royal Mounted? Certainly. He trains his vocal chords on a scientist's Death Ray and shatters it with eight octaves. Then he turns in his redcoat and signs with the New York Metropolitan Opera. All seriousness aside, this low-budgeter stars James Newill as the melodic hero. Directed by Ralph Staub. Louise Stanley, Dwight Frye, James Newill.

**SKY BIKE, THE (1968).** British version of Disney's MONKEY'S UNCLE, in which adorable youths rig a bicycle to a flying machine and pedal into the heavens, and the hearts of their fans. Lighter than air. Directed by Charles Frend. Liam Redmond, William Lucas, Ellen McIntosh.

**SKY PARADE, THE (1936).** Popular comic strip/radio show, THE AIR ADVENTURES OF JIMMIE ALLEN, was the basis for this programmer depicting youths and their inventions. This time Jimmie Allen invents a robot aircraft complete with cabaret show. Directed by Otho Lovering. William Gargan, Kent Taylor, Grant Withers, Katherine DeMille.

**SKY PIRATES (1986).** In 1945, John Hargreaves flies into a time warp near Easter Island and crashlands in the ocean . . . flash-ahead to his court martial where we learn he and other explorers are involved with a stone of magical powers brought to Earth by aliens. Indiana Jones-style adventure, directed by Colin Eggleston. Meredith Phillips, Max Phipps.

**SLAPSTICK (OF ANOTHER KIND) (1982).** Disastrous version of a Kurt Vonnegut novel by writer-producer-director Steven Paul. A misfire from the first frame, failing visually to translate Vonnegut's far-out literary concepts. An alien race watching over the Galaxies (Orson Welles' voice), sends "twin advisors" to Earth to prevent the Chinese from learning the secret of gravity and upsetting the Universe's balance. The parents chosen for impregnation are Jerry Lewis and Madeleine Kahn, whose ugly offspring grow up to look just like them. Played straight it might have worked—but not with the mugging of Lewis, Kahn, Marty Feldman (the family retainer), John Abbott (the doctor) and Pat Morita (Chinese spy). Jim Backus, as the President, looks pained as he explains why Air Force I is powered by chickenshit. Film director Samuel Fuller, as a colonel running a military academy for foul-ups, is a treat when he struts out dressed as a frontier scout. Otherwise, SLAPSTICK is the unfunniest comedy ever to hit your kisser with tasteless merengue. (VC)

**SLASHER IS A SEX MANIAC, THE.** See **PENETRATION.**

**SLAUGHTER HIGH.** See **APRIL FOOL'S DAY.** (The one with sexy Caroline Munro.)

**SLAUGHTER HOTEL (1973).** An expose of a popular hotel chain, as some business critics have claimed? Or just another beastly Italian horror film? Viewers will have to ponder subtleties and allegorical overtones for the answer . . . if they can stand the bloodletting and beheadings. The setting is an asylum for the insane run by Klaus Kinski. Directed by Fernando Di Leo. Margaret Lee. (VC)

## KURT VONNEGUT JR.: STUCK WITH A BAD SLAP

**SLAUGHTER OF THE VAMPIRES (1962).** Italian abomination about a Viennese bloodsucker who gives newlyweds a wedding-night surprise. Edited in 1969 and resold to TV as CURSE OF THE BLOOD GHOULS. Directed by Roberto Mauri. Dieter Eppler, Walter Brandi. (VC)

**SLAUGHTERHOUSE FIVE (1972).** Contemporary PILGRIM'S PROGRESS, based on Kurt Vonnegut's best-selling novel and directed by George Roy Hill, depicting the fire bombing of Dresden in 1945. But that is only one episode in the life of Billy Pilgrim, who is "unstuck" in time and leaps from time period to time period—or is he "traveling" in his mind? He and Hollywood starlet Montana Wildhack (Valerie Perrine) are captured by invisible beings and placed in a zoo on the planet Tralfamador. Wry commentary on the absurdity of human existence is presented in disjointed fashion by screenwriter Stephen Geller, but cleverly edited to produce a philosophical shrug of the shoulders. Michael Sacks, Ron Leibman, Perry King, Holly Near, John Dehner, Eugene Roche, Sorrell Booke, Perry King. (VC)

**SLAUGHTERERS.** See **CANNIBALS IN THE STREETS.**

**SLAVE GIRL (1947).** Camel with a Brooklyn accent narrates this sword-and-sandal adventure with Yvonne De Carlo as a Venetian slave. Youngsters will thoroughly enjoy the pirates and pashas; adults will be diverted by the dancing girls and a light-heartedness captured by director Charles Lamont. Sandy and dandy but not randy. Albert Dekker, George Brent, Broderick Crawford, Andy Devine, Lois Collier.

**SLAVE GIRLS.** See **PREHISTORIC WOMEN.**

**SLAVES OF THE INVISIBLE MONSTER (1950).** Chopped-up version of the 12-chapter Republic serial THE INVISIBLE MONSTER, directed by the unforgettable Fred C. Brannon—unforgettable because he also directed FLYING DISC MAN FROM MARS. The Phantom Ruler is a crummy crook who masters invisibility and locks horns with Lane Carson (Richard Webb), an insurance investigator. Fistfights, car chases, more fistfights. Aline Towne, Lane Bradford.

---

*"He's downright nasty, he's mean and he's gruesome/He'll make your threesome into a twosome/On the prowl, here and how, here comes the Yeti now."—The piano singer in SHRIEK OF THE MUTILATED.*

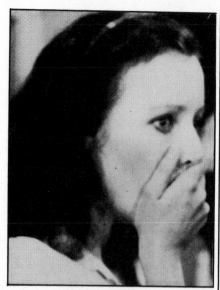

## 'SLEEPAWAY CAMP':
## WATCH AND SLEEP AWAY

**SLAYER, THE (1982).** On Georgia's Tybee Island, an actress who has been having really bad nightmares and some friends stay in an old house, soon to be stalked by a diabolical killer. Director J. S. Cardone brings an unusually talented intensity to this slash-bash and succeeds in creating an eerie electrical storm atmosphere. He also nicely builds up the gore murders, which include a man being decapitated by a trapdoor, a derelict being battered with a ship's oar and a woman being pitchforked through the breasts. The skimpy plot deals with the actress' childhood phobias, so at least there's someone to be interested in. Sarah Kendall, Frederick Flynn, Carol Kottenbrook, Alan McRae, Carl Kraines. On a double-bill cassette with **SCALPS.**

**SLEAZEMANIA: THE SPECIAL EDITION (1986).** Compilation of scenes from the worst exploitation movies ever (un)made, including ORGY OF THE DEAD, FLESH MERCHANTS, SMUT PEDDLER, and other crud wonders. (VC)

**SLEDGE HAMMER (1984).** Below par slasher thriller made on videotape about a hammer slammer who kills mom and lover at an early age and grows up to be an adult basher smasher when some teenagers come to the family home one weekend. Writer-director David A. Prior hammers home his point, nailing down the characters. Consider this critic a hammer damner. Ted Prior, Linda McGill, John Eastman. (VC)

**SLEEP OF DEATH (1979).** Beautiful Englishwomen pursues a nobleman, setting off a series of murders. Directed by Calvin Floyd. (VC)

**SLEEPAWAY CAMP (1983).** Weak-kneed slasher flick, without flair for gore. Oh, there are murders galore at Camp Arawak (sex pervert is scalded in vat of boiling water, boy drowns in overturned rowboat, youth is death-stung by angry bees, another kid is knived in the shower) but they're clumsily staged homicides. Mike Kellin runs the dilapidated camp, covering up the killings so his reputation won't suffer. So muddled, the surprise ending is meaningless. Written-directed by Robert Hiltzik with no understanding of what makes a horror film work. He should be sent to camp to sleep away his career. Felissa Rose, Karen Fields. (VC)

**SLEEPER (1973).** Life in America in 2173 as Woody Allen conceives it—he wrote, directed and starred as a man frozen alive in 1973 who awakens 200 years later in a Big Brother society. "I'm 2000 months behind in my rent," he cries. He and Diane Keaton search for the Dictator's Nose in order to

destroy the totalitarian society and help a revolutionary movement. Allen displays his talents in visual comedy (such as the giant vegetable scene), in mime as a jerking, jerky robot and in verbal gags that spare none of our institutions. One of Allen's best efforts. Marshall Brickman helped Allen write the script. John Beck, Mary Gregory. (VC)

**SLEEPING BEAUTY (1959).** Sentimental Disney cartoon, too cute in its depiction of good fairies and down-home folks and a bit grotesque in presenting Maleficient, her raven and the goblins. There is little story—just sweetness and honey. Voices by Mary Costa, Verna Felton, Barbara Luddy, Bill Shirley, Barbara Jo Allen, Taylor Holmes. (VC)

**SLEEPING BEAUTY (1966).** Full-length version of the Tchaikowsky ballet, danced by members of the Leningrad Kirov Ballet, with Alla Sizova in the role of Princess Aurora. Pure form and beauty in a rewarding series of uninterrupted dances. Directed by Appolinari Dupko and Konstantin Sergeyev. (VC)

**SLEEPING BEAUTY (1983).** FAIRIE TALE THEATER version of Tchaikovsky's ballet, directed by Jeremy Paul Kagan and starring Christopher Reeve, Bernadette Peters and Beverly D'Angelo. (VC)

**SLEEPING BEAUTY (1987).** An entry in the Cannon series of full-length features based on fairy tales, starring Morgan Fairchild in low-cut bodices which increase the tempo of the story. It's well acted in generous costuming and features David Holliday as the King, Tahnee Welch as Rosebud, Nicholas Clay as the Prince, Sylvia Miles as Red Fairy and Kenny Baker as an elf. Directed by David Irving. (VC)

**SLIGHTLY PREGNANT MAN, A (1973).** "You got knocked up?" a friend asks Marcello Mastroianni. He nods. Because of a hormone imbalance from chemicals in his food, Marcello is the world's first pregnant man. That should provide laughs and satire for French director Jacques Demy. Satire yes, laughs not so much. Even Demy has said the film was not ambitious enough. (Huh?) This exercise in unplanned parenthood co-stars Catherine Deneuve as the surprised—what else would you call her?—father. (VC)

**SLIME PEOPLE, THE (1963).** Robert Hutton runs through L.A. warning mankind that prehistoric monsters covered with viscous liquid matter, and climbing out of the sewers, are planning to erect a dome above the city to lower the temperature and create a climate suitable for fungi. Strictly for the crud-and-erosion crowd. Hutton directed. Susan Hart, Les Tremayne, Tom Laughlin, Robert Burton. (VC)

**SLIPPER AND THE ROSE, THE (1977).** Bryan Forbes' lavish musical-comedy version of CINDERELLA, moderately successful in lyrics, choreography and touching romance. Richard Chamberlain as Prince Charming and 24-year-old Gemma Craven as the brow-beaten scullery maid are the focus, yet it is often the character players (Annette Crosbie as the Fairy Godmother, Michael Hordern as the blustering King and Dame May Whitty as the crotchety Queen) who keep the story frothy. This free-wheeling interpretation deals with many facets of the famous storybook romance seldom plumbed before, giving the narrative freshness. Featuring Austrian castles, London's Southwark Cathedral and a dreamy Golden Coach. Christopher Gable, Kenneth More.

**SLITHIS (1978).** There's no way for us feeble humans to stop this hulking, anti-social monster—a mixture of radioactivity and organic mud from the Imperial Energy Plant off the L.A. coast. Now the slimy humanoid is stalking folks around Venice, Calif., and Marina Del Rey, tearing them limb from limb, chomping hungrily on their tasty flesh and slashing their faces to pulp. The monster (ex-Olympic swimmer Win Condict in a rubber suit) is a nice try by fledgling writer-producer-director Stephen Traxler, but the story, the overacting by Hy Pyke as the sheriff and the idiotic dialogue are Amateur City. On TV as **SPAWN OF THE SLITHIS.** (VC)

**SLUMBER PARTY MASSACRE (1982).** Call it SON OF DRILLER KILLER. A murderer escapes from an asylum and terrorizes L.A. teen-agers (well-stacked ones) with his portable battery-operated drill. The unusual aspect about an otherwise not-unusual slasher film: it was written by female activist Rita Mae Brown and produced-directed by a contemporary, Amy Jose. Yes, those who cried loudest about wanton exploitation of womanhood exploit it to the max! When it comes down to the wire, women as well as men are willing to exploit bare asses and titties and gobs of violence to make a fast buck. This features the ubiquitous drill churning through eyeballs, brains, shoulder blades and chest cavities, and slashing open an occasional throat or stomach. What is really sickeningly depressing is that once an innocent character has been forced to pick up a weapon for defense, he or she seems to enjoy using it as much as the frenzied, drooling killer. Michele Michaels, Robin Stille, Debra DeLiso. (VC)

**SMILING GHOST, THE (1941).** Weak comedy makes fun of haunted houses and features a Negro servant (Willie Best) seeking new ounces of bravery to face secret panels, hidden rooms and phony spooks. Wayne Morris is the "aw, gee" reporter hired by heiress Alexis Smith to find out why all her prospective husbands are dying like flies. Brenda Marshall has brunette hair to contrast Alexis' blonde coiffure. Directed by Lewis Seiler. Alan Hale, Lee Patrick, David Bruce.

**SMOKY MOUNTAIN CHRISTMAS, A (1986).** Tuneful TV-movie starring Dolly Parton as a country singing star (art imitates life?) who meets a witch (Anita Morris) and a backwoodsman (Lee Majors) in outback Tennessee. Ay-hoo. Bo Hopkins, Dan Hedaya. Directed by Henry Winkler.

**SMUGGLER'S COVE (1948).** Ersatz haunted-house mystery-comedy starring Leo Gorcey, Huntz Hall and the usual Bowery Boys, who fumble for a few laughs under William Beaudine's direction. Martin Kosleck, Gabriel Dell.

**SMURFS AND THE MAGIC FLUTE, THE (1984).** French-Belgian animated feature set in the Middle Ages in the land of the Smurfs, small bluish creatures. Into their kingdom comes an outlaw, Oilycreep, with the Magic Flute, an instrument which makes people dance wildly. Pursuing the bandit is Pee Wee from the king's castle. Enhanced by a Michel Legrand musical score. Produced-directed by Jose Dutillieu. Based on a popular series of books. (VC)

**SNAKE PEOPLE, THE (1971).** One of four Boris Karloff movies made in 1968, but unreleased for several years due to legal complications. Karloff is Karl Van Molder, a landowner whose daughter (Julissa) is kidnapped by a snake cult on Coaibai Island. Undistinguished fare. Co-directed and co-written by Jack Hill and Juan Ibanez.

**SNAKE PIT, THE.** See **BLOOD DEMON.** (Hiss!)

**SNAKE WOMAN, THE (1961).** What does a busty snake woman wear when she assumes human form? If you answered "co-bra," go to the center of the pit and hiss at director Sidney J. Furie. A poisonous venom is in the sinuous body of Susan Travis, injected there by her father years before, and she puts the bite on everyone in sight, turning into a cobra, until Scotland Yard inspector John McCarthy plays a snake charmer's flute to lure her into a trap. Actually, the inspector is a mongoose in disguise. The idea uncoiled from the snake-like imagination of Orville H. Hampton.

**SNOW CREATURE, THE (1954).** Abominable look at the Abominable Snowman of the Himalayas: The creature is dumb enough to nab the wife of a botanist, which leads to its capture and a journey that takes it to L.A., where it escapes its captors. Strictly a snow job by writer-director W. Lee Wilder, the brother of Billy Wilder. Some like it cold, apparently. Paul Langton, Rudolph Anders.

**SNOW DEVILS (1965).** You thought maybe it was the Abominable Snowman again? Aha, you're wrong. These are abominable spacemen from the planet Aytia, making a feeble attempt to take over our planet. Mediocre Italian science-fiction directed by Anthony Dawson. Giacomo Rossi-Stuart, Ombretta Colli, Renato Baldini, Archie Savage.

**SNOW QUEEN, THE (1959).** Hans Christian Andersen fairy tale animated by the Russians and intended for moppets, although adults might be touched by its sense of purity. Universal-International supplied a new soundtrack (featuring voices of Sandra Dee, Tommy Kirk and Patty McCormack) and tacked on an unnecessary prologue with Art Linkletter. Icy sliver in the eye of a young boy transforms him into an impish youth swept away to the chilly land of the Snow Queen. Nothing sophisticated or satiric, but visually attractive.

**SNOW QUEEN (1984).** Showtime's FAIRIE TALE THEATRE version of Hans Christian Andersen's story about a boy cursed by a goblin. Lance Derwin, Melissa Gilbert, Lee Remick (as the Queen). Directed by Peter Medak. (VC)

**SNOW WHITE (1987).** Yet another Cannon film based on a classic fairy tale. Diana Rigg shines through as the Mean Queen in this lively costume morality play, best remembered for the way Walt Disney handled the fable. Written-directed by Michael Berz and co-starring Billy Barty, Sarah Patterson, Nicola Stapleton and Mike Edmunds.

**SNOW WHITE AND THE SEVEN DWARFS (1938).** Unfettered version of the Brothers Grimm fairy tale, the first feature cartoon from Disney. A triumphant classic, its animation as fresh as the day it established new trends in cartooning. By now it's a familiar story—the stepdaughter of the wicked witch is marked for death but escapes to be befriended by seven little fellows mining jewels. Along comes the Poisoned Apple, Prince Charming, etc. An enchanting viewing experience child and adults never forget. (VC)

**SNOW WHITE AND THE THREE STOOGES (1961).** Brace yourself for the eye-gouging, scrambled-brains antics of Moe Howard, Joe De Rita and Larry Fine as the Three Stooges return in one of their best features. What makes this work is the beautiful color production and skating numbers featuring Carol Heiss as the lovely princess. Walter Lang directed the Noel Langley-Elwood Ullman script. Guy Rolfe, Buddy Baer, Patricia Medina, Edgar Barrier, Peter Coe. (VC)

**SNOWBEAST (1977).** Derivative TV-movie, inspired by JAWS, is set at a ski lodge where a Bigfoot creature is on the

**WALT DISNEY'S 'SNOW WHITE'**

prowl, inconsiderately killing vacationing customers. Owner Sylvia Sidney tries to keep it hushed up, but eventually panic prevails. There are excellent skiing sequences, but Joseph Stefano's script deals with too many cliches and never affords much of a look at the monster, going for the point of view technique. One hairy face at a ski lodge window is about all you see. Not exactly an avalanche of chills; snowbound. Directed by Herb Wallerstein. Bo Svenson, Yvette Mimieux, Clint Walker, Robert Logan.

**SO DARK THE NIGHT (1946).** Unusual lower birth feature dealing with schizophrenia from a completely oblique point of view. Steven Geray is a French detective on a holiday who is caught up in a series of murders. Brace for some surprising twists. Directed by Joseph H. Lewis. Micheline Cheirel, Eugene Borden, Gregory Gay, Egon Breecher.

**SO SAD ABOUT GLORIA (1973).** So sad about SO SAD ABOUT GLORIA, a sad statement of a sadistic shadowplay showing axe murders and the same sanguinary sad plot about driving a sad skirt into a state of sad insanity. Sad for director-producer Harry Thomason and sad for Dean Jagger, Lori Saunders, Lou Hoffman, Bob Ginnaven, and sad for you, the viewer. For sad-ists only.

**SOLARBABIES (1986).** In the post-Armageddon year 41, the world has been nuked into a desert where children are indoctrinated by a dictatorship called The Protectorate, who al-

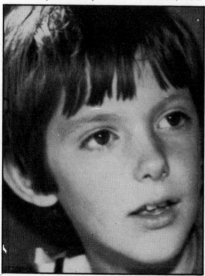

**LUKE HAAS IN 'SOLARBABIES'**

lows the young ones to act out their aggression with skateball teams. In Orphanage 43, ruled by the benevolent Charles Durning and reminiscent at times of the sports in ROLLERBALL, a group of youths finds Bohdi, a glowing white ball that is an alien life force. Possession of Bohdi becomes the pastime as it changes ownership several times. We have Nazilike policeman Richard Jordan, a gang called the Scorpions, killers known as "eco-warriors," and various tribes. Action on roller skates, with futuristic equipment (such as a robot named Terminec) involved. MAD MAX cliches makes you wish SOLARBABIES had more solar energy. Effects by Richard Edlund. Directed by Alan Johnson. Jami Gertz, Jason Patric, Lukas Haas, Claude Brooks. (VC)

**SOLARIS (1972).** Beautifully photographed Russian science-fiction film, but ponderous and philosophically obscure. On the planet Solaris, Earth has established an observation station. The planet's ocean is capable of sending "visitors" to the space station—who take on substance from the deepest guilt and memories of humans. Written-directed by Andrei Tarkovsky. Dontas Banionis, Natalia Bondarchuk.

**SOLE SURVIVOR, THE (1970).** When the wreckage of a World War II bomber is found in the Libyan desert, an investigating team discovers the only survivor of the crash might have lied about what happened in 1943. What the team cannot see are the ghosts of the crew, spirit-bound to the crash site until the truth is known. Guerdon Trueblood's script is literate (if occasionally verbose) and the production values of this Steve Shagan TV-movie are above average. Special praise to Vince Edwards, William Shatner and Richard Basehart, as well as director Paul Stanley.

**SOLE SURVIVOR (1982).** Offbeat supernatural horror thriller, thinking fan's fare that ultimately is too mystifying to bring satisfaction. Aging actress Anita Skinner has a premonition that her TV producer (Caren Larkey) will survive a catastrophic plane crash—and she does. Why is never made clear by writer-director Thom Eberhardt, but it it intimated that she was "overlooked" and weird forces of the undead will be coming to claim her. Yep, walking corpses turn up, but Eberhardt, in not providing adequate exposition, creates a murky tale, too slow-paced as he goes for ambience over visual shocks. Watch for death symbolism. (VC)

**SOMBRA THE SPIDER WOMAN (1947).** Whittled-down version of the Republic underworld action serial THE BLACK WIDOW, featuring 100 action-jamed minutes. Wow, gang, what excitement as the daughter of an asinine Asian tries to steal a new atomic rocket engine but is thwarted by criminologist Steve Colt at every cliffhanger. This despite the fact she's equipped with a shapely body, too. She's also got matter transmitters and other take-over-the-world gadgetry. Directed posthaste by Spencer Bennet and Fred C. Brannon. Virginia Lindley, Carol Forman, Bruce Edwards.

**SOME CALL IT LOVING (1973).** John Collier's fable, "Sleeping Beauty," about a girl asleep for eight years who is purchased from a carnival by a lonely man, was expanded by writer-producer-director James B. Harris, with Zalman King as the jazz player and Tisa Farrow as the sleeper. Richard Pryor plays a character on drugs. The full-length form, unfortunately, is more than the short story can bear. Some call it forgettable. Carol White, Logan Ramsey. (VC)

**SOME GIRLS DO (1967).** Splendid James Bond imitation starring Richard Johnson as Hugh "Bulldog" Drummond, a hard-working British detective graduated to superspy in this sequel (of sorts) to DEADLIER THAN THE MALE. The old Bulldog is after supervillain James Villiers, who has created an army of robotized sexy women to sabotage the SST-1, an experimental aircraft, and hold up Britain for eight million pounds. A voyeur's romp blending undercovered undercover females with such gadgets as a make-up kit that projects a soul-shattering "infrasonic" killer beam and powerboats operating on infrasupersonic speed devices. Director Ralph Thomas plays all the absurdities for the satire intended. The cast is either very British (Maurice Denham, Robert Morley) or very sensuous (Daliah Lavi, Beba Loncar, Sydney Rome, Virginia North). Never a dull moment, what?

**SOMEONE AT THE TOP OF THE STAIRS (1973).** Super-cheap TV-movie produced in Britain. Talk talk talk and few thrills as Donna Mills, Judy Carne, David Bekeyser, Brian McGrath and Francis Willis work with a creaky Brian Clemens plot about a man in the attic of an old mansion who absorbs the life force of ghosts and projects them as apparitions. There, that explains it. Directed by John Sichel.

**SOMEONE BEHIND THE DOOR (1971).** French psychothriller has a good cast (Anthony Perkins, Jill Ireland, Charles Bronson, Henri Garcin) but a mediocre plot about a brain surgeon trying to force an amnesia victim to commit murder. Directed by Nicolas Gessner. (VC)

**SOMEONE IS WATCHING ME (1978).** Hitchcockian TV thriller written and directed by John Carpenter in which Lauren Hutton is spied upon by a psycho Peeping Tom, and turns to fellow apartment highrise dweller Adrienne Barbeau for help. Taut, suspenseful tale co-starring David Birney.

**SOMETHING EVIL (1972).** Substantial TV-movie, an early work of director Steven Spielberg, who displays imaginative use of the camera to trick up some supernatural hokum taking place on a farm in Bucks County, Pa. The family af-

CREATURE FEATURES MOVIE GUIDE

## CHRISTOPHER REEVE: 'SOMEWHERE IN TIME'

fected consists of Sandy Dennis, Darren McGavin and Johnny Whittaker. The neighbors or townspeople include Jeff Corey, Ralph Bellamy and Bruno Ve Sota.

**SOMETHING IS CRAWLING IN THE DARK (1970).** Stranded travelers seek refuge in a haunted house, discovering evil all too quickly. Directed by Mario Colucci. Farley Granger, Stan Cooper. (VC)

**SOMETHING WEIRD (1968).** Not as awful as most Herschell Gordon Lewis exploitationers, but improvements can be measured on the head of a darning needle. An accident victim enters into a pact with a hideous witch and emerges with ESP powers, helping the police solve crimes. SOMETHING WEIRD is something wasted. Tony McCabe. (VC)

**SOMETHING WICKED THIS WAY COMES (1983).** Ray Bradbury's 1962 best-seller reached the screen a Disney production, with Bradbury writing his own screenplay and picking his own director, Jack Clayton, and star, Jason Robards. The result, alas, is not a classic (even Bradbury, apparently, has a hard time adpating Bradbury) but still recaptures the melancholy "dandelion wine" mood of Bradbury's youth in Illinois in 1932 and his poetic imagery. Two boys (one representing the daring side of Bradbury's schizophrenic soul, the other the conservative intellectual) encounter a sinister carnival operated by Mr. Dark, a delicious personification of evil. Dark and his midway freaks steal the youth of victims to replenish themselves (a theme originally explored in Bradbury's story, "The Dark Ferris") and it's up to the boys (aided by Robards as a librarian father) to resist the temptations of the insidious Dark, who is well etched by stage actor Jonathan Pryce. While the effects are often dazzling and offbeat, the relationship between the intellectual youth and the father doesn't build the fire it needs to consume the viewer. Still, this comes close to capturing the poetry and artistry of Bradbury's prose, and that is a remarkable achievement. Great character bits by Royal Dano as the Electric Man and Pam Grier as a witch. (VC)

**SOMEWHERE IN TIME (1980).** Sensitive adaptation of Richard Matheson's time travel novel, BID TIME RETURN. Christopher (Superman) Reeve is a romantic playwright fascinated with a turn-of-the-century stage actress (Jane Seymour). So intense is this fascination he overcomes time flow and travels back through the years to Michigan's Mackinac Island where he finds the actress and conducts a bittersweet love affair. Matheson adapted his book, Jeannot Szwarc directed. Teresa Wright, Christopher Plummer. (VC)

**SOMEWHERE TOMORROW (1983).** Sensitive, gentle love story, employing the lesser sensational elements of the ghost story. A teenager (Sarah Jesse Parker) is the first on the crash site of a small plane carrying two young men. One of the youths (Tom Shea) dies, but he returns from the spirit world to help the girl overcome personal problems, namely her refusal to accept the recent death of her father, and her mother's intentions to remarry. Tenderly told and intelligently written, but writer-producer-director Robert Wiemer fails to inject much excitement, nor is there any clever use of the ghost, so not even visual possibilities of special effects are explored. The ending is a cop-out and will disappoint fans of the supernatural. Nancy Addison, Rick Weber.

**SON OF ALI BABA (1952).** Just say the secret word— "Sesame"—and the door to the hidden cave will spring open and 40 thieves will pop out. What is more fantastic than that? How about Tony Curtis in the title role of this Universal-International Arabian fantasy actioner? If you can swallow his Brooklyn accent, there's a bridge he'd like to sell you. This Ross Hunter production was directed by Kurt Neumann with his scimitars crossed. Piper Laurie and Susan Cabot provide love interest, Victor Jory and Gerald Mohr provide villainy.

**SON OF BLOB.** Videocassette title for **BEWARE! THE BLOB.** (Beware! is the appropriate warning.)

**SON OF DR. JEKYLL, THE (1951).** Lightweight variation on the Jekyll-Hyde theme, with Louis Hayward as an experimenting scientist trying to prove dear old (dead) dad wasn't as evil as everyone claimed, especially that Robert Louis Stevenson chap. But then his own experiments go

## PAM GRIER: 'SOMETHING WICKED THIS WAY COMES'

awry and he turns bad. Some nights it just doesn't pay to mix those old secret chemicals. Directed by Seymour Friedman. Alexander Knox, Jody Lawrence, Gavin Muir.

**SON OF DRACULA (1943).** Universal's second sequel to DRACULA (after DRACULA'S DAUGHTER) focuses on Count Alucard (check that spelling, fans), a cloaked entity in Louisiana country who hypnotically draws Louise Albritton into vampirism. Loads of atmosphere, good make-up by Jack Pierce, nifty man-to-bat transitions (done with animation) and a sense of fun, with Chaney enjoying his role. Directed by Robert Siodmak, scripted by Eric Taylor. J. Edgar Bromberg, Evelyn Ankers, Robert Paige, Frank Craven.

**SON OF DRACULA (1974).** With Ringo Starr producing, and filling in as Merlin the Magician, this goes down in the annals as the only (we hope) rock 'n roll vampire flick. It vacillates between unamusing comedy and what Starr considers "outre." All the standard cliches are here, plus figures from the rock world, and while there is an obvious love for horror movies underlying the project, results are wishy washy. Directed by Freddie Francis. Dennis Price, Keith Moon, John Bonham, Suzanna Leigh, Freddie Jones. (VC)

**SON OF FLUBBER (1963).** Disney's sequel to THE AB-SENT-MINDED PROFESSOR revives Fred MacMurray as the forgetful scientist who doesn't know how to tie his shoes yet invents a "flubber gas" allowing him to control the weather (imagine an impromptu rainstorm inside a station wagon). Keenan Wynn is again the enemy of the college, trying to steal the gas, Nancy Olson is suffering Mom and Tommy Kirk is the son. Visually witty fantasy prevails. Directed by Robert Stevenson. Ed Wynn, Charles Ruggles, William Demarest, Paul Lynde, Stuart Erwin. (VC)

**SON OF FRANKENSTEIN (1939).** The third and final time Boris Karloff played the hulking Monster—and the last time the Monster evoked viewer sympathy. Director Rowland V. Lee, imitating James Whale, captures a surrealistic aura—Germanic in its expressionism—and there's a literate ring to the script by Willis Cooper, a famous radio writer (LIGHTS OUT, QUIET PLEASE). Bela Lugosi's Ygor the Shepherd is one of his more menacing roles—he escapes his own hamminess and type-casting. Basil Rathbone as the good doctor chews the scenery, but his histrionics are appropriate to the story. Lionel Atwill is unforgettable as the police chief with an artificial hand which clicks and jerks

like a mechanical monster. Superior effort in the series, one which no true-blooded horror fan should miss.

**SON OF GODZILLA (1968).** Bringing up junior can be trying, as this Japanese study in parenthood shows. Out of a giant egg pops a baby Godzilla dubbed Minya. The monster tyke has a slight disadvantage: He has harmless breath and is capable of blowing only smoke rings. Minya must be slapped around by father a bit until he learns good manners—such as how to hulk with style, shamble with grace and crush and maim with finesse. And then a giant praying mantis flies by, challenging the moppet monster to a duel. Children will find this delightful; adults will wonder if the Japanese are putting them on with a certain inept charm. Directed by Jun Fukuda. Tadao Takashima, Akira Kubo, Beverly Maeda. (VC)

**SON OF HERCULES IN THE LAND OF DARKNESS (1963).** More Italian grunt spectacle as Dan Vadis, in the muscle-bound role of Hercules, does battle with a wicked queen in an underground city. Spela Rozin.

**SON OF HERCULES IN THE LAND OF FIRE, THE (1963).** Ugh! Strain! Groan! This time Hercules is played by Ed Fury and he's up to his usual flexing, aiming his superstrength at unnatural forces. Directed by Giorgio Simonelli. Claudia Mori, Luciana Gilli, Adriano Micantoni, Nando Tamberlani.

**SON OF HERCULES VS. VENUS (1980).** Muscle heroes tackle Olympian Gods in the greatest Olympic Games of all. Directed by Marcello Baldi. (VC)

**SON OF INGAGA (1940).** Romantically-inclined giant ape runs through the jungle in search of his Caucasian heart throb, taking her back to the lab. Played for laughs . . . wasn't it? Let's give director Richard Kahn and writer Spencer Williams Jr. the benefit of the doubt, shall we? Zack Williams, Laura Bowman, Alfred Grant, Daisy Bufford.

**SON OF KONG, THE (1934).** King Kong creators Merian C. Cooper and Ernest B. Schoedsack concocted this sequel, unanimously panned by critics and disowned by its stop-motion animator, Willis O'Brien, who resented Ruth Rose's tongue-in-cheek script. That didn't stop it from making money, but it has never attained classic status, remaining in Kong's shadow. Still, it has comedy and adventure as Carl Denham (Robert Armstrong) returns to Skull Island in order to pay off debts incurred following Kong's destructive rampage through New York City. (Can you imagine the bill the Empire State Building owners handed him?) The offspring of Kong is a lovable, albino creature. Helen Mack replaces Fay Wray as the heroine, but returning are Frank Reicher, Noble Johnson and Victor Wong. Not as bad as some critics insist . . . certainly worth a look. (VC)

**SON OF SAMSON (1962).** Mark Forest is not playing Samson but Maciste. By any name he's a muscular dolt who falls prey to a wicked queen wearing a magical locket that puts thoughts of love into his feeble brain. Directed by Carlo Campogalliani. Chelo Alonso, Angelo Zanolli, Vira Silenti.

**SON OF SINBAD (1955).** Made in 3-D but released to theaters flat—you might use that same word to describe the impact this Howard Hughes-RKO release had on the movie market. Dale Robertson as Sinbad, with a Texas accent? Yech. More at home in this Hollywoodesque fantasy nonsense are Vincent Price (as Omar Khayyam the poet) and the sexually stimulating Mari Blanchard, who fills her scanty harem costumes with considerable pulchritude. Other women doing the same are Sally Forrest and Lili St. Cyr. The plot has to do with the secret of Green Fire, a forerunner to TNT, but the only fire this picture needed was under director Ted Tetzlaff. Arabian music by Victor Young. (VC)

**SONG OF BERNADETTE, THE (1943).** Film biography of a French woman who claimed to see visions of the Virgin Mary in 1858, and the ostracism, ordeal by trial and self-doubt she suffered until the Catholic Church accepted her experiences as a miracle and the healing waters of Lourdes were established. First-class Fox production directed by Henry King and written by George Seaton, with a wonderfully inspiring score by Alfred Newman. Jennifer Jones, Linda Darnell, Vincent Price, Lee J. Cobb, Gladys Cooper, Sig Ruman, Jerome Cowan, Alan Napier, Fritz Leiber Sr., Ian Wolfe.

**SONG OF THE SUCCUBUS (1975).** Leader of a rock group is haunted by a musical star who committed suicide around the turn of the century. TV-film stars Kim Milford, Stash Wagner, Gail Heideman. Directed by Glenn Jordan.

**SORCERERS, THE (1968).** One of the few films of wunderkind Michael Reeves before his untimely death . . . this adaptation of John Burke's novel depicts an elderly couple (Boris Karloff, Catherine Lacey) who devise a machine that enables them to experience the sensations of those under their control. Lacey goes a little whacky, feeling too many oats, and urges a mod-minded teenager to commit sadistic murders. It's an exciting idea, but Reeves was hampered by an almost non-existence budget and the film looks cheaper than it deserves. Ian Ogilvy, Susan George.

**SORCERESS, THE (1956).** Emphasis is on love and gorgeous settings in this French fantasy made in Sweden. The love affair is between a witch (Marina Vlady) and a young engineer (Maurice Ronet), who has been sent to the north woods to build a road. Overcoming the superstitious natives is about as heavy as the drama gets. Directed by Andre Michel. Nicole Courcel, Rune, Lindstrom.

**SORCERESS (1982).** High-camp sword-and-sorcery mishmesh produced by Jack Hill with the subtlety of a cauldron-stirring, cackling witch and directed by Brian Stuart as though he were hacking through bramblebrush with an axe. The dialogue by Jim Wynorski will have you howling as two sisters, endowed with supernatural strength as well as healthy chests (which they are inclined to reveal as often as possible, usually in the direction of the camera), search for the wicked wizard who murdered their mother. There's an interesting satyr-like character who bellows like a goat, a Viking swordsman and a young piece of beefcake who introduces the Siamese twins to nightly pleasures. Plus an army of zombie swordsmen and effects by John Carl Buechler, added by producer Roger Corman to save the picture from total disaster. Great bellylaughs. Bob Nelson, Bruno Rey. (VC)

**SORORITY HOUSE MASSACRE (1985).** Eternal fraternal is internal and infernal when a cackling knife killer, foaming at the mouth and wide of eyeballs within their sockets, slaughters daughters of the rich and seeks to make dead co-ed Angela O'Neill, who's been dreaming about an escaped psycho case. Written-directed by Carol Frank. (VC)

**S.O.S. COAST GUARD (1937).** Feature-length 1942 version of a 12-chapter Republic serial. A tepid affair, even when reduced to nonstop action, in which Bela Lugosi portrays a scientist (Boroff) who creates a deadly gas capable of disintegrating objects (in case you're wondering, the gas is composed of Arnaltite and Zanzoid, got it?). His opponent is Ralph Byrd (later to play Dick Tracy) as a Coast Guard undercover man. Directed breathlessly by William Witney and Alan James. Maxine Doyle, Carlton Young, Thomas Carr.

**S.O.S. INVASION (1969).** S.O.S.: Beware a certain Spanish science-fiction-terror film, directed by Silvio F. Balbuena,

about strange alien females who turn Earthlings into obeying automatons. S.O.S.: Sort of Shoddy.

**S.O.S. TIDAL WAVE (1939).** Outdated entertainment from Republic, set in the near future when television is a common device and used to scare everyone into thinking New York City is being overwashed by a colossal tidal wave (the flood scenes were lifted from DELUGE). Directed by John H. Auer. Ralph Byrd, Kay Sutton, Marc Laurence, Donald Barry.

**SOUL OF A MONSTER (1944).** Director Will Jason tries to make this potboiler special with tricked up camera angles, but results are still mediocre. George Macready portrays a millionaire on the verge of death, saved when his wife prays for help and salvation comes from female demon Rose Hobart. Jim Bannon, Jeanne Bates, Erik Rolf.

**SOUND OF HORROR (1967).** Spanish producer Gregory Siechristian keeps expenses down by making his monster (a prehistoric dinosaur) invisible. It only becomes "noticeable" by a bellowing cry on the soundtrack every time director Jose Anthonio Nieves Conde moves the camera. The roar sends the Greek expedition that stirred up the monster scurrying for new digs. Arturo Fernandez, Soledad Miranda.

**SOYLENT GREEN (1973).** Big-budgeted version of Harry Harrison's MAKE ROOM, MAKE ROOM that graphically, and depressingly, depicts life in 2022. A curious blending of the private eye genre with glimpses of a world to come, scripted by Stanley Greenberg without much faith to Harrison's story. Earth has become a smog-shrouded planet, hopelessly populated, and near-anarchy is at hand as Manhattan cop Charlton Heston solves a series of murders—perpetrated to protect a secret. This was Edgard G. Robinson's last film, and ironically he portrays a dying man who seeks a pleasant form of suicide in this downbeat world of tomorrow. Leigh Taylor-Young, Chuck Connors, Joseph Cotten, Brock Peters. Tautly directed by Richard Fleischer. (VC)

**SPACE CHILDREN, THE (1958).** Jack Arnold directed this as an allegory (about the ever-existing gap between adolescence and adulthood) and not just an escapist fantasy. Set in a seacoast desert community, which allows Arnold to duplicate some of the environmental mood effects from his earlier science-fiction films, the story concerns a family arriving at a rocket-launching center, where the children see a UFO land and later meet an intelligent rock-brain in a cave that takes

**MARI BLANCHARD: 'SON OF SINBAD'**

control of the youngsters so they can sabotage an atomic missile project. The telepathic alien, strangely enough, never communicates—it's all shown without exposition. This being a message picture first and an entertainment second, William Alland's production never builds to very much but flat-footed honorable intentions. Parents are depicted as dolts—children as wise pacifists. Whose side is Arnold on, anyway? Johnny Crawford, Russell Johnson, Sandy Descher.

**SPACE CRUISER (1977).** Animated Japanese space adventure (set in 2199) features interplanetary war between Earth and a wandering planet of evil, Gorgon. Not great animation; strictly for space-happy moppets. Directed-written by Yoshinobu Nishizaki, originally for an Oriental TV series. Voices by Marvin Miller, Rex Knolls and Mercy Goldman.

**SPACE CRUISER YAMATO PART II (1979).** Further depiction of warfare between our planet and Gorgon, designed by a team of Japanese animators under the writing and direction of Toshio Masuda.

**SPACE DEVILS. See SNOW DEVILS.**

**SPACE FIREBIRD 2772 (1980).** Japanese animated feature is a creative exercise in space adventure as adventurer Godoh and his robot Olga (pretty sexy) rocket into the void to circumvent the destructive activities of a firebird monster. Good job. Written-directed by Taku Sugiyama.

**SPACE INVASION OF LAPLAND. See INVASION OF THE ANIMAL PEOPLE.** (And lap it up!)

**SPACE KID. See MEATBALLS II.** (For meatheads)

**SPACE MASTER X-7 (1958).** Lower berth material of the "blob" school: Fungus off the hull of a space probe returned to Earth mixes with blood and becomes a "Blood Rust"—resembling an out-of-control batch of Jello—which goes on a killing spree. Quick, someone, decontaminate it before it spreads. The presence of Moe Howard in a minor role as a cabbie suggests director Edward Bernds might have intended this as comedy. But Bill Williams, Paul Frees and Joan Barry play it for serious.

**SPACE MISSION OF THE LOST PLANET. See VAMPIRE MEN OF THE LOST PLANET.** (For suckers)

**SPACE MONSTER (1965).** Of the "Rocky Jones, Space Ranger" school, in which space pilots argue among themselves while jockeying to another planet. The titular Space Monster is a rubbery-faced character (never explained) which the crew encounters halfway to its interstellar destination. Finally, after more bickering, the crew crashlands in the ocean of an alien world. Special effects consist of a model rocket floating in a tankful of crabs and lobsters, probably in an L.A. restaurant. Utterly unwatchable. James B. Brown, Russ Bender, Francine York. Producer-director Leonard Katzman went on to fame as producer of DALLAS.

**SPACE 1999.** Several episodes of this once-popular 1974-75 British TV series, starring Martin Landau and Barbara Bain as members of a moon station that is catapulted into space when the moon explodes, were repackaged as video features. In addition to this three-hour epic, there are **COSMIC PRINCESS, DESTINATION MOONBASE ALPHA** and **JOURNEY THROUGH THE BLACK SUN.**

**SPACE PATROL I and II (1955).** Early-day TV turkey about Buzz Corey and Cadet Happy fighting to clean up space for the United Planets. Each videocassette consists of three old kinescopes. You really have to be a fan of these old shows to endure its naivete and rock-bottom budget. Viewed as nostalgic camp, it passes . . . slightly. Directed by Dik Darley. Ed Kemmer, Lyn Osborne, Ken Mayer. (VC)

**SPACE RAIDERS (1983).** What might have been a classic kind of TREASURE ISLAND IN SPACE, with a castaway youth joining a band of star-roving renegades and merecenaries, is a humorless, leaden nonadventure in tedium, as characterless as the space pirates it depicts. This Roger Corman film is lacking in style and pace, unfolding mechanically, without heart, under writer-director Howard R. Cohen. Not one of the alien creatures looks like anything more than an actor wearing a rubber face mask, and the space battles are staged without excitement, obviously outtakes from earlier Corman space movies. One explosion is repeated over and over. When gang leader Vince Edwards (rough on the outside, all marshmallowy inside when it comes to the kid) goes against the Robot Death Ship, looking for a weak link in its defense, you know you've seen it all before, and you root for the bad guys. Thom Christopher, Patsy Pease, David Menderhall, Dick Miller. (VC)

**SPACE SOLDIERS. See FLASH GORDON (1936).**

**SPACE SOLDIERS CONQUER THE UNIVERSE.** Condensed version of the Buster Crabbe serial. See **FLASH GORDON CONQUERS THE UNIVERSE.**

**MEL BROOKS AS YOGA AND PRESIDENT SKOORB IN 'SPACEBALLS'**

**ROOKIES ADRIFT IN SPACE IN THE PLEASANT ADVENTURE 'SPACECAMP'**

**SPACE WARRIORS 2000 (1980).** Childeren's special effects science- fiction with a doll coming to life to join the Galaxy Council and fight alien invaders.

**SPACEBALLS (1987).** In spite of himself, writer-producer-director Mel Brooks manages to sprinkle some funny one-liners and puns throughout this out-and-out spoof of STAR WARS and other science-fiction classics. Remaining portions stand out as coarse and flat, especially since so much of this has an appeal for children and shouldn't have to be vulgar or resort to foul language. It begins with "Once upon a time warp . . ." with the rolling-style credits, then introduces us to Dark Helmet (villain), Lone Starr (young hero), Barf (dog-man, his own best friend), Princess Vespa (heroine), Yogurt (wise old sage with knowledge of that ethereal power, the Schwartz) and Pizza the Hut (monster). The plot has to do with Helmet and his Spaceballs trying to steal the oxygen from the atmosphere of the planet Druidia, but this is lam-poonery of the broadest kind, with non sequiturs, references (and even scenes) of the film crew and other Brooks' hooks, so plot is hardly important. Not all the characters work and the spoofery comes too long after the success of STAR WARS to seem relevant. (Didn't HARDWARE WARS do it better?) Still, the cast is bright: John Candy, Rick Moranis, Daphne Zuniga, Bill Pullman, Dick Van Patten, George Wyner. Brooks doubles as Yogurt and a human villain, Presi-dent Skoorb. Joan Rivers provides the voice of a female golden robot who "wants to talk."

**SPACECAMP (1986).** Spacecamp is where young would-be astronauts spend the summer undergoing simulated flights and learning the meaning of responsibility. A dingbat robot a la R2D2 causes a rocket to be launched when its young crew is aboard with adult trainer Kate Capshaw. How the kids face up to the rigors and perils of space flight make for an intrigu-ing premise enhanced by good special effects. Pleasant viewing, directed with a steady hand by Harry Winer. Lea Thompson, Tom Skerritt, Kelly Preston. (VC)

**SPACED OUT (1979).** British comedy about sexpots from a planet in the Betelgeuse star system who learn about the birds and the bees from Earthling male prisoners. Pretty cheap and pretty silly—and the women are pretty, too . . . pretty dumb . . . so don't expect much to challenge the intel-lect. Barry Stokes, Tony Maiden. Directed by Norman J. War-ren. (VC)

**SPACEFLIGHT 1C-1 (1965).** Giant spaceship carrying colonists to another world is the theme of this British adven-ture, with only so-so effects, and a so-so plot (by Harry Spalding) in which the travelers stage a revolt against RULE, a computer-controlled governmental system stifling creativity and freedom aboard ship. Bill Williams, Linda Marlowe.

**SPACEHUNTER: ADVENTURES IN THE FORBIDDEN ZONE (1983).** A $12 million space saga originally released in 3-D but with few "comin' at ya!" thrills. In the 22nd Century, interstellar mercenary Peter Strauss diverts his scow to the plague-riddled planet Terra 11 to rescue tourists in the clutches of the villainous Overdog (Michael Ironside), a half-human, half-machine entity who soaks up the psychic power of beautiful women (without, apparently, bothering with physi-cal contact). Production design is messy and funky with an eclectic assortment of costumes, weapons and vehicles. The screenplay never develops Strauss' Wolff character or his "Odd Couple" relationship with wandering waif Molly Ringwald. Ernie Hudson is wasted as the sidekick, Washington. Lamont Johnson directs with an eye to con-tinuous action, and there's a slam-bang conflagration with Overdog, but this ultimately fails to provide a memorable two hours at the movies. Andrea Marcovicci. (VC)

**SPACESHIP.** Videocassette title for **CREATURE WASN'T NICE, THE.** (How rude . . . !)

**SPACESHIP TO THE UNKNOWN (1936).** Newly re-edited version of the first half of the FLASH GORDON serial from Universal, which seems to be no better (or worse) than ear-lier chopped up versions. No amount of tampering can really take away the charm and fun of this, the best of all serials of the 1930s. See **FLASH GORDON.**

**SPACE-WATCH MURDERS, THE (1978).** When a spaceship returns to Earth with all but one of its crew mem-bers dead, a special Space Team investigates. Barbara Steele fans will enjoy their favorite heroine/villainess. Sam Groom, Tisha Sterling, Joan Caulfield.

**SPACEWAYS (1953).** Early Hammer foray into the fantastic, and an interesting twist it is. Howard Duff, space scientist, is suspected of placing the corpses of his wife and lover inside a satellite circling Earth. To clear himself, he blasts off in a rocket to recover the satellite. Early collaborative effort be-tween Michael Carreras (producer), Terence Fisher (director) and Jimmy Sangster (assistant director). Based on a radio play by Charles Eric Maine. Eva Bartok, Alan Wheatley.

**SPANIARD'S CURSE, THE (1958).** A British jury sends an innocent man to the gallows—he vows to get even. Sudden-ly, the jurors die one . . . heh heh . . . by one. Diabolical, isn't it? Directed by Ralph Kemplen. Tony Wright, Susan Beaumont, Lee Patterson, Basil Dignam, John Watson.

**SPARE PARTS (1984).** West German thriller, FLEISCH, is an offbeat, oft-intriguing medical mystery in which honeymooners become victims of a body organ transplant operation. The action drifts from Texas (where trucker Wolf Roth helps Nordic beauty Jutta Speidel find her missing hus-

THE DEADLY TAIPAN: FROM REAL LIFE, NOT THE CRUMMY MOVIE 'SPASMS'

band) to New York City for an unusual climax. Writer-director Rainer Erler avoids many of the usual cliches of this genre, and while it's a low budget B picture, it's a decent one. (VC)

**SPASMS (1983).** DEATH BITE, a chilling novel by Michael Maryk and Brent Monahan, depicted the horrible attacks in San Diego of a 19-foot-long taipan snake, a giant killer imported from the island of Narka-Pintu whose bite kills in three minutes. This Canadian adaptation alters the taipan to a demon serpent from the Gates of Hell, paralleling another Canadian film, JAWS OF SATAN. Oliver Reed, a hunter once bitten by the supernatural reptile, now has an ESP link to the demon and undergoes visions (filmed in black and white with a hand-held camera with distorted lens) of its vicious, gory, "cold-blooded" attacks. Peter Fonda is the snake expert who talks about "viral telepathy" with Reed to explain the link. Kerrie Keane is the obligatory female who just hangs around, Al Waxman is the uncouth villain who finally goes out with three "strikes" against him. Screenwriter Don Enright also introduces a pointless snake cult; his adaptation should have been exciting (the book certainly was) but it generates surprisingly little suspense and uncoils lethargically to a downright unsatisfying anticlimax. Tangerine Dream provides an unmemorable "serpent's love theme." Minimum special effects footage of the supernatural serpent—director William Fruet doesn't have the bite. (VC)

**SPAWN OF THE SLITHIS.** See SLITHIS.

**SPECIAL BULLETIN (1983).** Controversial TV-movie (by producer Don Ohlmeyer and writer-director Marshall Herskovitz) is a pastiche of a network news special. Scenes of an anchor news team at a network studio are interspersed with footage shot by "live" cameras on the scene. Suspense is ever-building and the effect of realism ever-numbing as antinuclear protestors kidnap five hostages and hold them prisoner in the harbor of Charleston, S.C. These well-intended but warped radicals have fashioned their own atomic device and threaten to set it off. The ending is a stunner. Ed Flanders, Kathryn Walker, David Clennon. (VC)

**SPECIAL EFFECTS (1984).** Unusually grim Larry Cohen film in which a film director murders an actress and tries to pin the rap on her husband. Dark and atmospheric, as only Cohen (GOD TOLD ME TO, THE STUFF) can be. (VC)

**SPECTERS (1987).** Italian chiller diller set in Rome, where professor Donald Pleasence digs up an ancient vault down in the catacombs which contains a monster from yesteryear. This film makes a specter-cle of itself. John Pepper, Katrine Michelsen, Massimo de Rossi. Directed by Marcello Avallone.

**SPECTRE (1977).** Intriguing Gene Roddenberry TV-pilot with Robert Culp and Gig Young as fighters of the supernatural who take on Asmodeus, a Prince of Evil controlling a Druid cult. Fans will find this delightful viewing. The Roddenberry-Samuel B. Peeples script full of surprises and Clive Donner's direction angled to capture the sexual side to the cult. Too bad the networks never picked up on this as a series—it

might have worked. John Hurt, Ann Bell, Jenny Runacre.

**SPECTRE OF EDGAR ALLAN POE, THE (1973).** Grieving over the loss of his loved one, a beauty who died before her time, Robert Walker Jr. (as Poe) seeks rest in the mansion of Cesar Romero, who just happens to be a sadist with a torture chamber of snakes. Director-producer-writer Mohy Quandour allegedly delves into phobias apparent in Poe's stories, but it's exploitation hokum shedding no insight into the real Poe. Tom Drake and Carol Ohmart run around the big drafty house to no avail. Nevermore, quoth viewers. (VC)

**SPELL, THE (1977).** Blatant steal from CARRIE . . . this TV-film is the story of a teenage girl who uses kinetic powers against her tormentors. Despite obvious parallels, this has a feel of its own and includes a coven of witches nurturing ESP powers in the young. The diabolical theme is finally overshadowed by a duel between daughter (Susan Myers) and mother (Lee Grant). The Brian Taggart script also makes salient comments on the Generation Gap and the lack of communication between children and parent. On that level, it is keenly interesting. Directed by Lee Philips.

**SPELL OF AMY NUGENT, THE (1940).** British supernatural thriller with a familiar plot (concocted by Miles Malleson) about a spiritualist bringing back a dead love to life evoke a mood of insouciance. Directed by John Harlow. Derek Farr, Felix Aylmer, Vera Lindsay, Frederick Leister.

**SPELL OF EVIL (1973).** Diane Cilento, reincarnation of a 16th Century witch, wields strange powers and inflicts terror on her husband and his secretary. Brian Clemens scripted this low-budget TV-movie, produced in Britain and directed by John Sichel. Jennifer Daniel, Edward De Souza.

**SPELL OF THE HYPNOTIST.** See FRIGHT.

**SPELLBOUND (1945).** Alfred Hitchcock walks "the dark corridors of the human mind," probing into guilt, fantasy, schizophrenia, paranoia and persecution complexes, but never forgetting this is a psychothriller. What a screenplay Ben Hecht has adapted from Francis Beeding's novel, THE HOUSE OF DR. EDWARDES. You're in for a couchful of tricks as headshrinker Ingrid Bergman attempts to unlock the brain of amnesia victim Gregory Peck. Watch how the "master of suspense" gradually reveals the Freudian clues, and see how he toys with the audience, leaving doubt if Peck is a murderer or not. The dream sequences were designed by Salvador Dali and include blank, staring eyes, mouthless-noseless faces, bizarre landscapes. Miklos Rozsa's music is the best "psychoanalytic" score ever written. Donald Curtis, Leo G. Carroll, Wallace Ford, Rhonda Fleming. (VC)

**SPIDER, THE (1958).** Producer-director Bert I. Gordon, who works harder than any other producer-director to save a buck, gets entangled in a web of ineptitude in presenting a giant mutant spider living in a cave outside of a town crawling with unbearable two-legged teenagers. Eight-legged monstrosity turns out to be eight times duller than most giant movie spiders. Ed Kemmer, of SPACE PATROL, stars as the adult who goes to the rescue. June Kenney, Gene Roth.

**SPIDER BABY (1970).** Revolting, black comedy sickie about cannibals who also breed with each other, and a threesome of child monsters. Written-directed without taste by Jack Hill. Carol Ohmart, Sig Haig, Lon Chaney Jr., Mantan Moreland, Quinn Redecker, Jill Banner. (VC)

**SPIDER RETURNS, THE (1941).** Feature version of the 15-chapter Columbia serial of the same title, based on a once-popular pulp magazine character who wore a mask and fought supercriminals. The Spider is out to stop The Gargoyle, a foreign saboteur seeking to subjugate mankind with a TV spying gadget called "The X-Ray Eye." Really exciting stuff, gang. Directed by James W. Horne. Warren Hull, Mary Ainslee, Dave O'Brien, Kenneth Duncay, Alden Chase.

**SPIDER WOMAN STRIKES BACK, THE (1946).** Dreary Universal thriller in which Gale Sondergaard recreates her portrayal from SHERLOCK HOLMES AND THE SPIDER WOMAN. Once again The Creeper (Rondo Hatton), who was introduced in THE PEARL OF DEATH, is scaring people to death with his malformed acromegalic face while Ms Spidey grows odd plants which feed on blood of young women. Who should happen along but young woman Brenda Joyce, who settles into the house of horror without realizing what awaits her. Milburn Stone and Kirby Grant are in the neighborhood, and maybe they can save her. Most movie fans struck back by avoiding this feature directed by Arthur Lubin.

**SPIDERMAN.** See **AMAZING SPIDERMAN, THE.**

**SPIDERMAN STRIKES BACK (1978).** Episodes of a two-part TV adventure from the short-lived series, THE AMAZING SPIDERMAN, recut for syndicated TV. In videocassette as **AMAZING SPIDERMAN, THE.** See **DEADLY DUST.**

**SPIDERMAN: THE DRAGON'S CHALLENGE.** See **CHINESE WEB, THE.**

**SPIES A-GO-GO.** See **NASTY RABBIT, THE.**

**SPIRAL STAIRCASE, THE (1946).** Nifty psychosuspense thriller in which speechless housemaid Dorothy McGuire is pursued through a New England mansion in 1906 by a killer who specializes in murdering women with physical deformities. There are tense sequences directed by Robert Siodmak, and Mel Dinelli's script emphasizes the more subtle psychological motivations. The whodunit aspects are well treated. Based on Ethel Lina White's SOME MUST WATCH. George Brent, Ethel Barrymore, Kent Smith, Elsa Lanchester, Rhonda Fleming, Rhys Williams. (VC)

**SPIRAL STAIRCASE, THE (1975).** Thoroughly botched version of Ethel Lina White's SOME MUST WATCH, capturing none of the suspense or mystery of this old-fashioned plot about a speechless nurse trapped in a house with a psycho-killer. There's no feeling of isolation (the house is in the suburbs, not the country) in Andrew Meredith's script and Peter Collinson's direction is as limp as the corpses. Jacqueline Bisset tries to make her part believable, but the identity of the murderer can be quickly discerned. Christopher Plummer and Sam Wanamaker certainly deserve better. Mildred Dunnock, Gayle Hunnicutt, Elaine Stritch, John Philip Law. (VC)

**SPIRIT IS WILLING, THE (1967).** Vacuous William Castle comedy-thriller in which a New England mansion is haunted by the victims of an axe murderer. Unfortunately, producer-director Castle did not know how to control comedians Sid Caesar and John Astin; the result made for unwilling audiences weak of viewing spirit. Ben Star adapted Nathaniel Benchley's THE VISITORS. Vera Miles, Cass Daley.

**SPIRIT OF THE BEEHIVE (1974).** In the year 1940, two Spanish children see FRANKENSTEIN and become obsessed with the Monster Myth. Because the moppets are isolated from their parents, their obsession and need to understand why the Monster killed the little girl in the pond draws them into a fantasy world where the Frankenstein Monster exists and treats them with kindness. Beautifully photographed film that, unfortunately, lacked broad appeal. Written-directed by Victor Erice. Fernando Fernan Gomez.

**SPIRIT OF THE DEAD.** Videocassette title for **ASPHYX, THE,** although it is also in videocassette as **ASPHYX, THE.**

**SPIRITISM (1965).** Mexican version of the famous story, "The Monkey's Paw," would have author W. W. Jacobs rising from his grave to throttle director Benito Alazaraki. This is the old tale of a mother granted three wishes when she comes in possession of the mummified paw. The wishes result in . . .

**SPIRITS OF THE DEAD (1969).** Three directors join talents to adapt Edgar Allan Poe tales. "Metzengerstein" is Roger Vadim's contribution, featuring Jane and Peter Fonda as a wanton countess and her cousin who attend orgies and fight among themselves. When she kills him, he returns as a black stallion. It's the weakest of the trio. The next is "William Wilson" (Louis Malle directed) with Alain Delon as a man with a dual personality who tries to win Brigitte Bardot in a card game. The third is the best: Federico Fellini's "Never Bet the Devil Your Head, or Toby Dammit," with Terence Stamp as a drunken British actor called to Rome to receive an award. Presented with a Ferrari, he races toward a fatal rendezvous. Narrated by Vincent Price. James Robertson Justice.

**SPIRITUALIST, THE (1948).** Of interest to seance attendees—not because this film has any ghosts or goblins but because it reveals how a fake medium (Turhan Bey) creates

# Hunting for the Underdog

**MICHAEL IRONSIDE AS OVERDOG; THE SCRAMBLER VEHICLE IN 'SPACEHUNTER'**

his supernatural illusions with projectors, recordings, sliding panels, etc. Meanwhile, gullible Lynn Bari thinks her dead husband has returned to chat over old times. Also known as THE AMAZING MR. X. Directed by Bernard Vorhaus. Richard Carlson, Cathy O'Donnell, Virginia Gregg.

**SPLASH (1984).** This comedy hits the water just right—a Disney release that is a gainer and a half. Released under the Touchstone banner, it was that studio's first film with a glimpse of female nudity. Daryl Hannah is a mermaid who leaves her Bermuda waters for Manhattan, where on dry land she falls in love with Tom Hanks and creates some hysterical scenes gnawing on lobsters in a restaurant or screeching fish notes that shatter a dozen TV screens at once. Ron Howard's direction never jackknives and the Lowell Ganz-Babaloo Mandel-Bruce Jay Friedman screenplay is a series of charming vignettes. John Candy as Hanks' produce district brother, Eugene Levy as the nerd trying to expose Hannah's secret and Richard Shull as Dr. Ross all contribute wonderful characterizations. And love those scenes of Hannah, tail and all, floating in a bathtub. Dody Goodman and Shecky Greene also contribute nice bits. (VC)

**SPLATTER . . . ARCHITECTS OF FEAR (1986).** Behind-the-scenes look at how low budget horror movie-makers prepare their grisly special effects. Interesting, informative; better than the movies the effects guys are working on, that's

for sure. Directed by Peter Rowe. (VC)

**SPLATTER UNIVERSITY (1984).** Described as "where the school colors are blood red" . . . another slasher flick with the usual line-up of victims. Directed by Richard W. Haines. Francine Forbes, Cathy Lacommare, Dick Biel. (Available in two different videocassette versions.)

**SPOOK BUSTERS (1946).** Huntz Hall's I.Q. approximates the intelligence of a chimpanzee, so surgeon Douglas Dumbrille (as The Mad Scientist) decides to implant Huntz's brain into the head of a gorilla. This Monogram lowbrower, directed by William Beaudine, is set in a haunted house. No doubt the title inspired GHOSTBUSTERS. Leo Gorcey, Gabriel Dell, Bobby Jordan, Billy Benedict.

**SPOOK CHASERS (1957).** Late-in-the-series Bowery Boys haunted house cheapie, with Stanley Clements (replacing Leo Gorcey, who had dropped out) and Huntz Hall meeting gorillas, ghosts and "apparitions" in a drafty mansion at the height of a thunderstorm. You'll need a chaser after watching this Allied Artists abortion directed by George Blair.

**SPOOKIES (1986).** Sorcerer Felix Ward, in bringing his long-dead bride back to life, uses some teenagers who just happen to drop by his mansion one night as sacrifices, conjuring up all manner of monsters and beasties to do the killing. Directed by Brendan Faulkner, Thomas Doran, Frank M.

# *Mermaid in America*

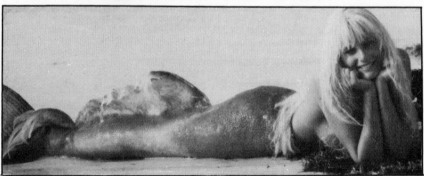

**DARYL HANNAH AS MADISON, THE GIRL WITH THE BIG TAIL IN 'SPLASH'**

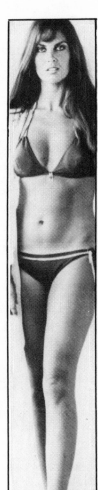

Farel. Dan Scott, Alec Nemser.

**SPOOKS RUN WILD (1941).** The East Side Kids meet Bela Lugosi in a Monogram lower berth comedy. The Carl Foreman-Charles Marion script features Lugosi as a killer called The Monster, who travels in a coffin and is pursued by Von Gorsch. Directed by Phil Rosen, produced by Sam Katzman. Huntz Hall, Leo Gorcey, Bobby Jordan.

**SPOOKY MOVIE SHOW, THE. See MASK, THE.**

**SPY IN THE GREEN HAT, THE (1966).** More MAN FROM U.N.C.L.E. TV episodes re-edited into a feature with Napoleon Solo (Robert Vaughn) stopping madman Jack Palance from diverting the Gulf Stream with a sound device. David McCallum is Vaughn's fellow agent and Leo G. Carroll is the assignment chief. The usual spy nonsense. Directed by Joseph Sargent. Janet Leigh, Maxie Rosenbloom, Allen Jenkins, Joan Blondell, Elisha Cook Jr.

**SPY IN YOUR EYE (1966).** The formula for a laser death beam is sought by a secret agent representing the major powers; that spy is Dana Andrews, unaware one of his eyeballs is actually a TV transmitting gadget. Here's mud in your eye. Italian spy shenanigans directed by Vittorio Sala. Brett Halsey, Pier Angeli, Gaston Moschin.

**SPY SMASHER (1942).** Spy Smasher was a regular character in Fawcett comic books during the 1940s . . . in this 12-chapter serial from Republic, the superhero is portrayed by Kane Richmond. He battles valiantly against The Mask, a German dastard heading a sabotage ring in America. Ongoing cliffhangers feature zap guns, supersonic skyplanes, and advanced forms of TV electronics. Directed by serial specialist William Witney. Marguerite Chapman, Tris Coffin, Sam Flint, Hans Schumm, Frank Corsaro. (VC)

**SPY SMASHER RETURNS.** Re-edited feature-length version of **SPY SMASHER** for syndicated TV.

**SPY SQUAD (1962).** Imbecilic espionage emptiness in which duped Commie-rat sneaks and undercover guys from other foreign powers chase after the nose-cone of a capsule. The masterwork of writer-producer-director Will Zens. Dick O'Neil, Dick Miller.

**SPY WHO LOVED ME, THE (1977).** The best James Bond adventure-fantasy following the retirement of Sean Connery. Bond is assigned to prevent the builder of an underwater city (Curt Jurgens) from stealing atomic subs and turning their missiles on the free world—an impossible mission made possible with the help of Soviet spy Barbara Bach. The action sequences are terrific, the full-scale freighter sets are impressive and overall the film has an expensive look. The sex jokes are leeringly sophomoric and the Christopher Wood-Richard Maibaum plot typically far-fetched, but you won't be bored. Richard Kiel almost steals the film as the indefatigable villain Jaws, who survives catastrophes without disrupting a hair on his head. The character, in fact, returned in MOONRAKER. Lewis Gilbert directed the action and mayhem with a straight face. Caroline Munro is featured in a bikini, chasing Bond along a road in her helicopter. (VC)

**SPY WITH MY FACE, THE (1966).** When U.N.C.L.E. agent Robert Vaughn thrusts a pistol between the breasts of Senta Berger, she remarks, "The one in the middle seems to be a gun." Yes, gang, another feature re-edited from one-hour TV shows. Senta is plotting to take over Project Earth Save (a weapon powerful enough to destroy Griffith Park in one afternoon) and substitute a lookalike Napoleon Solo. Then, for laughs, she plans to ransom the USA for 80 zillion bucks. Spy fun with microphones in the lipstick case and cyanide in the Kool cigarette pack. Directed by John Newland. David McCallum, Michael Evans, Sharon Farrell, Leo G. Carroll.

**SQUIRM (1976).** Just try to worm out of watching this one: electrically-charged earthworms, sandworms and bookworms (not to mention such bilateral invertebrates as acanthocephalans, nemertines, gordiaceans and annelids) wriggle, wiggle and squiggle into huge lumps prior to dawn, attacking dumb clucks (such as Don Scardino, Patricia Pearcy and Jean Sullivan) who drop by the swamp. Yep, it's the early worm that gets the bird. Made in Georgia by writer-director Jeff Lieberman with a tongue-in-cheek style.

**CAROLINE MUNRO**

**BARBARA BACH**

# 'These Are the Voyages . . .

THE STARSHIP ENTERPRISE, AS IT APPEARED IN THE ORIGINAL TV SERIES (1966)

WILLIAM SHATNER      LEONARD NIMOY      DeFOREST KELLEY

INTERGALACTIC FIREPOWER: 'STAR TREK: THE WRATH OF KHAN'

# ... *Where No Man Has Gone Before'*

THE BIRD OF PREY UNDER THE GOLDEN GATE: SCENE FROM THE FOURTH 'TREK' FILM

GEORGE TAKEI

JAMES DOOHAN

NICHELLE NICHOLS

WALTER KOENIG

ANGELIQUE PETTYJOHN

Ludicrous but fun cinema, allegedly populated by 250,000 real-life worms. Glow, worms, glow . . . (VC)

**SSSSS (1973).** Does the title refer to the sound made by slumped-over viewers 15 minutes into the picture? Or does it refer to the cobras mad scientist Strother Martin keeps in his laboratory on his farm outside town? It doesn't matter since producers Richard Zanuck and Dick Brown wanted only to prove they could make a picture with passable special effects and a ridiculous premise before going on to THE STING and JAWS. Turning a full-grown man into a common household cobra is a farce in the hands of writer Hal Dresden and director Bernard Kowalski. Would you believe a climax where a man-snake battles a mongoose? Oh well, life is one big snake pit. Dirk Benedict, Richard B. Shull.

**STAGE FRIGHT (1983).** Demented actress (Jenny Neumann) gets cold feet before the curtain rises, the first of several things that turn frigid during this British horror movie-within-a-movie. Drop your drapes!

**STAIRWAY TO HEAVEN (1946).** Philosophical fantasy from British producers-directors-writers Michael Powell and Emeric Pressburger that is literate, imaginative and profound in dealing with a man defying his own fate. Always maintaining a sense of humor, this British film (in black and white, with color sequences) follows an RAF pilot (David Niven) who leaps from his flaming bomber without a bloody parachute. But someone slips up in Heaven and he is allowed to survive. Conductor 71 (a French aristocrat who was guillotined) is dispatched to Earth but the pilot demands a trial by the higher celestial court and proceeds to tell the powers-that-be why he should continue to live. Kim Hunter, Marius Goring, Raymond Massey, Robert Coote, Richard Attenborough, Roger Livesey, Robert Atkins.

**STALK THE WILD CHILD (1976).** Another JUNGLE BOOK update in which Benjamin Bottoms portrays a toddler raised by wolves, who turns into older Joseph Bottoms by the time he's discovered and removed from the jungle. It's the job of psychiatrist David Janssen to get him ready for freeways, taco stands and late-night TV movies. Eventually this pilot became a short-lived TV series, LUCAN, that starred Kevin Brophy in the title role. Directed by William Hale.

**STALKER (1979).** Russia's Andrei Tarkovsky, who gave us SOLARIS, once again demonstrates daring style in this weird tale of a writer and scientist who enter a "mysterious zone" from which no one has ever returned. Their tour guide for this momentous event is called Stalker. Plenty of food for thought with enough messages to open a telegram service. Weighty but not unwieldy. Anatoly Solonitsyn, Alisa Freindlich.

**STANLEY (1972).** Awful exploitationer produced-directed by William Grefe asks the poignant question: Can a rattlesnake named Stanley find happiness with a Seminole Indian who bears a grudge against mankind? As the Indian, Chris Robinson is passable, destined for greater things as a TV soap star on GENERAL HOSPITAL, but Stanley, from Snake Central Casting, really sinks its teeth into Gary Crutcher's plot—and characters including crook Alex Rocco. Sufferers of ophidiophobia should beware of this movie. (VC)

**STAR CRYSTAL (1985).** "High-tech" science-fiction with good effects and spaceship interiors. It begins as a horror-mystery film in the vein of ALIEN when astronauts discover a strange crystal in the Olympus Mons crater of Mars. Later, when a crew of five is trapped aboard a shuttlecraft with a lifeform from the rock, director Lance Lindsay brings out all the horror cliches: tentacles that wrap around bodies of victims, drained corpses, etc. But after the creature taps into the computer system and gets Bible religion, it/him/she (?) goes straight and emerges a cute E.T. copy. This never makes up its mind what it is, and turns into a real anomaly. John W. Smith, Faye Bolt, C. Jutson Campbell. (VC)

**STAR MAIDENS (1976).** The planet Medusa is dominated by female chauvinist pigs who force men to grovel at their feet, pleading for equal rights. Needed: Men's Lib. Released to TV in two parts. Directed by Wolfgang Storch and James Gatward. Judy Geeson, Christiane Kruger, Pierre Brice, Norman Warwick.

**STAR ODYSSEY (1978).** In this Italian potboiler, aliens auction off "insignificant" planets, with Earth going for the highest price. The inheritors show up over the green planet in a death ship, blasting away. The only man who can save us is a psychic professor surrounded by adventurers, misfits and comedic robots, who seek to destroy the alien ship's metal, Indirium. The humanoids wear metallic suits and blond wigs, props left over from WAR OF THE ROBOTS, a spaghetti import also directed by Al Bradly. Screen science-fiction at its worst, with inane dialogue and a music track that is a joke. The funniest scenes involve a fight between a human and an android boxer and really stupid antics between man-and-wife robots. You have to see one of these to believe they exist. Yanti Somer, Gianni Garko, Sharon Baker.

**STAR PILOTS (1966).** As soon as STAR WARS became a roaring success, an Italian flop, 2+5 MISSION HYDRA, was dusted off, retitled and distributed to unwitting audiences. Three aliens from another galaxy land on Earth to kidnap homo sapiens for a zoo that will open soon in a solar system near you. Directed by Pietro Francisci. Kirk Morris, Gordon Mitchell, Roland Lesarfee, Leontine Snell.

**STAR SLAMMER.** See **PRISON SHIP.** (Captive viewing?)

**STAR TREK.** All the original TV episodes have been issued in cassette format, including five two-in-one specials, and are available in most video stores. So is the famous untelevised pilot; see **CAGE, THE.**

**STAR TREK—THE MOTION PICTURE (1979).** First movie version of the popular TV series was a $40 million epic. But did director Robert Wise pull off an epic? "Trekkies" came away disappointed, feeling it was too talkative and handicapped by weak concepts. Harold Livingston's screenplay—combining the TV episodes "The Changeling" and "The Doomsday Machine"—depicts a cloud-like object on a collision course with Earth and the USS Enterprise speeding from drydock to intercept. Attempts are made to rise above the mock heroics of STAR WARS but it still falls short of being a 2001: A SPACE ODYSSEY with its lack of a living villain and its cloudy characters. The effects are uneven—ranging from excellent (when depicting the cloud's interior) to less-than-adequate (when depicting a San Francisco shuttleport.) The original cast is: William Shatner, Leonard Nimoy, DeForest Kelley, James Doohan, George Takei, Walter Koenig, Nichelle Nichols and Grace Lee Whitney. Stephen Collins and Persis Khambatta are non-regulars. Despite its flaws, this was a worldwide box-office success and began a series of sequels continuing today. (VC)

**STAR TREK II: THE WRATH OF KHAN (1982).** Rejoice! This is truer to the TV series than the first film. A 1967 episode, "Space Seed," serves as the springboard, with the villainous Khan (Ricardo Montalban, playing a crazed superintelligent Earthman) wreaking revenge on Captain Kirk for stranding him years before on a God-forsaken planet. The crew is back (Shatner, Kelley, Doohan, Koenig, Takei, Nichols), but it's Leonard Nimoy who commands center stage with his death scene and burial in space. It was a brilliant gimmick by writer Jack B. Sowards that ensured the film's success and paved the way for a sequel, STAR TREK III: THE SEARCH FOR SPOCK. An enormous success for Paramount, producer Harv Bennett and director Nicholas Meyer. Non-regulars included Kirstie Alley, Bibi Besch, Paul Winfield and Ike Eisenmann. The one individual shoved into the background was creator Gene Roddenberry, who reportedly did not get along with Paramount during the making of the first film and was persona non grata. WRATH OF KHAN is not a classic but its clean-lined effects (by Ken Ralston and the Industrial Light & Magic team) and its unpretentious space-opera yarn make it an A effort worth going to the end of the Universe to see. (VC)

---

*"An avalanche of killer worms! Writhing across the land in a tidal wave of terror!"—Advertisement for **SQUIRM.***

**STAR TREK III: THE SEARCH FOR SPOCK (1984).** This begins where STAR TREK II: THE WRATH OF KHAN left off—with the USS Enterprise returning to Earth, its crew members still grieving over the death of science officer Spock. But while WRATH OF KHAN was almost classic in its depiction of the STAR TREK regulars, this smacks of standard TV plotting and writing. So that it finally resembles an over-inflated one-hour show, brimming with special effects you wish they could have done on TV back in the 1960s. It seems that before he died, Spock transferred the essence of his soul to Dr. McCoy, so they must now return to Genesis (a planet undergoing a speeded-up evolutionary cycle), recover Spock's corpse while fighting off sadistic Klingons, and get back to Vulcan in time to restore the eary alien to life. Almost pure potboiler, with little time for character development, although Trekkies will see plenty of the regulars in action. Leonard Nimoy does a fine job directing—one wishes the script by producer Harve Bennett had contained more emotion and sharp dialogue. Ken Ralston again heads the Industrial Light & Magic team, creating effects that reflect the state-of-the-art level to which this series has ascended. Guest appearances by Mark Lenard as Spock's father, Dame Judith Anderson as the High Priestess of Vulcan, Christopher Lloyd as the Klingon commander. At hand are the regulars: William Shatner, Nimoy, DeForest Kelley, Jimmy Doohan, George Takei, Nichelle Nichols, Walter Koenig. (VC)

**STAR TREK IV: THE VOYAGE HOME (1986).** Unquestionably this is the best of the STAR TREK features, a curiously satisfying blend of story and characters without the sadistic violence of the second and third films. Picking up where THE SEARCH FOR SPOCK ended, this depicts the regulars returning to Earth aboard the Klingon Bird of Prey, while Earth is under siege from an alien space probe. To save Earth, Kirk orders the ship around the sun to travel back in time to the 20th Century to kidnap two humpback whales. Most of the action takes place in San Francisco and the scenes of Kirk, Spock and the others adjusting to modern times are hilarious. A charming idea, beautifully directed by Leonard Nimoy, and a family film in the truest sense, with an ecology message not impinging on entertaining values. Catherine Hicks appears as a whale conservationist. William Shatner, Nimoy, DeForest Kelley, George Takei, James Doohan, Nichelle Nichols, Walter Koenig. (VC)

**STAR VIRGIN (1979).** Adult science-fiction flick set on a faraway planet where the only human left is a robot created by a race of machines. They show her assorted sex scenes, some of which involve a Dracula character. Directed by Linus Gator. Kari Klark, Johnny Harden, Tracy Walton.

**STAR WARS (1977).** Director-writer George Lucas' masterpiece of space opera adventure. Plotwise, it's nothing more than a rehash of FLASH GORDON narratives, but Lucas treats the material with $10 million of respect. Every penny shows in dazzling effects, futuristic gadgets and costumes. There are laser gun battles; a planet called Tatoonie; a hairy space freighter pilot named Chewbacca the Wookie; a spaceship squadron attack on a satellite known as the Death Star; Darth Vader, villainous Dark Lord of the Sith; ships moving at the speed of light; robots and more robots; and a spaceport bar sequence featuring a menagerie of grotesque extraterrestrial life. Laurel-and-Hardy robots (R2D2 and C3PO) provide comedy relief, in some ways becoming more human than the humans. A close look reveals that Lucas has a penchant for objects (call them "toys") and this is like an adolescent fantasy, wrought by adult technology. Lucas wisely chose a cast of refreshing unknowns (Mark Hamill as Luke Skywalker, Harrison Ford as Han Solo, Carrie Fisher as Princess Leia Organa) and added pros Alec Guinness as an aging space warrior and Peter Cushing as Darth Vader's right-hand henchman. John Dykstra supervised vast teams of effects artists; the popular music score is by John Williams. Followed by THE EMPIRE STRIKES BACK and RETURN OF THE JEDI, which completed the first trilogy Lucas has designed to trace the history of the Empire, the Skywalker family, the background of Darth Vader, etc. (VC)

**STARBIRDS (1982).** Space war explodes between Earth and winged creatures from a space station circling Jupiter in this animated U.S.-Japanese cartoon adventure. Focus is on a supership called Dynamo, launched to counter the attack. Directed by Tadao Nagahama and Michael Part.

**STARCHASER: THE LEGEND OF ORIN (1951).** Full-length 3-D cartoon feature (ballyhooed as the first) uneven in its execution, but visually powerful with breathtaking space battles, constant explosions and weapons of tomorrow. Many stereovision effects are outstanding, but characters and storyline smack of Saturday morning cartoons. And it's all too derivative of STAR WARS. It's certainly no Disneyesque film Steven Hahn produced-directed from a screenplay by Jeffrey Scott: Orin is a slave digging for power-giving crystals in Mineworld, ruled by robots with electric whips and the tyrant Zygon. Orin breaks out to the land above, undergoing adventures with an obligatory female, a blind youth, a roguish adventurer in the Han Solo vein and a spaceship operated by Arthur the Computer. Many background paintings are well conceived, others less so. Some panning effects, which should have been sensational in 3-D, tend to go jittery or blurry. Parts of the film, however, move at warp factor five, making up for technical and story defects. One of the best scenes has Orin being manhandled by a scraggly group of "mandroids," half-human, half-machine creatures in need of spare parts. This cartoon is a must for all 3-D addicts. Voices by Joe Colligan, Carmen Argenziano, Noelle North. (VC)

**STARCRASH (1979).** A return to the delightfully campy dialogue and plotlines of old-fashioned serials. The universe is in the grip of the evil, cackling Count Zarth Arn (Joe Spinell) and only Stella Starr, a space pilot who wears high-heeled boots while in warp drive, can stop him with the help of alien navigator Akton and Elle the Robot, who speaks like a mentally deficient Texan. As played by Caroline Munro, wearing black leather underwear, Stella stops the starshow. Marjoe Gortner is her male partner and Christopher Plummer is The Emperor of Space. A galactic wreck for adults, but kids 6 to 18 will shriek with delight. Flash Gordon never had a girl like Caroline . . . Directed by Lewis Coates, an Italian better known in his native land as Luigi Cozzi. (VC)

**STARCROSSED (1985).** TV-movie ripoff of STARMAN, only featuring a female E.T. in humanoid form being befriended by a sympathetic Earthling male. A secret government organization is after the stranded alien (Belinda Bauer) and there are also two of her own kind stalking her with super-deadly zap laser guns, which means plenty of explosions, car chases and other action fare from writer-director Jeffrey Bloom. There's an attempt at a poignant love story between Bauer and James Spader but the cheapness of the effects and the lack of an interesting production look doom this two-hour project to the graveyard of uninspired time killers. Jacqueline Brookes, Peter Kowanko, Clark Johnson.

**STARFLEET: THE THALIAN SPACE WARS (198?).** Animated science-fiction space adventures depicting interplanetary warfare.

**STARFLIGHT: THE PLANE THAT COULDN'T LAND (1983).** Mild science-fiction theme (a hypersonic transport aircraft) is overpowered by standard TV-movie plot gimmicks about passengers trapped in flight with time and oxygen running out and other suspense ploys that won't have anyone on the edge of their seats. Directed by Jerry Jameson. Lee Majors, Hal Linden, Lauren Hutton, Robert Webber, Ray Milland, Jocelyn Brando, Tess Harper, Gail Strickland.

**STARK MAD (1929).** Lloyd Bacon film, released in silent and sound versions; pretty hoary by today's standards, but an interesting piece nevertheless. A Mayan temple houses a giant ape, whose cries startle the obligatory jungle expedition. Also involved: a Hairy Taloned Monster, H. B. Warner, Irene Rich, Claude Gillingwater and Louise Fazenda.

**STARLIGHT SLAUGHTER. See EATEN ALIVE.** (Chomp!)

**STARMAN (1984).** One of the few science-fiction movies of the 1980s with as much "heart" and emotion as effects—not quite as triumphant as E.T. but working in that direction. When a ship crashlands on Earth, its pilot transforms into the embodiment of deceased Jeff Bridges, whose wife (Karen Allen) must now accompany on his odyssey to safety. Starman has the powers of resurrection, among other things, and there's a Jesus Christ parable in the Bruce A. Evans-Raynold

**KAREN ALLEN WATCHES A TRANSFORMATION IN 'STARMAN'**

Gideon screenplay. What builds is a love between Earthling and alien, which culminates in her impregnation—the first joining of two races. On their trail is sympathetic scientist Charles Martin Smith and a ruthless government agent, Richard Jaeckel, who's after Starman for the usual wrong reasons. John Carpenter directed with a feeling for his characters, injecting as much comedy as the serious theme allowed. A commendable effort, with Dick Smith, Stan Winston and Rick Baker contributing topnotch effects, many executed by Industrial Light & Magic. (VC)

**STARSHIP INVASIONS (1977).** Christopher Lee, playing a humanoid alien, Captain Ramses, in a silly costume, battles another race of extraterrestrials in order to invade Earth. Robert Vaughn is equally wasted as a UFO expert investigating a series of sightings followed by mass suicides. No one seems to be trying very hard to raise above the level of a juvenile Z movie. A tax shelter deal for writer-director Ed Hunt? Daniel Pilon, Victoria Johnson.

**STEEL KEY, THE (1953).** Drably conventional British thriller about spies trying to steal a process that hardens steel. Audiences should steel themselves against boredom. Directed by Robert Baker, scripted by John Gilling. Terence Morgan, Joan Rice, Raymond Lovell, Dianne Foster.

**STEPFORD WIVES, THE (1975).** Superior horror film with an intelligent William Goldman screenplay (from Ira Levin's fine novel) and thoughtful direction by Bryan Forbes. This says more about our society's obsession with mechanical things than dozens of so-called relevant movies, and it says it in a frightening way: In a complacent upper-crust community in New England a conspiracy is afoot among the men to replace their independent wives with robot-controlled humanoid imitations. And the mastermind is a former employee of Disney (think about that one). Katharine Ross discovers her friends (Paula Prentiss and Tina Louise, among others) are automated replacements and the suspense builds to a rousing finish right out of FRANKENSTEIN. Owen Roizman's cinematography adds to the atmosphere and dimension of this exciting, scary piece. Patrick O'Neal, Nanette Newman, Peter Masterson.

**STEPHEN KING'S NIGHT SHIFT COLLECTION.** Videocassette exclusive containing two half-hour adaptations from King's 1978 short story collection, NIGHT SHIFT. "Woman in the Room," written and directed by Frank Darabont, is the simple story of a young attorney whose mother is dying, and who contemplates euthanasia. A strong mood piece with little plot, produced in 1983. The second, "Boogeyman," written-directed by Jeffrey C. Schiro, is about a father (Michael Reid) who suspects a "boogeyman" murdered his children and put his wife into a nuthouse. He goes to a psychiatrist (Bert Linder) for help. Nice twist ending. Again heavy on ambience. Latter short produced in 1982 at the New York University School of Undergraduate Film. (VC)

**STEPHEN KING'S SILVER BULLET.** Videocassette title for SILVER BULLET. (Hi yo, King, away!)

**STEREO (1969).** A 65-minute, 16mm black and whiter shot for $3500 in Canada by David Cronenberg. This first effort is set in a bleak institution where Dr. Stringfellow conducts experiments in ESP. While the photography is crisp, the narrative is presented in voiceover, without synch dialogue or music. The pedantic passages are pieces of pseudoscientific information as if taken from a medical journal. Yet one can see the seminal beginnings for Cronenberg's later films. Stringfellow is operating on human guinea pigs to release their psychic powers and discovers that sexual activity results in better communications. He begins a new experiment to prove there can be love between subject and doctor. Very odd softcore love scenes follow. Strictly for completists. Others will be bewildered and/or bored.

**STILL OF THE NIGHT (1982).** Sophisticated, intelligent whodunit in the psychological vein, detailing how psychiatrist Roy Scheider tracks a slasher killer who murdered a patient. It's writer-director Robert Benton's homage to Hitchcock with a few slasher-flick touches added—a quiet, underplayed approach as Scheider suspects the killer is a beautiful blonde (Meryl Streep) who was having an affair with the murdered patient. The symbolic dream sequence is out of Hitchcock's SPELLBOUND; even the Streep character recalls Kim Novak in VERTIGO. Jessica Tandy contributes a small role as Scheider's mother, a fellow psychiatrist who helps him ferret out clues. Little gore or violence—this could be the only cerebral slasher movie ever made. Idea by Benton and David Newman. Joe Grifasi, Sara Botsford. (VC)

**STING OF DEATH (1966).** Mad biologist John Vella turns himself into an underwater monster with tentacles that strangle. The kind of horror drama it's impossible to get all wrapped up in. Directed by William Grefe. Neil Sedaka,

Valerie Hawkins, Joe Morrison, John Vella.

**STOLEN AIRSHIP (1969).** Czech fantasy directed by Karel Zeman is a loose adaptation of Jules Verne themes, depicting children at the turn of the century who steal an airship and encounter Captain Nemo. Michael Pospisil, Hanus Bor.

**STOP PRESS GIRL (1949).** Sally Ann Howes has a strong effect on men, but what she does to machinery you won't believe: After 15 minutes of exposure to the lovely lass, every gadget in sight breaks down. Jolly good British fun; our bowlers are off to director Michael Barry and supporting players Gordon Jackson, Basil Radford, Naunton Wayne, James Robertson Justice and Kenneth More.

**STORY OF MANKIND, THE (1957).** Debate rages between the Devil (Vincent Price in a cutaway and red ascot) and the Spirit of Man (the earnest Ronald Colman) as to whether or not Earth is worth keeping in the solar system. In flashbacks, Satan shows man's mistakes, Colman points out his admirable traits. The result is a spectacle of history in which Peter Lorre is nutty Nero, Dennis Hopper is Napoleon, Marie Wilson is a silly Marie Antoinette, Reginald Gardiner is an aging Shakespeare and Francis X. Bushman is a pompous Moses. Unfortunately, there is no sense of style on the part of producer-director Irwin Allen. Only when Harpo Marx portrays Sir Isaac Newton, slicing apples with his harp, and when Groucho Marx barters for Manhattan and ogles shapely squaws does this experiment have vitality or enchantment. The cast goes on and on: Cesar Romero, Henry Daniell, William Schallert, Ziva Rodann, Agnes Moorehead, John Carradine, Virginia Mayo, Charles Coburn, Helmut Dantine . . .

**STORY OF THREE LOVES, THE (1953).** Trilogy of romanticized tales, bittersweet and lyrical, is an excellent MGM vehicle for several stars, capturing an almost mystical quality that permeates the moonstruck characters. Although only one story is fantasy, the whole film has an undercurrent of magic, as if the characters are floating in a fantasy realm of true love. "Mademoiselle" is a whimsical vignette in which governess Leslie Caron recites love poetry while trying to teach young Ricky Nelson, who rebels against her smothering care. With the help of witch Ethel Barrymore, he turns into a full-grown man and, controlled by impulses he doesn't understand, proceeds to fall in love with Ms Caron. This is a wonderful segment directed by Vincent Minnelli, with Farley Granger as the starry-eyed "man-boy." The other stories, "The Jealous Lover" (James Mason, Moira Shearer) and

**KATHARINE ROSS IN
'THE STEPFORD WIVES'**

"Equilibrium" (Kirk Douglas, Pier Angeli), are more serious but still have a magical quality (enhanced by the lush music of Miklos Rozsa) that will find favor with fantasy lovers.

**STRAIGHT ON TILL MORNING (1972).** Obscure Hammer psychothriller designed for ambience and characterization as it unfolds leisurely. It is fascinating because of imaginative cross-cutting and its sympathy for a man who records the voices of his murder victims. Director Peter Collinson is trying to be arty yet it works—thanks not only to the editing tempo but to the moods of Rita Tushingham (as a mousy, shy young thing) and the killer, Shane Briant, a confused psychotic who befriends Rita, then draws her into his spider's lair. The film, unfortunately, has a downbeat, unsatisfying ending. Produced by Michael Carreras.

**STRAIT-JACKET (1964).** An original Robert Bloch screenplay and one of his favorites—producer-director William Castle left most of it intact. Less gimmicked up than most of Castle's films of the period, although it still has its share of red herrings. Joan Crawford allegedly chopped off the heads of her husband and lover several years ago and is now returning home in an attempt to start a fresh life. But new murders involving axes and rolling heads are committed and Crawford might be committed again—she thinks she's going bats. Ah, but you, discerning viewer, know better. Don't miss it, just for Crawford's performance. Diane Baker, Leif Erickson, Rochelle Hudson, George Kennedy. (VC)

**STRANGE ADVENTURE (1933).** Monogram quickie set in the typically strange house where a hooded killer strikes at victims. Too old to be either strange or an adventure. Directed by Phil Whitman. William V. Mong, Regis Toomey, Dwight Frye, June Clyde, Lucille LaVerne.

**STRANGE AND DEADLY OCCURRENCE, THE (1974).** Is the mansion of Robert Stack and Vera Miles haunted? Or is someone playing tricks on their hyper-imaginations? TV-movie from producer Sandor Stern creeps around the issue too long. John Llewellyn Moxie directed. L.Q. Jones, Herb Edelman, Margaret Willock, Dena Dietrich.

**STRANGE BEHAVIOR (1981).** Aussie-New Zealand production (also known as DEAD KIDS) in which a mad, vengeful doctor murders high school students after conducting weird experiments on their bodies. The acting is often overblown and the plotting by producer Michael Condon and director Michael Laughlin out of a horror pulp, but the film has a sense of freshness and features a strong cast: Michael Murphy, Louise Fletcher, Fiona Lewis, Scott Brady. (VC)

**STRANGE BREW (1983).** Dave Thomas and Rick Moranis portray Bob and Doug McKenzie, characters they created on TV, in this whacky roller-coaster-ride-of-a-movie in which mad doctor Max Von Sydow plans to conquer the world by addicting everyone with a new brand of beer. Uncontrolled chaos, directed by Thomas and Moranis, who also wrote (if it can be called that) the berserk script. (VC)

**STRANGE CARGO (1940).** Many were puzzled over this Joseph L. Mankiewicz production based on Richard Sale's allegorical novel, NOT TOO NARROW, TOO DEEP. While on the surface it is a Devil's Island prison picture, it is also a story in which each character is symbolic. Ian Hunter, for example, projects certain Jesus Christ characteristics. Now that we've given you an important clue, you figure out the rest. Joan Crawford, Clark Gable, Peter Lorre, Paul Lucas, Albert Dekker, Paul Fix. Directed by Frank Borzage.

**STRANGE CASE OF DR. JEKYLL AND MR. HYDE, THE (1968).** U.S.-Canadian TV production produced by Dan Curtis and starring Jack Palance as one of the most effective Jekyll-Hydes in the cinematic history of Robert Louis Stevenson's horror classic about schizophrenia and drugs. Directed by Charles Jarrott. The makeup is by Dick Smith. Denholm Elliott, Torin Thatcher, Oscar Homolka, Leo Genn, Billie Whitelaw, Duncan Lamont, Gillie Fenwich. (VC)

**STRANGE CASE OF DR. RX, THE (1942).** Insidious-type killing agents (poisoned needles, undetectable venom, etc.) are employed by a doctor who kills only those who have escaped imprisonment through legal loopholes. Predictable red herring-packaged Universasl potboiler finally has the self-ap-

**BLAST IT!: ONE OF THE STORMTROOPERS IN THE ORIGINAL 'STAR WARS' (1977)**

**THE JAWA CREATURE OF TATOOINE**

**DEATH INVADER DARTH VADER**

pointed avenger desiring to transfer the brain of Patric Knowles into the cranium of a gorilla. Lionel Atwill figures prominently as Dr. Fish. Directed by William Nigh. Anne Gwynne, Mantan Moreland, Shemp Howard.

**STRANGE CONFESSION** (1945). Another "Inner Sanctum" programmer from Universal, starring Lon Chaney Jr. as a tormented man being victimized by a drug manufacturer. Said to be based on the play THE MAN WHO RECLAIMED HIS HEAD, first adapted to the movies in 1934 with Claude Rains, but the M. Coates Webster script goes off in its own directions. Directed by John Hoffman. Brenda Joyce, Milburn Stone, Lloyd Bridges, Addison Richards, George Chandler.

**STRANGE DOOR, THE** (1951). Robert Louis Stevenson's "The Sire de Maletroit's Door" serves as the plot for this torture-chamber programmer, with Charles Laughton as an elegantly insane 18th Century nobleman who chews up the

Iron Maidens and rushes through his dialogue as though he wanted to get on to more prestigious projects. Quite histrionic, as subtle as a case of Bubonic Plague. Laughton so oozes evil that his henchman (Boris Karloff) turns out to be the good guy in comparison. Joseph Pevney directs with florid flourish. Sally Forrest, Michael Pate, Alan Napier.

**STRANGE EXORCISM OF LYNN HART, THE.** See **DADDY'S DEADLY DARLING.** (Oink! Oink!)

**STRANGE HOLIDAY, THE** (1942). This Arch Oboler film (he wrote and directed) is based on his LIGHTS OUT radio play, "This Precious Freedom," in which a vacationing businessman returns to his hometown to find a fascist dictatorship in power. The surprise ending will come as a disappointment to those who haven't already suspected a cheap trick is being played on them. Claude Rains, Barbara Bates.

**STRANGE ILLUSION, THE** (1945). Edgar G. Ulmer appreciators will be delighted to discover this minor PRC quickie in which teen-ager James Lydon dreams his father's death wasn't an accident. He suspects a man he sees in his dreams is also the man wooing his unsuspecting mother. Warren William, Regis Toomey, Sally Eiler, George Reed.

**STRANGE IMPERSONATION (1946).** Doctor experimenting with new pain- killing drug finds his patients undergo terrifying nightmares. Directed by Anthony Mann. Brenda Marshall, William Gargan, Hillary Brooke, Lyle Talbot.

**STRANGE INVADERS (1983).** In the style of monster invader movies of the 1950s, a fun-blend of comedy and thrills, special effects and chases in telling its genre-inspired tale of outer space creatures plotting our overthrow who have settled in a small midwestern town in 1958 to assume our bodies. Paul LeMat gets involved when he discovers his ex-wife is one of them and now her pals are coming to look for her daughter, who's an alien too. Well, half an alien. LeMat and Nancy Allen end up on the run, warning others of the plot. Good direction by Michael Laughlin, who co-wrote with William Condon. Michael Lerner, Louise Fletcher, Fiona Lewis, Kenneth Tobey, June Lockhart. (VC)

**STRANGE MR. GREGORY, THE (1946).** Weird magician Edmund Lowe, in love with beautiful Jean Rogers, stops at nothing to possess her—even undergoing a self-induced trance to simulate death. The cast (Frank Reicher, Don Douglas, Jonathan Hale) walks around Monogram sound stages in a similar stupor. Directed by Phil Rosen.

**STRANGE NEW WORLD (1975).** Episodic adventures in which astronauts—in suspended animation for 180 years in deep space—return to discover Earth has divided into odd cults following nuclear holocaust. Hence, three separate stories, pared from an original two-hour format to 90 minutes. Part of Gene Roddenberry's trilogy of pilot failures that include GENESIS II and PLANET EARTH. John Saxon, Kathleen Miller, James Olson. Directed by Robert Butler.

**STRANGE PEOPLE (1933).** Indeed, the people who have gathered in an old dark house are all members of a jury that once sentenced a man to death. Was that man innocent? Surely his returned spirit is angry as he warns the jury that death is at hand. Outside, wind and rain and lightning . . . as creaky as the staircase a dark figure descends . . . directed by Richard Thorpe. John Darrow, Hale Hamilton.

**STRANGE POSSESSION OF MRS. OLIVER, THE (1978).** Richard Matheson has fashioned an intriguing tale of dual personality. Karen Black is a bored housewife married to an equally boring husband-lawyer (George Hamilton). She begins to get the yen to wear a low-cut red blouse, blonde wig and slinky skirt. She is also compelled to buy a house in a beach community, where it would appear a woman who looks just like her once resided—before her tragic demise. Director Gordon Hessler builds the mystery with a deft camera, creating ambiguities to intrigue us: Is Black undergoing possession, reincarnation or what? Supernatural mood blends with psychological thrills. Nice twist ending.

**STRANGE TALES/RAY BRADBURY THEATER (1986).** Videocassette reissue of episodes shown on Showtime's RAY BRADBURY THEATER. Three literary classics have been handsomely adapted by Bradbury: "The Town Where No One Got Off" (with Jeffrey Goldblum), "The Screaming Woman" (Drew Barrymore) and "Banshee" (Peter O'Toole).

**STRANGE WORLD OF PLANET X.** See **COSMIC MONSTERS.** (X marks the splotch)

**STRANGENESS, THE (1985).** Inspired by THE BOOGENS, this is still uninspired "lost mine" stuff as a team of geologists enters the legendary Golden Spike Mine, closed years before when workmen mysteriously vanished. There's a cruel boss, a writer who talks in deathless prose, an experienced old mine hand and other cliched types. Long stretches of nothing, extended periods of ennui, with an occasional glimpse of a tentacled creature animated by stop motion. No feeling of menace as the film plods to a routine climax. Directed by David Michael Hillman, without any sense of "strangeness." Dan Lunham, Terri Berland. (VC)

**STRANGER, THE (1973).** Pilot for a proposed (but unsold) series as American astronaut Glenn Corbett, sole survivor of his space flight team, wakes up on a planet identical to Earth (but it's really an alien world on the far side of the sun). He tries to return to home with the help of turncoat scientist Lew Ayres and sympathetic femme Sharon Acker while corrupt power figures Cameron Mitchell and Steve Franken track him. Despite cliches and standard TV values, Gerald Sanford's script zips along and director Lee H. Katzin keeps his characters moving so you won't have much time to wonder why cars on an alien world have California plates. Cameos by George Coulouris and Dean Jagger.

**STRANGER FROM VENUS (1954).** Eerie British shocker in which Helmut Dantine is a Venusian who arrives to warn us we must straighten out our planetary conflicts—or else a galactic federation will blow us to bits. A lot like THE DAY THE EARTH STOOD STILL. Ironically, Patricia Neal stars in this film too. Directed by Burt Balaban. Derek Bond, Cyril Luckham, Marigold Russell. (VC)

**STRANGER IN OUR HOUSE (1978).** Exploitation director Wes Craven tones down his "taste" for this TV-movie of demonic possession. Although EXORCIST star Linda Blair doesn't levitate or spin her head 360 degrees, she is the victim again, this time of a cousin who uses supernatural powers against Linda's household. Lee Purcell, Jeremy Slate, Carol Lawrence. On video as **SUMMER OF FEAR.**

**STRANGER IN THE HOUSE.** See **BLACK CHRISTMAS.**

**STRANGER IS WATCHING, A (1982).** Unsettling mixture of suspense and excruciating violence, directed by Sean Cunningham, the mastermind behind FRIDAY THE 13TH, PART I. Even though this is a better-crafted movie and has a superior plot (from a book by Mary Higgins Clark), it was an utter flop. What Cunningham fails to realize is that audiences prefer slasher movies in which the killer is a faceless super-

*Spa Fon?*

*Squa Tront!*

**JUST TWO OF THE STRANGE INVADERS**

## KATE MULGREW:
## 'A STRANGER IS WATCHING'

natural killing machine. That rule is broken as we follow the killer (Rip Torn) step by step when he kidnaps a TV reporter and a young girl and hides them in the New York subway system. Also, the reporter (Kate Mulgrew) is so well drawn that it becomes unbearable to watch when a screwdriver is thrust into her stomach. Cunningham might have done better to stress the kidnaping plot and the capital punishment aspects, going for inherent suspense in the Hitchcock tradition. James Naughton, Barbara Baxley, Roy Poole. (VC)

**STRANGER ON THE THIRD FLOOR (1940).** Director Boris Ingster has a true sense of style and indulges in surrealistic camera angles for dream sequences in this horror thriller starring Peter Lorre as a homicidal maniac. Call it German Expressionistic. Lorre is excellent in the role and makes up for some of the weaknesses in Frank Partos' screenplay. There's a very strange trial sequence too. Elisah Cook Jr., John McGuire, Margaret Tallicet, Cliff Clark. (VC)

**STRANGER WITHIN, THE (1974).** Richard Matheson's teleplay concerns a woman (Barbara Eden) whose actions are controlled by her unborn baby. Is the child an alien? A supernatural force? Not one of Matheson's best . . . Standard TV-movie production values at a plodding pace. Directed by Lee Philips. George Grizzard is the puzzled husband. (VC)

**STRANGERS (1980).** Explorers in a Colorado cave come across strange blue stones linked to a recent space capsule mission— only to find something monstrous lurking in the dark. Hee hee hee hee hee. Belinda Mayne, Marc Bodin.

**STRANGER'S GUNDOWN, THE (1975).** Blazing-sixguns Western of the Spaghetti school, zeroing in on a cold-blooded gunfighter who blasts everyone in sight. Is this enigmatic holster-slapper a spirit from the grave, impervious to ordinary lead poisoning? He's called Django the Bastard, and lives up to his name. Part of an Italian series. Directed-written by Sergio Garrone.

**STRANGERS IN PARADISE (1986).** In 1939, a Nazi undergoes suspended animation, awakening in the 1980s to renew his terror. Written-produced-directed by Ulli Lommel. (VC)

**STRANGLER, THE (1963).** Misunderstood, insecure fat man with a mother's complex chokes nurses to death because they symbolize keeping his bedridden mother alive. Victor Buono and Ellen Corby are well cast in the roles and director

Burt Topper works diligently with Bill Ballinger's screenplay, but the low budget strangles everyone in the end. (VC)

**STRANGLER OF BLACKMOOR CASTLE, THE (1960).** Creaky Edgar Wallace thriller features assorted West German character types rushing through a drafty English castle trying to avoid a costumed neck-squeezer who cackles with glee as he murders them one by one. Directed by Harald Reinl. Karin Dor, Hans Nielsen, Ingmar Zeisberg.

**STRANGLER OF THE SWAMP (1946).** German director Frank Wisbar adapted his fantasy, FERRYMAN MARIA, into this PRC supernatural thriller, low on budget but high on style and decaying ambience. A ferryboat operator has been murdered and now the swamp country is terrorized by the "walking dead" shape of Charles Middleton (Ming of the FLASH GORDON serials) who, one by one, hangs those responsible for his death. Rosemary LaPlanche is a beautiful actress who overcomes the limited swamp sets and a perfunctory romance with Blake Edwards (later to become a producer-director) to help this rise out of the minor leagues to become a miniclassic in atmosphere. Given more money, Wisbar might have made it better. Frank Conlon, Effie Parnell.

**STRANGLERS OF BOMBAY (1959).** Dramatic recreation of the true story of the Kali devil cult and how the British in the 1820s finally put down the cult followers, who murdered for the sheer joy of spilling blood. A crisp, lean Hammer production, directed by Terence Fisher with a touch of the macabre and starring Allan Cuthbertson and Guy Rolfe. Not for the squeamish. Marne Maitland, Jan Holden.

**STREET TRASH (1987).** Strange booze making the rounds of New York's Skid Row turns derelicts and other alkies into bubbling puddles of goo in this low-budget feature shot in New York by director Jim Muro, who first made a 16mm short subject to get financing. It's pretty disgusting as the special effects team has a field day, but anyone with a modicum of good taste will avoid this like the Bubonic Plague. Mike Lackey, Vic Noto.

**STREETS OF FIRE (1984).** Odd rock-action movie, set in a U.S. city in an unspecified time that amalgamates many styles. A rock 'n roll star in this strange landscape, played by Diane Lane, is kidnapped by thugs called The Bombers. Boyfriend Michael Pare pursues with tough broad Amy Madigan tagging along, her dialogue some of the best ever written for a hard-boiled chick. The action is well staged by director Arthur Hill, who co-wrote the outre screenplay with Larry Gross, and the urban streets are a mixture of modish motifs, giving the film a unique ambience. There are ten original songs with a throbbing rock beat provided by Ry Cooder's music. Rick Moranis, Richard Lawson. (VC)

**STRONGEST MAN IN THE WORLD, THE (1975).** Disney teen comedy, sequel to THE COMPUTER WORE TENNIS SHOES. Kurt Russell discovers a formula for superhuman powers. There's funny weightlifting scenes, but it's predictable fun and games. Eve Arden, Cesar Romero (repeating his role as a crook who steals formulas), Phil Silvers, William Schallert. Directed by Vincent McEveety.

**STRYKER (1983).** Low-budget quickie from the typewriter of Howard R. Cohen (of SATURDAY THE 14TH and SPACE RAIDERS infamy) that is little more than a swipe of ROAD WARRIOR as we leap into a post-Armageddon world where tribes of strangely dressed survivors are fighting over water. Stryker (Steve Sandor) is a grotesque, unadorable hero along the lines of Mad Max and engenders absolutely zero sympathy. This mess was directed without care by Cirio H. Santiago in the Philippines, and it's one corny action scene after the other. Andria Savio, William Ostrander. (VC)

**STUDENT BODIES (1981).** Spoof on the slasher trend has the courage of its convictions, but its humor is on such a sophomoric level that this becomes unstomachable, as bad as the films it ribs. Interesting as a parody, but of little substance. Mickey Rose wrote-directed. Kristen Riter, Matt Goldsby, Richard Brando (as an off-screen menace called The Breather), Mimi Weddell, Joe Flood. (VC)

**STUDY IN TERROR, A (1966).** Who would be better qualified to deduce the identity of that chap who knives his way through the London streets, Jack the Ripper, than the in-domitable Sherlock Holmes and his sycophant, Dr. Watson. Ripping good show (written by Donald and Derek Ford) with busty prostitutes shrouded by the Whitechapel district fog and a somewhat conceited Holmes played by John Neville. Donald Houston assists as Dr. Watson. Quick, Watson, the Morning Express! Directed stylishly by James Hill.

**STUFF, THE (1985).** Another strange, strange satirical horror story from the bizarre, bizarre mind of writer-producer-director Larry Cohen. A bubbly, gooey substance pops up from the earth and becomes a delicious yogurt-like dessert called The Stuff. When industrial spy Michael Moriarty tries to learn the formula, he uncovers the real truth: The dreams that the Stuff are made of are nightmares. It's a living substance that takes over mind and body, oozing out of gaping mouths and attacking its enemies in a flowing wave of glup. It's kind of THE BLOB, sort of. Cohen treats this horror premise as a joke. One minute he's reminding us of fluoride in water and poisonous preservatives in food, in the next he's spoofing the military and advertising world. His concept is a hodgepodge of ideas never fully focused. Andrea Marcovicci portrays the marketing expert-love interest and Paul Sorvino is the carica-ture of an Army officer. Patrick O'Neal, Garrett Morris, Scott Bloom, Alexander Scourby (in his last role). Jim Danforth and David Allen worked on the goo-boo effects. (VC)

**SUCCUBUS (1969).** Beware heavy cuts by TV censors, for this German film directed by Jesus Franco is X-rated. Noth-ing hardcore, you understand, just bare bosoms and sugges-tions, rather than depictions, of sordid sexual acts surround-ing a night club entertainer who simulates torture and inter-course during her "number." The Devil arrives (shown in double exposure) and taunts her, forcing her to perform mur-der during her nitery routine. Howard Vernon, Jack Taylor, Adrian Hoven, Janine Reynaud, Nathalie Ford.

**SUDDENLY, LAST SUMMER (1960).** We include this be-cause of one of the most bizarre acts of cannibalism im-aginable—a homosexual youth who mistreats his sexual partners and is "eaten" alive. All symbolic, of course, since it is based on a Tennessee Williams play. Williams and Gore Vidal collaborated on the script for director Joseph L. Mankiewicz. Elizabeth Taylor, beautiful sister of the homosexual, is used to lure young boys to the beach in Mexico. Now she is in an insane asylum, threatened with a lobotomy operation because the youth's mother, Katharine

Hepburn, doesn't want the truth known about her son. Only headshrinker Montgomery Clift can get at the truth. Unforget-tably strange movie as only Williams can write them. Albert Dekker, Mercedes McCambridge, Gary Raymond. (VC)

**SUGAR COOKIES (1977).** After a pornie filmmaker tricks a sexy model to commit suicide in front of the camera, a friend of the dead girl wreaks her revenge. Directed by Theodore Gershuny. Lynn Lowry, Monique Van Vooren. (VC)

**SUGAR HILL (1974).** Black exploitation pic depicting black zombies getting revenge on Honkie White Bastards. Marki Bey (certainly not related to Turhan) seeks the vengeance after her boyfriend is knocked off by a Mafia group. Don Pedro Colley is the Baron called back from death as her in-strument of revenge. Robert (YORGA) Quarry is involved. Directed by Paul Maslansky. Betty Anne Rees.

**SUICIDE CULT (1977).** The CIA, using astrology as a science, discovers a way to forecast everyone's future. One mad scientist delves into the issue of Jesus Christ's Second Coming and finds himself doing battle with a devil cult. Directed by Jim Glickenhouse. Bob Byrd. (VC)

**SUICIDE MISSION (1971).** A Mexican wrestler in droopy trunks and a silver mask, Santo, grunts and groans through another hapless assignment—viewers will surely hope he won't come back alive. But no such luck. Directed by Federico Curiel. Lorena Velazquez, Elsa Cardenas.

**SUMMER OF FEAR.** Videocassette title for **STRANGER IN OUR HOUSE.** (Home from the chill?)

**SUMMER OF SECRETS (1976).** Australian film is difficult to categorize or describe—it begins as a psychological thriller about a boy and girl being terrorized by an eccentric, then shifts gears to probe a bizarre variance on the Frankenstein Monster theme. Too ponderous and talkative to be commer-cial, too unfocused and pseudointellectual to appeal to the thinking man. Directed by Jim Sharman, who helmed THE ROCKY HORROR PICTURE SHOW. Arthur Dignam, Rufus Colllins, Nell Campbell, Kate Fitzpatrick. (VC)

**SUPER FUZZ (1980).** U.S.-Italian production so dumb and innocuously good-natured that it becomes enjoyable as a Florida cop (Terence Hill, Italian spaghetti-Western star) is exposed to a rocketship explosion and develops superhuman powers—telepathy, rapid body movement, etc. Partner Ernest Borgnine flips trying to deal with these talents, and his

'THE STUFF': THE STUFFING THAT EXPLOITATION IS STUFFED WITH

comedy timing enhances an otherwise vapid, empty showcase. The film's climax degenerates into the broadest of chase slapstick; yet, somehow, that sense of playfulness prevents SUPER FUZZ from becoming totally negligible. Directed by Sergio Corbucci. Joanne Dru, Marc Lawrence. Borgnine starred in two TV pilots with a similar theme, FUTURE COP and COPS AND ROBIN. (VC)

**SUPER VAN (1977).** Lamar Card directed this obscure vehicle about a solar-powered vehicle equipped with a laser zap gun. Poor man's BIG BUS? Keith Saylor, Mark Schneider, Morgan Woodward, Katie Saylor.

**SUPERARGO AND THE FACELESS GIANTS (1967).** Better this should have been titled SUPERARGO AND THE BRAINLESS PRODUCERS. An Italian-Spanish potboiler—nonsense about a special agent mastering the art of mind control with the help of a one-time lama. Athletes turned into

interesting variation on "The Most Dangerous Game," but it's just superdull. Produced by Aubrey Schenck, written-directed by George Schenck. Viz Diaz, Jose Romulo.

**SUPERBUG, SUPER AGENT (1976).** Witless attempt by the Germans to rip off Disney's THE LOVE BUG. Dudu the Beetle is a computerized Volkswagen which can talk, swim and camouflage itself as a rock. Consider director Rudolf Zehetgruber's talents non-existent. The dubbing is atrocious, the editing is sloppy beyond belief, the acting totally indifferent. As dead as a disconnected battery.

**SUPERGIRL (1971).** Stacked chick from outer space tries to warn us of an alien invasion—Frenchmen get so carried away by her voluptuousness they forget the threat and try to get the babe in the sack for some uh-la-la. Just goes to prove that you *can* keep a good Frenchman down. Directed by Rudolf Thome. Iris Berben, Marquand Bohm.

**HELEN SLATER AS SUPERGIRL; FAYE DUNAWAY AS SELENA THE SLIMY VILLAINESS**

mummy robots are inflicting damage on the world—as much as this will damage your brain. A sequel to SUPERARGO VS. DIABOLICUS. Directed by Paolo Bianchini. Ken Wood (his real name is Giovanni Cianfriglia), Guy Madison, Liz Barrett, Diana Lorys, Thomas Blanco.

**SUPERARGO VS. DIABOLICUS (1968).** First in the Italo-Spanish SUPERARGO series, a heap of brainrot about a mind-controlling spy who also has the power of levitation in his fight against a uranium thief (Gerhard Tichey) plotting to take over the world. Ken (Giovanni Cianfriglia) Wood, as limber as the petrified forest, portrays Superargo. Empty cranium vs. dull uranium. Gerard Tichy, Monica Randall.

**SUPERBEAST (1972).** Antoinette Bower joins Harry Lauter in the Philippines for an unimaginative story about an experimenting doctor who turns criminals into wild beasts which then serve as targets for big-game hunters. Sounds like an

**SUPERGIRL (1984).** Wild and woolly Alexander Salkind production in the SUPERMAN—THE MOVIE tradition, featuring wonderful flying scenes and expensive effects. Kara (daughter of Zoltar, brother of Superman's father) accidentally loses the Omega Hedran, a life-giving object that spells doom for Argo City (on the planet Krypton) unless she can recover it. Jumping aboard the Binar Shoot, a vehicle for passing through the Sixth Dimension, Kara (Helen Slater) comes to Earth, assumes the guise of college girl Linda Lee and engages in adventures with Selena, a wicked witch (beautifully essayed by Faye Dunaway) who uses the Hedran to conjure up evil forces. What's lacking in David Odell's episodic script are strong relationships . . . it's just one incredible event after another, with no attempt at cohesive logic, and even a little logic is needed in the wildest of fantasies. What saves this is its visual style (thanks to cinematographer Alan Hume) and Dunaway's flamboyant

## He's a Real Super Fella

**GEORGE REEVES AND NOELL NEILL: THE TELEVISION SUPERMAN AND LOIS LANE**

sorceress. She proclaims herself "The ultimate siren of Endor," and becomes Hollywood's greatest greater-than-life villainess. The production is also aided by Peter O'Toole (as Kara's father) who reaches Shakespearean heights when he's lost in the Phantom Zone and turns to alcoholism. Slater performs well in her debut role, considering whom she's up against. Effects by Derek Meddings and Roy Fields. Music by Jerry Goldsmith. Directed by Jeannot Szwarc. Mia Farrow appears briefly as Supergirl's mother and Brenda Vaccaro is whimsical as Selena's right-hand gal. Peter Cook, Simon Ward, Hart Bochner, Mia Farrow. (VC)

**SUPERKIDS** (1978/79). Two British TV-movies for children, edited back-to-back, are strictly formula comedies about magical powers possessed by youngsters but coveted by scheming adults. In "Sammy's Super T-Shirt," a 12-year-old with the power to bound across the ground like a basketball is pursued by two nefarious, bumbling scientists; in "Electric Eskimo," an Alaskan youth is endowed with electrical energy. Strictly for the young set; adults beware.

**SUPERMAN** (1948). An 88-minute version of the 15-chapter Columbia serial directed by Spencer G. Bennet and Thomas Carr and starring Kirk Alyn as the Man of Steel, the sensational comic book creation of Jerome Siegel and Joe Schuster. The film begins with the origin of Superman and proceeds to his battle with the Spider Lady, who covets a deadly "reducer ray" that could destroy an entire city. Meanwhile, he's threatened by a piece of Kryptonite. Noel Neill is Lois Lane, Carol Forman is the Spider Lady.

**SUPERMAN—THE MOVIE** (1978). Super-spectacular $40 million Ilya Salkind production pays homage to the most famous superhero of the comic books, radio, and serials . . .

but never in a single style. This beautifully crafted film begins as a space adventure, depicting the origin of Superman, his father Jor-El (Marlon Brando) and the demise of the planet Krypton, all done seriously. It then shifts to our young hero landing on Earth as a baby and being tended to by the Kent family, and here a sentimental, pastoral, lyrical quality in the cornfields of Kansas prevails. The more traditional comic book ambience is generated when Kent shows up in Metropolis, writing for the Daily Planet, and falling in love with reporter Lois Lane. It's a great affair, with Superman carrying Lois through the skies of the city. And finally, we have Superman's adventures with Lex Luthor, evil mastermind who plans to create an earthquake that will send California into the Pacific. Mixture of styles may have been caused by so many writers: Mario Puzo, David Newman, Leslie Newman, Robert Benton. John Williams' musical score gives the film a true sense of grandeur. Richard Donner directed, and did a wonderful job. Christopher Reeve doubles as Superman and Clark Kent and he's perfect casting. Gene Hackman hams it up as Luthor, Ned Beatty likewise as his bumbling sidekick, and Margot Kidder is perfect as Lois. Pure entertainment, highly recommended. (VC)

**SUPERMAN II** (1981). Entertaining special-effects masterpiece translates the famous comic book to the screen without being totally camp. A rich mosaic of action, light-hearted romance ("mushy stuff") and a sense of stylistic spoofery, even if the individuality of director Richard Lester is somewhat dwarfed by the enormity of the story. The cast is wonderful, with Christopher Reeve again doubling as the Man of Steel and as Clark Kent, mild-mannered reporter, Margot Kidder again falling in love with Superman, and Gene Hackman returning as master villain Lex Luthor. Sarah

Douglas, Jack O'Halloran and Terence Stamp appear as Kryptonite heavies who turn the world topsy-turvy with their superpowers. Their destruction of downtown Metropolis is brilliantly conceived. The flying effects have been improved since the first film. The Mario Puzo-David Newman-Leslie Newman screenplay moves moves moves, and you'll love E. G. Marshall as our First Executive with a toupee. Ned Beatty (back as Otis), Jackie Cooper (back as Perry White) and Susannah York (back as Superman's mother) appear briefly in reprised roles. (VC)

**SUPERMAN III (1983).** Alexander and Ilya Salkind, the Brothers Whim of producers, have committed an unpardonable cinematic sin: After establishing high standards for effects and scripting in their first two Superman epics, they allowed mediocrity to set in. The David/Leslie Newman script is a half-witted affair in which the Man of Steel (Christopher Reeve again) pursues archcriminal Ross Webster (unctuously played by Robert Vaughn). But Superman doesn't seem to have his heart in it—and the same can be said for director Richard Lester, whose SUPERMAN II was so much more stylized. There's a dull love affair between Clark Kent (also Reeve) and his old high school flame Lana Lang (Annette O'Toole) that never builds, and Richard Pryor is plain stupid as computer whiz Gus Gorman, victimized by Vaughn to reprogram the world so there is a monopolistic hold on the world's oil supply. The only time the film comes to life is when Superman is weakened by a piece of ersatz Kryptonite and turns evil—you'll see Superman drinking whiskey and having an affair with Vaughn's sexy playmate, Annie Ross. Finally there's a great duel of alter egos when Kent and Superman square off against each other in a junkyard. But the humanity that enhanced the previous films is missing, and no amount of special-effects magic can make up for it. Jackie Cooper appears briefly as Perry White, and Margot Kidder is in just two scenes as Lois Lane, spending the rest of the picture on Bermuda on vacation. (VC)

**SUPERMAN IV: THE QUEST FOR PEACE (1987).** Superman is no longer so super--Menahem Golan and Yoram Globus took over the series from the Salkinds and instantly proved they were made of putty--not steel. The Harrison Ellenshaw special effects are so inferior as to be (1) laughable and (2) disappointing, and the Lawrence Konner-Mark Rosenthal script (based on a Christopher Reeve idea) is a spectacular mess, never leaping a single bound. Christopher Reeve as Clark Kent/Superman is so appealing you want to like this movie, but everything director Sidney J. Furie does gets in the way of a good time. Superman is on a kick to dump all our nuclear weapons into an outer space junkpile but returning to stop him is Lex Luther (Gene Hackman), who creates a solar mighty man to combat our stalwart hero with the S on his jumpsuit. This battle is straight out of a comic book, grunts and all, and is an insult to the three films that preceded it, whether you liked them or not. Mariel Hemingway as the new owner of the Daily Planet provides the film's only charm by exposing her beautiful gams. And that, fans, is the highlight of this distressingly disappointing movie. Sam Wanamaker portrays Mariel's greedy father, and he's more of an interesting villain than Luther. Jon Cryer, Marc McClure. Margo Kidder returns as Lois Lane, and except for one flying sequence with Superman seems to have been left out of the picture.

**SUPERMAN AND THE JUNGLE DEVIL (1954).** Episodes of the George Reeves TV series spliced into a feature movie, then promptly resold to TV. Noell Neill as Lois Lane.

**SUPERMAN AND THE MOLE MEN (1951).** George Reeves first played the Man of Steel in this Robert L. Lippert feature, later divided into two chapters and shown on the long-running TV series SUPERMAN in which Reeve starred for several years. Dwarves emerge frm the subterranean depths of Earth to throw a town into panic, but Superman appears to act as a go-between. Phyllis Coates appears as Lois Lane, a role she duplicated on TV. Jeff Corey, Walter Reed, Stanley Andrews. Directed by Lee Sholem. (VC)

**SUPERMAN FLIES AGAIN (1954).** Three episodes of the TV SUPERMAN series pasted together into feature length by producer Whitney Ellsworth. The Man of Steel breaks up a band of jewel thieves; he helps a private eye solve a caper;

he is exposed to Kryptonite, a piece of his home planet that weakens his superabilities. George Reeves leaps over tall buildings and speeding locomotives with ease. Directed by Thomas Carr and George Blair. Noel Neill, Jack Larson, Robert Shayne. Elisha Cook Jr., John Hamilton.

**SUPERNATURAL (1933).** After the success of WHITE ZOMBIE, Victor and Edward Halperin produced this tale for Paramount starring Carole Lombard as a woman possessed by an electrocuted villainess (Vivienne Osborne). Randolph Scott hangs around the periphary as the hero. Horribly antiquated. H.B. Warner, Vivienne Osborne, Alan Dinehart.

**SUPERNATURAL (1981).** Spanish production in which a deceased husband returns from the grave to avenge his wife's infidelity. An expert in ESP is called in and there's a lot of dialogue about paranormal activities and extrasensory perception. Parapsychology is finally used to repel the dead guy. Directed by Eugenio Martin. Cristina Galbo, Maximo Valverde. Naturally super-boring.

**SUPERNATURALS, THE (1986).** Well-produced Sandy Howard production that opens in 1865, when Confederate prisoners are forced to walk across a mine field by a Union sadist. A youth surviving that ordeal possesses magical powers that, a hundred years later, plague a detachment of Army recruits training in the area where the Civil War massacre took place. Dead rebels are on the march, killing the soldiers one by one, while the boy's mother, in beautiful form, falls for one of the troopers. Macabre, eerie imagery by director Armand Mastroianni richly enhances this offbeat, above-average horror thriller. Nichelle Nichols, Maxwell Caulfield, Talia Balsam, Scott Jacoby, Levar Burton. Excellent music by Robert O. Ragland. (VC)

**SUPERSONIC MAN (1979).** Spanish science-fantasy adventure for the kids as a poverty-stricken rocket man from another world, a fast-moving warrior who answers to Kronos, fights to save mankind from an evil scientist, Dr. Gulk (Cameron Mitchell). Supermoronic. Directed by Juan Piquer. Michael Coby, Richard Yesteran, Diana Polakov. (VC)

**SUPERSONIC SAUCER (1956).** Quaint British film for children in which moppets help a flying saucer from Venus out of a tight spot on Earth. Includes animated sequences. Directed by S. G. Ferguson. Marcia Monolescue, Fella Edmonds, Donald Gray, Gillian Harrison, Tony Lyons.

**SUPERSPEED (1935).** Uninspired "invention" flick in which a scientist has perfected a "superspeed" gadget that causes everyone to fight each other for its possession. Lambert Hillyer directed. Norman Foster, Mary Carlisle, Charles Grapewin, Florence Rice, Arthur Hohl.

**SUPERSTITION (1982).** Haunted house-exorcism package with plenty of gore special effects. Black Lake is haunted by the spirit of a witch drowned there in 1692, and she also haunts the mansion next door, allowing for bloody acts of violence that makes it appear the house is responsible. What we have here is an exploding head in a microwave oven, a body ripped open by a whirring skillsaw ("My, what teeth you have!"), a body gutted and chopped in half by a descending windowframe, the toes of a swimmer eaten off, a man hung by the neck in an elevator shaft, a man crushed by a wine press, and a woman nailed to the floor with giant spikes (including one through her brain). The characters are fodder for the deathmill in Donald G. Thompson's script, including Albert Salmi's inquisitive policeman, Larry Pennell's drunken, ineffectual husband, James Houghton's investigating hero and Lynn Carlin's heroine. James W. Robinson's direction is hampered by flat lighting. Double bill stuff. (VC)

**SUPERTRAIN (1979).** A GRAND HOTEL on rails and one of the worst TV premises ever. This pilot for a flop, derailed series (which eventually embarrassed the hell out of NBC) loses steam almost immediately as it depicts an atomic-powered choo choo that comes complete with swimming pool, discotheque and other modern and/or futuristic gadgets. But instead of being slick and streamlined, this chug-chug-chugs down the tracks—it's barely the little engine that could. A Dan Curtis production written by Earl W. Wallace and starring Keenan Wynn as the train's owner. Vicki Lawrence, George Hamilton, Fred Williamson, Alan Alda.

**SUPERWHEELS (1978).** Sequel to West Germany's SU-PERBUG SUPERAGENT features the continuing inept misadventures of the yellow Volkswagen nicknamed Dudu, computerized to talk and think like a human. Its programmer, Jim Bondi, is a cowboy-style roustabout who befriends two nuns taking part in a mountainous car race, helping them overcome the evil Count and his two accident-causing henchmen. The scenic snow-covered Alps are littered with junked cars—and this movie. Robert Marck, Sal Brogi.

**SURF NAZIS MUST DIE (1987).** Post-Armageddon time (what, again?) and the Samurai Surfers are at war with the Surf Nazis for control of the beaches of the world. As the title indicates, this is a total oddity from Troma (the company that gave us THE TOXIC AVENGER and NUKE 'EM HIGH) full of non sequiturs amidst its violent action and genre parody. Watch and wonder. Directed by Peter George. Barry Brenner, Gail Neely, Bobbie Bresee, Michael Sonye.

**SURF TERROR. See MONSTER FROM THE SURF.**

**SURF II (1982).** The big gag: There never was a SURF I. Ha ha ha ha . . . glub glub. New Wavers in black outfits are aliens who abduct teen-agers into an underwater UFO . . . Buzz Cola, a new soft drink, turns teens into zombies or women . . . this foolish sexploitation trash defies description. Foolish and dumb, it consists of unfunny jokes, such as eating seaweed, crunching on glass, jiggling bare breasts into the mouths of overweight boys and kidding a stupid sheriff, Chief Boyardit. The script by director Randall Badat is impossible to describe as genres and infantile jokes are blended like flotsam on the beach. Joshua Cadman, Linda Kerridge (the Marilyn Monroe lookalike from FADE TO BLACK), Cleavon Little, Ruth Buzzi, Lyle Waggoner. (VC)

**SURROGATE, THE (1984).** Unhappily married couple (Art Hindle and Shannon Tweed) seek help from a sex therapist (Carole Laure) who tries to free their repressed fantasies . . . second storyline focuses on a serial murderer specializing in stabbings . . . elements are linked by director Don Carmody. Michael Ironside, Marilyn Lightstone, Jim Bailey.

**SURVIVAL 1990 (198?).** Survivors of a nuclear holocaust scavage the devastated landscape in packs of mutants and still-ordinary men. Mad Max with Blood and his boy? (VC)

**SURVIVAL ZONE (1983).** Following nuclear holocaust, apocalypse and armageddon, marauding motorcycle gangs attack holed-up ranchers to claim the land in an orgy of blood and violence. Gary Lockwood, Morgan Stevens. (VC)

**SURVIVALIST, THE (1987).** When war with Russia appears iminent, some biker gangs in Texas take over the territory, terrorizing Steve Railsback and his son, who is on a scouting

**THIS 'STUDENT BODY'
WILL NEVER GRADUATE**

trip. Mindless action in the MAD MAX vein, but without style or interesting characters. This film can't possibly survive. Jason Healey, Marjoe Gortner, Cliff De Young, David Wayne, Susan Blakely.

**SURVIVOR, THE (1981).** Australian adaptation of James Herbert's novel about a plane crash that kills all passengers but one—and the strange events that follow. The cast is top-notch (Robert Powell, Jenny Agutter, Joseph Cotten) and the atmosphere thoroughly proper to this kind of "haunted" story. Directed by David Hemmings. Music by Brian May. (VC)

**SUSPIRIA (1977).** Short on logic but long on thrills, this is a fan's picture—an Italian import written-directed by Dario Argento, a cult favorite after DEEP RED. Jessica Harper is an American girl, enrolled in a German dance academy, when suddenly there's a thunderstorm, which sets the mood for a bat attack, falling maggots, a throat-ripping dog and a cackling coven of witches. Highly commendable "cheap thrills" with Joan Bennett and Alida Valli in supporting roles.

**SVENGALI (1931).** George du Maurier's TRILBY came to the screen with John Barrymore as the hypnotic, eye-rolling impresario who uses his evil powers to seduce Marian Marsh and turn her into a singing star. Directed by Archie Mayo. Marian Marsh, Donald Crisp, Lumsden Hare. (VC)

**SVENGALI (1955).** Baroque British version of George du Maurier's TRILBY, starring Donald Wolfit as a bearded hypnotist who sways the will of a beautiful singer and turns her into a brilliant performer—but he cannot force honey-haired Hildegarde Neff to love him. Director-writer Noel Langley emphasizes the love affair between Miss Neff and an artist (Terence Morgan). Weird, somber adaptation, preceded by a German attempt in 1927 and a Warner Bros. variation in 1931 with John Barrymore and Marian Marsh.

**SVENGALI (1983).** TV version of the George du Maurier classic, directed by Anthony Harvey and written by Frank Cucci. The cast is the thing here: Peter O'Toole as the vocal coach, Jodie Foster as Zoe Alexander the singer, with Elizabeth Ashley and Pamela Blair in supporting roles. Stripped of diabolical elements, this is an ordinary love story, without good vs. evil conflicts. (VC)

**SWAMP OF THE BLOOD LEECHES. See ALIEN DEAD, THE.** (Go ahead, be a sucker!)

**SWAMP OF THE LOST MONSTERS, THE (1964).** Mexico's cowboy star Gaston Santos and his Wonder Horse ride to the rescue of a screaming heroine when she is attacked by an amphibian creature in this Mexican-produced Saturday matinee fodder. American producer V. Gordon Murray re-released the film west-of-the-border with new footage shot by director Siem Segar. The rest of this mess, featuring inept comic relief (a fat Pancho-like character), stupid fistfights, lowbrow slapstick action and a superphony gillman suit, was directed by Raphael Baledon. It's "lost" all right—in every sense of the word. Manola Savedra, Manuel Dondi.

**SWAMP OF THE LOST SOULS, THE. See SWAMP OF THE LOST MONSTER, THE.** (Mired either way)

**SWAMP THING (1982).** Popular comic-book creature, half-man, half-slime, is the laughing stock of the Okefenokee in the hands of director-writer Wes Craven. The juvenile approach is an ironic shift from his LAST HOUSE ON THE LEFT and THE HILLS HAVE EYES and will disappoint fans expecting hardcore horror. The monster looks exactly like what it is—a strongarm actor in a rubber suit. And Craven lingers lovingly on the phony outfit, allowing us to wince for minutes at a stretch. Louis Jourdan has the thankless role of Arcane, Swamp Thing's nemesis, and Adrienne Barbeau streaks through the wilderness, screaming as she is pursued by the creature (for a moment she pauses to bear her lovely breasts). Though trying to play a "ballsy broad" and make Alice Cable a heroine, she ends up being decorative and rescuable. Nicholas Worth, David Hess, Don Knight. (VC)

**SWARM, THE (1978).** Lousiest of the "killer bees on the loose" movies, although based on a god book by Arthur Herzog. Sterling Silliphant's adaptation and Irwin Allen's direction dealt too much with cliches and not with Herzog's original concepts. The South American killer bees are moving northward, and threaten to destroy civilization. All that's stopping them are Michael Caine, as a bee specialist, Katharine Ross, Olivia de Havilland, Ben Johnson, Fred MacMurray, Richard Chamberlain, Richard Widmark and a slew of other Hollywood actors. You're in for a real stinging. The "swarmy" musical score is by John Williams. (VC)

**SWEENEY TODD (1971).** British TV version of THE DEMON BARBER OF FLEET STREET, reviving the old legendary plot about the strange alliance between a barber and the owner of a bakery shop located conveniently next door. Seems the hair-cutter also cuts throats, then turns over the bodies to the baker who puts them into his pastries. Here's pie in your eye. Produced by Sidney Pink. Freddie Jones stars.

**SWEENEY TODD (1984).** Angela Lansbury and George Hearn star in this TV version of the smash Broadway hit (based on the old British tale of

**SWAMP THING BATTLES THE ARCANE MONSTER (BIG DEAL!)**

a throat-cutter's union with a pie maker), which was nominated for several awards. It's a musical version, dark and atmospheric, not pleasant at all, for the bloodletting is extremely realistic for the stage. Just be ready to watch Lansbury and Hearn explore the sick side to the human appetite. (VC)

**SWEET SIXTEEN (1983).** Muddled mess of a horror movie, featuring too few murders to satisfy the slasher crowd and too much confusion in the final reel for anyone to make sense of it. Erwin Goldman's screenplay is at fault, for Jim Sotos has done a decent job of directing on a low budget and the cast is composed of many good B players, all trying valiantly to bring quality to a story they must realize is ill-conceived. Setting is a Texas town where a rash of murders seems to be centered around newcomer Melissa (Aleisa Shirley), just turning 16. Her sexual awakening is presumably the cause of the violence, but far more interesting is sheriff Bo Hopkins and his daughter Dana Kimmell, who bring vitality to their roles. A red herring subplot involves an Indian burial ground—which Patrick Macnee, as Melissa's father, is excavating—but it never dovetails. The odd cast includes Susan Strasberg, Henry Wilcoxon (as an old Indian), Sharon Farrell, Larry Storch and Michael Pataki. (VC)

**SWEET SOUND OF DEATH (1965).** Boy meets girl. Boy falls in love with girl. Boy and girl vow never to be parted. Girl vows, if need be, to return from grave. Girl dies. Girl keeps promise. Boy wonders if girl isn't carrying romantic infatuation to extremes, especially when he's down wind from her. Spanish boy Javier Seto directed and wrote script. Like girl, nothing sweet about it, stinks.

**SWEET SUGAR (1972).** Voodoo melodrama with the usual mad doctor up to some illegal experimentation with human beings. A bitter pill to take. Directed by Michel Levesque. Phyllis E. Davis, Ella Edwards, Timothy Brown. (VC)

**SWEET, SWEET RACHEL (1971).** Unseen presence tries to drive three lovely lasses out of their beautiful skulls. ESP expert Alex Dreier experiments, disturbing the unseen world around him. TV-movie has nice ambience and a feeling for the supernatural via director Sutton Rolley. Stefanie Powers, Pat Hingle, Brenda Scott, Chris Robinson, Steve Inhat.

**SWORD AND THE DRAGON, THE (1956).** The Russians celebrate a legendary swordsman, Ilya Mourometz, the slayer of creatures. In this adaptation of his career as a

monster carver, he wields a magic sword against an ogre; a "wind" monster; and a three-headed hydra. It'll slay you, too. Boris Andreyev is the gallant knight, erratic but errant. Directed by V. Kotochnev. Boris Andreyev, Andrei Abrikosov.

**SWORD AND THE SORCERER, THE (1982).** Producers Brandon Chase and Marianne Chase offer a fantasy reminiscent of Saturday matinee serials as Lee Horsley battles the forces of evil in a mythical kingdom (Eh-Dan) ruled over by the baddie Cromwell (Richard Lynch) and his demon (George Maharis). Prince Talon (Horsley) must also rescue Kathleen Beller. It was well directed by Albert Pyun and has bloody effects as well as great transformations of men into monsters (the work of Richard Washington). Cinematography is often muddy and too dark, but this really holds one's interest. (VC)

**SWORD IN THE STONE, THE (1963).** T. H. White's account of the early days of King Arthur was turned into a full-length animated Disney cartoon capturing the fantasy and excitement of how Arthur (called Wart) meets Merlin the Magician and undergoes several adventures before pulling the sword Excalibur from the stone and proving he is the rightful ruler of Britain. Young Arthur is changed into a fish so he might witness the wonders of the sea, and he joins in battle with sorcerers in a memorable sequence. Voices by Sebastian Cabot, Karl Swenson and Alan Napier. (VC)

**SYBIL (1976).** Sally Field as a woman with 17 personalities outrivals THE THREE FACES OF EVE in number but not quality. This TV-movie is nevertheless fascinating in exploring what makes her-her-her-her-her-her-her-her-her-her-her-her-her-her-her-her-her tick. Directed by Daniel Petrie. This time Joanne Woodward plays the psychiatrist. Brad Davis, Martine Bartlett, Jane Hoffman, William Prince. (VC)

**SWORD OF ALI BABA, THE (1965).** Cheap Howard Christie production for Universal with a script written around existing action footage from ALI BABA AND THE 40 THIEVES, a 1944 adventure flick. It's the same old plot set in bedazzling Bagdad, only now it's bedraggled Bagdad. Peter Mann is the son of the desert and Jocelyn Lane is the rose of the oasis. Others in turbans are Gavin MacLeod, Peter Whitney, Frank De Kova. Virgil Vogel directed the new footage, and may Allah curse him with a thousand camel fleas in the boidoir of his eldest daughter on her wedding night.

**SWORD OF HEAVEN (1985).** Magical blade, allegedly forged hundreds of years ago by Zen priests from a

**'THE SWORD AND THE SORCERESS'**

meteorite, becomes the subject of contention between the evil gang that possesses it and a Japanese policeman, naturally skilled in martial arts, visiting California. Directed by Byron Meyers. Tadashi Yamashita, Mel Novak, Bill (Superfoot) Wallace, Venus Jones. (VC)

**SWORD OF THE BARBARIANS, THE (1983).** Sangrai the adventurer, the son of Ator (hero of two Italian sorcery films), vows when his wife is murdered to destroy the followers of the Goddess Rani, and rides to the Ark of the Templars for a magical crossbow that will help him finish the job. Then he tangles with the baddies. Barbarically cheap Italian sword-and-sandal yarn, directed without flair by Michael E. Lemick. You've seen all the flailing swords before. Peter MacCoy, Sabrina Siani, Margarethe Christian, Yvonne Fraschetti.

**SWORD OF THE SPACE ARK (1977).** Really atrocious Japanese TV-movie clone of STAR WARS, consisting of horrible special effects, a dumb plot about an army of robots attacking the planet Kendall and a space freighter manned by some really dumb dudes, including a suave-voiced Wookie-type piloting the ship. Utterly unwatchable. Redubbed and produced for the U.S. market by Bunker Jenkins. Hence, Bunker junker and ultimately a clunker.

**SWORD OF THE VALIANT (1984).** Entertaining, swashbuckling interpretation of the Legend of Sir Gawain and the Green Knight, awash in colorful dialogue and characters. The Green Knight, a God-like supernatural entity, rides into King Arthur's court and challenges any brave knight to chop off his head. The only catch is, if the swinger misses, the Green Knight (Sean Connery) gets a return swing. A squire (Miles O'Keeffe) accepts the challenge, thus beginning an outre odyssey into adventure, myth and magic as he sets out on a one-year quest for the answer to a riddle of wisdom. His wanderings take him to the land of Leonette, where he finds love, imprisonment and a new enemy in the evil form of Ronald Lacey. The action is superbly reminiscent of an Errol Flynn swashbuckler and the story moves briskly. The sets and costumes in this Golan-Globus production are splendid as is the supporting cast: Trevor Howard as the disillusioned king, Lila Kedrova as the wife of the protector of Leonette, Peter Cushing as a roving fop, Cyrielle Claire as Sir Gawain's love. Wonderfully photographed by Freddie Young and Peter Hurst. Leigh Lawson, John Rhys-Davies. (VC)

**SWORDKILL. See GHOSTWARRIOR.**

**SWORDS OF WAYLAND, THE (1983).** Episode of cable TV's ROBIN HOOD THE LEGEND, starring Michael Praed as the hero of Sherwood who with his Merrie Men clashes with a devil-worship cult. (VC)

**SYLVIA AND THE PHANTOM (1945).** Alfred Adam's play was adapted by the French into a period comedy in which a lovely young woman meets the spirit of a long-dead gentleman. Directed by Claude Autant-Lara. Odette Joyeux, Jacques Tati, Francois Perier, Louis Salou. (VC)

**'SYLVIA AND THE PHANTOM'**

---

*"Of all the worlds, in all the galaxies, in all the universe . . . why did they have to pick this one?"—STRANGE INVADERS._*

*"Nefratis was a lot more terrifying than a fellow in a black cloak and dinner suit. Her supernatural powers were only matched by her cruelty. She would slaughter newborn babes and drink their blood from a cup. It was even said she ripped the hearts out of full-grown men. Brr."—John Carradine as Professor John J. Andoheb in* **THE TOMB.**

**T.A.G.—THE ASSASSINATION GAME (1983).** Curious off-shoot of the slasher genre, written-directed by Nick Castle. A game's afoot of make-believe assassination on college campuses, with students stalking each other armed with rubber dart guns. But one spoil sport goes psycho and kills opponents with a .45 (try to duck that dart), then stalks Linda Hamilton, while Robert Carradine tracks clues for the campus paper. There's a nice jazz score by Craig Safan, but little suspense or payoff to this slight offering. Ready or not, here it comes. Perry Lang, Frazer Smith, Kristine DeBell. (VC)

**TAKING TIGER MOUNTAIN (1983).** Independent production, in black and white, shot on a shoestring in Wales. The time is the near future, when the Soviet Union and U.S.A. are recovering from three mega-wars. While American boat people flee to Britain, draft dodger Bill Paxton is brainwashed to be an assassin by a hellfire feminist terror group. His target: a major in charge of selling white slaves. Moody, stark, low-budget grainy. Produced-written by Tom Huckabee.

**TALE OF THE FROG PRINCE (1982).** Shelley Duvall's FAERIE TALE THEATER originally presented this popular story of how a prince is turned into a frog by a fairy godmother. Directed by Eric Idle. Robin Williams, Teri Garr, Candy Clark. (VC)

**TALES FROM BEYOND THE GRAVE.** See **FROM BEYOND THE GRAVE.** (Graves of Wrath?)

**TALES FROM THE CRYPT (1972).** Adaptation of five E.C. comic stories published in the 1950s by Albert Feldstein/William Gaines (who still produce Mad Magazine). The famous panels (drawn by such artists as Johnny Craig, Graham Ingels and Jack Davis) have been recreated faithfully; and thanks to Milton Subotsky's script and Freddie Francis' direction, this comes off as a fun-filled horror film. Four individuals trapped with the Crypt Keeper (Sir Ralph Richardson) are told a narrative foreshadowing his/her destiny. "And All Through the House" deals with Joan Collins fighting off a Santa Claus madman on Christmas Eve; "Reflection of Death" is about a dead man who can't get used to the idea;

"Poetic Justice," deals with a St. Valentine's Day gift delivered by Peter Cushing, fresh from his grave; "Wish You Were Here" is a variation on "The Monkey's Paw"; and "Blind Alleys" has Nigel Patrick blundering through a mazework of razor blades. VAULT OF HORROR, the sequel, adapted four more shuddery E.C. yarns. (VC)

**TALES FROM THE DARKSIDE, VOLUME I (1984).** Three repackaged episodes of George Romero's half-hour TV series. "Word Processor of the Gods?" is a Stephen King story in which a writer changes history on a computer; a good idea that falls totally flat. "Djinn, No Chaser," based on a Harlan Ellison story, is a whimsical farce about a married couple (Colleen Camp, Charles Levin) encountering a genie in the form of Kareem Abdul Jabbar. "Slippage" depicts how David Patrick Kelly slips through the cracks of time and vanishes. Mediocre, limp material. (VC)

**TALES FROM THE DARKSIDE: VOL. 2 (1984).** Three more short shorts from George Romero's low-budget syndicated series: Danny Aiello stars as a gambler in "The Odds," making a bet with a ghost; Harry Anderson stars in "All a Clone by the Telephone" in which an answering machine drives him crazy; and "Anniversary Dinner" features a hitchhiker involved with cannibals. Average. (VC)

**TALES FROM THE DARKSIDE: VOL. 3 (1984-85).** More half-hour TV cheapies from George ("Living Dead") Romero: "Mookie and Pookie" is a good idea about two computers who is dying and reprograms himself to live; "It All Comes Out in the Wash" is an episode with Vince Edwards who seeks an idyllic lifestyle; and "Levitation" is a superb magic story starring Joseph Turkel as a stage magician who carries his sleight-of-brand too far. Best in the series. (VC)

**TALES FROM THE DARKSIDE: VOL. 4 (1984-85).** Three more quickies from the Romero series: "The New Man," the pilot episode, stars Vic Tayback as a heavy drinker who finds his past catching up to him in a strange way; "Snip, Snip" is a cute comedy with Bud Cort and Carol Kane as practitioners of magic who use their powers to win a lottery; and

**KIM NOVAK IN 'TALES THAT
WITNESS MADNESS'**

"Painkiller" is about a guy being nagged to death. (VC)

**TALES FROM THE DARKSIDE VOL. 5 (1984).** Three more episodes of the syndicated TV series: "Inside the Closet," in which a co-ed's dreamy world becomes a nightmare; "The False Prophet," about a horoscope addict with a Pisces complex; and "Grandma's Last Wish," showing how a neglected old lady gets her revenge. (VC)

**TALES OF HOFFMAN (1951).** Michael Powell/Emeric Pressburger version of Jacques Offenbach's opera, beautifully executed in Technicolor. Love and fantasy blend when Hoffman relates his past romances to travelers resting in an inn. In "Olympia," he falls in love with a dancing doll; in "Giulietta," Hoffman loves a girl under the spell of a witch; and in "Antonia," Hoffman struggles to save a girl who will die if he sings. The superb cast is headed by Moira Shearer, the exquisite dancer from another Powell-Pressburger classic, RED SHOES. Robert Helpman, Pamela Brown.

**TALES OF MYSTERY AND IMAGINATION. See SPIRITS OF THE DEAD.**

**TALES OF TERROR (1962).** Roger Corman at his producing-directing best, with Richard Matheson superbly adapting a trilogy of Poe stories, "rococo Gothic." In "Morella," maddened Vincent Price faces his wife's ghost . . . slow but eerie, with Price believably sinking into alcoholic insanity. A combination of "The Black Cat" and "The Cask of Amontillado" teams Price and Peter Lorre in a rollicking wine-tasting contest. This tale is played for laughs, and Lorre comes off in excellent form. In "The Case of M. Valdemar," Price is on his deathbed, kept alive by hypnotist Basil Rathbone. Handsomely mounted and entertaining in a preposterous way. Debra Paget, Wally Campo, Joyce Jameson. (VC)

**TALES OF THE HAUNTED.** Short-lived TV series, now re-edited as **EVIL STALKS THIS HOUSE.**

**TALES OF TOMORROW I (1953).** One of TV's earliest adult science-fiction series, which ran for three seasons on ABC. A milestone, even though it was cheaply produced, often featuring excellent casts. This contains four episodes: "Frankenstein," "Dune Roller," "Appointment on Mars" and "The Crystal Egg." Worth searching out. Lon Chaney Jr., Bruce Cabot. (VC)

**TALES OF TOMORROW II (1953).** Four more episodes of

TV's first important science-fiction series: "Past Tense," "A Child Is Crying," "Ice From Space" and "The Window." Boris Karloff, Paul Newman, Rod Steiger, Walter Abel. (VC)

**TALES THAT WITNESS MADNESS (1972).** British horror anthology in the style of TALES FROM THE CRYPT, directed by Freddie Francis and written by Jennifer Jayne. Donald Pleasence and Jack Hawkins are strolling through an insane asylum and meet four crazed souls who spill their yarns: "Mr. Tiger" is about a boy who creates imaginary beasts in the style of Bradbury's "The Veldt," and hence is quite unoriginal; "Mel" stars Joan Collins as a bitchy wife who resents her husband bringing a tree into the living room—a tree that is living in a terrifying sense; "Penny Farthing" is a time-travel tale involving a haunted bicycle; and "Luau" is a voodoo/cannibal story with Kim Novak as a rich doll whose daughter is a sacrificial lamb. The final shocker concerns what happens to Pleasence and Hawkins in the asylum. Involving and unusual. Georgia Brown, Donald Houston.

**TAM LIN (1971).** Roddy McDowall directed this feature which, according to him, was never theatrically released. William Spier's script (based on a Robert Burns' poem) is about an old witch involved with jet setters. A terrible fate (perhaps?) for a film starring Ava Gardner, Ian McShane, Cyril Cusack, Richard Wattis and Stephanie Beacham. Write your congressman and demand something be done . . .

**TANYA'S ISLAND (1980).** Exotic Canadian model D. D. Williams fantasizes she's on an island with a hairy beast—a man in a gorilla suit designed by Rick Baker and Rob Bottin. Obviously, producer-writer Pierre Brousseau had good intentions and hired a good director, Alfred Sole, to carry them out, but nothing quite meshes. Made in Puerto Rico. (VC)

**TARANTULA (1955).** Director Jack Arnold tries to recapture the moods of IT CAME FROM OUTER SPACE and CREATURE FROM THE BLACK LAGOON but this Universal-International "giant creature" thriller comes off as a lesser effort. Leo G. Carroll, seeking a nutrient to feed the increasing world population, turns a spider into a monster which, naturally, escapes. John Agar and Mara Corday have a perfunctory, dull romance which is soon forgotten so Clifford Stine's special effects can take over. But the effects are only mildly exciting and the film builds unspectacularly to a fiery climax as the ill-tempered arachnid continues its uninspired attacks on mankind. Clint Eastwood has a bit part as a jet pilot. Nestor Paiva, Ross Elliott, Eddie Parker.

**TARANTULAS: THE DEADLY CARGO (1977).** When an aircraft crashes in a California orange-growing region, banana spiders in a shipment of coffee beans from South

**PETER CUSHING IN
'TALES FROM THE CRYPT'**

America escape to begin a campaign of murder against everyone connected with oranges (except Anita Bryant). Claude Akins organizes the townspeople (overcoming the objections of dumb officials) and tracks the deadly critters to the local orange-packing plant. TV spiders act far more intelligent than the TV humans. Directed by Stuart Hagmann. Charles Frank, Howard Hesseman, Pat Hingle. (VC)

**TARGET EARTH (1954).** Cheapie Allied Artists-Herman Cohen release makes a clunking thud that matches the clunking of metal robots wandering through an American city after Earth has been zapped by a Death Ray and there are only a handful of survivors. At least it keeps the budget down. Richard Denning, Virginia Grey, Whit Bissell, Kathleen Crowley, House Peters Jr. and Arthur Space are among the boring types who behave foolishly while fighting off those clunker robot machines. Not even Paul Dunlap's music helps this exercise in tedium. Directed by Sherman A. Rose.

**TARGET . . . EARTH? (1980).** Victor Buono is an alien watching Earth with a computer's help and wondering about our reaction to the Siberian explosion of 1908. Lowbrown science-fiction that tries to mix in some pseudofact and quasiknowledge by having scenes with Isaac Asimov and Carl Sagan. Billions . . . and billions . . . of people tuned out. Produced-directed by Joost van Rees. (VC)

**TARGET FOR KILLING (1966).** A whole lot of brainwashing is going on in this Austrian-Italian production, and it has something to do with "electro-psychic massage." Routine spy action stuff but with a decent cast: Stewart Granger, Karin Dor, Curt Jergens, Adolfo Celi, Klaus Kinski, Erica Remberg, Rupert Davies. Directed by Manfred Kohler.

**TARGETS (1968).** Roger Corman came to Peter Bogdanovich with out-takes from THE TERROR (1963) and asked the director to construct a movie. Bogdanovich needed only a few scenes to concoct a tale about Byron Orlok, an aging horror star who feels he's passe (the real world's horrors are far worse, he believes) and wants to retire. Orlok is played by Boris Karloff in one of his best roles. Meanwhile, Tim O'Kelly, average and very American, murders his family in cold blood with a high-powered rifle and snipes at motorists. Later, these two divergent elements merge at a drive-in, where Orlok is delivering his farewell address. Bogdanovich co-stars as a young Sammy Fuller-type director. In recent years this unusual feature has taken on cult status. Sandy Baron, Mike Farrell, Jack Nicholson, Dick Miller. (VC)

**TARZAN AND THE AMAZONS (1945).** Entertaining Johnny Weissmuller entry in the Tarzan series. In this one the vine-swinger and his family (Brenda Joyce as Jane, Johnny Sheffield as Boy) encounter white amazon women led by an old lady, Maria Ouspenskaya, best known as the gypsy woman in the "Wolf Man" films at Universal. Kurt Neumann directed the action-packed script. Barton MacLane.

**TARZAN AND THE GREEN GODDESS (1938).** Feature version of the 1935 serial THE NEW ADVENTURES OF TARZAN, with Herman Brix (later Bruce Bennett) as the ape man who forsakes Africa for Guatemala to find a friend kidnapped by villainous Mayans. He locates a cache of jewels which also contains the formula for a revolutionary explosive. This did not revolutionize Tarzan movies, however, being a poorly directed (Edward Kull), horrendously written (Charles F. Royal) and atrociously acted formula jungle adventure.

**TARZAN AND THE LEOPARD WOMEN (1946).** Using long steel claws built into their leopard pelts, a cult of natives cuts out the hearts of victims and turns them over to their High Priestess (Acquanetta) to appease the angered Leopard God. Fun-filled potted-plant potboiler (28th in the Tarzan series) starring Johnny Weissmuller, Brenda Joyce, Johnny Sheffield, Edgar Barrier, Dennis Hoey, Anthony Caruso, Tommy Cook. Produced-directed by Kurt Neumann.

**TARZAN'S DESERT MYSTERY (1943).** Burroughs' jungle hero battles prehistoric monsters, but don't think producer Sol Lesser was spending money. He was swiping stock footage from ONE MILLION B.C. Tarzan wanders across sand dunes instead of jungle, looking for a plant that could cure malaria, and fighting off Nazis. Helpings of fun and

**JOHNNY WEISSMULLER AS TARZAN**

propaganda are packed into Edward T. Lowe's rousing screenplay directed by William Thiele. Nancy Kelly, Otto Kruger, Joe Sawyer, Robert Lowery, Johnny Sheffield.

**TARZAN'S MAGIC FOUNTAIN (1949).** Lex Barker became the first Tarzan listed in the New York Social Register, and the tenth actor to essay the Edgar Rice Burroughs role. When a long-lost aviatrix (Evelyn Ankers) is found wandering in the jungle, looking no older than 25, explorers penetrate Tarzan's domain in search of a Fountain of Youth, guarded by the ferocious Leopard People. Also note that Tarzan now wears moccasins. Brenda Joyce is a fetching Jane—dig those crazy jungle skins. Albert Dekker, Alan Napier, Elmo Lincoln, Charles Drake. Directed by Lee Sholem.

**TASTE OF BLOOD, A (1967).** Herschell Gordon Lewis' updating of the Dracula legend finds a descendant of the count drinking from a flagon of vampire wine. Whom should he seek out and mark for death? Why, the destroyers of his maligned ancestor. Gore specialist Lewis appears in the cast. Bill Rogers, Elizabeth Wilkinson, Otto Schlesinger. One draggin' flagon, this chalice from no palace. (VC)

**TASTE OF EVIL, A (1973).** Barbara Parkins, recovering from a rape attack, is either going crazy or is the victim of a diabolical plot. This Aaron Spelling TV-movie was written by

Jimmy Sangster, directed by John Llewellyn Moxey. Barbara Stanwyck, Roddy McDowall, Arthur O'Connell, William Windom, Bing Russell, Dawn Frame.

**TASTE OF SIN, A (1983).** German filmmaker Ulli Lommel (BOOGEYMAN) cast his real-life wife Suzanna Love as a woman who murders her male lovers on or near London Bridge because she's haunted by the nightmarish memory of her mother's death at the hands of a GI when she was only six. Much of this is derivative of Hitchcock and other suspense specialists, but Lommel does have his own unique way as a writer-director and sometimes-cinematographer. Ms Love is assisted by Robert Walker Jr., an architect restoring the bridge. Made in Arizona and London.

**TASTE THE BLOOD OF DRACULA (1970).** A tooth-bite above most of Hammer's Dracula films of the period, with Christopher Lee again conveying an aura of menace when three gentlemen in search of lust and thrills engage in a bit of satanism, inadvertently resurrecting the long-dead Count. These men and their families meet death in horrible albeit traditional vampiric fashion. Dracula, in a genuinely imaginative climax, faces a new form of death in a recently reconstructed church. Above average direction by Peter Sasdy, with screenwriter John Elder atoning for the horrible botch he made of EVIL OF FRANKENSTEIN.

**TEEN WOLF (1985).** Werewolf tale with a shaggy twist: Instead of an infected lycanthrope going kill crazy under a full moon, an underdog teenager (Michael J. Fox) learns from dad about his wolfish genealogy and copes with being hairy on the gymnasium floor during a basketball game. In that respect the Joseph Loeb III-Matthew Weisman screenplay is unique, but nothing is done with the premise, beyond Fox fighting within himself for the human half to succeed without resorting to the wolf, which is capable of break dancing and other physical feats. James Hampton, Scott Paulin, Jerry Levine, Susan Ursitti. Directed by Rod Daniel. (VC)

**TEENAGE CAVEMAN (1958).** Despite rock-age production values, an inept performance by Robert Vaughn and horrendous music by Albert Glasser, this is salvaged by the direction of Roger Corman and a strangely shaped script by R. Wright Campbell. Vaughn, from a primitive tribe forbidden to trespass where dwells The Monster That Kills With a Touch, enters the taboo zone anyway, where a surprise ending awaits him (but not you—you can see it coming). There is no truth to the rumor this was originally called I WAS A TEENAGE CAVEBOY. Jonathan Haze, Robert Shayne, Frank De Kova, Leslie Bradley, Darrah Marshall.

**TEENAGE MONSTER. See METEOR MONSTER.**

**TEENAGE PSYCHO MEETS BLOODY MAMA. See IN-**

**CHARLES BRONSON IN
RECEIVERSHIP: 'TELEFON'**

**MICHAEL J. FOX: 'TEEN WOLF'**

**CREDIBLY STRANGE CREATURES WHO STOPPED LIVING AND BECAME CRAZY MIXED-UP ZOMBIES, THE.**

**TEENAGE ZOMBIES (1960).** Hulking entities of evil, never exceeding 19, are created by a nerve gas—the brainstorm of a mad doctor (Katherine Victor) living on an island. Unfortunately, these vacationing teenage hulks look as vacuous and hollow-eyed as any teenager walking down a street, mesmerized by rock 'n roll music on a transistor. So this is less a horror film than a social document of unusual realism. Produced-directed by Jerry Warren who followed the inanities of Jacques Le Cotier's script.

**TEENAGERS FROM OUTER SPACE (1958).** Evil teenage aliens land on Earth in the company of Gargon, a lobster creature which walks on its hind legs and turns to jelly when the good-kid alien aims his Blaster Zap Gun. Strictly for the teenage set, if teenagers can sit through it. It's doubtful adults will want to. Produced-written-directed by Tom Graeff. David Love, Dawn Anderson, Bryan Grant.

**TELEFON (1977).** Much talent is wasted on a feeble premise: A phone call to programmed spies in the U.S. activates them with a post-hypnotic phrase and they carry out acts of sabotage. It's dirty Commie rats up to their usual world-conquering tricks . . . but special agent Charles Bronson is calling the long-distance operator for information, to track the baddies from Moscow. Why Don Siegel wanted to direct this, or why Sterling Silliphant and Peter Hyams got involved in writing the script . . . gee, was it for money? Lee Remick, Donald Pleasence, Tyne Daly, Alan Badel, Patrick Magee, Sheree North, John Mitchum. (VC)

**TELEPHONE BOOK, THE (1971).** Weird premise makes for an offbeat soft-core sex movie. Sultry Sarah Kennedy seeks the world's best obscene phone caller. The man with that talent is an astronaut who has suffered the loss of a vital body organ in space and now gets his jollies through Ma Bell. There's an animated cartoon sequence that is sexually explicit, so don't look for this on The Late Show. Written-directed by Nelson Lyon. Norman Rose, James Harder, Jill Clayburgh, Ondine, Barry Morse, Ultra Violet.

**TELEVISION SPY (1939).** Foreign spies covet the Iconoscope, a marvelous newfangled device that can transmit a picture 3000 miles and be viewed on a screen 6 x 8! That's no big deal today but imagine how audiences felt in 1939! Of mild interest, as it was directed by Edward Dmytryk. Anthony Quinn, Richard Denning, William Henry.

**TELL-TALE HEART, THE (1960).** Intensely acted, well photographed British horror film based loosely on Edgar

## ROMAN POLANSKI IN 'THE TENANT'

Allan Poe's classic short story. Laurence Payne portrays Poe, who drops off to sleep writing at his desk, and dreams he's Edgar Marsh, a librarian in a French town where he falls in love with a flowershop worker (Adrienne Corri), a femme fatale who would rather dally with Edgar's best friend (Dermot Walsh). The librarian, crazed with jealousy, murders his friend and places his body under the floorboards in the library. Soon, the exaggerated beating of a heart drives him to the threshold of madness. There's a very macabre sequence in which Payne cuts out the heart of his victim, holding the still-pumping organ in his bloody hands. A memorable sleeper directed by Ernest Morris and written by Brian Clemens and Elden Howard. Watch for subtle literary clues hinting at the surprise ending. (VC)

**TEMPTER, THE (1974).** Watch this Italian rip-off of THE EXORCIST and you won't eat for a week after seeing: possessed woman gulping down severed head of toad; possessed woman licking up spilt blood; possessed woman regurgitating wine; possesed woman vomiting scrambled eggs; possessed woman spitting up green slime; possessed woman spewing into the face of a relative. The plot has to do with reincarnation of a witch burnt at the stake hundreds of years ago. Demonic winds, flying furniture, far-flung objects. What the Devil are Mel Ferrer, Arthur Kennedy and George Coulouris doing in this Antichrist pasta? (VC)

**TEN LITTLE INDIANS (1965).** Inferior remake of AND THEN THERE WERE NONE, the classic Agatha Christie suspense mystery set on a lonely island where a handful of guests are stranded and stalked by a killer. Writers Harry Alan Towners and Peter Yeldham have changed the setting to a snowbound chateau and updated the characters. It doesn't work, making one thirst for the Rene Clair original. Hugh O'Brian, Shirley Eaton, Wilfrid Hyde-White, Fabian, Leo Genn, Daliah Lavi. Directed by George Pollock. Please, no Pollock jokes.

**TEN LITTLE INDIANS (1976).** Third film version of Agatha Christie's mystery play, and the least satisfying. Producer-screenwriter Harry Alan Towers has shifted the setting to Iran, of all places, into a posh Persian hotel. Orson Welles' voice supports a big cast (Elke Sommer, Oliver Reed, Gert Frobe, Herbert Lom, Charles Aznavour, Richard Attenborough) but ultimately it's the 1945 version (AND THEN THERE WERE NONE) you want. (VC)

**TEN TO MIDNIGHT (1983).** Slasher film with a message: American courts are too lenient on murderers and the law has become a search for loopholes, with defense lawyers having little concern for innocent citizens. Hardened cop Charles Bronson, a Dirty Harry of the 1980s, distressed when

the legal system thwarts him from taking a sex-crazed killer of women off the streets, plants incriminating evidence to put the killer away, but his conscience won't allow him to go through with it. The most interesting characters are Andrew Stevens as Bronson's inexperienced but well-meaning partner and Lisa Eilbacher as Bronson's daughter, chief target of the mad-dog slasher. The killer is chillingly played by Gene Dare (though his motives are often obscured); he murders while totally nude. Polished direction by J. Lee Thompson and a honed script by William Roberts make this a standout. Geoffrey Lewis, Wilford Brimley. (VC)

**TENANT, THE (1976).** In his REPULSION, Polish writer-director Roman Polanski dealt with the disintegration of a young woman into psychotic schizophrenia. This deals with a young man's perverse obsession with a dead woman who previously lived in his Parisian apartment. Polanksi portrays that man, a Polish exile, who slowly loses all sense of identity and takes on the traits of the dead woman. Is this spirit possession or is the man simply insane? A subtle question, not quickly or easily answered. Jo Van Fleet, Melvyn Douglas, Shelley Winters, Claude Dauphin, Lila Kedrova. (VC)

**TENDER DRACULA OR CONFESSIONS OF A BLOOD DRINKER (1974).** Peter Cushing portrays a movie actor playing a vampire who plays a count who plays . . . French production directed by Pierre Grunstein, scripted by Justin Lenoir. Alida Valli, Bernard Menez.

**TENDER FLESH. See WELCOME TO ARROW BEACH.**

**TENDERNESS OF THE WOLVES (1973).** Award-winning German film directed by Ulli Lommel, who tells this story of a mass murderer in avant garde, symbolic fashion. The public never took to Ulli's intellectual filmmaking, so he gave up in disgust and made BOOGEY MAN and BRAINWAVES. Here his intentions are honorable, if not rewarded. Jeff Roden, Margit Carstensen, Kurt Raab, Brigitte Mira.

**TENEBRAE (1982).** Lesser known Italian film written-directed by Dario Argento, best known for DEEP RED and SUSPIRIA. It features the well-photographed, graphic murders for which Argento is famed as a maniac pursues beautiful European babes down dark streets. The main character is a mystery writer who finds that these murders are conforming to the plot of one of his books. Pretty far out, but good Argento. John Saxon, Anthony Franciosa, Daria Nicolodi.

**TENNIS COURT (1984).** British Hammer TV production, made for "The Fox Mystery Theater," with some interesting supernatural twists: Hannah Gordon's ex-lover from the days of World War II, a victim of burns and unrequited love now confined to a recuperation center, projects his anger onto the

**ULLI LOMMEL IN HIS
PRE-COMMERCIAL DAYS**

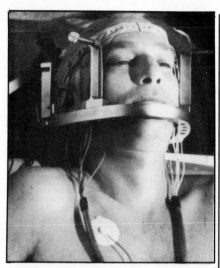

**GEORGE SEGAL IN 'THE TERMINAL MAN'**

family's old tennis court, where a variety of unpleasant events occur to Hannah's son and herself. She hires a parapsychologist to investigate, and he too is subjected to the phenomena. Peter Graves is on hand as a priest/former lover. The twist ending is nicely done, if somewhat predictable. Directed by Cyril Frankel.

**TENTACLES (1977).** Italian production is a steal of JAWS, jazzed up with a name cast headed by Henry Fonda, John Huston, Shelley Winters and Claude Akins. A killer octopus, an extremely unfrightening creature, terrorizes a seaside town. God, is this slow moving, dim-witted and thoroughly exasperating! Directed by Oliver Hellman, better known as Ovido Assonitis. Cesare Danova, Bo Hopkins. (VC)

**TENTH VICTIM, THE (1965).** In the 21st century, war has been outlawed and replaced by "The Big Hunt," a means of venting aggression wherein citizens are "licensed to kill," alternating as hunters and victims. Anyone surviving ten hunts is guaranteed financial rewards for life. The game idea sprang from the fertile imagination of Robert Sheckley, and under Elio Petri's direction is savagely satirical and suspenseful, with Ursula Andress as a "hunter" with a loaded bra (we kid you not) and Marcello Mastroianni as her prey. Plot is frequently erratic and hard to swallow, but the chase and ingenious weapons are engrossing. Not to mention Ursula's bod. Elsa Martinelli is also a shapely huntress. (VC)

**TERMINAL CHOICE (1982).** Riveting medical psychothriller, one of the best of its kind, intensively caring about holding you spellbound as its diabolical murder plot unfolds. Joe Spano's patients are dying at Dodson Medical Clinic in Toronto because someone is tampering with the computer system, programming life-and-death hospital equipment to kill patients. Investigators Diane Venora and Don Francks move in; suspicious-looking doctors and medical red herrings crop up in Neal Bell's script. Climactic scenes of Spano trapped in a hospital bed are unusually exciting. Strange blending of mystery, computerized science-fiction and whodunit. David McCallum portrays the clinic's owner. Watch director Sheldon Larry for better things. (VC)

**TERMINAL ISLAND (1973).** Stephanie Rothman directed this tale of the future, in which convicts endure ordeals of an inescapable prison. Typical behind-bars stuff—sleazy dialogue and people, ample nudity. Don Marshall, Phyllis Davis, Ena Hartman and Tom Selleck engage in overblown

conversations on seemingly relevant issues. A terminal case from beginning to end? (VC)

**TERMINAL MAN, THE (1974).** The first half of this version of Michael Crichton's best-seller is a compelling study in modern technology and surgical techniques. Neurosurgeons implant a miniaturized computer in the brain of George Segal, who's suffering from fits of rage (described as temporal lobe epilepsy) following an accident. But the film's second half, following Segal after he escapes the hospital staff, becomes a pointless series of homicides, ending in a graveyard sequence with a crucifixion. The pace is too lethargic for material that should be fast-moving, and the ambiguities of producer-director Mike Hodges' script become transparent as the terminal man terminates. Joan Hackett is fine as a doctor on the operating staff—the flaws are foggy characterizations and inappropriate directorial techniques. Jill Clayburgh, Ian Wolfe, Matt Clark, Richard Drysart. (VC)

**TERMINATOR, THE (1984).** One of the best action movies of the 1980s, blending fantasy with horror and suspense to create an incredibly satisfying viewing experience. Arnold Schwarzenegger portrays a humanoid robot from 2029 A.D., a time when man has been conquered by robot machines. Schwarzie travels back to present day to assassinate a young woman; one day she will give birth to a child who will overthrow the robot society. The machine-killer begins a cold-blooded reign of terror to find the woman, killing anyone in his way. The pacing is relentless as the intended victim (Linda Hamilton) flees with Michael Biehn's help. James Cameron directs with a real sense for pace, and the script by Cameron and producer Gale Anne Hurd not only has an abundance of action but even works in a relevant love story. Stan Winston's effects are wonderfully graphic; the whole thing is one big success. Schwarzenegger's simple line, "I'll be back," is a classic. Paul Winfield, Lance Henriksen, Rick Rossovich, Dick Miller, Earl Boen. (VC)

**TERRIBLE PEOPLE, THE (1960).** Edgar Wallace mystery is the basis for this West German thriller about an executed murderer who returns to kill those who prosecuted him. Or so it seems . . . familiar stuff, pretty ho hum. Joachim Fuchsberger, Karin Dor. Directed by Harald Reinl.

**TERRIFIED (1963).** Dreary, unbelievably bad Crown-International programmer depicting a crazed killer in a black mask who runs around a deserted mining town murdering boring teenagers. Passe even when it was produced. Directed by Lew Landers. Rod Lauren, Steve Drexel, Tracy Olsen, Denver Pyle, Barbara Luddy, Harry Lauter.

**TERROR, THE (1938).** British adaptation of an Edgar Wallace play, set in an old dark house, Monk's Hall Priory, when weird events might or might not be supernatural. Directed by Richard Bird. Wilfrid Lawson, Bernard Lee, Alastair Sim.

**TERROR, THE (1963).** History of this Roger Corman tricky quickie is more fascinating than the film: After finishing THE RAVEN, Corman realized Boris Karloff owed him two days work, so he fashioned a script and filmed Karloff's scenes back to back. Later, Francis Ford Coppola, Monte Hellman, Jack Hill and Dennis Jacob added new scenes. No wonder the Jack Hill-Leo Gordon script is a mess. Lost Napoleonic officer Jack Nicholson (who even directed some scenes) pursues ghostly Sandra Knight into an isolated seacliff mansion owned by Karloff. Erratic as hell. Supporting players in this anomaly: Jonathan Haze, Dick Miller. (VC)

**TERROR, THE (1978).** Low-budget British fare, directed by Norman J. Warren and written by David McGillivray, about a filmmaker who creates a film about his family, which once burned a witch at the stake. Suddenly the cast and crew are subjected to mysterious deaths. Carolyn Courage, John Nolan, James Aubrey, Sarah Keller. (VC)

**TERROR ABOARD (1933).** Graphic murders on an ocean liner lend this whodunit an uncompromising starkness, but there is nothing buoyant about director Paul Sloane. He

*"Hoodlums from another world on a ray-gun rampage!"— Advertisement for TEENAGERS FROM OUTER SPACE.*

**CREATURE FEATURES MOVIE GUIDE**

needed a lifesaver—but nobody threw him one. Charles Ruggles, Neil Hamilton, John Halliday, Shirley Grey.

**TERROR AT LONDON BRIDGE.** See **BRIDGE ACROSS TIME.** (And all fall down . . . dead!)

**TERROR AT RED WOLF INN (1972).** Young woman is lured to a seaside inn on the pretext of winning an all-expenses-paid holiday, only to discover that the elderly couple running the tourist house is into cannibalism, as is their mentally retarded son. Allen J. Actor's script is full of tongue-in-cheek subtleties and he keeps the horror visuals limited to PG. Only the nihilistic ending will leave one feeling let down. Otherwise, a good scare job, kind of a tame TEXAS CHAINSAW MASSACRE with similar macabre touches. Director Bud Townsend does an okay job, but don't make any reservations at the Red Wolf. The food tastes strange there . . . Linda Gillin, Arthur Space, Mary Jackson. (VC)

**TERROR BENEATH THE SEA (1966).** What's a Japanese monster movie without Godzilla or Ghidrah? Not much, if this is any indication. A mad doctor, the ruler of a vast underwater city, turns humans into water-breathing "cyborgs." A plot is afoot to Take Over the World but two reporters and a physicist turn the tide in the underwater experimental lab. U.S. version was shot simultaneously with the Japanese version and stars many English-speaking cast members. Its director is Hajime Sato, who goes by the name of Terence Ford. Shinichi Chiba, the star, is now better known as Sonny Chiba, martial arts specialist. Hideo Murota, Peggy Neal.

**TERROR CASTLE.** See **HORROR CASTLE.**

**TERROR CIRCUS (1973).** Step right up, ladies and gentlemen . . . see insane killer Andrew Prine capture beautiful women . . . observe beautiful women horribly tortured . . . see how producer-director Gerald Cormier handles blood and gore . . . step right up, ladies and gents, boys and girls . . . get away, kid, you bother me . . . yes, here it is . . . focus your orbs on Manuella Thiess, Jennifer Ashley and other lovelies screaming their lovely lungs at top octave . . . yes, kiddies, carnage, mayhem, all the things life is worth living for . . . Everything you've always wanted on the Monster Midway but were too afraid to pay your dime for . . . . step right this way . . . I said stop botherin' me, kid . . .

**TERROR CREATURES FROM THE GRAVE (1965).** Lackluster Italian chiller has the presence of Barbara Steele but not the presence of mind to tell a compelling story, or provide genuine scares. Instead, you're handed nonsense about a terrible plague and how victims are summoned from the dead to avenge an occultist. The photography is okay but what lousy direction by Ralph Zucker. Sure cure for insomnia. Walter Brandi, Marilyn Mitchell, Alfredo Rizzi.

**TERROR EYES.** See **NIGHT SCHOOL.**

**TERROR FACTOR.** See **SCARED TO DEATH.**

**TERROR FROM THE YEAR 5000 (1958).** Experimentation with a time machine brings objects from the future—including a malformed woman who needs males to procreate the human race in 5000 A.D. The line forms to the right, gents. She gets the guys she needs through hypnosis and other subterfuges. Real claptrack, a definite failure for writer-producer-director Robert Gurney Jr. Joyce Holden, Ward Costello, Beatrice Furdeaux, John Stratton.

**TERROR FROM WITHIN (1974).** Pamela Franklin undergoes psychic dreams, realizing a copse of elm trees, a photo hidden in a painting and a mysterious Rolls-Royce are clues to a mystery. A cheaply produced British TV-movie, a plodding thing without punch. Brian Clemens (creator of THE AVENGERS) gave his idea to telewriter Dennis Spooner. Franklin has little to do but look frightened and toss in her sleep; the real star is Ian Bannen as a strange man always

'I'LL BE BACK!' PROMISES ARNOLD SCHWARZENEGGER IN 'THE TERMINATOR'

**CREATURE FEATURES MOVIE GUIDE**

**JAMES MASON IN 'TERROR HOUSE'**

carving on wood. Very ho-hum bum. Directed by James Ormerod. Suzanne Neve, Oliver Tobias, Dallas Adams.

**TERROR HOUSE** (1943). Also known as THE NIGHT HAS EYES, this is a superior British gothic thriller of the damsel-in-distress school, in which lovely schoolteacher Mary Clare and a companion journey to the Yorkshire moors (fraught with perilous quicksand) where a friend disappeared a year earlier. During a storm they meet a sinister hermit of a man, James Mason, who believes he turns into a frenzied killer under the full moon, a result of a shock he sustained in the civil war in Spain. There's an odd psychological edge (taken from an Alan Kennington novel) and some heavy moor ambience thanks to director Leslie Arliss. After a lot of red herrings, there are some real graphic shocks and a satisfying ending, with stark images, peasoup fog and miasma. Wilfrid Lawson, Joyce Howard, Tucker McGuire.

**TERROR HOUSE.** See **TERROR AT RED WOLF INN.**

**TERROR IN THE AISLES** (1984). Compilation of shock scenes from horror, science-fiction and crime movies, a rehash of favorites and a look at recent material. Some is from classy or classic movies while other scenes were lifted from schlock. In short, a hodgepodge that does have its moments of intensity as we relive Hitchcock's PSYCHO and STRANGERS ON A TRAIN. Other films represented are Carpenter's version of THE THING, SUSPIRIA, WHEN A STRANGER CALLS, NIGHTHAWKS, THE EXORCIST, ROSEMARY'S BABY and DRESSED TO KILL. The cassette version has more gore than the TV version. Compiled by Andrew Kuehn and Stephen Netburn. (VC)

**TERROR IN THE CRYPT** (1963). Christopher Lee heads the cast of this Spanish-Italian supernatural yarn that approaches its subject leisurely, in a sincere effort to build suspense and atmosphere, and to pay homage to its inspiration, J. Sheridan Le Fanu's CARMILLA. Lee, a nobleman who fears his daughter is possessed by a witch, invites occult experts to his castle to observe her behavioral patterns. Several murders occur before the demon is exorcised. Directed by Thomas Miller. Jose Campos, Vera Valmont.

**TERROR IN THE FOREST.** See **FOREST, THE.**

**TERROR IN THE HAUNTED HOUSE** (1958). Newlyweds Cathy O'Donnell and Gerald Mohr reside in a lonely mansion in a mood of happiness, but soon the bride is haunted by dreams and memories of a murder she witnessed as a child—or is she hallucinating? Or is hubby Mohr up to something diabolical? The answers await your curiosity—should you have any after reading this description. Directed by producer William S. Edwards.

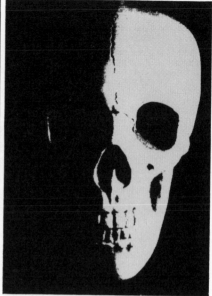

**'TERROR IN THE AISLES'**

**TERROR IN THE JUNGLE** (1968). Search party seeks a youth lost in the Amazon after a plane crash; the boy escapes cannibals and other unpleasantries of the steaming jungle with his toy tiger, which turns into the real thing to protect him. Mexican-U.S. co-production directed by that masterly trio: Tom De'Simone, Andy Janzack and Alex Graton. Henry Clayton Jr., Robert Burns, Fawn Silver.

**TERROR IN THE MIDNIGHT SUN.** See **INVASION OF THE ANIMAL PEOPLE.** (Reigning cats and dogs?)

**TERROR IN THE SWAMP** (1985). Poachers' Cave, now there's a place to stay away from, I'm warnin' ya. Seems folks 'round Houma, Louisiana, are turnin' up plumb dead. Course, the reason's mighty clear, them local scientists been tamperin' with the nutria water rodent, and danged if they haven't done created a giant moo-tation rat. Reckon it twern't gonna scare ya too much cause it's just oneathem extras in a hairy suit. Dad rat it. Soon's that picture was finished, folks ran that Joe Catalanotto and his'n crew smack outta town and told him and them high-falutin' actors, Billy Holliday, Chuck Long and Michael Tedesco, quit givin' us swamp folks a bad name or next time we'll sic them gators 'n cot'n moccasins on you city slickers, hot damn gotohell. (VC)

**TERROR IN THE WAX MUSEUM** (1973). Parade of character actors turns this shallow tallow HOUSE OF WAX pastiche into a passable film. If nothing else holds your interest, you can try identifying each of the familiar faces. A murderer with waxy build-up is adding new trophies to his waxy displays in Jameson Brewer's script, and it's all logically explained at the end. George Fenady directed. Broderick Crawford, Ray Milland, Elsa Lanchester, John Carradine, Louis Hayward, Maurice Evans, Patric Knowles, Lisa Lu.

**TERROR IS A MAN** (1959). Blood Island, not a suitable tourist attraction in the Philippines, is where the survivor of a sea disaster swims to meet a demented scientist (Francis Lederer) conducting experiments to turn a human into a leopard creature. First in the "Blood Island" series that later starred John Ashley. Directed by Gerry De Leon. Greta Thyssen, Richard Derr, Oscar Keesee, Lilia Duran.

---

*"A horror horde of crawl-and-crush Giants clawing out of the Earth from mile-deep catacombs!"—Advertisement for* **THEM.**

**TERROR OF DR. MABUSE, THE.** See **TESTAMENT OF DR. MABUSE, THE.**

**TERROR OF DR. FRANKENSTEIN.** See **VICTOR FRANKENSTEIN.** (To Victor belongs the spoiled)

**TERROR OF GODZILLA, THE.** See **TERROR OF MECHAGODZILLA.** (a mecha-nation, Japan!)

**TERROR OF MECHAGODZILLA (1978).** Giant robot monster attacks Earth, realizing the green planet isn't going to be a pushover when fire-snorting Godzilla shows up, slamming his tail in anger. Also involved in this Japanese mish mash (along with the kitchen sink) are mechanized cyborgs, Ghidrah, Ebirah, Rodan and a bird monster, Chitanoceras. Godzilla's creator, Inoshiro Honda, directed. This sequel to GODZILLA VS. THE COSMIC MONSTER was the 15th in the series. Katsuhiko Sasaki, Tomoke Ai.

**TERROR OF SHEBA (1974).** Superior psychological British thriller: Lana Turner is a vindictive mother subjecting her bastard son to persecution to get even for the way men in her life mistreated her. The boy turns crazy and drowns the family cats in bowls of milk, burying their bodies in a minigraveyard concealed in a labyrinth. As an adult (Ralph Bates), he still bears the brunt of mother's evil when she kills his child and arranges for his wife to find him in the arms of another

**LANA TURNER: NO QUEEN IN 'TERROR OF SHEBA'**

woman. But, Bates has his revenge. Stark, taut, well-produced film with first-rate performances by Turner (looking well-preserved), Bates, Trevor Howard as the secret father, Olga Georges-Picot as the seductress and Suzan Farmer as the wronged wife. Directed by Don Chaffey. On videocassette as **THE GRAVEYARD.**

**TERROR OF THE MAD DOCTOR.** See **TESTAMENT OF DR. MABUSE, THE.**

**TERROR OF THE TONGS (1961).** Opener in Hammer's Fu Manchu series with Christopher Lee as the ruthless tong leader surrounded by torture devices, diabolical weapons, insidious poisons, treacherous doctors, slave girls, opium dens and other pleasures of life. Okay nonsense—later films fluctuated between campiness and ineptitude. Directed by Anthony Bushell; written by Jimmy Sangster. Geoffrey Toone, Yvonne Monlaur, Burt Kwouk, Milton Reid.

**TERROR ON TAPE (1983).** Compilation of grisly scenes from horror/science-fiction exploitation films—we're talking

Gross City, men. Clips are frameworked around bits in which videostore owner Cameron Mitchell (resembling a ghoul) greets customers (a nerd, a macho construction worker, a sexpot in a revealing outfit) and pushes the sickening merchandise. Scenes are from VAMPIRE HOOKERS, RETURN OF THE ALIEN'S DEADLY SPAWN, BLOODTIDE, CATHY'S CURSE, FROZEN SCREAM, ALIEN PREY, COLOR ME BLOOD RED and 2000 MANIACS. You'll see baby alien monsters eating a human head, a hatchet sinking into a human brain, hairy hands strangling a father in a confessional booth, a needle plunging into an eye, a human arm being severed, a boulder being dropped on a woman's chest, impaling by pitchfork, a scalping, ad nauseum. For strong stomachs only, and we mean strong! The wraparound was directed by Robert A. Worms III and features Michelle Bauer as the hot tamale let's-romp chick. (VC)

**TERROR ON TOUR (1980).** Don Edmonds, noted for his sadistic films about Ilsa, female commadant of a Nazi death camp, helmed this uninvolving minor-league psychoslasher flick in which the stabber runs around murdering prostitutes while dressed as a member of a hard-rock group, The Clowns. It's up to the real Clowns to make fools of themselves while tracking the killer. Mainly an excuse for an abundance of feebly produced rock footage as the amateurish cast misses every beat of Del Lekus' script. Rick Styles, Chip Greeman, Rich Pemberton, Lisa Rodriguez. (VC)

**TERROR OUT OF THE SKY (1979).** Sequel to THE SAVAGE BEES, in which bumbling bumble bee experts Efrem Zimbalist Jr. and Dan Haggerty of the National Bee Center are attacked by stingers that go buzz in the night. Nicely directed by Lee H. Katzin. Ike Eisenmann, Steve Franken, Tovah Feldshuh. (VC)

**TERROR TRAIN (1980).** Unsavory college kids, holding a masquerade party aboard a speeding train, are knocked off one by one by a knife-wielding maniac. Muddled characters created by Y. T. Drake make it difficult to swallow the preposterous action. The only exciting moments come when Jamie Lee Curtis, scream queen from HALLOWEEN, is pursued by the maddened killer through the train. Ben Johnson as the sympathetic conductor and magician David Copperfield are derailed by one lousy script, as is director Roger Spottiswoode (who went on to better pictures).

**TERRORNAUTS, THE (1967).** British science-fiction is terror-not when an astronomer and his laboratory are teleported to another planet where several incidents, none of them making much sense, occur with monotonous repetition. Indifferently directed by Montgomery Tully. Simon Oates, Zena Marshall, Patricia Hayes. Amicus production adapted by John Brunner from a Murray Leinster novel. (VC)

**TERRORVISION (1986).** Failed comedy-satire from producer Charles Band, written-directed by Ted Nicolaou with no idea about how comedy should be played. It's a lowbrow insult to anyone's sense of humor when a garbage collector alien on the planet Pluton accidentally jettisons a monster into space, which comes to Earth on a lightning bolt and enters a home through its TV screens. The monster, designed by John Buechler, is a gross thing with big teeth and a long tongue and it hogs the camera too long. Folks in the invaded home are a swinging couple (Mary Woronov, Gerrit Graham), a militant grandfather (Bert Remsen) and an obnoxious kid (Chad Allen). An Elvira clone, Medusa, is another wasted character. Made in Italy so Band could save a buck. (VC)

**TERRORVISION (1985).** TV-anthology of horror short stories, lifted from a syndicated series that never got off the ground. Producers lacked TerrorVision. Bill Reilly, Kim Merril.

**TEST PILOT PIRX (1979).** Stories by Polish science-fiction writer Stanislaw Lem form the basis for this futuristic look at robots who look like humans. One is sent to Jupiter on an experimental assignment. Written-directed by Marek Piestrak.

**TESTAMENT (1983).** Powerful anti-war film, depicting in a low-key fashion the after-effects of nuclear holocaust. Hamelin is a small community in central California beyond the major blast area, escaping any detectable destruction. However, invisible gamma rays, radiation and fallout take their toll. Focus is on a mother and four children (the father is

# *One Big Happy Family . . .*

## MEET GRANDPA, LEATHERFACE, COOK, CHOP-TOP AND (SPRAWLED) MUPPET

away at the time of the blast) as she clutches for hope while despair grows around her. No devastation, no blood and only a few corpses wrapped in sheets—yet this is a gut-wrenching picture that has stunned many and made them weep. Based on a short short story by Carol Amen (who says the idea came to her in a vision); produced by Jonathan Bernstein and Lynne Littman (she also directed) for PBS. Jane Alexander is outstanding as the confused mother fighting to hold her family together. William Devane is strong in the brief father role. Mako, Leon Ames and Lurene Tuttle appear in cameos. Lukas Haas, Clete Roberts. (VC)

**TESTAMENT OF DR. CORDELIER, THE (1959).** Jean Renoir's version of Stevenson's "The Strange Case of Dr. Jekyll and Mr. Hyde," starring Jean-Louis Barrault in the dual role of Dr. Cordelier and the evil Opale. Not considered one of Renoir's better films. Micheline Gary, Teddy Bilis.

**TESTAMENT OF DR. MABUSE, THE (1933).** Sequel to Fritz Lang's 1922 DR. MABUSE, THE GAMBLER. The evil genius (Rudolf Klein-Rogge) dies broken and alone in a lunatic asylum. But the head of the sanitorium, Dr. Baum, becomes infected with megalomania and other Mabuse traits—he has inherited Mabuse's warped spirit. Shrewd inspector Lohmann (from Lang's M, also played by Otto Wernicke) tracks the surrogate criminal. Atmosphere, suspense, social melodrama in the best Lang tradition. Oscar Beregi.

**TESTAMENT OF DR. MABUSE, THE (1962).** First in a series of West German remakes based on Fritz Lang's early films about a math genius who turns his intellect to pursuits of crime against humanity. Confined to an insane asylum, Dr. Mabuse still works his devilish schemes through hypnosis and other acts of terror carried out by his henchmen—even after his demise. Hardly up to the quality of Lang's version, yet a sincere attempt by director Werner Klinger. Wolfgang Preiss is the doctor, Walter Rilla is in charge of the asylum and Gert Frobe is Lohmann, the policeman dedicated to stopping Mabuse. Senta Berger, Helmut Schmid.

**TESTAMENT OF ORPHEUS (1960).** French film written-directed by Jean Cocteau, who plays the central figure: a

poet of the 18th Century seeking the meaning of existence in strange landscapes, where reality cannot be distinguished from fantasy. He encounters Minerva, goddess of wisdom; a blind Oedipus and a bald receptionist (Yul Brynner). Imaginative, arresting mixture. Pablo Picasso, Charles Aznavour.

**TEXAS CHAINSAW MASSACRE, THE (1974).** Strictly an exercise in exploitation, but done with such a sense of grotesque style that it has become a cult classic in American Grand Guignol. Nowadays it might seem tame but in its day it was controversial, so cruel and sick seemed its macabre touches. Marilyn Burns establishes new screaming records as she is pursued through an orchard by a madman eager to sink his teeth into her neck—the teeth of his chainsaw, that is. Poor Marilyn. She's bound and gagged, beaten, cut with a razor blade, shoved into a canvas sack and forced to sit in an armchair made of real arms. The family of sick characters are played for grotesque comedy. Directed by that mild-mannered sentimentalist Tobe Hooper, who went on to make SALEM'S LOT and POLTERGEIST. Kim Henkel co-wrote the script with Hooper. Gunnar Hanse plays the crazy guy with the buzzing saw. The 1986 sequel is even greater. (VC)

**TEXAS CHAINSAW MASSACRE PART 2, THE (1986).** Lawman Lefty Enright (Dennis Hopper), father of one of the victims of the first film, is tracking the crazy chainsaw killers, using a radio disc jockey named Stretch (Caroline Williams) as bait. Tobe Hooper's new cut-and-tear adventures of the Sawyer family comprise one of the oddest movies ever made—a hip, flip comment on various forms of American mania, personified by the return of Leatherface (chainsaw-whacking specialist), Chop-Top (the idiot with a metal plate in his head) and Grandpa, still trying to hit victims over the head with a sledgehammer, but usually missing. Hooper captures a macabre sense of humor from L. M. Kit Carson's groovy albeit simplistic script which turns to surreal horror once Stretch is trapped in the underground caverns of an abandoned tourist attraction. Hooper turns Grand Guignol into farce and sociological subtext, and Hopper is a standout as the avenger with two chainsaws strapped to his side like six-shooters. Gory, not for the squeamish, but the satire makes it a must-see. (VC)

# ... Of Murderers and Preverts

**LEATHERFACE (BILL JOHNSON) GETS HIS FROM LEFTY ENRIGHT (DENNIS HOPPER)**

**THAT LADY IN ERMINE (1948).** Director Ernst Lubitsch died during filming of this Fox costume period comedy, so Otto Preminger helmed the last ten days of shooting without credit. The setting is southeast Europe in 1861 when Douglas Fairbanks Jr. steps from a painting in bodily form to pursue another solid body, Betty Grable. Swirling gowns, dashing colonels and gorgeous countesses in a never-never land of Bavarian customs. This light-hearted Technicolor affair doesn't make a lot of sense but it's visually appealing, its characters gallant and beautous. Cesar Romero, Walter Abel, Reginald Gardiner, Whit Bissell, Harry Davenport.

**THAT RIVIERA TOUCH (1966).** Rival gangs search for an emerald necklace in a haunted villa on the Riviera, with corpses all over the place and secret passageways allowing the cast to run wild in "old dark house" fashion. Directed by Cliff Owen. Eric Morecombe, Ernie Wise.

**THAT'S THE SPIRIT (1945).** Inoffensive, charming comedy starring Jack Oakie as a vaudeville trouper who returns from the dead and plays Pan-like music to bring happiness to his wife (June Vincent) and daughter (Peggy Ryan) who are dominated by Scrooge-like banker Gene Lockhart. It'll bolster your own spirits with its innocuous charm. Directed by Charles Lamont. Irene Ryan, Buster Keaton.

**THEATER OF BLOOD (1972).** Macabre black comedy (similar to the Dr. Phibes series with its sick jokes and bloodletting) starring Vincent Price as ham Shakespearean actor Edward Lionheart, who so murders scenes from the classics that London's critics murder him in the press. The "murdering" becomes literal when Lionheart has his revenge against the critics and murders them with the help of a band of bums (the true identity of which will surprise you). Death devices are borrowed from Shakespeare, a clever touch to Anthony Greville-Bell's script. Death's labor found, you might say. Diana Rigg, Jack Hawkins, Harry Andrews, Coral Browne, Diana Dors, Robert Morley, Michael Hordern, Dennis Price. Jolly good horror from director Douglas Hickox. (VC)

**THEATER OF DEATH (1967).** Whodunit-horror story with slasher murder overtones. Parisian theater presenting Grand Guignol is site of several murders committed by a ghoul or vampire. Could it be that Christoper Lee, head of the troupe, is responsible? Don't count on it, as there are a few surprises. Samuel Gallu directed. Lelia Goldoni, Julian Glover. Jenny Till, Ivor Dean. (VC)

**THEM (1954).** "Giant bug" movies of the 1950s tended to be cheapjack affairs, but not this Warner Bros. classic, which holds up as a science-fiction thriller and as a chase suspense-mystery story, wonderfully concocted by screenwriter Ted Sherdemann. Director Gordon Douglas captures a maximum of atmosphere in this taut tale of mutant ants (12 feet high) terrorizing the New Mexico desert near the Alamogordo atomic test sites. Superior effects by Ralph Ayers will convince you those giant ants are real and attacking! Intriguing chase to track down the queen bee and destroy her nest leads to the L.A. sewers—more opportunity for Douglas to build suspense as armies of men move into the slimy tubes. Edmund Gwenn is the aging expert in myrmecology, the science of ants; heroes are James Arness and James Whitmore, with Joan Weldon as Gwenn's daughter, who's also a scientist. William Schallert, Onslow Stevens, Dub Taylor, Leonard Nimoy, Fess Parker. (VC)

**THESE ARE THE DAMNED (1961).** Joseph Losey directed Hammer's low-key, uncompromising indictment of the misuse of atomic power. A government program headed by Alexander Knox is using children for experimental purposes—a cold, ruthless act reflecting the world's battle for political power through nuclear threat. All the themes have been cleverly blended by Evan Jones from H. L. Lawrence's novel, CHILDREN OF LIGHT. MacDonald Carey is the American who discovers the secret project, Oliver Reed is the leader of the youths, Shirley Anne Field is Reed's brother and Viveca Lindfors is a shattered woman.

**THEY ALL DIED LAUGHING (1964).** Scientist Leo McKern discovers a happiness-induced drug that kills once the laughter dies away. British film is a mixture of comedy and terror, but the title does not refer to the audience. It's not that funny. Directed by Don Chaffey. Janet Munro, Dennis Price, Miles Malleson, Leonard Rossiter, Jerome Willis.

## 'Them': They Scare the Femme and the Him to Make a Gem

**THEY CAME FROM BEYOND SPACE (1967).** Joseph Millard's novel, THE GODS HATE KANSAS, was adapted by Milton Subotsky and directed by Freddie Francis. It's a familiar Quatermass-style tale of extraterrestrials taking over human bodies on the outskirts of Cornwall in order to make repairs to their damaged spaceship, which has crashed on the Moon. Similar to NIGHT SLAVES. Jennifer Jayne, Michael Gough, Robert Hutton, Maurice Good. (VC)

**THEY CAME FROM WITHIN (1976).** First of several grisly Canadian films written-directed by David Cronenberg (RABID, SCANNERS, VIDEODROME) featuring graphic gore when body-eating parasites, roused by the sexual appetites of their hosts, eat through human bodies, munching on flesh with as much relish as patrons put on hotdogs. Great scenes of wormy creepies crawling out of bodies. Paul Hampton, Barbara Steele. Strong stomachs required. (VC)

**THEY MIGHT BE GIANTS (1971).** Escaping an intolerable life in which his wife has just died, lawyer George C. Scott retreats into a fantasy world in which he believes himself to

### JOAN WELDON'S PICNIC INTERRUPTED

be Sherlock Holmes, mankind's savior. This lovely, thoughtful premise unfortunately goes awry and becomes a disjointed allegory, so surrealistic in its unfolding that its initial hold dwindles and is lost in an enigmatic climax, where illusion and reality mingle to form a new madhouse. Joanne Woodward co-stars as Scott's psychiatrist, whose name happens to be Dr. Watson. Based on a play by James Goldman, who wrote the script. Directed by Anthony Harvey. Jack Gilford, Lester Rawlins. (VC)

**THEY SAVED HITLER'S BRAIN (1964).** Washed-up, has-been Nazis living on a Caribbean island keep the Fuehrer's head alive in a Special Solution in order to carry out their leader's Final Solution. New plans for world domination go badly when a neurobiologist and daughter (experts on a deadly nerve gas) intervene to schtick it to Schicklegrubber. Abominably directed by David Bradley, this has a reputation

**THE HEAVY-FOOTED GENIE IS A SOUL BROTHER TO SABU IN 'THE THIEF OF BAGDAD'**

for being among the worst movies ever made. By all means, don't miss it. John Holland, Nestor Paiva, Walt Stocker, Scott Peters, Audrey Caire, Carlos Rivas. (VC)

**THEY'RE COMING TO GET YOU (1972).** . . . but don't get carried away by this Italian-Spanish flicker about the efforts of a devil cult to possess the body of a cutie pie innocent. Same old sex, sadism, gore. Directed by Sergio Martino. Edwige Fenech, George Hilton, Susan Scott.

**THEY'RE PLAYING WITH FIRE (1984).** Minor whodunit that seriously attempts to be a suspense shocker, then deteriorates into a standard slasher film featuring a fiendish killer in a ski mask, wielding a wicked axe. The only real interesting asset of this low budget effort written-directed by Howard Avedis is Sybil Danning, the B-movie girl with the golden body, who wears skimpy bikinis and strips to make love to Eric Brown. She is one incredible woman. Supporting cast includes Andrew Prine, who is thoroughly wasted, Paul Clemens and K. T. Stevens. Marlene Schmidt co-produced with Avedis. And now back to Sybil . . . (VC)

**THIEF OF BAGDAD, THE (1940).** British producer Sir Alexander Korda's fantasy in the Arabian Nights tradition is still the best of its kind—an allegory of good vs. evil, a love story, an adventure of quest, retribution and restitution, a tale of black magic in which a wizard, tormented by his love for a woman, is driven to his doom. Above all, this blends metaphor of language with poetic visuals and lush, exotic music. Sabu possesses an ageless quality as the thief who joins deposed king John Justin to fight the wicked Vizier, played to perfection by Conrad Veidt, and to romance beautiful June Duprez. Screenwriter Miles Malleson doubles as the dopey but loveable sultan who collects the world's strangest toys. Rex Ingram is the towering, thunderous Djinni, who springs from a tiny bottle uncorked by Sabu. Visual effects and cinematography by William Cameron Menzies, music by Miklos Rozsa. Three directors were needed: Michael Powell, Ludwig Berger and Tim Whelan. Splendid Technicolor adventure; cannot be recommended too highly. (VC)

**THIEF OF BAGDAD, THE (1960).** Entertaining Arabian Nights adventure, but a thousand and one adventures away from the 1940 version. This Italian production, imported to America by Joseph Levine, stars Steve Reeves as a muscular hero who must pass seven tests to possess the Blue Rose, the only cure for an ailing princess. But why would anyone face so many dangers for such a flaccid character (played by Georgia Moll)? Made in Tunis and Italy. Directed by Arthur Lubin, Edy Vessel, Arturo Dominici. (VC)

**THIEF OF BAGDAD, THE (1978).** TV version of the Thousand and One Nights tales (directed by Clive Donner) in which a roguish beggar-thief battles the evil wizard, replete with magic carpet, bottled genie, veiled beauties, paradise gardens and magical lamp. Special effects by John (STAR WARS) Stears. Prince: Kabir Bedi; thief: Roddy McDowall; wizard: Terence Stamp. Others in the cast: Peter and Paula Ustinov, Frank Finlay, Ian Holm, Marina Vlady. (VC)

**THIEF OF DAMASCUS, THE (1952).** Sword-and-sandal scandal from flickie-quickie producer Sam Katzman stars Paul Henreid as an Arabian Nights hero consorting with Scheherazade, Sinbad and Ali Baba to put down an evil caliph. Same old "Open Sesame" seeds. John Sutton, Jeff Donnell, Lon Chaney Jr., Elena Verdugo. Directed by Will Jason; scripted by Robert E. Kent.

**THIN AIR.** See **BODY STEALERS, THE.** (Just doing what comes snatch-erally?)

**THING, THE . . . FROM ANOTHER WORLD (1951).** Christian Nyby is credited with directing this RKO version of John W. Campbell's "Who Goes There?" but it is generally known producer Howard Hawks was on the set as guiding benefactor. Certainly the technique of overlapping, fast-delivered dialogue is a tell-tale giveaway. No matter . . . because of its concern for a strong camaraderie among men (a standard Hawks trait), for sprightly dialogue (by Charles Lederer), for tingling suspense, and because it captures the frigid atmosphere of an Arctic research station, THE THING remains one of the best science-fiction thrillers of the 1950s. Another achievement is composer Dimitri Tiomkin's use of the theremin which creates an unholy chilling theme. A small band of men (and one woman) at an isolated outpost near the North Pole retrieves the frozen body of an alien which has come to Earth aboard a flying saucer. Once the creature (described as an emotionless vegetable monster) thaws out, it's on a destructive rampage, needing human blood to survive. The makeup for the creature (James Arness in a jumpsuit with putty nose) is a letdown, but glimpses of the monster are minimized, allowing tension to build unrelentingly. Kenneth Tobey heads the Air Force personnel, Douglas Spencer is great as the wise-cracking newsman, Robert Cornithwaite memorable as the misguided scientist. Margaret Sheridan, Dewey Martin, Eduard Franz, Paul Frees, John Dierkes, George Fenneman, Tom Steele, Robert Nichols. (VC)

**THING, THE (1982).** Outstanding John Carpenter-directed version of John W. Campbell's "Who Goes There?", the classic novella first brought to the screen by Howard Hawks in

1951. While that film is remembered for suspense and characterizations, and not for its monster or effects, Carpenter has striven for exactly the opposite values, stressing the shape-changing extraterrestrial beast at the expense of all else. Yet, it is this single facet that makes the film so compelling. Rob Bottin and a large team of tricksters have created remarkably grisly, gruesome effects—perhaps the most gruesome ever captured on film. According to Bottin, there are 45 different glimpses of the creature as it undergoes stages of change. The stuff of our worst nightmares, this will give children bad dreams and may even upset adults. The cast is topped by Kurt Russell, with strong support from Wilford Brimley, T. K. Carter, Richard Dysart and Richard Masur. This time the setting is an Antarctic research station where a team of scientists is isolated by a raging storm. Meanwhile The Thing, freed from its imprisonment in the ice, where it has been for 100,000 years (next to its crashed flying saucer), begins taking "shape." The screenplay by William Lancaster (son of Burt) is muddled but as a special effects classic, this is the greatest. (VC)

**THING THAT WOULDN'T DIE, THE (1958).** Universal-International, once the king of horror, was foundering when it produced this programmer, for David Duncan's script is wretched and Will Cowan's direction double-wretched, with studio composer Joseph Gershenson stealing themes from other films to keep the budget low. The back lot studio ranch is the setting for a feeble story about a girl with divining powers who finds the head of a 16th Century devil worshipper which maintains a hypnotic hoodoo over the cast as the long-dead dastard, once an enemy of Sir Francis Drake, tries to rejoin his severed head to its body. But believe us, this lacks body of any kind. William Reynolds, Andra Martin.

**THING WITH TWO HEADS, THE (1972).** Imagine the social satire that might have gone into this horror-fantasy about a hulking black convict (Rosey Grier) who wakes up from an operation to find the head of a bigoted white surgeon (Ray Milland) attached to his neck. But no . . . instead we are subjected to gross stupidities as Grier rushes around the L.A. landscape to clear himself of a murder charge and Milland acts like a redneck dolt. Every opportunity for something

# Showing Us a Thing or Two

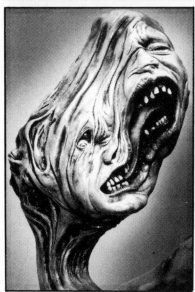

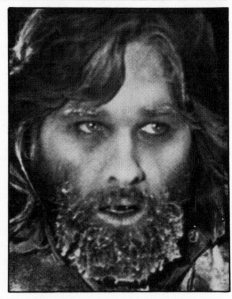

**KURT RUSSELL BATTLES EXTRATERRESTRIAL SHAPE-CHANGER IN 'THE THING' (1982)**

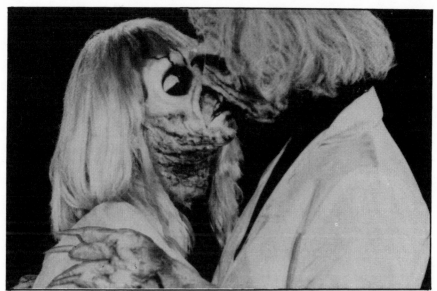

**TILL LIFE DO THEY PART: SMOOCHING SPIRITS IN CASTLE'S '13 GHOSTS'**

amusing or clever is missed by director Lee Frost. William Smith, Roger Perry, Chelsea Brown, Don Marshall.

**THINGS HAPPEN AT NIGHT (1948).** . . . but not much happens in this British version of a Frank Harvey play, THE POLTERGEIST, which depicts a young girl possessed by a mischievous demon. Directed by Francis Searle. Gordon Hacker, Garry Marsh, Olga Linda, Beatrice Campbell.

**THINGS TO COME (1936).** British production from Alexander Korda—directed by William Cameron Menzies from a screenplay by H. G. Wells, who adapted his own novel—is a minor classic in science-fiction set design and special effects, although its philosophies now seem muddled and naively outdated. The epic is broken into three prophetic sections. The first depicts war in 1940 which leads to the Dark Age, when pestilence (the Wandering Sickness) sweeps the world. The second section deals with a feudal system in which neighboring districts wage war. The third part, set in 2036, depicts man on a higher plane devoting himself to art and science. A rocket expedition to the moon is planned, but reactionaries fear man has advanced far enough and stage an uprising. Which leads to war. Thus, history is a cyclical process. Stunning achievement for its time, with a cast that does wonders with the oft-pedantic dialogue: Sir Cedric Hardwicke, Raymond Massey, Ralph Richardson, Margaretta Scott, Edward Chapman. (VC)

**THIRD FROM THE SUN (1972).** Bulgarian science-fiction trilogy: "Eden" is a tale about friendly aliens; "The Stranger" depicts another alien of lesser benevolence; and "My First Day" is a time-travel tale. Directed by Georgi Stoyanov.

**THIRST (1979).** Above-average Australian vampire tale that has a compelling, perverse nature in its bite as a young woman (Chantal Contouri) is taken to a country farm, where she is "fattened" for the kill by a vampire gang. Henry Silva has a great death scene and David Hemmings is outstanding in a surprise-twist role. Well directed by Rod Hardy, tautly writing by John Pinkney. THIRST will certainly quench your taste for a good horror movie. (VC)

**THIRSTY DEAD, THE (1974).** Philippine film could have used extra sips of energy, for "dead" sums it up all too well. Zealots of the jungle kidnap Manilan girls to inject blood into their veins that will give them eternal youth. They escape their captors, but for the viewer there is no escape from dreariness. Directed by Terry Becker. John Considine, Jennifer Billingsley, Judith McConnell. (VC)

**THIRTEEN GHOSTS (1960).** Campy, unimportant horror film produced and directed by William Castle, prophet of the great god Gimmick. Filmed in "Illusiono," for which viewers were provided "Ghost Finders": glasses with panels of red (enabling them to see the ghosts) and blue (blocking out the ghosts). Robb White's story: A family inherits a haunted house, unaware a fortune is hidden among the bric-a-brac. Ghosts come and go in tedious fashion. Thirteen was Castle's unlucky number this time out. Rosemary De Camp, Donald Woods, Martin Milner, Margaret Hamilton. (VC)

**THIRTEEN WOMEN (1932).** Myrna Loy, acting as if she were playing the evil daughter in THE MASK OF FU MANCHU, portrays an insidious half-caste who uses her hypnotic powers to evil ends. It's a battle of wills and wiles between her and Irene Dunne. Directed by George Archainbaud. Ricardo Cortez, C. Henry Gordon, Irene Dunne.

**THIRTEENTH CHAIR, THE (1937).** Outstanding MGM cast (Dame May Whitty, Lewis Stone, Henry Daniell) enhances a rickety story about a seance faked to elicit a murderer's confession. The film reveals how spiritualists pull off their shoddiest tricks. Based on Bayard Veillier's play; produced in 1929 by Tod Browning with Bela Lugosi and Conrad Nagel.

**THIRTEENTH GUEST, THE (1932).** As creaky as the unoiled doors in the drafty corridor . . . as dusty as the unswept corners of the secret rooms . . . yes, another "old dark house" imitation starring Ginger Rogers and Lyle Talbot among those trapped in the mansion with a black-caped killer equipped with strange weaponry and gadgets. Directed by Albert Ray. J. Farrell MacDonald, James Eagles.

**THIRTEENTH REUNION.** Videocassette version of an episode of HAMMER HOUSE OF HORROR. See **CHARLIE BOY/THIRTEENTH REUNION, THE.**

**THIRTY-FOOT BRIDE OF CANDY ROCK, THE (1959).** Lou Costello's last feature (sans partner Bud Abbott) stars Lou as a goofy inventor who transforms girlfriend Dorothy Provine into a gigantic representative of the feminist movement. A sad finale to the career of a once-popular film prankster. Directed by Sidney Miller. Robert Burton, Doodles Weaver, Gale Gordon, Jimmy Conlin, Charles Lane. (VC)

**THIS HOUSE POSSESSED (1981).** It's possessed all right—it wants to keep lovely Lisa Eilbacher to itself. It must have a perverted form of housekeeping in mind. TV-movie starring Parker Stevenson, Joan Bennett, Slim Pickens, Shelley Smith, K. Callan. Directed by William Wiard.

**THIS ISLAND EARTH (1955).** Sincere adaptation of Raymond F. Jones' novel resulted in a classy Universal-International science-fiction epic with abundant effects by Clifford Stine and Stanley Horsley. The Franklin Coen-Edward G. O'Callighan script is uneven but it's still a pleasure to ogle the space battles and interplanetary travel as Rex Reason and Faith Domergue are transported to the planet Metaluna by extraterrestrial humanoid Jeff Morrow to save the dying world from attack by its rival enemy, Zahgon. Sounds juvenile, but it was excitingly directed by Joseph Newman (aided by Jack Arnold and producer William Alland) and crisply edited by Virgil Vogel. The climax is heightened by a six-foot offspring of a giant bug with exposed brain, eyes as big as saucers and blood vessels outside the skin. Lance Fuller, Russell Johnson, Douglas Spencer, Robert Nichols. (VC)

**THIS STUFF'LL KILL YA! (1971).** Gore specialist Herschell Gordon Lewis special: Some revenooers turn up in an Oklahoma town where a local minister is behind the gore murders of college girls. Blood and brimstone, maybe? The last movie of cowboy actor Tim Holt. (VC)

Lang returned to West Germany to co-write and direct this resurrection of his 1932 classic, THE TESTAMENT OF DR. MABUSE, reactivating the evil genius who turns his intellect to nefarious pursuits. Not up to the original, but still damn good Lang as Commissioner Kraugs (Gert Frobe) tracks the criminal to the Hotel Luxor. This set off a wave of Mabuse remakes, all inferior to the original. Dawn Addams, Wolfgang Preiss, Peter Van Eyck, Howard Vernon.

**THREADS (1984).** Great Britain's answer to THE DAY AFTER, a semidocumentary docudrama (first shown on the BBC) depicting what happens to the city of Sheffield when the USA and the USSR spark a nuclear war. Horribly grim and terrifying, sparing none of the hopelessness and sense of despair that accompanies such a futile act. Hence, not a great joy to watch—but you won't forget it. Written-directed by Mick Jackson. (VC)

**THREE CASES OF MURDER (1955).** Superior British trilogy: While the second narrative is a standard police procedural, the first and third are of a macabre nature. "Lord Mountdrago," by Somerset Maugham, stars Orson Welles as

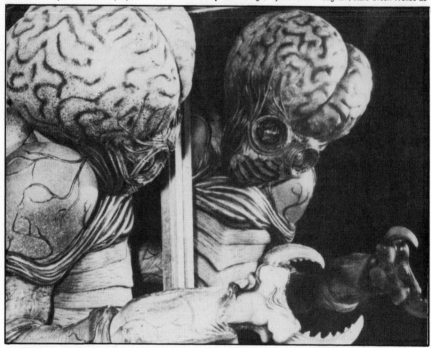

## THE MUTANT MONSTER THAT STALKS FAITH DOMERGUE IN 'THIS ISLAND EARTH'

**THOR THE CONQUERER (1982).** Italian sword-and-sorcery adventure directed by T. Ricci and starring Malisa Lang and Conrad Nichols. Usual stuff involving a magical sword in a fantasy kingdom, etc.

**THOSE FANTASTIC FLYING FOOLS. See BLAST OFF.**

**THOUSAND AND ONE NIGHTS, A (1945).** Cornel Wilde as Aladdin rubs the Magic Lamp and out pops Evelyn Keyes, as well-curved as his scimitar, a femme blade. After lurking through caves, peering at the brocade costumes of harem cuties and fighting off Phil Silvers' bad jokes, Wilde still falls short of 1001 delights. Watch for Shelley Winters—she's sexily positioned among the plotting viziers. And Rex Ingram, still rollicking with delight over THIEF OF BAGDAD, returns as a mighty genie. Hang on, little ones, we're about to fly across the world again on a Magic Carpet. Directed by Alfred E. Green. Nestor Paiva, Adele Jergens.

**THOUSAND EYES OF DR. MABUSE, THE (1960).** Fritz

a member of the House of Lords who continually dreams about a man he once humiliated, and that man's apparent revenge. Directed by George More O'Ferall, with Alan Badel and Andre Morell. "In the Picture" stars Badel as an insane painter trapped in his own painting in a museum; he entices browsers into the canvas so he can assume human form again. Directed by Wendy Toye; with Leueen MacGrath.

**THREE NUTS IN SEARCH OF A BOLT (1964).** Licentious comedy spiced up by busty Mamie Van Doren (as sexpot Saxie Symboll) who teams with Paul Gilbert and John Cronin to have a hambone actor (Tommy Noonan) pretend he's a famous psychiatrist (!) so he can analyze their sexual problems and bring them to new peaks of happiness. Whether she can act or not is immaterial as Mamie of the monumental mammaries proceeds to shed his clothing for reasons that would give Freud a complex. Judicious editing required for commercial TV. Ziva Rodann, Alvy Moore, L.Q. Jones. Noonan directed/co-wrote with Ian McGlashan.

**THREE ON A MEATHOOK (1973).** Writer-director Phillip Schuman, who shot a documentary about the making of RAIDERS OF THE LOST ARK, directed this pornie film with a cult following. Allegedly it's based on the true murder case of Ed Gein, the madman who wore the skin of his victims and had a mother complex. Yes, the same real-life homicidal maniac who inspired Robert Bloch to write PSYCHO. Charles Kissinger, James Pickett.

**THREE STOOGES IN ORBIT, THE (1962).** Your senses will be spinning too during this feature starring Moe Howard, Larry Fine and Joe De Rita as nitwits who meet crazy inventor Emil Sitka, designer of a submarine-tank combination. Complicating the plot are Martians out to steal the device. This cinematic idiocy is super-lowbrow yet now radiates a special nostalgic flavor, brought on by the fact that the Stooges have become entertainment icons, enduring beyond their own time. Even the phony monster masks seem quaint and amusing, rather than cheap. My, how time gives the darnedest things a patina of historical significance. Directed by Edward Bernds; produced by Norman Maurer, one-time editor of Three Stooges comic books. Carol Christensen, Nestor Paiva, Edson Stroll, George Neise.

**THREE STOOGES MEET HERCULES, THE (1962).** Spoof on musclemen epics, with Moe Howard, Larry Fine and Joe De Rita working in Ithaca, N.Y., in a soda shop, befriending the guy living next door who just happens to be inventing a time machine. They all travel back in time to Greece before Christ to that Ithaca to meet Ulysses, Hercules (portrayed here as a dumb grunt master) and Achilles the Heel. The funniest scenes feature the Stooges in drag in a harem, mistaken as hand maidens, and a Ben-Hur parody as they row a king's vessel on a "holiday cruise." Effacious and outrageous, with the Stooges trapped in a low budget continuum that ultimately sets them back two centuries extra. Directed by Edward Bernds. Emil Sitka, Gene Roth, Samson Burke. (VC)

**THREE WORLDS OF GULLIVER, THE (1960).** Following THE SEVENTH VOYAGE OF SINBAD, producer Charles H. Schneer and special effects artist Ray Harryhausen collaborated to bring Jonathan Swift's satire to the screen, and the results are impressive. Again, Kerwin Mathews portrays the young hero—a traveler who falls overboard and finds himself captive in the land of the Lilliputians, tiny people under the thumb of the Brobdingnags, unfriendly giants from a neighborhing island. Mathews befriends the Tiny Tims and battles the big guys. The wonderful effects capture more of a fairy tale quality than other Harryhausen efforts. Romance, action and comedy with the younger set better served. Directed by Jack Sher. Jo Morrow, Peter Bull, June Thorburn, Lee Patterson. Music by Bernard Herrmann.

**THRILL KILLERS, THE (1967).** Ray Dennis Steckler, an eccentric but likable low budget filmmaker, probably best known for THE INCREDIBLY STRANGE CREATURES WHO STOPPED LIVING AND BECAME CRAZY MIXED-UP ZOMBIES, directs and stars in this high-energy though often laughable psychokiller smasher-basher in which an escaped maniac, Mad Dog Glick, is terrorzing assorted passers-by when he runs into three other escaped nuts, one of whom carries a large axe wherever he goes. A lot of what Steckler does is crude satire and there's an underlying element of naivete that makes it palatable, if not classic. The film works best as a chase during its last half hour as Liz Renay runs (and repeatedly screams) for her life. Steckler has built up an odd cult following with his handful of films, of which this is one of the best. (VC)

**THRILLER (1983).** Granddaddy of rock music videos with horror and monster motifs inspired by the movies. This vehicle—written-directed by John Landis—shot Michael Jackson into the big time, and features a memorable song voiced by Vincent Price. The monsters and makeup are quite good, but it still never stops looking like a piece for MTV. Okay as a novelty item, but it's probable this will become quickly dated. A special video called THE MAKING OF THRILLER shows the behind-the-scenes view. (VC)

**THRONE OF FIRE, THE (1983).** Costume fantasy in which a sword-wielding muscleman must save the world from the son of the devil and a witch named Azira. Directed in Italy by

**MOE HOWARD, STOOGE TO THE GILLS**

Franco Prosperi. Sabrina Siani plays the daughter of King Egon. (VC)

**THUNDER RUN (1985).** Minor science fiction devices qualify this actioner set in the deserts of Nevada and Arizona when an aging trucker (Forrest Tucker in his final screen role) helms a Kenmore Supertruck (with indestructible tires, bulletproof windows and trick weapons) through a gauntlet of foreign agents who drive camouflaged Volkswagens (equipped with heat-seeking rockets) and other Road Warrior-style vehicles. There's nonsense about a computer code, a tunnelful of laser beams and a mysterious helicopter. Tuck is carrying a valuable cargo of plutonium for CIA security boss John Ireland and wheels the rig with the daring daffiness of Mad Max. The crashes are plentiful and well-photographed and there's a likeable quality about the characters that cancels out the absurd premise and the various contrivances. Directed vigorously by Gary Hudson. John Sheperd, Jill Whitlow, Marilyn O'Connor.

**THUNDERBALL (1965).** Stylish James Bond espionage adventure, set largely underwater and featuring exotic, sophisticated scuba equipment and weapons. Sean Connery, as 007, tracks one-eyed Largo (Adolf Celi) who has hijacked a NATO aircraft armed with atomic bombs and demands a ransom of one million pounds. Several quippish puns by 007 will bring a wince to your lips—blame it on Richard Maibaum and John Hopkins, who adapted the Ian Fleming novel. But the undersea photography and full-scale battles make this an outstanding contribution to the series (this story was remade loosely into NEVER SAY NEVER AGAIN.) Claudine Auger plays Domino, and Luciana Paluzzi is a palaluzzi of a woman in her bathing suits. Directed with real pizzazz by Terence Young. Rik Von Nutter, Martine Beswick. (VC)

**THUNDERBIRDS ARE GO (1966).** Gerry and Sylvia Anderson, who produced some top British TV science-fiction, first became known for THUNDERBIRDS, which featured realistic special effects and mature storylines around marionette characters. This full-length treatment is demonstrative of the excellent puppet-model work. The International Space Rescue Service blasts off for Mars but the project is threatened by saboteurs. See also REVENGE OF THE MYSTERONS FROM MARS. Directed by David Lane.

**THUNDERBIRDS: COUNTDOWN TO DISASTER (1981).** Marionette science-fiction from England with the space adventurers saving the Empire State Building and putting out an oil fire in the Atlantic. Directed by David Elliott, David Lane and Desmond Saunders. (VC)

**THUNDERBIRDS SIX (1968).** More puppet adventures as our heroes face the Black Phantom in their new spacecraft.

Gerry and Sylvia Anderson wrote and produced, David Lane directed. (VC)

**THUNDERBIRDS TO THE RESCUE (1980).** Home Box Office version of the British THUNDERBIRDS marionette series featuring some really imaginative model and puppet work. Novelty film worth watching.

**THX 1138 (1971).** In an underground society, in the distant future, man lives in a drugged stupor, ruled by a computerized police system which does not permit emotions or sexual desires. George Lucas, in his directing debut, creates an automated, trance-state world that is a visual experience but hardly an intellectual one. While the future technology and the emotionless behavior of the robots are fascinating, the Walter Murch-Lucas script never gives us more than a fleeting glimpse into another man's nightmare. Nor are there characters to identify with or root for, as captive Robert Duvall breaks loose from the system to escape to the unknown surface world. Produced by Francis Ford Coppola, who first admired Lucas' short 16mm film which he made at USC entitled THX 1138 4EB. Consider this a stepping stone to STAR WARS. Donald Pleasence, Maggie McOmie, Don Pedro Colley, Johnny Weissmuller Jr. (VC)

**TICKLED PINK.** See **MAGIC SPECTACLES, THE.**

**TIDAL WAVE (1975).** Roger Corman's Americanized version of SUBMERSION OF JAPAN, an Oriental epic depicting the sinking of the subcontinent of Japan by tidal waves, land catastrophies and assorted disasters and tragedies. Footage with Lorne Greene was added to give "local" appeal. Unfortunately, excessive U.S. editing destroyed much of the film's continuity. Still, director Shiro Moritani captures a feeling of doom unusual in Japanese films of this kind. American scenes directed by Andrew Meyer.

**THX 1138**

**THX 1138**

**TIGER FANGS (1943).** Obscure PRS quickie set in the Far East (on potted jungle sets) in which June Duprez is terrorized by what would appear to be killer humans who have assumed the form of tigers. Pretty stuffy and predictable; the horror elements are minimal. Directed by Sam Newfield. Frank Buck, Duncan Renaldo, Howard Banks.

**TIGER MAN.** See **LADY AND THE MONSTER, THE.**

**TIGHTROPE (1984).** Fascinating, perplexing study of a New Orleans policeman (Clint Eastwood) investigating the brutal sex murders of women involved in the kinky velvet underworld of perversion. Eastwood is lured into this sordid world and finds he enjoys it—but then discovers the killer has a vendetta against him. The subtext finds Eastwood examining his own values, although the main thrust remains the pursuit, craftily built to an exciting climax by writer-director Richard Tuggle, who treats this more like a slasher-horror thriller than a whodunit. Clint's romance with Genevieve Bujold mildly contributes to the theme. One of Eastwood's best. (VC)

**TILL DEATH (1978).** Tepid, lethargically paced supernatural-ghost tale, in need of editing. Keith Atkinson is locked in a mausoleum with the corpse of his recently deceased wife (Belinda Balaski), who died in a car crash which he caused. He's snared in a kind of "eternity" state of limbo, where the spouse rises from her crypt and tries to seduce him into joining her in the Great Beyond. None of this makes sense, and the ending, in which transparent entities menace the helpless couple, sheds no light on Gregory Dana's muddled script. Walter Stocker pointed the camera and co-produced with actor Marshall Reed. Not to have and to hold . . .

**TIME AFTER TIME (1979).** Ingenious time travel yarn directed by Nicholas Meyer in which Jack the Ripper flees Victorian London in a machine built by H. G. Wells, landing in San Francisco, November 1979. Wells, pur-

suing the slasher, becomes an amusing anachronism as he adjusts to 20th Century customs. David Warner is an intriguing Ripper, remarking to Wells, "We haven't gone ahead, we've gone back; man hasn't advanced beyond barbarism," flipping on the six o'clock news to prove it. Malcolm McDowell is the British idealist-writer and Mary Steenburgen the kooky but lovable bank executive who befriends him. This imaginative fantasy is enhanced by a rich Miklos Rozsa score. Charles Cioffi, Shelley Hack, Clete Roberts. (VC)

**TIME BANDITS (1981).** Thoroughly wacky time-travel comedy zanily directed by Terry Gilliam of Monty Python infamy. Destructive fun as a gang of dwarfs aids a youth (Craig Warnock) lost in a time hole. Gags fly fast and furious, and many stars show up in cameos: Sean Connery is Agamemnon, John Cleese is a hilarious Robin Hood, David Warner is wonderful as the Evil Genius of the Universe. Others featured in the Gilliam-Michael Palin script: Sir Ralph Richardson, Ian Holm, Kenny Baker, Shelley Duvall. Absolutely bananas at times, but you'll be too busy laughing to tell yourself none of this mayhem makes sense. Great effects by John Bunker, Ross King and Val Charlton. Producer George Harrison also provided songs. (VC)

**TIME FLIES (1944).** Rollicking time-travel spoof in which music hall comedians are transported to the days of Elizabeth I. The jokesters encounter William Shakespeare in the process of writing a classic play. Since the time-hoppers already know the lines, they feed them to Shakespeare whenever he gets stuck. Playing with time paradoxes makes this British production a real mind blower. Directed by Walter Forde. Tommy Handley, Evelyn Dall, George Moon, Felix Aylmer, Moore Marriott, Graham Moffatt.

**TIME MACHINE, THE (1960).** Stylish George Pal version of the famous H. G. Wells novel, charming in its depiction of 19th Century milieu and moving at a fast clip as Rod Taylor hops into

**NICHOLAS MEYER**        **RICHARD TUGGLE**

his ingenious apparatus and travels through several centuries. He arrives at a bleak world in the year 802,701 to find mankind's remnants: The rulers are the cannibalistic Morlocks and the Elois serve as slave labor and food, working in underground caverns. It's continuously exciting and still has a poignant message that avoids being overly preachy. Taylor is excellent and Yvette Mimieux is cuddly as the soft, warm heroine, Weena. The special effects by Gene Warren and Wah Chang were deserving of an Academy Award. Pal directed the David Duncan script. Alan Young, Sebastian Cabot, Whit Bissell, Doris Lloyd. (VC)

**TIME MACHINE, THE (1978).** Nothing to do with H. G. Wells' classic, just a cheapjack TV-movie, a pilot for an unsold series. And deservedly so. Scientist John Beck saves the world from a runaway missile even before he jumps into his gleaming time bus and races from zone to zone. Dreadful scripting by Wallace Bennett has Beck shooting it out with outlaws in a Western town, facing witchhunters in Salem and sailing into the far future to meet the Elois. Insulting to the memory of Wells and all self-respecting science-fiction enthusiasts. Director Henning Schallerup should get lost in another time zone. Priscilla Barnes, Rosemary De Camp, Whit Bissell, Jack Kruschen, John Hansen. (VC)

**TIME OF THE APES (1987).** Overly juvenile (and overly dumb) Japanese TV-movie in which some obnoxious children and a pampering adult are trapped in a PLANET OF THE APES world, where the Commander of the simians (a top banana?) has his monkey minions chasing after the interlopers. They manage to survive cliffhanger after cliffhanger, the dubbed voices seldom matching. Strictly for kiddies. Reiko Tokunaga, Hirito Saito.

**TIME OF THEIR LIVES, THE (1946).** Abbott and Costello comedy is a welcome change from their usual inanities. Lou is murdered and dumped in a well; the time is 1780 and Lou was on his way to warn George Washington of Benedict Arnold's treachery. Now he and fellow ghost Marjorie Reynolds must haunt a tavern in modern times to find a letter disclaiming their guilt. Special effects "Invisible Man"-style. Binne Barnes, Kirk Alyn and Gale Sondergaard enliven this

**DAVID WARNER IN 'TIME BANDITS'**

**MORLOCKS IN 'TIME MACHINE' (1960)**

wacky spoof directed by Charles Barton.

**TIME TRAVELERS, THE (1964).** German scientist Preston Foster and companions Merry Anders and Phil Carey are projected into the future to find Earth burned to a cinder by atomic war. Man-eating creatures ravage the surface (the lava beds near Barstow, Calif.) but underground is a colony of survivors using robots to build a spaceship for escape to another planet. Watch for Forrest J. Ackerman in a cameo. Written-directed by Ib Melchior. John Hoyt.

**TIME TRAVELERS, THE (1976).** Disappointing TV-movie created by Rod Serling for producer Irwin Allen, schlock king of lowbrow TV science-fiction. Scientists travel back in time to prevent the Chicago fire—but everything gets burned up anyway, including you, when you realize Allen stole the fire footage from IN OLD CHICAGO, the same trick he used in his 1966 series, TIME TUNNEL. Sam Groom, Richard Basehart, Trish Stewart, Francine York, Booth Coleman. Directed without inspiration by Alex Singer.

**TIME TUNNEL, THE.** In 1983, 20th Century-Fox released to TV five compilations of re-edited episodes of Irwin Allen's 1966-67 series. Each consists of two stories joined by Elmer's Glue-All: ALIENS FROM ANOTHER PLANET, KILL OR BE KILLED, OLD LEGENDS NEVER DIE, RAIDERS FROM OUTER SPACE and REVENGE OF THE GODS. The series was set at an underground laboratory (Tic Toc Base) where the U.S. Government is conducting experiments in time travel under General Heyward Kirk (Whit Bissell) and engineer Lee Meriwether. Scientists James Darren and Robert Colbert are trapped in the apparatus and emerge in time zones past, present and future. It wasn't a great series, but hardly anything Allen produced would be ranked as classic. Just ranked as "rank." Notable for its stock footage from epic 20th Century-Fox films and for stealing soundtrack music from said epics. It's more fun to identify the scenes and music than to follow the storylines.

**TIME WALKER (1982).** Science-fiction mummy yarn that gets so wrapped up in unbelievable plot developments, it unravels early in the action—or nonaction, since this is a lethargic, lumbering two-bit movie by inexperienced film makers. When archeologist Ben Murphy breaks into King Tut's tomb, he finds a sarcophagus containing an extraterrestrial under wraps. Back at the California Institute of the Sciences, dumb technician Kevin Brophy exposes the long-dead creature to too much gamma force—so the alien pops up alive, shambling around in search of five glowing "jewels," which will enable him to communicate with his home planet. "E.T., Phone Home"—get it? The rest of the cast shambles around like so many dummy mummies in need of a director. So where was director Tom Kennedy all this time? (VC)

**TIME WARP (1981).** Low-budget space adventure sold directly to TV in which an astronaut on a voyage to Jupiter is zapped by a time paradox malfunction. Mainly played for comedy. Adam West, Gretchen Corbett, Chip Johnson, Kirk Alyn. Directed by Allan Sandler and Robert Emenegger.

**TIMERIDER: THE ADVENTURES OF LYLE SWANN (1983).** Time-travel hogwash depicting how a Baja 500 race motorcyclist gets lost in the desert and passes through time portals, which scientists are experimenting with back at control center. Just a poor rehash of TIME TUNNEL as Fred Ward lands in the 1880s to be surrounded by outlaw leader Peter Coyote and his ornery gang of mavericks, who'd love to trade their hooves for wheels. Ample stunt riding and horse chases, but production values are those of a TV-movie and the script by producer Michael Nesmith and William Dear (the latter also directed) is predictable, including the time paradox "surprise" ending. Belinda Bauer provides interesting love interest—in fact, she's the only intriguing character. Ed Lauter, Richard Masur, L.Q. Jones. (VC)

**TIMESLIP. See ATOMIC MAN, THE.**

**TIN MAN (1983).** Youth incapable of speaking or hearing builds a machine that allows him to enjoy both senses. Tinny. Hollow. Directed by John G. Thomas. Timothy Bottoms, Deana Jurgens, John Philip Law, Troy Donahue. (VC)

**TINGLER, THE (1959).** Gimmicked-up fright flick from producer-director William Castle, with theaters originally wired to give audiences a "tingle" at "shocking" moments. Disregarding that hokum, though, this is fine Castle Macabre, enhanced by a tongue-in-cheek flavor. Scientist Vincent Price discovers each of us has a mysterious element brought to life by fear that takes possession of our backbones. Removed from the body, the spine becomes a lobster-like monster attaching itself to the nearest human and sucking away bone marrow. The best sequence in this camp-ish mini-classic is when The Tingler is loose in a movie theater and everyone runs like hell as the thing crawls through the projector aperture. There is a hand coming out of a tub of blood shot in color, but TV prints are in black and white. Robb White dreamed up the nifty idea. Daryl Hickman, Philip Coolidge, Judith Evelyn, Patricia Cutts.

**TINTIN AND THE BLUE ORANGES (1965).** Belgian adven-ture-comedy comic strip created by Herge (Georges Remi) comes to the screen with Jean-Pierre Talbot and Jean Bouise in an adventure involving a kidnapped professor and a magical fruit. Okay stuff for those familiar with the world-famous comic adventure. Directed by Philippe Condroyer.

**TINTORERA . . . BLOODY WATERS (1977).** Open wide . . . it's a British-Mexican ripoff of JAWS, full of chopped nuts created by director Rene Cardona Jr. Involved in the hunt for the Great White are Susan George, Hugo Stiglitz, Priscilla Barnes, Fiona Lewis and Jennifer Ashley. Wider please . . . we want to get the entire body in the fish's mouth . . . ah good, thank you . . . Chomp! Chew chew! Gulp! (VC)

**TO ALL A GOODNIGHT (1980).** Another slap at Santa Claus, depicting graphic murders at the Calvin (Klein?) Finishing School for Girls, performed by a homicidal yuletider in a St. Nick costume. Even the blood is slow-moving as the killer fires crossbow arrows into torsos, plants an axe blade in a forehead, hangs a severed head in a shower stall, shoves a knife into a back, and loops a garroting wire around a soft human throat. Undistinguished clone of FRIDAY THE 13th. Directed by David Hess. Jennifer Runyon, Forrest Swanson, William Lauer, Buck West. (VC)

**TO KILL A CLOWN (1972).** Young naive couple renting a beach cottage become prey to a crazed Vietnam veteran who unleashes his Dobermans on them. Alan Alda as the demented cripple delivers a chilling performance. While the ending is not satisfying, there are moments that ring true. Based on a story by Algis Budrys, "Master of the Hounds." Directed by George Bloomfield. Blythe Danner and Heath Lamberts are believable as the couple. (VC)

**TO KILL A STRANGER (1985).** When singer Angelica Maria is forced to murder sex maniac Donald Pleasence, does she report it to the cops? Hell no, the guy was a war hero. So she conceals the body. Meanwhile, there's long-suffering husband Dean Stockwell and a cop (Aldo Ray) and a military officer (Mad Magazine cartoonist Sergio Aragones). What the hell is a nice guy like Aragones doing in this flick? Directed by Juan Lopez-Moctezuma.

**TO LOVE A VAMPIRE (1970).** In the wake of the success of THE VAMPIRE LOVERS, a blatant amalgam of lesbian love and vampirism, Hammer produced this sequel in the Karnstein series, utilizing characters created by J.S. Le Fanu,

**THE HORROR IMAGES OF 'TIMEWALKER': NOT AS GOOD AS IT LOOKS**

**CREATURE FEATURES MOVIE GUIDE**

although any relationship to the original book was abandoned for commercial shock. A girls' finishing school next door to Karnstein Castle provides the perfect setting for dozens of nubile young woman exercising in flowing white robes and some exercising lesbian contact with a girl named Mircalla (Yvette Stensgaard). Jimmy Sangster directed Tudor Gates' script without subtlety, which forced U.S. distributors to cut this film heavily. In cassette as LUST FOR A VAMPIRE. Ralph Bates, Mike Raven, Pippa Steel, Suzanna Leigh, Erik Chitty.

**TO THE DEVIL . . . A DAUGHTER (1976).** Christopher Lee, evil satanist, wants to transform a young child into a devil goddess in this Hammer film based on a Dennis Wheatley novel and directed with a strong sense of evil by Peter Sykes. Richard Widmark (acting with unusual intensity) portrays an occult writer who tries to stop Lee with the help of a book, THE GRIMOIRE OF ASTAROTH. The 16-year-old is Nastassia Kinski, daughter of Klaus Kinski. Sykes zooms all over the gloomy landscapes and the final results are pretty good if somewhat muddled because of Chris Wicking's script. Honor Blackman, Denholm Elliott. (VC)

**TO TRAP A SPY (1966).** The very first MAN FROM U.N.C.L.E. TV pilot, re-edited to feature length. Robert Vaughn and David McCallum are undercover agents fighting a crime syndicate cashing in on the misery of an African nation. Don Medford directed producer Sam Rolfe's script. William Marshall, Fritz Weaver, Patricia Crowley, Luciana Paluzzi. Leo G. Carroll portrays the assignment chief, Mr. Waverly.

**TOBOR THE GREAT (1954).** Clanking sounds do not emanate from the mechanical man of the title, but from the rusty mind of director Lee Sholem and the unoiled typewriters of alleged screenwriters Phillip MacDonald and Dick Goldstone, who were responsible for this fiasco intended for six-year-old intellects. But even those so young will be bored

**MONSTERS.** (My, what great big . . . )

**TOMB, THE (1985).** Egyptian snake goddess Nefratis, nothing more than a vampire with fangs, is resurrected from her sarcophagus by young dumb adventurers and materializes in L.A. to recover a magical amulet in the possession of archeologist Cameron Mitchell. The acting is really bad, full of modern idiom when it should possess feeling for an ancient culture—blame poor direction on Fred Olen Ray. And the bad dialogue ("I've come to kill you, you mummufied bitch!") on Ken Hall. Sybil Danning and John Carradine have pointless cameos. Michelle Bauer is sexy as the vamp but she needs to take acting lessons. Susan Stokey, David Pearson, Richard Alan Hench. (VC)

**TOMB OF LIGEIA (1965).** Edgar Allan Poe's poem, in which the spirit of a dead woman returns through the corpse of her husband's second wife, becomes a Roger Corman film made in England. Many consider this one of Corman's best—Poe lovers, on the other hand, objected to its overuse of the walking corpse and the fact Vincent Price must kill it over and over again. The literacy of the production is attributable in part to screenwriter Robert Towne and Corman's direction. The 1820s of England are well captured in the set design. Elizabeth Shepherd, John Westbrook, Derek Francis. (VC)

**TOMBS OF THE BLIND DEAD.** First in a series of Spanish-Portuguese films from writer-director Amando De Ossorio. This is listed under **BLIND DEAD, THE**. Others in the series: HORROR OF THE ZOMBIES, NIGHT OF THE SEAGULLS, RETURN OF THE EVIL DEAD.

**TOMB OF THE LIVING DEAD (1969).** Sexy Angelique Pettyjohn (famed as gladiator Shahna on STAR TREK) is a terrific eyeful as she meets a green-eyed, green-skinned monster in this sequel to BEAST OF BLOOD, made in the Philippines with John Ashley co-starring. It's the chlorophyll

---

*"An intellectual carrot! The mind boggles!"—Scotty the newspaperman in* **THE THING (1951).**

---

by the spy antics and performances of Charles Drake, Karin Booth, Lyle Talbot, Robert Shayne, Taylor Holmes and William Schallert, who look as though they wanted to get oiled and forget the whole thing. Ask yourself: Tobor or not Tobor. TOBOR is a bore. (VC)

**TOM CORBETT, SPACE CADET: VOL. I.** Six 15-minute episodes of a TV science-fiction adventure series, produced around 1950-51 for live telecast. Crude space opera of interest only to historians and TV nostalgia freaks. Frankie Thomas, Al Markim, Jan Merlin, Frank Sutton. (VC)

**TOM CORBETT, SPACE CADET: VOL. II.** Four 30-minute episodes of the continuing space adventures of Corbett, Roger Manning and Astro, produced in the mid-1950s for live TV. Cast off this blast off unless you're into old-fashioned video nostalgia. (VC)

**TOM THUMB (1958).** Delightful George Pal fantasy-musical, based on the fairy tale by the Brothers Grimm about a woodsman, Honest John, who wishes for a child the size of his thumb—and literally gets it in the form of happy-go-lucky Russ Tamblyn, a trampoline star who bounces bubbly in the role. Enchanting, nonsensical mixture of live-action choreography, animation in the old Puppetoon style Pal introduced in the 1940s; and music and songs with a touch of sparkling magic. Terry-Thomas and Peter Sellers are wonderfully corny as the villains in the Black Swamp who misuse the minuscule Thumb to rob the King's Treasury. The plot (by director Ladislas Foder) is slight—it's Pal's ability to capture a cinematic lightheartedness that works. The music track is great. Alan Young, Jessie Mathews, June Thorburn. (VC)

**TOM THUMB (1958).** Spanish version of the Grimm fairy tale, directed by Rene Cardona and starring Maria Elena Marques and Cesare Quezadas. Narrated by Paul Tripp.

**TOM THUMB AND LITTLE RED RIDING HOOD VS. THE MONSTERS.** See **LITTLE RED RIDING HOOD AND THE**

creation of a typical mad movie doctor, but the creature with the real features remains undulating Ms. Pettyjohn. Eddie Romero and Gerardo de Leon co-directed.

**TOMB OF THE UNDEAD (1972).** Criminals return from the grave to avenge themselves on the guards and warden who mistreated them. Written-directed by John Hayes. John Dennis, Susan Charney. (VC)

**TOMB OF TORTURE (1966).** Corny Italian-German chiller about a dumb girl who thinks she is the reincarnation of a dead countess and undergoes traumatic nightmares. Torture only in the sense you have to sit and watch this Italian film badly repackaged for the U.S. market by Richard Gordon. Directed by Antonio Boccaci. Annie Albert plays the beleaguered girl. Thony Maky, William Gray.

**TOMB OF HORROR.** See **TERROR CREATURES FROM THE GRAVE.**

**TOMORROW MAN, THE (1979).** Canadian TV pilot for a series not unlike THE PRISONER in many ways: Stephen Markle is a political captive in a top-security prison tempted by his fascist-state jailers with various means of escape. Offbeat and odd. Worth a viewing. Directed by Tibor Takacs.

**TONIGHT'S THE NIGHT (1954).** Gentle, insignificant British comedy in which woman-chasing David Niven inherits a haunted castle in Ireland. The hauntings vacillate between real ones and fake ones. Tonight's not the night . . . unless you can think of nothing better to do. Yvonne DeCarlo, Barry Fitzgerald. Produced-directed by Mario Zampi.

**TOO SCARED TO SCREAM (1983).** PSYCHO lives when a knife-wielding murderer attacks assorted victims in a Manhattan apartment building. Obvious suspect is the doorman (Ian MacShane), a repressed ex-actor who spouts Shakespeare and lives with his invalid mother (played catatonically by Maureen O'Sullivan). Mother? Did we say Mother? Hmmmm . . . Cops Mike Connors and Anne Archer meet assorted suspects and sex perverts as director Tony Lo Bianco builds adequate suspense and throws in some smelly red herrings. Better developed than most slasher flicks. Leon Isaac Kennedy, Ruth Ford, John Heard, Murray Hamilton. (VC)

**TOOLBOX MURDERS, THE (1977).** Disgusting but imaginative use of power drill, nail gun, hammer and other electrically powered hand tools provides modus operandi for a fiendish killer, played with cackling relish by Cameron Mitchell. He's the manager of an apartment and by night he dons a mask to lay waste to the women he hates because of a mother complex. Strong stomachs required. Directed by Dennis Donnelly. Pamelyn Ferdin, Anita Corsaut. (VC)

**TOOMORROW (1970).** Olivia Newton-John and other pop singers are kidnapped by out-of-tune aliens who need music for their home planet. Offkey British musical-comedy, directed-written by Val Guest. Watch it tooday.

**TOPPER (1937).** Classically funny Hal Roach adaptation of the Thorne Smith comedy novel. Constance Bennett and Cary Grant portray a rich, happily-married couple killed in an accident, but fate decrees they remain on Earth until achieving a good deed. So they decide to straighten out the affairs of henpecked Cosmo Topper (Roland Young) and nagging wife Billie Burke. Delightfully madcap, jammed with visual tricks, utterly refreshing. This led to two sequels (TOPPER TAKES A TRIP and TOPPER RETURNS) and in the 1950s became a long-running TV series with Leo G. Carroll, Anne Jeffreys and Robert Sterling. (VC)

**TOPPER (1980).** Updated TV version of the classic Thorne Smith supernatural comedy, designed as a vehicle for hubby-wife team Kate Jackson and Andrew Stevens. But it's a slow, laborious affair compared to its inspiration, having none of the madcap charm of the 1930s. Totally tepid . . . a bottomer. Directed by Charles Dubin. Jack Warden, Rue McClanahan, James Karen, Charles Siebert.

**TOPPER RETURNS (1941).** Second Hal Roach sequel to TOPPER consists of more rollicking high jinks in the Thorne Smith tradition with Roland Young as the sophisticate who solves an "old dark house" murder mystery with the aid of a new ghost (Joan Blondell). The great supporting cast includes Carole Landis, Billie Burke (as Topper's goofy spouse), Dennis O'Keefe, Patsy Kelly and Eddie "Rochester" Anderson (who provides racist comedy typical of the period). Directed by Roy Del Ruth. (VC)

**TOPPER TAKES A TRIP (1939).** The first TOPPER sequel, again with Constance Bennet as the svelte Marion Kerby, a ghost who pops in and out of sight while trying to keep Cosmo (Roland Young) from divorcing pea-brained Mrs. Top-

per (Billie Burke) during their holiday in Europe. Stuffy characters (such as Alan Mowbray's butler) are an added treat, and once again Hal Roach's special effects department has objects moving mysteriously as the female ghost performs her mischievous deeds. Directed by Norman Z. McLeod. Irving Pichel, Alex D'Arcy, Franklin Pangborn.

**TORMENT (1986).** Made in San Francisco by writers-writers Samson Aslanian and John Hopkins, this psychothriller depicts a mad killer who terrorizes the policeman tracking him. Production values are better than the story. Taylor Gilbert, William Witt, Eve Brenner. (VC)

**TORMENTED (1960).** Bert I. Gordon-Joe Steinberg production—which means it's schlock time on the old tube tonight. A nice young man (Richard Carlson) turns out to be not so nice after he pushes his wife (Juli Reding) off a lighthouse platform. The woman's corpse materializes to haunt him. Instead of acting rational, he goes off the deep end to provide this film with a so-called surprise ending. Bert I. Gordon directed the George Worthing Yates script. Susan Gordon, Gene Roth, Joe Turkel, Lillian Adams, Lugene Sanders.

**TORMENTED. See EERIE MIDNIGHT SHOW, THE.**

**TORPEDO OF DOOM (1938).** Feature version of the Republic serial FIGHTING DEVIL DOGS, directed by that unbeatable triumvirate of action directors: William Witney, John English, Robert Beche. Marine Corps lieutenants Lee Powell and Herman Brix (to become Bruce Bennett) square off against The Lightning, a caped hooligan who specializes in destroying things with bolts of electricity. The artificial thunderbolt machine (a clap trap?) becomes their target and from that point on, the action is nonstop.

**TORSO (1973).** Italian gore murders galore with touches of sleazy lightcore pornography dominate this crude, rude sick flick. Suzy Kendall and a gang of glamour models are on the fringes of a series of hacksaw murders committed by a madman in a hood who strangles his female victims and then fondles their nude bodies with his bloody hands. Really upsetting stuff, climaxing when Kendall (one leg in a cast) is trapped in a villa with the killer as he saws up all of Suzy's beautiful friends. Moreso TORSO? Less-so messo. Written-directed by Sergio Martino. John Richardson, Tina Aumont, Luc Meranda. (VC)

**TORTURE CHAMBER OF BARON BLOOD.** Videocassette title of **BARON BLOOD.** (Baron wastes?)

**TORTURE CHAMBER OF DR. SADISM (1969).** German production patterned loosely on Poe's THE PIT AND THE PENDULUM, with similarities few and far between the swings of the blade. Christopher Lee portrays Count Regular, who regularly counts the drops when he goes after Karin Dor's blood for the serum of immortality. Good atmosphere and expressionistic settings offset the non-expressive screenplay by Manfred Kohler and the expressionless direction by Harald Reinl. Lex Barker, Carl Lange, Vladimir Medar, Christiane Rucker, Dieter Eppler. (VC)

**TORTURE DUNGEON (1969).** Andy Milligan, purveyor of blood and guts in living color, wishes to entertain you with mutilations, dissections, savage beatings and all-around bloodletting as seen from the eyes of the Duke of Norwich. Wallow in the sanguinary joy of it all as that medieval nobleman knocks off anyone in line for the throne he covets down in the old dank dungeon. That's entertainment? (VC)

**TORTURE GARDEN (1967).** Above-average horror anthology, skillfully written by Robert Bloch (he adapted four of his stories), and imaginatively directed by Freddie Francis. At a British carnival sideshow, barker Dr. Diablo (Burgess Meredith) offers "special terrors" to his visitors—a glimpse into their unpleasant futures. Hence, the Bloch Busters: "Enoch" is the Weird Tales classic about a demon cat who eats the heads of its victims; "Terror Over Hollywood" shows why all our favorite movie stars are so beautiful; "Mr. Steinway" is the bizarre look at a haunted piano; and "The Man Who Collected Poe" (the best of the lot) stars Jack Palance as a sorcerer who brings Poe back from the dead much to the shock of Poe collector Peter Cushing. And then, of course, there's the surprise ending with Dr. Diablo. Beverly

**THE QUIXOTIC 'TOXIC AVENGER'**

**THINNER-THAN-AIR CONSTANCE BENNETT AND CARY GRANT
PROP UP ROLAND YOUNG IN 'TOPPER'**

Adams, Robert Hutton, Barbara Ewing. (VC)

**TORTURE SHIP (1939).** Avoid passage aboard this floating carrier of tedium, bound for the port of boredom with ennui just off the starboard side. Although allegedly based on a Jack London story, "A Thousand Deaths," this Victor Halperin-directed production (he gave us WHITE ZOMBIE) is pure flotsam depicting a crazy doctor (Irving Pichel) experimenting with the glands of criminals aboard his floating lab of horror. Lyle Talbot, Sheila Bromley.

**TOUCH OF MELISSA, THE. See TOUCH OF SATAN, THE.**

**TOUCH OF SATAN, THE (1973).** Evil sisters on a farm chop up folks and make a pact with the Devil to prevent aging, and then when a young man happens along, one of the witches (Emby Mellay) falls in love. Foolish little thing. Directed by Don Henderson. (VC)

**TOURIST TRAP (1979).** Low-budget exploitation chiller borrows freely from PSYCHO, CARRIE and HALLOWEEN, and comes off powerfully with its games of cat-and-mouse terror, thanks to the imaginative direction of David Schmoeller. Four likable young travelers are lured to a deserted roadside wax museum owned by reclusive Chuck Connors. Stealing the show are numerous mannikins (with gaping, screaming mouths) and masks that litter a madman's torture chamber. The film sinks deeper and deeper into nightmare allegory until reality is nonexistent, and one needn't bother to sort out any sense of logic. Jocelyn Jones, Tanya Roberts. (VC)

**TOWER OF EVIL (1974).** Snape Island houses a lighthouse and a cache of ancient Phoenician treasures; it is also the romping ground for a murderer who severs hands and heads from corpses and leaves the remains for visitors (including Jill Haworth and Bryant Halliday) to stumble across. Graphic shocker has plenty of bare flesh and sexual activity in addition to its horrors to hold interest—and that's during the film's quieter moments. From British producer Richard Gordon; written-directed by Jim O'Connolly. Dennis Price, George Coulouris, Anna Palk, Jack Watson. (VC)

**TOWER OF LONDON (1939).** Boris Karloff's performance as Mord, executioner of the Duke of Gloucester (Richard III), alone warrants a viewing of this study in homicidal royalty. Bodies are strewn in the dungeons and dining halls of 15th Century London as the Duke and Mord knock off all those in their way—including Vincent Price, who is drowned in a vat

of wine, and two young children who are ruthlessly strangled. This is Merrie Olde England? Basil Rathbone is chilling as the power-hungry duke, and Karloff unforgettable when he pleads to fight in the battle of Tewksbury because "I've never killed in hot blood before." Literate script by Robert N. Lee; directed by Rowland V. Lee.

**TOWER OF LONDON (1962).** You thought the 1939 Basil Rathbone version was grotesque and bloody? It seems a children's fable compared to this Roger Corman adaptation with Vincent Price as Richard III, a hunchback cripple whose withered arm and twisted leg match his mind—a mind haunted by guilt as he schemes and murders for power to the British throne. Torture and death nonstop . . . the squeamish should beware. The Mord role is played by Michael Pate. Corman directed, his brother Gene produced. Joan Freeman, Sandra Knight, Bruce Gordon.

**TOWER OF SCREAMING VIRGINS (1971).** West German horror import full of soft-core nudity and dozens of cliches about an unsavory place called the Tower of Silenna, to which a French murderess entices noblemen for unpleasant bloodletting.

**TOWER OF TERROR (1941).** Insane lighthouse keeper creates horror for those around him; eerie setting; slow British pace. Wilfred Lawson, Michael Rennie, Movita, Morland Graham. Directed by Lawrence Huntington.

**TOWER OF TERROR. See ASSAULT.**

**TOWN THAT DREADED SUNDOWN, THE (1977).** In March, 1946, in Texarkana, a schizoid killer wearing a hood began a reign of terror that to this day remains unsolved. Writer-director Charles B. Pierce brings a touch of pseudo-realism to this true crime drama, but then spoils it with dumb comedy relief involving a maladroit deputy. Ben Johnson and Andrew Prine stand out as toughened lawmen in hot pursuit. The murders are unnerving as the Phantom strikes without mercy. Features elements that foreshadow the slasher films. Ben Johnson, Andrew Prine, Dawn Wells. (VC)

**TOXIC AVENGER, THE (1984).** Flaky farce on monster movies, a scattergun of visual gags with some pellets on target and others missing by miles. It's funky and ugly and gory and cruddy and yet eventually takes on a crude charm despite its excesses. Played for parody, TOXIC AVENGER is set in Tromaville, a center for toxic waste, where nerdish 90-

pound janitor Melvin falls into a barrel of atomic poison and emerges a mutated crusader who fights crime, his symbol a wet mop shoved into the face of an unconscious foe. Satirical vignettes ensue, depicting brutish fights and a romance between the dippy crime-fighter and a well-developed blind girl. Amidst this hodgepodge are some raunchy sex jokes and plenty of bouncing bare breasts. Produced-directed by Samuel Weis and Michael Hertz. Mitchell Cohen, Andree Maranda, Jennifer Babtist. (VC)

**TOXIC ZOMBIES (1984).** Poor man's imitation of NIGHT OF THE LIVING DEAD, in which hippie marijuana growers are sprayed by a herbicide, Dromax, which gives them hollow eyes and bloodlust. Type-0 flows and the gore spurts as the shamblers mindlessly attack picnickers and fishermen. A federal agent enters the area to investigate, discovering a government conspiracy that ordered the spraying. Writer-producer-director Charles McCrann offers little subtext or substance beyond the bloodletting, so this is your basic exercise in exploitation futility. Charles Austin, Beverly Shapiro, Dennis Helfend. (VC)

**TOY BOX, THE (1971).** Plaything from schlock exploitation producer Harry Novak has some monsters from outer space turning up on Earth and stimulating human beings sexually so they can then eat their delicious brains. Yes, it's Novak showing us the intellectual side to his charming character. Written-directed by Ron Garcia. Evan Steele, Ann Myers, Lisa Goodman, Deborah Osborne, T. E. Brown.

**TRACK OF THE MOONBEAST (1976).** An Indian talks about the legend of an Incredible Lizard God, then an asteroid shower falls on New Mexico, a fragment lodging in a young man's brain as he watches with his HotPants-wearing girlfriend. Yeah, you guessed it—the guy turns into a rubber-suited monster with a bad case of acne. Murder, mayhem and ample shots of the pretty girl's bare legs follow. Extremely poor in every way; low budget director Dick Ashe was not helped by Joe Blasco's make-up and phony suit. A real time waster. Chase Cordell, Donna Leigh Drake. (VC)

**TRACK OF THE VAMPIRE.** See **BLOOD BATH.**

**TRACKS (1976)** Avant garde writer-director Henry Jaglom (A SAFE PLACE) earnestly comments on the loss of the American Dream by depicting Vietnam veteran Dennis Hopper accompanying the corpse of a combat buddy to his burial place. The entire film is set aboard a train and zeroes in on the hallucinations and fantasies of Hopper, for the war has destroyed all his beliefs. This had little dramatic impact on audiences, but Jaglom's good intentions are boundless. Taryn Power, Dean Stockwell, Topo Swope, Zack Norman, Michael Emil. (VC)

**TRANCERS (1984).** Muddled cross between BLADE RUNNER and THE TERMINATOR, set in the 23rd Century when half of L.A. is underwater, and a war rages between police and zombie-like "Trancers." These human killers are trained by Whistler (Michael Stefani), whose adversary is hard-boiled "Angel City Trooper" Jack Deth (Tim Thomerson). Whistler has gone into the past to eliminate the relatives of a special peace council so the council will no longer exist. Deth follows him to modern-day L.A. where he often uses a time-stopping wristwatch so he can save the heroine. A mess of a storyline that director-producer Charles Band can't handle. Some of this is so bad, it's hard to believe. Helen Hunt, Anne Seymour, Richard Herd, Richard Erdman. (VC)

**TRANS-ATLANTIC TUNNEL, THE (1935).** In the vein of THINGS TO COME, a pseudorealistic prophecy film with Curt Siodmak helping in the adaptation for producer Michael Balcon. The time is the 1940s as a crew, under engineer-designer Richard Dix, gives their blood, sweat and tears to dig a tunnel under the Atlantic with a 50-foot radium drill. Interesting for its predominance of advanced technology. Walter Huston appears as the President, George Arliss is the Prime Minister officiating over tunnel-opening ceremonies and Madge Evans is Dix's long-suffering wife, enduring years of him digging under the ocean. Directed by Maurice Elvery. Leslie Banks, Helen Vinson, C. Aubrey Smith. (VC)

**TRANSFORMERS, THE (1986).** Feature version of the TV cartoon series in which the fighting robots save the Universe from a planet called Unicron and an army of baddies led by Megatron. The only distinguishing value is the film's voices: Orson Welles, Robert Stack, Leonard Nimoy, Eric Idle, Judd Nelson, Lionel Stander. Otherwise, it's Saturday morning all over again. (VC)

**TRANSFORMERS, THE: VOL. 1-7 (1984-85).** Animated series available in videocassette, depicting the autobots in their never-ending fight against the forces of evil. Moppets only. (VC)

**TRANSMUTATIONS.** New theatrical title for **UNDER-WORLD.**

**TRANSYLVANIA 6-5100 (1985).** Nutty newsmen Ed Begley Jr. and Jeff Goldblum are assigned to find Frankenstein in Transylvania by the editor of a sleazoid tabloid. What they dig up in a backlot Rumanian village are would-be monsters created by the quite insane Dr. Malavaqua (Joseph Bologna) and his assistants Lupi (Carol Kane) and Radu (John Byner), who pose as domestic help. There's a hunchback, vampire, Frankenstein hulker, mummy . . . but you'll be depressed to find out what they really are. An unfunny script by director

**ED BEGLEY JR. AND JEFF GOLDBLUM IN 'TRANSYLVANIA 6-5100': PHONING HOME?**

CREATURE FEATURES MOVIE GUIDE

**GENE QUINTANO, PRODUCER AND CO-STAR OF 'TREASURE OF THE FOUR CROWNS'**

Rudy DeLuca creates a major disappointment. Jeffrey Jones, Geena Davis, Michael Richards, Norman Fell. (VC)

**TRAPPED BY TELEVISION (1936).** Science-fiction only in its time—today a humdrum whodunit laughably outdated. Inventor Lyle Talbot perfects a new cathode ray tube and puts the squeeze on gangsters designing their own criminal network. It's merictully short (63 min.), its single saving grace. Directed by Del Lord. Thurston Hall, Mary Astor, Nat Pendleton, Marc Lawrence, Joyce Compton.

**TRAUMA (1962).** Sweet young girl (Lorrie Richards) witnesses the brutal murder of her socialite aunt and lapses into amnesia to escape reality. Supposedly cured, she returns to the lonely mansion to uncover the mystery of her lost years, aided by architect John Conte. Directed-written by Robert Malcolm Young. Lynn Bari portrays the murdered aunt. (VC)

**TRAUMA.** See **TERMINAL CHOICE.** (Melo-trauma?)

**TREACHERY AND GREED ON THE PLANET OF THE APES (1974).** Recycled TV episodes of the short-lived series that tried to recapture the glory of THE PLANET OF THE APES movies but failed miserably. Shoddy sets and special effects spell doom for Roddy McDowall, William Smith, John Hoyt, Zina Bethune, Victor Killian. A simian's delight? Directed by Don McDougall and Bernard McEveety.

**TREASURE OF THE FOUR CROWNS (1983).** Tony Anthony and Gene Quintano, who gave the world COMIN' AT YA! in 3-D, blend elements of MISSION: IMPOSSIBLE and RAIDERS OF THE LOST ARK to depict adventurers stealing valuable crystals from a cult of religious nuts. These crystals have magical and atomic powers of "good or evil," depending on who owns them. The main concern is the 3-D; some effects are good, but logic is discarded for cheap thrills. The caper portion provides some suspense, but otherwise it's silly and condescending. Directed by Ferdinando Baldi in Spain. Anthony and Quintano portray adventurers with Ana Obregon, Francisco Rabal and Kate Levan. (VC)

**TREASURE OF THE MOON GODDESS (1987).** Adventure-fantasy in the Indiana Jones mold, in which small-time night club singer Lu De Belle (Linnea Quigley) resembles a certain moon goddess, which shakes up some South American natives. Does she have magical powers or not? Boat captain Asher Brauner and sleazy manager Don Calfa are among the colorful characters. Directed by Joseph Louis Agraz.

**TRIAL, THE (1963).** An Orson Welles movie—he wrote, directed, portrayed a lawyer, sketched the sets, selected the music, served as cameraman, supervised dubbing and handled the editing. Whew! His artistry is detectable everywhere in this outre version of Franz Kafka's allegorical story of the nondescript bank clerk Joseph K. (Anthony Perkins), who is arrested without reason and placed on trial. There are several interpretations to this Kafka tale, made all the more rich by the Wellesian treatment. Intriguing cameos by Akim Tamiroff, Romy Schneider, Jeanne Moreau and Elsa Martinelli. Expect a very strange, enigmatic movie. (VC)

**TRIBE, THE (1974).** Boring TV-movie depicting Neanderthals (led by Victor French) and Cro-Magnons fighting it out 100,000 years ago. There's not a dinosaur in sight; just people in pelts sitting around or sneaking over hilltops, waiting for history to overtake them so mankind can begin making movies about prehistoric man. Dullest caveman movie ever made, directed by Richard A. Colla. Warren Vanders, Henry Wilcoxon, Andriana Shaw.

**TRICK FOR TRICK (1933).** Seance melodrama with a magician hosting the gathering of murder suspects so he can use the supernatural to get the goods on the guilty. One of those "is it a real ghost or a phony?" kind of pictures. Victor Jory, Ralph Morgan, Edward Van Sloan, Luis Alberni, Tom Dugan. Directed by Hamilton McFadden.

**TRICK OR TREAT (1986).** Ripoff of PHANTOM OF THE PARADISE, focusing on a heavy metal rocker (Sammi Curr, played by Tony Fields) who zaps dancers with electric bolts from his guitar. Curr, who uses sadism and death images in his act, has died and gone to rock heaven only to be brought back when a young fan (Marc Price) plays his last record backwards and is ordered to get out there and kick ass. Price finally realizes he's being manipulated by an evil force, and tries to stop Sammi's returned corpse with the help of girlfriend Lisa Orgolini. In a gag appearance, Ozzy Osbourne appears as a TV crusader against rock music. Good effects at the climax can't save this from its adolescent mentality. Directed by actor Charles Martin Smith.

**TRICK OR TREATS (1982).** Variation on HALLOWEEN, complete with baby-sitter and ghastly killer. A practical joke, carried out years ago, is the motivation for an act of violence on the night of the goblins. Produced-written-directed by Gary Graver, who also did the cinematography. Jackelyn Giroux, Peter Jason, David Carradine, Carrie Snodgress, Steve Railsback, Paul Bartel, Dan Pastorini. (VC)

*"Is it what men do that darkens the sky? Or do skies blacken the souls of men?"—TOWER OF LONDON.*

**TRILOGY (1970).** Frank Perry's film features three stories by Truman Capote: "A Christmas Memory," "Miriam" and "Among the Paths to Eden." Only "Miriam" will be of interest to horror fans, based on a famous ghost story. Unfortunately, this supernatural segment was heavily edited and it is difficult to tell if this is a journey into madness or a supernatural tale. Mildred Natwick, Susan Dunfee, Carol Gustafson.

**TRILOGY OF TERROR (1975).** Anthology TV-movie produced-directed by Dan Curtis. William F. Nolan has adapted stories by himself and Richard Matheson. The unusual feature is that Karen Black appears in all three in four leading roles. "Julie" is a witchcraft tale involving a sexually unhappy teacher being blackmailed by a student; "Millicent and Therese" permits Black to engage in schizophrenia as she portrays diametrically opposing sisters; and "Amelia" (from Matheson's "Prey") is a horrifying tale of a doll that terrorizes Black in her apartment. Gregory Harrison, Robert Burton, John Karlen, George Gaynes. (VC)

and forget. Morgan Upton, Nate Thurmond.

**TROLL (1986).** Unusually tame, G-rated Charles Band production directed with a sense of taste by John Carl Buechler, a special effects man making his directorial debut. The setting is a San Francisco apartment building where little Jenny Beck is possessed by a troll from another dimension. This ugly undroll troll has a magical ring that turns everyone into mythical creatures or rainforests. The creatures and effects are adequate but the characters are cardboard and the promising themes in Ed Naha's script never developed beyond embryos. Michael Moriarty and Shelley Hack as the parents are wasted, as is Sonny Bono in a cameo (he becomes the rainforest). The only standout is June Lockhart as the guardian over the Tolkien-like creatures, and her lovely real-life daughter, Anne Lockhart, who appears briefly. A sincere attempt to avoid the usual cliches that just never catches fire. Nice try, but no GREMLINS. (VC)

**TROLLENBERG TERROR, THE.** See **CRAWLING EYE,**

### JOHN CARL BUECHLER'S MONSTERS IN 'TROLL': BETTER THAN THE MOVIE

**TRIPODS (1985).** British adaptation of three John Christopher novels in which aliens called "Tripods" take over Earth in the year 2193 A.D. (VC)

**TRIUMPH OF THE SONS OF HERCULES (1963).** "Yuri Men" are beastly creatures, ripping apart human bodies as men pull wings off flies, but they're still no match for the might of Maciste in yet another Italian adventure bulging with beefcake in the form of Kirk Morris. Directed by Tanio Boccia. Ljuba Bodine, Cathia Caro.

**TROG (1970).** Super-ridiculous Herman Cohen production is a thorough time waster—it also wasted the talents of Joan Crawford as an anthropologist helping a caveman—a troglodyte, played by Joe Cornelius) find a place in contemporary society, and occasionally taking him to lunch. (This same idea was presented in a far more mature way in ICEMAN.) Michael Gough overacts terribly as the villain thwarting her research. Director Freddie Francis does what he can with Aben Kandel's stone-age screenplay, which isn't much. TROG is a dog. Robert Hutton, Bernard Kay.

**TROIKA (1969).** Avant garde film by San Francisco's Fred Hobbs saw minimal distribution, being of questionable commercial value. Much imagination and bizarre imagery including bug monsters, but too little discipline. Be prepared to see

**THE.** (Trolling for monsters?)

**TROMBA, THE TIGER MAN (1949).** German film is a pitiful affair about a lion trainer who utilizes a strange drug to maintain control over his creatures—and a beautiful woman. Directed by Helmut Weiss. Rene Deltgen, Gustav Knuth.

**TRON (1982).** Walt Disney's science-fiction adventure set in an electronic game world broke new cinematic territory with its splendid computer-generated images, but story and acting are so ineptly ridiculous that what emerges is a novelty piece with nowhere to go. A major problem is writer-director Steven Lisberger's plot. Instead of setting up the characters, he immediately plunges into the computerized Tron world, making one feel lost from the start. The plot concerns a corporate bigwig (David Warner) stealing the game ideas of designer Jeff Bridges. To find the evidence to prove Warner's conspiracy, Bridges and two pals (Cindy Morgan, Bruce Boxleitner) are zapped into the other-dimensional world of the computer. Wonderful blending of live action with computerized graphics, but at no time is there a genuine sense of menace—just a playfulness. Nice try, Steven, but no Pac-Man. Barnard Hughes, Dan Shor. (VC)

**TROUBLESOME DOUBLE (1971).** British comedy, sequel to EGGHEAD'S ROBOT, features whiz kids creating new things

**CREATURE FEATURES MOVIE GUIDE**

in the lab. Moppets only. Keith Chegwin, Julie Collins, Richard Wattis. Directed by Milo Lewis.

**TUCK EVERLASTING (1980).** Gentle, pastoral turn-of-the-century fantasy (based on Natalie Babbitt's novel) in which a young girl growing up in the South is befriended by a benevolent family that never ages. Its members, 104 years ago in the pioneer days, drank holy water from a spring and are destined to live forever, but their secret is threatened by a stranger. Director Frederick King Keller approaches this material with an autumnal quality, treating the characters with sensitivity and an understanding rare in movies. No special effects, very little violence; a lot of humor and warmth, though. Genuine family movie. Fred A. Keller, Paul Flessa, James McGuire, Margaret Chamberlain. (VC)

**TUNNEL, THE.** Alternative videocassette title for **TRANSATLANTIC TUNNEL.** (Is this tunnel vision?)

**TUNNELVISION (1976).** In 1985, the Senate accuses Tunnelvision, the People's TV Network, of altering the fabric of society through programming. An investigation serves as an excuse for dozens of parodies and satires on game shows, news telecasts, commercials, comedy series, etc. At least 50 actors and satirists appear in this spoof of contemporary video-watching. Irreverent and witty. Credit Neil Israel, direc-

Conway and Robert Montomgery Jr. are five. Tedium galore as Lunar Eagle One lands in the crater Menelaus to encounter lunatic creatures ruled by the Great Coordinator, who threatens to turn Earth into a giant popsicle. This movie sucks, all right. Directed by David Bradley. John Wengraf, Cory Devlin, Tema Bey and Michi Kobi are four more reasons why 12 TO THE MOON is less than classic.

**TWENTY MILLION MILES TO EARTH (1957).** Space probe returning from Venus, damaged by a meteor, crashes into the ocean off Sicily. A tiny dinosaur-like creature (a Venusian specimen) survives the impact but our atmosphere causes it to grow at an accelerated rate—all too quickly it assumes monstrous proportions, crashing through the Roman Forum and the Temple of Saturn while Army combat units pursue with flame-throwers. This Columbia low-budgeter (directed by Nathan Juran) has outstanding stop-motion work by Ray Harryhausen, whose Ymir creature is one of his finest; Harryhausen injects personality into the Ymir and evokes sympathy for its plight. Harryhausen's partner, Charles H. Schneer, produced this minor classic. Joan Taylor, William Hopper, Arthur Space, Frank Puglia, Tito Vuolo.

**27TH DAY, THE (1957).** Aliens wish to colonize Earth but cannot conduct warfare—it's against their religion—so they send an emissary (Arnold Moss) to abduct five Earthlings

**DAVID WARNER AS THE VILLAINOUS SARK IN THE COMPUTERIZED WORLD OF 'TRON'**

tor-co-writer-executive producer, for this channel hop into the future. Chevy Chase, Phil Proctor, Howard Hesseman, Edwina Anderson, James Bacon, Roger Bowen. (VC)

**TURKEY SHOOT.** See **ESCAPE 2000.**

**TURN OF THE SCREW (1974).** TV-movie, originally in two parts, is an adaptation of Henry James' classic horror novella, written by William F. Nolan and directed by Dan Curtis. The ambiguities of the story are faithfully retained and Lynn Redgrave, as the governess tutoring two children seemingly troubled (or possessed) by a dead spirit (or spirits), is superior. Megs Jenkins, Jasper Jacob, Eva Griffith. (VC)

**TURNABOUT (1940).** TOPPER creator Thorne Smith wrote the whacky novel on which this Hal Roach production is based. The gimmick here is that a married couple (Carole Landis and John Hubbard) exchange bodies. The single joke is stretched a little thin, although director Roach pads it with interesting visuals. Adolph Menjou, William Gargan, Mary Astor, Donald Meek, Joyce Compton, Marjorie Main.

**TUT AND TUTTLE (1981).** Time-travel TV-movie, designed as a comedy for the young uns, stars Chris Barnes as a fair-haired youth who is propelled through the centuries back to ancient Egypt, where he meets Tutankhame (Eric Green) and helps him save the Nile from total defile. Vic Tayback, Jo Anne Worley.

**TWELVE TO THE MOON (1960).** There are a dozen reasons why this poverty-stricken science-fiction thriller doesn't thrill, and Ken Clark, Anthony Dexter, Francis X. Bushman, Tom

from different countries. In his UFO, Moss gives each captive some capsules which could, on telepathic command, destroy all human life within 27 days. It's the aliens' way of giving us a chance to commit suicide. Or, if we don't use the capsules, we win and they'll go away. Realizing the power they hold, and how that power could be misused by less scrupulous individuals, the principals disperse to hide and contemplate. Main focus is on Gene Barry and Valerie French as they wrestle with their consciences and fall in love. Message science-fiction with strong anti-Communist overtones in the vein of RED PLANET MARS, adapted by John Mantley from his own novel. William Asher directed. George Voskovec, Stefan Schnabel, Paul Birch, Ralph Clanton.

**2069 A.D.—A SENSATION ODYSSEY (1969).** Men of the future travel into the past in a time machine to alter history. People of the present, beware. Directed by Cam Sopetsky. Harvey Foster.

**2069: A SEX ODYSSEY (1974).** West German-Austrian sex comedy in which women from Venus land on Earth to collect samples of male semen so they can impregnate folks on their dying planet. Directed by H. G. Keil. Nina Frederic, Catherina Conti, Heidrun Hankammer.

**2019: THE FALL OF NEW YORK.** See **AFTER THE FALL OF NEW YORK.**

**TWENTY THOUSAND LEAGUES UNDER THE SEA (1954).** Classic Disney adventure (based on the Jules Verne novel) spares no expense to re-create Captain Nemo's atomic sub,

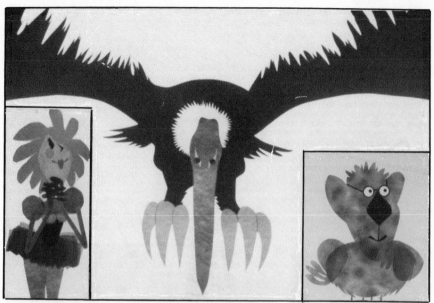

**A VULTURE MINION SWOOPS DOWN ON FLORA AND RALPH IN 'TWICE UPON A TIME'**

the underwater kingdoms, the giant squid and other Vernesque wonders. Kirk Douglas, Peter Lorre and Paul Lukas are survivors of a whaling ship sinking who find themselves on the Nautilus, under the command of the brilliant but demented Nemo (James Mason), who wages war against those who wage war. The effects are remarkably grand for their day, especially the squid attack as men armed with harpoons try to get the multi-tentacled giant off the sub's hull. This remains the film that best captures the flavor of Verne and his inventions despite all the imitations that followed. Directed by Richard Fleischer, written by Earl Fenton. (VC)

**TWICE TOLD TALES (1963).** Lushly photographed anthology highlighting three fantasy-horror tales by Nathaniel Hawthorne, Vincent Price in each. Writer-producer Robert E. Kent has selected: "Dr. Heidegger's Experiment," in which Price and Sebastian Cabot experiment with a rejuvenation serum that returns their youth and brings long-dead Mari Blanchard back from the grave; "Rappaccini's Daughter," a strange yarn in which a woman's touch brings instant death, and a plant that destroys any who touch it; and "The House of the Seven Gables," a traditional haunted house/family curse story (and weakest of the three). Director Sidney Salkow's pacing is slow, but rich detail and ensemble acting make the film work. Brett Halsey, Beverly Garland, Richard Denning.

**TWICE UPON A TIME (1983).** Unique albeit arcane animation piece by John Korty, utilizing the Lumage process, an improvement on the Eastern European technique of miniature cutouts photographed through clear sheets of glass (as opposed to the cel method of animation). This fanciful fairy tale is about the Rushers of Din, who each night dream sweet dreams from Sunny Frivoli—until the Murkworks intervene with their nightmares. It then becomes a race for control of the Cosmic Clock as two whimsical heroes, Ralph the All-Purpose Animal and his sidekick Mum (who speaks in sound effects), fight the raunchy Synonamess Botch, maniacal ruler of the Murkworks Nightmare Factory. Script concocted by Korty, Swenson, Suella Kennedy and Bill Couturie. Soundtrack voices by Paul Frees, Hamilton Camp, Julie Payne, James Cranna, Marshall Efron.

**TWILIGHT OF THE DEAD. See GATES OF HELL, THE.**

**TWILIGHT PEOPLE (1972).** Another deserted island, another demented doctor eager to experiment in the tradition of Dr. Moreau and another menagerie of half-human, half-

animal creatures. There's even a tree woman in this Roger Corman-David Cohen production, directed in the Philippines by Eddie Romero. Twilight for all concerned (on both sides of the camera) as darkness quickly settles. John Ashley, Pam Grier, Jan Merlin, Pat Woodell. (VC)

**TWILIGHT ZONE—THE MOVIE (1983).** Entertaining if not classic homage to the great Rod Serling TV series. Produced by Steven Spielberg and John Landis, this is made up of four tales (three based on TV episodes) and a clever prologue. Landis directed and wrote the prologue and first episode, which stars Vic Morrow as a bigot puzzlingly projected into situations where he is vilified (by Nazis, Ku Klux Klansmen, black American soldiers in Vietnam, etc.). While it has the moralistic turnaround Serling loved, Landis' script is weak and makes this the least of the quartet. Providing a warm glow is Spielberg's segment about how old folks in a rest home rediscover youth with the help of a traveling goodwill magician, Scatman Crothers. It's a spiritually uplifting fantasy. Third and best of the yarns is an adaptation of a Jerome Bixby story (scripted by Richard Matheson, directed by Joe Dante) about a youth with the ability to affect physical things by "willing" them. A good cast (Kathleen Quinlan, Jeremy Licht, Kevin McCarthy, Patricia Barry, William Schallert, Dick Miller) adds to the nostalgia. And there's some 1930s-style animation by Sally Cruikshank and a novel interpretation of life-size cartoon monsters by Rob Bottin. Final episode, directed by Australia's George Miller, is based on the famous TV episode: "Nightmare at 20,000 Feet," in which a neurotic (John Lithgow, in the role originated by William Shatner) sees a gnomelike monster on the wing of a jetliner and goes bananas to prevent it from making the plane crash. (VC)

**TWILIGHT'S LAST GLEAMING (1977).** In 1981, former Air Force officer Burt Lancaster and other prison escapees take over a SAC missile room and threaten mankind with nuclear destruction unless secret political documents (a la "The Pentagon Papers") are revealed. Director Robert Aldrich also focuses on the U.S. President (Charles Durning) and the dilemma he faces to satisfy Lancaster's unreasonable demands; also afoot is a conspiracy that allows for a shocking conclusion. Aldrich doesn't quite bring off this difficult theme, but there is ample food for political thought. Richard Widmark, Melvyn Douglas, Paul Winfield. (VC)

**TWINKLE, TWINKLE, KILLER KANE. See NINTH CONFIGURATION, THE.**

**TWINS OF EVIL (1971).** Predictably plotted sequel to Hammer's VAMPIRE LOVERS and LUST FOR A VAMPIRE, dealing with the Karnstein family and its vampiric curse. Peter Cushing is a witchhunter of the 19th Century seeking to help two "infected" 19-year-old beauties: Mary and Madeleine Collinson, altogether beauties who are seen in the altogether in several shots. Tudor Gates' script is heavy with heaving bosoms and unsubtle hints of lesbian love-biting. Directed by John Hough. Dennis Price, Isobel Black. (VC)

**TWISTED BRAIN (1973).** Harassed high school student Pat Cardi, too mousy to stand up for his own rights, transforms at night into a hairy beast who stalks his tormentors on campus in a tired worm-turns plot. An entire segment dealing with the boy's parents has nothing to do with the rest of the film; it was added as padding. Originally released as HORROR HIGH, but it's no high at all; in fact, it was an all-time low for director Larry Stouffer. (VC)

**TWISTED NERVE (1969).** Ray Boulting directed this British chiller about a psychopathic killer (Hywel Bennett) who plans to trap innocent, vulnerable Hayley Mills, and slit her throat. The young man has a Mongoloid brother and may be suffering from chromosome defects. Unfortunately, Bennett is never that menacing and the film moves at an ungodly lumbersome pace. Music by Bernard Herrmann. Billie Whitelaw, Phyllis Calvert, Frank Finlay, Thorley Walters.

**TWITCH OF THE DEATH NERVE. See CARNAGE.**

**TWO DEATHS OF SEAN DOOLITTLE (1975).** George Grizzard portrays a man who has no fear of dying for he thinks there is a doctor who can restore him to life. British TV-movie. Directed by Lela Swift. Barnard Hughes, Jeremiah Sullivan, Grayson Hall.

**TWO FACES OF DR. JEKYLL, THE (1961).** Hammer pulls a switch on the overworked Robert Louis Stevenson split personality plot: Instead of a good-looking doctor turning into an ugly brute, a not-so-handsome chap transmutates into a handsome playboy who falls for London's can-can girls. Directed by Terence Fisher. Keeping their best sides toward the camera are Paul Massie, Dawn Addams, Christopher Lee, Oliver Reed. Strictly a game of Hyde-and-seek.

**TWO FACES OF EVIL (1981).** Two one-hour episodes of the British telly's HAMMER HOUSE OF HORROR, re-edited for the U.S. In "Two Faces of Evil," a husband driving his family through a village is attacked by a hitchhiking Dracula, apparently a doppelganger of the husband. Director Alan Gibson wrings good performances from Anna Calder-Marshall and Gary Raymond. In "Rude Awakening," Denholm Elliott portrays a woman-chasing realtor who keeps returning to Lower Moat Manor in his nightmares. Gerald Savory has structured a savory script directed by another Hammer veteran, Peter Sasdy. Pat Heywood, James Laurenson, Lucy Gutteridge. Each is available separately in videocassette.

**TWO LITTLE BEARS, THE (1962).** Mild, child-pleasing fantasy fluff in which the two children of parents Eddie Albert and Jane Wyatt turn themselves into bear cubs at night. Now dad wishes they could hibernate for the winter. Directed by Randall F. Hood. Brenda Lee, Soupy Sales, Nancy Kulp, Butch Patrick, Jimmy Boyd, Donnie Carter.

**TWO LOST WORLDS (1950).** Hackneyed desert island non-thriller about 19th Century shipwrecked pirates who've kidnapped a girl and must face the wrath of prehistoric monsters and heroic James Arness, who's out to save the chick. The monsters are stock footage from ONE MILLION B.C. A case of lost opportunities. Directed by Norman Dawn. Bill Kennedy, Laura Elliott, Gloria Petroff, Tom Hubbard.

**TWO OF A KIND (1983).** Simply awful, revolting vehicle for Olivia Newton-John and John Travolta. It is unforgivable they chose this wimpy fantasy to continue their screen romance begun in GREASE. This is just plain turkey fat. Travolta's a down-at-the-heels nobody who robs a bank to pay off loan sharks, she's the bank teller he holds up. Meanwhile, Gene Hackman is the Voice of God in Heaven, where angels Charles Durning, Beatrice Straight and Scatman Crothers use the earthly couple to prove to God the world doesn't have to start all over again—there is still some good in the worst of mankind. In the hands of writer-director Vincent Bufino it's a botched mess, without warmth, humor or social redeeming value. Oh, we almost forgot: Oliver Reed turns up as the Devil, to tempt our heroes from the path of righteousness. One time when a joker could beat TWO OF A KIND. (VC)

**TWO ON A GUILLOTINE (1965).** Old-fashioned screamer produced-directed by William Conrad, with illusionist Cesar Romero promising daughter Connie Stevens an inheritance of $300,000 if she spends seven nights in an old estate. Ghostly events happen, but nothing that will frighten knowledgeable horror fans. Slanted for a younger audience,

**JOHN LITHGOW AND VIC MORROW IN THE ILL-FATED 'TWILIGHT ZONE—THE MOVIE'**

with unnecessary rock 'n roll music and Dean Jones as a newspaper reporter. John Hoyt, Virginia Gregg.

**TWO PLUS FIVE: MISSION HYDRA.** See **STAR PILOTS.**

**2001: A SPACE ODYSSEY (1968).** Stanley Kubrick's monumental venture into the realm of science-fiction is a landmark film combining visual fascinations with a plethora of ideas often left to individual interpretation. Special effects by Douglas Trumbull are an achievement for their time, the music by Johann and Richard Strauss and other classical composers lends the film distinction, and the screenplay (by Kubrick and Arthur C. Clarke) is stunning in its implications. The boggling story begins with a "Dawn of Man" sequence in which ape-like creatures (the beginnings of man) are given intelligence after touching a monolithic black slab. By 2001, man is on the moon and preparing to journey to other planets when a similar slab is uncovered which transmits a signal to Jupiter. Astronauts Gary Lockwood and Keir Dullea are assigned to investigate, but their odyssey is endangered by a ruthless, malfunctioning computer nicknamed HAL. How the machine is overcome makes for a suspenseful allegory of man vs. machine. Final journey through the Star Gate is a sensory experience of psychedelic colors and psychotic patterns, heightened to a fevery pitch with music to commit suicide to. The "Star Child" ending is enigmatic and complex. Stunning, intelligent film yet to be imitated or surpassed, even by the 1984 sequel. Best on a big screen. (VC)

**2010: THE YEAR WE MAKE CONTACT (1984).** If Stanley Kubrick's 2001: A SPACE ODYSSEY is the Bible of movie science-fiction, then this sequel (written-produced-directed-photographed by Peter Hyams) is blasphemy. Although this picks up nine years later as continuing adventures of Hal the malfunctioning computer, David Bowman (the astronaut who vanished into the Star Gate) and the abandoned Intrepid space vehicle, it has none of the epic sense of Kubrick's masterpiece—in fact, it mundanely starts on Earth and wastes a half-hour depicting needless scenes of Roy Scheider's home life, conversations about a Russian-U.S. rescue mis-

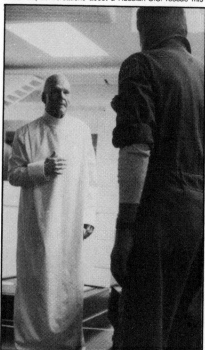

**KEIR DULLEA AS DAVID BOWMAN IN '2010'**

sion to Jupiter and other trivial junk. When the film finally gets into space to recount the important parts of Arthur C. Clarke's story, it must be rescued by Richard Edlund's effects. Credit him for one of the most exciting sequences set in space: the walk of two men transferring from the Russian spacecraft Leonov to the deserted Intrepid. That enigmatic "black monolith" is back, but the Kubrick ambiguities are gone—replaced by a simplified theme that tells, never suggests, that the floating slab belongs to God. Those who remember RED PLANET MARS will blanch at Clarke's pseudoreligious miracle which finishes the film—and hopefully the thought of any further irrelevant, irreverent sequels. Scheider, John Lithgow and Bob Balaban as the American spacers work with limited roles, but remain second best to Edlund's effects. Keir Dullea appears briefly as Bowman; among the Russian astronauts are Helen Mirren and Dana Elcar, who contribute little to the action. Major disappointment. (VC)

**2020 TEXAS GLADIATORS (1985).** Post-holocaust adventure of the MAD MAX school, featuring a band called "The Rangers" who go around rescuing innocent people from marauders. One of these good guys is found to be bad and exiled. He shows up years later with some sniveling motorcyclists and the action is hot and heavy. This Italian ROAD WARRIOR imitation is not much better or worse than other imitations, and went directly to TV. Directed by Kevin Mancuso. Harrison Muller, Al Cliver, Sabrina Siani.

**TWO THOUSAND MANIACS (1964).** Revolting exploitation material panders with scenes devoted to dismembered arms and legs, chopped-up bodies and heaped intestines. Setting is the modern South where rednecks are still fighting the Civil War by hacking to death any Northerners who wander through. Rednecks making red necks, get it? It turns out the town of Pleasant Valley, once wiped out by General Grant, periodically appears out of a time warp so the citizens can wreak revenge. Considered the "masterpiece" of gore purveyor Herschell Gordon Lewis. One watches at one's own risk. Connie Mason, Thomas Wood, Ben Moore. (VC)

**TWO THOUSAND YEARS LATER (1969).** Good intentions on the part of producer-director-writer Bert Tenzer make this worthwhile, even if the execution is occasionally faulty, and the satiric punches poorly delivered. The god Mercury, who has kept a Roman gladiator in suspensed animation, thaws him out and sends him into the future, to our time and place. The warrior warns us we're headed for the Big Fall, but he himself falls prey to the vultures of society. Terry-Thomas, Edward Everett Horton, Pat Harrington Jr.

**TWO WEEKS TO LIVE (1942).** Lum 'n Abner were a couple of rustic store managers popular on radio in the 1940s. In this feature version, Lum thinks Abner's dying, so he helps him find jobs to pay the hospital bill. Work includes flying a Martian rocket, clomping through a haunted house and drinking a Jekyll-Hyde formula. Innocuous, old-fashioned fun, as old as the hills of Tennessee. Directed by Malcolm St. Clair. Chester Lauk, Norris Goff, Franklin Pangborn, Charles Middleton, Rosemary LaPlanche.

**TWO WORLDS OF JENNIE LOGAN, THE (1979).** Plagued by her husband coming off an affair, unhappy housewife Lindsay Wagner finds an old dress in a Victorian home and slides into a time continuum, traveling back to the turn of the century to fall in love with Marc Singer. She passes back and forth between her two worlds, involved with murder, confused identities and the paradox of changing the past to ensure her future happiness. Nicely written by director Frank DeFelitta (he adapted David Williams' novel SECOND SIGHT) with well-etched performances by Wagner, Singer, Linda Gray, Joan Darling and Henry Wilcoxon. (VC)

**TWONKY, THE (1953).** Man's ultimate fate, that the TV set will one day take over his life, is allegorically expressed in this Arch Oboler film (he wrote-produced-directed) based on an amusing story by Henry Kuttner. A life force invades the video components in the home of Hans Conried and turns his set into a living thing. It hypnotizes others who would destroy it, until Hans wakes up to the reality of his nightmare. Strange, offbeat minor comedy. Billy Lynn, Gloria Blondell, Janet Warren, Ed Max, Al Jarvis, Norman Field.

**CREATURE FEATURES MOVIE GUIDE**

"Sing a song of graveyards / An acre full of germs / Four and twenty landlords / Dinner for the Worms. / And when the box was planted / The worms began to sing, / Wasn't that a dainty dish to sit before the Thing."—The gravedigger in **THE UNDEAD.**

**UFO (1956).** Investigative reporter wanders Washington D.C. interviewing Air Force personnel of Project Bluebook (a study of flying saucers). End result of this Ivan Tors-Clarence Greene pseudodocumentary is not a very close encounter, Francis Martin's script proving inconclusive. "Real life" footage of UFOs is out of focus, shaky and just as inconclusive. Actor Tom Powers narrates.

**UFO—EXCLUSIVE (1979).** Sheer speculation about unidentified flying objects, alien life forms walking our Earth and other exciting stuff like that, all presented in this phony baloney documentary narrated by Robert Morgan.

**UFO INCIDENT, THE (1975).** Fact or fiction? You must judge this intriguing TV-movie based on an alleged incident that occurred to Betty and Barney Hill while they drove through lonely countryside (an incident detailed in the book INTERRUPTED JOURNEY). They were hypnotized by alien creatures and led into a flying saucer to undergo biological testing. Only later, with a sympathetic psychiatrist's help, did the frightening details emerge. This unusually thoughtful treatment deals with the psychological trauma of UFO abductions but also leaves doubt as to exactly what happened. Provocatively directed by Richard A. Colla, with James Earl Jones and Estelle Parsons convincing as the racially-mixed couple. The doctor is excellently essayed by Barnard Hughes.

**UFO JOURNALS (1976).** 4-F way to OD on the ABCs of UFOs carrying DNA E.T.'s with ESP. On the QT, this 2-D job didn't have IQ or B.O. TNT. It was DOA. OK?

**UFO SYNDROME (1981).** Is the U.S. Government conspiring to cover up the true reason there are so many strange lights in the sky? Or are we seeing leftover footage from UFO JOURNALS? The possibilities are as endless as the Universe. Produced-directed by Richard Martin, narrated by Anthony Eisley.

**UFO: TARGET EARTH (1974).** Producer-director Michael A. deGaetano is responsible for this cheap ($70,000) off-target bore that misses Earth by miles. An electronics expert picks up signals of an alien craft submerged in a lake near town and tries to uncover its secrets, but this is an exercise in monumental tedium. Too much talk and not enough action. And no visible monster! Nick Plakias, Cynthia Cline.

**UFOS ARE REAL (1979).** UFOs are real boring, if this pseudodocumentary is any indication. It offers nothing to prove its title except the same old "evidence" of grainy, inconclusive film and still photographs, and keeps harping on how reliable all the eyewitnesses are, how sinister the Air Force is, etc. A lot of it is probably true, and some of the experts and witnesses are convincing, but other films have done it with greater style. Written-directed by Ed Hunt. Also known as ALIEN ENCOUNTERS.

**UFOS: IT HAS BEGUN (1976).** Rod Serling narrates this semidocumentary approach to the mystery of flying circular disc craft. Guest appearances by Burgess Meredith, Jose Ferrer and Dr. Jacques Vallee. Directed by Ray Rivas.

**UGETSU (1954).** Academy Award-winning Japanese film, based on stories by Akinari Ueda (an honorable 18th Century writer), is a weird, evanescent blend of violence and fantasy set against 16th Century Japan. Two parallel stories evolve around a potter and a farmer who abandon their wives to fulfill dreams of glory. The farmer turns Samurai warrior through singular circumstances, and the potter falls for a highborn woman who turns out to be a spirit. Acted in classic Japanese style, often as delicate as brush strokes on a vase, sometimes brutal in its sweaty action, but always beautifully photographed by Kazuo Miyagawa. Translated, the title means "Pale, mysterious moon after the rain." Directed by Kenji Mizoguchi. Machiko Kyo, Masayuki Mori.

**UGLY DUCKING, THE (1959).** Comedic Hammer treatment of the Jekyll-Hyde theme in which Bernard Bresslaw portrays a mentally defective descendant of Robert Louis Stevenson's scientist who concocts the old formula and turns into Teddy Hyde, colorful addition to the dance hall crowd and jewel robbery set. Undistinguished comedy, too corny to turn into a swan. Directed by Lance Comfort. Reginald Beckwith, Jon Pertwee, Michael Ripper, Richard Wattis.

**ULTIMATE IMPOSTOR, THE (1978).** Unsold TV pilot, based on William Zacha's THE CAPRICORN MAN, stars Joseph

Hacker as a U.S. agent whose memories are totally wiped out by the Chinese Reds. Back at headquarters, he is considered the perfect guinea pig for receiving alpha-10 wave lengths packed with computerized information, which in turn is transmitted into his brain cells. He can retain this information for only 36 hours, which adds suspense to his first assignment: find a defecting Russian submarine officer who has been kidnapped by Ruskie agents. Average TV actioner, scripted by producer Lionel E. Siegel. Directed by Paul Stanley. Keith Andes (with a totally bald scalp), Erin Gray, Tracy Brooks Swope, John Van Dreelen. (VC)

**ULTIMATE WARRIOR, THE (1975).** Science-fiction tale set in post-Armageddon America. Plagues have further decimated mankind as Max von Sydow leads survivors under his dictatorial rule. Yul Brynner as a "street fighter" guides his own survivors to a better life, battling through the debris. Written-directed by Robert Clouse. William Smith, Stephan McHattie, Joanna Miles, Richard Kelton. (VC)

**ULTRAMAN (1967).** Feature version of a Japanese TV comic strip, in which a befuddled Oriental turns into a man of steel to fight the monsters of the Universe that have managed to survive Godzilla movies. Strictly for the kiddiesans. Co-directed by special effects wizard Eiji Tsuburaya. Satoshi Furuya, Shoji Kobayashi.

**KIRK DOUGLAS RESISTING THE SIRENS OF THE ROCKS IN 'ULYSSES'**

**ULTRAMAN—MONSTER BIG BATTLE (1979).** More re-edited footage from the Japanese kiddie science-fiction television series, ULTRAMAN.

**ULYSSES (1955).** The Homeric touch has been lost in this Carlo Ponti-Dino de Laurentiis production, better described as a tribute to costume-sword adventures. Kirk Douglas brings a sense of quest and tragedy as the heroic Ithacan who sacks Troy and spends ten years making his way home. The Gods frown on Kirk as he battles from adventure to adventure, meeting the Cyclops, Circe the Enchantress (who turns Ulysses' crew into swine), and the Sirens of the Rocks. It ends in a bloodbath on Ithaca, where Ulysses slaughters suitors of wife Penelope (Silvana Mangano doubles as Circe and the long-suffering wife.) Irwin Shaw and Ben Hecht assisted several Italians with the script; Mario Camerini directed. Anthony Quinn, Rossana Podesta. (VC)

**ULYSSES AGAINST THE SON OF HERCULES (1963).** Mythological baloney in which the gods turn their anger against Ulysses and order Hercules to stop his earthly pursuits. The two musclemen join ranks to fight off the Bird People and the Troglodytes ruled by a wicked, insane king. And so it goes for 100 minutes of film, produced by one-eyed Italian and French producers, and directed by Mario Caiano. Georges Marchal, Michael Lane, Raffaella Carra.

**UNCANNY, THE (1977).** Writer Peter Cushing must convince a skeptical publisher that the behavior of felines is deadly by telling him three tales. This British-Canadian production was originally made as BRRRR! Three down . . . six lives to go. Directed by Denis Heroux. Ray Milland, Susan Penhaligon, Joan Greenwood, Roland Culver, Donald Pleasence, Samantha Eggar, John Vernon. (VC)

**UNCLE WAS A VAMPIRE (1960).** Italian variation on Dracula with touches of comedy—whether intended or not is not clear. An Italian nobleman is turned into the traditional nocturnal bloodsucker, but production values are as impoverished as the nobleman. Sylva Koscina is nice on the eyes, while Christopher Lee appears as "uncle." You'll want to cry uncle before the final fade. Directed by the avuncular Stefano Steno. Kai Fischer, Renato Rascel.

**UNDEAD, THE (1957).** Roger Corman film inspired by the Bridey Murphy craze of the 1950s: A psychiatrist (Richard Garland), through hypnosis, sends a prostitute (Pamela Duncan) into the past, where she is destined to be burned as a witch. Knowing the events to come, she tries to alter history . . . with unsettling results. Corman directed the Mark Hanna-Charles Griffith script. Allison Hayes, Val Dufour, Billy Barty, Dick Miller, Mel Welles, Richard Devon.

**UNDER THE SIGN OF CAPRICORN (1971).** U.S. scientists studying the aboriginals of the Australian outback are mysteriously murdered one by one, leading Barry Sullivan to think that perhaps one of the natives has cursed him. Martin Landau, Chuck Connors, Stella Stevens.

**UNDERCOVER LOVER.** See **MAN FROM S.E.X., THE.**

**UNDERSEA KINGDOM (1936).** Full-length version of the

Republic 12-chapter serial starring Ray "Crash" Corrigan as a naval officer possessing superstrength who finds himself on the Lost Continent of Atlantis, battling it out with Monte Blue, who has a disintegrator weapon that could destroy America. Robots, submarines and other fantastic weaponry keep the story moving, as does the lively direction of Joseph Kane and B. Reeves Eason. It's a gas! (2-vol. VC)

**UNDERTAKER AND HIS PALS, THE (1967).** Sickening black comedy (minus laughs) in which a mortician increases his profit margin by getting cadavers from motorcycle-riding murderers. Once he has dough for the funeral services, he picks up a little side money by turning the corpses over to a restaurant, where they are dished up a la carte for gourmet customers and served au Gratuitous. Robert Lowery, the Batman of 1943, must have been hard up for work when he accepted his role from producer-director David C. Graham, whose ineptitude as a filmmaker reaches classic proportions midway through the first reel.

**UNDERWATER CITY, THE (1962).** Alex Gordon's production is a sincere effort to splash up Deep Six excitement as scientist William Lundigan, Julia Adams, Roy Roberts and Carl Benton Reid build an underwater metropolis. But a low budget and a mediocre script by Owen Harris dampen the activities. Directed without style by Frank McDonald. Ultimately, it was consigned to Davy Jones' Locker.

**UNDERWORLD (1985).** Extremely strange British horror/science-fiction film based on a story by Clive Barker (famed for his BOOKS OF BLOOD) and James Caplin. A drug that allows its users to live out various fantasies also creates mutations in the body. These new mutants kidnap a prostitute and hold her hostage in order to get more of the drug, and then a gangster-chemist decides to bump off the whole bunch. Directed by George Pavlou. Denholm Elliott, Roy Bain, Hugo Motherskille. Shown theatrically in America as **TRANSMUTATIONS.**

**UNDYING MONSTER, THE (1942).** Odd offshoot of the werewolf genre, based on the perenially popular novel by Jessie Douglas Kerruish and starring James Ellison, Heather Angel and John Howard. Director John Brahm captures the Cornwall setting in this tale of a family haunted by a centuries-old lycanthropic curse. Mature and thoughtful, with emphasis on ambience rather than a great monster or special effects. Bramwell Fletcher, Heather Thatcher.

**UNEARTHLY, THE (1957).** Enjoyable sleaze, grade-Z fashion, with John Carradine as a mad scientist who discovers a 17th gland containing the secret of youth, "prolonging life for thousands of years." So naturally he kidnaps innocent people and exposes their bodies to electricity bolts and deformities. His assistant, Lobo, is lumbering Tor Johnson. Helping out in the thesping department are Myron Healy as a sympathetic criminal seeking refuge in the doc's recuperation center and sexy femme Allison Hayes as an intended victim. Carradine, always on the verge of hysteria, asks "Did you sterilize my #23 scalpel?" and plays morbid organ music during dinner. Producer-director Brooke L. Peters manages a silly "buried alive" sequence and there's a laughable twist ending. Roy Gordon, Arthur Batanides. (VC)

**UNEARTHLY STRANGER (1963).** John Neville wakes up to discover his lovely wife (Gabriella Lecudi) sleeps with her eyes open. Her peculiar traits increase—until Neville realizes he has married an extraterrestrial, sent to Earth to interfere in the space project he's working on by killing scientists. However, when the E.T. femme falls for Neville, the plan goes awry. Thoughtful British science-fiction thriller from producer Albert Fennell suggests and implies, rather than shows, the horrors at work. John Krish directed. Jean Marsh, Philip Stone, Warren Mitchell, Patrick Newell.

**UNHINGED (1983).** Old mansion in Oregon is the setting for this low budget regional film in which a series of murders are committed with a variety of horrendous weapons. Those squeaking sounds in the background are the unoiled hinges of the killer's mind. Written-produced-directed by Don Gronquist. Laurel Munsion, Sara Ansley.

**UNHOLY NIGHT (1929).** Ben Hecht's "Green Ghost" served as the basis for this early sound supernatural tale involving a

legend about a man who dies of a disease that taints his skin green. Directed by Lionel Barrymore. Ernest Torrence, Roland Young, Boris Karloff (as a Hindu servant), John Loder, Dorothy Sebastian, Polly Moran.

**UNHOLY QUEST, THE (1934).** Long-forgotten (and we're all the better for it) British chiller about an obsessed physician reviving the embalmed corpse of a Holy Crusader with the help of a blackmailer's body. Directed by R. W. Lotinga. Claude Bailey, Terence de Marney, John Milton.

**UNHOLY THREE (1925).** One of director Tod Browning's weird little silent films starring Lon Chaney Sr. as a ventriloquist who teams up with a midget, an ape and a muscleman to pull off an unusual caper. Victor McLaglen, Mae Busch, Matt Moore. Rare; pops up sometimes at revival houses.

**UNHOLY THREE (1930).** Sound (but not too sound) remake of Tod Browning's 1925 film, again with Lon Chaney Sr. as the leader of a colorful gang pulling off an ingenious caper. Jack Conway directed. Lila Lee, Elliott Nugent. (VC)

**UNIDENTIFIED FLYING ODDBALL (1979).** Walt Disney comedy update of Mark Twain's CONNECTICUT YANKEE IN KING ARTHUR'S COURT in which a space engineer and his robot are sent back in time to the Round Table milieu of King Arthur. Don Tait adapted this lighthearted fantasy (a U.S.-British production) and Russ Mayberry directed with the

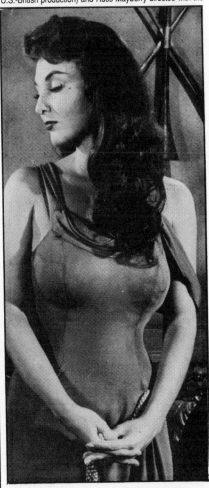

**ALLISON HAYES IN 'THE UNDEAD'**

"Glub

Glub

Bubble

Bubble

Gurgle

Pop"

—The soundtrack of
**UNDERWATER CITY.**

same spoofy touch he gave PETE'S DRAGON. Dennis Dugan, Jim Dale, Ron Moody (as Merlin the Magician), Kenneth More, John Le Mesurier. (VC)

**UNINVITED, THE (1944).** One of the few genuine supernatural classics of the cinema, based on a novel by Dorothy Macardle, in which Ray Milland and Ruth Hussey, as brother and sister, purchase an old house on the Cornish coast only to be subjected to weird phenomena: strange smells, a wilting flower, an ectoplasmic presence on the stairs. This Paramount production from Charles Brackett reeks with atmosphere (credit director Lewis Allen and writers Frank Partos and Dodie Smith) and is further intensified by medium Gail Russell who holds the key to the mystery. The best ghost movie of the 1940s. Alan Napier, Donald Crisp, Cornelia Otis Skinner, Dorothy Stickner, Barbara Everest.

**UNKNOWN, THE (1927).** Tod Browning's silent classic starring Lon Chaney Sr. as Alonzo the Armless Wonder, a circus freak who is actually a murderer hiding from the police. Alonzo becomes a knife-thrower after learning to toss blades with his feet. Abnormal sexuality leads Alonzo to cut off his arms for a woman's love. Perverted but fascinating. Joan Crawford, Norman Kerry, Nick de Ruiz.

**UNKNOWN, THE (1946).** Third and last entry in Columbia's cheap, short-lived series based on Carlton E. Morse's popular radio thriller, I LOVE A MYSTERY. Jim Bannon stars as ace adventurer Jack Packard and Barton Yarborough is Doc Young in this adaptation of the famous episode, "Faith, Hope and Charity Sisters," although the sisters have been simplified to one to save bucks. The investigators search for a cloaked entity in a haunted mansion in the South, to which Jeff Donnell has just returned as the wayward daughter. The phantom cries of a baby heighten the mystery. Henry Levin directed this film, which today is of only minor interest.

**UNKNOWN ISLAND (1948).** Paleological potboiler, straight out of a pulp magazine, throws together several prehistoric beasts on an uncharted island in the Pacific discovered by Barton MacLane (tough sea captain), Richard Denning (alcoholic beachcomber), Virginia Grey (obligatory skirt with pouting lips) and Philip Reed (returning war hero). The rubber-suited monsters shuffle around without ever attacking anyone. Threat factor is zero. There's also a ridiculous gorilla that battles a dinosaur—one of the most ludicrous moments in the history of lost-island movies. Directed turgidly by Jack Bernhard, scripted by Bob Shannon and Jack Harvey.

**UNKNOWN POWERS (1980).** Three half-hour episodes of a pseudodocumentary TV series witlessly spliced together to create this turgid study of extrasensory (non)perception. Samantha Eggar, Jack Palance, Will Geer and Roscoe Lee Browne are the Hollywood personalities who host-narrate these weak studies of occult science. Its power remains unknown. (VC)

**UNKNOWN TERROR, THE (1957).** The known terror, as discovered by critics, is Charles Marquis Warren's direction of this singularly unimaginative trash depicting an expedition in the Caribbean jungle to find the Cave of Death. Dr. Ramsey (Gerald Milton) has fungus-mold formula which he injects into patients—with more than athlete's foot as a result. Meanwhile, that expedition includes Mala Powers (she runs through phony foliage in flimsy negligees), John Howard (he climbs into the Cave of Death without even a flashlight) and Paul Richards (he watches the heaving bosom of Indian girl May Wynn). Now you know the real terror.

**UNKNOWN WORLD (1951).** Robert L. Lippert cheapie, filmed in the Carlsbad Caverns, depicts an expedition which corkscrews into the core of the earth with a giant duralunin-powered drill mounted on the front of their "mole ship." These human burrowers, searching for a new place for mankind to live so decent people can escape the threat of atomic attack, discover conditions at Earth's center to be harmful to reproduction. The Millard Kaufman script is neat and unpretentious. Directed by Terrell O. Morse with a sense of style. At least this is different. Bruce Kellogg, Victor Killian, Jim Bannon, Marilyn Nash, Otto Waldis.

**UNSEEN, THE (1945).** Nifty, low budget Paramount mystery with haunted house overtones which don't quite pan out, but the Raymond Chandler-Hagar Wilde storyline has fascinating characters and ghostly ambience, which director Lewis Allen brings full-bodied to the screen. What a great cast: Joel McCrea, Gail Russell, Herbert Marshall, Phyllis Brooks.

**UNSEEN, THE (1980).** Despite a trite-sounding plot (three beautiful TV newscasters are secluded in a house with a madman and, one by one, are brutalized and murdered), this is a strange, sometimes enthralling low budget flick, made in and around Solvang, Calif., a Danish-style village of windmills and smorgasbord restaurants. It takes one of the hoariest cliches of horror movies—the animalistic, "unseen" entity living in the cellar—and manages to give it a new sense of mystery, even compassion. Not that the film aspires to anything more than it is—it just does what it sets out to do well under Peter Foleg's direction. Barbara Bach, Sydney Lassick, Stephen Furst, Karen Lamm, Lelia Goldoni. (VC)

**UNTAMED WOMEN (1952).** An uncharted island is home for many gorgeous hunks of pulchritude called Druids (Doris Merrick, Midge Ware, Judy Brubaker, Carol Brewster) who specialize in modeling animal skins. The shapely femmes decide to introduce a new line of low-cut wear when shipwreck survivors are beached nearby. Roving the island are prehistoric beasts (outtakes from ONE MILLION B.C.), who dig the new fashions too. Part of the landscape includes man-eating plants and male slaves. Pulp material no longer fashionable; out of style. Lyle Talbot, Mikel Conrad, Morgan Jones, Autumn Rice. Directed by W. Merle Connell.

**UP FROM THE DEPTHS (1979).** "Down to the Depths of Despair" better describes this amateurish imitation of JAWS, which features ridiculous characters, phony special effects and a holiday feeling that betrays any cinematic drama. Charles Griffith, an old Roger Corman alumnus, directed on location in the Hawaiian Islands, hamstrung with a terrible script by Alfred Sweeny. Sam Bottoms wins worst acting award bottoms up. In this picture, you root for the killer fish and hope the dumb white-eyes get eaten.

**UP IN SMOKE (1957).** Huntz Hall sells his soul to the Devil in exchange for the names of winning horses. Our tip of the day: Sell your own soul to the Devil to avoid this lowbrow Allied Artists entry in the Bowery Boy series—one of the last ever made. Devil-doesn't-care direction by William Beaudine, I-don't-give-a-damnation script by Jack Townley.

**UPSTATE MURDERS, THE. See SAVAGE WEEKEND.**

**UTOPIA (1951).** One of the last films to feature Stan Laurel and Oliver Hardy, this is a French-Italian production in which an island pops up mysteriously from the sea. There, a new society is designed to be the ultimate in living. Far from the comedy team's best work—of interest to die-hard fans only. Also known as ATOLL K. Directed by Leo Joannon. (VC)

---

*"You don't believe in this superstitious rot, do you?"— Famous last words in THE UNDYING MONSTER.*

**CREATURE FEATURES MOVIE GUIDE**

K.D.

*"A whisper of warm desire becomes a shriek of chilling terror in the embrace of the blood-nymphs."—Advertising come-on for* **THE VAMPIRE LOVERS.**

**V (1983).** Four-hour miniseries written-produced-directed by Kenneth Johnson. Fifty giant saucer-shaped motherships from another galaxy appear, crewed by humanoids here to exchange precious commodities to save their dying planet. But these E.T.s are two-faced conquerors, wresting control of TV networks to take over the world. Guerrilla units led by Marc Singer fight back by zapping the humanoids with their own ray guns and stealing their shuttlecrafts. It is then that V (for victory in the old World War II phrase, V for Victory) deteriorates into mock heroics and a plot about bigotry and betrayal patterned on Nazi Germany. The special effects are good, but the art design is derivative. The best touch is when a high school marching band greets the first aliens to Earth with the theme from STAR WARS.

**V: THE FINAL BATTLE (1984).** Six-hour continuation of V, but without creator Kenneth Johnson. Producers Daniel H. Blatt-Robert Singer took the helm, hiring Richard Heffron to direct and a mess of hacks to carry on the story. Primarily action and intrigue in the TV vein, designed to introduce a weekly TV series that was short-lived. Jane Badler stands out as an alien bitch in charge of the invasion. Marc Singer is back at the hero, with Faye Grant.

**VALERIE AND THE WEEK OF WONDERS (1970).** Beautifully photographed Czech film directed by Jaromil Jires will baffle and infuriate any who attempt to decipher its disjointed plot involving a pair of earrings and a vampire bishop called The Weasel. Forget logic and enjoy the visual splendors in pastel colors and Freudian overtones. Jaroslava Musil, Helena Anyzkova.

**VALHALLA (1986).** Danish cartoon version of a popular comic strip in which two human youngsters are involved with Thor, god of Thunder, Loke, an evil counterpart, and a vicious baby giant named Quark in the land of Udgaard, where wicked giants dwell. Poorly done, in the vein of a Saturday morning cartoon. Directed without distinction by Peter Madsen.

**VALLEY OF GWANGI, THE (1969).** Excellent Charles H. Schneer production with brilliant stop motion effects by Ray Harryhausen and a romantically pleasing story by Willis O'Brien. It's an exciting turn-of-the-century Western (directed by James O'Connolly) in which cowboy James Franciscus discovers a forbidden valley of prehistoric creatures. A Tyrannosaurus rex is lassoed and hogtied in one helluva exciting sequence, then displayed in a traveling circus. Up there with the best of Harryhausen's work. Made in Spain. Gila Golan, Richard Carlson, Freda Jackson, Laurence Naismith.

**VALLEY OF THE DRAGONS (1961).** Jules Verne story (adapted by director Edward Bernds) served as the premise for this undistinguished adventure in which a comet swooping past Earth during the 19th Century sucks up two Earthmen in the process of fighting a duel. On their floating rock, Cesare Danova and Sean McClory find prehistoric monsters (or are we seeing outttakes from ONE MILLION B.C.?) and tribes of warring cave people. Verne was reduced to a lugubrious state. Joan Staley, Gregg Martel.

**VALLEY OF THE EAGLES (1952).** Good location photography and a suspenseful script by director Terence Young enhance this British production set in Lapland. An invention that converts sound into energy is stolen by a scientist's assistant, who also has an eye on the inventor's wife. A police inspector comes to the rescue. Jack Warner, Nadia Gray, Christopher Lee, John McCallum, Anthony Dawson.

**VALLEY OF THE STONE MEN.** See **MEDUSA VS. THE SON OF HERCULES.** (Stoned again?)

**VALLEY OF THE ZOMBIES (1946).** Republic Studio stinker with such a poor budget there aren't any zombies—only mad doctor Ian Keith, resurrected from beyond the pale and keeping himself alive with a blood transfusion. Robert Livingston and Adrian Booth creep around eerie graveyards and eerie mansions, while the cops are portrayed as the dumbest characters alive. Hopelessly outdated, but it has a special charm all its own—a charm of ineptitude. Directed by Philip Ford.

**VAMP (1986).** Above-average teenage comedy blending horror and laughs when members of a frat party step into the After Dark Club—and a comedy Twilight Zone—to meet Grace Jones (as Katrina, an Egyptian mummy goddess). She and her strippers are literal femme fatales who put the bite on the boys. New World comedy has a few scary-fun moments

**GRACE JONES VAMPING IN 'VAMP'**

as well as gore humor. Directed stylishly by Richard Wenk. Chris Makepeace, Sandy Baron, Robert Rusler, Billy Drago, Brad Logan. (VC)

**VAMPIRA.** See **OLD DRACULA.**

**VAMPIRE, THE (1956).** In modern Mexico, Count Lavud (German Robles) is forced to suck the blood of victims twice before they become truly undead. A bloodsucker sure has to work harder these days. Directed by Fernando Mendez. Imported by K. Gordon Murray. Abel Salazar is the co-star.

**VAMPIRE, THE (1957).** Also known as MARK OF THE VAMPIRE, this minor biter, strictly lower berth, depicts doctor John Beal pulling a Jekyll-Hyde routine after he swallows the inevitable pill. Coleen Gray, Kenneth Tobey, Dabbs Gear, Paul Brinegar. Directed by Paul Landres.

**VAMPIRE (1979).** Remarkably effective vampire tale—the best ever produced for TV—features the standard trappings of the Gothic thriller but crypt-oligizes them intelligently and chillingly. Jason Miller and E. G. Marshall are superb as vampire stalkers while Richard Lynch is menacing as an 800-year-old bloodsucker sleeping in San Francisco. Made on location, this is unresolved so the story would segue into a weekly series, but it was never picked up. Well directed by E. W. Swackhammer; written by Steve Bochco and Michael Kozell. Jessica Walter, Barrie Youngfellow.

**VAMPIRE AND THE BALLERINA (1963).** One vampire picture that keeps the characters on their toes. But dancing school was never like this, not even in Italy, where this nonsense takes place. When ballet artists are lost in the woods, they discover a castle owned by a vampire contessa. The only time in the history of vampire cinema a blooddrinker performed a pirouette while necking with his girlfriend. Helene Remy, Maria Luisa Rolando, Walter Brandi.

**VAMPIRE BAT, THE (1933).** Mad scientist Lionel Atwill (as that wonderfully dedicated but demented Dr. Otto von Niemann) sneaks around leaving puncture marks in the necks of victims—but is he a vampire? Edward T. Lowe's script and Frank Strayer's direction are hopelessly outdated, but this is worth seeing for the cast: Melvyn Douglas as leading man, Fay Wray as screaming heroine, Dwight Frye as crazy henchman.

**VAMPIRE BEAST CRAVES BLOOD, THE.** See **BLOOD BEAST TERROR** (but only if you have the craving).

**VAMPIRE CIRCUS (1972).** Three-ring Hammer midway of horror, set in 1810 Serbia in a small village wracked by plague. Paying a visit to the community is a big top with low entertainers: vampires and other types capable of transmutation into animals and grotesque night creatures. The owner of the circus, a vampire himself, is seeking revenge against those who murdered his cousin. Graphically gory in the Hammer tradition. Directed by Robert Young. Adrienne Cori, Laurence Payne, Thorley Walters, David Prowse (Darth Vader), Lynne Frederick, Skip Martin.

**VAMPIRE DOLL, THE (1970).** Japanese horror avoids cliches of the Dracula genre and deals with a girl with a damned soul. Too artistic for the schlock crowd. Kayo Matsuo, Akira Nakao. Directed by Michio Yamamoto.

**VAMPIRE HAPPENING (1971).** Not much about vampires is happening in this German comedy fiasco with uninspired performers who waste their time (and yours) stalking corridors of a dreary old castle. The star is Ferdy Mayne, who plays the Dracula spinoff. Directed by Freddie Francis. Yvor Murillo, Ingrid Van Bergen. (VC)

**VAMPIRE HOOKERS (1979).** John Carradine dons the cape of a bloodsucking vampire who uses shapely wenches to bring victims to the local cemetery, where he finishes them off. Don't get hooked watching this Filipino production. Directed by Cirio H. Santiago, scripted by Howard Cohen. Bruce Fairbairn, Trey Wilson, Karen Stride. (VC)

**VAMPIRE KILLERS.** See **FEARLESS VAMPIRE KILLERS, THE.** (What a cross to bear!)

**VAMPIRE LOVERS, THE (1970).** Initial entry in Hammer's Karnstein series with Ingrid Pitt as the beautiful, busty Lesbian-inclined Mircalla (sequels were LUST FOR A VAMPIRE and TWINS OF EVIL). It features a sensuous sex romp between two gorgeous babes (heavily edited by U.S. censors) who engage in streaking and breast-biting. Peter Cushing is General Spielsdorf, the exorcist who must behead the body of Mircilla (an anagram of Carmilla) before evil rests. Directed by Roy Ward Baker from a Tudor Gates script. Pippa Steele, Madeline Smith, Kate O'Meara, George Cole, Douglas Wilmer, Dawn Addams, Ferdy Mayne. (VC)

**VAMPIRE MEN OF THE LOST PLANET (1971).** Dr. Rynning (John Carradine) rockets to a faraway unknown planet inhabited by bloodsuckers, where he also meets serpent monsters, devil bats and Spectrum X. The latter are creatures from a Filipino horror movie which was re-edited, the new U.S. footage being produced and directed by Al Adamson. Robert Dix, Vicki Volante.

**VAMPIRE OF DR. DRACULA.** See **MARK OF THE WOLFMAN.**

**VAMPIRE OVER LONDON.** See **MY SON, THE VAMPIRE.**

**VAMPIRE PEOPLE.** See **BLOOD DRINKERS, THE.**

**VAMPIRE PLAYGIRLS.** See **CEMETERY GIRLS.**

**VAMPIRE'S COFFIN, THE (1958).** Campy Chubusco-Azteca Mexican pastiche of a Universal horror movie of the 1940s—stylish in its own ridiculous way, and more fun than some south-of-the-border imports. This one was Americanized by the infamous K. Gordon Murray. Enhanced by good black-and-white photography, the film depicts a pair of tomb defilers who unleash on the world a vampire drenched in salsa sauce. Bordering on a Bela Lugosi parody, the sanguinary count turns one of the defilers into an Igor-like minion and begins stalking beautiful women, who are always fainting so he can carry them away to his hideout. The climactic battle in a wax museum (reminiscent of HOUSE OF WAX) is a real gas, with the vampire needlessly turning into a bat to fool his human foe. There's a laugh-a-minute, enhanced by a score that tries to copy the work of Hans Salter. German Robles portrays the evil Count Lavud, Producer Abel Salazar doubles as a cast member to keep the budget down. Directed by Fernando Mendez.

**CREATURE FEATURES MOVIE GUIDE**

**INGRID PITT AND MADELINE SMITH IN 'THE VAMPIRE LOVERS'**

**VAMPIRE'S GHOST, THE (1945).** Republic Studio grade Z abomination (surpassed in cheapness only by VALLEY OF THE ZOMBIES) which had the distinction of being co-written by Leigh Brackett, a leading fantasy writer. Admittedly, there are unusual ingredients here: the setting is a saloon in Africa, operated by a vampire named Webb Fallon, who has been cursed for the last few hundred years, and John Abbott tries to bring a sense of pain to the character. The film was cursed the day it was produced by Rudy Abel, for it is slow and monotonous, directed without style by Lesley Selander. Grant Withers, Peggy Stewart, Adele Mara, Roy Barcroft.

**VAMPIRES IN HAVANA (1985).** Animated cartoon by Cuban writer-director Juan Padron may be presenting an allegory of the Castro takeover in this tale about a jazz trumpeter-vampire who is plotting the overthrow of a dictator. Nice try, Padron, but no Cuban cigar.

**VAMPIRE'S NIGHT ORGY, THE (1973).** Softcore Spanish flick in which an entire European town is taken over by vampires, eager to mix blood-drinking with sexual proclivity. Not exactly an orgy of excitement; call it "touching." Directed by Leon Klimovsky. Helga Line, Jack Taylor.

**VAMPYR (1932).** German masterpiece photographed by Rudolf Mate (he later became a Hollywood director) and directed by Carl Theodore Dreyer, based loosely on J. Sheridan Le Fanu's CARMILLA. It remains one of the few horror films ever to so well capture the nightmarish qualities of a dream. A visitor (Julian West) to a peculiar inn in a strange village is given a book on vampirism and plunged into a world of shadows, coffins and vampires. Only in recent years has VAMPYR taken on a cult following among aficionados and been recognized as a minor art classic. (VC)

**VAMPYRES—DAUGHTERS OF DARKNESS (1975).** R-rated version of the X-rated VAMPYRES. Lesbian bloodsuckers Fram and Miriam (Marianne Moore and Anulka) prey on campers vacationing on the lawn of their castle—until one of them makes the mistake of falling in love with handsome Murray Brown. The theme is: every lesbian vampire should own a castle. They certainly have a gay time in the crypt with Joseph Larraz directing.

**VANISHING POINT (1971).** Exciting chase film (with excellent stunt driving by Carey Loftin) has an intriguing metaphysical side under Richard Sarafian's direction. Barry Newman is Kowalski, a laconic, enigmatic race driver leading the police on a breathtaking race from Denver to Nevada. A psychic link is established between Kowalski and a blind black radio disc jockey (Cleavon Little), who makes him a superhero to listeners, seeing in Kowalski a symbol of rebellion against the Establishment. Symbolism surrounding an old desert rat (Dean Jagger) who collects rattlesnakes is a bit heavy but contributes to the odd existential philosophies about vanishing breeds. Written by Guillermo Cain. (VC)

**VARAN THE UNBELIEVABLE (1958).** Varan was described by one critic as a flying squirrel with jet-propelled nuts, by another as a prehistoric bat . . . what the hell is this thing called Varan? Beats the hell out of us, but kiddies will squeal with delight at this Americanized version of a Japanese monster movie directed by Inoshiro Honda. Pure action as the Godzilla carbon copy beelines toward Tokyo, encountering resistence from a naval officer. Scenes with Myron Healy were added for U.S. appeal. Effects by Honda's partner, Eiji Tsuburaya. Kozo Nomura, Akihiko Hirata. (VC)

**VAULT OF HORROR, THE (1973).** Sequel to TALES FROM THE CRYPT consists of stories adapted from the E.C. comics of the 1950s edited by William Gaines and Albert Feldstein. Milton Subotsky's black-macabre script recaptures only some of the E.C. flavor, but horror fans will still enjoy. Five people trapped in an underground tomb with the Vault Keeper listen as he spins five yarns that run the gamut: vampirism, limb dismemberment, body snatching, voodoo, satanism, etc. "Midnight Mess," stars Daniel and Anna Massey; "The Neat Job," Glynis Johns and Terry-Thomas; "This Trick'll Kill You," Curt Jurgens; "Bargain in Death," Edward Judd and Michael Craig; and "Drawn and Quartered," Tom Baker. Roy Ward Baker directed. (VC)

**VEIL, THE (1958).** Four vignettes from an unsold TV series, with Boris Karloff introducing each segment: "Crystal Ball," "The Doctor," "Genesis," and "What Happened to Peggy?" Directed by Herbert L. Strock. Patrick Macnee, Robert Griffin, Ray Montgomery. Other TV features built from THE VEIL are JACK THE RIPPER and DESTINATION NIGHTMARE.

**VEIL, THE.** See HAUNTS.

**VEIL OF BLOOD (1973).** Swiss vampire yarn written-

**OLINKA BOROVA IN 'VENGEANCE OF SHE'**

directed by Joe Sarno, about a baroness of blood whose soul is kept alive in the bodies of her descendants. Nadia Senkowa, Untel Syring, Ulrike Butz.

**VELVET HOUSE.** See CRUCIBLE OF HORROR.

**VELVET VAMPIRE, THE (1971).** Commendable attempt by director Stephanie Rothman to make an unusual vampire picture. Strong sexual overtones heighten the suspense when travelers Michael Blodgett and Sherry Miles stop at the ranchero of Celeste Yarnall, unaware she is a sensual vampire, being a descendant of horror writer Sheridan Le Fanu. There's time wasted with desert dunebuggy footage, but

once Yarnall focuses on her targets, male and female, the going gets sensuous. How the vampire is laid to rest belongs strictly to the Flower Child Generation. (VC)

**VENETIAN AFFAIR, THE (1966).** Predictable, cliched spy thriller about a nerve-destroying drug that turns men into controllable zombies . . . but done with a topnotch cast headed by Robert Vaughn as an undercover agent, Karl Boehm as the dastardly villain, Elke Sommer and Felicia Farr as sexy go-betweens and Boris Karloff as a mysterious inventor. The Venice location photography is pleasant and distracts from the muddled story by E. Jack Neuman, who adapted a novel by Helen MacInnes. Directed by Jerry Thorpe. Ed Asner, Luciana Paluzzi, Roger C. Carmel, Joe De Santos.

**VENGEANCE LAND (1986).** In the year 2030, the Hunters hunt the Hunted. Zap guns in desolation. Directed by Roderick Taylor.

**VENGEANCE OF FU MANCHU (1968).** Lackluster Harry Alan Towers production (third in the British series) with Christopher Lee as the Oriental mastermind who forces a surgeon to create an exact duplicate of Scotland Yard's Nayland Smith in an insidious plot to substitute the chief law enforcers with killer clones. Strangely lacking in action. Directed by Jeremy Summers. Howard Marion Crawford, Tsai Chin, Horst Frank, Maria Rohm, Tony Ferrer.

**VENGEANCE OF HERCULES.** See GOLIATH AND THE DRAGON.(Oh, Goliath down, Herc!)

**VENGEANCE OF SHE, THE (1968).** This sequel to H. Rider Haggard's SHE stars sexy Olinka Berova as a seductive woman inexorably drawn to a lost city where she is asked to enter the Eternal Flame by John Richardson, king of Kuma. Peter O'Donnell's screenplay is a deterioration of Haggard's concept, only half-heartedly executed for Hammer by director Cliff Owen. Edward Judd, Andre Morell, Colin Blakely.

**VENGEANCE OF THE MUMMY.** See MUMMY'S REVENGE, THE. (Mummy Deadest!)

**VENGEANCE OF THE ZOMBIES (1972).** Spanish fright job directed by Leon Klimovsky (the hombre who gave us SAGA OF DRACULA and VAMPYRES) and starring that Holy Toledo monster star Paul Naschy. Indian sage named Krisna (is his first name Harry?) arranges, through a magical chant, to raise a woman from the grave, who is turned into a killing machine for purposes of revenge. Montezuma's revenge could be next. Mirta Miller, Vic Winner, Luis Ciges.

**VENOM (1982).** Kidnapping-hostage-siege plot mixed with snake-menace subplot results in a taut suspenser despite melodramatic contrivances and one-dimensional characters. Martin Bregman's production maintains a compelling hold as a black mamba, the most lethal reptile around the house, is loose in a London mansion where kidnappers Oliver Reed, Susan George and Klaus Kinski hold a rich kid for ransom. Tension mounts as the killer snake slithers through the house, ready to strike. Meanwhile, policeman Nicol Williamson barricades the street to engage in standard hostage cliches. Director Piers Haggard keeps Robert Carrington's script uncoiling. Sterling Hayden is the boy's grandfather, a retired big-game hunter (hence knowledgeable about deadly serpents), and Sarah Miles portrays an expert in herpetology who is trapped in the house. (VC)

**VENUS AGAINST THE SON OF HERCULES (1962).** An entire planet against one lousy muscleman? Naw, just a sinewhappy warrior against mangy Italian meeklings as he fights to overcome magical incantations, monsters, man-eating plants and other stuff by writer-director Marcello Baldi. Massimo Serato, Roger Browne, Jackie Lane.

**VENUS IN FURS (1970).** Contrived Harry Alan Towers production features James Darren and Barbara McNair as ghosts unaware they are spirits as they become involved with

**KIM NOVAK BEING DIRECTED BY ALFRED HITCHCOCK FOR 'VERTIGO'**

the underworld of sex and sadism. Director Jesus Franco (who co-scripted with Malvin Wald) spins a weird story about weirdos and perverts. The title was lifted from Sacher-Masoch, but everything else was taken from Hunger. Just goes to prove you can't wrap a sow's ear in a mink stole. Klaus Kinski, Dennis Price, Maria Rohm, Margaret Lee. (VC)

**VERTIGO (1958).** Alfred Hitchcock classic reeking with a supernatural atmosphere that is greatly enhanced by Bernard Herrmann's eerie music. Even though suggestions of afterlife and reincarnation are explained logically, it's still a compelling story in which James Stewart, a detective who has survived a bad fall and suffers from a fear of heights, prevents mysterious Kim Novak from committing suicide in San Francisco Bay and falls in love with her as he tries to help her remember her past. The Alec Coppel-Samuel Taylor screenplay is based on an excellent French thriller by Pierre Boileau and Thomas Narcejac. Barbara Del Geddes, Henry Jones, Tom Helmore. (VC)

**VICE VERSA (1948).** Early Peter Ustinov effort (he wrote-produced-directed) is a comedy-fantasy in which an idol's evil eye turns son into father and . . . vice versa. Kay Walsh, Anthony Newley, Roger Livesey, Petula Clark.

**VICTOR FRANKENSTEIN (1977).** Irish-Swedish version of

**JIMMY STEWART FALLING IN LOVE WITH MYSTERIOUS, ELUSIVE NOVAK**

**CREATURE FEATURES MOVIE GUIDE**

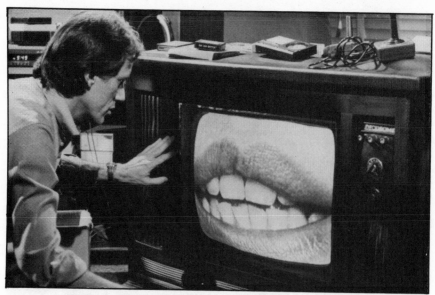

**JAMES WOODS (WATCHING A DENTAL SHOW?) IN 'VIDEODROME'**

Mary Shelley's FRANKENSTEIN starring Leon Vitali as the experimental doctor and Per Oscarsson as the Monster. Written-directed by Calvin Floyd, Stacey Dorning.

**VIDEO WARS (1984).** Incredibly inept Italian spy spoof, in which a dumb superspy named Scattergood (billed as George Diamond, but don't believe it), the head of SOB (Subversive Operations Bureau), is assigned by a video-happy President to stop a villain named Reichmonger, dictator of the kingdom of Vacabia who has programmed the video games of the world to brainwash everyone for conquest. Absolutely nothing happens in this Mario Giampaolo produced-directed fiasco except a bevy of beauties show off their breasts and legs, and a dumb Norwegian beauty (Joan Stenn, as Miss Hemisphere) tries to lay the hero. Lay it to rest and forget it. Zero entertainment. (VC)

**VIDEODROME (1983).** Badly bungled David Cronenberg picture, grotesque and repulsive. James Wood is a sleazy cable TV station owner, looking for porn programming, who stumbles across a sadistic series called VIDEODROME. Watch enough sex and violence and a new organ grows in your brain that creates hallucinations. Eventually your mind and body evolve into something more wholesome. It's a plot by the Moral Majority to cleanse the nation. If you're having trouble following this critique, wait until you see this botched mess. Rick Baker's effects are ugly, and much of the sex and violence were heavily cut by Universal so the film could be released with an R. Deborah Harry of Blondie is the beautiful female lead, but her character is so unsavory, she and Wood together as sadists are a turn off. (VC)

**VIEW TO A KILL, A (1985).** Something really misfired in Roger Moore's seventh (and last) 007 picture. Despite the massive destruction and opportunities for excitement, director John Glen's pacing is strangely lethargic. Part of the trouble is a minimum of offbeat gadgets and machines; a less-than-rugged Moore, whose quips have grown as weary as his physique; and a Richard Maibaum-Michael G. Wilson script lacking humor or freshness. Master villain Max Zorin plots to destroy Silicone Valley and the world micro-chip market by creating earthquakes to shake up the Andreas Fault. The film's only saving Grace is the lithe Ms Jones as May Day, a tigress who makes Christopher Walken's Zorin a wimp in comparison. Tanya Roberts as heroine Stacey Sutton is an attractive eyeful but her acting abilities are minimal. Patrick Macnee is pleasant as Bond's undercover companion

in the early scenes but he never gets a chance to display the ability of Steed the Avenger. There's a shootout on the Eiffel Tower, a high-speed fire engine chase down Market Street in San Francisco, a cliffhanging climax on the Golden Gate Bridge, and the blowing up of an underground cavern . . . but it just sits there and dies. (VC)

**VIKING WOMEN AND THE SEA SERPENT (1958).** Rock-bottom Roger Corman programmer (he produced-directed) depicts a water beast that functions as a deus ex machina by intervening at the last minute between bands of warring Vikings. Scenes are so dark, the ocean waves so phony and the position of man to beast so ambiguous, the only horror to be pondered is: Who designed the crummy monster? Too bad the creature didn't swallow the good guys along with the bad—that would really give him indigestion. The people are that tasteless. Abby Dalton, Gary Conway, Susan Cabot, Brad Jackson, Jonathan Haze, Richard Devon.

**VILLAGE OF EIGHT GRAVESTONES (1982).** What appears to be a murder mystery soon develops touches of the supernatural when the young heir to a fortune discovers there's a curse on his family, placed there four centuries ago by a band of eight samurai soldiers. Directed by Yoshitaro Nomura. Kenichi Hagiwara, Mayumi Ogawa.

**VILLAGE OF THE DAMNED (1960).** Faithful version of John Wyndham's MIDWICH CUCKOOS, thanks to director Wolf Rilla, who co-wrote the adaptation with Stirling Silliphant and George Barclay. A small community in England is isolated by a strange invisible shield and its inhabitants afflicted by prolonged sleep. Later, the village's pregnant women give birth to hollow-eyed children who possess irresistible hypnotic powers, and grow up to dominate adults, especially their fathers. Ultimately, these singular alien children will have a devastating effect on mankind. This British film was quite successful and generated a sequel, CHILDREN OF THE DAMNED, equally well done. George Sanders, Barbara Shelley, Michael Gwynn, Laurence Naismith. (VC)

**VILLAGE OF THE GIANTS (1965).** Bert I. Gordon on an unstoppable, unquenchable rampage—editing, writing, producing, directing, even contributing special effects. Is there no way this man can be chained? Is the world helpless against him? Must we be subjected to the blasphemous suggestion that this fantasy film is based on H. G. Wells' FOOD OF THE GODS? And must we be exposed to stupid teenagers who discover a food that makes them grow to amazing propor-

*"I don't know who I am. I'm a monster. I can't feel, I can't love. I'm not human . . . You can't love death."—Dr. Carl Lehman (David McIlwraith) in THE VINDICATOR.*

---

tions? And must we listen to such dialogue as "It's our world, not theirs" and "It's us against the adults"? Do we not all have the right to close our eyes rather than endure the varied acting styles of Tommy Kirk, Johnny Crawford, Beau Bridges, Ron Howard and Joy Harmon, all presented in Perceptovision? This is a mini among giants. (VC)

**VINCENT PRICE'S ONCE UPON A MIDNIGHT SCARY.** See **ONCE UPON A MIDNIGHT SCARY.**

**VINDICATOR, THE (1984).** Above-average, well-produced Canadian blend of horror and science-fiction (originally called FRANKENSTEIN '88) reminiscent of MAN-MADE MONSTER and THE INDESTRUCTIBLE MAN. Obsessed (and certainly mad) scientist Richard Cox takes the victim of an accident (David McIlwraith) and turns him into a cyborg, who escapes and commences a rampage of death and destruction because of his evil programming, even though he's basically a good guy who would rather go after the crooks. Bounty huntress Pam Grier (her name is Hunter) is hired to track the robot killer with a gun that fires "vaporized acid," and she's one ruthless bitch. There's some nice sewer sequences, good battles and destruction scenes, a violent rape and a sense of cinematic style emerging from director Jean-Claude Lord. Stan Winston created the cyborg look, which is more messy than dressy. Teri Austin, Maury Chaykin, Denis Simpson. (VC)

**VIOLENT MIDNIGHT.** See **PSYCHOMANIA.**

**VIRGIN AMONG THE LIVING DEAD (198?).** Young heiress is haunted by her family's secrets after arriving in the family's stomping grounds—where the stomping is literal. Christina Von Blanc, Britt Nichols. (VC)

**VIRGIN SPRING, THE (1960).** Superlative Ingmar Bergman classic based on an old Swedish song, "The Daughter of Tore of Vange," which tells of the rape-murder of an innocent girl, the revenge of the father and the gushing forth of a spring at the site of the heinous act. Bergman evokes 14th Century Sweden in memorable detail, his cast in turn capturing the simplicity, and desperation, of the grass-roots characters. Birgitta Petterson is the essence of purity and innocence as the murdered girl and Max von Sydow, as the outraged father, undergoes a strange ritual before pursuing the three rapists with his hunting knife. Powerful material, uncompromising in its depiction of rape, yet gentle in its reverence for the Swedish people. (VC)

**VIRGIN WITCH (1970).** British production focusing on black mass and witchcraft as two young women arrive in London to work as models, but soon find themselves in the velvet underground of lesbian sex and seduction. Directed by Roy Austin, scripted by Klaus Vogen from his novel. Ann Michelle, Vicky Michelle, Keith Buckley, Patricia Haines. (VC)

**VIRGINS AND VAMPIRES.** See **CAGED VIRGINS.**

**VIRUS (1980).** Well-produced, nihilistic U.S.-Japanese science-fiction thriller with pessimistic overtones, in which mankind is wiped out by a plague, except for a handful of survivors at the South Pole. A sub sails for Washington DC to

**MICHAEL IRONSIDE AND LEE GRANT IN 'VISITING HOURS'**

avert the automatic launching of U.S. nuclear missiles, with Bo Svenson and Sonny Chiba all that stand between another holocaust and salvation. The huge cast includes Glenn Ford, Henry Silva, Chuck Connors (as the sub captain), Robert Vaughn and Cec Linder. Directed-written by Kinji Fukasaku, from a novel by Sakyo Komatsu. (VC)

**VISIONS OF DEATH (1972).** Outstanding TV-movie, suspenseful as hell as physics professor Monte Markham is suddenly plagued by psychic visions in which he sees flashes of a mad bomber planning to blow up half of Denver. The tension mounts as policeman Telly Savalas first suspects Markham, then realizes his ESP is genuine. How they work together to capture the madman heaps on more suspense. Tautly written by Paul Playdon and directed with

Vidal must have had a little kitten. Joan Blackman, Fred Clark, Earl Holliman, Lee Patrick, Gale Gordon, Jerome Cowan, John Williams, Barbara Lawson. (VC)

**VISITING HOURS (1982).** Better-than-average slasher film that often follows killer Michael Ironside, so that we are as much with him as the victims. A Canadian production, this also focuses on Lee Grant as a TV reporter fighting for women's rights who is stalked by Colt Hawker (Ironside) in a hospital. Tautly directed by Jean Claude Lord and scripted with understanding of movie terror by Brian Taggert. Linda Purl, William Shatner, Lenore Zann, Harvey Atkin. (VC)

**VISITOR, THE (1980).** Offbeat imitation of THE OMEN, dealing with an Archangel who comes to Earth to ward off a force

---

## "*Get me the Zombies!*"—*Bela Lugosi as the utterly maniacal, scenery chewing Dr. Marlow in* **THE VOODOO MAN.**

---

style by Lee H. Katzin. Barbara Anderson provides solid love interest. Tim O'Connor, Joe Sirola, Lonny Chapman, Jim Antonio, Richard Erdman. Also known as **VISIONS.**

**VISIONS OF EVIL (1973).** Young woman just released from the fruitcake house is in fear of going back when she moves in with her husband and experiences nightmares of her doom. (VC)

**VISIT FROM A DEAD MAN (1974).** Low-budget videotape quickie shot in England. A triangular situation between a wealthy collector of statues, his gorgeous wife and a lawyer results first in murder, then in a supernatural visitation. Directed by Lela Swift. Alfred Drake, Stephen Collins, Heather MacRae.

**VISIT TO A SMALL PLANET (1960).** Producer Hal Wallis took Gore Vidal's Broadway play (a light-hearted affair that sparkled with ironic wit) and reshaped it into a shapeless, hapless vehicle for the slapstick of Jerry Lewis. As Kreton, an extraterrestrial who lands on Earth to observe the Civil War, Lewis discovers he has timed his arrival 100 years too late. He rectifies his mistake by becoming a Peeping Tom to observe American customs. The sight gags and inanities, of unimaginative proportions under Norman Taurog's direction, are set into feckless motion. Example: Lewis has the power to make people recite "Mary Had a Little Lamb" in baby talk.

of evil from Hell. This allegorical mumbo jumbo is told with odd camera angles, unexplainable effects and pseudo-religious symbolism that baffles rather than enlightens. Directed by Giulio Paradisi. An Italian-U.S. production with a top cast: Glenn Ford, Mel Ferrer, Shelley Winters, John Huston, Sam Peckinpah, Lance Henricksen. (VC)

**VISITOR FROM THE GRAVE (1982).** One-hour episode of the British series, HAMMER HOUSE OF HORROR, packaged as a videocassette. This can also be seen as half of a TV-movie coupled with "Children of the Full Moon." See **CHILDREN OF THE FULL MOON.**

**VOICE OF THE WHISTLER (1945).** Richard Dix is forced to commit murder by a post-hypnotic suggestion in this low budget film noir release, inspired by THE WHISTLER radio series. William Castle directed with a sense of doom. Lynn Merrick, Tom Kennedy, Rhys Williams, Donald Woods.

**VOICES (1973).** Little-known British film starring David Hemmings and Gayle Hunnicutt as a couple who arrive at an old mansion and imagine they see ghosts living there. Neat twist ending may catch viewers offguard. Directed by Kevin Billington. Lynn Farleigh, Peggy Ann Clifford.

**VOODOO BABY (1979).** Joe D'Amato directed this exploitationer involving black magic, demons and bizarre sexual

**MICHAEL CONNORS AND MARLA (BODY) ENGLISH IN 'VOODOO WOMAN'**

practices of the supernatural. Susan Scott, Richard Harrison, Lucia Ramirez.

**VOODOO BLOOD BATH.** See **I EAT YOUR SKIN** and **ZOMBIES.** (Everyone took a bath on this one!)

**VOODOO GIRL.** See **SUGAR HILL.**

**VOODOO HEARTBEAT (1972).** Minor indie feature, made in Las Vegas environs, about a voodoo formula ("serum of Satan") for eternal youth that turns users into vampires. Director Charles Nizet's script lacks logic, is heavy on cliches and features a cast of non-heartthrobs. Call it cardiac arrest. Philip Ahn, Ray Molina, Ern Dugo, Forrest Duke.

**VOODOO ISLAND (1957).** Scoffer of the supernatural (Boris Karloff) refuses to believe in the unexplained while investigating a tropical island plagued by voodoo curses. When Murvyn Vye is turned into a zombie, Karloff has first doubts . . . when a man-eating plant devours Jean Engstrom, Karloff decides that perhaps there are a few things unknown to man. It sure takes Boris a long time to get moving . . . the same could be said for this film, turgidity produced by Howard W. Koch and directed by Reginald Le Borg in Hawaii. Rhodes Reason, Beverly Tyler, Elisha Cook Jr.

**VOODOO MAN, THE (1944).** This is fun in a perverse way, it's so appallingly bad. George Zucco is a voodoo cult leader with a television "spy" device who works in cahoots with hypnotist Bela Lugosi and John Carradine, a drum-beating Igortype whose light bulbs are rather weak. Lugosi is kidnapping women with a phony roadblock detour, encasing them in sexy nightgowns and putting them into trances in the hopes that he can transfer one of their souls into the corpse of his wife, she who has been dead these past 22 years. This is attempted while Zucco utters some of the nuttiest mumbo jumbo ever created for a voodoo movie. Under William Beaudine's direction, Lugosi is the world's biggest hambone, with the Carradine character taking a close second. The Monogram production values (with Sam Katzman at the helm) are distressingly poor, and the acting is so bad it could put you into a catatonic state even if you find some of the elements in Robert Charles' script campy. Wanda McKay, Louise Currie, Henry Hall, Michael Ames.

**VOODOO WOMAN (1957).** Slow-moving, shopworn jungle thriller from producer Alex Gordon in which Marla English (whose body English is superb, even if she doesn't shape up much as an actress) falls under the spell of a mad doctor (Tom Conway) and resembles a "Living Dead" refugee with her fright wig and scare mask. Touch (Michael) Connors, Lance Fuller, Paul Dubov, Paul Blaisdell.

**VORTEX.** See **DAY TIME ENDED, THE.**

**VORTEX (1982).** Two hardware government corporations literally shoot it out for possession of a "Star Wars" laser weapon. James Russo, Lydia Lunch, Dick Miller, Bill Rice.

**VOYAGE INTO EVIL.** See **CRUISE INTO TERROR.**

**VOYAGE INTO SPACE (1968).** Japanese TV series re-edited to feature length and dubbed in English. Result: An outer space mess in which a youth and giant robot fight off imperialistic aliens. Mitsunobu Kaneko, Akio Tito.

**VOYAGE OF THE ROCK ALIENS (1984).** Science-fiction musical comedy featuring Chainsaw, Dee Dee, Frankie and Diane fighting off the invading extraterrestrials. Directed by James Fargo. Pia Zadora, Tom Nolan, Craig Sheffer, Ruth Gordon, Jimmy and the Mustangs.

**VOYAGE TO ARCTURUS (1971).** Cheapie space adventure

from writer-director B. J. Holloway, with all the usual outer space cliches. David Eldred, Tom Hastings, Susan Junge.

**VOYAGE TO THE BOTTOM OF THE SEA (1961).** Visually exciting, good-humored Irwin Allen production designed for the young set with big names to appeal to parents: Walter Pidgeon, Joan Fontaine, Peter Lorre, Robert Sterling. The biggest star remains the atomic sub Seaview, with panels of flashing lights and fluctuating gauges. (This set was later used in the long-running TV series of the same title.) The Van Allen Radiation Belt surrounding Earth has caught fire; the mission of Seaview is to fire a missile to put out the blaze. But complications erupt aboardship when it becomes evident there is a saboteur at work. Barbara Eden, Frankie Avalon, Michael Ansara, Henry Daniell, Regis Toomey. (VC)

**VOYAGE TO THE END OF THE UNIVERSE (1964).** Czech science-fiction has meritorious values, but these have been hampered by poor English dubbing and cropped Cinemascope format. Setting is a colossal spaceship carrying a colony to a new habitable world. Emphasis is on problems aboard the spacecraft, encounters with an alien craft and its dead crew, and an adventure in a space nebula. The surprise ending will fool no one, but director Jindrich Polak and cast work hard to pull it off. Zdenek Stepanek.

**VOYAGE TO THE PLANET OF PREHISTORIC WOMEN (1968).** Not a sequel to VOYAGE TO A PREHISTORIC PLANET, just more footage lifted from a 1962 Soviet film, PLANET OF STORMS, which Roger Corman repackaged for U.S. consumption. New footage directed by Peter Bogdanovich features Mamie Van Doren and other statuesque cuties in furry bikinis. These buxom dolls portray psychic humanoids who enjoy close encounters with stranded Earthnauts. And nauts to you, too, earthy ones.

**VOYAGE TO THE PREHISTORIC PLANET (1965).** Highlights from the Soviet science-fiction movie, PLANET OF STORMS, the story of cosmonauts exploring Venus. This has new footage shot by Curtis Harrington and features Basil Rathbone, Faith Domergue and Marc Shannon to give it international flavor. Roger Corman spliced it together with Elmer's Glue. Same old plot: Earthmen crashland on an alien world to face new dangers from extraterrestrials, robot men, centuries-old lizards, etc. Voyage to prehistoric tedium.

**VOYAGER FROM THE UNKNOWN (1982).** Episodes of the TV series VOYAGERS about travelers trapped in different time zones as they try to return to the present. Jon-Erik Hexum. (VC)

**VULCAN, SON OF JUPITER (1962).** Rod Flash flashes his biceps as he fights off lizard men and other standard monsters found in beefcake Italian fiascos. Directed by Emmimo Salvi. Gordon Mitchell, Bella Cortez, Furio Meniconi.

**VULTURE, THE (1967).** Akim Tamiroff as a creature with a bird's body, legs and wings, but retaining human head and arms? That's only the beginning, bird lovers. Dig the inept performances of Robert Hutton and Broderick Crawford, groove on the ersatz, belly-flopping suspense. Wonder how writer-producer-director Lawrence Huntington ever found another job in movies. They must be picking his bones, the movie vultures we mean.

**VULTURES (1985).** Jim Bailey in five roles (you figure out which characters) is the highpoint of this gore-murder thriller told in whodunit fashion. Yachtsman Stuart Whitman is accused of the crimes, but we know better as he pursues the clues. Average for its type. Written-produced-directed by Paul Leder. Yvonne De Carlo, Aldo Ray, Greg Mullavey, Maria Perschy. (VC)

---

*"This may not be The End!"—Closing credit of* **VOODOO WOMAN.**

*"I'm just your average horny little devil . . . (who) enjoys a little piece of pussy after lunch. How about it?"—Jack Nicholson (as Daryl Van Horne) to Susan Sarandon in **THE WITCHES OF EASTWICK.***

**WACKO (1981).** Producer-director Greydon Clark's parody of FRIDAY THE 13TH features The Halloween Lawn Mower Killer, a weirdo who wears a pumpkin for a face as he terrorizes Alfred Hitchcock High (where the Hitchcock Birds are about to face the De Palma Knives). It's all played strictly for laughs, but most of the gags fall flatter than pancakes—and flattery will get you nowhere. References (visual and verbal) to horror/science-fiction cinema might help buffs to enjoy this in a small way. Everyone else will wince as the town faces an unlucky Friday, 13 years after the original Lawn Mower Killing. Joe Don Baker plays a crazy cop named Dick Harbinger, George Kennedy and Stella Stevens play nutty parents (he a Peeping Tom, she a demented sexpot), Scott McGinnis plays the young heroic and Julia Duffy is a young virgin. (VC)

**WACKY WORLD OF DR. MORGUS (1962).** Regional film starring Dr. Morgus, one-time New Orleans horror movie host, as a doctor who invents a machine that turns people into sand and back again. Amateur city. Directed by Raoul Haig. Sid Noel, Thomas George, Dan Barton.

**WACKY WORLD OF MOTHER GOOSE, THE (1967).** Mother Goose characters twisted and reshaped into a story of spies, secret agents and undercover men. Featuring the voice of Margaret Rutherford.

**WAIT UNTIL DARK (1967).** Borderline psychothriller about a blind woman (Audrey Hepburn, who received an Oscar nomination) terrorized by killers who invade her New York apartment for a doll containing heroin. Director Terence Young treats the climax—killer Alan Arkin stalking the helpless woman—as though he wanted to outthrill Hitchcock, and for this sequence alone we recommend this shocker based on Frederick Knotts' Broadway play. Richard Crenna, Efrem Zimbalist Jr., Jack Weston, Samantha Jones. (VC)

**WALKING DEAD, THE (1936).** Recommended Warner Bros. chiller directed by Michael Curtiz and starring Boris Karloff as an ex-con who is framed for murder and electrocuted. Doctor Edmund Gwenn, experimenting on dead animals, restores Karloff to the living. As a hollow-eyed, hallow-faced cadaver, he pursues his framers, forcing them into situations where they meet violent deaths because of their own stupidity. Gruesome but fun. Ricardo Cortez, Marguerite Churchill,

Warren Hull, Barton MacLane, Henry O'Neill.

**WAR BETWEEN THE PLANETS (1965).** Wayward planet on a collision course with Earth creates tidal waves, land upheavals and panicky dialogue among Earthlings, giving Italian effects "artists" opportunity to play with cheap toy models. A giant brain controlling the asteroid must be entered by rescuers. Excessively unimpressive. Directed by Anthony Dawson. Giacomo Rossi-Stuart, Peter Martell.

**WAR GAME, THE (1966).** Shattering shocker by Peter Watkins depicts nuclear holocaust in a English village. Watkins doesn't spare graphic details: He deals with the human panic, fire storms, food shortages, atomic wounds, the maimed and the stunned and the dead. Objective, non-hysterical approach gives this TV-film (banned on the BBC for its realism) additional impact. Strikes close to home in the vein of THE DAY AFTER and THREADS. (VC)

**WAR GODS OF THE DEEP (1965).** Vernesque underwater fantasy quite fanciful, and watchable, as a band of intrepid heroes discovers the lost city of Lyonesse (off the Cornish coast) in 1903. Its smuggler inhabitants have survived for centuries as gillmen and their leader is Vincent Price, who thinks Susan Hart is the reincarnation of an old lover. Satisfying blend of action and humor, directed by Jacques Tourneur. Tab Hunter, David Tomlinson, Susan Hart.

**WAR IN SPACE (1977).** Japanese action with mediocre effects, overexcited cast members and a plot lifted out of Amazing Stories magazine circa 1942. A meteor swarm approaching Earth turns out to be a flotilla of space hardware from Venus, blasting us with lasers. The aliens are green-skinned humanoids, their leader a jerkola wearing a Roman-style helmet and commanding a giant mother ship. Oriental volunteers pursue the invaders back to Venus where they engage the enemy in guerrilla tactics and a final shootout that involves a man in a hairy suit armed with a laser. Plays like a service melodrama, with Jun Fukuda directing in the tradition of Inoshiro Honda. Kensaku Morita, Yuko Asano.

**WAR OF THE COLOSSAL BEAST (1958).** Bert I. Gordon's sequel to THE AMAZING COLOSSAL MAN finds the ever-growing 60-feet-tall Army Colonel Manning (played this time by Dean Parkin) not destroyed at Boulder Dam but down in

Mexico, snatching taco trucks off the highway in hopes of finding something that will stick to his king-size ribs. As in most Gordon films, the effects are at best pedantic, and the same could be said for the George Worthing Yates script. One of the soldier boys remarks, "There's no place in this civilization for a 60-foot man." He said it. Roger Pace, Sally Fraser, Russ Bender. Music by Albert Glasser.

**WAR OF THE GARGANTUAS (1967).** Sequel to FRANKENSTEIN CONQUERS THE WORLD was re-edited for the U.S., with a sequence explaining connection to the first film dropped; hence, connections are tenuous at best. With Inoshiro Honda directing and Eiji Tsuburaya at the effects helm, you're in for a monster extravaganza: A giant octopus battles another entity of green-hued evil and the greeny takes on a brown-hued beast. The only thing that happens by occident is Russ Tamblyn as a scientist.

**WAR OF THE MONSTERS (1966).** Toho's sequel to GAMMERA THE INVINCIBLE, with that friendly snapping turtle, Gammera, doing battle with Barugon the Dinosaur, a creature surrounded by a deadly forecefield. Kids will cheer the chest-pounding, noisy encounters; adults will snooze. Directed by Shigeo Tanaka. Kojiro Hongo.

**WAR OF THE PLANETS (1965).** In the next century, Tony Russell and Lisa Gastoni combat Martian invaders called Diaphanois, beings composed mainly of light rays. Weightless Italian science-fiction directed by Anthony Dawson, with only fair special effects. Carlo Giustini.

**WAR OF THE ROBOTS (1978).** Ambitious Italian space opera, but condescending and insulting to audiences. A race of robots (in metallic suits, wearing blond wigs) kidnap a beautiful woman; a squad of rocket jocks (including a Texan, yet) slip into warp drive and pursue across the galaxies, meeting weird alien races in papier mache rock caverns and firing laser beams hither and thither. Armies of extras, massive sets and tons of action can't compensate for Alfonso Brescia's inept direction (he's credited as Al Bradly). Special onions to Marcus Griffin for his awful electronics "shuffling" score, the dumbest ever, and to Alan Forsyth for inferior effects. Except for leading man Antonio Sabato, the credits would appear to be Angloized pseudonyms: Melissa Long, Patricia Gore, James Stuart, Robert Barnes and "a special performance" by Mickey Pilgrim. Pilgrim's Progress? We challenge you to sit through the whole 96 minutes. (VC)

**WAR OF THE SATELLITES (1958).** Aliens you never see (producer-director Roger Corman's economic ingenuity at work) don't want us fooling around in space, so one takes over the body of a scientist (Richard Devon) aboard a space satellite. But he (it) falls in love with fellow explorer Susan Cabot, a foolish act which makes him vulnerable to other Earthlings who suspect something is awry. Something is awry—the tepid screenplay by Lawrence Louis Goldman, who banged it out for Corman shortly after the Russians launched Sputnik. According to legend, Corman directed it in only eight days—one day longer than it took God to create the Universe. Dick Miller, Michael Fox, Robert Shayne.

**WAR OF THE WIZARDS. See PHOENIX, THE.**

**WAR OF THE WORLDS (1953).** George Pal's commendable version of H. G. Wells' novel of a Martian invasion—imaginatively depicted in the Oscar-winning effects of Gordon Jennings. Alien saucers land in isolated areas of California and zap everything in sight with greenish death rays. Barre Lyndon's script, focusing on research physicist Gene Barry and scientist Ann Robinson, sometimes sinks into cliches yet it unfolds with such compelling swiftness and breathless action, the invasion takes on epic proportions. One suspenseful sequence depicts a bug-eyed Martian, another shows Barry searching for his girl through war-ravaged L.A. The opening prologue is beautifully rendered, with the planets of our solar system described by the splendid voice of Sir Cedric Hardwicke. One of the few science-fiction classics of the cinema, directed by Byron Haskin. Carolyn Jones, Robert Cornthwaite, Paul Frees, Jack Kruschen, Les Tremayne, Alvy Moore, Charles Gemora (as the Martian). (VC)

**WAR OF THE ZOMBIES. See NIGHT STAR—GODDESS OF ELECTRA.**

**WARGAMES (1983).** Enthralling, suspense-packed fantasy in which teeners Matthew Broderick and Ally Sheedy accidentally gain access to the NORAD computer system and play a "game" of nuclear war between the U.S. and the Soviet Union that becomes the real thing back at control central. This is great edge-of-your-seat viewing with computer controller Dabney Coleman and Air Force General Barry Corbin working against the clock to avert nuclear holocaust. Wonderfully directed by John Badham. (VC)

**WARLOCK MOON (1973).** Weak witchcraft flick shot in the San Francisco-Bay Area by producer-director-editor Bill Herbert, who had the best intentions but a static directorial style that defeated him. The same can be said for the writing of John Sykes. The plot, which takes forever and a night to move, concerns Laurie Walters and Joe Spano fooling

**MARTIAN WAR MACHINE MODEL USED IN 'WAR OF THE WORLDS'**

around a strange house on the outskirts of Livermore (actually a deserted Army tuberculosis clinic), where some oddballs have established a witch cult. Only during the last minutes does real horror build, and there is a perverse twist ending, although it hardly seems worth sitting through to reach. Walters and Spano went on to better things in Hollywood as regulars in TV series. Edna Macafee, Ray K. Goman.

**WARLORDS OF ATLANTIS (1978).** Fourth and last film in a series of picturesque fantasy adventures from producer John Dark and director Kevin Connor, with Doug McClure starring. Here he portrays an intrepid hero transported via diving bell into an undersea kingdom of seven cities inhabited by treacherous Martians. Characters and situations in Brian Hayles' script are preposterous but Roger Dicken's monsters are visual delights: a giant octopus; a multi-armed mollusk with rolling eyeballs; a snake-fish; a thing with flippers called a Zarg; a flying fish with bad overbite; a scaly millipede. Cyd Charisse, as Atsil the High Priestess, fares well because she gets to display her shapely legs. Still, it's the octopus with the

plant, a bacteria is accidentally unleashed that infects the "rage" area of the brain and turns victims into homicidal maniacs. Trapped in the plant is security guard Kathleen Quinleen, while outside her sheriff-husband Sam Waterston tries to solve the mystery being kept hush-hush by government toady Yaphet Kotto. The performances are excellent, the script exciting, the action full of labyrinthian atwists and turns as they seek an antitoxin to stop the monsters. High tech, high excitement. (VC)

**WARP SPEED (1981).** Independent cheapie about a man endowed with ESP powers who realizes something strange is happening aboard a spacecraft. Camille Mitchell, Adam West, David Chandler.

**WARRIOR AND THE SORCERESS (1984).** One of the more interesting, and entertaining, Barbarian-and-sorcery Conan copies, with director John Broderick showing an influence of Japanese samurai movies. Here he copies YOJIMBO when The Dark One, a laconic warrior (and the only survivor of his race), hires out to two warring factions in the village of

**THE NORAD COMPUTER DISPLAY BOARD IN 'WARGAMES'**

real class. Shane Rimmer, Peter Gilmore.

**WARLORDS OF THE 21ST CENTURY (1981).** Gas now costs $59 a liter after the great Oil Wars and what's left of mankind on New Zealand (farmers and isolated groups) is subjected to roving bloodthirsty pirates, whose only nemesis is The Hunter (Michael Beck), an avenging warrior a la Mad Max. Originally made as BATTLETRUCK, for chief villain James Wainwright pillages with an armored oil carrier bristling with firepower. The story (co-written by director Harley Cokliss) centers on how The Hunter and Straker have their final showdown, with Straker's daughter (Annie McEnroe) caught in the middle. Randolph Powell. (VC)

**WARNING FROM SPACE (1956).** Japanese science-fiction message film, in which friendly extraterrestrials (shaped like starfish) land on Earth in human guise in order to warn us of dangers we face if we use atomic weapons, and to offer their help in stopping a planet that will soon collide with Earth. More mature than most Oriental films of this kind. Directed by Koji Shima.

**WARNING SIGN (1985).** Engrossing action thriller in the style of THE ANDROMEDA STRAIN, tautly directed by Hal Barwood, who co-wrote and co-produced with Matthew Robbins. At the isolated Utah plant of Biotek, an agricultural research center that is secretly a government germ warfare

Yabatar, shifting sides as fortunes of war shift. David Carradine is quite good in this variation on the wandering gunslinger. Oddities include The Protector (a giant octopus-monster), a green lizard that whispers into the ear of its master, a four-breasted dancing assassin and the sorceress, who forges the mighty sword of Ura for The Dark One and rushes about the entire picture, her glistening, beautiful breasts bared. Above average for Roger Corman these days. Luke Askew, Maria Socas. (VC)

**WARRIOR EMPRESS (1961).** Unimpressive Italian mythology-adventure wasting the looks and talent of Tina Louise and Kerwin Mathews. Setting is ancient Greece, where Mathews is taken to the underwater city of Poseidon, there to meet Sapho, Venus Lesbos. Feckless and sexless. Directed by Pietro Francisci. Riccardo Garrone, Albert Farnese.

**WARRIOR OF THE LOST WORLD (1985).** Silly MAD MAX ripoff, with the absurd premise that Earth has been devastated by radiation wars and now the evil Omegans, led by Prosser (Donald Pleasence), are fighting the good guys, the Outsiders. Robert Ginty comes riding by on a rocket-launching "supersonic speedcycle" equipped with Einstein the Computer, which espouses such comments as "Bad Mothers" (cops) and "Very Bad Mothers" (more cops). Ginty agrees to help Persis Khambatta rescue her father (Harrison Muller) from Prosser's stronghold, so there's plenty of explosive action that allows Fred Williamson (as Henchman) to crash the scene, guns blazing to synthesized music. Director David Worth's script makes little sense, but you can say that the action is nonstop. (VC)

**WARRIORS OF THE WASTELAND (1983).** Inferior, imbecilic MAD MAX ripoff by Italians finds two unlikable antiheroes (Timothy Brent, Fred Williamson) roving the nuked countryside 2019 A. H. (After Holocaust) in ridiculous-looking automobiles, seeking an evil band (The Templers, Administrators of Revenge) that is senselessly slaughtering innocent folks. Absurdly-dressed men ride redesigned motorbikes, fire silly zap guns (which give off inane electronic sounds) and no doubt wonder why director Enzo G. Castellari doesn't demand the Method style of acting. Suitable only for insomniacs in the wasteland of TV. George Eastman, Anna Kanakis, Thomas Moore, Mark Gregory, Giancarlo Prete. (VC)

**WARRIORS OF THE WIND (1985).** While portions of this Japanese animated feature resemble a typical Saturday morning science-fiction cartoon, it has an overriding style and air of excitement that sets it apart from its cheaper competitors. The setting is a post-holocaust world, where a race of people led by Queen Salina stand watch over The Valley of the Wind, inhabited by giant dragonflies and threatened by toxic poisoning. Giant centipede-like creatures with mystical healing powers were no doubt inspired by the sand worms in DUNE. Definitely worth seeing. Directed by Kazuo Komatsubara.

**WASP WOMAN, THE (1960).** Producer-director Roger Corman gives us a "stinker" in need of more production sting. Strictly a bottom-of-the-hive programmer (scripted by Leo Gordon) with Susan Cabot as a White Anglo-Saxon Protestant . . . a cosmetics manufacturer seeking an eternal youth formula from wasp enzymes. Once she's an oversized member of the Hymentopera clan, she turns predacious and goes on a murderous spree, sticking it to all the guys but good. It's the wasp-ish budget that finally does in THE WASP WOMAN. Anthony Eisley, Michael Mark, Frank Wolff.

**WATCHED! (1972).** This crime film about the downfall of a prosecuting attorney specializing in drug cases, who falls prey to cocaine and becomes a defense attorney, qualifies for this book only because of its surreal, hallucinatory scenes of Stacy Keach undergoing deterioration. Keach, who in later years would serve time in a British prison for possession of cocaine, is shown engulfed in the powdery drug, saying, "Cocaine! My mucus membrane is but a memory." Keach's adversary is drugbuster Harry Yulin, and the two have a compelling duel to the death. Writer-director John Parsons made this unusual film in San Francisco, capturing the Haight-Ashbury in the depressing aftermath of the drug culture that thrived there in the 1960s. A strange film, it requires patience but is worth seeing for the things it unwittingly prophesizes. Brigid Polk, Denver John Collins, Valerie Carter. (VC)

**WATCHER IN THE WOODS, THE (1980).** Disney attempted to escape formula kiddie movies with this adaptation of a Florence E. Randall novel, but the results are too silly to make it an adult movie and not silly enough to make it a kiddie treat. Music writer David McCallum, wife Carroll Baker and daughters Lynn-Holly Johnson and Kyle Richards move into a secluded mansion owned by a sinister old bat (Bette Davis). A strange psychic force is emanating from a nearby forest, but is never adequately explained as the teens, overwhelmed by ESP powers, try to help Davis' long-lost daughter. Apparently an alien probe has taken her, and there's a shower of fireworks by Harrison Ellenshaw that pas-

**SAM WATERSTON IN 'WARNING SIGN'**

ses as effects. The film, directed by John Hough, was never really released theatrically, even after it was revised and new footage was added. No one will be watching the Watcher, whatever it may be, except on video. Ian Bannen, Georgina Hale, Kyle Richards, Richard Pasco. (VC)

**WATER BABIES, THE (1978).** Charles Kingsley's novel was brought to the screen in a partly animated British film with James Mason, Billie Whitelaw and Joan Greenwood. Children escape into a watery kingdom—and once beneath the surface the film turns to animation. Actor Lionel Jeffries directed. Bernard Cribbins, David Tomlinson. (VC)

**WATER CYBORGS.** See **TERROR BENEATH THE SEA.**

**WATERMELON MAN (1970).** Unsophisticated, unrestrained comment on the undeclared war between blacks and whites, directed with a heavy hand by Melvin Van Peebles to entertain blacks and warn whites. Godfrey Cambridge, wearing "white-face," is a Caucasian bigot with a caustic tongue who suddenly turns Negro and is faced with unpleasant racial experiences. Seed-y morality play. Estelle Parsons, Howard Caine, Mantan Moreland, Kay Kimberley. (VC)

**WATERSHIP DOWN (1978).** Brilliantly animated version of Richard Adams' best-seller dramatizing the odyssey of rabbits fleeing their doomed warren and seeking a new home in the English countryside. Obeying but not understanding the psychic visions of a young rabbit, the creatures are threatened by a dictatorship under General Woundwort and flee for their lives. The tale is an analogy to the struggle of the British during World War II, ingeniously crafted by producer-director Martin Rosen. Even though there are violence and bloodletting when the fur flies, this offbeat cartoon is recommended to young and old for its many object lessons skillfully blended with an entertaining story. Voices by John Hurt, Ralph Richardson and Zero Mostel. (VC)

**WATTS MONSTER, THE.** See **DR. BLACK AND MR. HYDE.** (So Watts been happenin, man?)

---

*"Cocaine! My mucus membrane is but a memory."—Stacy Keach as a drug-craving lawyer in* **WATCHED**!

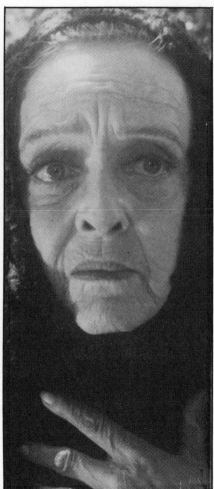

**LYNN-HOLLY JOHNSON, IAN BANNEN, BETTE DAVIS IN 'WATCHER IN THE WOODS'**

**WAVELENGTH (1983).** Thoughtful, sensitive morality tale thanks to writer-director Mike Gray, who has fashioned a philosophical story that indicts militaristic attitudes toward aliens. Robert Carradine, a burned-out guitarist in the Hollywood Hills, meets psychic Cherie Currie who mentally "hears" wails of help from E.T. humanoids (dubbed Beta, Delta and Gamma), captured from a downed UFO and secreted in a secret installation near Carradine's home. The couple penetrates the system to help the trio escape. Its one weakness is that youngsters with shaved heads play the aliens, when credibility calls for a more realistic rendering. Keenan Wynn is along to help the escape plan work. An effective soundtrack by Tangerine Dream. (VC)

**WAY . . . WAY OUT (1966).** So-so Jerry Lewis vehicle: In 1999 a replacement is needed to man a U.S. weather station on the moon. Lewis is selected, along with Connie Stevens, but domestic complications, even on the lunar surface, can be trying (and tiresome). Things perk up when Soviet astronaut Anita Ekberg appears, but veteran director Gordon Douglas can't prevent this from becoming weightless. Robert Morley, Dennis Weaver, Brian Keith, Dick Shawn.

**WEAPONS OF VENGEANCE (1963).** Disciple of Leonardo da Vinci creates a flying machine to fight evil. Italian-French adventure film is lackluster despite promising premise.

Directed by Leopoldo Savono. John Barrymore Jr., Giacomo Rossi-Stuart, Scilla Gabel, Jany Clair.

**WEB OF THE SPIDER (1972).** Stylish Italian supernatural thriller holds one's attention as it opens in a country tavern where Edgar Allan Poe (Klaus Kinski at his wildest) is telling one of his terror tales. A young journalist (Anthony Franciosa) is challenged by Poe and a landowner to spend one night in Blackwood Villa, a haunted castle. Once ensconced, Franciosa meets two beautiful women who fight over him. The redhead is a real knockout. What Franciosa is really seeing are spectral images of long-dead occupants of the castle, and he must relive the horror of their deeds. This remake of CASTLE OF BLOOD was directed by Anthony M. Dawson; based on Poe's "Danse Macabre."

**WEDNESDAY CHILDREN, THE (1973).** The Devil shows up on Earth in hippie form to show kids how to knock off bad adults. This is a morality play? Certainly not Saturday matinee fodder. Directed-written by Robert D. West. Marji Dodril, Donald E. Murray, Tom Kelly, Carol Cary.

**WEEKEND (1968).** Surrealistic French-Italian fantasy written-directed by Jean-Luc Godard, depicting Parisians out to have a good time on Saturday and Sunday, but encountering dead bodies all over the countryside and strange folks who claim to be historical personages. Hard to explain . . . some audiences were turned off by the unanswered enigmas of this art film. Strictly for the avant-garde crowd.

**WEIRD ONES, THE (1962).** Low budgeter from San Antonio, about which little is known. It has something to do with a pair of press agents who meet an alien creature. Written-produced-directed by Pat Boyette. Rudy Duran, Mike Braden, Lee Morgan.

**WEIRD SCIENCE (1985).** Absolutely awful teenage sex-fantasy comedy, more excruciating than titillating—a complete misfire from writer-director John Hughes. Two idiotic juvenile nerds (Anthony Michael Hall, Ilan Mitchell-Smith) feed a lot of ridiculous material into a computer to create a perfect woman. What comes out amidst a lot of pyrotechnic nonsense is Kelly LeBrock, a real beauty. The plot rambles on A.C. (After Creation) with no coherence and LeBrock possesses unexplained witch powers that make things come and go at will, including some appalling biker characters. The cast—Bill Paxton, Suzanne Snyder, Robert Downey—must still be trying to live down this fiasco. Final insult is the title, blatantly stolen from the E.C. comic that featured some of the best illustrated science-fiction stories of all time. Editors William Gaines and Albert Feldstein would have used Hughes' plot to line their garbage cans. (VC)

**WEIRD WOMAN (1944).** Entry in Universal's uninspired "Inner Sanctum" series again stars Lon Chaney Jr. In this one he's a professor in danger of being killed by witchcraft, but who refuses to believe his beautiful bride can protect him with her amulets and incantations. This version of Fritz Leiber's excellent novel, CONJURE WIFE, is inferior to the 1961 British remake, BURN, WITCH, BURN. Blame it on an oversimplified script by Brenda Weisberg and indifferent direction by Reginald Le Borg. Evelyn Ankers, Anne Gwynne, Ralph Morgan, Lois Collier, Kay Harding.

**WELCOME HOME, JOHNNY BRISTOL (1972).** Offbeat psychoanalytic TV-movie is reminiscent of CITIZEN KANE in style because its psychological clues are presented as a baffling mystery to a man's true identity. Recently returned from captivity in Vietnam, Johnny (Martin Landau) searches for the clues to his heritage, discovering his hometown has disappeared and the people from his past aren't who they should be. These perplexing puzzles are explained by Freudian symbolism. Has a compelling atmosphere and intriguing

**KELLY LeBROCK IN 'WEIRD SCIENCE'**

premise that pays off. Scripted by Stanley R. Greenberg, directed by George McGowan. Jane Alexander, Brock Peters, Martin Sheen, Pat O'Brien, Forrest Tucker, Mona Freeman.

**WELCOME TO ARROW BEACH (1973).** The last film to star Laurence Harvey, who also directed this main course in cannibalism. But excuse us if we don't stay for dinner—this is one entree that isn't very appetizing. Joanna Pettet, Stuart Whitman and John Ireland all look hungry for tastier material. Also known under its more appropriate title, TENDER FLESH. Meg Foster, Jesse Vint, Glory LeRoy.

**WELCOME TO BLOOD CITY (1977).** Eldritch Canadian psychological thriller best described as a kind of WESTWORLD in which a town is ruled by scientists. Doctors are building an army of assassins by subjecting the candidates to experiments that induce fantasies. Peter Sasdy directed. Jack Palance, Keir Dullea, Samantha Eggar, Barry Morse, Hollis McLaren. (VC)

**WEREWOLF, THE (1956).** Nifty low-budget monster flick from producer Sam Katzman in which Steven Ritch, suffering from radiation poisoning, is accidentally turned into a wolf man by thoughtless scientists. Rampage of death and destruction follows, in the vein typified by THE WOLF MAN. Location filming in and around Las Vegas by director Fred F. Sears gives this extra umph. If not a howling classic, certainly better than most werewolf movies of the 1950s, with the Robert E. Kent-James B. Gordon script creating sympathy for the misused wolf human. Don Megowan is the lawman who regretfully pursues Ritch.

**WEREWOLF (1987).** Totally derivative of the Rob Bottin-Rick Baker effects that earmarked THE HOWLING and AN AMERICAN WEREWOLF IN LONDON, so it doesn't have a single original bone in its imitative body. It's a two-hour pilot for a short-term syndicated TV series in which John York is

**EVELYN ANKERS IN 'WEIRD WOMAN'**

bitten by a wolfman, bleeds when his palm is (dis)graced by the sign of the pentagram and does battle with a master werewolf named Skorzeny, played grotesquely, in sickening make-up, by Chuck Connors. Stalking all the stalkers is a philosophical, grim-jawed bounty hunter imitating Clint Eastwood. Highlight of this below-standard fare is a battle between two furry monsters with jutting fangs, but even that doesn't build to much. Lance LeGault, Raphael Sbarge, Michelle Johnson, John Quade.

**WEREWOLF AND THE YETI, THE.** See **NIGHT OF THE HOWLING BEAST.** (Beast is Yeti to come!)

**WEREWOLF IN A GIRLS' DORMITORY (1963).** Good black-and-white photography, a competent cast and weird characters (crippled caretaker, haughty wife, teen-age blackmailer, cold secretary, sinister chauffeur) put this European horror film at the head of the class. Suggested menace (faces at windows, shadows on walls, etc.) as well as a heavy werewolf theme just when you want things to be hairy will keep you poised as murders occur in a girls' school that is finishing in more ways than one. Carl Schell, younger brother of Maximilian and Maria, heads the cast for director Richard Benson. Give this one the old college try.

**WEREWOLF OF LONDON (1935).** One of the earliest of Hollywood's werewolf films, not nearly as exciting as Universal's follow-up of 1941, THE WOLF MAN, which established the tradition this film failed to generate. Today it is very dated as Henry Hull portrays a botanist who seeks a strange plant that will only bloom in the Tibetan moonlight. During his expedition he is bitten by a savage beast. Returning to London, Hull turns into a four-legged monstrosity. Although Jack Pierce created the memorable make-up, Hull does little thesping to bring the role to life. Directed by Stuart Walker. Warner Oland, Valerie Hobson, Spring Byington.

**WEREWOLF OF WASHINGTON, THE (1973).** Clever mixture of werewolf horror and political satire by writer-director-editor Milton Moses Ginsberg. It begins in the vein of THE WOLF MAN with reporter-turned-press-aide Dean Stockwell bitten by a werewolf and warned by a gypsy woman about a curse. Back at the White House, Stockwell suspects a Communist conspiracy and confuses the "pentagram" (which appears in the palms of his victims-to-be) with "Pentagon," fearing a military plot. At night, on Capitol Hill, he looks for savory Senators and chewable Congressmen. The make-up is good, reminiscent of Universal's hairy man, and there's a good scene where Stockwell overturns a phone booth with a screaming woman inside. Meanwhile, the President (Biff McGuire)—an obvious parody of Nixon—has a wolfish appetite. When the President sees Stockwell as the wolf man, he says, "Down boy, heel." Different and amusing; recommended. Clifton James, Beeson Carroll, Jane House, Michael Dunn (as a scientist who would appear to be designing a Frankenstein Monster). Thayer David.

**WEREWOLF OF WOODSTOCK (1974).** Videotape TV-movie, one of the dumbest lycanthropy movies ever. Tige Andrews, of MOD SQUAD fame, portrays a farmer turned into a hippie-hating, beer-swilling monster that terrorizes music lovers by stalking the woods during the 1969 Woodstock Music Fair. Directed by John Moffitt. Meredith MacRae, Michael Parks, Ann Doran, Harold J. Stone.

**WEREWOLF VS. THE VAMPIRE WOMAN, THE (1972).** West German-Spanish fly-by-night werewolf film, with Paul Naschy as the monster with a silver bullet in his heart, resurrected by pathologists who would have known better if they had only seen THE WOLF MAN. The next thing you know, Waldemar Daninsky has paired with cuddly cuties to create a vampire baby. Writers Jacinto Molina and Hans Munkell mix up the legends a bit, but variety is the spice of death, and the images by director Leon Klimovsky are often quite striking if the story is not. Gaby Fuchs, Patty Shepard, Andres Resino.

Jacinto Molina, by the way, is really Naschy. (VC)

**WEREWOLVES ON WHEELS (1971).** With surfing music blaring on the soundtrack, a motorcycle gang roars through the countryside, curses, attends impromptu orgies, drinks barrels of beer and roughs up some monks. In retaliation, the cyclists are cursed with lycanthropy. What follows is some very unintentional comedy and very sleazy bloodletting and nudity. We're all for exploitation but please—do it with class. This extremely dumb release was directed by Michel Levesque. Stephen Oliver, D. J. Johnson, Billy Gray, Barry McGuire, Severn Darden. (VC)

**WEST OF ZANZIBAR (1929).** Tod Browning-MGM silent film starring Lon Chaney Sr. as a crippled, sadistic magician living in the Congo with plans to steal ivory with the help of a "monster." Lionel Barrymore, Warner Baxter, Mary Nolan.

**WESTWORLD (1973).** In terms of premise and visuals, this is superior science-fiction, written-directed by Michael (THE ANDROMEDA STRAIN) Crichton. What's missing are solid characterizations for Richard Benjamin and James Brolin and a reason for the malfunctioning of Westworld, an amusement center of the future, where vacationers enact fantasies. This is a rich man's Disneyland, consisting of environments with Western, medieval and Roman themes. The idea is to live the dangers of the periods without undergoing physical harm. But harm is in everyone's way when the center malfunctions and the robots kill the tourists. Yul Brynner portrays an android gunslinger who uses real bullets and begins a chase through the lavish, creative sets. But since we can care little for Benjamin, it's hard to take the horrors he faces all that seriously. FUTUREWORLD is a sequel which fared better as a story. Dick Van Patten, Steve Franken. (VC)

**WHAT? (1965).** Italian-French-British gothic, heavy with atmosphere and period costumes and set in an aristocratic mansion on a cliff, where everyone acts sinister or hysterical. Daliah Lavi is haunted by the visions of a murdered count (Christopher Lee as a sadistic chauvinist) and she flits about the castle in negligees, gasping at muddy footprints and a gnarly hand that's interminably reaching for her. For the U.S. market the sexual depravity scenes were heavily cut (What??), so what's left is a lot of skulking around under Mario Bava's direction. If you enjoy corny melodramas, by all means. Tony Kendall, Harriet White, Isli Oberon.

**WHAT A CARVE UP.** See **NO PLACE LIKE HOMICIDE.**

**WHAT A WHOPPER! (1961).** What a loser! Not even a quaint British sense of humor can salvage this tired joke about a dunderhead who creates a false Loch Ness monster only to have the real "Nessy" show up. Spike Milligan, Carole Lesley, Charles Hawtrey, Adam Faith, Sidney James. Directed by Gilbert Gunn, scripted by Terry Nation.

**WHAT EVER HAPPENED TO BABY JANE? (1962).** Contemporary Grand Guignol yarn directed by Robert Aldrich, which established a subgenre of horror films in the 1960s about batty old dames committing assorted crimes. It certainly helped to rejuvenate sagging careers. Bette Davis and Joan Crawford are sisters who have left acting to live in a gloomy old house. Bette gradually goes off her nut, torturing her crippled sister and driving herself to the brink of insanity. Nothing more horrible than a dead bird on a food tray is shown—the horrors here are psychotic ones implied by screenwriter Lukas Heller, taking off from a novel by Henry Farrell. Victor Buono, Anna Lee, Bert Freed. (VC)

**WHAT HAVE YOU DONE TO SOLANGE? (1971).** What have they done to this poor Italian-West German movie? It's dripping with gore and rampant with aberrant psychology, and completely ersatz and nonfrightening. Directed by Massimo Dallamano. Fabio Testi, Joachim Fuchsberger, Karin Baal, Gunther Stoll, Cristina Galbo.

**WHAT THE PEEPER SAW (1973).** Offbeat British psychodrama, most interesting for its ambiguities and hints of conspiracy. Mark Lester is a perverted little bastard who might have drowned his mother in the bathtub—or so suspects stepmother Britt Ekland, the only one to penetrate to the roots of the boy's "bad seed" tendencies. Father Hardy Kruger refuses to believe his son could have done it, so a psychiatrist (Lilli Palmer) makes it appear Britt is off her rocker and commits her. Screenwriter Trevor Preston is interested in the psychological interplay among his intriguing characters, and how they step in and out of shadows cast by the aberrant mind. Directed with only a minimum of flash and dash by James Kelly.

**WHAT WAITS BELOW (1983).** Intriguing fantasy-adventure with Robert Powell as a soldier of fortune called upon by a U.S. military unit in South America to help in the installation of a new sonar device in an underground cavern. Director Don Sharp captures tension and suspense as the expedition (including Timothy Bottoms, Anne Heywood, Richard Johnson, Lisa Blount) works its way ever deeper into the cavern's depths, only to discover (1) an ALIEN-like rock monster and (2) a race of Lemurians who are albino-skinned and speak in a strange tongue which is never translated. When the action finally erupts there's plenty of it. Producer Sandy Howard has put together a decent actioner. (VC)

**WHAT'S SO BAD ABOUT FEELING GOOD? (1968).** Gentle fable from director George Seaton, in the spirit of his MIRACLE ON 34th STREET. A toucan in New York harbor infects the city with a virus that brings about total euphoria. Cigarette and alcohol sales drop sharply, and politicians fear this universal friendliness will restructure American politics. But Seaton's approach is too inoffensive for effective Establishment satire. George Peppard, Mary Tyler Moore, Dom De Luise, Susan Saint James, Cleavon Little.

**WHAT'S THE MATTER WITH HELEN? (1971).** In the vein of WHAT EVER HAPPENED TO BABY JANE?, directed by Curtis Harrington with a tongue-in-cheek quality that alternates with the sharp suspense of Henry Farrell's script. Debbie Reynolds and Shelley Winters are mothers of murderers serving time who move to Hollywood during the 1930s to open a dancing school. Pretty soon Shelley, as Helen, gets religion from Agnes Moorehead and goes bonkers in her wonderfully unique way. Dennis Weaver, Pamelyn Ferdin.

**WHEELS OF FIRE (1984).** Armed with his nuclear-powered dune buggy, a Mad Max clone seeks his kidnapped sister, fighting off a horde of sadistic low-lifes. Even the dust off the wheels looks recycled. Directed by Chris Santiago. (VC)

**WHEN A STRANGER CALLS (1979).** Chilling premise: babysitter Carol Kane receives weird calls before realizing a killer is in the house with her, calling from an extension. After this shocking start, the story deteriorates into standard chase fare as cop Charles Durning, years later, pursues the killer after he escapes from an asylum. Finally, the story returns to the babysitter and again becomes a genre scare flick with moments that will make you leap with fright. Recommended to all babysitters. Directed by Fred Walton, who co-scripted with Steve Feke. Rachel Roberts, Colleen Dewhurst, Ron O'Neal, Tony Beckley. (VC)

**WHEN DINOSAURS RULED THE EARTH (1970).** Spectacularly built blonde Victoria Verti is some eyeful in this Hammer sequel to ONE MILLION B.C., which depicts early man squaring off against prehistoric creatures and the elements (including the formation of the moon). Jim Danforth headed a team of effects artists, while Val Guest wrote-directed. Ms Verti is a member of the Rock Tribe rescued by Robin Hawdon of the Sea Tribe. Cast out from their respective tribes, they rove the barren surface making sensuous love in caves and finding snakes, crabs and dinosaurs on plateaus and mesas. Effects are not up to the Harryhausen standard, but it's solid entertainment. Hammer-ed home.

**WHEN KNIGHTS WERE BOLD (1936).** British musical fantasy (of the CONNECTICUT YANKEE IN KING ARTHUR'S COURT school) in which commoner Jack Buchanan is transported in time to medieval days. Fay Wray is the damsel in need of rescuing. Directed by Jack Raymond. Martita Hunt, Robert Horton, Garry Marsh, Kate Cutler.

**WHEN MICHAEL CALLS (1969).** Compelling, sometimes intriguing TV-movie even if its outcome is predictable. Based on a John Farris novel, this walks that gossamer plotline between supernatural chiller and diabolical let's-drive-Sister-Jessica-to-Death as divorcee Elizabeth Ashley receives phone calls from her long-dead son, while ex-hubby Ben Gazzara investigates. The characters are interestingly etched by telewriter James Bridges and director Philip Leacock does his best on a limited budget. There are effective "dead boy" spectre scenes and a few chilling phone calls which drive Ashley hysterical. Michael Douglas, Marian Waldman, Albert S. Waxman and Karen Pearson.

**WHEN THE SCREAMING STOPS (1973).** Spanish horror film in which a seductress spirit cum reptilian rises from the Rhine River to munch on human beings, especially hearts. What delicacies, and so delicately handled by director Armando De Ossorio, the humanitarian who brought us THE BLIND DEAD. Would you believe the sword of Siegfried is brought into play in this mythical, gory shower of theatrics? . . . Would you believe the wicked sword of Conan? . . . Red Sonja . . . ? Tony Kendall, Helga Line. (VC)

**WHEN THE WIND BLOWS (1986).** Raymond Briggs' British cartoon book became the inspiration for this animated feature showcasing Hilda and Jim (average Britons represented by the voices of Peggy Ashcroft and John Mills) as they face nuclear holocaust with a stiff upper lip and all that. Decidedly offbeat. Directed by Jimmy Murakami.

**WHEN WOMEN HAD TAILS (1970).** Senta Berger stars in this Italian send-up of prehistoric monster movies and scantily clad cave people by portraying one of the latter, discovered by seven rock dwellers—seven being significant since this is a take-off on SNOW WHITE AND THE SEVEN DWARFS. It seems Ms Bergen wags her tail when she gets horny. Directed by Pasquale Festa Campanile, co-scripted by Lina Wertmuller. As for Ms Bergen: Va-va-voom! (VC)

**WHEN WOMEN LOST THEIR TAILS (1971).** Sequel to WHEN WOMEN HAD TAILS. Get it? Sizzling Senta Berger returns in her scanty animal skins in the continuing adven-

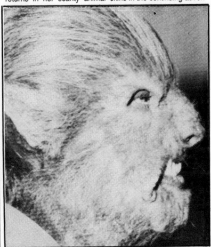

**LON CHANEY JR. AS 'THE WOLF MAN'**

tures of passionate women in days of volcanic, explosive sexuality. They truly love with a primitive passion! Again directed by Pasquale Festa Campanile, with Lina Wertmuller again rounding out the curvy storyline. (VC)

**WHEN WORLDS COLLIDE (1951).** Producer George Pal's respectable, above-average version of the Edwin Balmer-Philip Wylie novel, with an intelligent script by Sydney Boehm dealing with man's social disintegration when a star dubbed Bellus passes so close to Earth it causes destructive earthquakes, tidal waves and other forms of massive destruction. The only hope for mankind is to build a rocketship to take a handful of survivors to a satellite planet, Zyra—and thus begins the race to survive. Among those involved in the project are millionaire John Hoyt and lovers Richard Derr and Barbara Rush. Chesley Bonestell was technical advisor; Gordon Jennings won an Oscar for his effects. Directed by Rudolf Mate, who turned this into one of the best science-fiction films of the 1950s. Mary Murphy, Larry Keating. (VC)

**WHERE DO WE GO FROM HERE? (1945).** Effervescent, amusing 20th Century-Fox musical-comedy with costumed production numbers (lyrics by Ira Gershwin and Kurt Weill) and a sense of nonsensical fun as 4-F patriotic American Fred MacMurray finds Aladdin's Lamp, frees a genie named "Alley" (Gene Sheldon) and wishes himself in the army. But the genie with a magical watch fouls up and sends Fred back in time to join George Washington's army at Valley Forge. The non sequitur gags remind one of Mad Magazine at times, MacMurray does a ridiculous parody of Hitler in a barroom full of German stereotypes, and there's a delightful musical number aboard the Santa Maria when Mac winds up as part of Columbus' expedition to discover America. The silly casting includes Alan Mowbray as General Washington, Anthony Quinn as Chief Badger (who sells Manhattan to MacMurray for $24 dollars—the Badger Game, get it?) and June Haver and Joan Leslie as All-American beauties who fall for the bumbling, lovable Mac. Very American, very nostalgic. Directed by Gregory Ratoff.

**WHERE HAVE ALL THE PEOPLE GONE? (1974).** TV-film combines two bizarre elements: a solar fire that destroys all mechanical devices and a plague that decimates mankind, turning corpses into ashes. A typical video plod plot as a handful of survivors struggles to reach a home in Malibu . . . only science-fiction buffs will find the earthbound trek worth making. John Moxey directed the Lewis John Carlino-Sandor Stern script. Peter Graves, Verna Bloom, Kathleen Quinlan, George O'Hanlon Jr.

**WHERE THE BULLETS FLY (1967).** One dull cliffhanger after another as super-incredible superagent Tom Adams pursues the formula for a method of draining nuclear energy from a special alloy called spurium. This sequel to THE SECOND BEST SECRET AGENT IN THE WHOLE WIDE WORLD fluctuates from mediocrity to ineptitude and back again. Directed by John Gilling, scripted by Michael Pittock. Dawn Addams, Sidney James, Michael Ripper.

**WHERE THE DEVIL CANNOT GO (1960).** Czech fantasy in which Mephistopheles is played by a woman who tempts a modern equivalent of Faust. Directed by Zdenek Podskalsky.

**WHERE THE TRUTH LIES (1962).** Ambiguous, lugubrious French chiller adapted from a novel by suspense masters Pierre Boileau and Thomas Narcejac which fails to live up to its title. We never do find out the truth whether or not voodoo is responsible for a woman's catatonic, murderous condition. Written-directed by Henri Decoin. Juliette Greco, Jean-Marc Bory, Robert Dalban, Liselotte Pulver.

**WHERE TIME BEGAN (1977).** Spanish version of Jules Verne's novel by writer-director Juan Piquer is inferior to the 1959 adaptation, JOURNEY TO THE CENTER OF THE EARTH. The pace is sluggish, the characterizations dull. The film gains life when the monsters appear. Even though they are laughable dinosaur and King Kong imitations, they beat the monotony of the expedition into the bowels of Earth. Kenneth More stars as the professor in charge. Ivonne Sentis, Frank Brana, Pep Munne, Jack Taylor. (VC)

**WHILE I LIVE (1948).** British psychological supernatural thriller about a girl suffering from amnesia who sings a song

that could only have been known by a dead girl. This leads the dead girl's relatives to believe she's returned from the dead. Written-directed by John Harlow, from Robert Bell's play, THIS GAME GARDEN. Sonia Dresdel, Clifford Evans.

**WHIP HAND, THE (1951).** William Cameron Menzies, remembered for INVADERS FROM MARS and THE MAZE, designed and directed this "red menace thriller," a routine, uninspired RKO release with blatant touches of anti-Communist propaganda. Elliott Reid, Edgar Barrier and Raymond Burr labor against overwhelming odds with a crazy plot in which ex-Nazis hiding in a small northwestern town are searching for a germ that could wipe out civilization.

**WHIRLPOOL (1949).** Tense tale produced-directed by Otto Preminger about a hypnotist who puts himself into a trance to commit murder, scripted by Ben Hecht and Andrew Solt from a Guy Endore novel. Gene Tierney, Jose Ferrer, Richard Conte, Charles Bickford, Eduard Franz, Larry Keating.

**WHIRLPOOL (1970).** Danish pastry without any solid filling—it will leave a bad taste in your mouth. Orgiastic gore murders, necrophilia, that sort of sordidness. Starring Eddy Waters.

**WHISPERING GHOSTS (1942).** Old-fashioned, fun-filled mystery-comedy stuffed with ectoplasmic figures, spectral voices, a cursed ship—all logically explained away in the Philip MacDonald story scripted by Lou Breslow. Milton Berle is a radio program detective who seeks a killer with sidekick Willie Best, a comedy relief figure typically racist for the period. John Carradine, Brenda Joyce, Grady Sutton, Arthur Hohl. Directed by Alfred Werker.

**WHISTLING IN DIXIE (1942).** The Old Dark House again, this time with Red Skelton (in his recurring role as that radio detective, The Fox) scampering along eerie corridors, bumping into "ghosts" and hearing strange voices. The so-called "Whistling" series (this is a sequel to WHISTLING IN THE DARK) holds up well thanks to the comedic timing of the irascible Skelton, who was in his prime. Directed by S. Sylvan Simon. Ann Rutherford, George Bancroft, Guy Kibbee.

**WHISTLING IN THE DARK (1941).** Red Skelton's lovable albeit bumbling radio detective The Fox was to inspire a sequel, WHISTLING IN DIXIE. In this wild and woolly comedy mystery, Skelton bumps into a gang of moon worshippers. Fun from beginning to end with Skelton's undated slapstick a delight. And we're not just whistling, Dixie. Conrad Veidt, Ann Rutherford, Virginia Grey. Directed by S. Sylvan Simon.

**WHITE GORILLA, THE (1945).** Really bad piece of film patching, in which footage from a silent 1927 African adventure, PERILS OF THE JUNGLE, was inserted with new footage directed by Harry L. Fraser. A gorilla (Ray "Crash" Corrigan in a hairy white suit) clashes with a black gorilla in "the battle of the century"—but which century? So bad you might enjoy it, if you like punishing yourself.

**WHITE MARE'S SON, THE (1982).** Inexpensively produced, effective Hungarian animated feature, directed by Marcell Jankovics, based on an ancient Scythian legend about a dragon princess who disguises herself as a white horse to escape into exile where she can raise her son. Abstract and metaphoric in its imagery.

**WHITE PONGO (1945).** Laughable, nostalgic reminder of the killer-gorilla genre prolific to the 1940s. Pongo, a white ape believed to be the missing link between anthropod and man, carries off screaming Maris Nixon, threatening to mate with her in his lair. Cheer, don't wince, and have fun with this hoary old horror. Kick him where it hurts, Ms Wrixon. Directed by Sam Newfield, scripted by Raymond L. (Schlock) Schrock. Richard Fraser, Lionel Royce.

**WHITE REINDEER, THE (1953).** Offbeat Finnish film, extraordinary in its depiction of the Land of the Midnight Sun, and its superstitious people. Seeking a potion to keep her husband at home, a woman acquires the power to turn herself into a white reindeer and lure men to their deaths. Exotic detail and rare cinematic poetry. Directed by Eric Blomberg.

**WHITE ZOMBIE (1932).** Hailed in some quarters as a lost classic rediscovered in the 1960s—condemned in other quarters by fans who wish it had remained lost. Want the truth? It's creaky and awful, only occasionally enhanced by the symbolic imagery injected by producer Edward Halperin and director Victor Halperin. Bela Lugosi is in dire need of restraint as he overplays Legendre, a sweetless sugar plantation owner in the West Indies who holds sway over an army of zombies. Heavy-handed, turgid viewing, recommended only to die-hards or historians studying the decrepit films of yesteryear. Voodoo lore was borrowed by screenwriter Garnett Weston from William Seabrook's nonfictional MAGIC ISLAND. Madge Bellamy, John Harron. (VC)

**WHO? (1974).** Espionage-fantasy mixture in which a U.S. scientist undergoes Communist cybernetic surgery to become a counter-agent, only to endure an auto accident. The FBI sends Elliott Gould to investigate. John Gould's script is based on a novel by Algis Budrys. Trevor Howard, Joseph Bova, Ed Grover, Ivan Desny. Directed by Jack Gold.

**WHO DONE IT? (1956).** Above-average British comedy thriller (directed by Basil Deardon) in which an inept private detective saves the Empire from spies assigned to steal a weather-controlling device. Belinda Lee, Benny Hill, Ernest

**BRITT EKLAND IN 'THE WICKER MAN'**

Thesiger, Garry Marsh, George Margo.

**WHO KILLED AUNT MAGGIE? (1940).** Arthur Lubin directed this comedy mystery set in an old dark Southern plantation. It's the usual imagery of eerie corridors, secret panels, a black cat screeching in the night and a cotton clubber, who leaves several corpses on the floor. Nothing new, but kinda fun. John Hubbard, Wendy Barrie, Edgar Kennedy, Walter Abel, Onslow Stevens, Willie Best.

**WHO KILLED DOC ROBBIN? (1948).** Dated comedy of the Old Dark House school, complete with a man (actually a gorilla in a human suit), a gorilla (a man in a human suit) secret panels, drafty corridors, ectoplasmic manifestations and one very mad doctor. Only George Zucco, the crazy physician who has concocted an atomic apparatus, looks comfortable and relaxed in the haunted surroundings. Virginia Grey and Don Castle look lost, and stumble over the cliches. Directed by Bernard Carr with a revved engine.

**WHO KILLED MARY WHATS'ERNAME (1972).** It isn't the plot, it's the characters that bring to life this offbeat whodunit populated with strange, fascinating characters etched by a fine cast. Ex-boxer, diabetic Red Buttons—appalled at everyone's indifference to the ghastly murder of Mary Di Napoli, a New York streetwalker—decides to investigate. Aided by his feisty daughter (Alice Playten), Buttons begins meeting eccentric characters. There's whore Sylvia Miles, cop David Doyle, old partner Conrad Bain, sharp-tongued black patrolman Gilbert Lewis, suspicious landlord Dick Williams and weird 16mm filmmaker Sam Waterston. John O'Toole's story isn't much but he builds intriguing characters and director Ernie Pintoff gives the story added ambience by filming in sleazy, rundown city settings. An obscure movie worth digging up. (VC)

**WHO SLEW AUNTIE ROO? (1971).** Minor horror themes barely qualify this as a fright flick, yet it always evokes a rowdy response from viewers who recognize the Hansel-and-Gretel parallels to this modern tale of two children living with auntie Shelley Winters. She wants to toss them into the oven in what passes for a gingerbread house. The script (Gavin Lambert, Jimmy Sangster, Robert Blees) meanders but the cast works hard to make the feeble ideas work: Mark Lester, Ralph Richardson, Hugh Griffith, Lionel Jeffries. Despite its slightness, and only average treatment by director Curtis Harrington, this comes out a winner. (VC)

**WICKED, WICKED (1973).** Curiosity piece by writer-producer-director Richard L. Bare, projected in a split-screen process hyped as "Duo-Vision." Unfortunately, it's two bad movies in one as half of the screen shows mad killer Randolph Roberts wearing a fright mask, stalking beautiful women with his knife, and embalming them in cold-blooded fashion, the other half showing cop Scott Brady tracking him down. The split-screen concept allows for some suspense but that's about all. Rarely been shown since its first flop release. How is WICKED, WICKED? LOUSY, LOUSY. David Bailey, Tiffany Bolling, Edd Byrnes, Diane McBain.

**WICKER MAN, THE (1972).** This often-admired film sports a top British cast—Britt Ekland, Diane Cilento, Ingrid Pitt, Christopher Lee—but received poor distribution on two occasions: when initially released in a butchered form, and again in 1978-79 in re-edited form, with director Robin Hardy touring the U.S. to flack for the film. Despite the celluloid slaughter, this retains an unusual power in depicting the inhabitants of a Cornish village who act strangely when a constable turns up to investigate a disappearance. One of the highlights of this unusual story is an erotic nude sequence involving the comely Ms Ekland. And Lee considers it one of his best. The literate script is by Anthony Shaffer. Ian Campbell, Aubrey Morris, Edward Woodward. (VC)

**WILD IN THE SKY (1972).** Vietnam War protest film, depicting anti-heroes who hijack a U.S. bomber carrying an H-Bomb and threaten the government with Fort Knox's destruction. Brando De Wilde, Tim O'Connor, Keenan Wynn, Robert Lansing, James Daly. Directed by William T. Naud.

**WILD IN THE STREETS (1968).** Far-out premise, like man, dig this: Rock singer Max Frost (Christopher Jones), manipulated for political reasons, turns the tables on congressman

Hal Holbrook and manipulates Capitol Hill for his own devious goals. The result is a lower voting age (would you believe 14?) and an election in which the singer is elected President. His first act in Congress: to put everyone over 35 into concentration camps, where they are force-fed hallucinogens. Wild wild wild. Directed with youthful passion by Barry Shear and scripted with unbridled imagination by Robert Thom. Shelley Winters, Ed Begley, Millie Perkins, Diane Varsi, Richard Pryor, Dick Clark, Walter Winchell.

**WILD THING (1987).** Rob Knepper portrays an uncivilized youth living in the ruins of a ghetto and growing up to be a legendary defender of the oppressed and crime-stricken. It's an offbeat idea from a script by John Sayles, directed by Max Reid. Kathleen Quinlan appears as a social worker and love interest, and Robert Davi is the heavy.

**WILD WILD PLANET (1967).** Dull, dull Italian science-fiction

### ROSS MARTIN AS ARTEMUS GORDON

set in 2015 A.D. spends too much time setting up a premise that never jells—a miniaturized scientist (Massimo Serato) who plots to kidnap representatives of the United Democracies with the help of intergalactic robot female pirates. This unofficial sequel to WAR OF THE PLANETS was directed by Anthony Dawson. Tony Russell, Lisa Gastoni, Franco Nero, Massimo Serato, Charles Justin.

**WILD, WILD WEST REVISITED, THE (1979).** Another follow-up to the once-popular TV series, with Robert Conrad as secret agent James T. West and Ross Martin as his sidekick, Artemus Gordon. It's all cowboy fun and games with 19th Century clones, nuclear bombs and other out-of-time-and-place inventions springing from the wild, wild mind of scriptwriter William Bowers. Burt Kennedy directed purely for laughs. Jo Ann Harris, Paul Williams, Harry Morgan, Joyce Jameson, Shields and Yarnell, Rene Auberjonois.

**WILD WOMEN OF WONGO (1958).** Ten thousand years before Christ? That's what producer George R. Black, director James Wolcott and writer Cedric Rutherford would like you to believe as they present a film that truly belongs to the Stoned Age of Cinema. Wongo is indeed a world of "wild women" where prehistoric dames, in need of better hairdos, worship the Temple of the Dragon God. Meanwhile, Goona men wish they could get their beady hands on these luscious broads. An actress named Adrienne Bourbeau appears as one of the cave chicks, with the hots for Ed Fury. Wongo wongo bongo bongo slongo slongo.

**WILD WORLD OF BATWOMAN, THE (1966).** Cheapie writer-producer-director Jerry Warren makes Bert I. Gordon look like the John Huston of special effects with this regrettably floppish superheroine nonflick starring Katherine Victor

as a queen of costumed oddities fighting off the evil Dr. Neon and a companion named Ratfink. George Andre, Steve Brodie, Lloyd Nelson, Richard Banks.

**WILLARD (1971).** Stephen Gilbert's novel, RATMAN'S NOTEBOOKS, is material that proved a difficult mousetrap for director Daniel Mann and scripter Gilbert Ralston to set. You'll never be suckered in by its cheesiness. Too unbelievable in depicting how a 27-year-old failure (Bruce Davison) trains an army of 500 rats to do his evil bidding, which includes murdering a sadistic boss (Ernest Borgnine). Despite obvious shortcomings, WILLARD had box office snap, especially with black ghetto audiences who sided with the rats as they attacked honkies and Establishment figureheads. Sondra Locke plays Bruce's girlfriend in a miniskirt, Elsa Lanchester is the demanding, dying mother and Michael Dante is a fellow office worker. The sequel, BEN, was also a money-maker but just as mousy. (VC)

**WILLY/MILLY (1986).** Teenage girl turns herself into a teenage boy and faces a new lesson in sexual roles and growing up. A mature comedy in the hands of director Paul Schneider. Pamela Segall, Eric Gurry, Mary Tanner.

**WILLY McBEAN AND HIS MAGIC MACHINE (1965).** Japanese puppet feature in AniMagic, which approximates a 3-D look. McBean, a bright child who joins forces with Mexican monkey Pablo, travels through time to prevent Professor Rasputin von Rotten from tinkering with the fabric of history. Quaint and charming. Written-produced-directed by Arthur Rankin Jr. Voices by Larry Mann, Billie Richards, Alfie Scopp, Paul Kligman.

**WILLY WONKA AND THE CHOCOLATE FACTORY (1971).** Visually attractive adaptation of Roald Dahl's children's book, with enough whimsical humor and satire for adults too. It's a fantasy odyssey through a candy factory conducted by Gene Wilder, a fluffy concoction complete with morality lessons and a superb cast that includes Jack Albertson, Leonard Stone, Peter Ostrum, Denise Nickerson and Roy Kennear. Impressionistic sets of the chocolate factory almost steal away the Hershey bar. It'll melt in your mouth . . . (VC)

**WINGED SERPENT, THE.** See **Q.** (Queue up to see it!)

**WIRED TO KILL (1986).** The futuristic post-holocaust world in this low-low-budget actioner is different from Mad Max's, so at least it strives for some originality. The time is 1998, and while there is a similance of law and order, the world is still pretty screwed up when a young woman (Emily Longstreth) freshly kicked out of her home teams up with an electronics inventor (Devin Hoelscher) who's just had his legs broken by a sadist (Merritt Butrick) and his ruthless band of rapists and perverts. The gimmick here is that the incapacitated Hoelscher must use the girl to carry out his dirty work with the help of a robot named Winston. Directed-written by Franky Schaeffer. Frank Collison, Tommy Lister Jr., Kim Milford. A little better than usual for this stuff. (VC)

**WISHBONE CUTTER.** See **SHADOW OF CHIKARA.**

**WITCH, THE (1966).** Redundantly named Damiano Damiani directed and co-wrote this Italian tale that depicts Richard Johnson, as a historian working in a castle, who is caught up in psychological mystery with horrific overtones and touches of black magic and witchcraft. Rosanna Schiaffino, Gian Maria Volonte, Sarah Ferrati.

**WITCH BENEATH THE SEA, THE (1962).** Who is the alluring, legendary Amazon, her loins throbbing with passion, who attracts men and puts them into a frenzy of lustful desire? Who is the novelist who falls under the spell of her licentious urges? Is the legend of Marizinia true or is there a simpler explanation? Low budget stuff(ing) for lowbrow viewers. John Sutton, Gina Albert.

**WITCH IN LOVE.** See **WITCH, THE.**

**WITCH KILLER OF BROADMOOR.** See **NIGHT OF THE BLOOD MONSTER.** (Broadmoor: land for a dame?)

**WITCH WHO CAME FROM THE SEA (1976).** Insightful if gory portrait of a demented, sexually perverted woman who calls herself Molly the Mermaid. Millie Perkins is no witch; she's a homicidal killer of two muscular, sexy football stars, slashing them with a razorblade. She's haunted by memories of her sea captain father, who brutally raped her as a child, and now she attacks her lovers, often slicing up their sexual organs. Obviously, this low budget film directed by Matt Cimber on the beaches of L.A. is not for children. Richard Thom, Perkins' husband, has written a symbolic screenplay as disturbing as it is enlightening. Some of the murders are graphic, with Millie rubbing blood all over the mermaid tattooed on her stomach, and other scenes are very erotic as Perkins sheds her clothing to make sex to a TV commercial star. Supporting players are good: Vanessa Brown as a friend, Lonny Chapman as Long John, the owner of a bar; Peggy Feury as an equally crazy sister; and a bizarre tattooist named Jack Dracula. Unpleasant, yet it has an intelligence behind it that is compelling. (VC)

**WITCH WITHOUT A BROOM, A (1967).** Jeffrey Hunter, in one of his last roles before his untimely death, keeps seeing witch Maria Perschy pop up in his classroom. Fantasy turns to comedy as she ineptly casts spells which never quite work properly. Amusing Spanish-U.S. co-oper produced by Sidney Pink, directed by Jose El Lorietta.

**WITCHBOARD (1986).** A sincere effort to tell a story with more than passing characterizations underlies this low budget supernatural thriller utilizing the ouija board as a device for terror. Unfortunately, the first half could be called WITCHBORED, with writer-director Kevin S. Tenney in need of more panache for his planchette. Finally, the murders begin after a young wife (Tawny Kitaen) dabbles with a ten-year-old spirit, unaware she is communicating with a mass murderer back from the grave and stalking prey with his favorite weapon, an axe. The gore is light but the impact is still there at the chaotic climax, a blending of slasher-horror and EXORCIST-type thrills. Todd Allen, Stephen Nichols.

**WITCHCRAFT (1964).** British quickie, reportedly made in only 20 days under director Don (KISS OF THE VAMPIRE) Sharp, transcends its speedy Robert L. Lippert production values to become a sustaining (albeit minor) chiller starring Lon Chaney Jr. as a man who seeks vengeance after his family plot has been bulldozed. Yvette Rees, Jack Hedley, Jill Dixon, Viola Keats, David Weston.

**WITCHCRAFT GENERAL, THE.** See **CONQUEROR WORM.** (Death wormed over?)

**WITCHCRAFT '70 (1970).** Italian documentary written-directed-edited by Luigi Scattini, with English narration by Edmund Purdom, which explores contemporary witchcraft and various forms practiced throughout the world. Heavily edited for TV, since originally released with an X.

**WITCHCRAFT THROUGH THE AGES.** Videocassette title for **HAXAN.**

**WITCHES, THE.** See **DEVIL'S OWN, THE.**

**WITCHES AND THE GRINNYGOG, THE (1983).** British children's TV series re-edited for the U.S. telly. It's the supernatural misadventures of a coven and a magic statue. Zoe Loftin, Giles Harper, Heidi Mayo.

**WITCHES' BREW (1985).** Originally shot in 1978 as WHICH WITCH IS WHICH?, this failed to make the grade and underwent reshooting before being thrown away on cable TV. A comedy rendering of Fritz Leiber's BURN WITCH BURN (though uncredited), showing the humorous side to suburban witchcraft. Richard Benjamin is a university professor whose wife (Teri Garr) uses her witch's powers to help him get ahead, but he forces her to throw away her good-luck charms . . . leaving him wide open to the wives/witches of two job rivals and their mentor, an older witch played by Lana Turner. The old biddy conspires to enter Teri's body, allowing for a few cheap effects. The jokes are thin, the production qualities cheap. The cauldron never boils, and the broom is only for sweeping. Directed by Richard Shorr with additional footage shot by Herbert L. Strock. A Strock of bad luck? (VC)

**WITCHES MOUNTAIN, THE (198?).** Coven of cackling crones and hideous hags terrorize a young couple in the Pyrenees Mountains. Patty Shepard. (VC)

**WITCHES OF EASTWICK, THE (1987).** Three divorced women living in a New England village steeped in American tradition discover they have witch-like powers and, one by one, are willingly seduced by a newcomer to town, Daryl Van Horne, who is none other than the Devil incarnate, here to engage in a battle of the sexes that is intellectual and visually exciting thanks to the special effects of Rob Bottin. Nicholson is brilliant as the seductive chauvinist male who employs supernatural tricks (such as levitation) to tease his three conquests. The women, in turn, are equally talented for the occasion: Susan Sarandon is a suppressed music teacher who is turned into a passionate redhead; Cher is a sculptress, again showing her strong dramatic and comedic acting

**THE OUIJA BOARD THAT LEADS TO THE UNKNOWN IN 'WITCHBOARD'**

## JACK NICHOLSON WITH CHER, SUSAN SARANDON AND MICHELLE PFEIFFER IN 'THE WITCHES OF EASTWICK'

abilities; and Michele Pfeiffer is a local newspaper reporter, beautiful and vulnerable. Veronica Cartwright should also be singled out for her unusual performance as the woman of the town who realizes what Van Horne is up to and tries to stop him. There's some wonderfully witty dialogue by screenwriter Michael Cristofer, who adapted John Updike's novel, and director George Miller treats the material on an epic scale, suggesting we are seeing the supreme battle of good over evil, man against woman, and other cosmic themes. It is, however, Nicholson's performance that will endure and make this film memorable. One could be critical of the ending, which goes a bit berserk and overemploys some nauseating special effects (it's the Road Warrior coming out in Miller, perhaps?) but all in all this is a superior entertainment, with enough meat for any segment of the viewing audience. Richard Jenkins, Keith Jochim, Carel Struycken.

**WITCHFIRE (1985).** Shelley Winters fans, here it is, another film in which your favorite actress goes bonkers in grand style, cackling with a madness that will delight your perverse soul. She and two other old broads (Frances De Sapio, Corrine Chateau) crash out of an Asylum for the Utterly Insane, thinking they have the powers of witches. Taking refuge in an old mansion, they find Gary Swanson and begin to torment him as only witches can. It's the dialogue by director Vincent J. Privitera that makes this a classic among the World's Most Beloved and Awful Shelley Winters flicks. (VC)

**WITCHING, THE.** Videocassette title for **NECROMANCY.**

**WITCHING TIME (1980).** Two repackaged episodes from the British series, HAMMER HOUSE OF HORROR. In the title story, directed by Don Leaver, Patricia Quinn plays a witch of the 17th Century who time travels to the present. In the second, "The Silent Scream," directed by Alan Gibson, Peter Cushing portrays a scientist conducting experiments in human behavior—on man and animals. Jon Finch, Brian Cox, Ian McCulloch. Music by James Bernard. (VC)

**WITCHMAKER, THE (1969).** William O. Brown wrote-produced-directed this poor man's glimpse at witches and warlocks sneaking through the Louisiana bayou for producers L.Q. Jones and Alvy Moore. Much of this is ludicrous exploitation, especially the scenes in which Luther the Berserk (John Lodge) hangs up women by their heels, slices their throats and lets the blood drip to the ground. There's some chilling, atmospheric sequences filmed in the swamp country. Brown's plot has psychic researchers Moore, Anthony Eisley and the beautiful dolls investigating the bogland. Before long the gals are drifting through the misty

landscape in sexy negligees, which stirs the blood of the creeps back in the cave—and those creeps include horror movie host Seymour. (VC)

**WITCH'S CURSE, THE. See MACISTE IN HELL.**

**WITCH'S MIRROR, THE (1961).** The old Haunted Mirror Plot: The ghost of a murdered woman emerges from the accursed glass to wreak revenge on her husband, who acts dumber than most husbands in Mexican horror films produced by Abel Salazar. Seven year's bad luck guaranteed if you watch to the bitter end. Directed with a sense of self-reflection by Chano Urveta. Rosita Arenas.

**WITHOUT WARNING. See IT CAME WITHOUT WARNING.**

**WIZ, THE (1978).** The idea was to take THE WIZARD OF OZ, cast it with blacks and inject it into a modern setting. The springboard for this expensive Universal film musical was a Broadway smash by William Brown and Charles Smalls, but

*"Imagine what happens to posterity without Columbus, / No New York and Fiorello, / No Abbott and Costello."*—Fred MacMurray singing to Christopher Columbus aboard the Santa Maria in
# WHERE DO WE GO FROM HERE?

drastic changes were made by screenwriter Joel Schumacher and director Sidney Lumet, and critics were not enamored. The songs and music (by Smalls and Quincy Jones) vary in effectiveness, but all the picture seems to achieve is to cast a dark (no pun intended) pall over one's memories of the vivacious MGM musical of 1939. Here the plot is enmeshed in urban impressionism with the Wicked Witch's monkeys, for example, equipped with motorcycles. Diana Ross, Michael Jackson, Nipsey Russell, Lena Horne, Richard Pryor, Ted Ross, Mabel King. (VC)

**WIZARD, THE (1927).** Silent screen predecessor to those mad-scientist-tampering-with-an-ape pictures. Gaston Leroux's story, "Balaoo," directed by Richard Rosson, has insane physician Edmund Lowe sewing the head of a human onto a gorilla's body. A study in needlepoint?

**WIZARD OF BAGHDAD, THE (1961).** Sam Katzman production, which means its cheap, with script by Jesse L. Lasky Jr., which means he must have needed the money, with direction by George Sherman, which means it at least has good action sequences. It's your basic Arabian Nights Plot no. 7890: Prince overthrows vizar with the help of a drunken genie who finally gets his powers back after a long magicless hiatus. Dick Shawn, Diane Baker, Barry Coe, Don Beddoe, John Van Dreelen, Robert F. Simon.

**WIZARD OF GORE (1970).** One of the great gore classics from the king of blood and guts, producer-director Herschell Gordon Lewis. The Allan Kahn script has a mad magician (Ray Sager) cutting a woman in half and spiking another, and then hypnotizing the audience. Strong stomachs required. Ray Sager, Judy Cler, Wayne Ratay. (VC)

**WIZARD OF MARS, THE (1964).** Low-budget slop of the "gee whiz" school, its schlocky story borrowed from THE WIZARD OF OZ. Three astronauts and one femmenaut rocket to the Red Planet, crash-landing in a wilderness. By following a "golden road" they find a long-dead civilization ruled by wizard John Carradine, who is no longer capable of physical movement. Time on the planet is frozen, and only by unfreezing it can the Earthlings return home. The effects are totally inadequate to the ambitions of screenwriter David Hewitt, whose chores extended to producing-directing. Forrest J. Ackerman served as technical adviser, but to what avail is unclear. Turgidly acted by Roger Gentry, Vic McGee, Eve Bernhardt, Jerry Rannow. (VC)

**WIZARD OF OZ, THE (1939).** Perennial MGM classic (produced by Mervyn LeRoy, directed by Victor Fleming) continues to be enjoyed by new generations enthralled with the magical story-telling of L. Frank Baum, whose fairy tale was adapted by Noel Langley. Judy Garland is the young Kansan Judy who is knocked out during a tornado (in black and white) and wakes up (in color) in a fantasy kingdom. Taking the Yellow Brick Road to adventure, she meets the scarecrow (Ray Bolger), the Tin Man (Jack Haley), the Cowardly Lion (Bert Lahr). The fantastic kingdom of Oz is ruled by Frank Morgan and threatened by the wicked witch (Margaret Hamilton) and a swarm of deadly flying monkeys. Then, of course, there are the Munchkins. Cedric Gibbons' art design always looks fresh and vibrant, the songs and music are unforgettable and the exaggerated acting perfectly captures the proper note. Enjoy the Munchkin merriment, because you will never discover a film quite as wonderful as this one. Billie Burke, Charles Grapewin. (VC)

**WIZARDS (1976).** Tolkienesque masterpiece of animation by Ralph Bakshi, depicting a future when mankind, following a period of atomic holocaust mutation, is divided into two camps: the mechanized armies of Blackwolf the Tyrant, whose followers are a motley collection of frog creatures and demons, and the peace-loving elves who practice wizardry. The art work is stunning, especially the brutal clash of armies

in which Bakshi combines animation with live action stock footage. The influences of comic book artists Wally Wood, Frank Frazetta, Berni Wrightson and Al Williamson are pronounced. The narrative by Bakshi is sometimes garbled and the characterizations uneven, but these minor problems do not distract from the film's visual power. Bakshi's best!

**WIZARDS OF THE LOST KINGDOM (1984).** Cliche-riddled, amateurish sword-and-sorcery nonsense, distinguished only by the blase, tongue-in-cheek performance of Bo Svenson as Kor the Conqueror, a wandering swordsman who befriends a youth who is "Simon, song of the good wizard Wilford, magician of the Kingdom of Axum." Simon and his "fuzzface" companion, a furry thing called Goldpack, are searching for a magical ring, and so is Chirka the evil sorcerer. They throw rays of light at each other but the conflict is minimal and forced, and even Svenson can't sustain his performance for long under Hector Olivera's feeble direction. There's a hobgoblin, an insect woman who turns into a monster, five dead walking corpses and assorted STAR WARS-style aliens. As the kid says, "Pretty neat stuff, huh?" Vidal Peterson, Thom Christopher, Barbara Stock, Dolores Michaels. (VC)

**WOLF MAN, THE (1941).** Classic Universal horror thriller set the mood and lore for the werewolf genre, and presented an unusually sympathetic Lon Chaney Jr. He plays Lawrence Talbot, a young student attacked by a werewolf (Bela Lugosi) who, under the full moon, turns into a marauding, slavering monster. Jack Pierce's time-lapse make-up is outstanding for its time (though now outmoded) and Curt Siodmak's script explores the trauma and torment of lycanthropy. Maria Ouspenskaya recites the famous "werewolf curse" poem and Claude Rains portrays the father who gropes to understand his son's malady. Produced-directed by George Waggoner.

**WOLF PACK/THE KIRKWOOD HAUNTING (1978).** Two episodes of the SPIDERMAN TV show recut into a video feature. In the first episode, directed by Joe Manduke, a mind-expanding drug falls into the hands of a criminal who uses it

**PRODUCER SAM KATZMAN, KING OF Bs**

to turn men into zombies. In the second, directed by Don Mc-Dougall, a seance crowd stages a phony haunted house to bilk a millionairess. Nicholas Hammond, Robert F. Simon, Paul Carr, Marlyn Mason.

**WOLFEN (1981).** This adaptation of the Whitley Streiber horror novel might have been a winner, but . . . if you excite an audience's expectations for a monster, you'd damn well better pay off. When it's time for the titular entities (mutant wolves with superintelligent tracking abilities) to reveal themselves, the film falls faster than dog doo-doo. Instead of creatures capable of the ghastly gore murders for which they are credited, we are shown ordinary wolves with slight makeup. The disappointment is devastating. Up to then, WOLFEN is a graphically suspenseful thriller about a killer pack running wild in the ruins of the Bronx. Director Michael Wadleigh, who co-wrote with David Frye, also made bad changes in Streiber's plot. There's some business about American Indians (they were once pushed off their land, just like earlier

**ALBERT FINNEY IN 'WOLFEN'**

generations of wolves) but that remains secondary to Albert Finney as the cop in pursuit of the four-legged killers. The Steadicam point-of-view shots in the Bronx ruins are marvelous; if only the payoff had paid . . . Gregory Hines, Diane Venora, Edward James Olmos, Tom Noonan. (VC)

**WOLFMAN—A LYCANTHROPE (1978).** Although his films rarely play outside the South, Earl Owensby is a successful producer of money-making genre flicks, usually in which he stars in a Clint Eastwood guise. In this one, set in Georgia near the turn of the century, Earl has inherited the Curse of the Glasgow Family and turns into a hairy killer under the full moon. Tepid production, written-directed by Worth Keeter without style. But Owensby made money. He was howlin' all the way to the bank. (VC)

**WOLFWOMAN.** Videocassette title for **LEGEND OF THE WOLFWOMAN.** (Lobo Lady Lopes Loosely!)

**WOMAN EATER, THE (1957).** Unchewy, cheap British im-port from producer Richard Gordon with George Coulouris as a mad doctor who feeds females to a tree. Is its bark worse than its bite? In turn, the tree provides the insane Coulouris with a serum for bringing the dead to life. Below usual British nourishment standards . . . it will eat up your valuable time and give you severe indigestion. Burp! . . . See? Directed by Charles Saunders on an empty stomach, maybe?

**WOMAN IN THE MOON (1929).** Silent Fritz Lang film, depicting man's first trip to the moon and a lunar landscape of sand dunes. Lang was one of the best directors of the 1920s in handling science-fiction material, as METROPOLOS so richly proves. (VC)

**WOMAN WHO CAME BACK, THE (1945).** Arthritic Republic witchcraft thriller in which a woman suspected of being the reincarnation of a 300-year-old witch returns to New England. Undistinguished material from director Walter Colmes. The cast—Otto Kruger, John Loder, Nancy Kelly, Ruth Ford—deserved a helluva lot better.

**WOMAN WHO WOULDN'T DIE, THE (1964).** Murderer is tricked into thinking he is pursued by the ghost of a victim. Or is it merely a trick by the living to make him talk? For Gary Merrill, it was the British movie that wouldn't live. Directed by Gordon Hessler, adapted by Daniel Mainwaring from Jay Bennett's CATACOMBS. Jane Merrow, Neil McCallum.

**WOMANHUNT, THE (1972).** John Ashley-Eddie Romero schlockaroo, made in the Philippines, copies "The Most Dangerous Game," but this time with a mad hunter who prefers blondes, brunettes and redheads in pith-helmeted pursuits on his private little island. No males need apply. Lisa Todd, of HEE HAW, is one of the curvaceous creatures the madman pursues. Oglers, pay attention. Ashley also co-stars and Romero directed. Sid Haig, Pat Woodell.

**WOMBLING FREE (1977).** British children's concoction (in the style of The Muppets, but without half the charm or fun) depicting how some cutie creatures called Wombles set out to clean up dirty old London. BBC special based on a popular book by Bernard Spear. Directed by Lionel Jeffries. David Tomlinson, Ken Baker, Frances De La Tour, Marcus Powell.

**WOMEN OF THE PREHISTORIC PLANET (1966).** Space opera on a TV budget: space travelers (led by stalwarts John Agar and Wendell Corey) land on an alien world inhabited by prehistoric people and stock-footage giant lizards. Writer-director Arthur C. Pierce tries to make up for all the defects by tacking on a surprise ending which is no surprise. Night club comedian Paul Gilbert appropriately plays for laughs—the rest of the cast should have followed spacesuit. Directed tackily by George Gilbert. Merry Anders, Stu Margolin, Adam Roarke, Lyle Waggoner, Stuart Lasswell. (VC)

**WONDER MAN (1944).** Delightful Samuel Goldwyn comedy, showcasing the multi-talents of Danny Kaye under Bruce Humberstone's fluid direction. Danny plays twins—one of whom is murdered by gangsters. His ghost returns to help his brother overcome complications with the underworld. Kaye has a romp, flashing his multitalents. Virginia Mayo, Vera-Ellen, Steve Cochran, Otto Kruger, Huntz Hall, S.Z. Sakall.

**WONDER WOMAN (1974).** First TV pilot depicting Charles Moulton's comic book heroine was a failure. John D. F. Black's script updated Wonder Woman and placed her in a liberated society instead of stressing the period of the original strip (the 1940s, when a woman really had to fight chauvinistic attitudes as well as forces of evil). Cathy Lee Crosby just didn't have enough "wonder" to be the busty supergal with bullet-bouncing bracelets as she battles villain Abner Smith (Ricardo Montalban) with the help of her companion Steve Trevor (Kaz Garas). A superior series concept starring Lynda Carter (now talk about a busty supergal!) was introduced in 1975 and became a hit series. Directed by Vincent Mc-

---

*"Know what? Life's a bitch. First the New Plague killed my mom along with 120 million other people. Now my dad kicks me out of the house so he can screw around. What is this? The Dark Ages?"—Emily Longstreth's narration for* **WIRED TO KILL.**

# W Is for Wondrous Writers . . .

ISAAC ASIMOV

RAY BRADBURY

PETER STRAUB

ARTHUR C. CLARKE AT WORK ON THE SCRIPT FOR '2110'

CORNELL WOOLRICH

STEPHEN KING

CLIVE BARKER

Eveety. Andrew Prine, Richard X. Slattery.

**WONDER WOMEN (1973).** Filipino hunk of horror with the insane scientist being a beautiful woman, Dr. Su (Nancy Kwan), and her victims being athletes whom she kidnaps so she can use them as spare parts to sell to aging or dying millionaires. The producer, Ross Hagen, doubles as a hero who arrives on Dr. Su's island to investigate the disappearances. Suzy Wong was really on the skids. Directed by Robert O'Neill. Maria De Aragon, Robert Collins.

**WONDERFUL WORLD OF THE BROTHERS GRIMM, THE (1962).** The first wide-screen Cinerama film to have a plotline, this George Pal production uses the process to wonderful advantage in recounting the story of the brothers Grimm (Laurence Harvey and Karl Boehm) and three of the fairy tales they concocted despite their own personal biographical hardships. These stories are "The Cobbler and the Elves," featuring animated puppets; "The Dancing Princess" with Yvette Mimieux, Jim Backus and Russ Tamblyn; and "The Singing Bone," with Terry-Thomas, Buddy Hackett and Otto

Kruger. There is also a memorably sentimental sequence in which one of the brothers imagines the characters he has created visiting him in his sick room. Claire Bloom, Walter Slezak, Ian Wolfe, Barbara Eden, Arnold Stang. Directed by Pal and Henry Levin, scripted by Charles Beaumont, David Harmon, William Roberts.

**WONDERS OF ALADDIN, THE (1961).** Wonderless, pathetic US.-Italian attempt by producer Joseph E. Levine to cash in on the Arabian Nights genre, with Donald O'Connor hopelessly miscast as the possessor of the magic lamp. Vittorio De Sica makes an appearance as the genie, but there's nothing wondrous about this comedic swashbuckling bomb directed by Henry Levin and Mario Bava, Aldo Fabrizi, Milton Reid. Michelle Mercier, Noelle Adam. (VC)

**WON'T WRITE HOME, MOM—I'M DEAD.** See **TERROR FROM WITHIN.** (Horror you? I'm slime!)

**WORK IS A FOUR-LETTER WORD (1968).** British fantasy-comedy directed by Peter Hall set in the near future, where worker David Warner is involved with strange drug-filled

**THE AVENGING EVIL FORCE, AN UNEARTHLY POWER, IN 'THE WRAITH'**

mushrooms, odd machines that take on the personality of their own, etc. Based on a Henry Livings play called EH? How's that again? Cilla Black, Elizabeth Spriggs.

**WORLD BEYOND, THE (1978).** Unsold TV pilot has promising premises (writer dies on the operating table and is revived; is lured by strange, compelling voices to a deserted island where a mud monster is killing people) but the execution is amateurish. Granville van Dusen.

**WORLD BEYOND THE MOON, THE (1953).** SPACE PATROL was one of TV's earliest science-fiction shows, designed chiefly for juvenile watchers and done live in the studio, which didn't permit many rocketship take-offs or astonishing effects. The series is nostalgically remembered by those growing up at the time, although a re-reviewing reveals terrible plots, cardboard sets and an acting of a low caliber. It may have had a charm in its own time and place, but not out of that context. Regulars were Ed Kemmer as Commander Buzz Corey and Lyn Osborn as Cadet Happy. See **SPACE PATROL.**

**WORLD OF DRACULA (1979).** Re-edited episodes of a TV series about a modern-day 512-year-old vampire living in San Francisco who is pursued by a descendant of Von Helsing. Corny but colorful stuff, with a lot of memorable lines of dialogue as the vampire-hunter and his girlfriend (whose mother was a victim of Dracula) constantly close in on the articulate, often-poetic bloodsucker. Directed by Kenneth Johnson (producer and co-writer), Sutton Roley and Jeffrey Hayden. Bever-leigh Banfield, Louise Sorel.

**WORLD OF HORROR (1968).** Polished Polish TV-film comprised of three famous literary horror stories: Oscar Wilde's "Lord Arthur Saville's Crime," Wilde's "The Canterville Ghost" and Wilkie Collins' "A Terribly Strange Bed."

**WORLD OF THE VAMPIRES, THE (1960).** Abel Salazar production, imported from Mexico by American-International for TV, is unique in that music played on a piano built with bones and skulls is used to destroy the bloodsucking monsters. Not the same old tune, amigo. Directed by Alfonso Corona Blake. Mauricio Garces, Jose Baviera. (VC)

**WORLD, THE FLESH AND THE DEVIL, THE (1959).** Allegory dealing with the morality and racial prejudice of man, set within the framework of an "end-of-the-world" story. Miner Harry Belafonte survives atomic attack and, moving on to New York City, finds other survivors: Inger Stevens and Mel Ferrer, the latter a candidate for the Ku Klux Klan with his racial hatreds. The most striking scenes are those of Belafonte wandering through the deserted streets of New York. Writer-director Ranald MacDougall based his provocative script loosely on M. P. Shiel's THE PURPLE CLOUD. The fine musical score is by Miklos Rozsa.

**WORLD WAR III (1982).** Political-military science-fiction dominates this TV-movie in which Russia invade Alaska with an eye on seizing the oil pipeline. Should the U.S. go to war or not? President Rock Hudson must decide. This provocative venture was written by Robert L. Joseph (being based on a best-selling novel) and directed by David Greene and Boris Sagal. The latter was killed during filming when he backed into the rotor blade of a helicopter. David Soul, Brian Keith, Cathy Lee Crosby, Katherine Helmond, James Hampton (VC).

**WORLD WITHOUT END (1956).** Entertaining grade-B actioner in which a rocket crew passes thorugh a time warp into 2508 A.D. The Earth has been destroyed by atomic war, and the inhabitants are mutant cave types. But underground lives a race of humanoid survivors led by Rod Taylor. Nothing new, but fast-moving with its many fights, monsters, etc. Written-directed by Edward Bernds. Hugh Marlowe, Lisa Montell, Paul Brinegar, Nancy Gates, Nelson Leigh.

**WORLD'S GREATEST ATHLETE, THE (1973).** Typically innocuous Disney comedy, in which Roscoe Lee Browne must resort to playing a witch doctor and Tim Conway is his usual

**CADET HAPPY IN 'SPACE PATROL'**

dumb-cluck self. Jan-Michael Vincent portrays the superathlete. Of course, he gets caught up in voodoo and body shrinking. Silly but enjoyable; for the family. Directed by Robert Scheerer. John Amos, Billy De Wolfe, Nancy Walker, Howard Cosell, Dayle Haddon.

**WORM EATERS, THE (1981).** Crazy Guy (Herb Robins, who also wrote-directed this sleazy exploitationer) talks to worms and forces people to eat them (remarkably disgusting, wouldn't you say?) and turns them into worm monsters. Could have been intended as a horror comedy, although with the eccentric Robins at the helm, and T. V. Mikels producing, anything was possible. Worm your way out of watching unless you have a taste for wriggling, crawly things. (VC)

**WORST SECRET AGENTS, THE.** See **OH, THOSE SECRET AGENTS.** (Oh, the worst!)

**WORST WITCH, THE (1986).** Children's TV-movie, never elevating itself out of the silly league, set at a training school for witches, where recruit Fairuza Balk is an ugly duckling razzed by fellow pupils. Director Robert Young treats the whole thing like a juvenile joke, never allowing head witchmistress Diana Rigg or Grand Wizard Tim Curry the opportunity to soar in their roles (pun intended). The flying broom effects are lousy, the acting belongs to the Arched Eyebrow school. Kids might cheer, but adults will surely wince (and please don't call me Shirley).

**WRAITH, THE (1986).** Boy, is Nick Cassavetes (son of John) a mean mother as he leads his gang of sadistic hotrodders into the jaws of Hell. But he gets his when a ghostly spirit (Charlie Sheen) turns up in a haunted Turbo Interceptor and Nick baby can't dodge the Dodge. One by one, the mean guys are killed in car crashes. Griffin O'Neal, Randy Quaid, David Sherrill, Clint Howard.

**WRESTLING WOMEN VS. THE AZTEC MUMMY (1965).** Female wrestling champions of Mexico battle a supernatural being—in this case a mummy that turns into a vampire when the correct incantation is mumbled. This Mexican film was designed by director Rene Cardona and writer Abel Salazar to jack up interest in the Aztec Mummy by surrounding it with shapely, grunting femmes. Still shapeless. (VC)

---

*"My God! It's eating the windshield!"—A trapped human in*
*WITHOUT WARNING.*

KENN DAVIS '87

# X

*"If thine eye offends thee, pluck it out."*—Preacher John Dierkes to Ray Milland in **X—THE MAN WITH X-RAY EYES.**

**X FROM OUTER SPACE (1967).** X for xcruciating . . . yet again another Japanese creature bonanza for moppets produced by adults with children's minds. Guilala, a giant stegosaurus which spits steel spears (instead of radioactive fire) grows from a single cell into a monster after being brought from outer space attached to the hull of a spacecraft. The monster goes on the same old rampage, destroying the nearest city, which again happens to be destruction-prone Tokyo. Directed by Kazui Nihonmatsu. Starring the impulsive Eiji Okada and the erratic Shinichi Yanagisawa.

**X17 TOP SECRET (1965).** Nothing top secret about it—this is a bottom-of-the-trash-heap spy thriller produced by Spaniards and Italians hoping to make fast bucks by spending as few of their own as possible. Lang Jeffries and other espionage imbeciles are after a special glass that burns through steel when sunlight reflects off its surface. Viewers got burned, too. Directed by Amerigo Anton.

**X-RAY (1982).** Like HALLOWEEN II, this is set almost entirely in a city hospital in which a mad slasher is on the loose, murdering without discrimination. Director Boaz Davidson's stylishness is weakened by a chamberpot of cliches thrown together into a flimsy plot by Marc Behm. Still, there's a greater sense of fun than in most slasher flicks, thanks to a cast overemphasizing hysteria and paranoia. A flashback shows a 1961 Valentine's Day murder witnessed by an adolescent girl. Flash forward to Barbi Benton entering "massacre hospital" for a check-up—and the body count begins. There are effective images of horror and death, and Davidson captures an eerie ambience that takes one's attention off the countless story holes. Barbi does well with her characterless role and is the only non-suspicious member of the cast. Chip Lucia, Jon Van Ness, Guy Austin, Lanny Duncay and John Warner Williams always look and sound as if they could

**OLIVIA NEWTON-JOHN IN 'XANADU'**

be the killer. Nice music by Arlon Ober, even if it is all cliches. In videocassette as **MASSACRE HOSPITAL.**

**X—THE MAN WITH X-RAY EYES (1963).** One of Roger Corman's strangest films, hampered by inadequate effects and budget yet singularly compelling as it unfolds an allegorical plot about Dr. Xavier (Ray Milland) who discovers a way of seeing through objects—all the way to the heart of the Universe! The climax to the Robert Dillon-Ray Russell script was inspired by the Bible and is utterly gross, yet producer-director Corman succeeds in jolting you. John Hoyt, Don Rickles, Dick Miller, Diana Van Der Vlis, John Dierkes. (VC)

**X—THE UNKNOWN (1957).** This Hammer rammer is sometimes confused as part of the Quatermass series, and although Dean Jean portrays a sympathetic scientist similar to Quatermass, it is a vehicle unto itself, featuring Jimmy Sangster's first screenplay. It is science-fiction reeking with eerie atmosphere as a sludge monster rises from the depths of a Scottish bogland to seek out radioactive materials on which to feed. Good effects and great gloominess invoked by director Leslie Norman. Leo McKern, Anthony Newley, Edward Judd, Edward Chapman, William Lucas.

**XANADU (1980).** Musical fantasy, directed by Robert Greenwald, in which Olivia Newton-John is one of the nine Muses, roller skating in the park and into the life of artist Michael Beck in an effort to have his dreams come true. With such a weak premise on which to base a feature, one would hope the singing and dancing to be of an unforgettable quality. Alas, poor dork, that's not the case. Definitely not something to muse over. Gene Kelly, James Sloyan, Katie Hanley, Sandahl Bergman. A remake of DOWN TO EARTH. (VC)

**XTRO (1982).** A touch of ALIEN, a little blending of POLTERGEIST and a modicum of VENOM—in short, just your average everyday ripoff movie with nothing original thrown into the bargain. This British science-fictioner starts with Philip Sayer being abducted by E.T.s, then returning to Earth three years later, reprogrammed to suck on other people's flesh and give his young son psychic powers. There's silly baloney about toy soldiers coming to life that seems strangely at odds with the ALIEN imitations. One doesn't know whether to laugh, scream at the gooey, horrendous effects or just go blind. Is masturbation the answer? A few hideous moments might have your skin crawling, but in general a waste of time and talent. Directed with little imagination by Harry Davenport. (VC)

**BARBI BENTON IN 'X-RAY'**

*"At least he died on the job."—A policeman observing James Bond's naked corpse in a bed in* **YOU ONLY LIVE TWICE.**

**YAMBAO (1956).** Ramon Gay acts queerly as a sugar plantation boss bewitched into romancing an old crone's granddaughter in this Mexican flambe directed by Alfredo Crevena. Ninon Sevilla, Ricardo Roman.

**YEAR OF THE CANNIBALS (1971).** Patterned loosely on Sophocles' ANTIGONE, with Britt Ekland caught up in bizarre social changes following World War III. It is now against the law to bury the bodies of insurgents who are slaughtered by the hundreds but Britt and Pierre Clementi do so under the threat of death. This Italian film gets littered with as many platitudes as there are bodies strewn on the post-Armageddon avenues. Written-directed by Liliana Cavani.

**YEAR 2889.** See **IN THE YEAR 2889.**

**YELLOW CAB MAN, THE (1949).** Unimportant but pleasantly diverting Red Skelton vehicle (pun intended) has the comedian inventing a glass that can't be shattered and then speeding for his life with spies in pursuit. This MGM comedy

immediately shifts into high and stays there, the meter running all the way. Directed by Jack Donohue. Gloria De Haven, Walter Slezak, Edward Arnold, James Gleason, Paul Harvey, Jay C. Flippen, John Butler.

**YELLOW PHANTOM (1936).** Feature version of the SHADOW OF CHINATOWN serial starring Bela Lugosi as Victor Poten, an insane Eurasian scientist whose racial hatred for Caucasians and Orientals leads him to slink around Chinatown in a cape, committing supposedly clever murders and hypnotizing innocent people with a remote-controlled "You-are-in-my-power" device. Actually, this is clumsily handled by director Robert F. Hill and must have looked archaic even when it was first released. Dreadful thesping. Herman (Bruce Bennett) Brix, Joan Barclay, Luana Walters, Charles King, Forrest Taylor, George Chan.

**YELLOW SUBMARINE (1968).** Full-length cartoon featuring the music of the Beatles and the Beatles as their animated

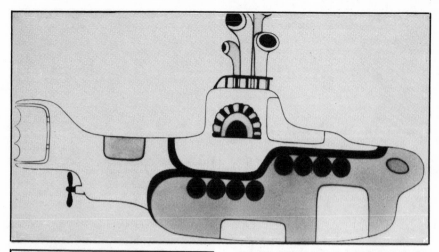

## THE BEATLES' 'YELLOW SUBMARINE'

here surrounds a legendary tribe of Comanches (Tulpan Warriors) who turn to plastic when they're shot. There's the imitative snake attack scenes and temple sequences, and a magic horn. Its light-heartedness makes it palatable. (VC)

**YESTERDAY MACHINE, THE (1965).** Obscure regional film from Texas in which a mad scientist named Von Hauser invents a time travel device and helps Adolf Hitler escape into the time continuum. Tim Holt sets out to stop him from tampering with history. Written-directed by Russ Marker. James Britton, Ann Pellegrino.

**YETI (1977).** Italian view of the Abominable Snowman of the Himalayas quickly deteriorates into a kiddie show in which a poorly designed creature helps a mute boy and an insufferable collie who looks like she accidentally wandered off the set of LASSIE. YETI, in the hands of director Frank Kramer, is yucky. Phoenix Grant, Jim Sullivan.

**YOG—MONSTER FROM SPACE (1971).** Also known as SPACE AMOEBA, this Japanese sci-fi sukiyaki depicts an alien amoeba that comes from outer space on the hull of a space probe, infecting various life forms on Earth and turning them into Godzilla-like destructors who bear such names as Ganime, Kamoeba and Gezora. Scientists work day and night to devise a method of stopping the infection, finally settling on bat cries from old DRACULA soundtracks. (Sorry, we were only kidding . . . we're just getting punchy as we near the end of this massive book.) What really gets them in the end is an erupting volcano. Oops, did we give something away? Directed by Inoshiro Honda.

**YONGARY, MONSTER FROM THE DEEP (1967).** South Koreans joined with the Japanese to produce this "horror" about a hulking monster (who looks not unlike Godzilla) freed from its centuries-old cave by an atomic blast who destroys Seoul, the capital of South Korea. Yongary is different from Godzilla in that he drinks gasoline for breakfast, lunch and dinner . . . but Yongary still runs out of petrol before the first reel is over. You really have to like men-in-monster-suits to tune in. Directed by Kiduck Kim. Starring the unflappable Yugil Oh and the undiscouraged Chungim Nam.

**YOR: THE HUNTER FROM THE FUTURE (1983).** Lowbrow fantasy escapism, but energetically on the level of a Saturday serial and hence palatable entertainment. Italian director Anthony Dawson, a master at cheap imitatons of whatever trend is popular, never aspires to more than he delivers. At least the noisy soundtrack will keep you alert, even if the acting will deaden your brain cells. YOR starts as a caveman pastiche with muscular hunk Reb Brown rescuing beautiful Corinne Clery from a prickly dinosaur and fighting off hairy Neander-

selves, who board Young Fred's submarine to help him defeat the Blue Meanies and the Ferocious Flying Glove in Pepperland. Imaginative pop and op art set new trends at the time of the film's release, and the satiric and verbal humor is rollicking. Live-action-with-animation, etchings and footage of the Beatles as well as a soundtrack lovingly loaded with the wonderful Beatles sound make for a masterpiece that will undoubtedly sustain itself for decades to come. Directed by George Dunning, who made it all come together.

**YELLOWHAIR AND THE FORTRESS OF GOLD (1984).** Mixture of spaghetti Western violence and Indiana Jones humor when a white woman raised by Indians (Laurene Landon) and Pecos Bill (Ken Roberson) search for the "Treasure of Kings" while pursued by an outlaw gang and Mexican federales, both led by sadistic brutes. The fantasy element

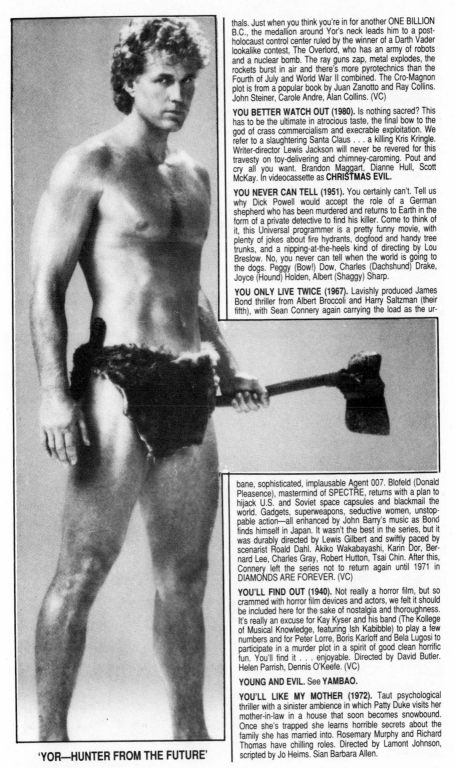

thals. Just when you think you're in for another ONE BILLION B.C., the medallion around Yor's neck leads him to a post-holocaust control center ruled by the winner of a Darth Vader lookalike contest, The Overlord, who has an army of robots and a nuclear bomb. The ray guns zap, metal explodes, the rockets burst in air and there's more pyrotechnics than the Fourth of July and World War II combined. The Cro-Magnon plot is from a popular book by Juan Zanotto and Ray Collins. John Steiner, Carole Andre, Alan Collins. (VC)

**YOU BETTER WATCH OUT (1980).** Is nothing sacred? This has to be the ultimate in atrocious taste, the final bow to the god of crass commercialism and execrable exploitation. We refer to a slaughtering Santa Claus . . . a killing Kris Kringle. Writer-director Lewis Jackson will never be revered for this travesty on toy-delivering and chimney-caroming. Pout and cry all you want. Brandon Maggart, Dianne Hull, Scott McKay. In videocassette as **CHRISTMAS EVIL.**

**YOU NEVER CAN TELL (1951).** You certainly can't. Tell us why Dick Powell would accept the role of a German shepherd who has been murdered and returns to Earth in the form of a private detective to find his killer. Come to think of it, this Universal programmer is a pretty funny movie, with plenty of jokes about fire hydrants, dogfood and handy tree trunks, and a nipping-at-the-heels kind of directing by Lou Breslow. No, you never can tell when the world is going to the dogs. Peggy (Bow!) Dow, Charles (Dachshund) Drake, Joyce (Hound) Holden, Albert (Shaggy) Sharp.

**YOU ONLY LIVE TWICE (1967).** Lavishly produced James Bond thriller from Albert Broccoli and Harry Saltzman (their fifth), with Sean Connery again carrying the load as the ur-bane, sophisticated, implausable Agent 007. Blofeld (Donald Pleasence), mastermind of SPECTRE, returns with a plan to hijack U.S. and Soviet space capsules and blackmail the world. Gadgets, superweapons, seductive women, unstoppable action—all enhanced by John Barry's music as Bond finds himself in Japan. It wasn't the best in the series, but it was durably directed by Lewis Gilbert and swiftly paced by scenarist Roald Dahl. Akiko Wakabayashi, Karin Dor, Bernard Lee, Charles Gray, Robert Hutton, Tsai Chin. After this, Connery left the series not to return again until 1971 in DIAMONDS ARE FOREVER. (VC)

**YOU'LL FIND OUT (1940).** Not really a horror film, but so crammed with horror film devices and actors, we felt it should be included here for the sake of nostalgia and thoroughness. It's really an excuse for Kay Kyser and his band (The Kollege of Musical Knowledge, featuring Ish Kabibble) to play a few numbers and for Peter Lorre, Boris Karloff and Bela Lugosi to participate in a murder plot in a spirit of good clean horrific fun. You'll find it . . . enjoyable. Directed by David Butler. Helen Parrish, Dennis O'Keefe. (VC)

**YOUNG AND EVIL. See YAMBAO.**

**YOU'LL LIKE MY MOTHER (1972).** Taut psychological thriller with a sinister ambience in which Patty Duke visits her mother-in-law in a house that soon becomes snowbound. Once she's trapped she learns horrible secrets about the family she has married into. Rosemary Murphy and Richard Thomas have chilling roles. Directed by Lamont Johnson, scripted by Jo Heims. Sian Barbara Allen.

**'YOR—HUNTER FROM THE FUTURE'**

# A Youthful Mad Doctor . . .

GENE WILDER RESURRECTING PETER BOYLE IN 'YOUNG FRANKENSTEIN'

MARTY FELDMAN AS IGGOR

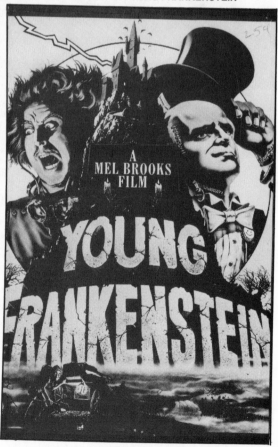

CREATURE FEATURES MOVIE GUIDE

# . . . and Sherlock Holmes

**YOUNG FRANKENSTEIN (1974).** Hysterically funny Mel Brooks take-off on the Universal horror films of the 1930s, in particular THE BRIDE and SON OF FRANKENSTEIN, since entire sequences of those films are parodied. Brooks, who directed/co-wrote the script with Gene Wilder, is wild and ingeniously creative, though some of the satire works and some falls flat. Peter Boyle is the singularly inane creature created by Dr. Frankenstein (Wilder), while Marty Feldman is the hunchbacked Iggor, Cloris Leachman the daffy woman hanging around the Frankenstein castle and Madeleine Kahn the eventual "bride." Watch for Gene Hackman as the blind hermit in the forest. You'll scream—with delight. (VC)

**YOUNG SHERLOCK HOLMES (1985).** Rousing Steven Spielberg-produced action-adventure, perfect in all technical aspects, and handsomely cast. It's a tribute to the Victorian detective by portraying him and Watson as students at a boys' school, solving a mystery that seems in the Sir Arthur Conan Doyle tradition. At least the first third, which captures the antecedents of the Holmes canon and the restraint of Doyle's story-telling and has some of Chris Columbus' best writing. The Holmes stories were, after all, studies in ratiocination and deduction and only occasionally lapsed into wild and woolly adventure. But when the gaslit "Rover Boys" stumble across a secret Egyptian death cult in the heart of London, it slides into an Indiana Jones adventure with mock

derring-do and heroics. And because there's nightmarish hallucinations, Spielberg and gang have an excuse to drag out special effects: a dead squab that comes to life on the dinner plate like some killer buzzard; gargoyles that attack an old inventor in a curio shop; a tray of French pastries that become animated cutesy-pie imps; graveyard horrors with rotting corpses; etc. Spielberg twice apologizes in the credits for taking liberties but apparently had permission to use the characters (or was it just a blessing?). Many Holmesian props (pipe, Inverness cape, violin, deerstalker's cap) are cleverly introduced. Conan Doyle is spinning . . . (VC)

**YOUNG, THE EVIL AND THE SAVAGE, THE (1968).** Michael Rennie makes one of his last screem appearances in this Italian exploitation thriller, and it's an unremarkable closing to his otherwise fine career. A girls' dormitory is the setting for several gore murders. Rennie and Mark Damon lurk on the premises. Directed by Anthony Dawson (Antonio Margherti). Eleanor Brown, Sally Smith.

**YOU'RE TELLING ME (1934).** There's no way to puncture a newfangled tire invented by W. C. Fields, and there's no way the marvelous air in this old Paramount comedy will ever leak completely out. The studio pumped all it could into it. Directed by Erle C. Kenton. Larry "Buster" Crabbe, Joan Marsh, Adrienne Ames, Louise Carter.

---

*"Arf! Arf! Arf! Arf! Arf!"—A German shepherd just before it turns into Dick Powell in* **YOU NEVER CAN TELL.**

# Z

*"But the visitors would not so happy be/If they could see what's behind the tree./If they could see the eyes that are watching them/They would leave this island of evil men./But if they wait till the full moon comes/To shine on the hands of the voodoo drums,/The chance to leave may come too late/And blood on the ground will mark their fate." —The Calypso Singer in ZOMBIES ON BROADWAY.*

**ZAAT** (1973). See **BLOOD WATERS OF DR. Z**.

**ZACARIAH** (1971). Say, viewin' pardners, it's "the first electric Western" with them high-falutin' rock personalities Country Joe MacDonald, Elvin Jones and Doug Kershaw. Them jaspers're packin' six-shooters 'n rovin' through 1880 quippin' in hip lingo and spoutin' modern homilies, with some grits throwed in. But rein up there, amigo . . . them shootin' irons're loaded with blanks 'n the script by that there Firesign Theater, it's a misfire, you betchum. Reckon it's time to put this gang out to pasture. Empty saddles in the ole corral tonight, pardners. 'N now, amigos 'n compadres, like tah strum 'n hum a little song for ya . . . (VC)

**ZAMBA THE GORILLA** (1949). Beau Bridges, in an early juvenile role, portrays a pre-teener lost in the jungle and living with a gorilla. When his mother comes looking for him, Zamba demands more than cookies and milk to relinquish his ape-hold on the 6-year-old. Eagle Lion sepiatone flick, directed by action specialist William Berke and starring Jon Hall as a jungle hero and June Vincent as a woman who feels the passions of the veldt.

**ZAPPED** (1982). Pathetic comedy that falls repeatedly on its face as Scott Baio (a TV boy star) discovers he has telekinetic powers after a high school lab explosion. The intellectual height of this undernourishment is to have Baio cause a girl's blouse to pop open or have her dress fly off. Willy Aames, also a TV boy star, is around as a cardboard character to say "Gee Whiz." So belabored that not even teen-agers, for whom producer Jeffrey D. Apple intended it, will sit still for long. Director Robert J. Rosenthal was defeated before he started. Scatman Crothers, Roger Bowen and Sue Ane Langdon have really dumb cameos. (VC)

**ZARDOZ** (1973). Odd, visually exciting science-fiction/fantasy tale set in 2293. But writer-producer-director John Boorman too frequently is heavy-handed and unnecessarily symbolic when Sean Connery (as an Exterminator, one of the few men of the future entitled to impregnate women) infiltrates a region called The Vortex, an intellectual society segregated from the rest of the world's savagery. It evolves into a political-social allegory (with esoteric literary overtones) and is often composed of incongruous, unfathomable elements that create a sludgy pace. For hardcore fans who will appreciate experiments in the outre—general audiences may find this unbearable, enigmatic viewing. Charlotte Rampling, Sally Anne Newton, Sara Kestelman. (VC)

**ZEBRA FORCE, THE** (1977). Well-produced cops-and-robbers action film set in L.A. locations spotlights a squad of Vietnam vets who take on the Mob to rid society of drug-dealers. The twist here is that the Caucasian soldiers turn into Negroes when they strike against Richard X. Slattery and his guys, then revert back to Caucasians afterward in the blink of an eye. Without explanation! Their leader is a one-armed Lieutenant who needs a sound tube against his throat to speak. An implausible twist ending rounds out the action of this unusual film, the gimmick of which may destroy for you the otherwise-good chase and caper excitement. Odd, and a bit disconcerting, to say the least. Written and directed by Joe Tornaturi. Mike Lane, Rockne Tarkington, Glenn Wilder, Anthony Caruso. (VC)

**ZELIG** (1983). Brilliant Woody Allen pastiche of biographical-documentary films comprised of historical black-and-white footage, staged footage and real scenes into which Allen has been matted. It's a startling job of bringing to life a ridiculous fictional character, Leonard Zelig, a schmuck of the first order, whose shyness and alienation from society have given him a unique talent: the chameleon ability to take on the bodily characteristics of those around him. This wonderful parody spotlights Allen with Eugene O'Neill, Herbert Hoover, the crowd at Hearst's Castle, and even Adolf Hitler during a Munich rally. It's a classic Allen gag carried off ingeniously (it took him five years to re-create the look and feel of the 1920s and '30s). Mia Farrow is compellingly believable as the mousy psychiatrist who tries to break Zelig of his malady, and you'll see real-life people (such as Susan Sontag) making fun of themselves by participating in this colossal movie lampoon. Three cheers for the klutzy Mr. Zelig, and four cheers for the unprecedented Allen. (VC)

**ZEDER** (1984). See **REVENGE OF THE DEAD**.

**ZERO BOYS, THE** (1987). Well-armed band of one-time nerds now-heroic studs is still susceptible to knife-wielding murderers in another undistinguished FRIDAY THE 13TH clone, without redeeming social values. Directed by Nico Mastorakis. Daniel Hirsch, Kelli Maroney, Tom Shell.

**SEAN CONNERY IN 'ZARDOZ'**

> *"I am the supreme Zodiac. I must not let the animal notions of man block the way to my spiritual progress. If I'm to be happy in paradise, I must collect my slaves now. All those I kill in this life will be my slaves and be reborn in paradise."*—The murderer talking to himself in
### THE ZODIAC KILLER.

**ZETA ONE (1969).** Outer space cuties called Angvians battle drab undercover operatives in this British production from Tony Tenser, which is best described as soft-core pornography. Writer-director Michael Cort adapted his story from a comic strip. Robin Hawdon, James Robertson Justice, Dawn Addams, Charles Hawtrey, Anna Gael.

**ZODIAC KILLER, THE (1971).** A chintzy, amateurish rendering of a true murder case that rocked San Francisco in the late 1960s, and which remains unsolved to this day. Several citizens were indiscriminately murdered by a man who played a dangerous cat-and-mouse game by taunting police with cyphers and other clues. This version, concocted with the help of one-time S.F. Chronicle reporter Paul Avery, is wretchedly conceived, with little directorial style from producer Tom Hanson. A couple of the murders are graphically effective—especially a pair of sunbathers being stabbed to death by the hooded killer—but otherwise the staging and editing are quite poor. Oddly enough, the closing voice-over narration of the killer is chilling as he describes how the law works to protect him. Hal Reed, Bob Jones, Ray Lynch and Tom Pittman comprise the nonprofessional cast, which is aided briefly by the appearance of Doodles Weaver, of all people. Note: Another Chronicle employee, former political cartoonist Robert Graysmith, later wrote a best-selling account of his own personal investigation of the case, and at presstime a movie was planned based on that book's unusual findings. Considering the insignificance of this film, the field is wide open for the Graysmith project.

**ZOLTAN, HOUND OF HELL.** Videocassette title for **DRACULA'S DOG.**

**ZOMBIE (1979).** Unauthorized sequel to Romero's DAWN OF THE DEAD, set on St. Thomas Island where Tisha Farrow and Ian McCulloch battle an army of zombies, which have been resurrected via voodoo rituals by fiendish doctor Richard Johnson. Heads are blown off in abundance (that's the only way to stop a zombie, remember?) and director Lucio Fulci allows this Italian exploitationer to reach ridiculous extremes—such as having a zombie attack and bite a killer shark and having a human eyeball punctured. But that's what this "walking dead" genre is all about, right? (VC)

**ZOMBIE FLESH EATERS.** See **ZOMBIE.** (Yummy!)

**ZOMBIE ISLAND MASSACRE (1984).** Mistitled film has nothing to do with zombies and the only massacre that takes place is between criminals and the law, for this is about smuggling and stuff like that. Directed by John N. Carter. David Broadnax, Rita Jenrette.

**ZOMBIES (1961).** Crude, dumbly conceived junk piece about a Miami Beach writer lured to a Caribbean island to solve the mystery of some fright-faced natives. This exemplifies sleazy thrills as William Joyce runs around with floozy Heather Hewitt to solve the unmysterious mystery. Credit (or discredit) Del Tenny for writing-producing-directing this mess. Assistant director was William Grefe, who went on to direct STANLEY and other losers.

**ZOMBIES' LAKE (1985).** Corpses of Nazi soldiers violently slaughtered in a World War II battle rise from the depths of a very unpicturesque lake to attack nude women swimmers, who spread wide their legs while the camera photographs them from below. The rotting troopers fondle the bare breasts and asses. Gee, an art horror movie with redeeming values. Howard Vernon, Britt Carva, Fred Sanders. (VC)

**ZOMBIES OF MORA TAU (1957).** Columbia producer Sam Katzman must have been in a trance-like state when he read Raymond T. Marcus' script. Edward L. Cahn must have also been in a deep sleep when he accepted the assignment to direct. Otherwise, why bother? Gregg Palmer and Allison Hayes (the 50-Foot Woman) sleepwalk through roles as adventurers in search of a fortune in diamonds guarded over in an underwater hiding place by hollow-eyed insomniacs. Ray Corrigan, Morris Ankrum, Gregg Palmer . . . zzzzzzz. (VC)

**ALLISON HAYES IN 'THE ZOMBIES OF MORA TAU'**

*"Do you have any women with you? Like blondes from Venus, maybe?"*
*—A horny G.I. dogface meeting with aliens in ZONE TROOPERS.*

**ZOMBIES OF THE STRATOSPHERE (1952).** Complete version of Republic's 12-chapter with a rocketman of the Inter-Planetary Patrol (Judd Holdren), a watchdog of the solar system, looking like a reject from KING OF THE ROCKETMEN as he flies through the skies fighting crime. Space zombies Marex and Narab persuade an evil scientist to help construct a hydrogen bomb and explode it, forcing Earth out of its orbit. Fred C. Brannon directed the superexciting stuff. Aline Towne, Lane Bradford, Stanley Waxman, Leonard Nimoy, Tom Steele, Wilson Wood, Jack Shea. (VC)

**ZOMBIES ON BROADWAY (1945).** When the owners of the Zombie Hut, a night club on the Big Street, announce they'll have real-life dead zombies performing on stage, they're forced to send schmucks Wally Brown and Allen Carney to the West Indies island of San Sebastian to bring back the real dead McCoy. Darby Jones, the wonderful bug-eyed zombie corpse in I WALKED WITH A ZOMBIE, is back for more shenanigans, this time strictly for laughs, as he stalks Anne Jeffreys and the two idiots through potted jungles, occasionally carrying off a body. Bela Lugosi portrays Dr. Renault, the madman perfecting his walking dead, in his usual wide-eyed style. Taken as a period piece, it's quite funny with Sheldon Leonard in a good role as the night club owner. Director Gordon Douglas guides the cast through the inanities quite well. Ian Wolfe, Frank Jenks.

**ZOMBIETHON (1986).** Compilation videocassette special of the goriest scenes imaginable from zombie movies of the past, with new wraparound footage produced-directed by Ken Dixon. Various young women pursued by walking dead enter the El Rey Theater to sit in a crowd of movie-watching zombies and see clips from ZOMBIE (1979), which include the infamous eye-gouging and shark-biting sequences; ZOMBIES' LAKE, with emphasis on bare flesh and wide-open legs; OASIS OF THE ZOMBIES, a foreign film with Afrika Corps soldiers stalking the living; and ASTRO-ZOMBIES. Only with this final camp classic does this videotape take on a fun quality; otherwise, you really have to love zombies to find much enjoyment. Other clips from THE INVISIBLE DEAD, A VIRGIN AMONG THE LIVING DEAD and FEAR. (VC)

**ZONE TROOPERS (1986).** Simple-minded, mildly enjoyable World War II fantasy from Empire International, which resembles a segment of TV's COMBAT when GI dogfaces in Italy shoot it out with German troops. Four survivors flee into the forest to meet "Bug," an extraterrestrial creature with an insect's head who evaporates a few Nazi war machines with his disintegrator zap ray. "Bug" is part of a band of alien troopers stranded on our planet and since they understand war, and the good guys from the bad guys, they side up with the dogfaces to blast dirty Nazi rats into another dimension. Unusually gentle for a Charles Band production, with nostalgic '40s tunes on the soundtrack. Not bad. Directed by Danny Bilson; okay effects by John Buechler. Tim Thomerson, Timothy Van Patten, Biff Manard. (VC)

**ZONTAR: THE THING FROM VENUS (1968).** Described as a new version of Roger Corman's IT CONQUERED THE WORLD . . . but why resurrect that old turkey? Well, don't laugh because this film is so inept, it's a minor cult favorite among those who love really good bad movies. The story reaches new lows in screen science-fiction as John Agar opposes a space monster capable of dominating the human mind. Too bad a spark of creativity didn't dominate the mind of writer-director Larry Buchanan. See it. You won't believe it.

**ZOO SHIP (1985).** Huge spaceship, carrying specimens from all over the Universe, crashlands on Earth, and you know what that means. Special effects by Jim Danforth and Sydney Dutton. Directed by Richard Shorr. James Whitmore,

Craig Wasson, Keenan Wynn, Audra Lindley, Roddy Mc-Dowell.

**ZOTZ! (1962).** Walter Karig's popular 1940's novel was finally produced by William Castle, with screenplay by Ray Russell, but the results, despite all those years of waiting, were negligible. An old coin possesses strange powers once its holder utters the word "Zotz!" Karig's neat twist on the Aladdin's Lamp theme has been reduced to cinematic cliches, with enemy spies coming after the owner of the coin, Tom Poston. ZOTZ to you, William Castle. Jim Backus, Fred Clark, Cecil Kellaway, Louis Nye.

**Z.P.G. (1972).** Which stands for Zero Population Growth, in case you haven't been following Earth's current population problems. And which stands for Zero Picture Grabber, if you've already seen the film. Geraldine Chaplin plays a wife

# S.E.X.Y. E.T.'s

**CUTIE ANGVIAN IN 'ZETA ONE'**

of the 21st Century who defies anti-birth laws and has her baby anyway (hubby Oliver Reed helped, of course). The city is surrounded by a deadly smog, forcing most of the cast to wear gas masks, but masks might be more in order for the audience to prevent them from gagging on this turgid sociological science-fiction. Directed by Michael Campus, scripted by Max Ehrlich and Frank DeFelitta.

**Z-7 OPERATION REMBRANDT (1967).** Lang Jeffries, who thrilled you to no end in X-17 TOP SECRET, returns in another internationally financed spy adventure set in Tangier, dealing with a cosmic death ray that could destroy all the asparagus crops throughout the world unless Z-7 starts zinging it to the bad guys. The film also depicts in pseudo-documentary fashion how the mayonnaise industry tries to prevent such a disaster. Written-directed by Giancarlo Romitelli. Laura Valenzuela, Carlo Hinterman.

---

*"The Zombies are at the door!" They're coming in! Arrgghh!'— A victim*
*in ZOMBIE FLESH EATERS.*

# Don't Be Cruel!
# BUY AN EXTRA COPY
# OF THIS BOOK TODAY
# FOR A FRIEND!

"The Creature Features Movie Guide" makes a great gift for Christmas, Halloween, Public Hangings and Monster Mashes and Bashes

Also, look carefully at this book. Is it dogeared? Torn on the edges cause you thumb it all the time? Maybe you need a new copy for you!

## ORDER COPIES WHILE THEY LAST!

You can order the trade edition for $12.95 (Californians add 78 cents for State sales tax) or the Deluxe Signed Edition for $41 (Californians add $2.60 for State sales tax). Send checks or money orders to:

## CREATURES AT LARGE PRESS
### P.O. Box 687 • Pacifica CA 94044

**The Oddest Video Library
Anywhere on Earth**

# THE CINEMA SHOP

- **BLACK FILMS OF THE '40s**
- **TEENAGE EXPLOITATION**
- **WORLD WAR II DOCUMENTARIES**
- **SCIENCE-FICTION AND HORROR**
- **SLEAZE CLASSICS**
- **B WESTERNS**
- **INDESCRIBABLE ODDITIES**

## Owner: DAN FARIS
## Manager: STEVE IMURA

**604 Geary Street
San Francisco**

**(415) 885-6785**

# COLLECTORS BOOK STORE

## MOVIE STILLS - POSTERS - MAGAZINES

### ORIGINAL 8x10" BLACK AND WHITE MOVIE PHOTOS

Over two million 1915-1980's glossy photographs are available by FILM TITLE (actual movie scenes with the stars) and by STAR NAME (portraits).

### STILL PRICES

| DECADE | SCENE STILLS | PORTRAITS | DECADE | SCENE STILLS | PORTRAITS |
|---|---|---|---|---|---|
| 1980's —— | $3.00 each | $3.50 each | 1940's —— | $5.00 each | $6.00 each |
| 1970's —— | $3.50 each | $4.00 each | 1930's —— | $6.00 each | $7.50 each |
| 1960's —— | $4.00 each | $4.50 each | 1920's —— | $10.00 each | $15.00 each |
| 1950's —— | $4.50 each | $5.00 each | 1910's —— | $15.00 each | $20.00 each |

Color photos - $5.00-$7.50; Reprint - $3.50
Photo prices may vary according to rarity

### MOVIE POSTERS, LOBBY CARDS, AND PRESSBOOKS

A fine selection of 27x41" one-sheet movie posters, 11x14" color lobby cards, and movie pressbooks is available. Please send your wantlist.

### MOVIE AND TELEVISION SCRIPTS

Thousands of movie scripts are available from the 1920's to date. Many television scripts are also available. Please send your wantlist.

### MOVIE FAN MAGAZINES

Back issues of PHOTOPLAY, MODERN SCREEN, MOVIE STORY, SCREENLAND, and many other titles are available from 1912 through 1969 in fine, uncut condition. Customers should order by magazine title and exact date.

## HOW TO ORDER BY MAIL

1. $10.00 minimum purchase through the mail.
2. $3.00 postage & handling charge per domestic order.
   $5.50 minimum charge for foreign orders, surface mail.
   Orders shipped by U.S. Post Office and/or UPS.
3. Insurance charge, if insurance is desired:
   Orders worth       $5.00 to  $50.00  -   include $1.10
   Orders worth       $51.00 to $100.00  -   include $1.40
   Orders worth       $101.00 to $150.00  -   include $1.80
4. Payment accepted by VISA, MasterCard, American Express, or personal check. Checks may be held for two weeks for clearance. If sending cash, use registered mail.
5. California residents please add 6½% State Sales Tax on all items except magazines.
6. Money-back guarantee on all mail-order items if merchandise is immediately returned in good order. Phone orders welcome (213) 467-3296
7. Xeroxing of stills for your inspection, 20¢ each.
8. For individuals or companies desiring very obscure material (for instance, scenes of people throwing snowballs or church interiors, etc.) which requires extensive research on our part, a research fee of $25.00 in advance will apply.

Collectors Book Store, located at the famous intersection of Hollywood and Vine, is a California corporation and has been in business since 1965. The store phone number is (213) 467-3296. Business hours are 11:00 - 5:00 P.M. Monday through Friday, and 10:00 - 5:30 P.M. Saturday. Closed Sundays. We are also the home of the famous COLLECTORS SHOWCASE monthly mail auction.

COLLECTORS BOOK STORE, 1708 N. Vine St., Hollywood, California 90028-6003

## Movie Material Purchased - Auction Consignments Invited

# ROSE
# PUBLISHING

35106 Millwood Court • Newark, California, 94560 • (415) 793-7554

## LOW-COST PUBLISHING

Rose Publishing uses Xerox® Ventura Publisher™ to paginate manuscripts from your IBM®-compatible word processor. A wide range of fonts is available to suit your individual needs.

Our typesetting is done on the Linotronic 300 for the best-quality professional look, or on a 300 dpi laser printer for budget products and proofs.

This book was typeset entirely by Rose Publishing. Please give us a call to discuss your low-cost publishing needs.

# INCREDIBLY STRANGE FILMS!

A functional guide to important territory neglected by the film-criticism establishment, spotlighting unhailed directors—**Herschell Gordon Lewis, Russ Meyer, Larry Cohen, Ray Dennis Steckler, Ted V. Mikels, Joe Sarno,** and others—who have been critically consigned to the ghettos of gore and sexploitation films. Genre overviews explore subjects as **Biker films, LSD films, J.D films, Beach Party films, Mondo & Educational** films. In-depth interviews focus on philosophy while anecdotes entertain as well as illuminate theory. Includes biographies, filmographies, bibliography, quotations, an A-Z of film personalities, lists of recommended films, sources, etc. 8½x11", 172 photos, 224 pages. **$17** postpaid, **$18** sea mail or Canada (**$24** air overseas).

Name _____

Address _____

_____

Amount enclosed: _____ Quantity: _____

**MAIL TO:** Re/Search Film Book, 1529 Grant Ave., San Francisco, CA 94133